T0238807

Lecture Notes in Computer Science   9813

Commenced Publication in 1973
Founding and Former Series Editors:
Gerhard Goos, Juris Hartmanis, and Jan van Leeuwen

More information about this series at http://www.springer.com/series/7410

Benedikt Gierlichs · Axel Y. Poschmann (Eds.)

Cryptographic Hardware and Embedded Systems – CHES 2016

18th International Conference
Santa Barbara, CA, USA, August 17–19, 2016
Proceedings

 Springer

Editors
Benedikt Gierlichs
KU Leuven
Leuven
Belgium

Axel Y. Poschmann
NXP Semiconductors Germany GmbH
Hamburg
Germany

ISSN 0302-9743   ISSN 1611-3349   (electronic)
Lecture Notes in Computer Science
ISBN 978-3-662-53139-6   ISBN 978-3-662-53140-2   (eBook)
DOI 10.1007/978-3-662-53140-2

Library of Congress Control Number: 2016946628

LNCS Sublibrary: SL4 – Security and Cryptology

Printed on acid-free paper

This Springer imprint is published by Springer Nature
The registered company is Springer-Verlag GmbH Berlin Heidelberg

Preface

The 18th Conference on Cryptographic Hardware and Embedded Systems (CHES 2016) was held at the University of California at Santa Barbara, California, USA, August 17–19, 2016. The conference was sponsored by the *International Association for Cryptologic Research* and—after 2010 and 2013—it was the third time that CHES was co-located with CRYPTO.

CHES 2016 received a record 148 submissions. Each paper was anonymously reviewed by at least four Program Committee members in a double-blind peer-review process. Submissions co-authored by PC members received at least five reviews. With the help of 210 external reviewers our 47 Program Committee members wrote an impressive total of 623 reviews. This year CHES continued the policy that submissions needed to closely match the final versions published by Springer in length and format. Additionally, we implemented a new paper submission policy whereby authors needed to indicate conflicts of interest with Program Committee members. This mutual indication process led to the upfront identification of roughly five times more conflicts of interest, and, consequently, to a more fair and smooth review process. The Program Committee selected 30 papers for publication in these proceedings, corresponding to a 20% acceptance rate.

Several papers were nominated for the CHES 2016 best paper award. After voting, the Program Committee gave the award to *Differential Computation Analysis: Hiding Your White-Box Designs Is Not Enough* by Joppe W. Bos, Charles Hubain, Wil Michiels, and Philippe Teuwen. The runners-up were *Cache Attacks Enable Bulk Key Recovery on the Cloud* by Mehmet S. Inci, Berk Gulmezoglu, Gorka Irazoqui, Thomas Eisenbarth, and Berk Sunar, and *Software Implementation of Koblitz Curves Over Quadratic Fields* by Thomaz Oliveira, Julio López, Francisco Rodríguez-Henríquez. All three were invited to submit extended versions to the *Journal of Cryptology*.

The technical program was completed by a panel discussion that provided valuable feedback to the academic and industrial communities, and by an excellent invited talk (jointly with CRYPTO 2016) by Paul Kocher from Cryptography Research, a Division of Rambus.

As a continued tradition, CHES 2016 also featured a poster session and we are very grateful to Billy Bob Brumley for chairing this aspect of the program. In addition, two tutorials were given on the day preceding the conference: one by Victor Lomné on *Common Criteria Certification of a Smartcard: A Technical Overview* and one by Yuval Yarom on *Micro-Architectural Side-Channel Attacks*. For the second time a CHES challenge was organized. We are very grateful to Ryad Benadjila, Emmanuel Prouff, and Adrian Thillard for chairing the challenge selection process, and to Colin O'Flynn for running the CHES 2016 challenge.

The review process was a challenging and time-consuming task. We sincerely thank the Program Committee members as well as their external reviewers for the hard work and many hours spent reviewing, assessing, and discussing. The submission process, the review process, and the editing of the final proceedings were greatly simplified by the software written by Shai Halevi and we thank him for his kind and immediate support throughout the whole process.

We would also like to thank the General Chairs, Çetin Kaya Koç and Erkay Savaş, local organizers Sally Vito and Whitney Morris (of UCSB Conference Services), Juan Manuel Escalante, who designed the CHES 2016 memorabilia, and the webmaster, Thomas Eisenbarth. Our thanks also go out to Matt Robshaw and Jonathan Katz, the Program Chairs of CRYPTO 2016, for the successful collaboration and alignment of the programs of CHES and CRYPTO. We are very grateful for the financial support received from our many generous sponsors.

Finally, among the numerous people that contributed to the success of CHES 2016, above all others are the authors who submitted their research papers to the conference. Without them, this conference would not exist. We enjoyed chairing the Program Committee and we hope you will enjoy these proceedings.

June 2016

Benedikt Gierlichs
Axel Y. Poschmann

CHES 2016

18th Conference on Cryptographic Hardware and Embedded Systems

Santa Barbara, California, USA
August 17–19, 2016

Sponsored by the *International Association for Cryptologic Research*

General Chairs

Çetin Kaya Koç	University of California at Santa Barbara, USA
Erkay Savaş	Sabanci University, Turkey

Program Chairs

Benedikt Gierlichs	KU Leuven, Belgium
Axel Y. Poschmann	NXP Semiconductors, Germany

Program Committee

Josep Balasch	KU Leuven, Belgium
Lejla Batina	Radboud University, The Netherlands
Daniel J. Bernstein	University of Illinois at Chicago, USA and Technische Universiteit Eindhoven, The Netherlands
Guido Bertoni	STMicroelectronics, Italy
Chen-Mou Cheng	National Taiwan University, Taiwan
Hermann Drexler	Giesecke & Devrient, Germany
Orr Dunkelman	University of Haifa, Israel
Junfeng Fan	Open Security Research, China
Sebastian Faust	Ruhr-Universität Bochum, Germany
Viktor Fischer	Jean Monnet University Saint-Etienne, France
Wieland Fischer	Infineon Technologies, Germany
Henri Gilbert	ANSSI, France
Christophe Giraud	Oberthur Technologies, France
Daniel Holcomb	University of Massachusetts Amherst, USA
Naofumi Homma	Tohoku University, Japan
Michael Hutter	Cryptography Research, USA
Kimmo Järvinen	Aalto University, Finland
Marc Joye	Technicolor, France
Lars R. Knudsen	Technical University of Denmark, Denmark
Kerstin Lemke-Rust	Bonn-Rhein-Sieg University of Applied Sciences, Germany
Tancrède Lepoint	CryptoExperts, France

Yang Li	Nanjing University of Aeronautics and Astronautics, China
Roel Maes	Intrinsic-ID, The Netherlands
Mitsuru Matsui	Mitsubishi Electric, Japan
Marcel Medwed	NXP Semiconductors, Austria
Amir Moradi	Ruhr-Universität Bochum, Germany
Debdeep Mukhopadhyay	Indian Institute of Technology Kharagpur, India
Elke De Mulder	Cryptography Research, USA
David Naccache	École normale supérieure, France
Elisabeth Oswald	University of Bristol, UK
Daniel Page	University of Bristol, UK
Thomas Peyrin	Nanyang Technological University, Singapore
Emmanuel Prouff	Safran Identity & Security, France
Francesco Regazzoni	ALaRI, Lugano, Switzerland
Matthieu Rivain	CryptoExperts, France
Alexander Schlösser	NXP Semiconductors, Germany
Sergei Skorobogatov	University of Cambridge, UK
Meltem Sönmez Turan	NIST, USA
Marc Stöttinger	Continental Teves, Germany
Berk Sunar	Worcester Polytechnic Institute, USA
Hugues Thiebeauld	eshard, France
Olivier Thomas	Texplained, France
Mehdi Tibouchi	NTT Secure Platform Laboratories, Japan
Steve Trimberger	Xilinx, USA
Ingrid Verbauwhede	KU Leuven, Belgium
Andre Weimerskirch	University of Michigan, USA
Brecht Wyseur	NAGRA, Switzerland

External Reviewers

Martin R. Albrecht	Sonia Belaïd	Martin Butkus
Guilherme Almeida	Ryad Benadjila	Rodrigo Portella do Canto
Gilles Van Assche	Florent Bernard	Claude Carlet
Jean-Philippe Aumasson	Régis Bevan	Pierre-Louis Cayrel
Aydin Aysu	Shivam Bhasin	Gizem Selcan Cetin
Reza Azarderakhsh	Sarani Bhattacharya	Thomas Chabrier
Florian Bache	Russ Bielawski	Rajat Subhra Chakraborty
Thomas Baignères	Begül Bilgin	Ayantika Chatterjee
Subhadeep Banik	Markus Bockes	Urbi Chatterjee
Guillaume Barbu	Joppe Bos	Ricardo Chaves
Guy Barwell	Lilian Bossuet	Chien-Ning Chen
Alberto Battistello	Claudio Bozzato	Cong Chen
Sven Bauer	Jakub Breier	Abdelkarim Cherkaoui
Georg T. Becker	Billy Bob Brumley	Jean-Michel Cioranesco
Steffen Becker	Samuel Burri	Ruan de Clercq

Thomas De Cnudde
Brice Colombier
Jean-Sébastien Coron
Guillaume Dabosville
Joan Daemen
Wei Dai
Poulami Das
Nicolas Debande
Jeroen Delvaux
Jintai Ding
Yarkin Doroz
Emmanuelle Dottax
Baris Ege
Thomas Eisenbarth
Guangjun Fan
Claudio Favi
Peter Felber
Magnus Gausdal Find
Matthieu Finiasz
Daisuke Fujimoto
Georges Gagnerot
Adriano Gaibotti
Jake Longo Galea
Benoit Gerard
Cezary Glowacz
Gilbert Goodwill
Louis Goubin
Aurélien Greuet
Vincent Grosso
Daniel Gruss
Frank K. Gürkaynak
Mike Hamburg
Ghaith Hammouri
Bill Hass
Wei He
Annelie Heuser
Lars Hoffmann
Yuan-Che Hsu
Ilia Iliashenko
Gorka Irazoki
Dirmanto Jap
Eliane Jaulmes
Tommi Junttila
Elif Bilge Kavun

Osnat Keren
Mehran Mozaffari
Kermani
Ilya Kizhvatov
Patrick Klapper
Miroslav Knezevic
Markus Kuhn
Tanja Lange
Sam Lauzon
Jenwei Lee
Gaëtan Leurent
Wen-Ding Li
Zhe Liu
Zheng Liu
Susanne Lohmann
Cuauhtemoc Mancillas
Lopez
Atul Luykx
Pieter Maene
Houssem Maghrebi
Cedric Marchand
Daniel Martin
Marco Martinoli
Daniel Masny
Pedro Maat Massolino
Luke Mather
Sanu Mathew
Ingo von Maurich
Silvia Mella
Filippo Melzani
Bart Mennink
Rafael Misoczki
Nicolas Moro
Zakari Najm
Ousmane Ndiaye
Ventzislav Nikov
Tobias Nink
Tobias Oder
Brisbane Ovilla
Erdinc Ozturk
Clara Paglialonga
Paolo Palmieri
Louiza Papachristodoulou
Kostas Papagiannopoulos

Sikhar Patranabis
Sylvain Pelissier
Hervé Pelletier
Jan Pelzl
Bo-Yuan Peng
Peter Pessl
Antonio de la Piedra
Thomas Prest
Christian Pilato
Gilles Piret
Thomas Plos
Ilia Polian
Thomas Pöppelmann
Frédéric de Portzamparc
Jürgen Pulkus
Christof Rempel
Joost Renes
Oscar Reparaz
Thomas Ricosset
Lionel Riviere
Molka ben Romdhane
Franck Rondepierre
Debapriya Basu Roy
Sujoy Sinha Roy
Markku-Juhani
O. Saarinen
Durga Prasad Sahoo
Kazuo Sakiyama
Peter Samarin
Fabrizio De Santis
Pascal Sasdrich
Falk Schellenberg
Werner Schindler
Tobias Schneider
Okan Seker
Hwajeong Seo
Siang Meng Sim
Daniel Smith-Tone
Martijn Stam
Francois-Xavier Standaert
Takeshi Sugawara
Ruggero Susella
Daisuke Suzuki
Pawel Swierczynski

Contents

Side Channel Analysis

Correlated Extra-Reductions Defeat Blinded Regular Exponentiation   3
  Margaux Dugardin, Sylvain Guilley, Jean-Luc Danger, Zakaria Najm,
  and Olivier Rioul

Horizontal Side-Channel Attacks and Countermeasures on the ISW
Masking Scheme.   23
  Alberto Battistello, Jean-Sébastien Coron, Emmanuel Prouff,
  and Rina Zeitoun

Towards Easy Leakage Certification   40
  François Durvaux, François-Xavier Standaert,
  and Santos Merino Del Pozo

Simple Key Enumeration (and Rank Estimation) Using Histograms:
An Integrated Approach.   61
  Romain Poussier, François-Xavier Standaert, and Vincent Grosso

Automotive Security

Physical Layer Group Key Agreement for Automotive Controller Area
Networks.   85
  Shalabh Jain and Jorge Guajardo

– vatiCAN – Vetted, Authenticated CAN Bus 106
  Stefan Nürnberger and Christian Rossow

Invasive Attacks

Mitigating SAT Attack on Logic Locking 127
  Yang Xie and Ankur Srivastava

No Place to Hide: Contactless Probing of Secret Data on FPGAs 147
  Heiko Lohrke, Shahin Tajik, Christian Boit, and Jean-Pierre Seifert

Side Channel Countermeasures I

Strong 8-bit Sboxes with Efficient Masking in Hardware 171
  Erik Boss, Vincent Grosso, Tim Güneysu, Gregor Leander,
  Amir Moradi, and Tobias Schneider

Masking AES with $d + 1$ Shares in Hardware   194
  Thomas De Cnudde, Oscar Reparaz, Begül Bilgin, Svetla Nikova,
  Ventzislav Nikov, and Vincent Rijmen

New Directions

Differential Computation Analysis: Hiding Your White-Box Designs is Not
Enough   215
  Joppe W. Bos, Charles Hubain, Wil Michiels, and Philippe Teuwen

Antikernel: A Decentralized Secure Hardware-Software Operating System
Architecture   237
  Andrew Zonenberg and Bülent Yener

Software Implementations

Software Implementation of Koblitz Curves over Quadratic Fields   259
  Thomaz Oliveira, Julio López, and Francisco Rodríguez-Henríquez

QcBits: Constant-Time Small-Key Code-Based Cryptography   280
  Tung Chou

μKummer: Efficient Hyperelliptic Signatures and Key Exchange
on Microcontrollers   301
  Joost Renes, Peter Schwabe, Benjamin Smith, and Lejla Batina

Cache Attacks

Flush, Gauss, and Reload – A Cache Attack on the BLISS Lattice-Based
Signature Scheme   323
  Leon Groot Bruinderink, Andreas Hülsing, Tanja Lange,
  and Yuval Yarom

CacheBleed: A Timing Attack on OpenSSL Constant Time RSA   346
  Yuval Yarom, Daniel Genkin, and Nadia Heninger

Cache Attacks Enable Bulk Key Recovery on the Cloud   368
  Mehmet Sinan İnci, Berk Gulmezoglu, Gorka Irazoqui,
  Thomas Eisenbarth, and Berk Sunar

Physical Unclonable Functions

Strong Machine Learning Attack Against PUFs with No Mathematical
Model   391
  Fatemeh Ganji, Shahin Tajik, Fabian Fäßler, and Jean-Pierre Seifert

Efficient Fuzzy Extraction of PUF-Induced Secrets: Theory and
Applications.. 412
  Jeroen Delvaux, Dawu Gu, Ingrid Verbauwhede, Matthias Hiller,
  and Meng-Day (Mandel) Yu

Run-Time Accessible DRAM PUFs in Commodity Devices............ 432
  Wenjie Xiong, André Schaller, Nikolaos A. Anagnostopoulos,
  Muhammad Umair Saleem, Sebastian Gabmeyer, Stefan Katzenbeisser,
  and Jakub Szefer

Side Channel Countermeasures II

On the Multiplicative Complexity of Boolean Functions and Bitsliced
Higher-Order Masking....................................... 457
  Dahmun Goudarzi and Matthieu Rivain

Reducing the Number of Non-linear Multiplications in Masking Schemes ... 479
  Jürgen Pulkus and Srinivas Vivek

Faster Evaluation of SBoxes via Common Shares.................. 498
  Jean-Sébastien Coron, Aurélien Greuet, Emmanuel Prouff,
  and Rina Zeitoun

Hardware Implementations

FourQ on FPGA: New Hardware Speed Records for Elliptic Curve
Cryptography over Large Prime Characteristic Fields............... 517
  Kimmo Järvinen, Andrea Miele, Reza Azarderakhsh, and Patrick Longa

A High Throughput/Gate AES Hardware Architecture by Compressing
Encryption and Decryption Datapaths — Toward Efficient CBC-Mode
Implementation.. 538
  Rei Ueno, Sumio Morioka, Naofumi Homma, and Takafumi Aoki

Efficient High-Speed WPA2 Brute Force Attacks Using Scalable Low-Cost
FPGA Clustering 559
  Markus Kammerstetter, Markus Muellner, Daniel Burian,
  Christian Kudera, and Wolfgang Kastner

Fault Attacks

EnCounter: On Breaking the Nonce Barrier in Differential Fault Analysis
with a Case-Study on PAEQ.................................. 581
  Dhiman Saha and Dipanwita Roy Chowdhury

Curious Case of Rowhammer: Flipping Secret Exponent Bits Using Timing
Analysis. 602
    Sarani Bhattacharya and Debdeep Mukhopadhyay

A Design Methodology for Stealthy Parametric Trojans and Its Application
to Bug Attacks 625
    Samaneh Ghandali, Georg T. Becker, Daniel Holcomb,
    and Christof Paar

Author Index 649

Side Channel Analysis

Correlated Extra-Reductions Defeat Blinded Regular Exponentiation

Margaux Dugardin[1,2(✉)], Sylvain Guilley[2,3], Jean-Luc Danger[2,3], Zakaria Najm[4], and Olivier Rioul[2,5]

[1] CESTI, Thales Communications and Security, 31000 Toulouse, France
[2] LTCI, CNRS, Télécom ParisTech, Université Paris-Saclay, 75013 Paris, France
{margaux.dugardin,sylvain.guilley,jean-luc.danger,
olivier.rioul}@telecom-paristech.fr
[3] Secure-IC SAS, 35510 Cesson-Sévigné, France
{sylvain.guilley,jean-luc.danger}@secure-ic.com
[4] ST-Microelectronics, 13790 Rousset, France
zakaria.najm@st.com
[5] CMAP, Ecole Polytechnique, Université Paris-Saclay, 91128 Palaiseau, France
olivier.rioul@polytechnique.edu

Abstract. Walter and Thomson (CT-RSA '01) and Schindler (PKC '02) have shown that extra-reductions allow to break RSA-CRT even with message blinding. Indeed, the extra-reduction probability depends on the type of operation (square, multiply, or multiply with a constant). Regular exponentiation schemes can be regarded as protections since the operation sequence does not depend on the secret.

In this article, we show that there exists a strong negative correlation between extra-reductions of two consecutive operations, provided that the first feeds the second. This allows to mount successful attacks even against blinded asymmetrical computations with a regular exponentiation algorithm, such as Square-and-Multiply Always or Montgomery Ladder. We investigate various attack strategies depending on the context—known or unknown modulus, known or unknown extra-reduction detection probability, etc.—and implement them on two devices: a single core ARM Cortex-M4 and a dual core ARM Cortex M0-M4.

Keywords: Side-channel analysis · Montgomery modular multiplication · Extra-reduction leakage · Message blinding · Regular exponentiation

1 Introduction

State of the Art of Timing Attacks. Any cryptographic algorithm in an embedded system is vulnerable to side-channel attacks. Timing attacks on the RSA Straightforward Method (RSA-SFM) were pioneered by Kocher [12]. The attack consists in building "templates" whose distributions are compared to that of the response. It is required that the cryptographic parameters be known since the attack is profiled.

© International Association for Cryptologic Research 2016
B. Gierlichs and A.Y. Poschmann (Eds.): CHES 2016, LNCS 9813, pp. 3–22, 2016.
DOI: 10.1007/978-3-662-53140-2_1

Schindler [16] extended timing attacks to RSA with Chinese Remainder Theorem (RSA-CRT) using chosen messages. This attack exploits a conditional extra-reduction at the end of modular multiplications. Schindler and co-authors carried out numerous improvements [1,2,17–20] in the case where the exponentiation uses windows or exponent randomization.

Walter and Thompson [21] remarked that even when data is blinded, the distribution of extra-reductions is different for a square and for a multiply. They assumed that side-channel measurements such as power or timing during exponentiation are sufficiently clean to detect the presence or absence of an extra-reduction at each individual operation. Schindler [17] improved this attack by also distinguishing multiplications by a constant from squarings and multiplications by non-fixed parameters.

Today's Solutions. In order to protect the implementation from the above attacks, a first solution consists in exponent randomization on top of message blinding. Such a protection, however, is sensitive to carry leakage [9] and amenable to other attacks like simple power analysis [7] (SPA). A second solution relies on regular exponentiation like Square-and-Multiply-Always (SMA, see Algorithm 1) or Montgomery Ladder (ML, see Algorithm 2). Both algorithms consist in a square and a multiply operation in each iteration i, yielding no leakage to SPA.

Algorithm 1. Square and Multiply Always Left-to-Right	**Algorithm 2.** Montgomery Ladder Left-to-Right
Input: $m, k = (k_l k_{l-1} \ldots k_0)_2, p \quad (k_l = 1)$	**Input:** $m, k = (k_l k_{l-1} \ldots k_0)_2, p \quad (k_l = 1)$
Output: $m^k \bmod p$	**Output:** $m^k \bmod p$
1: $R_0 \leftarrow 1$	1: $R_0 \leftarrow m$
2: $R_1 \leftarrow m$	2: $R_1 \leftarrow R_0 \times R_0 \bmod p \qquad \triangleright$ FS
3: **for** $i = l - 1$ **downto** 0 **do**	3: **for** $i = l - 1$ **downto** 0 **do**
4: $\quad R_1 \leftarrow R_1 \times R_1 \bmod p \qquad \triangleright S_i$	4: $\quad R_{\neg k_i} \leftarrow R_0 \times R_1 \bmod p \qquad \triangleright M_i$
5: $\quad R_{k_i} \leftarrow R_1 \times m \ \bmod p \qquad \triangleright M_i$	5: $\quad R_{k_i} \leftarrow R_{k_i} \times R_{k_i} \bmod p \qquad \triangleright S_i$
6: **end for**	6: **end for**
7: **return** R_1	7: **return** R_0

Contributions of This Paper. We show that despite message blinding and regular exponentiation, it is still possible for an attacker to take advantage of extra-reductions: A new bias is found, namely a strong negative correlation between the extra-reduction of two consecutive operations. As shown in this paper, the bias can be easily leveraged to recover which registers are written to (at line 5 of Algorithm 1 or at lines 4 and 5 of Algorithm 2) which eventually leads to retrieve the secret key. The advantages of this method are the following:

- messages are unknown; this captures general situations such as RSA with OAEP or PSS padding and RSA input blinding [11, Sect. 10];
- RSA parameters can be unknown; hence RSA-CRT is also vulnerable;

- all binary exponentiation algorithms are vulnerable, even the regular ones like Square and Multiply Always, Montgomery Ladder, etc.;
- our attack can also be applied to Elliptic Curve Cryptography (ECC).

From a mathematical viewpoint, we also provide a comprehensive framework for studying the joint probabilities of extra-reductions in a sequence of multiplies and squares.

Related Works. The "horizontal/vertical" side-channel attacks against blinded exponentiation described in [6,10,24] also use the dependency between the input/output of operands in square and multiply algorithms. Such attacks exploit the *vertical* amplitude of the signal during the time duration. Our work is thus complementary to these ideas since it considers a novel *horizontal* exploitable bias.

Outline. The rest of the paper is organized as follows[1]. Section 2 recalls known biases induced by extra-reductions in modular multiplication algorithms such as the Montgomery modular multiplication. Our contribution starts at Sect. 3, where the theoretical rationale for the strong negative correlation between extra-reductions of two chained operations is presented. Section 4 shows how this bias can be turned into a key recovery attack. Experimental validations for synthetic and practical traces are in Sect. 5. Section 6 concludes.

2 State of the Art of Extra-Reductions Probabilities

This section reviews known results about extra-reductions and their probability distributions. The results can be adapted easily to Barrett reduction or multiplication followed by reduction using the extended Euclid algorithm.

2.1 Montgomery Modular Multiplication: Definitions and Notations

Given two integers a and b, the classical modular multiplication $a \times b \bmod p$ computes the multiplication $a \times b$ followed by the modular reduction by p. Montgomery Modular Multiplication (MMM) transforms a and b into special representations known as their Montgomery forms.

Definition 1 (Montgomery Transformation [14]). *For any prime modulus p, the Montgomery form of $a \in \mathbb{F}_p$ is $\phi(a) = a \times R \bmod p$ for some constant R greater than and co-prime with p.*

In order to ease the computation, R is usually chosen as the smallest power of two greater than p, that is $R = 2^{\lceil \log_2(p) \rceil}$. Using the Montgomery form of integers, modular multiplications used in modular exponentiation algorithms (recall Algorithms 1 and 2) can be carried out using the Montgomery Modular Multiplication (MMM):

---

[1] A complete version containing auxiliary information is available in [8].

Definition 2 Montgomery Modular Multiplication [14]). *Let $\phi(a)$ and $\phi(b)$ two elements of $\mathbb{F}_p$ in Montgomery form. The MMM of $\phi(a)$ and $\phi(b)$ is $\phi(a) \times \phi(b) \times R^{-1} \bmod p$.*

Algorithm 3 below shows that the MMM can be implemented in two steps: (i) compute $D = \phi(a) \times \phi(b)$, then (ii) reduce D using Montgomery reduction which returns $\phi(c)$. In Algorithm 3, the pair (R^{-1}, v) is such that $RR^{-1} - vp = 1$.

Algorithm 3. Montgomery Reduction (Algorithm 14.32 of [13])

Input: $D = \phi(a) \times \phi(b)$
Output: $\phi(c) = \phi(a) \times \phi(b) \times R^{-1} \bmod p$
1: $m \leftarrow (D \bmod R) \times v \bmod R$
2: $U \leftarrow (D + m \times p) \div R$ ▷ Invariant: $0 \leq U < 2p$
3: **if** $U \geq p$ **then**
4:     $C \leftarrow U - p$ ▷ Extra-reduction
5: **else**
6:     $C \leftarrow U$
7: **end if**
8: **return** C

Definition 3 (Extra-Reduction). *In Algorithm 3, when the intermediate value U is greater than p, a subtraction named eXtra-reduction occurs so as to have a result C of the Montgomery multiplication between 0 and $p - 1$. We set $X = 1$ in the presence of the eXtra-reduction, and $X = 0$ in its absence.*

Most software implementations of modular arithmetic for large numbers (such as OpenSSL and mbedTLS) use the MMM, where there is a final extra-reduction. In mbedTLS, this extra-reduction is compensated. However, as shown below in Sect. 5.2, an attacker is still able in practice to detect using some side-channel which branch has been used (either line 4 or 6 of Algorithm 3).

2.2 A Bias to Differentiate a Multiply from a Square

Proposition 1 (Probability of Extra-Reduction in a Multiply and a Square Operation [16, **Lemma 1]).** *Assuming uniform distribution of operands, the probabilities of an extra-reduction in a multiply X_{M_i} and in a square X_{S_i} at iteration i are*

$$\mathbb{P}(X_{M_i} = 1) = \frac{p}{4R} \qquad and \qquad \mathbb{P}(X_{S_i} = 1) = \frac{p}{3R}. \qquad (1)$$

We note that extra-reductions are 33 % more likely when the operation is a square than when it is a multiply, irrespective of the ratio $\frac{p}{R} \in]\frac{1}{2}, 1[$. This allows one to break unprotected exponentiation algorithms.

3   A Bias to Test the Dependency of Operations

3.1   Principle of Correlated Extra-Reductions

In regular exponentiation algorithms, differentiating a multiply from a square does not allow SPA to distinguish the value of the exponent bits. Indeed, at every iteration i ($l - 1 \geq i > 0$ where i is decremented after each iteration), multiply and square operations are carried out unconditionally. However, the input value of each operation depends on the current exponent bit value k_i. Figure 1 illustrates the dependence or independence between the input/output values of multiplication M_i and the input value of the following square S_{i-1} as a function of the bit value k_i during the SMA algorithm (Algorithm 1). Intuitively, when the output of M_i is equal to the input of S_{i-1}, we can expect that the extra-reductions in both operation are strongly correlated.

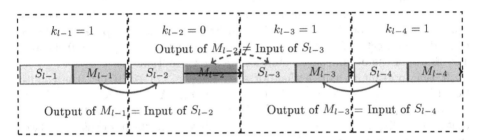

Fig. 1. Comparison between the output value of multiplication with the input of the following square in the Square-and-Multiply-Always exponentiation algorithm (Algorithm 1).

For the ML algorithm (Algorithm 2), the M_i and S_{i-1} operations depends directly on the two consecutive key bit values k_i and k_{i-1}. If the bit value k_{i-1} and its previous bit value k_i are different then the output of multiplication M_i and the input of square S_{i-1} are equal and yield strongly correlated extra-reductions; in the opposite case they yield uncorrelated extra-reductions.

Definition 4 (Guess Notation). *Let $\mathcal{G}_i$ be the "guess' Boolean random variable defined to be* **True** *(T) if the output of an operation at iteration i is equal to the input of the next operation at iteration $i - 1$, and* **False** *(F) otherwise.*

Also let X_{M_i} be a random variable corresponding to the eXtra-reduction of the MMM multiplication at iteration i and $X_{S_{i-1}}$ be a random variable corresponding to the eXtra-reduction during the MMM square at iteration $(i - 1)$.

Then $\mathbb{P}(X_{M_i}, X_{S_{i-1}} | \mathcal{G}_i = T)$ is their joint probability when the output value of the multiplication is equal to the input value of the square, and $\mathbb{P}(X_{M_i}, X_{S_{i-1}} | \mathcal{G}_i = F)$ is their joint probability when the output value of the multiplication is not equal to the input value of the square.

Table 1. Example of probabilities of eXtra-reduction X_{M_i} of multiply operation and $X_{S_{i-1}}$ of square operation knowing the Boolean value $\mathcal{G}_i$ for RSA-1024-p. The first line (correct guess) is applicable for both SMA and ML.

$(x_{M_i}, x_{S_{i-1}})$	(0,0)	(1,0)	(0,1)	(1,1)
$\mathbb{P}(x_{M_i}, x_{S_{i-1}} \mid \mathcal{G}_i = T)$	0.541575	0.191615	0.258276	0.008532
$\mathbb{P}(x_{M_i}, x_{S_{i-1}} \mid \mathcal{G}_i = F)$ for SMA	0.612756	0.120158	0.186803	0.080281
$\mathbb{P}(x_{M_i}, x_{S_{i-1}} \mid \mathcal{G}_i = F)$ for ML	0.586105	0.147246	0.213521	0.053128

The guess value $\mathcal{G}_i$ is linked to the key value depending on the regular exponentiation algorithm. For SMA and for a bit k_i, an attacker is able to estimate the probabilities $\hat{\mathbb{P}}(X_{M_i}, X_{S_{i-1}})$. This probability can be used to find the bit k_i as illustrated in Fig. 1 and explained in Sect. 4 below. For ML, $\mathcal{G}_i$ depends on two consecutive key bits as explained also in Sect. 4.

We have estimated the joint probabilities $\mathbb{P}(X_{M_i}, X_{S_{i-1}} \mid \mathcal{G}_i)$ using 1.000.000 random values for both SMA and ML algorithms and the example RSA-1024-p defined in [8, Sect. 2.2] for this modulus for which the ratio $p/R \simeq 0.800907$. The values of the obtained probabilities are shown in Table 1.

It is important to notice that for each $(x_{M_i}, x_{S_{i-1}}) \in \{0,1\}^2$, the conditional joint probabilities are distinct: $\mathbb{P}(X_{M_i} = x_{M_i}, X_{S_{i-1}} = x_{S_{i-1}} \mid \mathcal{G}_i = F) \neq \mathbb{P}(X_{M_i} = x_{M_i}, X_{S_{i-1}} = x_{S_{i-1}} \mid \mathcal{G}_i = T)$. Also for $\mathcal{G}_i = F$ in ML, it can be observed that $\mathbb{P}(X_{M_i}, X_{S_{i-1}} \mid \mathcal{G}_i) = \frac{p}{4R} \times \frac{p}{3R} = \mathbb{P}(X_{M_i}) \times \mathbb{P}(X_{S_{i-1}})$, which is consistent with the fact the two operations X_{M_i} and $X_{S_{i-1}}$ should be independent since they are completely unrelated.

It should be emphasized that the leakage identified in Table 1 is fairly large, since the Pearson correlations ρ of the two randoms variables are[2]:

$$\rho(X_{M_i}, X_{S_{i-1}} \mid \mathcal{G}_i = T) \approx -0.2535, \tag{2}$$
$$\rho(X_{M_i}, X_{S_{i-1}} \mid \mathcal{G}_i = F) \approx +0.1510 \text{ in SMA}, \tag{3}$$
$$\rho(X_{M_i}, X_{S_{i-1}} \mid \mathcal{G}_i = F) \approx -0.0017 \text{ in ML}. \tag{4}$$

To the best of our knowledge, such correlations have not been observed previously. A few observations are in order:

- when a square follows a multiply, and if there has been an extra-reduction in the multiplication, the result should be short, hence there is less chance for an extra-reduction to occur in the following square. This accounts for the negative correlation $\rho(X_{M_i}, X_{S_{i-1}} \mid \mathcal{G}_i = T)$;
- from Fig. 1 iteration $i = l - 2$ where $k_i = 0$, we can see that one input of the multiplication M_i equals the input of the following squaring S_{i-1}. Since a square and a multiplication share a common operand, provided it is sufficiently large, both operations are likely to have an extra-reduction at the same time, which accounts for the positive correlation $\rho(X_{M_i}, X_{S_{i-1}} \mid \mathcal{G}_i = F)$ for SMA;

---

2 $\rho(X_{M_i}, X_{S_{i-1}}) = \dfrac{Cov(X_{M_i}, X_{S_{i-1}})}{\sigma_{X_{M_i}} \sigma_{X_{S_{i-1}}}} = \dfrac{\mathbb{P}(X_{M_i}=1, X_{S_{i-1}}=1) - (\mathbb{P}(X_{M_i}=1) \times \mathbb{P}(X_{S_{i-1}}=1))}{\sqrt{\mathbb{P}(X_{M_i}=1)(1-\mathbb{P}(X_{M_i}=1))} \sqrt{\mathbb{P}(X_{S_{i-1}}=1)(1-\mathbb{P}(X_{S_{i-1}}=1))}}$.

– when a square and a multiply handle independent data, the extra-reductions are clearly also independent of each other, which explains the small value of $\rho(X_{M_i}, X_{S_{i-1}} | \mathcal{G}_i = F)$ for ML.

As explained next, when extra-reductions can be detected reliably, the data-flow can be analyzed accurately thereby defeating regular exponentiation protections.

3.2 Methodology to Analyze the Bias

In order to estimate the probability $\mathbb{P}(X_{M_i}, X_{S_{i-1}} | \mathcal{G}_i)$, we first determine the distribution of the output value after one MMM (following the method described by Sato et al. [15]) and then compute the joint probability for each case.

Let A, B be two independent random variables uniformly distributed in $[0, p[$ (represented in Montgomery form); let C be equal to the MMM product of A and B and U corresponds to the MMM product of A and B before eXtra-reduction (if any). Variables C and U coincide with that of Algorithm 3. As a matter of fact, an attacker cannot observe values, only extra-reductions which occur during Montgomery reduction (at line 4 of Algorithm 3). We use notations $\mathbb{P}$ for probabilities and f for probability density functions (p.d.f.'s).

Figure 2 shows histograms for C and U obtained from one million simulations; the binning consists of 100 bins of the interval $[0, 2p[$. It can be observed that

– the p.d.f. of C is uniform on $[0, p[$;
– the p.d.f. of U is a piecewise continuous function composed of a strictly increasing part, a constant part and a strictly decreasing part;
– the two conditional p.d.f.'s of C knowing $X_{M_i} \in \{0, 1\}$ (resp. $X_{S_i} \in \{0, 1\}$) are not uniform;
– for $c \in [0, p[$, one has $f(C = c) = f(U = c) + f(U = c + p)$ by definition of U;
– the maximum value of U is $p + p^2/R$, which is strictly smaller than $2p$.

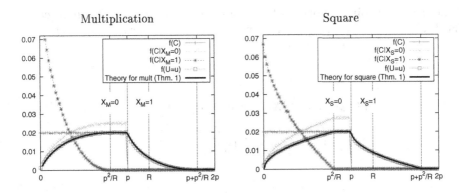

Fig. 2. Distribution of the output value of Montgomery multiplication (*left*) and square (*right*) for RSA-1024-p.

Recall that we use the Montgomery reduction described in Algorithm 3, where the reduction modulo p is carried out after every multiplication. This is also the case in [16,17], but *not* in [20,21] where the multiplicands lie in $[0, R[$. To complement those works, we now derive a closed-form expression of the output distribution of the Montgomery multiplication product and square (not found in [16,17]).

3.3 Mathematical Derivations

This subsection provides a mathematical justification of the biases observed in Table 1. In particular, it shows that such biases hold for all values of p and $R = 2^{\lceil \log_2(p) \rceil}$. Our closed-form expressions are derived as limits in distribution when $p \to +\infty$ that we shall write as approximations.

Theorem 1 (P.d.f. of MMM Before Extra-Reduction[3]). *Asymptotically when modulus p is large, the result of a Montgomery multiplication before the final extra-reduction (at line 2 of Algorithm 3) have piecewise p.d.f. given by*

$$
f_U(u) = \begin{cases}
\frac{Ru}{p^3}\left(1 - \ln(\frac{Ru}{p^2})\right) & \text{if } 0 \le u \le \frac{p^2}{R}; \\
\frac{1}{p} & \text{if } \frac{p^2}{R} \le u \le p; \\
\frac{1}{p} - \frac{R(u-p)}{p^3}\left(1 - \ln(\frac{R(u-p)}{p^2})\right) & \text{if } p \le u \le p + \frac{p^2}{R}; \\
0 & \text{otherwise.}
\end{cases}
\tag{5}
$$

The corresponding p.d.f. for the square is also in four pieces with the same intervals for u, and differs only from the multiplication in that it is equal to $\sqrt{Ru}/p^2$ when $0 \le u \le \frac{p^2}{R}$, and $1/p - \sqrt{R(u-p)}/p^2$ when $p \le u \le p + \frac{p^2}{R}$.

The theoretical values of Theorem 1 nicely superimpose with experimentally estimated p.d.f.'s as shown in Fig. 2.

Theorem 2 (Joint Probability of Extra-Reduction in Multiplication Followed by a Square [see Footnote 3]). *The following joint probabilities do not depend on the iteration index i, where $l - 1 \ge i > 0$.*
When $\mathcal{G}_i = T$:

$\mathbb{P}(X_{M_i}, X_{S_{i-1}})$	$X_{S_{i-1}} = 0$	$X_{S_{i-1}} = 1$
$X_{M_i} = 0$	$1 - \frac{7}{12}\frac{p}{R} + \frac{1}{48}\left(\frac{p}{R}\right)^4$	$\frac{p}{3R} - \frac{1}{48}\left(\frac{p}{R}\right)^4$
$X_{M_i} = 1$	$\frac{p}{4R} - \frac{1}{48}\left(\frac{p}{R}\right)^4$	$\frac{1}{48}\left(\frac{p}{R}\right)^4$

---

[3] Proof of this theorem is given in [8].

When $\mathcal{G}_i = F$ *in SMA:*

$\mathbb{P}(X_{M_i}, X_{S_{i-1}})$	$X_{S_{i-1}} = 0$	$X_{S_{i-1}} = 1$
$X_{M_i} = 0$	$1 - \frac{7}{12}\frac{p}{R} + \frac{1}{8}\left(\frac{p}{R}\right)^2$	$\frac{p}{3R} - \frac{1}{8}\left(\frac{p}{R}\right)^2$
$X_{M_i} = 1$	$\frac{p}{4R} - \frac{1}{8}\left(\frac{p}{R}\right)^2$	$\frac{1}{8}\left(\frac{p}{R}\right)^2$

When $\mathcal{G}_i = F$ *in ML:*

$\mathbb{P}(X_{M_i}, X_{S_{i-1}})$	$X_{S_{i-1}} = 0$	$X_{S_{i-1}} = 1$
$X_{M_i} = 0$	$1 - \frac{7}{12}\frac{p}{R} + \frac{1}{12}\left(\frac{p}{R}\right)^2$	$\frac{p}{3R} - \frac{1}{12}\left(\frac{p}{R}\right)^2$
$X_{M_i} = 1$	$\frac{p}{4R} - \frac{1}{12}\left(\frac{p}{R}\right)^2$	$\frac{1}{12}\left(\frac{p}{R}\right)^2$

It can be easily checked that Theorem 2 accurately matches experimental probability estimations given in Table 1.

Corollary 1. *The corresponding correlation coefficients are*

$$\rho(X_{M_i}, X_{S_{i-1}} | \mathcal{G}_i = T) = \frac{\frac{p^4}{48R^4} - \frac{p^2}{12R^2}}{\sqrt{\frac{p}{4R}\left(1 - \frac{p}{4R}\right)\frac{p}{3R}\left(1 - \frac{p}{3R}\right)}},$$

$$\rho(X_{M_i}, X_{S_{i-1}} | \mathcal{G}_i = F) = \frac{\frac{p^2}{24R^2}}{\sqrt{\frac{p}{4R}\left(1 - \frac{p}{4R}\right)\frac{p}{3R}\left(1 - \frac{p}{3R}\right)}} \text{ in SMA,}$$

$$\rho(X_{M_i}, X_{S_{i-1}} | \mathcal{G}_i = F) = 0 \text{ in ML.}$$

Proof. Apply Pearson's correlation definition on the results of Theorem 2.   □

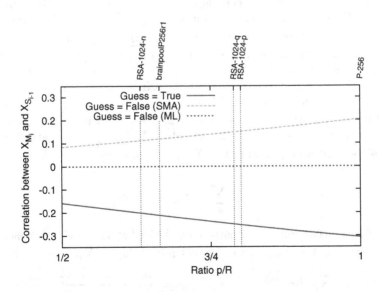

Fig. 3. Pearson's correlation between X_{M_i} and $X_{S_{i-1}}$.

When the guess is correct, $\rho(X_{M_i}, X_{S_{i-1}} | \mathcal{G}_i = T)$ is negative and increasingly negative as p/R increases, where

$$-\tfrac{3}{16}\sqrt{\tfrac{5}{7}} \approx -0.158 \quad \leq \quad \rho(X_{M_i}, X_{S_{i-1}} | \mathcal{G}_i = T) \quad \leq \quad -\tfrac{3}{4\sqrt{6}} \approx -0.306.$$

When the guess is incorrect, either the correlation is null (in the case of ML), or it is positive and increasing with p/R, where for $1/2 \leq p/R \leq 1$,

$$\tfrac{1}{2\sqrt{5\times 7}} \approx 0.085 \quad \leq \quad \rho(X_{M_i}, X_{S_{i-1}} | \mathcal{G}_i = F) \quad \leq \quad \tfrac{1}{2\sqrt{6}} \approx 0.204.$$

The variations of the correlation coefficients between X_{M_i} and $X_{S_{i-1}}$ in the three scenarios of Corollary 1 are plotted in Fig. 3.

Figure 3 shows that the correlation difference between guesses True/False is greater for the SMA algorithm than for the ML algorithm. Thus our attack on SMA should outperform that on ML. Also notice that the larger the ratio p/R, the larger the correlation difference; hence, we expect P-256 to be easier to break than brainpoolP256r1 with our attack.

4   Exploiting the Bias Using Our Attack

The difference between the two Pearson correlations according to the guess value $\mathcal{G}_i$ (Corollary 1) allows us to test whether some data produced by an operation is fed into the next operation. The bit value k_i can be estimated using the Pearson correlation ρ as a distinguisher, a threshold $\mathcal{T}$ depending of the knowledge of the attacker and a decision function denoted by $\mathcal{F}_{ALG}$ which depends of the regular exponentiation algorithm and the used distinguisher.

Attacker's Method. An attacker calls Q times the cryptographic operation with a static key k and measures the corresponding side-channel trace. For each trace $q \in \{1, \ldots, Q\}$, $(l-1)$ pairs of extra-reductions $(x^q_{M_i}, x^q_{S_{i-1}})_{l-1 \geq i > 0}$ are captured. The complete acquisition campaign is denoted $(\underline{x}_{M_i}, \underline{x}_{S_{i-1}})$, and is a matrix of size $Q \times (l-1)$ pairs of bits. Notice that neither the input nor the output of the cryptographic algorithm is required. For all $i \in \{l-1, \ldots, 1\}$ and $q \in \{1, \ldots, Q\}$, $x^q_{M_i}$ is equal to 1 (resp. 0) if the eXtra-reduction is present (resp. missing) during the multiplication M_i for query q. Similarly, $x^q_{S_{i-1}}$ is equal to 1 (resp. 0) if the eXtra-reduction is present (resp. missing) during the square S_{i-1} for query q. For each pair of random variable $(X_{M_i}, X_{S_{i-1}})$, the attacker first computes the estimated probability $\hat{\mathbb{P}}(X_{M_i}, X_{S_{i-1}})$, using:

$$\hat{\mathbb{P}}(X_{M_i}, X_{S_{i-1}}) = \frac{1}{Q}\sum_{q=1}^{Q} \mathbb{1}_{(X_{M_i}=x^q_{M_i}) \wedge (X_{S_{i-1}}=x^q_{S_{i-1}})}. \tag{6}$$

The attacker then computes the Pearson correlation[4] $\hat{\rho}(X_{M_i}, X_{S_{i-1}})$ for each pair $(x_{M_i}, x_{S_{i-1}}) \in \{0,1\}^2$ using the estimated probability $\hat{\mathbb{P}}(X_{M_i}, X_{S_{i-1}})$. Finally,

---

[4] $\hat{\rho}(X_{M_i}, X_{S_{i-1}}) = \dfrac{\hat{Cov}(X_{M_i}, X_{S_{i-1}})}{\hat{\sigma}_{X_{M_i}} \hat{\sigma}_{X_{S_{i-1}}}} = \dfrac{\hat{\mathbb{P}}(X_{M_i}=1, X_{S_{i-1}}=1) - (\hat{\mathbb{P}}(X_{M_i}=1) \times \hat{\mathbb{P}}(X_{S_{i-1}}=1))}{\sqrt{\hat{\mathbb{P}}(X_{M_i}=1)(1-\hat{\mathbb{P}}(X_{M_i}=1))}\sqrt{\hat{\mathbb{P}}(X_{S_{i-1}}=1)(1-\hat{\mathbb{P}}(X_{S_{i-1}}=1))}}.$

she estimates the exponent bit k_i with her knowledge corresponding to threshold $\mathcal{T}$ and decision function $\mathcal{F}_{\mathcal{ALG}}$.

Attacker's Knowledge. In public key cryptography, the attacker wants to recover the private exponent in RSA or the private scalar in ECC. In our attacks, we assume these secret values are static, as for instance in RSA-CRT decryption or static Diffie-Hellman key agreement protocol.

- In RSA-SFM and ECC, the attacker knows the parameters p and R defined in Sect. 2.1. In RSA-SFM, p is equal to the public modulus n_{RSA}. In ECC, p equals the characteristic of the finite field over which the elliptic curve is defined. The attacker can compute the Pearson correlations $\rho(X_{M_i}, X_{S_{i-1}}|\mathcal{G}_i = T)$ and $\rho(X_{M_i}, X_{S_{i-1}}|\mathcal{G}_i = F)$ using corollary 1. The threshold for the successful attack is defined by:

$$\mathcal{T} = \frac{\rho(X_{M_i}, X_{S_{i-1}}|\mathcal{G}_i = T) + \rho(X_{M_i}, X_{S_{i-1}}|\mathcal{G}_i = F)}{2}. \tag{7}$$

- In RSA-CRT, the attacker does not know the parameters p and R defined in Sect. 2.1, because the prime factors p_{RSA} and q_{RSA} are secret parameters. Hence the determination of the probabilities by theory or simulation are impossible. However, using the Q measurements $(x_{M_i}, x_{S_{i-1}})$, the attacker is able to determine the mean estimated probability $\hat{\mathbb{E}}_i \hat{\mathbb{P}}(X_{M_i}, X_{S_{i-1}})$ by[5]:

$$\hat{\mathbb{E}}_i \hat{\mathbb{P}}(X_{M_i}, X_{S_{i-1}}) = \frac{\sum_{i=1}^{l-1} \hat{\mathbb{P}}(X_{M_i}, X_{S_{i-1}})}{l-1}. \tag{8}$$

The attacker then computes the mean estimated Pearson correlations using the mean estimated probability (8), and the threshold for the successful attack is defined by:

$$\mathcal{T} = \frac{\hat{\mathbb{E}}_i \hat{\mathbb{P}}(X_{M_i} = 1, X_{S_{i-1}} = 1) - (\hat{\mathbb{E}}_i \hat{\mathbb{P}}(X_{M_i} = 1) \times \hat{\mathbb{E}}_i \hat{\mathbb{P}}(X_{S_{i-1}} = 1))}{\sqrt{\hat{\mathbb{E}}_i \hat{\mathbb{P}}(X_{M_i} = 1)\hat{\mathbb{E}}_i \hat{\mathbb{P}}(X_{M_i} = 0)} \sqrt{\hat{\mathbb{E}}_i \hat{\mathbb{P}}(X_{S_{i-1}} = 1)\hat{\mathbb{E}}_i \hat{\mathbb{P}}(X_{S_{i-1}} = 0)}}. \tag{9}$$

In fact, the threshold value $\mathcal{T}$ computed in (7) or (9) does not depend on i. The indication of index i was kept as a reminder that the multiplication M_i is done in the iteration which precedes that of the square S_{i-1}.

Decision Function. The decision function depending of the regular algorithm and the used distinguisher ρ is denoted as $\mathcal{F}_{\mathcal{ALG}}$. We detail this function for the SMA (Algorithm 1) and ML (Algorithm 2) algorithms.

---

[5] Notice that in some cases, e.g. if the key bits happen not to be balanced, $\hat{\mathbb{E}}_i \hat{\mathbb{P}}(X_{M_i}, X_{S_{i-1}})$ can be estimated in a less biased way using $\max_i\{\hat{\mathbb{P}}(X_{M_i}, X_{S_{i-1}})\} - \min_i\{\hat{\mathbb{P}}(X_{M_i}, X_{S_{i-1}})\}$.

- In the SMA algorithm, the scalar bit k_i decides whether the output of M_i is the input of S_{i-1} or not (see Fig. 1). If the bit value k_i equals 1, then the square S_{i-1} depends on M_i ($\mathcal{G}_i = T$), otherwise the output value of M_i is different from the input value of S_{i-1} ($\mathcal{G}_i = F$). Using the Sect. 3, we see that $\rho(X_{M_i}, X_{S_{i-1}}|\mathcal{G}_i = T) < \rho(X_{M_i}, X_{S_{i-1}}|\mathcal{G}_i = F)$, so the decision function $\mathcal{F}_{SMA}$ is defined by:

$$\hat{k}_i = \mathcal{F}_{SMA}(\rho, \mathcal{T}) = \begin{cases} 0 & \text{if } \hat{\rho}(X_{M_i}, X_{S_{i-1}}) \geq \mathcal{T}, \\ 1 & \text{otherwise.} \end{cases} \qquad (10)$$

- For the Montgomery Ladder (ML) algorithm, the M_i and S_{i-1} operations do not depend directly on the key bit value k_i. The dependence comes from the bit value k_{i-1} and the previous bit value k_i. If the two bits value k_{i-1} and k_i are different then the output of multiplication M_i and the input of square S_{i-1} are equal ($\mathcal{G}_i = T$), otherwise these output/input are different ($\mathcal{G}_i = F$). Using Sect. 3, we see that $\rho(X_{M_i}, X_{S_{i-1}}|\mathcal{G}_i = T) < \rho(X_{M_i}, X_{S_{i-1}}|\mathcal{G}_i = F)$, so the decision function $\mathcal{F}_{ML}$ using the previously estimated bit $\hat{k}_{i-1}$ is defined for each i ($l - 1 > i \geq 1$) by:

$$\hat{k}_i = \mathcal{F}_{ML}(\hat{k}_{i-1}, \rho, \mathcal{T}) = \begin{cases} \hat{k}_{i-1} & \text{if } \hat{\rho}(X_{M_i}, X_{S_{i-1}}) \geq \mathcal{T}, \\ \neg\hat{k}_{i-1} & \text{otherwise.} \end{cases} \qquad (11)$$

Regarding the second most significant bit k_{l-1} of the exponent, either both values $k_{l-1} = 0$ and $k_{l-1} = 1$ are tested to recover the full secret key, or our attack can be applied between the first square FS (defined at line 2 of Algorithm 2) and the square S_{l-1} (line 5 of Algorithm 2).

Algorithm 4. ρ-attack

Input: $(x_{M_i}, x_{S_{i-1}})$, a set of Q pairs of $(l - 1)$ bits

Output: An estimation $\hat{k} \in \{0, 1\}^{l-1}$ of the secret exponent

1: **for** $i = l - 1$ **downto** 1 **do**
2:     $\hat{\mathbb{P}}(X_{M_i}, X_{S_{i-1}}) \leftarrow 0$
3:     **for** $q = 1$ **to** Q **do**
4:         $\hat{\mathbb{P}}(X_{M_i} = x_{M_i}^q, X_{S_{i-1}} = x_{S_{i-1}}^q) \leftarrow \hat{\mathbb{P}}(X_{M_i} = x_{M_i}^q, X_{S_{i-1}} = x_{S_{i-1}}^q) + 1$
5:     **end for**
6:     $\hat{\mathbb{P}}(X_{M_i}, X_{S_{i-1}}) \leftarrow \hat{\mathbb{P}}(X_{M_i}, X_{S_{i-1}}) / Q$ ▷ Normalization
7:     Compute $\hat{\rho}(X_{M_i}, X_{S_{i-1}})$ using $\hat{\mathbb{P}}(X_{M_i}, X_{S_{i-1}})$
8: **end for**
9: Compute $\mathcal{T}$ depending on the attacker's knowledge
10: **for** $i = l - 1$ **downto** 1 **do**
11:     $\hat{k}_i \leftarrow \mathcal{F}_{ALG}(\hat{\rho}(X_{M_i}, X_{S_{i-1}}), \mathcal{T})$ ▷ Threshold
12: **end for**
13: **return** $\hat{k}$

Summary of the Attack. To estimate the exponent k by $\hat{k}$, we define two attacks:

- The attack named "ρ-attack-Hard", knowing the values of $\mathbb{P}(X_{M_i}, X_{S_{i-1}} | \mathcal{G}_i = T)$ and $\mathbb{P}(X_{M_i}, X_{S_{i-1}} | \mathcal{G}_i = F)$, using the threshold T computed by (7).
- The attack named "ρ-attack-Soft", when the theoretical value $\mathbb{P}(X_{M_i}, X_{S_{i-1}} | \mathcal{G}_i)$ is unknown. It uses the estimated probability $\hat{\mathbb{P}}(X_{M_i}, X_{S_{i-1}})$ to compute the threshold T by (9).

Algorithm 4 describes the attack to recover a full key. Lines 1-8 correspond to the computation of the estimated probabilities for each bit k_i defined by (6). Line 9 is the computation of the threshold: if the attack is ρ-attack-Hard the attacker uses (7), otherwise the attack is ρ-attack-Soft and she uses (9). The lines 10-12 compute the full estimated key using the decision function $\mathcal{F}_{ALG}$, defined by the Eqs. (10) or (11).

5 Experimental Results

In the first part of this section, we detail a simulated attack which exploits the bias (explained in Corollary 1) to determine the number of queries necessary for the success of the attack. Then, we detail the side-channel part (*local timing analysis* using power consumption and electromagnetic analysis to distinguish *functional vs dummy subtractions*) in order to detect whether an eXtra-reduction is performed ($X = 1$) or not ($X = 0$) during the Montgomery reduction (Algorithm 3).

5.1 Simulations

Let RSA-1024-p defined at [8, Sect. 2.2] the modulus p used in the SMA algorithm (Algorithm 1). We generated one thousand random queries and saved for all MMM the information whether an extra-reduction is done or not. The length of static key k is 512 bits. As detailed in the ρ-attack (Algorithm 4) we computed the estimated probabilities $\hat{\mathbb{P}}(X_{M_i}, X_{S_{i-1}})$ and the estimated Pearson correlation $\hat{\rho}(X_{M_i}, X_{S_{i-1}})$ to retrieve each k_i. The estimated threshold T computed by (9) in our simulation is equal to -0.06076, which is an excellent approximation of the theoretical threshold (7). To retrieve each bit if the exponent, we used the decision function $\mathcal{F}_{SMA}$ described for ρ-attack in SMA by (10).

Figure 4 shows the estimated Pearson correlation values $\hat{\rho}(X_{M_i}, X_{S_{i-1}})$ for the first iterations. It can be easily seen that the estimated key value by this sequence corresponds to $0 \times 1000111110101110111010011\ldots = 0 \times 11f5dd3\ldots$ Our ρ-attack retrieves the 511 bits of the exponent using 1000 randoms queries with success rate 100%.

Success Rate Curves. We implemented ρ-attack-Hard and ρ-attack-Soft in the ideal case, i.e., without noise. The success rate to recover one bit of the exponent is represented in Fig. 5, for both SMA and ML cases. Interestingly,

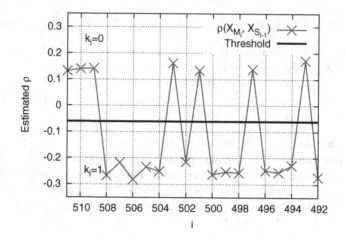

Fig. 4. Estimated Pearson correlations using 1000 randoms queries for RSA-1024-p for the first 20 iterations.

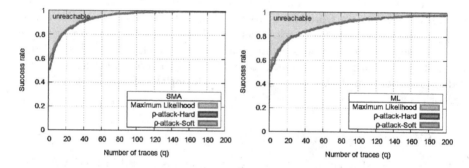

Fig. 5. Evolution of the success rate for the ρ-attack-Soft and the ρ-attack-Hard as a function of the number Q of queries (upper bound is the maximum likelihood), for RSA-1024-p.

ρ-attack-Hard and ρ-attack-Soft yield the same success rate, which happens to be (very close to) the optimal value. This optimal value is that obtained with the maximum likelihood distinguisher derived in [8].

The reason for the hard and soft attacks to have similar success probability is that the online estimation of the threshold is very good. Indeed, in the example of Fig. 5, the threshold T (Eq. (9)) is estimated based on $512Q$ traces, which is huge (one needs only to estimate 4 probabilities to get the estimation of T). So, in the rest of this section, we make no difference between the hard and soft versions of the attacks from a success rate point of view.

The ρ-attacks are very close to the Maximum Likelihood attack for a similar reason. Estimating the difference between two random variables of very little dimensionality (recall that $(X_{M_i}, X_{S_{i-1}})$ lives in $\{0,1\}^2$) can be done almost

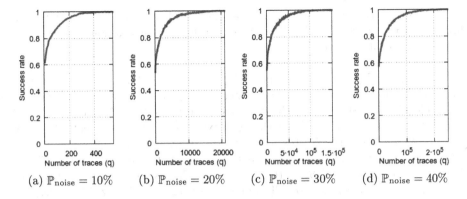

Fig. 6. Evolution of the success rate for the ρ-attack in function of queries Q using $p = \mathtt{RSA-1024-p}$ for four increasing noise values.

equivalently in the proportional scale [23] (Pearson correlation) as in the context of information theoretic attacks (maximum likelihood attack) [8].

We may also notice that as the *distinguisher margin* [22] is larger for SMA than for ML (recall Fig. 3), the former attack requires less traces to reach a given success rate.

In practical cases, detecting an extra-reduction using only one acquisition can lead to errors. The probability to have an error is denoted by $\mathbb{P}_{\mathrm{noise}}$. We show in Fig. 6 that the attack continues to be successful (albeit with more traces) over a large range of $\mathbb{P}_{\mathrm{noise}}$ values. Evidently when $\mathbb{P}_{\mathrm{noise}} = 50\,\%$ the attack becomes infeasible.

5.2   Experimental Detection of Extra-Reductions

Two Montgomery reduction implementations will be analyzed in this section. We raise the following questions.

1. How to exploit the *local timing* to distinguish the eXtra-reduction using power consumption measurements, on OpenSSL v1.0.1k-3 ([6])?
2. How to exploit the difference between a *real* and a *dummy* final subtraction using electromagnetic (EM) emanations, on mbedTLS v 2.2.0 ([7])?

(1a) Experiment Setup in Power. The target is a dual core LPC43S37 micro-controller fabricated in CMOS 90 nm Ultra Low Leakage process soldered on an LPCXpresso4337 board, and running at its maximum frequency (208 MHz). The side-channel traces where obtained measuring the instantaneous power consumption with a PICOSCOPE 6402C featuring 256 MB of memory, 500 MHz bandwidth and 5 GS/s sampling rate. We executed the private function of RSA

---

[6] Latest stable version at the time of submission.
[7] Latest version at the time of submission.

in OpenSSL with the private primes parameters defined by RSA-1024-p and
RSA-1024-q in [8, Sect. 2.2]. The private modular exponentiation is RSA-CRT
with a regular algorithm.

(1b) OpenSSL Experiment. In OpenSSL (see Listing 1.1 in Appendix A), the
final subtraction is made when U is greater than p like described in Algorithm 3.
A simple power analysis using the delay (referred to as "SPA-Timing") between
two MMM operations found whether the extra-reduction is present $(X = 1)$
or not $(X = 0)$. On the Cortex M4 core, the delay between the M_i and S_{i-1}
when $X_{M_i} = 1$ is $41.4952\,\mu s$, whereas the delay when $X_{M_i} = 0$ is $41.1875\,\mu s$.
For the square operation S_{i-1}, the delay is $41.5637\,\mu s$ when $X_{S_{i-1}} = 1$ and it
is $41.2471\,\mu s$ when $X_{S_{i-1}} = 0$. All in one, the observable timing differences are
respectively $308\,ns$ and $317\,ns$. When OpenSSL is offloaded on the Cortex M0
core of the LPC43S37, the timing difference is respectively $399\,ns$ and $411\,ns$.
The success rate of this detection attack is $100\,\%$, hence $\mathbb{P}_{noise} = 0$.

(2a) Experiment Setup in EM. The target device is an STM32F4 microcontroller, which contains an ARM Cortex-M4 processor running at its maximum
frequency (168 MHz). For the acquisition, we used a Tektronix oscilloscope and
a Langer near field probe. The sampling frequency is $1\,GSa/s$ with $50\,MHz$ hardware input low-pass filter enabled. The position of the probe was determined to
maximize the signal related to the activity of the hardware 32×32 processor.
We executed the private function of RSA in mbedTLS, with the private primes
parameters defined by RSA-1024-p and RSA-1024-q in [8, Sect. 2.2]. The private
modular exponentiation is RSA-CRT with a regular algorithm.

(2b) mbedTLS Experiment. In order to achieve constant-time MMM, mbedTLS
library implements a countermeasure using a dummy subtraction (see Listing 1.2
in Appendix A). In order to test the efficiency of the countermeasure, the duration
of the real and dummy subtraction were compared as shown in Fig. 7. The dura-
tions are the same. Therefore, the SPA-Timing attack is not practical anymore.

In a view to differentiate the two patterns, we use a horizontal side-channel
analysis [3], namely Pearson correlation (max-corr) [4] or the sum of the absolute
differences (min-abs-diff). We build two reference patterns of the real subtraction $RP(X = 1)$ and dummy subtraction $RP(X = 0)$, and compare these
patterns with one acquisition.

For this experiment, we use 500 acquisitions to build template $RP(X = 1)$
and again 500 acquisitions to make $RP(X = 0)$. The detection attack using one
acquisition $\mathcal{A}_x$ where the extra-reduction $X = x$ is considered successful:

– when $\rho(\mathcal{A}_x, RP(X = x)) > \rho(\mathcal{A}_x, RP(X = \neg x))$ for max-corr, and
– when $\mathbb{E}(|\mathcal{A}_x - RP(X = x)|) < \mathbb{E}(|\mathcal{A}_x - RP(X = x)|)$ for min-abs-diff.

The success rate of the extra-reduction detection using 30000 acquisitions is
$82.50\,\%$ for max-corr and $83.47\,\%$ for min-abs-diff, hence $\mathbb{P}_{noise} < 20\,\%$.

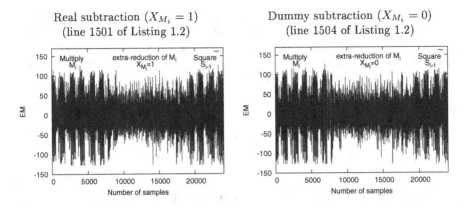

Fig. 7. Electromagnetic acquisition focus on one real subtraction (*left*) and pattern of one dummy subtraction (*right*) between two consecutive MMM operations.

5.3   Conclusions on Experiments

By combining the detection of extra-reductions using side-channel analysis (Sect. 5.2) and the theoretical attack to decide whether or not there is a dependency between various MMMs (Sect. 4), we deduce the number of queries Q needed to recover the secret exponent k. Table 2 summaries the results.

Table 2. Summary of the number of queries (see Fig. 6(b)) to retrieve all key bits of a secret exponent, as a function of side-channel detection method and regular exponentiation algorithm.

Type of attack side-channel for detection	SPA-Timing	max-corr	min-abs-diff
Detection probability for one query $= 1 - \mathbb{P}_{noise}$	100 %	82.50 %	83.47 %
Number of queries (SMA)	≈ 200	≈ 10000	≈ 10000
Number of queries (ML)	≈ 400	≈ 20000	≈ 20000

6   Conclusion

This paper has presented a new theoretical and practical attack against asymmetrical computation with regular exponentiation using extra-reductions as a side-channel. The working factor is the existence of a strong bias between the extra-reductions during the Montgomery Modular Multiplication of two consecutive operations. This new bias can be exploited in each regular binary algorithm, because each iteration consists in a square and a multiply whose inputs depend on the outputs of an operation from the previous iteration.

The new attacks have been detailed on RSA but are also applicable to ECC with appropriate customizations for various ECC implementations. As an example [5] for addition `madd-2004-hmv`, the Z-coordinate in output of addition is computed by a multiplication $Z3 = Z1 \times T1$ and for doubling `dbl-2007-bl`, the Z-coordinate in input of doubling is a square $ZZ = Z1 \times Z1$.

Acknowledgements. The authors would like to thank the anonymous reviewers for their useful comments that improved the quality of the paper. The first author would also like to thank François Dassance, Jean-Christophe Courrège and her colleagues for the suggestion of the main idea of this paper and their valuable insights.

A   Analysis of Extra-Reduction in OpenSSL and MbedTLS Source Codes

The extra-reduction is explicit in the source code of OpenSSL, as shown in Listing 1.1.

Listing 1.1. Extra-reduction in OpenSSL code. File `crypto/bn/bn_mont.c`

```
309  if (BN_ucmp( ret , &(mont->N)) >= 0)
310  {
311      if (!BN_usub( ret , ret ,&(mont->N))) goto err;
312  }
```

The big-number library of mbedTLS implements a protection against timing attacks. A subtraction is also carried out: it is either functional or dummy, as shown in Listing 1.2.

Listing 1.2. Extra-reduction in mbedTLS code. File `library/bignum.c`, function `mpi_montmul`

```
1500  if( mpi_cmp_abs( A, N ) >= 0 )
1501      mpi_sub_hlp( n, N->p, A->p );
1502  else
1503      /* prevent timing attacks */
1504      mpi_sub_hlp( n, A->p, T->p );
```

References

1. Acıiçmez, O., Schindler, W.: A vulnerability in RSA implementations due to instruction cache analysis and its demonstration on openSSL. In: Malkin, T. (ed.) CT-RSA 2008. LNCS, vol. 4964, pp. 256–273. Springer, Heidelberg (2008)
2. Acıiçmez, O., Schindler, W., Koç, Ç.K.: Improving Brumley and Boneh timing attack on unprotected SSL implementations. In: Atluri, V., Meadows, C., Juels, A. (eds.) CCS 2005, pp. 139–146. ACM, New York (2005)
3. Bauer, A., Jaulmes, É., Prouff, E., Reinhard, J.-R., Wild, J.: Horizontal collision correlation attack on elliptic curves - extended version. Cryptogr. Commun. **7**(1), 91–119 (2015)
4. Belgarric, P., Bhasin, S., Bruneau, N., Danger, J.-L., Debande, N., Guilley, S., Heuser, A., Najm, Z., Rioul, O.: Time-frequency analysis for second-order attacks. In: Francillon, A., Rohatgi, P. (eds.) CARDIS 2013. LNCS, vol. 8419, pp. 108–122. Springer, Heidelberg (2014)
5. Bernstein, D.J., Lange, T.: Explicit formulas database. http://www.hyperelliptic.org/EFD/
6. Clavier, C., Feix, B., Gagnerot, G., Roussellet, M., Verneuil, V.: Horizontal correlation analysis on exponentiation. In: Soriano, M., Qing, S., López, J. (eds.) ICICS 2010. LNCS, vol. 6476, pp. 46–61. Springer, Heidelberg (2010)
7. Courrège, J.-C., Feix, B., Roussellet, M.: Simple power analysis on exponentiation revisited. In: Gollmann, D., Lanet, J.-L., Iguchi-Cartigny, J. (eds.) CARDIS 2010. LNCS, vol. 6035, pp. 65–79. Springer, Heidelberg (2010)
8. Dugardin, M., Guilley, S., Danger, J.-L., Najm, Z., Rioul, O.: Correlated extra-reductions defeat blinded regular exponentiation - extended version. Cryptology ePrint Archive, Report 2016/597 (2016). http://eprint.iacr.org/2016/597
9. Fouque, P.-A., Réal, D., Valette, F., Drissi, M.: The carry leakage on the randomized exponent countermeasure. In: Oswald, E., Rohatgi, P. (eds.) CHES 2008. LNCS, vol. 5154, pp. 198–213. Springer, Heidelberg (2008)
10. Hanley, N., Kim, H.S., Tunstall, M.: Exploiting collisions in addition chain-based exponentiation algorithms using a single trace. In: Nyberg, K. (ed.) CT-RSA 2015. LNCS, vol. 9048, pp. 429–446. Springer, Heidelberg (2015)
11. Kocher, P.C.: Timing attacks on implementations of Diffie-Hellman, RSA, DSS, and other systems. In: Koblitz, N. (ed.) CRYPTO 1996. LNCS, vol. 1109, pp. 104–113. Springer, Heidelberg (1996)
12. Kocher, P.C.: On certificate revocation and validation. In: Hirschfeld, R. (ed.) FC 1998. LNCS, vol. 1465, pp. 172–177. Springer, Heidelberg (1998)
13. Menezes, A.J., van Oorschot, P.C., Vanstone, S.A.: Handbook of Applied Cryptography. CRC Press, Boca Raton (1996). http://www.cacr.math.uwaterloo.ca/hac/
14. Peter, L.: Montgomery: modular multiplication without trial division. Math. Comput. **44**(170), 519–521 (1985)
15. Sato, H., Schepers, D., Takagi, T.: Exact analysis of montgomery multiplication. In: Canteaut, A., Viswanathan, K. (eds.) INDOCRYPT 2004. LNCS, vol. 3348, pp. 290–304. Springer, Heidelberg (2004)
16. Schindler, W.: A timing attack against RSA with the Chinese Remainder Theorem. In: Paar, C., Koç, Ç.K. (eds.) CHES 2000. LNCS, vol. 1965, pp. 109–124. Springer, Heidelberg (2000)
17. Schindler, W.: A combined timing and power attack. In: Naccache, D., Paillier, P. (eds.) PKC 2002. LNCS, vol. 2274, pp. 263–279. Springer, Heidelberg (2002)

18. Schindler, W.: Exclusive exponent blinding may not suffice to prevent timing attacks on RSA. In: Güneysu, T., Handschuh, H. (eds.) CHES 2015. LNCS, vol. 9293, pp. 229–247. Springer, Heidelberg (2015)
19. Schindler, W., Koeune, F., Quisquater, J.-J.: Improving divide and conquer attacks against cryptosystems by better error detection/correction strategies. In: Honary, B. (ed.) Cryptography and Coding 2001. LNCS, vol. 2260, pp. 245–267. Springer, Heidelberg (2001)
20. Schindler, W., Walter, C.D.: More detail for a combined timing and power attack against implementations of RSA. In: Paterson, K.G. (ed.) Cryptography and Coding 2003. LNCS, vol. 2898, pp. 245–263. Springer, Heidelberg (2003)
21. Walter, C.D., Thompson, S.: Distinguishing exponent digits by observing modular subtractions. In: Naccache, D. (ed.) CT-RSA 2001. LNCS, vol. 2020, pp. 192–207. Springer, Heidelberg (2001)
22. Whitnall, C., Oswald, E.: A comprehensive evaluation of mutual information analysis using a fair evaluation framework. In: Rogaway, P. (ed.) CRYPTO 2011. LNCS, vol. 6841, pp. 316–334. Springer, Heidelberg (2011)
23. Whitnall, C., Oswald, E., Standaert, F.-X.: The myth of generic DPA..and the magic of learning. In: Benaloh, J. (ed.) CT-RSA 2014. LNCS, vol. 8366, pp. 183–205. Springer, Heidelberg (2014)
24. Witteman, M.F., van Woudenberg, J.G.J., Menarini, F.: Defeating RSA multiply-always and message blinding countermeasures. In: Kiayias, A. (ed.) CT-RSA 2011. LNCS, vol. 6558, pp. 77–88. Springer, Heidelberg (2011)

Horizontal Side-Channel Attacks and Countermeasures on the ISW Masking Scheme

Alberto Battistello[1]([✉]), Jean-Sébastien Coron[2], Emmanuel Prouff[3], and Rina Zeitoun[1]

[1] Oberthur Technologies, Colombes, France
{a.battistello,r.zeitoun}@oberthur.com
[2] University of Luxembourg, Luxembourg, Luxembourg
jean-sebastien.coron@uni.lu
[3] Laboratoire d'Informatique de Paris 6 (LIP6), Sorbonne Universités,
UPMC Univ Paris 06, CNRS, INRIA, Équipe PolSys, 4 place Jussieu,
75252 Paris Cedex 05, France

Abstract. A common countermeasure against side-channel attacks consists in using the masking scheme originally introduced by Ishai, Sahai and Wagner (ISW) at Crypto 2003, and further generalized by Rivain and Prouff at CHES 2010. The countermeasure is provably secure in the probing model, and it was showed by Duc, Dziembowski and Faust at Eurocrypt 2014 that the proof can be extended to the more realistic noisy leakage model. However the extension only applies if the leakage noise σ increases at least linearly with the masking order n, which is not necessarily possible in practice.

In this paper we investigate the security of an implementation when the previous condition is not satisfied, for example when the masking order n increases for a constant noise σ. We exhibit two (template) horizontal side-channel attacks against the Rivain-Prouff's secure multiplication scheme and we analyze their efficiency thanks to several simulations and experiments.

Eventually, we describe a variant of Rivain-Prouff's multiplication that is still provably secure in the original ISW model, and also heuristically secure against our new attacks.

1 Introduction

Side-channel analysis is a class of cryptanalytic attacks that exploit the physical environment of a cryptosystem to recover some *leakage* about its secrets. To secure implementations against this threat, security developers usually apply techniques inspired from *secret sharing* [Bla79, Sha79] or *multi-party computation* [CCD88]. The idea is to randomly split a secret into several shares such that the adversary needs all of them to reconstruct the secret. For these schemes, the

---

E. Prouff—Part of this work has been done at Safran Identity and Security, and while the author was at ANSSI, France.

© International Association for Cryptologic Research 2016
B. Gierlichs and A.Y. Poschmann (Eds.): CHES 2016, LNCS 9813, pp. 23–39, 2016.
DOI: 10.1007/978-3-662-53140-2_2

number of shares n in which the key-dependent data are split plays the role of a security parameter.

A common countermeasure against side-channel attacks consists in using the masking scheme originally introduced by Ishai, Sahai and Wagner (ISW) [ISW03]. The countermeasure achieves provable security in the so-called *probing security model* [ISW03], in which the adversary can recover a limited number of intermediate variables of the computation. This model has been argued to be practically relevant to address so-called *higher-order* side-channel attacks and it has been the basis of several efficient schemes to protect block ciphers.

More recently, it has been shown in [DDF14] that the probing security of an implementation actually implies its security in the more realistic *noisy leakage model* introduced in [PR13]. More precisely, if an implementation obtained by applying the compiler in [ISW03] is secure at order n in the probing model, then [DFS15, Theorem3] shows that the success probability of distinguishing the correct key among $|\mathbb{K}|$ candidates is bounded above by $|\mathbb{K}| \cdot 2^{-n/9}$ if the leakage L_i on each intermediate variable X_i satisfies:

$$I(X_i; L_i) \leqslant 2 \cdot (|\mathbb{K}| \cdot (28n + 16))^{-2},$$

where $I(\cdot; \cdot)$ denotes the *mutual information* and where the index i ranges from 1 to the total number of intermediate variables.

In this paper we investigate what happens when the above condition is not satisfied. Since the above mutual information $I(X_i; L_i)$ can be approximated by $k/(8\sigma^2)$ in the Hamming weight model in $\mathbb{F}_{2^k}$, where σ is the noise in the measurement (see the full version of this paper [BCPZ16]), this amounts to investigating the security of Ishai-Sahai-Wagner's (ISW) implementations when the number of shares n satisfies:

$$n > c \cdot \sigma$$

As already observed in previous works [VGS14, CFG+10], the fact that the same share (or more generally several data depending on the same sensitive value) is manipulated several times may open the door to new attacks which are not taken into account in the probing model. Those attacks, sometimes called *horizontal* [CFG+10] or *(Template) algebraic* [ORSW12, VGS14] exploit the algebraic dependency between several intermediate results to discriminate key hypotheses.

In this paper, we exhibit two (horizontal) side channel attacks against the ISW multiplication algorithm. These attacks show that the use of this algorithm (and its extension proposed by Rivain and Prouff in [RP10]) may introduce a weakness with respect to horizontal side channel attacks if the sharing order n is such that $n > c \cdot \sigma^2$, where σ is the measurement noise. While the first attack is too costly (even for low noise contexts) to make it applicable in practice, the second attack, which essentially iterates the first one until achieving a satisfying likelihood, shows very good performances. For instance, when the leakages are simulated by noisy Hamming weights computed over $\mathbb{F}_{2^8}$ with $\sigma = 1$, it recovers all the shares of a 21-sharing. We also confirm the practicality of our attack with a real life experiment on a development platform embedding the ATMega328 processor (see the full version of this paper [BCPZ16]). Actually, in this context where the leakages are multivariate and not univariate as in our theoretical analyses and simulations, the attack appears to be more efficient than expected and recovers all the shares of a n-sharing when $n \geqslant 40$.

Eventually, we describe a variant of Rivain-Prouff's multiplication that is still provably secure in the original ISW model, and also heuristically secure against our new attacks. Our new countermeasure is similar to the countermeasure in [FRR+10], in that it can be divided in two steps: a "matrix" step in which starting from the input shares x_i and y_j, one obtains a matrix $x_i \cdot y_j$ with n^2 elements, and a "compression" step in which one uses some randomness to get back to a n-sharing c_i. Assuming a leak-free component, the countermeasure in [FRR+10] is proven secure in the noisy leakage model, in which the leakage function reveals all the bits of the internal state of the circuit, perturbed by independent binomial noise. Our countermeasure does not use any leak-free component, but is only heuristically secure in the noisy leakage model (see Sect. 8.2 for our security analysis).

2 Preliminaries

For two positive integers n and d, a (n, d)-*sharing* of a variable x defined over some finite field $\mathbb{F}_{2^k}$ is a random vector $(x_1, x_2, \ldots, x_n)$ over $\mathbb{F}_{2^k}$ such that $x = \sum_{i=1}^{n} x_i$ holds (*completeness equality*) and any tuple of $d-1$ shares x_i is a uniform random vector over $(\mathbb{F}_{2^k})^{d-1}$. If $n = d$, the terminology simplifies to n-*sharing*. An algorithm with domain $(\mathbb{F}_{2^k})^n$ is said to be $(n - 1)$th-order secure in the probing model if on input an n-sharing $(x_1, x_2, \ldots, x_n)$ of some variable x, it admits no tuple of $n - 1$ or fewer intermediate variables that depends on x.

We refer to the full version of this paper [BCPZ16] for the definitions of Signal to Noise Ratio (SNR), Gaussian distribution, entropy and differential entropy.

3 Secure Multiplication Schemes

In this section, we recall the secure multiplication scheme over $\mathbb{F}_2$ introduced in [ISW03] and its extension to any field $\mathbb{F}_{2^k}$ proposed in [RP10].

Ishai-Sahai-Wagner's Scheme [ISW03]. Let $x^\star$ and $y^\star$ be binary values from $\mathbb{F}_2$ and let $(x_i)_{1 \leq i \leq n}$ and $(y_i)_{1 \leq i \leq n}$ be n-sharings of $x^\star$ and $y^\star$ respectively. To securely compute a sharing of $c = x^\star \cdot y^\star$ from $(x_i)_{1 \leq i \leq n}$ and $(y_i)_{1 \leq i \leq n}$, the ISW method works as follows:

1. For every $1 \leq i < j \leq n$, pick up a random bit $r_{i,j}$.
2. For every $1 \leq i < j \leq n$, compute $r_{j,i} = (r_{i,j} + x_i \cdot y_j) + x_j \cdot y_i$.
3. For every $1 \leq i \leq n$, compute $c_i = x_i \cdot y_i + \sum_{j \neq i} r_{i,j}$.

The above multiplication scheme achieves security at order $\lfloor n/2 \rfloor$ in the probing security model [ISW03].

The Rivain-Prouff Scheme. The ISW countermeasure was extended to $\mathbb{F}_{2^k}$ by Rivain and Prouff in [RP10]. As showed in [BBD+15], the SecMult algorithm below is secure in the ISW probing model against t probes for $n \geq t + 1$ shares; the authors also show that with some additional mask refreshing, the Rivain-Prouff countermeasure for the full AES can be made secure with $n \geq t + 1$ shares.

Algorithm 1. SecMult

Input: the n-sharings $(x_i)_{i \in [1..n]}$ and $(y_j)_{j \in [1..n]}$ of $x^\star$ and $y^\star$ respectively
Output: the n-sharing $(c_i)_{i \in [1..n]}$ of $x^\star \cdot y^\star$
1: **for** $i = 1$ **to** n **do**
2:    **for** $j = i + 1$ **to** n **do**
3:      $r_{i,j} \xleftarrow{\$} \mathbb{F}_{2^k}$
4:      $r_{j,i} \leftarrow (r_{i,j} + x_i \cdot y_j) + x_j \cdot y_i$
5:    **end for**
6: **end for**
7: **for** $i = 1$ **to** n **do**
8:    $c_i \leftarrow x_i \cdot y_i$
9:    **for** $j = 1$ **to** n, $j \neq i$ **do** $c_i \leftarrow c_i + r_{i,j}$
10: **end for**
11: **return** $(c_1, c_1, \ldots, c_n)$

In Algorithm 1, one can check that each share x_i or y_j is manipulated n times, whereas each product $x_i y_j$ is manipulated a single time. This gives a total of $3n^2$ manipulations that can be observed through side channels.

4   Horizontal DPA Attack

4.1   Problem Description

Let $(x_i)_{i \in [1..n]}$ and $(y_i)_{i \in [1..n]}$ be respectively the n-sharings of $x^\star$ and $y^\star$ (namely, we have $x^\star = x_1 + \cdots + x_n$ and $y^\star = y_1 + \cdots + y_n$). We assume that an adversary gets, during the processing of Algorithm 1, a single observation of each of the following random variables for $1 \leq i, j \leq n$:

$$L_i = \varphi(x_i) + B_i \tag{1}$$
$$L'_j = \varphi(y_j) + B'_j \tag{2}$$
$$L''_{ij} = \varphi(x_i \cdot y_j) + B''_{ij} \tag{3}$$

where φ is an unknown function which depends on the device architecture, where B_i, B'_j are Gaussian noise of standard deviation $\sigma/\sqrt{n}$, and B''_{ij} is Gaussian noise with standard deviation σ. Namely we assume that each x_i and y_j is processed n times, so by averaging the standard deviation is divided by a factor $\sqrt{n}$, which gives $\sigma/\sqrt{n}$ if we assume that the initial noise standard deviation is σ. The random variables associated to the ith share x_i and the jth share y_j are respectively denoted by X_i and Y_j. Our goal is to recover the secret variable $x^\star$ (and/or $y^\star$).

4.2   Complexity Lower Bound: Entropy Analysis of Noisy Hamming Weight Leakage

For simplicity, we first restrict ourselves to a leakage function φ equal to the Hamming weight of the variable being manipulated. In that case, the mutual information $I(X; L)$ between the Hamming weight of a uniform random variable X defined over $\mathbb{F}_{2^k}$ and a noisy observation L of this Hamming weight can be approximated as:

$$I(X; L) \simeq \frac{k}{8\sigma^2}, \tag{4}$$

if the noise being modeled by a Gaussian random variable has standard deviation σ. This approximation, whose derivation is given in the full version of this paper [BCPZ16], is only true for large σ.

To recover a total of $2n$ shares (n shares of $x^\star$ and $y^\star$ respectively) from $3n^2$ Hamming weight leakages (namely each manipulation leaks according to (1)-(3) with $\varphi = HW$), the total amount of information to be recovered is $2n \cdot k$ if we assume that the shares are i.i.d. with uniform distribution over $\mathbb{F}_{2^k}$. Therefore, since we have a total of $3n^2$ observations during the execution of Algorithm 1, we obtain from (4) that the noise standard deviation σ and the sharing order n must satisfy the following inequality for a side channel attack to be feasible:

$$3 \cdot n^2 \cdot \frac{k}{8\sigma^2} > 2n \cdot k. \tag{5}$$

We obtain an equality of the form $n > c \cdot \sigma^2$ for some constant c, as in a classical (vertical) side channel attack trying to recover $x^\star$ from n observations of intermediate variables depending on $x^\star$ [CJRR99]. This analogy between horizontal and vertical attacks has already been noticed in previous papers like [CFG+10] or [BJPW13]. Note that in principle the constant c is independent of the field degree k (which has also been observed in previous papers, see for instance [SVO+10]).

4.3   Attack with Perfect Hamming Weight Observations

In the full version of this paper [BCPZ16], we consider the particular case of perfect Hamming weight measurements (no noise), using a maximum likelihood approach. We show that even with perfect observations of the Hamming weight, depending on the finite-field representation, we are not always guaranteed to recover the secret variable $x^\star$; however for the finite field representation used in AES the attack enables to recover the secret $x^\star$ for a large enough number of observations.

4.4   Maximum Likelihood Attack: Theoretical Attack with the Full ISW State

For most field representations and leakage functions, the maximum likelihood approach used in the previous section recovers the i-th share of $x^\star$ from an observation of L_i and an observation of (L'_j, L''_{ij}) for every $j \in [1..n]$. It extends straightforwardly to noisy scenarios and we shall detail this extension in Sect. 5.1. However, the disadvantage of this approach is that it recovers each share separately, before rebuilding $x^\star$ and $y^\star$ from them. From a pure information theoretic point of view this is suboptimal since (1) the final purpose is not to recover all the shares perfectly but only the shared values and (2) only $3n$ observations are used to recover each share whereas the full tuple of $3n^2$ observations brings more information. Actually, the most efficient attack in terms of leakage exploitation consists in using the joint distribution of $(L_i, L'_j, L''_{ij})_{i,j \in [1..n]}$ to distinguish the correct hypothesis about $x^\star = x_1 + x_2 + \cdots + x_n$ and $y^\star = y_1 + y_2 + \cdots + y_n$.

As already observed in Sect. 3, during the processing of Algorithm 1, the adversary may get a tuple $(\ell_{ij})_{j \in [1..n]}$ (resp. $(\ell'_{ij})_{i \in [1..n]}$) of n observations for each L_i (resp. each L'_j) and one observation ℓ''_{ij} for each L''_{ij}. The full tuple of observations $(\ell_{ij}, \ell'_{ij}, \ell''_{ij})_{i,j}$ is denoted by $\boldsymbol{\ell}$, and we denote by $\boldsymbol{L}$ the corresponding random variable[1]. Then, to recover $(x^\star, y^\star)$ from $\boldsymbol{\ell}$, the *maximum likelihood approach* starts by estimating the pdfs $f_{\boldsymbol{L}|X^\star=x^\star, Y^\star=y^\star}$ for every possible $(x^\star, y^\star)$, and then estimates the following vector of distinguisher values for every hypothesis (x, y):

$$\mathrm{d}^\star_{\mathrm{ML}}(\boldsymbol{\ell}) \doteq \big(f_{\boldsymbol{L}|(X^\star, Y^\star)}(\boldsymbol{\ell}, (x, y)) \big)_{(x,y) \in \mathbb{F}^2_{2^k}} \tag{6}$$

The pair (x, y) maximizing the above probability is eventually chosen.

At a first glance, the estimation of the pdfs $f_{\boldsymbol{L}|X^\star=x^\star, Y^\star=y^\star}$ seems to be challenging. However, it can be deduced from the estimations of the pdfs associated to the manipulations of the shares. Indeed, after denoting by $\mathrm{p}_{x,y}$ each probability value in the right-hand side of (6), and by using the law of total probability together with the fact that the noises are independent, we get:

$$2^{2kn} \cdot \mathrm{p}_{x,y} =$$

$$\sum_{\substack{x_1, \cdots, x_n \in \mathbb{F}_{2^k} \\ x = x_1 + \cdots + x_n}} \sum_{\substack{y_1, \cdots, y_n \in \mathbb{F}_{2^k} \\ y = y_1 + \cdots + y_n}} \prod_{i,j=1}^{n} f_{L_i|X_i}(\ell_{ij}, x_i) \cdot f_{L'_j|Y_j}(\ell'_{ij}, y_j) \cdot f_{L''_{ij}|X_iY_j}(\ell''_{ij}, x_iy_j).$$

Unfortunately, even if the equation above shows how to deduce the pdfs $f_{\boldsymbol{L}|(X^\star, Y^\star)}(\cdot, (x^\star, y^\star))$ from characterizations of the shares' manipulations, a direct processing of the probability has complexity $O(2^{2nk})$. By representing the sum over the x_i's as a sequence of convolution products, and thanks to Walsh transforms processing, the complexity can be easily reduced to $O(n2^{n(k+1)})$. The latter complexity stays however too high, even for small values of n and k, which led us to look at alternatives to this attack.

---

[1] In (1)–(3), it is assumed that the observations $(\ell_{ij})_{j \in [1..n]}$ and $(\ell'_{ij})_{i \in [1..n]}$ are averaged to build a single observation with noise divided by $\sqrt{n}$. This assumption is not done here in order to stay as general as possible.

5   First Attack: Maximum Likelihood Attack on a Single Matrix Row

5.1   Attack Description

In this section, we explain how to recover each share x_i of $x^\star$ separately, by observing the processing of Algorithm 1. Applying this attack against all the shares leads to the full recovery of the sensitive value $x^\star$ with some success probability, which is essentially the product of the success probabilities of the attack on each share separately.

Given a share x_i, the attack consists in collecting the leakages on $(y_j, x_i \cdot y_j)$ for every $j \in [1..n]$. Therefore the attack is essentially a horizontal version of the classical (vertical) second-order side-channel attack, where each share x_i is multiplicatively masked over $\mathbb{F}_{2^k}$ by a random y_j for $j \in [1..n]$.

The most efficient attack to maximize the amount of information recovered on X_i from a tuple of observations $\boldsymbol{\ell} \doteq \ell_i, (\ell'_j, \ell''_{ij})_{j \in [1..n]} \hookleftarrow \boldsymbol{L} \doteq L_i, (L'_j, L''_{ij})_{j \in [1..n]}$ consists in applying a *maximum likelihood approach* [CJRR99, GHR15], which amounts to computing the following vector of distinguisher values:

$$\mathrm{d_{ML}}(\boldsymbol{\ell}) \doteq \left(f_{\boldsymbol{L}|X_i}(\boldsymbol{\ell}, \hat{x}_i) \right)_{\hat{x}_i \in \mathbb{F}_{2^k}} \tag{7}$$

and in choosing the candidate $\hat{x}_i$ which maximizes the probability. We refer to the full version of this paper [BCPZ16] for the derivation of each score $f_{\boldsymbol{L}|X_i}(\boldsymbol{\ell}, \hat{x}_i)$ in (7); we obtain:

$$f_{(L'_j, L''_{ij})|X_i}((\ell'_j, \ell''_{ij}), \hat{x}_i) = \sum_{y \in \mathbb{F}_{2^k}} f_{(L'_j, L''_{ij})|(X_i, Y_j)}((\ell'_j, \ell''_{ij}), (\hat{x}_i, y)) \cdot \mathrm{p}_{Y_j}(y) \ , \tag{8}$$

and similarly:

$$f_{(L_i, L''_{ij})|Y_j}((\ell_i, \ell''_{ij}), \hat{y}_j) = \sum_{x \in \mathbb{F}_{2^k}} f_{(L_i, L''_{ij})|(X_i, Y_j)}((\ell_i, \ell''_{ij}), (x, \hat{y}_j)) \cdot \mathrm{p}_{X_i}(x) \ . \tag{9}$$

5.2   Complexity Analysis

As mentioned previously, given a share x_i, the attack consists in collecting the leakages on $(y_j, x_i \cdot y_j)$ for every $j \in [1..n]$. Therefore the attack is essentially an horizontal version of the classical (vertical) second-order side-channel attack. In principle the number n of leakage samples needed to recover x_i with good probability (aka the attack complexity) should consequently be $n = \mathcal{O}(\sigma^4)$ [CJRR99, GHR15, SVO+10]. This holds when multiplying two leakages both with noise having σ as standard deviation. However here the leakage on y_j has a noise with a standard deviation $\sigma/\sqrt{n}$ instead of σ (thanks to the averaging step). Therefore the noise of the product becomes $\sigma^2/\sqrt{n}$ (instead of σ^2), which gives after averaging with n measurements a standard deviation of σ^2/n, and therefore an attack complexity satisfying $n = \mathcal{O}(\sigma^2)$, as in a classical first-order side-channel attack.

5.3 Numerical Experiments

The attack presented in Sect. 5.1 has been implemented against each share x_i of a value x, with the leakages being simulated according to (1)–(3) with $\varphi = \mathrm{HW}$. For the noise standard deviation σ and the sharing order n, different values have been tested to enlighten the relation between these two parameters. We stated that an attack succeeds iff the totality of the n shares x_i have been recovered, which leads to the full recovery of $x^\star$. We recall that, since the shares x_i are manipulated n times, measurements for the leakages L_i and L'_j have noise standard deviations $\sigma/\sqrt{n}$ instead of σ. For efficiency reasons, we have chosen to work in the finite field $\mathbb{F}_{2^4}$ (namely $k = 4$ in previous analyses).

For various noise standard deviations σ with SNR $= k(2\sigma)^{-2}$ (*i.e.* SNR $= \sigma^{-2}$ for $k = 4$), Table 1 gives the average minimum number n of shares required for the attack to succeed with probability strictly greater than 0.5 (the averaging being computed over 300 attack iterations). The attack complexity $n = \mathcal{O}(\sigma^2)$ argued in Sect. 5.2 is confirmed by the trend of these numerical experiments. Undeniably, this efficiency is quickly too poor for practical applications where n is small (clearly lower than 10) and the SNR is high (smaller than 1).

Table 1. First attack: number of shares n as a function of the noise σ to succeed with probability > 0.5

σ (SNR)	0 ($+\infty$)	0.2 (25)	0.4 (6.25)	0.6 (2.77)	0.8 (1.56)	1 (1)
n	12	14	30	73	160	284

6 Second Attack: Iterative Attack

6.1 Attack Description

From the discussions in Sect. 4.4, and in view of the poor efficiency of the previous attack, we investigated another strategy which targets all the shares simultaneously. Essentially, the core idea of our second attack described below is to apply several attacks recursively on the x_i's and y_j's, and to refine step by step the likelihood of each candidate for the tuple of shares. Namely, we start by applying the attack described in Sect. 5.1 in order to compute, for every i, a likelihood probability for each hypothesis $X_i = x$ (x ranging over $\mathbb{F}_{2^k}$); then we apply the same attack in order to compute, for every j, a likelihood probability for each hypothesis $Y_j = y$ (y ranging over $\mathbb{F}_{2^k}$) with the single difference that the probability $\mathrm{p}_{X_i}(x)$ in (9) is replaced by the likelihood probability which was just computed[2]. Then, one reiterates the attack to refine the likelihood probabilities $(\mathrm{p}_{X_i}(x))_{x \in \mathbb{F}_{2^k}}$, by evaluating (8) with the uniform distribution $\mathrm{p}_{Y_j}(y)$

---

[2] Actually to get the probability of $X_i \mid \boldsymbol{L}$ instead of $\boldsymbol{L} \mid X_i$, Bayes' Formula is applied which explains the division by the sum of probabilities in the lines 14 and 19 in Algorithm 2.

being replaced by the likelihood probability new-$p_{Y_j}(y)$ which has been previously computed. The scheme is afterwards repeated until the maximum taken by the pdfs of each share X_i and Y_j is greater than some threshold β. In order to have better results, we perform the whole attack a second time, by starting with the computation of the likelihood probability for each hypothesis $Y_j = y$ instead of starting by $X_i = x$.

We give the formal description of the attack processing in Algorithm 2 (in order to have the complete attack, one should perform the while loop a second time, by rather starting with the computation of new-$p_{Y_j}(y)$ instead of new-$p_{X_i}(x)$).

6.2 Numerical Experiments

The iterative attack described in Algorithm 2 has been tested against leakages simulations defined exactly as in Sect. 5.3. As previously we stated that an attack succeeds if the totality of the n shares x_i have been recovered, which leads to the full recovery of $x^\star$. For various noise standard deviations σ with SNR $= k(2\sigma)^{-2}$, Table 2 gives the average minimum number of shares n required for the attack to succeed with probability strictly greater than 0.5 (the averaging being computed over 300 attack iterations). The first row corresponds to $k = 4$, and the second row to $k = 8$ (the corresponding SNRs are SNR$_4 = \sigma^{-2}$ and SNR$_8 = (\sqrt{2}\sigma^2)^{-1}$). Numerical experiments yield greatly improved results in comparison to those obtained by running the basic attack. Namely, in $\mathbb{F}_{2^4}$, for a noise $\sigma = 0$, the number of shares required is 2, while 12 shares were needed for the basic attack, and the improvement is even more confirmed with a growing σ: for a noise $\sigma = 1$, the number of shares required is 25, while 284 shares were needed for the basic attack. It can also be observed that the results for shares in $\mathbb{F}_{2^4}$ and $\mathbb{F}_{2^8}$ are relatively close, the number of shares being most likely slightly smaller for shares in $\mathbb{F}_{2^4}$ than in $\mathbb{F}_{2^8}$. This observation is in-line with the lower bound in (5), where the cardinality 2^k of the finite field plays no role.

Table 2. Iterative attack: number of shares n as a function of the noise σ to succeed with probability > 0.5 in $\mathbb{F}_{2^4}$ (first row) and in $\mathbb{F}_{2^8}$ (second row).

σ (SNR$_4$, SNR$_8$)	0 ($+\infty, +\infty$)	0.2 (25, 17.67)	0.4 (6.25, 4.41)	0.6 (2.77, 1.96)	0.8 (1.56, 1.10)	1 (1, 0.7071)
n (for $\mathbb{F}_{2^4}$)	2	2	3	6	13	25
n (for $\mathbb{F}_{2^8}$)	5	6	8	11	16	21

7   Practical Results

In the full version of this paper [BCPZ16], we describe the result of practical experiments of our attack against a development platform embedding the ATMega328 processor.

Algorithm 2. Iterative Maximum Likelihood Attack

Input: a threshold β, an observation ℓ_i of each L_i, an observation ℓ'_j of each L'_j and
    one observation ℓ''_{ij} of each L''_{ij} (the random variables being defined as in (1)-(3))
Output: a n-tuple of pdfs $(\mathrm{p}_{X_i})_i$ (resp. $(\mathrm{p}_{Y_i})_i$) such that, for every $i \in [1..n]$,
    at least one $\hat{x}_i$ (resp. $\hat{y}_j$) satisfies $\mathrm{p}_{X_i}(\hat{x}_i) \geqslant \beta$ (resp. $\mathrm{p}_{Y_i}(\hat{y}_j) \geqslant \beta$)

1: **for** $i = 1$ **to** n **do**
2:    **for** $x \in \mathbb{F}_{2^k}$ **do**   # Initialize the likelihood of each candidate for X_i
3:       $\mathrm{p}_{X_i}(x) = f_{L_i|X_i}(\ell_i, x)$
4:    **end for**
5:    **for** $y \in \mathbb{F}_{2^k}$ **do**   # Initialize the likelihood of each candidate for Y_i
6:       $\mathrm{p}_{Y_i}(y) = f_{L'_i|Y_i}(\ell'_i, y_i)$
7:       new-$\mathrm{p}_{Y_i}(y) = \mathrm{p}_{Y_i}(y)$
8:    **end for**
9: **end**   **for**

10: **while end** $\neq n$ **do**
11:    end $\leftarrow 0$
12:    **for** $i = 1$ **to** n **do**
13:       **for** $x \in \mathbb{F}_{2^k}$ **do** # Compute/Update the likelihood of each candidate for X_i
14:          new-$\mathrm{p}_{X_i}(x) = 2^{-(2n+1)k} \dfrac{\mathrm{p}_{X_i}(x)}{\sum_{x' \in \mathbb{F}_{2^k}} \mathrm{p}_{X_i}(x')} \prod_{j=1}^{n} \sum_{y \in \mathbb{F}_{2^k}} \dfrac{\text{new-}\mathrm{p}_{Y_j}(y)}{\sum_{y' \in \mathbb{F}_{2^k}} \text{new-}\mathrm{p}_{Y_j}(y')} \cdot$
               $f_{L''_{ij}|X_iY_j}(\ell''_{ij}, x \cdot y)$
15:       **end for**
16:    **end for**
17:    **for** $i = 1$ **to** n **do**
18:       **for** $y \in \mathbb{F}_{2^k}$ **do** # Compute/Update the likelihood of each candidate for Y_i
19:          new-$\mathrm{p}_{Y_i}(y) = 2^{-(2n+1)k} \dfrac{\mathrm{p}_{Y_i}(y)}{\sum_{y' \in \mathbb{F}_{2^k}} \mathrm{p}_{Y_i}(y')} \prod_{j=1}^{n} \sum_{x \in \mathbb{F}_{2^k}} \dfrac{\text{new-}\mathrm{p}_{X_j}(x)}{\sum_{x' \in \mathbb{F}_{2^k}} \text{new-}\mathrm{p}_{X_j}(x')} \cdot$
               $f_{L''_{ij}|X_iY_j}(\ell''_{ij}, x \cdot y)$
20:       **end for**
21:    **end for**
22:    **for** $i = 1$ **to** n **do**
23:       **if** $\max_x(\text{new-}\mathrm{p}_{X_i}(x)) \geqslant \beta$ **and** $\max_y(\text{new-}\mathrm{p}_{Y_i}(y)) \geqslant \beta$ **then**
24:          end $++$
25:       **end if**
26:    **end for**
27: **end while**

---

8   A Countermeasure Against the Previous Attacks

8.1   Description

In the following, we describe a countermeasure against the previous attack against
the Rivain-Prouff algorithm. More precisely, we describe a variant of Algorithm 1,
called RefSecMult, to compute an n-sharing of $c = x^\star \cdot y^\star$ from $(x_i)_{i \in [1..n]}$
and $(y_i)_{i \in [1..n]}$. Our new algorithm is still provably secure in the original ISW

Algorithm 3. RefSecMult

Input: n-sharings $(x_i)_{i \in [1..n]}$ and $(y_j)_{j \in [1..n]}$ of $x^\star$ and $y^\star$ respectively
Output: an n-sharing $(c_i)_{i \in [1..n]}$ of $x^\star \cdot y^\star$
1: $M_{ij} \leftarrow \mathsf{MatMult}((x_1, \ldots, x_n), (y_1, \ldots, y_n))$
2: **for** $i = 1$ to n **do**
3:    **for** $j = i + 1$ to n **do**
4:       $r_{i,j} \leftarrow^{\$} \mathbb{F}_{2^k}$
5:       $r_{j,i} \leftarrow (r_{i,j} + M_{ij}) + M_{ji}$
6:    **end for**
7: **end for**
8: **for** $i = 1$ to n **do**
9:    $c_i \leftarrow M_{ii}$
10:    **for** $j = 1$ to n, $j \neq i$ **do** $c_i \leftarrow c_i + r_{i,j}$
11: **end for**
12: **return** $(c_1, c_1, \ldots, c_n)$

---

probing model, and heuristically secure against the horizontal side-channel attacks described the in previous sections.

As observed in [FRR+10], the ISW and Rivain-Prouff countermeasures can be divided in two steps: a "matrix" step in which starting from the input shares x_i and y_j, one obtains a matrix $x_i \cdot y_j$ with n^2 elements, and a "compression" step in which one uses some randomness to get back to a n-sharing c_i. Namely the matrix elements $(x_i \cdot y_j)_{1 \leq i,j \leq n}$ form a n^2-sharing of $x^\star \cdot y^\star$:

$$x^\star \cdot y^\star = \left(\sum_{i=1}^{n} x_i\right) \cdot \left(\sum_{j=1}^{n} y_j\right) = \sum_{1 \leq i,j \leq n} x_i \cdot y_j \tag{10}$$

and the goal of the compression step is to securely go from such n^2-sharing of $x^\star \cdot y^\star$ to a n-sharing of $x^\star \cdot y^\star$.

Our new countermeasure (Algorithm 3) uses the same compression step as Rivain-Prouff, but with a different matrix step, called MatMult (Algorithm 4), so that the shares x_i and y_j are not used multiple times (as when computing the matrix elements $x_i \cdot y_j$ in Rivain-Prouff). Eventually the MatMult algorithm outputs a matrix $(M_{ij})_{1 \leq i,j \leq n}$ which is still a n^2-sharing of $x^\star \cdot y^\star$, as in (10); therefore using the same compression step as Rivain-Prouff, Algorithm 3 outputs a n-sharing of $x^\star \cdot y^\star$, as required.

As illustrated in Fig. 1, the MatMult algorithm is recursive and computes the $n \times n$ matrix in four sub-matrix blocs. This is done by splitting the input shares x_i and y_j in two parts, namely $\boldsymbol{X}^{(1)} = (x_1, \ldots, x_{n/2})$ and $\boldsymbol{X}^{(2)} = (x_{n/2+1}, \ldots, x_n)$, and similarly $\boldsymbol{Y}^{(1)} = (y_1, \ldots, y_{n/2})$ and $\boldsymbol{Y}^{(2)} = (y_{n/2+1}, \ldots, y_n)$, and recursively processing the four sub-matrix blocs corresponding to $\boldsymbol{X}^{(u)} \times \boldsymbol{Y}^{(v)}$ for $1 \leq u, v \leq 2$. To prevent the same share x_i from being used twice, each input block $\boldsymbol{X}^{(u)}$ and $\boldsymbol{Y}^{(v)}$ is refreshed before being used a second time, using a mask refreshing algorithm. An example of such mask refreshing, hereafter called RefreshMasks, can for instance be found in [DDF14]; see Algorithm 5. Since the mask refreshing

Algorithm 4. MatMult

Input: the n-sharings $(x_i)_{i \in [1..n]}$ and $(y_j)_{j \in [1..n]}$ of $x^\star$ and $y^\star$ respectively
Output: the n^2-sharing $(M_{ij})_{i \in [1..n], j \in [1..n]}$ of $x^\star \cdot y^\star$
1: **if** $n = 1$ **then**
2:     $M \leftarrow [x_1 \cdot y_1]$
3: **else**
4:     $X^{(1)} \leftarrow (x_1, \ldots, x_{n/2})$, $X^{(2)} \leftarrow (x_{n/2+1}, \ldots, x_n)$
5:     $Y^{(1)} \leftarrow (y_1, \ldots, y_{n/2})$, $Y^{(2)} \leftarrow (y_{n/2+1}, \ldots, y_n)$
6:     $M^{(1,1)} \leftarrow \mathsf{MatMult}(X^{(1)}, Y^{(1)})$
7:     $X^{(1)} \leftarrow \mathsf{RefreshMasks}(X^{(1)})$, $Y^{(1)} \leftarrow \mathsf{RefreshMasks}(Y^{(1)})$
8:     $M^{(1,2)} \leftarrow \mathsf{MatMult}(X^{(1)}, Y^{(2)})$
9:     $M^{(2,1)} \leftarrow \mathsf{MatMult}(X^{(2)}, Y^{(1)})$
10:    $X^{(2)} \leftarrow \mathsf{RefreshMasks}(X^{(2)})$, $Y^{(2)} \leftarrow \mathsf{RefreshMasks}(Y^{(2)})$
11:    $M^{(2,2)} \leftarrow \mathsf{MatMult}(X^{(2)}, Y^{(2)})$
12:    $M \leftarrow \begin{bmatrix} M^{(1,1)} & M^{(1,2)} \\ M^{(2,1)} & M^{(2,2)} \end{bmatrix}$
13: **end if**
14: **return** M

does not modify the xor of the input $n/2$-vectors $X^{(u)}$ and $Y^{(v)}$, each sub-matrix block $M^{(u,v)}$ is still a $n^2/4$-sharing of $(\oplus X^{(u)}) \cdot (\oplus X^{(v)})$, and therefore the output matrix M is still a n^2-sharing of $x^\star \cdot y^\star$, as required. Note that without the RefreshMasks, we would have $M_{ij} = x_i \cdot y_j$ as in Rivain-Prouff.

Algorithm 5. RefreshMasks

Input: $a_1, \ldots, a_n$
Output: $c_1, \ldots, c_n$ such that $\sum_{i=1}^n c_i = \sum_{i=1}^n a_i$
1: **For** $i = 1$ to n **do** $c_i \leftarrow a_i$
2: **for** $i = 1$ to n **do do**
3:     **for** $j = i + 1$ to n **do do**
4:         $r \leftarrow \{0,1\}^k$
5:         $c_i \leftarrow c_i + r$
6:         $c_j \leftarrow c_j + r$
7:     **end for**
8: **end for**
9: **return** $c_1, \ldots, c_n$

Since the RefreshMask algorithm has complexity $\mathcal{O}(n^2)$, it is easy to see that the complexity of our RefSecMult algorithm is $\mathcal{O}(n^2 \log n)$ (instead of $\mathcal{O}(n^2)$ for the original Rivain-Prouff countermeasure in Algorithm 1). Therefore for a circuit of size $|C|$ the complexity is $\mathcal{O}(|C| \cdot n^2 \log n)$, instead of $\mathcal{O}(|C| \cdot n^2)$ for Rivain-Prouff. The following lemma shows the soundness of our RefSecMult countermeasure.

Lemma 1 (Soundness of RefSecMult). *The* RefSecMult *algorithm, on input n-sharings $(x_i)_{i \in [1..n]}$ and $(y_j)_{j \in [1..n]}$ of $x^\star$ and $y^\star$ respectively, outputs an n-sharing $(c_i)_{i \in [1..n]}$ of $x^\star \cdot y^\star$.*

Proof. We prove recursively that the MatMult algorithm, taking as input n-sharings $(x_i)_{i \in [1..n]}$ and $(y_j)_{j \in [1..n]}$ of $x^\star$ and $y^\star$ respectively, outputs an n^2-sharing M_{ij} of $x^\star \cdot y^\star$. The lemma for RefSecMult will follow, since as in Rivain-Prouff the lines 2 to 12 of Algorithm 3 transform a n^2-sharing M_{ij} of $x^\star \cdot y^\star$ into a n-sharing of $x^\star \cdot y^\star$.

The property clearly holds for $n = 1$. Assuming that it holds for $n/2$, since the RefreshMasks does not change the xor of the input $n/2$-vectors $\boldsymbol{X}^{(u)}$ and $\boldsymbol{Y}^{(v)}$, each sub-matrix block $\boldsymbol{M}^{(u,v)}$ is still an $n^2/4$-sharing of $(\oplus \boldsymbol{X}^{(u)}) \cdot (\oplus \boldsymbol{X}^{(v)})$, and therefore the output matrix $\boldsymbol{M}$ is still an n^2-sharing of $x^\star \cdot y^\star$, as required. This proves the lemma. ∎

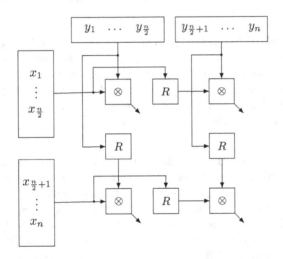

Fig. 1. The recursive MatMult algorithm, where R represents the RefreshMasks Algorithm, and $\otimes$ represents a recursive call to the MatMult algorithm.

Remark 1. The description of our countermeasure requires that n is a power of two, but it is easy to modify the countermeasure to handle any value of n. Namely in Algorithm 4, for odd n it suffices to split the inputs x_i and y_j in two parts of size $(n - 1)/2$ and $(n + 1)/2$ respectively, instead of $n/2$.

8.2   Security Analysis

Proven Security in the ISW Probing Model. We prove that our RefSecMult algorithm achieves at least the same level of security of Rivain-Prouff, namely it is secure in the ISW probing model against t probes for $n \geq t+1$ shares. For this we use the refined security model against probing attacks recently introduced in [BBD+15], called t-SNI security. This stronger definition of t-SNI security enables to prove that a gadget can be used in a full construction with $n \geq t + 1$ shares, instead of $n \geq 2t + 1$ for the weaker definition of t-NI security (corresponding to the original ISW security proof). The authors of [BBD+15] show that the ISW (and Rivain-Prouff) multiplication gadget does satisfy this stronger t-SNI security definition. They also show that with some additional mask refreshing satisfying the t-SNI property (such as RefreshMasks), the Rivain-Prouff countermeasure for the full AES can be made secure with $n \geq t+1$ shares.

The following lemma shows that our RefSecMult countermeasure achieves the t-SNI property; we provide the proof in Appendix A. The proof is essentially the same as in [BBD+15] for the Rivain-Prouff countermeasure; namely the compression step is the same, and for the matrix step, in the simulation we can assume that all the randoms in RefreshMasks are given to the adversary. The t-SNI security implies that our RefSecMult algorithm is also composable, with $n \geq t + 1$ shares.

Lemma 2 (t-SNI of RefSecMult). *Let $(x_i)_{1 \leq i \leq n}$ and $(y_i)_{1 \leq i \leq n}$ be the input shares of the SecMult operation, and let $(c_i)_{1 \leq i < n}$ be the output shares. For any set of t_1 intermediate variables and any subset $|\mathcal{O}| \leq t_2$ of output shares such that $t_1 + t_2 < n$, there exists two subsets I and J of indices with $|I| \leq t_1$ and $|J| \leq t_1$, such that those t_1 intermediate variables as well as the output shares $c_{|\mathcal{O}}$ can be perfectly simulated from $x_{|I}$ and $y_{|J}$.*

Heuristic Security Against Horizontal-DPA Attacks. We stress that the previous lemma only proves the security of our countermeasure against t probes for $n \geq t + 1$, so it does not prove that our countermeasure is secure against the horizontal-DPA attacks described in the previous sections, since such attacks use information about n^2 intermediate variables instead of only $n - 1$.

As illustrated in Fig. 1, the main difference between the new RefSecMult algorithm and the original SecMult algorithm (Algorithm 1) is that we keep refreshing the x_i shares and the y_j shares blockwise between the processing of the finite field multiplications $x_i \cdot y_j$. Therefore, as opposed to what happens in SecMult, we never have the same x_i being multiplied by all y_j's for $1 \leq j \leq n$. Therefore an attacker cannot accumulate information about a specific share x_i, which heuristically prevents the attacks described in this paper.

Acknowledgments. We are very grateful to the anonymous CHES reviewers for pointing a flaw in a previous version of our countermeasure in Sect. 8.

A   Proof of Lemma 2

Our proof is essentially the same as in [BBD+15]. We construct two sets I and J corresponding to the input shares of $x^\star$ and $y^\star$ respectively. We denote by

M_{ij} the result of the subroutine MatMult($(x_1, \ldots, x_n), (y_1, \ldots, y_n)$). From the definition of MatMult and RefreshMasks, it is easy to see that each M_{ij} can be perfectly simulated from x_i and y_j; more generally any internal variable within MatMult can be perfectly simulated from x_i and/or y_j for some i and j; for this it suffices to simulate the randoms in RefreshMasks exactly as they are generated in RefreshMasks.

We divide the internal probes in 4 groups. The four groups are processed separately and sequentially, that is we start with all probes in Group 1, and finish with all probes in Group 4.

- Group 1: If M_{ii} is probed, add i to I and J.
- Group 2: If $r_{i,j}$ or $c_{i,j}$ is probed (for any $i \neq j$), add i to I and J.

Note that after the processing of Group 1 and 2 probes, we have $I = J$; we denote by U the common value of I and J after the processing of Group 1 and 2 probes.

- Group 3: If $M_{ij} \oplus r_{i,j}$ is probed: if $i \in U$ or $j \in U$, add $\{i, j\}$ to both I and J.
- Group 4: If M_{ij} is probed (for any $i \neq j$), then add i to I and j to J. If some probe in MatMult requires the knowledge of x_i and/or y_j, add i to I and/or j to J.

We have $|I| \leq t_1$ and $|J| \leq t_1$, since for every probe we add at most one index in I and J. The simulation of probed variables in groups 1 and 4 is straightforward. Note that for $i < j$, the variable r_{ij} is used in all partial sums c_{ik} for $k \geq j$; moreover r_{ij} is used in $r_{ij} \oplus M_{ij}$, which is used in r_{ji}, which is used in all partial sums c_{jk} for $k \geq i$. Therefore if $i \notin U$, then r_{ij} is not probed and does not enter in the computation of any probed c_{ik}; symmetrically if $j \notin U$, then r_{ji} is not probed and does not enter in the computation of any probed c_{jk}.

For any pair $i < j$, we can now distinguish 4 cases:

- Case 1: $\{i, j\} \in U$. In that case, we can perfectly simulate all variables r_{ij}, M_{ij}, $M_{ij} \oplus r_{ij}$, M_{ji} and r_{ji}. In particular, we let $r_{ij} \leftarrow \mathbb{F}_{2^k}$, as in the real circuit.
- Case 2: $i \in U$ and $j \notin U$. In that case we simulate $r_{ij} \leftarrow \mathbb{F}_{2^k}$, as in the real circuit. If $M_{ij} \oplus r_{i,j}$ is probed (Group 3), we can also simulate it since $i \in U$ and $j \in J$ by definition of the processing of Group 3 variables.
- Case 3: $i \notin U$ and $j \in U$. In that case r_{ij} has not been probed, nor any variable c_{ik}, since otherwise $i \in U$. Therefore r_{ij} is not used in the computation of any probed variable (except r_{ji}, and possibly $M_{ij} \oplus r_{i,j}$). Therefore we can simulate $r_{ji} \leftarrow \mathbb{F}_{2^k}$; moreover if $M_{ij} \oplus r_{ij}$ is probed, we can perfectly simulate it using $M_{ij} \oplus r_{ij} = M_{ji} \oplus r_{ji}$, since $j \in U$ and $i \in J$ by definition of the processing of Group 3 variables.
- Case 4: $i \notin U$ and $j \notin U$. If $M_{ij} \oplus r_{i,j}$ is probed, since r_{ij} is not probed and does not enter into the computation of any other probed variable, we can perfectly simulate such probe with a random value.

From cases 1, 2 and 3, we obtain that for any $i \neq j$, we can perfectly simulate any variable r_{ij} such that $i \in U$. This implies that we can also perfectly simulate all partial sums c_{ik} when $i \in U$, including the output variables c_i. Finally, all probed variables are perfectly simulated.

We now consider the simulation of the output variables c_i. We must show how to simulate c_i for all $i \in \mathcal{O}$, where $\mathcal{O}$ is an arbitrary subset of $[1, n]$ such that $t_1 + |\mathcal{O}| < n$. For $i \in U$, such variables are already perfectly simulated, as explained above. We now consider the output variables c_i with $i \notin U$. We construct a subset of indices V as follows: for any probed Group 3 variable $M_{ij} \oplus r_{ij}$ such that $i \notin U$ and $j \notin U$ (this corresponds to Case 4), we put j in V if $i \in \mathcal{O}$, otherwise we put i in V. Since we have only considered Group 3 probes, we must have $|U| + |V| \leq t_1$, which implies $|U| + |V| + |\mathcal{O}| < n$. Therefore there exists an index $j^\star \in [1, n]$ such that $j^\star \notin U \cup V \cup \mathcal{O}$. For any $i \in \mathcal{O}$, we can write:

$$c_i = M_{ii} \oplus \bigoplus_{j \neq i} r_{ij} = r_{i,j^\star} \oplus \left(M_{ii} \oplus \bigoplus_{j \neq i, j^\star} r_{ij} \right)$$

We claim that neither $r_{i,j^\star}$ nor $r_{j^\star,i}$ do enter into the computation of any probed variable or other $c_{i'}$ for $i' \in \mathcal{O}$. Namely $i \notin U$ so neither $r_{i,j^\star}$ nor any partial sum c_{ik} was probed; similarly $j^\star \notin U$ so neither $r_{j^\star,i}$ nor any partial sum $c_{j^\star,k}$ was probed, and the output $c_{j^\star}$ does not have to be simulated since by definition $j^\star \notin \mathcal{O}$. Finally if $i < j^\star$ then $M_{i,j^\star} \oplus r_{i,j^\star}$ was not probed since otherwise $j^\star \in V$ (since $i \in \mathcal{O}$); similarly if $j^\star < i$ then $M_{j^\star,i} \oplus r_{j^\star,i}$ was not probed since otherwise we would have $j^\star \in V$ since $j^\star \notin \mathcal{O}$. Therefore, since neither $r_{i,j^\star}$ nor $r_{j^\star,i}$ are used elsewhere, we can perfectly simulate c_i by generating a random value. This proves the Lemma.

References

[BBD+15] Barthe, G., Belaïd, S., Dupressoir, F., Fouque, P.-A., Grégoire, B.: Compositional verification of higher-order masking: application to a verifying masking compiler. Cryptology ePrint Archive, Report 2015/506 (2015). http://eprint.iacr.org/

[BCPZ16] Battistello, A., Coron, J.-S., Prouff, E., Zeitoun, R.: Horizontal side-channel attacks, countermeasures on the ISW masking scheme. Cryptology ePrint Archive, Report 2016/540 (2016). Full version of this paper http://eprint.iacr.org/

[BJPW13] Bauer, A., Jaulmes, E., Prouff, E., Wild, J.: Horizontal and vertical side-channel attacks against secure RSA implementations. In: Dawson, E. (ed.) CT-RSA 2013. LNCS, vol. 7779, pp. 1–17. Springer, Heidelberg (2013)

[Bla79] Blakely, G.R.: Safeguarding cryptographic keys. In: National Computer Conference, vol. 48, pp. 313–317. AFIPS Press, New York, June 1979

[CCD88] Chaum, D., Crépeau, C., Damgård, I.: Multiparty unconditionally secure protocols (extended abstract). In: Simon, J. (ed.) Proceedings of 20th Annual ACM Symposium on Theory of Computing, Chicago, Illinois, USA, pp. 11–19. ACM, 2–4 May 1988

[CFG+10] Clavier, C., Feix, B., Gagnerot, G., Roussellet, M., Verneuil, V.: Horizontal correlation analysis on exponentiation. In: Soriano, M., Qing, S., López, J. (eds.) ICICS 2010. LNCS, vol. 6476, pp. 46–61. Springer, Heidelberg (2010)

[CJRR99] Chari, S., Jutla, C.S., Rao, J.R., Rohatgi, P.: Towards sound approaches to counteract power-analysis attacks. In: Wiener, M. (ed.) CRYPTO 1999. LNCS, vol. 1666, pp. 398–412. Springer, Heidelberg (1999)

[DDF14] Duc, A., Dziembowski, S., Faust, S.: Unifying leakage models: from probing attacks to noisy leakage. In: Nguyen, P.Q., Oswald, E. (eds.) EUROCRYPT 2014. LNCS, vol. 8441, pp. 423–440. Springer, Heidelberg (2014)

[DFS15] Duc, A., Faust, S., Standaert, F.-X.: Making masking security proofs concrete. In: Oswald, E., Fischlin, M. (eds.) EUROCRYPT 2015. LNCS, vol. 9056, pp. 401–429. Springer, Heidelberg (2015)

[FRR+10] Faust, S., Rabin, T., Reyzin, L., Tromer, E., Vaikuntanathan, V.: Protecting circuits from leakage: the computationally-bounded and noisy cases. In: Gilbert, H. (ed.) EUROCRYPT 2010. LNCS, vol. 6110, pp. 135–156. Springer, Heidelberg (2010)

[GHR15] Guilley, S., Heuser, A., Rioul, O.: A key to success - success exponents for side-channel distinguishers. In: Biryukov, A., Goyal, V. (eds.) INDOCRYPT 2015. LNCS, vol. 9462, pp. 270–290. Springer, Heidelberg (2015)

[ISW03] Ishai, Y., Sahai, A., Wagner, D.: Private circuits: securing hardware against probing attacks. In: Boneh, D. (ed.) CRYPTO 2003. LNCS, vol. 2729, pp. 463–481. Springer, Heidelberg (2003)

[ORSW12] Oren, Y., Renauld, M., Standaert, F.-X., Wool, A.: Algebraic side-channel attacks beyond the hamming weight leakage model. In: Prouff, E., Schaumont, P. (eds.) CHES 2012. LNCS, vol. 7428, pp. 140–154. Springer, Heidelberg (2012)

[PR13] Prouff, E., Rivain, M.: Masking against side-channel attacks: a formal security proof. In: Johansson, T., Nguyen, P.Q. (eds.) EUROCRYPT 2013. LNCS, vol. 7881, pp. 142–159. Springer, Heidelberg (2013)

[RP10] Rivain, M., Prouff, E.: Provably secure higher-order masking of AES. In: Mangard, S., Standaert, F.-X. (eds.) CHES 2010. LNCS, vol. 6225, pp. 413–427. Springer, Heidelberg (2010)

[Sha79] Shamir, A.: How to share a secret. Commun. ACM **22**(11), 612–613 (1979)

[SVO+10] Standaert, F.-X., Veyrat-Charvillon, N., Oswald, E., Gierlichs, B., Medwed, M., Kasper, M., Mangard, S.: The world is not enough: another look on second-order DPA. In: Abe, M. (ed.) ASIACRYPT 2010. LNCS, vol. 6477, pp. 112–129. Springer, Heidelberg (2010)

[VGS14] Veyrat-Charvillon, N., Gérard, B., Standaert, F.-X.: Soft analytical side-channel attacks. In: Sarkar, P., Iwata, T. (eds.) ASIACRYPT 2014. LNCS, vol. 8873, pp. 282–296. Springer, Heidelberg (2014)

Towards Easy Leakage Certification

François Durvaux[(⊠)], François-Xavier Standaert, and Santos Merino Del Pozo

ICTEAM/ELEN/Crypto Group, Université catholique de Louvain,
Louvain-la-Neuve, Belgium
francois.durvaux@gmail.com, {fstandae,santos.merino}@uclouvain.be

Abstract. Side-channel attacks generally rely on the availability of good leakage models to extract sensitive information from cryptographic implementations. The recently introduced leakage certification tests aim to guarantee that this condition is fulfilled based on sound statistical arguments. They are important ingredients in the evaluation of leaking devices since they allow a good separation between engineering challenges (how to produce clean measurements) and cryptographic ones (how to exploit these measurements). In this paper, we propose an alternative leakage certification test that is significantly simpler to implement than the previous proposal from Eurocrypt 2014. This gain admittedly comes at the cost of a couple of heuristic (yet reasonable) assumptions on the leakage distribution. To confirm its relevance, we first show that it allows confirming previous results of leakage certification. We then put forward that it leads to additional and useful intuitions regarding the information losses caused by incorrect assumptions in leakage modeling.

1 Introduction

Side-channel attacks are an important threat against the security of modern embedded devices. As a result, the search for efficient approaches to secure cryptographic implementations against such attacks has been an ongoing process over the last 15 years. Sound tools for quantifying physical leakages are a central ingredient for this purpose, since they are necessary to balance the implementation cost of concrete countermeasures with the security improvements they provide. Hence, while early countermeasures came with proposals of security evaluations that were sometimes specialized to the countermeasure, more recent works have investigated the possibility to consider evaluation methods that generally apply to any countermeasure. The unified evaluation framework proposed at Eurocrypt 2009 is a popular attempt in this direction [23]. It suggests to analyze cryptographic implementations with a combination of information theoretic and security metrics. The first ones aim at measuring the (worst-case) information leakage independent of the adversary exploiting it, and are typically instantiated with the Mutual Information (MI). The second ones aim at quantifying how efficiently an adversary can take advantage of this leakage in order to turn it into (e.g.) a key recovery, and are typically instantiated with a success rate.

In this context, an important observation is that most side-channel attacks, and in particular any standard Differential Power Analysis (DPA) attack, require

B. Gierlichs and A.Y. Poschmann (Eds.): CHES 2016, LNCS 9813, pp. 40–60, 2016.
DOI: 10.1007/978-3-662-53140-2_3

a leakage model [13]. This model usually corresponds to an estimation of the leakage Probability Density Function (PDF), possibly simplified to certain statistical moments. Since the exact distribution of (e.g.) power consumption or electromagnetic radiation measurements is generally unknown, it raises the problem that any physical security evaluation is possibly biased by model errors. In other words, security evaluations ideally require a perfect leakage model (so that all the information is extracted from the measurements). But in practice models are never perfect, so that the quality of the evaluation may highly depend on the quality of the evaluator. This intuition can be captured with the notion of Perceived Information (PI), that is nothing else than an estimation of the MI biased by the side-channel evaluator's model [19]. Namely, the MI captures the worst-case security level of an implementation, as it corresponds to an (hypothetical) adversary who can perfectly profile the leakage PDF. By contrast, the PI captures its practical counterpart, where actual (statistical) estimation procedures are used by an evaluator, in order to profile the leakage PDF.

Picking up on this problem, Durvaux et al. introduced first "leakage certification" methods at Eurocrypt 2014 [8]. Intuitively, leakage certification starts from the fact that actual leakage models are obtained via PDF estimation, which may lead to both estimation and assumption errors. As a result, and since it seems hard to enforce that such estimated models are perfect, the best that one can hope is to guarantee that they are "good enough". For estimation errors, this is easily verified using standard cross–validation techniques (in general, estimation errors can anyway be made arbitrarily small by measuring more). For assumption errors, things are more difficult since detecting them requires to find out whether the estimated model is close to an (unknown) perfect model. Interestingly, the Eurocrypt 2014 paper showed that indirect approaches allow determining if this condition is respected, essentially by comparing the model errors caused by incorrect assumptions to estimation errors. That is, let us assume that an evaluator is given a set of leakage measurements to quantify the security of a leaking implementation. As long as the assumption errors measured from these traces remain small in front of the estimation errors, the evaluator is sure that any improvement of his (possibly imperfect) assumptions will not lead to noticeable degradations of the estimated security level – since the impact of improved assumptions will essentially be hidden by the estimation errors. By contrast, once the assumption errors become significant in front of estimation ones, it means that an improved model is required to extract all the information from the measurements. Hence, leakage certification allows ensuring that the modeling part of an evaluation is sound (i.e. only depends on the implementation – not the evaluator).

In practice, the leakage certification test in [8] requires a number of technical ingredients. Namely, the evaluator first has to characterize the leakages of the target implementation with a sampled (cumulative) distance distribution, and to characterize his model with a simulated (cumulative) distance distribution. Working with distances allows exploiting a univariate goodness–of–fit test even for leakages of large dimensionalities (i.e. it allows comparing the univariate distances between multivariate leakages rather than comparing the multivariate leakages directly). The Cramér–von–Mises divergence is used as a comparison tool in the Eurocrypt 2014 paper. Qualitatively, large divergences between the sampled and simulated distributions essentially mean that the assumptions are imperfect. Quantitatively, the evaluator then has to determine whether such divergences are significant, by verifying whether they can be explained by assumption errors. This essentially requires computing the p-values when testing the hypothesis that the estimated model is correct (which again requires computing many simulated cumulative distance distributions). Summarizing, the beauty of this approach lies in the fact that it only relies on non-parametric estimations and requires no assumptions on the underlying leakage distributions. But this also comes at the cost of quite computationally intensive tools.

In this paper, we analyze solutions to mitigate the latter drawback, by investigating whether (computationally) cheaper and (conceptually) simpler certification procedures can be obtained at the cost of mild assumptions on the statistical distributions in hand. Two natural options directly come to mind for this purpose, that both aim to avoid dealing with the (expensive to characterize) cumulative leakage distributions directly. One possibility is to "summarize" the leakage distribution with its MI/PI estimates (since they can be used as indicators of the side-channel security level, as now proven in [7]). Another one is to analyze this distribution "moments by moments", motivated by the recent results in [16]. In both cases, and following the approach in [8], the main idea remains to compare actual leakage samples generated by a leaking implementation with hypothetical ones generated with the evaluator's model. Surprisingly, we show that the first approach cannot work, because of situations where model errors in one statistical moment (e.g. the mean) are reflected in another statistical moment (e.g. the variance), which typically arises when using the popular stochastic models in [20], and actually corresponds to the context of epistemic noise discussed in [12]. More interestingly, we also show that a moment-based approach provides excellent results under reasonable assumptions, and can borrow from the "leakage detection tests" that are already used by evaluation laboratories [11,14]. The resulting leakage certification method is significantly faster than the Eurocrypt 2014 one (and allows reproducing its experiments). We also show that it easily generalizes to masked implementations, and enables extracting very useful intuitions on the origin of the leakages. Eventually, our new tools lead to simple heuristics to approximate the information loss due to incorrect leakage models, which remained an open problem in [8]. Summarizing, we simplify leakage certification into a set of easy–to–implement procedures, hopefully more attractive for evaluation laboratories, of which we make the prototype implementations available as open source to facilitate their dissemination [1].

Cautionary Note. This paper is about *leakage certification*, which is a different problem than the *leakage detection* one discussed in [11,14] (despite we indeed borrow some tools from leakage detection to simplify leakage certification). In this respect, Goodwill et al.'s non specific t-test is a natural approach to leakage detection, and allows determining if there is "some" leakage in an implementation, independent of whether it can be exploited (e.g. how many traces do you need to attack). By contrast, leakage certification aims to guarantee that a leakage model that can be exploited in an attack (and, e.g. can be used to determine a key recovery success rate) is close enough to the true leakage model. That is, it aims to make evaluators confident that their attacks are close enough to the worst-case ones. So leakage detection and certification are essentially complementary. Note that leakage models (and certification) are needed in any attempt to connect side-channel analysis with cryptographic security guarantees (e.g. in leakage resilience [10]), where we will always need an accurate evaluation of the security level, or to build security graphs such as introduced in [27].

2 Background

2.1 Measurement Setup

We will consider both software and hardware experiments.

Our software experiments are based on measurements of an AES Furious implementation[1] run by an 8-bit Atmel AVR (ATMega644P) microcontroller at a 20 MHz clock frequency. We monitored the voltage variations across a 22 Ω resistor introduced in the supply circuit of our target chip. Acquisitions were performed using a Lecroy WaveRunner HRO 66 oscilloscope running at 625 Msamples/second and providing 8-bit samples. In practice, our evaluations focused on the leakage of the first AES master key byte (but would apply identically to any other enumerable target). Leakage traces were produced according to the following procedure. Let x and s be our target input plaintext byte and subkey, and $y = x \oplus s$. For each of the 256 values of y, we generated 1000 encryption traces, where the rest of the plaintext and key was random (i.e. we generated 256 000 traces in total, with plaintexts of the shape $p = x||r_1|| \ldots ||r_{15}$, keys of the shape $\kappa = s||r_{16}|| \ldots ||r_{30}$, and the r_i's denoting uniformly random bytes). In order to reduce the memory cost of our evaluations, we only stored the leakage corresponding to the 2 first AES rounds (as the dependencies in our target byte $y = x \oplus s$ typically vanish after the first round, because of the strong diffusion properties of the AES). We will denote the 1000 encryption traces obtained from a plaintext p including the target byte x under a key κ including the subkey s as: $\mathsf{AES}_{\kappa_s}(p_x) \rightsquigarrow l_y^i$ (with $i \in [1; 1000]$). Eventually, whenever accessing the points of these traces, we will use the notation $l_y^i(\tau)$ (with $\tau \in [1; 10\ 000]$, typically). Subscripts and superscripts are omitted when clear from the context.

Our hardware experiments are based on a similar setup, but consider a threshold implementation of PRESENT similar to the *Profile-4* design described in [17]. The leakage in such hardware implementations is mostly determined by the distance between two consecutive values in a target register R. Hence, we generated traces l_t^i (with $i \in [1; 100\ 000]$) for the 256 possible transitions $t =: R(x_1 \oplus s) \rightarrow R(x_2 \oplus s)$ between 4-bit intermediate results of the PRESENT S-box computations. This larger evaluation set was motivated by the protected

---

[1] Available at http://point-at-infinity.org/avraes/.

nature and larger noise of this implementation. Because of similar memory constraints as in the software case, we limited our measurements to the first PRESENT round. These measurements were taken at a 500 Msamples/second, using the SAKURA-G board [2]. Our target device is a SPARTAN-6 FPGA.

2.2   PDF Estimation Methods

Side-channel attacks such as the standard DPA described in [13] require a leakage model. In general, such models correspond to estimations of the leakage PDF (possibly simplified to certain statistical moments). In the following, we will consider two important PDF estimation techniques for this purpose. For convenience, we describe them with a profiling based on intermediate values y's as considered in our software experiments, but these tools can be applied similarly to the transitions t's considered in our hardware experiments.

Gaussian Templates. The Template Attack (TA) in [5] approximates the leakages using a set of normal distributions. It assumes that each intermediate computation generates Gaussian-distributed samples. In our typical scenario where the targets follow a key addition, we consequently use: $\hat{\Pr}_{\mathsf{model}}[l_y|s, x] \approx \hat{\Pr}_{\mathsf{model}}[l_y|s \oplus x] \sim \mathcal{N}(\mu_y, \sigma_y^2)$, where the "hat" notation is used to denote the estimation of a statistic. This approach requires estimating the sample means and variances for each value $y = x \oplus s$ (and mean vectors / covariance matrices in case of multivariate attacks). We denote the construction of such a model with $\hat{\Pr}_{\mathsf{model}}^{\mathsf{ta}} \leftarrow \mathcal{L}_Y^p$, where $\mathcal{L}_Y^p$ is a set of N_p traces used for profiling.

Regression-Based Models. To reduce the data complexity of the profiling, an alternative approach proposed by Schindler et al. is to exploit Linear Regression (LR) [20]. In this case, a stochastic model $\hat{\theta}(y)$ is used to approximate the leakage function and built from a linear basis $\mathbf{g}(y) = \{\mathbf{g}_0(y), ..., \mathbf{g}_{B-1}(y)\}$ chosen by the adversary/evaluator (usually $\mathbf{g}_i(y)$ are monomials in the bits of y). Evaluating $\hat{\theta}(y)$ boils down to estimating the coefficients α_i such that the vector $\hat{\theta}(y) = \sum_i \alpha_i \mathbf{g}_i(y)$ is a least-square approximation of the measured leakages L_y. In general, an interesting feature of such models is that they allow trading profiling efforts for online attack complexity, by adapting the basis $\mathbf{g}(y)$. That is, a simpler model with fewer parameters will converge for smaller values of N_p, but a more complex model can potentially approximate the real leakage function more accurately. Compared to Gaussian templates, another feature of this approach is that only a single variance (or covariance matrix) is estimated for capturing the noise (i.e. it relies on an assumption of homoscedastic errors). Again, we denote the constructions of such a model with $\hat{\Pr}_{\mathsf{model}}^{\mathsf{lr}} \leftarrow \mathcal{L}_Y^p$.

2.3   Evaluation Metrics

In this subsection, we recall a couple of useful evaluation metrics that have been introduced in previous works on side-channel attacks and countermeasures.

For convenience, we again express these metrics for software (value-based) profiling. But they can straightforwardly adapted to the transition-based case.

Correlation Coefficient. In view of the popularity of the Correlation Power Analysis (CPA) distinguisher in the literature [4], a natural candidate evaluation metric is Pearson's correlation coefficient. In the non-profiled setting, an a-priori (e.g. Hamming weight) model is used for computing the metric. The evaluator then estimates the correlation between his measured leakages and the modeled leakages of a target intermediate value. In our AES example, it would lead to $\hat{\rho}(L_Y(\tau), \mathsf{model}_{\mathsf{cpa}}(Y))$. In practice, this estimation is performed by sampling (i.e. measuring) N_t test traces from the leakage distribution (we denote the set of these N_t test traces as $\mathcal{L}_Y^t$). Next, and in order to avoid possible biases due to an incorrect a-priori choice of leakage model, a natural solution is to extend the previous proposal to the profiled setting. In this case, the evaluator will start by estimating a model from N_p profiling traces: $\mathsf{model}_{\mathsf{cpa}} \leftarrow \mathcal{L}_Y^p$ (with $\mathcal{L}_Y^p \perp\!\!\!\perp \mathcal{L}_Y^t$). In practice, $\mathsf{model}_{\mathsf{cpa}}$ can be seen as a simplification of the previous Gaussian templates, that only includes estimates for the first-order moments of the leakages. That is, for any time sample τ, we have $\mathsf{model}_{\mathsf{cpa}}(y) = \hat{m}_y^1(\tau) = \hat{\mathsf{E}}_i(L_y^i(\tau))$, with $\hat{m}_y^1$ a first-order moment and $\hat{\mathsf{E}}$ the sample mean operator.

Mutual and Perceived Information. In theory, the worst-case security level of an implementation can be measured with a MI metric. Taking advantage of the notations in Sect. 2.1 and considering the standard case where a key byte S is targeted, it amounts to estimate the following quantity:

$$\mathrm{MI}(S; X, L) = \mathrm{H}[S] + \sum_{s \in \mathcal{S}} \Pr[s] \sum_{x \in \mathcal{X}} \Pr[x] \sum_{l_y^i \in \mathcal{L}_t} \Pr_{\mathsf{chip}}[l_y^i | s, x] . \log_2 \Pr_{\mathsf{chip}}[s | x, l_y^i].$$

When summing over all s and x values, and a sufficiently large number of leakages, the estimation tends to the correct MI. Yet, as mentioned in introduction, the chip distribution $\Pr_{\mathsf{chip}}[l_y^i | s, x]$ is generally unknown to the evaluator. So in practice, the best that we can hope is to compute the following PI:

$$\hat{\mathrm{PI}}(S; X, L) = \mathrm{H}[S] + \sum_{s \in \mathcal{S}} \Pr[s] \sum_{x \in \mathcal{X}} \Pr[x] \sum_{l_y^i \in \mathcal{L}_t} \Pr_{\mathsf{chip}}[l_y^i | s, x] . \log_2 \hat{\Pr}_{\mathsf{model}}[s | x, l_y^i],$$

where $\hat{\Pr}_{\mathsf{model}} \leftarrow \mathcal{L}_Y^p$ is typically obtained using the previous Gaussian templates or LR-based models. Under the assumption that the model is properly estimated, it is shown in [13] that the CPA and PI metrics are essentially equivalent in the context of standard univariate side-channel attacks (i.e. exploiting a single leakage point $l_y^i(\tau)$ at a time). By contrast, only the PI naturally extends to multivariate attacks. It can be interpreted as the amount of information leakage that will be exploited by an adversary using an estimated model. So just as the MI is a good predictor for the success rate of an ideal TA exploiting the perfect model $\Pr_{\mathsf{chip}}$, the PI is a good predictor for the success rate of an actual TA exploiting the "best available" model $\hat{\Pr}_{\mathsf{model}}$ obtained thanks to profiling.

Moments-Correlating DPA. Eventually, and in order to extend the CPA distinguisher to higher-order moments, the Moments-Correlating Profiled DPA (MCP-DPA) has been introduced in [16]. It features essentially the same steps as a profiled CPA. The only difference is that the adversary first estimates dth-order statistical moments with his profiling traces, and then uses $\hat{\text{model}}^d_{\text{mcp-dpa}}(y) = \hat{m}^d_y(\tau)$, with $\hat{m}^d_y$ a dth-order moment. For concreteness, we will consider d's up to four (i.e. the sample mean for $d = 1$, variance for $d = 2$, skewness for $d = 3$ and kurtosis for $d = 4$), which allows us discussing the relevant case-study of a masked implementation with two shares. Yet, the tool naturally extends to any d. One useful feature of this distinguisher is that it embeds the same "metric" intuition as CPA: the higher the correlation estimated with MCP-DPA, the more efficient the corresponding attack exploiting a moment of given order.

2.4 Estimating a Metric with Cross-validation

Estimating a metric α from a leaking implementation holds in two steps. First, a model has to be estimated from a set of profiling traces $\mathcal{L}_p$: $\text{model} \leftarrow \mathcal{L}_p$. Second, a set of test traces $\mathcal{L}_t$ (following the true distribution $\Pr_{\text{chip}}$) is used to estimate the metric: $\hat{\alpha} \leftarrow (\mathcal{L}_t, \text{model})$. As a result, two main types of errors can arise. First, the number of traces in the profiling set may be too low to estimate the model accurately (which corresponds to estimation errors). Second, the model may not be able to accurately predict the distribution of samples in the test set, even after intensive profiling (which then corresponds to assumption errors).

In order to verify that estimations in a security evaluation are sufficiently accurate, the solution used in [8] is to exploit cross-validation. In general, this technique allows gauging how well a predictive (here leakage) model performs in practice. For k-fold cross-validations, the set of evaluation traces $\mathcal{L}$ is first split into k (non overlapping) sets $\mathcal{L}^{(i)}$ of approximately the same size. Let us define the profiling sets $\mathcal{L}_p^{(j)} = \bigcup_{i \neq j} \mathcal{L}^{(i)}$ and the test sets $\mathcal{L}_t^{(j)} = \mathcal{L} \setminus \mathcal{L}_p^{(j)}$. The sample metric is then repeatedly computed k times for $1 \leq j \leq k$ as follows. First, we build a model from a profiling set: $\text{model}^{(j)} \leftarrow \mathcal{L}_p^{(j)}$. Then we estimate the metric with the associated test set $\hat{\alpha}^{(j)} \leftarrow (\mathcal{L}_t^{(j)}, \text{model}^{(j)})$. Cross-validation protects evaluators from obtaining too optimistic sample metric values due to over-fitting, since the test computations are always performed with an independent data set. Finally, the k outputs can be averaged in order to get an unbiased metric estimate, and their spread characterizes the result's accuracy.

3   A Motivating Negative Result

As mentioned in introduction, detecting assumption errors is generally more challenging than detecting estimation errors (which is easily done with the previous cross-validation). Intuitively, it requires to investigate the likelihood that samples obtained from a leaking device can indeed be explained by an estimated model, which requires a (multivariate) goodness-of-fit test. Since such tests are computationally intensive, an appealing alternative would be to check whether the samples obtained from the leaking device lead to a PI that is at least close enough to the MI: this would guarantee a good estimation of the security level. But we again face the problem that the MI is unknown, which imposes trying indirect approaches. That is, we would need an metric counterpart to the sampled simulated distance distribution in [8], which would typically correspond to the following Hypothetical (mutual) Information (HI):

$$\hat{\text{HI}}(S; X, L) = \text{H}[S] + \sum_{s \in \mathcal{S}} \Pr[s] \sum_{x \in \mathcal{X}} \Pr[x] \sum_{l_y^i \in \mathcal{L}_t} \hat{\Pr}_{\text{model}}[l_y^i | s, x] \cdot \log_2 \hat{\Pr}_{\text{model}}[s | x, l_y^i].$$

Intuitively, this HI corresponds to the amount of information that would be extracted from an hypothetical implementation that would exactly leak according to the model $\hat{\Pr}_{\text{model}}$. In itself, the HI is useless to the evaluator, as it is actually disconnected from the chip distribution. For example, even a totally incorrect model (i.e. leading to a negative PI) would lead to a positive HI. By contrast, we could hope that as long as the HI and PI are "close", the assumption errors are "small enough" for the number of measurements considered in the security evaluation. Furthermore, we could use a simple hypothesis test to detect non-closeness. For a number of traces N in the evaluation set, this would require to compute estimates $\hat{\text{PI}}(S; X, L)^{(j)}$ and $\hat{\text{HI}}(S; X, L)^{(j)}$ with cross–validation, and to check whether these estimates come from different (univariate) distributions. If they significantly differ, we would conclude that the model exhibits assumption errors that degrade the estimated security level, in a similar fashion as in [8].

Unfortunately, and despite it can detect certain assumption errors, this approach cannot succeed in general. A simple counter–example can be explained in the context of LR. Say an adversary estimates a model with a linear basis, which leads to significant differences between the actual (mean) leakages and the ones suggested by the model. Then, because of the homoscedastic error assumption, the single variance of the LR-based model will reflect this error (i.e. capture both physical noise and model error). As a result, whenever this type of error increases, the PI will decrease (as expected) but the HI will also decrease (contrary to the MI). So testing the consistency between the PI and HI estimates will not reveal the inconsistencies between the PI estimates and the true MI.

4   A New Method to Detect Assumption Errors

Despite negative, the previous counter–example suggests two interesting tracks for simplifying leakage certification tests. First, summarizing a complete distribution into representative metrics (e.g. such as the PI) allows taking advantage of simpler statistical tests. Second, since the fact that the homoscedastic errors assumption is not fulfilled implies that errors made in the estimation of certain statistical moments (or more generally, parameters) of a distribution are reflected in other statistical moments of this distribution, a natural approach is to test the relevance of a model "moment by moment". That is, for a number of traces N in an evaluation set, one could verify that the moments estimated from actual leakage samples are hard to tell apart from the moments estimated from the model (with the same number of samples N). Based on this idea, our simplified method to detect assumption errors will be based on the following two hypotheses (one strictly necessary and the other optional but simplifying).

1. *The leakage distribution is well represented by its statistical moments.* This corresponds to the classical "moment problem" in statistics, for which there exist counter-examples (e.g. the log-normal distribution is not uniquely characterized by its moments). So our (informal) assumption is that these counter-examples will not be significant for our experimental case-studies.

2. *The sampled estimates of our statistical moments are approximately Gaussian-distributed.* This directly derives from the central limit theorem and actually depends on the number of samples used in the estimations (which will become sufficient as the leakages become more noisy, e.g. in the case of protected implementations that are most relevant for concrete investigations).

Let us add a couple of words of motivation for those assumptions.

First recall that we know from the previous results in [8] that leakage certification is possible without such assumptions, at the cost of somewhat involved statistical reasoning and estimations. So it seems natural to investigate alternative (heuristic) paths allowing to reach similar conclusions. As will be shown next, this is indeed the case of our simplified approach for a couple of relevant scenarios. Second, statistical moments are at the core of the reasoning regarding the masking countermeasure. That is, the security order of an implementation is generally defined as the lowest informative moment in the leakage distribution (minus one) – see [7] for an extensive discussion of this issue. Besides, many concrete (profiled and non-profiled) side-channel attacks are based (implicitly or explicitly) on parametric PDF estimation techniques that rely on the estimation of moments (e.g. the Gaussian templates and LR-based models in Sect. 2.2, but also second-order attacks such as [6,18]). So a certificative approach based on an analysis of moments seems well founded in these cases.[2] Eventually, contradictions of this first hypothesis imply potential false negatives in leakage certification, but no false positives. So it remains that any detected assumption error requires model improvement by the evaluator. Overall, and maybe most importantly, we believe that the following tools open interesting research avenues regarding the intuitive evaluation of leaking devices based on their moments.

---

[2] Note that theoretical approches to guarantee that a distribution is well characterized by its moments (such as Carleman's condition [22]) typically apply when considering an infinite number of them and in general, no distribution is determined by a finite number of moments. So the restriction of our reasoning to specific classes of meaningful distributions is in fact necessary for our approach to be sound. Besides, note also that non-parametric PDF estimations may not suffer from assumption errors (at the cost of a significantly increased estimation cost), so are out of scope here.

As for the Gaussian assumption, our motivation is even more pragmatic, and relates to the observation that simple t-tests are becoming de facto standards in the preliminary evaluation of leaking devices [11,14,21]. So we find it appealing to rely on statistical tools that are already widespread in the CHES community, and to connect them with leakage certification. As will be clear next, this allows us to use the same evaluation method for statistical moments of different orders. However, we insist that it is perfectly feasible to refine our approach by using a well adapted test for each statistical moment (e.g. F-test for variances, . . .).

4.1   Test Specification

The main idea behind our new leakage certification method is to compare (actual) dth-order moments $\hat{m}_y^d$ estimated from the leakages with (simulated) dth-order moments $\tilde{m}_y^d$ estimated from the evaluator's model $\hat{\mathrm{Pr}}_{\mathrm{model}}$ (by sampling this model). Thanks to our second assumption, this comparison can simply be performed based on Student's t-test. For this purpose, we need multiple estimations of the moments $\hat{m}_y^d$ and $\tilde{m}_y^d$, that we will obtain thanks to an approach inspired from Sect. 2.4 (although there is no cross–validation involved here).

More precisely, we start by splitting the full set of evaluation traces $\mathcal{L}$ into k (non overlapping) sets of approximately the same size $\mathcal{L}^{(j)}$, with $1 \le j \le k$. From these k subsets, we produce k estimates of (actual) d^{th}-order moments $\hat{m}_y^{d,(j)}$, each of them from a set $\mathcal{L}^{(j)}$. We then produce a set of simulated traces $\tilde{\mathcal{L}}$ that has the same size and corresponds to the same intermediate values as the real evaluation set $\mathcal{L}$, but where the leakages are sampled according to the model that we want to evaluate. In other words, we first build the model $\hat{\mathrm{Pr}}_{\mathrm{model}} \leftarrow \mathcal{L}$, and then generate a simulated set of traces $\tilde{\mathcal{L}} \leftarrow \hat{\mathrm{Pr}}_{\mathrm{model}}$. Based on $\tilde{\mathcal{L}}$, we produce k estimates of (simulated) d^{th}-order moments $\tilde{m}_y^{d,(j)}$, each of them from a set $\tilde{\mathcal{L}}^{(j)}$, as done for the real set of evaluation traces. From these real and simulated moments estimates, we compute the following quantities:

$$\hat{\mu}_y^d = \hat{\mathsf{E}}_j(\hat{m}_y^{d,(j)}), \qquad \hat{\sigma}_y^d = \sqrt{\hat{\mathsf{var}}_j(\hat{m}_y^{d,(j)})},$$

$$\tilde{\mu}_y^d = \hat{\mathsf{E}}_j(\tilde{m}_y^{d,(j)}), \qquad \tilde{\sigma}_y^d = \sqrt{\hat{\mathsf{var}}_j(\tilde{m}_y^{d,(j)})},$$

where $\hat{\mathsf{var}}$ is the sample variance operator. Eventually, we simply estimate the t statistic (next denoted with Δ_y^d) as follows:

$$\Delta_y^d = \frac{\hat{\mu}_y^d - \tilde{\mu}_y^d}{\sqrt{\frac{(\hat{\sigma}_y^d)^2 + (\tilde{\sigma}_y^d)^2}{k}}}.$$

The p-value of this t statistic within the associated Student's distribution returns the probability that the observed difference is the result of estimations issues:

$$p = 2 \times (1 - \mathsf{CDF}_{\mathsf{t}}(|\Delta_y^d|, d_f)),$$

where $\mathsf{CDF_t}$ is the Student's t cumulative distribution function, and d_f is its number of freedom degrees.[3] In other words, a small p-value indicates that the model is incorrect with high probability. Concretely, the only parameter to set in this test is the number of non overlapping sets k. Following [8], we used $k = 10$ which is a rather standard value in the literature. Note that increasing k has very limited impact on the accuracy of our conclusions since all variance estimates in the t-test are normalized by k. By contast it increases the time complexity of the test (so keeping k reasonably small is in general a good strategy).

5   Simulated Experiments

In order to validate our moment-based certification method, we first analyze a couple of simulated experiments, where we can control the assumption errors. In particular, and in order to keep these simulations reasonably close to concrete attacks, we consider four distinct scenarios. In the first one (reported in Fig. 1) we investigate errors in the mean of the model distribution. The upper part of the figure represents a non-parametric estimate of the true leakage distribution (with histograms) and a leakage model $\hat{\mathrm{Pr}}_{\mathtt{model}}$ following a Gaussian distribution. The middle part of the figure represents the estimated moments $\hat{m}_y^{d,(j)}$ (in blue) and $\tilde{m}_y^{d,(j)}$ (in red), in function of the number of traces used for their estimation, from which we clearly see the error in the mean. The lower part of the figure represents the evolution of our test's p-value in function of the number of traces used for certification. As expected, we directly detect an error in the mean (reflected by a very small p-value for this moment), whereas the p-values of the other moments remain erratic, reflecting the fact that (hypothetical) assumption errors are not significant in front of estimation errors (i.e. do not lead to significant information losses) for those moments. Similar figures corresponding to model errors in the variance, skewness and kurtosis are reported in the ePrint version of this work [9]. The last two cases typically correspond to the setting of a masked implementation for which the true distribution is a mixture [25].

These results confirm the simplicity of the method. That is, as the number of measurements in the evaluation set increases, we are able to detect the assumption errors in all cases. The only difference between the applications to different moments is that errors on higher-order moments may be more difficult to detect as the noise increases. This difference is caused by the same argument that justifies the relevance of the higher-order masking countermeasure. Namely, the sampling complexity when estimating the moments of a sufficiently noisy distribution increases exponentially in d. However, this is not a limitation of the certification test: if such errors are not detected for a given evaluation set, it just means that their impact is still small in front of assumption errors at this stage of the evaluation. Besides, we note that the respective relevance of the model errors on different moments will be further discussed in Sect. 7.

---

[3] Student's t distribution is a parametric probability density function whose only parameter is its number of freedom degrees, that can be directly derived from k and the previous σ estimates as: $d_f = (k-1) \times [(\hat{\sigma}_y^d)^2 + (\tilde{\sigma}_y^d)^2]^2 / [(\hat{\sigma}_y^d)^4 + (\tilde{\sigma}_y^d)^4]$.

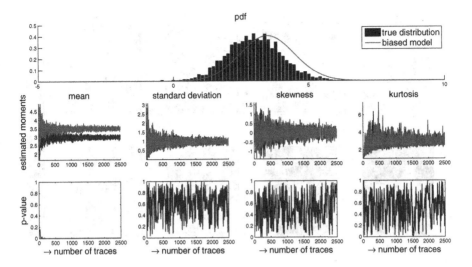

Fig. 1. Gaussian leakages, Gaussian model, error in the estimated mean. (Color figure online)

6 Software Experiments

In order to obtain a fair comparison with the results provided in [8], we first applied our new leakage certification method to the same case-study. Namely, we used the measurement setup from Sect. 2.1 and evaluated the relevance of two important profiling methods, namely the Gaussian TA and LR, for the most informative time sample in our leakage traces (i.e. with maximum PI).

The main difference with the previous simulated experiments is that we now have to test 256 models independently (each of them corresponding to a target intermediate value $y = x \oplus s$). Our results are represented in Fig. 2, where we plot the p-values output by our different t-tests in greyscale, for four statistical moments (i.e. the mean, variance, skewness and kurtosis). That is, each line in this plot corresponds to the lower part of the previous Fig. 1. A look at the first two moments essentially confirms the conclusions of Durvaux et al. More precisely, the Gaussian templates capture the measured leakages quite accurately (for the 256,000 traces in our evaluation set). By contrast, the linear regression quickly exhibits inconsistences. Interestingly, assumption errors appear both in the means and in the variances, which corresponds to the expected intuition. That is, errors in the means are detected because for most target intermediate values, the actual leakage cannot be accurately predicted by a linear combination of the S-box output bits.[4] And errors in the variances appear because the

---

[4] This happens for the selected time sample because of pipelining effects in the AVR microcontroller. Note that as in [8], the linear model did not exhibit any assumption error for other time samples given the amount of measured traces.

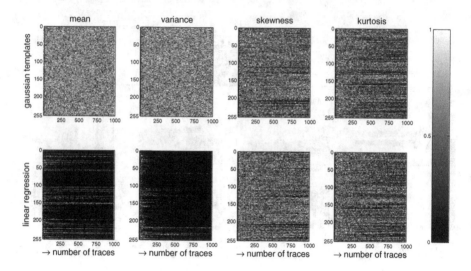

Fig. 2. Results of the new leakage certification test for software measurements.

LR-based models rely on the homoscedastic error assumption and capture both physical noise and noise due to assumption errors in a single term.

By contrast, and quite intriguingly, a look at the last two moments (i.e. skewness and kurtosis) also shows some differences with the results in [8]. That is, we remark that even for Gaussian templates, small model errors appear in these higher-order moments. This essentially corresponds to the fact that our measured leakages do not have perfectly key-independent skewness and kurtosis, as we assume in Gaussian PDF estimations. This last observation naturally raises the question whether these errors are significant, i.e. do they contradict the results of the Eurocrypt 2014 leakage certification test? In the next section, we show that it is not the case, and re-conciliate both approaches by investigating the respective informativeness of the four moments in our new test.

7 Quantifying the Information Loss

Since Fig. 2 suggests the existence of (small) model errors in our Gaussian templates, that are due to an incorrect characterization of the third- and fourth-order moments in our leakage traces, we now want to investigate whether these errors are leading to significant information losses. Fortunately, our "per-moment" approach to leakage certification also allows simple investigations in this direction (which heuristically answers one of the open questions in [8], about the information loss due to model errors). In particular, we can simply use the MCP-DPA mentioned in Sect. 2.3 for this purpose. Roughly, this tool computes the correlation between a simplified model (that corresponds to dth-order moments of the leakage distribution) to samples raised to the power d (centered or standardized if we consider centered and standardized moments). As discussed in [16], the resulting estimated correlation features a "metric intuition": the higher the value of the MCP-DPA distinguisher computed for an order d, the more efficient the MCP-DPA attack exploiting this statistical order of the leakage distribution. Hence, computing the value of the MCP-DPA distinguisher for different values of d should solve our problem, i.e. determine whether the moments for which assumption errors are detected are (among) the most informative ones.

Concretely, we start by applying MCP-DPA in the traditional sense and exploit cross–validation for this purpose, this time following exactly Sect. 2.4. That is, the set of evaluation traces $\mathcal{L}$ is again split into k (non overlapping) sets $\mathcal{L}^{(i)}$ of approximately the same size, and we use profiling sets $\mathcal{L}_p^{(j)} = \bigcup_{i \neq j} \mathcal{L}^{(i)}$ and test sets $\mathcal{L}_t^{(j)} = \mathcal{L} \backslash \mathcal{L}_p^{(j)}$. We then repeatedly compute the dth-order moments $\hat{m}_y^{d,(j)} \leftarrow \mathcal{L}_p^{(j)}$, and the dth-order MCP-DPA distinguisher:

$$\text{MCP-DPA}^{(j)}(d) = \hat{\rho}\Big(\hat{M}_Y^{d,(j)}, (L_y)^d \leftarrow \mathcal{L}_t^{(j)}\Big).$$

As previously mentioned, it corresponds to the sample correlation between the random variable representing the estimated moments $\hat{M}_Y^d$, and the random variable corresponding to the leakage samples coming from the test set $L_y \leftarrow \mathcal{L}_t^{(j)}$, raised to power d (possibly centered or standardized if we consider centered and standardized moments). The $k = 10$ estimates for this MCP-DPA metric are represented in the top part of Fig. 3. We additionally considered two slightly tweaked versions of MCP-DPA, where we rather estimate Gaussian TA (resp. LR-based) models $\hat{\text{Pr}}_{\text{model}}^{\text{ta}}$ (resp. $\hat{\text{Pr}}_{\text{model}}^{\text{lr}}$), and consider the two (resp. one) key-dependent moments from these models to compute the metric. These tweaked MCP-DPAs are represented in the middle (resp. lower) part of the figure.

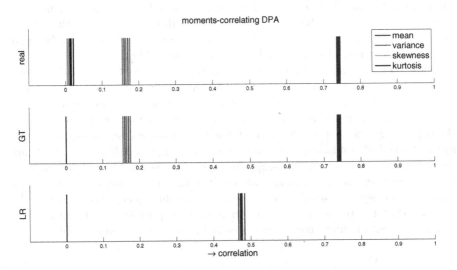

Fig. 3. MCP-DPA results for software measurements (with 256×1000 traces).

Our main observations are as follows. First, the upper part of the figure suggests that the most informative moments in our leakage traces are the mean and variance. There is indeed a small amount of information in the skewness and kurtosis. But by considering the classical rule–of–thumb that the number of samples N_s required to perform a successful correlation-based attack is inversely proportional to the square of its correlation coefficient, that is:

$$N_s \approx \frac{c}{\hat{\rho}\left(\hat{M}_Y^d, (L_y)^d\right)^2},$$

with c a small constant, we can see that the additional information gain in these higher-order moments is very limited in our context. For example the value of the mean-based MCP-DPA distinguisher (for which no assumption errors are detected) is worth ≈ 0.74 in the figure, and the value of the kurtosis-based MCP-DPA distinguisher (for which assumption errors are detected) is worth ≈ 0.02. Considering these two moments as independent information channels, the loss caused by the assumption errors on the kurtosis can be approximated as $\frac{0.74^2}{0.74^2+0.02^2} \approx 0.999$, meaning that improving the model so that the kurtosis is well characterized could only (and ideally) lead to an attack requiring this fraction of N_s to succeed (that is close to 1). This observation backs up the conclusions of the generic leakage certification test in [8] that Gaussian templates are sufficiently accurate for our evaluation set. Next, we see that TA-based and LR-based MCP-DPA yield no information in the higher-order moments, which trivially derives from the fact that they rely on a Gaussian assumption. Eventually, and quite interestingly, we note that the information loss between LR-based models and TA-based models can be approximated thanks to the correlation between their moments. For example, and considering the means in Fig. 3, we can compute the value of the LR-based MCP-DPA distinguisher – worth ≈ 0.48 in the figure – by multiplying the value of the TA-based MCP-DPA distinguisher – worth ≈ 0.74 – by $\hat{\rho}(\hat{M}_Y^{d,\mathsf{ta}}, \hat{M}_Y^{d,\mathsf{lr}})$ – worth ≈ 0.65 in our experiments (i.e. by taking advantage of the "product rule" for the correlation coefficient in [24]).

Those last tools are admittedly informal. Yet, we believe they provide a useful variety of heuristics allowing evaluators to analyze the results of their certification tests. In particular, they lead to easy–to–exploit intuitions regarding the impact of model errors detected in moments of a given order. As discussed in the beginning of Sect. 4, further formalizing these findings, and possibly putting forward relevant scenarios where our simplified approach leads to significant shortcomings, is an interesting scope for further research. Meanwhile, the next section describes an open source code to demonstrate the implementation efficiency of our new certification tests, and Sect. 9 complements these findings by showing that the proposed certification method applies too in the more challenging context of (unprotected and) masked hardware implementations.

8 Open Source Code

The previous experiments can be carried out thanks to five scripts and function files (in the Matlab format .m) available from [1] and described next:

1. **main.m.** This top-level script loads the leakage samples, changes their format, and calls the certification and display functions. The samples need to be formatted because the code is vectorised for efficiency: samples usually come as a disordered vector, i.e. regardless of the target intermediate values. We reshape this sample vector into a matrix of which each column corresponds to an intermediate value. That is, a N_t-by-256 matrix is created if 8-bit values are investigated (with N_t the number of samples per target value).
2. **moment_based_analysis.m.** This function detects assumption errors with our new certification test. For a given number of samples, the first four moments are computed from the leakage samples and then compared to the moments simulated from the two considered models, i.e. Gaussain templates and LR-based. In order to avoid overfitting, cross-validation is involved at each iteration. This function produces the results reported in Fig. 2.
3. **plot_grey_graphs.m.** This script displays the p-values as in Fig. 2.
4. **mcpdpa.m.** This function performs the MCP-DPA part of our analysis, which is only computed for the maximum number of samples per target intermediate values (i.e. N_t). Cross-validation is again exploited in order to avoid overfitting. This function produces the results reported in Fig. 3.
5. **plot_mcpdpa.m.** This scripts displays the MCP-DPA analysis of Fig. 3.

Two files in the Matlab data format .mat are also included in the demonstration code. The first file, **aes_sbox.mat**, is a table corresponding to the AES S-box execution, and is solely used to build the linear regression model. The second file, **traces.mat**, is a file containing the leakage samples in a vector **traces**, and the associated target intermediate value $y = x \oplus k$ in a vector **y**.

From the time complexity point–of–view, this code is considerably more efficient than the previous solution from [8]. Strict comparisons are hard to obtain since our current implementations are prototype ones, and further optimizations could be investigated. But roughly speaking, generating leakage certification plots for 256 leakage models as in Fig. 2 is completed in seconds of computations on a standard desktop computer, whereas it typically took hours with the Eurocrypt 2014 tools. Since the cost of our heuristic leakage certification method is essentially similar to the one of a CPA, it can easily be applied on full leakage traces, in particular if some high performance computing can be exploited to take advantage of the parallel nature of the certification problem [15].

9 Hardware Experiments

As usual in the evaluation of masked implementations, we first ran a preliminary test by setting the masks to constant null values, which actually corresponds to the case of an unprotected FPGA implementation of PRESENT. As mentioned

in Sect. 2, the main difference between this hardware case study and the previous
software one is that the leakages now depend on transitions between consecutive
values in a target register. For the rest, the details about such attacks and their
relation with the underlying architecture (that can be found in [16,17]) are not
necessary to understand our following discussions.

As expected, the results of this preliminary test were essentially similar to
the ones of the unprotected software case. That is, we did not detect assumption
errors for the Gaussian templates with up to 256,000 measurements, while some
errors could be detected in the LR-based attacks. The only interesting bit of
information from this context is the lower MCP-DPA values observed (see the
Appendix in [9]), which can be associated to a higher noise level.

We next moved to the more meaningful case with random masks activated,
for which the leakage certification results are given in Fig. 4. Two main observations can be extracted from these plots. First, and as previously, LR-based
attacks exhibit model errors in the first two moments, that are not detected
with Gaussian templates. Second, and more importantly, we see that strong
errors are detected for the skewness and kurtosis, already quite early in our
evaluation set. This is expected since these two moments are not captured at all,
neither by our Gaussian templates, nor by LR-based attacks. However, since the
information in a (first-order) threshold implementation should lie in higher-order
(at least > 1) statistical moments, it naturally raises the question whether this
model imperfection is critical from a security evaluation point–of–view.

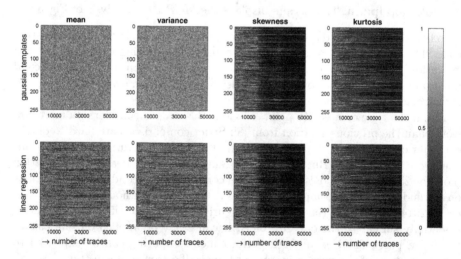

Fig. 4. Results of the new leakage certification test for masked hardware.

In order to answer this question, we again performed MCP-DPA attacks for
different statistical orders, as represented in Fig. 5. Interestingly, the upper plot
shows that, while there is no information in the first-order moments (as guaranteed by the first-order security property of threshold implementations), there is

indeed information in all the other moments. So we are actually in a case where the leakage certification test suggests improvements, and tells the evaluator that his (Gaussian) templates are not sufficient to extract all the information, while LR-based attacks could not succeed at all (since they do estimate a single variance for all the profiled transitions). This raises interesting scopes for further research, since profiling methods that easily incorporate such higher-moments have not been much explored in the side-channel literature so far [3].

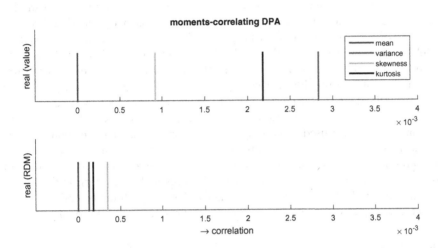

Fig. 5. MCP-DPA results for masked hardware (with 256 × 50,000 traces)

Besides, another interesting observation arises if, rather than simply plotting the asymptotic MCP-DPA values, we also plot the Relative Distinguishing Margin (RDM), defined in [28] as the distance between the correct key distinguisher value and the value for the highest ranked alternative. As illustrated by the lower plot of Fig. 5, this RDM is larger for the skewness than for the variance. This means that while the variance is the most informative moment overall (i.e. assuming some enumeration is possible as a post-processing after the attack [26]), the skewness is more useful in case the adversary has to recover the key thanks to side-channel measurements exclusively (since the nearest rival captured by the RDM is usually the most difficult to distinguish from the good key).

Summarizing, these experiments confirm the applicability of our easy leakage certification tests in a practically-relevant case study (i.e. a threshold implementation that is representative of state–of–the–art masking schemes). They also put forward that combining MCP-DPA evaluations with the estimation of a RDM metric allows extracting additional intuitions regarding the information vs. computation tradeoff that is inherent to any side-channel attack.

10   Conclusion

The evaluation of leaking devices against DPA attacks exploiting statistical models of leakage distributions implies answering two orthogonal questions:

1. Is the model used in the attack/evaluation correct?
2. How informative is the model used in the attack/evaluation?

The second question is highly investigated. It relates to the concrete security level of an implementation *given* a model, e.g. measured with a number of samples needed to recover the key. The first question is much less investigated and relates to the risk of a "false sense of security", i.e. evaluations based on non-informative models despite informative leakages. Leakage certification allows evaluators to guarantee that the models used in their DPA attacks are sufficiently accurate. The simple tests we provide in this paper makes it possible to easily integrate leakage certification in actual toolchains. We hope these results open the way towards globally sound evaluations for leaking devices, where one first guarantees that the models used in the attacks are correct, and then evaluates their informativeness, which boil downs to compute their corresponding PI [7].

Interesting scopes for further research include the extension of the tools in this paper to more case studies of protected implementations with higher-order and multivariate leakages, and the investigation of the profiling errors due to the characterization of different devices, possibly affected by variability [19].

Acknowledgements. François-Xavier Standaert Standaert is a research associate of the Belgian Fund for Scientific Research (FNRS-F.R.S.). This work has been funded in parts by the European Commission through the ERC project 280141 (acronym CRASH) and by the ARC project NANOSEC.

References

1. http://perso.uclouvain.be/fstandae/PUBLIS/171.zip
2. http://satoh.cs.uec.ac.jp/sakura/index.html
3. Batina, L., Gierlichs, B., Prouff, E., Rivain, M., Standaert, F.-X., Veyrat-Charvillon, N.: Mutual information analysis: a comprehensive study. J. Cryptol. **24**(2), 269–291 (2011)
4. Brier, E., Clavier, C., Olivier, F.: Correlation power analysis with a leakage model. In: Joye, M., Quisquater, J.-J. (eds.) CHES 2004. LNCS, vol. 3156, pp. 16–29. Springer, Heidelberg (2004)
5. Chari, S., Rao, J.-R., Rohatgi, P.: Template attacks. In: Kaliski Jr., B.S., Kaya Koç, Ç.K., Paar, C. (eds.) CHES 2002. LNCS, vol. 2523, pp. 13–28. Springer, Heidelberg (2003)
6. Dabosville, G., Doget, J., Prouff, E.: A new second-order side channel attack based on linear regression. IEEE Trans. Comput. **62**(8), 1629–1640 (2013)
7. Duc, A., Faust, S., Standaert, F.-X.: Making masking security proofs concrete - or how to evaluate the security of any leaking device. In: Oswald, E., Fischlin, M. (eds.) EUROCRYPT 2015. LNCS, vol. 9056, pp. 401–429. Springer, Heidelberg (2015)

8. Durvaux, F., Standaert, F.-X., Veyrat-Charvillon, N.: How to certify the leakage of a chip? In: Nguyen, P.Q., Oswald, E. (eds.) EUROCRYPT 2014. LNCS, vol. 8441, pp. 459–476. Springer, Heidelberg (2014)
9. Durvaux, F., Standaert, F.-X., Del Pozo, S.M.: Towards easy leakage certification. Cryptology ePrint Archive, Report 2015/537 (2015). http://eprint.iacr.org/
10. Dziembowski, S., Pietrzak, K.: Leakage-resilient cryptography. In: 49th Annual IEEE Symposium on Foundations of Computer Science, FOCS 2008, 25-28 October 2008, Philadelphia, PA, USA, pp. 293–302. IEEE Computer Society (2008)
11. Goodwill, G., Jun, B., Jaffe, J., Rohatgi, P.: A testing methodology for side channel resistance validation. NIST Non-invasive Attack Testing Workshop (2011). http://csrc.nist.gov/news_events/non-invasive-attack-testing-workshop/papers/08_Goodwill.pdf
12. Heuser, A., Rioul, O., Guilley, S.: Good is not good enough - deriving optimal distinguishers from communication theory. In: Batina, L., Robshaw, M. (eds.) CHES 2014. LNCS, vol. 8731, pp. 55–74. Springer, Heidelberg (2014)
13. Mangard, S., Oswald, E., Standaert, F.-X.: One for all - all for one: unifying standard differential power analysis attacks. IET Inf. Secur. 5(2), 100–110 (2011)
14. Mather, L., Oswald, E., Bandenburg, J., Wójcik, M.: Does my device leak information? An a priori statistical power analysis of leakage detection tests. In: Sako, K., Sarkar, P. (eds.) ASIACRYPT 2013, Part I. LNCS, vol. 8269, pp. 486–505. Springer, Heidelberg (2013)
15. Mather, L., Oswald, E., Whitnall, C.: Multi-target DPA attacks: pushing DPA beyond the limits of a desktop computer. In: Sarkar, P., Iwata, T. (eds.) ASIACRYPT 2014. LNCS, vol. 8873, pp. 243–261. Springer, Heidelberg (2014)
16. Moradi, A., Standaert, F.-X.: Moments-correlating DPA. IACR Cryptology ePrint Archive 2014:409 (2014)
17. Poschmann, A., Moradi, A., Khoo, K., Lim, C.-W., Wang, H., Ling, S.: Side-channel resistant crypto for less than 2, 300 GE. J. Cryptol. 24(2), 322–345 (2011)
18. Prouff, E., Rivain, M., Bevan, R.: Statistical analysis of second order differential power analysis. IEEE Trans. Comput. 58(6), 799–811 (2009)
19. Renauld, M., Standaert, F.-X., Veyrat-Charvillon, N., Kamel, D., Flandre, D.: A formal study of power variability issues and side-channel attacks for nanoscale devices. In: Paterson, K.G. (ed.) EUROCRYPT 2011. LNCS, vol. 6632, pp. 109–128. Springer, Heidelberg (2011)
20. Schindler, W., Lemke, K., Paar, C.: A stochastic model for differential side channel cryptanalysis. In: Rao, J.R., Sunar, B. (eds.) CHES 2005. LNCS, vol. 3659, pp. 30–46. Springer, Heidelberg (2005)
21. Schneider, T., Moradi, A.: Leakage assessment methodology. In: Güneysu, T., Handschuh, H. (eds.) CHES 2015. LNCS, vol. 9293, pp. 495–513. Springer, Heidelberg (2015)
22. Spanos, A.: Probability Theory and Statistical Inference: Econometricmodeling with Observational Data. Cambridge University Press, Cambridge (1999)
23. Standaert, F.-X., Malkin, T.G., Yung, M.: A unified framework for the analysis of side-channel key recovery attacks. In: Joux, A. (ed.) EUROCRYPT 2009. LNCS, vol. 5479, pp. 443–461. Springer, Heidelberg (2009)
24. Standaert, F.-X., Peeters, E., Rouvroy, G., Quisquater, J.-J.: An overview of power analysis attacks against field programmable gate arrays. Proc. IEEE 94(2), 383–394 (2006)
25. Standaert, F.-X., Veyrat-Charvillon, N., Oswald, E., Gierlichs, B., Medwed, M., Kasper, M., Mangard, S.: The world is not enough: another look on second-order

DPA. In: Abe, M. (ed.) ASIACRYPT 2010. LNCS, vol. 6477, pp. 112–129. Springer, Heidelberg (2010)
26. Veyrat-Charvillon, N., Gérard, B., Renauld, M., Standaert, F.-X.: An optimal key enumeration algorithm and its application to side-channel attacks. In: Wu, H., Knudsen, L.R. (eds.) SAC 2012. LNCS, vol. 7707, pp. 390–406. Springer, Heidelberg (2013)
27. Veyrat-Charvillon, N., Gérard, B., Standaert, F.-X.: Security evaluations beyond computing power. In: Nguyen, P.Q., Johansson, T. (eds.) EUROCRYPT 2013. LNCS, vol. 7881, pp. 126–141. Springer, Heidelberg (2013)
28. Whitnall, C., Oswald, E.: A fair evaluation framework for comparing side-channel distinguishers. J. Cryptogr. Eng. 1(2), 145–160 (2011)

Simple Key Enumeration (and Rank Estimation) Using Histograms: An Integrated Approach

Romain Poussier[1(✉)], François-Xavier Standaert[1], and Vincent Grosso[1,2]

[1] ICTEAM/ELEN/Crypto Group, Université catholique de Louvain,
Louvain-la-Neuve, Belgium
{romain.poussier,fstandae}@uclouvain.be
[2] Horst Görtz Institute for IT Security,
Ruhr-Universität Bochum, Bochum, Germany
vincent.grosso@ruhr-uni-bochum.de

Abstract. The main contribution of this paper, is a new key enumeration algorithm that combines the conceptual simplicity of the rank estimation algorithm of Glowacz et al. (from FSE 2015) and the parallelizability of the enumeration algorithm of Bogdanov et al. (SAC 2015) and Martin et al. (from ASIACRYPT 2015). Our new algorithm is based on histograms. It allows obtaining simple bounds on the (small) rounding errors that it introduces and leads to straightforward parallelization. We further show that it can minimize the bandwidth of distributed key testing by selecting parameters that maximize the factorization of the lists of key candidates produced by the enumeration, which can be highly beneficial, e.g. if these tests are performed by a hardware coprocessor. We also put forward that the conceptual simplicity of our algorithm translates into efficient implementations (that slightly improve the state-of-the-art). As an additional consolidating effort, we finally describe an open source implementation of this new enumeration algorithm, combined with the FSE 2015 rank estimation one, that we make available with the paper.

1 Introduction

Key enumeration and rank estimation algorithms have recently emerged as an important part of the security evaluation of cryptographic implementations, which allows post-processing the side-channel attack outcomes and determine the computational security of an implementation after some leakage has been observed. In this respect, key enumeration can be seen as an adversarial tool, since it allows testing key candidates without knowledge of the master key [4,8,10] (for example, it was an important ingredient of the best attack submitted to the DPA Contest v2 [5]). By contrast, rank estimation as an evaluation tool since it requires the knowledge of the master key. Its main advantage is that it allows efficiently gauging the security level of implementations for which enumeration is beyond reach (and therefore are not trivially insecure) [3,7,8,11,12].

Concretely, state-of-the-art solutions for key rank estimation are essentially sufficient to analyze any (symmetric) cryptographic primitive. Algorithms such

© International Association for Cryptologic Research 2016
B. Gierlichs and A.Y. Poschmann (Eds.): CHES 2016, LNCS 9813, pp. 61–81, 2016.
DOI: 10.1007/978-3-662-53140-2_4

as [3,7,8] typically allow estimating the rank of a 128- or 256-bit key with an accuracy of less than one bit, within seconds of computation. By contrast, efficiency remained a concern for key enumeration algorithms for some time, in particular due to the inherently serial nature of the optimal algorithm of Veryat et al. [10]. This situation evolved with the recent (heuristic) work of Bogdanov et al. [4] and the more formal solution of Martin et al. [8]. In these papers, the authors exploit the useful observation that by relaxing (a little bit) the optimality requirements of enumeration algorithms (as one actually does in rank estimation), it is possible to significantly improve their efficiency, and to make them parallelizable. Since this relaxation is done by rounding the key (log) probabilities (or scores) output by a side-channel attack, it directly suggests to try adapting the histogram-based rank estimation algorithm from Glowacz et al. to the case of key enumeration based on similar principles.

In this paper, we follow this track, and describe a new enumeration algorithm based on histogram convolutions. As for rank estimation, using such simple tools brings conceptual simplicity as an important advantage. Interestingly, we show next that this simplicity also leads to several convenient features and natural optimizations of the enumeration problem. First, it directly leads to simple bounds on the rounding errors introduced by our histograms (hence on the additional workload needed to guarantee optimal enumeration up to a certain rank). Second, it allows straightforward parallelization between cores, since the workload of each core is directly available as the number of elements in each bin of our histograms. Third, it outputs the keys as factorized lists, such that by adequately tuning the enumeration parameters (i.e. the number of bins, essentially), we are able to use our enumeration algorithm for distributed key testing with minimum bandwidth (which is typically desirable if hardware/FPGA implementations are used). In this respect, our experiments show that the best strategy is not always to maximize the accuracy of the enumeration (especially when enumerating up to large key ranks). We note that such features could also be integrated to other recent enumeration algorithms (i.e. [8], and to some extent [4]). Yet, this would require some adaptations while it naturally comes for free in our histogram-based case. Eventually, the same observation essentially holds for the performances of our algorithm, which slightly improve the state-of-the-art.

In view of the consolidating nature of this work, an important additional contribution is an open source implementation of our key enumeration algorithm, combined with the histogram-based rank estimation algorithm of FSE 2015, that we make available with this paper in order to facilitate the dissemination of these tools for evaluation laboratories [1].

2   Background

2.1   Algorithms Inputs

Details on how a side-channel attack extracts information from leakage traces are not necessary to understand the following analysis. We only assume that for a n-bit master key k, an attacker recovers information on N_s subkeys $k_0, ..., k_{N_s-1}$ of length $a = \frac{n}{N_s}$ bits (for simplicity, we assume that a divides n). The side-channel adversary uses the leakages corresponding to a set of q inputs $\mathcal{X}_q$ leading to a set of q leakages $\mathcal{L}_q$. As a result of the attack, he obtains N_s lists of 2^a probabilities $P_i = \Pr[k_i^* | \mathcal{X}_q, \mathcal{L}_q]$, where $i \in [0, N_s - 1]$ and k_i^* denotes a subkey candidate among the 2^a possible ones. TA (Template Attacks) and LR (Linear Regression)-based attacks directly output such probabilities. For other attacks such as DPA (Differential Power Analysis) or CPA (Correlation Power Analysis), one can use Bayesian extensions [10] or perform the enumeration directly based on the scores. Note that in this last case, the enumeration result will be correct with respect to the scores, but the corresponding side-channel attack is not guaranteed to be optimal [9]. For simplicity, our following analyses are based only on the optimal case where we enumerate based on probabilities. We leave the investigation of the overheads due to score-based enumeration as an interesting scope for further investigation. Eventually, the lists of probabilities are turned into lists of log probabilities, denoted as $LP_i = \log(P_i)$. This final step is used to get an additive relation between probabilities instead of a multiplicative one.

2.2 Preprocessing

Key enumeration (and rank estimation) algorithms generally benefit from the preprocessing which consists of merging m lists of probabilities P_i of size 2^a in order to generate a larger list $P_i' = \mathsf{merge}(P_0, P_1, \ldots, P_{m-1})$, such that P_i' contains the $2^{m \cdot a}$ product of probabilities of the lists $P_0, P_1, \ldots, P_{m-1}$. Taking again the previous notations where the n bits of master key are split in N_s subkeys of a bits, it allows to split them into $N_s' = N_s/m$ subkeys of $m \cdot a$ bits (or close to it when m does not divide N_s). We denote the preprocessing merging m lists as merge_m, with merge_1 meaning no merging. In the following, we assume that such a preprocessing is performed by default and therefore always use the notation N_s' for the number of subkeys.

2.3 Toolbox

We now introduce a couple of tools that we use to describe our algorithms, using the following notations: H will denote an histogram, N_b will denote a number of bins, b will denote a bin and x a bin index.

Linear histograms. The function $H = \mathsf{hist\_lin}(LP, N_b)$ creates a standard histogram from a list of (e.g.) log probabilities LP and N_b linearly-spaced bins. This is the same function as introduced in [9].

Convolution. This is the usual convolution algorithm which from two histograms H_1 and H_2 of sizes n_1 and n_2 computes $H_{1,2} = \mathsf{conv}(H_1, H_2)$ where $H_{1,2}[k] = \sum_{i=0}^{k} H_1[i] \times H_2[k-i]$. It is efficiently implemented with a FFT in time $\mathcal{O}(n \log n)$. In the rest of the paper we consider that the indexes start at 0.

Getting the size of a histogram. We defined by $\mathsf{size\_of}(H)$ the function that returns the number of bins of an histograms H.

Getting subkey candidates from a bin. We define $\mathcal{K} = \mathbf{get}(H, x)$ as a function that outputs the set of all subkeys contained in the bin of index x of an histogram H. Such a set can contain up to $2^{m \cdot a}$ elements depending on the merging value.

3   Enumeration Algorithm

In this section, we describe our new key enumeration algorithm. Since we join an open source code of this algorithm to the paper, our primary goal is to explain its main intuition. For this purpose, we combine a specification of the different enumeration steps with simple examples to help their understanding.

Concretely, our new key enumeration algorithm is an adaptation of the rank estimation algorithm of Glowacz et al. [7]. As in this previous work, we use histograms to efficiently represent the key log probabilities, and the first step of the key enumeration is a convolution of histograms modeling the distribution of our N'_s lists of log probabilities. This step is detailed in Algorithm 1. In the rest of the paper we will denote the initial histograms $H_0, ..., H_{N'_s - 1}$ and the convoluted histograms $H_{0:1}, ..., H_{0:N'_s - 1}$ as written in the output of Algorithm 1. For illustration, Fig. 1 shows an example of its application in the case of two 4-bit subkeys of which the log probabilities are represented by a 7-bin histogram, which are convoluted in the lower part of the figure.

Algorithm 1. Convolution.

Input. N'_s lists of log probabilities LP_i's, and number of bins N_b.
Output. Histograms of the log probabilities of each sub-key: $H_0, \ldots, H_{N'_s - 1}$,
        and their convolutions $H_{0:1}, \ldots, H_{0:N'_s - 1}$.
  $H_0 \leftarrow \mathsf{hist\_lin}(LP_0, N_b)$;
  $H_1 \leftarrow \mathsf{hist\_lin}(LP_1, N_b)$;
  $H_{0:1} \leftarrow \mathsf{conv}(H_0, H_1)$;
  for $i = 2$ to $N'_s - 1$ **do**
    $H_i \leftarrow \mathsf{hist\_lin}(LP_i, N_b)$;
    $H_{0:i} \leftarrow \mathsf{conv}(H_i, H_{0,i-1})$;
  end for **return** $H = [H_0, \ldots, H_{N'_s - 1}, H_{0:1}, \ldots, H_{0:N'_s - 1}]$.

Based on this first step, our algorithm allows to enumerate keys that are ranked between two bounds B_{start} and B_{stop}. In the standard situation where the adversary wants to enumerate starting from the most likely key, we set $B_{start} = 0$. However, there are at least two cases where other starting bounds can be useful. First, it is possible that one wishes to continue an enumeration that has been started previously. Second, and more importantly, the selection of these bounds directly allows efficient parallel key enumeration, where the amount of computation performed by each core is well balanced.

In order to enumerate all keys ranked between the bounds B_{start} and B_{stop}, the corresponding indexes of $H_{0:N'_s - 1}$ have to be computed, as described in Algorithm 2. It simply sums the number of keys contained in the bins starting

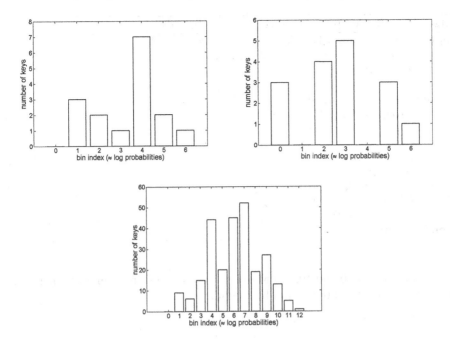

Fig. 1. Histograms representing the log probabilities of two 4-bit subkeys and their convolution. Upper left: $H_0 = [0, 3, 2, 1, 7, 2, 1]$. Upper right: $H_1 = [3, 0, 4, 5, 0, 3, 1]$. Bottom: $H_{0:1} = [0, 9, 6, 15, 44, 20, 45, 52, 19, 27, 13, 5, 1]$.

from the most likely one, until we exceed B_{start} and B_{stop}, and returns the corresponding indexes x_{start} and x_{stop}. That is, x_{start} (resp. x_{stop}) refers to the index of the bin where B_{min} (resp. B_{max}) is achieved (thus $x_{start} \geq x_{stop}$).

As in [7], a convenient feature of the histograms we use to represent the key log probabilities is that they lead to simple bounds on the "enumeration error" that is due to their rounding, hence on the additional workload needed to compensate this error. Namely, if one wants to be sure to enumerate all the keys of which the rank is between the bounds, then he should add $\lceil \frac{N'_s}{2} \rceil$ to x_{start} and substract it to x_{stop}.[1]

Figure 2 illustrates the computation of these indexes using the same example as in Fig. 1. In this case, the user wants to find the bins where the keys are ranked between 10 and 100. By summing up the number of keys contained in the bins of $H_{0:1}$ from the right to the left, we find that the bin indexed 10 starts with the rank 7 and the bin indexed 7 ends with the rank 117. Since the bin indexes 11 and 6 are out of the bounds (10 and 100), we know that the dark grey bins approximately contains the keys we want to enumerate, up to rounding errors. Furthermore, by adding the light grey bins, we are sure that all the keys

---

[1] The authors of [7] had a slightly worst bound of N'_s instead of $\lceil \frac{N'_s}{2} \rceil$. Indeed, they rounded the sum of all the subkeys' log probabilities, instead of summing the rounded subkeys' log probabilities.

Algorithm 2. Computation of the indexes' bounds.

Input. Lower and upper bounds on the key rank B_{start}, B_{stop}.
Output. Indexes of the bins between the bounds x_{start}, x_{stop}.

$x_{start} \leftarrow$ size_of$(H_{0:N'_s-1}) - 1$;
$cnt_{start} \leftarrow 0$;
while $cnt_{start} < B_{start}$ **do**
    $cnt_{start} \leftarrow cnt_{start} + H_{0:N'_s-1}(x_{start})$;
    $x_{start} \leftarrow x_{start} - 1$;
end while
$cnt_{stop} \leftarrow cnt_{start}$;
$x_{stop} \leftarrow x_{start}$;
while $cnt_{stop} < B_{stop}$ **do**
    $cnt_{stop} \leftarrow cnt_{stop} + H_{N'_s-1}(x_{stop})$;
    $x_{stop} \leftarrow x_{stop} - 1$;
end whilereturn x_{start}, x_{stop}.

---

between the ranks 10 and 100, as would be produced by an optimal enumeration algorithm (like [10]), are covered by the bins.

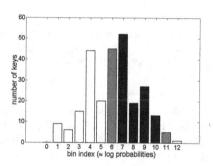

Fig. 2. Computation of the indexes' bounds for $B_{min} = 10$ and $B_{max} = 100$.

Given the histogram of the key log probabilities and the indexes of the bounds between which we want to enumerate, the enumeration simply consists in performing a backtracking over all the bins between x_{start} and x_{stop}. More precisely, during this phase we recover the bins of the initial histograms (i.e. before convolution) that we used to build a bin of the convoluted histogram $H_{0:N'_s-1}$. For a given bin b with index x of $H_{0:N'_s-1}$ corresponding to a certain log probability, we have to run through all the non-empty bins $b_0, ...b_{N'_s-1}$ of indexes $x_0, ...x_{N'_s-1}$ of $H_0, ..., H_{N'_s-1}$ such that $x_0 + ... + x_{N'_s-1} = x$. Each b_i will then contain at least one and at most $2^{m \cdot a}$ subkey(s) that we must enumerate. This leads to a *key factorization* which is a table containing N'_s subkey lists, such that each of these lists contains up to $2^{m \cdot a}$ subkeys associated to the bin b_i of the histogram H_i. Any combination of N'_s subkeys, each one being picked in a different list, results in a master key having the same rounded probability. Eventually, each time a factorization is completed, we call a fictive function process_key which takes as input the result of this factorization. This function could test the keys on-the-fly or send them to a third party for testing (this function is essentially independent of the enumeration process).

Algorithm 3 describes more precisely this bin decomposition process. From a bin index $x_{0:i}$ of $H_{0:i}$, we find all the non empty bins of indexes x_i of H_i such that the corresponding bin of index $x_{0:i} - x_i$ of $H_{0:i-1}$ is non empty as well. All the bins b_i following this property will lead to valid subkeys for k_i that we add to the key factorization using the function $\mathsf{get}(H_i, b_i)$. This is done for all convolution results from the last histogram $H_{0:N'_s-1}$ to the first $H_{0:1}$, which then leads to a full key factorization.

Algorithm 3. Bin decomposition.

Input. H: the structure containing all the histograms output by Algorithm 1;

    csh (*current_small_hist*): the index i of the current histogram H_i we target;

    x_{bin}: The bin index of $H_{0:i}$ we want to decompose.

Output. kf (*key_factorization*): the array of N'_s subkey lists containing factorized keys.

Inline comments are given in Table 1

    if $csh == 1$ **then**

        $x \leftarrow \mathsf{size\_of}(H_0) - 1$;

        while $(x \geq 0)$ & $(x + \mathsf{size\_of}(H_1)) \geq x_{bin})$ **do**   ▷ (1) and (2)

            if $H_0(x) > 0$ & $H_1(x_{bin} - x) > 0$ **then**   ▷ (3)

                $kf(1) \leftarrow \mathsf{get}(H_0, x)$;

                $kf(0) \leftarrow \mathsf{get}(H_1, x_{bin} - x)$;

                $\mathsf{process\_key}(kf)$;

            end if

            $x \leftarrow x - 1$;

        end while

    else

        $x \leftarrow \mathsf{size\_of}(H_{csh}) - 1$;

        while $(x \geq 0)$ & $(x + \mathsf{size\_of}(H_{0:csh-1}) \geq x_{bin})$ **do**   ▷ (4) and (5)

            if $H_{csh}(x) > 0$ & $H_{0:csh-1}(x_{bin} - x) > 0$ **then**   ▷ (6)

                $kf(csh) \leftarrow \mathsf{get}(H_i, x)$;

                $\mathsf{Decompose\_bin}(csh - 1, x_{bin} - x, H, kf)$;

            end if

            $x \leftarrow x - 1$;

        end while

    end if

In order to help the understanding of Algorithm 3, we provide an example of bin decomposition in Fig. 3. In this example, we want to enumerate all the keys having their log probability in the 7th bin of $H_{0:1}$ (represented with black stripes in the bottom part of the figure). Since this bin is not empty, we know that such keys exist. Hence, in order to enumerate all of them, we iterate over all the bins b_0 with indexes x_0 of H_0 and look if the corresponding bins b_1 with indexes $7 - x_0$ of H_1 are non-zero (i.e. contain at least one key). Whenever this

Table 1. Comments for Algorithm 3.

(1)	If $x < 0$ we looked at all the bins of H_0
(2)	If $x > x_{bin} - \text{size\_of}(H_1)$ we looked at all the bins of H_1.
(3)	If $H_0(x) > 0$ & $H_1(x_{bin} - x) > 0$ we have two non-zero bins such that the sum of the indexes matches, thus we found valid subkeys lists for k_0 and k_1.
(4)	If $x < 0$ we looked at all the bins of H_{csh}.
(5)	If $x > x_{bin} - \text{size\_of}(H_{0:csh})$ we looked at all the bins of $H_{0:csh}$.
(6)	If $H_{csh}(x) > 0$ & $H_{0:csh-1}(x_{bin} - x) > 0$ we have two non-zero bins such that the sum of the indexes matches, thus we found a valid subkeys list for k_{csh}

happens, we found a key factorization which corresponds to all the combinations of the subkeys contained in the bin b_0 of H_0 and the bin b_1 of H_1. These possible bin combinations are represented in the same color for H_0 (resp. H_1) in the top left (resp. top right) part of the figure. The bins in white are those for which no such combination is possible. For example, subkeys with log probability in the fourth bin of H_0 would require subkeys with log probability in the fifth bin of H_1 (so that $3 + 4 = 7$), but this fifth bin of H_1 is empty.

The generalization of this algorithm simply follows a recursive decomposition. That is, in order to enumerate all the keys within a bin b of index x in $H_{0:N_s'-1}$, we find two indexes $x_{N_s'-1}$ and $x - x_{N_s'-1}$ of $H_{N_s'-1}$ and $H_{0:N_s'-2}$ such that the corresponding bins are not empty. All the keys in the bin index $x_{N_s'-1}$ of $H_{N_s'-1}$ will be added to the key factorization. We then continue the recursion with the bin $x - x_{N_s'-1}$ of $H_{0:N_s'-2}$ by finding two non-empty bin indexes $x_{N_s'-2}$ and $x - x_{N_s'-1} - x_{N_s'-2}$ of $H_{0:N_s'-3}$, etc.

Finally, the main loop of our new enumeration is given in Algorithm 4. It simply calls Algorithm 3 for all the bins of $H_{0:N_s'-1}$ which are between the enumeration bounds.

Algorithm 4. Histogram-based enumeration.

Input. H: the structure containing all the histograms output by Algorithm 1;
  x_{start}: the bin index of $H_{0:N_s'-1}$ from which we start the enumeration;
  x_{stop}: the bin index of $H_{0:N_s'-1}$ from which we end the enumeration.
Output. kf (*key_factorization*) :the array of N_s' subkey lists containing the factorized keys.

  for $x = x_{start}$ to x_{stop} **do**
    Decompose_bin($N_s' - 1, x, H, kf$);
  end for

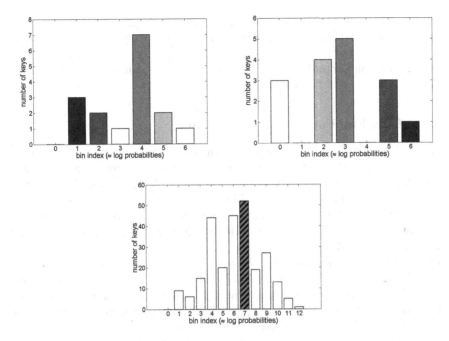

Fig. 3. Enumeration with histogram for a (shifted) log probability of 7.

4   Open Source Code

For usability, we join an open source implementation of our key enumeration algorithm to this paper. For completeness and in view of the similarity of the techniques they exploit, we also include the key rank estimation algorithm of [7] in this tool. The corresponding program is compiled using G++ and uses the NTL library [2] in order to compute the histogram convolutions. It works on Windows and Linux operating systems (and probably on MAC). In this section, we describe the inputs and outputs that have to be set before running key enumeration and rank estimation. The code is provided as supplementary material to the paper, with an example of utilization.

Note that while the previous section only describes the general idea of the algorithm, its implementation contains a couple of additional optimizations, typically involving precomputations, iterating only over non-zero bins of the histograms and ordering the convolution, which allows significant performance improvements.

Inputs of the Rank Estimation Algorithm.

- log_proba: the $N_s \times 2^a$ matrix encoded in double precision containing the subkey log probabilities obtained during thanks to the attack.
- real_key: the N_s-element vector containing the real subkeys values.

- nb_bin : the number of bins for the initial histograms H_i.
- merge: the value of merging. A value of 1 will not do any merging. A value of 2 will merge lists by two, this gives us $N'_s = \lceil \frac{N_s}{2} \rceil$ lists of 2^{2a} elements. The current version supports only a maximum merging value of 3, which means $N'_s = \lceil \frac{N_s}{3} \rceil$ lists of 2^{3a} subkeys.

Inputs of the Key Enumeration Algorithm.

- All the inputs of the rank estimation algorithm (with real_key being optional).
- bound_start: the starting bound of the enumeration. If this is e.g. set to 2^{10}, the enumeration will start from the closest bin of $H_{0:N'_s}$ such that at most 2^{10} keys are contained in the next bins.
- bound_stop: the ending bound of the enumeration. If this is e.g. set to 2^{32}, the enumeration will start from the closest bin of $H_{0:N'_s}$ such that at least 2^{32} keys are contained in the next bins.
- test_key: this is a boolean value. If set to 1, the enumeration algorithm will test the keys on-the-fly using an AES implementation, by recombining them from the factorizations (and stop when the key is found); if set to 0, it will keep the keys factorized, and the user should implement himself the way he wants to test the keys in the process_key function.
- texts: a $4 \times N_s$ matrix containing two plaintexts and their associated ciphertexts. These two plaintexts/ciphertexts are used to test on-the-fly if the correct key is found. This parameter does not have to be initialized if test_key is set to 0.
- to_bound: This is a boolean value. If set to 1, the enumeration algorithm will remove (resp. add) $\frac{N'_s}{2}$ to $index\_max$ (resp. $index\_min$) as described in the previous section, to ensure that we enumerate all the keys between bound_start and bound_stop.
- to_real_key: additional parameter for comparisons with previous works, that can take 4 values in $[0, 4]$. If set to 0, this parameter is ignored. If set to to $1, 2, 3$, it allows the user to measure the timing of enumerating up to the real key in different settings, ignore the value of bound_start and test_key and enumerate up to the bin that contains the real key. It then requires real_key to be initialized. If set to 1, the keys will neither be recombined nor tested. If set to 2, the keys are recombined but not tested with AES (it simply tests if the key is equal to the real one provided by the user). If set to 3, the keys are recombined and tested with the AES. If the real key rank is bigger than bound_end, the enumeration is aborted.

Algorithms Outputs.

- **Rank estimation informations:** returns the rank of the real key according to its rounded log probabilities and the min and max bounds on the actual rank of the real key. Also returns the time needed for rank estimation (including the preprocessing time).

– **Enumeration informations:** If the key has been found, returns the rank of the real key according to its rounded log probabilities and the min and max bounds on the actual rank of the real key. Also returns the time needed for preprocessing and the time needed for enumeration.

Examples. Together with our code, we provide different examples of key enumeration which are written in a file main_example.cpp and listed in Table 2. The first example (first line in the table) enumerates all the keys of rounded rank between 2^{10} and 2^{40} (taking the rounding bounds into account) and tests them using a reference AES-128 software implementation. The second example enumerates all the keys of rounded rank between 2^0 and 2^{40} without testing them. A user would then have to define the way he wants to implement the process_key function (e.g. by sending the factorized lists to a powerful third testing party). The last three examples enumerate all the keys up to the real one if its rounded rank is lower than 2^{32}. For the third one, the recorded timing will correspond to the enumeration time with factorization. For the fourth one, the recorded timing will correspond to the enumeration time including the recombination of the factorized lists. For the last one, the recorded timing will correspond to the enumeration time with key testing (with our reference AES-128 implementation) and thus with recombination.

Table 2. Running examples for key enumeration

to_real_key	real_key	test_key	to_bound	texts	bound_start	bound_stop	
0	*optional*	1	1	*given*	2^{10}	2^{40}	(1)
0	*optional*	0	0	–	2^0	2^{40}	(2)
1	*needed*	–	–	–	–	2^{32}	(3)
2	*needed*	–	–	–	–	2^{32}	(4)
3	*needed*	–	–	–	–	2^{32}	(5)

5   Performance Evaluations

In this section we evaluate the performances of our enumeration algorithm and discuss its pros and cons compared to previous proposals. For this purpose, we consider a setting of simulated leakages for an AES-128 implementation, which has been previously used for comparison of other enumeration algorithms [4,8, 10]. Namely, we target the output of an AES S-box, leading to 16 leakages of the form $l_i = \mathsf{HW}(\mathsf{S}(x_i, k_i)) + N$ for $i \in [0, 15]$, with HW the Hamming weight leakage function and N a random noise following a Gaussian distribution. We stress that the main experimental criteria influencing the complexity of an enumeration is the rank of the key (that we can control thanks to the noise variance). So other experimental settings would not lead to significantly different conclusions with respect to the performances of the enumeration algorithm.

Besides, the two main parameters of our algorithm are the number of bins and the amount of merging. Intuitively, a smaller number of bins leads to a faster execution time at the cost of an increased quantization error, and merging accelerates the enumeration at the cost of more memory requirements and pre-processing time. All the following experiments were performed with 256, 2048 and 65536 bins, and for an amount of merging of 1, 2 and 3. These values were chosen to allow comparisons with the results of [8]. That is, 256 (resp. 2048 and 65536) bins is similar to choosing a precision of 8 (resp. 11 and 16) bits for their algorithm. We limited the amount of merging to 3 because the memory requirements of this preprocessing then becomes too large for our AES-128 case study (a merging of 4 would require to store $4 \times 2^{32} \times 8$ bytes for the lists of log probabilities in double precision).

5.1   Enumeration Accuracy

One convenient feature of our algorithm is its ability to compute easily the quantization bounds related to the mapping from floating to integers. Since accuracy is usually the main concern when enumerating keys, we start our evaluations by analyzing the impact of the number of bins on these quantization bounds. For this purpose, we first recall that these quantization errors are related to the rounding, which was the key idea to improve the performance and parallelism of recent works on enumeration. Hence, our goal is to find the level of quantization errors that are acceptable from the enumeration accuracy point-of-view.

Figure 4 illustrates this impact for a precision of 256, 2048 and 65536 bins. Since the impact of merging is minor for such experiments, we only report the results with a merge_1 preprocessing. The Y-coordinate represents the number of keys one has to enumerate in order to guarantee an enumeration up to an exact key rank given by the X-coordinate. Optimal enumeration is shown in black (for which $X = Y$) and corresponds to the application of the algorithm in [10]. The red, blue and green curves respectively represent the maximum, average and minimum results we found based on a sampling of 1000 enumeration experiments. These experiments lead to two interesting observations. First, a lower precision (e.g. 256 bins) leads to larger enumeration overheads for small key ranks, but these overheads generally vanish as the key ranks increase. Second, increasing the number of bins rapidly makes the enumeration (rounding) error low enough (e.g. less than one bit) which is typically observed for the 2048- and 65536-bin cases, especially for representative ranks (e.g. beyond 2^{32}) where the enumeration cost becomes significant. This is in line with the observations made with histogram-based rank estimation [7].

Note that other algorithms such as [4,8] lead to similar accuracies with similar parameters (e.g. our 2048-bin case roughly corresponds to their 11-bit precision case). Besides, finding bounds on the rounding error should be feasible for [8] too, despite probably more involved than with histograms for which such bounds come for free.

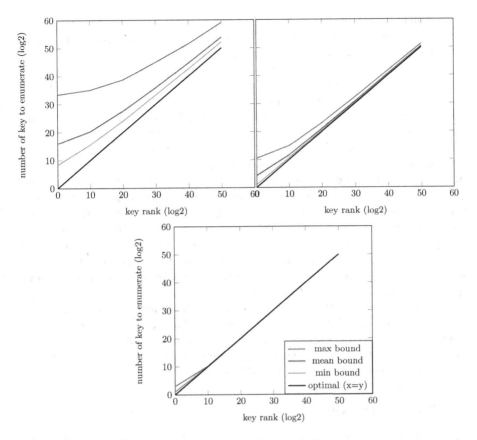

Fig. 4. Enumeration overheads due to rounding errors with merge$_1$ (i.e. no merging). Upper left: 256 bins. Upper right: 2048 bins. Bottom: 65536 bins. (Color figure online)

5.2 Factorization

Another important feature of our method is its intrinsic ability to output factorized keys instead of a single key at a time. Studying why and how this factorization evolves with our main parameters is important for two reasons. Firstly, it allows a better understanding of how our main parameters affect the performances of histogram-based enumeration, since a better factorization always reduces its amount of processing. Secondly, the number of keys per factorization may be important for the key testing phase, e.g. in case one wants to distribute the lists of key candidates to multiple (hardware) devices and therefore minimize the bandwidth of this distributed part of the computations. This second point will be discussed in Sect. 6.

Intuitively, increasing the amount of merging or decreasing the number of bins essentially creates more collisions in the initial histograms, thus increases the size of the factorized keys, and thus accelerates the enumeration process.

Interestingly, increasing the merging does not decrease the accuracy (by contrast with decreasing of the number of bins). Hence, this type of preprocessing should (almost) always be privileged up to the memory limits of the device on which the enumeration algorithms is running.

To confirm this intuition, Fig. 5 illustrates an evaluation of the factorization results for 256 (left) and 2048 (right) bins, and merging values from 1 to 3. The top figures represent the number of keys per factorization (Y-coordinate). The bottom figures represent the memory cost of the corresponding lists in bytes (Y-coordinate). The dashed curves represent the average value (over 1000 experiments) and the plain curves represent the maximum that occurred on our 1000 experiments. As we can see, using 256 bins leads to a lot of collisions and the merging value always amplifies the number of collisions. This increases the number of keys per factorization along with the memory size of the corresponding lists. The memory cost is anyway bounded by $N'_s \times 2^{m \cdot a}$, and the number of keys per factorization by $2^n = 2^{N'_s \cdot m \cdot a}$ (this extreme case would occur if all the subkeys have the same rounded probability and thus are within the same bins for all histograms H_i). We did not plot the results for 65536 bins since few collisions appear (and thus not many of factorizations).

Note that the algorithm in [8] has a similar behavior as it stores the keys having the same probabilities within a tree. So although the open source implementation joined to this previous work recombines the keys, it could also convert this tree representation into a factorized representation that is more convenient for distributed key testing with limited bandwidth.

5.3   Time Complexity

We finally discuss the performances of our algorithm in terms of timing. For this purpose, all our experiments were performed using i7-3770 CPU running at 3.40 GHz with 16 GB of RAM on Ubuntu. We start by comparing our results to the C++ implementation of the optimal key enumeration algorithm of Veyrat et al. [10], and consider the costs of enumeration only (i.e. we exclude the key testing and measure the time it takes to output factorized lists of keys). We then discuss the comparison with the work of Martin et al. at the end of the section.

Results for 256 and 65536 bins are given in Fig. 6. The Y-coordinate represents the time (in seconds) taken to enumerate keys until finding the correct one, for different ranks represented in the X-coordinate (in log2). As expected, the enumeration time without key testing is extremely fast for a (low) precision of 256 bins (in the upper part of the figure). For a merge$_1$ preprocessing, it takes less than 10 s to enumerate up to 2^{35} on average. For a merge$_2$ preprocessing, it does not even take a second. The bottom part of the figure then shows the results for 65536 bins with merge$_1$ and merge$_2$ preprocessings. Interestingly (and exceptionally), using the merge$_2$ preprocessing is worst than using merge$_1$ in this case. This is due to the fact that the 65536 bins do not bring enough collisions.

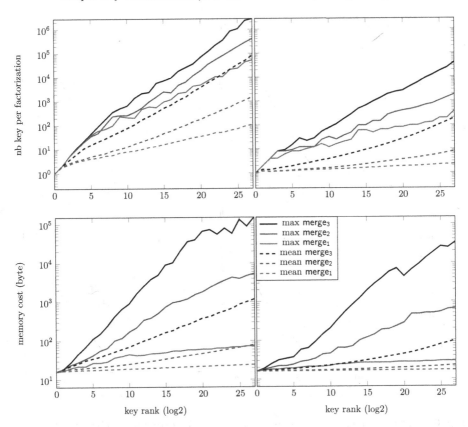

Fig. 5. Key factorization for different levels of merging and number of bins. Left: number of keys per factorization (top) and memory cost of the associated list in bytes (bottom) for 256 bins. Right: same plots for 2048 bins.

Hence, we loose more by iterating over all the non-empty bins than what we win from the collisions. Additional results for 2048 bins and other merging values are given in Appendix A.

We next discuss a number of additional issues related to these performances.

Preprocessing and Memory. The preprocessing time and the memory requirements of the algorithm are almost null for $merge_1$ and $merge_2$ preprocessings (i.e. less than a second and less than 30 Mb). However, $merge_3$ is more expensive in time and memory. Indeed, the algorithm has to keep the merged scores and the subkeys lists that fall into each bins in memory. In our experiments done for an AES-128 implementation, we have to process 5 lists of 2^{24} elements and one of 2^8. This requires approximatively 3.5 Gb of memory and 45 s of preprocessing. As for the other key enumeration algorithm based on rounded log probabilities (i.e. [4,8]), the memory requirements are independent of the enumeration depth.

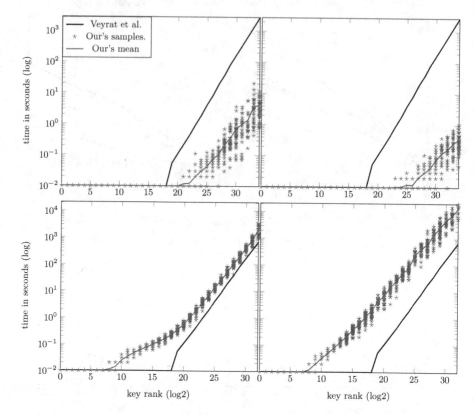

Fig. 6. Execution time for 256 and 65536 bins with factorized lists. The blue stars are the samples for our algorithm, the red curve is the corresponding mean, and the black curve is for the optimal enumeration algorithm in [10]. Upper left: 256 bins / merge$_1$. Upper right: 256 bins / merge$_2$. Bottom left: 65536 bins / merge$_1$. Bottom right: 65536 bins / merge$_2$. (Color figure online)

Parallelization. Our algorithm allows a very natural parallelization with minimum communication. Namely, after $H_{0:N'_s-1}$ has been computed, if the user wants to parallelize the enumeration among c cores, he simply has to split the bins into c sets which will contain approximatively the same amount of keys, so that each core will have approximatively the same workload. From our preliminary experiments, the gain of such a parallelization is linear in the number of threads, as expected.

Note that other key enumeration algorithms such as [4,8] can also be easily parallelized, but balancing the effort done by each core may be slightly more involved. This difference is again due to our treatment with histograms. That is, while we can directly select the ranks between which we want to enumerate with our starting and ending bounds, the solution in [8] rather has to select the minimum and maximum probabilities of the keys between which we want to enumerate, without a priori knowledge of the amount of keys it represents.

So good balance between the cores requires an (admittedly light) preprocessing to estimate the workload of the different cores. Besides, the heuristic nature of [4] (which is not aimed at optimal enumeration) also makes it difficult to compare from this point of view.

Comparison with the Enumeration Algorithm of Martin et al. To conclude this section, we add a comparison with the work in [8] and produce performance evaluations using their Java open source (using their "shift to 1 trick" to speed up the enumeration). We insist that this comparison is informal, since comparing implementations with different programming languages and optimization efforts, and therefore is only aimed to highlight that the simplicity of our enumeration algorithm reasonably translates into efficient implementations compared to the best state-of-the-art enumeration algorithms.

Figure 7 shows our comparison results for both 8 and 11 bits of precision (corresponding to 256 and 2048 bins for our algorithm). Since the implementation of Martin et al. measures the time to output the keys one by one (represented by the red curve in the figure), we consider a similar scenario for our algorithm (represented by the green curve in the figure). After some (quite irrelevant) time overheads of the implementation from [8] for low key ranks, we see that both algorithms reach a similar slope when the key ranks increase – yet with a sight constant gain for our implementation. Furthermore, increasing the precision and number of bins amplifies the initial overheads of the implementation from [8] while making the performances of both algorithms more similar for larger ranks. The additional black curve corresponds to the Java adaptation of the algorithm in [10], which allows us to check consistency with the previous comparisons from Martin et al. Since our algorithm allows to output factorized keys, we plotted in blue the associated timing. Eventually, we have no timing comparison with the work of [4] since the authors did not release their implementation. Extending the comparing enumeration algorithms in a more systematic manner is anyway an interesting scope for further research.

6   Application Scenarios

In this section we finally discuss the impact of our findings for an adversary willing to exploit enumeration in concrete application scenarios, which complements the similar discussion that can be found in [4]. Without loss of generality we focus on the case of the AES. We separate this discussion in the cases of adversaries having either a small or big computing infrastructure to mount an attack.

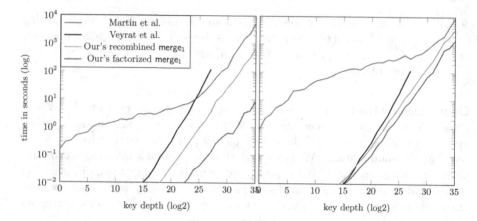

Fig. 7. Execution time for the java implementation of Veyrat et al., Martin et al. and ours with 8 bits of precision (left) and 11 bits of precision (right). (Color figure online)

In the first case we assume a local attacker with only one "standard" computer. Roughly, his computing power will be bounded by 2^{40}. In that case, he will simply use all his available cores to launch the key enumeration with key testing on-the-fly. Since it is likely that it will take more time to compute an AES encryption than to output a key candidate, this adversary will prefer a higher precision than a higher number of collisions. In that respect, and depending on the AES implementation's throughput, using 2048 bins could be a good tradeoff. Indeed, as the adversary's computing power is bounded and as the AES computation is the costly part, he should minimize the bounds overhead as seen in Sect. 5.1. Since the merging value has no impact on the accuracy, this value should always be maximized (ensuring we do not fall in a case where it slows down the enumeration process as shown in Sect. 5.3).

By contrast, the strategy will be quite different if we assume the adversary is an organization having access to a big computing infrastructure. For example, let assume that this organization has powerful computer(s) to launch the key enumeration along with many hardware AES implementations with limited memory. The adversary's computing power is now bounded by a much higher capability (e.g. 2^{64}). As we saw in Sect. 5.1, the gap between the optimal enumeration and the efficient one (using less bins) vanishes as we consider deeper key ranks. In that case, the attacker should maximize the enumeration throughput and minimize the bandwidth requirement (per single key), which he can achieve by decreasing the number of bins and increasing the merging value as much as possible (e.g. 256 bins with merge$_3$). All the key factorizations would then be sent to the hardware devices for efficient key testing. This could be done easily since a factorized key can be seen as a small effort distributor as in [9,12].

7   Related Work

A recent work from David et al. available on ePrint [6] allows one to enumerate keys from real probabilities without the memory issue of the original optimal algorithm from [10]. This gain comes at the cost of a loss of optimality which is different from the one introduced by the rounded log-probabilities.

8   Conclusion

This paper provides a simple key enumeration algorithm based on histograms along with an open source code implementing both the new enumeration method and the rank estimation algorithm from FSE 2015. In addition to its simplicity, this construction allows a sound understanding of the parameters influencing the performances of enumeration based on rounded probabilities. Additional convenient features include the easy computation of bounds for the rounding errors, and easy to balance parallelization. Our experiments also illustrate how to tune the enumeration for big distributed computing efforts with hardware co-processors and limited bandwidth. We believe the combination of efficient key enumeration and rank estimation algorithms are a tool of choice to help evaluators to understand the actual security level of concrete devices, and the actual capabilities of computationally enhanced adversaries.

Acknowledgements. François-Xavier Standaert is a research associate of the Belgian Fund for Scientific Research. This work has been funded in parts by the ERC project 280141 (acronym CRASH), the ERA-Net CHIST-ERA project SECODE and the DFG Research Training Group GRK 1817 Ubicrypt.

A   Additional Time Complexites

Figure 8 shows timing results for different number of bins and amounts of merging. The two figures on the top are the results for 256 (left) and 65536 (right) bins with $merge_3$ which are lacking in Fig. 6. As for the 65536-bin case, we saw in Fig. 6 that the merging can be detrimental (e.g. using $merge_1$ was better than using $merge_2$) when not enough collision are occur. However we see that we still benefit from using $merge_3$ in that case. The 3 other figures show the results of experiments with 2048 bins and a $merge_1$ preprocessing (middle left), $merge_2$ preprocessing (middle right) and $merge_3$ preproicessing (bottom).

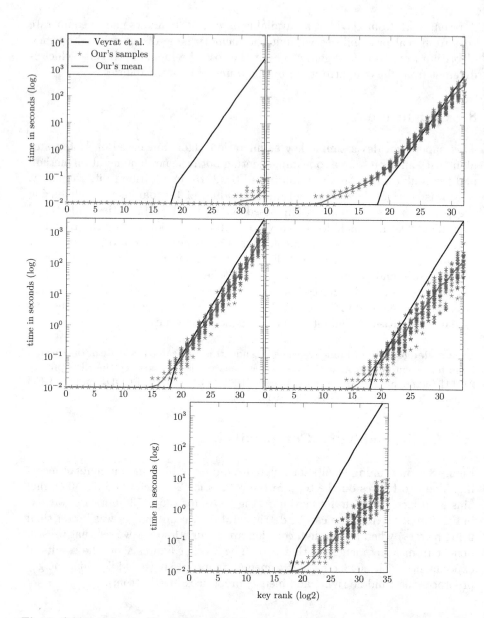

Fig. 8. Additional execution times with factorized lists. Upper left: 256 bins / merge$_3$. Upper right: 65536 bins / merge$_3$. Middle left: 2048 bins / merge$_1$. Middle right: 2048 bins / merge$_2$. Bottom: 2048 bins / merge$_3$.

References

1. http://perso.uclouvain.be/fstandae/PUBLIS/172.zip
2. http://www.shoup.net/ntl/
3. Bernstein, D.J., Lange, T., van Vredendaal, C.: Tighter, faster, simpler side-channel security evaluations beyond computing power. IACR Cryptol. ePrint Arch. **2015**, 221 (2015)
4. Bogdanov, A., Kizhvatov, I., Manzoor, K., Tischhauser, E., Witteman, M.: Fast and memory-efficient key recovery in side-channel attacks. IACR Cryptol. ePrint Arch. **2015**, 795 (2015)
5. Clavier, C., Danger, J.-L., Duc, G., Elaabid, M.A., Gérard, B., Guilley, S., Heuser, A., Kasper, M., Li, Y., Lomné, V., Nakatsu, D., Ohta, K., Sakiyama, K., Sauvage, L., Schindler, W., Stöttinger, M., Veyrat-Charvillon, N., Walle, M., Wurcker, A.: Practical improvements of side-channel attacks on AES: feedback from the 2nd DPA contest. J. Cryptograph. Eng. **4**(4), 259–274 (2014)
6. David, L., Wool, A.: A bounded-space near-optimal key enumeration algorithm for multi-dimensional side-channel attacks. IACR Cryptol. ePrint Arch. **2015**, 1236 (2015)
7. Glowacz, C., Grosso, V., Poussier, R., Schüth, J., Standaert, F.-X.: Simpler and more efficient rank estimation for side-channel security assessment. In: Leander, G. (ed.) FSE 2015. LNCS, vol. 9054, pp. 117–129. Springer, Heidelberg (2015)
8. Martin, D.P., O'Connell, J.F., Oswald, E., Stam, M.: Counting keys in parallel after a side channel attack. In: Iwata, T., et al. (eds.) ASIACRYPT 2015. LNCS, vol. 9453, pp. 313–337. Springer, Heidelberg (2015)
9. Poussier, R., Grosso, V., Standaert, F.-X.: Comparing approaches to rank estimation for side-channel security evaluations. In: Homma, N. (ed.) CARDIS 2015. LNCS, vol. 9514, pp. 125–142. Springer, Heidelberg (2016). doi:10.1007/978-3-319-31271-2_8
10. Veyrat-Charvillon, N., Gérard, B., Renauld, M., Standaert, F.-X.: An optimal key enumeration algorithm and its application to side-channel attacks. In: Knudsen, L.R., Wu, H. (eds.) SAC 2012. LNCS, vol. 7707, pp. 390–406. Springer, Heidelberg (2013)
11. Veyrat-Charvillon, N., Gérard, B., Standaert, F.-X.: Security evaluations beyond computing power. In: Johansson, T., Nguyen, P.Q. (eds.) EUROCRYPT 2013. LNCS, vol. 7881, pp. 126–141. Springer, Heidelberg (2013)
12. Ye, X., Eisenbarth, T., Martin, W.: Bounded, yet sufficient? How to determine whether limited side channel information enables key recovery. In: Joye, M., Moradi, A. (eds.) CARDIS 2014. LNCS, vol. 8968, pp. 215–232. Springer, Heidelberg (2015)

Automotive Security

Physical Layer Group Key Agreement for Automotive Controller Area Networks

Shalabh Jain$^{(\boxtimes)}$ and Jorge Guajardo

Robert Bosch LLC, Research and Technology Center,
Pittsburgh, PA 15203, USA
{shalabh.jain,jorge.guajardomerchan}@us.bosch.com

Abstract. Distribution of cryptographic keys between devices communicating over a publicly accessible medium is an important component of secure design for networked systems. In this paper, we consider the problem of group key exchange between Electronic Control Units (ECUs) connected to the Controller Area Network (CAN) within an automobile. Typically, existing solutions map schemes defined for traditional network systems to the CAN. Our contribution is to utilize *physical properties* of the CAN bus to generate group keys. We demonstrate that *pairwise interaction* between ECUs over the CAN bus can be used to efficiently derive group keys in both authenticated and non-authenticated scenarios. We illustrate the efficiency and security properties of the proposed protocols. The scalability and security properties of our scheme are similar to multi-party extensions of Diffie-Hellman protocol, without the computational overhead of group operations.

Keywords: Automotive security · ECU keys · CAN bus · Group keys

1 Introduction

Modern automobiles, in conjunction with mechanical components, utilize several electronic components (ECUs) for sensing, actuation, user interface and control. The ECUs communicate over a shared medium known as the CAN bus. Over the past decade, several ECUs that connect to external networks, e.g. via a Bluetooth, cellular or a wired interface, have been added to the CAN bus. Such interfaces enable remote access to the components on the internal network of the car. While these may be utilized to enable several useful functions for the users, e.g. emergency messaging systems, remote ignition, they can easily be misused by a malicious attacker. The ease of attack, and damage due to adversarial behavior has been demonstrated by several researchers over the past few years in [6,19,22,24,28].

A common observation by the attackers in [6,22], is the lack of security mechanisms in the CAN architecture. Traditional automobiles were designed as standalone systems, intended for autonomous operation. Thus, latency and reliability were the dominant criterion for network design. However, with increased

© International Association for Cryptologic Research 2016
B. Gierlichs and A.Y. Poschmann (Eds.): CHES 2016, LNCS 9813, pp. 85–105, 2016.
DOI: 10.1007/978-3-662-53140-2_5

connectivity, there is a need to secure the internal network from external attackers. The current automobile manufacturers utilize traditional network security principles at the periphery (firewalls, access control), to secure the CAN access. However, as demonstrated recently in [28], these techniques may not offer sufficient protection. Further, such methods do not address the fundamental lack of security in CAN messages.

Generally speaking, the attacks demonstrated thus far may be roughly divided into two stages. First, the attackers compromise an ECU with a remote interface and the ability to inject arbitrary messages on the CAN bus. Secondly, the attackers communicate with a critical ECU over the CAN bus and influence its behavior. The second stage is enabled by the broadcast nature of the internal network and the lack of authentication. Typically, any operation in the second stage requires knowledge of the internal bus protocol and message structure, which has been simplified by the lack of encryption on the network.

It is clear that any security solution for CAN should include fundamental protections such as source authentication and packet level encryption. Several researchers, e.g. [8,14,26], have proposed methods to include these primitives in the current CAN architecture. One of the fundamental requirements to enable these primitives is the existence of cryptographic keys shared between the communicating ECUs. However, it is challenging to pre-install group keys during production of the ECU or securely manage the keys over the long lifetime of a vehicle. Thus, we require an efficient key generation and exchange protocol that can be executed during the operation of the car to agree on secret keys.

To ensure minimal disturbance to critical operations on the CAN bus, the key exchange protocol must be bandwidth efficient. Further, it must incur a low computational overhead to accommodate a variety of ECU capabilities. Since CAN messages are multicast, it is necessary for the protocol to support the generation and update of group keys. In this paper, we propose such a protocol by utilizing the physical properties of the CAN bus.

1.1   Our Contributions

We extend the two-party protocol proposed in [23] to the generalized group scenario. Our contributions are as follows,

- We utilize the physical properties of the CAN bus to construct a group key exchange protocol that is secure in the information-theoretic sense from eavesdroppers.
- For the restricted scenario of computationally bounded adversaries, we propose a highly efficient tree based structure for our protocol that has logarithmic complexity for node addition and deletion.
- We propose an efficient authenticated group key exchange protocols that utilizes only the pre-established trust between the individual ECUs and the gateway.

1.2   Related Work

CAN Security: In this work, we utilize the physical properties of the CAN bus for exchange of keys. To the best of our knowledge, the first to utilize such properties for key agreement are Müller and Lothspeich in [23]. Their work forms the basis for our constructions and it will be reviewed in detail in Sect. 3. Security for CAN networks, particularly authentication and integrity of messaging, has been considered previously in [8, 11, 14, 26, 27]. However, this line of work assumes that a shared key already exists.

(Group) Key Agreement: Distribution of group keys for both authenticated and unauthenticated scenarios has been explored in literature for well over three decades. Several schemes have been proposed based on varying assumptions of adversarial behavior and initial setup. One of the earliest results in this direction, Diffie-Hellman (DH) key exchange [7], uses the hardness of computing discrete-log over prime order groups to generate keys between a pair of nodes. Steiner et al. in [25] proposed an extension of DH to groups that uses a mixture of point-to-point messages and broadcast messages. This was modified by authors in [16–18, 25], who utilize a tree based structure to improve communication efficiency and support efficient addition/deletion of nodes. Authors in [29] reduce communication and storage overhead by performing these group operations over elliptic curves.

Several methods have also been proposed to generate authenticated group keys, either by extension of the two-party protocols to groups or by using ideas based on secret-sharing, e.g. [2, 4, 12, 15]. These schemes have several desirable properties such as provable security, perfect forward secrecy (PFS) and key independence. Most schemes, e.g. [2, 4, 15, 25, 29], involve expensive group operations over prime fields, and thus are not suitable for computationally constrained devices on the CAN bus. Other protocols, e.g. [12], fail to provide security against an adversary that can compromise the pre-shared secrets. This property is desirable for automotive networks, where some nodes may be easily compromised due to open accessibility or lack of protections. Our protocol provides these security properties. Our main differentiation from these lies in utilization of the physical properties of the CAN bus as a substitute for the expensive operations.

1.3   Organization

The remainder of the paper is organized as follows. In Sect. 2, we describe the system assumptions and the adversarial model. We present the scheme from [23] in Sect. 3. We propose two extensions of this scheme that are secure against passive adversaries in Sect. 4. In Sect. 5, we propose two alternative protocols that provide cryptographic guarantees against active adversaries. We discuss the security and performance issues of our schemes in Sect. 6.

2   Preliminaries

2.1   Notation

We adhere to the following notation for the paper. We denote a random n bit value x sampled uniformly from the set $\{0,1\}^n$, consisting of all possible binary strings of n bits, as $x \leftarrow \{0,1\}^n$. We denote by $x := y$, the assignment of the value y to x.

For a binary string $x \in \{0,1\}^*$, $|x|$ represents the length of string and x' represent the complement of the string. For an index set $L \subseteq \{1,\ldots,|x|\}$, $x(L)$ refers to the substring with indices in L. If L consists of a single element, $x(L)$ simply refers to the Lth bit. Given two strings $x, y \in \{0,1\}^*$, $x \parallel y$ denotes the concatenation of the strings.

We denote by $I(X \wedge Y)$, the mutual information between random variables X and Y. $I(X \wedge Y) = H(X) - H(X|Y)$, where $H(X)$ is the entropy of X.

2.2   System Model and Assumptions

We consider the typical automotive network, comprising of ECUs connected via a shared wired bus that acts as a broadcast medium. During arbitration, the CAN bus allows multiple nodes to write simultaneously to the bus and observe the *overlapped* bus output. This feature, typically used for contention resolution, is essential for our scheme. Note that the current ECU design allows simultaneous read and write only during the *arbitration phase*, and not in the data phase. We assume that the CAN controller is sufficiently modified to allow this functionality for the entire packet. This can be achieved either via hardware or software modifications.

The typical CAN bus has two logical states, the dominant '0' state, where the bus is driven by a voltage, and the recessive '1' state, where the bus is grounded. If two nodes transmit a bit simultaneously, the effective state of the bus is dominant '0' if any of the nodes transmits a dominant signal. Thus, the bus acts as a logical AND gate between inputs from the nodes. This property, identified by authors in [23] to share sequence of bits between a pair of nodes, forms the basis of our scheme and hence a central assumption for our work. Note that though this work is in context of automotive networks, the scheme can be applied to any wired bus architecture that exhibits this property.

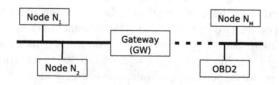

Fig. 1. Example of nodes connected by a shared medium

The typical CAN architecture, illustrated in Fig. 1, consists of one or more powerful nodes that act as gateway nodes (**GW**). As described by the authors in [22], current CAN architectures allow ECUs across different subnets to communicate transparently through the gateway. For our work, we assume each node shares a trust relationship with the gateway in the form of a pre-shared symmetric key. Thus nodeN_i shares key K_i with the gateway (**GW**). Such a relationship can be established during the vehicle manufacturing process, or during ECU installation by a mechanic.

For communication within a group, we assume a pre-existing communication ordering between the nodes. In typical automotive scenarios, different ECUs have well defined priority. Thus, the communication order may be pre-assigned based on ECU identity/priority, or assigned by random arbitration over the shared medium. Alternately, it can be defined in a common file, e.g. FIBEX file, and shared with the ECUs. We assume that for any group configuration, the member ECUs can determine their communication order.

Our protocols are based on simultaneous transmission by two nodes. Thus, all interactions in our system are between ECU pairs. We refer to the node that is earlier in the communication order as the primary or initiator node and the other node as the secondary or responding node. CAN messages are organized in frames that consist of an identifier field followed by the data field. We assume that the initiator uses the identifier to specify information about the key exchange session (e.g. session identifier) and the responder uses this to initiate simultaneous transmission of its message in the data field transmission phase. This identifier allows the protocol to be resumed in case of interruption by a ECU transmitting a 'critical' message for the automobile.

2.3   Adversarial Model

Several adversarial models have been proposed for key exchange protocols in literature, e.g. CK model [5], or BR model [3]. It is typically assumed that the adversary can record all messages transmitted on the bus, modify them, or insert its own messages.

Here, we consider two adversarial scenarios. For the schemes in Sect. 4, we restrict the adversarial behavior to passive observations. This model, though unrealistic for typical networks, can be sufficient for all attacks on the CAN bus. This is due to the inherent robustness that the CAN bus provides to active adversaries. Detailed analysis for this is presented in Sect. 6.1.

For schemes in Sect. 5, we consider a powerful adversarial scenario, wherein the adversary has complete control over the protocol execution. There, we argue that our schemes provides cryptographic guarantees against such adversaries. Due to the dependence of our scheme on physical properties of the bus, an adversary with a high resolution oscilloscope may be able to obtain the keys by probing the bus. Further, since our scheme does not have a practical implementation yet, it has not been analyzed for timing or power side-channels. We consider such attacks outside the scope of this paper.

2.4   Cryptographic Assumptions

For our protocol, we assume the existence of an indexed family of pseudorandom functions (PRF) [9], defined as,

Definition 1. *For the security parameter n, the function $g : \{0,1\}^n \times \{0,1\}^n \to \{0,1\}^n$ is a family of pseudorandom functions, indexed by the first parameter that satisfies the following conditions,*

- *For a randomly selected index $k \leftarrow \{0,1\}^n$, the function efficiently maps an element from the domain $\{0,1\}^n$ to the range $\{0,1\}^n$.*
- *(Security Condition). For an adversary that runs in polynomial (in security parameter) time, the output of the PRF, where the first parameter is randomly selected, is indistinguishable from random.*

In practice, PRFs can be realized either via a block cipher or by a well-designed efficient hash function with a random seed (as the index) as a part of the input.

Further, we utilize the definition of computational entropy of a random variable X from [13], defined as $H_C(X) = k \iff \{X \sim_C Y \text{ and } H(Y) \geq k\}$, i.e. For a PPT process, X is computationally indistinguishable from a random variable Y with true entropy greater than k. Clearly the following Lemma follows from Definition 1.

Lemma 1. *For a randomly selected $k \leftarrow \{0,1\}^n$, let $X_i = g(k,i)$. Then $H_C(X_i) = n$, $\forall i \in \{0,1\}^n$. Further, for $I \subset \{0,1\}^n$, where $|I| = r$, $H_C(X_I) = rn$, where X_I denotes the concatenation of all X_i, $i \in I$.*

2.5   Security Definition

We define the security of a key exchange scheme Π using the information theoretic notion from [21] as follows,

Definition 2. *A key agreement protocol $\{S_A, S_B\} = \Pi^{A,B}(1^k)$ between two parties A and B results in secret key outputs S_A, S_B at the respective parties. If the protocol terminates correctly, we have $|S_A| = k$, otherwise $S_A = S_B = \emptyset$. The protocol can be said to be secure if the following hold*

P1: The keys derived at the end match, $Pr(S_A \neq S_B) = 0$.
P2: If the observations of the adversary is characterized as Z, we have $I(S_A \wedge Z) = 0$.
P3: The key has entropy $H(S_A) = k$.

Here, we make no assumptions about the computational capability of the adversary. We argue a similar notion can be defined for computationally bounded adversaries by replacing the quantities in Definition 2 with their computational equivalent.

Definition 3. *A key agreement protocol $\{S_A, S_B\} = \Pi^{A,B}(1^k)$ is ϵ-secure for computationally bounded passive adversaries if the Definition 2 holds using the notion of computational entropy, i.e. $I_C(S_A \wedge Z) \doteq H_C(S_A) - H_C(S_A \mid Z) \leq \epsilon$, and $H_C(S_A) \geq k - \epsilon$.*

3 Two Party Plug-and-Secure (PnS) Protocol

The wired AND property of the CAN bus was first utilized by the authors in [23] for key agreement between a pair of nodes. Since our protocols are based on their scheme, we briefly describe it here. Our notation here differs from the original work to maintain uniformity with the remainder of our protocols. For details about implementation issues and synchronization, the reader is encouraged to read [23].

Function: $RetVal := \mathbf{f_x}(\mathbf{1^n})$, $x \in \{A, B\}$

$r \leftarrow \{0, 1\}^n$
$RetVal := r$

Protocol: $\mathbf{PnS(1^n, nodeA, nodeB, f_A, f_B)}$

1. nodeA and nodeB initialize secret strings as null, i.e. $s_A, s_B := \emptyset$.
2. nodeA and nodeB obtain random values $a := f_A(1^n)$ and $b := f_B(1^n)$.
3. Both nodes simultaneously write a, b to the bus and observe the bus output y.
4. Next similarly they write a', b' to the bus and observe the bus output z.
5. Let $\mathcal{G} = \{1 \leq j \leq n \mid y(j) = 0 \ AND \ z(j) = 0\}$. This represents the set of secret bits.
6. It can be easily verified that $a(\mathcal{G}) = b(\mathcal{G})'$. The primary node (nodeA here) sets $s_A := s_A \parallel a(\mathcal{G})$. The secondary node (nodeB here) sets the complementary bits, i.e. $s_B := s_B \parallel b(\mathcal{G})'$.
7. The string $s_A = s_B$ is shared secret between nodeA and nodeB and is the result of the subroutine.
   When used as a subroutine, the protocol halts here.
8. If the length of the string is insufficient, i.e. $|s_A| = |s_B| < n$, the protocol repeats from Step (2).
9. The final string $s_A = s_B$ is shared secret between nodeA, nodeB of length n.

Protocol 1. Two party PnS protocol from [23]

Let $PnS(1^n, nodeA, nodeB, f_A, f_B)$ denote the Plug-and-Secure protocol between nodeA and nodeB, where the security parameter 1^n denotes the length, n, of the shared secret key produced when the protocol terminates. We have chosen to parameterize the random number generation (RNG) by the nodes nodeA and nodeB, using the functions f_A and f_B respectively. This allows for a uniform presentation of the protocols, while providing the flexibility to alter the instantiation of the RNG across them. This advantage will become more evident in the group protocols. The random number generators are private for each of the nodes and maintain an independent and persistent state through the protocol. This state is typically expressed as a counter that is initialized during the first execution and incremented upon successive executions. We illustrate the sequence of operations of the protocol from [23] as Protocol 1.

In the description of Protocol 1, we assumed that nodeA was the initiator (primary node) and nodeB was the secondary node. Each node discards bits that are leaked to the adversary. It can be seen from Step 5 that the bit positions where either y or z are 1, correspond to indices of strings a and b that can be determined by any eavesdropper. Thus they are no longer secret.

$$y(i) = 1 \Leftrightarrow a(i) = 1 \ AND \ b(i) = 1,$$
$$z(i) = 1 \Leftrightarrow a(i) = 0 \ AND \ b(i) = 0.$$

The messages to initiate the protocol, and the parameter negotiation to determine the desired key length are omitted here. Similarly, we do not specify the key verification approach at the end of the protocol. A number of existing initialization and verification techniques can be used with the protocols. Here, our goal is to present the fundamental building block that is the basis for our group key protocol.

It is clear from the description that Protocol 1 is very efficient and it does not require any expensive cryptographic operations. Further, it inherits the properties of contributory protocols such as Diffie-Hellman. This makes it highly suitable for the constrained ECU environments. Several properties of Protocol 1 will be inherited by our group key protocols. We illustrate a few key properties here.

Security: We demonstrate that Protocol 1 is secure against computationally unbounded *passive* adversaries.

Theorem 1. *The protocol $\Pi_{Prot1}^{A,B}(1^n)$ satisfies Definition 2, where $\Pi_{Prot1}^{A,B}(1^n)$ denotes Protocol 1 between nodeA and nodeB.*

Proof. Denote by s_A, the secret key at nodeA and by Y, Z, the complete observations of the adversary corresponding to Steps (3) and (4) respectively. The Property (P2) can be simply verified by the correctness of the protocol upon termination. Further, $H(s_A) = n$, as the samples were uniformly selected. Denote by L as the set of indices of the random values output on the channel that contributed to the bits of the key. Then we show Property (P2) as follows,

$$\begin{aligned} I(s_A \wedge \{Y, Z\}) &= I(s_A \wedge \{Y(L), Z(L)\}) &&\text{(bits are iid)} \\ &= nI(s_A(l_1) \wedge \{Y(l_1), Z(l_1)\}), \ l_1 \in L &&\text{(key bits are iid)} \\ &= n(H(s_A(l_1)) - H(s_A(l_1) \mid Y(l_1), Z(l_1))) = 0. \end{aligned}$$

Key Independence: Successive invocation of f_A and f_B produce independent random strings. Since each instance of key generation depends only on the outputs of f_A, f_B, the current key reveals no information about the past keys or future keys.

Computational Definition: We define a computational version of Protocol 1 by using PRFs to generate the random values a and b. The changes required are briefly summarized in Protocol 2. This protocol can be proved to be secure against computationally bounded *passive* adversaries.

Function: $RetVal := \mathbf{f_x}(\mathbf{1^n}, \mathbf{s})$, $x \in \{A, B\}$

i: local persistent counter initialized to 0 during the first execution
$RetVal := g(s, i)$
$i := i + 1$

Protocol: **CompPnS$(1^n$, nodeA, nodeB, $\mathbf{f_A}$, $\mathbf{f_B}$)**
All steps of Protocol (1) remain the same except Step 2 which changes to the following
2(a). nodeA and nodeB compute local random values $t_a \leftarrow \{0, 1\}^n$, $t_b \leftarrow \{0, 1\}^n$.
2(b). The nodes obtain the random values for the protocol execution as
    $a := f_A(1^n, t_a)$ and $b := f_B(1^n, t_b)$.
8 (new). The protocol repeats from 2(b) of the new protocol.

Protocol 2. Computational version of the two party PnS

Theorem 2. *The protocol $\Pi_{Prot2}^{A,B}(1^n)$, satisfies Definition 3, where $\Pi_{Prot2}^{A,B}(1^n)$ denotes Protocol 2 between nodeA and nodeB.*

Proof. The proof follows from the proof of Theorem 1, by applying the computational definition of to conditional entropy. It will be included in the extended version of this paper.

4 Group Key Agreement Schemes

In this section we introduce two new group key agreement protocols without authentication. Though these can be viewed as a special case of the authenticated protocol, they warrant separate treatment due to different complexity and security properties.

The protocols presented here require a linear (in size of the group) number of interactions for initial key establishment. Intuitively, the broadcast nature of the CAN bus allows pairwise PnS interaction between successive nodes to be sufficient for global key agreement. Once two nodes execute the PnS protocol, they may be viewed as a single logical entity for any further transmissions by one of these nodes, based the PnS output. Thus, each successive interaction increases the size of the logical entity by one, until the whole group is created.

For the remainder of this paper, we assume that the group consists of M nodes, $\{\text{nodeN}_1, \ldots, \text{nodeN}_M\}$. For simplicity, we assume the communication sequence to be based on the lexicographic order, i.e. nodeN_1-nodeN_2-...-nodeN_M. We assume that the protocol initiation is triggered by the gateway node with information about the group members and parameters. The ECUs can determine their communication priority in a distributed manner based on the group configuration.

4.1 Simple Group Protocol

We first consider the simple extension of Protocol 1 to the M node scenario. The flow of messages to agree on the group key is illustrated in Protocol 3. The correctness of the protocol can be understood by examining Step (3) of Protocol 3. The first time this step is executed between nodeN$_2$ and nodeN$_3$, there exists a shared secret t_{N_2} between nodeN$_1$ and nodeN$_2$. Since t_{N_2} is the only value used by nodeN$_2$ in the PnS execution, the view of nodeN$_1$ is the same as nodeN$_2$. Thus the secret shared by PnS execution between nodeN$_2$ and nodeN$_3$ can be computed by nodeN$_1$ independently, based on the observed bus outputs. Also note that the bits of t_{N_3} obtained at the end of this step is a subset of the bits of t_{N_1}, i.e. $\exists I \subseteq \{1, \ldots, |t_{N_1}|\}$, $s.t$ $t_{N_3} = t_{N_1}(I)$.

Function: $RetVal := \mathbf{f_{N_i}}(\mathbf{1^n}, \mathbf{s})$, $1 \leq i \leq M$

    if $s \neq \emptyset$, $RetVal := s$
    otherwise $r \leftarrow \{0,1\}^n$, $RetVal := r$

Protocol: $\mathbf{SimpleGroup}(\mathbf{1^n}, \{\mathbf{nodeN_1}, \ldots, \mathbf{nodeN_M}\}, \{f_{N_1}, \ldots, f_{N_M}\})$

1. Each node initializes the secret key string $s_{N_i} = \emptyset$, $1 \leq i \leq M$.
2. The first pair of nodes executes PnS *subroutine* with a target string length $l = n \cdot 2^{(M-1)}$, to obtain the shared secret as

$$t_{N_{1,2}} := \mathrm{PnS}(1^l, \mathrm{nodeN_1}, \mathrm{nodeN_2}, f_{N_1}(1^l, \emptyset), f_{N_2}(1^l, \emptyset)).$$

    Each node maintains the temporary value of the PnS as $t_{N_1} = t_{N_2} := t_{N_{1,2}}$ respectively.

3. The next pair of nodes (nodeN$_2$, nodeN$_3$) executes PnS with the target length $l = |t_{N_2}|$ to obtain the private results (or update the private results) as

$$t_{N_{2,3}} := \mathrm{PnS}(1^l, \mathrm{nodeN_2}, \mathrm{nodeN_3}, f_{N_2}(1^l, t_{N_2}), f_{N_3}(1^l, \emptyset)).$$

4. All nodes prior to the currently active nodes update their private strings as the output of the PnS result. In this case, as nodeN$_1$ is the only node preceding (nodeN$_2$, nodeN$_3$), it updates its private string t_{N_1} as the output of the PnS protocol between nodeN$_2$ and nodeN$_3$. Thus $t_{N_1} = t_{N_2} = t_{N_3}$.
5. Protocol is repeated from Step (3) for each successive pair of nodes (nodeN$_3$, nodeN$_4$), ..., (nodeN$_{M-2}$, nodeN$_{M-1}$), (nodeN$_{M-1}$, nodeN$_M$).
6. All nodes update the shared keys as $s_{N_i} = s_{N_i} \| t_{N_i}$, $1 \leq i \leq M$.
7. If $|s_{N_M}| < n$, the protocol is repeated from Step (2) using $l = (n - |s_{N_M}|) \cdot 2^{(M-1)}$.

Protocol 3. Simple group key protocol for M nodes

For each repetition of this step between successive pairs of nodes, all nodes prior to the active pair can derive the result of the protocol. Thus, once nodeN$_M$ completes execution, all nodes share a common string. Though the implicit backward-sharing of keys is a desirable property, the overall communication efficiency of the protocol is low. To see this, observe that at each successive execution of Step 3, additional bits are leaked to an eavesdropper. Consider the ith bit of the string sampled by $\text{node}N_1$, $a_{N_1} := f_{N_1}(1^n, \emptyset)$. The probability that this bit does not leak by the end of the protocol is simply $2^{-(M-1)}$. Thus we obtain that the expected communication complexity to generate a n bit secret is exponential in the number of group elements, i.e. $\mathcal{O}(n \cdot 2^{(M-1)})$.

Node Arrival and Departure: At the end of the protocol, each node knows all random bits selected during the protocol. Thus, the departure of any node requires re-execution of the complete protocol. For node arrival, it may appear that the new node can simply be appended to the end of the chain. However, the execution of PnS with the new node would leak several bits (half on average). Thus, the whole protocol needs to be re-executed to compensate for the lost bits. Thus, both addition and deletion operations incur exponential communication cost, i.e. $\mathcal{O}(n \cdot 2^{(M-1)})$. However, the new key maintains the property of key independence.

Note that an alternative, more efficient protocol using PnS with information theoretic security guarantees could be envisaged if we do not require the protocol to be contributory, i.e. each node contributes to the randomness of the key. A selected leader can simply engage in pairwise PnS with all other nodes and use the derived keys as one-time pads to distribute a secret value. It is easy to see that the computational complexity for key generation, node departure and arrival for such a scheme would be linear, i.e. $\mathcal{O}(n \cdot M)$. However all protocols presented here are 'contributory' protocols.

Security: Since Protocol 3 simply extends Protocol 1, it has the advantage of inheriting the security properties of Protocol 1. As each stage of the protocol is secure against *passive* adversaries, the information theoretic security extends to the whole protocol. Similarly, it can be simply observed that the key independence property extends from each stage to the eventual protocol result.

4.2 Tree Based Group Protocol

The scheme presented in Sect. 4.1 provides ideal security guarantees at the cost of efficiency. However, security against computationally bounded adversaries is sufficient for practical systems. This relaxation enables the utilization of efficient topologies for key agreement.

For key generation, the nodes are organized in a binary tree structure, e.g. as shown in Fig. 2. The physical nodes (ECUs) are assigned to the leaf nodes of the tree. The virtual nodes correspond to logical entities that can be emulated by *any* physical leaf node in the subtree rooted at that node. For the algorithms in this paper, we assume that the physical messages triggered by the virtual node are sent by the leaf node in the subtree with the highest priority (leftmost node of the tree in our model). The message flow for the key generation scheme is detailed in Protocol 4.

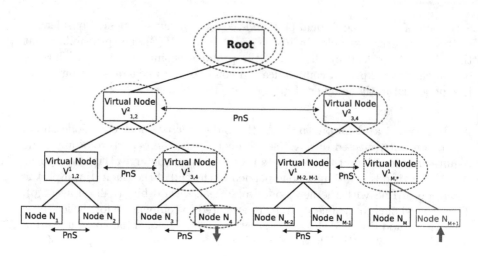

Fig. 2. Tree structure of PnS operations

The structure of the scheme is similar to the previous protocol. However, using the function $g(\cdot, \cdot)$ isolates successive PnS stages. Since the output of $g(\cdot, \cdot)$ is indistinguishable from random, it can be used in place of the random sampling in the original protocol. Secondly, as the leakage of output bits of $g(\cdot, \cdot)$ leaks no information about the inputs, bits leaked at any stage do not influence the prior stages. As a result of these properties, this scheme incurs a linear communication overhead for initial key generation, i.e. $\mathcal{O}(n \cdot M)$. The tree structure further optimizes node addition and deletion.

Node Departure: A node in the network has knowledge of all the random values generated and exchanged along the path, denoted as $\mathcal{P}_{dr}$, from the node to the root. Thus deletion of a node involves updating all the values known to the node and re-execution of PnS with the updated values. For example in Fig. 2, if nodeN$_4$ departs the network, it is sufficient to update the random values at nodeN$_3$ and the virtual nodes $V_{3,4}^1, V_{1,2}^2$, root.

We assume that the departing node broadcasts its identity to the group. Thus the nodes along $\mathcal{P}_{dr}$ and their siblings flag their values for updating. The update progresses upwards from the affected leaf node. If a node lies directly along $\mathcal{P}_{dr}$, it uses the new PnS result from the child node for all future protocol execution. All other nodes simply execute the PnS protocol with updated index values (in $f(\cdot)$).

At the end of the protocol, the value of the final PnS interaction is used as the group secret shared by all nodes. The statistical independence of the output of $g(\cdot, \cdot)$ for different inputs ensures that the new key is independent of the prior shared sequence and unknown to the departing node. Further, it can be observed that the computational complexity of this stage is simply $\mathcal{O}(n \cdot \log M)$.

Function: $Retval := \mathbf{f_{N_i}}(\mathbf{1}^n, \mathbf{s}),\ 1 \leq i \leq M$

   i: local persistent counter initialized to 0 during the first execution

   $RetVal := g(s, i)$

   $i := i + 1$

Protocol: **TreeGroup**$(\mathbf{1}^n, \{\mathbf{nodeN_1}, \dots, \mathbf{nodeN_M}\}, \{f_{N_1}, \dots, f_{N_M}\})$

1. Each leaf node initializes the private string $t_{N_i} \leftarrow \{0,1\}^n,\ 1 \leq i \leq M$.
2. The process starts at the leaf nodes. Each pair of siblings execute the complete PnS protocol with target string length n, and the result is assigned to the private string of the parent as

$$t_{V_{i,i+1}^1} := \mathrm{PnS}(\mathbf{1}^n, \mathrm{nodeN}_i, \mathrm{nodeN}_{i+1}, f_{N_i}(\mathbf{1}^n, t_{N_i}), f_{N_{i+1}}(\mathbf{1}^n, t_{N_{i+1}})),$$

   where $i = 1, 3, \dots$. Note: Here, we execute the complete PnS protocol. Thus the output is of length n, i.e. $|t_{V_{i,i+1}^1}| = n$.
3. Step (2) is repeated at the next level of hierarchy, i.e. first level of virtual nodes here, $V_{i,i+1}^1$, to generate the private strings for their parents.
4. The process of Step (3) continues till the virtual root node is reached. The private string of the root node t_{root} is the shared secret key between all nodes.

Protocol 4. Tree based group key protocol for M nodes

Node Arrival: Similar to the node departure scenario, a node arrival requires creation of a path to the root and executing the PnS protocol with siblings of the nodes along the new path.

For simplicity, we assume that the new node is temporarily assigned the priority equivalent to a recently departed node or the lowest priority among existing nodes in the group. This minimizes the changes to the tree structure and the re-computations required to add a node. In cases where this is not possible, we may add a node in the 'pre-assigned' order and modify the tree hierarchy accordingly.

Consider the example in Fig. 2, where nodeN_{M+1} joins the network. This requires updating the random values at nodeN_M and the virtual nodes $V_{M,M+1}^1, V_{3,4}^2$, root. This may be performed in a manner identical to the departing scenario. Thus, it can be observed that the new key will be independent of the old key and the computational complexity is simply $\mathcal{O}(n \cdot \log M)$.

Security Discussion: The organization of the nodes in a tree structure does not alter the role of the adversary. It simply modifies the order of participation of the nodes. Intuitively, we argue that similar to Protocol 3, the security of the series of PnS stages against a computationally bounded adversary can be derived directly from Theorem 2.

5 Authenticated Group Key Agreement Schemes

We now consider the scenario where group members must be authenticated prior to participation in the protocol. This requires some pre-established notion of trust or identity that can be verified. As described in Sect. 2.2, we consider the minimalistic scenario where each node shares a symmetric key with the gateway.

In our schemes, the gateway simply acts as a passive verifier of the operations. The broadcast channel allows the gateway to monitor the protocol execution. We ensure that the messages are a function of the shared keys K_i's. This allows the gateway to verify whether the messages used for the PnS protocol are from the expected parties. We present two implementations of this approach that provide a tradeoff between security and efficiency.

5.1 Authenticated Tree Based Protocol

First we utilize the efficient tree structure of Protocol 4 and add an authentication mechanism to it. This can be achieved via a simple modification to the method of selection of random values by the leaf nodes. In Protocol 4, the leaf nodes choose arbitrary random values for the initial sequence of PnS operations. Here, we assume that **GW** provides a random value and all nodes use a function of this random value and their shared key to bootstrap the PnS procedure.

Since the **GW** is aware of the random value and the shared keys, it can recreate and thus verify all random strings used in the PnS operations. Note that after the initiation of the protocol by **GW**, it only participates passively. If an error is detected, the **GW** halts the protocol by transmitting an error message. The detailed flow of messages for this is presented in Protocol 5.

As the structure of the protocol is similar to Protocol 4, it inherits the low complexity and security properties of the unauthenticated protocol. However, authenticated key exchange protocols may have an additional security requirement of Perfect Forward Secrecy (PFS), wherein the group key remains secret even in the event of compromise of trust credentials, i.e. K_i. Protocol 5 however fails to meet this requirement. In the event that an adversary compromises the shared secret, it can reconstruct the random values used for PnS (similar to **GW**) and hence learn the secret key from the transcripts. In the next section, we provide a solution to this problem.

5.2 Authenticated Linear Group Protocol

In Protocol 5, all inputs used for computing the random values for PnS were available to an adversary that compromises K_i. This was because one of the inputs was broadcast by **GW** to initiate the protocol. Here instead of the broadcast message, the **GW** transfers the initial random value to nodeN_1 through the PnS protocol. This ensures that *atleast* one of the inputs is never leaked to the adversary. However, as this requires the secret to be passed down the authentication chain, it forces us to use a linear structure. The flow of the protocol is illustrated as Protocol 6.

Function: $RetVal := \mathbf{f_{N_i}}(\mathbf{1^n}, \mathbf{s})$, $1 \le i \le M$

i: local persistent counter initialized to 0 during the first execution
Output $RetVal := g(s, i)$
$i := i + 1$

Protocol: **AuthTreeGroup(1^n, {nodeN$_1$, ..., nodeN$_M$}, $\{f_{N_1}, \ldots, f_{N_M}\}$)**

1. **GW** select a random sequence of n bits, i.e. $t_{gw} \leftarrow \{0,1\}^n$ and broadcasts it to all group members.
2. Each leaf node of the tree initializes the private string $t_{N_i} = g(K_i, t_{gw})$, $1 \le i \le M$. Here, K_i is the key shared between nodeN$_i$ and the **GW**.
3. The process starts at the leaf nodes. Each pair of siblings execute the PnS protocol with target string length n, and the result is assigned to the private string of the parent as

$$t_{V^1_{i,i+1}} := \text{PnS}(1^n, \text{nodeN}_i, \text{nodeN}_{i+1}, f_{N_i}(1^n, t_{N_i}), f_{N_{i+1}}(1^n, t_{N_{i+1}})),$$

where $i = 1, 3, \ldots$. Note that we execute the complete PnS protocol here so that the output is of length n, i.e. $|t_{V^1_{i,i+1}}| = n$.
4. Step (3) is repeated at the next level of hierarchy, i.e. first level of virtual nodes here, $V^1_{i,i+1}$, to generate the private strings for the parents of the virtual nodes.
5. The process of Step (4) continues till the virtual root node is reached. The private string of the root node t_{root} is the shared secret key between all nodes.
6. The gateway monitors the broadcast messages and verifies the correctness. It transmits an error message if the verification fails at any stage.

· **Protocol 5.** Authenticated tree based group key protocol for M nodes

---

Whenever two nodes engage in the PnS protocol, the first node uses a function of the random value from the previous stage, while the second node uses a fresh random value concatenated with some authentication credentials. The value used by the first node ensures that all nodes prior to it can re-create the PnS execution and learn its outputs. The value of the second node will be authenticated by the passively monitoring **GW**, before it is included in the chain.

To ensure security against compromise of K_i and still ensure verifiability, it is required that the second node use some fresh randomness, unknown to everyone else and the key K_i. It should be observed that successful authentication of the messages of the second node requires the PnS protocol to be internally executed atleast twice. In the first round, the fresh random value is extracted by **GW** and in the second round it is authenticated. We argue that this will always be the case as the probability that the PnS protocol is executed only once is 2^{-n}, i.e. when all bits of both the parties are complements of each other. Thus the authentication process does not add communication overhead. Similar to the previous schemes, the initial key generation has linear complexity, i.e. $\mathcal{O}(n \cdot M)$.

Function: $RetVal := \mathbf{f_x}(1^n, \mathbf{K}, \mathbf{ctr}, \mathbf{state})$, $x \in \{\mathbf{GW}, \text{nodeN}_1, \ldots, \text{nodeN}_M\}$

    i: local persistent counter initialized to 0 during the first execution
    l_state: local persistent flag initialized to 0 during the first execution
    if($l\_state \neq state$)
        if($state == 2$) $i := -1$
        if($state == 1$) $i := 0$
        $l\_state := state$
    if($i == -1$) $RetVal := ctr$
    else $RetVal := g(K, ctr + i)$
    $i := i + 1$

Protocol: $\mathbf{AuthLinearGroup}(1^n, \{\text{nodeN}_1, \ldots, \text{nodeN}_M\}, \{f_{N_1}, \ldots, f_{N_M}\})$

1. The **GW** is begins the protocol by acting as the first link in the PnS chain. The **GW** chooses $t_{GW} \leftarrow \{0,1\}^n$ and nodeN_1 chooses $t_{N_1} \leftarrow \{0,1\}^n$ to execute the PnS protocol as

$$t_{GW,N_1} = \text{PnS}(1^n, \mathbf{GW}, \text{nodeN}_1, f_{GW}(1^n, t_{GW}, 0, 1), f_{N_1}(1^n, K_{N_1}, t_{N_1}, 2)).$$

2. Next, nodeN_2 chooses a random value $t_{N_2} \leftarrow \{0,1\}^n$. nodeN_1 performs PnS with nodeN_2 as

$$t_{N_1,N_2} = \text{PnS}(1^n, \text{nodeN}_1, \text{nodeN}_2, f_{N_1}(1^n, t_{GW,N_1}, 0, 1), f_{N_2}(1^n, K_{N_2}, t_{N_2}, 2)).$$

3. Step (2) is repeated between successive pairs of nodes till the final node is reached. Denote by t_{N_{M-1},N_M}, the result of the final PnS operation. This is the group key shared by all nodes.

4. The gateway monitors the broadcast messages and verifies the correctness. It transmits an error message if the verification fails at any stage.

Protocol 6. Authenticated linear group key protocol for M nodes

---

Node Arrival and Departure: The addition of a node in a linear structure is simple. We assume that the added node is temporarily (for the group) assigned a lower priority than all other elements and thus, is to be added at the end of the chain. Thus the addition of a new member simply requires one PnS operation between the last node and the new member, i.e. complexity of $\mathcal{O}(1)$.

A departing node knows the secrets associated with all nodes that follow it. Thus a node departure requires all nodes following the departing node to update their key parameters. This may be performed by simply re-executing the PnS protocol with updated index values, without the need of sampling fresh random strings. Thus this incurs linear communication cost, i.e. $\mathcal{O}(n \cdot M)$.

6   Discussion

6.1   Security Properties

Though Sect. 5 describes schemes that are robust against arbitrary active adversaries, we argue that such an adversarial model is too restrictive for the automotive scenarios. Operations of our protocol and the architecture of the CAN bus restrict the actions of the adversary in our system. We argue that an active adversary cannot successfully perform any operation, except eavesdropping, without detection. Consider the following

1. **Modification of a packet** - The properties of the CAN bus allow only one type of modification to the messages transmitted by the nodes. An adversary can flip a recessive bit '1' to a dominant bit '0' by transmitting a voltage, however not vice-versa. It can be verified that this simply results in a mismatched key at both parties. This can easily be detected by any key verification method.
2. **Inserting messages for active nodes** - An active node, executing a pairwise session of the protocol, only accepts outputs on the bus that result from superposition of its own signals with that of the partner. Thus consider an adversary that attempts to compromise a session between $nodeN_1$ and $nodeN_2$ by inserting a 'specific' message for $nodeN_2$. However, this requires that the adversary initiate a transmission from $nodeN_2$. Assume that the message transmitted by the adversary is m_{adv}, and that by $nodeN_2$ is m_{N_2}. Thus the message recorded by $nodeN_2$ is the logical AND of these messages, i.e. $m_{adv} \wedge m_{N_2}$. However, as the adversary has no control over m_{N_2}, it cannot insert a 'specific' packet. It can however choose and force bits to be 0. This can be detected by key verification.
3. **Inserting messages for passive nodes** - In the group protocols, nodes that have engaged in one pairwise session may update their local parameters based on the output of the future sessions. An adversary may falsely emulate such sessions. However, it can be demonstrated that the probability of 'successfully' inserting a n bit packet, i.e. a packet that is accepted as a valid input by the passive node, is less than $\left(\frac{3}{4}\right)^n$.

Theorem 3. *Let the adversary activate the protocol of a passive node by inserting an arbitrary pair of strings b_1, b_2, where $|b_1| = |b_2| = n$, marked with the session identifier of the currently active nodes. The passive nodes detect the adversary with a probability greater than $1 - \left(\frac{3}{4}\right)^n$.*

Proof. Consider the scenario where $nodeN_2$ and $nodeN_3$ are actively engaging in PnS and $nodeN_1$ is the passive observer. Let $t_{N_{1,2}}$ be the string at $nodeN_1$ as a result of its interaction with $nodeN_2$. As described in Protocol 1, $nodeN_2$ uses that string for interaction with $nodeN_3$. Thus $nodeN_1$ can simply verify the bus output to and identify 'unexpected' behavior of the adversary as follows. Consider the set of indices L where $t_{N_{1,2}} = 0$, $L = \{l \leq |t_{N_{1,2}}| | t_{N_{1,2}}(i) = 0\}$.

The output on the bus as a result of the first PnS operation, corresponding to indices in the set L, should be 0. This results simply from the *AND* operation of the bus. Any deviation from this results in an error by nodeN_1. Thus for the message by adversary to be accepted, $b_1(L)$ should be 0, i.e. the adversary should be able to estimate the position of all 0s in the string $t_{N_{1,2}}$. Thus we obtain

$$Pr\left(\{b_1, b_2\} \text{ accepted}\right) = \sum_k Pr\left(\text{Adv covers all 0 positions} \mid |L| = k\right) \cdot$$

$$\underbrace{= \sum_{k=0}^n \left(\frac{1}{2}\right)^k \cdot \binom{n}{k}\left(\frac{1}{2}\right)^k \left(\frac{1}{2}\right)^{n-k}}_{Pr(|L| = k)} = \left(\frac{3}{4}\right)^n$$

4. **Impersonation** - The broadcast nature of the CAN bus ensures that any transmitted message is delivered to all the nodes. Thus any spoofed or replayed message by the adversary can be detected by the victim node and an error flag can be raised. We assume that such detection can occur due to the session IDs described earlier.

It is clear that Properties 1, 2, 3 are guaranteed by any PnS based key agreement scheme for the CAN bus. A cryptographic method to guarantee Property (4) is by utilizing the trust relation established with the gateway. An alternate way is to increase ECU robustness and include a mechanism to identify spoofed messages in the individual ECUs. For such cases, schemes that are secure against a passive eavesdropper would also be secure against an active adversary. Thus the efficient tree-based structure of Sect. 4 can be utilized to provide security against active adversaries.

6.2   Performance

One of the main benefits of the our approach is its computational advantage over the modular multiplications, as required for group schemes based on DH or ECDH. The variants of the our protocols allow a tradeoff between the complexity and bandwidth. Further, our schemes are based on pseudorandom functions, which can be practically implemented either via the SHA family of hash functions or a block cipher such as AES. Both these primitives are better suited for resource constrained devices, compared to modular multiplication.

To understand the performance comparison of our scheme, consider the scenario where the M nodes wish to generate a n bit key. Clearly, Protocol 3 requires no cryptographic primitives, but has a high bandwidth overhead. Each round of PnS using n bit inputs requires transmission of $2n$ bits on the bus (normal and the complement). Further, scenarios that use the cryptographic primitives use 2 invocations of the function for each round. We summarize the overhead and some properties of the protocols in Table 1. Authors in [10] evaluate the performance of various cryptographic primitives on various automotive microcontrollers, namely the S12X, a low end 16-bit automotive microcontroller from Freescale and the TriCore chip, a high end 32-bit microcontroller from the AUDO family of Infineon. The S12X family operates at 40 MHz while the Tricore chips can operate up to 180 MHz. For generating a key of length $n = 128$, we may utilize the SHA-256 hash function in place of the PRF. It can be seen that performance of the PRFs adds very little overhead of 3.145 ms and 0.045 ms respectively for each invocation for our target input lengths.

Table 1. Performance of the proposed schemes

Property	Protocol			
	3	4	5	6
	Simple unauth.	Tree-based unauth.	Tree based auth.	Linear auth.
Avg. no. of bits Tx on bus	$4n(2^{M-1} - 1)$	$4n(M - 1)$	$4n(M - 1)$	$4nM$
Avg. of PRF invocations	0	$4(M - 1)$	$5M - 4$	$4M - 2$
Node addition	$\mathcal{O}(n2^M)$	$\mathcal{O}(n \log M)$	$\mathcal{O}(n \log M)$	$\mathcal{O}(n)$
Node deletion	$\mathcal{O}(n2^M)$	$\mathcal{O}(n \log M)$	$\mathcal{O}(n \log M)$	$\mathcal{O}(nM)$

Due to the lack of implementation of state-of-the art key exchange schemes based on ECDH, e.g. MQV [20], on comparable automotive microcontrollers, we cannot present performance benchmarks for the group operations. However, to the best of our knowledge, in all performance benchmarks in literature, the group operations for ECDH with a comparable keysize (256 bits), implemented in software without any dedicated hardware support, consume atleast one to two orders higher time. Thus, we would assume that such a scaling would be expected for the automotive microcontrollers as well, i.e. overhead of ≈100 ms. Thus the performance advantage of our scheme is clear.

A typical implementation of the CAN bus operates at a rate of 125 kbits/s, i.e. 1000 frames per second. Each frame of frame contains 8 bytes of data. Thus on average, a PnS session between two nodes to generate a $n = 128$ bit key would last over 8 frames, i.e. 8 ms, which is similar to the overhead using ECDH.

With improvements in technology, it is expected that the recommended length of parameters for ECDH will increase significantly in the foreseeable future [1]. The computational overhead of group operations due to such changes has poor scaling in comparison to our group key protocols, which would scale linearly with the key length. Further, as physicists bring quantum computing into the practical realm, traditional EC-DH based schemes may be rendered insecure. By contrast, PnS based schemes would remain secure.

6.3   Conclusion

We presented methods to efficiently generate group keys for nodes connected via a shared bus, using physical layer properties. The methods utilize the natural wired AND operation provided by the bus architecture, in place of expensive modular exponentiation operations typically required. The algorithmic complexity of our scheme is equivalent to the most efficient key-agreement algorithm available today. One of the most promising applications for this schemes is in context of ECU networks inside an automobile. However, our assumptions are sufficiently generic to map to a variety of wired networks. Thus, these schemes can be utilized in different systems where low capability devices are present.

References

1. Cryptographic key length recommendations. http://www.keylength.com. Accessed 09 Feb 2016
2. Ateniese, G., Steiner, M., Tsudik, G.: Authenticated group key agreement and friends. In: Proceedings of Conference on Computer and Communications Security, pp. 17–26. ACM, New York (1998)
3. Bellare, M., Rogaway, P.: Entity authentication and key distribution. In: Stinson, D.R. (ed.) CRYPTO 1993. LNCS, vol. 773, pp. 232–249. Springer, Heidelberg (1994)
4. Bresson, E., Chevassut, O., Pointcheval, D.: Provably secure authenticated group Diffie-Hellman key exchange. ACM Trans. Inf. Syst. Secur. 10(3), July 2007
5. Canetti, R., Krawczyk, H.: Analysis of key-exchange protocols and their use for building secure channels. In: Pfitzmann, B. (ed.) EUROCRYPT 2001. LNCS, vol. 2045, pp. 453–474. Springer, Heidelberg (2001)
6. Checkoway, S., McCoy, D., Kantor, B., Anderson, D., Shacham, H., Savage, S., Koscher, K., Czeskis, A., Roesner, F., Kohno, T.: Comprehensive experimental analyses of automotive attack surfaces. In: Proceedings of the USENIX Security Symposium, August 2011
7. Diffie, W., Hellman, M.: New directions in cryptography. IEEE Trans. Inf. Theor. 22(6), 644–654 (1976)
8. Glas, B., Guajardo, J., Hacioglu, H., Ihle, M., Wehefritz, K., Yavuz, A.: Signal-based automotive communication security and its interplay with safety requirements. In: Embedded Security in Cars (ESCAR), Europe, November 2012
9. Goldreich, O., Goldwasser, S., Micali, S.: How to construct random functions. J. ACM 33(4), 792–807 (1986)
10. Groza, B., Murvay, S.: Efficient protocols for secure broadcast in controller area networks. IEEE Trans. Ind. Inf. 9(4), 2034–2042 (2013)
11. Groza, B., Murvay, S., van Herrewege, A., Verbauwhede, I.: LiBrA-CAN: a lightweight broadcast authentication protocol for controller area networks. In: Pieprzyk, J., Sadeghi, A.-R., Manulis, M. (eds.) CANS 2012. LNCS, vol. 7712, pp. 185–200. Springer, Heidelberg (2012)
12. Harn, L., Lin, C.: Authenticated group key transfer protocol based on secret sharing. IEEE Trans. Comput. 59(6), 842–846 (2010)
13. Hastad, J., Impagliazzo, R., Levin, L.A., Luby, M.: A pseudorandom generator from any one-way function. SIAM J. Comput. 28(4), 1364–1396 (1999)
14. Herrewege, A.V., Verbauwhede, I.: CANAuth - a simple, backward compatible broadcast authentication protocol for CAN bus. In: ECRYPT Workshop on Lightweight Cryptography 2011, Louvain-la-Neuve, BE, pp. 229–235 (2011)
15. Katz, J., Yung, M.: Scalable protocols for authenticated group key exchange. In: Boneh, D. (ed.) CRYPTO 2003. LNCS, vol. 2729, pp. 110–125. Springer, Heidelberg (2003)

16. Kim, Y., Perrig, A., Tsudik, G.: Group key agreement efficient in communication. IEEE Trans. Comput. **53**(7), 905–921 (2004)
17. Kim, Y., Perrig, A., Tsudik, G.: Communication-efficient group key agreement. In: Proceedings of the Annual Working Conference on Information Security, pp. 229–244 (2001)
18. Kim, Y., Perrig, A., Tsudik, G.: Tree-based group key agreement. ACM Trans. Inf. Syst. Secur. **7**(1), 60–96 (2004)
19. Koscher, K., Czeskis, A., Roesner, F., Patel, S., Kohno, T., Checkoway, S., McCoy, D., Kantor, B., Anderson, D., Shacham, H., Savage, S.: Experimental security analysis of a modern automobile. In: Proceedings of the Symposium on Security and Privacy, pp. 447–462, May 2010
20. Law, L., Menezes, A., Qu, M., Solinas, J., Vanstone, S.: An efficient protocol for authenticated key agreement. Des. Codes Crypt. **28**(2), 119–134 (2003)
21. Maurer, U.M.: Information-theoretically secure secret-key agreement by NOT authenticated public discussion. In: Fumy, W. (ed.) EUROCRYPT 1997. LNCS, vol. 1233, pp. 209–225. Springer, Heidelberg (1997)
22. Miller, C., Valasek, C.: A survey of remote automotive attack surfaces. Technical report, IOActive Inc., Online Whitepaper: Accessed 09 Feb 2016
23. Müller, A., Lothspeich, T.: Plug-and-secure communication for CAN. CAN Newsletter, pp. 10–14, December 2015
24. Rouf, I., Miller, R.D., Mustafa, H.A., Taylor, T., Oh, S., Xu, W., Gruteser, M., Trappe, W., Seskar, I.: Security and privacy vulnerabilities of in-car wireless networks: a tire pressure monitoring system case study. In: Proceedings of the USENIX Security Symposium, pp. 323–338, August 2010
25. Steiner, M., Tsudik, G., Waidner, M.: Key agreement in dynamic peer groups. IEEE Trans. Parallel Distrib. Syst. **11**(8), 769–780 (2000)
26. Szilagyi, C., Koopman, P.: Low cost multicast authentication via validity voting in time-triggered embedded control networks. In: Proceedings of the Workshop on Embedded Systems Security. ACM, New York (2010)
27. Szilagyi, C., Koopman, P.: Flexible multicast authentication for time-triggered embedded control network applications. In: Proceedings of the International Conference on Dependable Systems and Networks, pp. 165–174. IEEE, June 2009
28. Valasek, C., Miller, C.: Remote exploitation of an unaltered passenger vehicle. Technical report, IOActive Inc., Online Whitepaper: Accessed 09 Feb 2016
29. Wang, Y., Ramamurthy, B., Zou, X.: The performance of elliptic curve based group Diffie-Hellman protocols for secure group communication over ad hoc networks. In: Proceedings of the International Conference on Communications, vol. 5, pp. 2243–2248 (2006)

– vatiCAN –
Vetted, Authenticated CAN Bus

Stefan Nürnberger[(✉)] and Christian Rossow

CISPA, Saarland University, Saarbrücken, Germany
nuernberger@cs.uni-saarland.de, crossow@mmci.uni-saarland.de

Abstract. In recent years, several attacks have impressively demonstrated that the software running on embedded controllers in cars can be successfully exploited – often even remotely. The fact that components that were hitherto purely mechanical, such as connections to the brakes, throttle, and steering wheel, have been computerized makes digital exploits life-threatening. Because of the interconnectedness of sensors, controllers and actuators, any compromised controller can impersonate any other controller by mimicking its control messages, thus effectively depriving the driver of his control.

The fact that carmakers develop vehicles in evolutionary steps rather than as revolution, has led us to propose a backward-compatible authentication mechanism for the widely used *CAN* vehicle communication bus. vatiCAN allows recipients of a message to verify its authenticity via HMACs, while not changing CAN messages for legacy, non-critical components. In addition, vatiCAN detects and prevents attempts to spoof identifiers of critical components. We implemented a vatiCAN prototype and show that it incurs a CAN message latency of less than 4 ms, while giving strong guarantees against non-authentic messages.

1 Introduction

In the highly competitive field of automobile manufacturing, only those have survived who have adopted the art of extreme cost savings by establishing a well-coordinated concert of manufacturers, suppliers and assemblers. It is this fragile chain, which now turns out to be too static when it comes to cross-sectional changes as would be needed by a radically new, secure architecture.

Even though security experts agree that an overhauled, security-focused architecture is much-needed [2, 10, 16, 17], carmakers simply cannot easily change established designs. Arguably, two major obstacles are (1) the industry-wide "never touch a running system" attitude, which originates in legislative burdens and safety concerns, and (2) the overwhelming complexity of regulations in different jurisdictions of the world, which have fostered the outsourcing to highly specialized suppliers. This effect is even more amplified due to the tendency of acquisition rather than in-house innovation. As a result, desired functionalities are put out to tender and the hardware and software is instead developed by a long chain of suppliers. For example, Porsche claims to have the lowest manufacturing depth in the automotive industry with more than 80 % of production

© International Association for Cryptologic Research 2016
B. Gierlichs and A.Y. Poschmann (Eds.): CHES 2016, LNCS 9813, pp. 106–124, 2016.
DOI: 10.1007/978-3-662-53140-2_6

cost spent for supplier's parts, while the remaining 20 % are spent on engine production, the assembly, quality control and sale of their vehicles [3].

This is in contrast with the needed extensive architectural changes to implement at least some level of security. The lack of automotive security engineering principles as opposed to the desktop computer world is not surprising. The most widely used automotive communication protocol CAN^1 was designed to run in isolation stowed away behind panels. Faulty hardware or damaged wires were the only likely threat to such an isolated system. A deliberate manipulation could only happen with physical access to the inside of the car. While these design principles were absolutely adequate for safety requirements back then, modern cars have meanwhile reached an almost incomprehensive complexity and moreover violate the ancient isolation assumptions due to their promiscuous connectivity such as Bluetooth audio, 3G Internet, WiFi, wireless sensors, RDS^2, and TMC^3.

It is not only potentially possible but it has been practically shown that vulnerabilities in these wireless connections exist [2]. An attacker can then write arbitrary messages on the CAN bus, which connects the car's computers, the so-called *Electronic Control Units* (ECUs). While the culprit is indeed a vulnerable ECU that can be compromised, the exploited fact is that the CAN topology is a bus. This broadcast topology allows any connected device, including a compromised ECU, to send arbitrary control messages. The receivers have no way of verifying the authenticity of the sender or the control data.

Contributions. In this paper, we propose vatiCAN, a framework for embedded controllers connected to the CAN bus, which allows both senders and receivers to authenticate exchanged data. First and most importantly, receivers can check the authenticity of a received message. Second, senders can monitor the bus for their own messages to detect fraudulent messages. In detail, vatiCAN provides

- **Sender and message authentication** in the CAN bus broadcast topology, which prevents fake messages from illegitimate senders from being processed.
- Security against **replay-attacks** by incorporating a global nonce.
- **Spoof detection** of own messages in software by bus monitoring.
- Full **backward compatibility** as message payloads, sender IDs and most importantly CAN transceiver chips are left unmodified, which allows legacy devices to work without modifications.
- **Spoof prevention** of own messages is possible in hardware by changing bus arbitration.

While the possible improvements on a legacy architecture are somewhat limited by the intended backward compatibility, this paper shows what can be achieved when backward compatibility is the utmost goal. It thereby lays the foundation for automakers to increase the status quo of security while adhering to the established structures of minimal change.

---

[1] Controller Area Network - Developed by BOSCH and Mercedes-Benz in 1983.
[2] Radio Data System - digital payload for FM radio broadcast, e.g. station name.
[3] Traffic Message Channel - Traffic information over FM radio for navigation systems.

2   Background

To address the need to connect different sensors, actuators and their controllers with each other so that they can make informed decisions, BOSCH developed a new communication bus in 1983 [7,13]. For example, the widespread traction control system (TCS[4]) could use CAN to connect the necessary sensors (wheel rotation) and actuators (brakes). The TCS monitors the wheel spin on each of the four wheels and intentionally brakes individual wheels to get traction back (see Fig. 1).

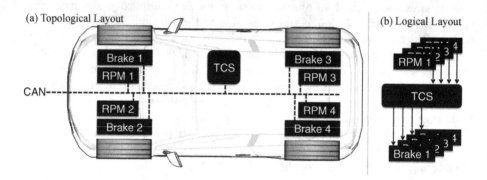

Fig. 1. Bus Topology on the example of the Traction Control System (TCS): Sensors (wheel RPM) are read as input while actuators (brakes) work as output.

CAN transmits so-called *CAN frames* consisting of a *priority*, the actual message *payload*, its *length* (1 to 8 bytes), and a *CRC checksum* followed by an *acknowledgment flag* (see Fig. 2).

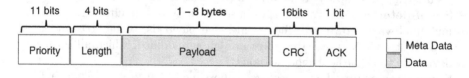

Fig. 2. A single CAN frame.

What makes CAN so widespread, are two important safety requirements it fulfils:

(1) the acknowledgement of reception and
(2) the arbitration of sending order.

---

[4] Also known as *ESP* - Electronic Stability Program.

	Priority/ Sender ID	Length	Data
Airbag	0x050	4	E0 F0 00 FF
Brake (Front Left)	0x1A0	8	10 F0 01 00 00 30 00 E1

Fig. 3. Example CAN messages from the airbag and brake captured on a 2005 Volkswagen Passat B6.

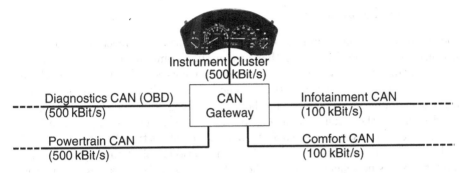

Fig. 4. Interconnected CAN buses through a CAN gateway in a VW Passat B6. (source: "Volkswagen erWin Online")

The acknowledgement of reception (1) is important because the sender of a critical message must be sure that it has been processed. Additionally, messages, which can only be sent one after the other, must be prioritized based on how important they are (2). This ensures the hard real-time requirements of the whole system.

The CAN bus achieves those two properties in hardware by using the electrical concept of so-called *dominant* and *recessive* bits. Bits are always transmitted synchronously at fixed time slots and dominant (logical 0) bits can overwrite recessive bits (logical 1). This simple principle allows the sender to check if at least one ECU has received the frame by reading the acknowledgement bit. Similarly, the prioritization of frames is solved: Since each frame starts with its 11-bit priority, the dominant bits overwrite the recessive priority bits of other frames transmitted at the same time. Only the highest priority frame is received by all the connected nodes, while a lower priority device automatically backs off when a recessive bit has been overwritten by somebody else. The priority is at the same the time CAN sender ID. Hence, if the airbag has sender ID 0x050 and front left brakes have ID 0x1A0, then the airbag has a *higher* priority because 0x050 is numerically lower than 0x1A0 (see Fig. 3).

CAN buses have different standardized speeds ranging from 5 to 1000 kBit/s. Most common are 500 kBit/s and 100 kBit/s, while 500 kBit/s networks have higher demands in terms of cables and CAN bus tranciever chips. Depending on the make and model, there are several CAN buses in a modern car.

The most prominent reasons for having more than one CAN bus are (1) Clear separation for safety reasons, (2) fault-tolerance in case one bus fails, (3) cost reduction due to lower speed CAN buses where high-speed CAN buses are not needed. An exemplary CAN bus network and its interconnectedness is depicted in Fig. 4.

3   Design

3.1   Problem Statement

The steadily increasing number of components that are connected on the CAN bus introduce a high likelihood that any of such components may be compromised [4]. Unfortunately, such a compromise may have severe security (and therefore also safety) implications to the automotive network. Of all possible threats, message spoofing remains one of the largest unsolved issued on the current CAN bus designs. In the worst case, a compromised component may inject fake CAN messages, e.g., messages that make the parking assistant turn the steering wheel.

In the current CAN design, there is no protection against these threats. First of all, CAN has no scheme to verify the *authenticity* of the messages, i.e., neither the sender information, nor the actual message payload. In principle, an attacker that controls any component on the CAN bus, can thus

(a) spoof the identity of any other component (e.g., to escalate privileges), or
(b) send arbitrary payload (e.g., to perform malicious actions).

Our goal is to introduce authenticity schemes to CAN. First, we aim to add *sender authenticity* to guarantee that CAN components can protect their identity by denying messages that spoof their identity. Second, we plan to add *content authenticity* to guarantee that a message was intentionally sent and its content was neither manipulated nor replayed.

It may seem trivial to redesign CAN such that those features are added. However, a practical solution faces several challenges:

C1 CAN has been designed primarily to match real-time characteristics of the communication. Any security mechanism must not add unacceptable overheads that significantly increase latency or lead to message collisions.
C2 ECUs are typically microcontrollers with very constrained computational power and storage space. Thus, heavy-duty crypto operations cannot be performed as they would add an unacceptable overhead.
C3 CAN messages are limited to 8 bytes, which requires us to either squeeze secure crypto into 64 bits or to use a higher level transmission protocol that re-assembles longer messages that are spread across several CAN frames.
C4 Cryptographic keys must be individual per car to render extracting keys in one car useless. Moreover, key agreement between ECUs must be dynamic to allow for broken parts to be replaced.

C5 Adapting all ECUs and all messages would be disproportionate as many ECUs are non-critical and do not need to be protected. Further, changing messages would result in compatibility problems and enormous costs as mass-produced components could otherwise no longer be used. To keep cost down, as few ECUs as possible should be modified.

C6 Authenticated messages should be immune to replay attacks. However, introducing a global state is against the design principle of CAN, which is stateless in order to tolerate packet loss.

Instead, our goal is to retrofit vatiCAN to CAN by adding a backward-compatible security add-on for selected senders and messages. Our vatiCAN add-on should not influence components that do not support the new security mechanisms. Components that *do* support vatiCAN, on the other hand, will benefit from the authenticity checks. Such a model allows for a gradual, evolutionary change towards a more secure CAN standard and can at the same time protect vital components, such as power steering, brakes and airbag, from the beginning.

3.2 Threat Model

We assume an attacker who does not have physical access to the car but she can fully compromise one (or a few) wireless ECUs that usually use several ID_k $k \in \{0, \ldots, 2^{11}\}$ to send on the CAN bus. The attacker's goal is to impersonate another ECU with ID_x with $k \neq x$. After the compromise of ECU with ID_k, the attacker has full flexibility in sending arbitrary messages to the CAN bus, i.e., she can fake sender identities and chose any message payloads.

The attacker is assumed not to compromise the ECU for which she intends to fake the packets—otherwise the attacker would already be using the genuine sender and can likely extract any cryptographic key material from the compromised devices and thus fake the identity regardless of any cryptographic scheme. Instead, we protect the identities of critical devices that might be impersonated (and not compromised) by an attacker.

In addition, we consider an attacker that can passively monitor the CAN bus. She can observe and record all messages that have been broadcasted on the CAN bus. This way, the attacker can also learn about components' identities.

3.3 High Level Concept

In this section, we describe the individual features of vatiCAN that address the challenges C1 through C5.

Message Organisation (C1, C5). The cryptographic authentication mechanism that vatiCAN uses must be decoupled from the actual message to remain backward compatibility. We opted for a separate message with a different sender ID such that legacy devices still see the original message content from the sender

ID they expect (C5). As a side effect, the induced cryptographic performance and bandwidth overhead only applies to critical messages that have been manually selected at development time. For those selected messages, their additional authentication message is then sent from a different ID for which only vatiCAN-aware recipients listen. The separation of messages also has the advantage that the recipient experiences no delay when receiving the original, unmodified message (C1) and can compute the necessary cryptographic authentication in parallel to the reception of the authentication message.

Special care must be taken when selecting the sender ID for the additional authentication message from ID_j for each legacy sender ID_i. Since senders correspond to priorities on the CAN bus, a careless selection of a new j may result in other messages being delayed if the priority is too high or may lead to the priority inversion problem if the priority is too low. We therefore choose the new $j = i + 1$, which lowers the authentication's priority by the smallest granularity possible. Under the assumption that this new ID is not taken, this effectively assigns the same priority to the authentication message as all other message priorities are still lower or higher, respectively.

Message Authentication (C2, C3). vatiCAN supports content authenticity, which cryptographically ensures that the sender was in possession of the required and correct cryptographic key. As a cryptographic primitive, we chose a light-weight keyed-Hash Message Authentication Code (HMAC) since symmetric cryptography fulfils our requirements and is more suitable for embedded resource-constrained devices with real-time requirements. As underlying hash function for the HMAC construction, we chose the Keccak algorithm that has been standardized as SHA-3. According to the performance evaluation of hash functions on the popular Atmel embedded microcontroller [1], Keccak is the fastest hash function (C2). We chose the Keccak parameters to produce 64 bit output with 128 bits of rate and capacity ($r = c = 128$). The input size of 128 bits was chosen to accommodate the original payload of up to 64 bits, the sender ID and a nonce (see below).

For messages that have been selected for authentication at development time, an additional HMAC CAN frame is sent from the sender j. The recipients can then verify if the HMAC matches the content received earlier, and if so, accept the message. This two-step process can also be used to pre-condition the upcoming action (e.g. move brakes to the disk) as soon as the first un-authenticated, legacy content has been received and then defer the actual command execution (e.g., brake) until the authentication approval arrives. If the HMAC is invalid or has not been received in a given time frame, the recipient can discard the message and potentially issue a warning.

3.4 Replay Attacks (C6)

To prevent **replay attacks**, vatiCAN incorporates a nonce in the HMAC computation. Otherwise an attacker could record a vital message and its HMAC and then replay both later. In contrast to other authentication schemes, we do not require the nonce to be non-predictable but we require the nonce not to produce two messages with the same HMAC. Since we opted for not modifying the original payload, we cannot distribute the nonce for each authenticated message. To avoid an additional broadcast of the nonce, the sender and all receivers must implicitly agree on the same nonce that must be different for each message. For this purpose, we introduce a counter c_j, which is specific for each sender j and is incremented with each message sent by ID_j. This ensures that the HMAC of recurring CAN payloads is different each time. We chose sender-specific counters rather than a global counter because some ECUs might not be online all the time and most ECUs implement a hardware ID filter that only forwards CAN frames from those IDs that are of interest to this particular ECU.

To account for the fact that messages might get lost or ECUs are temporarily in power-safe mode, we additionally introduce the global Nonce Generator (NG). The NG periodically broadcasts a random global nonce g, which shall be used by all counters c_j as their new value. This way, counters get synced up again across different ECUs. In other words, on each broadcast of g, all ECUs reset their $c_j = g$ and start counting from there with each message they send.

Consequently, the HMAC of the each message m is computed by the sender (recall that i is the ID of the legacy sender, and $j = i + 1$ is the ID of the HMAC message) and by the recipient as follows:

$$h = \mathrm{HMAC}(i \mid m \mid c_j)$$

We incorporate the legacy sender i in the HMAC, such that no identical payloads from different senders produce the same HMAC if they happen to share the same key. Since messages on the CAN bus are received in the same order for all nodes, choosing the right g is deterministic for all nodes. The g that was valid before the legacy message from i was sent has to be used to verify the HMAC sent by j in order to avoid race conditions.

The overall timing and message exchange is exemplified in Fig. 5, in which the throttle sends a message that the engine validates. First, the NG broadcasts the new nonce (761). Next, the throttle broadcasts the legacy message. Afterwards, it computes the HMAC, using its legacy ID, the legacy message payload (30) and the nonce. Simultaneously, the engine also computes the HMAC over the message payload sent by the throttle. Finally, after the throttle broadcasts the HMAC, the engine will verify if the computed HMAC values match.

Even though the attacker can receive the current nonce g, she is not in possession of the necessary key to compute the HMAC. In other words, g is not secret.

A nonce introduces a "state" in a protocol that is designed to be stateless to accommodate for packet loss. Should a packet loss occur (e.g., damaged cables) all subsequent HMACs could not be verified anymore until the next global nonce g is broadcasted by the NG. Hence, the interval at which the NG broadcasts g at the same time sets the *deaf* time, which is the maximum time an ECU might see invalid HMACs after a hardware failure. A suggested frequency is every 50 ms, which corresponds to an additional bus utilization of $\approx 1\,\%$ at $500\,\mathrm{kBit/s}$.

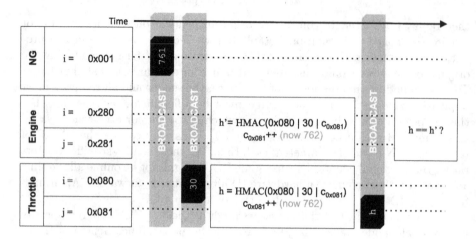

Fig. 5. Timing of interaction between NG, legacy and authenticated messages.

Spoof Detection and Prevention. A first primitive of vatiCAN is to mitigate the risk that compromised components can fake the identity of other components. To this end, we leverage the fact that CAN is a bus-oriented network, and components thus receive messages from all other components on the bus. In fact, if a component monitors the CAN communication, it can identify spoofed messages by monitoring messages with its own sender identification. If a component detects a message with its own sender ID, it must be a spoofed message. Since messages transmitted by a CAN transceiver are not considered received messages, this can be clearly distinguished. Once detected, this issue is made available in software in the form of an exception. However, other recipients might have already processed this message. This software solution is only suitable for detecting and, e.g., displaying a message to the driver. Alternatively, it is also possible to drop a detected spoofed message by intentionally destroying the CRC checksum. However, the CRC checksum part is usually processed in hardware and hence deliberate destruction is only possible when the CAN transceiver chip is modified. A difficulty of this approach is that the CAN messages have to be destroyed before the transmission of the spoofed frame is completed. Luckily, the sender information is at the start of each frame and is synchronously processed for bus arbitration anyway. This means an early detection stage is possible by invalidating the CRC bits using dominant bits (e.g. all zeros) while a CAN frame is still being processed. This approach is similar to the already implemented acknowledgement (see Sect. 2) in the CAN bus standard, which is also set at the correct timing of the *ACK* bit during transmission. We assume that (at least) the NG—which is the only component that needs to be added for vatiCAN—is protected with such a hardware-assisted spoofing prevention mechanism. Hence an attacker cannot impersonate the NG and inject arbitrary nonces.

Should a sender ID be shared between ECUs, the spoof detection described above cannot be applied. A shared sender ID could be used for door ECUs that simply send a message that the door is open. Each door has an ECU that uses the same sender ID because it only matters *that* a door is open but not which.

Key Distribution (C4). According to the HMAC construction, the used cryptographic key is either padded to the length of the hash function's input block size, or it is hashed if it is longer than the block size. To avoid an additional hashing operation, we recommend setting the length of the cryptographic key exactly to the length of the input block size of the hash function: 128 bits.

We also chose not to use one global key, but individual keys per ECU. Of course, it is also possible to group ECUs that share the same key. This saves precious flash memory at the expense of reduced security. Typically, ECUs form logical clusters, e.g., all four wheel rotation sensor ECUs, and all four brake ECUs form a logical cluster of *traction control*. vatiCAN leverages this and supports assigning sets of IDs the same cryptographic key, bonding them to a group.

The most critical aspect is the key provisioning: the process of getting keys into ECUs in the first place. The cryptographic key for each ECU or group needs to be provisioned to each ECU that is part of that logical cluster. Generally, two possibilities exist:

(a) **During Assembly.** The keys could be generated randomly during production and automatically be injected into the flash memory of the corresponding ECUs. However, this makes replacing ECUs after a fault or accident more involved, as either keys have to be extracted from other ECUs or new keys need to be generated and distributed to all clusters that the faulty ECU communicates with.

(b) **Key Agreement.** Alternatively, keys can also be agreed upon using Diffie-Hellman key exchange every time the car is turned on. However, this option has several disadvantages: ECUs that switch on on-demand have to re-run the key agreement. Moreover, man-in-middle attacks are possible without certificates stored in the ECUs, which is not practical. And lastly, multi-party key exchange is non-trivial for an embedded microcontroller.

This is why we chose option (a) to provision the keys during production of an ECU. In case an ECU needs to be replaced, all other ECUs need to be updated with the new key. Luckily, software updates through the on-board diagnostics (OBD) port are commonplace and supported by most ECUs. This allows for re-programming of keys without physically removing the ECUs from the car. To protect against malicious key updates by compromised ECUs, the key provisioning could be protected using asymmetric cryptography. For example, signed updates are a viable option, despite the fact that they are relatively slow.

4   Implementation

We implemented a proof-of-concept of vatiCAN on the popular Atmel AVR microcontrollers and used off-the-shelf automotive components, such as an instrument cluster, that act as legacy devices. Our implementation is also available as download in the form of a library for the popular Arduino development environment (see Appendix A).

4.1 Hardware Platform

As hardware platform, we used Atmel AVR microcontrollers, each of which is connected to a Microchip MCP2515 CAN bus controller over SPI [11]. The CAN bus is built on a work bench top and connects an off-the-shelf automobile instrument cluster as symbolic legacy device. The bench top CAN test network resembles a *Hardware-in-the-Loop-Test* (HIL), which is common in the automobile industry [5]. We used this hardware to build the prototype (see Fig. 6):

Atmel AVR ATMega328p   8 bit microcontroller
                             (32 kB of flash, 2 kB of SRAM, 16 MHz)
Microchip MCP2515   CAN bus controller chip (3 TX / 2 RX
                             buffers)
Seat Ibiza instrument cluster From the 2009 model 6J
Logitech Formula GP   Accelerator and brake pedals

Components of the topology of the HIL setup shown in Fig. 7 are:

(a) Electronic Throttle Control (ETC)
(b) Powertrain Control Module (PCM)
(c) Instrument cluster (speed, RPM, airbag warning, ABS warning).
(d) Auxiliary Simulator (AS) for airbag, brakes, and wheels.

The ETC reads the analog potentiometer mounted to the accelerator pedal (0 % to 100 % pressed) and broadcasts the value on the CAN bus so that it can be interpreted by the PCM. The PCM in turn simulates an internal combustion engine and broadcasts engine RPM and oil temperature on the CAN bus. The Seat Ibiza instrument cluster shows the engine RPM using an analog dial.

Fig. 6. Bench HIL setup with original instrument cluster ECU and re-engineered ETC and PCM ECUs.

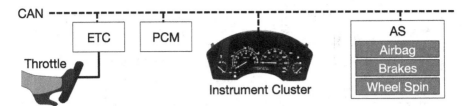

Fig. 7. Hardware-in-the-Loop Test (HIL): ETC, PCM and AS.

The corresponding speed that the speedometer dial shows is being sent by the AS and calculated from the engine RPM and currently selected (simulated) gear.

4.2 Secure Message Selection

The strong-suit of vatiCAN is its interoperability and backward-compatibility with legacy devices that do not understand authenticated messages. For this reason, we chose the original instrument cluster from a 2009 Seat Ibiza, which shows speed and engine RPM despite being secured by vatiCAN. Not all exchanged messages in the HIL were secured, because not all messages are vital. We chose to secure the (1) throttle position message, (2) engine RPM, (3), wheel rotation (vehicle speed), and (4) anti-lock brake controller

All the other messages needed to operate properly (see Appendix B) are not authenticated as they are not vital.

4.3 Software Architecture

The vatiCAN library abstracts CAN bus access to sending and receiving messages, while received messages incorporate the notion of being authenticated or not. The application using vatiCAN registers known sender IDs for authenticated messages and two callbacks. One callback for receiving messages (legacy and authenticated) and one for errors (authentication mismatch, timeouts).

For this purpose, the vatiCAN library keeps a list of authenticated sender IDs i and thus can perform a look-up based on the sender ID for every received CAN frame. Then, vatiCAN knows whether to expect an additional authentication CAN frame from j. All CAN frames are delivered immediately to the application using the provided call-backs. However, CAN bus frames originating from senders not in the list of authenticated senders are flagged *insecure* while frames originating from senders that should authenticate their messages are flagged as *not authenticated yet*. If authentication messages are expected, the HMAC calculation is started in the background. The application code using vatiCAN can then decide whether to prepare or pre-compute intermediate steps until the authentication message arrived and was verified. If the authentication message arrives, vatiCAN automatically compares the computed HMAC to the received authentication message and either invokes the message reception

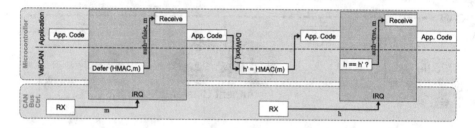

Fig. 8. CAN bus frame reception, message processing and the application.

call-back indicating an authenticated message, or invokes the error call-back if the HMAC comparison failed. The message verification is designed in such a way that the order of internal HMAC computation and authentication message reception does not matter. Whichever completes last, triggers the comparison and forwards either the message or an error to the application.

Since AVR ATmega microcontrollers do not support hardware multi-threading, the background HMAC computation is implemented as an interrupt service routine (ISR), which is triggered on CAN frame reception and defers computations to a later point indicated by the application code. The interaction diagram shown in Fig. 8 depicts the processing of a single, authenticated message.

The implemented code consists of a vatiCAN CAN bus interface library written in C++ and a hash function that currently uses the Keccak (SHA-3) implementation in assembler that was adapted from [1]. The C++ library consists of only 314 lines of code, while the hash function in assembler consists of 250 lines of code. The compiled code sizes can be found in the evaluation in Sect. 5.

5   Performance Evaluation

We evaluated the performance in terms of message reception delay, bus congestion due to added CAN frames and in terms of memory footprint. The evaluation was conducted on the hardware presented in Sect. 4. To obtain time measurements, we used the internal ATmega timer with a pre-scaler of 64, which divides the used 16 Mhz clock speed in 250 kHz accuracy (4 μs accuracy). All experiments have been conducted on the very common 500 kBit/s bus speed.

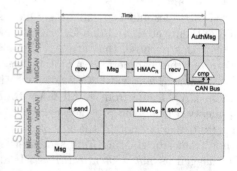

Fig. 9. Parallel computation of HMACs

We then measured the time it takes to calculate a single HMAC for a CAN frame, given *nonce* and sender ID as additional input. The HMAC calculation takes about 47,600 clock cycles or 2.95 ms for the used clock speed of 16 Mhz. The total time the reception of a message is deferred due to the calculation of the HMAC and comparison with the received authentication CAN frame is 3.3 ms. That means, the look-up if the sender ID is in the list of secure senders plus the string comparison of calculated and received HMAC make up for 0.35 ms. Note that the application gets notified immediately after reception of the payload and can start precomputations. This means that both the sender and receiver can compute the HMAC of the payload *in parallel*.

Figure 9 illustrates the parallel computation. $HMAC_S$ is the sender's computation of the HMAC including the currently valid nonce, while $HMAC_R$ is the receiver's computation of the received message Msg. The HMAC computations take place simultaneously on the receiver's and sender's side, as the receiver starts computing the HMAC as soon as the plain text message Msg arrives. The receiver then compares $HMAC_R$ against $HMAC_S$ to check if they match. This parallel computation is a major benefit of HMAC compared to asymmetric cryptographic message signatures, for which the receiver has to wait for the signature before further validations.

Next, we measure the round-trip time for legacy vs. vatiCAN-secured CAN frames. In case of legacy frames, one microcontroller broadcasts an 8-byte CAN frame and another microcontroller receives the message and immediately broadcasts another message. The time measured is the interval between sending the first message and after receiving the response. For plain, unauthenticated 8-byte CAN frames, the ping-pong time interval is 1.08 ms and consequently 2 messages were exchanged in total. For vatiCAN, 2 messages have to be sent and 2 messages have to be received. Both microcontrollers must calculate 2 HMACs (one for sending, one for verification). The total time between sending the secure message until after reception of the secure response is 4.5 ms.

Please note that the used ATmega 8 bit microcontrollers represent the lower bound of an automotive performance evaluation. The common v850 32 bit microcontrollers offer ≈2.6× the performance.

5.1 Bus Congestion

For safety reasons, it is important to know the limits of the CAN bus network in terms of throughput in order to ensure that no messages get lost. Car manufacturers also use HIL tests to ensure a safety margin such that under all conceivable conditions the maximum bandwidth and thus the maximum intended latency is never exceeded. To measure the typical utilization of a heavily used bus, we chose the 500 kBit/s instrument cluster CAN (see Fig. 4) because it combines messages from the powertrain CAN bus, the infotainment CAN bus, and the comfort CAN bus. Appendix B lists all recorded messages and their frequency of occurrence in the VW Passat B6.

Due to the re-occurring nature of CAN messages, every 100 ms the same messages were seen on the bus. Per second, 560 messages are sent with a total payload of 4,230 bytes (33,840 bits). Due to the CAN frame overhead (start bit, length bits, CRC, stuff bits etc.) each frame needs an additional 47 bits to be transmitted. Hence, per second a total of $33,840 + 560 \cdot 47 = 60,160$ bits are transmitted. We tested the maximum possible bandwidth under realistic conditions by flooding the bus with 8-byte CAN frames. Counting whole CAN frames (payload + header bits) we achieved a throughput of 448 kBit/s. Thus, the measured utilization of 60.2 kBit/s corresponds to 13.4 % utilization. With 3 out of 13 senders protected by vatiCAN, per second 110 messages of the 560 total messages are protected. This accounts for additional $110 \cdot (47 + 64)$ bits $= 12,210$ bits. Thus, the total bus utilization increases to 72.4 kBit/s (16.2 %).

5.2 Memory Footprint

The total vatiCAN library size is 2152 bytes of AVR instructions of which 678 bytes are attributed to the Keccak implementation and the remaining 1474 bytes are the surrounding vatiCAN message verification, HMAC and interrupt logic. In addition, vatiCAN has to store an additional 32-bit word for the sender's nonce (4 byte) per sender ID. Even in the unlikely case that an ECU expects 100 different vatiCAN sender IDs, this would result in mere 100*4=400 bytes.

6   Security Evaluation

The goal of an attacker is to inject a specific, potentially dangerous CAN frame and to forge its HMAC. Since the attacker needs to forge an HMAC for one specific message (or a few specific messages), it does not suffice to find an arbitrary collision in the underlying hash. Instead, the attacker's goal is to find a concrete collision or the actual cryptographic key.

We chose the Keccak (SHA-3) parameters ($r = c = 128$, $n = 64$) such that it projects its input to 64 bits (8 byte CAN frame) output. While an output size of merely 64 bits is significantly shorter than the typical length of SHA3's 224 bits, the increased advantage of the attacker is offset by the limited validity of a message due to the cyclic message nature of CAN bus and the invalidation through the Nonce Generator NG.

The cryptographic strength of the used HMAC construction depends on the length of the secret key and on the chosen output size. An attacker could record a payload message and its corresponding HMAC. Using the known sender j and the calculated nonce c_j, she can then brute-force all possible keys until she finds an input that matches the recorded HMAC. Because of the fixed 128 bit key, an attacker would need 2^{127} tries on average. Hence, the success probability $P_{key} = 2^{-127}$. The other option, to guess the output of the HMAC correctly is $P_{out} = 2^{-63}$ due to the 64 bit output length. Please note that the birthday paradox in finding an arbitrary hash collision does not apply here, since the attacker has to match a specific plaintext legacy payload. On the Atmega328p running at 16 MHz, the computation of 2^{32} HMACs would need $2^{32} \cdot 2.95\ ms = 12,670,154\ s = 146$ days, which is well outside the validity period set by the NG. Although a faster ECU could brute-force the HMAC quicker, this is likely not fast enough. Even though a dual-core 32-bit ARM 1 GHz (e.g., the infotainment system) would be about 100x faster, it still takes 24 h to brute-force for a nonce update interval of 50 ms.

It should be considered that an attacker might successfully compromise an ECU on which a key is stored that is used for vatiCAN. If keys are grouped and used on multiple ECUs, the attacker can use this key to generate valid HMACs for any sender to which the group key belongs.

7   Related Work

The first paper that extensively demonstrated practical vulnerabilities of a modern automobile [10] was published in 2010 and has been cited many times in academia and the press since. The authors demonstrated that it is possible to inject code into ECUs, which are connected to various CAN buses. Further, they demonstrated that bridging the CAN gateway is possible, effectively connecting a less-critical to a highly-critical CAN bus. Further, they demonstrated that even remote attacks exist that do not require physical access to the car [2].

Despite the ECUs being the culprit in terms of vulnerabilities, the underlying CAN bus makes a life-threatening attack feasible since a compromised ECU may affect any other connected system. In recent years, several authentication methods for broadcast buses have been introduced. The closest related work to vatiCAN is *CANAuth* [16]. CANAuth proposes a similar HMAC-based authentication scheme, however, their goal was to incorporate the HMAC into the payload CAN frame itself. They achieve this by basing their solution on CAN+, a physical layer modification of the CAN protocol to achieve higher data rates [18]. Since the additional CAN+ bits are stuffed in-between legacy CAN bits, it is backward-compatible to CAN controllers, which do not support CAN+. However, CAN+ would require new hardware to be used for the nodes that should support CANAuth, and no such hardware exists yet. Our goal was to update software only and to re-use existing hardware and CAN controllers.

Also purely theoretical work on the topic of CAN bus sender authentication exists [17] that formalizes which cryptographic primitives are required to guarantee secure communication between different ECUs – even across different buses. The authors consider key distribution, PKIs and encrypted communication. In contrast to our solution, their sender authenticity is proven using signature, i.e. asymmetric cryptography. A similar solution to our spoofed message detection has been presented in [12]. In contrast to invalidating the spoofed message by destroying the CRC, the authors detect the spoofed message and immediately send an error frame on the bus.

More general, the TESLA protocols [14,15] are designed to authenticate a broadcast sender with symmetric cryptography. However, they use delayed disclosure of keys, i.e. the sender uses uses a symmetric key for the HMAC that nobody else knows. Consequently, at reception time, no receiver is able to authenticate the packet until the key will be made available in a later packet. This clearly violates our real-time challenge C1. While the improved version of

TESLA [14] supports immediate disclosure of the key, each packet incorporates a hash of the succeeding packet to build a chain. This is clearly unsuited for highly lively but predictable CAN bus traffic.

Finally, the AUTOSAR standard [6] also supports an HMAC-based message authentication scheme. In contrast to vatiCAN, Autosar is not backward compatible, as Autosar uses higher level communication (PDUs) to which an HMAC is appended. Moreover, Autosar does not support spoofing prevention.

8   Limitations and Future Work

Due to the rather restrictive payload of 8 bytes maximum, several protocols have emerged that build on top of CAN to implement higher layers, such as longer payloads and transmission control. Popular examples are KWP2000 [9] or ISO TP [8], which are commonly used for software updates and ECU diagnostics. Using vatiCAN, especially for software updates originating from outside the vehicle, makes sense. However, the current implementation which authenticates every single CAN frame would induce an impractical bandwidth overhead. A more elegant solution would be to authenticate the payload on the KWP2000 or ISO TP layer by attaching a digital signature.

While the achieved latency of only 3.3 ms on a simple microcontroller is seemingly fast, for high motorway speeds, a few milliseconds make a difference between life and death. Should vatiCAN be applied to active safety functions of a car (e.g., collision avoidance through active braking), the induced latency of 3.3 ms results in a traveling distance of 0.9 m at motorway speed of 100 $\frac{km}{h}$.

9   Conclusion

The adaptation of new technology in the automobile sector is a cautious and slow process. It is therefore important to change only a few parts, while the established and reliable majority of components can be re-used. Therefore, vatiCAN is designed to be backward-compatible to allow tried and trusted components to rely on the same CAN messages without need for modification. However, those parts for which a manufacturer decides to enhance security can be easily protected by means of a software upgrade, which uses vatiCAN instead of another CAN bus interface library. Our vatiCAN implementation is able to deliver real-time protection to ensure that a compromised ECU cannot be leveraged to fake messages, which are potentially life-threatening. The induced latency of 3.3 ms for authenticated messages is fast enough for most situations and shows the practicality and feasibility of the approach. However, for highly timing-critical functions, such as brakes, a millisecond delay might be unacceptable.

While the presented results should encourage automakers to implement what is currently possible given a dated CAN bus architecture, it also shows the need for a novel design to achieve stronger security claims and better performance.

Acknowledgments. This work was supported by the German Ministry for Education and Research (BMBF) through funding for the Center for IT-Security, Privacy and Accountability (CISPA).

A   Availability

Our vatiCAN implementation is available as free software download published under the LGPL v2. We provide a library for the popular Arduino development environment for Atmel's AVR microcontrollers. Its source code is publicly available at http://automotive-security.net/securecan

B   VW Passat B6 CAN Messages

The following messages were captured on the instrument cluster CAN bus on a VW Passat B6 and are reproduced in the HIL to have realistic bus utilization.

Function	CAN ID	Every	Frequ.	Length	Bytes/s	Exemplary Payload	vatiCAN
Airbag	050	20 ms	50 Hz	4 bytes	200	E0:F0:00:FF	⊘
Steering	0C2	20 ms	50 Hz	8 bytes	400	F0:00:00:00:80:40:00:CF	⊘
Electronic Power Steering (EPS)	0D0	50 ms	20 Hz	6 bytes	120	D7:C0:61:08:5E:20	⊘
ABS1	1A0	10 ms	100 Hz	8 bytes	800	00:00:00:00:FE:FE:00:00	⊘
ABS2	4A0	10 ms	100 Hz	8 bytes	800	00:00:00:00:FE:FE:00:00	⊘
Brakes	1AC	20 ms	50 Hz	8 bytes	400	00:80:7F:7F:69:A1:00:C2	☑
ETC / Engine RPM	280	20 ms	50 Hz	8 bytes	400	49:00:20:20:00:FA:36:00	☑
Engine Status	35B	100 ms	10 Hz	8 bytes	80	0F:00:00:B8:28:19:02:96	⊘
Coolant	288	20 ms	50 Hz	8 bytes	400	43:78:00:04:00:56:00:00	⊘
Instrument Cluster	320	20 ms	50 Hz	8 bytes	400	02:00:00:ff:ff:cd:ff:96	⊘
Vehicle Speed	5A0	100 ms	10 Hz	8 bytes	80	00:00:00:00:5B:B6	☑
Instrument Cluster	621	100 ms	10 Hz	7 bytes	70	04:00:01:00:02:00:00	⊘
Instrument Cluster	727	100 ms	10 Hz	8 bytes	80	02:00:00:ff:ff:c6:ff:9e	⊘

Throughput (net)	**33840** bits/s
Throughput (overhead)	**26320** bits/s
Throughput (gross)	**60160** bits/s
Average Utilization	**13.4%**

References

1. Balasch, J., et al.: Compact implementation and performance evaluation of hash functions in ATtiny devices. In: Mangard, S. (ed.) CARDIS 2012. LNCS, vol. 7771, pp. 158–172. Springer, Heidelberg (2013)
2. Checkoway, S., McCoy, D., Kantor, B., Anderson, D.,Shacham, H., Savage, S., Koscher, K., Czeskis, A., Roesner, F., Kohno, T., et al.: Comprehensive experimental analyses of automotive attack surfaces. In: USENIX Security Symposium (2011)
3. Dr. Ing. h.c. F. Porsche Aktiengesellschaft: Annual report 2004/2005. http://www.porsche.com/filestore.aspx?default.pdf?pool=uk&type=download&id=annualreport-200405&lang=none&filetype=default
4. Ebert, C., Jones, C.: Embedded software: facts, figures, and future. Computer **4**, 42–52 (2009)
5. Hanselmann, H.: Hardware-in-the loop simulation as a standard approach for development, customization, and production test of ECUs. Technical report, SAE Technical Paper (1993)

6. AUTOSAR Specifications 4.2 (2016). http://autosar.org
7. ISO. ISO 11898-1:2003 Road Vehicles – Controller Area Network (CAN) – Part 1: Data Link Layer and Physical Signalling. International Organization for Standardization (ISO), Geneva (1993)
8. ISO. ISO/DIS 15765-2 Road Vehicles – Diagnostic Communication Over Controller Area Network (DoCAN) – Part 2: Transport Protocol and Network Layer Services. International Organization for Standardization (ISO), Geneva (2011)
9. ISO. ISO 14230-2:2013 Road Vehicles – Diagnostic Communication Over K-Line (DoK-Line) – Part 2: Data Link Layer. International Organization for Standardization (ISO), Geneva (2013)
10. Koscher, K., Czeskis, A., Roesner, F., Patel, S., Kohno, T., Checkoway, S., McCoy, D., Kantor, B., Anderson, D., Shacham, H., et al.: Experimental security analysis of a modern automobile. In: IEEE Symposium on Security and Privacy, pp. 447–462 (2010)
11. Leens, F.: An introduction to I2C and SPI protocols. IEEE Instrum. Meas. Mag. **12**(1), 8–13 (2009)
12. Matsumoto, T., Hata, M., Tanabe, M., Yoshioka, K., Oishi, K.: A method of preventing unauthorized data transmission in controller area network. In: Vehicular Technology Conference (VTC), pp. 1–5. IEEE (2012)
13. Navet, N., Simonot-Lion, F.: Automotive embedded systems handbook, CRC Press (2008)
14. Perrig, A., Canetti, R., Song, D., Tygar, J.D.: Efficient and secure source authentication for multicast. Netw. Distrib. Syst. Secur. Symp. (NDSS) **1**, 35–46 (2001)
15. Perrig, A., Canetti, R., Tygar, J.D., Song, D.: Efficient authentication and signing of multicast streams over lossy channels. In: IEEE Symposium on Security and Privacy, pp. 56–73. IEEE (2000)
16. Van Herrewege, A., Singelee, D., Verbauwhede, I.: CANAuth – a simple, backward compatible broadcast authentication protocol for CAN bus. In: 2011 ECRYPT Workshop on Lightweight Cryptography (2011)
17. Wolf, M., Weimerskirch, A., Paar, C.: Security in automotive bus systems. In: Proceedings of the Workshop on Embedded Security in Cars (ESCAR) (2004)
18. Ziermann, T., Wildermann, S., Teich, J.: CAN+: a new backward-compatible controller area network (CAN) protocol with up to 16× higher data rates. In: 2009 Design, Automation & Test in Europe Conference & Exhibition, DATE 2009, pp. 1088–1093. IEEE (2009)

Invasive Attacks

Mitigating SAT Attack on Logic Locking

Yang Xie[✉] and Ankur Srivastava

University of Maryland, College Park, USA
{yangxie,ankurs}@umd.edu

Abstract. Logic locking is a technique that has been proposed to protect outsourced IC designs from piracy and counterfeiting by untrusted foundries. A locked IC preserves the correct functionality only when a correct key is provided. Recently, the security of logic locking is threatened by a new attack called SAT attack, which can decipher the correct key of most logic locking techniques within a few hours [12] even for a reasonably large number of keys. This attack iteratively solves SAT formulas which progressively eliminate the incorrect keys till the circuit unlocked. In this paper, we present a circuit block (referred to as Anti-SAT block) to thwart the SAT attack. We show that the number of SAT attack iterations to reveal the correct key in a circuit comprising an Anti-SAT block is an exponential function of the key-size thereby making the SAT attack computationally infeasible. Through our experiments, we illustrate the effectiveness of our approach to securing modern chips fabricated in untrusted foundries.

Keywords: Logic locking · SAT attack · Hardware IP protection

1   Introduction

Outsourced fabrication of integrated circuit (IC) enables IC design companies to access advanced semiconductor technology at a low cost. Although it is cost-effective, the outsourced design faces various security threats since the offshore foundry might not be trustworthy. Without close monitoring and direct control, the outsourced designs are vulnerable to various attacks such as Intellectual Property (IP) piracy [10] and counterfeiting [3]. The malicious foundry can reverse-engineer a GDSII layout file to obtain its gate-level netlist and claim the ownership of the hardware IP design, or it can overbuild the IC and sell illegal copies into the market. These security threats (also known as supply chain attacks) pose a significant economic risk to most commercial IC design companies.

Logic locking is a technique that is proposed to thwart the aforementioned supply chain attacks. The basic idea is to insert additional key-controlled logic gates (key-gates), key-inputs and an on-chip memory into an IC design to hide its original functionality, as shown in Fig. 1. The key-inputs are connected to the on-chip memory and the locked IC preserves the correct functionality only when a correct key is set to the on-chip memory. To prevent the untrusted foundry from probing internal signals of a running chip, a tamper-proof chip protection

© International Association for Cryptologic Research 2016
B. Gierlichs and A.Y. Poschmann (Eds.): CHES 2016, LNCS 9813, pp. 127–146, 2016.
DOI: 10.1007/978-3-662-53140-2_7

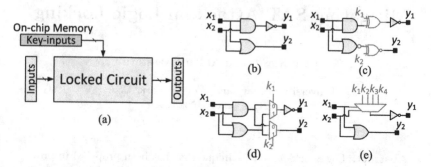

Fig. 1. Logic locking techniques: (a) Overiew; (b) An original netlist; (c) XOR/XNOR based logic locking; (d) MUX based logic locking; (e) LUT based logic locking.

shall be implemented. Recent years have seen various logic locking techniques based on different key-gate types and key-gate insertion algorithms. According to the key-gate types, they can be classified into three major categories: XOR/XNOR based logic locking [8,9,11], MUX based logic locking [7,9,13] and Look-Up-Table (LUT) based logic locking [1,5,6], as shown in Fig. 1 (b-e). Among all, the XOR/XNOR based logic locking has received the most attention mainly due to its simple structure and low performance overhead. Various XOR/XNOR based logic locking algorithms have been proposed to identify the optimal locations for inserting the key-gates, such as fault-analysis based insertion [9] and interference-analysis based insertion [8]. *The security objective of these logic locking techniques is to increase the output corruptibility (i.e., produce more incorrect outputs for more input patterns) given an incorrect key, and to prevent effective key-learning attacks.*

The security of logic locking is threatened if the correct key values into the key-gates are accessible to or can be learned within a practical time by the malicious foundries. To learn the correct key, Subramanyan *et al.* [12] proposed a satisfiability checking based attack (*SAT attack*) algorithm that can effectively break most logic locking techniques proposed in [1,2,8,9,11] within a few hours even for a reasonably large number of keys. The insight of SAT attack is to infer the correct key using a small number of carefully selected input patterns and their correct outputs observed from an activated functional chip (which can be obtained from the open market). This set of correct input/output pairs together ensures that only the correct key will be consistent with these observations. The process of finding such input/output pairs is iteratively formalized as a sequence of SAT formulas that can be solved by state-of-the-art SAT solvers. In each of these iterations, the SAT formulation rules out a bunch of wrong key combinations till it reaches a point where all the wrong keys have been removed. The SAT attack is powerful as it guarantees that upon termination it can always reveal the correct key. This guarantee can't be achieved by other attacks on logic locking such as the EPIC attack [7]. Hence in this paper we focus on the SAT attack on logic locking.

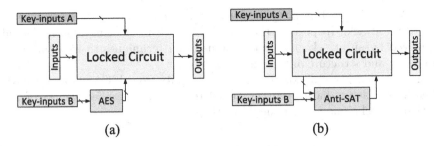

Fig. 2. SAT attack mitigation techniques: (a) Adding an AES circuit to increase the time for solving a SAT formula [14]; (b) Adding our proposed Anti-SAT circuit block to increase the number of SAT attack iterations.

Since the SAT attack needs to iteratively solve a set of circuit-based SAT formulas to reveal the correct key, its efficiency is determined by two aspects: (a) the execution time for solving a SAT formula in one iteration and (b) the number of iterations required to reveal the correct key. The first aspect depends on whether a locked circuit is easily solvable by a SAT solver (*i.e.*, finding a satisfiable assignment for the SAT formula based on this circuit). Based on this idea, Yasin *et al.* [14] proposed adding an AES circuit (with a fixed AES key) to enhance a locked circuit's resistance to the SAT attack. The insight underlying this proposal is shown in Fig. 2(a). A portion of key-inputs is firstly connected to the AES inputs and the outputs of the AES are the actual key-inputs into the locked circuit. As the AES circuit is hard to be solved by a SAT solver, the SAT attack will fail to find a satisfiable assignment for the SAT attack formula within a practical time limit. Although this approach can effectively increase the SAT attack execution time, the AES circuit results in a significant performance overhead since a standard AES circuit implementation requires a large number of gates [4]. This makes the approach in [14] impractical.

In this paper, we propose a relatively lightweight circuit block (referred to as Anti-SAT block) that can be embedded into a design to efficiently mitigate the SAT attack. The basic structure of our Anti-SAT block is shown in Fig. 2(b). While a portion of keys (key-inputs A) is connected to the original circuit to obfuscate its functionality, another portion of keys (key-inputs B) is connected to the Anti-SAT block to thwart the key-learning of SAT attack. *The Anti-SAT block is designed in a way that the total number of SAT attack iterations (and thus the total execution time) to reveal the correct key in the Anti-SAT block is an exponential function of the key-size in the Anti-SAT block.* Therefore, it can be integrated into a design to enhance its resistance to the SAT attack. The contributions of this paper are summarized as follows:

- We propose an Anti-SAT circuit block to mitigate the SAT attack on logic locking. We illustrate how to construct the functionality of the Anti-SAT block and use a mathematically rigorous approach to prove that if chosen correctly, the Anti-SAT block makes SAT attack computationally infeasible (exponential in key-size).

- The Anti-SAT block is integrated into a circuit to increase its resistance to the SAT attack. To prevent the Anti-SAT block from being identified (and removed by an attacker) we apply obfuscation techniques to hide the functionality and structure of the Anti-SAT block.
- Rigorous analysis and experiments on 6 circuits from ISCAS85 and MCNC benchmark suites have been conducted to validate the effectiveness of our proposed technique against the SAT attack.

2   Background: SAT Attack

2.1   Attack Model

The SAT attack model [12] assumes that the attacker is an untrusted foundry whose objective is to obtain the correct key of a locked circuit. The malicious foundry has access to the following two components:

- A locked gate-level netlist, which can be obtained by reverse-engineering a GDSII layout file. This is available because the fabrication is done by the untrusted foundry which has the design details. The locked netlist is represented as $Y = f_l(X, K)$ with primary inputs X, key inputs K and primary outputs Y. Its SAT formula in conjunctive normal form (CNF) is represented as $C(X, K, Y)$.
- An activated functional chip, which can be obtained from open market. This IC can be used to evaluate a set of input patterns and observe their correct output patterns as a black box model $Y = eval(X)$.

2.2   Attack Insight

The key idea of the SAT attack is to reveal the correct key using a small number of carefully selected inputs and their correct outputs observed from an activated functional chip. These special input/output pairs are referred to as *distinguishing input/output (I/O) pairs*. Each distinguishing I/O pair can identify a subset of *wrong key combinations* and all together they guarantee that only the correct key can be consistent with these correct I/O pairs. This implies that a key that correctly matches the inputs to the outputs for all the distinguishing I/O pairs must be the correct key. The crux of the SAT attack is to find this set of distinguishing I/O pairs by solving a sequence of SAT formulas.

Definition 1: (Wrong key combination). Consider the logic function $Y = f_l(X, K)$ and its CNF SAT formula $C(X, K, Y)$. Let $(X, Y) = (X_i, Y_i)$, where (X_i, Y_i) is a correct I/O pair. The set of key combinations WK_i which result in an incorrect output of the logic circuit (*i.e.,* $Y_i \neq f_l(X_i, K)$, $\forall K \in WK_i$) is called the set of wrong key combinations identified by the I/O pair (X_i, Y_i). In terms of SAT formula, it can be represented as $C(X_i, K, Y_i) = False$, $\forall K \in WK_i$.

Definition 2: (Distinguishing input/output pair). As noted above, the SAT attack shall solve a set of SAT formulas iteratively. In each iteration, it shall find a correct I/O pair to identify a subset of wrong key combinations until none of these are left. An I/O pair at i-th iteration is a distinguishing I/O pair $(\boldsymbol{X}_i^d, \boldsymbol{Y}_i^d)$, if it can identify a "unique" subset of wrong key combinations that cannot be identified by the previous $i-1$ distinguishing I/O pairs, $i.e.$, $WK_i \not\subset (\cup_{j=1}^{j=i-1} WK_j)$, where WK_i is the set of wrong key combinations identified by the distinguishing I/O pair at i-th iteration.

The crux of the SAT attack algorithm relies on finding the distinguishing I/O pairs iteratively to identify $unique$ wrong key combinations (see Definition 2) until no further ones can be found. At this point, the set of all distinguishing I/O pairs $together$ identifies all wrong key combinations thereby unlocking the circuit. Then, the correct key is the one that satisfies the following SAT formula G:

$$G := \bigwedge_{i=1}^{\lambda} C(\boldsymbol{X}_i^d, \boldsymbol{K}, \boldsymbol{Y}_i^d) \qquad (1)$$

where $(\boldsymbol{X}_i^d, \boldsymbol{Y}_i^d)$ is the distinguishing I/O pair from i-th iteration and λ is the total number of iterations. Basically it finds a key $\boldsymbol{K}$ which satisfies the correct functionality for all the identified distinguishing I/O pairs. This must be the correct key since no other distinguishing I/O pairs exist (see Definition 2).

Take the XOR/XNOR based locked circuit in Fig. 1(c) as an example. At first iteration, the I/O pair $(\boldsymbol{X}_1^d, \boldsymbol{Y}_1^d) = (00, 10)$ is a distinguishing I/O pair because it can rule out wrong key combinations $\boldsymbol{K} = (01), (10),$ and (11) as these key combinations will result in incorrect outputs $(y_1 y_2) = (11), (00)$ and (01), respectively. Since this single I/O observation has already ruled out all incorrect key combinations, we have revealed the correct key $\boldsymbol{K} = (00)$. In general, a small number of correct I/O pairs (compared to all possible I/O pairs) are usually enough to infer the correct key [12]. As a result, the SAT attack is efficient because it only requires a small number of iterations to find these distinguishing I/O pairs.

2.3 Attack Algorithm

As noted above, the central theme of SAT attack algorithm is to iteratively find distinguishing I/O pairs till no new ones can be found. To find such distinguishing I/O pairs, the SAT attack algorithm iteratively formulates a SAT formula that can be solved by SAT solvers. The SAT formula F_i at i-th iteration is:

$$F_i := C(\boldsymbol{X}, \boldsymbol{K}_1, \boldsymbol{Y}_1) \wedge C(\boldsymbol{X}, \boldsymbol{K}_2, \boldsymbol{Y}_2) \wedge (\boldsymbol{Y}_1 \neq \boldsymbol{Y}_2)$$
$$(\bigwedge_{j=1}^{j=i-1} C(\boldsymbol{X}_j^d, \boldsymbol{K}_1, \boldsymbol{Y}_j^d)) \wedge (\bigwedge_{j=1}^{j=i-1} C(\boldsymbol{X}_j^d, \boldsymbol{K}_2, \boldsymbol{Y}_j^d)) \qquad (2)$$

where $C(\boldsymbol{X}, \boldsymbol{K}, \boldsymbol{Y})$ is the SAT formula (CNF form) for a locked circuit and $(\boldsymbol{X}_{\{1...i-1\}}^d, \boldsymbol{Y}_{\{1...i-1\}}^d)$ are the distinguishing I/O pairs that are found in previous $i-1$ iterations. If satisfiable, an assignment for variables $\boldsymbol{X}, \boldsymbol{K}_1, \boldsymbol{K}_2,$

Algorithm 1. SAT Attack Algorithm [12]

Input: C and $eval$
Output: $\boldsymbol{K}_C$
1: $i := 1$;
2: $G_i := True$;
3: $F_i := C(\boldsymbol{X}, \boldsymbol{K}_1, \boldsymbol{Y}_1) \wedge C(\boldsymbol{X}, \boldsymbol{K}_2, \boldsymbol{Y}_2) \wedge (\boldsymbol{Y}_1 \neq \boldsymbol{Y}_2)$;
4: **while** sat$[F_i]$ **do**
5: $\quad \boldsymbol{X}_i^d := $ sat_assignment$_X[F_i]$;
6: $\quad \boldsymbol{Y}_i^d := eval(\boldsymbol{X}_i^d)$;
7: $\quad G_{i+1} := G_i \wedge C(\boldsymbol{X}_i^d, \boldsymbol{K}, \boldsymbol{Y}_i^d)$;
8: $\quad F_{i+1} := F_i \wedge C(\boldsymbol{X}_i^d, \boldsymbol{K}_1, \boldsymbol{Y}_i^d) \wedge C(\boldsymbol{X}_i^d, \boldsymbol{K}_2, \boldsymbol{Y}_i^d)$;
9: $\quad i := i + 1$;
10: **end while**
11: $\boldsymbol{K}_C := $ sat_assignment$_K(G_i)$;

$\boldsymbol{Y}_1, \boldsymbol{Y}_2$ will be generated. The first line in the formula (2) evaluates the circuit functionality for a specific $\boldsymbol{X} = \boldsymbol{X}_i^d$ at two different key values $\boldsymbol{K}_1$ and $\boldsymbol{K}_2$ such that the outputs are different (see $\boldsymbol{Y}_1 \neq \boldsymbol{Y}_2$). This guarantees that the input $\boldsymbol{X} = \boldsymbol{X}_i^d$ is capable of identifying two keys $\boldsymbol{K}_1, \boldsymbol{K}_2$ which produce different outputs. Hence at least one of the two keys must be wrong. This in itself is not enough to call $\boldsymbol{X} = \boldsymbol{X}_i^d$ as a distinguishing input because previous iteration may have found another input assignment that could have differentiated between $\boldsymbol{K}_1$ and $\boldsymbol{K}_2$. According to Definition 2, a distinguishing input in the i-th iteration must find "unique" wrong key combinations that have not been identified by previous $i - 1$ distinguishing I/O pairs. This condition is checked by the SAT clauses in the second line. In the second line $\boldsymbol{X}_j^d$ is the distinguishing input identified in the previous j-th iteration and $\boldsymbol{Y}_j^d$ is the corresponding correct output. This correct output is know from the activated functional chip obtained from the open market. The clauses in the second line guarantee that the keys $\boldsymbol{K}_1$ and $\boldsymbol{K}_2$ which result in "different"outputs in line 1 of this formula produce the "correct" outputs for all previous distinguishing I/O pairs. Hence in this iteration we could identify at least one incorrect key combination which previous iterations could not. Therefore by Definition 2 the input $\boldsymbol{X}_i^d$ (obtained from the SAT solver) and the corresponding "correct" output $\boldsymbol{Y}_i^d = eval(\boldsymbol{X}_i^d)$ (obtained from the activated chip) represent the i-th distinguishing I/O pair.

The SAT attack algorithm is shown in Algorithm 1. Basically it starts by first solving the line one of the formula (2) and as iterations progress it adds the clauses comprised in line two of the formula (2). It stops when the resulting SAT formula is unsatisfiable indicating no further distinguishing I/O pairs exist. The correct key is obtained by finding a key value which satisfies the correct I/O behavior of all the distinguishing I/O pairs. This algorithm is guaranteed to find the correct key. Please refer to [12] for any further theoretical details.

3   Efficiency Analysis of SAT Attack

The efficiency of SAT attack can be evaluated by the total execution time:

$$T = \sum_{i=1}^{\lambda} t_i \tag{3}$$

where λ is the total number of SAT attack iterations and t_i is the SAT solving time for i-th iteration. Consequently, the SAT attack can be mitigated if t_i is large and/or λ is large.

The SAT solving time t_i is dependent on benchmark characteristics as well as the efficiency of the SAT solver used. To increase t_i, Yasin et al. [14] proposed to add an AES circuit to protect the locked circuit, as shown in Fig. 2(a). As the AES circuit is hard to be solved by a SAT solver, the SAT attack will fail to find a satisfiable assignment for the SAT attack formula. Although this approach is effective, the AES circuit leads to a large performance overhead since a standard AES circuit implementation requires a large number of gates [4].

Increasing the number of iterations λ is another approach to mitigate the SAT attack. λ depends on the key-size and key location in the locked circuit. However, simply increasing the key-size or trying different key locations may not effectively thwart the SAT attack. As shown in the SAT attack results [12], even with large number of keys (50 % area overhead), for six previously proposed key-gate insertion algorithms [1,2,8,9,11], 86 % benchmarks on average can still be unlocked in 10 h.

4   Anti-SAT Block Design

To mitigate the SAT attack, we propose to insert a relatively light-weight circuit block (referred to as Anti-SAT block) that can efficiently increase the number of iterations λ so as to increase the total execution time T. Figs. 3(a) and 3(b) illustrate two configurations of the proposed Anti-SAT block. They consist of two logic blocks $B_1 = g_{l1}(\boldsymbol{X}, \boldsymbol{K}_{l1})$ and $B_2 = \overline{g_{l2}(\boldsymbol{X}, \boldsymbol{K}_{l2})}$. These two logic blocks share the same set of inputs $\boldsymbol{X}$ and their original functionalities (before locking) g and $\overline{g}$ are complementary, but are locked with different keys ($\boldsymbol{K}_{l1}$ and $\boldsymbol{K}_{l2}$) at different locations ($l1$ and $l2$). The one-bit output Y is the AND (for Fig. 3(a)) or OR (for Fig. 3(b)) operation of two logic blocks.

Constant-output Property: one basic property of Anti-SAT block is that when the key vector is correctly set, the output Y is a constant (*e.g.* always equals to 0 for Fig. 3(a) or 1 for Fig. 3(b)). Otherwise, Y can output either 1 or 0 depending on the inputs. This property enables it to be integrated into the original circuit. As shown in Fig. 3(c), the inputs of Anti-SAT block $\boldsymbol{X}$ are from the wires in the original circuit. The output Y is connected into the original circuit using an XOR gate (or a XNOR gate + inverter). When a correct key is provided, the output Y always equals to 0 (XOR gate behaves as a buffer) and thus will not affect the functionality of the original circuit. If a wrong key is provided, Y can

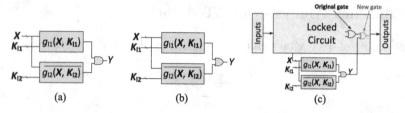

Fig. 3. Anti-SAT block configuration: (a) An Anti-SAT block that always outputs 0 if key values are correct; (b) An Anti-SAT block that always outputs 1 if key values are correct. (c) Integrating the Anti-SAT block into a circuit.

be 1 for some inputs (XOR gate behaves as an inverter) and thus can produce a fault in the original circuit.

In the subsequent sections, we provide details on constructing the Anti-SAT block (*i.e.*, the functionality of g) and its impact on SAT attack complexity. We provide a rigorous mathematical analysis which give a provable lower bound to the number of SAT attack iterations. For some constructions of g, this lower bound is exponential in the number of keys thereby making the SAT-attack complexity very high. In the remaining of this paper, we take Fig. 3(a) as the configuration in our analysis and experiments (without loss of generality).

4.1   Construction of Anti-SAT Block

Now we describe how the Anti-SAT block can be constructed. Note that this construction may not be unique and other constructions may also be feasible. Consider the circuit illustrated in Fig. 4(a). Here a set of key-gates (XORs) are inserted at the inputs of two logic blocks, so $B_1 = g(\boldsymbol{X} \oplus \boldsymbol{K}_{l1})$ and $B_2 = \overline{g(\boldsymbol{X} \oplus \boldsymbol{K}_{l2})}$, where $|\boldsymbol{K}_{l1}| = |\boldsymbol{K}_{l2}| = n$. Hence the key-size is $2n$. The outputs B_1 and B_2 are fed into an AND gate and produce an output Y. As a result, we have $Y = g(\boldsymbol{X} \oplus \boldsymbol{K}_{l1}) \wedge \overline{g(\boldsymbol{X} \oplus \boldsymbol{K}_{l2})}$.

Note that here we are using only XOR gates as key-gates for the sake of ease of explanation. The key-gates used in Fig. 4(a) could be either XOR or XNOR gates based on a user-defined key. Similar to conventional XOR/XNOR base logic locking [9], if a correct key-bit is 0, the key-gate can be XOR or XNOR + inverter. If the key-bit is 1, the key-gate can be XNOR or XOR + inverter. The usage of inverters can remove the association between key-gate types and key-values (*e.g.* the correct key into an XOR gate can now be either 0 or 1). Moreover, as discussed in [9], the synthesis tools can "bubble push" the inverters to their fan-out gates and an attacker cannot easily identify which inverters are part of the key-gates. Besides, the XOR/XNOR gates can be synthesized using other gate types. Combined with obfuscation techqniues which will be discussed in Sect. 4.4, the attacker cannot obtain the correct key-values based on the types of gates connected to the key-inputs.

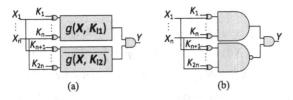

(a)   (b)

Fig. 4. Anti-SAT block construction: (a) basic Anti-SAT block construction and (b) one possible construction to ensure large number of SAT attack iterations.

Since the Anti-SAT block has $2n$ keys, the total number of wrong key combinations is $2^{2n} - c$, assuming there exists c correct key combinations. Because correct key input (for Fig. 4(a)) happens when i-th key from $\boldsymbol{K}_{l1}$ and i-th key from $\boldsymbol{K}_{l2}$ have the same value, the number of correct key combinations $c = 2^n$.

4.2   SAT Attack Complexity Analysis

Here we analyze the complexity of a SAT attack on the Anti-SAT block construction of Fig. 4(a) (assuming this is the circuit being attacked to decode the $2n$ key bits).

Terminology. Given a Boolean function $g(\boldsymbol{L})$ with n inputs, assuming there exists p input vectors that make g equal to one (denote p as *output-one count*, $1 \le p \le 2^n - 1$), we can classify the input vectors $\boldsymbol{L}$ into two groups L^T and L^F, where one group makes $g = 1$ and another makes $g = 0$:

$$L^T = \{\boldsymbol{L}|g(\boldsymbol{L}) = 1\}, \quad (|L^T| = p)$$
$$L^F = \{\boldsymbol{L}|g(\boldsymbol{L}) = 0\}, \quad (|L^F| = 2^n - p) \tag{4}$$

The function g and its complementary function $\overline{g}$ are used to construct the Anti-SAT block as shown in Fig. 4(a).

Theorem 1: *Assuming the output-one count p of function g is sufficiently close to 1 or sufficiently close to $2^n - 1$, the number of iterations needed by the SAT attack (see λ in Eq. 3) to decipher the correct key is lower bounded by 2^n.*

Proof: As described in Sect. 2, the SAT attack algorithm will iteratively find a distinguishing I/O pair $(\boldsymbol{X}_i^d, Y_i^d)$ to identify wrong key combinations in the Anti-SAT block until all wrong key combinations are identified. In the i-th iteration, the corresponding distinguishing I/O pair can identify a subset of wrong key combinations, denoted as WK_i. Notice that for any input combinations (including the distinguishing inputs $\boldsymbol{X}_i^d$), the correct output (when provided the correct key) is 0. Therefore, a wrong key combination $\boldsymbol{K} = (\boldsymbol{K}_{l1}, \boldsymbol{K}_{l2}) \in WK_i$ which was identified by $(\boldsymbol{X}_i^d, Y_i^d)$ must produce the Anti-SAT block output as 1. This condition is described below.

$$Y_i^d = g(\boldsymbol{X}_i^d \oplus \boldsymbol{K}_{l1}) \wedge \overline{g(\boldsymbol{X}_i^d \oplus \boldsymbol{K}_{l2})} = 1.$$

$$\Leftrightarrow (g(\boldsymbol{X}_i^d \oplus \boldsymbol{K}_{l1}) = 1) \wedge (g(\boldsymbol{X}_i^d \oplus \boldsymbol{K}_{l2}) = 0) \qquad (5)$$

$$\Leftrightarrow ((\boldsymbol{X}_i^d \oplus \boldsymbol{K}_{l1}) \in L^T) \wedge ((\boldsymbol{X}_i^d \oplus \boldsymbol{K}_{l2}) \in L^F)$$

Basically Eq. (5) states that the wrong key identified in the i-th iteration must be such that its corresponding output Y should be 1. This implies that both g and $\bar{g}$ must evaluate to 1. This means that the input to g, which is $\boldsymbol{X}_i^d \oplus \boldsymbol{K}_{l1}$, should be in L^T and the input to $\bar{g}$, which is $\boldsymbol{X}_i^d \oplus \boldsymbol{K}_{l2}$, should be in L^F.

Since $\boldsymbol{X}_i^d \oplus \boldsymbol{K}_{l1}$ is the input vector to g, for any given $\boldsymbol{X}_i^d$, we can always find a key $\boldsymbol{K}_{l1}$ such that $\boldsymbol{X}_i^d \oplus \boldsymbol{K}_{l1} \in L^T$. Basically $\boldsymbol{X}_i^d \oplus \boldsymbol{K}_{l1}$ flips some of the bits of $\boldsymbol{X}_i^d$ (for which corresponding $\boldsymbol{K}_{l1}$ bits are 1) while keeping other bits the same (for which corresponding $\boldsymbol{K}_{l1}$ bits are 0). Hence for a given $\boldsymbol{X}_i^d$, we can always choose $\boldsymbol{K}_{l1}$ such that the resulting input to g is in L^T. However note that $|L^T| = p$ in (4). Hence for any given $\boldsymbol{X}_i^d$, we can select $\boldsymbol{K}_{l1}$ in p different ways such that $\boldsymbol{X}_i^d \oplus \boldsymbol{K}_{l1} \in L^T$.

Similarly, for any given $\boldsymbol{X}_i^d$, we can always find a key $\boldsymbol{K}_{l2}$ such that $\boldsymbol{X}_i^d \oplus \boldsymbol{K}_{l2} \in L^F$. Note that $|L^F| = 2^n - p$ in (4). Hence for any given $\boldsymbol{X}_i^d$, we can select $\boldsymbol{K}_{l2}$ in $2^n - p$ different ways such that $\boldsymbol{X}_i^d \oplus \boldsymbol{K}_{l2} \in L^F$.

Now, as noted above, for a given $\boldsymbol{X}_i^d$, a wrong key $\boldsymbol{K} = (\boldsymbol{K}_{l1}, \boldsymbol{K}_{l2})$ should be such that $\boldsymbol{X}_i^d \oplus \boldsymbol{K}_{l1} \in L^T$ and $\boldsymbol{X}_i^d \oplus \boldsymbol{K}_{l2} \in L^F$. The total number of ways in which we can select a wrong key $\boldsymbol{K} = (\boldsymbol{K}_{l1}, \boldsymbol{K}_{l2})$ are $p \cdot (2^n - p)$.

Now in any given iteration i, for a given X_i^d, the *maximum* number of incorrect keys identified is $p \cdot (2^n - p)$. This follows naturally from the discussion above. The reason this is the *maximum* number because it is very much possible that some of these keys were identified in previous iterations. Hence the total number of "unique" incorrect keys UK_i identified in iteration i is bounded by $p \cdot (2^n - p)$. This is noted in the equation below.

$$p \cdot (2^n - p) \geq UK_i \qquad (6)$$

where UK_i is the number of unique incorrect keys identified at iteration i. The SAT attack works by iteratively removing all incorrect keys till only the correct ones are left (assuming after λ iterations). Hence the following holds true.

$$\lambda(p \cdot (2^n - p)) \geq \sum_{i=1}^{\lambda} UK_i \qquad (7)$$

Since $\sum_{i=1}^{\lambda} UK_i$ is the total number of incorrect key combinations, its value must be $= 2^{2n} - c$. The equation above can be rewritten as follows.

$$\lambda \geq \lambda_l = \frac{2^{2n} - c}{p(2^n - p)} \qquad (8)$$

Here λ_l is the lower bound on λ. As noted in Fig. 4(a) the correct key happens when the i-th bit from K_1 and i-th bit from K_2 have the same value. Hence $c = 2^n$. When $p \rightarrow 1$ or $p \rightarrow 2^n - 1$, we have the lower bound as follows:

$$\lambda_l = \frac{2^{2n} - 2^n}{p(2^n - p)} \rightarrow \frac{2^{2n} - 2^n}{1 \times (2^n - 1)} = 2^n \tag{9}$$

Hence Proved. Therefore, if we choose a g function such that p is either very low or very high then the SAT attack would at least require an exponential number of iterations in n. One possible choice of g is indicated in Fig. 4(b) where g is chosen to be a simple AND gate. For AND gates $p = 1$ which clearly results in exponential complexity of SAT attack. Experimental results to indicate that shall be indicated subsequently. Moreover, we can see that the lower bound λ_l is tight when $p = 1$ or $p = 2^n - 1$. This is because that for a n-input Anti-SAT block, the total number of input combinations is 2^n so the number of iterations to find distinguishing inputs is upper-bounded $\lambda \leq 2^n$. This combined with the Eq. (9) shows that the lower bound is tight when $p = 1$ or $p = 2^n - 1$.

4.3 Anti-SAT Block Location

When the Anti-SAT block is integrated into a circuit, a set of wires in the original circuit are connected to the inputs X of the Anti-SAT block and the output Y of the Anti-SAT block is integrated to a wire in the original circuit (as shown in Fig. 3(c)). If X are connected to wires that are highly correlated (e.g. two nets with identical logic), then the overall security of the block shall be reduced because less possible input combinations can occur at the input of the Anti-SAT block. The location for Y is also important. An incorrect key causes $Y = 1$ for some inputs. This incorrect output must impact the overall functionality of the original circuit. Otherwise the logic will continue to function correctly despite wrong key inputs. In conclusion, the best location of the Anti-SAT block is such the inputs X are highly independent and Y has high observability at the POs (i.e., change in Y can be observed by the POs of the original circuit). The impact of Anti-SAT block location on the overall security shall be evaluated in the experiments.

4.4 Anti-SAT Block Obfuscation

Since the Anti-SAT block is independent of the locked circuit, it may be removed or nullified by an attacker if it is identified, thereby leaving only the locked circuit. Then, the SAT attack can be launched to unlock the circuit without the Anti-SAT block. Note that a similar criticism is possible for the AES based logic locking approach [14] which is very strong in presence of SAT attack but might be easily circumvented by an attacked due to its large footprint. To prevent such an identification and nullification, we apply both functional and structural obfuscation techniques to obfuscate the Anti-SAT block such that it can be covertly embedded in the original design.

Functional Obfuscation. In the Anti-SAT block, the logic blocks g and $\bar{g}$ have complementary functionality. An attacker can simulate the circuit and find potential complementary pairs of signals leading to potential identification of the Anti-SAT block. To prevent such attacks, we propose to insert additional key-gates at internal wires of two logic blocks (and the internal wires of $2n$ XOR/XNORs at the inputs since they can be synthesized using other gates) to obfuscate their functionalities. With an incorrect key, the functionalities of these two logic blocks are different and an attacker will fail to find the complementary pairs of signals through simulation. Besides, the logic blocks g and $\bar{g}$ and the key-gates can be synthesized using different logic gates to reduce their similarity.

Structural Obfuscation. Besides functional obfuscation, we need to obfuscate the structure of the Anti-SAT block to prevent any structure-based attacks which are independent of functionality. In the Anti-SAT block, the internal wires in g and $\bar{g}$ do not have connections with the locked circuit. This makes the Anti-SAT block a relatively isolated and separable structure. When the size of the Anti-SAT block is roughly known, it's possible for an attacker to utilize a partitioning algorithm to partition the whole circuit into two parts while ensuring that small partition has about the same size as the Anti-SAT block. If a large portion of gates of the Anti-SAT block is moved to the small partition, then the attacker will have less difficulty to identify the Anti-SAT block. In order to prevent such attacks, we utilize the MUX-based logic locking (as shown in Fig. 1(d)) to increase the inter-connectivity between the locked circuit and the Anti-SAT block. A set of two-input MUX gates is utilized to connect these two parts. One input of the MUX is from a random wire w_1 of the locked circuit and the other input is from a random wire w_2 of the Anti-SAT block. The output of MUX replace the original signal (either w_1 or w_2) and is connected to the fan-outs of either w_1 or w_2. The selection bit of MUX is the key-input. After inserting the MUXes, the whole circuit is re-synthesized so as to obscure the boundary between two parts. With more MUXes inserted, the interconnections between the Anti-SAT block and the locked circuit will be increased and it's difficult for an attacker to partition and isolate the Anti-SAT block from the locked circuit, which will be validated in Sect. 5.3.

Combined with Conventional Logic Locking Techniques. As noted before, conventional logic locking techniques as indicated in Fig. 1 try to avoid an unauthorized user who does not have a key from accessing the chip's functionality. They attempt to insert key gates in a way to force the chip to deviate substantially from the actual functionality whenever a wrong key is provided. These techniques are not immune to SAT attack (as noted in [12] and also indicated in our simulations). While our Anti-SAT block can provide provable measures to increasing the SAT attack complexity, they may not necessarily cause substantial deviation in the chip functionality for incorrect keys. Hence an unauthorized end user may still be able to use the chip correctly for "many" inputs (but not all). Therefore, conventional logic locking techniques need to be

Table 1. Impact of output-one count p on the security level of the $n = 16$-bit baseline Anti-SAT block. Timeout is 10 h.

p	1	81	243	2187	30375	63349	65293	65455	65535
# Iteration	-	10675	4760	901	273	898	4647	-	-
Time (s)	timeout	16555.8	8746.12	174.743	3.24	307.104	12932.3	timeout	timeout

Table 2. Impact input-size n on the security level of the baseline Anti-SAT block (output-one count $p = 1$). Timeout is 10 h.

n	8	10	12	14	16
# Iteration	255	1023	4095	16383	-
Time (s)	1.14569	20.024	324.727	4498.03	timeout

combined with our Anti-SAT block designs for achieving foolproof logic locking. Moreover, the key-gates inserted at the original circuit can make the Anti-SAT block less distinguishable with the original circuit. Without these key-gates in the original circuit, an attacker has less difficulty to locate the Anti-SAT block by inspecting the only key-inputs into the Anti-SAT block.

5 Experiments and Results

In this section, we evaluate the security level of our proposed Anti-SAT blocks. The security level is evaluated by the number of *SAT attack iterations* as well as the *execution time* to infer the correct key. The SAT attack tools and benchmarks used are from [12]. The CPU time limit is set to 10 h as [12]. The experiments are running on an Intel Core i5-2400 CPU with 16 GB RAM.

5.1 Anti-SAT Block Design

We firstly evaluate the security level of the Anti-SAT block with respect to different design parameters: (a) the input-size n and output-one count p of function g and (b) the Anti-SAT block location. The **n-bit baseline Anti-SAT (BA) block** is constructed using a n-input AND gate and a n-input NAND gate (output-one count $p = 1$) as g and $\bar{g}$ to ensure large number of iterations. However notice that this is not the only possible choice for g and $\bar{g}$. As we have shown in Sect. 4.2, other function g that has sufficiently large n and sufficiently small (or large) p can also guarantee large number of iterations. The key-gates (XOR/XNOR) are inserted at the inputs of g and $\bar{g}$ with key-size $|K_{l1}| = |K_{l2}| = n$. Obfuscation techniques proposed in Sect. 4.4 are not applied here but they will be evaluated in the Sect. 5.3 when the Anti-SAT block is integrated into a circuit.

Table 3. Impact of Anti-SAT block location on security level of the baseline n-bit Anti-SAT blocks ($n = 8, 12, 16$) inserted at c1355 circuit. Timeout is 10 h. The random case is averaged over 5 trials.

	$|K_{l1}| = |K_{l2}| = n$	8	12	16
Random	Avg. # Iteration	151	1748	11461
	Avg. Time (s)	1.4296	162.529	10272.4
Secure	# Iteration	255	4095	-
	Time (s)	3.452	759.924	timeout

Input-size n and output-one count p. As shown in Eq. (8), the lower bound of SAT attack iterations λ_l to unlock the Anti-SAT block is related to the input-size n and output-one count p of function g.

If n is fixed, λ_l is maximized when $p \to 1$ or $p \to 2^n - 1$. To evaluate the impact of p, we replace some 2-input AND gates with 2-input OR gates in a $n = 16$-bit baseline Anti-SAT block to gradually increase p. Table 1 illustrates the impact of p on the security level of the 16-bit Anti-SAT block. For $p = 1$ and $p = 2^{16} - 1 = 65535$, the SAT attack algorithm fails to unlock the Anti-SAT block in 10 h. This is because that it requires a large number of iterations ($\approx 2^{16}$) to rule out all the incorrect key combinations. As $p \to 2^{16}/2$ (the worst case), the SAT attack begins to succeed using less and less iterations and execution time. This result validates that when p is very small or very large for a fixed n, the iterations λ will be large and the SAT attack will fail within a practical time limit.

Moreover, as described in Sect. 4.2, λ_l is an exponential function of n when p is very low ($p \to 1$) or very high ($p \to 2^n - 1$). Table 2 shows the exponential relationship between λ and n when $p = 1$ for five baseline Anti-SAT block ($n = 8, 10, 12, 14, 16$). It can be seen that as n increases, the simulated SAT iterations and execution time grows exponentially. Besides, the number of iterations validates that the lower bound λ_l is tight when $p = 1$, as discussed in Sect. 4.2.

Anti-SAT Block Location. As noted in Sect. 4.3, the Anti-SAT block location may impact the its security in terms of SAT attack iterations and execution time. We compare two approaches of integrating the Anti-SAT block with the original circuit, namely *secure integration* and *random integration*. For the *secure integration*, n inputs of the Anti-SAT block X are connected to n PIs of the original circuit. The output Y is connected to a wire which is randomly selected from wires that have the top 30 % observability. The randomness of the location of Y can assist in hiding the output of the Anti-SAT block. For the *random integration*, the inputs X are connected to random wires of the original circuit, and the output Y is connected to a random wire. For both cases, the wire for Y has a latter topological order than that of the wires for X to prevent combinational loop. Table 3 compares two integration approaches when three baseline Anti-SAT block of different sizes ($n = 8, 12, 16$) are integrated into the c1355 circuit from ISCAS85. It can be seen that for three Anti-SAT blocks, secure integration is more secure than random integration as the former requires more iterations ($\sim 2\times$) and execution time ($\sim 3\times$) for the SAT attack algorithm to reveal the key. Therefore, in the following experiments, we adopt the secure integration as the way to integrate the Anti-SAT block into a circuit.

5.2 Anti-SAT Block Application

We evaluate the security level of the Anti-SAT block when it's applied to 6 circuits of different sizes from ISCAS85 and MCNC benchmark suites. The benchmark information is shown in Table 4. We compare three logic locking configurations as follows:

- **TOC13**: The original circuit is locked using TOC13 logic locking algorithm [9] which inserts XOR/XNOR gates into the circuit to obfuscate its functionality. Figure 5 shows that TOC13 is effective in increasing the output corruptibility (in terms of the Hamming distance (HD) between the output of an original circuit and a locked circuit given a random key). Also, it can be seen that 5 % overhead (ratio between # key-gates and # original gates) is roughly enough to approach 50 % HD for all benchmarks.
- **TOC13(5 %) + n-bit BA**: In this configuration, the original circuit is locked with TOC13 with 5 % overhead. Besides, we integrate a n-bit baseline Anti-SAT (BA) block into the locked circuit using the *secure integration, i.e.*, the n inputs of the Anti-SAT block are connected to n PIs of the original circuit, and the output of the Anti-SAT block is connected to a wire in the original circuit which is randomly selected from the wires that have the top 30 % observability. For a n-bit BA, its key-size is $k_{BA} = 2n$ because $2n$ keys are inserted at the inputs of g and $\bar{g}$.
- **TOC13(5 %) + n-bit OA**: In this configuration, the obfuscation techniques proposed in Sect. 4.4 are applied to make the baseline Anti-SAT block less distinguishable from the locked circuit. In our experiment, we insert n MUXes to increase the inter-connectivity between a n-bit baseline Anti-SAT block and the locked circuit. Besides, we insert additional n XOR/XNOR gates at random internal wires of the logic blocks g and $\bar{g}$ to obfuscate their functionality to prevent the detection of complementary pairs of signals. Thus, the keys in a n-bit obfuscated Anti-SAT (OA) block is $k_{OA} = 4n$.

We compare the security level of three configurations when the same number of keys are used in each configuration. We investigate the sensitivity of SAT attack complexity on the increase of key-size. For TOC13, the increased keys are inserted to the original circuit. For TOC13 (5 %) + n-bit BA/OA, the increased keys are used in the Anti-SAT block and increasing the key-size also indicates increasing the Anti-block size (in terms of input-size n) because we construct the BA and OA with $k_{BA} = 2n$ and $k_{OA} = 4n$, respectively. In this experiment, we integrate the baseline Anti-SAT blocks of input-size $n_{BA} = 8, 10, 12, 14, 16, 18, 20$

Table 4. Benchmark information of 6 circuits from ISCAS85 and MCNC benchmark suites and the key-sizes of three logic locking configurations.

Circuit	#PI	#PO	#Gates	Key-size		
				TOC13 (5%)	n-bit BA	n-bit OA
c1355	41	32	546	29	2n	4n
c1908	33	25	880	46		
c3540	50	22	1669	86		
dalu	75	16	2298	119		
des	256	245	6473	336		
i8	133	81	2464	130		

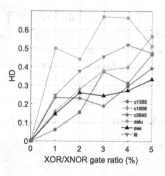

Fig. 5. HD v.s. key-gate ratio for TOC13 logic locking.

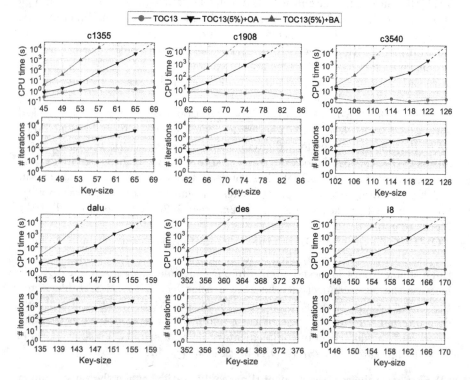

Fig. 6. SAT attack results on 6 benchmarks with three logic locking configurations: TOC13 only, TOC13(5%) + BA, and TOC13(5%) + OA. Timeout is 10 h (3.6×10^4 s). The dashed line in the top figure (execution time) is the curve fitting result when the SAT attack has time-outed after certain key-size.

and the obfuscated Anti-SAT blocks of input-size $n_{OA} = 4, 5, 6, 7, 8, 9, 10$. The input-size of BA is twice the size of OA ($n_{BA} = 2n_{OA}$) when their key-sizes are the same $k_{BA} = k_{OA}$.

Table 5. Percentage of a 14-bit obfuscated Anti-SAT block isolated to a small partition when a min-cut partitioning algorithm is utilized. Area estimation error is percentage error of an attacker's estimation about the size of the Anti-SAT block.

Circuits	Area estimation error							
	0 %		5 %		15 %		25 %	
	NO MUX	With MUX	No MUX	With MUX	No MUX	With MUX	No MUX	With MUX
c1355	99.07 %	0.00 %	99.07 %	0.93 %	40.74 %	0.93 %	0.00 %	0.00 %
c1908	99.07 %	0.93 %	99.07 %	0.00 %	0.00 %	0.93 %	0.00 %	0.00 %
c3540	0.00 %	0.00 %	0.00 %	0.00 %	0.00 %	0.00 %	0.00 %	0.00 %
dalu	99.07 %	0.00 %	99.07 %	0.00 %	99.07 %	0.00 %	0.00 %	0.00 %
des	0.00 %	0.00 %	0.00 %	0.00 %	0.00 %	0.00 %	0.00 %	0.00 %
i8	100.00 %	0.00 %	100.00 %	0.00 %	0.00 %	0.00 %	0.00 %	0.00 %
Average	66.20 %	0.16 %	66.20 %	0.15 %	23.30 %	0.31 %	0.00 %	0.00 %

The SAT attack result on three configurations w.r.t increasing key-size are shown in Fig. 6. For each benchmark, the top figure shows the SAT attack execution time and the bottom figure shows the number of SAT attack iterations, both in log scale. It can be seen that for TOC13, increasing the key-size cannot effectively increase SAT attack complexity. For all benchmarks locked with TOC13, they can be easily unlocked using at most 48 iterations and 8.48 s. On the other hand, when the Anti-SAT blocks are integrated, the SAT attack complexity increases exponentially with the key-size in the Anti-SAT block. This holds for both the baseline Anti-SAT block and the obfuscated Anti-SAT block. Also the results show that with the same key-size, the grow rate of n-bit OA is slower than n-bit BA. This is because that for OA, a portion of keys are utilized to obfuscate the design and the resulting OA is half the size as the BA (in terms of n) as described earlier. Finally, we can see that for all benchmarks, the SAT attack fails to unlock the circuits within 10 h when a 14-bit BA ($k_{BA} = 28$) is inserted or when a 10-bit OA ($k_{OA} = 40$) is inserted.

5.3   Anti-SAT Obfuscation

In Sect. 4.4, we claim that the Anti-SAT block has a separable structure because it has few interconnections with the locked circuit. When the size of the Anti-SAT block is roughly known, it's possible for an attacker to utilize a min-cut partitioning algorithm to partition the whole circuit into two parts while ensuring that small partition has about the same size as the Anti-SAT block. If a large portion of gates of the Anti-SAT block is moved to the small partition, an attacker will have less difficulty to identify the Anti-SAT block. In order to prevent the Anti-SAT block from being identified, we propose to use MUX-based logic locking to increase the inter-connectivity between the locked circuit and the Anti-SAT block. Table 5 shows the percentage of gates of a $n = 14$-bit OA (with or without MUXes) that are isolated to the small partition after min-cut partitioning. The reason for using a 14-bit OA is because that it can achieve a sufficiently large SAT attack time (according to the fitting result in Fig. 7 which will be discussed later). Because the Anti-SAT block can be synthesized with different types of gates, it's difficult for an attacker to obtain the exact size of the Anti-SAT block. Therefore, we perform the partitioning algorithm while assuming a certain area estimation error for the Anti-SAT block and analyze its impact on the attack results.

As shown in Table 5, when the area estimation error is 0 % and no MUXes are inserted, the Anti-SAT block in 4 circuits (c1355, c1908, dalu, and i8) can be isolated. In these circuits, the percentages of gates of the Anti-SAT block isolated by the partitioning algorithm are almost 100 %. However, with the increase of area estimation error, the partitioning fails to isolate the Anti-SAT block. Besides, when $n = 14$ MUXes are inserted to increase the inter-connectivity between the Anti-SAT block and the locked circuit, the percentages of isolated Anti-SAT block are almost 0 % for four assumptions of area estimation error. This is because that the number of interconnections between the Anti-SAT block and the locked circuit is increased and partitioning them will result in a large cut-size, so the partitioning algorithm will avoid to separate the Anti-SAT block.

5.4 Performance Overhead of the Anti-SAT Block

In our construction, a n-bit obfuscated Anti-SAT block consists of logic blocks g and $\bar{g}$, a 2-input AND gate, $3n + 1$ XOR/XNOR gates and n 2-input MUX gates. These extra logic gates will introduce performance overhead such as area, power and delay. Different implementation of g and $\bar{g}$ will result in different overhead. The performance overhead will be increased when sub-optimal synthesis is utilized to obfuscate the Anti-SAT block. In our experiments, we utilize a n-bit AND gate and a n-bit NAND gate to implement the function g and $\bar{g}$. The estimated SAT attack complexity and area overhead of inserting a n-bit OA into the des circuit are shown in Fig. 7. The overhead is evaluated in terms of the ratio between the total size of extra gates and the total size of original gates. It can be seen that a slight increase in area overhead can result in exponential increase in SAT attack's computation complexity. It's also important to notice that the design of the Anti-SAT block does not scale with the benchmark size; it only scales with the attacker's computation power. Compared to the technique

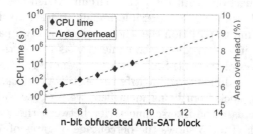

Fig. 7. SAT attack execution time (in log scale) and area overhead for the des circuit integrated with n-bit obfuscated Anti-SAT. The original circuit is locked with TOC13 (5 % overhead). The blue dashed line is the fitting curve for CPU time.

proposed in [14] which inserts an AES circuit to defend the SAT attack, our proposed technique has much less overhead.

6 Conclusion

In this paper, we present a circuit block called Anti-SAT to mitigate the SAT attack on logic locking. We show that the iterations required by the SAT attack to reveal the correct key in the Anti-SAT block is an exponential function of the key-size in the Anti-SAT block. The Anti-SAT block is integrated to a locked circuit to increase its resistance against SAT attack. Compared to adding a large hard-SAT circuit (*e.g.* AES), our proposed Anti-SAT block has a much smaller overhead, which makes it a cost-effective technique to mitigate the SAT attack.

Acknowledgments. This work was supported by NSF under Grant No. 1223233 and AFOSR under Grant FA9550-14-1-0351.

References

1. Baumgarten, A., Tyagi, A., Zambreno, J.: Preventing IC piracy using reconfigurable logic barriers. IEEE Des. Test Comput. **27**(1), 66–75 (2010)
2. Dupuis, S., Ba, P.S., Di Natale, G., Flottes, M.L., Rouzeyre, B.: A novel hardware logic encryption technique for thwarting illegal overproduction and hardware trojans. In: 2014 IEEE 20th International On-Line Testing Symposium (IOLTS), pp. 49–54. IEEE (2014)
3. Guin, U., Huang, K., DiMase, D., Carulli, J.M., Tehranipoor, M., Makris, Y.: Counterfeit integrated circuits: a rising threat in the global semiconductor supply chain. Proc. IEEE **102**(8), 1207–1228 (2014)
4. HelionTechnology: High performance AES (Rijndael) cores for ASIC (2015). http://www.heliontech.com/downloads/aes_asic_helioncore.pdf
5. Khaleghi, S., Da Zhao, K., Rao, W.: IC piracy prevention via design withholding and entanglement. In: 2015 20th Asia and South Pacific Design Automation Conference (ASP-DAC), pp. 821–826. IEEE (2015)
6. Liu, B., Wang, B.: Embedded reconfigurable logic for ASIC design obfuscation against supply chain attacks. In: Proceedings of the Conference on Design, Automation and Test in Europe, p. 243. European Design and Automation Association (2014)
7. Plaza, S.M., Markov, I.L.: Solving the third-shift problem in IC piracy with test-aware logic locking. IEEE Trans. Comput.-Aided Des. Integr. Circuits Syst. **34**(6), 961–971 (2015)
8. Rajendran, J., Pino, Y., Sinanoglu, O., Karri, R.: Security analysis of logic obfuscation. In: Proceedings of the 49th Annual Design Automation Conference, pp. 83–89. ACM (2012)
9. Rajendran, J., Zhang, H., Zhang, C., Rose, G.S., Pino, Y., Sinanoglu, O., Karri, R.: Fault analysis-based logic encryption. IEEE Trans. Comput. **64**(2), 410–424 (2015)
10. Rostami, M., Koushanfar, F., Karri, R.: A primer on hardware security: models, methods, and metrics. Proc. IEEE **102**(8), 1283–1295 (2014)

11. Roy, J.A., Koushanfar, F., Markov, I.L.: Epic: Ending piracy of integrated circuits. In: Proceedings of the Conference on Design, Automation and Test in Europe, pp. 1069–1074. ACM (2008)
12. Subramanyan, P., Ray, S., Malik, S.: Evaluating the security of logic encryption algorithms. In: 2015 IEEE International Symposium on Hardware Oriented Security and Trust (HOST), pp. 137–143. IEEE (2015)
13. Wendt, J.B., Potkonjak, M.: Hardware obfuscation using PUF-based logic. In: Proceedings of the 2014 IEEE/ACM International Conference on Computer-Aided Design, pp. 270–277. IEEE Press (2014)
14. Yasin, M., Rajendran, J., Sinanoglu, O., Karri, R.: On improving the security of logic locking. IEEE Trans. Comput.-Aided Des. Integr. Circuits Syst. $\mathbf{PP}$(99), 1 (2015)

No Place to Hide: Contactless Probing of Secret Data on FPGAs

Heiko Lohrke[1]([✉]), Shahin Tajik[2]([✉]), Christian Boit[1], and Jean-Pierre Seifert[2]

[1] Semiconductor Devices, Technische Universität Berlin, Berlin, Germany
lohrke@mailbox.tu-berlin.de, christian.boit@tu-berlin.de
[2] Security in Telecommunications, Technische Universität Berlin, Berlin, Germany
{stajik,jpseifert}@sec.t-labs.tu-berlin.de

Abstract. Field Programmable Gate Arrays (FPGAs) have been the target of different physical attacks in recent years. Many different countermeasures have already been integrated into these devices to mitigate the existing vulnerabilities. However, there has not been enough attention paid to semi-invasive attacks from the IC backside due to the following reasons. First, the conventional semi-invasive attacks from the IC backside — such as laser fault injection and photonic emission analysis — cannot be scaled down without further effort to the very latest nanoscale technologies of modern FPGAs and programmable SoCs. Second, the more advanced solutions for secure storage, such as controlled Physically Unclonable Functions (PUFs), make the conventional memory-readout techniques almost impossible. In this paper, however, novel approaches have been explored: Attacks based on Laser Voltage Probing (LVP) and its derivatives, as commonly used in Integrated Circuit (IC) debug for nanoscale low voltage technologies, are successfully launched against a 60 nanometer technology FPGA. We discuss how these attacks can be used to break modern bitstream encryption implementations. Our attacks were carried out on a Proof-of-Concept PUF-based key generation implementation. To the best of our knowledge this is the first time that LVP is used to perform an attack on secure ICs.

Keywords: FPGA security · Laser voltage probing · Physically unclonable function · Semi-invasive backside attack.

1 Introduction

Modern Field Programmable Gate Arrays (FPGAs) and programmable System on Chips (SoCs) are used nowadays in different critical applications. Since most FPGAs and programmable SoCs store their configuration in SRAM cells, they have to be configured in an untrusted field through bitstreams stored in an external non-volatile memory (NVM) upon each power-on. Due to the lack of protection against side-channel leakage in an adversarial environment,

---

H. Lohrke and S. Tajik— These authors contributed equally to this work.

B. Gierlichs and A.Y. Poschmann (Eds.): CHES 2016, LNCS 9813, pp. 147–167, 2016.
DOI: 10.1007/978-3-662-53140-2_8

the transmission of the bitstream (even in an encrypted format) can expose the design [23,30,31,46]. Furthermore, volatile Battery Backed RAMs (BBRAMs) and eFuses, which can be used to store the secret key for decryption of the bitstream, are unreliable and vulnerable to scanning electron microscopy (SEM) [46].

FPGA vendors always attempt to add more advanced countermeasures to their devices, to effectively mitigate physical attacks. While DPA vulnerabilities of the decryption cores can be solved by DPA-resistant IP cores and asymmetric authentication schemes, Physically Unclonable Functions (PUFs) can mitigate the insecurity of eFuses and BBRAMs [46]. Moreover, different physical sensors inside the FPGAs can monitor the environmental changes to detect glitching and fault injection attacks. However, a proper physical protection against semi- and fully-invasive attacks from the IC backside is still missing on these modern platforms.

There are good reasons for FPGA vendors to be less concerned about the security of the IC backside. First, the latest generations of SRAM-based FPGAs are manufactured with 20 nm technology and the next generation of FPGAs will be built with 16 and 14 nm technologies [13,19]. Yet, it has already been demonstrated that, even for larger FPGA technologies such as 45 nm and 60 nm, conventional semi-invasive attacks from the IC backside, such as Laser Fault Injection (LFI) [39] and Photonic Emission Analysis (PEM) [41], are onerous tasks. Therefore, such attacks cannot be scaled down efficiently along with the trend of shrinking transistor technologies. Second, FPGA vendors believe that integration of new storage solutions, such as PUFs, raises the security level of key storage against backside attacks [7,25,35], as no key is stored permanently on the chip to be read-out by the adversary.

Our Contribution. In this work we introduce a novel semi-invasive attack against FPGAs using a known failure analysis technique, called Laser Voltage Probing (LVP) [24]. We demonstrate how the attacker can use LVP and derivatives to locate circuitry of interest, such as registers and ring oscillators (ROs), by knowing or estimating the frequency of different operations. Estimation of aforementioned frequency characteristics can be achieved by either having knowledge of implementations or by performing power analysis in the frequency domain. Moreover, we explain how LVP enables us to probe different *volatile* and *on-die-only* signals and data streams on the chip without having any physical contact to the wires or transistors. Besides, with the help of LVP one can characterize high frequency signals, such as the output of ROs, which are used in RO PUFs and True Random Number Generators (TRNGs). For our practical evaluation, we consider a PUF in key generation mode inside an FPGA to decrypt the bitstream. The PoC implementation was realized on an FPGA manufactured in a 60 nm process technology. Due to lack of proper protection, we were able to perform our analysis from the IC backside. This work is presenting the first results to evaluate the potential of LVP for possible future attacks on small technologies, where conventional backside semi-invasive attacks, such as PEM and LFI, would require much more efforts.

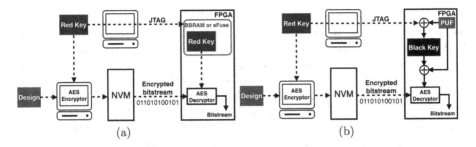

Fig. 1. (a) Bitstream encryption and decryption using a red key [46]. (b) Bitstream encryption and decryption using a black key, PUF key and red key [35].

2 Background

2.1 FPGA Security During Configuration

Bitstream encryption is a conventional solution to prevent the piracy of IPs during FPGA configuration. In this case a secret "red key" (i.e., an unencrypted key) is transferred to the FPGA in a safe environment, see Fig. 1(a). This key will be stored either in the Battery Backed RAM (BBRAM) or eFuses on the chip. At the same time, the application design is encrypted by the red key and stored in an external non-volatile memory (NVM). Each time the FPGA is powered up in the untrusted field, the encrypted bitstream is transmitted to the chip and it will be decrypted by the stored red key inside the chip. Although this technique raises the security of the bitstream transmission against interception, it has been shown that the decryption cores on different FPGAs, responsible for decoding the bitstream, are vulnerable to electromagnetic (EM) and differential power analysis (DPA) [23,30,31]. Moreover, the key storage technologies on FPGAs such as eFuses are vulnerable to semi-invasive attacks and can be read out with a scanning electron microscope (SEM) [46].

Utilizing updatable protected soft decryption cores and asymmetric authentication can defeat non-invasive side-channel attacks, such as differential power analysis (DPA) [35]. Moreover, Physically Unclonable Functions (PUFs) [15,34] can remedy the shortcomings of insecure storage in modern FPGAs [46]. Instead of storing the secret key in an insecure memory, PUFs exploit the manufacturing variability on identical devices to generate virtually unique secret keys for each device. Therefore, PUFs can be used for secure key generation and key obfuscation in an untrusted environment, where the adversary has access to the device and is able to launch a physical attack. In addition to key generation, PUFs can be utilized as unique identifiers to restrict access to FPGAs and prevent cloning and spoofing attacks [16,17,26,40].

PUF and DPA-resistant decryptors can be implemented either by dedicated logic inside the FPGA (i.e., hard cores) or by configuring the FPGA logic cells (i.e., soft cores). Although the principle of using PUFs for key obfuscation and DPA-resistant decryptors to defeat physical attacks are similar among different

FPGA vendors, the implementation details differ. In this work, we explain the red key wrapping technique using soft PUFs and soft decryptors, which is used by Xilinx SoCs [35]. The main idea is to generate a "black key" (i.e., an encrypted key, which in itself is useless to an attacker), to generate the secret red key on the fly during configuration. This black key can then be stored safely in an insecure NVM and the red key will only exist as volatile, internal-only data. The preparations for this technique are as follows. In the trusted field a boot loader containing the red key and a soft PUF IP is transferred into the volatile configuration SRAM of the FPGA. After the boot loader is loaded, the PUF is configured on the programmable logic of the device and its responses are used in conjunction with the red key to generate the black key [35], see Fig. 1(b). The black key generated in this way can only be converted back to the red key with the correct, chip-specific, internal-only PUF response (i.e., PUF key). In the untrusted field an encrypted first stage boot loader with the black key, the same soft PUF IP and a DPA-resistant decryption IP core is loaded into the device. The chip-specific PUF response is then used to unwrap the black key and generate the red key on the fly. Finally, the encrypted configuration bitstream is transferred to the device and will be decrypted by the red key inside the FPGA. In this way the decryption IP core can be updated against future side-channel analysis threats. Furthermore, the soft PUF in conjunction with the black key provides volatile, internal-only and updatable key storage, and therefore, the red key is in memory only during the configuration of the device.

2.2 Current PUF Implementations

Current FPGA market leaders have already started to integrate PUFs into their latest products [7,25,35]. Hard SRAM PUFs from Intrinsic-ID Inc. have already been integrated into the Microsemi SmartFusion2 and IGLOO2 FPGAs [7] and are going to be implemented on Altera Stratix 10 SoCs and FPGAs [25]. Moreover, Xilinx has patented a key generation technique based on hard RO PUFs which might be used in their next generation FPGAs and SoCs [45]. Currently, the Xilinx Zynq-7000 SoCs enables the user to implement soft PUF IP cores as well as DPA-resistant soft decryptor IPs to protect the red key during configuration [35]. Furthermore, selected Microsemi flash-based SmartFusion2 and IGLOO2 FPGAs can be utilized as a Root of Trust to transfer soft PUF IP cores to target SRAM-based FPGAs for secure authentication [26]. Soft PUFs can be purchased from third-party developers, such as Verayo Inc. [6], Intrisic-ID Inc. [4], Lewis Innovative Technology Inc. [5] and Helion Technology Limited. [3].

Since the implemented soft or hard PUFs inside of FPGAs are controlled PUFs, where a non-invasive electrical access to the challenges and responses of the PUFs is restricted by either physical or algorithmic countermeasures, most of the reported modeling [9,14,37] and semi-invasive [29,33,42,43] attacks in the literature are ineffective. In this case the unprocessed challenges can be transmitted with the first stage boot loader to the FPGA, which will be processed later on the device by non-linear functions and applied to the PUF. The response of the PUF will also be generated and processed inside the device and cannot be observed in a non-invasive way.

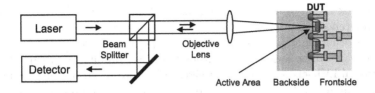

Fig. 2. Simplified illustration of LVP signal acquisition.

2.3   Laser Voltage Probing and Laser Voltage Imaging

Several techniques have been introduced into failure analysis to allow contactless probing of Devices Under Test (DUTs). One category of such techniques uses optical beams and is therefore, referred to as *contactless optical probing*. These techniques allow failure analysis engineers to probe electrical signals through the silicon backside and to also create 2D activity maps of active circuitry. Turnkey solutions for optical probing are readily available from different manufacturers, among them Hamamatsu Photonics, Checkpoint Technologies, DCG Systems (now part of FEI) and Semicaps. In the literature optical probing can be referred to as Laser Voltage Probing (LVP), Electro Optical Probing (EOP), Laser Timing Module (LTM) or Laser Time Probe (LTP). Acquisition of 2D activity maps is similarly referred to as Laser Voltage Imaging (LVI), Electro Optical Frequency Mapping (EOFM) or Signal Mapping Image (SMI). In this paper we choose to refer to waveform probing as Laser Voltage Probing (LVP) and to acquisition of 2D activity maps as Laser Voltage Imaging (LVI). Both techniques together will be referred to as LVx.

The actual technical realisation of LVx varies depending on the manufacturer, however, the basic principles remain the same. For optical probing as used in LVP a laser beam is focussed through the silicon backside, traverses the active device area, is reflected of, for instance, metal structures and leaves the device again through the silicon backside, see Fig. 2. The returning beam is then fed to an optical detector to measure its intensity. Usually near infrared (NIR) wavelengths are used to prevent the absorption of light by the silicon. Inside the active area the electrical parameters of the device, such as electrical fields and currents, lead to changes in the absorption coefficient and refractive index. Because of this, the optical beam intensity is altered either directly through absorption or in some cases indirectly through interference effects because of the changed refractive index. Empirical studies have shown, that a linear approximation is often sufficient to describe the relationship between the voltage at the electrical node and the reflected light signal. Therefore, the detector signal waveform recreates the electrical waveform from inside the device. This allows optical probing of electrical waveforms by just pointing the laser beam at the electrical node of interest. However, since the light modulation is very small (on the order of 100 ppm) the detector signal usually needs to be averaged while the device is running in a triggered loop to achieve a decent signal to noise ratio. As this is just a rough sketch of the principles of optical probing, readers interested in a detailed discussion of the underlying physical interactions are referred to [24] and the references mentioned therein.

On the other hand, optical frequency mapping, as used in Laser Voltage Imaging (LVI), can be seen as an extension to optical probing as explained above. In one typical LVI setup, the detector signal is not averaged but instead fed into a spectrum analyzer, which is set to some frequency of interest and zero span. Therefore, the spectrum analyzer effectively acts as a narrow frequency filter with adjustable bandwidth. Using galvanometric x/y mirrors the laser beam is then scanned across the device and the filter output of the spectrum analyzer is sampled for every scanned pixel. Afterwards, a PC with appropriate software is used to assemble the sampled frequency filter values into a 2D picture using a grey-scale representation. If an electrical node operates at the frequency of interest, it will modulate the light reflected of it with said frequency. This will in turn lead to a detector signal modulated with this frequency, which will be able to pass through the frequency filtering spectrum analyzer. Therefore all nodes operating at this frequency will show up as white spots in the LVI image. All nodes operating at a different frequency or areas which are not modulating the laser light will stay black. It should be noted that it is enough if some frequency component of the waveform present at the node can pass the frequency filter. Hence, this method can be used to detect nodes operating with arbitrary waveforms, as long as the first harmonic frequency or other strong frequency components of that waveform can be determined. As soon as the nodes of interest are found in this way, the galvanometric mirrors can be set to directly probe the waveform of one specific node with Laser Voltage Probing using a stationary beam within seconds. An advantage of LVI over LVP is, that for LVP waveform acquisition a loop trigger signal is always needed, whereas for LVI the device can be free-running.

In practice LVx systems are often incorporated into Laser Scanning Microscopes (LSMs). LSMs acquire optical images by scanning a laser beam across a sample and detecting the reflected light. They are therefore already equipped with scanning mirrors and an optical illumination and detection path, and thus, LVx systems can be used as an add-on.

3 Attack Scenario

We propose two LVP-based attacks against FPGAs during configuration. In the first attack scenario we demonstrate how the adversary can probe the red, black and PUF key using Laser Voltage Imaging (LVI). This allows the attacker to extract the red key, and therefore, enables her to decrypt the encrypted bitstream offline, which can lead to reverse engineering or cloning of the design. In the second attack, we will show how the attacker can characterize an RO PUF based on a combination of LVI, Laser Voltage Probing (LVP) and power analysis. Characterization of the individual oscillators of the RO PUF enables the attacker to model the PUF, and therefore, to clone its functionality. Knowing the *approximate* location of the key registers and the PUF components on the chip is the main assumption of our proposed attacks.

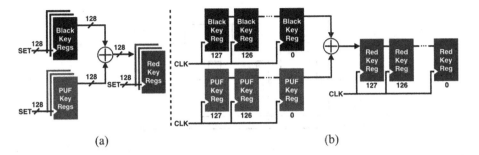

Fig. 3. (a) Parallel generation of the red key, (b) serial generation of the red key.

3.1   Key Extraction

The principle of key generation inside an FPGA has been discussed in Sect. 2.1. All three key values can be either shifted serially through a shift register or they can be loaded into the registers in parallel based on the implementation, see Fig. 3. We will first discuss the case, where the register values are loaded and processed in parallel. In this case the attacker can utilize LVI directly to extract all three values. As discussed in Sect. 2.3, LVI reveals nodes switching with a certain frequency, or more precisely, having certain frequency components. Therefore, to locate registers of interest, the attacker has to know a frequency or frequency component, which reveals the registers and is ideally data-dependent. Thus, she will need to take a look at the switching frequencies during red key generation. It is evident that after power-on all registers are first initialized to their default value by the reset circuitry. Following that, all black key registers are loaded in parallel and the PUF circuit is started. As soon as the PUF has finished generating its output, its values are also loaded onto the corresponding registers simultaneously. In a final step, the red key, which is now available at the XOR output, can be loaded onto all red key registers. Consequently, we can see that all register blocks of interest (black key, PUF key, red key) receive data — exactly once per power-on. This can be exploited to generate suitable frequency components by placing the device in a reset loop. In such a scenario, the first harmonic of the waveforms on these registers will be the reset frequency, as they change their states once per reset. If we now take a detailed look at the data dependency of these waveforms, we notice that there is a fundamental difference between registers carrying a zero bit and registers carrying a one bit. In Fig. 4 the waveforms of two registers receiving a one and a zero bit as well as the reset signal RST are depicted. For the register receiving a one bit (REG_A) it is evident that the register starts at logic low level and then changes its state, as soon as the time needed for the preceding calculations (T_{CALC}) has elapsed. As soon as the reset input goes high, the register is reset and afterwards the power-on cycle is restarted once reset goes low again. Since we can expect T_{CALC} to be constant for consecutive power-ons we can see that REG_A's period will be T_{RST} and we can expect its first harmonic to be at $1/T_{RST}$. For register REG_B,

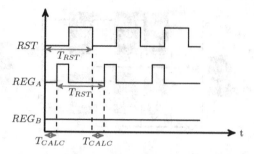

Fig. 4. Waveforms of the reset signal (RST) and two registers, receiving a one (REG_A) and a zero (REG_B) bit.

carrying a zero, the case is much simpler. REG_B will not change its value at all, and therefore, will not to have any harmonics at the reset frequency. Thus the attacker can expect the registers carrying a one to modulate the reflected light with a first harmonic of $1/T_{RST}$. Registers carrying a zero are expected to not modulate the reflected light at all. The interaction will be the same for black key, PUF key and red key register blocks. Although T_{CALC} will change for each register block, the first harmonic will still be at $1/T_{RST}$ for all of them. Therefore, to extract the register values the attacker can perform an LVI measurement on the register block of interest while setting the spectrum analyzer filter frequency to the reset loop frequency. If the LVI measurement is then grayscale encoded, registers carrying a one are expected to show up white while registers carrying a zero will remain black.

For the case of the serial implementation the situation is slightly different. Here the data will be processed bit by bit and the individual registers in the relevant register blocks will be connected together to form one shift register for each block. The data bits will then be shifted out of the black key and PUF key shift registers, passed through the XOR and shifted into the red key shift register. As a result, each individual register would show a different waveform depending on its position in the shift register and the actual data values. The waveforms of the individual registers would still have the reset frequency as their first harmonic, however, detecting the bit values can not be broken down to a simple black/white distinction as for the parallel case. Nevertheless, the attacker will still detect the registers of interest in an LVI image, although with varying signal strength. Since she is able to determine the precise register locations this way, she can then move on to directly probe the waveforms of individual registers using Laser Voltage Probing (LVP). This might be a tedious task, depending on the number of bits, however, she should be able to find the first register of each shift register this way. As soon as the first register of the red key shift register is found, the attacker can extract the key from its waveform, as the complete key gets shifted through this register during calculation.

Therefore, using just LVI or a combination of LVI and LVP the attacker should be able extract the key data regardless of the chosen implementation.

3.2 RO PUF Characterization

In order to characterize an RO PUF, the attacker has to be able to measure the frequencies of the ring oscillators (ROs) with high precision. PUF characterization enables the attacker to clone the RO PUF. If the attacker can estimate the frequency of the ROs at least approximately, she will be able to directly take an LVI measurement at that specific frequency. This can be achieved by electromagnetic or power analysis in the frequency domain. Using one of these methods the attacker will not be able to observe individual RO frequencies, but rather the superposition of all running ROs. Nevertheless, if she performs an LVI measurement at this approximate frequency with a large enough bandwidth, she should be able to see the nodes of the ROs in the LVI image. As soon as the nodes of the ROs are identified in this way the attacker can proceed to probe them individually. However, since the ROs are free-running, there is no trigger signal available for waveform acquisition, and therefore conventional Laser Voltage Probing (LVP) will fail. Yet, the attacker is free to connect the reflected light signal of the LVP directly to the spectrum analyzer of the LVP/LVI setup while probing one individual RO. Through setting the spectrum analyzer to conventional frequency sweep mode she will then be able to see the spectrum of the reflected light signal. As the laser beam will just probe one node of one RO, the waveform of that specific RO will be modulated onto the reflected light signal. Thus, the precise frequency of that individual RO will be visible on the spectrum analyzer. This will eliminate the need for a trigger signal and allow the attacker to characterize that specific RO. She can then proceed to characterize the whole RO PUF by pointing the laser at the nodes of the remaining individual ROs.

4 Setup

4.1 Device Under Test

The samples used for our experiments were Altera Cyclone IV FPGAs with part number EP4CE6E22C8N manufactured in a 60 nm process [8]. In this sample all Logic Elements (LEs) contain 4-input Lookup Tables (LUTs) and a dedicated register. The device contains 6272 Logic Array Blocks (LAB) with 16 LEs each. We chose the 144 pin TQFP package in order to simplify the sample preparation. The first step of preparation was the removal of the exposed ground pad on the backside of the package. The samples were then thinned by an Ultratec ASAP-1 polishing machine to a remaining silicon thickness of 25 μm. However this step would not have been necessary. Modern ICs only have to be depackaged and are sufficiently thin as-is for NIR analysis, just leading to a lower signal level if used directly. In the second step, the prepared samples were inversely soldered to a custom PCB. Bond wires originally leading to the exposed ground pad were then reconnected using silver conductive paint. A JTAG connection was used for configuring the FPGA after power-on.

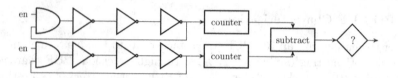

Fig. 5. A simplified schematic of an RO pair in the RO PUF construction. After a predefined period of oscillation, the states of both counters are compared to each other to generate a binary response.

4.2 PoC FPGA Implementation

For our Proof-of-Concept we have implemented an RO PUF and a red key (See Sect. 2.1.) calculation. To make the design less complex, we have connected the outputs of the ROs directly to individual counters, see Fig. 5. Each RO in our design has been realized with 21 inverters. All components of the ROs and the counters have been placed manually inside the FPGA using the Altera Quartus II integrated development environment. The LEs in every RO were placed as close as possible, directly next to each other. We have emulated the rebooting and configuration of the FPGA by adding a reset signal to our implementation. The black key and PUF key in our design have 8-bit length. As discussed in Sect. 3, unwrapping the black key can be carried out either in a parallel or serial way. Hence, for the first scenario, we have implemented the red key generation by XORing all values of the black key with the PUF key in parallel, see Fig. 3. For the second scenario, we have realized two shift registers for the black key and PUF key, where those values are shifted serially to an XOR gate and the result is shifted into the red key registers.

4.3 Measurement Setup

The core of our optical setup (Fig. 6(a)) is a Hamamatsu "PHEMOS-1000" laser scanning microscope. The PHEMOS is equipped with an optical probing and frequency mapping option. This option consists of a highly stable laser light source (Hamamatsu C12993), a Laser Voltage Probing and Laser Voltage Imaging preamplifier (Hamamatsu C12323), an Agilent "Acqiris" digitizer card and an Advantest U3851 spectrum analyzer. The laser light source emits radiation at 1319 nm which is input into the optical path, deflected by galvanometric mirrors and then focussed through an objective lens into the backside of the DUT. The reflected light from the DUT is passed on to a detector and the detector signal is fed into the preamplifier. The signal leaving the preamplifier can then either be routed to the spectrum analyzer for LVI or to the digitizer card for acquisition of LVP waveforms. For all measurements shown in this paper a Hamamatsu 50x/0.76NA lens with silicon thickness correction was used. The approximate laser power with this lens on the DUT is 50 mW for 100 % laser power. Additionally 5x and 20x objective lenses were used for navigation. The whole optical setup is controlled by a PC running the PHEMOS control software.

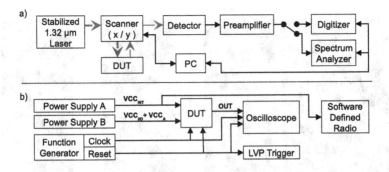

Fig. 6. Optical (a) and electrical (b) setup block diagram

Our electrical setup (Fig. 6(b)) is as follows: Two power supplies are connected to the DUT. The first one (Agilent E3645A) provides $V_{CCINT} = 1.2V$ (internal logic), the second one (Power Designs Inc. 2005) supplies $V_{CCIO} = 2.5V$ (I/O) and $V_{CCA} = 2.5V$ (PLL and analog). All voltages were within recommended levels [8]. A Rigol DG4162 two channel function generator produces clock and reset signals which are fed into the DUT. The clock and reset signals as well as an auxiliary DUT output are also connected to a LeCroy WaveMaster 8620 A oscilloscope for testing and control purposes. The reset signal is furthermore fed into the Laser Voltage Probing (LVP) trigger input. To be able to conduct basic power analysis in the frequency domain, a Software Defined Radio (SDR) is AC-coupled to the V_{CCINT} power rail. The SDR is an inexpensive USB dongle which uses a Realtek RTL2832U chipset and a Rafael Micro R820T tuner. For controlling the SDR, free and open source software is used. "Gqrx" [2] is used for measurements with a spectral bandwidth below 2.4 MHz and the python script "RTLSDR Scanner" [1] for higher bandwidths.

5 Results

5.1 Key Extraction

For our first measurements we used a parallel implementation as described in Sect. 4.2. The black key was set to 10101101, the PUF key to 11011011 and the resulting red key was 01110110. The measurement was conducted with 5 MHz reset frequency and 50 MHz clock. Both were 50 % duty cycle and 2.4 V high level and 0 V low level. The laser power was 10 % and the pixel dwell time 3.3 ms. The filter frequency for LVI was set to the reset frequency and the bandwidth to 300 Hz.

First, we performed an overview LVI image of an area containing all three register blocks, see Fig. 7(a). There are clearly nodes whose waveforms contain frequency components at the reset frequency, and therefore, give rise to an LVI signal. Since it is known in which LABs the black key, PUF key and red key registers have been placed, it is now straight forward to assign the blocks to their

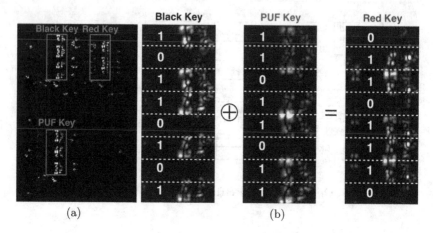

Fig. 7. LVI images of the parallel implementation. (a) All three register blocks taking part in the red key calculation. (b) Detail view of the individual register blocks. Dashed lines denote the LE boundaries. Each LE is approx. 6 μm in height.

respective keys. To analyze the data content of the registers, a higher resolution is helpful. The measurement has thus been repeated on each register block while applying a scanner zoom. The resulting LVI images can be seen in Fig. 7(b) and the expected behaviour discussed in Sect. 3.1 is observed. As expected, registers carrying a zero do not contribute to the LVI signal while registers carrying a one can clearly contribute. We can see that there are slight differences in the appearance of the nodes from measurement to measurement, which are probably due to focus drift. Nevertheless, we can observe that the attacker is easily able to extract the relevant values of the black key, PUF key and red key directly from these LVI images. For the serial implementation we used the same basic measurement setup. However, the reset signal and LVI frequency were modified to be 1 MHz, as the serial implementation needs more clock cycles to execute. The reset duty cycle was set to 58 % as a makeshift trigger delay, causing only full bits to show up in the result before reset assertion. The laser power was increased to 15 % and the pixel dwell time decreased to 1 ms. Following that, an LVI image of the red key register block was taken, which is shown in Fig. 8. It is evident that there is no simple black/white data dependency, as discussed in Sect. 3.1. Still, we can see a difference in signal strength for the registers, with the ones at the top giving less signal than the ones at the bottom. To get a rough idea of which points could be promising for Laser Voltage Probing (LVP) we used a fast Fourier transform calculator to analyze the amplitude of the first harmonic component for different expected waveforms. We observed that for our case of one to eight bits shifted with a comparatively large reset "dead time" following, the waveforms with more bit shifts gave us a stronger first harmonic component. Our conclusion was therefore that the lower half area was the most promising to probe. Direct probing of the lower-half registers was successful and revealed the lowest register to be the "shift-in" register. However, it was noticed that

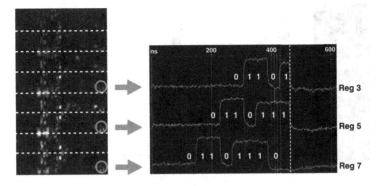

Fig. 8. LVI image of the red key register block and probed waveforms for the serial implementation. Reset assertion is marked by a dashed vertical line.

waveforms with a better signal to noise ratio could be acquired on the locations right of the actual register area. We assume that these locations are associated with routing and therefore the signal has already been buffered before reaching them. Furthermore, these locations are more isolated signal-wise which also leads to a better signal waveform. Hence, the final measurements were carried out on these locations for the shift-in register and two other registers further down the signal path. The resulting waveforms can be seen in Fig. 8. It is obvious that the red key can be extracted from the lowest LVP waveform of the shift-in register by an attacker. We acquired further waveforms while setting the integration number down to 100.000 loops, which is the current limit in the PHEMOS software, and were still able to distinguish the bit states easily. Therefore, we expect this approach to work with even less loop counts, as soon as the limit is removed from the software.

5.2 RO Characterization

For characterisation of the ring oscillators (ROs) we used the approach discussed in 3.2. In this section we will demonstrate the frequency measurement for one of the ROs. We first used the Software Defined Radio (SDR) to get a rough estimation for the LVI frequency by taking a look at the superposition of all RO frequencies in the spectral domain on the power rail. By slight adjustments of this estimate we were then able to create LVI overview images of the LEs forming the different ROs, one of which is depicted in Fig. 9(a). The parameters used for this LVI measurement were: 127.3539 MHz spectrum analyzer filter frequency, 60 % laser power, and 0.33 ms pixel dwell time. The ROs showed much more short term frequency fluctuations than the previously used conventional clock sources. Therefore, the LVI filter bandwidth had to be set to 100 kHz to account for the more widespread RO spectrum. After being able to identify the nodes of interest inside the LEs in this way, the beam was held stationary on one of them and the preamplified light detector signal was fed into the spectrum analyzer. The spectrum analyzer was then configured to show

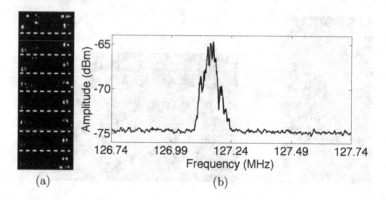

Fig. 9. (a) LVI image of 8 LEs of an RO, each approx. 6 μm in height. Dashed lines denote the LE boundaries. Each LE shows multiple potential probing locations. (b) LVP spectrum of the same RO.

the spectrum of this signal, which was modulated by the RO waveform present at the electrical node. For this measurement the laser power was set slightly higher, to 73 %, the spectrum analyzer frequency span to 1 MHz, resolution bandwidth to 30 kHz and video bandwidth to 10 Hz. The resulting spectrum in Fig. 9(b) shows the RO frequency approximately 10 dBm above the noise floor. Thus, the attacker is able to determine the current RO frequency precisely using only contactless optical probing methods. It should be noted that the resolution bandwidth mentioned before is not the resolution to be expected for the frequency measurement. As the attacker will only be interested in the average frequency of the RO, she is free to use multiple frequency sweeps to get a smooth spectrum and determine its peak value. The frequency of this peak value will then deliver the average frequency with a precision only depending on the number of averaged sweeps. By analysing the average frequency acquired this way it can be seen that the RO frequency was shifted by approximately 0.15 % when the laser power was increased from 60 % to 73 %. As long as the individual ROs are probed in the same way with the same laser power, this should not lead to problems for the attacker. Since the important question for the attacker is just which RO is faster, characterizing the RO PUF will still be successful if she takes care to probe all ROs in the same way, generating the same shift. Nevertheless, we will discuss this aspect in detail in Sect. 6.

6   Discussion

6.1   Locating the Registers and IP Cores on the Chip

As mentioned in Sect. 3, knowing the approximate location of the key registers and PUF IP core is the main assumption of our proposed attacks. Different scenarios can be considered to understand how realistic this assumption is.

As discussed in Sect. 2.1, the soft PUF IP cores, black key and their placements are transmitted in the first stage boot loader. If the first stage boot loader or Boot0 is not encrypted, the attacker can intercept the boot loader on the board and gain knowledge about the configuration of the PUF and the red and black key registers. For instance, the Microsemi Root of Trust solution [26] permits either the transfer of unencrypted or encrypted first stage boot loaders to the target SRAM-based FPGA. If the boot loader is encrypted, it will be decrypted by the hard dedicated AES core inside the target FPGA. While in the unencrypted case the boot loader can be easily intercepted, for the encrypted case DPA vulnerabilities of dedicated AES cores might be used to extract the encryption key and decrypt the boot loader [23,30–32]. However, in the case of asymmetric authentication as used by Xilinx SoCs, it is much harder for the attacker to expose the boot loader configuration [32]. Because of the authentication, the attacker cannot launch a DPA attack against the hard AES core and therefore might not be able to decrypt the first stage boot loader.

If the first stage boot loader cannot be intercepted, the attacker has to have access to the used IP cores prior to the attack. Though difficult, it is conceivable that the adversary can get access to the IP cores via an insider or by posing as a potential customer to IP core suppliers. Having the IP cores, the attacker can synthesize the PUF on an identical FPGA model and analyze the design either in the IDE (if no obfuscation is used) or by looking at the generated bitstream to find the circuitry of the interest.

If the attacker cannot get access to the IP cores, the attack will be more difficult due to the unknown location of the circuitry of interest. In this case, if the utilized soft PUF is an RO PUF, one could launch the attack proposed in Sect. 3.2 to find the ROs and the counters connected to them on the chip. The location of the RO PUF can then be a reference point to localize other parts of the design inside the FPGA. Furthermore, one can estimate the operational frequency of different registers to apply LVI and localize the related registers individually on the chip. After a successful localization of the key registers, the attacker can extract data from them by LVP/LVI based on the implementation (See Sect. 5.1). In the case of a parallel implementation, if the key registers are naively implemented in the right order (i.e., from LSB to MSB), the attacker can easily extract the key by using LVI. Otherwise, if the keys are latched in an obfuscated way, the attacker can only read the state of the permuted registers and might not find the right order of the registers to assemble the key. For a serial implementation, if the order of the registers is obfuscated, the attacker can probe all registers to find the one through which the whole key is shifted.

The proposed attacks to key registers can in principle also be applied, if a hard PUF and a hard AES are in use. In this case, the attacker has to reverse-engineer the ASIC configuration circuit of the FPGA to locate the circuitry of interest. Although the search space for the region of interest might be reduced, the attacker has to probe and reverse-engineer more compact and dense ASIC circuits in comparison to FPGA logic cells, which might be challenging.

6.2 Feasibility and Scalability of the Attack

The process technology of FPGAs and programmable SoCs, which are supporting partial reconfiguration for soft PUF implementation, are equal to or smaller
than 60 nm. Since our LVI and LVP experiments have been carried out on an
FPGA with 60 nm technology, the question of the applicability of the same technique on smaller technologies might be raised. The real size of the transistors
is normally 7 to 8 times larger than the nominal technology node [18]. Besides,
the size of the LEs and the routing (intra and inter LEs) of FPGAs is much
larger than the size of the transistors, see Fig. 7. Hence, the optical resolution
requirements for data extraction are much less severe than for probing individual
transistors. Based on our measurements, the LE height in an Altera Cyclone IV
is about 6 μm. The theoretical expected resolution of our laser spot is approximately 1 μm^2. Thus, optical probing should still be possible on an LE approx.
six times smaller. It is worth mentioning that for LVP and LVI typical FPGAs
are an advantageous target, as multiple transistors close together will carry the
same waveform in an LE.

There are also solutions for increasing the optical resolution of LVP and LVI
techniques. For instance, one can use solid immersion lenses (SILs) to get 2
to 3 times better resolution, which already enables *single transistor* probing at
14 nm [18]. Moreover, lasers with shorter wavelengths (e.g., in the visible light
spectrum) can be used to further increase the resolution [10,12]. However, in
the latter case, the substrate of the chip has to be thinned to 10μm or less to
prevent the absorption of the photons.

Meanwhile, it is still interesting to understand why other backside semi-
invasive attacks, such as PEM or LFI, have limited efficiency on small technologies in comparison to LVP and LVI. In the case of PEM, the photon emission
rate is proportional to the core voltage of the chip. However, the core voltage
of technologies smaller than 60 nm is too low [41] and the attacker therefore
has to integrate over a large number of iterations to capture enough photons for
analysis. LFI attacks on the other hand target mostly single memory cells, which
requires the system used for the attack to be able to resolve single transistors
on the chip.

6.3 Tamper Evidence

Tamper evidence is believed to be one of the main advantages of PUFs [27].
In other words, it is assumed that semi-invasive and fully-invasive attacks on
the PUF implementation alter the challenge-response behavior of the PUF, and
therefore, the secret information is lost. Tamper-evidence against fully-invasive
attacks is experimentally verified only for optical and coating PUF so far [36,47].
However, the core of most soft and hard PUFs are *intrinsic* PUFs (i.e., delay-
based PUFs and memory-based PUFs) [27]. Unfortunately, for these constructions limited information on tamper-evidence is available in the PUF-related
literature. Fortunately, results on constructions similar to delay-based PUFs can
be found in the failure analysis literature. For instance, it has been reported that

mechanical stress from depackaging and substrate thinning have negligible effects on the absolute and relative frequencies of ring oscillators (ROs) [11]. In another experiment, it has been shown that removing most of the bulk silicon, down to the bottom of the n-wells, does not alter the delays of the inverter chains [38]. Additionally, without affecting the challenge-response behavior of the PUFs, different successful semi-invasive attacks have been reported on silicon intrinsic PUF instances in the literature [20,29,33,43,44]. On the other hand, PUF developers do their best to mitigate the noisy response of the PUF by different error correction techniques [22,28]. Therefore, if few CRPs are changed by the physical tampering, they will be corrected by such error correction techniques. Based on these results, depackaging the chip and thinning the substrate does not destruct the target PUF.

Although passive semi-invasive attacks do not affect the behavior of the PUF, the laser beam in our proposed attack can change the temperature of the transistors. Temperature variations have transient and reversible effects on the delay and frequency of the inverter chains in arbiter PUFs and RO PUFs. In our experiments, a shift of frequency has been observed while performing LVI and LVP on the ROs. However, the attacker is still able to precisely characterize and measure the frequencies of the ROs by performing LVI and LVP, if she takes care to probe all ring oscillators under the same conditions. If the attacker is not able to fulfill this requirement, she might also probe the registers of the counters which are connected to the RO output. Assuming the counters or other circuitry connected to the RO PUFs are located far enough away she will be able to mount her attack without influencing the ROs. Finally she might take measurements of one individual RO frequency for different laser powers and extrapolate from that to the frequency for zero laser power. Therefore, a precise physical characterization of the RO PUF is certainly feasible.

6.4   Countermeasures

Silicon light sensors have been proposed to detect the photons of the laser beam. However, in our experiments we have used a laser beam which has a longer wavelength than the silicon band gap. Hence, no electron-hole pairs will be generated by the laser photons. A silicon photo sensor is therefore unlikely to trigger.

A potential algorithmic countermeasure can be randomization of the reset states of the registers for the parallel implementation. As a result, the simple black/white data distinction (see Sect. 3.1) would be severely impeded, as there now would be switching activity during the reset loop on all registers. For the serial case, a randomization of the relation of the outer reset signal to the internal reset signal would destroy the needed trigger relationship and make waveform probing on the registers impossible. Another simple countermeasure includes the obfuscation of the key registers by randomizing their order, see Sect. 6.1.

Finally, the ROs in a ring oscillator network with virtually equal frequencies can be placed in different areas of the FPGA. Using LVP will then slightly shift the frequencies of ROs which are in or close to the probed area. Hence, the frequency deviation of these ROs in comparison to the mean frequency of all

ROs can be used to raise an alarm. Similarly, delay-based PUFs might be useful as sensors, if their elements are placed in different regions of the chip.

7   Conclusion

In this paper, we have proposed novel semi-invasive attacks from the IC backside using LVP and LVI techniques. We have demonstrated that these techniques can be potentially used against modern FPGAs and programmable SoCs during configuration. Based on these considerations, it becomes apparent that replacing the eFuses or BBRAMS with controlled PUFs does not raise the security level of key storage as high as one would expect in the first place. Even recent controlled stateless PUF constructions [22] are vulnerable to contactless probing. Moreover, while the size of the transistors is shrinking, novel inexpensive failure analysis techniques are developed to debug and probe nanoscale manufactured circuits in a semi-invasive and contactless way. It is worth mentioning that much less time is required for optical contactless probing of different signals than for conventional techniques, such as FIB microprobing [21]. Using our approach the amount of time needed to probe multiple nodes is on the order of minutes while for FIB microprobing it will be on the order of days. Furthermore, it is obvious that our attack technique has the potential to directly probe the bitstream after on-chip decryption, circumventing all security measures in place. However, there are several requirements for probing such a large amount of data and finding a suitable probing location in the much smaller and denser ASIC area, which might not be fulfilled by a standard LVP setup. Nevertheless, we strongly believe that future generations of FPGAs remain vulnerable to contactless probing, if proper protections or countermeasures for the IC backside are not implemented.

Acknowledgements. This research was supported by the German Federal Ministry of Education and Research in the project Photon FX^2 and by the Helmholtz Research School on Security Technologies. We would also like to acknowledge Hamamatsu Photonics for support. We gratefully thank Andreas Eckert and Helmar Dittrich at TU Berlin for sample and PCB preparation.

References

1. Ear to Ear Oak. http://eartoearoak.com/software/rtlsdr-scanner/. Accessed 6 June 2016
2. Gqrx SDR. http://gqrx.dk. Accessed 6 June 2016
3. Helion Technology Limited. http://www.heliontech.com. Accessed 6 June 2016
4. Intrisic-ID Inc. https://www.intrinsic-id.com. Accessed 6 June 2016
5. Lewis Innovative Technology Inc. http://lewisinnovative.com. Accessed 6 June 2016
6. Verayo Inc. http://www.verayo.com. Accessed 6 June 2016
7. White Paper: Overview of Data Security Using Microsemi FPGAs and SoC FPGAs. Microsemi Corporation, Aliso Viejo, CA (2013)

8. Altera: Cyclone IV Device Handbook. Altera Corporation, San Jose (2014)
9. Becker, G.T.: The gap between promise and reality: on the insecurity of XOR arbiter PUFs. In: Güneysu, T., Handschuh, H. (eds.) CHES 2015. LNCS, vol. 9293, pp. 535–555. Springer, Heidelberg (2015)
10. Beutler, J.: Visible light LVP on bulk silicon devices. In: 41st International Symposium for Testing and Failure Analysis, 1–5 November 2015. ASM (2015)
11. Boit, C., Kerst, U., Schlangen, R., Kabakow, A., Le Roy, E., Lundquista, T., Pauthnerb, S.: Impact of back side circuit edit on active device performance in bulk silicon ICs. In: International Test Conference. vol. 2, p. 1236 (2005)
12. Boit, C., Lohrke, H., Scholz, P., Beyreuther, A., Kerst, U., Iwaki, Y.: Contactless visible light probing for nanoscale ICs through 10 μm bulk silicon. In: Proceedings of the 35th Annual NANO Testing Symposium - NANOTS 2015, pp. 215–221 (2015)
13. Davidson, A.: WP-01220-1.1: A New FPGA Architecture and Leading-Edge FinFET Process Technology Promise to Meet Next-Generation System Requirements. Altera Corporation, San Jose (2015)
14. Ganji, F., Tajik, S., Seifert, J.-P.: Why attackers win: on the learnability of XOR arbiter PUFs. In: Conti, M., Schunter, M., Askoxylakis, I. (eds.) TRUST 2015. LNCS, vol. 9229, pp. 22–39. Springer, Heidelberg (2015)
15. Gassend, B., Clarke, D., Van Dijk, M., Devadas, S.: Silicon physical random functions. In: Proceedings of the 9th ACM Conference on Computer and Communications Security. pp. 148–160. ACM (2002)
16. Guajardo, J., Kumar, S.S., Schrijen, G.-J., Tuyls, P.: FPGA intrinsic PUFs and their use for IP protection. In: Paillier, P., Verbauwhede, I. (eds.) CHES 2007. LNCS, vol. 4727, pp. 63–80. Springer, Heidelberg (2007)
17. Güneysu, T., Markov, I., Weimerskirch, A.: Securely sealing multi-FPGA systems. In: Choy, O.C.S., Cheung, R.C.C., Athanas, P., Sano, K. (eds.) ARC 2012. LNCS, vol. 7199, pp. 276–289. Springer, Heidelberg (2012)
18. von Haartman, M.: Optical fault isolation and nanoprobing techniques for the 10nm technology node and beyond. In: 41st International Symposium for Testing and Failure Analysis, November 1–5, 2015. ASM (2015)
19. Hansen, L.: White Paper WP470: Unleash the Unparalleled Power and Flexibility of Zynq UltraScale+ MPSoCs. Xilinx, Inc., San Jose, CA (2015)
20. Helfmeier, C., Boit, C., Nedospasov, D., Seifert, J.P.: Cloning physically unclonable functions. In: 2013 IEEE International Symposium on Hardware-Oriented Security and Trust (HOST), pp. 1–6. IEEE (2013)
21. Helfmeier, C., Nedospasov, D., Tarnovsky, C., Krissler, J.S., Boit, C., Seifert, J.P.: Breaking and entering through the silicon. In: Proceedings of the 2013 ACM SIGSAC Conference on Computer Communications Security, pp. 733–744. ACM (2013)
22. Herder, C., Ren, L., van Dijk, M., Yu, M.D.M., Devadas, S.: Trapdoor computational fuzzy extractors and stateless cryptographically-secure physical unclonable functions. IEEE Trans. Dependable Secur. Comput. 2016(99), 1–1 (2016)
23. Hori, Y., Katashita, T., Sasaki, A., Satoh, A.: Electromagnetic side-channel attack against 28-nm FPGA device. In: Pre-proceedings of WISA (2012)
24. Kindereit, U., Woods, G., Tian, J., Kerst, U., Leihkauf, R., Boit, C.: Quantitative Investigation of laser beam modulation in electrically active devices as used in laser voltage probing. IEEE Trans. Device Mater. Reliab. 7(1), 19–30 (2007)
25. Lu, T., Kenny, R., Atsatt, S.: White Paper WP-01252-1.0: Stratix 10 Secure Device Manager Provides Best-in-Class FPGA and SoC Security. Altera Corporation, San Jose, CA (2015)

26. Luis, W., Richard Newell, G., Alexander, K.: Differential power analysis counter-measures for the configuration of SRAM FPGAs. In: IEEE Military Communications Conference, MILCOM 2015–2015. pp. 1276–1283. IEEE (2015)

27. Maes, R.: Physically Unclonable Functions: Constructions: Properties and Applications. Springer, Heidelberg (2013)

28. Maes, R., van der Leest, V., van der Sluis, E., Willems, F.: Secure key generation from biased PUFs. In: Güneysu, T., Handschuh, H. (eds.) CHES 2015. LNCS, vol. 9293, pp. 517–534. Springer, Heidelberg (2015)

29. Merli, D., Schuster, D., Stumpf, F., Sigl, G.: Semi-invasive EM attack on FPGA RO PUFs and countermeasures. In: Proceedings of the Workshop on Embedded Systems Security, p. 2. ACM (2011)

30. Moradi, A., Barenghi, A., Kasper, T., Paar, C.: On the vulnerability of FPGA bitstream encryption against power analysis attacks: extracting keys from xilinx virtex-II FPGAs. In: Proceedings of the 18th ACM Conference on Computer and Communications Security. pp. 111–124. ACM (2011)

31. Moradi, A., Oswald, D., Paar, C., Swierczynski, P.: Side-channel attacks on the bitstream encryption mechanism of altera stratix II: facilitating black-box analysis using software reverse-engineering. In: Proceedings of the ACM/SIGDA International Symposium on Field Programmable Gate Arrays. pp. 91–100. ACM (2013)

32. Moradi, A., Schneider, T.: Improved Side-Channel Analysis Attacks on Xilinx Bitstream Encryption of 5, 6, and 7 Series, COSADE 2016, Graz, Austria, 14 April 2016

33. Nedospasov, D., Seifert, J.P., Helfmeier, C., Boit, C.: Invasive PUF analysis. In: 2013 Workshop on Fault Diagnosis and Tolerance in Cryptography (FDTC), pp. 30–38. IEEE (2013)

34. Pappu, R., Recht, B., Taylor, J., Gershenfeld, N.: Physical one-way functions. Science 297(5589), 2026–2030 (2002)

35. Peterson, E.: White Paper WP468: Leveraging Asymmetric Authentication to Enhance Security-Critical Applications Using Zynq-7000 All Programmable SoCs. Xilinx, Inc., San Jose (2015)

36. Ravikanth, P.S.: Physical one-way functions. Ph.D. thesis, Massachusetts Institute of Technology (2001)

37. Rührmair, U., Sehnke, F., Sölter, J., Dror, G., Devadas, S., Schmidhuber1, J.: Modeling attacks on physical unclonable functions. In: Proceedings of the 17th ACM Conference on Computer and Communications Security. pp. 237–249 (2010)

38. Schlangen, R., Leihkauf, R., Kerst, U., Lundquist, T., Egger, P., Boit, C.: Physical analysis, trimming and editing of nanoscale IC function with backside FIB processing. Microelectron. Reliab. 49(9), 1158–1164 (2009)

39. Selmke, B., Brummer, S., Heyszl, J., Sigl, G.: Precise laser fault injections into FPGA BRAMs in 90 nm and 45 nm feature size. In: 14th Smart Card Research and Advanced Application Conference - CARDIS 2015 (2015)

40. Simpson, E., Schaumont, P.: Offline hardware/software authentication for reconfigurable platforms. In: Goubin, L., Matsui, M. (eds.) CHES 2006. LNCS, vol. 4249, pp. 311–323. Springer, Heidelberg (2006)

41. Tajik, S., Dietz, E., Frohmann, S., Dittrich, H., Nedospasov, D., Helfmeier, C., Seifert, J.P., Boit, C., Hübers, H.W.: Photonic side-channel analysis of arbiter PUFs. J. Cryptol. 1–22 (2016). doi:10.1007/s00145-016-9228-6

42. Tajik, S., Dietz, E., Frohmann, S., Seifert, J.-P., Nedospasov, D., Helfmeier, C., Boit, C., Dittrich, H.: Physical characterization of arbiter PUFs. In: Batina, L., Robshaw, M. (eds.) CHES 2014. LNCS, vol. 8731, pp. 493–509. Springer, Heidelberg (2014)

43. Tajik, S., Ganji, F., Seifert, J.P., Lohrke, H., Boit, C.: Laser fault attack on physically unclonable functions. In: 2015 Workshop on Fault Diagnosis and Tolerance in Cryptography (FDTC), IEEE (2015)
44. Tajik, S., Nedospasov, D., Helfmeier, C., Seifert, J.P., Boit, C.: Emission analysis of hardware implementations. In: 2014 17th Euromicro Conference on Digital System Design (DSD), pp. 528–534. IEEE (2014)
45. Trimberger, S.M.: Copy protection without non-volatile memory. US Patent 8,416,950 (2013)
46. Trimberger, S.M., Moore, J.J.: FPGA security: motivations, features, and applications. Proc. IEEE **102**(8), 1248–1265 (2014)
47. Tuyls, P., Schrijen, G.-J., Škorić, B., van Geloven, J., Verhaegh, N., Wolters, R.: Read-proof hardware from protective coatings. In: Goubin, L., Matsui, M. (eds.) CHES 2006. LNCS, vol. 4249, pp. 369–383. Springer, Heidelberg (2006)

Side Channel Countermeasures I

Strong 8-bit Sboxes with Efficient Masking in Hardware

Erik Boss[1], Vincent Grosso[1], Tim Güneysu[2], Gregor Leander[1],
Amir Moradi[1(✉)], and Tobias Schneider[1]

[1] Horst Görtz Institute for IT Security,
Ruhr-Universität Bochum, Bochum, Germany
{erik.boss,vincent.grosso,gregor.leander,amir.moradi,
tobias.schneider-a7a}@rub.de
[2] University of Bremen and DFKI, Bremen, Germany
tim.gueneysu@uni-bremen.de

Abstract. Block ciphers are arguably the most important cryptographic primitive in practice. While their security against mathematical attacks is rather well understood, physical threats such as side-channel analysis (SCA) still pose a major challenge for their security. An effective countermeasure to thwart SCA is using a cipher representation that applies the threshold implementation (TI) concept. However, there are hardly any results available on how this concept can be adopted for block ciphers with large (i.e., 8-bit) Sboxes. In this work we provide a systematic analysis on and search for 8-bit Sbox constructions that can intrinsically feature the TI concept, while still providing high resistance against cryptanalysis. Our study includes investigations on Sboxes constructed from smaller ones using Feistel, SPN, or MISTY network structures. As a result, we present a set of new Sboxes that not only provide strong cryptographic criteria, but are also optimized for TI. We believe that our results will found an inspiring basis for further research on high-security block ciphers that intrinsically feature protection against physical attacks.

1 Introduction

Block ciphers are among the most important cryptographic primitives. Although they usually follow ad-hoc design principles, their security with respect to known attacks is generally well-understood. However, this is not the case for the security of their implementations. The security of an implementation is often challenged by physical threats such as side-channel analysis or fault-injection attacks. In many cases, those attacks render the mathematical security meaningless. Hence, it is essential that a cipher implementation incorporates appropriate countermeasures against physical attacks. Usually, those countermeasures are developed retroactively for a given, fully specified block cipher. A more promising approach is including the possibility of adding efficient countermeasures into the design from the very start.

© International Association for Cryptologic Research 2016
B. Gierlichs and A.Y. Poschmann (Eds.): CHES 2016, LNCS 9813, pp. 171–193, 2016.
DOI: 10.1007/978-3-662-53140-2_9

For software implementations, this has been done. Indeed, a few ciphers have been proposed that aim to address the issue of protection against physical attacks by facilitating a masked Sbox by design. The first example is certainly NOEKEON [18], other examples include Zorro [20], Picarro [33] and the LS-design family of block ciphers [21].

For hardware implementations, the situation is significantly different. Here, simple masking is less effective due to several side-effects, most notably glitches (see [27]). As an alternative to simple masking, a preferred hardware countermeasure against side-channel attacks is the so-called threshold implementation (TI) [32], as used for the cipher FIDES [6]. TI is a masking variant that splits any secret data into several shares, using a simple secret-sharing scheme. Those shares are then grouped in non-complete subsets to be separately processed by individual subfunctions. All subfunctions jointly correspond to the target function (i.e., the block cipher). Since none of the subfunctions depends on all shares of the secret data at any time, it is intuitive to see that it is impossible to reconstruct the secret by first-order side-channel observations. We provide a more detailed description of the functionality of threshold implementations in Sect. 2.

Unfortunately, it is not trivial to apply the TI concept to a given block cipher. The success of this process strongly depends on the complexity of the cipher's round function and its internal components. While the linear aspects of any cipher are typically easy to convert to TI, this is not generally true for the non-linear Sbox. For 4-bit Sboxes, it is possible to identify a corresponding TI representation by exhaustive search [10]. However, for larger Sboxes, in particular 8-bit Sboxes, the situation is very different. In this case, the search space is far too large to allow an exhaustive search. In fact, 8-bit Sboxes are far from being fully understood, from both a cryptographic and an implementation perspective.

With respect to cryptographic strength against differential and linear attacks, the AES Sbox (and its variants) can be seen as holding the current world record. We do not know of any Sbox with better properties, but those might well exist. Unfortunately, despite considerable effort, no TI representation is known for the AES Sbox that does not require any additional external randomness [7,9,31].

Our Contribution. In this paper we approach this problem of identifying cryptographically strong 8-bit Sboxes that provide a straightforward TI representation. More precisely, our goal is to give examples of Sboxes that come close to the cryptanalytic resistance of the AES Sbox. Also, the straight application of the TI concept to an Sbox should still lead to minimal resource and area costs. This enables an efficient and low-cost implementation in hardware as well as bit-sliced software.

In our work we systematically investigate 8-bit Sboxes that are constructed based on what can be seen as a mini-cipher. Concretely, we construct Sboxes based on either a Feistel-network (operating with two 4-bit branches and a 4-bit Sbox as the round function), a substitution permutation network or the MISTY network. This general approach has already been used and studied extensively. Examples of Sboxes constructed like this are used for example in the ciphers

Crypton [25,26], ICEBERG [40], Fantomas [21], Robin [21] and Khazad [3]. A more theoretical study was most recently presented by Canteaut *et al.* in [16].

Our idea extends the previous work by combining those constructions aiming at achieving strong cryptographic criteria with small Sboxes that are easy to share and intrinsically support the TI concept. As a result of our investigation, we present a set of different 8-bit Sboxes. These Sboxes are either (a) superior to the known constructions from a cryptographic perspective but can still be implemented with moderate resource requirements or (b) outperform all known constructions in terms of efficiency in the application of the TI concept to the Sbox, while still maintaining a comparable level of cryptographic strength with respect to other known Sboxes. All our findings are detailed in Table 1.

Outline. This work is structured as follows. Preliminaries on well-known strategies to construct Sboxes as well as the TI concept are given in Sect. 2. We discuss the applicability of TI on known 8-bit Sboxes in Sect. 3. The details and results of the search process are given in Sects. 4 and 5, respectively. We conclude with Sect. 6.

2   Preliminaries

2.1   Cryptanalytic Properties for Sboxes

In this subsection we recall the tools used for evaluating the strength of Sboxes with respect to linear, differential and algebraic properties. For this purpose, we consider an n-bit Sbox S as a vector of Boolean functions: $S = (f_0, \ldots, f_{n-1})$, $f_i : \mathbb{F}_2^n \to \mathbb{F}_2$. We denote the cardinality of a set A by $\#A$ and the dot product between two elements $a, b \in \mathbb{F}_2^n$ by: $\langle a, b \rangle = \sum_{i=0}^{n-1} a_i b_i$.

Non-linearity. To be secure against linear cryptanalysis [28] a cipher must not be well-approximated by linear or affine functions. As the Sbox is generally the only non-linear component in an SP-network, it has to be carefully chosen to ensure a design is secure against linear attacks. For a given Sbox, the main criterium here is the Hamming distance of any component function, i.e. a linear combination of the f_i, to the set of all affine functions. The greater this distance, the stronger the Sbox with respect to linear cryptanalysis. The Walsh transform $W_S(a, b)$, defined as

$$W_S(a, b) := \sum_{x \in \mathbb{F}_2^n} (-1)^{\langle a, x \rangle + \langle b, S(x) \rangle},$$

can be used to evaluate the correlation of a linear approximation $(a, b) \neq (0, 0)$. More precisely,

$$P(\langle b, S(x) \rangle = \langle a, x \rangle) = \frac{1}{2} + \frac{W_S(a, b)}{2^{n+1}}.$$

The larger the absolute value of $W_S(a, b)$, the better the approximation by the linear function $\langle a, x \rangle$ (or the affine function $\langle a, x \rangle + 1$, in case $W_S(a, b) < 0$). This motivates the following well known definition.

Definition 1 (Linearity). *Given a vectorial Boolean function S, its* linearity *is defined as*

$$\text{Lin}(S) = \max_{a,b\neq 0} |W_S(a,b)|.$$

The smaller $\text{Lin}(S)$, the stronger the Sbox is against linear cryptanalysis.

It is known that for any function S from $\mathbb{F}_2^n$ to $\mathbb{F}_2^n$ it holds that $\text{Lin}(S) \geq 2^{\frac{n+1}{2}}$ [17]. Functions that reach this bound are called Almost Bent (AB) functions. However, in the case $n > 4$ and n even, we do not know the minimal value of the linearity that can be reached. In particular, for $n = 8$ the best known non-linearity is achieved by the AES Sbox with $\text{Lin}(S) = 32$.

Differential Uniformity. A cipher must also be resistant against differential cryptanalysis [5]. To evaluate the differential property of an Sbox, we consider the set of all non-zero differentials and their probabilities (up to a factor 2^{-n}). That is, given $a, b \in \mathbb{F}_2^n$ we consider

$$\delta_S(a,b) := \#\{x \in \mathbb{F}_2^n \,\|\, S(x + a) = S(x) + b\},$$

which corresponds to 2^n times the probability of an input difference a propagating to an output difference b through the function S. This motivates the following well known definition.

Definition 2 (Differential Uniformity). *Given a vectorial Boolean function S, its* differential uniformity *is defined as*

$$\text{Diff}(S) = \max_{a\neq 0,b} |\delta_S(a,b)|.$$

The smaller $\text{Diff}(S)$, the stronger the Sbox regarding differential cryptanalysis.

It is known that for Sboxes S that have the same number of input and output bits it holds that $\text{Diff}(S) \geq 2$. Functions that reach that bound are called Almost Perfect Nonlinear (APN). While APN functions are known for any number n of input bits, APN *permutations* are known only in the case of n odd and $n = 6$.

In particular, for $n = 8$ the best known case is $\text{Diff}(S) = 4$, e.g., AES Sbox.

Algebraic Degree. The algebraic degree is generally considered as a good indicator of security against structural attacks, such as integral, higher-order differential or, most recently, attacks based on the division property.

Recall that any Boolean function f can be uniquely represented using its Algebraic Normal Form (ANF):

$$f(x) = \sum_{u \in \mathbb{F}_2^n} a_u x^u,$$

where $x^u = \prod_{i=0}^{n-1} x_i^{u_i}$, with the convention $0^0 = 1$. Now, the algebraic degree can be defined as follows.

Definition 3 (Algebraic Degree). *The algebraic degree of f is defined as:*

$$\deg(f) = \max_{u \in \mathbb{F}_2^n} \left\{ \sum_i u_i, a_u \neq 0 \right\}.$$

This definition can be extended to vectorial Boolean functions (Sboxes) as follows

$$\deg(S) = \max_{0 \leq i \leq n} \deg(f_i).$$

For a permutation on $\mathbb{F}_2^n$ the maximum degree is $n - 1$. Lots of permutations over $\mathbb{F}_2^n$ achieve this maximal degree. Again the AES Sbox is optimal in this respect, i.e., the AES Sbox has the maximal degree of 7 for 8-bit permutations.

Affine Equivalence. An important tool in our search for good Sboxes is the notion of affine equivalence. We say that two functions f and g are affine equivalent if there exists two affine permutations A_1 and A_2 such that $f = A_1 \circ g \circ A_2$. The importance of this definition is given by the well-known fact that both the linearity and the differential uniformity are invariant under affine equivalence. That is, two functions that are affine equivalent have the same linear and differential criteria.

2.2   Construction of 8-Bit Sboxes.

Apart from the AES Sbox, which is basically the inversion in the finite field $\mathbb{F}_{2^8}$, hardly any primary construction for useful, cryptographically strong, 8-bit Sboxes is known.

However, several secondary constructions have been applied successfully. Here, the idea is to build larger Sboxes from smaller Sboxes. For block ciphers this principle was first introduced in MISTY [29].

Later, this approach was modified and extended. In particular, it was used by several lightweight ciphers to construct Sboxes with different optimization criteria, e.g., smaller memory requirements, more efficient implementation, involution, and easier software-level masking.

There are basically three known constructions, all of which can be seen as mini-block ciphers: Feistel networks, the MISTY construction and SP-networks. Figure 1 shows how these constructions build larger Sboxes from smaller Sboxes. Note that the MISTY construction is a special case of the SPN. Indeed, the MISTY construction is equivalent to SPN when $F_1 = Id$ and the matrix $\mathcal{A} = \left(\begin{smallmatrix} 1 & 1 \\ 1 & 0 \end{smallmatrix} \right)$.

For a small number of rounds, we can systematically analyze the cryptographic properties of those constructions (see [16] for the most recent results). However, for a larger number of rounds, a theoretical understanding becomes increasingly more difficult in most cases.

Table 1 shows the different characteristics of 8-bit Sboxes known in the literature that are built from smaller Sboxes. We excluded the PICARO Sbox [33]

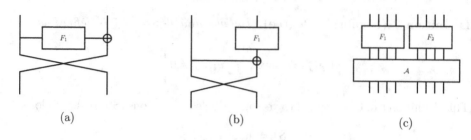

Fig. 1. (a) Feistel (b) MISTY (c) SPN

from the list, since it is not a bijection. Furthermore, Zorro is also excluded since the exact specifications of its structure are not publicly known. We refer often to this table as it summarizes all our findings and achievements.

2.3   Threshold Implementations

The first attempts to realize Boolean masking in hardware were unsuccessful, mainly due to glitches [27,30]. Combinatorial circuits which receive both the mask and the masked data, i.e., secret sharing with 2 shares, most likely exhibit first-order leakage. Threshold Implementation (TI) has been introduced to deal with this issue and realize masking in glitchy circuits [32].

The TI concept has been extended to higher orders [8], but our target, in this work, is resistance against first-order attacks. Hence, we give the TI specifications only with respect to first-order resistance. Let us assume a k-bit intermediate value x of a cipher as one of its Sbox inputs (at any arbitrary round) and represent it as $\boldsymbol{x} = \langle x_1, \ldots, x_k \rangle$. For $n-1$ order Boolean masking, x is represented by $(\boldsymbol{x}^1, \ldots, \boldsymbol{x}^n)$, where $\boldsymbol{x} = \bigoplus_{i=1}^{n} \boldsymbol{x}^i$ and each $\boldsymbol{x}^i$ similarly denotes a k-bit vector $\langle x_1^i, \ldots, x_k^i \rangle$.

Applying linear functions over Boolean-masked data is trivial, since $\mathsf{L}(\boldsymbol{x}) = \bigoplus_{i=1}^{n} \mathsf{L}(\boldsymbol{x}^i)$. However, realization of the masked non-linear functions (Sbox) is generally non-trivial and is thus the main challenge for TI. As per the TI concepts, at least $n = t + 1$ shares should be used to securely mask an Sbox with algebraic degree t. Moreover, TI defines three additional properties:

Correctness. The masked Sbox should provide the output in a shared form $(\boldsymbol{y}^1, \ldots, \boldsymbol{y}^m)$ with $\bigoplus_{i=1}^{m} \boldsymbol{y}^i = \boldsymbol{y} = \mathsf{S}(\boldsymbol{x})$ and $m \geq n$.

Non-completeness. Each output share $\boldsymbol{y}^{j \in \{1, \ldots, m\}}$ is provided by a component function $\mathsf{f}^j(.)$ over a subset of the input shares. Each component function $\mathsf{f}^{j \in \{1, \ldots, m\}}(.)$ must be independent of at least one input share.

Uniformity. The security of most masking schemes relies on the uniform distribution of the masks. Since in this work we consider only the cases with $n = m$ and bijective Sboxes, we can define the uniformity as follows. The masked Sbox with $n \times k$ input bits and $n \times k$ output bits should form a bijection. Otherwise, the output of the masked Sbox (which is not uniform) will appear at the input of the next masked non-linear functions (e.g., the Sbox at the next cipher round), and lead to first-order leakage.

Indeed, the challenge is the realization of the masked Sboxes with high algebraic degree. If $t > 2$, we can apply the same trick used in [32,34], i.e., by decomposing the Sbox into quadratic bijections. In other words, if we can write $S : G \circ F$, where both G and F are bijections with $t = 2$, we are able to implement the first-order TI of F and G with the minimum number of shares $n = 3$. Such a construction needs registers between the masked F and G to isolate the corresponding glitches.

After the decomposition, fulfilling all the TI requirements except *uniformity* is straightforward. As a solution, the authors of [10] proposed to find affine functions A_1 and A_2 in such a way that $F : A_2 \circ Q \circ A_1$. If we are able to represent a uniform sharing of the quadratic function Q, applying A_1 on all input shares, and A_2 on all output shares gives us a uniform sharing of F.

TI of 4-bit Permutations. In [11] the authors analyze 4-bit permutations and identify 302 equivalence classes. In the following, we use the same notation as in [11] to refer to these classes. Out of these 302, six classes are quadratic. These six quadratic functions, whose uniform TI can be achieved by *direct sharing* or with simple *correction terms* (see [11]) are listed in Table 2. We included their minimum area requirements as the basis of our investigations in the next sections. In contrast to the others, Q_{300} also needs to be decomposed for uniform sharing.

2.4   Design Architectures

Due to the high area overhead of threshold implementations (particularly the size of the shared Sbox), serialized architectures are favored, e.g. in [9,31,34,38]. Our main target in this work is a serialized architecture in which one instance of the Sbox is implemented. Furthermore, we focus on byte-wise serial designs due to our underlying 8-bit Sbox target. In such a scenario, the state register forms a shift register, that at each clock cycle shifts the state bytes through the Sbox and makes use of the last Sbox output as feedback. Figure 2 depicts three different architectures which we can consider. Note that extra logic is not shown in this figure, e.g. the multiplexers to enable other operations like ShiftRows.

A shared Sbox with 3 shares should contain registers, e.g., PRESENT [34] and AES [9,31]. As an example, if the shared Sbox contains 4 stages (see Fig. 2(a)) and forms a pipeline, all of the Sbox computations can be done in $n + 3$ clock cycles, with n as the number of state bytes. We refer to this architecture as *raw* in later sections. Note that realizing a pipeline is desirable. Otherwise, the Sbox computations would take $3n + 1$ clock cycles.

As an alternative, we can use the state registers as intermediate registers of the shared Sbox. Figure 2(b) shows the corresponding architecture, where more multiplexers should be integrated to enable the correct operation (as an example in Skinny [4]). In this case, all n shared Sboxes can be computed in n clock cycles. It is noteworthy that such an optimization is not always fully possible if intermediate registers of the shared Sbox are larger than the state registers (e.g., in case of AES [9,31]).

If the Sbox has been constructed by k times iterating a function F, it is possible to significantly reduce the area cost. Figure 2(c) shows an example. Therefore, similar to a raw architecture without pipeline, $(k-1)\,n+1$ clock cycles are required for n Sboxes. This is not efficient in terms of latency, but is favorable for low-throughput applications, where very low area is available and in particular when SCA protection is desired. We refer to this architecture as *iterative*.

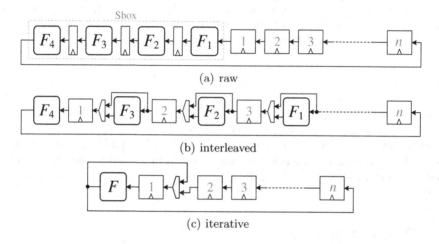

(a) raw

(b) interleaved

(c) iterative

Fig. 2. Different serialized design architectures

3   Threshold Implementation of Known 8-bit Sboxes

Amongst 8-bit Sboxes, the AES TI Sbox has been widely investigated while nothing about the TI of other Sboxes can be found in public literature. The first construction of the AES TI Sbox was reported in [31]. The authors made use of the tower-field approach of Canright [15] and represented the full circuit by quadratic operations. By applying second-order Boolean masking, i.e., three shares as minimum following the TI concept, all operations are independently realized by TI. On the other hand, the interconnection between (and concatenation of) uniform TI functions may violate the uniformity. Therefore, the authors integrated several fresh random masks – known as remasking or applying virtual shares [11] – to maintain the uniformity, in total 48 bits for each full Sbox. Since the AES TI Sbox has been considered for a serialized architecture, the authors formed a 4-stage pipeline design, which also increased the area by 138 registers.

Later in [9] three more efficient variants of the AES TI Sbox were introduced. The authors applied several tricks, e.g., increasing the number of shares to 4 and 5 and reduce them back to 3 in order to relax the fresh randomness requirements. Details of all different designs are listed in Table 1. In short, the most efficient design (called *nimble*) forms a 3-stage pipeline, where 92 extra registers and 32 fresh random bits are required.

CLEFIA. makes use of two 8-bit Sboxes S_0 and S_1. The first one is formed by utilizing four different 4-bit bijections and multiplication by 2 in $GF(2^4)$ defined by polynomial $X^4 + X + 1$. The entire SS_0 : E6CA872FB14059D3[1], SS_1 : 640D2BA39CEF8751, SS_2 : B85EA64CF72310D9, and SS_3 : A26D345E0789BFC1 are cubic and – based on the classification given in [11] – belong to classes C_{210}, C_{163}, C_{160}, and C_{160} respectively. Unfortunately, all these classes are of non-alternating group and cannot be shared with 3 shares, i.e., no solution exists either by decomposition or remasking[2]. We should use at least 4 shares (which is out of our focus), and its uniform sharing with 4 shares also needs to be done in at least 3 stages. Therefore, a 4-share version of TI S_0 can be realized in 6 stages.

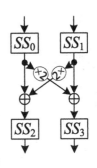

The second one is constructed following the AES Sbox, i.e., inversion in $GF(2^8)$, but with a different primitive polynomial and affine transformations. Based on the observations in [2,36], inversion in one field can be transformed to another field by linear isomorphisms. Therefore, S_1 and the AES Sbox are affine equivalent and all difficulties to realize the AES TI Sbox hold true for S_1.

Crypton V0.5. utilizes two 8-bit Sboxes, S_0 and S_1, in a 3-round Feistel, as shown here. By swapping P_0 and P_2 the Sbox S_0 is converted to its inverse S_1. P_1 : AF4752E693C8D1B0 belongs to the cubic class C_{295}. Similar to the sub functions of CLEFIA, it belongs to the non-alternating group and cannot be shared with 3 shares. In short, at least 4 shares in 3 stages should be used. Further, P_0 : F968994C626A135F and P_2 : 04842F8D11F72BEF are quadratic, non-bijective functions, but that does not necessarily mean that their uniform sharing with 4 shares

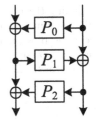

does not exist. We have examined this issue by applying *direct sharing* [11], and we could not find their uniform sharing with either 3 or 4 shares. In this case, remasking is a potential solution. However, due to the underlying Feistel structure of S_0 and S_1, the non-uniformity of the shared P_0 and P_2 does not affect the uniformity of the resulting Sbox as long as the sharing of the *Sbox input* is uniform. More precisely, P_0 output is XORed with the left half of the Sbox input. If the input is uniformly shared, the input of P_1 is uniform regardless of the uniformity of the P_0 output. See [8] and [11], where it is shown that $a \cdot b$

---

[1] In the following we denote functions by a hexadecimal-string in which the first letter denotes the first element of the look-up table implementing the function.

[2] Alternatively, one can apply the technique presented in [24].

Table 1. Criteria for the 8-bit Sboxes

	Diff.	Lin.	Deg.	Iter. #b	AND #c	Unprotected Area [GE] itera.d	raw e	Delay ns	Threshold implementation a Area [GE] itera.d	raw f	Delay ns	Stage #g	Mask #h	Type
AES [19]	4	32	7		32 [13]		236	5.69		4244 [31]		5	48	Inversion
										3708 [9]		3	44	
										3653 [9]		3	44	
										2835 [9]		3	32	
CLEFIA (S0) [39]	10	56	7							4 shares		6	0	SPN
CLEFIA (S1) [39]	4	32	7							like AES		3	32	Inversion
Crypton V0.5 [25]	8	64	5				68	1.76		4 shares		5	0	Feistel
Crypton V1 [26]	10	64	6				111	2.40		4 shares		6	0	SPN
ICEBERG [40]	8	64	7				151	2.39		2115	1.67	9	0	SPN
Fantomas [21]	16	64	5		11		130	2.43		766	1.72	4	0	MISTY
Khazad [3]	8	64	7				154	2.48		2062	1.87	9	0	SPN
Robin [21]	16	64	6	3	12	28	79	2.37	319	1180	1.73	6	0	Feistel
Scream v3 [22]	8	64	6		12		87	2.38		2204	2.00	6	0	Feistel
Whirlpool [37]	8	56	7				146	2.37		2203	2.08	9	0	SPN
SB1	16	64	6	8	16	8	57	1.38	51	1189	1.09	8	0	SPN (BitP)
SB2	16	64	4	2	12	46	99	1.99	253	631	1.70	2	0	SPN (Mat)
SB3	8	60	7	4	24	48	198	3.98	273	1498	2.10	4	0	SPN (Mat)
SB4	8	56	7	5	30	29	140	4.09	202	1507	2.10	5	0	Feistel
SB5	10	60	7	9	27	12	95	3.19	78	1583	1.10	9	0	SPN (BitP)
SB6	10	60	7	4	20	49	174	4.78	226	1247	1.95	4	0	SPN (Mat)

[a] With 3 shares
[b] Number of iterations of a unique function
[c] Number of AND gates, important for masked bit-sliced software implementations
[d] Excluding the required extra logic, e.g., multiplexers and registers
[e] Fully combinatorial
[f] Including pipeline registers
[g] Number of stages in the pipeline
[h] Number of fresh mask bits required for each full Sbox

(AND gate) cannot be uniformly shared with 3 shares, but $a \cdot b + c$ (AND+XOR) can be uniform if a, b, and c are uniformly shared. Therefore, a 4-share version of TI S_0 (resp. S_1) can be realized in 5 stages.

Crypton V1. Sboxes are made of two 4-bit bijections P_0 : FEA1B58D9327064C, P_1 : BAD78E05F634192C and their inverse in addition to a linear layer in between. P_0 and its inverse P_0^{-1} belong to the cubic class $\mathcal{C}_{278}$, which can be uniformly shared with 3 and 4 shares but in 3 stages. Both P_1 and its inverse P_1^{-1} are affine equivalent to the non-alternating cubic class $\mathcal{C}_{295}$, that – as given above – must be shared at least with 4 shares. Therefore, in order to share each Crypton V1 Sbox, 4 shares in a construction with 6 stages should be used.

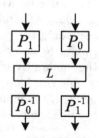

ICEBERG. is formed by two 4-bit bijections S_0 : D7329AC1F45E60B8 and S_1 : 4AFC0D9BE6173582 in a 3-round SPN structure, where permutation P_8 is a bit permutation. Both S_0 and S_1 are affine equivalent to the cubic class $\mathcal{C}_{270}$, which needs at least 3 stages to be uniformly shared with 3 shares. Therefore, a uniform sharing of the ICEBERG Sbox with 3 shares can be realized in 9 stages without any fresh randomness. Amongst the smallest decompositions, we suggest $A_4 \circ \mathcal{Q}_{294} \circ A_3 \circ \mathcal{Q}_{294} \circ A_2 \circ \mathcal{Q}_{294} \circ A_1$ for S_0 with A_1 : B038F47CD65E921A, A_2 : C6824E0AD7935F1B, A_3 : 3DB50E8679F14AC2, A_4 : AC24E860BD35F971, and for S_1 with A_1 : 63EB50D827AF149C, A_2 : D159F37BC048E26A, A_3 : 2AE608C43BF719D5, A_4 : C5814D09E7A36F2B, and $\mathcal{Q}_{294}$: 0123456789BAEFDC.

Fantomas. utilizes one 3-bit bijection S_3 : 03615427 and one 5-bit bijection S_5 : 00, 03, 12, 07, 14, 17, 04, 11, 0C, 0F, 1F, 0B, 19, 1A, 08, 1C, 10, 1D, 02, 1B, 06, 0A, 16, 0E, 1E, 13, 0D, 15, 09, 05, 18, 01 in a 3-round MISTY construction. S_3 is affine equivalent to the quadratic class $\mathcal{Q}_3^3$, which can be uniformly shared with 3 shares in at least 2 stages. As a decomposition, we considered S_3 : $A_3 \circ \mathcal{Q}_1 \circ A_2 \circ \mathcal{Q}_2 \circ A_1$ with A_1 : 07342516, A_2 : 02461357, A_3 : 01235476, $\mathcal{Q}_1$: 01234576, and $\mathcal{Q}_2$: 01234675.

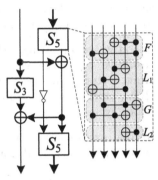

The construction of S_5, as shown here, consists of 4 Toffoli gates and 4 XORs. The quadratic F and G, as well as linear parts L_1 and L_2 are correspondingly marked. Hence, we can decompose S_5 : $L_2 \circ G \circ L_1 \circ F$. The uniform sharing of both F and G can be found by direct sharing. Therefore, the Fantomas Sbox can be uniformly shared with 3 shares in 4 stages, without any fresh mask. Figure 3(a) depicts the block diagram representation, and the area requirements are listed in Table 1. Each Sbox cannot be implemented iteratively, and each Sbox computation has a latency of 4 clock cycles. However, a pipeline design can send out Sbox results in consecutive clock cycles, but with a 4-clock-cycle latency.

Khazad. utilizes the Anubis Sbox, which is also based on a 3-round SPN. Two 4-bit bijections P : 3FE054BCDA967821 and Q : 9E56A23CF04D7B18 in addition to a bit permutation layer form the 8-bit Sbox. Similar to ICEBERG, both P and Q belong to the cubic class $\mathcal{C}_{270}$. Therefore, the uniform sharing of the Khazad (resp. Anubis) Sbox can be realized in 9 stages without fresh masks. For the decomposition, we suggest $A_4 \circ \mathcal{Q}_{294} \circ A_3 \circ \mathcal{Q}_{294} \circ A_2 \circ \mathcal{Q}_{294} \circ A_1$ for P with A_1 : 04C862AE15D973BF, A_2 : A2E680C4B3F791D5, A_3 : 842EA60CB71D953F, A_4 : 80D5C491A2F7E6B3, and for

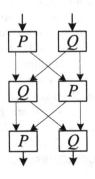

Q with A_1 : 082A3B194C6E7F5D, A_2 : 3FB71D952EA60C84, A_3 : 19D53BF708C42AE6, A_4 : 0B38291A4F7C6D5E.

Robin. is constructed based on the 3-round Feistel, similar to Crypton V0.5, but a single 4-bit bijection S_4 plays the role of all functions P_1, P_2, and P_3. Although the swap of the nibbles in the last Feistel round is omitted, the Robin Sbox is the only known 8-bit Sbox which can be implemented in an iterative fashion. S_4 : 086D5F7C4E2391BA has been taken from [41], known as the Class 13 Sbox. S_4 is affine equivalent to the cubic class C_{223} and, as stated above, can be uniformly shared with 3 shares in 2 stages. As one of the smallest solutions we considered $A_3 \circ Q_{294} \circ A_2 \circ Q_{294} \circ A_1$ with A_1 : AE268C04BF379D15, A_2 : C480A2E6D591B3F7, A_3 : 20A8B93164ECFD75. Therefore, with no extra fresh randomness we can realize uniform sharing of the Robin Sbox with 3 shares in 6 stages.

In order to implement this construction, we have four different options. A block diagram of the design is shown in Fig. 3(b) (the registers filled by the gray color are essential for pipeline designs).

- Iterative, w/o pipeline, each Sbox in 6 clock cycles.
- Iterative, pipeline, each two Sboxes in 6 clock cycles.
- Raw, w/o pipeline, each Sbox in 6 clock cycles.
- Raw, pipeline, each 6 Sboxes in 6 clock cycles, each one with a latency of 6 clock cycles.

Note that extra control logic (such as multiplexers) is required for all iterative designs which is excluded from Fig. 3(b) and Table 1 for the sake of clarity.

Scream V3. is similar to that of Crypton V0.5, i.e., 3-round Feistel. P_0, and P_2 are replaced by two *almost perfect nonlinear* (APN) functions $APN1$: 020B300A1E06A452 and $APN2$: 20B003A0E1604A25, and P_1 by S_1 : 02C75FD64E8931BA. Similar to Crypton V0.5, the two APN functions are not bijective. However, they are cubic rather than quadratic. The source of these two APNs is the construction given in [16]. We can decompose both of them into two quadratic functions as $APN1 : F \circ G$ and $APN2 : F \circ (\oplus 1) \circ G$, with F : 020B30A01E06A425 and G : 0123457689ABCDFE. By $(\oplus 1)$ we represent an identity followed by XOR with constant 1, i.e., flipping the least significant bit. Uniform sharing of G with 3 shares can be easily achieved by direct sharing. F, however, cannot be easily shared. F consists of three 2-input AND gates which directly give three output bits. To the best of our knowledge, F cannot be uniformly shared without applying remasking. However, as stated for Crypton V0.5, the non-uniformity of F (in general $APN1$ and $APN2$) does not play any role if S_1 is uniformly shared.

S_1 is affine equivalent to the cubic class C_{223} which can be uniformly shared in 2 stages with 3 shares. Therefore, the Scream V3 Sbox can be shared by 3 shares in 6 stages, without any fresh random masks. There are many options to decompose S_1; as one of the smallest solutions we suggest S_1 : $A_3 \circ Q_{294} \circ A_2 \circ Q_{294} \circ A_1$ with A_1 : 26AE159D37BF048C, A_2 : 4C086E2A5D197F3B, A_3 : 082A3B194C6E7F5D.

Whirlpool. employs three different 4-bit bijections E, E^{-1} and R in a customized SPN. E : 1B9CD6F3E874A250 and its inverse are affine equivalent to the cubic class $\mathcal{C}_{278}$, which can be uniformly shared with 3 shares in at least 3 stages. R : 7CBDE49F638A2510 also belongs to the cubic class $\mathcal{C}_{270}$. As given for ICE-BERG and Khazad, $\mathcal{C}_{270}$ needs 3 stages for a uniform sharing with 3 shares. Hence, the entire Whirlpool Sbox can be uniformly shared with 3 shares in 9 stages, without any extra randomness. The decomposition of R is similar to that of Khazad, i.e., R : $A_4 \circ \mathcal{Q}_{294} \circ A_3 \circ \mathcal{Q}_{294} \circ A_2 \circ \mathcal{Q}_{294} \circ A_1$ with A_1 : 02138A9BCEDF4657, A_2 : 0C48A6E21D59B7F3, A_3 : C509E72BD418F63A, A_4 : 0A1B4E5F28396C7D. However, the decomposition of E and E^{-1} are more costly. One of the cheapest solutions is $A_4 \circ \mathcal{Q}_{294} \circ A_3 \circ \mathcal{Q}_{293} \circ A_2 \circ \mathcal{Q}_{294} \circ A_1$ for E with A_1 : 048CAE2673FBD951, A_2 : 80C4B3F7A2E691D5, A_3 : 0B834FC71A925ED6, A_4 : 014589CD2367ABEF, and for E^{-1} with A_1 : A2F76E3B80D54C19, A_2 : A280E6C4B391F7D5, A_3 : 95F31D7B84E20C6A, A_4 : 2736AFBE05148D9C, and $\mathcal{Q}_{293}$: 0123457689CDEFBA.

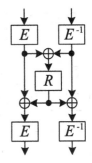

Due to their required minimum 4 shares, except for CLEFIA, Crypton V0.5, and Crypton V1, we have implemented TI for all the aforementioned Sboxes, and have given their area requirements as well as the number of stages (clock cycles) in Table 1. For the synthesis, we used Synopsys Design Compiler with the UMC-L18G212T3 [42] ASIC standard cell library, i.e., UMC 0.18μm technology node. It is noteworthy that amongst all the Sboxes we covered, the Robin Sbox is the only one which can be iteratively implemented. We should also emphasize that Midori [1] and Skinny [4] (in their 128-bit versions) make use of 8-bit Sboxes. Midori 8-bit Sboxes are made by concatenating two 4-bit Sboxes and the Skinny one by four times iterating an 8-bit quadratic bijection. In both cases their differential and linear properties are 64 and 128 respectively, which are notably less compared to the strong 8-bit Sboxes listed in Table 1. Therefore, we did not consider them in our investigations.

Table 2. Performance figures of 4×4 quadratic bijections with respect to their TI cost

	Table	Area [GE]	# of stages
$\mathcal{Q}_4^4$	0123456789ABDCFE	27	1
$\mathcal{Q}_{12}^4$	0123456789CDEFAB	63	1
$\mathcal{Q}_{293}^4$	0123457689CDEFBA	84	1
$\mathcal{Q}_{294}^4$	0123456789BAEFDC	51	1
$\mathcal{Q}_{299}^4$	012345678ACEB9FD	114	1
$\mathcal{Q}_{300}^4$	0123458967CDEFAB	151	2 ($\mathcal{Q}_{12} \circ \mathcal{Q}_4$)

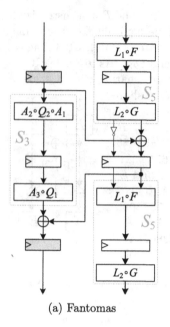

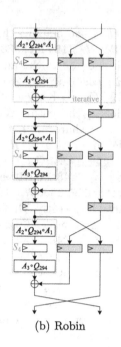

(a) Fantomas   (b) Robin

Fig. 3. Threshold implementation of Robin and Fantomas Sboxes, each signal represents 3 shares, the gray registers for pipeline variants

4   Finding TI-Compliant 8-bit Sboxes

Our goal is to find strong 8-bit Sboxes which can be efficiently implemented as threshold implementations. To this end, we incorporate the idea of building an 8-bit Sbox from smaller Sboxes in our search. In particular we aim to construct a round function that can be easily shared and iterated to generate a cryptographically strong Sbox. Easily shareable in our context refers to functions for which an efficient uniform shared representation is known. Thus, if we find a function with these properties, the resulting sequence of round functions will be a good cryptographic Sbox which can be efficiently masked. As done previously, we concentrate on the three basic constructions mentioned above: Feistel, SPN, and MISTY. As the number of possible choices for SPN is too large for an exhaustive search, we focus on two special cases for the linear layer of the SP-network. First, instead of allowing general linear layers we focus on bit-permutations only. Those have the additional advantage of being basically for free, both in hardware and in a (bitsliced) software implementation. Second, we focus on linear layers which correspond to matrix multiplications over $\mathbb{F}_{16}$. Those cover the MISTY construction as a special case.

In all cases, the building blocks for our round function are 4-bit Sboxes. As described in Sect. 2, those Sboxes are well-analyzed and understood regarding both their threshold implementation [11] and their cryptographic properties. To minimize the number of required shares, we mainly consider functions with a maximum degree of two. Additional shares, otherwise, may increase the area or randomness requirements for the whole circuit. In [11], six main quadratic permutation classes are identified which are listed in Table 2. All existing quadratic 4-bit permutations are affine equivalent to one of those six. However, it should be noted that permutations of class $\mathcal{Q}_{300}^4$ cannot be easily shared with three shares without decomposition or additional randomness. Therefore, we mainly focus on the other classes from our search. Note that we include the identity function $\mathcal{A}_0^4$ in the case of the SPN construction. Since the identity function does not require any area, round functions based on a combination of identity and one quadratic 4-bit permutation can result in very lightweight designs.

One important difference to all previous constructions listed in Table 1 is that we do consider higher number of iterations for our constructions. This is motivated by two observations. First, it might allow to improve upon the cryptographic criteria and second it might be beneficial to actually use a simpler round function, in particular those that can be implemented in one stage, more often than a more complicated round function with a smaller number of iterations. As can be seen in Table 1 this approach of increasing the number of iterations is quite successful in many cases.

Next we describe in detail the search for good Sboxes for each of the three constructions we considered.

4.1 Feistel-Construction

As a first construction, we examine round functions using a Feistel-network similar to Fig. 1(a). By the basic approach described below, we were able to exhaustively investigate all possible constructions based on any 4-bit to 4-bit function for any number of iterations between 1 and 5. This can be seen as an extension (in the case of $n = 4$ and for identical round functions) to the results given in [16] where up to 3 rounds have been studied.

However, such an exhaustive search is not possible in a naive way. As there are 2^{64} 4-bit functions and checking the cryptographic criteria of an n-bit Sbox requires roughly 2^{2n} basic operations, a naive approach would need more than 2^{80} operations.

Fortunately, this task can be accelerated by exploiting the distinct structure of Feistel-networks while still covering the entire search space.

We recall the definition of a Feistel round for the function $F : \mathbb{F}_2^n \to \mathbb{F}_2^n$:

$$\text{Feistel}_F^1 : \mathbb{F}_2^n \times \mathbb{F}_2^n \to \mathbb{F}_2^n \times \mathbb{F}_2^n, \qquad (L, R) \mapsto (R \oplus F(L), L).$$

We denote by Feistel_F^n the nth functional power of Feistel_F^1, i.e.,

$$\text{Feistel}_F^n = \text{Feistel}_F^1 \circ \text{Feistel}_F^1 \circ \cdots \circ \text{Feistel}_F^1 \, .$$

To reduce the search space, we show below that if $G = A \circ F \circ A^{-1}$ for an invertible affine function A, then Feistel_F^n is affine equivalent to Feistel_G^n.

Thus, we can reduce our search space from all 2^{64} functions, to roughly XY functions. Indeed, Brinkmann classified all 4 to 4 bit functions up to extended affine equivalence [14]. There are 4713 equivalence classes up to extended affine equivalence. Now, with the results given in the full version of the paper [12], it is enough to consider all functions of the form $A_1 \circ F + C$, where A_1 is an affine permutation and C is any linear mapping on 4 bits. As $\text{Feistel}^n_{A_1 \circ F \circ A_2 + C'}$ is affine equivalent to the function $\text{Feistel}^n_{A_2 \circ A_1 \circ F \circ A_2 \circ A_2^{-1} + C' \circ A_2^{-1}} = \text{Feistel}^n_{A_2 \circ A_1 \circ F + C'}$, this will exhaust all possibilities up to affine equivalence. Doing so, we reduce the search space to:

$$\#Sboxes = 4713 \cdot 2^4 \cdot |\text{GL}(2,4)| \cdot 2^{16} \simeq 2^{46.50}. \tag{1}$$

As this is still a large search space, we emplyed GPUs to tackle this task.

4.2   SPN-Construction with Bit-Permutations as the Linear Layer

In addition to Feistel-networks, we examined round functions which are similar to Fig. 1(c). However, $\mathcal{A}$ is replaced by an XOR with a constant followed by an 8-bit permutation. Depending on F_1 and F_2, this construction can lead to very lightweight round functions since constant addition and simple bit permutations are very efficient in hardware circuits. For F_1 and F_2 we consider the five quadratic permutations (listed in Table 2) as well as the identity function (denoted by $\mathcal{A}_0^4$). Obviously, we exclude the combination $F_1 = F_2 = \mathcal{A}_0^4$. There are 8! different 8-bit permutations and 256 possibilities for the constant addition. If we looked for all combinations of all affine equivalents of the chosen functions, we would have to test

$$\#Sboxes = 256 \cdot 8! \cdot 35 \cdot 322560^4 \cdot 10 \simeq 2^{105} \tag{2}$$

Sboxes. This is clearly not feasible. Therefore, we decide to restrict the number of possibilities for each of the two functions. In particular, we only consider the representative for each class as presented in [11] without affine equivalents. This reduces the search space to

$$\#Sboxes = 256 \cdot 8! \cdot 35 \cdot 10 \simeq 2^{32}, \tag{3}$$

which can be completely processed.

Similar to the Feistel-network, it is possible to further reduce the complexity of the search. To this end, we first define the round function for this type of Sbox as

$$\text{BitPerm}^1_{F_1,F_2,C,P} : \mathbb{F}_2^n \times \mathbb{F}_2^n \to \mathbb{F}_2^{2n}$$
$$(L,R) \mapsto P\big((F_1(L)\|F_2(R)) \oplus C \big),$$

where $\|$ denotes the concatenation of the two parts. Furthermore, it can be trivially seen that for every combination of an 8-bit permutation P_1 and an 8-bit constant C_1 there exist a complementary combination of an 8-bit permutation P_2 and an 8-bit constant C_2 with

$$P_1\big((L\|R)\oplus C_1\big) = P_2\big((R\|L)\oplus C_2\big), \quad \forall\ R, L \in \mathbb{F}_2^n.$$

Thus, the search can be speeded up since $\mathrm{BitPerm}^1_{F_1,F_2,C_1,P_1}$ is the same as $\mathrm{BitPerm}^1_{F_2,F_1,C_2,P_2}$. Therefore, we only need to check

$$\#Sboxes = 256 \cdot 8! \cdot 20 \cdot 10 \simeq 2^{31} \tag{4}$$

Sboxes for this type of round function.

4.3   SPN-Construction with $\mathbb{F}_{16}$-linear Layers only

For the last type of construction, we consider another special case of the construction depicted in Fig. 1(c). Here we restrict ourselves to the case where $\mathcal{A}$ corresponds to a multiplication with a 2×2 matrix with elements from $\mathbb{F}_{16}$. Additionally, a constant is again added to the outputs of F_1 and F_2. As noted before, a special case of this construction is the MISTY technique.

For F_1 and F_2 we consider the five quadratic functions and the identity function. Just like for the bit permutation round function, it is not feasible to check all affine equivalents. Therefore, we limit our search to these functions. The field multiplication is performed with the commonly used polynomial $X^4 + X + 1$ [23]. Given that the matrix needs to be invertible and provide some form of mixture between the two halves, this leaves us with 61200 possibilities for the matrix multiplication. It is further possible to apply the same optimization as for permutation-based round functions. Therefore, we need to check

$$\#Sboxes = 256 \cdot 61200 \cdot 20 \cdot 10 \simeq 2^{31.5} \tag{5}$$

Sboxes for this type of round function.

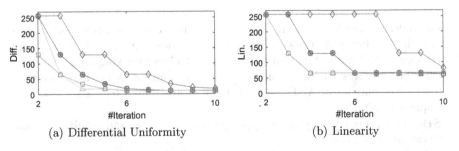

(a) Differential Uniformity   (b) Linearity

Fig. 4. The smallest achievable differential uniformity and linearity for each number of iterations for round functions with $\mathbb{F}_{16}$-linear layers and $F_1 = \mathcal{A}_0^4$ and $(\diamond)F_2 = \mathcal{Q}_4^4$, $(*)F_2 = \mathcal{Q}_{12}^4$, $(\triangle)F_2 = \mathcal{Q}_{293}^4$, $(\circ)F_2 = \mathcal{Q}_{294}^4$, $(\square)F_2 = \mathcal{Q}_{299}^4$.

5   Results

We completed the search for the three aforementioned types of round functions with up to ten iterations.

The search for Feistel-networks for all 4713 classes takes around two weeks on a machine with four NVIDIA K80s for a specific set of parameters. In particular, the performance depends on the bounds defined by cryptographic properties (differential uniformity) as well as the iteration count of the network. Note that, with respect to cryptographic criteria, our search shows that for iterations ≤ 5 *no 8-bit balanced Feistel with identical round functions* can have a linearity below 56 *and* a differential uniformity below 8.

Furthermore, the search for SPNs with bit permutations (resp. with $\mathbb{F}_{16}$-linear layer) required around 48 h (resp. 54 h) on one Intel Xeon CPU with 12 cores. It was possible to detect some very basic relations between the security, number of iterations and area of the Sbox. Figure 4 shows the smallest differential uniformity and linearity values which can be achieved for a specific number of iterations using a round function based on the $\mathbb{F}_{16}$-linear layer with constant addition. As expected, the more iterations are applied, the higher resistance against linear and differential cryptanalysis could be achieved. The size of each of the considered quadratic permutations is given in Table 2. Bigger functions like $\mathcal{Q}_{293}^4$ and $\mathcal{Q}_{299}^4$ achieve good cryptographic properties with fewer iterations than smaller functions like $\mathcal{Q}_4^4$. For the other combinations of (F_1, F_2) and types of round functions the graphs behave similarly. Depending on the remaining layers of the cipher and the targeted use case, a designer needs to find a good balance between the parameters. In the following, we present a few selected Sboxes optimized for different types of applications.

In our evaluation, we only consider Sboxes with differential uniformity at most 16 and linearity of at most 64. These are the worst properties between the observed constructed 8-bit Sboxes in Table 1. From the cryptographic standpoint, our Sboxes should not be inferior to these functions. We identified the following strong Sboxes that cover the most important scenarios.

- $\mathbf{SB}_1$: This Sbox possesses a very small round function. In a serial design the round function is usually implemented only once to save area.
- $\mathbf{SB}_2$: This Sbox is selected to enable an efficient implementation in a round-based design. For this not only the size of the round function is important but also the number of iterations. Additional iterations require additional instantiations of the round function with a dedicated register stage. Furthermore, this Sbox requires the least number of iterations and can be implemented with a very low number of AND gates. Thus, it is also suited to masked software implementations.
- $\mathbf{SB}_3$: This Sbox has very good cryptographic properties and requires one less iteration than $\mathbf{SB}_4$.
- $\mathbf{SB}_4$: This Sbox has very good cryptographic properties.
- $\mathbf{SB}_5$: This Sbox is similar to $\mathbf{SB}_1$ which has a small round function. However, it trades area for better cryptographic properties.

– $\mathbf{SB}_6$: This Sbox is similar to $\mathbf{SB}_2$ that is optimized for raw implementations. However, it trades area for better cryptographic properties.

5.1   Selected Sboxes

In this section, we supply the necessary information to implement the selected Sboxes. For this, we first recall the basic structure of the round functions. Table 1 shows that our selected round functions consists of bit permutations and $\mathbb{F}_{16}$-linear layers. The structure of both types is similar to Fig. 1(c). We denote the most (resp. least) significant four bits as L (resp. R). The round function $Round$: $\mathbb{F}_2^4 \times \mathbb{F}_2^4 \mapsto \mathbb{F}_2^8$ is then defined as

$$\text{Round}(L, R) = P\big((F_1(L)\|F_2(R)) \oplus C\big),$$

where C is an 8-bit constant and $P(.)$ denotes either an 8-bit permutation or an $\mathbb{F}_{16}$-linear layer. In Table 3, we describe a specific bit permutation with an eight-element vector where each element denotes the new bit position, e.g., no permutation is 01234567 whereas complete reversal is 76543210. The $\mathbb{F}_{16}$-linear layer is realized as a multiplication with a 2×2 matrix with elements in $\mathbb{F}_{16}$. Let us denote the most (resp. least) significant four input bits to the matrix multiplication as L_M (resp. R_M). The multiplication is then defined as

$$\text{MatMul}(L_M, R_M) = (E_1 \cdot L_M \oplus E_2 \cdot R_M \| E_3 \cdot L_M \oplus E_4 \cdot R_M),$$

where $E_1, E_2, E_3, E_4 \in \mathbb{F}_{16}$ are the elements of the chosen matrix. To describe the linear layers of our Sboxes we give the specific $[E_1, E_2, E_3, E_4]$ for each matrix in Table 3.

These parameters combined with the number of iterations enable the realizations of each Sbox. To increase efficiency of the TI the constant is added to only one of the shares. In some cases, the area of the design can be reduced by adding a particular constant to the two remaining shares. This is based on the fact that an additional NOT gate can turn e.g., an AND gate to a smaller NAND gate [35]. The following linear layer still needs to be applied to all shares. Table 3 contains this condensed description of the selected Sboxes. Further details for each of them can be found in the full version of the paper [12].

For $\mathbf{SB}_4$, since it uses a Feistel-network, we construct the Sbox using the round function $H(x) = G(F(x)) \oplus A(x)$, where F is taken from the 4713 equivalence classes; G and A represent the linear and affine parts respectively. H, F, G and A are all 4-bit to 4-bit functions. The full definition of the round is then simply $(L, R) \mapsto (R \oplus H(L), L)$.

5.2   Comparison

Table 1 gives an overview of our results and we summarize the most important observations in the following. The first observation is that our proposed designs do not require fresh mask bits to achieve uniformity. This is an improvement over

Table 3. Specifics of the selected Sboxes.

	F_1	F_2	Const. (Hex)	Parameter	Type	Iterations
SB_1	$\mathcal{A}_0^4$	$\mathcal{Q}_{294}^4$	04	62750413	Perm.	8
SB_2	$\mathcal{Q}_{293}^4$	$\mathcal{Q}_{293}^4$	EE	[2, 4, 4, 2]	Matrix	2
SB_3	$\mathcal{Q}_{293}^4$	$\mathcal{Q}_{299}^4$	6C	[2, 2, 3, 11]	Matrix	4
SB_5	$\mathcal{Q}_4^4$	$\mathcal{Q}_{294}^4$	85	20647135	Perm.	9
SB_6	$\mathcal{Q}_{293}^4$	$\mathcal{Q}_{294}^4$	F8	[0, 5, 13, 15]	Matrix	4

	F	G	A	Type	Iterations
SB_4	0001024704638EAD	028A9B1346CEDF57	6273627351405140	Feistel	5

all TI types of the AES Sbox and some other Sboxes from Table 1. They need up to 64 bits of randomness for one full Sbox. Given that modern ciphers usually include multiple rounds with many Sboxes, this can add up to a significant amount of randomness which needs to be generated.

Furthermore, all of our proposed Sboxes can be implemented iteratively. This comes with the advantage that even the more complex designs, e.g., SB_4 and SB_5, can be realized with very few gates depending on the design architecture. From all the other Sboxes in Table 1 this is only possible for Robin and its round function requires more area than any of our proposed Sboxes.

In particular, SB_1 and SB_2 require the least area in their respective target architectures (i.e., iterative and raw) out of all considered 8-bit Sboxes. The difference for the iterative architecture is especially large where SB_1 needs roughly six times less area than the Robin Sbox.

SB_2 requires the least number of stages. Additionally, it requires only 12 AND gates for the whole Sbox which is very close to the best number, i.e., 11 for Fantomas. This is an advantage for masked bit-sliced implementations making SB_2 suitable for software and hardware designs. A more detailed discussion of this aspect is given in the full version of the paper [12].

As expected, we did not find any Sbox with better cryptographic properties than the AES Sbox. However, SB_3 and SB_4 can still provide better resistance against cryptanalysis attacks than most of the other considered Sboxes. This comes at the cost of an increased area for the raw implementations. Nevertheless, the required area is still smaller than any AES TI and their round function is still smaller than Robin for iterative designs.

As depicted in Fig. 4, a trade-off between resources and cryptographic properties is possible. If SB_1 and SB_2 do not provide the desired level of security and SB_3 and SB_4 are too large, SB_5 and SB_6 might be the best solution. Their cryptographic properties are still better or equal than the competitors while the area is significantly smaller than SB_3 and SB_4. For the sake of completeness, we included the area requirement of the unprotected implementation as well as the latency of different designs in Table 1.

Decryption usually requires the inverse of the Sbox. Therefore, it is important that the Sbox inverse has comparably good properties to the original Sbox. For SB_4 this is obvious since the Feistel-structure makes it straightforward to construct the inverse. Therefore, inverse SB_4 has exactly the same properties as SB_4. For the other cases, this is not trivial. Nevertheless, the inverse of each of our-considered quadratic functions is self-affine equivalent. For more information the interested reader is referred to the full version of the paper [12].

6 Conclusion and Future Work

In this work we identified a set of six 8-bit S-boxes with highly useful properties using a systematic search on a range of composite Sbox constructions. Our findings include 8-bit Sboxes that provide comparable or even higher resistance against linear and differential cryptanalysis with respect to other 8-bit Sbox but intrinsically support the TI concept without any external randomness. At the same time our selected Sboxes come with a range of useful implementation properties, such as a highly efficient serialization option, or a very low area requirement. Future work comprises extended criteria for the Sbox composition, including diffusion layers beyond permutations.

Acknowledgements. This work is partly supported by the DFG Research Training Group GRK 1817 Ubicrypt and the European Union's Horizon 2020 research and innovation programme under grant agreement No. 643161 (ECRYPT-NET).

References

1. Banik, S., Bogdanov, A., Isobe, T., Shibutani, K., Hiwatari, H., Akishita, T., Regazzoni, F.: Midori: a block cipher for low energy. In: Iwata, T., et al. (eds.) ASIACRYPT 2015. LNCS, vol. 9453, pp. 411–436. Springer, Heidelberg (2015). doi:10.1007/978-3-662-48800-3_17

2. Barkan, E., Biham, E.: In how many ways can you write Rijndael? In: Zheng, Y. (ed.) ASIACRYPT 2002. LNCS, vol. 2501, pp. 160–175. Springer, Heidelberg (2002)

3. Barreto, P.S.L.M., Rijmen, V.: The Khazad legacy-level block cipher. Primitive Submitted to NESSIE, 97 (2000)

4. Beierle, C., Jean, J., Kölbl, S., Leander, G., Moradi, A., Thomas Peyrin, Y., Sasaki, P.S., Sim, S.M.: The Skinny family of block ciphers and its low-latency variant mantis. CRYPTO 2016. LNCS. Springer, Berlin (2016). (to appear)

5. Biham, E., Shamir, A.: Differential cryptanalysis of DES-like cryptosystems. In: Menezes, A., Vanstone, S.A. (eds.) CRYPTO 1990. LNCS, vol. 537, pp. 2–21. Springer, Heidelberg (1991)

6. Bilgin, B., Bogdanov, A., Knežević, M., Mendel, F., Wang, Q.: FIDES: lightweight authenticated cipher with side-channel resistance for constrained hardware. In: Bertoni, G., Coron, J.-S. (eds.) CHES 2013. LNCS, vol. 8086, pp. 142–158. Springer, Heidelberg (2013)

7. Bilgin, B., Gierlichs, B., Nikova, S., Nikov, V., Rijmen, V.: A more efficient AES threshold implementation. In: Pointcheval, D., Vergnaud, D. (eds.) AFRICACRYPT. LNCS, vol. 8469, pp. 267–284. Springer, Heidelberg (2014)
8. Bilgin, B., Gierlichs, B., Nikova, S., Nikov, V., Rijmen, V.: Higher-order threshold implementations. In: Sarkar, P., Iwata, T. (eds.) ASIACRYPT 2014, Part II. LNCS, vol. 8874, pp. 326–343. Springer, Heidelberg (2014)
9. Bilgin, B., Gierlichs, B., Nikova, S., Nikov, V., Rijmen, V.: Trade-offs for threshold implementations illustrated on AES. IEEE Trans. CAD Integr. Circ. Syst. **34**(7), 1188–1200 (2015)
10. Bilgin, B., Nikova, S., Nikov, V., Rijmen, V., Stütz, G.: Threshold implementations of all 3×3 and 4×4 S-boxes. In: Prouff, E., Schaumont, P. (eds.) CHES 2012. LNCS, vol. 7428, pp. 76–91. Springer, Heidelberg (2012)
11. Bilgin, B., Nikova, S., Nikov, V., Rijmen, V., Tokareva, N., Vitkup, V.: Threshold implementations of small S-boxes. Cryptogr. Commun. **7**(1), 3–33 (2015)
12. Boss, E., Grosso, V., Güneysu, T., Leander, G., Moradi, A., Schneider, T.: Strong 8-bit Sboxes with efficient masking in hardware. Cryptology ePrint Archive, Report 2016/647 (2016). http://eprint.iacr.org/2016/647
13. Boyar, J., Peralta, R.: A new combinational logic minimization technique with applications to cryptology. In: Festa, P. (ed.) SEA 2010. LNCS, vol. 6049, pp. 178–189. Springer, Heidelberg (2010)
14. Brinkmann, M.: EA classification of all 4 bit functions. Personal Communication (2008)
15. Canright, D.: A very compact S-box for AES. In: Rao, J.R., Sunar, B. (eds.) CHES 2005. LNCS, vol. 3659, pp. 441–455. Springer, Heidelberg (2005)
16. Canteaut, A., Duval, S., Leurent, G.: Construction of lightweight S-boxes using Feistel and MISTY structures. In: Dunkelman, O., et al. (eds.) SAC 2015. LNCS, vol. 9566, pp. 373–393. Springer, Heidelberg (2016). doi:10.1007/978-3-319-31301-6_22
17. Chabaud, F., Vaudenay, S.: Links between differential and linear cryptanalysis. In: De Santis, A. (ed.) EUROCRYPT 1994. LNCS, vol. 950, pp. 356–365. Springer, Heidelberg (1995)
18. Daemen, J., Peeters, M., Van Assche, G., Rijmen, V.: Nessie proposal: NOEKEON. In: 1st Open NESSIE Workshop, pp. 213–230 (2000)
19. Daemen, J., Rijmen, V.: The Design of Rijndael: AES - The Advanced Encryption Standard. Information Security and Cryptography. Springer, Berlin (2002)
20. Gérard, B., Grosso, V., Naya-Plasencia, M., Standaert, F.-X.: Block ciphers that are easier to mask: how far can we go? In: Bertoni, G., Coron, J.-S. (eds.) CHES 2013. LNCS, vol. 8086, pp. 383–399. Springer, Heidelberg (2013)
21. Grosso, V., Leurent, G., Standaert, F.-X., Varıcı, K.: LS-designs: bitslice encryption for efficient masked software implementations. In: Cid, C., Rechberger, C. (eds.) FSE 2014. LNCS, vol. 8540, pp. 18–37. Springer, Heidelberg (2015)
22. Grosso, V., Leurent, G., Standaert, F.-X., Varici, K., Journault, A., Durvaux, F., Gaspar, L., Kerckhof, S.: SCREAM side-channel resistant authenticated encryption with masking - Version 3. Submission to CAESAR Competition of Authenticated Ciphers. https://competitions.cr.yp.to/round2/screamv3.pdf
23. Guo, J., Peyrin, T., Poschmann, A., Robshaw, M.: The LED block cipher. In: Preneel, B., Takagi, T. (eds.) CHES 2011. LNCS, vol. 6917, pp. 326–341. Springer, Heidelberg (2011)
24. Kutzner, S., Nguyen, P.H., Poschmann, A.: Enabling 3-share threshold implementations for all 4-bit S-boxes. In: Lee, H.-S., Han, D.-G. (eds.) ICISC 2013. LNCS, vol. 8565, pp. 91–108. Springer, Heidelberg (2014)

25. Lim, C.H.: CRYPTON: a new 128-bit block cipher - specification and analysis. NIST AES Proposal (1998)
26. Lim, C.H.: A revised version of CRYPTON - CRYPTON V1.0. In: Knudsen, L.R. (ed.) FSE 1999. LNCS, vol. 1636, pp. 31–45. Springer, Heidelberg (1999)
27. Mangard, S., Pramstaller, N., Oswald, E.: Successfully attacking masked AES hardware implementations. In: Rao, J.R., Sunar, B. (eds.) CHES 2005. LNCS, vol. 3659, pp. 157–171. Springer, Heidelberg (2005)
28. Matsui, M.: Linear cryptanalysis method for DES cipher. In: Helleseth, T. (ed.) EUROCRYPT 1993. LNCS, vol. 765, pp. 386–397. Springer, Heidelberg (1994)
29. Matsui, M.: New block encryption algorithm MISTY. In: Biham, E. (ed.) FSE 1997. LNCS, vol. 1267, pp. 54–68. Springer, Heidelberg (1997)
30. Moradi, A., Mischke, O., Eisenbarth, T.: Correlation-enhanced power analysis collision attack. In: Mangard, S., Standaert, F.-X. (eds.) CHES 2010. LNCS, vol. 6225, pp. 125–139. Springer, Heidelberg (2010)
31. Moradi, A., Poschmann, A., Ling, S., Paar, C., Wang, H.: Pushing the limits: a very compact and a threshold implementation of AES. In: Paterson, K.G. (ed.) EUROCRYPT 2011. LNCS, vol. 6632, pp. 69–88. Springer, Heidelberg (2011)
32. Nikova, S., Rijmen, V., Schläffer, M.: Secure hardware implementation of nonlinear functions in the presence of glitches. J. Cryptol. 24(2), 292–321 (2011)
33. Piret, G., Roche, T., Carlet, C.: PICARO – a block cipher allowing efficient higher-order side-channel resistance. In: Bao, F., Samarati, P., Zhou, J. (eds.) ACNS 2012. LNCS, vol. 7341, pp. 311–328. Springer, Heidelberg (2012)
34. Poschmann, A., Moradi, A., Khoo, K., Lim, C.-W., Wang, H., Ling, S.: Side-channel resistant crypto for less than 2,300 GE. J. Cryptol. 24(2), 322–345 (2011)
35. Poschmann, A.Y.: Lightweight cryptography: cryptographic engineering for a pervasive world. Ph.D. thesis, Ruhr University Bochum (2009)
36. Raddum, H.: More dual Rijndaels. In: Dobbertin, H., Rijmen, V., Sowa, A. (eds.) AES 2005. LNCS, vol. 3373, pp. 142–147. Springer, Heidelberg (2005)
37. Rijmen, V., Barreto, P.S.L.M.: The WHIRLPOOL hash function. World-Wide Web document, p. 72 (2001)
38. Shahverdi, A., Taha, M., Eisenbarth, T.: Silent simon: a threshold implementation under 100 slices. In: HOST 2015, pp. 1–6. IEEE (2015)
39. Shirai, T., Shibutani, K., Akishita, T., Moriai, S., Iwata, T.: The 128-bit blockcipher CLEFIA (extended abstract). In: Biryukov, A. (ed.) FSE 2007. LNCS, vol. 4593, pp. 181–195. Springer, Heidelberg (2007)
40. Standaert, F.-X., Piret, G., Rouvroy, G., Quisquater, J.-J., Legat, J.-D.: ICEBERG: an involutional cipher efficient for block encryption in reconfigurable hardware. In: Roy, B., Meier, W. (eds.) FSE 2004. LNCS, vol. 3017, pp. 279–299. Springer, Heidelberg (2004)
41. Ullrich, M., De Cannière, C., Indesteege, S., Küçük, Ö., Mouha, N., Preneel, B.: Finding optimal bitsliced implementations of 4 × 4-bit S-boxes. In: Symmetric Key Encryption Workshop, p. 20 (2011)
42. Virtual Silicon Inc.: 0.18 μm VIP Standard Cell Library Tape Out Ready, Part Number: UMCL18G212T3, Process: UMC Logic 0.18 μm Generic II Technology: 0.18 μm, July 2004

Masking AES with $d + 1$ Shares in Hardware

Thomas De Cnudde[1]([✉]), Oscar Reparaz[1], Begül Bilgin[1], Svetla Nikova[1],
Ventzislav Nikov[2], and Vincent Rijmen[1]

[1] KU Leuven, ESAT-COSIC and iMinds, Leuven, Belgium
{thomas.decnudde,oscar.reparaz,begul.bilgin,svetla.nikova,
vincent.rijmen}@esat.kuleuven.be
[2] NXP Semiconductors, Leuven, Belgium
venci.nikov@gmail.com

Abstract. Masking requires splitting sensitive variables into at least
$d + 1$ shares to provide security against DPA attacks at order d. To this
date, this minimal number has only been deployed in software implementations of cryptographic algorithms and in the linear parts of their
hardware counterparts. So far there is no hardware construction that
achieves this lower bound if the function is nonlinear and the underlying
logic gates can glitch. In this paper, we give practical implementations
of the AES using $d + 1$ shares aiming at first- and second-order security
even in the presence of glitches. To achieve this, we follow the conditions presented by Reparaz et al. at CRYPTO 2015 to allow hardware
masking schemes, like Threshold Implementations, to provide theoretical higher-order security with $d + 1$ shares. The decrease in number of
shares has a direct impact in the area requirements: our second-order
DPA resistant core is the smallest in area so far, and its S-box is 50 %
smaller than the current smallest Threshold Implementation of the AES
S-box with similar security and attacker model. We assess the security
of our masked cores by practical side-channel evaluations. The security
guarantees are met with 100 million traces.

Keywords: AES · DPA · Masking · Threshold implementation

1 Introduction

When cryptography is naively deployed in embedded devices, secrets can leak
through side-channel information such as instantaneous power consumption,
electromagnetic emanations or timing of the device. Ever since attacks based
on side-channels were discovered and investigated [3,17,18], several studies have
been performed to counter the exploitation of these vulnerabilities.

A popular way to strengthen cryptographic implementations against such
physical cryptographic attacks is masking [10]. It randomizes the internal computation and hence detaches the side-channel information from the secret-dependent
intermediate values. Masking is both provable secure [10,23] and practical. Masking has been shown to increase the difficulty of mounting side-channel attacks on
a wide range of cryptographic algorithms.

© International Association for Cryptologic Research 2016
B. Gierlichs and A.Y. Poschmann (Eds.): CHES 2016, LNCS 9813, pp. 194–212, 2016.
DOI: 10.1007/978-3-662-53140-2_10

The basic principle of masking is to split each sensitive intermediate variable of the cryptographic algorithm into multiple shares using secret sharing, and to perform computations on these shares. From the moment that the input is split until the shared output of the cryptographic algorithm is released, shares of the sensitive intermediate variables are never combined in a way that these variables are unmasked, i.e. the unshared sensitive variables are never revealed. Only after the calculation has finished, the shared output is reconstructed to disclose its unmasked value.

Masking is not unconditionally secure. A dth-order masked implementation can be broken by a $(d+1)^{\mathrm{th}}$-order DPA attack. However, attacks of higher orders are more difficult to carry out in practice due to the exponential increase in number of measurements needed, so one typically guarantees only security up to a certain order. We use the standard convention that a dth-order attack exploits the dth-order statistical moment. This covers both univariate and multivariate attacks.

Although provable secure, masking is in practice often not straightforward to implement securely. In hardware, masking is delicate to implement since many assumptions on the leakage behavior of logic gates are not fully met in practice. In standard CMOS technology, glitches can diminish the security of a straightforward masked implementation [19]. There are masking schemes that cope with this non-ideal behavior and can provide security under more realistic and easier to meet assumptions. One example is Threshold Implementations.

1.1   Related Work

The Threshold Implementation (TI) technique which is based on Boolean masking has minimal assumptions on the underlying hardware platform [21]. More precisely, it assumes that logic gates will glitch, and provides security even if this happens. Due to its cost effectiveness, it has been applied to many cryptographic algorithms including KECCAK [7] and the standardized AES [14,20] and PRESENT [22] symmetric-key algorithms. Recently, the security level of TI has been extended to resist univariate attacks at any order [5]. To further increase the security of TI against multivariate attacks, the use of remasking was suggested in [26].

This consolidated masking scheme, hereon CMS, inherits all TI properties and uses the remasking of ISW [16] to break the multivariate correlation between the different clock cycles. Moreover, it has been shown in [26] that d^{th}-order security of any function can be achieved by only $d+1$ input shares using CMS which is the theoretical lower bound in masking schemes. Until then, it was believed that d^{th}-order security on a non-ideal circuit can only be achieved by using more than $d+1$ shares if the function is nonlinear [5,24]. This bound on the number of input shares s_{in} was given as $s_{in} \geq td+1$ for a function of algebraic degree t in TI and $s_{in} \geq 2d+1$ for a field multiplication in a complementary scheme [24] which provides the same level of security using Shamir's secret sharing. In this paper, we use the words CMS and TI interchangeably.

There exist plenty masked AES implementations, hence we limit our introduction to TIs. The first TI of AES presented in [20] requires 11.1 kGE. Later, the hardware footprint of TI-AES is reduced to 8.1 kGE in a sequence of publications [4,6]. All these first-order TIs use functions with at least three input shares, with the exception of the smallest TI-AES which uses two shares for linear operations. A second-order TI of the AES S-box using six input shares is presented in [14] and is shown to require 7.8 kGE. We emphasize that in all these TIs, the number of input shares of the nonlinear operations are chosen to be $s_{in} \geq td + 1$.

1.2 Contribution

We present the first Threshold Implementations in the form of the Consolidated Masking Scheme using $d+1$ input shares. We present both a first-order (6.6 kGE) and a second-order (10.4 kGE) secure implementation of AES. Our construction is generic and can be extended to higher orders. The area reduction of our new TIs compared to the smallest TIs of AES presented so far is shown to be 18 % for first-order and approximately 45 % for second-order security at the cost of an increase in the amount of required internal randomness. We observe negligible (first-order) or no (second-order) difference in throughput compared to prior TIs. We show the results of leakage detection tests with 100 million traces collected from an FPGA implementation to back up the security claims.

Organization. In Sect. 2, we provide the notation and the theory of CMS. In Sect. 3, we unfold the steps taken to mask AES using $d + 1$ shares. We present the results of the side-channel analysis in Sect. 4. In Sect. 5, we discuss the implementation cost of our designs. We conclude the paper and propose directions for future work in Sect. 6.

2 Preliminaries

2.1 Notation

We use small and bold letters to describe elements of $\mathbb{GF}(2^n)$ and their sharing respectively. We assume that any possibly sensitive variable $a \in \mathbb{GF}(2^n)$ is split into s shares $(a_1, \ldots, a_s) = \mathbf{a}$, where $a_i \in \mathbb{GF}(2^n)$, in the initialization phase of the cryptographic algorithm. A possible way of performing this initialization, which we inherit, is as follows: the shares $a_1, \ldots, a_{s-1}$ are selected randomly from a uniform distribution and a_s is calculated such that $a = \sum_{i \in \{1,\ldots,s\}} a_i$. We refer to the jth bit of a as a^j unless $a \in \mathbb{GF}(2)$. We use the same notation to share a function f to s shares $\mathbf{f} = (f_1, \ldots, f_s)$.

The number of input and output shares of $\mathbf{f}$ are denoted by s_{in} and s_{out} respectively. We refer to field multiplication, addition and concatenation as $\otimes$, $\oplus$ and $\oplus\!\!\!\!\bigcirc$ respectively.

2.2   Consolidated Masking Scheme

We now give an overview of the construction of CMS. Figure 1 illustrates the construction steps for the second-order sharing of a two input AND gate ($ab = \sum_{i=1}^{s_{in}} \sum_{j=1}^{s_{in}} a_i b_j$) using $s_{in} = td + 1 = 5$ shares on the left, with $\mathbf{a} = (a_1, a_2, a_3, a_4, a_5)$ and $\mathbf{b} = (b_1, b_2, b_3, b_4, b_5)$, and using $s_{in} = d + 1 = 3$ shares on the right, where we have $\mathbf{a} = (a_1, a_2, a_3)$ and $\mathbf{b} = (b_1, b_2, b_3)$. The CMS construction is divided in several layers that we detail in the sequel.

Nonlinear layer $\mathcal{N}$. This layer is composed of all the linear and nonlinear terms ($a_i b_j$ for the AND-gate example) of the shared function, and hence responsible for the *correctness* of the sharing. A requirement is that this layer must see uniformly shared inputs.

Linear layer $\mathcal{L}$. This layer inherits *non-completeness*, the essence of TI. It ensures that no more than d shares of a variable are used within each group of terms to be XORed. If the number of input shares is limited to $d + 1$, the non-completeness implies the use of only one share per unmasked value in each group. We refer to [26] for more details.

Refreshing layer $\mathcal{R}$. The multivariate security of a dth-order masking scheme depends on the proper insertion of additional randomness to break dependency between intermediates potentially appearing in different clock cycles. One way of remasking is using s_{out} bits of randomness for s_{out} shares at the end of $\mathcal{L}$ in a circular manner. The restriction of this layer can be relaxed when first-order or univariate security is satisfactory.

Synchronization layer $\mathcal{S}$. In a circuit with non-ideal gates, this layer ensures that non-completeness is satisfied in between nonlinear operations. It is depicted with a bold line in Fig. 1 and is typically implemented as a set of registers in hardware. The lack of this layer causes leakage in subsequent nonlinear operations.

Compression layer $\mathcal{C}$. This layer is used to reduce the number of shares synchronized in $\mathcal{S}$. It is especially required when the number of shares after $\mathcal{S}$ is different from the number of input shares of $\mathcal{N}$.

For further clarification, we also describe the concept of uniformity, the difference between using $d + 1$ shares or more and the limitations brought by using $d + 1$ shares in the rest of this section.

Uniformity. Uniformity plays a role in the composition of sharings in the first-order scenario. If the output of a shared function $\mathbf{f}$ is used as an input to a nonlinear function $\mathbf{g}$, the fact that $\mathbf{f}$ is a uniform sharing means that the input of $\mathbf{g}$ is uniform without remasking. Thus, in this case, $\mathcal{R}$ is not required. Note that satisfying uniformity when the outputs of multiple possibly uniformly shared functions are combined has shown to be a difficult task [4].

The situation is very different in the higher-order scenario, and security issues with composition can arise [26]. In this paper, we resort to $\mathcal{R}$ instead of focusing on the gains of satisfying uniformity, even in the first-order case.

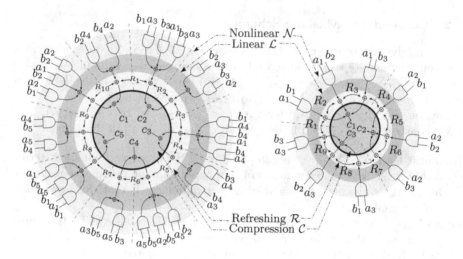

Fig. 1. Second-order masking of a two-input AND gate with $td + 1 = 5$ shares (left) and $d + 1 = 3$ shares (right)

Number of Input Shares. Using $td+1$ input shares originates from the rule-of-thumb "combinations of up to d component functions f_i should be independent of at least one input share". However, this is an overly strict requirement to fulfill non-completeness. One can construct a sharing such that combinations of up to d component functions are independent of at least one input share *of each variable*, without imposing any condition on the index i. The resulting sharing **f** is clearly secure since no combinations of up to d component functions reveals all shares of a variable.

In this paper, we benefit from this observation and use $d + 1$ shares. This incurs a significantly smaller area footprint, as will be shown later on. It is however not obvious at first sight whether a construction with $d + 1$ shares is necessarily smaller. As a matter of fact, there are many factors that work in the opposite direction, i.e. the number of component functions f_k is increased, and there is a need for additional circuitry for the refreshing and compression of the output shares. On the other hand, the shares f_k are significantly smaller, since they depend on fewer input bits. A classic result from Shannon [28] states that almost all Boolean functions with d input bits require a circuit of size $\Theta(2^d/d)$. One can assume that the size of the component functions f_k follows this exponential dependency regarding the number of input shares. Thus, it may pay off to have more component functions f_k and additional circuitry to obtain a smaller overall sharing.

Independent Input Sharing. Going from $td + 1$ to $d + 1$ shares imposes slightly stronger conditions on the input shares. The most important additional requirement compared to $td+1$ sharings is that the shared variables at the input of a nonlinear function should be independent. The following extreme example illustrates the problem: assume a first-order sharing of an AND gate with shared inputs (a_1, a_2) and (b_1, b_2) which necessarily calculates the terms $a_1 b_2$ and $a_2 b_1$. If these sharings are dependent, for the sake of the example say $\mathbf{a} = \mathbf{b}$, the term $a_1 b_2 = a_1 a_2$ obviously leaks a. This example clearly breaks the joint uniformity rule for $\mathbf{a}$ and $\mathbf{b}$. Note that this does not necessarily imply the requirement of unshared values to be independent.

3   Masking AES with $d + 1$ Shares

In what follows, we first describe in detail how the AES is masked with 3 shares using TI to achieve second-order security. The same principle applies to higher orders, but care is required when applying the refreshing and compression layer [26]. Then, we scale this construction down to achieve a first-order secure implementation, and detail some further optimizations we can apply specifically to the first-order secure case. As the following paragraph suggests, masking of linear operations is straightforward and therefore, our discussion will focus on the AES S-box.

Linear Components. The masking of the linear components of AES such as ShiftRows, MixColumns and AddRoundKey are achieved by instantiating $d + 1$ state and key arrays. Each pair of state and key array is responsible for one single share of the plaintext and key. Such a $d + 1$ sharing for linear operations has already been used in prior masked AES implementations and hence we do not provide further detail.

3.1   Second-Order TI of the AES S-box with 3 Shares

As in all previous TIs of the AES S-box [4,6,14,20], our masked implementation is based on Canright's Very Compact S-box [9]. This allows for a fairer comparison of the area reduction that comes from our masking strategy.

Figure 2 depicts the unmasked S-box with the specific subfield decompositions we adopt. Although it is possible to reduce the number of pipeline stages of one S-box by merging Stage 3 and Stage 4 into an inversion in $\mathbb{GF}(2^4)$ [4,6], we choose to rely on multiplications alone, since the number of component functions equals $(d + 1)^t$, i.e. we can achieve a lower area and a reduced randomness consumption by using multiplications ($t = 2$) instead of inversions ($t = 3$). We now go over the masked design in a stage by stage manner, where the stages are separated by pipeline registers. The complete masked S-box is depicted in Fig. 3.

First Stage. The first operation occurring in the decomposed S-box performs a change of basis through a linear map. Its masking requires instantiating this linear map once for each share i. This mapping is implemented in combinational logic and it maps the 8-bit input $(a_i^1, \ldots, a_i^8)$ to the 8-bit output $(y_i^1, \ldots, y_i^8)$ for each share i as follows:

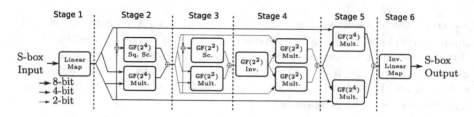

Fig. 2. Operations in the unmasked AES Sbox

$$y_i^1 = a_i^8 \oplus a_i^7 \oplus a_i^6 \oplus a_i^3 \oplus a_i^2 \oplus a_i^1 \qquad y_i^5 = a_i^8 \oplus a_i^5 \oplus a_i^4 \oplus a_i^2 \oplus a_i^1$$
$$y_i^2 = a_i^7 \oplus a_i^6 \oplus a_i^5 \oplus a_i^1 \qquad y_i^6 = a_i^1$$
$$y_i^3 = a_i^7 \oplus a_i^6 \oplus a_i^2 \oplus a_i^1 \qquad y_i^7 = a_i^7 \oplus a_i^6 \oplus a_i^1$$
$$y_i^4 = a_i^8 \oplus a_i^7 \oplus a_i^6 \oplus a_i^1 \qquad y_i^8 = a_i^7 \oplus a_i^4 \oplus a_i^3 \oplus a_i^2 \oplus a_i^1$$

Note that synchronizing the output values of the first stage with registers is required for security. For simplicity, we explain what can go wrong in the absence of these registers for the first-order case, but the same can be expressed for any order d. Let's consider the y^2 and y^6 bits of the output of the linear map. The shares corresponding to those bits are then given by (y_1^2, y_2^2) and (y_1^6, y_2^6) respectively. These two bits will go through the AND gates of the subsequent $\mathbb{GF}(2^4)$ multiplier, which leads to the following term being computed at one point:

$$y_1^2 y_2^6 = (a_1^7 + a_1^6 + a_1^5 + a_1^1)a_2^1$$

If there is no register between the linear map and the $\mathbb{GF}(2^4)$ multiplier, the above expression is realized by combinational logic, which deals with a_1^1 and a_2^1 in a nonlinear way and causes leakage on $\mathbf{a}^1 = (a_1^1, a_2^1)$. Note that the problem mentioned above does not happen in TIs with $s_{in} = td + 1$ shares, since the conservative non-completeness condition makes sure that each component function is independent of at least one share (for $d = 1$). Hence, linear functions before and after nonlinear component functions can be used without synchronization. No remasking is required after this stage since the computed function is linear.

Second Stage. We consider the parallel application of nonlinear multiplication and affine Square Scaling (Sq. Sc.) as one single function $\mathbf{d} = \mathbf{b} \otimes \mathbf{c} \oplus SqSc(\mathbf{b} \oplus \mathbf{c})$. For the second order, the resulting equations are given by:

$$\mathbf{d}_1 = \mathbf{b}_1 \otimes \mathbf{c}_1 \oplus SqSc(\mathbf{b}_1 \oplus \mathbf{c}_1)$$
$$\mathbf{d}_2 = \mathbf{b}_1 \otimes \mathbf{c}_2$$
$$\mathbf{d}_3 = \mathbf{b}_1 \otimes \mathbf{c}_3$$
$$\mathbf{d}_4 = \mathbf{b}_2 \otimes \mathbf{c}_1$$
$$\mathbf{d}_5 = \mathbf{b}_2 \otimes \mathbf{c}_2 \oplus SqSc(\mathbf{b}_2 \oplus \mathbf{c}_2)$$
$$\mathbf{d}_6 = \mathbf{b}_2 \otimes \mathbf{c}_3$$
$$\mathbf{d}_7 = \mathbf{b}_3 \otimes \mathbf{c}_1$$
$$\mathbf{d}_8 = \mathbf{b}_3 \otimes \mathbf{c}_2$$
$$\mathbf{d}_9 = \mathbf{b}_3 \otimes \mathbf{c}_3 \oplus SqSc(\mathbf{b}_3 \oplus \mathbf{c}_3)$$

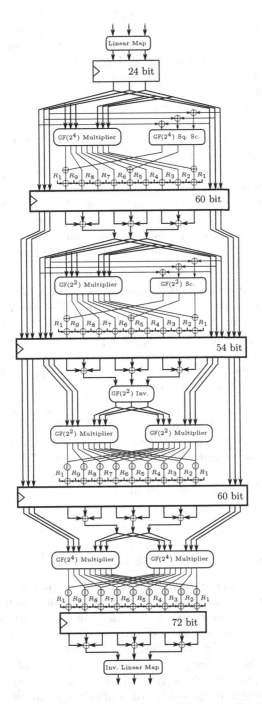

Fig. 3. Structure of the second-order TI of the AES S-box

It is important to add the affine contribution from the Square Scaling to the multiplier output in such a way that the non-completeness property is not broken, which leaves only one possibility for the construction. In previous works [4, 6, 20], these two functions are treated separately, leading to more outputs at this stage. By approaching the operations in the second stage in parallel, we obtain two advantages. Firstly, we omit the extra registers for storing the outputs of both sub-functions separately. Secondly, less randomness is required to achieve uniformity for the inputs of the next stage.

Before the new values are clocked in the register, we need to perform a mask refreshing. This serves two purposes for higher-order TI. Firstly, it is required to make the next stage's inputs uniform and secondly, we require new masks for the next stage's inputs to provide multivariate security. The mask refreshing uses a ring structure and has the advantage that the sum of fresh masks does not need to be saved in an extra register. In addition, we use an equal number of shares and fresh masks, which leads to a randomness consumption of 36 bits for this stage. After the mask refreshing, a compression is applied to reduce the number of output shares back to $d + 1$.

Third Stage. This stage is similar to the second stage. Here, the received nibbles are split in 2-bit couples for further operation. The Scaling operation (Sc) replaces the similar affine Square Scaling and is executed alongside the multiplication in $GF(2^2)$. By combining both operations, we can share the total function by taking again the non-completeness into account. Since a nonlinear multiplication is performed on the 2-bit shares, remasking is required on its 9 outputs, consuming a total of 18 bits of randomness.

Fourth Stage. The fourth stage is composed of an inversion and two parallel multiplications in $GF(2^2)$. The inversion in $GF(2^2)$ is linear and is implemented by swapping the bits using wires and comes at no additional cost. The outputs of the multiplications are concatenated, denoted by ⓪ in Fig. 3, to form 4-bit values in $GF(2^4)$. The concatenated 4-bit values of the 9 outputs of the multipliers are remasked with a total of 36 fresh random bits.

Fifth Stage. Stage 5 is similar to Stage 4. The difference of the two stages lies in the absence of the inversion operation and the multiplications being performed in $GF(2^4)$ instead of $GF(2^2)$. The concatenation of its outputs results in byte values, which are remasked with 72 fresh random bits.

Sixth Stage. In the final stage of the S-box, the inverse linear map is performed. By using a register between Stage 5 and Stage 6, we can remask the shares and perform a compression before the inverse linear map is performed resulting in only three instead of nine instances of inverse linear maps. As with the linear map, no uniform sharing of its inputs is required for security. However, in the full AES, this output will at some point reappear at the input of the S-box, where it undergoes nonlinear operations again. This is why we insert the remasking. Note that this register and the register right after the linear map can be merged with the AES state registers.

3.2 First-Order TI of the AES S-Box with 2 Shares

To achieve a very compact first-order TI, we can scale down the general structure from Sect. 3.1. We can apply some optimizations to reduce the amount of randomness consumed for the first-order implementation, since multivariate security is not required anymore.

We start with the previous construction with the number of shares reduced from $s_{in} = 3$ to $s_{in} = 2$. We now highlight the particular optimizations: parallel operations in Stage 2 and 3 and modified refreshing.

Parallel Operations. The parallel linear and nonlinear operations from Stage 2 and 3 are altered in the following way:

$$\mathbf{d}_1 = \mathbf{b}_1 \otimes \mathbf{c}_1 \oplus SqSc(\mathbf{b}_1 \oplus \mathbf{c}_1)$$
$$\mathbf{d}_2 = \mathbf{b}_1 \otimes \mathbf{c}_2$$
$$\mathbf{d}_3 = \mathbf{b}_2 \otimes \mathbf{c}_1$$
$$\mathbf{d}_4 = \mathbf{b}_2 \otimes \mathbf{c}_2 \oplus SqSc(\mathbf{b}_2 \oplus \mathbf{c}_2)$$

Again, the ith output of both SqSc and Sc operations are combined with output $\mathbf{b}_i \otimes \mathbf{c}_i$ of the multiplier in order to preserve non-completeness. While this structure is similar to our second-order design, we consider this parallel operation an optimization compared to other first-order TIs [4,6,20].

Modified Refreshing. The ring structure of the refreshing in the general, higher-order case can be substituted with a less costly structure for first-order security. This structure of the refreshing is shown in Fig. 4. This modification lowers the randomness requirements from 4 to 3 units of randomness.[1]

4 Side-Channel Analysis Evaluation

In this section, we report on the practical side-channel analysis evaluation we performed on our two designs: one core aiming at first-order security and the other aiming at second-order security.

Preliminary Tests. A preliminary evaluation was carried out with the tool from [25] in a simulated environment, allowing to refine our design. We then proceed with the side-channel evaluation based on actual measurements.

4.1 Experimental Setup

Platform. We use a SASEBO-G board [2]. The SASEBO-G features two Xilinx Virtex-II Pro FPGAs: an XC2VP7 to hold our cryptographic implementations and an XC2VP30 for handling the communication between the board and the measurement PC.

---

[1] A unit of randomness is defined as a set of independent and uniformly distributed bits with the field size of the wire as its cardinality.

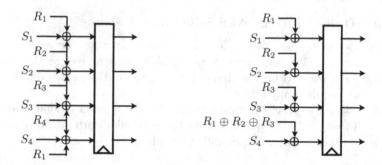

Fig. 4. Ring versus additive refreshing

Low Noise. We did our best to keep the measurement noise to the lowest possible level. The platform itself is very low noise (DPA on an unprotected AES succeeds with few tens of traces). We clock our designs at 3 MHz with a very stable clock and sample at 1 GS/s with a Tektronix DPO 7254C oscilloscope. The measurements cover 1.5 rounds of AES.

Synthesis. We used standard design flow tools (Xilinx ISE) to synthetize our designs. We selected the KEEP_HIERARCHY option during synthesis to prevent optimizations over module boundaries that would destroy our (security critical) design partitioning.

Randomness. The randomness required by our design is supplied by a PRNG that runs on the crypto FPGA. The PRNG consists of a fully unrolled round-reduced PRINCE [8] in OFB mode with a fresh key each masked AES execution. Since our second-order implementation requires 162 fresh mask bits per clock cycle, three parallel instantiations of the PRNG are used to supply the randomness. In the first-order case, one instance suffices. We interleave the execution of the PRNG (in a single cycle) with every clock cycle of the masked AES in order to decrease the impact of noise induced by the PRNG.

4.2 Methodology

We use leakage detection tests [11–13, 15, 27] to test for any power leakage of our masked implementations. The fix class of the leakage detection is chosen as the zero plaintext in all our evaluations.

Procedure. We follow the standard practice when testing a masked design. Namely, we first turn off the PRNG to switch off the masking countermeasure. The design is expected to show leakage in this setting, and this serves to confirm that the experimental setup is sound (we can detect leakage). We then proceed by turning on the PRNG. If we do not detect leakage in this setting, the masking countermeasure is deemed to be effective.

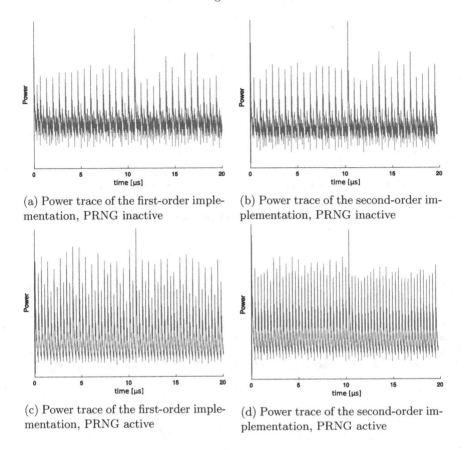

(a) Power trace of the first-order implementation, PRNG inactive

(b) Power trace of the second-order implementation, PRNG inactive

(c) Power trace of the first-order implementation, PRNG active

(d) Power trace of the second-order implementation, PRNG active

Fig. 5. Average power traces

4.3   First-Order TI of AES

We first evaluate the first-order secure masked AES. Figures 5a and 5c show an example of power traces when the PRNG is inactive and active respectively for the first-order implementations. It is clear that the interleaved PRNG does not overlap with AES. We now apply the leakage detection test.

PRNG Off. Fig. 6a shows the result of the t-test on the implementation without randomness. First- (top) and second-order (bottom) results clearly show leaks that surpass the confidence threshold of ±4.5. Thus, as expected, this setting is not secure.

PRNG On. When we turn on the random number generator, our design shows no first-order leakage with up to 100 million traces. The t-test statistic for the first and second orders are plotted in Fig. 6b. In agreement with the security claim of the design, the first-order trace does not show leakage. The second-order does.

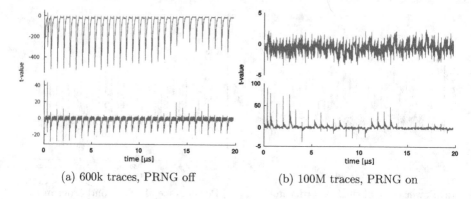

(a) 600k traces, PRNG off

(b) 100M traces, PRNG on

Fig. 6. First- (top) and second-order (bottom) leakage detection test results for the first-order implementation

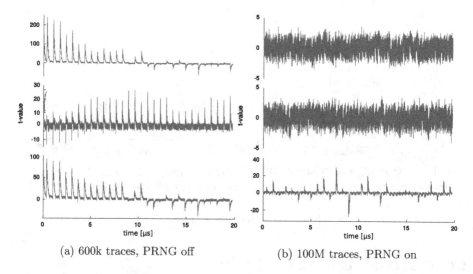

(a) 600k traces, PRNG off

(b) 100M traces, PRNG on

Fig. 7. First- (top), second- (middle) and third-order (bottom) leakage detection test results for the second-order implementation

This is expected since the design does not provide second-order security (note that sensitive variables are split among two shares).

4.4 Second-Order TI of AES

Figs. 5b and d show an average power consumption trace of the second-order implementation for an inactive PRNG and for an active PRNG respectively. We proceed with the evaluation using the leakage detection test.

PRNG Off. The evaluation results of the implementation without randomness are given in Fig. 7a. As expected, first- (top), second- (middle) and third-order (bottom) leaks are present.

PRNG On. When the masking is turned on by enabling the PRNG, we expect our design to show no leakage in the first and second order.

The results of the t-test with 100 million traces are shown in Fig. 7b. As expected, we only observe leakage in the third order. The t-values of the first- and second-order tests never exceed the confidence threshold of ±4.5.

Bivariate Analysis. We also performed a second-order bivariate leakage detection test with centered product pre-processing. To alleviate the computational complexity of this analysis, measurements span only one full S-box execution and the sampling rate is lowered to 200 MS/s.

PRNG Off. The lower left corner of Fig. 8 shows the absolute t values for the bivariate analysis of the unmasked implementation. As expected, leakages of considerable magnitude (t values exceeding 100) are present and we conclude that the measurement setup for the bivariate analysis is sound.

PRNG On. When the PRNG is switched on, the outcome of the test is different. The absolute value of the resulting bivariate leakage when the masks are switched on with 100 million traces is depicted in the upper right corner of Fig. 8. No excursions of the t-values beyond ±4.5 occur and thus the test is passed.

One might ask if 100 million traces are enough. To gain some insight that this (arbitrary) number is indeed enough, we refer back to the performed third-order tests of Fig. 7b. We can see that third-order leakage is detectable, and thus we can assert that bivariate second-order attacks are not the cheapest strategy for an adversary. Therefore, the masking is deemed effective.

5 Implementation Cost

Table 1 lists the area costs of the individual components of our designs. Table 2 gives the full implementation costs of our designs and of related TIs. The area estimations are obtained with Synopsys 2010.03 and the NanGate 45 nm Open Cell Library [1].

Discussion. We now discuss the increase in implementation costs when going from first- to second-order security and compare the results with similar designs w.r.t. the area, the speed and the required randomness for an AES encryption. Note that this discussion does not necessarily apply to other ciphers or implementations, e.g. lightweight block ciphers with small S-boxes might benefit from keeping $s_{in} \geq td+1$ in nonlinear functions. For future comparisons, Table 3 gives the implementation cost per S-box stage in function of the security order d.

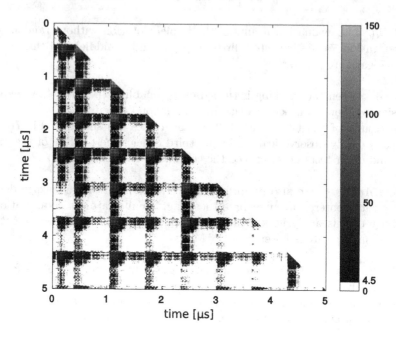

Fig. 8. Bivariate analysis of second-order implementation, 100k traces, PRNG off (bottom left), 100M traces, PRNG on (top right)

Area. Both the first- and the second-order masked AES cores are the smallest available to this date. Moving from first-order to second-order security requires an increase of 50 % in GE for linear functions and an increase of around 100 % for nonlinear functions. The larger increase for nonlinear functions stems from the quadratic increase of output shares as function of an increment in input shares, resulting in more registers per stage.

Table 1. Area of different functions of the masked AES

	Area [GEs]	
	Compile	Compile ultra
First-order TI		
S-box	1977	1872
AES key & State array	4472	4238
AES control	232	230
Total AES	6681	6340
Second-order TI		
S-box	3796	3662
AES key & State array	6287	6258
AES control	366	356
Total AES	10449	10276

Table 2. Implementation cost of different TIs of AES

AES	Area [GE][a]	S-box area [GE][a]	S-box	Randomness[b] [bit]	Clock cyles
Unprotected [20]	2601/2421	233	1	-	226
1st-order					
[20]	11114/11031	- /4244	5	48	266
[4]	9102/8172	3708/3004	4	44	246
[6]	11221/10167	3653/2949	4	44	246
[6]	8119/7282	2835/2224	4	32	246
This paper	6681/6340	1977/1872	6	54	276
2nd-order					
[14][c]	18602/14872	11174/7849	6	126	276
This paper	10449/10276	3796/3662	6	162	276

[a]Using compile/compile_ultra option. (The compile_ultra option requires careful application. To avoid optimizing over share boundaries, each submodule is compiled using compile_ultra. The resulting netlists are then given to a top module and synthesized with the regular compile option. This way, the gates from the ASIC library are instantiated conform to the KEEP_HIERARCHY option.)
[b]Per S-box lookup
[c]Area estimation of a non-tested AES with tested S-box

Speed. The number of clock cycles for an AES encryption is equal for our first- and second-order implementations. All previous first-order TIs have a faster encryption because they have less pipeline stages in the S-box.

Randomness. Our first-order AES requires 54 bits of randomness per S-box execution. For our second-order implementation, this number increases to 162 bits of randomness. These numbers are higher than previous TIs for both the

Table 3. Implementation cost per pipeline stage in function of the order $d > 1$

AES	Number of masked bits	Number of register bits
Stage 1	0	$8(d + 1)$
Stage 2	$4(d + 1)^2$	$4(d + 1)^2 + 8(d + 1)$
Stage 3	$2(d + 1)^2$	$2(d + 1)^2 + 12(d + 1)$
Stage 4	$4(d + 1)^2$	$4(d + 1)^2 + 8(d + 1)$
Stage 5	$8(d + 1)^2$	$8(d + 1)^2$
Stage 6	0	$8(d + 1)$
Total	$18(d + 1)^2$	$18(d + 1)^2 + 44(d + 1)$

first- and second-order implementations. For the first-order implementation, this increase can be explained by noting that for a minimal sharing, no correction terms can be applied to make the sharing uniform, hence explaining the need for mask refreshing. For the second-order implementation, even more randomness is required per output share to achieve bivariate security. All shares of one stage require randomness for both satisfying the uniformity and for statistical independence of its following stage.

6 Conclusion

In this paper, two new hardware implementations of AES secure against differential power analysis attacks were described. Both implementations use the theoretical minimum number of shares in the linear and nonlinear operations by following the conditions from Reparaz et al. [26]. The security of both designs were validated by leakage detection tests in lab conditions.

In summary, our first-order implementation of AES requires 6340 GE, 54 bits of randomness per S-box and a total of 276 clock cycles. In comparison to the previously smallest TI of AES by Bilgin et al. [6], an area reduction of 15% is obtained. The number of clock cycles for an encryption is increased by 11% and the required randomness is raised with 68%. The presented second-order implementation of AES requires 10276 GE, 162 bits of randomness per S-box and 276 clock cycles. Compared to the second-order TI-AES of [14], we obtain a 53% reduction in area at the cost of a 28% increase in required randomness. The number of clock cycles for an encryption stays the same.

While the area of these implementations are the smallest published for AES to this date, the required randomness is substantially increased. Investigating ways of reducing the randomness is essential for lightweight application. In future work, paths leading to minimizing this cost will be researched. A second direction for future work is to compare the security in terms of number of traces required to perform a successful key retrieval between our implementations and the AES in [6]. This can lead to better insights in the trade-off between security and implementation costs for TIs with $s_{in} = d + 1$ and $s_{in} = td + 1$ shares.

Acknowledgments. The authors would like to thank the anonymous reviewers for providing constructive and valuable comments. This work was supported in part by NIST with the research grant 60NANB15D346, in part by the Research Council KU Leuven (OT/13/071 and GOA/11/007) and in part by the European Unions Horizon 2020 research and innovation programme under grant agreement No. 644052 HECTOR. Begül Bilgin is a Postdoctoral Fellow of the Fund for Scientific Research - Flanders (FWO). Oscar Reparaz is funded by a PhD fellowship of the Fund for Scientific Research - Flanders (FWO). Thomas De Cnudde is funded by a research grant of the Institute for the Promotion of Innovation through Science and Technology in Flanders (IWT-Vlaanderen).

References

1. NanGate Open Cell Library. http://www.nangate.com/
2. Research Center for Information Security, National Institute of AdvancedIndustrial Science and Technology, Side-channel Attack Standard EvaluationBoard SASEBO-G Specification. http://satoh.cs.uec.ac.jp/SASEBO/en/board/sasebo-g.html
3. Agrawal, D., Archambeault, B., Rao, J.R., Rohatgi, P.: The EM side-channel(s). In: Kaliski, B.S., Koç, Ç.K., Paar, C. (eds.) CHES 2002. LNCS, vol. 2523, pp. 29–45. Springer, Heidelberg (2002). http://dx.doi.org/10.1007/3-540-36400-5_4
4. Bilgin, B., Gierlichs, B., Nikova, S., Nikov, V., Rijmen, V.: A more efficient AES threshold implementation. In: Pointcheval, D., Vergnaud, D. (eds.) AFRICACRYPT 2014. LNCS, vol. 8469, pp. 267–284. Springer, Heidelberg (2014). http://dx.doi.org/10.1007/978-3-319-06734-6_17
5. Bilgin, B., Gierlichs, B., Nikova, S., Nikov, V., Rijmen, V.: Higher-order threshold implementations. In: Sarkar, P., Iwata, T. (eds.) ASIACRYPT 2014. LNCS, vol. 8874, pp. 326–343. Springer, Heidelberg (2014). http://dx.doi.org/10.1007/978-3-662-45608-8_18
6. Bilgin, B., Gierlichs, B., Nikova, S., Nikov, V., Rijmen, V.: Trade-offs for threshold implementations illustrated on AES. IEEE Trans. CAD Integr. Circ. Syst. **34**(7), 1188–1200 (2015). http://dx.doi.org/10.1109/TCAD.2015.2419623
7. Bilgin, B., Daemen, J., Nikov, V., Nikova, S., Rijmen, V., Van Assche, G.: Efficient and first-order DPA resistant implementations of KECCAK. In: Francillon, A., Rohatgi, P. (eds.) CARDIS 2013. LNCS, vol. 8419, pp. 187–199. Springer, Heidelberg (2014). http://dx.doi.org/10.1007/978-3-319-08302-5_13
8. Borghoff, J., Canteaut, A., Güneysu, T., Kavun, E.B., Knezevic, M., Knudsen, L.R., Leander, G., Nikov, V., Paar, C., Rechberger, C., Rombouts, P., Thomsen, S.S., Yalçin, T.: PRINCE - a low-latency block cipher for pervasive computing applications (full version). IACR Cryptology ePrint Archive 2012/529 (2012). http://eprint.iacr.org/2012/529
9. Canright, D.: A very compact S-box for AES. In: Rao, J.R., Sunar, B. (eds.) CHES 2005. LNCS, vol. 3659, pp. 441–455. Springer, Heidelberg (2005). http://dx.doi.org/10.1007/11545262_32
10. Chari, S., Jutla, C.S., Rao, J.R., Rohatgi, P.: Towards sound approaches to counteract power-analysis attacks. In: Wiener, M. (ed.) CRYPTO 1999. LNCS, vol. 1666, pp. 398–412. Springer, Heidelberg (1999). http://dx.doi.org/10.1007/3-540-48405-1_26
11. Cooper, J., DeMulder, E., Goodwill, G., Jaffe, J., Kenworthy, G., Rohatgi, P.: Test vector leakage assessment (TVLA) methodology in practice. In: International Cryptographic Module Conference (2013). http://icmc-2013.org/wp/wp-content/uploads/2013/09/goodwillkenworthtestvector.pdf
12. Coron, J.-S., Kocher, P.C., Naccache, D.: Statistics and secret leakage. In: Frankel, Y. (ed.) FC 2000. LNCS, vol. 1962, pp. 157–173. Springer, Heidelberg (2001). http://dx.doi.org/10.1007/3-540-45472-1_12
13. Coron, J., Naccache, D., Kocher, P.C.: Statistics and secret leakage. ACM Trans. Embed. Comput. Syst. **3**(3), 492–508 (2004). http://doi.acm.org/10.1145/1015047.1015050
14. De Cnudde, T., Bilgin, B., Reparaz, O., Nikov, V., Nikova, S.: Higher-order threshold implementation of the AES S-box. In: Homma, N., et al. (eds.) CARDIS 2015. LNCS, vol. 9514, pp. 259–272. Springer, Heidelberg (2016). doi:10.1007/978-3-319-31271-2_16

15. Goodwill, G., Jun, B., Jaffe, J., Rohatgi, P.: A testing methodology for side-channel resistance validation. In: NIST Non-Invasive Attack Testing Workshop (2011). http://csrc.nist.gov/news_events/non-invasive-attack-testing-workshop/papers/08_Goodwill.pdf

16. Ishai, Y., Sahai, A., Wagner, D.: Private circuits: securing hardware against probing attacks. In: Boneh, D. (ed.) CRYPTO 2003. LNCS, vol. 2729, pp. 463–481. Springer, Heidelberg (2003). http://dx.doi.org/10.1007/978-3-540-45146-4_27

17. Kocher, P.C.: Timing attacks on implementations of Diffie-Hellman, RSA, DSS, and other systems. In: Koblitz, N. (ed.) CRYPTO 1996. LNCS, vol. 1109, pp. 104–113. Springer, Heidelberg (1996). http://dx.doi.org/10.1007/3-540-68697-5_9

18. Kocher, P.C., Jaffe, J., Jun, B.: Differential power analysis. In: Wiener, M. (ed.) CRYPTO 1999. LNCS, vol. 1666, pp. 388–397. Springer, Heidelberg (1999). http://dx.doi.org/10.1007/3-540-48405-1_25

19. Mangard, S., Pramstaller, N., Oswald, E.: Successfully attacking masked AES hardware implementations. In: Rao, J.R., Sunar, B. (eds.) CHES 2005. LNCS, vol. 3659, pp. 157–171. Springer, Heidelberg (2005). http://dx.doi.org/10.1007/11545262_12

20. Moradi, A., Poschmann, A., Ling, S., Paar, C., Wang, H.: Pushing the limits: a very compact and a threshold implementation of AES. In: Paterson, K.G. (ed.) EUROCRYPT 2011. LNCS, vol. 6632, pp. 69–88. Springer, Heidelberg (2011). http://dx.doi.org/10.1007/978-3-642-20465-4_6

21. Nikova, S., Rijmen, V., Schläffer, M.: Secure hardware implementation of non-linear functions in the presence of glitches. J. Cryptol. 24(2), 292–321 (2011). http://dx.doi.org/10.1007/s00145-010-9085-7

22. Poschmann, A., Moradi, A., Khoo, K., Lim, C., Wang, H., Ling, S.: Side-channel resistant crypto for less than 2, 300 GE. J. Cryptol. 24(2), 322–345 (2011). http://dx.doi.org/10.1007/s00145-010-9086-6

23. Prouff, E., Rivain, M.: Masking against side-channel attacks: a formal security proof. In: Johansson, T., Nguyen, P.Q. (eds.) EURO-CRYPT 2013. LNCS, vol. 7881, pp. 142–159. Springer, Heidelberg (2013). http://dx.doi.org/10.1007/978-3-642-38348-9_9

24. Prouff, E., Roche, T.: Higher-order glitches free implementation of the AES using secure multi-party computation protocols. In: Preneel, B., Takagi, T. (eds.) CHES 2011. LNCS, vol. 6917, pp. 63–78. Springer, Heidelberg (2011). http://dx.doi.org/10.1007/978-3-642-23951-9_5

25. Reparaz, O.: Detecting flawed masking schemes with leakage detection tests. In: Peyrin, T. (ed.) FSE 2016. LNCS, vol. 9813, pp. xx–yy. Springer, Heidelberg (2016)

26. Reparaz, O., Bilgin, B., Nikova, S., Gierlichs, B., Verbauwhede, I.: Consolidating masking schemes. In: Gennaro, R., Robshaw, M. (eds.) CRYPTO 2015. LNCS, vol. 9215, pp. 764–783. Springer, Heidelberg (2015). http://dx.doi.org/10.1007/978-3-662-47989-6_37

27. Schneider, T., Moradi, A.: Leakage assessment methodology. In: Güneysu, T., Handschuh, H. (eds.) CHES 2015. LNCS, vol. 9293, pp. 495–513. Springer, Heidelberg (2015). http://dx.doi.org/10.1007/978-3-662-48324-4_25

28. Shannon, C.: The synthesis of two-terminal switching circuits. Bell Syst. Tech. J. 28(1), 59–98 (1949)

New Directions

Differential Computation Analysis: Hiding Your White-Box Designs is Not Enough

Joppe W. Bos[1(✉)], Charles Hubain[2], Wil Michiels[1,3], and Philippe Teuwen[2]

[1] NXP Semiconductors, Leuven, Belgium
{joppe.bos,wil.michiels}@nxp.com
[2] Quarkslab, Paris, France
{chubain,pteuwen}@quarkslab.com
[3] Technische Universiteit Eindhoven, Eindhoven, The Netherlands

Abstract. Although all current scientific white-box approaches of standardized cryptographic primitives are broken, there is still a large number of companies which sell "secure" white-box products. In this paper, we present a new approach to assess the security of white-box implementations which requires *neither* knowledge about the look-up tables used *nor* any reverse engineering effort. This *differential computation analysis* (DCA) attack is the software counterpart of the differential power analysis attack as applied by the cryptographic hardware community.

We developed plugins to widely available dynamic binary instrumentation frameworks to produce *software execution traces* which contain information about the memory addresses being accessed. To illustrate its effectiveness, we show how DCA can extract the secret key from numerous publicly (non-commercial) available white-box programs implementing standardized cryptography by analyzing these traces to identify secret-key dependent correlations. This approach allows one to extract the secret key material from white-box implementations significantly faster and without specific knowledge of the white-box design in an automated manner.

1 Introduction

The widespread use of mobile "smart" devices enables users to access a large variety of ubiquitous services. This makes such platforms a valuable target (cf. [48] for a survey on security for mobile devices). There are a number of techniques to protect the cryptographic keys residing on these mobile platforms. The solutions range from unprotected software implementations on the lower range of the security spectrum, to tamper-resistant hardware implementations on the other end. A popular approach which attempts to hide a cryptographic key inside a software program is known as a *white-box implementation*.

Ch. Hubain and Ph. Teuwen—This work was performed while the second and fourth author were an intern and employee in the Innovation Center Crypto & Security at NXP Semiconductors, respectively.

B. Gierlichs and A.Y. Poschmann (Eds.): CHES 2016, LNCS 9813, pp. 215–236, 2016.
DOI: 10.1007/978-3-662-53140-2_11

Traditionally, people used to work with a security model where implementations of cryptographic primitives are modeled as "black boxes". In this black box model the internal design is trusted and only the in- and output are considered in a security evaluation. As pointed out by Kocher et al. [32] in the late 1990s, this assumption turned out to be false in many scenarios. This black-box may leak some meta-information: e.g., in terms of timing or power consumption. This side-channel analysis gave rise to the gray-box attack model. Since the usage of (and access to) cryptographic keys changed, so did this security model. In two seminal papers from 2002, Chow, Eisen, Johnson and van Oorschot introduce the white-box model and show implementation techniques which attempt to realize a white-box implementation of symmetric ciphers [16,17].

The idea behind the white-box attack model is that the adversary can be the owner of the device running the software implementation. Hence, it is assumed that the adversary has full control over the execution environment. This enables the adversary to, among other things, perform static analysis on the software, inspect and alter the memory used, and even alter intermediate results (similar to hardware fault injections). This white-box attack model, where the adversary is assumed to have such advanced abilities, is realistic on many mobile platforms which store private cryptographic keys of third-parties. White-box implementations can be used to protect which applications can be installed on a mobile device (from an application store). Other use-cases include the protection of digital assets (including media, software and devices) in the setting of digital rights management, the protection of Host Card Emulation (HCE) and the protection of credentials for authentication to the cloud. If one has access to a "perfect" white-box implementation of a cryptographic algorithm, then this implies one should not be able to deduce any information about the secret key material used by inspecting the internals of this implementation. This is equivalent to a setting where one has only black-box access to the implementation. As observed by [19] this means that such a white-box implementation should resist all existing and future side-channel attacks.

As stated in [16], "*when the attacker has internal information about a cryptographic implementation, choice of implementation is the sole remaining line of defense.*" This is exactly what is being pursued in a white-box implementation: the idea is to embed the secret key in the implementation of the cryptographic operations such that it becomes difficult for an attacker to extract information about this secret key even when the source code of the implementation is provided. Note that this approach is different from anti-reverse-engineering mechanisms such as code obfuscation [5,36] and control-flow obfuscation [25] although these are typically applied to white-box implementations as an additional line of defense. Although it is conjectured that no long-term defense against attacks on white-box implementations exist [16], there are still a significant number of companies selling secure white-box solutions. It should be noted that there are almost no known published results on how to turn any of the standardized public-key algorithms into a white-box implementation, besides a patent by Zhou and Chow proposed in 2002 [61]. The other published white-box techniques exclusively focus on symmetric cryptography. However, all such published approaches have been theoretically broken (see Sect. 2 for an overview). A disadvantage of these published attacks is that it requires detailed information on how the white-box implementation is constructed. For instance, knowledge about the exact location of the S-boxes or the round transitions might be required together with the format of the applied encodings to the look-up tables (see Sect. 2 on how white-box implementations are generally designed). Vendors of white-box implementations try to avoid such attacks by ignoring Kerckhoffs's principle and keeping the details of their design secret (and change the design once it is broken).

Our Contribution. All current cryptanalytic approaches require detailed knowledge about the white-box design used: e.g. the location and order of the S-boxes applied and how and where the encodings are used. This preprocessing effort required for performing an attack is an important aspect of the value attributed to commercial white-box solutions. Vendors are aware that their solutions do not offer a long term defense, but compensate for this by, for instance, regular software updates. Our contribution is an attack that works in an automated way, and it is therefore a major threat for the claimed security level of the offered solutions compared to the ones that are already known.

In this paper we use dynamic binary analysis (DBA), a technique often used to improve and inspect the quality of software implementations, to access and control the intermediate state of the white-box implementation. One approach to implement DBA is called dynamic binary instrumentation (DBI). The idea is that additional analysis code is added to the original code of the client program at run-time in order to aid memory debugging, memory leak detection, and profiling. The most advanced DBI tools, such as Valgrind [46] and Pin [37], allow one to monitor, modify and insert instructions in a binary executable. These tools have already demonstrated their potential for behavioral analysis of obfuscated code [52].

We have developed plugins for both Valgrind and Pin to obtain *software traces*[1]: a trace which records the read and write accesses made to memory. These software traces are used to deduce information about the secret embedded in a white-box implementation by correlating key guesses to intermediate results. For this we introduce *differential computation analysis* (DCA), which can be seen as the software counterpart of the differential power analysis (DPA) [32] techniques as applied by the cryptographic hardware community. There are, however, some important differences between the usage of the software and hardware traces as we outline in Sect. 4.

We demonstrate that DCA can be used to efficiently extract the secret key from white-box implementations which apply at most a single remotely handled external encoding. We apply DCA to the publicly available white-box challenges

---

[1] The entire software toolchain ranging from the plugins, to the GUI, to the individual scrips to target the white-box challenges as described in this paper is released as open-source software: see https://github.com/SideChannelMarvels.

of standardized cryptographic algorithms we could find; concretely this means extracting the secret key from four white-box implementations of the symmetric cryptographic algorithms AES and DES. In contrast to the current cryptanalytic methods to attack white-box implementations, this technique does not require any knowledge about the implementation strategy used, can be mounted without much technical cryptographic knowledge in an automated way, and extract the key significantly faster. Besides this cryptanalytic framework we discuss techniques which could be used as countermeasures against DCA (see Sect. 6).

The main reason why DCA works is related to the choice of (non-) linear encodings which are used inside the white-box implementation (cf. Sect. 2). These encodings do not sufficiently hide correlations when the correct key is used and enables one to run side-channel attacks (just as in gray-box attack model). Sasdrich et al. looked into this in detail [50] and used the Walsh transform (a measure to investigate if a function is a balanced correlation immune function of a certain order) of both the linear and non-linear encodings applied in their white-box implementation of AES. Their results show extreme unbalance where the correct key is used and this explain why first-order attacks like DPA are successful in this scenario.

Independently, and after this paper appeared online, Sanfelix, de Haas and Mune also presented attacks on white-box implementations [49]. On the one hand they confirmed our findings and on the other hand they considered software fault attacks which is of independent interest.

2   Overview of White-Box Cryptography Techniques

The white-box attack model allows the adversary to take full control over the cryptographic implementation and the execution environment. It is not surprising that, given such powerful capabilities of the adversary, the authors of the original white-box paper [16] conjectured that no long-term defense against attacks on white-box implementations exists. This conjecture should be understood in the context of code-obfuscation, since hiding the cryptographic key inside an implementation is a form of code-obfuscation. It is known that obfuscation of *any* program is impossible [3], however, it is unknown if this result applies to a specific subset of white-box functionalities. Moreover, this should be understood in the light of recent developments where techniques using multilinear maps are used for obfuscation that may provide meaningful security guarantees (cf. [2,10,22]). In order to guard oneself in this security model in the medium- to long-run one has to use the advantages of a software-only solution. The idea is to use the concept of *software aging* [27]: this forces, at a regular interval, updates to the white-box implementation. It is hoped that when this interval is small enough, this gives insufficient computational time to the adversary to extract the secret key from the white-box implementation. This approach makes only sense if the sensitive data is only of short-term interest, e.g. the DRM-protected broadcast of a football match. However, the practical challenges of enforcing these updates on devices with irregular internet access should be noted.

External Encodings. Besides its primary goal to hide the key, white-box implementations can also be used to provide additional functionality, such as putting a fingerprint on a cryptographic key to enable traitor tracing or hardening software against tampering [42]. There are, however, other security concerns besides the extraction of the cryptographic secret key from the white-box implementation. If one is able to extract (or copy) the entire white-box implementation to another device then one has copied the functionality of this white-box implementation as well, since the secret key is embedded in this program. Such an attack is known as *code lifting*. A possible solution to this problem is to use external encodings [16]. When one assumes that the cryptographic functionality E_k is part of a larger ecosystem then one could implement $E'_k = G \circ E_k \circ F^{-1}$ instead. The input (F) and output (G) encoding are randomly chosen bijections such that the extraction of E'_k does not allow the adversary to compute E_k directly. The ecosystem which makes use of E'_k must ensure that the input and output encodings are canceled. In practice, depending on the application, input or output encodings need to be performed locally by the program calling E'_k. E.g. in DRM applications, the server may take care of the input encoding remotely but the client needs to revert the output encoding to finalize the content decryption.

In this paper, we can mount successful attacks on implementations which apply *at most a single remotely handled external encoding*. When both the input is received with an external encoding applied to it remotely and the output is computed with another encoding applied to it (which is removed remotely) then the implementation is not a white-box implementation of a standard algorithm (like AES or DES) but of a modified algorithm (like $G \circ \text{AES} \circ F^{-1}$ or $G \circ \text{DES} \circ F^{-1}$).

General Idea. The general approach to implement a white-box program is presented in [16]. The idea is to use look-up tables rather than individual computational steps to implement an algorithm and to encode these look-up tables with random bijections. The usage of a fixed secret key is embedded in these tables. Due to this extensive usage of look-up tables, white-box implementations are typically orders of magnitude larger and slower than a regular (non-white-box) implementation of the same algorithm. It is common to write a program that automatically generates a random white-box implementation given the algorithm and the fixed secret key as input. The randomness resides in the randomly chosen bijections to hide the secret key usage in the various look-up tables.

2.1 White-Box Results

White-Box Data Encryption Standard (WB-DES). The first publication attempting to construct a WB-DES implementation dates back from 2002 [17] in which an approach to create white-box implementations of Feistel ciphers is discussed. A first attack on this scheme, which enables one to unravel the obfuscation mechanism, took place in the same year and used fault injections [26] to extract the secret key by observing how the program fails under certain errors. In 2005, an improved WB-DES design, resisting this fault attack, was presented in [35]. However, in 2007, two differential cryptanalytic attacks [6] were presented which can extract the secret key from this type of white-box [23,59]. This latter approach has a time complexity of only 2^{14}.

White-Box Advanced Encryption Standard (WB-AES). The first approach to realize a WB-AES implementation was proposed in 2002 [16]. In 2004, the authors of [8] present how information about the encodings embedded in the look-up tables can be revealed when analyzing the lookup tables composition. This approach is known as the BGE attack and enables one to extract the key from this WB-AES with a 2^{30} time complexity. A subsequent WB-AES design introduced perturbations in the cipher in an attempt to thwart the previous attack [12]. This approach was broken [45] using algebraic analysis with a 2^{17} time complexity in 2010. Another WB-AES approach which resisted the previous attacks was presented in [60] in 2009 and got broken in 2012 with a work factor of 2^{32} [44].

Another interesting approach is based on using the different algebraic structure for the same instance of an iterative block cipher (as proposed originally in [7]). This approach [28] uses dual ciphers to modify the state and key representations in each round as well as two of the four classical AES operations. This approach was shown to be equivalent to the first WB-AES implementation [16] in [33] in 2013. Moreover, the authors of [33] built upon a 2012 result [57] which improves the most time-consuming phase of the BGE attack. This reduces the cost of the BGE attack to a time complexity of 2^{22}. An independent attack, of the same time complexity, is presented in [33] as well.

2.2 Prerequisites of Existing Attacks

In order to put our results in perspective, it is good to keep in mind the exact requirements needed to apply the white-box attacks from the scientific literature. These approaches require at least a basic knowledge of the scheme which is white-boxed. More precisely, the adversary needs to (1) know the type of encodings that are applied on *the intermediate results*, and (2) know which *cipher operations* are implemented by which *(network of) lookup tables*. The problem with these requirements is that vendors of white-box implementations are typically reluctant in sharing any information on their white-box scheme (the so-called "security through obscurity"). If that information is not directly accessible but only a binary executable or library is at disposal, one has to invest a significant amount of time in reverse-engineering the binary manually. Removing several layers of obfuscation before retrieving the required level of knowledge about the implementations needed to mount this type of attack successfully can be cumbersome. This additional effort, which requires a high level of expertise and experience, is illustrated by the sophisticated methods used as described in the write-ups of the publicly available challenges as detailed in Sect. 5. The differential computational analysis approach we outline in Sect. 4 does not need to remove the obfuscation layers nor requires reverse engineering of the binary executable.

3   Differential Power Analysis

Since the late 1990s it is publicly known that the (statistical) analysis of a power trace obtained when executing a cryptographic primitive might correlate to, and hence reveal information about, the secret key material used [32]. Typically, one assumes access to the hardware implementation of a known cryptographic algorithm. With $I(p_i, k)$ we denote a target intermediate state of the algorithm with input p_i and where only a small portion of the secret key is used in the computation, denoted by k. One assumes that the power consumption of the device at state $I(p_i, k)$ is the sum of a data dependent component and some random noise, i.e. $\mathcal{L}(I(p_i, k)) + \delta$, where the function $\mathcal{L}(s)$ returns the power consumption of the device during state s, and δ denotes some leakage noise. It is common to assume (see e.g., [39]) that the noise is random, independent from the intermediate state and is normally distributed with zero mean. Since the adversary has access to the implementation he can obtain triples (t_i, p_i, c_i). Here p_i is one plaintext input chosen arbitrarily by the adversary, the c_i is the ciphertext output computed by the implementation using a fixed unknown key, and the value t_i shows the power consumption over the time of the implementation to compute the output ciphertext c_i. The measured power consumption $\mathcal{L}(I(p_i, k)) + \delta$ is just a small fraction of this entire power trace t_i.

The goal of an attacker is to recover the part of the key k by comparing the real power measurements t_i of the device with an estimation of the power consumption under all possible hypotheses for k. The idea behind a Differential Power Analysis (DPA) attack [32] (see [31] for an introduction to this topic) is to divide the measurement traces in two distinct sets according to some property. For example, this property could be the value of one of the bits of the intermediate state $I(p_i, k)$. One assumes — and this is confirmed in practice by measurements on unprotected hardware — that the distribution of the power consumptions for these two sets is different (i.e., they have different means and standard deviations). In order to obtain information about part of the secret key k, for each trace t_i and input p_i, one enumerates all possible values for k (typically $2^8 = 256$ when attacking a key-byte), computes the intermediate value $g_i = I(p_i, k)$ for this key guess and divides the traces t_i into two sets according to this property measured at g_i. If the key guess k was correct then the difference of the subsets' averages will converge to the difference of the means of the distributions. However, if the key guess is wrong then the data in the sets can be seen as a random sampling of measurements and the difference of the means should converge to zero. This allows one to observe correct key guesses if enough traces are available. The number of traces required depends, among other things, on the measurement noise and means of the distributions (and hence is platform specific).

While having access to output ciphertexts is helpful to validate the recovered key, it is not strictly required. Inversely, one can attack an implementation where only the output ciphertexts are accessible, by targeting intermediate values in the last round. The same attacks apply obviously to the decryption operation.

The same technique can be applied on other traces which contain other types of side-channel information such as, for instance, the electromagnetic radiations of the device. Although we focus on DPA in this paper, it should be noted that there exist more advanced and powerful attacks. This includes, among others, higher order attacks [41], correlation power analyses [11] and template attacks [15].

4   Software Execution Traces

To assess the security of a binary executable implementing a cryptographic prim-itive, which is designed to be secure in the white-box attack model, one can execute the binary on a CPU of the corresponding architecture and observe its power consumption to mount a differential power analysis attack (see Sect. 3). However, in the white-box model, one can do much better as the model implies that we can observe everything without any measurement noise. In practice such level of observation can be achieved by instrumenting the binary or instrument-ing an emulator being in charge of the execution of the binary. We chose the first approach by using some of the available Dynamic Binary Instrumentation (DBI) frameworks. In short, DBI usually considers the binary executable to analyze as the bytecode of a virtual machine using a technique known as just-in-time com-pilation. This recompilation of the machine code allows performing transforma-tions on the code while preserving the original computational effects. DBI frame-works, like Pin [37] and Valgrind [46], perform another kind of transformation: they allow to add custom callbacks in between the machine code instructions by writing plugins or tools which hook into the recompilation process. These callbacks can be used to monitor the execution of the program and track specific events. The main difference between Pin and Valgrind is that Valgrind uses an architecture independent Intermediate Representation (IR) called VEX which allows to write tools compatible with any architecture supported by the IR. We developed (and released) such plugins for both frameworks to trace execution of binary executables on x86, x86-64, ARM and ARM64 platforms and record the desired information: namely, the memory addresses being accessed (for read, write or execution) and their content. It is also possible to record the content of CPU registers but this would slow down acquisition and increase the size of traces significantly; we succeeded to extract the secret key from the white-box implementations without this additional information. This is not surprising as table-based white-box implementations are mostly made of memory look-ups and make almost no use of arithmetic instructions (see Sect. 2 for the design rationale behind many white-box implementations). In some more complex con-figurations e.g. where the actual white-box is buried into a larger executable it might be desired to change the initial behavior of the executable to call directly the block cipher function or to inject a chosen plaintext in an internal applica-tion programming interface (API). This is trivial to achieve with DBI, but for the implementations presented in Sect. 5, we simply did not need to resort to such methods.

The following steps outline the process how to obtain software traces and mount a DPA attack on these software traces.

First Step. Trace a single execution of the white-box binary with an arbitrary plaintext and record all accessed addresses and data over time. Although the tracer is able to follow execution everywhere, including external and system libraries, we reduce the scope to the main executable or to a companion library if the cryptographic operations happen to be handled there. A common computer security technique often deployed by default on modern operating systems is the Address Space Layout Randomization (ASLR) which randomly arranges the address space positions of the executable, its data, its heap, its stack and other elements such as libraries. In order to make acquisitions completely reproducible we simply disable the ASLR, as the white-box model puts us in control over the execution environment. In case ASLR cannot be disabled, it would just be a mere annoyance to realign the obtained traces.

Second Step. Next, we visualize the trace to understand where the block cipher is being used and, by counting the number of repetitive patterns, determine which (standardized) cryptographic primitive is implemented: e.g., a 10-round AES-128, a 14-round AES-256, or a 16-round DES. To visualize a trace, we decided to represent it graphically similarly to the approach presented in [43]. Figure 1 illustrates this approach: the virtual address space is represented on the x-axis, where typically, on many modern platforms, one encounters the text segment (containing the instructions), the data segment, the uninitialized data (BSS) segment, the heap, and finally the stack, respectively. The virtual address space is extremely sparse so we display only bands of memory where there is something to show. The y-axis is a temporal axis going from top to bottom. Black represents addresses of instructions being executed, green represents addresses of memory locations being read and red when being written. In Fig. 1 one deduces that the code (in black) has been unrolled in one huge basic block, a lot of memory is accessed in reads from different tables (in green) and the stack is comparatively so small that the read and write accesses (in green and red) are barely noticeable on the far right without zooming in.

Third Step. Once we have determined which algorithm we target we keep the ASLR disabled and record multiple traces with random plaintexts, optionally using some criteria e.g. in which instructions address range to record activity. This is especially useful for large binaries doing other types of operations we are not interested in (e.g., when the white-box implementation is embedded in a larger framework). If the white-box operations themselves take a lot of time then we can limit the scope of the acquisition to recording the activity around just the first or last round, depending if we mount an attack from the input or output of the cipher. Focusing on the first or last round is typical in DPA-like attacks since it limits the portion of key being attacked to one single byte at once,

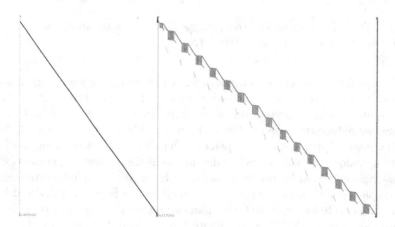

Fig. 1. Visualization of a software execution trace of a white-box DES implementation. (Color figure online)

as explained in Sect. 3. In the example given in Fig. 1, the read accesses pattern make it trivial to identify the DES rounds and looking at the corresponding instructions (in black) helps defining a suitable instructions address range. While recording all memory-related information in the initial trace (first step), we only record a single type of information (optionally for a limited address range) in this step. Typical examples include recordings of bytes being read from memory, or bytes written to the stack, or the least significant byte of memory addresses being accessed.

This generic approach gives us the best trade-off to mount the attack as fast as possible and minimize the storage of the software traces. If storage is not a concern, one can directly jump to the third step and record traces of the full execution, which is perfectly acceptable for executables without much overhead, as it will become apparent in several examples in Sect. 5. This naive approach can even lead to the creation of a fully automated acquisition and key recovery setup.

Fourth Step. In step 3 we have obtained a set of software traces consisting of lists of (partial) addresses or actual data which have been recorded whenever an instruction was accessing them. To move to a representation suitable for usual DPA tools expecting power traces, we serialize those values (usually bytes) into vectors of ones and zeros. This step is essential to exploit all the information we have recorded. To understand it, we compare to a classical hardware DPA setup targeting the same type of information: memory transfers.

When using DPA, a typical hardware target is a CPU with one 8-bit bus to the memory and all eight lines of that bus will be switching between low and high voltage to transmit data. If a leakage can be observed in the variations of the power consumption, it will be an analog value proportional to the sum of bits equal to one in the byte being transferred on that memory bus.

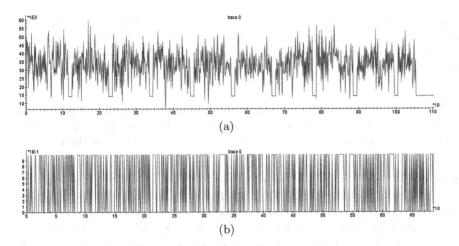

Fig. 2. Figure (a) is a typical example of a (hardware) power trace of an unprotected AES-128 implementation (one can observe the ten rounds). (b) is a typical example of a portion of a serialized software trace of stack writes in an AES-128 white-box, with only two possible values: zero or one.

Therefore, in such scenarios, the most elementary leakage model is the Hamming weight of the bytes being transferred between CPU and memory. However, in our software setup, we know the exact 8-bit value and to exploit it at best, we want to attack each bit individually, and not their sum (as in the Hamming weight model). Therefore, the serialization step we perform (converting the observed values into vectors of ones and zeros) is as if in the hardware model each corresponding bus line was leaking individually one after the other.

When performing a DPA attack, a power trace typically consists of sampled analog measures. In our software setting we are working with *perfect* leakages (i.e., no measurement noise) of the individual bits that can take only two possible values: 0 or 1. Hence, our software tracing can be seen from a hardware perspective as if we were probing each individual line with a needle, something requiring heavy sample preparation such as chip decapping and Focused Ion Beam (FIB) milling and patching operations to dig through the metal layers in order to reach the bus lines without affecting the chip functionality. Something which is much more powerful and invasive than external side-channel acquisition.

When using software traces there is another important difference with traditional power traces along the time axis. In a physical side-channel trace, analog values are sampled at a fixed rate, often unrelated to the internal clock of the device under attack, and the time axis represents time linearly. With software execution traces we record information only when it is relevant, e.g. every time a byte is written on the stack if that is the property we are recording, and moreover bits are serialized as if they were written sequentially. One may observe that given this serialization and sampling on demand, our time axis does not represent an actual time scale. However, a DPA attack does not require a proper time axis. It only requires that when two traces are compared, corresponding events that occurred at the same point in the program execution are compared against each other. Figure 2a and b illustrate those differences between traces obtained for usage with DPA and DCA, respectively.

Fifth Step. Once the software execution traces have been acquired and shaped, we can use regular DPA tools to extract the key. We show in the next section what the outcome of DPA tools look like, besides the recovery of the key.

Optional Step. If required, one can identify the exact points in the execution where useful information leaks. With the help of *known-key correlation* analysis one can locate the exact "faulty" instruction and the corresponding source code line, if available. This can be useful as support for the white-box designer.

To conclude this section, here is a summary of the prerequisites of our differential computation analysis, in opposition to the previous white-box attacks' prerequisites which were detailed in Sect. 2.2: (1) Be able to run several times (a few dozens to a few thousands) the binary in a controlled environment. (2) having knowledge of the plaintexts (before their encoding, if any), or of the ciphertexts (after their decoding, if any).

5   Analyzing Publicly Available White-Box Implementations

5.1   The Wyseur Challenge

As far as we are aware, the first public white-box challenge was created by Brecht Wyseur in 2007. On his website[2] one can find a binary executable containing a white-box DES encryption operation with a fixed embedded secret key. According to the author, this WB-DES approach implements the ideas from [17,35] (see Sect. 2.1) plus "some personal improvements". The interaction with the program is straight-forward: it takes a plaintext as input and returns a ciphertext as output to the console. The challenge was solved after five years (in 2012) independently by James Muir and "SysK". The latter provided a detailed description [54] and used differential cryptanalysis (similar to [23,59]) to extract the embedded secret key.

Figure 3a shows a full software trace of an execution of this WB-DES challenge. On the left one can see the loading of the instructions (in black), since the instructions are loaded repeatedly from the same addresses this implies that loops are used which execute the same sequence of instructions over and over again. Different data is accessed fairly linearly but with some local disturbances as indicated by the large diagonal read access pattern (in green). Even to the trained eye, the trace displayed in Fig. 3a does not immediately look familiar to DES. However, if one takes a closer look to the address space which represents

---

[2] See http://whiteboxcrypto.com/challenges.php.

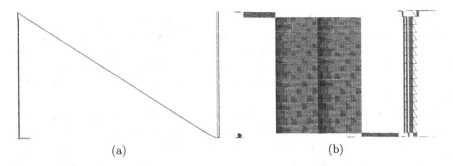

(a)   (b)

Fig. 3. (a) Visualization of a software execution trace of the binary Wyseur white-box challenge showing the entire accessed address range. (b) A zoom on the stack address space from the software trace shown in (a). The 16 rounds of the DES algorithm are clearly visible. (Color figure online)

the stack (on the far right) then the 16 rounds of DES can be clearly distinguished. This zoomed view is outlined in Fig. 3b where the y-axis is unaltered (from Fig. 3a) but the address-range (the x-axis) is rescaled to show only the read and write accesses to the stack.

Due to the loops in the program flow, we cannot just limit the tracer to a specific memory range of instructions and target a specific round. As a trace over the full execution takes a fraction of a second, we traced the entire program without applying any filter. The traces are easily exploited with DCA: e.g., if we trace the bytes written to the stack over the full execution and we compute a DPA over this entire trace without trying to limit the scope to the first round, the key is completely recovered with as few as 65 traces when using the output of the first round as intermediate value.

The execution of the entire attack, from the download of the binary challenge to full key recovery, including obtaining and analyzing the traces, took less than an hour as its simple textual interface makes it very easy to hook it to an attack framework. Extracting keys from different white-box implementations based on this design now only takes a matter of seconds when automating the entire process as outlined in Sect. 4.

5.2   The Hack.lu 2009 Challenge

As part of the Hack.lu 2009 conference, which aims to bridge ethics and security in computer science, Jean-Baptiste Bédrune released a challenge [4] which consisted of a *crackme.exe* file: an executable for the Microsoft Windows platform. When launched, it opens a GUI prompting for an input, redirects it to a white-box and compares the output with an internal reference. It was solved independently by Eloi Vanderbéken [58], who reverted the functionality of the white-box implementation from encryption to decryption, and by "SysK" [54] who managed to extract the secret key from the implementation.

Our plugins for the DBI tools have not been ported to the Windows operating system and currently only run on GNU/Linux and Android. In order to use our tools directly we decided to trace the binary with our Valgrind variant and Wine [1], an open source compatibility layer to run Windows applications under GNU/Linux. Due to the configuration of this challenge we had full control on the input to the white-box.

Visualizing the traces using our software framework clearly shows ten repetitive patterns on the left interleaved with nine others on the right. This indicates (with high probability) an AES encryption or decryption with a 128-bit key. The last round being shorter as it omits the *MixColumns* operation as per the AES specification. We captured a few dozen traces of the entire execution, without trying to limit ourselves to the first round. Due to the overhead caused by running the GUI inside Wine the acquisition ran slower than usual: obtaining a single trace took three seconds. Again, we applied our DCA technique on traces which recorded bytes written to the stack. The secret key could be completely recovered with only 16 traces when using the output of the first round *SubBytes* as intermediate value of an AES-128 encryption. As "SysK" pointed out in [54], this challenge was designed to be solvable in a couple of days and consequently did not implement any internal encoding, which means that the intermediate states can be observed directly. Therefore in our DCA the correlation between the internal states and the traced values get the highest possible value, which explains the low number of traces required to mount a successful attack.

5.3   The SSTIC 2012 Challenge

Every year for the SSTIC, *Symposium sur la sécurité des technologies de l'information et des communications* (Information technology and communication security symposium), a challenge is published which consists of solving several steps like a Matryoshka doll. In 2012, one step of the challenge [40] was to validate a key with a Python bytecode "check.pyc": i.e. a marshalled object[3]. Internally this bytecode generates a random plaintext, forwards this to a white-box (created by Axel Tillequin) *and* to a regular DES encryption using the key provided by the user and then compares both ciphertexts. Five participants managed to find the correct secret key corresponding to this challenge and their write-ups are available at [40]. A number of solutions identified the implementation as a WB-DES without encodings (naked variant) as described in [17]. Some extracted the key following the approach from the literature while some performed their own algebraic attack.

Tracing the entire Python interpreter with our tool, based on either PIN or Valgrind, to obtain a software trace of the Python binary results in a significant overhead. Instead, we instrumented the Python environment directly. Actually, Python bytecode can be decompiled with little effort as shown by the write-up of Jean Sigwald. This contains a decompiled version of the "check.pyc" file where the white-box part is still left serialized as a pickled object[4]. The white-

---

[3] https://docs.python.org/2/library/marshal.html
[4] https://docs.python.org/2/library/pickle.html

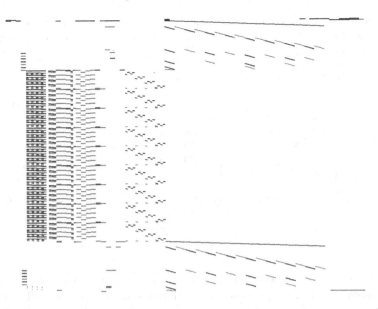

Fig. 4. Visualization of the stack reads and writes in the software execution trace portion limited to the core of the Karroumi WB-AES.

box makes use of a separate *Bits* class to handle its variables so we added some hooks to record all new instances of that particular class. This was sufficient. Again, as for the Hack.lu 2009 WB-AES challenge (see Sect. 5.2), 16 traces were enough to recover the key of this WB-DES when using the output of the first round as intermediate value. This approach works with such a low number of traces since the intermediate states are not encoded.

5.4   A White-Box Implementation of the Karroumi Approach

A white-box implementation of both the original AES approach [16] and the approach based on dual ciphers by Karroumi [28] is part of the Master thesis by Dušan Klinec [30][5]. As explained in Sect. 2.1, this is the latest academic variant of [16]. Since there is no challenge available, we used Klinec's implementation to create two challenges: one with and one without external encodings. This implementation is written in C++ with extensive use of the Boost[6] libraries to dynamically load and deserialize the white-box tables from a file. An initial software trace when running this white-box AES binary executable shows that the white-box code itself constitutes only a fraction of the total instructions (most of the instructions are from initializing the Boost libraries). From the stack trace (see Fig. 4) one can recognize the nine *MixColumns* operating on the four columns. Therefore we used instruction address filtering to focus on the white-box core and skip all the Boost C++ operations.

---

[5] The code be found at https://github.com/ph4r05/Whitebox-crypto-AES.
[6] http://www.boost.org/.

Table 1. DCA ranking for a Karroumi white-box implementation when targeting the output of the *SubBytes* step in the first round based on the least significant address byte on memory reads.

target bit	key byte															
	0	1	2	3	4	5	6	7	8	9	10	11	12	13	14	15
0	1	256	255	256	255	256	253	1	256	256	239	256	1	1	1	255
1	1	256	256	256	1	255	256	1	1	5	1	256	1	1	1	1
2	256	1	255	256	1	256	226	256	256	256	1	256	22	1	256	256
3	256	255	251	1	1	1	254	1	1	256	256	253	254	256	255	256
4	256	256	74	256	256	256	255	256	254	256	256	256	1	1	256	1
5	1	1	1	1	1	1	50	256	253	1	251	256	253	1	256	256
6	254	1	1	256	254	256	248	256	252	256	1	14	255	256	250	1
7	1	256	1	1	252	256	253	256	256	255	256	1	251	1	254	1
All	✓	✓	✓	✓	✓	✓	✗	✓	✓	✓	✓	✓	✓	✓	✓	✓

The best results were obtained when tracing the lowest byte of the memory addresses used in read accesses (excluding stack). Initially we followed the same approach as before: we targeted the output of the *SubBytes* in the first round. But, in contrast to the other challenges considered in this work, it was not enough to immediately recover the entire key. For some of the tracked bits of the intermediate value we observed a significant correlation peak: this is an indication that the first key candidate is very probably the correct one. Table 1 shows the ranking of the right key byte value amongst the guesses after 2000 traces, when sorted according to the difference of means (see Sect. 3). If the key byte is ranked at position 1 this means it was properly recovered by the attack. In total, for the first challenge we constructed, 15 out of 16 key bytes were ranked at position 1 for at least one of the target bits and one key byte (key byte 6 in the table) did not show any strong candidate. However, recovering this single missing key-byte is trivial using brute-force.

It is interesting to observe in Table 1 that when a target bit of a given key byte does not leak (i.e. is not ranked first) it is very often *the worst* candidate (ranked at the 256th position) rather than being at a random position. This observation, that still holds for larger numbers of traces, can also be used to recover the key. In order to give an idea of what can be achieved with an *automated* attack against new instantiations of this white-box implementation with other keys, we provide some figures: The acquisition of 2000 traces takes about 800s on a regular laptop (dual-core i7-4600U CPU at 2.10 GHz). This results in 3328 kbits (416 kB) of traces when limited to the execution of the first round. Running the attack requires less than 60 s. Attacking the second challenge with external encodings gave similar results. This was expected as there is no difference, from our adversary perspective, when applying external encodings or omitting them since in both cases we have knowledge of the original plaintexts before any encoding is applied.

5.5 The NoSuchCon 2013 Challenge

In April 2013, a challenge designed by Eloi Vanderbéken was published for the occasion of the NoSuchCon 2013 conference[7]. The challenge consisted of a Windows binary embedding a white-box AES implementation. It was of "keygen-me" type, which means one has to provide a name and the corresponding *serial* to succeed. Internally the serial is encrypted by a white-box and compared to the MD5 hash of the provided name.

The challenge was completed by a number of participants (cf. [38,53]) but without ever recovering the key. It illustrates one more issue designers of white-box implementations have to deal with in practice: one can convert an encryption routine into a decryption routine without actually extracting the key.

For a change, the design is not derived from Chow [16]. However, the white-box was designed with external encodings which were *not* part of the binary. Hence, the user input was considered as encoded with an unknown scheme and the encoded output is directly compared to a reference. These conditions, without any knowledge of the relationship between the real AES plaintexts or ciphertexts and the effective inputs and outputs of the white-box, make it infeasible to apply a meaningful DPA attack, since, for a DPA attack, we need to construct the guesses for the intermediate values. Note that, as discussed in Sect. 2, this white-box implementation is *not* compliant with AES anymore but computes some variant $E'_k = G \circ E_k \circ F^{-1}$. Nevertheless we did manage to recover the key and the encodings from this white-box implementation with a new algebraic attack, as described in [56]. This was achieved after a painful de-obfuscation of the binary (almost completely performed by previous write-ups [38,53]), a step needed to fulfill the prerequisites for such attacks as described in Sect. 2.2.

The same white-box is found among the CHES 2015 challenges[8] in a Game-Boy ROM and the same algebraic attack is used successfully as explained in [55] once the tables got extracted.

6 Countermeasures Against DCA

In hardware, counter-measures against DPA typically rely on a random source. The output can be used to mask intermediate results, to re-order instructions, or to add delays (see e.g. [14,24,51]). For white-box implementations, we cannot rely on a random source since in the white-box attack model such a source can simply be disabled or fixed to a constant value. Despite this lack of *dynamic* entropy, one can assume that the implementation which generates the white-box implementation has access to sufficient random data to incorporate in the generated source code and look-up tables. How to use this *static* random data embedded in the white-box implementation?

---

[7] See http://www.nosuchcon.org/2013/.

[8] https://ches15challenge.com/static/CHES15Challenge.zip, preserved at https://archive.org/details/CHES15Challenge

Adding (random) delays in an attempt to misalign traces is trivially defeated by using an address instruction trace beside the memory trace to realign traces automatically. In [18] it is proposed to use *variable* encodings when accessing the look-up tables based on the affine equivalences for bijective S-boxes (cf. [9] for algorithms to solve the affine equivalence problem for arbitrary permutations). As a potential countermeasure against DCA, the embedded (and possibly merged with other functionality) static random data is used to select which affine equivalence is used for the encoding when accessing a particular look-up table. This results in a variable encoding (at run-time) instead of using a fixed encoding. Such an approach can be seen as a form of masking as used to thwart classical first-order DPA.

One can also use some ideas from threshold implementations [47]. A threshold implementation is a masking scheme based on secret sharing and multi-party computation. One could also split the input in multiple shares such that not all shares belong to the same affine equivalence class. If this splitting of the shares and assignment to these (different) affine equivalence classes is done pseudorandomly, where the randomness comes from the static embedded entropy and the input message, then this might offer some resistance against DCA-like attacks.

In practice, one might resort to methods to make the job of the adversary more difficult. Typical software counter-measures include obfuscation, antidebug and integrity checks. It should be noted, however, that in order to mount a successful DCA attack one does not need to reverse engineer the binary executable. The DBI frameworks are very good at coping with those techniques and even if there are efforts to specifically detect DBI [21,34], DBI becomes stealthier too [29].

7 Conclusions and Future Work

As conjectured in the first papers introducing the white-box attack model, one cannot expect long-term defense against attacks on white-box implementations. However, as we have shown in this work, all current publicly available white-box implementations do not even offer any short-term security since the differential computation analysis (DCA) technique can extract the secret key within seconds. We did not investigate the strength of commercially available white-box products since no company, as far as we are aware, made a challenge publicly available similar to, for instance, the RSA factoring challenge [20] or the challenge related to elliptic curve cryptography [13].

Although we sketched some ideas on countermeasures, it remains an open question how to guard oneself against these types of attacks. The countermeasures against differential power analysis attacks applied in the area of high-assurance applications do not seem to carry over directly due to the ability of the adversary to disable or tamper with the random source. If medium to long term security is required then tamper resistant hardware solutions, like a secure element, seem like a much better alternative.

Another interesting research direction is to see if the more advanced and powerful techniques used in side-channel analysis from the cryptographic hardware community obtain even better results in this setting. Examples include correlation power analysis and higher order attacks.

References

1. Amstadt, B., Johnson, M.K.: Wine. Linux J. **1994**(4) (1994). http://dl.acm.org/citation.cfm?id=324681.324684, ISSN: 1075-3583
2. Barak, B., Garg, S., Kalai, Y.T., Paneth, O., Sahai, A.: Protecting obfuscation against algebraic attacks. In: Nguyen, P.Q., Oswald, E. (eds.) EUROCRYPT 2014. LNCS, vol. 8441, pp. 221–238. Springer, Heidelberg (2014)
3. Barak, B., Goldreich, O., Impagliazzo, R., Rudich, S., Sahai, A., Vadhan, S.P., Yang, K.: On the (im)possibility of obfuscating programs. In: Kilian, J. (ed.) CRYPTO 2001. LNCS, vol. 2139, pp. 1–18. Springer, Heidelberg (2001)
4. Bédrune, J.-B.: Hack.lu 2009 reverse challenge 1 (2009). http://2009.hack.lu/index.php/ReverseChallenge
5. Bhatkar, S., DuVarney, D.C., Sekar, R.: Address obfuscation: an efficient approach to combat a broad range of memory error exploits. In: Proceedings of the 12th USENIX Security Symposium. USENIX Association (2003)
6. Biham, E., Shamir, A.: Differential cryptanalysis of Snefru, Khafre, REDOC-II, LOKI and Lucifer. In: Feigenbaum, J. (ed.) CRYPTO 1991. LNCS, vol. 576, pp. 156–171. Springer, Heidelberg (1992)
7. Billet, O., Gilbert, H.: A traceable block cipher. In: Laih, C.-S. (ed.) ASIACRYPT 2003. LNCS, vol. 2894, pp. 331–346. Springer, Heidelberg (2003)
8. Billet, O., Gilbert, H., Ech-Chatbi, C.: Cryptanalysis of a white box AES implementation. In: Handschuh, H., Hasan, M.A. (eds.) SAC 2004. LNCS, vol. 3357, pp. 227–240. Springer, Heidelberg (2004)
9. Biryukov, A., Cannière, C., Braeken, A., Preneel, B.: A toolbox for cryptanalysis: linear and affine equivalence algorithms. In: Biham, E. (ed.) EUROCRYPT 2003. LNCS, vol. 2656, pp. 33–50. Springer, Heidelberg (2003)
10. Brakerski, Z., Rothblum, G.N.: Virtual black-box obfuscation for all circuits via generic graded encoding. In: Lindell, Y. (ed.) TCC 2014. LNCS, vol. 8349, pp. 1–25. Springer, Heidelberg (2014)
11. Brier, E., Clavier, C., Olivier, F.: Correlation power analysis with a leakage model. In: Joye, M., Quisquater, J.-J. (eds.) CHES 2004. LNCS, vol. 3156, pp. 16–29. Springer, Heidelberg (2004)
12. Bringer, J., Chabanne, H., Dottax, E.: White box cryptography: another attempt. Cryptology ePrint Archive, Report 2006/468 (2006). http://eprint.iacr.org/2006/468
13. Certicom: The certicom ECC challenge. https://www.certicom.com/index.php/the-certicom-ecc-challenge
14. Chari, S., Jutla, C.S., Rao, J.R., Rohatgi, P.: Towards sound approaches to counteract power-analysis attacks. In: Wiener, M. (ed.) CRYPTO 1999. LNCS, vol. 1666, pp. 398–412. Springer, Heidelberg (1999)
15. Chari, S., Rao, J.R., Rohatgi, P.: Template attack. In: Kaliski Jr., B.S., Koç, Ç.K., Paar, C. (eds.) CHES 2002. LNCS, vol. 2523, pp. 13–28. Springer, Heidelberg (2003)

16. Chow, S., Eisen, P.A., Johnson, H., van Oorschot, P.C.: White-box cryptography and an AES implementation. In: Nyberg, K., Heys, H.M. (eds.) SAC 2002. LNCS, vol. 2595, pp. 250–270. Springer, Heidelberg (2003)

17. Chow, S., Eisen, P., Johnson, H., van Oorschot, P.C.: A white-box DES implementation for DRM applications. In: Feigenbaum, J. (ed.) DRM 2002. LNCS, vol. 2696, pp. 1–15. Springer, Heidelberg (2003)

18. de Mulder, Y.: White-box cryptography: analysis of white-box AES implementations. Ph.D. thesis, KU Leuven (2014)

19. Delerablée, C., Lepoint, T., Paillier, P., Rivain, M.: White-box security notions for symmetric encryption schemes. In: Lange, T., Lauter, K., Lisoněk, P. (eds.) SAC 2013. LNCS, vol. 8282, pp. 247–264. Springer, Heidelberg (2014)

20. EMC Corporation: The RSA factoring challenge. http://www.emc.com/emc-plus/rsa-labs/historical/the-rsa-factoring-challenge.htm

21. Falco, F., Riva, N.: Dynamic binary instrumentation frameworks: I know you're there spying on me. In: REcon (2012). http://recon.cx/2012/schedule/events/216.en.html

22. Garg, S., Gentry, C., Halevi, S., Raykova, M., Sahai, A., Waters, B.: Candidate indistinguishability obfuscation and functional encryption for all circuits. In: 54th Annual IEEE Symposium on Foundations of Computer Science, FOCS, pp. 40–49. IEEE Computer Society (2013)

23. Goubin, L., Masereel, J.-M., Quisquater, M.: Cryptanalysis of white box DES implementations. In: Adams, C., Miri, A., Wiener, M. (eds.) SAC 2007. LNCS, vol. 4876, pp. 278–295. Springer, Heidelberg (2007)

24. Goubin, L., Patarin, J.: DES and differential power analysis. In: Koç, Ç.K., Paar, C. (eds.) CHES 1999. LNCS, vol. 1717, pp. 158–172. Springer, Heidelberg (1999)

25. Huang, Y., Ho, F.S., Tsai, H., Kao, H.M.: A control flow obfuscation method to discourage malicious tampering of software codes. In: Lin, F., Lee, D., Lin, B.P., Shieh, S., Jajodia, S. (eds.) Proceedings of the 2006 ACM Symposium on Information, Computer and Communications Security, ASIACCS 2006, p. 362. ACM (2006)

26. Jacob, M., Boneh, D., Felten, E.W.: Attacking an obfuscated cipher by injecting faults. In: Feigenbaum, J. (ed.) DRM 2002. LNCS, vol. 2696, pp. 16–31. Springer, Heidelberg (2003)

27. Jakobsson, M., Reiter, M.K.: Discouraging software piracy using software aging. In: Sander, T. (ed.) DRM 2001. LNCS, vol. 2320, pp. 1–12. Springer, Heidelberg (2002)

28. Karroumi, M.: Protecting white-box AES with dual ciphers. In: Rhee, K.-H., Nyang, D.H. (eds.) ICISC 2010. LNCS, vol. 6829, pp. 278–291. Springer, Heidelberg (2011)

29. Kirsch, J.: Towards transparent dynamic binary instrumentation using virtual machine introspection. In: REcon (2015). https://recon.cx/2015/schedule/events/20.html

30. Klinec, D.: White-box attack resistant cryptography. Master's thesis, Masaryk University, Brno, Czech Republic (2013). https://is.muni.cz/th/325219/fi_m/

31. Kocher, P., Jaffe, J., Jun, B., Rohatgi, P.: Introduction to differential power analysis. J. Cryptogr. Eng. 1(1), 5–27 (2011)

32. Kocher, P.C., Jaffe, J., Jun, B.: Differential power analysis. In: Wiener, M. (ed.) CRYPTO 1999. LNCS, vol. 1666, pp. 388–397. Springer, Heidelberg (1999)

33. Lepoint, T., Rivain, M., De Mulder, Y., Roelse, P., Preneel, B.: Two attacks on a white-box AES implementation. In: Lange, T., Lauter, K., Lisoněk, P. (eds.) SAC 2013. LNCS, vol. 8282, pp. 265–286. Springer, Heidelberg (2014)

34. Li, X., Li, K.: Defeating the transparency features of dynamic binary instrumentation. In: BlackHat US (2014). https://www.blackhat.com/docs/us-14/materials/us-14-Li-Defeating-The-Transparency-Feature-Of-DBI.pdf
35. Link, H.E., Neumann, W.D.: Clarifying obfuscation: improving the security of white-box DES. In: International Symposium on Information Technology: Coding and Computing (ITCC 2005), pp. 679–684. IEEE Computer Society (2005)
36. Linn, C., Debray, S.K.: Obfuscation of executable code to improve resistance to static disassembly. In: Jajodia, S., Atluri, V., Jaeger, T. (eds.) Proceedings of the 10th ACM Conference on Computer and Communications Security, CCS 2003, pp. 290–299. ACM (2003)
37. Luk, C., Cohn, R.S., Muth, R., Patil, H., Klauser, A., Lowney, P.G., Wallace, S., Reddi, V.J., Hazelwood, K.M.: Pin: building customized program analysis tools with dynamic instrumentation. In: Sarkar, V., Hall, M.W. (eds.) Proceedings of the ACM SIGPLAN 2005 Conference on Programming Language Design and Implementation, pp. 190–200. ACM (2005)
38. Maillet, A.: Nosuchcon 2013 challenge - write up and methodology (2013). http://kutioo.blogspot.be/2013/05/nosuchcon-2013-challenge-write-up-and.html
39. Mangard, S., Oswald, E., Standaert, F.: One for all - all for one: unifying standard differential power analysis attacks. IET Inf. Secur. 5(2), 100–110 (2011)
40. Marceau, F., Perigaud, F., Tillequin, A.: Challenge SSTIC 2012 (2012). http://communaute.sstic.org/ChallengeSSTIC2012
41. Messerges, T.S.: Using second-order power analysis to attack DPA resistant software. In: Paar, C., Koç, Ç.K. (eds.) CHES 2000. LNCS, vol. 1965, pp. 238–251. Springer, Heidelberg (2000)
42. Michiels, W.: Opportunities in white-box cryptography. IEEE Secur. Priv. 8(1), 64–67 (2010)
43. Mougey, C., Gabriel, F.: Désobfuscation de DRM par attaques auxiliaires. In: Symposium sur la sécurité des technologies de l'information et des communications (2014). http://www.sstic.org/2014/presentation/dsobfuscation_de_drm_par_attaques_auxiliaires
44. De Mulder, Y., Roelse, P., Preneel, B.: Cryptanalysis of the Xiao–Lai white-box AES implementation. In: Knudsen, L.R., Wu, H. (eds.) SAC 2012. LNCS, vol. 7707, pp. 34–49. Springer, Heidelberg (2013)
45. De Mulder, Y., Wyseur, B., Preneel, B.: Cryptanalysis of a perturbated white-box AES implementation. In: Gong, G., Gupta, K.C. (eds.) INDOCRYPT 2010. LNCS, vol. 6498, pp. 292–310. Springer, Heidelberg (2010)
46. Nethercote, N., Seward, J.: Valgrind: a framework for heavyweight dynamic binary instrumentation. In: Ferrante, J., McKinley, K.S., (eds.) Proceedings of the ACM SIGPLAN 2007 Conference on Programming Language Design and Implementation, pp. 89–100. ACM (2007)
47. Nikova, S., Rechberger, C., Rijmen, V.: Threshold implementations against side-channel attacks and glitches. In: Ning, P., Qing, S., Li, N. (eds.) ICICS 2006. LNCS, vol. 4307, pp. 529–545. Springer, Heidelberg (2006)
48. Polla, M.L., Martinelli, F., Sgandurra, D.: A survey on security for mobile devices. IEEE Commun. Surv. Tutor. 15(1), 446–471 (2013)
49. Sanfelix, E., de Haas, J., Mune, C.: Unboxing the white-box: practical attacks against obfuscated ciphers. In: BlackHat Europe 2015 (2015). https://www.blackhat.com/eu-15/briefings.html
50. Sasdrich, P., Moradi, A., Güneysu, T.: White-box cryptography in the gray box - a hardware implementation and its side channels. In: FSE 2016, LNCS. Springer, Heidelberg (2016, to appear)

51. Schramm, K., Paar, C.: Higher order masking of the AES. In: Pointcheval, D. (ed.) CT-RSA 2006. LNCS, vol. 3860, pp. 208–225. Springer, Heidelberg (2006)
52. Scrinzi, F.: Behavioral analysis of obfuscated code. Master's thesis, University of Twente, Twente, Netherlands (2015). http://essay.utwente.nl/67522/1/Scrinzi_MA_SCS.pdf
53. Souchet, A.: AES whitebox unboxing: No such problem (2013). http://0vercl0k.tuxfamily.org/bl0g/?p=253
54. SysK: Practical cracking of white-box implementations. Phrack 68: 14. http://www.phrack.org/issues/68/8.html
55. Teuwen, P.: CHES2015 writeup (2015). http://wiki.yobi.be/wiki/CHES2015_Writeup#Challenge_4
56. Teuwen, P.: NSC writeups (2015). http://wiki.yobi.be/wiki/NSC_Writeups
57. Tolhuizen, L.: Improved cryptanalysis of an AES implementation. In: Proceedings of the 33rd WIC Symposium on Information Theory. Werkgemeenschap voor Inform.-en Communicatietheorie (2012)
58. Vanderbéken, E.: Hacklu reverse challenge write-up (2009). http://baboon.rce.free.fr/index.php?post/2009/11/20/HackLu-Reverse-Challenge
59. Wyseur, B., Michiels, W., Gorissen, P., Preneel, B.: Cryptanalysis of white-box DES implementations with arbitrary external encodings. In: Adams, C., Miri, A., Wiener, M. (eds.) SAC 2007. LNCS, vol. 4876, pp. 264–277. Springer, Heidelberg (2007)
60. Xiao, Y., Lai, X.: A secure implementation of white-box AES. In: 2nd International Conference on Computer Science and its Applications 2009, CSA 2009, pp. 1–6 (2009)
61. Zhou, Y., Chow, S.: System and method of hiding cryptographic private keys. 15 December 2009. US Patent 7,634,091

Antikernel: A Decentralized Secure Hardware-Software Operating System Architecture

Andrew Zonenberg[1](✉) and Bülent Yener[2]

[1] IOActive Inc., Seattle, WA 98105, USA
andrew.zonenberg@ioactive.com
[2] Rensselaer Polytechnic Institute, Troy, NY 12180, USA
yener@cs.rpi.edu

Abstract. The "kernel" model has been part of operating system architecture for decades, but upon closer inspection it clearly violates the principle of least required privilege. The kernel is a single entity which provides many services (memory management, interfacing to drivers, context switching, IPC) having no real relation to each other, and has the ability to observe or tamper with all state of the system. This work presents *Antikernel*, a novel operating system architecture consisting of both hardware and software components and designed to be fundamentally more secure than the state of the art. To make formal verification easier, and improve parallelism, the Antikernel system is highly modular and consists of many independent hardware state machines (one or more of which may be a general-purpose CPU running application or systems software) connected by a packet-switched network-on-chip (NoC). We create and verify an FPGA-based prototype of the system.

Keywords: Network on chip · System on chip · Security · Operating systems · Hardware accelerators

1 Introduction

The Antikernel architecture is intended to be more, yet less, than simply a "kernel in hardware". By breaking up functionality and decentralizing as much as possible we aim to create a platform that allows applications to pick and choose the OS features they wish to use, thus reducing their attack surface dramatically compared to a conventional OS (and potentially experiencing significant performance gains, as in an exokernel).[1]

Antikernel is a decentralized architecture with no system calls; all OS functionality is accessed through message passing directly to the relevant service. To create a process, the user sends a message to the CPU core he wishes to run it on. To allocate memory, he sends a message to the RAM controller.

---

[1] This paper is based on author 1's doctoral dissertation research [1].

© International Association for Cryptologic Research 2016
B. Gierlichs and A.Y. Poschmann (Eds.): CHES 2016, LNCS 9813, pp. 237–256, 2016.
DOI: 10.1007/978-3-662-53140-2_12

Each of these nodes is self-contained and manages its own state internally (although nodes are free to, and many will, request services from other nodes).

There is no "all-powerful" software; all functionality normally implemented by a kernel is handled by unprivileged software or hardware. Even the hardware is limited in capability; for example the flash controller has no access to RAM owned by the CPU. By formally verifying the isolation and interprocess communication, we can achieve a level of security which exceeds even that of a conventional separation kernel: even arbitrary code execution on a CPU grants no privileges beyond those normally available to userspace software. Escalation to "ring 0" or "kernel mode" is made impossible due to the complete lack of such privileges; unprivileged userspace runs directly on "bare metal".

Thus Antikernel architecture unifies two previously orthogonal fields - hardware accelerators and operating system (OS) security - in order to create a new OS architecture which can enforce OS security policy at a much lower level than previously possible. In contrast to the classical OS model, our system blurs or eliminates many of the typical boundaries between software, hardware, kernels, and drivers. Most uniquely, there is no single piece of software or hardware in our architecture which corresponds to the kernel in a classical OS. The operating system is instead an emergent entity arising out of the collective behavior of a series of distinct hardware modules connected via message passing, which together provide all of the services normally provided by a kernel and drivers. Each hardware device includes state machines which implement low-level resource management and security for that particular device, and provides an API via message passing *directly to userspace*. Applications software may either access this API directly (as in an exokernel [2]) or through server software providing additional abstractions (as in a microkernel).

By decentralizing to this extent, and creating natural chokepoints for dataflow between functional subsystems (as in a separation kernel [3,4]), we significantly reduce the portion of the system which is potentially compromised in the event of a vulnerability in any one part, and render API-hooking rootkits impossible (since there is no syscall table to tamper with). In order to avoid difficult-to-analyze side channels between multiple modules accessing shared memory, we require that all communication between modules take place via message passing (as in a multikernel [5]). This modular structure allows piecewise formal verification of the system since the dataflow between all components is constrained to a single well-defined interface.

Unlike virtualization-based separation platforms (such as Qubes [6]), our architecture does not require massive processing and memory overhead for each security domain, and is thus well suited to running many security domains on an embedded system with limited resources. Our architecture also scales to a large number of mutually untrusting security domains, unlike platforms such as ARM TrustZone [7] which provide one-way protection of a single domain.

We have tested the feasibility of the architecture by creating a proof-of-concept implementation targeting a Xilinx FPGA, and report experimental results including formal correctness proofs for several key components. The prototype is open source [8] to encourage verification of our results and further research.

2 Related Work

There are many examples in the literature of operating system components being moved into hardware[2] however the majority of these systems are focused on performance and do not touch on the security implications of their designs at all.

Fundamentally, any hard-wired OS component has an intrinsic *local* security benefit over an equivalent software version - it is physically impossible for software to tamper with it. This brings an unfortunate corollary - it cannot be patched if a design error, possibly with security implications, is discovered. Extremely careful testing and validation of both the design and implementation is thus required. Furthermore, hardware OSes may not provide any *global* benefits to security: If the hardware component does not perform adequate validation or authentication on commands passed to it from software, compromised or malicious software can simply coerce the hardware into doing its bidding. Next we briefly review some of the related work in this domain.

2.1 Security Agnostic Hardware Accelerations

Several researchers implemented hardware accelerators for various RTOS functions: [9] proposes a distributed OS built into a network-on-chip, or NoC; [10] proposes a basic RTOS which contains a simple hardware microkernel implementing a scheduler, semaphores, and timers; [11] describes a microkernel-based OS using a 2D mesh NoC. Each node is a CPU with a microkernel on it, running user processes and/or servers. [12] proposes a "hardware OS kernel", or HOSK, which is connected to a conventional (unmodified) RISC processor and functions as an accelerator. [13] describes BORPH, an operating system for a reconfigurable platform containing one or more CPUs and one or more reconfigurable components such as FPGAs. It introduces the concept of a "hardware process", which is functionally equivalent to a conventional OS process.

While these approaches provide significant performance benefits compared to a software-only implementation, there are no authentication or protection capabilities built into them, thus they provide no security benefits.

2.2 Security-Focused Designs

[14] presents an FPGA-based implementation of a separation kernel. It describes a distributed OS based on a "time-triggered network on chip" (TTNoC) connecting a series of IP cores, each considered a separate partition within the system.

---

[2] This paper uses the term "hardware OS" to refer to a series of state machines implemented in silicon which provide operating system services to a computer. Some other authors use the same term to refer to a very different concept: a component of an operating system (which is typically implemented in software) responsible for managing partitions of an FPGA or other reconfigurable computing device.

While the TTNoC provides complete and deterministic isolation between hosts (i.e., no traffic sent by any other host can ever impact the ability of another to communicate and thus there are no timing/resource exhaustion side channels) it suffers from the lack of burst capabilities and does not scale well to systems involving a large number of hosts (in a system with N nodes each one can only use 1/N of the available bandwidth).

[15] describes a "zero-kernel operating system" or ZKOS. The general guiding principles of "no all-powerful component", "hardware-software codesign", and "safe design" are very similar to our work, as well as the conclusion that privilege rings are an archaic and far too coarse-grained concept. The main difference is that their system relies on "streams" (point-to-point one-way communications links) and "gates" (similar to a syscall vector, allows one security domain to call into another) for IPC and does not support arbitrary point-to-point communication. Furthermore, while threading and message passing are implemented in hardware, the ZKOS architecture appears to be primarily software based with minimal hardware support and does not support hardware processes/drivers. Finally, BiiN [16] was the result of a joint Intel-Siemens project to develop a fault-tolerant computer, which could be configured in several fault-tolerant modes including paired lock-step CPUs. A capability-based security system is used to control access to particular objects in memory or disk. The system architecture advocates heavy compartmentalization with each program divided up as much as possible, and using protected memory between compartments (although the goal was reliability against hardware faults through means such as error correcting codes and lock-stepped CPUs, not security against tampering). No mention of formal verification could be found in any published documentation.

3 Antikernel Network Architecture

At the highest logical level, an Antikernel-based system consists of a series of nodes (userspace processes or hardware peripherals) organized in a quadtree[3] and connected by a packet-switched NoC with 16-bit addressing.[4] Hardware and software components are indistinguishable to developers and are addressed using the same message passing interface.

Each bottom-level leaf node is assigned a /16 subnet (a single address) and corresponds to a single hardware module. The next level nodes are routers for /14

---

[3] The choice of a quadtree was made purely for convenience of prototyping. Other implementations of the Antikernel architecture could use an octree, 2D grid, add direct sibling-to-sibling links to reduce load on the root, or use more esoteric topologies depending on system requirements.

[4] For the remainder of this paper, NoC routing addresses are written in IPv6-style hexadecimal CIDR notation. For example the subnet consisting of all possible addresses is denoted 0000/0, 8002/16 is a single host, etc. The architecture can be scaled to larger address sizes in the future if needed, however it is unlikely that more than 65536 unique IP cores will be present in any SoC in the near future and smaller addresses require less FPGA resources.

subnets, followed by routers for /12 subnets, and so on. Routers are instantiated as needed to cover active subnets only; if there are only four nodes in the system the network will consist of a single top-level router with four children rather than an eight-level tree. Nodes may also be allocated a subnet larger than a /16 if they require multiple addresses: perhaps a CPU with support for four hardware threads, with each thread as its own security domain, would use a /14 sized subnet so that the remainder of the system can distinguish between the threads.

"The network" is actually two parallel networks specialized for different purposes, as shown in Fig. 1. The RPC network transports fixed-size datagrams consisting of one header word and three data words, and is optimized for low-latency control-plane traffic. The DMA network transports variable size datagrams, and is optimized for high-throughput data-plane traffic. Each node uses the same address on both networks to ensure consistency, although individual nodes are free to only use one network and disable their associated port on the other (for example, node "n8002/16"). Entire routers for one network or the other may be optimized out by the code generator if they have no children (for example, there is no RPC router for the subnet 8004/14 as all nodes in that subnet are DMA-only).

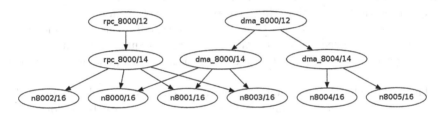

Fig. 1. Example routing topology showing RPC and DMA

A full link for either network contains two independent unidirectional links, each consisting of a 32-bit data bus[5] and several status flags. Since the prototype is FPGA-based all network links are system-synchronous, however they could fairly easily be converted to source-synchronous for a globally-asynchronous/locally synchronous (GALS) ASIC clocking structure.

Packets for both networks begin with a single-word layer-2 routing header containing the 16-bit source and destination node addresses, followed by protocol-specific layer-3 headers.[6] Each network guarantees strict FIFO ordering, as well as reliable delivery, for any two endpoints.

---

[5] Links could potentially scale to 64, 128, or larger multiples of 32 bits if higher bandwidth is needed, however our prototype does not implement this.

[6] There is no layer-2 header field to distinguish RPC and DMA traffic; since the networks are physically distinct the protocol can be trivially determined from context. Alternate implementations of the architecture could potentially merge both protocols into a single network with an additional header to specify the protocol.

3.1   Remote Procedure Call (RPC)

An RPC message consists of the standard layer-2 routing header followed by an ID indicating the operation to be performed ("call"), a type field ("op"), and the message payload.

Any RPC transaction involves two nodes. The node which initiates the transaction is designated the *master*; the other is designated the *slave*. These roles are not fixed and any node may choose to act as a master or slave at any time.

Interrupts. The simplest kind of RPC transaction is an *interrupt*[7]: a unidirectional notification from master to slave. RPC interrupts are typically sent to inform the slave that some long-running operation (such as a backgrounded DMA write to slow flash memory) has completed at the master, or that an external event took place (such as an Ethernet frame arriving, or a button pressed). The `call` field of an interrupt packet is set to a value chosen by the master describing the specific type of event; the data fields may or may not be significant depending on the specific master's application-layer protocol.

Function Calls. The second major kind of RPC transaction is a function call: a request by the master that the slave take some action, followed by a result from the slave. This result may be either a success/fail return value indicating that the remote procedure call completed, or a retry request indicating that the slave is too busy to accept new requests and that the call should be repeated later.

The `call` field of a function call packet is set to a slave-dependent value describing one of 256 functions the master wishes the slave to perform. The meaning of the data fields is dependent on the slave's application-layer protocol.

A return packet (including a retry) must have the same `call` value as the incoming function call request to allow matching of requests to responses. The meaning of the data fields is dependent on the slave's application-layer protocol.

Although not implemented by any current slaves, the RPC call protocol allows out-of-order (OoO) transaction processing (handling multiple requests in the most efficient order, rather than that in which they were received).

Flow Control/Routing. The RPC protocol will function over links with arbitrary latency (and thus register stages may be added at any point on a long link to improve timing), however a round-trip delay of more than one packet time will reduce throughput since the transmitter must block until an ACK arrives from the next-hop router before it can send the next packet. We plan to solve this issue with credit-based flow control in a future revision.

---

[7] Note that the term "interrupt" was chosen because these messages convey roughly the same information that IRQs do in classical computer architecture. While the slave node is free to interrupt its processing and act on the incoming message immediately, it may also choose to buffer the incoming message and handle it later.

The RPC router is a full crossbar which allows any of the five ports to send to any other, with multiple packets in flight simultaneously. Each exit queue maintains a round-robin counter which increments mod 5 each time a packet is sent. In the event that two ports wish to send out the same port simultaneously, the port identified by the counter is given max priority; otherwise the lowest numbered source port wishing to send wins. This ensures baseline quality of service (each port is guaranteed 20% of the available bandwidth) while still permitting bursting (a port can use up to 100% of available bandwidth if all others are idle).

3.2 Direct Memory Access (DMA)

Packet Structure and Semantics. A DMA packet consists of the standard layer-2 routing header followed by a type field, data length, and a 32-bit address indicating the target of the DMA operation. This is then followed by message content (up to 512 32-bit words in our current prototype) for "read data" and "write data" packets. The "read request" packet has no data field.

All write operations must be to an integral number of 32-bit words; byte masking is not supported (although it could potentially be added in the future by using some of the reserved bits in the DMA header). If byte-level write granularity is required this is typically implemented with a read-modify-write.

Since the DMA address field is 32 bits, a maximum of 4 GB may be addressed within a single device (/16 subnet). Nodes requiring >4 GB of address space may be assigned to larger subnets; for example a SD card controller might use a /14 subnet (4 routing addresses) to permit use of cards up to 16 GB (4 × 4 GB). When sending pointers between nodes it is necessary to send both the 16-bit routing address and the 32-bit pointer. The resulting 48-bit physical address uniquely identifies a single byte of data within the system.

Memory Read/Write. A memory read transaction consists of one packet from master to slave, with the type field set to "read request", the address set to the location of the data being requested, and the length set to the number of words being read. If the request is permitted by the slave's security policy, it responds with a packet of type "read data". Address and length are set as in the requested packet, and the data field contains the data being returned. If the request is not permitted by policy, the slave returns an error code so that the master knows no response is forthcoming.

A memory write consists of one packet from master to slave, with the type field set to "write data" and length/address set appropriately. If the request is permitted by the slave's security policy, it responds with a "write complete" RPC interrupt. This allows the master to implement memory-fencing semantics for interprocess communication: to avoid potential race conditions, one cannot send the pointer to another node (or change access controls on it) until the in-flight write has completed. If the request is not permitted, the slave returns an RPC error interrupt so that the master knows the underlying physical memory has not been modified.

Flow Control and Routing. The current DMA flow control scheme expects a fixed single-cycle latency between routers with lock-step acknowledgement[8]. The DMA router uses the same arbiter and crossbar modules as the RPC router, although the buffers are somewhat larger.

4   Memory Management

One of the most critical services an operating system must provide is allowing applications to allocate, free, and manipulate RAM. In the minimalistic environment of an exokernel there is no need for an OS to provide sub-page allocation granularity, so we require nodes to allocate full pages of memory and manage sub-page regions (such as for C's `malloc()` function) in a userspace heap. If a block larger than a page is required, the node must allocate multiple single pages and map them sequentially to its internal address space.

Antikernel's memory management enforces a "one page, one owner" model. Shared memory is intentionally not supported, however data may be transferred from one node to another in a zero-copy fashion by changing ownership of the page(s) containing the data to the new user.

The Antikernel memory management API is extremely simple, in keeping with the exokernel design philosophy. It consists of four RPC calls for manipulating pages ("get free page count", "allocate page", "free page", and "change ownership of page") as well as DMA reads and writes. A "write complete" RPC interrupt is provided to allow nodes to implement memory fencing semantics before `chown()`ing a page.

The data structures required to implement this API are extremely simple, and thus easy to formally verify: a FIFO queue of free pages and an array mapping page IDs to owner IDs. When the memory subsystem initializes, the FIFO is filled with the IDs of all pages not used for the internal metadata and the ownership array records all pages as owned by the memory manager.

Requesting the free page count simply returns the size of the free list FIFO. Allocating a page fails if the free list is empty. If not, the first page address on the FIFO is popped and returned to the caller; the ownership records are also updated to record the caller as the new owner of the page. Freeing a page is essentially the allocation procedure run in reverse. After checking that the caller is the owner of the page, it is zeroized to prevent any data leakage between nodes, then pushed onto the free list and the ownership records updated to record the memory manager as the new owner of the page. Changing page ownership does not touch the free list at all; after verifying that the caller is the owner of the page the ownership records are simply updated with the new owner.

DMA reads and writes perform ownership checks and, if successful, return or update the contents of the requested range. The current memory controller API requires that all DMA transactions be aligned to 128-bit (4 word) boundaries, be a multiple of 4 words in size, and not cross page boundaries.

---

[8] We plan to extend this in the future in order to support variable latency for long-range cross-chip links, as was done for RPC.

The current prototype codebase contains two compatible implementations of the Antikernel memory management API: BlockRamAllocator (backed by on-die block RAM, parameterizable size) and NetworkedDDR2Controller (backed by DDR2, currently fixed at 128 MB capacity with a 16-bit bus). A parameterizable-depth allocator backed by DDR3 or QDR-II+ is planned, but has not yet been implemented.

Since Antikernel's architecture is inherently NUMA, multiple memory controllers may be instantiated without causing problems as long as full 48-bit pointers are used to avoid ambiguity.

5   SARATOGA Processor and Threading

The prototype CPU for Antikernel (named SARATOGA) is a high-performance dual-issue in-order barrel processor using a modified version of the the MIPS-1 instruction set with an 8-stage pipeline[9] and a parameterizable number of hardware threads.[10] This produces the net effect of 8 virtual CPUs at 1/8 the core clock rate, time-sharing the same two execution units.

The CPU can easily reach around 180 MHz on a Xilinx Artix-7 FPGA (-2 speed), and can be pushed to 200 with careful floorplanning of the L1 caches and register file. Area is 5700 flipflops, 6400 LUTs, 2570 slices, and 44 RAMs for the CPU itself. The reference system is 12800 flipflops, 15100 LUTs, 5900 slices, and 77 RAMs.[11] This includes the standard Antikernel infrastructure (name server, JTAG debug bridge, system info core), as well as a packet sniffer observing the CPU's RPC uplink to aid in system bring-up.

In addition to allocating one NoC address per hardware thread, the CPU has a dedicated management address used for out-of-band control functionality. This allows applications to request services from the CPU (for example starting a new process, quitting, or modifying their page table). The first address of the CPU's subnet is used as the OoB management address. This ensures that any node which queries the name server for the hostname of the processor will get the management address. The high half of the subnet is used for thread addresses; all other addresses in the low half of the subnet are unused and incoming packets are dropped.

5.1   Thread Scheduler

The processor begins in the idle state; the run queue (a circular linked list) is empty, with no threads running. A free-list of thread IDs is initialized to contain every valid thread ID, and a bitmap of thread IDs is initialized to the "unallocated" state. When a "create new process" message is received by the

---

[9] The pipeline has two stages of instruction fetch, two of decode/register fetch, and four of execution.

[10] Any power of two ≥ 8 is legal; the default for synthesis is 32.

[11] These numbers are for the default configuration with 32 threads, 2-way cache associativity, 16 lines of 8 words per cache bank.

CPU on its management address the free list is popped, the bitmap is updated to reflect that this thread ID is allocated, and the thread ID is now available for use (but is not yet scheduled). A simple hardware state machine loads the statically linked ELF executable at the provided physical address, initializes the thread, and requests that the scheduler append it to the run queue.

During execution, the CPU reads the current thread from the linked list and schedules it for execution if possible, then goes on to the next thread in the linked list the following cycle. If the thread is already in the pipeline (which may be true if less than 8 threads are currently runnable) then it waits for one cycle and tries again. If the thread is not in the run queue at all (which may be true if the thread was just canceled, or if no threads are currently runnable), then the CPU goes to the next thread and tries again the next cycle.

To delete a thread, it is removed from the linked list and pushed into the free list, and the bitmaps are updated to reflect its state as free. The linked-list pointers for the deleted thread are not changed; this ensures that if the CPU is about to execute the thread being deleted it will correctly read the "next" pointer and continue to a runnable thread the next clock cycle. (There are no use-after-free problems possible due to the multi-cycle latency of the allocate and free routines; by the time the freshly deleted thread can be reallocated the CPU is guaranteed to have continued to a runnable thread.)

The architecture allows for a thread to very quickly remove itself from the run queue without terminating (although the thread management API does not currently provide a means for doing this). This will allow threads blocking on IO or an L1 cache miss to be placed in a "sleep" state from which they can quickly awake, but which does not waste CPU time.

5.2   Execution Units

SARATOGA has two execution units connected to separate ports on the register file. Both are copies of the same Verilog module however some functionality is left unconnected (and thus optimized out) in execution unit 1. Each execution unit takes in two values from the register file during EXEC0, and outputs one value to the register file during EXEC3.

During EXEC0, unit 0 may dispatch an RPC send or receive, or a memory transaction. Results from RPC receives (if data is available), as well as memory operations (in case of an L1 cache hit) are available during EXEC2. All ALU operations other than integer division complete by EXEC1.

5.3   L1 Cache

The L1 cache for SARATOGA is split into independent I- and D-side banks, and is fully parameterizable for levels of associativity, words per line, and lines per thread. The default configuration is 2-way set associative and 16 lines of 8 32-bit words, for a total size of 1 KB instruction and 1 KB data cache per thread (plus tag bits) and 32 KB overall. The cache is virtually addressed and there is no coherency between the I- and D-side caches.

The current cache is quite small per thread, which is likely to lead to a high miss rate, but this is somewhat made up for by the ability of multithreading to hide latency - if all 32 threads are active, a 31-cycle miss latency can be tolerated with a penalty of only one skipped instruction. We have not yet implemented performance counters for measuring cache performance; after this is added there are likely to be numerous optimizations to the cache structure.

5.4   MMU

In order to speed prototyping a very simple MMU was created, consisting of a software-controlled TLB with no external page tables. It supports a parameterizable number (the default is 32) of 2 KB pages of virtual memory per thread, mapped consecutively starting at virtual address 0x40000000. Each thread has a fully independent virtual address space, meaning that the total amount of virtual memory addressable by all threads combined in the default configuration is 32*32 pages, or 2 MB. This has been sufficient for initial prototyping; a full MMU with a TLB and external page tables in RAM is planned for the future. Since software accesses the MMU using an abstracted API via the CPU management port, it is possible to make arbitrary changes to the internal MMU and TLB structure without breaking software compatibility.

Each page table entry consists of a valid bit, R/W/X permission flags, a 16-bit node ID, and a 21-bit upper address within that node (low bits are implicit zero). This allows the full 48 bits of physical address space to be used.

5.5   RPC Network Interface

In order to send an RPC message, the high half of the a0 register is loaded with the "send" opcode; the low half of a0, as well as a1, a2, and a3, store the RPC message. This is identical to the standard C calling convention for MIPS, which makes implementation of the syscall() library function trivial. (The high half of a0 is used as the opcode since this would normally be the source address of the packet, but this is added by hardware). A syscall instruction then actually sends the message.

Receiving an RPC message is essentially the same process in reverse. The high half of a0 is loaded with the "receive" opcode and a syscall instruction is executed. When a message is ready, it is written to v1, v0, k0, and k1. This places the success/fail code and the first half-word of the return data in v0, typically used for integer results in the MIPS C calling convention.

Since a new application starting up on a SARATOGA core does not necessarily know the management address of its host CPU, we provide a means for doing so through the syscall instruction. At any time, an application may perform a syscall with the high half of a0 set to "get management address" to set the v0 register to the current CPU's management address. All other CPU management operations are accessed via RPCs to the management address.

5.6   ELF Loader with Code Signature Checking

To create a new process, a node sends a "create process" call to the CPU's OoB management port, specifying the physical address of the executable to run. The management system begins by allocating a new thread context, returning failure if all are currently in use.

If a thread ID was successfully obtained, the ELF loader then issues a DMA read for sizeof(Elf32_Ehdr) bytes to the supplied physical address, expecting to find a well formed ELF executable header. If the header is invalid (wrong magic numbers, incorrect version, or not a big-endian MIPS executable file) an error is returned.

If the header is well formed, the loader then looks at the e_entry field to find the address of the program's entry point. This is fed into a FIFO of data to be processed by the signature engine.[12] It is important to hash headers, as well as the contents of all executable pages, in order to ensure that a signed application cannot be modified to start at a different address within the code, potentially performing undesired actions.

The loader then checks the e_phoff field to find the address of the program header table, which stores the addresses of all segments in the program's memory image. It loops over the program header table and checks the p_type field for each entry. If the type is PT_LOAD (meaning the segment is part of the loadable memory image) then the loader reads the contents of the segment and feeds them into the hashing engine and stores the virtual and physical addresses in a buffer for future mapping. If the type is 0x70000005 (an unused value in the processor-defined region of the ELF program header type specification) then the segment is read into a buffer holding the expected signature. After all loadable segments have been hashed, the signature is compared to the expected value. If they do not match an error is returned and the allocated thread context is freed.

If the signature is valid, the list of address mappings is then fed to the MMU. Note that the ELF loader is the only part of the processor which has permission to set the PAGE_EXECUTE permission on a memory page; permissions for pages mapped by software through the OoB interface are ANDed with PAGE_READ_WRITE before being applied. This means that it is impossible by design for any unsigned code to ever execute as long as the physical memory backing the executable cannot be modified externally (for example, by modifying the contents of an external flash chip while the program is executing). With appropriate choices of access controls for on-chip memory, and use of encryption to prevent tampering with off-chip memory, this risk can be mitigated. After the initial memory mappings are created the program counter for the newly created thread is set to the entry point address from the ELF header and the thread is added to the run queue.

---

[12] We used HMAC-SHA256 in the prototype due to FPGA capacity limitations, as well as difficulty finding a suitable open source public key signature core. An actual ASIC implementation would presumably use RSA or ECC signatures.

5.7   Remote Attestation

SARATOGA supports a simple form of remote attestation. When an application is loaded by the ELF loader, the signature is stored in a buffer associated with the thread ID. At any time in the future, any NoC node may ask the CPU (via RPC to the management interface) to return the signature associated with a given thread context.

6   Security Analysis

6.1   Threat Model

Antikernel's primary goal is to enforce compartmentalization between user-space processes, and between user-space and the operating system. The focus is on damage control, rather than preventing initial penetration. The attacker is assumed to be remote so physical attacks are not considered. Existing antitemper techniques can, of course, be used along with the Antikernel architecture to produce a system with some degree of robustness against physical tampering; but it is important to note that no physical security is perfect and an attacker with unrestricted physical access to the system is likely to be able to penetrate any security given sufficient time and budget.

Antikernel is designed to ensure that following are not possible given that an attacker has gained unprivileged code execution within the context of a user-space application or service: (i) download a backdoor payload and configure it to run after system restart, (ii) modify executable code in memory or persistent storage, intercept/spoof/modify system calls or IPC of another process, (iii) read or write private state of another process, or (iv) gain access to handles belonging to another process by any means.

We consider an abstract RTL-level model of the system with ideal digital signals in which it is not possible for the state of one register or input pin to observe or modify the state of another except if they are connected through combinatorial logic in the RTL netlist.[13]

6.2   Methodology and Goals

We have performed fairly extensive verification on the current prototype system using a mix of simulation, hardware-in-loop (HiL) testing on our test cluster, and formal methods. All tests are fully automated and re-run before every commit. The general verification methodology begins by creating at least one HiL test

---

[13] In practice it is sometimes possible for this property to be violated (for example by DRAM read disturbance, as described in [17,18]). Such attacks exploit subtle layout-vs-schematic (LVS) mismatches which are not picked up by automated tools. While detecting these bugs is certainly an important task, it requires a level of solid-state physics better suited to a journal of electrical engineering so we leave it as an open research problem and focus on the computer science problem: ensuring safety of the pre-layout netlist.

for each module or subsystem being verified, supplemented by simulation tests in some cases to speed the design cycle. The focus of this level of verification is catching obvious bugs that occur when the module is used as intended. 100 % of the modules in the project receive at least this level of verification.

In addition, the most critical subsystems are provably verified against a formal model of the desired behavior. The choice of modules to verify is determined by several factors including their importance to the security model (the worse the impact of a bug, the more important provable correctness is) and their complexity (simpler modules are easier to prove correct).[14] The Verilog source for formal/simulation testbenches, as well as the C++ test cases and top-level modules for HiL testing, is included under the "tests" directory of the source distribution.

6.3   Assumptions

All of the low-level proofs of correctness were performed on post-synthesis RTL netlists using yosys [19]. We assume correctness of the temporal induction proof system in yosys and the SAT solver.[15] In other words, we assume that if the post-synthesis netlist is inconsistent and one or more of the assertions in the netlist are violated, that the solver will correctly detect the error and declare the proof to not hold.

These proofs are only valid down to the RTL level for the current prototype. The actual synthesis and place-and-route (PAR) of the prototype systems were performed using Xilinx's proprietary tools; correctness of these tools and the FPGA silicon is assumed.[16]

It is assumed that the RPC network consists of a series of RPCv2Router objects connected in a quadtree, with nodes under the routers. All of these nodes must connect to the RPC network with either an RPCv2Router-Transceiver or an RPCv2Transceiver object, configured as a leaf node (with the exception of the multithreaded CPUs such as SARATOGA, which are treated as multiple nodes under one router for the scope of the network-level proofs).

The DMA network is assumed to consist of a series of DMARouter objects connected in a quadtree, and nodes under the routers. Each node must connect to the DMA network with a DMATransceiver or DMARouterTransceiver object, configured as a leaf node. As with the RPC network, multithreaded CPUs are a special case and handled separately.

---

[14] While full verification of the entire implementation is of course desirable, and a goal we are working toward, it would require many man-years of additional effort. Additionally, several components of the design are still being optimized and improved, making a correctnesss proof of the current code a waste of time.

[15] MiniSAT by default, although different solvers can be configured at run time.

[16] Since the FPGA microarchitecture is undocumented, equivalence checking on the actual FPGA bitstream would not be possible without extensive reverse engineering of the silicon. While an interesting problem, and one that researchers including author 1 are actively working on [20], it is beyond the scope of this paper.

Furthermore, it is assumed that if any node connects to both networks it uses the same address on each, and that there is no information flow between nodes outside of the NoC (for example, by wires that do not pass through a NoC router, or off-die paths on the printed circuit board).

All of the test SoCs created as part of this paper were generated by our nocgen tool, which is intended to enforce these requirements for the top-level module, however its correctness has not yet been proven. Verifying that any particular generated source file (and the instantiated modules) meet these requirements is relatively easy to do by inspection. In the future we intend to create a DRC tool which uses yosys to parse the actual RTL source for a particular SoC and verifies that all of the on-chip topology requirements are met.

6.4   Networks

All four combinations of RPC and DMA transceivers (node or router at each end) for a layer-2 link were formally verified using yosys.[17]

Each test case instantiates one transmitter and one receiver of the appropriate types, as well as testbench code. yosys is then run on each testbench to synthesize to RTLIL intermediate representation, followed by invoking the SAT solver to prove the assertions in the testbenches. If the solver declares that all assertions pass, the proof is considered to hold.

While the testbenches are all slightly different due to the differences in interface between router/client transceivers and RPC/DMA network protocols, their basic operation is the same. When the test starts, all outputs are in the idle state and remain so in the absence of external stimuli. When a transmit is requested, the test logic stores the signals at the transceiver's inputs and asserts that the same data exits the receiver a fixed time later. The test also verifies that attempts to transmit while the receiver is busy block until the receiver is free (thus preventing dropped packets) and that the transceiver fully resets to its original state after sending a packet.

It is also necessary to prove that packets are correctly forwarded to the desired layer-3 destination by routers. We can map the quadtree directly to routing addresses by allocating two bits of the address to each level of the tree. Each router simply checks if the high bits match its subnet, forwards out the downstream port identified by the next two bits if so, and otherwise forwards out the upstream port. It is easy to see by inspection that this algorithm will always lead to a correct tree traversal.

---

[17] It is important to note that due to the large maximum packet size (512 words) it was not possible to run the DMA network proofs to a steady state, thus the proof is not complete. The current proof is artificially limited to examining state for the first 64 cycles and shows that no assertions are violated during this time. Running the solver on each proof takes about ten minutes on a single CPU core and uses between three and ten gigabytes of RAM; given a sufficiently large amount of CPU time and RAM there is no reason why the proof cannot be extended until a steady state is reached.

Since correct routing at the hop level combined with a valid quadtree topology implies correct routing at the network level, and the previous proofs show that link-layer forwarding is correct, the proof for correct end-to-end forwarding thus reduces to showing that the router correctly implements the routing algorithm, which is shown by another of our proofs (for the RPC network only).[18]

6.5   Name Server

Even if the layer-3 links between nodes are secure and packet misrouting is impossible, if a rogue node can trick a target node into sending its traffic to the wrong address, by causing the name server to report incorrect data, then MITM attacks can still occur.

Avoiding this requires proving two properties: First, the name server must always return the correct entry (if one exists) from its table when queried, or an error if none exists. Second, the name server must only insert names into the table, or remove them, if authorized by system security policy.

The top-level NOCNameServer module consists of several RAM blocks, an RPC transceiver, an HMAC-SHA256 engine, a "target matching" system (which compares outputs of the RAMs against a value being searched for), a mutex, and the main control state machine.

We assume correctness of the RAM and prove correctness of the transceiver separately. The mutex, target matching logic, and HMAC cores have undergone conventional validation but do not have correctness proofs as of this writing. Several correctness properties have been proven on the control state machine, as described below.

We currently have a partial liveness proof on the name server, which shows that two of the RPC calls will always terminate in constant time and return the name server to the idle condition. It also shows that these two calls will always behave as specified by the formal model, and will never modify any other state. A liveness proof for the remaining opcodes in progress however it was not complete as of this writing.

We have verified correct operation of the name server's registration and lookup functionality via conventional verification techniques, including automated unit testing, but have not yet completed a formal correctness proof.

Names for hardware nodes that are "baked" into the name table at logic synthesis time require no further authentication since the source code of the SoC

---

[18] Aside from the transceivers, the majority of the DMA network router is identical to that of RPC, instantiating the same modules with the same configuration. The only changes were adding an additional SRAM buffer and multiplexer for each port since the DMA transceiver has separate memory channels for headers and packet bodies, as opposed to the single channel for RPC. We believe that these changes are sufficiently non-intrusive that the probability of them containing a security-critical bug is very low. Although a full part-wise verification of the router (as was done for RPC) is certainly possible, and should be performed before an Antikernel system is actually deployed in a critical application, we believe that doing so at this stage of development would be an inefficient use of research time.

is trusted implicitly (and an attacker has no way to modify these addresses short of an invasive silicon attack). Names being registered by a random NoC node at run time, however, are not inherently trusted. In order to prevent malicious name registrations, the name server requires a cryptographic signature to be presented and validated before the name can be registered.

6.6 RAM Controller

There are two implementations of the RAM controller API, `BlockRAMAllocator` and `NetworkedDDR2Controller`. Both are covered by an extensive conventional (non-formal) verification suite in the current codebase. In order to ensure interoperability, the same compiled test binary is run on bitstreams containing both RAM controller implementations and is verified to work properly with both.

7 Conclusions and Future Work

The overall goal of this research was to determine whether moving operating system functionality into hardware is a practical means for improving operating system security. We define a high-level architecture, Antikernel, for an operating system which freely mixes hardware and software components as equal peers connected by a packet-switched network. The architecture takes the ideal of "least required privilege" to the extreme by having each node in the network be a fully encapsulated system which manages its own security policy, and only allows access to its internal state through a well-defined API.

The architecture draws inspiration from numerous existing operating system architectures, such as the microkernel (minimal privileged functionality with most services in userspace), the exokernel (drivers as very thin wrappers around hardware providing nothing but security and sharing), and the separation kernel (enforcing strong isolation between processes except through a defined interface).

Additionally, the modular structure of an Antikernel system is highly amenable to piecewise formal verification. If we define security of the entire system as the condition where all security properties of each node are upheld, we can then prove security by proving security of the interconnect, as well as proving that every node's security policy is internally consistent (in other words, policy cannot be violated by sending arbitrary messages to the NoC interface or any external communications interfaces).

We hope that this work will serve to inspire future research at the intersection of computer architecture and security, and lead to more convergent full-stack design of critical systems. Blurring the lines between hardware and software appears to be a promising architectural model and one warranting further study. By releasing all of our source code we hope to encourage future work building on our design. We intend to continue actively developing the project.

While the current prototype does show that hardware-based operating systems are practical and can be highly secure, it is far from usable in real-world applications. Many features which are necessary in a real-world operating system could not be implemented due to limited manpower so effort was focused on the most critical core features such as memory and process management.

The current prototype relies on the initialization code starting all software applications in the same order (and thus receiving the same thread ID since these are allocated in FIFO order every boot). A more stable system for binding processes to IDs is, of course, desirable.

As of this writing, neither of the memory controller implementations have been formally verified. No part of the CPU (other than the NoC transceivers) has been formally verified to date. While SARATOGA's architecture was designed to minimize the risk of accidental data leakage between thread contexts, until full verification is completed we cannot rule out the possibility that such a bug exists. Eventually we would like to verify that the CPUs themselves correctly implement the semantics of our reduced MIPS-1 instruction set. If we then compiled our application code with a formally verified C compiler (such as CompCert C [21,22]) we could have full equivalency proofs from C down to RTL.[19] This could then be combined with verification of the C source code, resulting in fully verified correct execution from application software all the way down to RTL.

Finally, our prototype is intended to be a proof of concept for hardware-based compartmentalization at the OS level. As a result, we do not incorporate any of the numerous defensive techniques in the literature for guarding against physical tampering, hardware faults, or software-based exploits targeting userland. Currently, implementation of many useful subsystems (such as the networking stack and filesystem) are missing major features or entirely absent. Although many of the core components (such as the NoC) have been formally verified, many higher-level components and peripherals have received basic functional testing only and the full system should be considered research-grade. Further work could explore integrating existing software-based mitigations with Antikernel.

The prototype prioritizes ease of verification and implementation over performance: for example, the SARATOGA CPU uses a simple barrel scheduler which has poor single-threaded performance, lacks support for out-of-order execution, and has very unoptimized logic for handling L1 cache misses. Although these factors combine to cause a significant (order of magnitude) performance reduction compared to a legacy system running the same ISA, these are due to implementation choices rather than any inherent limitations of the architecture. We conjecture that a more optimized Antikernel implementation could match or even exceed the performance of existing OS/hardware combinations due to the streamlined, exokernel-esque design.

Additionally, although backward compatibility with existing operating systems was explicitly *not* a design goal, we have done a small amount of work on a POSIX compatibility layer. This is unlikely to ever reach "recompile and run" compatibility with legacy software due to inherent architecture differences, but we hope that it will help minimize porting effort.

---

[19] The current CompCert compiler does not support the MIPS instruction set - only x86, ARM, and PowerPC. We plan to explore adding formally verified MIPS code generation to this or another verified C compiler in the future.

References

1. Zonenberg, A.D.: Antikernel: a decentralized secure hardware-software operating system architecture. Ph.D. dissertation, Rensselaer Polytechnic Institute (2015)
2. Engler, D.R., et al.: Exokernel: an operating system architecture for application-level resource management. SIGOPS Oper. Syst. Rev. **29**(5), 251–266 (1995)
3. Rushby, J.M.: Design and verification of secure systems. In: Proceedings of the 8th ACM Symposium on Operating Systems Principles, pp. 12–21 (1981)
4. Martin, W., White, P., Taylor, F.S., Goldberg, A.: Formal construction of the mathematically analyzed separation kernel. In: 15th IEEE International Conference Automated Software Engineering, ASE 2000, pp. 133–141 (2000)
5. Baumann, A., et al.: The multikernel: a new OS architecture for scalable multicore systems. In: Proceedings of the ACM SIGOPS 22nd Symposium Operating Systems Principles, New York, NY, USA, pp. 29–44 (2009)
6. Rutkowska, J., Wojtczuk, R.: Qubes OS Architecture, January 2010. http://files.qubes-os.org/files/doc/arch-spec-0.3.pdf
7. ARM Ltd. TrustZone Technology (2014). http://www.arm.com/products/processors/technologies/trustzone.php. Accessed 09 Apr 2015
8. Zonenberg, A.: Antikernel source repository, 18 March 2016. http://redmine.drawersteak.com/projects/achd-soc/repository. Accessed 18 Mar 2016
9. Engel, M., Spinczyk, O.: A radical approach to network-on-chip operatingsystems. In: 42nd Hawaii International Conference on System Sciences, HICSS 2009, pp. 1–10, January 2009
10. Nordstrom, S., et al.: Application specific real-time microkernel in hardware. In: 14th IEEE-NPSS Real Time Conference 2005, p. 4, June 2005
11. Hu, W., Ma, J., Wu, B., Ju, L., Chan, T.: Distributed on-chip operating systemfor network on chip. In: 2010 IEEE 10th International Conference on Computer and Information Technology (CIT), pp. 2760–2767, 1 July 2010
12. Park, S., et al.: A hardware operating system kernel for multi-processor systems. IEICE Electron. Express **5**(9), 296–302 (2008)
13. So, H.K.-H., et al.: A unified hardware/software runtime environment for FPGA-based reconfigurable computers using BORPH. In: Proceedings of the 4th International Conference Hardware/Software Codesign Systems Synthesis CODES+ISSS 2006, pp. 259–264 (2006)
14. Wasicek, V., et al.: A system-on-a-chip platform for mixed-criticality applications. In: 2010 13th IEEE International Symposium on Object/Component/Service-Oriented Real-Time Distributed Computing (ISORC), pp. 210–216, May 2010
15. Thomas, A., et al.: Towards a Zero-Kernel Operating System, 10 January 2013. http://www.infsec.cs.uni-saarland.de/hritcu/publications/zkos_draft_jan10_2013.pdf. Accessed 09 Apr 2015
16. BiiN Corporation. BiiN Systems Overview, Portland, OR, July 1988. http://bitsavers.informatik.uni-stuttgart.de/pdf/biin/BiiN_Systems_Overview.pdf. Accessed 09 Apr 2015
17. Kim, Y., et al.: Flipping bits in memory without accessing them: an experimental study of DRAM disturbance errors. In: 2014 ACM/IEEE 41st International Symposium on Computer Architecture (ISCA), pp. 361–372, June 2014
18. Evans, C.: Project Zero: Exploiting the DRAM rowhammer bug to gain kernel privileges, 9 March 2015. http://googleprojectzero.blogspot.com/2015/03/exploiting-dram-rowhammer-bug-to-gain.html. Accessed 09 Apr 2015
19. Wolf, C.: Yosys open synthesis suite. http://www.clifford.at/yosys/

20. Zonenberg, A.: From Silicon to Compiler: Reverse-Engineering the Xilinx XC2C32A, 22 July 2015. https://recon.cx/2015/slides/recon2015-18-andrew-zonenberg-From-Silicon-to-Compiler.pdf. Accessed 02 Mar 2016
21. Blazy, S., Dargaye, Z., Leroy, X.: Formal verification of a C Compiler front-end. In: Misra, J., Nipkow, T., Sekerinski, E. (eds.) FM 2006. LNCS, vol. 4085, pp. 460–475. Springer, Heidelberg (2006)
22. Boldo, S., et al.: A formally-verified C compiler supporting floating-point arithmetic. In: 21st IEEE International Symposium Computer Arithmetic ARITH, pp. 107–115. IEEE Computer Society Press (2013)

Software Implementations

Software Implementation of Koblitz Curves over Quadratic Fields

Thomaz Oliveira[1]([✉]), Julio López[2], and Francisco Rodríguez-Henríquez[1]

[1] Computer Science Department, CINVESTAV-IPN, Mexico, Mexico
thomaz.figueiredo@gmail.com, jlopez@ic.unicamp.br
[2] Institute of Computing, University of Campinas, Campinas, Brazil
francisco@cs.cinvestav.mx

Abstract. In this work, we retake an old idea presented by Koblitz in his landmark paper [21], where he suggested the possibility of defining anomalous elliptic curves over the base field $\mathbb{F}_4$. We present a careful implementation of the base and quadratic field arithmetic required for computing the scalar multiplication operation in such curves. In order to achieve a fast reduction procedure, we adopted a redundant trinomial strategy that embeds elements of the field $\mathbb{F}_{4^m}$, with m a prime number, into a ring of higher order defined by an almost irreducible trinomial. We also report a number of techniques that allow us to take full advantage of the native vector instructions of high-end microprocessors. Our software library achieves the fastest timings reported for the computation of the timing-protected scalar multiplication on Koblitz curves, and competitive timings with respect to the speed records established recently in the computation of the scalar multiplication over prime fields.

1 Introduction

Anomalous binary curves, generally referred to as Koblitz curves, are binary elliptic curves satisfying the Weierstrass equation, $E_a : y^2 + xy = x^3 + ax^2 + 1$, with $a \in \{0, 1\}$. Since their introduction in 1991 by Koblitz [21], these curves have been extensively studied for their additional structure that allows, in principle, a performance speedup in the computation of the elliptic curve point multiplication operation. As of today, the research works dealing with standardized Koblitz curves in commercial use, such as the binary curves standardized by NIST [23] or the suite of elliptic curves supported by the TLS protocol [4,9], have exclusively analyzed the security and performance of curves defined over binary extension fields $\mathbb{F}_{2^m}$, with m a prime number (for recent examples see [1,5,32,36]).

Nevertheless, Koblitz curves defined over $\mathbb{F}_4$ were also proposed in [21]. We find interesting to explore the cryptographic usage of Koblitz curves defined over

----

T. Oliveira, F. Henríquez—The authors would like to thank CONACyT (project number 180421) for their funding of this research.

J. López—The author was supported in part by the Intel Labs University Research Office and by a research productivity scholarship from CNPq Brazil.

B. Gierlichs and A.Y. Poschmann (Eds.): CHES 2016, LNCS 9813, pp. 259–279, 2016.
DOI: 10.1007/978-3-662-53140-2_13

$\mathbb{F}_4$ due to their inherent usage of quadratic field arithmetic. Indeed, it has been recently shown [3,25] that quadratic field arithmetic is extraordinarily efficient when implemented in software. This is because one can take full advantage of the Single Instruction Multiple Data (SIMD) paradigm, where a vector instruction performs simultaneously the same operation on a set of input data items.

Quadratic extensions of a binary finite field $\mathbb{F}_{q^2}$ can be defined by means of a monic polynomial $h(u)$ of degree two irreducible over $\mathbb{F}_q$. The field $\mathbb{F}_{q^2}$ is isomorphic to $\mathbb{F}_q[u]/(h(u))$ and its elements can be represented as $a_0 + a_1 u$, with $a_0, a_1 \in \mathbb{F}_q$. The addition of two elements $a, b \in \mathbb{F}_{q^2}$, can be performed as $c = (a_0 + b_0) + (a_1 + b_1)u$. By choosing $h(u) = u^2 + u + 1$, the multiplication of a, b can be computed as, $d = a_0 b_0 + a_1 b_1 + ((a_0 + a_1) \cdot (b_0 + b_1) + a_0 b_0)u$. By carefully organizing the code associated to these arithmetic operations, one can greatly exploit the pipelines and their inherent instruction-level parallelism that are available in contemporary high-end processors.

Our Contributions. In this work we designed for the first time, a 128-bit secure and timing attack resistant scalar multiplication on a Koblitz curve defined over $\mathbb{F}_4$, as they were proposed by Koblitz in his 1991 seminal paper [21]. We developed all the required algorithms for performing such a computation. This took us to reconsider the strategy of using redundant trinomials (also known as almost irreducible trinomials), which were proposed more than ten years ago in [6,10]. We also report what is perhaps the most comprehensive analysis yet reported of how to efficiently implement arithmetic operations in binary finite fields and their quadratic extensions using the vectorized instructions available in high-end microprocessors. For example, to the best of our knowledge, we report for the first time a 128-bit AVX implementation of the linear pass technique, which is useful against side-channel attacks.

The remaining of this paper is organized as follows. In Sect. 2 we formally introduce the family of Koblitz elliptic curves defined over $\mathbb{F}_4$. In Sects. 3 and 4 a detailed description of the efficient implementation of the base and quadratic field arithmetic using vectorized instructions is given. We present in Sect. 5 the scalar multiplication algorithms used in this work, and we present in Sect. 6 the analysis and discussion of the results obtained by our software library. Finally, we draw our concluding remarks and future work in Sect. 7.

2   Koblitz Curves over $\mathbb{F}_4$

Koblitz curves over $\mathbb{F}_4$ are defined by the following equation

$$E_a : y^2 + xy = x^3 + a\gamma x^2 + \gamma, \tag{1}$$

where $\gamma \in \mathbb{F}_{2^2}$ satisfies $\gamma^2 = \gamma + 1$ and $a \in \{0, 1\}$. Note that the number of points in the curves $E_0(\mathbb{F}_4)$ and $E_1(\mathbb{F}_4)$ are, $\#E_0(\mathbb{F}_4) = 4$ and $\#E_1(\mathbb{F}_4) = 6$, respectively. For cryptographic purposes, one uses Eq. (1) operating over extension fields of the form $\mathbb{F}_q$, with $q = 4^m$, and m a prime number. The set of affine points $P = (x, y) \in \mathbb{F}_q \times \mathbb{F}_q$ that satisfy Eq. (1) together with a point at infinity represented as $\mathcal{O}$, forms an abelian group denoted by $E_a(\mathbb{F}_{4^m})$, where its group law is defined by the point addition operation.

Since for each proper divisor l of k, $E(\mathbb{F}_{4^l})$ is a subgroup of $E(\mathbb{F}_{4^k})$, one has that $\#E(\mathbb{F}_{4^l})$ divides $\#E(\mathbb{F}_{4^k})$. Furthermore, by choosing prime extensions m, it is possible to find $E_a(\mathbb{F}_{4^m})$ with almost-prime order, for instance, $E_0(\mathbb{F}_{2^{2 \cdot 163}})$ and $E_1(\mathbb{F}_{2^{2 \cdot 167}})$. In the remaining of this paper, we will show that the aforementioned strategy can be used for the efficient implementation of a 128-bit secure scalar multiplication on software platforms counting with 64-bit carry-less native multipliers, such as the ones available in contemporary personal desktops.

The Frobenius map $\tau : E_a(\mathbb{F}_q) \to E_a(\mathbb{F}_q)$ defined by $\tau(\mathcal{O}) = \mathcal{O}$, $\tau(x, y) = (x^4, y^4)$, is a curve automorphism satisfying $(\tau^2 + 4)P = \mu\tau(P)$ for $\mu = (-1)^a$ and all $P \in E_a(\mathbb{F}_q)$. By solving the equation $\tau^2 + 4 = \mu\tau$, the Frobenius map can be seen as the complex number $\tau = (\mu \pm \sqrt{-15})/2$.

2.1 The τ-adic Representation

Given a Koblitz curve $E_a/\mathbb{F}_{2^{2m}}$ with group order $\#E_a(\mathbb{F}_{2^{2m}}) = h \cdot \rho \cdot r$, where h is the order $\#E_a(\mathbb{F}_4)$, r is the prime order of our subgroup of interest, and ρ is the order of a group of no cryptographic interest.[1] We can express a scalar $k \in \mathbb{Z}_r$ as an element in $\mathbb{Z}[\tau]$ using the now classical partial reduction introduced by Solinas [31], with a few modifications. The modified version is based on the fact that $\tau^2 = \mu\tau - 4$.

Given that the norm of τ is $N(\tau) = 4$, $N(\tau - 1) = h$, $N(\tau^m - 1) = h \cdot \rho \cdot r$ and $N((\tau^m - 1)/(\tau - 1)) = \rho \cdot r$, the subscalars r_0 and r_1 resulting from the partial modulo function will be both of size approximately $\sqrt{\rho \cdot r}$. As a consequence, the corresponding scalar multiplication will need more iterations than expected, since it will consider the order ρ of a subgroup which is not of cryptographic interest.

For that reason, we took the design decision of considering that the input scalar of our point multiplication algorithm is already given in the $\mathbb{Z}[\tau]$ domain. As a result, a partial reduction of the scalar k is no longer required, and the number of iterations in the point multiplication will be consistent with the scalar k size. If one needs to retrieve the equivalent value of the scalar k in the ring $\mathbb{Z}_r$, this can be easily computed with one multiplication and one addition in $\mathbb{Z}_r$. This strategy is in line with the degree-2 scalar decomposition method within the GLS curves context as suggested in [12].

2.2 The Width-w τNAF Form

Assuming that the scalar k is specified in the $\mathbb{Z}[\tau]$ domain, one can represent the scalar in the regular width-w τNAF form as shown in Algorithm 1. The length of the representation width-w τNAF of an element $k \in \mathbb{Z}[\tau]$ is discussed in [30].

---

[1] Usually the order ρ is composite. Also, every prime factor of ρ is smaller than r.

Algorithm 1. Regular width-w τ-recoding for m-bit scalar

Input: $w, t_w, \alpha_v = \beta_v + \gamma_v \tau$ for $v = \{\pm 1, \pm 3, \pm 5, \ldots, \pm 4^{w-1} - 1\}, \rho = r_0 + r_1 \tau \in \mathbb{Z}[\tau]$
with odd r_0, r_1

Output: $\rho = \displaystyle\sum_{i=0}^{\lceil \frac{m+2}{w-1} \rceil} v_i \tau^{i(w-1)}$

```
 1: for i ← 0 to ⌈(m+2)/(w-1)⌉ - 1 do     14: if r₀ ≠ 0 and r₁ ≠ 1 then
 2:    if w = 2 then                        15:    vᵢ ← r₀ + r₁τ
 3:       vᵢ ← ((r₀ - 4·r₁) mod 8) - 4     16: else
 4:       r₀ ← r₀ - vᵢ                     17:    if r₁ ≠ 0 then
 5:    else                                 18:       vᵢ ← r₁
 6:       u ← (r₀ + r₁tw mod 2^(2w-1)) - 2^(2(w-1))   19:    else
 7:       if v > 0 then s ← 1 else s ← -1   20:       vᵢ ← r₀
 8:       r₀ ← r₀ - sβᵥ, r₁ ← r₁ - sγᵥ, vᵢ ← sαᵥ   21:    end if
 9:    end if                               22: end if
10:    for j ← 0 to (w - 2) do
11:       t ← r₀, r₀ ← r₁ + (μ·r₀)/4, r₁ ← -t/4
12:    end for
13: end for
```

Given a width w, after running Algorithm 1, we have $2^{2(w-1)-1}$ different digits.[2] As a result, it is necessary to be more conservative when choosing the width w, when compared to the Koblitz curves defined over $\mathbb{F}_2$. For widths $w = 2, 3, 4, 5$ we have to pre- or post-compute $2, 8, 32$ and 128 points, respectively. For the 128-bit point multiplication, we estimated that the value of the width w must be at most four, otherwise, the costs of the point pre/post-processing are greater than the addition savings obtained in the main iteration.

In addition, we must find efficient expressions of $\alpha_v = v \bmod \tau^w$. The method for searching the best expressions in Koblitz curves over $\mathbb{F}_2$ [33] cannot be directly applied in the $\mathbb{F}_4$ case. Because of this, we manually provided α_v representations for $w \in \{2, 3, 4\}$ and $a = 1$, which are our implementation parameters. The main rationale for our representation choices was to minimize the number of field arithmetic operations. In practice, we strive for reducing the required number of full point additions by increasing the number of point doublings and mixed additions, which have a cheaper computational cost.[3] In Table 1 we present the α_v representatives along with the operations required to generate the multiples of the base point.[4]

Therefore, one point doubling and one full addition are required to generate the points $\alpha_v \cdot P$ for $w = 2$, one point doubling, four full additions, three

---

[2] We are considering only positive digits, since the cost of computing the negative points in binary elliptic curves is negligible.

[3] Full addition is defined as the addition of two points given in projective coordinates. The mixed addition operation adds one point given in projective coordinates with another given in affine coordinates.

[4] Notice that the multiples $\alpha_v \cdot P$ as shown in Table 1, must be computed out of order. The order for computing the multiples is shown in roman numbers.

Table 1. Representations of $\alpha_v = v \bmod \tau^w$, for $w \in \{2,3,4\}$ and $a = 1$ and the required operations for computing α_v. Here we denote by D, FA, MA, T the point doubling, full addition, mixed addition and the Frobenius map, respectively. In addition, we consider that the point $\alpha_1 P$ is represented in affine coordinates. The order for computing the points is given in roman numbers

w	v	$v \bmod \tau^w$	α_v	Operations	Order
2	1	1	1	n/a	I
	3	3	3	$t_0 \leftarrow 2\alpha_1, \alpha_3 \leftarrow t_0 + \alpha_1\ (D + FA)$	II
3	1	1	1	n/a	I
	3	3	3	$t_0 \leftarrow 2\alpha_1, \alpha_3 \leftarrow t_0 + \alpha_1\ (D + FA)$	II
	5	5	$-\tau - \alpha_{15}$	$\alpha_5 \leftarrow -t_1 - \alpha_{15}\ (MA)$	VIII
	7	$3\tau + 3$	$\tau^2\alpha_3 + \alpha_3$	$\alpha_7 \leftarrow \tau^2\alpha_3 + \alpha_3\ (FA + 2T)$	III
	9	$3\tau + 5$	$\alpha_7 + 2$	$\alpha_9 \leftarrow \alpha_7 + t_0\ (FA)$	IV
	11	$3\tau + 7$	$\alpha_9 + 2$	$\alpha_{11} \leftarrow \alpha_9 + t_0\ (FA)$	V
	13	$-\tau - 7$	$\tau^2 - \alpha_3$	$\alpha_{13} \leftarrow t_2 - \alpha_3\ (MA)$	VII
	15	$-\tau - 5$	$\tau^2 - 1$	$t_1 \leftarrow \tau\alpha_1, t_2 \leftarrow \tau t_1, \alpha_{15} \leftarrow t_2 - \alpha_1\ (MA + 2T)$	VI
4	1	1	1	n/a	I
	3	3	$-\tau^3 - \alpha_{61}$	$\alpha_3 \leftarrow -t_4 - \alpha_{61}\ (MA)$	XXVI
	5	5	$-\tau^3 - \alpha_{59}$	$\alpha_5 \leftarrow -t_4 - \alpha_{59}\ (MA)$	XXVII
	7	7	$-\tau^3 - \alpha_{57}$	$\alpha_7 \leftarrow -t_4 - \alpha_{57}\ (MA)$	XXVIII
	9	9	$-\tau^3 - \alpha_{55}$	$\alpha_9 \leftarrow -t_4 - \alpha_{55}\ (MA)$	XXIX
	11	11	$-2\tau^2 + \alpha_{43}$	$\alpha_{11} \leftarrow -t_2 + \alpha_{43}\ (FA)$	XXX
	13	13	$-2\tau^2 + \alpha_{45}$	$\alpha_{13} \leftarrow -t_2 + \alpha_{45}\ (FA)$	XXXI
	15	15	$-2\tau^2 + \alpha_{47}$	$\alpha_{15} \leftarrow -t_2 + \alpha_{47}\ (FA)$	XXXII
	17	$5\tau - 11$	$-\tau^3 - \alpha_{47}$	$t_4 \leftarrow \tau^2 t_3, \alpha_{17} \leftarrow -t_4 - \alpha_{47}\ (MA + 2T)$	XIX
	19	$5\tau - 9$	$-\tau^3 - \alpha_{45}$	$\alpha_{17} \leftarrow -t_4 - \alpha_{47}\ (MA)$	XX
	21	$5\tau - 7$	$-\tau^3 - \alpha_{43}$	$\alpha_{17} \leftarrow -t_4 - \alpha_{45}\ (MA)$	XXI
	23	$5\tau - 5$	$-\tau^3 - \alpha_{41}$	$\alpha_{17} \leftarrow -t_4 - \alpha_{43}\ (MA)$	XXII
	25	$5\tau - 3$	$-\tau^3 - \alpha_{39}$	$\alpha_{17} \leftarrow -t_4 - \alpha_{41}\ (MA)$	XXIII
	27	$5\tau - 1$	$-\tau^3 - \alpha_{37}$	$\alpha_{17} \leftarrow -t_4 - \alpha_{39}\ (MA)$	XXIV
	29	$5\tau + 1$	$-\tau^3 - \alpha_{35}$	$\alpha_{17} \leftarrow -t_4 - \alpha_{37}\ (MA)$	XXV
	31	$-2\tau - 9$	$2\tau^2 - 1$	$t_2 \leftarrow \tau t_1, \alpha_{31} \leftarrow t_2 - \alpha_1\ (MA + T)$	XII
	33	$-2\tau - 7$	$2\tau^2 + 1$	$\alpha_{33} \leftarrow t_2 + \alpha_1\ (MA)$	XIII
	35	$-2\tau - 5$	$-2\tau - 5$	$\alpha_{35} \leftarrow \alpha_{37} - t_0\ (FA)$	VI
	37	$-2\tau - 3$	$-2\tau - 3$	$\alpha_{37} \leftarrow \alpha_{39} - t_0\ (FA)$	IV
	39	$-2\tau - 1$	$-2\tau - 1$	$t_0 \leftarrow 2\alpha_1, t_1 \leftarrow \tau t_0, \alpha_{39} \leftarrow -t_1 - \alpha_1\ (D + MA + T)$	II
	41	$-2\tau + 1$	$-2\tau + 1$	$\alpha_{41} \leftarrow -t_1 + \alpha_1\ (MA)$	III
	43	$-2\tau + 3$	$-2\tau + 3$	$\alpha_{43} \leftarrow \alpha_{41} + t_0\ (FA)$	V
	45	$-2\tau + 5$	$-2\tau + 5$	$\alpha_{45} \leftarrow \alpha_{43} + t_0\ (FA)$	VII
	47	$-2\tau + 7$	$-2\tau + 7$	$\alpha_{47} \leftarrow \alpha_{45} + t_0\ (FA)$	VIII
	49	$-2\tau + 9$	$-2\tau + 9$	$\alpha_{49} \leftarrow \alpha_{47} + t_0\ (FA)$	IX
	51	$-2\tau + 11$	$-2\tau + 11$	$\alpha_{51} \leftarrow \alpha_{49} + t_0\ (FA)$	X
	53	$-2\tau + 13$	$-2\tau + 13$	$\alpha_{53} \leftarrow \alpha_{51} + t_0\ (FA)$	XI
	55	$3\tau - 13$	$3\tau - 13$	$t_3 \leftarrow \tau\alpha_1, \alpha_{55} \leftarrow t_3 - \alpha_{53}\ (MA + T)$	XIV
	57	$3\tau - 11$	$3\tau - 11$	$\alpha_{57} \leftarrow t_3 - \alpha_{51}\ (MA)$	XV
	59	$3\tau - 9$	$3\tau - 9$	$\alpha_{59} \leftarrow t_3 - \alpha_{49}\ (MA)$	XVI
	61	$3\tau - 7$	$3\tau - 7$	$\alpha_{61} \leftarrow t_3 - \alpha_{47}\ (MA)$	XVII
	63	$3\tau - 5$	$3\tau - 5$	$\alpha_{63} \leftarrow t_3 - \alpha_{45}\ (MA)$	XVIII

mixed additions and four applications of the Frobenius map for the $w = 3$ case and one point doubling, twenty full additions, eleven mixed additions and five applications of the Frobenius map for the $w = 4$ case.

2.3   Security of the Koblitz Curves Defined over $\mathbb{F}_4$

Since the Koblitz curves defined over $E_a(\mathbb{F}_{4^m})$ operate over quadratic extensions fields, it is conceivable that Weil descent attacks [13,16] could possibly be efficiently applied on these curves. However, Menezes and Qu showed in [22] that the GHS attack cannot be implemented efficiently for elliptic curves defined over binary extension fields $\mathbb{F}_q$, with $q = 2^m$, and m a prime number in $[160, \dots, 600]$. Further, a specialized analysis for binary curves defined over fields of the form $\mathbb{F}_{4^m}$ reported in [14], proved that the only vulnerable prime extension in the range $[80, \dots, 256]$, is $m = 127$. Therefore, the prime extension used in this work, namely, $m = 149$, is considered safe with respect to the state-of-the-art knowledge of the Weil descent attack classes.

For a comprehensive survey of recent progress in the computation of the elliptic curve discrete problem in characteristic two, the reader is referred to the paper by Galbraith and Gaudry [11].

3   Base Field Arithmetic

In this section, we present the techniques used in our work in order to implement the binary field arithmetic. We selected a Koblitz curve with the parameter $a = 1$ defined over $\mathbb{F}_{4^m}$ with $m = 149$. This curve was chosen because the order of its subgroup of interest is of size 2^{254}, which yields a security level roughly equivalent to a 128-bit secure scalar multiplication.

3.1   Modular Reduction

One can construct a binary extension field $\mathbb{F}_{2^m}$ by taking a polynomial $f(x) \in \mathbb{F}_2[x]$ of degree m which is irreducible over $\mathbb{F}_2$. It is very important that the form of the polynomial $f(x)$, admits an efficient modular reduction. The criteria for selecting $f(x)$ depends on the architecture where the implementation will be executed as it was extensively discussed in [29].

For our field extension choice, we do not have degree-149 trinomials which are irreducible over $\mathbb{F}_2$. An alternative solution is to construct the field through irreducible pentanomials. Given an irreducible pentanomial $f(x) = x^m + x^a + x^b + x^c + 1$, the efficiency of the shift-and-add reduction method depends mostly on the fact that the term-degree differences $m - a$, $m - b$ and $m - c$, are all equal to 0 modulo W, where W is the architecture word size in bits.

Using the terminology of [29], lucky irreducible pentanomials are the ones where the three previously mentioned differences are equal to 0 modulo W. Fortunate irreducible pentanomials are the ones where two out of the three above differences are equal to 0 modulo W. The remaining cases are called ordinary irreducible pentanomials. Performing an extensive search with $W = 8$, we found no lucky pentanomials, 189 fortunate pentanomials and 9491 ordinary pentanomials for the extension $m = 149$.

The problem is that fortunate pentanomials make the modular reduction too costly if we compare it with the field multiplication computed with carry-less instructions. This is because we need to perform four shift-and-add operations per reduction step. Besides, two of those operations require costly shift instructions, since they are shifts not divisible by 8.

3.2 Redundant Trinomials

As a consequence of the above analysis, we resorted to the redundant trinomials strategy introduced in [6,10], also known as almost irreducible trinomials. Given a non-irreducible trinomial $g(x)$ of degree n that factorizes into an irreducible polynomial $f(x)$ of degree $m < n$, the idea is to perform the field reduction modulo $g(x)$ throughout the scalar multiplication and, at the end of the algorithm, reduce the polynomials so obtained modulo $f(x)$. In a nutshell, throughout the algorithm we represent the base field elements as polynomials in the ring $\mathbb{F}_2[x]$ reduced modulo $g(x)$. At the end of the algorithm, the elements are reduced modulo $f(x)$ in order to bring them back to the target field $\mathbb{F}_{2^{149}}$. For the sake of simplicity, throughout this paper, we will refer to those elements as field elements.

Since our target software platform counts with a native 64-bit carry-less multiplier, an efficient representation of the field elements must have at most 192 bits, *i.e*, three 64-bit words. For that reason, we searched for redundant trinomials of degree at most 192.

We selected the trinomial, $g(x) = x^{192} + x^{19} + 1$, for two reasons. First, since our target architecture contains 128-bit vectorized registers, the difference $(m - a) > 128$ allows us to perform the shift-and-add reduction in just two steps. Second, the property $m \bmod 64 = 0$, which allows us to perform efficiently the first part of the shift-and-add reduction. The steps to perform the modular reduction are described in Algorithm 2.[5] The reduction using 128-bit registers is presented in Sect. 4, where we discuss our strategy for implementing the arithmetic in the quadratic field extension.

Algorithm 2. Modular reduction by the trinomial $g(x) = x^{192} + x^{19} + 1$

Input: A 384-bit polynomial $r(x) = F \cdot x^{320} + E \cdot x^{256} + D \cdot x^{192} + C \cdot x^{128} + B \cdot x^{64} + A$ in $\mathbb{F}_2[x]$ stored into six 64-bit registers (A - F).
Output: A 192-bit polynomial $s(x) = r(x) \bmod g(x) = I \cdot x^{128} + H \cdot x^{64} + G$ stored into three 64-bit registers (G - I).

1: $G \leftarrow A \oplus D \oplus (F \gg 45) \oplus ((D \oplus (F \gg 45)) \ll 19)$
2: $H \leftarrow B \oplus E \oplus (E \ll 19) \oplus (D \gg 45)$
3: $I \leftarrow C \oplus F \oplus (F \ll 19) \oplus (E \gg 45)$

---

[5] The symbols $\ll, \gg$ stand for bitwise shift of packed 64-bit integers.

The overall cost of the modular reduction is ten xors and five bitwise shifts. At the end of the scalar multiplication, we have to reduce the 192-bit polynomial to an element of the field $\mathbb{F}_{2^{149}}$. Note that the trinomial $g(x) = x^{192} + x^{19} + 1$ factorizes into a 69-term irreducible polynomial $f(x)$ of degree 149.

The final reduction is performed via the mul-and-add reduction which, experimentally, performed more efficiently than the shift-and-add reduction.[6] Concisely, the mul-and-add technique consists in a series of steps which includes shift operations (in order to align the bits in the registers), carry-less multiplications and xor operations for eliminating the extra bits.

The basic mul-and-add step is described in Algorithm 3. Here, besides the usual notation, we represent the 64-bit carry-less multiplication by the symbol $\times_{ij}$, where $i, j = \{L, H\}$, with L and H representing the lowest and highest 64-bit word packed in a 128-bit register, respectively. For example, if one wants to multiply the 128-bit register A lowest 64-bit word by the 128-bit register B highest 64-bit word, we would express this operation as $T \leftarrow A \times_{LH} B$.

Algorithm 3. Basic step of the mul-and-add reduction modulo the 69-term irreducible polynomial $f(x)$

Input: A j-bit polynomial $r(x) = B \cdot x^{128} + A$ stored into two 128-bit registers (A, B), for $j \in [191, 148]$, the irreducible polynomial $f(x) = F \cdot x^{128} + E$ stored into two 128-bit registers (E, F).

Output: A $(j-3)$-bit polynomial $s(x) = D \cdot x^{128} + C$ stored into two 128-bit registers (C, D).

1: $T_0 \leftarrow B \gg 21$ (64-bit alignment)　　5: $T_1 \leftarrow T_1 \oplus (T_2 \ll 64)$
2: $T_1 \leftarrow E \times_{LL} T_0$　　　　　　　　　6: $T_0 \leftarrow T_0 \oplus (T_2 \gg 64)$
3: $T_2 \leftarrow E \times_{HL} T_0$　　　　　　　　　7: $C \leftarrow A \oplus T_1$
4: $T_0 \leftarrow F \times_{LL} T_0$　　　　　　　　　8: $D \leftarrow B \oplus T_0$

Algorithm 3 requires four xors, three bitwise shifts and three carry-less multiplications. In our particular case, the difference between the degrees of the two most significant monomials of $f(x)$ is three. Also, note that we need to reduce 43 bits (191–148). As a result, it is required $\lceil \frac{43}{3} \rceil = 15$ applications of the Algorithm 3 in order to conclude this reduction.

4   Quadratic Field Arithmetic

In this Section, the basic arithmetic operations in the quadratic field are presented. As usual, the quadratic field $\mathbb{F}_{2^{2 \cdot 149}}$ was constructed by the degree two monic polynomial $h(u) = u^2 + u + 1$, and its elements are represented as $a_0 + a_1 u$, with $a_0, a_1 \in \mathbb{F}_{2^{149}}$.

---

[6] For a more detailed explanation of the shift-and-add and the mul-and-add reduction methods to binary fields, see [5].

4.1 Register Allocation

The first aspect to be considered is the element allocation into the architecture's available registers. In our case, we have to store two polynomials of 192 bits into 128-bit registers in such a way that it allows an efficient modular reduction and, at the same time, it generates a minimum overhead in the two main arithmetic operations, namely, the multiplication and squaring.

Let us consider an element $a = (a_0 + a_1 u) \in \mathbb{F}_{2^{2 \cdot 149}}$, where $a_0 = C \cdot x^{128} + B \cdot x^{64} + A$ and $a_1 = F \cdot x^{128} + E \cdot x^{64} + D$ are 192-bit polynomials, each one of them stored into three 64-bit words (A-C, D-F). Also, let us have three 128-bit registers R_i, with $i \in \{0, 1, 2\}$, which can store two 64-bit words each. In this Section, we adopted the following notation, given a 128-bit register R, its most and least significant packed 64-bit words, denoted respectively by S and T, are represented as $R = S|T$. The first option is to rearrange the 384-bit element $a = (a_0 + a_1 u)$ as,

$$R_0 = A|B, \quad R_1 = C|D, \quad R_2 = E|F.$$

The problem with this representation is that a significant overhead is generated in the multiplication function, more specifically, in the pre-computation phase of the Karatsuba procedure (cf. Sect. 4.2 with the computation of $V_{0,1}$, $V_{0,2}$ and $V_{1,2}$). Besides, in order to efficiently perform the subsequent reduction phase, we must temporarily store the polynomial terms into four 128-bit vectors, which can cause a register overflow. A better method for storing the element a is to use the following arrangement,

$$R_0 = D|A, \quad R_1 = E|B, \quad R_2 = F|C.$$

Using this setting, there still exists some overhead in the multiplication and squaring arithmetic operations, even though the penalty on the latter operation is almost negligible. In the positive side, the terms of the elements a_0, a_1 do not need to be rearranged and the modular reduction of these two base field elements can be performed in parallel, as discussed next.

4.2 Multiplication

Given two $\mathbb{F}_{2^{2 \cdot 149}}$ elements $a = (a_0 + a_1 u)$ and $b = (b_0 + b_1 u)$, with a_0, a_1, b_0, b_1 in $\mathbb{F}_{2^{149}}$, we perform the multiplication $c = a \cdot b$ as,

$$\begin{aligned} c = a \cdot b &= (a_0 + a_1 u) \cdot (b_0 + b_1 u) \\ &= (a_0 b_0 \oplus a_1 b_1) + (a_0 b_0 \oplus (a_0 \oplus a_1) \cdot (b_0 \oplus b_1)) u, \end{aligned}$$

where each element $a_i, b_i \in \mathbb{F}_{2^{149}}$ is composed by three 64-bit words. The analysis of the Karatsuba algorithm cost for different word sizes was presented in [35]. There, it was shown that the most efficient way to multiply three 64-bit word polynomials $s(x) = s_2 x^2 + s_1 x + s_0$ and $t(x) = t_2 x^2 + t_1 x + t_0$ as $v(x) = s(x) \cdot t(x)$ is through the one-level Karatsuba method,

$$V_0 = s_0 \cdot t_0, \quad V_1 = s_1 \cdot t_1, \quad V_2 = s_2 \cdot t_2,$$

$$V_{0,1} = (s_0 \oplus s_1) \cdot (t_0 \oplus t_1), \quad V_{0,2} = (s_0 \oplus s_2) \cdot (t_0 \oplus t_2) \quad V_{1,2} = (s_1 \oplus s_2) \cdot (t_1 \oplus t_2),$$

$$v(x) = V_2 \cdot x^4 + (V_{1,2} \oplus V_1 \oplus V_2) \cdot x^3 + (V_{0,2} \oplus V_0 \oplus V_1 \oplus V_2) \cdot x^2 + (V_{0,1} \oplus V_0 \oplus V_1) \cdot x + V_0,$$

which costs six multiplications and twelve additions. The Karatsuba algorithm as used in this work is presented in Algorithm 4.[7]

Algorithm 4. Karatsuba algorithm for multiplying three 64-bit word polynomials $s(x)$ and $t(x)$

Input: Six 128-bit registers R_i, with $i \in \{0 \ldots 5\}$, containing the elements $R_0 = t_0|s_0, R_1 = t_1|s_1, R_2 = t_2|s_2, R_3 = (t_0 \oplus t_1)|(s_0 \oplus s_1), R_4 = (t_0 \oplus t_2)|(s_0 \oplus s_2), R_5 = (t_1 \oplus t_2)|(s_1 \oplus s_2).$

Output: Three 128-bit registers R_i, with $i \in \{6 \ldots 8\}$, which store the value $v(x) = s(x) \cdot t(x) = v_5 \cdot x^{320} + v_4 \cdot x^{256} + v_3 \cdot x^{192} + v_2 \cdot x^{128} + v_1 \cdot x^{64} + v_0$ as $R_6 = v_1|v_0, R_7 = v_3|v_2, R_8 = v_5|v_4.$

1: $tmp_0 \leftarrow R_0 \times_{HL} R_0$
2: $tmp_1 \leftarrow R_1 \times_{HL} R_1$
3: $tmp_2 \leftarrow R_2 \times_{HL} R_2$
4: $tmp_3 \leftarrow R_3 \times_{HL} R_3$
5: $tmp_4 \leftarrow R_4 \times_{HL} R_4$
6: $tmp_5 \leftarrow R_5 \times_{HL} R_5$
7: $tmp_5 \leftarrow tmp_5 \oplus tmp_1$
8: $tmp_5 \leftarrow tmp_5 \oplus tmp_2$

9: $tmp_1 \leftarrow tmp_1 \oplus tmp_0$
10: $tmp_4 \leftarrow tmp_4 \oplus tmp_1$
11: $tmp_4 \leftarrow tmp_4 \oplus tmp_2$
12: $tmp_3 \leftarrow tmp_3 \oplus tmp_1$
13: $R_6 \leftarrow (tmp_3 \ll 64)$
14: $R_8 \leftarrow (tmp_5 \gg 64)$
15: $R_7 \leftarrow ((tmp_5, tmp_3) \rhd 64)$

Algorithm 4 requires six carry-less instructions, six vectorized xors and three bitwise shift instructions. In order to calculate the total multiplication cost, it is necessary to include the Karatsuba pre-computation operations at the base field level (twelve vectorized xors and six byte interleaving instructions) and at the quadratic field level (six vectorized xors). Also, we must consider the reorganization of the registers in order to proceed with the modular reduction (six vectorized xors).

4.3 Modular Reduction

The modular reduction of an element $a = (a_0 + a_1 u)$, where a_0 and a_1 are 384-bit polynomials, takes nine vectorized xors and six bitwise shifts. The computational savings of the previously discussed register configuration can be seen when we compare the reduction of quadratic field elements, presented in Algorithm 5 with the modular reduction of the base field elements (see Algorithm 2). The cost of reducing an element in $\mathbb{F}_{2^{149}}$ in 64-bit registers is about the same as the cost of the reduction of an element in $\mathbb{F}_{2^{2 \cdot 149}}$ stored into 128-bit registers. Thus, we achieved a valuable speedup of 100 %.

---

[7] As before, the symbols $\ll, \gg$ stand for bitwise shift of packed 64-bit integers. The symbol $\rhd$ stands for bytewise multi-precision shift.

Algorithm 5. Modular reduction of the terms a_0, a_1 of an element $a = (a_0 + a_1 u)$ modulo $g(x) = x^{192} + x^{19} + 1$

Input: An element $a = a_0 + a_1 u = (F \cdot x^{320} + E \cdot x^{256} + D \cdot x^{192} + C \cdot x^{128} + B \cdot x^{64} + A) + (L \cdot x^{320} + K \cdot x^{256} + J \cdot x^{192} + I \cdot x^{128} + H \cdot x^{64} + G)u$, with the 64-bit words (A-L) arranged in six 128-bit registers as $R_0 = G|A, R_1 = H|B, R_2 = I|C, R_3 = J|D, R_4 = K|E, R_5 = L|F$

Output: Elements $(a_0, a_1) \mod g(x) = M \cdot x^{128} + N \cdot x^{64} + O, P \cdot x^{128} + Q \cdot x^{64} + R$, with the 64-bit words (M-R) organized in three 128-bit registers as $R_6 = R|O, R_7 = Q|N, R_8 = P|M$

1: $R_8 \leftarrow R_2 \oplus R_5$
2: $R_7 \leftarrow R_1 \oplus R_4$
3: $R_8 \leftarrow R_8 \oplus (R_5 \ll 19)$
4: $R_7 \leftarrow R_7 \oplus (R_4 \ll 19)$
5: $R_8 \leftarrow R_8 \oplus (R_4 \gg 45)$

6: $R_7 \leftarrow R_7 \oplus (R_3 \ll 45)$
7: $R_6 \leftarrow R_3 \oplus (R_5 \gg 45)$
8: $R_6 \leftarrow R_6 \oplus (R_6 \ll 19)$
9: $R_6 \leftarrow R_6 \oplus R_0$

4.4 Squaring

Squaring is a very important function in the Koblitz curve point multiplication algorithm, since it is the building block for computing the τ endomorphism. In our implementation, we computed the squaring operation through carry-less multiplication instructions which, experimentally, was an approach less expensive than the bit interleaving method (see [15, Sect. 2.3.4]). The pre-processing phase is straightforward, we just need to rearrange the 32-bit packed words of the 128-bit registers in order to prepare them for the subsequent modular reduction.

The pre- and post-processing phases require three shuffle instructions, three vectorized xors and three bitwise shifts. The complete function is described in Algorithm 6. Given 128-bit registers R_i, we depict the SSE 32-bit shuffle operation as $R_0 \leftarrow R_1 \ \backslash\!\backslash \ xxxx$. For instance, if we compute $R_0 \leftarrow R_1 \ \backslash\!\backslash \ 3210$, it just maintains the 32-bit word order of the register R_1, in other words, it just copies R_1 to R_0. The operation $R_0 \leftarrow R_1 \ \backslash\!\backslash \ 2103$ rotates the register R_1 to the left by 32-bits. See [17,18] for more details.

4.5 Inversion

The inversion operation is computed via the Itoh-Tsujii method [19]. Given an element $c \in \mathbb{F}_{2^m}$, we compute $c^{-1} = c^{(2^{m-1}-1) \cdot 2}$ through an addition chain, which in each step computes the terms $(c^{2^i-1})^{2^j} \cdot c^{2^j-1}$ with $0 \le j \le i \le m-1$. For the case $m = 149$, the following chain is used,

$$1 \to 2 \to 4 \to 8 \to 16 \to 32 \to 33 \to 66 \to 74 \to 148.$$

This addition chain is optimal and was found through the procedure described in [7]. Note that although we compute the inversion operation over polynomials in $\mathbb{F}_2[x]$ (reduced modulo $g(x) = x^{192} + x^{19} + 1$), we still have to perform the addition chain with $m = 149$, since we are in fact interested in the embedded $\mathbb{F}_{2^{149}}$ field element.

Algorithm 6. Squaring of an element $a = (a_0 + a_1 u) \in \mathbb{F}_{2^{2 \cdot 149}}$

Input: Element $a = a_0 + a_1 u = (C \cdot x^{128} + B \cdot x^{64} + A) + (F \cdot x^{128} + E \cdot x^{64} + D)u \in \mathbb{F}_{2^{2 \cdot 149}}$, with the 64-bit words (A-F) arranged in three 128-bit registers as $R_0 = D|A, R_1 = E|B, R_2 = F|C$

Output: Element $a^2 = c = c_0 + c_1 u = (I \cdot x^{128} + H \cdot x^{64} + G) + (L \cdot x^{128} + K \cdot x^{64} + J)u \in \mathbb{F}_{2^{2 \cdot 149}}$, where both elements $(c_0, c_1) \in \mathbb{F}_2[x]$ are reduced modulo $x^{192} + x^{19} + 1$. The 64-bit words (G-L) are arranged in three 128-bit registers as $R_3 = J|G, R_4 = H|K, R_5 = I|L$.

1: $tmp_0 \leftarrow R_0 \oslash 3120$	9: $aux_5 \leftarrow tmp_2 \times_{HH} tmp_2$
2: $tmp_1 \leftarrow R_1 \oslash 3120$	10: $R_3, R_4, R_5 \leftarrow \texttt{ModularReduction}(aux_{0...5})$
3: $tmp_2 \leftarrow R_2 \oslash 3120$	11: $tmp_0 \leftarrow R_3 \gg 64$
4: $aux_0 \leftarrow tmp_0 \times_{LL} tmp_0$	12: $tmp_1 \leftarrow R_4 \gg 64$
5: $aux_1 \leftarrow tmp_0 \times_{HH} tmp_0$	13: $tmp_2 \leftarrow R_5 \gg 64$
6: $aux_2 \leftarrow tmp_1 \times_{LL} tmp_1$	14: $R_3 \leftarrow R_3 \oplus tmp_0$
7: $aux_3 \leftarrow tmp_1 \times_{HH} tmp_1$	15: $R_4 \leftarrow R_4 \oplus tmp_1$
8: $aux_4 \leftarrow tmp_2 \times_{LL} tmp_2$	16: $R_5 \leftarrow R_5 \oplus tmp_2$

As previously discussed, in each step of the addition chain, we must calculate an exponentiation c^{2^j} followed by a multiplication, where the value j represents the integers that form the addition chain. Experimentally, we found that when $j \geq 4$, it is cheaper to compute the exponentiation through table look-ups instead of performing consecutive squarings. Our pre-computed tables process four bits per iteration, therefore, it is required $\lceil \frac{192}{4} \rceil = 48$ table queries in order to complete the multisquaring function.

5 τ-and-add Scalar Multiplication

In this Section we discuss the single-core algorithms that compute a timing-resistant scalar multiplication through the τ-and-add method over Koblitz curves defined over $\mathbb{F}_4$. There are two basic approaches, the right-to-left and the left-to-right algorithms.

5.1   Left-to-right τ-and-add

This algorithm is similar to the traditional left-to-right double-and-add method. Here, the point doubling operation is replaced by the computationally cheaper τ endomorphism. In addition, we need to compute the width w-τNAF representation of the scalar k and perform linear passes (cf. Sect. 5.3) in the accumulators in order to avoid cache attacks [26,34]. The method is shown in Algorithm 7.

The main advantage of this method is that the sensitive data is indirectly placed in the points P_{v_i}. However, those points are only read and then added to the unique accumulator Q. As a consequence, only one linear pass per iteration is required before reading P_{v_i}. On the other hand, the operation $\tau^{w-1}(Q)$ must be performed by successive squarings, since computing it through look-up tables could leak information about the scalar k.

Algorithm 7. Left-to-right regular w-TNAF τ-and-add on Koblitz curves defined over $\mathbb{F}_4$

Input: A Koblitz curve $E_a/\mathbb{F}_{2^{2m}}$, a point $P \in E_a(\mathbb{F}_{2^{2m}})$ of order r, $k \in \mathbb{Z}_r$
Output: $Q = kP$

1: Compute $\rho = r_0 + r_1\tau = k$ partmod $\left(\frac{\tau^m-1}{\tau-1}\right)$
2: Ensure that r_0 and r_1 are odd.
3: Compute the width-w regular τ-NAF of $r_0 + r_1\tau$ as $\sum_{i=0}^{\lceil\frac{m+2}{w-1}+1\rceil} v_i\tau^{i(w-1)}$
4: **for** $v \in \{1,3,\ldots 4^{w-1}-1\}$ **do** Compute $P_v = \alpha_v \cdot P$ **end for**
5: $Q \leftarrow \mathcal{O}$
6: **for** $i = \frac{m+2}{w-1} + 1$ **to** 0 **do**
7:     $Q \leftarrow \tau^{w-1}(Q)$
8:     Perform a linear pass to recover P_{v_i}
9:     $Q \leftarrow Q \pm P_{v_i}$
10: **end for**
11: Subtract $P, \tau(P)$ from Q if necessary
12: **return** $Q = kP$

5.2 Right-to-left τ-and-add

This other method processes the scalar k from the least to the most significant digit. Taking advantage of the τ endomorphism, the GLV method is brought to its full extent. This approach is presented in Algorithm 8.

Algorithm 8. Right-to-left regular w-TNAF τ-and-add on Koblitz curves defined over $\mathbb{F}_4$

Input: A Koblitz curve $E_a/\mathbb{F}_{2^{2m}}$, a point $P \in E_a(\mathbb{F}_{2^{2m}})$ of order r, $k \in \mathbb{Z}_r$
Output: $Q = kP$

1: Compute $\rho = r_0 + r_1\tau = k$ partmod $\pmod{\frac{\tau^m-1}{\tau-1}}$
2: Ensure that r_0 and r_1 are odd.
3: Compute the width-w regular τ-NAF of $r_0 + r_1\tau$ as $\sum_{i=0}^{\lceil\frac{m+2}{w-1}+1\rceil} v_i\tau^{i(w-1)}$
4: **for** $i \in \{1,3,\ldots 4^{w-1}-1\}$ **do** $Q_i = \mathcal{O}$
5: **for** $i = 0$ **to** $\frac{m+2}{w-1} + 1$ **do**
6:     Perform a linear pass to recover Q_i
7:     $Q_i \leftarrow Q_i \pm P$
8:     Perform a linear pass to store Q_i
9:     $P \leftarrow \tau^{w-1}(P)$
10: $Q \leftarrow \mathcal{O}$
11: **for** $u \in \{1,3,\ldots 4^{w-1}-1\}$ **do** $Q = Q + \alpha_v \cdot Q_i$
12: Subtract $P, \tau(P)$ from Q if necessary
13: **return** $Q = kP$

Here, we have to perform a post-computation in the accumulators instead of precomputing the points P_i as in the previous approach. Also, the τ endomorphism is applied to the point P, which is usually public. For that reason, we can compute τ with table look-ups instead of performing squarings multiple times.

The downside of this algorithm is that the accumulators carry sensitive information about the digits of the scalar. Also, the accumulators are read and written. As a result, it is necessary to apply the linear pass algorithm to the accumulators Q_i twice per iteration.

5.3   Linear Pass

The linear pass is a method designed to protect sensitive information against side-channel attacks associated with the CPU cache access patterns. Let us consider an array A of size l. Before reading a value $A[i]$, with $i \in [0, l-1]$, the linear pass technique reads the entire array A but only stores, usually into an output register, the requested data $A[i]$. In that way, the attacker does not know which array index was accessed just by analyzing the location of the cache-miss in his own artificially injected data. However, this method causes a considerable overhead, which depends on the size of the array.

In this work, we implemented the linear pass method using 128-bit SSE vectorized instructions and registers. For each array index j, we first copy j to a register and compare this value with the current scalar k τNAF digit. The SSE instruction pcmpeqq compares the values of two 128-bit registers A and B and sets the resulting register C with bits one, if A and B are equal, and bits zero otherwise. For that reason, we can use the register C as a mask: if j is equal to the scalar k digit, the register C will contain only bits one. Then, by performing logical operations between C and each of the array values $A[j]$, we can retrieve the requested data.

Experimental results shown that the implementation of the linear pass technique with SSE registers is more efficient than using 64-bit conditional move instructions [25] by a factor of 2.125. The approach just described is presented in Algorithm 9.

Algorithm 9. Linear pass using 128-bit AVX vectorized instructions

---

Input: An array A of size l, a requested index d, SSE 128-bit registers tmp, dst.
Output: The register dst containing $A[d]$.
1: $dst \leftarrow 0$
2: **for** $i \in \{0, \dots, l-1\}$ **do**
3:     $tmp \leftarrow i$
4:     $tmp \leftarrow$ compare(tmp, d)
        (compare returns 1^{128} if the operands are equal and 0^{128} otherwise.)
5:     $tmp \leftarrow tmp \wedge A[i]$
6:     $dst \leftarrow dst \oplus tmp$
7: **end for**

---

6   Results and Discussion

Our software library can be executed in any Intel platform, which comes with the SSE 4.1 vector instructions and the 64-bit carry-less multiplier instruction pclmulqdq. The benchmarking was executed in an Intel Core i7 4770k 3.50 GHz machine (Haswell architecture) with the TurboBoost and HyperThreading features disabled. Also, the library was coded in the GNU11 C and Assembly languages.

Regarding the compilers, we performed an experimental analysis on the performance of our code compiled with different systems: GCC (Gnu Compiler Collection) versions 5.3, 6.1; and the clang frontend for the LLVM compiler infrastructure versions 3.5 and 3.8. All compilations were done with the flags -O3 -march=haswell -fomit-frame-pointer. For the sake of comparison, we reported our timings for all of the previously mentioned compilers. However, when comparing our code with the state-of-the-art works, we opted for the *clang/llvm* 3.8, since it gave us the best performance.

6.1   Parameters

Given $q = 2^m$, with $m = 149$, we constructed our base binary field $\mathbb{F}_q \cong \mathbb{F}_2[x]/(f(x))$ with the 69-term irreducible polynomial $f(x)$ described in Sect. 4. The quadratic extension $\mathbb{F}_{q^2} \cong \mathbb{F}_q[u]/(h(u))$ was built through the irreducible quadratic $h(u) = u^2 + u + 1$. However, our base field arithmetic was computed modulo the redundant trinomial $g(x) = x^{192} + x^{19} + 1$, which has among its irreducible factors, the polynomial $f(x)$.

Our Koblitz curve was defined over $\mathbb{F}_{q^2}$ as $E_1/\mathbb{F}_{q^2} : y^2 + xy = x^3 + ux^2 + u$, and the group $E_1(\mathbb{F}_{q^2})$ contains a subgroup of interest of order

$$r = \text{0x637845F7F8BFAB325B85412FB54061F148B7F6E79AE11CC843ADE1470F7E4E29},$$

which corresponds to approximately 255 bits. In addition, throughout our scalar multiplication, we represented the points in λ-affine [20,28] and λ-projective [25] coordinates. We selected an order-r base point P at random represented in λ-affine coordinates.

6.2   Field and Elliptic Curve Arithmetic Timings

In Table 2, we present the timings for the base and the quadratic field arithmetic. The multisquaring operation is used to support the Itoh-Tsujii addition chain, therefore, it is implemented only in the field $\mathbb{F}_{2^{149}}$ (actually, in a 192-bit polynomial in $\mathbb{F}_2[x]$). In addition, we gave timings to reduce a 192-bit polynomial element in $\mathbb{F}_2[x]$ modulo $f(x)$. Finally, all timings of operations in the quadratic field include the subsequent modular reduction.

Applying the techniques presented in [27], we saw that our machine has a margin of error of four cycles. This range is not of significance when considering the timings of the point arithmetic or the scalar multiplication. Nevertheless, for inexpensive functions such as multiplication and squaring, it is recommended to consider it when comparing the timings between different compilers.

Table 2. Timings (in clock cycles) for the finite field operations in $\mathbb{F}_{2^{2 \cdot 149}}$ using different compiler families

Compilers	Multiplication	Squaring	Multi-squaring	Inversion	Reduction modulo $f(x)$
GCC 5.3	52	20	100	2,392	452
GCC 6.1	52	20	104	2,216	452
clang 3.5	64	24	100	1,920	452
clang 3.8	60	20	96	1,894	452

Table 3. The ratio between the arithmetic and multiplication in $\mathbb{F}_{2^{149}}$. The timings were taken from the code compiled with the *clang 3.8* compiler

Operations	Squaring	Multisquaring	Inversion	Reduction modulo $f(x)$
operation / multiplication	0.33	1.60	31.56	7.53

In the following, we compare in Table 3 the base arithmetic operation timings with the multiplication operation, which is the main operation of our library. The ratio squaring/multiplication is relatively expensive. This is because the polynomial $g(x) = x^{192} + x^{19} + 1$, does not admit a reduction specially designed for the squaring operation. Furthermore, the multisquaring and the inversion operations are also relatively costly. A possible explanation is that here, we are measuring timings in a Haswell architecture, which has a computationally cheaper carry-less multiplication when compared with the Sandy Bridge platform [18].

In Table 4 we give the timings of the point arithmetic functions. There, we presented the costs of applying the τ endomorphism to an affine point (two coordinates) and a λ-projective point (three coordinates). The reason is that, depending on the scalar multiplication algorithm, one can apply the Frobenius map on the accumulator (projective) or the base point (affine). In addition, we report in Table 4, the *mixed point doubling* operation, which is defined as follows. Given a point $P = (x_P, y_P)$, the mixed-doubling function computes, $R = (X_R, L_R, Z_R) = 2P$. In other words, it performs a point doubling on an affine point and returns the resulting point in projective representation. Such primitive is useful in the computation of the τNAF representations $\alpha_v = v \bmod \tau^w$ (see Sect. 2.2).

Table 4 also shows the superior performance of the *clang* compiler in the point arithmetic timings, since the only operations where it has a clear disadvantage are the full and mixed point doubling. However, those functions are rarely used throughout a Koblitz curve scalar multiplication. In fact, they are used only in the precomputing phase. Next, in Table 5, we show the relation of the point arithmetic timings with the field multiplication.

Table 4. Timings (in clock cycles) for point addition over a Koblitz curve E_1/q^2 using different compiler families

Compilers	Full Addition	Mixed Addition	Full Doubling	Mixed Doubling	τ endomorphism 2 coord	3 coord
GCC 5.3	792	592	372	148	80	120
GCC 6.1	796	588	368	148	80	120
clang 3.5	768	580	404	164	84	124
clang 3.8	752	564	384	160	84	120

Table 5. The ratio between the timings of point addition and the field multiplication. The timings were taken from the code compiled with the *clang 3.8* compiler

Operations	Full Addition	Mixed Addition	Full Doubling	Mixed Doubling	τ endomorphism 2 coord	3 coord
operation / multiplication	12.53	9.39	6.40	2.66	1.40	2.00

6.3 Scalar Multiplication Timings

Here the timings for the left-to-right regular w-τNAF τ-and-add scalar multiplication, with $w = 2, 3, 4$ are reported. The setting $w = 2$ is presented in order to analyze how the balance between the pre-computation and the main iteration costs works in practice. Our main result lies in the setting $w = 3$. Also, among the scalar multiplication timings, we show, in Table 6, the costs of the regular recoding and the linear pass functions.

Table 6. A comparison of the scalar multiplication and its support functions timings (in clock cycles) between different compiler families

Compilers	Regular recoding w=2	w=3	w=4	Linear pass w=2	w=3	w=4	Scalar multiplication w=2	w=3	w=4
GCC 5.3	1,656	2,740	2,516	8	40	240	100,480	72,556	90,020
GCC 6.1	1,792	2,688	2,480	8	44	240	99,456	71,728	89,740
clang 3.5	1,804	2,680	2,396	8	44	272	96,812	69,696	86,632
clang 3.8	1,808	2,704	2,376	8	40	264	95,196	68,980	85,244

Regarding the regular recoding function, we saw an increase of about 46 % in the 3-τNAF timings when comparing with the $w = 2$ case. The reason is that, for the $w = 3$ case, we must compute a more complicated arithmetic. Also, when selecting the digits, we must perform a linear pass in the array that stores them. Otherwise, an attacker could learn about the scalar k by performing a timing-attack based on the CPU cache.

The linear pass function also becomes more expensive in the $w = 3$ case, since we have more points in the array. However, in the $m = 149$ case, we have to process 64 more iterations with the width $w = 2$, when compared with the 3-τNAF point multiplication (since the number of iterations depends on m and w: $\frac{m+2}{w-1} + 2$). As a result, the linear pass function overhead is mitigated by the savings in mixed additions and applications of τ endomorphisms in the main loop. Finally, our scalar multiplication measurements consider that the point $Q = kP$ is returned in the λ-projective coordinate representation. If the affine representation is required, it is necessary to add about 2,000 cycles to the total scalar multiplication timings.

6.4   Comparisons

In Table 7, we compare our implementation with the state-of-the-art works. Our 3-τNAF left-to-right τ-and-add point multiplication outperformed by 29.64% the work in [24], which is considered the fastest protected 128-bit secure Koblitz implementation. When compared with prime curves, our work is surpassed by 15.29 % and 13.06 % by the works in [8] and [2], respectively.

Table 7. Scalar multiplication timings (in clock cycles) on 128-bit secure ellitpic curves

Curve/Method	Architecture	Timings
Koblitz over $\mathbb{F}_{2^{283}}$ (τ-and-add, 5-τNAF [24])	Haswell	99,000
GLS over $\mathbb{F}_{2^{2 \cdot 127}}$ (double-and-add, 4-NAF [25])	Haswell	61,712
Twisted Edwards over $\mathbb{F}_{(2^{127}-1)^2}$ (double-and-add [8])	Haswell	59,000
Kummer genus-2 over $\mathbb{F}_{2^{127}-1}$ (Kummer ladder [2])	Haswell	60,556
Koblitz over $\mathbb{F}_{4^{149}}$ (τ-and-add, 2-τNAF (this work))	Haswell	96,822
Koblitz over $\mathbb{F}_{4^{149}}$ (τ-and-add, 3-τNAF (this work))	Haswell	69,656
Koblitz over $\mathbb{F}_{4^{149}}$ (τ-and-add, 4-τNAF (this work))	Haswell	85,244

Skylake architecture. In addition, we present timings for our scalar multiplication algorithms, also compiled with *clang* 3.8, in the Skylake architecture (Intel Core i7 6700K 4.00 GHz). The results (in clock cycles) for the cases $w = 2, 3, 4$ are, respectively, 71,138, 51,788 and 66,286.

7   Conclusion

We have presented a comprehensive study of how to implement efficiently Koblitz elliptic curves defined over quaternary fields $\mathbb{F}_{4^m}$, using vectorized instructions on the Intel micro-architectures codename Haswell and Skylake.

As a future work, we plan to investigate the use of 256-bit AVX2 registers to improve the performance of our code. In addition, we intend to implement the scalar multiplication algorithms in other architectures such as the ARMv8. Finally, we would like to design a version of our point multiplication in the multi-core and known point scenarios.

References

1. Aranha, D.F., Faz-Hernández, A., López, J., Rodríguez-Henríquez, F.: Faster implementation of scalar multiplication on Koblitz curves. In: Hevia, A., Neven, G. (eds.) LatinCrypt 2012. LNCS, vol. 7533, pp. 177–193. Springer, Heidelberg (2012)
2. Bernstein, D.J., Chuengsatiansup, C., Lange, T., Schwabe, P.: Kummer strikes back: new DH speed records. In: Sarkar, P., Iwata, T. (eds.) ASIACRYPT 2014. LNCS, vol. 8873, pp. 317–337. Springer, Heidelberg (2014)
3. Birkner, P., Longa, P., Sica, F.: Four-dimensional Gallant-Lambert-Vanstone scalar multiplication. Cryptology ePrint Archive, Report 2011/608 (2011). http://eprint.iacr.org/
4. Blake-Wilson, S., Bolyard, N., Gupta, V., Hawk, C., Moeller, B.: Elliptic Curve Cryptography (ECC) cipher suites for Transport Layer Security (TLS). RFC 4492. Internet Engineering Task Force (IETF) (2006). https://tools.ietf.org/html/rfc4492
5. Bluhm, M., Gueron, S.: Fast software implementation of binary elliptic curve cryptography. J. Cryptogr. Eng. 5(3), 215–226 (2015)
6. Brent, R.P., Zimmermann, P.: Algorithms for finding almost irreducible and almost primitive trinomials. In: Primes and Misdemeanours: Lectures in Honour of the Sixtieth Birthday of Hugh Cowie Williams, Fields Institute, p. 212 (2003)
7. Clift, N.M.: Calculating optimal addition chains. Computing 91(3), 265–284 (2011)
8. Costello, C., Longa, P.: FourQ: four-dimensional decompositions on a Q-curve over the mersenne prime. In: Iwata, T., et al. (eds.) ASIACRYPT 2015. LNCS, vol. 9452, pp. 214–235. Springer, Heidelberg (2015). doi:10.1007/978-3-662-48797-6_10
9. Dierks, T., Rescorla, E.: The Transport Layer Security (TLS) Protocol version 1.2. RFC 5246. Internet Engineering Task Force (IETF) (2008). https://tools.ietf.org/html/rfc5246
10. Doche, C.: Redundant trinomials for finite fields of characteristic 2. In: Boyd, C., González Nieto, J.M. (eds.) ACISP 2005. LNCS, vol. 3574, pp. 122–133. Springer, Heidelberg (2005)
11. Galbraith, S.D., Gaudry, P.: Recent progress on the elliptic curve discrete logarithm problem. Des. Codes Cryptogr. 78(1), 51–72 (2016)
12. Galbraith, S.D., Lin, X., Scott, M.: Endomorphisms for faster elliptic curve cryptography on a large class of curves. In: Joux, A. (ed.) EUROCRYPT 2009. LNCS, vol. 5479, pp. 518–535. Springer, Heidelberg (2009)
13. Gaudry, P., Hess, F., Smart, N.P.: Constructive and destructive facets of Weil descent on elliptic curves. J. Cryptol. 15, 19–46 (2002)
14. Hankerson, D., Karabina, K., Menezes, A.: Analyzing the Galbraith-Lin-Scott point multiplication method for elliptic curves over binary fields. IEEE Trans. Comput. 58(10), 1411–1420 (2009)
15. Hankerson, D., Menezes, A.J., Vanstone, S.: Guide to Elliptic Curve Cryptography. Springer, Secaucus (2003)

16. Hess, F.: Generalising the GHS attack on the elliptic curve discrete logarithm problem. LMS J. Comput. Math. **7**, 167–192 (2004)
17. Intel Corporation: Intel Intrinsics Guide. https://software.intel.com/sites/landingpage/IntrinsicsGuide/. Accessed 18 Feb 2016
18. Intel Corporation: Intel 64 and IA-32 Architectures Software Developers Manual 325462–056US (2015)
19. Itoh, T., Tsujii, S.: A fast algorithm for computing multiplicative inverses in $GF(2^m)$ using normal bases. Inf. Comput. **78**(3), 171–177 (1988)
20. Knudsen, E.W.: Elliptic scalar multiplication using point halving. In: Lam, K.-Y., Okamoto, E., Xing, C. (eds.) ASIACRYPT 1999. LNCS, vol. 1716, pp. 135–149. Springer, Heidelberg (1999)
21. Koblitz, N.: CM-curves with good cryptographic properties. In: Feigenbaum, J. (ed.) CRYPTO 1991. LNCS, vol. 576, pp. 279–287. Springer, Heidelberg (1992)
22. Menezes, A., Qu, M.: Analysis of the Weil descent attack of Gaudry, Hess and smart. In: Naccache, D. (ed.) CT-RSA 2001. LNCS, vol. 2020, pp. 308–318. Springer, Heidelberg (2001)
23. National Institute of Standards and Technology: Recommended elliptic curves for federal government use. NIST Special Publication (1999). http://csrc.nist.gov/csrc/fedstandards.html
24. Oliveira, T., Aranha, D.F., López, J., Rodríguez-Henríquez, F.: Fast point multiplication algorithms for binary elliptic curves with and without precomputation. In: Joux, A., Youssef, A. (eds.) SAC 2014. LNCS, vol. 8781, pp. 324–344. Springer, Heidelberg (2014)
25. Oliveira, T., López, J., Aranha, D.F., Rodríguez-Henríquez, F.: Two is the fastest prime: lambda coordinates for binary elliptic curves. J. Cryptogr. Eng. **4**(1), 3–17 (2014)
26. Page, D.: Theoretical use of cache memory as a cryptanalytic side-channel. Cryptology ePrint Archive, Report 2002/169 (2002). http://eprint.iacr.org/
27. Paoloni, G.: How to benchmark code execution times on intel IA-32 and IA-64 instruction set architectures. Technical report, Intel Corporation (2010)
28. Schroeppel, R.: Cryptographic elliptic curve apparatus and method (2000). US patent 2002/6490352 B1
29. Scott, M.: Optimal irreducible polynomials for $GF(2^m)$ arithmetic. Cryptology ePrint Archive, Report 2007/192 (2007). http://eprint.iacr.org/
30. Solinas, J.A.: An improved algorithm for arithmetic on a family of elliptic curves. In: Kaliski Jr., B.S. (ed.) CRYPTO 1997. LNCS, vol. 1294, pp. 357–371. Springer, Heidelberg (1997)
31. Solinas, J.A.: Efficient arithmetic on Koblitz curves. Des. Codes Cryptogr. **19**(2–3), 195–249 (2000)
32. Taverne, J., Faz-Hernández, A., Aranha, D.F., Rodríguez-Henríquez, F., Hankerson, D., López, J.: Software implementation of binary elliptic curves: impact of the carry-less multiplier on scalar multiplication. In: Preneel, B., Takagi, T. (eds.) CHES 2011. LNCS, vol. 6917, pp. 108–123. Springer, Heidelberg (2011)
33. Trost, W.R., Xu, G.: On the optimal pre-computation of window τ-NAF for Koblitz curves. Cryptology ePrint Archive, Report 2014/664 (2014). http://eprint.iacr.org/
34. Tsunoo, Y., Tsujihara, E., Minematsu, K., Miyauchi, H.: Cryptanalysis of block ciphers implemented on computers with cache. In: International Symposium on Information Theory and Its Applications, pp. 803–806. IEEE Information Theory Society (2002)

35. Weimerskirch, A., Paar, C.: Generalizations of the Karatsuba algorithm for efficient implementations. Cryptology ePrint Archive, Report 2006/224 (2006). http://eprint.iacr.org/

36. Wenger, E., Wolfger, P.: Solving the discrete logarithm of a 113-bit Koblitz curve with an FPGA cluster. In: Joux, A., Youssef, A. (eds.) SAC 2014. LNCS, vol. 8781, pp. 363–379. Springer, Heidelberg (2014)

Qcbits: Constant-Time Small-Key
Code-Based Cryptography

Tung Chou$^{(\boxtimes)}$

Department of Mathematics and Computer Science, Technische Universiteit
Eindhoven, P.O. Box 513, 5600 MB Eindhoven, The Netherlands
blueprint@crypto.tw

Abstract. This paper introduces a constant-time implementation for
a quasi-cyclic moderate-density-parity-check (QC-MDPC) code based
encryption scheme. At a 2^{80} security level, the software takes 14 679 937
Cortex-M4 and 1 560 072 Haswell cycles to decrypt a short message, while
the previous records were 18 416 012 and 3 104 624 (non-constant-time)
cycles. Such speed is achieved by combining two techniques: 1) perform-
ing each polynomial multiplication in $\mathbb{F}_2[x]/(x^r - 1)$ and $\mathbb{Z}[x]/(x^r - 1)$
using a sequence of "constant-time rotations" and 2) bitslicing.

Keywords: McEliece · Niederreiter · QC-MDPC codes · Bitslicing ·
Software implementation

1 Introduction

In 2012, Misoczki et al. proposed to use QC-MDPC codes for code-based cryptography [3]. The main benefit of using QC-MDPC codes is that they allow
small key sizes, as opposed to using binary Goppa codes as proposed in the original McEliece paper [1]. Since then, implementation papers for various platforms
have been published; see [4,5] (for FPGA and AVR), [7,9] (for Cortex-M4), and
[11] (for Haswell, includes results from [4,5,7]).

One problem of QC-MDPC codes is that the most widely used decoding
algorithm, when implemented naively, leaks information about secrets through
timing. Even though decoding is only used for decryption, the same problem can
also arise if the key-generation and encryption are not constant-time. Unfortunately, the only software implementation paper that addresses the timing-attack
issue is [7]. [7] offers constant-time encryption and decryption on a platform
without caches (for writable-memory).

This paper presents Qcbits (pronounced "quick-bits"), a fully constant-time
implementation of a QC-MDPC-code-based encryption scheme. Qcbits provides

This work was supported by the Netherlands Organisation for Scientic Research
(NWO) under grant 639.073.005 and by the Commission of the European Communities through the Horizon 2020 program under project number 645622 PQCRYPTO.
Permanent ID of this document: 172b0e150c3b6be91b0bdaa0870c1e7d. Date:
2016.03.13.

B. Gierlichs and A.Y. Poschmann (Eds.): CHES 2016, LNCS 9813, pp. 280–300, 2016.
DOI: 10.1007/978-3-662-53140-2_14

Table 1. Performance results for QcBits, [7,9], and the vectorized implementation in [11]. The "key-pair" column shows cycle counts for generating a key pair. The "encrypt" column shows cycle counts for encryption. The "decrypt" column shows cycle counts for decryption. For performance numbers of Qcbits, 59-byte plaintexts are used to follow the eBACS [16] convention. For [9] 32-byte plaintexts are used. Cycle counts labeled with * mean that the implementation for the operation is not constant-time on the platform, which means that the worst-case performance can be much worse (especially for decryption). Note that all the results are for 2^{80} security ($r = 4801, w = 90, t = 84$; see Sect. 2.1).

platform	key-pair	encrypt	decrypt	reference	implementation	scheme
Haswell	784 192	82 732	1 560 072	(new) QcBits	clmul	KEM/DEM
	20 339 160	225 948	2 425 516	(new) QcBits	ref	KEM/DEM
	*14 234 347	*34 123	*3 104 624	[11]		McEliece
Sandy Bridge	2 497 276	151 204	2 479 616	(new) QcBits	clmul	KEM/DEM
	44 180 028	307 064	3 137 088	(new) QcBits	ref	KEM/DEM
Cortex-A8	61 544 763	1 696 011	16 169 673	(new) QcBits	ref	KEM/DEM
Cortex-M4	140 372 822	2 244 489	14 679 937	(new) QcBits	no-cache	KEM/DEM
	*63 185 108	*2 623 432	*18 416 012	[9]		KEM/DEM
	*148 576 008	7 018 493	42 129 589	[7]		McEliece

constant-time key-pair generation, encryption, and decryption for a wide variety of platforms, including platforms with caches. QcBits follows the McBits paper [17] to use a variant of the hybrid (KEM/DEM) Niederreiter encryption scheme proposed in [13,14]. (The variant does not exactly follow the KEM/DEM construction since there is an extra "KEM failed" bit passed from the KEM to the DEM; see [17]) As a property of the KEM/DEM encryption scheme, the software is protected against adaptive chosen ciphertext attacks, as opposed to the plain McEliece or Niederreiter [2] encryption scheme. The code is written in C, which makes it easy to understand and verify. Moreover, QcBits outperforms the performance results achieved by all previous implementation papers; see below.

The reader should be aware that QcBits, in the current version, uses a 2^{80}-security parameter set from [3]. Note that with some small modifications QcBits can be used for a 2^{128} security parameter. However, I have not found good "thresholds" for the decoder for 2^{128} security that achieves a low failure rate and therefore decide not to include the code for 2^{128} security in the current version. Also, the key space used is smaller than the one described in [3]. However, this is also true for all previous implementation papers [4,5,7,9,11]. These design choices are made to reach a low decoding failure rate; see Sects. 2.1 and 7 for more discussions.

Performance Results. The performance results of QcBits are summarized in Table 1, along with the results for [7,9], and the vectorized implementation in [11]. In particular, the table shows performance results of the implementations contained in Qcbits for different settings. The implementation "ref" serves as the reference implementation, which can be run on all reasonable 64/32-bit platforms. The implementation "clmul" is a specialized implementation that relies on the PCLMULQDQ instruction, i.e., the $64 \times 64 \rightarrow$ 128-bit carry-less multiplication instruction. The implementation "no-cache" is similar to ref except that it does not provide full protection against cache-timing attacks. Both "ref" and "clmul" are constant-time, even on platforms with caches. "no-cache" is constant-time only on platforms that do not have cache for *writable* memory. Regarding previous works, both the implementations in [11] for Haswell and [9] for Cortex-M4 are not constant-time. [7] seems to provide constant-time encryption and decryption, even though the paper argues about resistance against simple-power analysis instead of being constant-time.

On the Haswell microarchitecture, QcBits is about twice as fast as [11] for decryption and an order of magnitude faster for key-pair generation, even though the implementation of [11] is not constant-time. QcBits takes much more cycles on encryption. This is mainly because QcBits uses a slow source of randomness; see Sect. 3.1 for more discussions. A minor reason is that KEM/DEM encryption requires intrinsically some more operations than McEliece encryption, e.g., hashing.

For tests on Cortex-M4, STM32F407 is used for QcBits and [7], while [9] uses STM32F417. Note that there is no cache for writable memory (SRAM) on these devices. QcBits is faster than [9] for encryption and decryption. The difference is even bigger when compared to [7]. The STM32F407/417 product lines provide from 512 kilobytes to 1 megabyte of flash. [9] reports a flash usage of 16 kilobytes, while the implementation no-cache uses 62 kilobytes of flash when the symmetric primitives are included and 38 kilobytes without symmetric primitives. See Sect. 2.3 for more discussions on the symmetric primitives.

It is important to note that, since the decoding algorithm is probabilistic, each implementation of decryption comes with a failure rate. For QcBits no decryption failure occurred in 10^8 trials. I have not found "thresholds" for the decoding algorithm that achieves the same level of failure rate at a 2^{128} security level, which is why QcBits uses a 2^{80}-security parameter set. For [11], no decryption failure occurred in 10^7 trials. For [9] the failure rate is not indicated, but the decoder seems to be the same as [11]. It is unclear what level of failure rate [7] achieves. See Sect. 7 for more discussions about failure rates.

Table 2 shows performance results for 128-bit security. Using thresholds derived from the formulas in [3, Section A] leads to a failure rate of $6.9 \cdot 10^{-3}$ using 12 decoding iterations. Experiments show that there are some sets of thresholds that achieve a failure rate around 10^{-5} using 19 decoding iterations, but this is still far from 10^{-8}; see Sect. 6 for the thresholds. Note that [9,11] did not specify the failure rates they achieved for 128-bit security, and [7] does not have implementation for 128-bit security. It is reported in [3] that no decryption failure occurred in 10^7 trials for all the parameter sets presented in the paper (including the ones used for Tables 1 and 2), but they did not provide details such as how many decoding iterations are required to achieve this.

Table 2. Performance results for `QcBits`, [9], and the vectorized implementation in [11] for 128-bit security ($r = 9857, w = 142, t = 134$; see Sect. 2.1). The cycle counts for `QcBits` decryption are underlined to indicate that these are cycle counts for one decoding iteration. Experiments show that `QcBits` can achieve a failure rate around 10^{-5} using 19 decoding iterations (see Sect. 6).

platform	key-pair	encrypt	decrypt	reference	implementation	scheme
Haswell	5 824 028	196 836	<u>1 363 948</u>	(**new**) QcBits	clmul	KEM/DEM
	*54 379 733	*106 871	*18 825 103	[11]		McEliece
Cortex-M4	750 584 383	6 353 732	<u>7 436 655</u>	(**new**) QcBits	no-cache	KEM/DEM
	*251 288 544	*13 725 688	*80 260 696	[9]		KEM/DEM

Comparison with Other Post-Quantum Public-Key Systems. In 2013, together with Bernstein and Schwabe, I introduced `McBits` (cf. [17]), a constant-time implementation for the KEM/DEM encryption scheme using binary Goppa code. At a 2^{128} security level, the software takes only 60493 Ivy Bridge cycles to decrypt. It might seem that `QcBits` is far slower than `McBits`. However, the reader should keep in mind that `McBits` relies on external parallelism to achieve such speed: the cycle count is the result of dividing the time for running 256 decryption instances in parallel by 256. The speed of `QcBits` relies only on internal parallelism: the timings presented in Table 1 are all results of running only one instance.

Lattice-based systems are known to be pretty efficient, and unfortunately `QcBits` is not able to compete with the best of them. For example, the eBACS website reports that `ntruees439ep1`, at a 2^{128} security level, takes 54940 Haswell cycles (non-constant-time) for encryption and 57008 for Haswell cycles (non-constant-time) for decryption. Also, the recently published "Newhope" paper [32] for post-quantum key exchange, which targets a 2^{128} quantum security level, reports 115414 Haswell cycles (constant-time) for server-side key generation, 23988 Haswell cycles (constant-time) for server-side shared-secret computation, and 144788 Haswell cycles (constant-time) for client-side key generation plus shared-secret computation.

It is worth noticing that using QC-MDPC codes instead of binary Goppa codes allows smaller key sizes. [3] reports a public-key size of 601 bytes for a 2^{80}-security parameter set (the one used for Table 1), 1233 bytes for a 2^{128}-security parameter set (the one used for Table 2), 4097 bytes for a 2^{256}-security parameter set. [17] reports 74624 bytes for a 2^{80}-security parameter set and 221646 bytes for a 2^{128}-security parameter set, and 1046739 bytes for a 2^{256}-security parameter set. The public-key size is 609 bytes for `ntruees439ep1`. The "message sizes" for Newhope are 1824 bytes (server to client) and 2048 bytes (client to server).

The usage of binary Goppa code was proposed by McEliece in [1] in 1978, along with the McEliece cryptosystem. After almost 40 years, nothing has really changed the practical security of the system. The NTRU cryptosystem is almost 20 years old now. QC-MPDC-code-based cryptosystems, however, are still quite young and thus require some time to gain confidence from the public.

2   Preliminaries

This section presents preliminaries for the following sections. Section 2.1 gives a brief review on the definition of QC-MDPC codes. Section 2.2 describes the "bit-flipping" algorithm for decoding QC-MDPC codes. Section 2.3 gives a specification of the KEM/DEM encryption scheme implemented by QcBits.

2.1   QC-MDPC Codes

"MDPC" stands for "moderate-density-parity-check". As the name implies, an MDPC code is a linear code with a "moderate" number of non-zero entries in a parity-check matrix H. For ease of discussion, in this paper it is assumed $H \in \mathbb{F}_2^{r \times n}$ where $n = 2r$, even though some parameter sets in [3] use $n = 3r$ or $n = 4r$. H is viewed as the concatenation of two square matrices, i.e., $H = H^{(0)}|H^{(1)}$, where $H^{(i)} \in \mathbb{F}_2^{r \times r}$.

"QC" stands for "quasi-cyclic". Being quasi-cyclic means that each $H^{(i)}$ is "cyclic". For ease of discussion, one can think this means

$$H^{(k)}_{(i+1) \bmod r,\, (j+1) \bmod r} = H^{(k)}_{i,j},$$

even though the original paper allows a row permutation on H. Note that being quasi-cyclic implies that H has a fixed row weight w. The following is a small parity-check matrix with $r = 5, w = 4$:

$$\begin{pmatrix} 1\,0\,1\,0\,0 & 0\,1\,0\,0\,1 \\ 0\,1\,0\,1\,0 & 1\,0\,1\,0\,0 \\ 0\,0\,1\,0\,1 & 0\,1\,0\,1\,0 \\ 1\,0\,0\,1\,0 & 0\,0\,1\,0\,1 \\ 0\,1\,0\,0\,1 & 1\,0\,0\,1\,0 \end{pmatrix}.$$

The number of errors a code is able to correct is often specified as t. Since there is no good way to figure out the minimum distance for a given QC-MDPC code, t is usually merely an estimated value.

Qcbits uses $r = 4801$, $w = 90$, and $t = 84$ matching a 2^{80}-security parameter set proposed in [3]. However, Qcbits further requires that $H^{(0)}$ and $H^{(1)}$ have the same row weight, namely $w/2$. This is not new, however, as all the previous implementation papers [4,5,7,9,11] also restrict H in this way. For QcBits this is a decision for achieving low failure rate; see Sect. 7 for more discussions on this issue. Previous implementation papers did not explain why they restrict H in this way.

2.2   Decoding (QC-)MDPC Codes

As opposed to many other linear codes that allow efficient deterministic decoding, the most popular decoder for (QC-)MDPC code, the "bit-flipping" algorithm, is a probabilistic one. The bit-flipping algorithm shares the same idea with so-called "statistical decoding" [19,21]. (The term "statistical decoding" historically come later than "bit-flipping", but "statistical decoding" captures way better the idea behind the algorithm.)

Given a vector that is at most t errors away from a codeword, the algorithm aims to output the codeword (or equivalently, the error vector) in a sequence of iterations. Each iteration decides statistically which of the n positions of the input vector v might have a higher chance to be in error and flips the bits at those positions. The flipped vector then becomes the input to the next iteration. In the simplest form of the algorithm, the algorithm terminates when Hv becomes zero.

The presumed chance of each position being in error is indicated by the count of unsatisfied parity checks. The higher the count is, the higher the presumed chance a position is in error. In other words, the chance of position i being in error is indicated by

$$u_i = |\{i \mid H_{i,j} = (Hv)_i = 1\}|.$$

In this paper the syndrome Hv will be called the *private syndrome*.

Now the remaining problem is, which bits should be flipped given the vector u? In [3] two possibilities are given:

- Flip all positions that violate at least $\max(\{u_i\}) - \delta$ parity checks, where δ is a small integer, say 5.
- Flip all positions that violate at least T_i parity checks, where T_i is a precomputed threshold for iteration i.

In previous works several variants have been invented. For example, one variant based on the first approach simply restarts decoding with a new δ if decoding fails in 10 iterations.

QcBits uses precomputed thresholds. The number of decoding iterations is set to be 6, and the thresholds are

$$29, 27, 25, 24, 23, 23.$$

These thresholds are obtained by interactive experiments. I do not claim that these are the best thresholds. With this list of thresholds, no iteration failure occurs in 10^8 decoding trials. See Sect. 6 for more details about the trials.

The best results in previous implementation papers [4,5,7,9,11] are achieved by a variant of the precomputed-threshold approach. In each iteration of the variant, the u_i's are computed in order. If the current u_i is greater than or equal to the precomputed threshold, v_i is flipped and the syndrome is directly updated by adding the i-th column of H to the syndrome. With this variant, [11] reports that the average number of iterations is only 2.4.

QcBits always takes 6 decoding iterations, which is much more than 2.4. However, the algorithms presented in the following sections allow QcBits to run each iteration very quickly, albeit being constant-time. As the result, Qubits still achieves much better performance results in decryption.

2.3 The Hybrid Niederreiter Encryption System for QC-MDPC Codes

The KEM/DEM encryption uses the Niederreiter encryption scheme for KEM. Niederreiter encryption is used to encrypt a *random* vector e of weight t, which is then fed into a key-derivation function to obtain the symmetric encryption and authentication key. The ciphertext is then the concatenation of the Niederreiter ciphertext, the symmetric ciphertext, and the authentication tag for the symmetric ciphertext. The decryption works in a similar way as encryption; see for example [17] for a more detailed description. By default QcBits uses the following symmetric primitives: Keccak [23], Salsa20 [25], and Poly1305 [24]. To be more precise, QcBits uses Keccak with 512-bit outputs to hash e, and the symmetric encryption and authentication key are defined to be the first and second half of the hash value. For symmetric encryption and authentication, QcBits uses Salsa20 with nonce 0 and Poly1305. Note that QcBits does not implement Keccak, Salsa20, and Poly1305; it only provides an interface to call these primitives. For the experiments results in Table 1, the implementations of the symmetric primitives are from the SUPERCOP benchmarking toolkit. The user can use their own implementations for the primitives, or even use some other symmetric primitives (in this case the user has to change the hard-coded parameters, such as key size of the MAC).

The secret key is a representation of a random parity-check matrix H. Since the first row H gives enough information to form the whole matrix, it suffices to represent H using an array of indices in $\{j \mid H_{0,j}^{(0)} = 1\}$ and an array of indices in $\{j \mid H_{0,j}^{(1)} = 1\}$. In each array the indices should not repeat, but they are *not* required to be sorted. QcBits represents each array as a byte stream of length w, where the i-th double byte is the little-endian representation of the i-th index in the array. The secret key is then defined as the concatenation of the two byte streams.

The public key is a representation of the row reduced echelon form of H. The row reduced matrix is denoted as P. Niederreiter requires $P^{(0)}$ to be the identity matrix I_r, or the key pair must be rejected. (Previous papers such as [7] use $P^{(1)} = I_r$, but using $P^{(0)} = I_r$ is equivalent in terms of security.) In other words, $P^{(1)}$ contains all information of P (if P is valid). Note that P is also quasi-cyclic; QcBits thus defines the public key as a byte stream of length $\lfloor (r+7)/8 \rfloor$, where the byte values are

$$(P_{7,0}^{(1)} P_{6,0}^{(1)} \dots P_{0,0}^{(1)})_2, \ (P_{15,0}^{(1)} P_{14,0}^{(1)} \dots P_{8,0}^{(1)})_2, \ \dots$$

The encryption process begins with generating a random vector e of weight t. The ciphertext for e is then the public syndrome $s = Pe$, which is represented as a byte stream of length $\lfloor (r+7)/8 \rfloor$, where the byte values are

$$(s_7 s_6 \dots s_0)_2, \ (s_{15} s_{14} \dots s_8)_2, \ \dots$$

For hashing, e is represented as a byte stream of length $\lfloor (n+7)/8 \rfloor$ in a similar way as the public syndrome. The 32-byte symmetric encryption key and the

32-byte authentication key are then generated as the first and second half of the 64-byte hash value of the byte stream. The plaintext m is encrypted and authenticated using the symmetric keys. The ciphertext for the whole KEM/DEM scheme is then the concatenation of the public syndrome, the ciphertext under symmetric encryption, and the tag. In total the ciphertext takes $\lfloor (r + 7)/8 \rfloor + |m| + 16$ bytes.

When receiving an input stream, the decryption process parses it as the concatenation of a public syndrome, a ciphertext under symmetric encryption, and a tag. Then an error vector e' is computed by feeding the public syndrome into the decoding algorithm. If $Pe' = s$, decoding is successful. Otherwise, a decoding failure occurs. The symmetric keys are then generated by hashing e' to perform symmetric decryption and verification. QcBits reports a decryption failure if and only if the verification fails or the decoding fails.

3 Key-Pair Generation

This section shows how QcBits performs key-pair generation using multiplications in $\mathbb{F}_2[x]/(x^r - 1)$. Section 3.1 shows how the private key is generated. Section 3.2 shows how key-pair generation is viewed as multiplications in $\mathbb{F}_2[x]/(x^r - 1)$. Section 3.3 shows how multiplications in $\mathbb{F}_2[x]/(x^r - 1)$ are implemented. Section 3.4 shows how squarings in $\mathbb{F}_2[x]/(x^r - 1)$ are implemented.

3.1 Private-Key Generation

The private-key is defined to be an array of w random 16-bit indices. QcBits obtains random bytes by first reading 32 bytes from a source of randomness and then expands the 32 bytes into the required length using salsa20. QcBits allows the user to choose any source of randomness. To generate the performance numbers on Ivy Bridge, Sandy Bridge, and Cortex-A8 in Table 1, /dev/urandom is used as the source of randomness. To generate the performance numbers on Cortex-M4 in Table 1, the TRNG on the board is used as in [9]. The RDRAND instruction used by [11] is not considered for there are security concerns about the instruction; see the Wikipedia page of RDRAND [26]. One can argue that there is no evidence of a backdoor in RDRAND, but I decide not to take the risk.

3.2 Polynomial View: Public-Key Generation

For any matrix M, let $M_{i,:}$ denote the vector $(M_{i,0}, M_{i,1}, \dots)$ and similarly for $M_{:,i}$. In Sect. 2, the public key is defined as a sequence of bytes representing $P_{:,0}^{(1)}$, where P is the row reduced echelon form of the parity-check matrix H. A simple way to implement constant-time public-key generation is thus to generate H from the private key and then perform a Gaussian elimination. It is not hard to make Gausssian elimination constant-time; see for example, [17]. However, public-key generation can be made much more time- and memory-efficient when considering it as polynomial operations, making use of the quasi-cyclic structure.

For any vector v of length r, let $v(x) = v_0 + v_1 x + \cdots + v_{r-1} x^{r-1}$. As a result of $H^{(0)}$ being cyclic, we have

$$H_{j,:}^{(i)}(x) = x^j H_{0,:}^{(i)}(x) \in \mathbb{F}_2[x]/(x^r - 1).$$

The Gaussian elimination induces a linear combination of the rows of $H^{(0)}$ that results in $P_{0,:}^{(0)}$. In other words, there exists a set I of indices such that

$$1 = \sum_{i \in I} x^i H_{0,:}^{(0)}(x) = (\sum_{i \in I} x^i) H_{0,:}^{(0)}(x),$$

$$P_{0,:}^{(1)}(x) = \sum_{i \in I} x^i H_{0,:}^{(1)}(x) = (\sum_{i \in I} x^i) H_{0,:}^{(1)}(x).$$

In other words, the public key can be generated by finding the inverse of $H_{0,:}^{(0)}(x)$ in $\mathbb{F}_2[x]/(x^r - 1)$ and then multiplying the inverse by $H_{0,:}^{(1)}(x)$. The previous implementation papers [4,5,7,9,11] compute the inverse using the extended Euclidean algorithm. The algorithm in its original form is highly non-constant-time. [30] provides a way to make extended Euclidean algorithm constant-time; so far it is unclear to me whether their algorithm is faster than simply using exponentiation (see below).

In order to be constant-time, QcBits computes the inverse by carrying out a fixed sequence of polynomial multiplications. To see this, first consider the factorization of $x^r - 1 \in \mathbb{F}_2[x]$ as $\prod_i \left(f^{(i)}(x)\right)^{p_i}$, where each $f^{(i)}$ is irreducible. $\mathbb{F}_2[x]/(x^r - 1)$ is then equivalent to

$$\prod_i \mathbb{F}_2[x] \big/ \left(f^{(i)}(x)\right)^{p_i}$$

Since

$$\left| \left(\mathbb{F}_2[x] \big/ \left(f^{(i)}(x)\right)^{p_i}\right)^* \right| = 2^{\deg(f^{(i)}) \cdot p_i} \cdot (2^{\deg(f^{(i)})} - 1)/2^{\deg(f^{(i)})}$$

$$= 2^{\deg(f^{(i)}) \cdot p_i} - 2^{\deg(f^{(i)}) \cdot (p_i - 1)},$$

one may compute the inverse of an element in $\mathbb{F}_2[x]/(x^r - 1)$ by raising it to power

$$\mathrm{lcm}\left(2^{\deg(f^{(1)}) \cdot p_1} - 2^{\deg(f^{(1)}) \cdot (p_1 - 1)}, 2^{\deg(f^{(2)}) \cdot (p_2 - 1)} - 2^{\deg(f^{(2)}) \cdot (p_2 - 1)}, \ldots\right) - 1.$$

QcBits uses $r = 4801$. The polynomial $x^{4801} - 1$ can be factored into

$$(x + 1) f^{(1)} f^{(2)} f^{(3)} f^{(4)} \in \mathbb{F}_2[x],$$

where each $f^{(i)}$ is an irreducible polynomial of degree 1200. Therefore, QcBits computes the inverse of a polynomial modulo $x^{4801} - 1$ by raising it to the power $\mathrm{lcm}(2 - 1, 2^{1200} - 1) - 1 = 2^{1200} - 2$.

Raising an element in $\mathbb{F}_2[x]/(x^{4801}-1)$ to the power $2^{1200}-2$ can be carried out by a sequence of squarings and multiplications. The most naive way is to use the square-and-multiply algorithm, which leads to 1199 squarings and 1198 multiplications. QcBits does better by finding a good addition chain for $2^{1200}-2$. First note that there is a systematic way to find a good addition chain for integers of the form 2^k-1. Take $2^{11}-1$ for example, the chain would be

$$1 \rightarrow 10_2 \rightarrow 11_2 \rightarrow 1100_2 \rightarrow 1111_2 \rightarrow 11110000_2 \rightarrow 11111111_2 \rightarrow 1111111100_2$$
$$\rightarrow 1111111111_2 \rightarrow 11111111110_2 \rightarrow 11111111111_2.$$

This takes 10 doublings and 5 additions. Using the same approach, it is easy to find an addition chain for $2^{109}-1$ that takes 108 doublings and 10 additions. QcBits then combines the addition chains for $2^{11}-1$ and $2^{109}-1$ to form an addition chain for $2^{11\cdot109}-1 = 2^{1199}-1$, which takes $10\cdot109+108 = 1198$ doubling and $5+10 = 15$ additions. Once the $(2^{1199}-1)$-th power is computed, the $(2^{1200}-2)$-th power can be computed using one squaring. In total, computation of the $(2^{1200}-2)$-th power takes 1199 squarings and 15 multiplications in $\mathbb{F}_2[x]/(x^{4801}-1)$.

Finally, with the inverse, $P_{0,:}^{(1)}(x)$ can be computed using one multiplication. The public key is defined to be a representation of $P_{:,0}^{(1)}$ instead of $P_{0,:}^{(1)}$. Qcbits thus derives $P_{0,:}^{(1)}$ from $P_{:,0}^{(1)}$ by noticing

$$P_{0,j}^{(1)} = \begin{cases} P_{0,r-j}^{(1)} & \text{if } j > 0 \\ P_{0,0}^{(1)} & \text{if } j = 0. \end{cases}$$

Note that the conversion from $P_{:,0}^{(1)}$ to $P_{0,:}^{(1)}$ does not need to be constant-time because it can be easily reversed from public data.

3.3   Generic Multiplication in $\mathbb{F}_2[x]/(x^r-1)$

The task here is to compute $h = fg$, where $f, g \in \mathbb{F}_2[x]/(x^r-1)$. In QcBits, the polynomials are represented using an array of $\lceil r/b \rceil$ b-bit words in the natural way. Take f for example (the same applies to g and h), the b-bit values are:

$$(f_{b-1}f_{b-2}\cdots f_0)_2, (f_{2b-1}f_{2b-2}\cdots f_b)_2, \ldots.$$

The user can choose b to be 32 or 64, but for the best performance b should be chosen according to the machine architecture. Let $y = x^b$. One can view this representation as storing each coefficient of the radix-y representation of f using one b-bit integer. In this paper this representation is called the "dense representation".

Using the representation, we can compute the coefficients (each being a $2b$-bit value) of the radix-y representation of h, using carry-less multiplications on the b-bit words of f and g. Once the $2b$-bit values are obtained, the dense representation of h can be computed with a bit of post-processing. To be precise, given two b-bit numbers $(\alpha_{b-1}\alpha_{b-2}\cdots\alpha_0)_2$ and $(\beta_{b-1}\beta_{b-2}\cdots\beta_0)_2$, a carry-less multiplication computes the $2b$-bit value (having actually only $2b - 1$ bits)

$$\left(\bigoplus_{i+j=2b-2} \alpha_i\beta_j \quad \bigoplus_{i+j=2b-3} \alpha_i\beta_j \cdots \bigoplus_{i+j=0} \alpha_i\beta_j \right)_2.$$

In other words, the input values are considered as elements in $\mathbb{F}_2[x]$, and the output is the product in $\mathbb{F}_2[x]$.

The implementations clmul uses the PCLMULQDQ instruction to perform carry-less multiplications between two 64-bit values. For the implementation ref and no-cache, the following C code is used to compute the higher and lower b bits of the $2b$-bit value:

```
low = x * ((y >> 0) & 1);
v1 = x * ((y >> 1) & 1);
low  ^= v1 << 1;
high = v1 >> (b-1);
for (i = 2; i < b; i+=2)
{
        v0 = x * ((y >> i) & 1);
        v1 = x * ((y >> (i+1)) & 1);
        low  ^= v0 << i;
        low  ^= v1 << (i+1);
        high ^= v0 >> (b-i);
        high ^= v1 >> (b-(i+1));
}
```

3.4 Generic Squaring in $\mathbb{F}_2[x]/(x^r - 1)$

Squarings in $\mathbb{F}_2[x]/(x^r - 1)$ can be carried out as multiplications. However, obviously squaring is a much cheaper operation as only $\lceil r/b \rceil$ carry-less multiplications (actually squarings) are required.

The implementation clmul again uses the PCLMULQDQ instruction to perform carry-less squarings of 64-bit polynomials. Following the section for interleaving bits presented in the "Bit Twiddling Hacks" by Sean Eron Anderson [12], the implementations ref and no-cache use the following C code twice to compute the square of a 32-bit polynomial represented as 32-bit word:

```
x = (x | (x << 16)) & 0x0000FFFF0000FFFF;
x = (x | (x <<  8)) & 0x00FF00FF00FF00FF;
x = (x | (x <<  4)) & 0x0F0F0F0F0F0F0F0F;
x = (x | (x <<  2)) & 0x3333333333333333;
x = (x | (x <<  1)) & 0x5555555555555555;
```

By using the code twice we can also compute the square of a 64-bit polynomial.

4 KEM Encryption

This section shows how QcBits performs the KEM encryption using multiplications in $\mathbb{F}_2[x]/(x^r - 1)$. Section 4.1 shows how the error vector is generated. Section 4.2 shows how public-syndrome computation is viewed as multiplications in $\mathbb{F}_2[x]/(x^r - 1)$. Section 4.3 shows how these multiplications are implemented.

4.1 Generating the Error Vector

The error vector e is generated in essentially the same way as the private key. The only difference is that for e we need t indices ranging from 0 to $n - 1$, and there is only one list of indices instead of two. Note that for hashing it is still required to generate the dense representation of e.

4.2 Polynomial View: Public-Syndrome Computation

The task here is to compute the public syndrome Pe. Let $e^{(0)}$ and $e^{(1)}$ be the first and second half of e. The public syndrome is then

$$s = P^{(0)}e^{(0)} + P^{(1)}e^{(1)}$$
$$= \sum_i P^{(0)}_{:,i} e^{(0)}_i + \sum_i P^{(1)}_{:,i} e^{(1)}_i.$$

Since P is quasi-cyclic, we have

$$s(x) = \sum_i x^i P^{(0)}_{:,0}(x) e^{(0)}_i + \sum_i x^i P^{(1)}_{:,0}(x) e^{(1)}_i$$
$$= P^{(0)}_{:,0}(x) e^{(0)}(x) + P^{(1)}_{:,0}(x) e^{(1)}(x)$$
$$= e^{(0)}(x) + P^{(1)}_{:,0}(x) e^{(1)}(x).$$

In other words, the private syndrome can be computed using one multiplication in $\mathbb{F}_2[x]/(x^r - 1)$. The multiplication is not generic in the sense that $e^{(1)}(x)$ is sparse. See below for how the multiplication is implemented in QcBits.

4.3 Sparse-Times-Dense Multiplications in $\mathbb{F}_2[x]/(x^r - 1)$

The task here can be formalized as computing $f^{(0)} + f^{(1)}g^{(1)} \in \mathbb{F}_2[x]/(x^r - 1)$, where $g^{(1)}$ is represented in the dense representation. $f^{(0)}$ and $f^{(1)}$ are represented together using an array of indices in $I = \{i \mid f^{(0)}_i = 1\} \cup \{i+r \mid f^{(1)}_i = 1\}$, where $|I| = t$.

One can of course perform this multiplication between $f^{(1)}$ and $g^{(1)}$ in a generic way, as shown in Sect. 3.3. The implementation clmul indeed generates the dense representation of $f^{(1)}$ and then computes $f^{(1)}g^{(1)}$ using the PCLMULQDQ instruction. [11] uses essentially the same technique. The implementations ref and `no-cache` however, make use of the sparsity in $f^{(0)}$ and $f^{(1)}$; see below for details.

Now consider the slightly simpler problem of computing $h = fg \in \mathbb{F}_2[x]/(x^r - 1)$, where f is represented as an array of indices in $I = \{i \mid f_i = 1\}$, and g is in the dense representation. Then we have

$$fg = \sum_{i \in I} x^i g.$$

Therefore, the implementations `ref` and `no-cache` first set $h = 0$. Then, for each $i \in I$, $x^i g$ is computed and then added to h. Note that $x^i g$ is represented as an array of $\lceil r/b \rceil$ b-bit words, so adding $x^i g$ to h can be implemented using $\lceil r/b \rceil$ bitwise-`XOR` instructions on b-bit words.

Now the remaining problem is how to compute $x^i g$. It is obvious that $x^i g$ can be obtained by rotating g by i bits. In order to perform a constant-time rotation, the implementation `ref` makes use of the idea of the Barrel shifter [27]. The idea is to first represent i in binary representation

$$(i_{k-1} i_{k-2} \cdots i_0)_2.$$

Since $i \leqslant r - 1$, it suffices to use $k = \lfloor \lg(r-1) \rfloor + 1$. Then, for j from $k-1$ to $\lg b$, a rotation by 2^j bits is performed. One of the unshifted vector and the shifted vector is chosen (in a constant-time way) and serves as the input for the next j. After dealing with all $i_{k-1}, i_{k-2}, \ldots, i_{\lg b}$, a rotation of $(i_{\lg b-1} i_{\lg b-2} \cdots i_0)_2$ bits is performed using a sequence of logical instructions.

To clarify the idea, here is a toy example for the case $n = 40, b = 8$. The polynomial g is

$$(x^8 + x^{10} + x^{12} + x^{14}) + (x^{16} + x^{17} + x^{20} + x^{21}) + (x^{24} + x^{25} + x^{26} + x^{27})$$
$$+ (x^{36} + x^{37} + x^{38} + x^{39}),$$

which is represented in an array of 5 bytes as

$$00000000_2, 01010101_2, 00110011_2, 00001111_2, 11110000_2.$$

The goal is to compute $x^i g$ where $i = 010011_2$. Since $\lfloor \lg(40 - 1) \rfloor + 1 = 6$, the algorithm begins with computing a rotation of $100000_2 = 32$ bits, which can be carried out by moving around the bytes. The result is

$$01010101_2, 00110011_2, 00001111_2, 11110000_2, 00000000_2.$$

Since the most significant bit is not set, the unshifted polynomial is chosen. Next we proceed to perform a rotation of $010000_2 = 16$ bits. The result is

$$00001111_2, 11110000_2, 00000000_2, 01010101_2, 00110011_2.$$

Since the second most significant bit is set, we choose the rotated polynomial. The polynomial is then shifted by $001000_2 = 8$ bits. However, since the third most significant bit is not set, the unshifted polynomial is chosen. To handle the least significant $\lg b = 3$ bits of i, a sequence of logical instructions are used to combine the most significant 011_2 and the least significant 101_2 bits of the bytes, resulting in

$$01100001_2, 11111110_2, 00000000_2, 00001010_2, 10100110_2.$$

Note that in [3] r is required to be a prime (which means r is not divisible by b), so the example is showing an easier case. Roughly speaking, the implementation **ref** performs a rotation as if the vector length is $r - (r \bmod b)$ and then uses more instructions to compensate for the effect of the $r \bmod b$ extra bits. The implementation **no-cache** essentially performs a rotation of $(i_{k-1} i_{k-2} \cdots i_{\lg b} 0 \cdots 0)_2$ bits and then performs a rotation of $(i_{\lg b-1} i_{\lg b-2} \cdots i_0)_2$ bits.

With the constant-time rotation, we can now deal with the original problem of computing $f^{(0)} + f^{(1)} g^{(1)} \in \mathbb{F}_2[x]/(x^r - 1)$. QcBits first sets $h = 0$. Then for each $i \in I$, one of either 1 or $g^{(1)}$ is chosen according to whether $i < r$ or not, which has to be performed in a constant-time way to hide all information about i. The chosen polynomial is then rotated by $i \bmod r$ bits, and the result is added to h. Note that this means the implementations **ref** and **no-cache** perform a dummy polynomial multiplication to hide information about $f^{(0)}$ and $f^{(1)}$.

5   KEM Decryption

This section shows how **QcBits** performs the KEM decryption using multiplications in $\mathbb{F}_2[x]/(x^r - 1)$ and $\mathbb{Z}[x]/(x^r - 1)$. The KEM decryption is essentially a decoding algorithm. Each decoding iteration computes

- the private syndrome Hv and
- the counts of unsatisfied parity checks, i.e., the vector u, using the private syndrome.

Positions in v are then flipped according the counts. Section 5.1 shows how private-syndrome computation is implemented as multiplications in $\mathbb{F}_2[x]/(x^r - 1)$. Section 5.2 shows how counting unsatisfied parity checks is viewed as multiplications in $\mathbb{Z}[x]/(x^r - 1)$. Section 5.3 shows how these multiplications in $\mathbb{Z}[x]/(x^r - 1)$ are implemented. Section 5.4 shows how bit flipping is implemented.

5.1   Polynomial View: Private-Syndrome Computation

The public syndrome and the private syndrome are similar in the sense that they are both computed by matrix-vector products where the matrices are quasi-cyclic. For the public syndrome the matrix is P and the vector is e. For the private syndrome the matrix is H and the vector is v. Therefore, the computation of the private syndrome can be viewed as polynomial multiplication in the same way as the public syndrome. That is, the private syndrome can be viewed as

$$H^{(0)}_{:,0}(x) v^{(0)}(x) + H^{(1)}_{:,0}(x) v^{(1)}(x) \in \mathbb{F}_2[x]/(x^r - 1).$$

The computations of the public syndrome and the private syndrome are still a bit different. For encryption the matrix P is dense, whereas the vector e is sparse. For decryption the matrix H is sparse, whereas the vector v is dense. However, the multiplications $H_{:,0}^{(i)}(x) v^{(i)}(x)$ are still sparse-times-dense multiplications. QcBits thus computes the private syndrome using the techniques described in Sect. 4.3.

Since the secret key is a sparse representation of $H_{0,:}^{(i)}$, we do not immediately have $H_{:,0}^{(i)}$. This is similar to the situation in public-key generation, where $P_{:,0}^{(1)}$ is derived from $P_{0,:}^{(1)}$. QcBits thus computes $H_{:,0}^{(i)}$ from $H_{0,:}^{(i)}$ by adjusting each index in the sparse representation in constant time.

5.2 Polynomial View: Counting Unsatisfied Parity Checks

Let $s = Hv$. The vector u of counts of unsatisfied parity checks can be viewed as

$$u_j = \sum_i H_{i,j} \cdot s_i \in \mathbb{Z}^n,$$

where $H_{i,j}$ and s_j are treated as integers. In other words,

$$u = \sum_i H_{i,:} \cdot s_i \in \mathbb{Z}^n.$$

Let $u^{(0)}$ and $u^{(1)}$ be the first and second half of u, respectively. Now we have:

$$
\left(u^{(0)}(x), u^{(1)}(x) \right) = \left(\sum_i x^i H_{0,:}^{(0)}(x) \cdot s_i, \sum_i x^i H_{0,:}^{(1)}(x) \cdot s_i \right)
$$
$$
= \left(H_{0,:}^{(0)}(x) \cdot s(x), H_{0,:}^{(1)}(x) \cdot s(x) \right) \in (\mathbb{Z}[x]/(x^r - 1))^2 .
$$

In other words, the vector u can be computed using 2 multiplications in $\mathbb{Z}[x]/(x^r - 1)$. Note that the multiplications are not generic: $H_{0,:}^{(i)}(x)$ is always sparse, and the coefficients of $H_{0,:}^{(i)}(x)$ and $s(x)$ can only be 0 or 1. See below for how such multiplications are implemented in QcBits.

5.3 Sparse-Times-Dense Multiplications in $\mathbb{Z}[x]/(x^r - 1)$

The task can be formalized as computing $fg \in \mathbb{Z}[x]/(x^r - 1)$, where $f_i, g_i \in \{0, 1\}$ for all i, and f is of weight only w. f is represented as an array of indices in $I_f = \{i | f_i = 1\}$. g is naturally represented as an array of $\lceil r/b \rceil$ b-bit values as usual. Then we have

$$fg = \sum_{i \in I_f} x^i g.$$

Even though all the operations are now in $\mathbb{Z}[x]/(x^r - 1)$ instead of $\mathbb{F}_2[x]/(x^r - 1)$, each $x^i g$ can still be computed using a constant-time rotation as in Sect. 4.3.

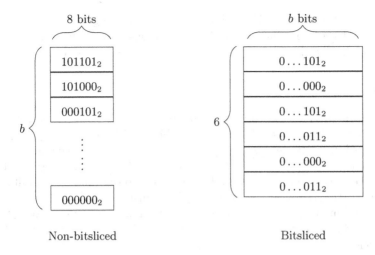

8 bits b bits

Non-bitsliced   Bitsliced

Fig. 1. Storage of b numbers of unsatisfied parity checks in non-bitsliced form and bitsliced format.

Therefore, QcBits first sets $h = 0$, and then for each $i \in I$, $x^i g$ is computed using the constant-time rotation and then added to h. After all the elements in I are processed, we have $h = fg$. Note that $x^i g$ is represented as an array of $\lceil r/b \rceil$ b-bit words.

Now the remaining problem is how to add $x^i g$ to h. A direct way to represent h is to use an array of r bytes (it suffices to use 1 byte for each coefficient when $w/2 < 256$, which is true for all parameter sets in [3] with $n = 2r$), each storing one of the r coefficients. To add $x^i g$ to h, the naive way is for each coefficient of h to extract from the corresponding b-bit word the bit required using one bitwise-AND instruction and at most one shift instruction, and then to add the bit to the byte using one addition instruction. In other words, it takes around 3 instructions on average to update each coefficient of h.

QcBits does better by bitslicing the coefficients of h: Instead of using b bytes, QcBits uses several b-bit words to store a group of b coefficients, where the i-th b-bit word stores the i-th least significant bits of the b coefficients. Since the column weight of H is $w/2$, it suffices to use $\lfloor \lg w/2 \rfloor + 1$ b-bit words. To update b coefficients of h, a sequence of logical operations is performed on the $\lfloor \lg w/2 \rfloor + 1$ b-bit words and the corresponding b-bit word in $x^i g$. These logical instructions simulate b copies of a circuit for adding a 1-bit number into a $(\lfloor \lg w/2 \rfloor + 1)$-bit number. Such a circuit requires roughly $\lfloor \lg w/2 \rfloor + 1$ half adders, so updating b coefficients takes roughly $2(\lfloor \lg w/2 \rfloor + 1)$ logical instructions on b-bit words.

Figure 1 illustrates how the b coefficients are stored when $w = 90$. In the non-bitsliced approach b bytes are used. In the bitsliced approach $\lfloor \lg(90/2) \rfloor + 1 = 6$ b-bit words are used, which account for $6b/8$ bytes. Note that this means bitslicing saves memory. Regarding the number of instructions, it takes $(6 \cdot 2)/b$ logical instructions on average to update each coefficient. For either $b = 32$ or $b = 64$, $(6 \cdot 2)/b$ is much smaller than 3. Therefore, bitslicing also helps to enhance performance.

The speed that McBits [17] achieves relies on bitslicing as well. However, the reader should keep in mind that QcBits, as opposed to McBits, makes use of parallelism that lies intrinsically in one single decryption instance.

5.4 Flipping Bits

The last step in each decoding iteration is to flip the bits according to the counts. Since QcBits stores the counts in a bitsliced format, bit flipping is also accomplished in a bitsliced fashion. At the beginning of each decoding iteration, the bitsliced form of b copies of $-t$ is generated and stored in $\lfloor \lg w/2 \rfloor + 1$ b-bit words. Once the counts are computed, $-t$ is added to the counts in parallel using logical instructions on b-bit words. These logical instructions simulate copies of a circuit for adding $(\lfloor \lg w/2 \rfloor + 1)$-bit numbers. Such a circuit takes $(\lfloor \lg w/2 \rfloor + 1)$ full adders. Therefore, each $u_i + (-t)$ takes roughly $5(\lfloor \lg w/2 \rfloor + 1)/b$ logical instructions.

The additions are used to generate sign bits for all $u_i - t$, which are stored in two arrays of $\lceil r/b \rceil$ b-bit words. To flip the bits, QcBits simply XORs the complement of b-bit words in the two arrays into $v^{(0)}$ and $v^{(1)}$. It then takes roughly $1/b$ logical instructions to update each v_i.

For $w = 90$, we have $5(\lfloor \lg w/2 \rfloor + 1)/b + 1b = 31/b$, which is smaller than 1 for either $b = 32$ or $b = 64$. In contrast, when the non-bitsliced format is used, the naive approach is to use at least one subtraction instruction for each $u_i - t$ and one XOR instruction to flip the bit. One can argue that for the non-bitsliced format there are probably better ways to compute u and perform bit flipping. For example, one can probably perform several additions/subtractions of bytes in parallel in one instruction. However, such an approach seems much more expensive than one might expect as changes of formats between a sequence of bits and bytes are required.

6   Experimental Results for Decoding

This section shows experimental results for QC-MDPC decoding under different parameter sets. The decoding algorithm used is the precomputed-threshold approach introduced in Sect. 2.2. The codes are restricted: $H^{(0)}$ and $H^{(1)}$ are required to have the same row weight. r, w, t have same meaning as in Sect. 2.1. sec indicates the security level. T is the list of thresholds. If not specified otherwise, the thresholds are obtained using the formulas in [3, Appendix A]. S is a list that denotes how many iterations the tests take. The summation of the numbers in S is the total number of tests, which is set to either 10^8 first the first three cases and 10^6 for the last case. The 10^8 (10^6) tests consist of 10^4 (10^3) decoding attempts for each of 10^4 (10^3) key pairs. The first number in the list indicates the number of tests that fail to decode in #T iterations (i.e., in the total number of iterations). The second number indicates the number of tests that succeed after 1 iteration. The third number indicates the number of tests that succeed after 2 iterations; etc. `avg` indicates the average number of iterations for the successful tests.

```
r = 4801
w = 90
t = 84
sec = 80
T = [29, 27, 25, 24, 23, 23]
S = [0, 0, 752, 69732674, 30232110, 34417, 47]
avg = 3.30
```

The thresholds are obtained by interactive experiments. `QcBits` uses this setting.

```
r = 4801
w = 90
t = 84
sec = 80
T = [28, 26, 24, 23, 23, 23, 23, 23, 23, 23]
S = [40060, 0, 9794, 87815060, 12079266, 51387, 3833, 519, 70, 10,
1]
avg = 3.12
```

```
r = 9857
w = 142
t = 134
sec = 128
T = [44, 42, 40, 37, 36, 36, 36, 36, 36, 36, 36, 36]
S = [689298, 0, 0, 86592, 53307303, 42797368, 2856446, 235479,
24501, 2651, 333, 26, 3]
avg = 4.46
```

```
r = 9857
w = 142
t = 134
sec = 128
T = [48, 47, 46, 45, 44, 43, 42, 42, 41, 41, 40, 40, 39, 39, 38,
38, 37, 37, 36]
S = [12, 0, 0, 0, 0, 0, 142, 78876, 578963, 290615, 43180, 6363,
1309, 336, 108, 54, 27, 7, 4, 4]
avg = 8.33
```

The thresholds are obtained by interactive experiments.

7   The Future of QC-MDPC-Based Cryptosystems

QcBits provides a way to perform constant-time QC-MDPC decoding, even on platforms with caches. Moreover, decoding in QcBits is much faster than that in previous works. However, the fact that the bit-flipping algorithm is probabilistic can be a security issue. The security proofs in [13,14] do assume that the KEM is able to decrypt a KEM ciphertext with "overwhelming probability". As there is no good way to estimate the failure rate for a given QC-MDPC code, the best thing people can do is to run a large number of experiments. QcBits manages to achieve no decoding failures in 10^8 trials. Indeed, 10^8 is not a trivial number, but whether such level of failure rate is enough to keep the system secure remains unclear, not to mention that this is for 80-bit security only. See Sect. 6 for more detailed experimental results on failure rates.

One can probably mitigate the problem by reducing the failure rate. This may be achieved by improving decoding algorithms or designing better parameter sets. However, a more fundamental problem that has not been answered is how low the failure rate should be in order to be secure.

Another probably less serious problem is that QcBits and all previous implementation papers [4,5,7,9,11] force the parity check matrix H to have equal weights in $H^{(0)}$ and $H^{(1)}$, which is not the same as what was described in [3]. QcBits restricts the key space in this way to reduce the failure rate. Of course, one can argue that even if the key space is not restricted, for a very high probability $H^{(0)}$ and $H^{(1)}$ would still have the same weight. However, such an argument is valid only if the adversary can only target one system. For an adversary who aims to break one out of many systems, it is still unclear whether such restriction affects the security. Hopefully researchers will spend time on this problem also.

References

1. McEliece, R.J.: A public-key cryptosystem based on algebraic coding theory. JPL DSN Progress Report, pp. 114–116 (1978). http://ipnpr.jpl.nasa.gov/progress_report2/42-44/44N.PDF
2. Niederreiter, H.: Knapsack-type cryptosystems and algebraic coding theory. Probl. Control Inf. Theor. **15**, 159–166 (1986)
3. Misoczki, R., Tillich, J.-P., Sendrier, N., Barreto, P.S.L.M.: MDPC-McEliece: new McEliece variants from moderate density parity-checkcodes, In: IEEE International Symposium on Information Theory, pp. 2069–2073 (2013). http://eprint.iacr.org/2012/409.pdf
4. Heyse, S., von Maurich, I., Güneysu, T.: Smaller keys for code-based cryptography: QC-MDPC McEliece implementations on embedded devices. In: Bertoni, G., Coron, J.-S. (eds.) CHES 2013. LNCS, vol. 8086, pp. 273–292. Springer, Heidelberg (2013)
5. von Maurich, I., Güuneysu, T.: Lightweight code-based cryptography: QC-MDPC McEliece encryption on reconfigurable devices. In: DATE 2014 [6], pp. 1–6 (2014). https://www.sha.rub.de/media/sh/veroeffentlichungen/2014/02/11/Lightweight_Code-based_Cryptography.pdf

6. Fettweis, G., Nebel, W. (eds.): Design, Automation and Test in Europe Conference and Exhibition, DATE 2014, Dresden, Germany, 24–28 March 2014. European Design and Automation Association (2014). ISBN 978-3-9815370-2-4, See [5]

7. von Maurich, I., Güneysu, T.: Towards side-channel resistant implementations of QC-MDPC McEliece encryption on constrained devices. In: Mosca, M. (ed.) PQCrypto 2014. LNCS, vol. 8772, pp. 266–282. Springer, Heidelberg (2014)

8. Mosca, M. (ed.): Post-Quantum Cryptography. LNCS, vol. 8772. Springer, Berlin (2014). See [7]

9. von Maurich, I., Heberle, L., Güneysu, T.: IND-CCA secure hybrid encryption from QC-MDPC Niederreiter. In: PQCrypto 2016 [10] (2016)

10. Takagi, T. (ed.): Post-Quantum Cryptography. LNCS, vol. 9606. Springer, Berlin (2016). See [9]

11. von Maurich, I., Oder, T., Güneysu, T.: Implementing QC-MDPC McEliece encryption. ACM Trans. Embed. Comput. Syst. **14**, 44 (2015)

12. Anderson, S.E.: Bit Twiddling Hacks (1997–2005). https://graphics.stanford.edu/~seander/bithacks.html

13. Persichetti, E.: Improving the efficiency of code-based cryptography. Ph.D. thesis, University of Auckland (2012). http://persichetti.webs.com/publications .

14. Persichetti, E.: Secure and anonymous hybrid encryption from coding theory. In: Gaborit, P. (ed.) PQCrypto 2013. LNCS, vol. 7932, pp. 174–187. Springer, Heidelberg (2013)

15. Gaborit, P. (ed.): Post-Quantum Cryptography. LNCS, vol. 7932. Springer, Berlin (2013). See [14]

16. Bernstein, D.J., Lange, T. (eds.): eBACS: ECRYPT Benchmarking of Cryptographic Systems (2016). http://bench.cr.yp.to. Accessed 2 Feb 2016

17. Bernstein, D.J., Chou, T., Schwabe, P.: McBits: fast constant-time code-based cryptography. In: Bertoni, G., Coron, J.-S. (eds.) CHES 2013. LNCS, vol. 8086, pp. 250–272. Springer, Heidelberg (2013)

18. Bertoni, G., Coron, J.-S. (eds.): CHES 2013. LNCS, vol. 8086. Springer, Heidelberg (2013). ISBN 978-3-642-40348-4

19. Al Jabri, A.K.: A statistical decoding algorithm for general linear block codes. In: [20], pp. 1–8 (2001)

20. Honary, B. (ed.): Cryptography and Coding. LNCS, vol. 2260. Springer, Heidelberg (2001). ISBN 3-540-43026-1, See [19]

21. Overbeck, R.: Statistical decoding revisited. In: Batten, L.M., Safavi-Naini, R. (eds.) ACISP 2006. LNCS, vol. 4058, pp. 283–294. Springer, Heidelberg (2006)

22. Batten, L.M., Safavi-Naini, R. (eds.): ACISP 2006. LNCS, vol. 4058. Springer, Heidelberg (2006). ISBN 3-540-35458-1, See [21]

23. Bertoni, G., Daemen, J.: Peeters, M., Van Assche, G.: Keccak and the SHA-3 standardization (2013). http://csrc.nist.gov/groups/ST/hash/sha-3/documents/Keccak-slides-at-NIST.pdf

24. Bernstein, D.J.: The Poly1305-AES message-authentication code. In: FSE 2005 [28], pp. 32–49 (2005). http://cr.yp.to/papers.html#poly1305

25. Bernstein, D.J.: The Salsa20 family of stream ciphers. In: [29], pp. 84–97 (2008). http://cr.yp.to/papers.html#salsafamily

26. Wikipedia: RdRand — Wikipedia. The Free Encyclopedia (2016). https://en.wikipedia.org/wiki/RdRand. Accessed 2 Feb 2016

27. Wikipedia: Barrel Shifter — Wikipedia. The Free Encyclopedia (2016). https://en.wikipedia.org/wiki/Barrel_shifter. Accessed 2 Feb 2016

28. Gilbert, H., Handschuh, H. (eds.): FSE 2005. LNCS, vol. 3557. Springer, Heidelberg (2005). ISBN:3-540-26541-4, See [24]

29. Robshaw, M., Billet, O. (eds.): New Stream Cipher Designs. LNCS. Springer, Heidelberg (2008). ISBN:978-3-540-68350-6, See [25]
30. Georgieva, M., de Portzamparc, F.: Toward secure implementation of McEliece decryption, In: COSADE 2015 [31], pp. 141–156 (2015). http://eprint.iacr.org/2015/271.pdf
31. Mangard, S., Poschmann, A.Y. (eds.): Constructive Side-Channel Analysis and Secure Design. LNCS, vol. 9064. Springer, Heidelberg (2015). See [30]
32. Alkim, E., Ducas, L., Pöppelmann, T., Schwabe, P.: Post-Quantum key Exchange—A New Hope, The IACR ePrint Archive (2015). https://eprint.iacr.org/2015/1092

μKummer: Efficient Hyperelliptic Signatures and Key Exchange on Microcontrollers

Joost Renes[1(✉)], Peter Schwabe[1], Benjamin Smith[2], and Lejla Batina[1]

[1] Digital Security Group, Radboud University, Nijmegen, The Netherlands
{j.renes,lejla}@cs.ru.nl, peter@cryptojedi.org
[2] INRIA and Laboratoire d'Informatique de l'École polytechnique (LIX),
Palaiseau, France
smith@lix.polytechnique.fr

Abstract. We describe the design and implementation of efficient signature and key-exchange schemes for the AVR ATmega and ARM Cortex M0 microcontrollers, targeting the 128-bit security level. Our algorithms are based on an efficient Montgomery ladder scalar multiplication on the Kummer surface of Gaudry and Schost's genus-2 hyperelliptic curve, combined with the Jacobian point recovery technique of Chung, Costello, and Smith. Our results are the first to show the feasibility of software-only hyperelliptic cryptography on constrained platforms, and represent a significant improvement on the elliptic-curve state-of-the-art for both key exchange and signatures on these architectures. Notably, our key-exchange scalar-multiplication software runs in under 9520k cycles on the ATmega and under 2640k cycles on the Cortex M0, improving on the current speed records by 32 % and 75 % respectively.

Keywords: Hyperelliptic curve cryptography · Kummer surface · AVR ATmega · ARM Cortex M0

1 Introduction

The current state of the art in asymmetric cryptography, not only on microcontrollers, is elliptic-curve cryptography; the most widely accepted reasonable security is the 128-bit security level. All current speed records for 128-bit secure key exchange and signatures on microcontrollers are held—until now—by elliptic-curve-based schemes. Outside the world of microcontrollers, it is well known that genus-2 hyperelliptic curves and their Kummer surfaces present an attractive alternative to elliptic curves [1,2]. For example, at Asiacrypt 2014 Bernstein, Chuengsatiansup, Lange and Schwabe [3] presented speed records for timing-attack-protected 128-bit-secure scalar multiplication on a range of architectures

L. Batina— This work has been supported by the Netherlands Organisation for Scientific Research (NWO) through Veni 2013 project 13114 and by the Technology Foundation STW (project 13499 - TYPHOON &ASPASIA), from the Dutch government. Permanent ID of this document: b230ab9b9c664ec4aad0cea0bd6a6732. Date: 2016-04-07.

© International Association for Cryptologic Research 2016
B. Gierlichs and A.Y. Poschmann (Eds.): CHES 2016, LNCS 9813, pp. 301–320, 2016.
DOI: 10.1007/978-3-662-53140-2_15

with Kummer-based software. These speed records are currently only being surpassed by the elliptic-curve-based FourQ software by Costello and Longa [4] presented at Asiacrypt 2015, which makes heavy use of efficiently computable endomorphisms (i.e., of additional structure of the underlying elliptic curve). The Kummer-based speed records in [3] were achieved by exploiting the computational power of vector units of recent "large" processors such as Intel Sandy Bridge, Ivy Bridge, and Haswell, or the ARM Cortex-A8. Surprisingly, very little attention has been given to Kummer surfaces on embedded processors. Indeed, this is the first work showing the feasibility of software-only implementations of hyperelliptic-curve based crypto on constrained platforms. There have been some investigations of binary hyperelliptic curves targeting the much lower 80-bit security level, but those are actually examples of software-hardware co-design showing that using hardware acceleration for field operations was necessary to get reasonable performance figures (see eg. [5,6]).

In this paper we investigate the potential of genus-2 hyperelliptic curves for both key exchange and signatures on the "classical" 8-bit AVR ATmega architecture, and the more modern 32-bit ARM Cortex-M0 processor. The former has the most previous results to compare to, while ARM is becoming more relevant in real-world applications. We show that not only are hyperelliptic curves competitive, they clearly outperform state-of-the art elliptic-curve schemes in terms of speed and size. For example, our variable-basepoint scalar multiplication on a 127-bit Kummer surface is 31 % faster on AVR and 26 % faster on the M0 than the recently presented speed records for Curve25519 software by Düll et al. [7]; our implementation is also smaller, and requires less RAM.

We use a recent result by Chung, Costello, and Smith [8] to also set new speed records for 128-bit secure signatures. Specifically, we present a new signature scheme based on fast Kummer surface arithmetic. It is inspired by the EdDSA construction by Bernstein, Duif, Lange, Schwabe, and Yang [9]. On the ATmega, it produces shorter signatures, achieves higher speeds and needs less RAM than the Ed25519 implementation presented in [10].

Table 1. Cycle counts and stack usage in bytes of all functions related to the signature and key exchange schemes, for the AVR ATmega and ARM Cortex M0 microcontrollers.

	ATmega		Cortex M0	
	Cycles	Stack bytes	Cycles	Stack bytes
keygen	10 206 181	812	2 774 087	1 056
sign	10 404 033	926	2 865 351	1 360
verify	16 240 510	992	4 453 978	1 432
dh_exchange	9 739 059	429	2 644 604	584

Our routines handling secret data are constant-time, and are thus naturally resistant to timing attacks. These algorithms are built around the Montgomery ladder, which improves resistance against simple-power-analysis (SPA) attacks. Resistance to DPA attacks can easily be added to the implementation by randomizing the scalar and/or Jacobian points. Re-randomizing the latter after each ladder step would also guarantee resistance against horizontal types of attacks.

Source code. We place all of the software described in this paper into the public domain, to maximize the reuseability of our results. The software is available at http://www.cs.ru.nl/~jrenes/.

2 High-Level Overview

We begin by describing the details of our signature and Diffie–Hellman schemes, explaining the choices we made in their design. Concrete implementation details appear in Sects. 3 and 4 below. Experimental results and comparisons follow in Sect. 5.

2.1 Signatures

Our signature scheme, defined at the end of this section, adheres closely to the proposal of [8, Sect. 8], which in turn is a type of Schnorr signature [11]. There are however some differences and trade-offs, which we discuss below.

Group structure. We build the signature scheme on top of the group structure from the Jacobian $\mathcal{J}_{\mathcal{C}}(\mathbb{F}_q)$ of a genus-2 hyperelliptic curve $\mathcal{C}$. More specifically, $\mathcal{C}$ is the Gaudry–Schost curve over the prime field $\mathbb{F}_q$ with $q = 2^{127} - 1$ (cf. Sect. 3.2). The Jacobian is a group of order $\#\mathcal{J}_{\mathcal{C}}(\mathbb{F}_q) = 2^4 N$, where

$$N = 2^{250} - \texttt{0x334D69820C75294D2C27FC9F9A154FF47730B4B840C05BD}$$

is a 250-bit prime. For more details on the Jacobian and its elements, see Sect. 3.3.

Hash function. We may use any hash function H with a 128-bit security level. For our purposes, $H(M) = \texttt{SHAKE128}(M, 512)$ suffices [12]. While $\texttt{SHAKE128}$ has variable-length output, we only use the 512-bit output implementation.

Encoding. At the highest level, we operate on points Q in $\mathcal{J}_{\mathcal{C}}(\mathbb{F}_q)$. To minimize communication costs, we compress the usual 508-bit representation of Q into a 256-bit encoding $\underline{Q}$ (see Sect. 3.3). (This notation is the same as in [9].)

Public generator. The public generator can be any element P of $\mathcal{J}_{\mathcal{C}}(\mathbb{F}_q)$ such that $[N]P = 0$. In our implementation we have made the arbitrary choice $P = (X^2 + u_1 X + u_0, v_1 X + v_0)$, where

$u_1 = \texttt{0x7D5D9C3307E959BF27B8C76211D35E8A},$ $u_0 = \texttt{0x2703150F9C594E0CA7E8302F93079CE8},$

$v_1 = \texttt{0x444569AF177A9C1C721736D8F288C942},$ $v_0 = \texttt{0x7F26CFB225F42417316836CFF8AEFB11}.$

This is the point which we use the most for scalar multiplication. Since it remains fixed, we assume we have its decompressed representation precomputed, so as to avoid having to perform the relatively expensive decompression operation whenever we need a scalar multiplication; this gives a low-cost speed gain. We further assume we have a "wrapped" representation of the projection of P to the Kummer surface, which is used to speed up the xDBLADD function. See Sect. 4.1 for more details on the xWRAP function.

Public keys. In contrast to the public generator, we assume public keys are compressed: they are communicated much more frequently, and we therefore benefit much more from smaller keys. Moreover, we include the public key in one of the hashes during the sign operation [13,14], computing $h = H(\underline{R}||\underline{Q}||M)$ instead of the $h = H(\underline{R}||M)$ originally suggested by Schnorr [11]. This protects against adversaries attacking multiple public keys simultaneously.

Compressed signatures. Schnorr [11] mentions the option of compressing signatures by hashing one of their two components: the hash size only needs to be $b/2$ bits, where b is the key length. Following this suggestion, our signatures are 384-bit values of the form $(h_{128}||s)$, where h_{128} means the lowest 128 bits of $h = H(\underline{R}||\underline{Q}||M)$, and s is a 256-bit scalar. The most obvious upside is that signatures are smaller, reducing communication overhead. Another big advantage is that we can exploit the half-size scalar to speed up signature verification. On the other hand, we lose the possibility of efficient batch verification.

Verification efficiency. The most costly operation in signature verification is the two-dimensional scalar multiplication $T = [s]P \oplus [h_{128}]Q$. In [8], the authors propose an algorithm relying on the differential addition chains presented in [15]. However, since we are using compressed signatures, we have a small scalar h_{128}. Unfortunately the two-dimensional algorithm in [8] cannot directly exploit this fact, therefore not obtaining much benefit from the compressed signature. On the other hand, we can simply compute $[s]P$ and $[h_{128}]Q$ separately using the fast scalar multiplication on the Kummer surface and finally add them together on the Jacobian. Here $[s]P$ is a 256-bit scalar multiplication, whereas $[h_{128}]Q$ is only a 128-bit scalar multiplication. Not only do we need fewer cycles compared to the two-dimensional routine, but we also reduce code size by reusing the one-dimensional scalar multiplication routine.

The scheme. We now define our signature scheme, taking the above into account.

Key generation (keygen). Let d be a 256-bit secret key, and P the public generator. Compute $(d'||d'') \leftarrow H(d)$ (with d' and d'' both 256 bits), then $Q \leftarrow [16d']P$. The public key is Q.

Signing (sign). Let M be a message, d a 256-bit secret key, P the public generator, and Q a compressed public key. Compute $(d'||d'') \leftarrow H(d)$ (with d' and d'' both 256 bits), then $r \leftarrow H(d''||M)$, then $R \leftarrow [r]P$, then $h \leftarrow H(\underline{R}||\underline{Q}||M)$, and finally $s \leftarrow (r - 16h_{128}d') \bmod N$. The signature is $(h_{128}||s)$.

Verification (verify). Let M be a message with a signature $(h_{128}\|s)$ corresponding to a public key Q, and let P be the public generator. Compute $T \leftarrow [s]P \oplus [h_{128}]Q$, then $g \leftarrow H(\underline{T}\|\underline{Q}\|M)$. The signature is correct if $g_{128} = h_{128}$, and incorrect otherwise.

Remark 1. We note that there may be faster algorithms to compute the "one-and-a-half-dimensional" scalar multiplication in verify, especially since we do not have to worry about being constant-time. One option might be to adapt Montgomery's PRAC [16, Sect. 3.3.1] to make use of the half-size scalar. But while this may lead to a speed-up, it would also cause an increase in code size compared to simply re-using the one-dimensional scalar multiplication. We have chosen not to pursue this line, preferring the solid benefits of reduced code size instead.

2.2 Diffie-Hellman Key Exchange

For key exchange it is not necessary to have a group structure; it is enough to have a pseudo-multiplication. We can therefore carry out our the key exchange directly on the Kummer surface $\mathcal{K}_\mathcal{C} = \mathcal{J}_\mathcal{C}/\langle\pm\rangle$, gaining efficiency by not projecting from and recovering to the Jacobian $\mathcal{J}_\mathcal{C}$. If Q is a point on $\mathcal{J}_\mathcal{C}$, then its image in $\mathcal{K}_\mathcal{C}$ is $\pm Q$. The common representation for points in $\mathcal{K}_\mathcal{C}(\mathbb{F}_q)$ is a 512-bit 4-tuple of field elements. For input points (i.e. the generator or public keys), we prefer the 384-bit "wrapped" representation (see Sect. 3.5). This not only reduces key size, but it also allows a speed-up in the core xDBLADD subroutine. The wrapped representation of a point $\pm Q$ on $\mathcal{K}_\mathcal{C}$ is denoted by $\underline{\pm Q}$.

Key exchange (dh_exchange). Let d be a 256-bit secret key, and $\underline{\pm P}$ the public generator (respectively public key). Compute $\underline{\pm Q} \leftarrow \underline{\pm[d]P}$. The generated public key (respectively shared secret) is $\underline{\pm Q}$.

Remark 2. While it might be possible to reduce the key size even further to 256 bits, we would then have to pay the cost of compressing and decompressing, and also wrapping for xDBLADD (see the discussion in [8, App. A]). We therefore choose to keep the 384-bit representation, which is consistent with [3].

3 Building Blocks: Algorithms and Their Implementation

We begin by presenting the finite field $\mathbb{F}_{2^{127}-1}$ in Sect. 3.1. We then define the curve $\mathcal{C}$ in Sect. 3.2, before giving basic methods for the elements of $\mathcal{J}_\mathcal{C}$ in Sect. 3.3. We then present the fast Kummer $\mathcal{K}_\mathcal{C}$ and its differential addition operations in Sect. 3.4.

3.1 The Field $\mathbb{F}_q$

We work over the prime finite field $\mathbb{F}_q$, where q is the Mersenne prime

$$q := 2^{127} - 1.$$

We let $\mathbf{M}$, $\mathbf{S}$, $\mathbf{a}$, $\mathbf{s}$, $\mathbf{neg}$, and $\mathbf{I}$ denote the costs of multiplication, squaring, addition, subtraction, negation, and inversion in $\mathbb{F}_q$. Later, we will define a special operation for multiplying by small constants: its cost is denoted by $\mathbf{m_c}$.

For complete field arithmetic we implement modular reduction, addition, subtraction, multiplication, and inversion. We comment on some important aspects here, giving cycle counts in Table 2.

We can represent elements of $\mathbb{F}_q$ as 127-bit values; but since the ATmega and Cortex M0 work with 8- and 32-bit words, respectively, the obvious choice is to represent field elements with 128 bits. That is, an element $g \in \mathbb{F}_q$ is represented as $g = \sum_{i=0}^{15} g_i 2^{8i}$ on the AVR ATmega platform and as $g = \sum_{i=0}^{3} g_i' 2^{32i}$ on the Cortex M0, where $g_i \in \{0, \ldots, 2^8 - 1\}$, $g_i' \in \{0, \ldots, 2^{32} - 1\}$.

Working with the prime field $\mathbb{F}_q$, we need integer reduction modulo q; this is implemented as `bigint_red`. Reduction is very efficient because $2^{128} \equiv 2 \bmod q$, which enables us to reduce using only shifts and integer additions. Given this reduction, we implement addition and subtraction operations for $\mathbb{F}_q$ (as `gfe_add` and `gfe_sub`, respectively) in the obvious way.

The most costly operations in $\mathbb{F}_q$ are multiplication (`gfe_mul`) and squaring (`gfe_sqr`), which are implemented as 128×128-bit integer operations (`bigint_mul` and `bigint_sqr`) followed by a call to `bigint_red`. Since we are working on the same platforms as [7] in which both of these operations are already highly optimized, we took the necessary code from those implementations:

- On the AVR ATmega: The authors of [17] implement a 3-level Karatsuba multiplication of two 256-bit integers, representing elements f of $\mathbb{F}_{2^{255}-19}$ as $f = \sum_{i=0}^{31} f_i 2^{8i}$ with $f_i \in \{0, \ldots, 2^8 - 1\}$. Since the first level of Karatsuba relies on a 128×128-bit integer multiplication routine named `MUL128`, we simply lift this function out to form a 2-level 128×128-bit Karatsuba multiplication. Similarly, their 256×256-bit squaring relies on a 128×128-bit routine `SQR128`, which we can (almost) directly use. Since the 256×256-bit squaring is 2-level Karatsuba, the 128×128-bit squaring is 1-level Karatsuba.
- On the ARM Cortex M0: The authors of [7] use optimized Karatsuba multiplication and squaring. Their assembly code does not use subroutines, but fully inlines 128×128-bit multiplication and squaring. The 256×256-bit multiplication and squaring are both 3-level Karatsuba implementations. Hence, using these, we end up with 2-level 128×128-bit Karatsuba multiplication and squaring.

The function `gfe_invert` computes inversions in $\mathbb{F}_q$ as exponentiations, using the fact that $g^{-1} = g^{q-2}$ for all g in $\mathbb{F}_q^{\times}$. To do this efficiently we use an addition chain for $q - 2$, doing the exponentiation in $10\mathbf{M} + 126\mathbf{S}$.

Finally, to speed up our Jacobian point decompression algorithms, we define a function `gfe_powminhalf` which computes $g \mapsto g^{-1/2}$ for g in $\mathbb{F}_q$ (up to a choice of sign). To do this, we note that $g^{-1/2} = \pm g^{-(q+1)/4} = \pm g^{(3q-5)/4}$ in $\mathbb{F}_q$; this exponentiation can be done with an addition chain of length 136, using $11\mathbf{M} + 125\mathbf{S}$. We can then define a function `gfe_sqrtinv`, which given (x, y) and a bit b, computes $(\sqrt{x}, 1/y)$ as $(\pm xyz, xyz^2)$ where $z = $ `gfe_powminhalf`(xy^2), choosing the sign so that the square root has least significant bit b. Including the `gfe_powminhalf` call, this costs $15\mathbf{M} + 126\mathbf{S} + 1\mathbf{neg}$.

Table 2. Cycle counts for our field implementation (including function-call overhead).

	AVR ATmega	ARM Cortex M0	Symbolic cost
bigint_mul	1 654	410	
bigint_sqr	1 171	260	
bigint_red	438	71	
gfe_mul	1 952	502	$\mathbf{M}$
gfe_sqr	1 469	353	$\mathbf{S}$
gfe_mulconst	569	83	$\mathbf{m_c}$
gfe_add	400	62	$\mathbf{a}$
gfe_sub	401	66	$\mathbf{s}$
gfe_invert	169 881	46 091	$\mathbf{I}$
gfe_powminhalf	169 881	46 294	$11\mathbf{M} + 125\mathbf{S}$
gfe_sqrtinv	178 041	48 593	$15\mathbf{M} + 126\mathbf{S} + 1\mathbf{neg}$

3.2 The Curve $\mathcal{C}$ and Its Theta Constants

We define the curve $\mathcal{C}$ "backwards", starting from its (squared) theta constants

$$a := -11, \quad b := 22, \quad c := 19, \quad \text{and} \quad d := 3 \quad \text{in } \mathbb{F}_q.$$

From these, we define the dual theta constants

$$A := a + b + c + d = 33, \qquad B := a + b - c - d = -11,$$
$$C := a - b + c - d = -17, \qquad D := a - b - c + d = -49.$$

Observe that projectively,

$$(1/a : 1/b : 1/c : 1/d) = (114 : -57 : -66 : -418),$$
$$(1/A : 1/B : 1/C : 1/D) = (-833 : 2499 : 1617 : 561).$$

Crucially, all of these constants can be represented using just 16 bits each. Since Kummer arithmetic involves many multiplications by these constants, we implement a separate 16×128-bit multiplication function `gfe_mulconst`. For the AVR ATmega, we store the constants in two 8-bit registers. For the Cortex M0, the values fit into a halfword; this works well with the 16×16-bit multiplication. Multiplication by any of these 16-bit constants costs $\mathbf{m_c}$.

Continuing, we define $e/f := (1 + \alpha)/(1 - \alpha)$, where $\alpha^2 = CD/AB$ (we take the square root with least significant bit 0), and thus

$$\lambda := ac/bd = \texttt{0x15555555555555555555555555555552},$$
$$\mu := ce/df = \texttt{0x73E334FBB315130E05A505C31919A746},$$
$$\nu := ae/bf = \texttt{0x552AB1B63BF799716B5806482D2D21F3}.$$

These are the *Rosenhain invariants* of the curve $\mathcal{C}$, found by Gaudry and Schost [18], which we are (finally!) ready to define as

$$\mathcal{C} : Y^2 = f_{\mathcal{C}}(X) := X(X-1)(X-\lambda)(X-\mu)(X-\nu).$$

The curve constants are the coefficients of $f_{\mathcal{C}}(X) = \sum_{i=0}^{5} f_i X^i$: so $f_0 = 0$, $f_5 = 1$,

$f_1 = $ 0x1EDD6EE48E0C2F16F537CD791E4A8D6E, $f_2 = $ 0x73E799E36D9FCC210C9CD1B164C39A35,

$f_3 = $ 0x4B9E333F48B6069CC47DC236188DF6E8, $f_4 = $ 0x219CC3F8BB9DFE2B39AD9E9F6463E172.

We store the squared theta constants $(a : b : c : d)$, along with $(1/a : 1/b : 1/c : 1/d)$, and $(1/A : 1/B : 1/C : 1/D)$; the Rosenhain invariants λ, μ, and ν, together with $\lambda\mu$ and $\lambda\nu$; and the curve constants f_1, f_2, f_3, and f_4, for use in our Kummer and Jacobian arithmetic functions. Obviously, none of the Rosenhain or curve constants are small; multiplying by these costs a full **M**.

3.3   Elements of $\mathcal{J}_{\mathcal{C}}$, compressed and decompressed

Our algorithms use the usual Mumford representation for elements of $\mathcal{J}_{\mathcal{C}}(\mathbb{F}_q)$: they correspond to pairs $\langle u(X), v(X) \rangle$, where u and v are polynomials over $\mathbb{F}_q$ with u monic, $\deg v < \deg u \le 2$, and $v(X)^2 \equiv f_{\mathcal{C}}(X) \pmod{u(X)}$. We compute the group operation $\oplus$ in $\mathcal{J}_{\mathcal{C}}(\mathbb{F}_q)$ using a function ADD, which implements the algorithm found in [19] (after a change of coordinates to meet their Assumption 1)[1] at a cost of $28\mathbf{M} + 2\mathbf{S} + 11\mathbf{a} + 24\mathbf{s} + 1\mathbf{I}$.

For transmission, we compress the 508-bit Mumford representation to a 256-bit form. Our functions compress (Algorithm 1) and decompress (Algorithm 2) implement Stahlke's compression technique (see [20] and [8, Appendix A] for details).

Algorithm 1. compress: compresses points on $\mathcal{J}_{\mathcal{C}}$ to 256-bit strings. Symbolic cost: $3\mathbf{M} + 1\mathbf{S} + 2\mathbf{a} + 2\mathbf{s}$. ATmega: $8\,016$ cycles. Cortex M0: $2\,186$ cycles.

Input: $\langle X^2 + u_1 X + u_0, v_1 X + v_0 \rangle = P \in \mathcal{J}_{\mathcal{C}}$.
Output: A string $b_0 \cdots b_{255}$ of 256 bits.
1 $w \leftarrow 4((u_1 \cdot v_0 - u_0 \cdot v_1) \cdot v_1 - v_0^2)$;   // $3\mathbf{M} + 1\mathbf{S} + 2\mathbf{a} + 2\mathbf{s}$
2 $b_0 \leftarrow$ LeastSignificantBit(v_1) ;
3 $b_{128} \leftarrow$ LeastSignificantBit(w) ;
4 **return** $b_0 \| u_0 \| b_{128} \| u_1$

3.4   The Kummer Surface $\mathcal{K}_{\mathcal{C}}$

The Kummer surface of $\mathcal{C}$ is the quotient $\mathcal{K}_{\mathcal{C}} := \mathcal{J}_{\mathcal{C}}/\langle\pm 1\rangle$; points on $\mathcal{K}_{\mathcal{C}}$ correspond to points on $\mathcal{J}_{\mathcal{C}}$ taken up to sign. If P is a point in $\mathcal{J}_{\mathcal{C}}$, then we write

$$(x_P : y_P : z_P : t_P) = \pm P$$

---

[1] We only call ADD once in our algorithms, so for lack of space we omit its description.

Algorithm 2. `decompress`: decompresses 256-bit string to a point on $\mathcal{J}_C$.
Symbolic cost: $46\mathbf{M} + 255\mathbf{S} + 17\mathbf{a} + 12\mathbf{s} + 6\mathbf{neg}$. ATmega: $386\,524$ cycles
Cortex M0: $106\,013$ cycles

Input: A string $b_0 \cdots b_{255}$ of 256 bits.
Output: $\langle X^2 + u_1 X + u_0, v_1 X + v_0 \rangle = P \in \mathcal{J}_C$.

1 $U_1 = b_{129} \cdots b_{256}$ as an element of $\mathbb{F}_q$
2 $U_0 = b_1 \cdots b_{127}$ as an element of $\mathbb{F}_q$
3 $T_1 \leftarrow U_1^2$ // 1S
4 $T_2 \leftarrow U_0 - T_1$ // 1s
5 $T_3 \leftarrow U_0 + T_2$ // 1a
6 $T_4 \leftarrow U_0 \cdot (T_3 \cdot f_4 + (U_1 \cdot f_3 - 2f_2))$ // 3M + 1a + 2s
7 $T_3 \leftarrow -T_3$ // 1neg
8 $T_1 \leftarrow T_3 - U_0$ // 1s
9 $T_4 \leftarrow 2(T_4 + (T_1 \cdot U_0 + f_1) \cdot U_1)$ // 2M + 3a
10 $T_1 \leftarrow 2(T_1 - U_0))$ // 1a + 1s
11 $T_5 \leftarrow ((U_0 - (f_3 + U_1 \cdot (U_1 - f_4))) \cdot U_0 + f_1)^2$ // 2M + 1S + 2a + 2s
12 $T_5 \leftarrow T_4^2 - 2T_5 \cdot T_1$ // 1M + 1S + 1a + 1s
13 $(T_6, T_5) \leftarrow \texttt{gfe\_sqrtinv}(T_5, T_1, b_1)$ // 19M + 127S + 2neg
14 $T_4 \leftarrow (T_5 - T_4) \cdot T_6$ // 1M + 1s
15 $T_5 \leftarrow -f_4 \cdot T_2 - ((T_3 - f_3) \cdot U_1) + f_2 + T_4$ // 2M + 2s + 2a + 1neg
16 $T_6 = \texttt{gfe\_powminhalf}(4T_6)$ // $= 1/(2v_1)$. 11M + 125S + 2a
17 $V_1 \leftarrow 2T_5 \cdot T_6$ // 1M + 1a
18 **if** $b_0 \neq \texttt{LeastSignificantBit}(V_1)$ **then** $(V_1, T_6) \leftarrow (-V_1, -T_6)$ // 2neg
19 $T_5 \leftarrow (U_1 \cdot f_4 + (T_2 - f_3)) \cdot U_0$ // 2M + 1a + 1s
20 $V_0 \leftarrow (U_1 \cdot T_4 + T_5 + f_1) \cdot T_6$ // 2M + 2a
21 **return** $\langle X^2 + U_1 X + U_0, V_1 X + V_0 \rangle$

for its image in $\mathcal{K}_C$. To avoid subscript explosion, we make the following convention: when points P and Q on $\mathcal{J}_C$ are clear from the context, we write

$$(x_\oplus : y_\oplus : z_\oplus : t_\oplus) = \pm(P \oplus Q) \quad \text{and} \quad (x_\ominus : y_\ominus : z_\ominus : t_\ominus) = \pm(P \ominus Q).$$

The Kummer surface of this C has a "fast" model in $\mathbb{P}^3$ defined by

$$\mathcal{K}_C : E \cdot xyzt = \left(\begin{array}{c} (x^2 + y^2 + z^2 + t^2) \\ -F \cdot (xt + yz) - G \cdot (xz + yt) - H \cdot (xy + zt) \end{array} \right)^2$$

where

$$F = \frac{a^2 - b^2 - c^2 + d^2}{ad - bc}, \quad G = \frac{a^2 - b^2 + c^2 - d^2}{ac - bd}, \quad H = \frac{a^2 + b^2 - c^2 - d^2}{ab - cd},$$

and $E = 4abcd\,(ABCD/((ad - bc)(ac - bd)(ab - cd)))^2$ (see eg. [21**?**,22]). The identity point $\langle 1, 0 \rangle$ of $\mathcal{J}_C$ maps to

$$\pm 0_{\mathcal{J}_C} = (a : b : c : d).$$

Algorithm 3 (`Project`) maps general points from $\mathcal{J}_{\mathcal{C}}(\mathbb{F}_q)$ into $\mathcal{K}_{\mathcal{C}}$. The "special" case where u is linear is treated in [8, Sect. 7.2]; this is not implemented, since `Project` only operates on public generators and keys, none of which are special.

Algorithm 3. Project: $\mathcal{J}_{\mathcal{C}} \to \mathcal{K}_{\mathcal{C}}$. Symbolic cost: $8\mathbf{M} + 1\mathbf{S} + 4\mathbf{m_c} + 7\mathbf{a}$ $+ 4\mathbf{s}$. ATmega: 20 205 cycles. Cortex M0: 5 667 cycles.

Input: $\langle X^2 + u_1 X + u_0, v_1 X + v_0 \rangle = P \in \mathcal{J}_{\mathcal{C}}$.
Output: $(x_P : y_P : z_P : t_P) = \pm P \in \mathcal{K}_{\mathcal{C}}$.

1 $(\mathsf{T}_1, \mathsf{T}_2, \mathsf{T}_3, \mathsf{T}_4) \leftarrow (\mu - u_0, \lambda\nu - u_0, \nu - u_0, \lambda\mu - u_0)$ // 4s
2 $\mathsf{T}_5 \leftarrow \lambda + u_1$ // 1a
3 $\mathsf{T}_7 \leftarrow u_0 \cdot ((\mathsf{T}_5 + \mu) \cdot \mathsf{T}_3)$ // 2M + 1a
4 $\mathsf{T}_5 \leftarrow u_0 \cdot ((\mathsf{T}_5 + \nu) \cdot \mathsf{T}_1)$ // 2M + 1a
5 $(\mathsf{T}_6, \mathsf{T}_8) \leftarrow (u_0 \cdot ((\mu + u_1) \cdot \mathsf{T}_2 + \mathsf{T}_2), u_0 \cdot ((\nu + u_1) \cdot \mathsf{T}_4 + \mathsf{T}_4))$ // 4M + 4a
6 $\mathsf{T}_1 \leftarrow v_0^2$ // 1S
7 $(\mathsf{T}_5, \mathsf{T}_6, \mathsf{T}_7, \mathsf{T}_8) \leftarrow (\mathsf{T}_5 - \mathsf{T}_1, \mathsf{T}_6 - \mathsf{T}_1, \mathsf{T}_7 - \mathsf{T}_1, \mathsf{T}_8 - \mathsf{T}_1)$ // 4s
8 **return** $(a \cdot \mathsf{T}_5 : b \cdot \mathsf{T}_6 : c \cdot \mathsf{T}_7 : d \cdot \mathsf{T}_8)$ // 4m_c

---

3.5 Pseudo-addition on $\mathcal{K}_{\mathcal{C}}$

While the points of $\mathcal{K}_{\mathcal{C}}$ do not form a group, we have a pseudo-addition operation (differential addition), which computes $\pm(P \oplus Q)$ from $\pm P$, $\pm Q$, and $\pm(P \ominus Q)$. The function `xADD` (Algorithm 4) implements the standard differential addition. The special case where $P = Q$ yields a pseudo-doubling operation.

To simplify the presentation of our algorithms, we define three operations on points in $\mathbb{P}^3$. First, $\mathcal{M} : \mathbb{P}^3 \times \mathbb{P}^3 \to \mathbb{P}^3$ multiplies corresponding coordinates:

$$\mathcal{M} : ((x_1 : y_1 : z_1 : t_1), (x_2 : y_2 : z_2 : t_2)) \longmapsto (x_1 x_2 : y_1 y_2 : z_1 z_2 : t_1 t_2).$$

The special case $(x_1 : y_1 : z_1 : t_1) = (x_2 : y_2 : z_2 : t_2)$ is denoted by

$$\mathcal{S} : (x : y : z : t) \longmapsto (x^2 : y^2 : z^2 : t^2).$$

Finally, the Hadamard transform[2] is defined by

$$\mathcal{H} : (x : y : z : t) \longmapsto (x' : y' : z' : t') \quad \text{where} \quad \begin{cases} x' = x + y + z + t, \\ y' = x + y - z - t, \\ z' = x - y + z - t, \\ t' = x - y - z + t. \end{cases}$$

Clearly $\mathcal{M}$ and $\mathcal{S}$ cost $4\mathbf{M}$ and $4\mathbf{S}$, respectively. The Hadamard transform can easily be implemented with $4\mathbf{a} + 4\mathbf{s}$. However, the additions and subtractions are relatively cheap, making function call overhead a large factor. To minimize this we inline the Hadamard transform, trading a bit of code size for efficiency.

---

[2] Note that $(A : B : C : D) = \mathcal{H}((a : b : c : d))$ and $(a : b : c : d) = \mathcal{H}((A : B : C : D))$.

Algorithm 4. xADD: Differential addition on $\mathcal{K}_{\mathcal{C}}$. Symbolic cost: $14\mathbf{M} + 4\mathbf{S} + 4\mathbf{m_c} + 12\mathbf{a} + 12\mathbf{s}$. ATmega: $34\,774$ cycles. Cortex M0: $9\,598$ cycles.

Input: $(\pm P, \pm Q, \pm(P \ominus Q)) \in \mathcal{K}_{\mathcal{C}}^3$ for some P and Q on $\mathcal{J}_{\mathcal{C}}$.
Output: $\pm(P \oplus Q) \in \mathcal{K}_{\mathcal{C}}$.

1 $(V_1, V_2) \leftarrow (\mathcal{H}(\pm P), \mathcal{H}(\pm Q))$	// 8a + 8s
2 $V_1 \leftarrow \mathcal{M}(V_1, V_2)$	// 4M
3 $V_1 \leftarrow \mathcal{M}(V_1, (1/A : 1/B : 1/C : 1/D))$	// 4m_c
4 $V_1 \leftarrow \mathcal{H}(V_1)$	// 4a + 4s
5 $V_1 \leftarrow \mathcal{S}(V_1)$	// 4S
6 $(C_1, C_2) \leftarrow (z_\ominus \cdot t_\ominus, x_\ominus \cdot y_\ominus)$	// 2M
7 $V_2 \leftarrow \mathcal{M}((C_1 : C_1 : C_2 : C_2), (y_\ominus : x_\ominus : t_\ominus : z_\ominus))$	// 4M
8 **return** $\mathcal{M}(V_1, V_2)$	// 4M

Lines 5 and 6 of Algorithm 4 only involve the third argument, $\pm(P \ominus Q)$; essentially, they compute the point $(y_\ominus z_\ominus t_\ominus : x_\ominus z_\ominus t_\ominus : x_\ominus y_\ominus t_\ominus : x_\ominus y_\ominus z_\ominus)$ (which is projectively equivalent to $(1/x_\ominus : 1/y_\ominus : 1/z_\ominus : 1/t_\ominus)$, but requires no inversions; note that this is generally *not* a point on $\mathcal{K}_{\mathcal{C}}$). In practice, the pseudoadditions used in our scalar multiplication all use a fixed third argument, so it makes sense to precompute this "inverted" point and to scale it by $x_\ominus$ so that the first coordinate is 1, thus saving $7\mathbf{M}$ in each subsequent differential addition for a one-off cost of $1\mathbf{I}$. The resulting data can be stored as the 3-tuple $(x_\ominus/y_\ominus, x_\ominus/z_\ominus, x_\ominus/t_\ominus)$, ignoring the trivial first coordinate: this is the *wrapped* form of $\pm(P \ominus Q)$. The function xWRAP (Algorithm 5) applies this transformation.

Algorithm 5. xWRAP: $(x : y : z : t) \mapsto (x/y, x/z, x/t)$. Symbolic cost: $7\mathbf{M} + 1\mathbf{I}$ ATmega: $182\,251$ cycles. Cortex M0: $49\,609$ cycles.

Input: $(x : y : z : t) \in \mathbb{P}^3$
Output: $(x/y, x/z, x/t) \in \mathbb{F}_q^3$.

1 $V_1 \leftarrow y \cdot z$	// 1M
2 $V_2 \leftarrow x/(V_1 \cdot t)$	// 2M + 1I
3 $V_3 \leftarrow V_2 \cdot t$	// 1M
4 **return** $(V_3 \cdot z, V_3 \cdot y, V_1 \cdot V_2)$	// 3M

Algorithm 6 combines the pseudo-doubling with the differential addition, sharing intermediate operands, to define a differential double-and-add xDBLADD. This is the fundamental building block of the Montgomery ladder.

4 Scalar Multiplication

All of our cryptographic routines are built around scalar multiplication in $\mathcal{J}_{\mathcal{C}}$ and pseudo-scalar multiplication in $\mathcal{K}_{\mathcal{C}}$. We implement pseudo-scalar multiplication using the classic Montgomery ladder in Sect. 4.1. In Sect. 4.2, we extend this to full scalar multiplication on $\mathcal{J}_{\mathcal{C}}$ using the point recovery technique proposed in [8].

Algorithm 6. xDBLADD: Combined differential double-and-add. The difference point is wrapped. Symbolic cost: $7M + 12S + 12m_c + 16a + 16s$. ATmega: 36 706 cycles. Cortex M0: 9 861 cycles.

Input: $(\pm P, \pm Q, (x_\ominus/y_\ominus, x_\ominus/z_\ominus, x_\ominus/t_\ominus)) \in \mathcal{K}_\mathcal{C}^2 \times \mathbb{F}_q$.
Output: $(\pm[2]P, \pm(P \oplus Q)) \in \mathcal{K}_\mathcal{C}^2$.

1 $(V_1, V_2) \leftarrow (\mathcal{S}(\pm P), \mathcal{S}(\pm Q))$ // 8S
2 $(V_1, V_2) \leftarrow (\mathcal{H}(V_1), \mathcal{H}(V_2))$ // 8a + 8s
3 $(V_1, V_2) \leftarrow (\mathcal{S}(V_1), \mathcal{M}(V_1, V_2))$ // 4M+4S
4 $(V_1, V_2) \leftarrow (\mathcal{M}(V_1, (\frac{1}{A} : \frac{1}{B} : \frac{1}{C} : \frac{1}{D})), \mathcal{M}(V_2, (\frac{1}{A} : \frac{1}{B} : \frac{1}{C} : \frac{1}{D})))$ // 8m$_c$
5 $(V_1, V_2) \leftarrow (\mathcal{H}(V_1), \mathcal{H}(V_2))$ // 8a + 8s
6 **return** $(\mathcal{M}(V_1, (\frac{1}{a} : \frac{1}{b} : \frac{1}{c} : \frac{1}{d})), \mathcal{M}(V_2, (1 : \frac{x_\ominus}{y_\ominus} : \frac{x_\ominus}{y_\ominus} : \frac{x_\ominus}{t_\ominus})))$ // 3M + 4m$_c$

Table 3. Operation and cycle counts of basic functions on the Kummer and Jacobian.

	M	S	m$_c$	a	s	neg	I	ATmega	Cortex M0
ADD	28	2	0	11	24	0	1	228 552	62 886
Project	8	1	4	7	8	0	0	20 205	5 667
xWRAP	7	0	0	0	0	0	1	182 251	49 609
xUNWRAP	4	0	0	0	0	0	0	7 297	2 027
xADD	14	4	4	12	12	0	0	34 774	9 598
xDBLADD	7	12	12	16	16	0	0	36 706	9 861
recoverGeneral	77	8	0	19	10	3	1	318 910	88 414
fast2genPartial	11	0	0	9	0	0	0	21 339	6 110
fast2genFull	15	0	0	12	0	0	0	29 011	8 333
recoverFast	139	12	4	70	22	5	1	447 176	124 936
compress	3	1	0	2	2	0	0	8 016	2 186
decompress	46	255	0	17	12	6	0	386 524	106 013

4.1 Pseudomultiplication on $\mathcal{K}_\mathcal{C}$

Since $[m](\ominus P) = \ominus[m]P$ for all m and P, we have a pseudo-scalar multiplication operation $(m, \pm P) \longmapsto \pm[m]P$ on $\mathcal{K}_\mathcal{C}$, which we compute using Algorithm 7 (the Montgomery ladder), implemented as crypto_scalarmult. The loop of Algorithm 7 maintains the following invariant: at the end of iteration i we have

$$(V_1, V_2) = (\pm[k]P, \pm[k+1]P) \quad \text{where} \quad k = \sum_{j=i}^{\beta-1} m_j 2^{\beta-1-i}.$$

Hence, at the end we return $\pm[m]P$, and also $\pm[m+1]P$ as a (free) byproduct. We suppose we have a constant-time conditional swap routine CSWAP$(b, (V_1, V_2))$, which returns (V_1, V_2) if $b = 0$ and (V_2, V_1) if $b = 1$. This makes the execution of Algorithm 7 uniform and constant-time, and thus suitable for use with secret m.

Our implementation of crypto_scalarmult assumes that its input Kummer point $\pm P$ is wrapped. This follows the approach of [3]. Indeed, many calls

---

Algorithm 7. crypto_scalarmult: Montgomery ladder on $\mathcal{K}_\mathcal{C}$. Uniform and constant-time: may be used for secret scalars. The point is wrapped. Symbolic cost: $(4+7\beta)\mathbf{M}+12\beta\mathbf{S}+12\beta\mathbf{m_c}+16\beta\mathbf{a}+16\beta\mathbf{s}$, where β = scalar bitlength. ATmega: 9 513 536 cycles. Cortex: 2 633 662 cycles.

Input: $(m = \sum_{i=0}^{\beta-1} m_i 2^i, (x_P/y_P, x_P/z_P, x_P/t_P)) \in [0, 2^\beta) \times \mathbb{F}_q^3$ for $\pm P$ in $\mathcal{K}_\mathcal{C}$.
Output: $(\pm[m]P, \pm[m+1]P) \in \mathcal{K}_\mathcal{C}^2$.
1 $V_1 \leftarrow (a : b : c : d)$
2 $V_2 \leftarrow \text{xUNWRAP}(x_P/y_P, x_P/z_P, x_P/t_P)$ $// = \pm P$. 4M
3 **for** $i = 250$ *down to* 0 **do** $// 7\beta\text{M} + 12\beta\text{S} + 12\beta m_c + 16\beta\text{a} + 16\beta\text{s}$
4      $(V_1, V_2) \leftarrow \text{CSWAP}(m_i, (V_1, V_2))$
5      $(V_1, V_2) \leftarrow \text{xDBLADD}(V_1, V_2, (x_P/y_P, x_P/z_P, x_P/t_P))$
6      $(V_1, V_2) \leftarrow \text{CSWAP}(m_i, (V_1, V_2))$
7 **return** (V_1, V_2)

---

to crypto_scalarmult involve Kummer points that are stored or transmitted in wrapped form. However, crypto_scalarmult does require the unwrapped point internally—if only to initialize one variable. We therefore define a function xUNWRAP (Algorithm 8) to invert the xWRAP transformation at a cost of only 4M.

Algorithm 8. xUNWRAP: $(x/y, x/z, x/t) \mapsto (x : y : z : t)$. Symbolic cost: 4M. ATmega: 7 297 cycles. Cortex: 2 027 cycles.

Input: $(u, v, w) \in \mathbb{F}_q^3$ s.t. $u = x_P/y_P, v = x_P/z_P, w = x_P/t_P$ for $\pm P \in \mathcal{K}_\mathcal{C}$
Output: $(x_P : y_P : z_P : t_P) \in \mathbb{P}^3$
1 $(T_1, T_2, T_3) \leftarrow (v \cdot w, u \cdot w, u \cdot v)$ $// 3M$
2 **return** $(T_3 \cdot w : T_1 : T_2 : T_3)$ $// 1M$

4.2 Point Recovery from $\mathcal{K}_\mathcal{C}$ to $\mathcal{J}_\mathcal{C}$

Point recovery means efficiently computing $[m]P$ on $\mathcal{J}_\mathcal{C}$ given $\pm[m]P$ on $\mathcal{K}_\mathcal{C}$ and some additional information. In our case, the additional information is the base point P and the second output of the Montgomery ladder, $\pm[m+1]P$. Algorithm 9 (Recover) implements the point recovery described in [8]. This is the genus-2 analogue of the elliptic-curve methods in [24–26].

We refer the reader to [8] for technical details on this method, but there is one important mathematical detail that we should mention (since it is reflected in the structure of our code): point recovery is more natural starting from the general Flynn model $\widetilde{\mathcal{K}}_\mathcal{C}$ of the Kummer, because it is more closely related to the Mumford model for $\mathcal{J}_\mathcal{C}$. Algorithm 9 therefore proceeds in two steps: first Algorithms 10 (fast2genFull) and 11 (fast2genPartial) map the problem into $\widetilde{\mathcal{K}}_\mathcal{C}$, and then we recover from $\widetilde{\mathcal{K}}_\mathcal{C}$ to $\mathcal{J}_\mathcal{C}$ using Algorithm 12 (recoverGeneral).

Algorithm 9. Recover: From $\mathcal{K}_{\mathcal{C}}$ to $\mathcal{J}_{\mathcal{C}}$. Symbolic cost: $139M + 12S + 4m_c + 70a + 22s + 3neg + 1I$. ATmega: $447\,176$ cycles. Cortex: $124\,936$ cycles.

Input: $(P, \pm P, \pm Q, \pm(P \oplus Q)) \in \mathcal{J}_{\mathcal{C}} \times \mathcal{K}_{\mathcal{C}}^3$ for some P, Q in $\mathcal{J}_{\mathcal{C}}$.
Output: $Q \in \mathcal{J}_{\mathcal{C}}$.

1	gP ← fast2genPartial($\pm P$)	// 11M + 9a
2	gQ ← fast2genFull($\pm Q$)	// 15M + 12a
3	gS ← fast2genPartial($\pm(P \oplus Q)$)	// 11M + 9a
4	xD ← xADD($\pm P, \pm Q, \pm(P \oplus Q)$)	// 14M + 4S + 4m_c + 12a + 12s
5	gD ← fast2genPartial(xD)	// 11M + 9a
6	**return** recoverGeneral(P, gP, gQ, gS, gD)	// 77M+8S+19a+10s+3neg+1I

Since the general Kummer $\widetilde{\mathcal{K}}_{\mathcal{C}}$ only appears briefly in our recovery procedure (we never use its relatively slow arithmetic operations), we will not investigate it in detail here—but the curious reader may refer to [27] for the general theory. For our purposes, it suffices to recall that $\widetilde{\mathcal{K}}_{\mathcal{C}}$ is, like $\mathcal{K}_{\mathcal{C}}$, embedded in $\mathbb{P}^3$; and the isomorphism $\mathcal{K}_{\mathcal{C}} \to \widetilde{\mathcal{K}}_{\mathcal{C}}$ is defined (in eg. [8, Sect. 7.4]) by the linear transformation

$$(x_P : y_P : z_P : t_P) \longmapsto (\tilde{x}_P : \tilde{y}_P : \tilde{z}_P : \tilde{t}_P) := (x_P : y_P : z_P : t_P)L,$$

where L is (any scalar multiple of) the matrix

$$\begin{pmatrix} a^{-1}(\nu - \lambda) & a^{-1}(\mu\nu - \lambda) & a^{-1}\lambda\nu(\mu - 1) & a^{-1}\lambda\nu(\mu\nu - \lambda) \\ b^{-1}(\mu - 1) & b^{-1}(\mu\nu - \lambda) & b^{-1}\mu(\nu - \lambda) & b^{-1}\mu(\mu\nu - \lambda) \\ c^{-1}(\lambda - \mu) & c^{-1}(\lambda - \mu\nu) & c^{-1}\lambda\mu(1 - \nu) & c^{-1}\lambda\mu(\lambda - \mu\nu) \\ d^{-1}(1 - \nu) & d^{-1}(\lambda - \mu\nu) & d^{-1}\nu(\lambda - \mu) & d^{-1}\nu(\lambda - \mu\nu) \end{pmatrix},$$

which we precompute and store. If $\pm P$ is a point on $\mathcal{K}_{\mathcal{C}}$, then $\widetilde{\pm P}$ denotes its image on $\widetilde{\mathcal{K}}_{\mathcal{C}}$; we compute $\widetilde{\pm P}$ using Algorithm 10 (fast2genFull).

Algorithm 10. fast2genFull: The map $\mathcal{K}_{\mathcal{C}} \to \widetilde{\mathcal{K}}_{\mathcal{C}}$. Symbolic cost: $15M + 12a$. ATmega: $29\,011$ cycles. Cortex: $8\,333$ cycles.

Input: $\pm P \in \mathcal{K}_{\mathcal{C}}$
Output: $\widetilde{\pm P} \in \widetilde{\mathcal{K}}_{\mathcal{C}}$.

1	$\tilde{x}_P \leftarrow x_P + (L_{12}/L_{11})y_P + (L_{13}/L_{11})z_P + (L_{14}/L_{11})t_P$	// 3M + 3a
2	$\tilde{y}_P \leftarrow (L_{21}/L_{11})x_P + (L_{22}/L_{11})y_P + (L_{23}/L_{11})z_P + (L_{24}/L_{11})t_P$	// 4M + 3a
3	$\tilde{z}_P \leftarrow (L_{31}/L_{11})x_P + (L_{32}/L_{11})y_P + (L_{33}/L_{11})z_P + (L_{34}/L_{11})t_P$	// 4M + 3a
4	$\tilde{t}_P \leftarrow (L_{41}/L_{11})x_P + (L_{42}/L_{11})y_P + (L_{43}/L_{11})z_P + (L_{44}/L_{11})t_P$	// 4M + 3a
5	**return** $(\tilde{x}_P : \tilde{y}_P : \tilde{z}_P : \tilde{t}_P)$	

Sometimes we only require the first three coordinates of $\widetilde{\pm P}$. Algorithm 11 (fast2genPartial) saves $4M + 3a$ per point by not computing $\tilde{t}_P$.

Algorithm 11. `fast2genPartial`: The map $\mathcal{K}_{\mathcal{C}} \to \mathbb{P}^2$. Symbolic cost: $11\mathrm{M} + 9\mathrm{a}$. ATmega: $21\,339$ cycles. Cortex: $8\,333$ cycles.

Input: $\pm P \in \mathcal{K}_{\mathcal{C}}$.
Output: $(\tilde{x}_P : \tilde{y}_P : \tilde{z}_P) \in \mathbb{P}^2$
1 $\tilde{x}_P \leftarrow x_P + (L_{12}/L_{11})y_P + (L_{13}/L_{11})z_P + (L_{14}/L_{11})t_P$ // $3\mathrm{M} + 3\mathrm{a}$
2 $\tilde{y}_P \leftarrow (L_{21}/L_{11})x_P + (L_{22}/L_{11})y_P + (L_{23}/L_{11})z_P + (L_{24}/L_{11})t_P$ // $4\mathrm{M} + 3\mathrm{a}$
3 $\tilde{z}_P \leftarrow (L_{31}/L_{11})x_P + (L_{32}/L_{11})y_P + (L_{33}/L_{11})z_P + (L_{34}/L_{11})t_P$ // $4\mathrm{M} + 3\mathrm{a}$
4 **return** $(\tilde{x}_P : \tilde{y}_P : \tilde{z}_P)$

Algorithm 12. `recoverGeneral`: From $\widetilde{\mathcal{K}}_C$ to $\mathcal{J}_C$. Symbolic cost: $77\mathrm{M} + 8\mathrm{S} + 19\mathrm{a} + 10\mathrm{s} + 3\mathrm{neg} + 1\mathrm{I}$. ATmega: $318\,910$ cycles. Cortex: $88\,414$ cycles.

Input: $(P, \widetilde{\pm P}, \widetilde{\pm Q}, \pm \widetilde{(P \oplus Q)}, \pm \widetilde{(P \ominus Q)})) \in \mathcal{J}_C \times \widetilde{\mathcal{K}}_C^4$ for some P and Q in $\mathcal{J}_C$. The values of $\tilde{t}_P$, $\tilde{t}_{\oplus}$, and $\tilde{t}_{\ominus}$ are not required.
Output: $Q \in \mathcal{J}_C$.
1 $(Z1, Z2) \leftarrow (\tilde{y}_P \cdot \tilde{x}_Q - \tilde{x}_Q \cdot \tilde{y}_P, \tilde{x}_P \cdot \tilde{z}_Q - \tilde{z}_P \cdot \tilde{x}_Q)$ // $4\mathrm{M}{+}2\mathrm{s}$
2 $T1 \leftarrow Z1 \cdot \tilde{z}_P$ // $1\mathrm{M}$
3 $mZ3 \leftarrow Z2 \cdot \tilde{y}_P + T1$ // $1\mathrm{M} + 1\mathrm{a}$
4 $D \leftarrow Z2^2 \cdot \tilde{x}_P + mZ3 \cdot Z1$ // $2\mathrm{M} + 1\mathrm{S} + 1\mathrm{a}$
5 $T2 \leftarrow Z1 \cdot Z2$ // $1\mathrm{M}$
6 $T3 \leftarrow \tilde{x}_P \cdot \tilde{x}_Q$ // $1\mathrm{M}$
7 $E \leftarrow T3 \cdot (T3 \cdot (f_2 \cdot Z2^2 - f_1 \cdot T2) + \tilde{t}_Q \cdot D)$ // $5\mathrm{M} + 1\mathrm{S} + 1\mathrm{a} + 1\mathrm{s}$
8 $E \leftarrow E + mZ3 \cdot \tilde{x}_Q^2 \cdot (f_3 \cdot Z2 \cdot \tilde{x}_P + f_4 \cdot mZ3)$ // $5\mathrm{M} + 1\mathrm{S} + 2\mathrm{a}$
9 $E \leftarrow E + mZ3 \cdot \tilde{x}_Q \cdot (mZ3 \cdot \tilde{y}_P - Z2 \cdot \tilde{x}_P \cdot \tilde{z}_Q)$ // $5\mathrm{M} + 1\mathrm{a} + 1\mathrm{s}$
10 $X1 \leftarrow \tilde{x}_P \cdot (Z2 \cdot v_1(P) - Z1 \cdot v_0(P))$ // $3\mathrm{M} + 1\mathrm{s}$
11 $T4 \leftarrow Z1 \cdot \tilde{y}_P + Z2 \cdot \tilde{x}_P$ // $2\mathrm{M} + 1\mathrm{a}$
12 $X2 \leftarrow T1 \cdot v_1(P) + T4 \cdot v_0(P)$ // $2\mathrm{M} + 1\mathrm{a}$
13 $C5 \leftarrow Z1^2 - T4 \cdot \tilde{x}_Q$ // $1\mathrm{M} + 1\mathrm{S} + 1\mathrm{s}$
14 $C6 \leftarrow T1 \cdot \tilde{x}_Q + T2$ // $1\mathrm{M} + 1\mathrm{a}$
15 $T5 \leftarrow \tilde{z}_{\oplus} \cdot \tilde{x}_{\ominus} - \tilde{x}_{\oplus} \cdot \tilde{z}_{\ominus}$ // $2\mathrm{M} + 1\mathrm{s}$
16 $X3 \leftarrow X1 \cdot T5 - X2 \cdot (\tilde{x}_{\oplus} \cdot \tilde{y}_{\ominus} - \tilde{y}_{\oplus} \cdot \tilde{x}_{\ominus})$ // $4\mathrm{M} + 2\mathrm{s}$
17 $(X5, X6) \leftarrow (X3 \cdot C5, X3 \cdot C6)$ // $2\mathrm{M}$
18 $X4 \leftarrow T3 \cdot (X1 \cdot (\tilde{z}_{\oplus} \cdot \tilde{y}_{\ominus} - \tilde{y}_{\oplus} \cdot \tilde{z}_{\ominus}) + T5 \cdot X2)$ // $5\mathrm{M} + 1\mathrm{a} + 1\mathrm{s}$
19 $(X7, X8) \leftarrow (X5 + Z1 \cdot X4, X6 + Z2 \cdot Z4)$ // $2\mathrm{M} + 2\mathrm{a}$
20 $T6 \leftarrow \tilde{x}_{\oplus} \cdot \tilde{x}_{\ominus}$ // $1\mathrm{M}$
21 $E \leftarrow -T6 \cdot T3 \cdot (E \cdot \tilde{x}_P^2 + (X1 \cdot T3)^2)$ // $5\mathrm{M} + 2\mathrm{S} + 1\mathrm{a} + 1\mathrm{neg}$
22 $(X9, X10) \leftarrow (E \cdot X7, E \cdot X8)$ // $2\mathrm{M}$
23 $F \leftarrow X2 \cdot (\tilde{x}_{\oplus} \cdot \tilde{y}_{\ominus} + \tilde{y}_{\oplus} \cdot \tilde{x}_{\ominus}) + X1 \cdot (\tilde{z}_{\oplus} \cdot \tilde{x}_{\ominus} + \tilde{x}_{\oplus} \cdot \tilde{z}_{\ominus})$ // $6\mathrm{M} + 3\mathrm{a}$
24 $F \leftarrow X1 \cdot F + 2(X2^2 \cdot T6)$ // $2\mathrm{M} + 1\mathrm{S} + 2\mathrm{a}$
25 $F \leftarrow -2(F \cdot D \cdot T6 \cdot T3 \cdot T3^2 \cdot \tilde{x}_P)$ // $5\mathrm{M} + 1\mathrm{S} + 1\mathrm{a} + 1\mathrm{neg}$
26 $(U1, U0) \leftarrow (-F \cdot \tilde{y}_Q, F \cdot \tilde{z}_Q)$ // $2\mathrm{M} + 1\mathrm{neg}$
27 $Fi \leftarrow 1/(F \cdot \tilde{x}_Q)$ // $1\mathrm{M} + 1\mathrm{I}$
28 $(u_1', u_0', v_1', v_0') \leftarrow (Fi \cdot U1, Fi \cdot U0, Fi \cdot X9, Fi \cdot X10)$ // $4\mathrm{M}$
29 **return** $\langle X^2 + u_1'X + u_0', v_1'X + v_0' \rangle$

4.3   Full Scalar Multiplication on $\mathcal{J}_\mathcal{C}$

We now combine our pseudo-scalar multiplication function crypto_scalarmult with the point-recovery function Recover to define a full scalar multiplication function jacobian_scalarmult (Algorithm 13) on $\mathcal{J}_\mathcal{C}$.

Algorithm 13. jacobian_scalarmult: Scalar multiplication on $\mathcal{J}_\mathcal{C}$, using the Montgomery ladder on $\mathcal{K}_\mathcal{C}$ and recovery to $\mathcal{J}_\mathcal{C}$. Assumes wrapped projected point as auxiliary input. Symbolic cost: $(7\beta+143)\mathbf{M}+(12\beta+12)\mathbf{S}+(12\beta+4)\mathbf{m_c}+(70+16\beta)\mathbf{a}+(22+16\beta)\mathbf{s}+3\mathbf{neg}+\mathbf{I}$. ATmega: 9 968 127 cycles. Cortex: 2 709 401 cycles.

Input: $(m, P, (x_P/y_P, x_P/z_P, x_P/t_P)) \in [0, 2^\beta) \times \mathcal{J}_\mathcal{C}$
Output: $[m]P \in \mathcal{J}_\mathcal{C}$

1 $(\mathsf{X}_0, \mathsf{X}_1) \leftarrow$ crypto_scalarmult$(m, (x_P/y_P, x_P/z_P, x_P/t_P))$
                                             // $(7\beta + 4)\mathrm{M}+12\beta\mathrm{S}+12\beta m_c+16\beta\mathrm{a}+16\beta\mathrm{s}$
2 $\mathsf{xP} \leftarrow$ xUNWRAP$((x_P/y_P, x_P/z_P, x_P/t_P))$ // $4\mathrm{M}$
3 **return** Recover$(P, \mathsf{xP}, \mathsf{X}_0, \mathsf{X}_1)$ // $139\mathrm{M}+12\mathrm{S}+4m_c+70\mathrm{a}+22\mathrm{s}+3\mathrm{neg}+1\mathrm{I}$

Remark 3. jacobian_scalarmult takes not only a scalar m and a Jacobian point P in its Mumford representation, but also the wrapped form of $\pm P$ as an auxiliary argument: that is, we assume that $\mathsf{xP} \leftarrow$ Project(P) and xWRAP(xP) have already been carried out. This saves redundant Project and xWRAP calls when operating on fixed base points, as is often the case in our protocols. Nevertheless, jacobian_scalarmult could easily be converted to a "pure" Jacobian scalar multiplication function (with no auxiliary input) by inserting appropriate Project and xWRAP calls at the start, and removing the xUNWRAP call at Line 2, increasing the total cost by $11\mathbf{M} + 1\mathbf{S} + 4\mathbf{m_c} + 7\mathbf{a} + 8\mathbf{s} + 1\mathbf{I}$.

5   Results and Comparison

The high-level cryptographic functions for our signature scheme are named keygen, sign and verify. Their implementations contain no surprises: they do exactly what was specified in Sect. 2.1, calling the lower-level functions described in Sects. 3 and 4 as required. Our Diffie-Hellman key generation and key exchange use only the function dh_exchange, which implements exactly what we specified in Sect. 2.2: one call to crypto_scalarmult plus a call to xWRAP to convert to the correct 384-bit representation. Table 1 (in the introduction) presents the cycle counts and stack usage for all of our high-level functions.

Code and compilation. For our experiments, we compiled our AVR ATmega code with `avr-gcc -O2`, and our ARM Cortex M0 code with `clang -O2` (the optimization levels `-O3`, `-O1`, and `-Os` gave fairly similar results). The total program size is 20242 bytes for the AVR ATmega, and 19606 bytes for the ARM Cortex M0. This consists of the full signature and key-exchange code, including the reference implementation of the hash function `SHAKE128` with 512-bit output.[3]

Basis for comparison. As we believe ours to be the first genus-2 hyperelliptic curve implementation on both the AVR ATmega and the ARM Cortex M0 architectures, we can only compare with elliptic curve-based alternatives at the same 128-bit security level: notably [7,29–31]. This comparison is not superficial: the key exchange in [7,29,30] uses the highly efficient x-only arithmetic on Montgomery elliptic curves, while [31] uses similar techniques for Weierstrass elliptic curves, and x-only arithmetic is the exact elliptic-curve analogue of Kummer surface arithmetic. To provide full scalar multiplication in a group, [31] appends y-coordinate recovery to its x-only arithmetic (using the approach of [26]); again, this is the elliptic-curve analogue of our methods.

Results for ARM Cortex M0. As we see in Table 4, genus-2 techniques give great results for Diffie–Hellman key exchange on the ARM Cortex M0 architecture. Compared with the current fastest implementation [7], we reduce the number of clock cycles by about 27 %, while roughly halving code size and stack space. For signatures, the state-of-the-art is [31]: here we reduce the cycle count for the underlying scalar multiplications by a very impressive 75 %, at the cost of an increase in code size and stack usage.

Table 4. Comparison of scalar multiplication routines on the ARM Cortex M0 architecture at the 128-bit security level. **S** denotes signature-compatible full scalar multiplication; **DH** denotes Diffie–Hellman pseudo-scalar multiplication.

	Implementation	Object	Clock cycles	Code size	Stack
S,DH	Wenger et al. [31]	NIST P-256	≈ 10 730 000	7 168 bytes	540 bytes
DH	Düll et al. [7]	Curve25519	3 589 850	7 900 bytes	548 bytes
DH	This work	$\mathcal{K}_\mathcal{C}$	2 633 662	≈ 4 328 bytes	248 bytes
S	This work	$\mathcal{J}_\mathcal{C}$	2 709 401	≈ 9 874 bytes	968 bytes

Results for AVR ATmega. Looking at Table 5, on the AVR ATmega architecture we reduce the cycle count for Diffie–Hellman by about 32 % compared with the current record [7], again roughly halving the code size, and reducing stack usage by about 80 %. The cycle count for Jacobian scalar multiplication (for signatures) is reduced by 71 % compared with [31], while increasing the stack usage by 25 %.

---

[3] We used the reference C implementation for the Cortex M0, and the assembly implementation for AVR; both are available from [28]. The only change required is to the padding, which must take domain separation into account according to [12, p. 28].

Table 5. Comparison of scalar multiplication routines on the AVR ATmega architecture at the 128-bit security level. **S** denotes signature-compatible full scalar multiplication; **DH** denotes Diffie–Hellman pseudo-scalar multiplication. The implementation marked * also contains a fixed-basepoint scalar multiplication routine, whereas the implementation marked † does not report code size for the separated scalar multiplication.

	Implementation	Object	Cycles	Code size	Stack
DH	Liu et al. [29]	256-bit curve	$\approx 21\,078\,200$	14 700 bytes*	556 bytes
S,DH	Wenger et al. [31]	NIST P-256	$\approx 34\,930\,000$	16 112 bytes	590 bytes
DH	Hutter, Schwabe [30]	Curve25519	22 791 579	n/a†	677 bytes
DH	Düll et al. [7]	Curve25519	13 900 397	17 710 bytes	494 bytes
DH	This work	$\mathcal{K}_\mathcal{C}$	9 513 536	$\approx 9\,490$ bytes	99 bytes
S	This work	$\mathcal{J}_\mathcal{C}$	9 968 127	$\approx 16\,516$ bytes	735 bytes

Finally we can compare to the current fastest full signature implementation [10], shown in Table 6. We almost halve the number of cycles, while reducing stack usage by a decent margin (code size is not reported in [10]).

Table 6. Comparison of signature schemes on the AVR ATmega architecture at the 128-bit security level.

Implementation	Object	Function	Cycles	Stack
Nascimento et al. [10]	Ed25519	sig. gen	19 047 706	1 473 bytes
Nascimento et al. [10]	Ed25519	sig. ver	30 776 942	1 226 bytes
This work	$\mathcal{J}_\mathcal{C}$	sign	10 404 033	926 bytes
This work	$\mathcal{J}_\mathcal{C}$	verify	16 240 510	992 bytes

References

1. Bernstein, D.J.: Elliptic vs. hyperelliptic, part 1 (2006). http://cr.yp.to/talks/2006.09.20/slides.pdf
2. Bos, J.W., Costello, C., Hisil, H., Lauter, K.: Fast cryptography in genus 2. In: Johansson, T., Nguyen, P.Q. (eds.) EUROCRYPT 2013. LNCS, vol. 7881, pp. 194–210. Springer, Heidelberg (2013). https://eprint.iacr.org/2012/670.pdf
3. Bernstein, D.J., Chuengsatiansup, C., Lange, T., Schwabe, P.: Kummer strikes back: new DH speed records. In: Sarkar, P., Iwata, T. (eds.) ASIACRYPT 2014. LNCS, vol. 8873, pp. 317–337. Springer, Heidelberg (2014). https://cryptojedi.org/papers/#kummer
4. Costello, C., Longa, P.: Fourℚ: four-dimensional decompositions on aℚ-curve over the mersenne prime. In: Iwata, T., Cheon, J.H. (eds.) ASIACRYPT 2015. LNCS, vol. 9452, pp. 214–235. Springer, Heidelberg (2015). https://eprint.iacr.org/2015/565

5. Batina, L., Hwang, D., Hodjat, A., Preneel, B., Verbauwhede, I.: Hardware/Software Co-design for Hyperelliptic Curve Cryptography (HECC) on the 8051 μP. In: Rao, J.R., Sunar, B. (eds.) CHES 2005. LNCS, vol. 3659, pp. 106–118. Springer, Heidelberg (2005). https://www.iacr.org/archive/ches2005/008.pdf
6. Hodjat, A., Batina, L., Hwang, D., Verbauwhede, I.: HW/SW co-design of a hyperelliptic curve cryptosystem using amicrocode instruction set coprocessor. Integr. VLSI J. **40**, 45–51 (2007). https://www.cosic.esat.kuleuven.be/publications/article-622.pdf
7. Düll, M., Haase, B., Hinterwälder, G., Hutter, M., Paar, C., Sánchez, A.H., Schwabe, P.: High-speed curve25519 on 8-bit, 16-bit and 32-bit microcontrollers. Des. Codes Crypt. **77**, 493–514 (2015). http://cryptojedi.org/papers/#mu25519
8. Costello, C., Chung, P.N., Smith, B.: Fast, uniform, and compact scalar multiplication for elliptic curves and genus 2 Jacobians with applications to signature schemes.Cryptology ePrint Archive, Report 2015/983 (2015). https://eprint.iacr.org/2015/983
9. Bernstein, D.J., Duif, N., Lange, T., Schwabe, P., Yang, B.Y.: High-speed high-security signatures. J. Cryptogr. Eng. **2**, 77–89 (2012). https://cryptojedi.org/papers/ed25519
10. Nascimento, E., López, J., Dahab, R.: Efficient and secure elliptic curve cryptography for 8-bit AVR microcontrollers. In: Chakraborty, R.S., Schwabe, P., Solworth, J. (eds.) SPACE 2015. LNCS, vol. 9354, pp. 289–309. Springer, Heidelberg (2015)
11. Schnorr, C.-P.: Efficient identification and signatures for smart cards. In: Brassard, G. (ed.) CRYPTO 1989. LNCS, vol. 435, pp. 239–252. Springer, Heidelberg (1990)
12. Dworkin, M.J.:SHA-3 standard: Permutation-based hash and extendable-outputfunctions.Technical report, National Institute of Standards and Technology(NIST) (2015). http://www.nist.gov/manuscript-publication-search.cfm?pub_id=919061
13. Katz, J., Wang, N.: Efficiency improvements for signature schemes with tight securityreductions.In: Proceedings of the 10th ACM Conference on Computer and Communications Security, CCS 2003, pp. 155–164. ACM (2003). https://www.cs.umd.edu/~jkatz/papers/CCCS03_sigs.pdf
14. Vitek, J., Naccache, D., Pointcheval, D., Vaudenay, S.: Computational alternatives to random number generators. In: Tavares, S., Meijer, H. (eds.) SAC 1998. LNCS, vol. 1556, pp. 72–80. Springer, Heidelberg (1999). https://www.di.ens.fr/ pointche/Documents/Papers/1998_sac.pdf
15. Bernstein, D.J.: Differential addition chains (2006). http://cr.yp.to/ecdh/diffchain-20060219.pdf
16. Stam, M.: Speeding up subgroup cryptosystems. Ph.D. thesis, Technische Universiteit Eindhoven (2003). http://alexandria.tue.nl/extra2/200311829.pdf?q=subgroup
17. Hutter, M., Schwabe, P.: Multiprecision multiplication on AVR revisited. J. Cryptogr. Eng. **5**, 201–214 (2015). http://cryptojedi.org/papers/#avrmul
18. Gaudry, P., Schost, E.: Genus 2 point counting over prime fields. J Symb Comput **47**, 368–400 (2012). https://cs.uwaterloo.ca/~eschost/publications/countg2.pdf
19. Hisil, H., Costello, C.: Jacobian coordinates on genus 2 curves. In: Sarkar, P., Iwata, T. (eds.) ASIACRYPT 2014. LNCS, vol. 8873, pp. 338–357. Springer, Heidelberg (2014). https://eprint.iacr.org/2014/385.pdf
20. Stahlke, C.: Point compression on jacobians of hyperelliptic curves over$\mathbb{F}_q$.Cryptology ePrint Archive, Report 2004/030 (2004). https://eprint.iacr.org/2004/030

21. Chudnovsky, D.V., Chudnovsky, G.V.: Sequences of numbers generated by addition in formal groups and new primality and factorization tests. Adv. Appl. Math. **7**, 385–434 (1986)
22. Cosset, R.: Applications of theta functions for hyperelliptic curvecryptography.Ph.D. thesis, Université Henri Poincaré - Nancy I (2011). https://tel. archives-ouvertes.fr/tel-00642951/file/main.pdf
23. Gaudry, P.: Fast genus 2 arithmetic based on theta functions. J. Math. Cryptol. **1**, 243–265 (2007). https://eprint.iacr.org/2005/314/
24. López, J., Dahab, R.: Fast multiplication on elliptic curves over $GF(2_m)$ without precomputation. In: Koç, Ç.K., Paar, C. (eds.) CHES 1999. LNCS, vol. 1717, pp. 316–327. Springer, Heidelberg (1999)
25. Okeya, K., Sakurai, K.: Efficient elliptic curve cryptosystems from a scalar multiplication algorithm with recovery of the y-Coordinate on a Montgomery-Form Elliptic Curve. In: Koç, Ç.K., Naccache, D., Paar, C. (eds.) CHES 2001. LNCS, vol. 2162, pp. 126–141. Springer, Heidelberg (2001)
26. Brier, E., Joye, M.: Weierstra elliptic curves and side-channel attacks. In: Naccache, D., Paillier, P. (eds.) PKC 2002. LNCS, vol. 2274, pp. 335–345. Springer, Heidelberg (2002). http://link.springer.com/content/pdf/10.1007%2F3-540-45664-3_24.pdf
27. Cassels, J.W.S., Flynn, E.V.: Prolegomena to a Middlebrow Arithmetic of Curves of Genus 2, vol. 230. Cambridge University Press, Cambridge (1996)
28. Bertoni, G., Daemen, J., Peeters, M., Assche, G.V.: The KECCAK sponge function family (2016). http://keccak.noekeon.org/
29. Liu, Z., Wenger, E., Großschädl, J.: MoTE-ECC: energy-scalable elliptic curve cryptography for wireless sensor networks. In: Boureanu, I., Owesarski, P., Vaudenay, S. (eds.) ACNS 2014. LNCS, vol. 8479, pp. 361–379. Springer, Heidelberg (2014). https://online.tugraz.at/tug_online/voe_main2. getvolltext?pCurrPk=77985
30. Hutter, M., Schwabe, P.: NaCl on 8-bit AVR microcontrollers. In: Youssef, A., Nitaj, A., Hassanien, A.E. (eds.) AFRICACRYPT 2013. LNCS, vol. 7918, pp. 156–172. Springer, Heidelberg (2013). http://cryptojedi.org/papers/#avrnacl
31. Wenger, E., Unterluggauer, T., Werner, M.: 8/16/32 shades of elliptic curve cryptography on embedded processors. In: Paul, G., Vaudenay, S. (eds.) INDOCRYPT 2013. LNCS, vol. 8250, pp. 244–261. Springer, Heidelberg (2013). https://online.tugraz.at/tug_online/voe_main2.getvolltext?pCurrPk=72486

Cache Attacks

Flush, Gauss, and Reload – A Cache Attack on the BLISS Lattice-Based Signature Scheme

Leon Groot Bruinderink[1]([⊠]), Andreas Hülsing[1]([⊠]), Tanja Lange[1]([⊠]), and Yuval Yarom[2,3]([⊠])

[1] Department of Mathematics and Computer Science,
Technische Universiteit Eindhoven, P.O. Box 513, 5600 MB Eindhoven, Netherlands
l.groot.bruinderink@tue.nl, andreas@huelsing.net, tanja@hyperelliptic.org
[2] The University of Adelaide, Adelaide, Australia
[3] NICTA, Sydney, Australia
yval@cs.adelaide.edu.au

Abstract. We present the first side-channel attack on a lattice-based signature scheme, using the FLUSH+RELOAD cache-attack. The attack is targeted at the discrete Gaussian sampler, an important step in the Bimodal Lattice Signature Schemes (BLISS). After observing only 450 signatures with a perfect side-channel, an attacker is able to extract the secret BLISS-key in less than 2 minutes, with a success probability of 0.96. Similar results are achieved in a proof-of-concept implementation using the FLUSH+RELOAD technique with less than 3500 signatures.

We show how to attack sampling from a discrete Gaussian using CDT or Bernoulli sampling by showing potential information leakage via cache memory. For both sampling methods, a strategy is given to use this additional information, finalize the attack and extract the secret key. We provide experimental evidence for the idealized perfect side-channel attacks and the FLUSH+RELOAD attack on two recent CPUs.

Keywords: SCA · FLUSH+RELOAD · Lattices · BLISS · Discrete Gaussians

1 Introduction

The possible advent of general purpose quantum computers will undermine the security of all widely deployed public key cryptography. Ongoing progress towards building such quantum computers recently motivated standardization bodies to set up programs for standardizing post-quantum public key primitives, focusing on schemes for digital signatures, public key encryption, and key exchange [7,18,23].

This work was supported in part by the Commission of the European Communities through the Horizon 2020 program under project number 645622 PQCRYPTO. Permanent ID of this document: da245c8568290e4a0f45c704cc62a2b8.

© International Association for Cryptologic Research 2016
B. Gierlichs and A.Y. Poschmann (Eds.): CHES 2016, LNCS 9813, pp. 323–345, 2016.
DOI: 10.1007/978-3-662-53140-2_16

A particularly interesting area of post-quantum cryptography is lattice-based cryptography; there exist efficient lattice-based proposals for signatures, encryption, and key exchange [1,3,9,15,21,26,37] and several of the proposed schemes have implementations, including implementations in open source libraries [34]. While the theoretical and practical security of these schemes is under active research, security of implementations is an open issue.

In this paper we make a first step towards understanding implementation security, presenting the first side-channel attack on a lattice-based signature scheme. More specifically, we present a cache-attack on the Bimodal Lattice Signature Scheme (BLISS) by Ducas, Durmus, Lepoint, and Lyubashevsky from CRYPTO 2013 [9], attacking a research-oriented implementation made available by the BLISS authors at [8]. We present attacks on the two implemented methods for sampling from a discrete Gaussian and for both successfully obtain the secret signing key.

Note that most recent lattice-based signature schemes use noise sampled according to a discrete Gaussian distribution to achieve provable security and a reduction from standard assumptions. Hence, our attack might be applicable to many other implementations. It is possible to avoid our attack by using schemes which avoid discrete Gaussians at the cost of more aggressive assumptions [14].

1.1. The Attack Target. BLISS is the most recent piece in a line of work on identification-scheme-based lattice signatures, also known as signatures without trapdoors. An important step in the signature scheme is blinding a secret value in some way to make the signature statistically independent of the secret key. For this, a blinding (or noise) value $\mathbf{y}$ is sampled according to a discrete Gaussian distribution. In the case of BLISS, $\mathbf{y}$ is an integer polynomial of degree less than some system parameter n and each coefficient is sampled separately. Essentially, $\mathbf{y}$ is used to hide the secret polynomial $\mathbf{s}$ in the signature equation $\mathbf{z} = \mathbf{y} + (-1)^b(\mathbf{s} \cdot \mathbf{c})$, where noise polynomial $\mathbf{y}$ and bit b are unknown to an attacker and $\mathbf{c}$ is the challenge polynomial from the identification scheme which is given as part of the signature $(\mathbf{z}, \mathbf{c})$.

If an attacker learns the noise polynomials $\mathbf{y}$ for a few signatures, he can compute the secret key using linear algebra and guessing the bit b per signature. Actually, the attacker will only learn the secret key up to the sign but for BLISS $-\mathbf{s}$ is also a valid secret key.

1.2. Our Contribution. In this work we present a FLUSH+RELOAD attack on BLISS. We implemented the attack for two different algorithms for Gaussian sampling. First we attack the *CDT sampler with guide table*, as described in [29] and used in the attacked implementation as default sampler [8]. CDT is the fastest way of sampling discrete Gaussians, but requires a large table stored in memory. Then we also attack a rejection sampler, specifically the Bernoulli-based sampler that was proposed in [9], and also provided in [8].

On a high level, our attacks exploit cache access patterns of the implementations to learn a few coefficients of $\mathbf{y}$ per observed signature. We then develop mathematical attacks to use this partial knowledge of different $\mathbf{y}_j$s together with the public signature values $(\mathbf{z}_j, \mathbf{c}_j)$ to compute the secret key, given observations from sufficiently many signatures.

In detail, there is an interplay between requirements for the offline attack and restrictions on the sampling. First, restricting to cache access patterns that provide relatively precise information means that the online phase only allows to extract a few coefficients of $\mathbf{y}_j$ per signature. This means that trying all guesses for the bits b per signature becomes a bottleneck. We circumvent this issue by only collecting coefficients of $\mathbf{y}_j$ in situations where the respective coefficient of $\mathbf{s} \cdot \mathbf{c}_j$ is zero as in these cases the bit b_j has no effect.

Second, each such collected coefficient of $\mathbf{y}_j$ leads to an equation with some coefficients of $\mathbf{s}$ as unknowns. However, it turns out that for CDT sampling the cache patterns do not give exact equations. Instead, we learn equations which hold with high probability, but might be off by ± 1 with non-negligible probability. We managed to turn the computation of $\mathbf{s}$ into a lattice problem and show how to solve it using the LLL algorithm [20]. For Bernoulli sampling we can obtain exact equations but at the expense of requiring more signatures.

We first tweaked the BLISS implementation to provide us with the exact cache lines used, modeling a perfect side-channel. For BLISS-I, designed for 128 bits of security, the attack on CDT needs to observe on average 441 signatures during the online phase. Afterwards, the offline phase succeeds after 37.6 seconds with probability 0.66. This corresponds to running LLL once. If the attack does not succeed at first, a few more signatures (on average a total of 446) are sampled and LLL is run with some randomized selection of inputs. The combined attack succeeds with probability 0.96, taking a total of 85.8 seconds. Similar results hold for other BLISS versions. In the case of Bernoulli sampling, we are given exact equations and can use simple linear algebra to finalize the attack, given a success probability of 1.0 after observing 1671 signatures on average and taking 14.7 seconds in total.

To remove the assumption of a perfect side-channel we performed a proof-of-concept attack using the FLUSH+RELOAD technique on a modern laptop. This attack achieves similar success rates, albeit requiring 3438 signatures on average for BLISS-I with CDT sampling. For Bernoulli sampling, we now had to deal with measurement errors. We did this again by formulating a lattice problem and using LLL in the final step. The attack succeeds with a probability of 0.88 after observing an average of 3294 signatures.

1.3. Structure. In Section 2, we give brief introductions to lattices, BLISS, and the used methods for discrete Gaussian sampling as well as to cache-attacks. In Section 3, we present two information leakages through cache-memory for CDT sampling and provide a strategy to exploit this information for secret key extraction. In Section 4, we present an attack strategy for the case of Bernoulli sampling. In Section 5, we present experimental results for both strategies assuming a perfect side-channel. In Section 6, we show that realistic experiments also succeed, using FLUSH+RELOAD attacks.

2   Preliminaries

This section describes the BLISS signature scheme and the used discrete Gaussian samplers. It also provides some background on lattices and cache attacks.

2.1. Lattices. We define a *lattice* Λ as a discrete subgroup of $\mathbb{R}^n$: given $m \leq n$ linearly independent vectors $\mathbf{b}_1, \ldots, \mathbf{b}_m \in \mathbb{R}^n$, the lattice Λ is given by the set $\Lambda(\mathbf{b}_1, \ldots, \mathbf{b}_m)$ of all integer linear combinations of the $\mathbf{b}_i$'s:

$$\Lambda(\mathbf{b}_1, \ldots, \mathbf{b}_m) = \left\{ \sum_{i=1}^{m} x_i \mathbf{b}_i \mid x_i \in \mathbb{Z} \right\}.$$

We call $\{\mathbf{b}_1, \ldots, \mathbf{b}_m\}$ a basis of Λ and define m as the rank. We represent the basis as a matrix $\mathbf{B} = (\mathbf{b}_1, \ldots, \mathbf{b}_m)$, which contains the vectors $\mathbf{b}_i$ as column vectors. In this paper, we mostly consider full-rank lattices, i.e. $m = n$, unless stated otherwise. Given a basis $\mathbf{B} \in \mathbb{R}^{n \times n}$ of a full-rank lattice Λ, we can apply any unimodular transformation matrix $\mathbf{U} \in \mathbb{Z}^{n \times n}$ and $\mathbf{UB}$ will also be a basis of Λ. The LLL algorithm [20] transforms a basis $\mathbf{B}$ to its LLL-reduced basis $\mathbf{B}'$ in polynomial time. In an LLL-reduced basis the shortest vector $\mathbf{v}$ of $\mathbf{B}'$ satisfies $\|\mathbf{v}\|_2 \leq 2^{\frac{n-1}{4}} (|\det(\mathbf{B})|)^{1/n}$ and there are looser bounds for the other basis vectors. Here $\|\cdot\|_2$ denotes the Euclidean norm. Besides the LLL-reduced basis, NTL's [33] implementation of LLL also returns the unimodular transformation matrix $\mathbf{U}$, satisfying $\mathbf{UB} = \mathbf{B}'$.

In cryptography, lattices are often defined via polynomials, e.g., to take advantage of efficient polynomial arithmetic. The elements in $R = \mathbb{Z}[x]/(x^n + 1)$ are represented as polynomials of degree less than n. For each polynomial $f(x) \in R$ we define the corresponding vector of coefficients as $\mathbf{f} = (f_0, f_1, \ldots, f_{n-1})$. Addition of polynomials $f(x) + g(x)$ corresponds to addition of their coefficient vectors $\mathbf{f} + \mathbf{g}$. Additionally, multiplication of $f(x) \cdot g(x) \mod (x^n + 1)$ defines a multiplication operation on the vectors $\mathbf{f} \cdot \mathbf{g} = \mathbf{gF} = \mathbf{fG}$, where $\mathbf{F}, \mathbf{G} \in \mathbb{Z}^{n \times n}$ are matrices, whose columns are the rotations of (the coefficient vectors of) $\mathbf{f}, \mathbf{g}$, with possibly opposite signs. Lattices using polynomials modulo $x^n + 1$ are often called *NTRU lattices* after the NTRU encryption scheme [15].

An *integer lattice* is a lattice for which the basis vectors are in $\mathbb{Z}^n$, such as the NTRU lattices just described. For integer lattices it makes sense to consider elements modulo q, so basis vectors and coefficients are taken from $\mathbb{Z}_q$. We represent the ring $\mathbb{Z}_q$ as the integers in $[-q/2, q/2)$. We denote the quotient ring $R/(qR)$ by R_q. When we work in $R_q = \mathbb{Z}_q[x]/(x^n + 1)$ (or R_{2q}), we assume n is a power of 2 and q is a prime such that $q \equiv 1 \mod 2n$.

2.2. BLISS. We provide the basic algorithms of BLISS, as given in [9]. Details of the motivation behind the construction and associated security proofs are given in the original work. All arithmetic for BLISS is performed in R and possibly with each coefficient reduced modulo q or $2q$. We follow notation of BLISS and also use boldface notation for polynomials.

By D_σ we denote the discrete Gaussian distribution with standard deviation σ. In the next subsection, we will zoom in on this distribution and how to sample from it in practice. The main parameters of BLISS are dimension n, modulus q and standard deviation σ. BLISS uses a cryptographic hash function H, which outputs binary vectors of length n and weight κ; parameters d_1 and d_2 determining the density of the polynomials forming the secret key; and d, determining the length of the second signature component.

Algorithm 2.1. BLISS Key Generation

Output: A BLISS key pair $(\mathbf{A}, \mathbf{S})$ with public key $\mathbf{A} = (\mathbf{a}_1, \mathbf{a}_2) \in R_{2q}^2$ and secret key
$\mathbf{S} = (\mathbf{s}_1, \mathbf{s}_2) \in R_{2q}^2$ such that $\mathbf{AS} = \mathbf{a}_1 \cdot \mathbf{s}_1 + \mathbf{a}_2 \cdot \mathbf{s}_2 \equiv q \bmod 2q$.
1: choose $\mathbf{f}, \mathbf{g} \in R_{2q}$ uniformly at random with exactly d_1 entries in $\{\pm 1\}$ and d_2
   entries in $\{\pm 2\}$
2: $\mathbf{S} = (\mathbf{s}_1, \mathbf{s}_2) = (\mathbf{f}, 2\mathbf{g} + 1)$
3: **if S** violates certain bounds (details in [9]), **then** restart
4: $\mathbf{a}_q = (2\mathbf{g} + 1)/\mathbf{f} \bmod q$ (restart if $\mathbf{f}$ is not invertible)
5: **return** $(\mathbf{A}, \mathbf{S})$ where $\mathbf{A} = (2\mathbf{a}_q, q - 2) \bmod 2q$

Algorithm 2.1 generates correct keys because

$$\mathbf{a}_1 \cdot \mathbf{s}_1 + \mathbf{a}_2 \cdot \mathbf{s}_2 = 2\mathbf{a}_q \cdot \mathbf{f} + (q-2) \cdot (2\mathbf{g}+1) \equiv 2(2\mathbf{g}+1) + (q-2)(2\mathbf{g}+1) \equiv q \bmod 2q.$$

Note that when an attacker has a candidate for key $\mathbf{s}_1 = \mathbf{f}$, he can validate correctness by checking the distributions of $\mathbf{f}$ and $\mathbf{a}_q \cdot \mathbf{f} \equiv 2\mathbf{g} + 1 \bmod 2q$, and lastly verifying that $\mathbf{a}_1 \cdot \mathbf{f} + \mathbf{a}_2 \cdot (\mathbf{a}_q \cdot f) \equiv q \bmod 2q$, where $\mathbf{a}_q$ is obtained by halving $\mathbf{a}_1$.

Signature generation (Algorithm 2.2) uses $p = \lfloor 2q/2^d \rfloor$, which is the highest order bits of the modulus $2q$, and constant $\zeta = \frac{1}{q-2} \bmod 2q$. In general, with $\lfloor . \rceil_d$ we denote the d highest order bits of a number. In Step 1 of Algorithm 2.2, two integer vectors are sampled, where each coordinate is drawn independently and according to the discrete Gaussian distribution D_σ. This is denoted by $\mathbf{y} \leftarrow D_{\mathbb{Z}^n, \sigma}$.

In the attacks, we concentrate on the first signature vector $\mathbf{z}_1$, since $\mathbf{z}_2^\dagger$ only contains the d highest order bits and therefore lost information about $\mathbf{s}_2 \cdot \mathbf{c}$; furthermore, $\mathbf{A}$ and $\mathbf{f}$ determine $\mathbf{s}_2$ as shown above. So in the following, we only consider $\mathbf{z}_1, \mathbf{y}_1$ and $\mathbf{s}_1$, and thus will leave out the indices.

In lines 5 and 6 of Algorithm 2.2, we compute $\mathbf{s} \cdot \mathbf{c}$ over R_{2q}. However, since secret $\mathbf{s}$ is sparse and challenge $\mathbf{c}$ is sparse and binary, the absolute value of $\|\mathbf{s} \cdot \mathbf{c}\|_\infty \le 5\kappa \ll 2q$, with $\|\cdot\|_\infty$ the ℓ_∞-norm. This means these computations are simply additions over $\mathbb{Z}$, and we can therefore model this computation as a

---

Algorithm 2.2. BLISS Signature Algorithm

Input: Message μ, public key $\mathbf{A} = (\mathbf{a}_1, q - 2)$, secret key $\mathbf{S} = (\mathbf{s}_1, \mathbf{s}_2)$
Output: A signature $(\mathbf{z}_1, \mathbf{z}_2^\dagger, \mathbf{c}) \in \mathbb{Z}_{2q}^n \times \mathbb{Z}_p^n \times \{0, 1\}^n$ of the message μ
1: $\mathbf{y}_1, \mathbf{y}_2 \leftarrow D_{\mathbb{Z}^n, \sigma}$
2: $\mathbf{u} = \zeta \cdot \mathbf{a}_1 \cdot \mathbf{y}_1 + \mathbf{y}_2 \bmod 2q$
3: $\mathbf{c} = H(\lfloor \mathbf{u} \rceil_d \bmod p, \mu)$
4: choose a random bit b
5: $\mathbf{z}_1 = \mathbf{y}_1 + (-1)^b \mathbf{s}_1 \cdot \mathbf{c} \bmod 2q$
6: $\mathbf{z}_2 = \mathbf{y}_2 + (-1)^b \mathbf{s}_2 \cdot \mathbf{c} \bmod 2q$
7: **continue** with a probability based on $\sigma, \|\mathbf{Sc}\|, \langle \mathbf{z}, \mathbf{Sc} \rangle$ (details in [9]), **else** restart
8: $\mathbf{z}_2^\dagger = (\lfloor \mathbf{u} \rceil_d - \lfloor \mathbf{u} - \mathbf{z}_2 \rceil_d) \bmod p$
9: **return** $(\mathbf{z}_1, \mathbf{z}_2^\dagger, \mathbf{c})$

---

vector-matrix multiplication over $\mathbb{Z}$:

$$\mathbf{s} \cdot \mathbf{c} = \mathbf{sC},$$

where $\mathbf{C} \in \{-1, 0, 1\}^{n \times n}$ is the matrix whose columns are the rotations of challenge $\mathbf{c}$ (with minus signs matching reduction modulo $x^n + 1$). In the attacks we access individual coefficients of $\mathbf{s} \cdot \mathbf{c}$; note that the jth coefficient equals $\langle \mathbf{s}, \mathbf{c}_j \rangle$, where $\mathbf{c}_j$ is the jth column of C.

For completeness, we also show the verification procedure (Algorithm 2.3), although we do not use it further in this paper. Note that reductions modulo $2q$ are done before truncating and reducing modulo p.

Algorithm 2.3. BLISS Verification Algorithm

Input: Message μ, public key $\mathbf{A} = (\mathbf{a}_1, q - 2) \in R_{2q}^2$, signature $(\mathbf{z}_1, \mathbf{z}_2^\dagger, \mathbf{c})$
Output: Accept or reject the signature
1: **if** $\mathbf{z}_1, \mathbf{z}_2^\dagger$ violate certain bounds (details in [9]), **then** reject
2: accept iff $\mathbf{c} = H(\lfloor \zeta \cdot \mathbf{a}_1 \cdot \mathbf{z}_1 + \zeta \cdot q \cdot \mathbf{c} \rceil_d + \mathbf{z}_2^\dagger \bmod p, \mu)$

2.3. Discrete Gaussian Distribution. The probability distribution of a (centered) discrete Gaussian distribution is a distribution over $\mathbb{Z}$, with mean 0 and standard deviation σ. A value $x \in \mathbb{Z}$ is sampled with probability:

$$\frac{\rho_\sigma(x)}{\sum_{y=-\infty}^{\infty} \rho_\sigma(y)},$$

where $\rho_\sigma(x) = \exp\left(\frac{-x^2}{2\sigma^2}\right)$. Note that the sum in the denominator ensures that this is actually a probability distribution. We denote the denominator by $\rho_\sigma(\mathbb{Z})$.

To make sampling practical, most lattice-based schemes use three simplifications: First, a tail-cut τ is used, restricting the support of the Gaussian to a finite interval $[-\tau\sigma, \tau\sigma]$. The tail-cut τ is chosen such that the probability of a real discrete Gaussian sample landing outside this interval is negligible in the security parameter. Second, values are sampled from the positive half of the support and then a bit is flipped to determine the sign. For this the probability of obtaining zero in $[0, \tau\sigma]$ needs to be halved. The resulting distribution on the positive numbers is denoted by D_σ^+. Finally, the precision of the sampler is chosen such that the statistical distance between the output distribution and the exact distribution is negligible in the security parameter.

There are two generic ways to sample from a discrete Gaussian distribution: using the cumulative distribution function [25] or via rejection sampling [11]. Both these methods are deployed with some improvements which we describe next. These modified versions are implemented in [8]. We note that there are also other ways [5,10,30,31] of efficiently sampling discrete Gaussians.

CDT Sampling. The basic idea of using the cumulative distribution function in the sampler, is to approximate the probabilities $p_y = \mathbb{P}[x \leq y \mid x \leftarrow D_\sigma]$, computed with λ bits of precision, and save them in a large table. At sampling time, one samples a uniformly random $r \in [0, 1)$, and performs a binary search through the table to locate $y \in [-\tau\sigma, \tau\sigma]$ such that $r \in [p_{y-1}, p_y)$. Restricting to the non-negative part $[0, \tau\sigma]$ corresponds to using the probabilities $p_y^* = \mathbb{P}[|x| \leq y \mid x \leftarrow D_\sigma]$, sampling $r \in [0, 1)$ and locating $y \in [0, \tau\sigma]$. While this is the most efficient approach, it requires a large table. We denote the method that uses the approximate cumulative distribution function with tail cut and the modifications described next, as the *CDT sampling* method.

One can speed up the binary search for the correct sample y in the table, by using an additional *guide table* I [6,19,29]. The BLISS implementation we attack uses I with 256 entries. The guide table stores for each $u \in \{0, \ldots, 255\}$ the smallest interval $I[u] = (a_u, b_u)$ such that $p_{a_u}^* \leq u/256$ and $p_{b_u}^* \geq (u+1)/256$. The first byte of r is used to select $I[u]$ leading to a much smaller interval for the binary search. Effectively, r is picked byte-by-byte, stopping once a unique value for y is obtained. The CDT sampling algorithm with guide table is summarized in Algorithm 2.4.

Bernoulli Sampling (Rejection Sampling). The basic idea behind rejection sampling is to sample a uniformly random integer $y \in [-\tau\sigma, \tau\sigma]$ and accept this sample with probability $\rho_\sigma(y)/\rho_\sigma(\mathbb{Z})$. For this, a uniformly random value $r \in [0, 1)$ is sampled and y is accepted iff $r \leq \rho_\sigma(y)$. This method has two huge downsides: calculating the values of $\rho_\sigma(y)$ to high precision is expensive and the rejection rate can be quite high.

In the same paper introducing BLISS [9], the authors also propose a more efficient Bernoulli-based sampling algorithm. We recall the algorithms used (Algorithms 2.5, 2.6, and 2.7), more details are given in the original work. We denote this method as *Bernoulli sampling* in the remainder of this paper.

The basic idea is to first sample a value x, according to the binary discrete Gaussian distribution D_{σ_2}, where $\sigma_2 = \frac{1}{2\ln 2}$ (Step 1 of Algorithm 2.5). This can be done efficiently using uniformly random bits [9]. The actual sample $y = Kx + z$, where $z \in \{0, \ldots, K - 1\}$ is sampled uniformly at random and

---

Algorithm 2.4. CDT Sampling With Guide Table

Input: Big table $T[y]$ containing values p_y^* of the cumulative distribution function of the discrete Gaussian distribution (using only non-negative values), omitting the first byte. Small table I consisting of the 256 intervals

Output: Value $y \in [-\tau\sigma, \tau\sigma]$ sampled with probability according to D_σ

1: pick a random byte r
2: let $(I_{\min}, I_{\max}) = (a_r, b_r)$ be the left and right bounds of interval $I[r]$
3: **if** $(I_{\max} - I_{\min} = 1)$:
4:      generate a random sign bit $b \in \{0, 1\}$
5:      **return** $y = (-1)^b I_{\min}$
6: let $i = 1$ denote the index of the byte to look at
7: pick a new random byte r
8: **while** (1):
9:      $I_z = \lfloor \frac{I_{\min} + I_{\max}}{2} \rfloor$
10:      **if** $(r > (i$th byte of $T[I_z]))$:
11:         $I_{\min} = I_z$
12:      **else if** $(r < (i$th byte of $T[I_z]))$:
13:         $I_{\max} = I_z$
14:      **else if** $(I_{\max} - I_{\min} = 1)$:
15:         generate a random sign bit $b \in \{0, 1\}$
16:         **return** $y = (-1)^b I_{\min}$
17:      **else:**
18:         increase i by 1
19:         pick new random byte r

Algorithm 2.5. Sampling from $D_{K\sigma}^+$ for $K \in \mathbb{Z}$

Input: Target standard deviation σ, integer $K = \lfloor \frac{\sigma}{\sigma_2} + 1 \rfloor$, where $\sigma_2 = \frac{1}{2\ln 2}$

Output: An integer $y \in \mathbb{Z}^+$ according to $D_{K\sigma_2}^+$

1: sample $x \in \mathbb{Z}$ according to $D_{\sigma_2}^+$
2: sample $z \in \mathbb{Z}$ uniformly in $\{0, \ldots, K - 1\}$
3: $y \leftarrow Kx + z$
4: sample b with probability $\exp\left(-z(z + 2Kx)/(2\sigma^2)\right)$
5: **if** $b = 0$ **then** restart
6: **return** y

Algorithm 2.6. Sampling from $D_{K\sigma}$

Output: An integer $y \in \mathbb{Z}$ according to $D_{K\sigma_2}$

1: sample integer $y \leftarrow D_{K\sigma}^+$ (using Algorithm 2.5)
2: **if** $y = 0$ **then** restart with probability $1/2$
3: generate random bit b and **return** $(-1)^b y$

$K = \lfloor \frac{\sigma}{\sigma_2} + 1 \rfloor$, is then distributed according to the target discrete Gaussian distribution D_σ, by rejecting with a certain probability (Step 4 of Algorithm 2.5). The number of rejections in this case is much lower than in the original method. This step still requires computing a bit, whose probability is an exponential

Algorithm 2.7. Sampling a bit with probability $\exp(-x/(2\sigma^2))$ for $x \in [0, 2^\ell)$

Input: $x \in [0, 2^\ell)$ an integer in binary form $x = x_{\ell-1} \ldots x_0$. Table ET with precomputed values $\mathrm{ET}[i] = \exp(-2^i/(2\sigma^2))$ for $0 \le i \le \ell - 1$
Output: A bit b with probability $\exp(-x/(2\sigma^2))$ of being 1
1: **for** $i = \ell - 1$ **to** 0:
2:     **if** $x_i = 1$ **then**
3:         sample A_i with probability $\mathrm{ET}[i]$.
4:         **if** $A_i = 0$ **then return** 0
5: **return** 1

---

value. However, it can be done more efficiently using Algorithm 2.7, where ET is a small table.

2.4. Cache Attacks. The cache is a small bank of memory which exploits the temporal and the spatial locality of memory access to bridge the speed gap between the faster processor and the slower memory. The cache consists of *cache lines*, which, on modern Intel architectures, can store a 64-byte aligned *block* of memory of size 64 bytes.

In a typical processor there are several cache *levels*. At the top level, closest to the execution core, is the *L1 cache*, which is the smallest and the fastest of the hierarchy. Each successive level (L2, L3, etc.) is bigger and slower than the preceding level.

When the processor accesses a memory address it looks for the block containing the address in the L1 cache. In a *cache hit*, the block is found in the cache and the data is accessed. Otherwise, in a *cache miss*, the search continues on lower levels, eventually retrieving the memory block from the lower levels or from the memory. The cache then *evicts* a cache line and replaces its contents with the retrieved block, allowing faster future access to the block.

Because cache misses require searches in lower cache levels, they are slower than cache hits. Cache timing attacks exploit this timing difference to leak information [2,13,22,24,27]. In a nutshell, when an attacker uses the same cache as a victim, victim memory accesses change the state of the cache. The attacker can then use the timing variations to check which memory blocks are cached and from that deduce which memory addresses the victim has accessed. Ultimately, the attacker learns the cache line of the victim's table access: a range of possible values for the index of the access.

In this work we use the FLUSH+RELOAD attack [13,36]. A FLUSH+RELOAD attack uses the `clflush` instruction of the x86-64 architecture to evict a memory block from the cache. The attacker then lets the victim execute before measuring the time to access the memory block. If during its execution the victim has accessed an address within the block, the block will be cached and the attacker's access will be fast. If, however, the victim has not accessed the block, the attacker will reload the block from memory, and the access will take much longer. Thus, the attacker learns whether the victim accessed the memory block during its execution. The FLUSH+RELOAD attack has been used to attack implementations of RSA [36], AES [13,17], ECDSA [28,35] and other software [12,38].

3   Attack 1: CDT Sampling

This section presents the mathematical foundations of our cache attack on the CDT sampling. We first explain the phenomena we can observe from cache misses and hits in Algorithm 2.4 and then show how to exploit them to derive the secret signing key of BLISS using LLL. Sampling of the first noise polynomial $y \in D_{\mathbb{Z}^n,\sigma}$ is done coefficientwise. Similarly the cache attack targets coefficients y_i for $i = 0, \ldots, n-1$ independently.

3.1. Weaknesses in Cache. Sampling from a discrete Gaussian distribution using both an interval table I and a table with the actual values T, might leak information via cache memory. The best we can hope for is to learn the cache-lines of index r of the interval and of index I_z of the table lookup in T. Note that we cannot learn the sign of the sampled coefficient y_i. Also, the cache line of $T[I_z]$ always leaves a range of values for $|y_i|$. However, in some cases we can get more precise information combining cache-lines of table lookups in both tables. Here are two observations that narrow down the possibilities:

Intersection: We can intersect knowledge about the used index r in I with the knowledge of the access $T[I_z]$. Getting the cache-line of $I[r]$ gives a range of intervals, which is simply another (bigger) interval of possible values for sample $|y_i|$. If the values in the range of intervals are largely non-overlapping with the range of values learned from the access to $T[I_z]$, then the combination gives a much more precise estimate. For example: if the cache-line of $I[r]$ reveals that sample $|y_i|$ is in set $S_1 = \{0,1,2,3,4,5,7,8\}$ and the cache-line of $T[I_z]$ reveals that sample $|y_i|$ must be in set $S_2 = \{7,8,9,10,11,12,13,14,15\}$, then by intersecting both sets we know that $|y_i| \in S_1 \cap S_2 = \{7,8\}$, which is much more precise information.

Last-Jump: If the elements of an interval $I[r]$ in I are divided over two cache-lines of T, we can sometimes track the search for the element to sample. If a small part of $I[r]$ is in one cache-line, and the remaining part of $I[r]$ is in another, we are able to distinguish if this small part has been accessed. For example, interval $I[r] = \{5,6,7,8,9\}$ is divided over two cache-lines of T: cache-line $T_1 = \{0,1,2,3,4,5,6,7\}$ and line $T_2 = \{8,9,10,11,12,13,14,15\}$. The binary search starts in the middle of $I[r]$, at value 7, which means line T_1 is always accessed. However, only for values $\{8,9\}$ also line T_2 is accessed. So if both lines T_1 and T_2 are accessed, we know that sample $|y_i| \in \{8,9\}$.

We will restrict ourselves to only look for cache access patterns that give even more precision, at the expense of requiring more signatures:

1. The first restriction is to only look at cache weaknesses (of type Intersection or Last-Jump), in which the number of possible values for sample $|y_i|$ is two. Since we do a binary search within an interval, this is the most precision one can get (unless an interval is unique): after the last comparisons (table lookup in T), one of two values will be returned. This means that by picking either of these two values we limit the error of $|y_i|$ to at most 1.

2. The probabilities of sampling values using CDT sampling with guide table I are known to match the following probability requirement:

$$\sum_{r=0}^{255} \mathbb{P}[X = x \mid X \in I[r]] = \frac{\rho_\sigma(x)}{\rho_\sigma(\mathbb{Z})}. \tag{1}$$

Due to the above condition, it is possible that adjacent intervals are partially overlapping. That is, for some r, s we have that $I[r] \cap I[s] \neq \emptyset$. In practice, this only happens for $r = s+1$, meaning adjacent intervals might overlap. For example, if the probability of sampling x is greater than $1/256$, then x has to be an element in at least two intervals $I[r]$. Because of this, it is possible that for certain parts of an interval $I[r]$, there is a biased outcome of the sample.

The second restriction is to only consider cache weaknesses for which additionally one of the two values is significantly more likely to be sampled, i.e., if $|y_i| \in \{\gamma_1, \gamma_2\} \subset I[r]$ is the outcome of cache access patterns, then we further insist on

$$\mathbb{P}[|y_i| = \gamma_1 \mid |y_i| \in \{\gamma_1, \gamma_2\} \subset I[r]] \gg \mathbb{P}[|y_i| = \gamma_2 \mid |y_i| \in \{\gamma_1, \gamma_2\} \subset I[r]]$$

So we search for values γ_1 so that $\mathbb{P}[|y_i| = \gamma_1 \mid |y_i| \in \{\gamma_1, \gamma_2\} \subset I[r]] = 1 - \alpha$ for small α, which also matches access patterns for the first restriction. Then, if we observe a matching access pattern, it is safe to assume the outcome of the sample is γ_1.

3. The last restriction is to only look at cache-access patterns, which reveal that $|y_i|$ is larger than $\beta \cdot \mathbb{E}[\langle \mathbf{s}, \mathbf{c} \rangle]$, for some constant $\beta \geq 1$, which is an easy calculation using the distributions of $\mathbf{s}, \mathbf{c}$. If we use this restriction in our attack targeted at coefficient y_i of $\mathbf{y}$, we learn the sign of $|y_i|$ by looking at the sign of coefficient z_i of $\mathbf{z}$, since:

$$\text{sign}(y_i) \neq \text{sign}(z_i) \leftrightarrow \langle \mathbf{s}, \mathbf{c} \rangle > (y_i + z_i)$$

So by requiring that $|y_i|$ must be larger than the expected value of $\langle \mathbf{s}, \mathbf{c} \rangle$, we expect to learn the sign of y_i. We therefore omit the absolute value sign in $|y_i|$ and simply write that we learn $y_i \in \{\gamma_1, \gamma_2\}$, where the γ's took over the sign of y_i (which is the same as the sign of z_i).

There is some flexibility in these restrictions, in choosing parameters α, β. Choosing these parameters too restrictively, might lead to no remaining cache-access patterns, choosing them too loosely makes other parts fail.

In the last part of the attack described next, we use LLL to calculate short vectors of a certain (random) lattice we create using BLISS signatures. We noticed that LLL works very well on these lattices, probably because the basis used is sparse. This implies that the vectors are already relatively short and orthogonal. The parameter α determines the shortness of the vector we look for, and therefore influences if an algorithm like LLL finds our vector. For the experiments described in Section 5, we required $\alpha \leq 0.1$. This made it possible for every parameter set we used in the experiments to always have at least one cache-access pattern to use.

Parameter β influences the probability that one makes a huge mistake when comparing the values of y_i and z_i. However, for the parameters we used in the experiments, we did not find recognizable cache-access patterns which correspond to small y_i. This means, we did not need to use this last restriction to reject certain cache-access patterns.

3.2. Exploitation. For simplicity, we assume we have one specific cache access pattern, which reveals if $y_i \in \{\gamma_1, \gamma_2\}$ for $i = 0, \ldots, n-1$ of polynomial $\mathbf{y}$, and if this is the case, y_i has probability $(1 - \alpha)$ to be value γ_1, with small α. In practice however, there might be more than one cache weakness, satisfying the above requirements. This would allow the attacker to search for more than one cache access pattern done by the victim. For the attack, we assume the victim is creating N signatures[1] $(\mathbf{z}_j, \mathbf{c}_j)$ for $j = 1, \ldots, N$, and an attacker is gathering these signatures with associated cache information for noise polynomial $\mathbf{y}_j$. We assume the attacker can search for the specific cache access pattern, for which he can determine if $y_{ji} \in \{\gamma_1, \gamma_2\}$. For the cases revealed by cache access patterns, the attacker ends up with the following equation:

$$z_{ji} = y_{ji} + (-1)^{b_j} \langle \mathbf{s}, \mathbf{c}_{ji} \rangle, \tag{2}$$

where the attacker knows coefficient z_{ji} of $\mathbf{z}_j$, rotated coefficient vectors $\mathbf{c}_{ji}$ of challenge $\mathbf{c}_j$ (both from the signatures) and $y_{ji} \in \{\gamma_1, \gamma_2\}$ of noise polynomial $\mathbf{y}_j$ (from the side-channel attack). Unknowns to the attacker are bit b_j and $\mathbf{s}$.

If $z_{ji} = \gamma_1$, the attacker knows that $\langle \mathbf{s}, \mathbf{c}_{ji} \rangle \in \{0, 1, -1\}$. Moreover, with high probability $(1 - \alpha)$ the value will be 0, as by the second restriction y_{ji} is biased to be value γ_1. So if $z_{ji} = \gamma_1$, the attacker adds $\xi_k = \mathbf{c}_{ji}$ to a list of *good* vectors. The restriction $z_{ji} = \gamma_1$ means that the attacker will in some cases not use the information in Eq. (2), although he knows that $y_{ji} \in \{\gamma_1, \gamma_2\}$.

When the attacker collects enough of these vectors $\xi_k = \mathbf{c}_{ji}$; $0 \leq i \leq n-1, 1 \leq j \leq N, 1 \leq k \leq n$, he can build a matrix $\mathbf{L} \in \{-1, 0, 1\}^{n \times n}$, whose columns are the ξ_k's. This matrix satisfies:

$$\mathbf{s}\mathbf{L} = \mathbf{v} \tag{3}$$

for some unknown but short vector $\mathbf{v}$. The attacker does not know $\mathbf{v}$, so he cannot simply solve for $\mathbf{s}$, but he does know that $\mathbf{v}$ has norm about $\sqrt{\alpha n}$, and lies in the lattice spanned by the rows of $\mathbf{L}$. He can use a lattice reduction algorithm, like LLL, on $\mathbf{L}$ to search for $\mathbf{v}$. LLL also outputs the unimodular matrix $\mathbf{U}$ satisfying $\mathbf{U}\mathbf{L} = \mathbf{L}'$. The attack tests for each row of $\mathbf{U}$ (and its rotations) whether it is

---

[1] Here $\mathbf{z}_j$ refers to the first signature polynomial $\mathbf{z}_{j1}$ of the jth signature $(\mathbf{z}_{j1}, \mathbf{z}_{j2}^\dagger, \mathbf{c}_j)$.

sparse and could be a candidate for $\mathbf{s} = \mathbf{f}$. As stated before, correctness of a secret key guess can be verified using the public key.

This last step does not always succeed, just with high probability. To make sure the attack succeeds, this process is randomized. Instead of collecting exactly n vectors $\xi_k = \mathbf{c}_{ji}$, we gather $m > n$ vectors, and pick a random subset of n vectors as input for LLL. While we do not have a formal analysis of the success probability, experiments (see Section 5) confirm that this method works and succeeds in finding the secret key (or its negative) in few rounds of randomization.

A summary of the attack is given in Algorithm 3.1.

Algorithm 3.1. Cache-attack on BLISS with CDT Sampling

Input: Access to cache memory of a victim with a key-pair $(\mathbf{A}, \mathbf{S})$. Input parameters n, σ, q, κ of BLISS. Access to signature polynomials $(\mathbf{z}_1, \mathbf{z}_2^\dagger, \mathbf{c})$ produced using $\mathbf{S}$. Victim uses CDT sampling with tables T, I for noise polynomials $\mathbf{y}$. Cache weakness that allows to determine if coefficient $y_i \in \{\gamma_1, \gamma_2\}$ of $\mathbf{y}$, and when this is the case, the value of y_i is biased towards γ_1

Output: Secret key $\mathbf{S}$

1: let $k = 0$ be the number of vectors collected so far and let $M = []$ be an empty list of vectors
2: **while** $(k < m)$:   // collect m vectors ξ_k before randomizing LLL
3:    collect signature $(\mathbf{z}_1, \mathbf{z}_2^\dagger, \mathbf{c})$, together with cache information for each coefficient y_i of noise polynomial $\mathbf{y}$
4:    **for each** $i = 0, \ldots, n - 1$:
5:       **if** $y_i \in \{\gamma_1, \gamma_2\}$ (determined via cache information) and $z_{1i} = \gamma_1$:
6:          add vector $\xi_k = \mathbf{c}_i$ to M and set $k = k + 1$
7: **while** (1):
8:    choose random subset of n vectors from M and construct matrix $\mathbf{L}$ whose columns are those vectors from M
9:    perform LLL basis reduction on $\mathbf{L}$ to get: $\mathbf{UL} = \mathbf{L}'$, where $\mathbf{U}$ is a unimodular transformation matrix and $\mathbf{L}'$ is LLL reduced
10:    **for each** $j = 1, \ldots, n$:
11:       check if row $\mathbf{u}_j$ of $\mathbf{U}$ has the same distribution as $\mathbf{f}$ and if $(\mathbf{a}_1/2) \cdot \mathbf{u}_j \bmod 2q$ has the same distribution as $2\mathbf{g} + 1$. Lastly verify if $\mathbf{a}_1 \cdot \mathbf{u}_j + \mathbf{a}_2 \cdot (\mathbf{a}_1/2) \cdot \mathbf{u}_j \equiv q \bmod 2q$
12:       **return** $\mathbf{S} = (\mathbf{u}_j, (\mathbf{a}_1/2) \cdot \mathbf{u}_j \bmod 2q)$ if this is the case

---

4 Attack 2: Bernoulli Sampling

In this section, we discuss the foundations and strategy of our second cache attack on the Bernoulli-based sampler (Algorithms 2.5, 2.6, and 2.7). We show how to exploit the fact that this method uses a small table ET, leaking very precise information about the sampled value.

4.1. Weaknesses in Cache. The Bernoulli-sampling algorithm described in Section 2.3 uses a table with exponential values $ET[i] = \exp(-2^i/(2\sigma^2))$ and inputs of bit-size $\ell = O(\log K)$, which means this table is quite small. Depending on bit i of input x, line 3 of Algorithm 2.7 is performed, requiring a table look-up for value $ET[i]$. In particular when input $x = 0$, no table look-up is required. An attacker can detect this event by examining cache activity of the sampling process. If this is the case, it means that the sampled value z equals 0 in Step 2 of Algorithm 2.5. The possible values for the result of sampling are $y \in \{0, \pm K, \pm 2K, \ldots\}$. So for some cache access patterns, the attacker is able to determine if $y \in \{0, \pm K, \pm 2K, \ldots\}$.

4.2. Exploitation. We will use the same methods as described in Section 3.2, but now we know that for a certain cache access pattern the coefficient $y_i \in \{0, \pm K, \pm 2K, \ldots\}$, $i = 0, \ldots, n-1$, of the noise polynomial $\mathbf{y}$. If $\max |\langle \mathbf{s}, \mathbf{c} \rangle| \leq \kappa < K$, (which is something anyone can check using the public parameters and which holds for typical implementations), we can determine y_i completely using the knowledge of signature vector $\mathbf{z}$. When more signatures[2] $(\mathbf{z}_j, \mathbf{c}_j); j = 1, \ldots, N$ are created, the attacker can search for the specific access pattern and verify whether $y_{ji} \in \{0, \pm K, \pm 2K, \ldots\}$, where y_{ji} is the i'th coefficient of noise polynomial $\mathbf{y}_j$.

If the attacker knows that $y_{ji} \in \{0, \pm K, \pm 2K, \ldots\}$ and it additionally holds that $z_{ji} = y_{ji}$, where z_{ji} is the i'th coefficient of signature polynomial $\mathbf{z}_j$, he knows that $\langle \mathbf{s}, \mathbf{c}_{ji} \rangle = 0$. If this is the case, the attacker includes coefficient vector $\zeta_k = \mathbf{c}_{ji}$ in the list of *good* vectors. Also for this attack the attacker will discard some known y_{ji} if it does not satisfy $z_{ji} = y_{ji}$.

Once the attacker has collected n of these vectors $\xi_k = \mathbf{c}_{ji}; 0 \leq i \leq n-1, 1 \leq j \leq N, 1 \leq k \leq n$, he can form a matrix $\mathbf{L} \in \{-1, 0, 1\}^{n \times n}$, whose columns are the ξ_k's, satisfying $\mathbf{sL} = 0$, where 0 is the all-zero vector. With very high probability, the ξ_k's have no dependency other than introduced by $\mathbf{s}$. This means $\mathbf{s}$ is the only kernel vector. Note the subtle difference with Eq. (3): we do not need to randomize the process, because we know the right-hand side is the all-zero vector. The attack procedure is summarized in Algorithm 4.1.

4.3. Possible Extensions. One might ask why we not always use the knowledge of y_{ji}, since we can completely determine its value, and work with a non-zero right-hand side. Unfortunately, bits b_j from Eq. 2 of the signatures are unknown. This means an attacker has to use a linear solver 2^N times, where N is the number of required signatures (grouping columns appropriately if they come from the same signature). For large N this becomes infeasible and N is typically on the scale of n. By requiring that $z_{ji} = y_{ji}$, we remove the unknown bit b_j from the Eq. (2).

---

[2] Again, $\mathbf{z}_j$ refers to the first signature polynomial $\mathbf{z}_{j1}$ of the jth signature $(\mathbf{z}_{j1}, \mathbf{z}_{j2}^\dagger, \mathbf{c}_j)$.

Algorithm 4.1. Cache-attack on BLISS with Bernoulli sampling

Input: Access to cache memory of victim with a key-pair $(\mathbf{A}, \mathbf{S})$. Input parameters n, σ, q, κ of BLISS, with $\kappa < K$. Access to signatures $(\mathbf{z}_1, \mathbf{z}_2^\dagger, \mathbf{c})$ produced using $\mathbf{S}$. Victim uses Bernoulli sampling with the small exponential table to sample noise polynomial $\mathbf{y}$.

Output: Secret key $\mathbf{S}$

1: let $k = 0$ be the number of vectors gained so far and let $M = []$ be an empty list of vectors

2: **while**$(k < n)$:

3:     collect signature $(\mathbf{z}_1, \mathbf{z}_2^\dagger, \mathbf{c})$ together with cache information for each coefficient y_i of noise polynomial $\mathbf{y}$

4:     **for each** $i = 1, \ldots, n$ do:

5:         **if** $y_i \in \{0, \pm K, \pm 2K, ..\}$ (according to cache information), and $z_{1i} = y_i$ **then** add coefficient vector $\xi_k = \mathbf{c}_i$ as a column to M and set $k = k + 1$

6: form a matrix $\mathbf{L}$ from the columns in M. Calculate kernel space of $\mathbf{L}$. This gives a matrix $\mathbf{U} \in \mathbf{Z}^{\ell \times n}$ such that $\mathbf{UL} = 0$, where 0 is the all-zero matrix

7: **for each** $j = 1, \ldots, \ell$ do: // we expect $\ell = 1$

8:     check if row $\mathbf{u}_j$ of $\mathbf{U}$ has the same distribution as $\mathbf{f}$ and if $(\mathbf{a}_1/2) \cdot \mathbf{u}_j \bmod 2q$ has the same distribution as $2\mathbf{g} + 1$. Lastly verify if $\mathbf{a}_1 \cdot \mathbf{u}_j + \mathbf{a}_2 \cdot (\mathbf{a}_1/2) \cdot \mathbf{u}_j \equiv q \bmod 2q$

9:     **return** $\mathbf{S} = (\mathbf{u}_j, (\mathbf{a}_1/2) \cdot \mathbf{u}_j \bmod 2q)$ if this is the case

10: remove a random entry from M, put $k = k - 1$, **goto** step 2

Similar to the first attack, an attacker might also use vectors $\xi_k = \mathbf{c}_{ji}$, where $\langle \mathbf{s}, \mathbf{c}_{ji} \rangle \in \{-1, 0, 1\}$, in combination with LLL and possibly randomization. This approach might help if fewer signatures are available, but the easiest way is to require exact knowledge, which comes at the expense of needing more signatures, but has a very fast and efficient offline part. Section 6.3 deals with this approximate information.

5   Results with a Perfect Side-Channel

In this section we provide experimental results, where we assume the attacker has access to a perfect side-channel: no errors are made in measuring the table accesses of the victim. We apply the attack strategies discussed in the previous two sections and show how many signatures are required for each strategy.

5.1. Attack Setting. Sections 3 and 4 outline the basic ideas behind cache attacks against the two sampling methods for noise polynomials $\mathbf{y}$ used in the target implementation of BLISS. We now consider the following idealized situation: the victim is signing random messages and an attacker collects these signatures. The attacker knows the exact cache-lines of the table look-ups done by the victim while computing the noise vector $\mathbf{y}$. We assume cache-lines have size 64 bytes and each element is 8 bytes large (type LONG). To simplify exposition, we assume the cache-lines are divided such that element i of any table is in cache-line $\lfloor i/8 \rfloor$.

Our test machine is an AMD FX-8350 Eight-Core CPU running at 4.1 GHz. We use the *research oriented* C++ implementation of BLISS, made available by the authors on their webpage [8]. Both of the analyzed sampling methods are provided by the implementation, where the tables T, I and ET are constructed dependent on σ. We use the NTL library [33] for LLL and kernel calculations.

The authors of BLISS [9] proposed several parameter sets for the signature scheme (see full version [4, Table A.1]). We present attacks against all combinations of parameter sets and sampling methods; the full results of the perfect side-channel attacks are given in the full version [4, Appendix B].

5.2. CDT Sampling.

When the signing algorithm uses CDT sampling as described in Algorithm 2.4, the perfect side-channel provides the values of $\lfloor r/8 \rfloor$ and $\lfloor I_z/8 \rfloor$ of the table accesses for r and I_z in tables I and T. We apply the attack strategy of Section 3.

We first need to find cache-line patterns, of type intersection or last-jump, which reveal that $|y_i| \in \{\gamma_1, \gamma_2\}$ and $\mathbb{P}[|y_i| = \gamma_1 \mid |y_i| \in \{\gamma_1, \gamma_2\}] = 1 - \alpha$ with $\alpha \leq 0.1$. One way to do that is to construct two tables: one table that lists elements $I[r]$, that belong to certain cache-lines of table I, and one table that lists the accessed elements I_z inside these intervals $I[r]$, that belong to certain cache-lines of table T. We can then brute-force search for all cache weaknesses of type intersection or last-jump. For example, in BLISS-I the first eight elements of I (meaning $I[0], \dots, I[7]$) belong to the first cache-line of I, but for the elements in $I[7] = \{7, 8\}$, the sampler accesses element $I_z = 8$, which is part of the second cache-line of T. This is an intersection weakness: if the first cache-line of I is accessed and the second cache-line of T is accessed, we know $y_i \in \{7, 8\}$. Similarly, one can find last-jump weaknesses, by searching for intervals $I[r]$ that access multiple cache-lines of T. Once we have these weaknesses, we need to use the biased restriction with $\alpha \leq 0.1$. This can be done by looking at all bytes except the first of the entry $T[I_z]$ (this is already used to determine interval $I[r]$). If we denote the integer value of these 7 bytes by $T[I_z]_{\text{byte} \neq 1}$, then we need to check if $T[I_z]$ has property

$$(T[I_z])_{\text{byte} \neq 1} / (2^{56} - 1) \leq \alpha$$

(or $(T[I_z])_{\text{byte} \neq 1} / (2^{56} - 1) \geq (1 - \alpha)$). If one of these properties holds, then we have $y_i \in \{I_z - 1, I_z\}$ and $\mathbb{P}[|y_i| = I_z \mid |y_i| \in \{I_z - 1, I_z\}] = 1 - \alpha$ (or with I_z and $I_z - 1$ swapped). For each set of parameters we found at least one of these weaknesses using the above method (see the full version [4, Table B.1] for the values).

We collect m (possibly rotated) coefficient vectors $\mathbf{c}_j$ and then run LLL at most $t = 2(m - n) + 1$ times, each time searching for $\mathbf{s}$ in the unimodular transformation matrix using the public key. We consider the experiment failed if the secret key is not found after this number of trials; the randomly constructed lattices have a lot of overlap in their basis vectors which means that increasing t further is not likely to help. We performed 1000 repetitions of each experiment (different parameters and sizes for m) and measured the success probability p_{succ}, the average number of required signatures $\overline{N}$ to retrieve m usable challenges, and the average length of $\mathbf{v}$ if it was found. The expected number of required signatures $\mathbb{E}[N]$ is also given, as well as the running time for the LLL trials. This expected number of required signatures can be computed as:

$$\mathbb{E}[N] = \frac{m}{n \cdot \mathbb{P}[\mathrm{CP}] \cdot \mathbb{P}[\langle \mathbf{s}_1, \mathbf{c}\rangle = 0]},$$

where CP is the event of a usable cache-access pattern for a coordinate of $\mathbf{y}$.

From the results (given in the full version [4, Table B.2]) we see that, although BLISS-0 is a toy example (with security level $\lambda \leq 60$), it requires the largest average number $\overline{N}$ of signatures to collect m columns, i.e., before the LLL trials can begin. This illustrates that the cache-attack depends less on the dimension n, but mainly on σ. For BLISS-0 with $\sigma = 100$, there is only one usable cache weakness with the restrictions we made.

For all cases, we see that a small increase of m greatly increases the success probability p_{succ}. The experimental results suggest that picking $m \approx 2n$ suffices to get a success probability close to 1.0. This means that one only needs more signatures to always succeed in the offline part.

5.3. Bernoulli Sampling. When the signature algorithm uses Bernoulli sampling from Algorithm 2.6, a perfect side-channel determines if there has been a table access in table ET. Thus, we can apply the attack strategy given in Section 4. We require $m = n$ (possibly rotated) challenges $\mathbf{c}_i$ to start the kernel calculation. We learn whether any element has been accessed in table ET, e.g., by checking the cache-lines belonging to the small part of the table. We performed only 100 experiments this time, since we noticed that $p_{\mathrm{succ}} = 1.0$ for all parameter sets with a perfect side-channel. This means that the probability that n random challenges $\mathbf{c}$ are linearly independent is close to 1.0. We state the average number $\overline{N}$ of required signatures in the full version [4, Table B.3]. This time, the expected number is simply:

$$\mathbb{E}[N] = \left(\left(\frac{1}{\rho_\sigma(\mathbb{Z})} \sum_{x=-\lfloor \tau\sigma/K \rfloor}^{\lfloor \tau\sigma/K \rfloor} \rho_\sigma(xK) \right) \cdot \mathbb{P}[\langle \mathbf{s}_1, \mathbf{c}\rangle = 0] \right)^{-1}$$

for $K = \lfloor \frac{\sigma}{\sigma_2} + 1 \rfloor$ and tail-cut $\tau \geq 1$. Note that the number of required signatures is smaller for BLISS-II than for BLISS-I. This might seem surprising as one might expect it to increase or be about the same as BLISS-I because the dimensions and security level are the same for these two parameter sets. However, σ is chosen a lot smaller in BLISS-II, which means that also value K is smaller. This influences $\overline{N}$ significantly as the probability to sample values xK is larger for small σ.

6   Proof-of-Concept Implementation

So far, the experimental results were based on the assumption of a perfect side-channel: we assumed that we would get the cache-line of every table look-up in the CDT sampling and Bernoulli sampling. In this section, we reduce the assumption and discuss the results of more realistic experiments using the FLUSH+RELOAD technique.

When moving to real hardware some of the assumptions made in Section 5 no longer hold. In particular, allocation does not always ensure that tables are aligned at the start of cache lines and processor optimizations may pre-load memory into the cache, resulting in false positives. One such optimization is the *spatial prefetcher*, which pairs adjacent cache lines into 128-byte chunks and prefetches a cache line if an access to its pair results in a cache miss [16].

6.1. FLUSH+RELOAD on CDT Sampling. Due to the spatial prefetcher, FLUSH+RELOAD cannot be used consistently to probe two paired cache lines. Consequently, to determine access to two consecutive CDT table elements, we must use a pair that spans two unpaired cache lines. In the full version [4, Table C.3], we show that when the CDT table is aligned at 16 bytes, we can always find such a pair for BLISS-I. Although this is not a proof that our attack works in all scenarios, i.e. for all σ and all offsets, it would also not be a solid defence to pick exactly those scenarios for which our attack would not work, e.g., because α could be increased.

The attack was carried out on an HP Elite 8300 with an i5-3470 processor. running CentOS 6.6. Before sampling each coordinate y_i, for $i = 0, \ldots, n - 1$, we flush the monitored cache lines using the `clflush` instruction. After sampling the coordinate, we reload the monitored cache lines and measure the response time. We compare the response times to a pre-defined threshold value to determine whether the cache lines were accessed by the sampling algorithm.

A visualization of the FLUSH+RELOAD measurements for CDT sampling is given in Fig. 6.1. Using the intersection and last-jump weakness of the CDT sampler in cache-memory, we can determine which value is sampled by the victim by probing two locations in memory. To reduce the number of false positives, we focus on one of the weaknesses (given in the full version [4, Table B.1]) as a target for the FLUSH+RELOAD. This means that the other weaknesses are not detected and we need to observe more signatures than with a perfect side-channel, before we collect enough columns to start with the offline part of the attack.

We executed 50 repeated attacks against BLISS-I, probing the last-jump weakness for $\{\gamma_1, \gamma_2\} = \{55, 56\}$. We completely recovered the private key in 46 out of the 50 cases. On average we require 3438 signatures for the attack, to collect $m = 2n = 1024$ equations. We tried LLL five times after the collection and considered the experiment a failure if we did not find the secret key in these five times. We stress that this is not the optimal strategy to minimize the number of required signatures or to maximize the success probability. However, it is an indication that this proof-of-concept attack is feasible.

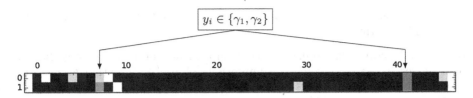

Fig. 6.1. Visualization of FLUSH+RELOAD measurements of table look-ups for BLISS-I using CDT sampling with guide table I. Two locations in memory are probed, denoted in the vertical axis by $0, 1$, and they represent two adjacent cache-lines. For interval $I[51] = [54, 57]$, there is a last-jump weakness for $\{\gamma_1, \gamma_2\} = \{55, 56\}$, where the outcome of $|y_i|$ is biased towards $\gamma_1 = 55$ with $\alpha = 0.0246$. For each coordinate (the horizontal axis), we get a response time for each location we probe: dark regions denote a long response time, while lighter regions denote a short response time. When both of the probed locations give a fast response, it means the victim accessed both cache-lines for sampling y_i. In this case the attacker knows that $|y_i| \in \{55, 56\}$; here for $i = 8$ and $i = 41$.

6.2. Other Processors. We also experimented with a newer processor (Intel core i7-5650U) and found that this processor has a more aggressive prefetcher. In particular, memory locations near the start and the end of the page are more likely to be prefetched. Consequently, the alignment of the tables within the page can affect the attack success rate. We find that in a third of the locations within a page the attack fails, whereas in the other two thirds it succeeds with probabilities similar to those on the older processor. We note that, as demonstrated in the full version [4, Table B.1], there are often multiple weaknesses in the CDT. While some weaknesses may fall in unexploitable memory locations, others may still be exploitable.

6.3. FLUSH+RELOAD on Bernoulli Sampling. For attacking BLISS using Bernoulli sampling, we need to measure if table ET has been accessed at all. Due to the spatial prefetcher we are unable to probe all of the cache lines of ET. Instead, we flush all cache lines containing ET before sampling and reload only even cache lines after the sampling. Flushing even cache lines is required for the FLUSH+RELOAD attack. We flush the odd cache lines to trigger the spatial prefetcher, which will prefetch the paired even cache lines when the sampling accesses an odd cache line. Thus, flushing all of the cache lines gives us a complete coverage of the table even though we only reload half of the cache lines.

Since we do not get error-free side-channel information, we are likely to collect some c with $\langle s, c_i \rangle \neq 0$ as columns in $\mathbf{L}$. Instead of computing the kernel (as in the idealized setting) we used LLL (as in CDT) to handle small errors and we gathered more than n columns and randomized the selection of $\mathbf{L}$.

We tested the attack on a MacBook air with the newer processor (Intel core i7-5650U) running Mac OS X El Capitan. We executed 50 repeated attacks against BLISS-I, probing three out of the six cache lines that cover the ET table. We completely recovered the private key in 44 of these samples. On average we required 3294 signatures for the attack to collect $m = n + 100 = 612$ equations.

The experiment is considered a failure if we did not find the secret key after trying LLL five times.

6.4. Conclusion. Our proof-of-concept implementation demonstrates that in many cases we can overcome the limitations of processor optimizations and perform the attack on BLISS. The attack, however, requires a high degree of synchronization between the attacker and the victim, which we achieve by modifying the victim code. For a similar level of synchronization in a real attack scenario, the attacker will have to be able to find out when each coordinate is sampled. One possible approach for achieving this is to use the attack of Gullasch et al. [13] against the Linux Completely Fair Scheduler. The combination of a cache attack with the attack on the scheduler allows the attacker to monitor each and every table access made by the victim, which is more than required for our attacks.

7   Discussion of Candidate Countermeasures

In this paper we presented cache attacks on two different discrete Gaussian samplers. In the following we discuss some candidate countermeasures against our specific attacks but note that other attacks might still be possible. A standard countermeasure against cache-attacks are constant-time accesses.

Constant-time table accesses, meaning accessing *every element of the table for every coordinate* of the noise vector, were also discussed (and implemented) by Bos et al. [3] for key exchange. This increased the number of table accesses by about two orders of magnitude. However, in the case of signatures the tables are much larger than for key exchange: a much larger standard deviation for the discrete Gaussian distribution is required. For 128 bits of security, a standard deviation $\sigma = 8/\sqrt{2\pi} \approx 3.19$ suffices for key exchange, resulting in a table size of 52 entries. In contrast, BLISS-I uses a standard deviation of $\sigma = 215$, resulting in a table size of 2580 entries. It therefore seems that this countermeasure induces significant overhead for signatures: at least as much as for the key exchange. It might be the case that constant-time accesses to a certain part of the table is already sufficient as a countermeasure against our attack, but it is unclear how to do this precisely. One might think that constant-time accesses to table I in the CDT sampler is already sufficient as a countermeasure. In this case, the overhead is somewhat smaller, since I contains 256 entries. However, the last-jump weakness only uses the knowledge of accesses in the T table, which is still accessible in that case.

In the case of the Bernoulli-based sampler, doing constant-time table accesses does not induce that much overhead: the size of table ET is about $\ell \approx 2 \log K$. This means swapping line 2 and 3 of Algorithm 2.7 might prevent our attack as all elements of ET are always accessed. Note that removing line 4 of Algorithm 2.7 (and returning 0 or 1 at the end of the loop) does not help as a countermeasure. It does make the sampler constant-time, but we do not exploit that property. We exploit the fact that table accesses occur, depending on the input.

A concurrent work by Saarinen [32] discusses another candidate countermeasure: the VectorBlindSample procedure. The VectorBlindSample procedure basically samples m vectors of discrete Gaussian values with a smaller standard deviation, shuffles them in between, and adds the results. The problem of directly applying our attack is that we need side-channel information of all summands for a coefficient. The chances for this are quite small. However, it does neither mean that other attacks are not possible nor that it is impossible to adapt our attack.

Acknowledgements. The authors would like to thank Daniel J. Bernstein and Léo Ducas for fruitful discussions and suggestions.

References

1. Alkim, E., Ducas, L., Pöppelmann, T., Schwabe, P.: Post-quantum key exchange - a new hope. IACR Cryptology ePrint Archive 2015/1092 (2015)
2. Bernstein, D.J.: Cache-timing attacks on AES (2005). Preprint available at http://cr.yp.to/antiforgery/cachetiming-20050414.pdf
3. Bos, J.W., Costello, C., Naehrig, M., Stebila, D.: Post-quantum key exchange for the TLS protocol from the ring learning with errors problem. In: S&P 2015, pp. 553–570. IEEE Computer Society (2015)
4. Groot Bruinderink, L., Hülsing, A., Lange, T., Yarom, Y.: Flush, Gauss, and reload - a cache attack on the BLISS lattice-based signature scheme. IACR Cryptology ePrint Archive 2016/300 (2016)
5. Buchmann, J., Cabarcas, D., Göpfert, F., Hülsing, A., Weiden, P.: Discrete Ziggurat: a time-memory trade-off for sampling from a Gaussian distribution over the integers. In: Lange, T., Lauter, K., Lisoněk, P. (eds.) SAC 2013. LNCS, vol. 8282, pp. 402–418. Springer, Heidelberg (2014)
6. Chen, H.-C., Asau, Y.: On generating random variates from an empirical distribution. AIIE Trans. **6**(2), 163–166 (1974)
7. Chen, L., Liu, Y.-K., Jordan, S., Moody, D., Peralta, R., Perlner, R., Smith-Tone, D.: Report on post-quantum cryptography. NISTIR 8105, Draft, February 2016
8. Ducas, L., Durmus, A., Lepoint, T., Lyubashevsky, V.: BLISS: Bimodal Lattice Signature Schemes (2013). http://bliss.di.ens.fr/
9. Ducas, L., Durmus, A., Lepoint, T., Lyubashevsky, V.: Lattice signatures and bimodal Gaussians. In: Canetti, R., Garay, J.A. (eds.) CRYPTO 2013, Part I. LNCS, vol. 8042, pp. 40–56. Springer, Heidelberg (2013)
10. Dwarakanath, N.C., Galbraith, S.D.: Sampling from discrete Gaussians for lattice-based cryptography on a constrained device. Appl. Algebra Eng. Commun. Comput. **25**(3), 159–180 (2014)
11. Gentry, C., Peikert, C., Vaikuntanathan, V.: Trapdoors for hard lattices and new cryptographic constructions. In: Dwork, C. (ed.) STOC 2008, pp. 197–206. ACM (2008)
12. Gruss, D., Spreitzer, R., Mangard, S.: Cache template attacks: Automating attacks on inclusive last-level caches. In: Jung, J., Holz, T. (eds.) USENIX Security 2015, pp. 897–912. USENIX Association (2015)
13. Gullasch, D., Bangerter, E., Krenn, S.: Cache games – bringing access-based cache attacks on AES to practice. In: S&P 2011, pp. 490–505. IEEE Computer Society (2011)

14. Güneysu, T., Lyubashevsky, V., Pöppelmann, T.: Practical lattice-based cryptography: a signature scheme for embedded systems. In: Prouff, E., Schaumont, P. (eds.) CHES 2012. LNCS, vol. 7428, pp. 530–547. Springer, Heidelberg (2012)
15. Hoffstein, J., Pipher, J., Silverman, J.H.: NTRU: a ring-based public key cryptosystem. In: Buhler, J.P. (ed.) ANTS 1998. LNCS, vol. 1423, pp. 267–288. Springer, Heidelberg (1998)
16. Intel Corporation. Intel 64 and IA-32 Architectures Optimization Reference Manual, April 2012
17. Irazoqui, G., Inci, M.S., Eisenbarth, T., Sunar, B.: Wait a minute! A fast, cross-VM attack on AES. In: Stavrou, A., Bos, H., Portokalidis, G. (eds.) RAID 2014. LNCS, vol. 8688, pp. 299–319. Springer, Heidelberg (2014)
18. ETSI Quantum-Safe Cryptography (QSC) ISG. Quantum-safe cryptography. ETSI working group (2015). http://www.etsi.org/technologies-clusters/technologies/quantum-safe-cryptography
19. L'Ecuyer, P.: Non-uniform random variate generations. In: Lovric, M. (ed.) International Encyclopedia of Statistical Science, pp. 991–995. Springer, Heidelberg (2011)
20. Lenstra, A.K., Lenstra, H.W., Lovász, L.: Factoring polynomials with rational coefficients. Math. Ann. 261(4), 515–534 (1982)
21. Lindner, R., Peikert, C.: Better key sizes (and attacks) for LWE-based encryption. In: Kiayias, A. (ed.) CT-RSA 2011. LNCS, vol. 6558, pp. 319–339. Springer, Heidelberg (2011)
22. Liu, F., Yarom, Y., Ge, Q., Heiser, G., Lee, R.B.: Last-level cache side-channel attacks are practical. In: S&P 2015, pp. 605–622. IEEE Computer Society (2015)
23. NSA. NSA Suite B Cryptography. NSA website (2015). https://www.nsa.gov/ia/programs/suiteb_cryptography/
24. Osvik, D.A., Shamir, A., Tromer, E.: Cache attacks and countermeasures: the case of AES. In: Pointcheval, D. (ed.) CT-RSA 2006. LNCS, vol. 3860, pp. 1–20. Springer, Heidelberg (2006)
25. Peikert, C.: An efficient and parallel Gaussian sampler for lattices. In: Rabin, T. (ed.) CRYPTO 2010. LNCS, vol. 6223, pp. 80–97. Springer, Heidelberg (2010)
26. Peikert, C.: Lattice cryptography for the internet. In: Mosca, M. (ed.) PQCrypto 2014. LNCS, vol. 8772, pp. 197–219. Springer, Heidelberg (2014)
27. Percival, C.: Cache missing for fun and profit. In: BSDCan 2005 (2005)
28. van de Pol, J., Smart, N.P., Yarom, Y.: Just a little bit more. In: Nyberg, K. (ed.) CT-RSA 2015. LNCS, vol. 9048, pp. 3–21. Springer, Heidelberg (2015)
29. Pöppelmann, T., Ducas, L., Güneysu, T.: Enhanced lattice-based signatures on reconfigurable hardware. In: Batina, L., Robshaw, M. (eds.) CHES 2014. LNCS, vol. 8731, pp. 353–370. Springer, Heidelberg (2014)
30. Pöppelmann, T., Güneysu, T.: Towards practical lattice-based public-key encryption on reconfigurable hardware. In: Lange, T., Lauter, K., Lisoněk, P. (eds.) SAC 2013. LNCS, vol. 8282, pp. 68–86. Springer, Heidelberg (2014)
31. Roy, S.S., Vercauteren, F., Verbauwhede, I.: High precision discrete Gaussian sampling on FPGAs. In: Lange, T., Lauter, K., Lisoněk, P. (eds.) SAC 2013. LNCS, vol. 8282, pp. 383–401. Springer, Heidelberg (2014)
32. Saarinen, M.-J.O.: Arithmetic coding and blinding countermeasures for ring-LWE. IACR Cryptology ePrint Archive 2016/276 (2016)
33. Shoup, V.: NTL: a library for doing number theory (2015). http://www.shoup.net/ntl/
34. strongSwan. strongSwan 5.2.2 released, January 2015. https://www.strongswan.org/blog/2015/01/05/strongswan-5.2.2-released.html

35. Yarom, Y., Benger, N.: Recovering OpenSSL ECDSA nonces using the FLUSH+ RELOAD cache side-channel attack. IACR Cryptology ePrint Archive 2014/140 (2014)

36. Yarom, Y., Falkner, K.: FLUSH+RELOAD: a high resolution, low noise, L3 cache side-channel attack. In: Fu, K., Jung, J. (eds.) USENIX Security 2014, pp. 719–732. USENIX Association (2014)

37. Zhang, J., Zhang, Z., Ding, J., Snook, M., Dagdelen, Ö.: Authenticated key exchange from ideal lattices. In: Oswald, E., Fischlin, M. (eds.) EUROCRYPT 2015. LNCS, vol. 9057, pp. 719–751. Springer, Heidelberg (2015)

38. Zhang, Y., Juels, A., Reiter, M.K., Ristenpart, T.: Cross-tenant side-channel attacks in PaaS clouds. In: CCS 2014, pp. 990–1003. ACM (2014)

CacheBleed: A Timing Attack on OpenSSL Constant Time RSA

Yuval Yarom[1](✉), Daniel Genkin[2], and Nadia Heninger[3]

[1] The University of Adelaide and NICTA, Adelaide, Australia
yval@cs.adelaide.edu.au
[2] Technion and Tel Aviv University, Tel Aviv, Israel
danielg3@cs.technion.ac.il
[3] University of Pennsylvania, Philadelphia, USA
nadiah@cis.upenn.edu

Abstract. The scatter-gather technique is a commonly implemented approach to prevent cache-based timing attacks. In this paper we show that scatter-gather is not constant time. We implement a cache timing attack against the scatter-gather implementation used in the modular exponentiation routine in OpenSSL version 1.0.2f. Our attack exploits cache-bank conflicts on the Sandy Bridge microarchitecture. We have tested the attack on an Intel Xeon E5-2430 processor. For 4096-bit RSA our attack can fully recover the private key after observing 16,000 decryptions.

Keywords: Side-channel attacks · Cache attacks · Cryptographic implementations · Constant-time · RSA

1 Introduction

1.1 Overview

Side-channel attacks are a powerful method for breaking theoretically secure cryptographic primitives. Since the first works by Kocher [33], these attacks have been used extensively to break the security of numerous cryptographic implementations. At a high level, it is possible to distinguish between two types of side-channel attacks, based on the methods used by the attacker: hardware-based attacks, which monitor the leakage through measurements (usually using dedicated lab equipment) of physical phenomena such as electromagnetic radiation [43], power consumption [31,32], or acoustic emanation [22], and software-based attacks, which do not require additional equipment but rely instead on the attacker software running on or interacting with the target machine. Examples of the latter include timing attacks which measure timing variations of cryptographic operations [7,16,17] and cache attacks which observe cache access patterns [40,41,49].

Percival [41] published in 2005 a *cache attack*, which targeted the OpenSSL [39] 0.9.7c implementation of RSA. In this attack, the attacker and the victim programs are colocated on the same machine and processor, and thus share the

© International Association for Cryptologic Research 2016
B. Gierlichs and A.Y. Poschmann (Eds.): CHES 2016, LNCS 9813, pp. 346–367, 2016.
DOI: 10.1007/978-3-662-53140-2_17

same processor cache. The attack exploits the structure of the processor cache by observing minute timing variations due to cache contention. The cache consists of fixed-size *cache lines*. When a program accesses a memory address, the cache-line-sized block of memory that contains this address is stored in the cache and is available for future use. The attack traces the changes that the victim program execution makes in the cache and, from this trace, the attacker is able to recover the private key used for the decryption.

In order to implement the modular exponentiation routine required for performing RSA public and secret key operations, OpenSSL 0.9.7c uses a sliding-window exponentiation algorithm [11]. This algorithm precomputes some values, called *multipliers*, which are used throughout the exponentiation. The access pattern to these precomputed multipliers depends on the exponent, which, in the case of decryption and digital signature operations, should be kept secret. Because each multiplier occupies a different set of cache lines, Percival [41] was able to identify the accessed multipliers and from that recover the private key. To mitigate this attack, Intel implemented a countermeasure that changes the memory layout of the precomputed multipliers. The countermeasure, often called *scatter-gather*, interleaves the multipliers in memory to ensure that the same cache lines are accessed irrespective of the multiplier used [14]. While this countermeasure ensures that the same cache lines are always accessed, the offsets of the accessed addresses within these cache lines depend on the multiplier used and, ultimately, on the private key.

Both Bernstein [7] and Osvik et al. [40] have warned that accesses to different offsets within cache lines may leak information through timing variations due to cache-bank conflicts. To facilitate concurrent access to the cache, the cache is often divided into multiple *cache banks*. Concurrent accesses to different cache banks can always be handled, however each cache bank can only handle a limited number of concurrent requests—often a single request at a time. A *cache-bank conflict* occurs when too many requests are made concurrently to the same cache bank. In the case of a conflict, some of the conflicting requests are delayed. While timing variations due to cache-bank conflicts are documented in the Intel Optimization Manual [28], no attack exploiting these has ever been published. In the absence of a demonstrated risk, Intel continued to contribute code that uses scatter-gather to OpenSSL [23,24] and to recommend the use of the technique for side-channel mitigation [12,13]. Consequently, the technique is in widespread use in the current versions of OpenSSL and its forks, such as LibreSSL [35] and BoringSSL [10]. It is also used in other cryptographic libraries, such as the Mozilla Network Security Services (NSS) [38].

1.2 Our Contribution

In this work we present CacheBleed, the first side-channel attack to systematically exploit cache-bank conflicts. In Sect. 3 we describe how CacheBleed creates contention on a cache bank and measures the timing variations due to conflicts and in Sect. 4 we use CacheBleed in order to attack the scatter-gather implementation of OpenSSL's modular exponentiation routine. After observing 16,000

RSA decryptions or signing operations, we are able to recover 60 % of the secret exponent bits. To find the remaining bits we adapt the Heninger-Shacham algorithm [25] for the information we collect with CacheBleed. In order to achieve full key extraction, our attack requires about two CPU hours. Parallelizing across multiple CPUs, we achieved key extraction in only a few minutes. See Sect. 5 for a more complete discussion.

1.3   Targeted Software and Hardware

Software. In this paper we target the modular exponentiation operation as implemented in OpenSSL version 1.0.2f which was the latest version of OpenSSL prior to our disclosure to OpenSSL. As mentioned above, similar (and thus potentially vulnerable) code can be found in several forks of OpenSSL such as LibreSSL [35] and BoringSSL [10]. Other cryptographic libraries, such as the Mozilla Network Security Services (NSS) [38] use similar techniques and may be vulnerable as well.

Hardware. Our attacks exploit cache-bank conflicts present in Intel Sandy Bridge Processor family. We ran our experiments on an Intel Xeon E5-2430 processor which is a six-core Sandy Bridge machine with a 2.20 GHZ clock. Our target machine is running CentOS 6.7 installed with its default parameters and with huge pages enabled.

Disclosure and Mitigation. We have reported our results to the developers of OpenSSL, LibreSSL, NSS, and BoringSSL. We worked with the OpenSSL developers to evaluate and deploy countermeasures to prevent the attacks described in this paper (CVE-2016-0702). These countermeasures were subsequently incorporated into OpenSSL 1.0.2g and BoringSSL. The LibreSSL development team notified us that they are still working on a patch. The current version (2.4.0) appears to remain vulnerable. For NSS, our attack was documented under Mozilla bug 1252035. The bug documentation indicates that the fix is scheduled to be included in version 3.24.

2   Background

2.1   OpenSSL's RSA Implementation

RSA [44] is a public-key cryptosystem which supports both encryption and digital signatures. To generate an RSA key pair, the user generates two prime numbers p, q and computes $N = pq$. Next, given a public exponent e (OpenSSL uses $e = 65537$), the user computes the secret exponent $d \equiv e^{-1} \bmod \phi(N)$. The public key is the integers e and N and the secret key is d and N. In textbook RSA encryption, a message m is encrypted by computing $m^e \bmod N$ and a ciphertext c is decrypted by computing $c^d \bmod N$.

Algorithm 1. Fixed-window exponentiation

---

input : window size w, base a, modulus k, n-bit exponent $b = \sum_{i=0}^{\lceil n/w \rceil} 2^{wi} \cdot b_i$
output: $a^b \bmod k$

// Precomputation
$a_0 \leftarrow 1$
for $j = 1, \ldots, 2^w - 1$ **do**
$\quad | \quad a_j \leftarrow a_{j-1} \cdot a \bmod k$
end

// Exponentiation
$r \leftarrow 1$
for $i = \lceil n/w \rceil - 1, \ldots, 0$ **do**
$\quad$ **for** $j = 1, \ldots, w$ **do**
$\quad \quad | \quad r \leftarrow r^2 \bmod k$
$\quad$ **end**
$\quad r \leftarrow r \cdot a_{b_i} \bmod k$
end
return r

RSA-CRT. RSA decryption is often implemented using the Chinese remainder theorem (CRT), which provides a speedup over exponentiation mod n. Instead of computing $c^d \bmod n$ directly, RSA-CRT splits the secret key d into two parts $d_p = d \bmod (p-1)$ and $d_q = d \bmod (q-1)$, and then computes two parts of the message as $m_p = c^{d_p} \bmod p$ and $m_q = c^{d_q} \bmod q$. The message m can then be recovered from m_p and m_q using Garner's formula [21]:

$$h = (m_p - m_q)(q^{-1} \bmod p) \bmod p \quad \text{and} \quad m = m_q + hq.$$

The main operation performed during RSA decryption is the modular exponentiation, that is, calculating $a^b \bmod k$ for some secret exponent b. Several algorithms for modular exponentiation have been suggested. In this work we are interested in the two algorithms that OpenSSL has used.

Fixed-Window Exponentiation. In the *fixed-window exponentiation* algorithm, also known as *m-ary exponentiation*, the n-bit exponent b is represented as an $\lceil n/w \rceil$ digit integer in base 2^w for some chosen *window size* w. That is, b is rewritten as $b = \sum_{i=0}^{\lceil n/w \rceil - 1} 2^{wi} \cdot b_i$ where $0 \leq b_i < 2^w$. The pseudocode in Algorithm 1 demonstrates the fixed-window exponentiation algorithm. In the first step, the algorithm precomputes a set of *multipliers* $a_j = a^j \bmod k$ for $0 \leq j < 2^w$. It then scans the base 2^w representation of b from the most significant digit ($b_{\lceil n/w \rceil - 1}$) to the least significant (b_0). For each digit b_i it squares an intermediate result w times and then multiplies the intermediate result by a_{b_i}. Each of the square or multiply operations is followed by a modular reduction.

Sliding-Window Exponentiation. The *sliding-window algorithm* represents the exponent b as a sequence of digits b_i such that $b = \sum_{i=0}^{n-1} 2^i \cdot b_i$, with b_i

being either 0 or an odd number $0 < b_i < 2^w$. The algorithm first precomputes $a_1, a_3, \ldots a_{2^w-1}$ as in the fixed-window case. It then scans the exponent from the most significant to the least significant digit. For each digit, the algorithm squares the intermediate result. For non-zero digit b_i, it also multiplies the intermediate result by a_{b_i}.

The main advantages of the sliding-window algorithm over the fixed-window algorithm are that, for the same window size, sliding window needs to precompute half the number of multipliers, and that fewer multiplications are required during the exponentiation. The sliding-window algorithm, however, leaks the position of the non-zero multipliers to adversaries who can distinguish between squaring and multiplication operations. Furthermore, the number of squaring operations between consecutive multipliers may leak the values of some zero bits. Up to version 0.9.7c, OpenSSL used sliding-window exponentiation. As part of the mitigation of the Percival [41] cache attack, which exploits these leaks, OpenSSL changed their implementation to use the fixed-window exponentiation algorithm.

Since both algorithms precompute a set of multipliers and access them throughout the exponentiation, a side-channel attack that can discover which multiplier is used in the multiplication operations can recover the digits b_i and from them obtain the secret exponent b.

2.2   The Intel Cache Hierarchy

We now turn our attention to the cache hierarchy in modern Intel processors. The cache is a small, fast memory that exploits the temporal and spatial locality of memory accesses to bridge the speed gap between the faster CPU and slower memory. In the processors we are interested in, the cache hierarchy consists of three levels of caching. The top level, known as the *L1 cache*, is the closest to the execution core and is the smallest and the fastest cache. Each successive cache level is larger and slower than the preceding one, with the *last-level cache* (LLC) being the largest and slowest.

Cache Structure. The cache stores fixed-sized chunks of memory called *cache lines*. Each cache line holds 64 bytes of data that come from a 64-byte aligned *block* in memory. The cache is organized as multiple *cache sets*, each consisting of a fixed number of *ways*. A block of memory can be stored in any of the ways of a single cache set. For the higher cache levels, the mapping of memory blocks to cache sets is done by selecting a range of address bits. For the LLC, Intel uses an undisclosed hash function to map memory blocks to cache sets [30,37,50]. The L1 cache is divided into two sub caches: the *L1 data cache* (L1-D) which caches the data the program accesses, and the *L1 instruction cache* (L1-I) which caches the code the program executes. In multi-core processors, each of the cores has a dedicated L1 cache. However, multithreaded cores share the L1 cache between the two threads.

Cache Sizes. In the Intel Sandy Bridge microarchitecture, each of the L1-D and L1-I caches has 64 sets and 8 ways to a total capacity of $64 \cdot 8 \cdot 64 = 32,768$ bytes. The L2 cache has 512 sets and 8 ways, with a size of 256 KiB. The L2 cache is *unified*, storing both data and instructions. Like the L1 cache, each core has a dedicated L2 cache. The L3 cache, or the LLC, is shared by all of the cores of the processor. It has 2,048 sets *per core*, i.e. the LLC of a four core processor has 8,192 cache sets. The number of ways varies between processor models and ranges between 12 and 20. Hence the size of the LLC of a small dual core processor is 3 MiB, whereas the LLC of an 8-cores processor can be in the order of 20 MiB. The Intel Xeon E5-2430 processor we used for our experiments is a 6-core processor with a 20-way LLC of size 15 MiB. More recent microarchitectures support more cores and more ways, yielding significantly larger LLCs.

Cache Lookup Policy. When the processor attempts to access data in memory, it first looks for the data in the L1 cache. In a *cache hit*, the data is found in the cache. Otherwise, in a *cache miss*, the processor searches for the data in the next level of the cache hierarchy. By measuring the time to access data, a process can distinguish cache hits from misses and identify whether the data was cached prior to the access.

2.3   Microarchitectural Side-Channel Attacks

In this section we review related works on microarchitectural side-channel timing attacks. These attacks exploit timing variations that are caused by contention on microarchitectural hardware resources in order to leak information on the usage of these resources, and indirectly on the internal operation of the victim. Acıiçmez and Seifert [5] distinguish between two types of channels: those that rely on a persistent state and those that exploit a transient state. Persistent-state channels exploit the limited storage space within the targeted microarchitectural resource. Transient-state channels, in contrast, exploit the limited bandwidth of the targeted element.

Persistent-State Attacks. The PRIME+PROBE attack [40,41] is an example of a persistent-state attack. The attack exploits the limited storage space in cache sets to identify the sets used for the victim's data. The attacker preloads data to the cache and allows the victim to execute before measuring the time to access the preloaded data. When the victim accesses its data it is loaded into the cache, replacing some of the attacker's preloaded data. Accessing data that has been replaced will take longer than accessing data still in the cache. Thus the attacker can identify the cache sets that the victim has accessed. Persistent-state channels have targeted the L1 data cache [7,15,40,41], the L1 instruction cache [1,4, 51], the branch prediction buffer [2,3], the last-level cache [27,29,36,46,49], and DRAM open rows [42]. The PRIME+PROBE attack was used to recover the accessed multipliers in the sliding-window exponentiation of OpenSSL 0.9.7c [41] and of GnuPG 1.4.18 [27,36].

Transient-State Attacks. Transient-state channels have been investigated mostly within the context of covert channels, where a *Trojan* process tries to covertly exfiltrate information. The idea dates back to Lampson [34] who suggests that processes can leak information by modifying their CPU usage. Covert channels were also observed with shared bus contention [26,48], Acıiçmez and Seifert [5] are the first to publish a side-channel attack based on a transient state. The attack monitors the usage of the multiplication functional unit in a hyperthreaded processor. Monitoring the unit allows an attacker to distinguish between the square and the multiply phases of modular exponentiation. The attack was tested on a victim running fixed-window exponentiation, so no secret information was obtained.

Another transient-state channel uses bus contention to leak side-channel information [47]. By monitoring the capacity of the memory bus allocated to the attacker, the attacker is able to distinguish the square and the multiply steps. Because the attack of [47] was only demonstrated in a simulator, the question of whether actual hardware leaks such high-resolution information is still open.

2.4   Scatter-Gather Implementation

One of the countermeasures Intel recommends against side-channel attacks is to avoid secret-dependent memory access *at coarser than cache line granularity* [12, 13]. This approach is manifested in the patch Intel contributed to the OpenSSL project to mitigate the Percival [41] attack. The patch[1] changes the layout of the multipliers in memory. Instead of storing the data of each of the multipliers in consecutive bytes in memory, the new layout scatters each multiplier across multiple cache lines [14]. Before use, the fragments of the required multiplier are gathered to a single buffer which is used for the multiplication. Figure 1 contrasts the conventional memory layout of the multipliers with the layout used in the scatter-gather approach. This scatter-gather design ensures that the order of accessing cache lines when performing a multiplication is independent of the multiplier used.

Because Intel cache lines are 64 bytes long, the maximum number of multipliers that can be used with scatter-gather is 64. For large exponents, increasing the number of multipliers reduces the number of multiply operations performed during the exponentiations. Gopal et al. [23] suggest dividing the multipliers into 16-bit fragments rather than into bytes. This improves performance by allowing loads of two bytes in a single memory access, at the cost of reducing the maximum number of multipliers to 32. Gueron [24] recommends 32-bit fragments, thus reducing the number of multipliers to 16. He shows that the combined savings from the reduced number of memory accesses and the smaller cache footprint of the multipliers outweighs the performance loss due to the added multiplications required with less multipliers.

---

[1] https://github.com/openssl/openssl/commit/46a643763de6d8e39ecf6f76fa79b
4d04885aa59.

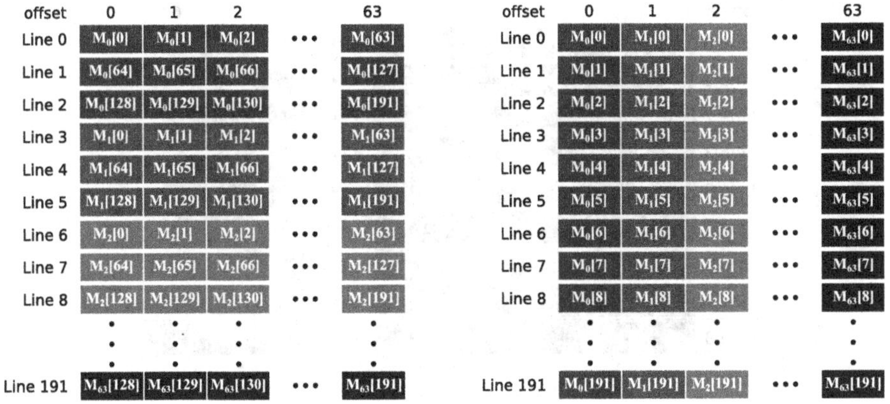

Fig. 1. Conventional (left) vs. scatter-gather (right) memory layout.

The OpenSSL Scatter-Gather Implementation. The implementation of exponentiation in the current version of OpenSSL (1.0.2f) deviates slightly from the layout described above. For 2048-bit and 4096-bit key sizes the implementation uses a fixed-window algorithm with a window size of 5, requiring 32 multipliers. Instead of scattering the multipliers in each cache line, the multipliers are divided into 64-bit fragments, scattered across groups of four consecutive cache lines. (See Fig. 2.) That is, the table that stores the multipliers is divided into groups of four consecutive cache lines. Each group of four consecutive cache lines stores one 64-bit fragment of each multiplier. To avoid leaking information on the particular multiplier used in each multiplication, the gather process accesses all of the cache lines and uses a bit mask pattern to select the ones that contain fragments of the required multiplier. Furthermore, to avoid copying the multiplier data, the implementation combines the gather operation with the multiplication. This spreads the access to the scattered multiplier across the multiplication.

Key-Dependent Memory Accesses. Because the fragments of each multiplier are stored in a fixed offset within the cache lines, all of the scatter-gather implementations described above have memory accesses that depend on the multiplier used and thus on the secret key. For a pure scatter-gather approach, the multiplier is encoded in the low bits of the addresses accessed during the gather operation. For the case of OpenSSL's implementation, only the three least significant bits of the multiplier number are encoded in the address while the other two bits are used as the index of the cache line within the group of four cache lines that contains the fragment.

We note that because these secret-dependent accesses are at a finer than cache line granularity, the scatter-gather approach has been considered secure against side-channel attacks [24].

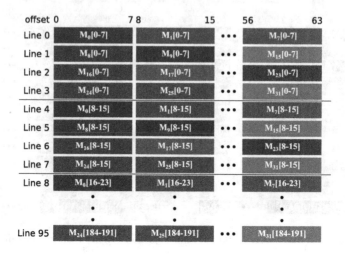

Fig. 2. The memory layout of the multipliers table in OpenSSL

2.5   Intel L1 Cache Banks

With the introduction of superscalar computing in Intel processors, cache bandwidth became a bottleneck for processor performance. To alleviate the issue, Intel introduced a cache design consisting of multiple *banks* [6]. Each of the banks serves part of the cache line specified by the offset in the cache line. The banks can operate independently and serve requests concurrently. However, each bank can only serve one request at a time. When multiple accesses to the same bank are made concurrently, only one access is served, while the rest are delayed until the bank can handle them.

Fog [18] notes that cache-bank conflicts prevent instructions from executing simmultaneously on Pentium processors. Delays due to cache-bank conflicts are also documented for other processor versions [19,20,28].

Both Bernstein [7] and Osvik et al. [40] mention that cache-bank conflicts cause timing variations and warn that these may result in a timing channel which may leak information about low address bits. Tromer et al. [45] note that while scatter-gather has no secret-dependent accesses to cache lines, it does have secret-dependent access to cache banks. Bernstein and Schwabe [8] demonstrate timing variations due to conflicts between read and write instructions on addresses within the same cache bank and suggest these may affect cryptographic software. However, although the risk of side-channel attacks based on cache-bank conflicts has been identified long ago, no attacks exploiting them have ever been published.

3   The CacheBleed Attack

We now proceed to describe CacheBleed, the first side-channel attack to systematically exploit cache-bank conflicts. The attack identifies the times at which a victim accesses data in a monitored cache bank by measuring the delays caused by contention on the cache bank.

In our attack scenario, we assume that the victim and the attacker run concurrently on two hyperthreads of the same processor core. Thus, the victim and the attacker share the L1 data cache. Recall that the Sandy Bridge L1 data cache is divided into multiple banks and that the banks cannot handle concurrent load accesses. The attacker issues a large number of load accesses to a cache bank and measures the time to fulfill these accesses. If during the attack the victim also accesses the same cache bank, the victim accesses will contend with the attacker for cache bank access, causing delays in the attack. Hence, when the victim accesses the monitored cache bank the attack will take longer than when the victim accesses other cache banks.

To implement CacheBleed we use the code in Listing 1. The bulk of the code (Lines 4–259) consists of 256 addl instructions that read data from addresses that are all in the same cache bank. (The cache bank is selected by the low bits of the memory address in register r9.) We use four different destination registers to avoid contention on the registers themselves. Before starting the accesses, the code takes the value of the current cycle counter (Line 1) and stores it in register r10 (Line 2). After performing 256 accesses, the previously stored value of the cycle counter is subtracted from the current value, resulting in the number of cycles that passed during the attack.

```
1    rdtscp
2    movq     %rax , %r10
3
4    addl     0x000(%r9) , %eax
5    addl     0x040(%r9) , %ecx
6    addl     0x080(%r9) , %edx
7    addl     0x0c0(%r9) , %edi
8    addl     0x100(%r9) , %eax
9    addl     0x140(%r9) , %ecx
10   addl     0x180(%r9) , %edx
11   addl     0x1c0(%r9) , %edi
         .
         .
         .
256  addl     0xf00(%r9) , %eax
257  addl     0xf40(%r9) , %ecx
258  addl     0xf80(%r9) , %edx
259  addl     0xfc0(%r9) , %edi
260
261  rdtscp
262  subq     %r10 , %rax
```

Listing 1. Cache-Bank Collision Attack Code

We run the attack code on an Intel Xeon E5-2430 processor—a six-core Sandy Bridge processor, with a clock rate of 2.20 GHz. Figure 3 shows the histogram of the running times of the attack code under several scenarios.[2]

Scenario 1: Idle. In the first scenario, *idle hyperthread*, the attacker is the only program executing on the core. That is, one of the two hyperthreads executes the attack code while the other hyperthread is idle. As we can see, the attack takes around 230 cycles, clearly showing that the Intel processor is superscalar and that the cache can handle more than one access in a CPU cycle.

Scenario 2: Pure Compute. The second scenario has a victim running a computation on the registers, without any memory access. As we can see, access in this scenario is slower than when there is no victim. Because the victim does not perform memory accesses, cache-bank conflicts cannot explain this slowdown. Hyperthreads, however, share most of the resources of the core, including the execution units, read and write buffers and the register allocation and renaming resources [20]. Contention on any of these resources can explain the slowdown we see when running a pure-compute victim.

Scenario 3: Pure Memory. At the other extreme is the *pure memory* victim, which continuously accesses the cache bank that the attacker monitors. As we can see, the attack code takes almost twice as long to run in this scenario. The distribution of attack times is completely distinct from any of the other scenarios. Hence identifying the victim in this scenario is trivial. This scenario is, however, not realistic—programs usually perform some calculation.

Scenarios 4 and 5: Mixed Load. The last two scenarios aim to measure a slightly more realistic scenario. In this case, one in four victim operations is a memory access, where all of these memory accesses are to the same cache bank. In this scenario we measure both the case that the victim accesses the monitored cache line (*mixed-load*) and when there is no cache-bank contention between the victim and the attacker (*mixed-load–NC*). We see that the two scenarios are distinguishable, but there is some overlap between the two distributions. Consequently, a single measurement may be insufficient to distinguish between the two scenarios.

In practice, even this mixed-load scenario is not particularly realistic. Typical programs will access memory in multiple cache banks. Hence the differences between measurement distributions may be much smaller than those presented in Fig. 3. In the next section we show how we overcome this limitation and correctly identify a small bias in the cache-bank access patterns of the victim.

---

[2] For clarity, the presented histograms show the envelope of the measured data.

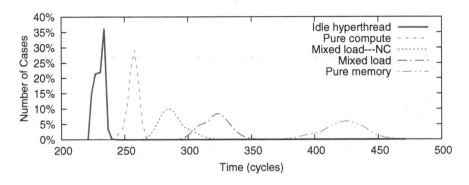

Fig. 3. Distribution of time to read 256 entries from a cache bank.

4 Attacking the OpenSSL Modular Exponentiation Implementation

To demonstrate the technique in a real scenario, we use CacheBleed to attack the implementation of the RSA decryption in the current version of OpenSSL (version 1.0.2f). This implementation uses a fixed-window exponentiation with $w = 5$. As discussed in Sect. 2.4 OpenSSL uses a combination of the scatter-gather technique with masking for side-channel attack protection. Recall that the multipliers are divided into 64-bit fragments. These fragments are scattered into 8 *bins* along the cache lines such that the three least significant bits of the multiplier select the bin. The fragments of a multiplier are stored in groups of four consecutive cache lines. The two most significant bits of the multiplier select the cache line out of the four in which the fragments of the multiplier are stored. See Fig. 2. The multiplication code selects the bin to read using the least significant bits of the multiplier. It then reads a fragment from the selected bin in each of the four cache lines and uses masking to select the fragment of the required multiplier. Because the multiplication code needs to access the multiplier throughout the multiplication, the cache banks of the bin containing the multiplier are accessed more often than other cache banks. We use CacheBleed to identify the bin and, consequently, to find the three least significant bits of the multiplier.

Identifying Exponentiations. We begin by demonstrating that it is possible to identify the exponentiation operations using cache-bank conflicts. Indeed, using the code in Listing 1, we create a sequence of measurements of cache-bank conflicts. As mentioned in Sect. 3, the difference between the distributions of measurements in similar scenarios may be very small. Consequently, a single measurement is unlikely to be sufficient for identifying the bin used in each multiplication. To distinguish the distributions, we create multiple sequences and average the measurements at each trace point to get a trace of the average measurement time. Figure 4 shows the traces of measurements of two bins, each averaged over 1,000 decryptions using a 4096-bit key.

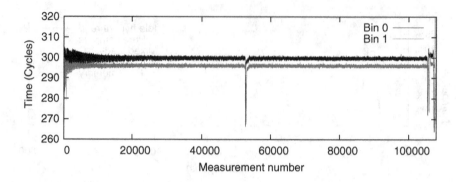

Fig. 4. Measurement trace of OpenSSL RSA decryption

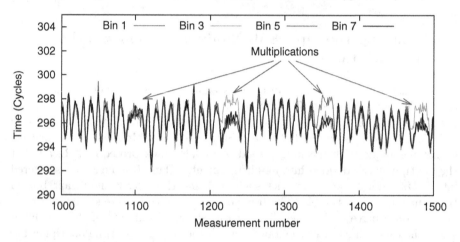

Fig. 5. Measurement trace of OpenSSL RSA decryption—detailed view (Color figure online)

The figure clearly shows the two exponentiations executed as part of the RSA-CRT calculation. Another interesting feature is that the measurements for the two bins differ by about 4 cycles. The difference is the result of the OpenSSL modular reduction algorithm, which accesses even bins more often than odd bins. Consequently, there is more contention on even bins, and measurements on even bins take slightly longer than those on odd bins.

Identifying Multiplication Operations. Next, we show that is also possible to identify the individual multiplication operations performed during the modular exponentiation operation. Indeed, Fig. 5 shows a small section of the traces of the odd bins. In these traces, we can clearly see the multiplication operations (marked with arrows) as well as the spikes for each of the squaring and modular reduction operations. Recall that the OpenSSL exponentiation repeatedly calculate sequences of five modular squaring and reduction operations followed by a modular multiplication.

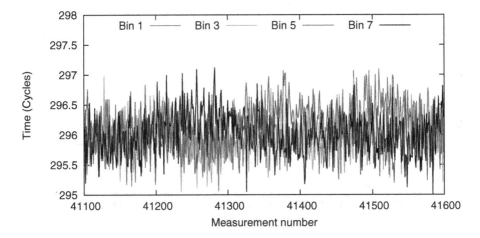

Fig. 6. CacheBleed average trace towards the end of the exponentiation

Identifying Multiplier Values. Note that in the second and fourth multiplications, the measurements in the trace of bin 3 (yellow) take slightly longer than the measurements of the other bins. This indicates that the three least significant digits of the multiplier used in these multiplications are 011. Similarly, the spike in the green trace observed during the third multiplication indicates that the three least significant bits of the multiplier used are 001. This corresponds to the ground truth where the multipliers used in the traced sections are 2, 11, 1, 11.

As we can see, we can extract the multipliers from the trace. However, there are some practical challenges that complicate both the generation of the traces and their analysis. We now discuss these issues.

Aligning CacheBleed Measurement Sequences for Averaging. Recall that the traces shown in Fig. 5 are generated by averaging the sequences of CacheBleed measurements over 1,000 decryptions. When averaging, we need to ensure that the sequences align with each other. That is, we must ensure that each measurement is taken in the same relative time in each multiplication.

To ensure that the sequences are aligned, we use the FLUSH+RELOAD attack [49] to find the start of the exponentiation. Once found, we start collecting enough CacheBleed measurements to cover the whole exponentiation. FLUSH+RELOAD has a resolution of about 500 cycles, ensuring that the sequences start within 500 cycles, or up to two measurements, of each other.

Relative Clock Drift. Aligning the CacheBleed sequences at the start of the exponentiation does not result in a clean signal. This is because both the victim and the attacker are user processes, and they may be interrupted by the operating system. The most common interruption is due to timer interrupts, which

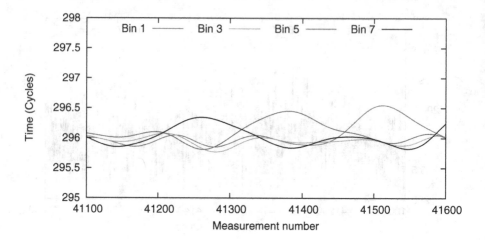

Fig. 7. Measurement trace after a lowpass filter

on Linux-based operating systems happen every millisecond. Since each modular exponentiation in the calculation of a 4096-bit RSA-CRT decryption takes 5 ms, we experience 5 to 6 timer interrupts during the exponentiation. Timer interrupts can be easily identified because serving them takes over 5,000 cycles, whereas non-interrupted measurements take around 300 cycles. Consequently, if a measurement takes more than 1,000 cycles, we assume that it was interrupted and therefore discard it.

The attacker, however, does not have exact information on the interrupts that affect the victim, resulting in clock drift between the attacker and the victim. As we progress through the exponentiation, the signal we capture becomes more noisy. Figure 6 shows the signal towards the end of the exponentiation. As we can see, the multiplications are barely visible.

To reduce noise, we pass the signal through a low-pass filter, which removes high frequencies from the signal and highlights the behavior at the resolution of one multiplication. Figure 7 shows the result of passing the above trace through the filter. It is possible to clearly identify three multiplications, using bins 7, 5 and 1.

Aligning Traces of Multiple Bins. As discussed above, measurements in even bins are slower on average than measurements in odd bins. This creates two problems. The first is that we need to normalize the traces before comparing them to find the multiplier. The second problem is that we use the measurements as a virtual clock. Consequently, when we measure over a fixed period of time, traces of even bins will be shorter, i.e., have fewer measurements, than traces of odd bins. This create a clock shift between traces belonging to even bins and traces belonging to odd bins, which increases as the exponentiation progresses. In order to normalize the trace length, we remove element 0 of the

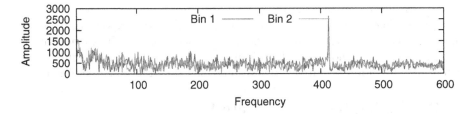

Fig. 8. The frequency spectrum of a trace

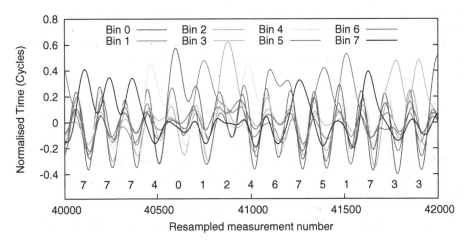

Fig. 9. Normalized resampled traces

frequency domain. This effectively subtracts the trace's average from each trace measurement, thereby making all the traces be at the same length.

We then find the frequency of multiplications in the trace by looking at the frequency domain of the trace. Figure 8 shows the frequency spectrum of two of the traces. For a 4096-bit key, OpenSSL performs two exponentiations with 2048-bit exponents. With a window size of 5, there are $2048/5 \approx 410$ multiplications. As we can see, there is a spike around the frequency 410 matching the number of multiplications. Using the frequency extracted from the trace, rather than the expected number of multiplications, allows us to better adjust to the effects of noise at the start and end of the exponentiation which might otherwise result in a loss of some multiplications.

Partial Key Extraction. We use CacheBleed to collect 16 traces, one for each of the 8 bins in each of the two exponentiations. Each trace is the average of 1,000 sequences of measurements, totalling 16,000 decryption operations. Figure 9 shows a sample of the analyzed traces, i.e. after averaging, passing through a low-pass filter, normalizing the signal and resampling. As we can see, the used bins are clearly visible in the figure.

We manage to recover the three least significant bits of almost all of the multipliers. Due to noise at the start and the end of the exponentiations, we miss one or two of the leading and trailing multiplications of each exponentiation. Next, in Sect. 5, we show that the information we obtain about the three least significant bits of almost all of the multipliers is enough for key extraction.

5   Recovering the RSA Private Key

Successfully carrying out the attack in the previous sections for a 4096-bit modulus allowed us to learn the three least significant bits of every window of five bits for the Chinese remainder theorem coefficients $d_p = d \bmod p - 1$ and $d_q = d \bmod q - 1$. In this section, we describe how to use this knowledge to recover the full private RSA key. We use the techniques of Heninger and Shacham [25] and İnci et al. [27].

Solving for the Modular Multipliers. We have partial knowledge of the bits of d_p and d_q, where each satisfies the relation $ed_p = 1 + k_p(p - 1)$ and $ed_q = 1 + k_q(q - 1)$ for positive integers $k_p, k_q < e$. In the common case of $e = 65537$, this leaves us with at most 2^{32} possibilities for pairs of k_p, k_q to test. Following [27], the k_p and k_q are related, so we only need to search 65,537 possible values of k_p.

We start by rearranging the relations on d_p and d_q to obtain $ed_p - 1 - k_p = k_p p$ and $ed_q - 1 - k_q = k_q q$. Multiplying these together, we obtain the relation

$$(ed_p - 1 + k_p)(ed_q - 1 + k_q) = k_p k_q N. \tag{1}$$

Reducing modulo e yields $(k_p - 1)(k_q - 1) \equiv k_p k_q N \bmod e$.

Thus, given a value for k_p we can solve for the unique value of $k_q \bmod e$. We do not have enough information about d_p and d_q to deduce further information, so we must test all e values of k_p.

Branch and Prune Algorithm. For each candidate k_p and k_q, we will use Eq. 1 to iteratively solve for d_p and d_q starting from the least or most significant bits, branching to generate multiple potential solutions when bits are unknown and pruning potential solutions when known bits contradict a given solution. In contrast to [25], the bits we know are not randomly distributed. Instead, they are synchronized to the three least significant bits of every five, with one or two full windows of five missing at the least and most significant positions of each exponent. This makes our analysis much simpler: when a bit of d_p and d_q is unknown at a location i, we branch to generate two new solutions. When a bit of d_p and d_q is known at a particular location, using the same heuristic assumption as in [25], an incorrect solution will fail to match the known bit of d_p and d_q with probability 0.5. When k_p and k_q are correct, we expect our algorithm to generate four new solutions for every pair of unknown bits, and prune these to a single correct solution at every string of three known bits. When k_p and k_q are incorrect, we expect no solutions to remain after a few steps.

Empirical Results. We tested key recovery on the output of our attack run on a 4096-bit key, which correctly recovered the three least significant bits of every window of five, but missed the two least significant windows and one most significant window for both d_p and d_q. We implemented this algorithm in Sage and ran it on a Cisco UCS Server with two 2.30 GHz Intel E5-2699 processors and 128 GiB of RAM. For the correct values of k_p and k_q, our branch-and-prune implementation recovered the full key in 1 second on a single core after examining 6,093 candidate partial solutions, and took about 160 ms to eliminate an incorrect candidate pair of k_p and k_q after examining an average of 1,500 candidate partial solutions. A full search of all 65,537 candidate pairs of k_p and k_q parallelized across 36 hyperthreaded cores took 3.5 min. We assumed the positions of the missing windows at the most and least significant bits were known. If the relative positions are unknown, searching over more possible offsets would increase the total search time by a factor of 9.

6   Mitigation

Countermeasures for the CacheBleed attack can operate at the hardware, the system or the software level. Hardware-based mitigations include increasing the bandwidth of the cache banks. Our attack does not work on Haswell processors, which do not seem to suffer from cache-bank conflicts [20,28]. But, as Haswell does show timing variations that depend on low address bits [20], it may be vulnerable to similar attacks. Furthermore, this solution does not apply to the Sandy Bridge processors currently in the market.

Disabling Hyperthreading. The simplest countermeasure at the system level is to disable hyperthreading. Disabling hyperthreading, or only allowing hyperthreading between processes within the same protection domain, prevents any concurrent access to the cache banks and eliminates any conflicts. Unlike attacks on persistent state, which may be applicable when a core is time-shared, the transient state that CacheBleed exploits is not preserved during a context switch. Hence the core can be time-shared between non-trusting processes. The limited security of hyperthreading has already been identified [5]. We recommend that hyperthreading be disabled even on processors that are not vulnerable to CacheBleed for security-critical scenarios where untrusted users share processors.

Constant-Time Implementations. At the software level, the best countermeasure is to use a *constant-time* implementation, i.e. one that does not have secret-dependent branches or memory accesses. A common technique for implementing constant-time table lookup is to use a combination of arithmetic and bitwise operations to generate a mask that depends on the secret value. The whole table is then accessed and the mask is used to select the required table entry. Mozilla's fix for CacheBleed uses this approach.

Modifying Memory Accesses. Rather than using to a constant-time implementation, OpenSSL mitigates CacheBleed through a combination of two changes. The first change is to use 128-bit memory accesses, effectively halving the number of bins used. The second change is to modify the memory access pattern during the gathering process so that the software accesses a different offset in each of the four cache lines.

Combining the four different offsets with the 128-bit accesses means that when gathering a multiplier fragment, OpenSSL accesses all 16 of the cache banks. The order of accessing the cache banks depends on the value of the multiplier, so the design leaks secret key information to adversaries that can recover the order of the accesses. We note, however, that our attack does not have the resolution required to determine the order of successive memory accesses and that we are not currently aware of any technique for exploiting this leak.

Furthermore, using 128-bit memory accesses means that the potential leakage created by the order of accessing the cache banks is only two bits for each multiplier, or 40 % of the bits of the exponents for the 5-bit windows used by OpenSSL for both 2048 and 4096-bit exponents. Our key recovery technique will produce exponentially many solutions in this case: heuristically, we expect it to branch to produce two solutions for each multiplier. In this case, the attacker could use the branch-and-prune method to produce exponentially many candidates up to half the length of each Chinese remainder theorem exponent d_p or d_q, and then use the method of Blömer and May [9] to recover the remaining half in polynomial time. Thus even if an adversary is able to exploit the leak, full key recovery may only be feasible for very small keys without further algorithmic improvements.

While we are not aware of a practical exploit of the leak in the OpenSSL code, we believe that leaving a known timing channel is an undue risk. We have conveyed information about the leak and our concerns to the OpenSSL development team.

7 Conclusions

In this work, we presented CacheBleed, the first timing attack to recover low address bits from secret-dependent memory accesses. We demonstrate that the attack is effective against state-of-the-art cryptographic software, widely thought to be immune to timing attacks.

The timing variations that underlie this attack and the risk associated with them have been known for over a decade. Osvik et al. [40] warn that *"Cache bank collisions (e.g., in Athlon 64 processors) likewise cause timing to be affected by low address bits."* Bernstein [7] mentions that *" For example, the Pentium 1 has similar cache-bank conflicts."* A specific warning about the cache-bank conflicts and the scatter-gather technique appears in Footnote 38 of Tromer et al. [45].

Our research illustrates the risk to users when cryptographic software developers dismiss a widely hypothesized potential attack merely because no proof-of-concept has yet been demonstrated. This is the prevailing approach for security vulnerabilities, but we believe that for cryptographic vulnerabilities, this approach is risky, and developers should be proactive in closing potential vulnerabilities even in the absence of a fully practical attack. To that end we observe that OpenSSL's decision to use an ad-hoc mitigation techniques, instead of deploying a constant-time implementation, continues to follow such a risky approach.

Acknowledgements. We would like to thank Daniel J. Bernstein for suggesting the name CacheBleed and for helpful comments.

NICTA is funded by the Australian Government through the Department of Communications and the Australian Research Council through the ICT Centre of Excellence Program. This material is based upon work supported by the U.S. National Science Foundation under Grants No. CNS-1408734, CNS-1505799, and CNS-1513671, a gift from Cisco, the Blavatnik Interdisciplinary Cyber Research Center, the Check Point Institute for Information Security, a Google Faculty Research Award, the Israeli Centers of Research Excellence I-CORE program (center 4/11), the Leona M. & Harry B. Helmsley Charitable Trust, and by NATO's Public Diplomacy Division in the Framework of "Science for Peace".

References

1. Acıiçmez, O.: Yet another microarchitectural attack: exploiting I-cache. In: CSAW, Fairfax, VA, US (2007)
2. Acıiçmez, O., Gueron, S., Seifert, J.-P.: New branch prediction vulnerabilities in openSSL and necessary software countermeasures. In: Galbraith, S.D. (ed.) Cryptography and Coding 2007. LNCS, vol. 4887, pp. 185–203. Springer, Heidelberg (2007)
3. Acıiçmez, O., Koç, Ç.K., Seifert, J.-P.: Predicting secret keys via branch prediction. In: Abe, M. (ed.) CT-RSA 2007. LNCS, vol. 4377, pp. 225–242. Springer, Heidelberg (2006)
4. Acıiçmez, O., Brumley, B.B., Grabher, P.: New results on instruction cache attacks. In: Mangard, S., Standaert, F.-X. (eds.) CHES 2010. LNCS, vol. 6225, pp. 110–124. Springer, Heidelberg (2010)
5. Acıiçmez, O., Seifert, J.-P.: Cheap hardware parallelism implies cheap security. In: 4th International Workshop on Fault Diagnosis and Tolerance in Cryptography, Vienna, AT, pp. 80–91 (2007)
6. Alpert, D.B., Choudhury, M.R., Mills, J.D.: Interleaved cache for multiple accesses per clock cycle in a microprocessor. US Patent 5559986, September 1996
7. Bernstein, D.J.: Cache-timing attacks on AES (2005). Preprint http://cr.yp.to/papers.html#cachetiming
8. Bernstein, D.J., Schwabe, P.: A word of warning. In: CHES 2013 Rump Session, August 2013
9. Blömer, J., May, A.: New partial key exposure attacks on RSA. In: Boneh, D. (ed.) CRYPTO 2003. LNCS, vol. 2729, pp. 27–43. Springer, Heidelberg (2003)
10. BoringSSL. https://boringssl.googlesource.com/boringssl/
11. Bos, J.N.E., Coster, M.J.: Addition chain heuristics. In: Brassard, G. (ed.) CRYPTO 1989. LNCS, vol. 435, pp. 400–407. Springer, Heidelberg (1990)
12. Brickell, E.: Technologies to improve platform security. In: CHES 2011 Invited Talk, September 2011. http://www.iacr.org/workshops/ches/ches2011/presentations/Invited%201/CHES2011_Invited_1.pdf

13. Brickell, E.: The impact of cryptography on platform security. In: CT-RSA 2012 Invited Talk, February 2012. http://www.rsaconference.com/writable/presentations/file_upload/cryp-106.pdf
14. Brickell, E., Graunke, G., Seifert, J.-P.: Mitigating cache/timing based side-channels in AES and RSA software implementations. In: RSA Conference 2006 Session DEV-203, February 2006
15. Brumley, B.B., Hakala, R.M.: Cache-timing template attacks. In: Matsui, M. (ed.) ASIACRYPT 2009. LNCS, vol. 5912, pp. 667–684. Springer, Heidelberg (2009)
16. Brumley, B.B., Tuveri, N.: Remote timing attacks are still practical. In: Atluri, V., Diaz, C. (eds.) ESORICS 2011. LNCS, vol. 6879, pp. 355–371. Springer, Heidelberg (2011)
17. Brumley, D., Boneh, D.: Remote timing attacks are practical. In: 12th USENIX Security, Washington, DC, US, pp. 1–14 (2003)
18. Fog, A.: How to optimize for the Pentium processor, August 1996. https://notendur.hi.is/hh/kennsla/sti/h96/pentopt.txt
19. Fog, A.: How to optimize for the Pentium family of microprocessors, April 2004. https://cr.yp.to/2005-590/fog.pdf
20. Fog, A.: The microarchitecture of Intel, AMD and VIA CPUs: an optimization guide for assembly programmers and compiler makers, January 2016. http://www.agner.org/optimize/microarchitecture.pdf
21. Garner, H.L.: The residue number system. IRE Trans. Electron. Comput. EC–8(2), 140–147 (1959)
22. Genkin, D., Shamir, A., Tromer, E.: RSA key extraction via low-bandwidth acoustic cryptanalysis. In: Garay, J.A., Gennaro, R. (eds.) CRYPTO 2014, Part I. LNCS, vol. 8616, pp. 444–461. Springer, Heidelberg (2014)
23. Gopal, V., Guilford, J., Ozturk, E., Feghali, W., Wolrich, G., Dixon, M.: Fast and constant-time implementation of modular exponentiation. In: Embedded Systems and Communications Security, Niagara Falls, NY, US (2009)
24. Gueron, S.: Efficient software implementations of modular exponentiation. J. Crypt. Eng. 2(1), 31–43 (2012)
25. Heninger, N., Shacham, H.: Reconstructing RSA private keys from random key bits. In: Halevi, S. (ed.) CRYPTO 2009. LNCS, vol. 5677, pp. 1–17. Springer, Heidelberg (2009)
26. Wei-Ming, H.: Reducing timing channels with fuzzy time. In: 1991 Computer Society Symposium on Research Security and Privacy, Oakland, CA, US, pp. 8–20 (1991)
27. İnci, M.S., Gülmezoğlu, B., Irazoqui, G., Eisenbarth, T., Sunar, B.: Seriously, get off my cloud! Cross-VM RSA key recovery in a public cloud. IACR Cryptology ePrint Archive, Report 2015/898, September 2015
28. Intel 64 & IA-32 AORM: Intel 64 and IA-32 Architectures Optimization Reference Manual. Intel Corporation, April 2012
29. Irazoqui, G., Eisenbarth, T., Sunar, B.: S$A: a shared cache attack that works across cores and defies VM sandboxing - and its application to AES. In: S&P, San Jose, CA, US (2015)
30. Irazoqui, G., Eisenbarth, T., Sunar, B.: Systematic reverse engineering of cache slice selection in Intel processors. IACR Cryptology ePrint Archive, Report 2015/690, July 2015
31. Kocher, P.C., Jaffe, J., Jun, B.: Differential power analysis. In: Wiener, M. (ed.) CRYPTO 1999. LNCS, vol. 1666, pp. 388–397. Springer, Heidelberg (1999)
32. Kocher, P., Jaffe, J., Jun, B., Rohatgi, P.: Introduction to differential power analysis. J. Cryptogr. Eng. 1, 5–27 (2011)

33. Kocher, P.C.: Timing attacks on implementations of Diffie-Hellman, RSA, DSS, and other systems. In: Koblitz, N. (ed.) CRYPTO 1996. LNCS, vol. 1109, pp. 104–113. Springer, Heidelberg (1996)
34. Lampson, B.W.: A note on the confinement problem. Commun. ACM **16**, 613–615 (1973)
35. LibreSSL Project. https://www.libressl.org
36. Liu, F., Yarom, Y., Ge, Q., Heiser, G., Lee, R.B.: Last-level cache side-channel attacks are practical. In: S&P, San Jose, CA, US, pp. 605–622, May 2015
37. Maurice, C., Le Scouarnec, N., Neumann, C., Heen, O., Francillon, A.: Reverse engineering intel last-level cache complex addressing using performance counters. In: Bos, H., et al. (eds.) RAID 2015. LNCS, vol. 9404, pp. 48–65. Springer, Heidelberg (2015). doi:10.1007/978-3-319-26362-5_3
38. Mozilla: Network security services. https://developer.mozilla.org/en-US/docs/Mozilla/Projects/NSS
39. OpenSSL Project. https://openssl.org
40. Osvik, D.A., Shamir, A., Tromer, E.: Cache attacks and countermeasures: the case of AES. In: 2006 CT-RSA (2006)
41. Percival, C.: Cache missing for fun and profit. In: BSDCan 2005, Ottawa, CA (2005)
42. Pessl, P., Gruss, D., Maurice, C., Schwarz, M., Mangard, S.: Reverse engineering Intel DRAM addressing and exploitation (2015). arXiv Preprint arXiv:1511.08756
43. Quisquater, J.-J., Samyde, D.: Electromagnetic analysis (EMA): measures and counter-measures for smart cards. In: E-Smart 2001, Cannes, FR, pp. 200–210, September 2001
44. Rivest, R.L., Shamir, A., Adleman, L.: A method for obtaining digital signatures and public-key cryptosystems. CACM **21**, 120–126 (1978)
45. Tromer, E., Osvik, D.A., Shamir, A.: Efficient cache attacks on AES, and countermeasures. J. Cryptol. **23**(1), 37–71 (2010)
46. van de Pol, J., Smart, N.P., Yarom, Y.: Just a little bit more. In: Nyberg, K. (ed.) CT-RSA 2015. LNCS, vol. 9048, pp. 3–21. Springer, Heidelberg (2015)
47. Wang, Y., Suh, G.E.: Efficient timing channel protection for on-chip networks. In: 6th NoCS, Lyngby, Denmark, pp. 142–151 (2012)
48. Zhenyu, W., Zhang, X., Wang, H.: Whispers in the hyper-space: high-speed covert channel attacks in the cloud. In: 21st USENIX Security, Bellevue, WA, US (2012)
49. Yarom, Y., Falkner, K.: Flush+Reload: a high resolution, low noise, L3 cache side-channel attack. In: 23rd USENIX Security, San Diego, CA, US, pp. 719–732 (2014)
50. Yarom, Y., Ge, Q., Liu, F., Lee, R.B., Heiser, G.: Mapping the Intel last-level cache, September 2015. http://eprint.iacr.org/
51. Zhang, Y., Juels, A., Reiter, M.K., Ristenpart, T.: Cross-VM side channels and their use to extract private keys. In: 19th CCS, Raleigh, NC, US, pp. 305–316, October 2012

Cache Attacks Enable Bulk Key Recovery
on the Cloud

Mehmet Sinan İnci[✉], Berk Gulmezoglu, Gorka Irazoqui, Thomas Eisenbarth,
and Berk Sunar

Worcester Polytechnic Institute, Worcester, MA, USA
{msinci,bgulmezoglu,girazoki,teisenbarth,sunar}@wpi.edu

Abstract. Cloud services keep gaining popularity despite the security
concerns. While non-sensitive data is easily trusted to cloud, security
critical data and applications are not. The main concern with the cloud
is the shared resources like the CPU, memory and even the network
adapter that provide subtle side-channels to malicious parties. We argue
that these side-channels indeed leak fine grained, sensitive information
and enable key recovery attacks on the cloud. Even further, as a quick
scan in one of the Amazon EC2 regions shows, high percentage – 55 % –
of users run outdated, leakage prone libraries leaving them vulnerable to
mass surveillance.

The most commonly exploited leakage in the shared resource systems
stem from the cache and the memory. High resolution and the stability
of these channels allow the attacker to extract fine grained information.
In this work, we employ the `Prime and Probe` attack to retrieve an RSA
secret key from a co-located instance. To speed up the attack, we reverse
engineer the cache slice selection algorithm for the Intel Xeon E5-2670
v2 that is used in our cloud instances. Finally we employ noise reduction
to deduce the RSA private key from the monitored traces. By processing
the noisy data we obtain the complete 2048-bit RSA key used during the
decryption.

Keywords: Amazon EC2 · Co-location detection · RSA key recovery ·
Virtualization · Prime and Probe attack

1 Motivation

Cloud computing services are more popular than ever with their ease of access,
low cost and real-time scalability. With increasing adoption of cloud, concerns
over cloud specific attacks have been rising and so has the number of research
studies exploring potential security risks in the cloud domain. A main enabler
for cloud security is the seminal work of Ristenpart et al. [40]. The work demonstrated the possibility of co-location as well as the security risks that come
with it. The co-location is the result of resource sharing between tenant Virtual
Machines (VMs). Under certain conditions, the same mechanism can also be

© International Association for Cryptologic Research 2016
B. Gierlichs and A.Y. Poschmann (Eds.): CHES 2016, LNCS 9813, pp. 368–388, 2016.
DOI: 10.1007/978-3-662-53140-2_18

exploited to extract sensitive information from a co-located victim VM, resulting in security and privacy breaches. Methods to extract information from VMs have been intensely studied in the last few years however remain infeasible within public cloud environments, e.g. [29,37,41,48]. The potential impact of attacks on crypto processes can be even more severe, since cryptography is at the core of any security solution. Consequently, extracting cryptographic keys across VM boundaries has also received considerable attention lately. Initial studies explored the Prime and Probe technique on L1 cache [19,49]. Though requiring the attacker and the victim to run on the same physical CPU core simultaneously, the small number of cache sets and the simple addressing scheme made the L1 cache a popular target. Follow up works have step by step removed restrictions and increased the viability of the attacks. The shared Last Level Cache (LLC) now enables true cross-core attacks [8,30,45] where the attacker and the victim share the CPU, but not necessarily the CPU core. Most recent LLC Prime and Probe attacks no longer rely on de-duplication [14,26] or core sharing, making them more widely applicable.

With the increasing sophistication of attacks, participants of the cloud industry ranging from Cloud Service Providers (CSPs), to hypervisor vendors, up all the way to providers of crypto libraries have fixed many of the newly exploitable security holes through patches [1,3,4]—many in response to published attacks. However, many of the outdated cryptographic libraries are still in use, opening the door for exploits. A scan over the entire range of IPs in the South America East region yields that 55% of TLS hosts installed on Amazon EC2 servers have not been updated since 2015 and are vulnerable to an array of more recently discovered attacks. Consequently, a potential attacker such as a nation state, hacker group or a government organization can exploit these vulnerabilities for bulk recovery of private keys. Besides the usual standard attacks that target individuals, this enables mass surveillance on a population thereby stripping the network from any level of privacy. Note that the attack is enabled by our trust in the cloud. The cloud infrastructure already stores the bulk of our sensitive data. Specifically, when an attacker instantiates multiple instances in a targeted availability zone of a cloud, she co-locates with many vulnerable servers. In particular, an attacker trying to recover RSA keys can monitor the LLC in each of these instances until the pattern expected by the exploited hardware level leakage is observed. Then the attacker can easily scan the cloud network to build a public key database and deduce who the recovered private key belongs to. In a similar approach, Heninger et al. [21] scan the network for public keys with shared or similar RSA modulus factors due to poor randomization. Similarly Bernstein et al. [10] compiled a public key database and scanned for shared factors in RSA modulus commonly caused by broken random number generators.

In this work, we explore the viability of full RSA key recovery in the Amazon EC2 cloud. More precisely, we utilize the LLC as a covert channel both to co-locate and perform a cross-core side-channel attack against a recent cryptographic implementation. Our results demonstrate that even with complex and resilient infrastructures, and with properly configured random number generators, cache attacks are a big threat in commercial clouds.

370 M.S. İnci et al.

Our Contribution

This work presents a full key recovery attack on a modern implementation of RSA in a commercial cloud and explores all steps necessary to successfully recover both the key and the identity of the victim. This attack can be applied under two different scenarios:

1. **Targeted Co-location:** In this scenario, we launch instances until we co-locate with the victim as described in [24,42]. Upon co-location the secret is recovered by a cache enabled cross-VM attack.
2. **Bulk Key Recovery:** We randomly create instances and using cross-VM cache attacks recover imperfect private keys. These keys are subsequently checked and against public keys in public key database. The second step allows us to eliminate noise in the private keys and determine the identity of the owner of the recovered key.

Unlike in earlier bulk key recovery attacks [10,21] we do not rely on faulty random number generators but instead exploit hardware level leakages.

Our specific technical contributions are as follows:

- We first demonstrate that the LLC contention based co-location detection tools are plausible in public clouds
- Second, we reverse-engineer the undocumented non-linear slice selection algorithm implemented in Intel Xeon E5-2670 v2 [2] used by our Amazon EC2 instances, and utilize it to automate and accelerate the attack
- Third, we describe how to apply the `Prime and Probe` attack to the LLC and obtain RSA leakage information from co-located VMs
- Last, we present a detailed analysis of the necessary post-processing steps to cope with the noise observed in a real public cloud setup, along with a detailed analysis on the CPU time (at most 30 core-hours) to recover both the noise-free key and the owner's identity (IP).

2 Related Work

This work combines techniques needed for co-location in a public cloud with state-of-the art techniques in cache based cross-VM side channel attacks.

Co-location Detection: In 2009 Ristenpart et al. [40] demonstrated that a potential attacker has the ability to co-locate and detect co-location in public IaaS clouds. In 2011, Zhang et al. [47] demonstrated that a tenant can detect co-location in the same core by monitoring the L2 cache. Shortly after, Bates et al. [7] implemented a co-location test based on network traffic analysis. In 2015, Zhang et al. [48] demonstrated that de-duplication enables co-location detection from co-located VMs in PaaS clouds. In follow-up to Ristenpart et al.'s work [40], Zhang et al. [44] and Varadarajan et al. [42] explored co-location detection in commercial public cloud in 2015. Both studies use the memory bus contention channel explored by Wu et al. in 2012 [43] to detect co-location. Finally in 2016, İnci et al. [24] explored co-location detection on Amazon EC2, Microsoft Azure and Google Compute Engine using three detection methods namely memory bus locking, LLC covert channel and LLC software profiling.

Recovering Cache Slice Selection Methods: A basic technique based on hamming distances for recovering and exploiting **linear** cache slice selection was introduced in [23]. Irazoqui et al. [27] and Maurice et al. [36] used a more systematic approach to recover linear slice selection algorithms in a range of processors, the latter pointing out the coincidence of the functions across processors. Recently, Yarom et al. [46] recovered a 6 core slice selection algorithm with a similar technique as the one presented in this work.

Side-Channel Attacks: RSA have been widely studied and explored with regards to diverse covert channels such as time [12,33], power [32], EM emanations [15,16], and even acoustic channels [17]. Micro-architectural side-channel attacks also succeeded on recovering secret keys used in symmetric cryptography. After the first theoretical [22,39] and practical [9,38] attacks utilizing micro-architectural covert channels, Aciiçmez et al. [5,6] demonstrated the possibility of recovering RSA secret keys using the instruction cache and the branch prediction unit as covert channels. Later, Zhang et al. [49] recovered El-Gamal secret keys across co-located VMs exploiting leakage in the upper level caches.

While all the previously mentioned side-channel attacks used a private core resource (i.e., attacker needs to be running in the same CPU core as the victim), in 2014 Yarom et al. [45] proved to be able to recover RSA secret keys across co-located VMs by using the `Flush and Reload` attack in the presence of memory de-duplication. Recently Liu et al. [14] implemented an attack against El-Gamal using the `Prime and Probe` attack in the LLC, whereas Bhattacharya et al. [11] utilized the branch prediction performance counters to recover RSA keys.

In addition to the attacks on public key cryptography schemes cache attacks also have been applied to AES [26,30], ECDSA [8], TLS messages [31], the number of items in a shopping cart [48] or even the key strokes typed in a keyboard [18]. Even further, they recently have been applied to PaaS clouds [48], across processors [28] and in smartphones [35].

3   Prime and Probe in the LLC

In computer systems, the physical memory is protected and not visible to the user, who only sees the virtual addresses that the data resides at. Therefore a memory address translation stage is required to map virtual addresses to physical. However, there are some bits of the virtual address that remain untranslated, i.e., the least significant p_{low} bits with $2^{p_{low}}$ size memory pages. These are called the *page offset*, while the remaining part of the address is called the *page frame number* and their combination make the physical address. The location of a memory block in the cache is determined by its physical address. Usually the physical address is divided in three different sections to access *n-way* caches: the byte field, the set field and the tag field. The length of the byte and set fields are determined by the cache line size and the number of sets in the cache, respectively. The more sets a cache has, more bits are needed from the *page frame number* to select the set that a memory block occupies in the cache.

The `Prime and Probe` attack has been widely studied in upper level caches [5,49], but was first introduced for the LLC in [14,26] with the use of **hugepages**. Unlike regular memory pages that reveal only 12 bits of the physical address, hugepages reveal 21 bits, allowing the LLC monitoring. Also, profiling the LLC in contrast to the L1 or L2 cache has various advantages. Firstly, unlike the upper level caches, the LLC is shared across cores, providing a cross-core covert channel. Moreover, the time distinguishability of accesses in upper level caches is much lower than those between the LLC and memory. On the other hand, due to the size of LLCs, we cannot simultaneously profile the whole cache, but rather a small portion of it at a time. In addition to that, modern processors divide their LLC into slices with a non-public hash algorithm, making it difficult to predict where the data will be located. Taking all these into account, the `Prime and Probe` attack is divided in two main stages:

Prime Stage: The attacker fills a portion of the LLC with his own data and waits for a period of time for the victim to access the cache.

Probe Stage: The attacker probes (reloads) the primed data. If the victim accessed the monitored set of the cache, one (or more) of the attacker's lines will not reside in the cache anymore, and will have to be retrieved from the memory.

As stated before, profiling a portion of the cache becomes more difficult when the LLC is divided into slices. However, as observed by [14] we can create an *eviction set* without knowing the algorithm implemented. This involves a step prior to the attack where the attacker finds the memory blocks colliding in a specific set/slice. This can be done by creating a large pool of memory blocks, and access them until we observe that one of them is fetched from the memory. The procedure will be further explained in Sect. 4. A group of memory blocks that fill one set/slice in the LLC will form an *eviction set* for that set/slice.

4   Co-locating on Amazon EC2

In order to perform our experiments across co-located VMs we first need to make sure that they are running in the same server. We present the LLC as an exploitable covert channel with the purpose of detecting co-location between two instances. For the experiments, we launched 4 accounts (named A, B, C and D) on the South American Amazon EC2 region and launched 20 m3.medium instances in each of these accounts, 80 instances in total.

On these instances, we performed our LLC co-location detection test and obtained co-located instance pairs. In total, out of 80 instances launched from different accounts, we were able to obtain 7 co-located pairs and one triplet. Account A had 5 co-located instances out of 20 while B and C had 4 and 7 respectively. As for the account D, we had no co-location with instances from other accounts. Overall, assuming that the account A is the target, next 60 instances launched in accounts B, C, D have 8.3 % probability of co-location with the target. Note that all co-locations were between machines from different accounts. The experiments did not aim at obtaining co-location with a single instance, for which the probability of obtaining co-location would be lower.

4.1   The LLC Co-location Method

The LLC is shared across all cores of most modern Intel CPUs, including the Intel Xeon E5-2670 v2 used (among others) in Amazon EC2. Accesses to LLC are thus transparent to all VMs co-located on the same machine, making it the perfect domain for covert communication and co-location detection.

Our LLC test is designed to detect cache lines that are needed to fill a specific set in the cache. In order to control the location that our data will occupy in the cache, the test allocates and works with hugepages.[1] In normal operation with moderate noise, the number of lines to fill one set is equal to LLC associativity, which is 20 in Intel Xeon E5-2670 v2 used in our Amazon EC2 instances. However, with more than one user trying to fill the same set at the same time, one will observe that fewer than 20 lines are needed to fill one set. By running this test concurrently on a co-located VM pair, both controlled by the same user, it is possible to verify co-location with high certainty. The test performs the following steps:

- Prime one memory block b_0 in a set in the LLC
- Access additional memory blocks $b_1, b_2, \ldots, b_n$ that occupy the same set, but can reside in a different slice.
- Reload the memory block b_0 to check whether it has been evicted from the LLC. A high reload time indicates that the memory block b_0 resides in the RAM. Therefore we know that the required m memory blocks that fill a slice are part of the accessed additional memory blocks $b_1, b_2, \ldots, b_n$.
- Subtract one of the accessed additional memory blocks b_i and repeat the above protocol. If b_0 is still loaded from the memory, b_i does not reside in the same slice. If b_0 is now located in the cache, it can be concluded that b_i resides in the same cache slice as b_0 and therefore fill the set.
- Count the number of memory blocks needed to fill a set/slice pair. If the number is significantly different than the associativity, it can be concluded that we have cache contention across co-located VMs.

The LLC is not the only method that we have tried in order to verify co-location (see extended version of this paper for more information [25]). However, the experiments show that the LLC test is the only decisive and reliable test that can detect whether two of our instances are running in the same CPU in Amazon EC2. We performed the LLC test in two steps as follows:

---

[1] The co-location test has to be implemented carefully, since the heavy usage of hugepages may yield into performance degradation. In fact, while trying to achieve a quadruple co-location Amazon EC2 stopped our VMs due to performance issues. For a more detailed explanation, see [25].

1. **Single Instance Elimination:** The first step of the LLC test is the elimination of single instances i.e. the ones that are not co-located with any other in the instance pool. To do so, we schedule the LLC test to run at all instances at the same time. Instances not detecting co-location is retired. For the remaining ones, the pairs need to be further processed as explained in the next step. Note that without this preliminary step, one would have to perform $n(n-1)/2$ pair detection tests to find co-located pairs, i.e. 3160 tests for 80 instances. This step yielded 22 co-located instances out of 80.
2. **Pair Detection:** Next we identify pairs for the possibly co-located instances. The test is performed as a binary search tree where each instance is tested against all the others for co-location.

4.2   Challenges and Tricks of Co-location Detection

During our experiments on Amazon EC2, we have observed various problems and interesting events related to the underlying hardware and software. Here we discuss what to expect when experimenting on Amazon EC2.

Instance Clock Decay: In our experiments using Amazon EC2, we have noticed that instance clocks degrade slowly over time. More interestingly, after detecting co-location using the LLC test, we discovered that co-located instances have the same clock degradation with 50 ns resolution. We believe that this information can be used for co-location detection.

Hardware Complexity: Modern Amazon EC2 instances have much more advanced and complex hardware components like 10 core, 20 thread CPUs and SSDs. Thus, our cache profiling techniques have to be adapted to handle servers with multiple slices that feature non-linear slice selection algorithms.

Co-located VM Noise: Compute cloud services including Amazon EC2 maintain a variety of services and servers. Most user-based services, however, quiet down when users quiet down, i.e. after midnight. Especially between 2 a.m. and 4 a.m. Internet traffic as well as computer usage is significantly lower than the rest of the day. We confirmed this assumption by measuring LLC noise in our instances and collected data from 6 instances over the course of 4 week days. Results are shown in Fig. 1. LLC noise and thus server load are at its peak around 8 p.m. and lowest at 4 a.m. We also measured the noise observed in the first 200 sets of the LLC for one day in Fig. 2. The y-axis shows the probability of observing a cache access by a co-located user other than victim during a `Prime and Probe` interval of the spy process (i.e. the attacker cannot detect the cache access of the victim process). The measurements were taken every 15 min. A constant noise floor at approx. 4.5 % is present in all sets. Sets 0 and 3 feature the highest noise, but high noise (11 %)is observed at the starting points of other pages as well. In fact, certain set numbers (0, 3, 26, 39, 58) mod 64 seem to be predictably more noisy and not well suited for the attack.

Dual Socket Machines: We did not find evidence of dual socket machines among the medium instances that we used in both co-location and attack steps. Indeed once co-located, our LLC co-location test always succeeded over time,

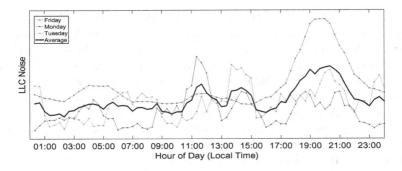

Fig. 1. LLC noise over time of day, by day (dotted lines) and on average (bold line).

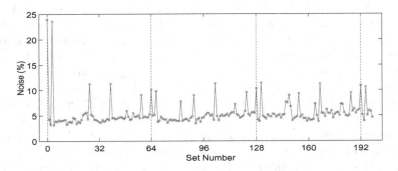

Fig. 2. Average noise for the first 200 sets in a day. Red lines are the starting points of pages. Sets 0 and 3 feature the highest amount of noise, with a repeating pattern every 64 sets (which is the width of a page in the LLC). (Color figure online)

even after a year. If the instances were to reside in dual socket machines and the VM processes moved between CPUs, the co-location test would have failed. However, even in that case, repeated experiments would still reveal co-location just by repeating the test after a time period enough to allow a socket migration.

5   Obtaining the Non-linear Slice Selection Algorithm

The LLC attack that will later be performed is based on the ability of generating colliding memory blocks, i.e., blocks that collide for a specific set and slice. In modern processors, each set in the LLC is divided into slices (usually one slice per core) to respond to multiple requests at a time. The usage of a sliced LLC as a covert channel becomes simpler when we deal with a power of two number of slices. In these cases, due to the linearity, the set bits does not affect the slice bits in the eviction set created for one of the slices. Thus, we could create an eviction set for a specific set-slice pair composed by $b1, b2, ..bn$ memory blocks choosing a random set s. If we later want to target a different set, we could still use $b1, b2, ...bn$ by changing only the set bits and they will fill the same slice.

This fact was used in [14, 26] to perform LLC side channel attacks. This peculiarity is not observed in non-linear slices, i.e., the same $b1, b2, .., bn$ will only slice-collide for a small number of sets. The slice colliding blocks can either be empirically observed for each set, or guessed if the non-linear slice selection algorithm is known. Our particular EC2 instance type utilizes a Intel Xeon E5-2670 v2, which features a 25 MB LLC distributed over 10 LLC slices (i.e., non power of two). We decide to reverse-engineer the non-linear slice selection algorithm to speed up our eviction set creation algorithm. Note that the approach that we follow can be utilized to reverse engineer *any* non-linear slice selection algorithm.

We describe the slice selection algorithm as

$$H(p) = h_3(p) \| h_2(p) \| h_1(p) \| h_0(p) \tag{1}$$

where each $H(p)$ is a concatenation of 4 different functions corresponding to the 4 necessary bits to represent 10 slices. Note that $H(p)$ will output results from 0000 to 1001 if we label the slices from 0–9. Thus, a non-linear function is needed that excludes outputs 10–15. Further note that p is the physical address and will be represented as a bit string: $p = p_0 p_1 \ldots p_{35}$. In order to recover the non-linear hash function implemented by the Intel Xeon E5-2670 v2, we use a fully controlled machine featuring the same Intel Xeon E5-2670 v2 found in Amazon's EC2 servers. We first generate ten equation systems (one per slice) based on slice colliding addresses by applying the same methodology explained to achieve co-location and generating up to 100,000 additional memory blocks.

Up to this point, one can solve the non-linear function after a re-linearization step given sufficiently many equations. Since we are not be able to recover enough addresses (due to RAM limitations) we take a different approach. Figure 3 shows the distribution of the 100,000 addresses over the 10 slices. Note that 8 slices are mapped to by 81.25 % of the addresses, while 2 slices get only about 18.75 %, i.e., a 3/16 proportion. We will refer to these two slices as the *non-linear slices*.

We proceed to first solve the first 8 slices and the last 2 slices separately using linear functions. For each we try to find solutions to the equation systems

$$P_i \cdot \hat{H}_i = \hat{0}, \tag{2}$$

$$P_i \cdot \hat{H}_i = \hat{1} . \tag{3}$$

Here P_i is the equation system obtained by arranging the slice colliding addresses into a matrix form, $\hat{H}_i$ is the matrix containing the slice selection functions and $\hat{0}$ and $\hat{1}$ are the all zero and all one solutions, respectively. This outputs two sets of linear solutions both for the first 8 linear slices and the last 2 slices.

Given that we can model the slice selection functions separately using linear functions, and given that the distribution is non-uniform, we model the hash function is implemented in two levels. In the first level a non-linear function chooses between either of the 3 linear functions describing the 8 linear slices or the linear functions describing the 2 non-linear slices. Therefore, we speculate that the 4 bits selecting the slice looks like:

$$H(p) = \begin{cases} h_0(p) = h_0(p) & h_1(p) = \neg(nl(p)) \cdot h_1'(p) \\ h_2(p) = \neg(nl(p)) \cdot h_2'(p) & h_3(p) = nl(p) \end{cases}$$

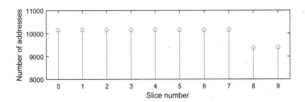

Fig. 3. Number of addresses that each slice takes out of 100,000. The non-linear slices take less addresses than the linear ones.

Table 1. Results for the hash selection algorithm implemented by the Intel Xeon E5-2670 v2

f	Hash function	$H(p) = h_0(p) \| \neg(nl(p)) \cdot h_1'(p) \| \neg(nl(p)) \cdot h_2'(p) \| nl(p)$
h_0	$p_{18} \oplus p_{19} \oplus p_{20} \oplus p_{22} \oplus p_{24} \oplus p_{25} \oplus p_{30} \oplus p_{32} \oplus p_{33} \oplus p_{34}$	
h_1'	$p_{18} \oplus p_{21} \oplus p_{22} \oplus p_{23} \oplus p_{24} \oplus p_{26} \oplus p_{30} \oplus p_{31} \oplus p_{32}$	
h_2'	$p_{19} \oplus p_{22} \oplus p_{23} \oplus p_{26} \oplus p_{28} \oplus p_{30}$	
nl	$v_0 \cdot v_1 \cdot \neg(v_2 \cdot v_3)$	
v_0	$p_9 \oplus p_{14} \oplus p_{15} \oplus p_{19} \oplus p_{21} \oplus p_{24} \oplus p_{25} \oplus p_{26} \oplus p_{27} \oplus p_{29} \oplus p_{32} \oplus p_{34}$	
v_1	$p_7 \oplus p_{12} \oplus p_{13} \oplus p_{17} \oplus p_{19} \oplus p_{22} \oplus p_{23} \oplus p_{24} \oplus p_{25} \oplus p_{27} \oplus p_{31} \oplus p_{32} \oplus p_{33}$	
v_2	$p_9 \oplus p_{11} \oplus p_{14} \oplus p_{15} \oplus p_{16} \oplus p_{17} \oplus p_{19} \oplus p_{23} \oplus p_{24} \oplus p_{25} \oplus p_{28} \oplus p_{31} \oplus p_{33} \oplus p_{34}$	
v_3	$p_7 \oplus p_{10} \oplus p_{12} \oplus p_{13} \oplus p_{15} \oplus p_{16} \oplus p_{17} \oplus p_{19} \oplus p_{20} \oplus p_{23} \oplus p_{24} \oplus p_{26} \oplus p_{28} \oplus p_{30}$ $\oplus p_{31} \oplus p_{32} \oplus p_{33} \oplus p_{34}$	

where h_0, h_1 and h_2 are the hash functions selecting bits 0,1 and 2 respectively, h_3 is the function selecting the 3rd bit and nl is a nonlinear function of an unknown degree. We recall that the proportion of the occurrence of the last two slices is 3/16. To obtain this proportion we need a degree 4 nonlinear function where two inputs are negated, i.e.:

$$nl = v_0 \cdot v_1 \cdot \neg(v_2 \cdot v_3) \tag{4}$$

where nl is 0 for the 8 linear slices and 1 for the 2 non-linear slices. Observe that nl will be 1 with probability 3/16 while it will be zero with probability 13/16, matching the distributions seen in our experiments. Consequently, to find v_0 and v_1 we only have to solve Eq. (3) for slices 8 and 9 together to obtain a 1 output. To find v_2 and v_3, we first separate those addresses where v_0 and v_1 output 1 for the linear slices $0 - 7$. For those cases, we solve Eq. (3) for slices $0 - 7$. The result is summarized in Table 1. We show both the non-linear function vectors v_0, v_1, v_2, v_3 and the linear functions h_0, h_1, h_2. These results describe the behavior of the slice selection algorithm implemented in the Intel Xeon E5-2670 v2. With this result, we can now easily predict the slice selection on the target processor in the EC2 cloud.

6   Cross-VM RSA Key Recovery

To prove the viability of the Prime and Probe attack in Amazon EC2 across co-located VMs, we present an expanded version of the attack implemented in [14] by showing its application to RSA. It is important to remark that the attack *is not* processor specific, and can be implemented in any processor with inclusive last level caches. In order to perform the attack:

- We make use of the fact that the offset of the address of each table position entry does not change when a new decryption process is executed. Therefore, we only need to monitor a subsection of all possible sets, yielding a lower number of traces.
- Instead of the monitoring both the multiplication and the table entry set (as in [14] for El-Gamal), we *only monitor a table entry set in one slice*. This avoids the step where the attacker has to locate the multiplication set and avoids an additional source of noise.

The attack targets a sliding window implementation of RSA-2048 where each position of the pre-computed table will be recovered. We will use Libgcrypt 1.6.2 as our target library, which not only uses a sliding window implementation but also uses CRT and message blinding techniques [34]. The message blinding process is performed as a side channel countermeasure for chosen-ciphertext attacks, in response to studies such as [16,17].

We use the Prime and Probe side channel technique to recover the positions of the table T that holds the values $c^3, c^5, c^7, \ldots, c^{2^W-1}$ where W is the window size. For CRT-RSA with 2048 bit keys, $W = 5$ for both exponentiations d_p, d_q. Observe that, if all the positions are recovered correctly, reconstructing the key is a straightforward step.

Recall that we do not control the victim's user address space. This means that we do not know the location of each of the table entries, which indeed changes from execution to execution. Therefore we will monitor a set hoping that it will be accessed by the algorithm. However, our analysis shows a special behavior: each time a new decryption process is started, even if the location changes, the offset field does not change from decryption to decryption. Thus, we can *directly* relate a monitored set with a specific entry in the multiplication table.

The knowledge of the processor in which the attack is going to be carried out gives an estimation of the probability that the set/slice we monitor collides with the set/slice the victim is using. For each table entry, we fix a specific set/slice where not much noise is observed. In the Intel Xeon E5-2670 v2 processors, the LLC is divided in 2048 sets and 10 slices. Therefore, knowing the lowest 12 bits of the table locations, we will need to monitor *one* set/slice that solves $s \bmod 64 = o$, where s is the set number and o is the offset for a table location. This increases the probability of probing the correct set from $1/(2048 \cdot 10) = 1/20480$ to $1/((2048 \cdot 10)/64) = 1/320$, reducing the number of traces to recover the key by a factor of 64. Thus our spy process will monitor accesses to *one* of the 320 set/slices related to a table entry, hoping that the RSA encryption accesses it when we run repeated decryptions. Thanks to the knowledge of the non linear slice selection algorithm, we can easily change our monitored set/slice if we see a high amount of noise in one particular set/slice. Since we also have to monitor a different set per table entry, it also helps us to change our eviction set accordingly. The threshold is different for each of the sets, since the time to access different slices usually varies. Thus, the threshold for each of the sets has to be calculated before the monitoring phase. In order to improve the applicability of the attack the LLC can be monitored to detect whether there are RSA decryptions or not in the co-located VMs as proposed in [24]. After it is proven that there are RSA decryptions the attack can be performed.

In order to obtain high quality timing leakage, we synchronize the spy process and the RSA decryption by initiating a communication between the victim and attacker, e.g. by sending a TLS request. Note that we are looking for a particular pattern observed for the RSA table entry multiplications, and therefore processes scheduled before the RSA decryption will not be counted as valid traces. In short, the attacker will communicate with the victim before the decryption. After this initial communication, the victim will start the decryption while the attacker starts monitoring the cache usage. In this way, we monitor 4,000 RSA decryptions with the same key and same ciphertext for each of the 16 different sets related to the 16 table entries.

We investigate a hypothetical case where a system with dual CPU sockets is used. In such a system, depending on the hypervisor CPU management, two scenarios can play out; processes moving between sockets and processes assigned to specific CPUs. In the former scenario, we can observe the necessary number of decryption samples simply by waiting over a longer period of time. In this scenario, the attacker would collect traces and only use the information obtained during the times the attacker and the victim share sockets and discard the rest as missed traces. In the latter scenario, once the attacker achieves co-location, as we have in Amazon EC2, the attacker will always run on the same CPU as the target hence the attack will succeed in a shorter span of time.

7   Leakage Analysis Method

Once the online phase of the attack has been performed, we proceed to analyze the leakage observed. There are three main steps to process the obtained data. The first step is to identify the traces that contain information about the key. Then we need to synchronize and correct the misalignment observed in the chosen traces. The last step is to eliminate the noise and combine different graphs to recover the usage of the multiplication entries. Among the 4,000 observations for each monitored set, only a small portion contains information about the multiplication operations with the corresponding table entry. These are recognized because their exponentiation trace pattern differs from that of unrelated sets. In order to identify where each exponentiation occurs, we inspected 100 traces and created the timeline shown in Fig. 4(b). It can be observed that the first exponentiation starts after 37 % of the overall decryption time. Note that among

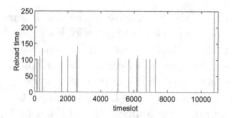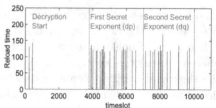

Fig. 4. Different sets of data where we find (a) trace that does not contain information (b) trace that contains information about the key

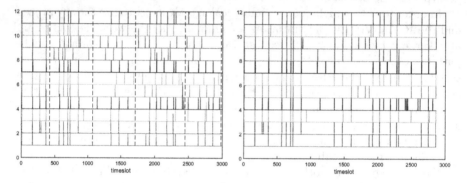

Fig. 5. 10 traces from the same set where (a) they are divided into blocks for a correlation alignment process (b) they have been aligned and the peaks can be extracted

all the traces recovered, only those that have more than 20 and less than 100 peaks are considered. The remaining ones are discarded as noise. Figure 4 shows measurements where no correct pattern was detected (Fig. 4(a)), and where a correct pattern was measured (Fig. 4(b)).

In general, after the elimination step, there are 8−12 correct traces left per set. We observe that data obtained from each of these sets corresponds to 2 consecutive table positions. This is a direct result of CPU cache prefetching. When a cache line that holds a table position is loaded into the cache, the neighboring table position is also loaded due to cache locality principle.

For each graph to be processed, we first need to align the creation of the look-up table with the traces. Identifying the table creation step is trivial since each table position is used twice, taking two or more time slots. Figure 5(a) shows the table access position indexes aligned with the table creation. In the figure, the top graph shows the true table accesses while the rest of the graphs show the measured data. It can be observed that the measured traces suffer from misalignment due to noise from various sources e.g. RSA or co-located neighbors.

To fix the misalignment, we take most common peaks as reference and apply a correlation step. To increase the efficiency, the graphs are divided into blocks and processed separately as seen in Fig. 5(a). At the same time, Gaussian filtering is applied to peaks. In our filter, the variance of the distribution is 1 and the

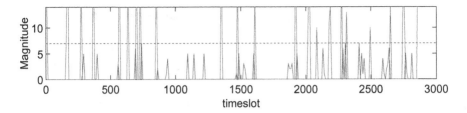

Fig. 6. Eliminating false detections using a threshold (red dashed line) on the combined detection graph. (Color figure online)

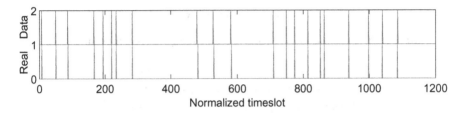

Fig. 7. Comparison of the final obtained peaks with the correct peaks with adjusted timeslot resolution

mean is aligned to the peak position. Then for each block, the cross-correlation is calculated with respect to the most common hit graph i.e. the intersection set of all graphs. After that, all graphs are shifted to the position where they have the highest correlation and aligned with each other. After the cross-correlation calculation and the alignment, the common patterns are observable as in Fig. 5(b). Observe that the alignment step successfully aligns measured graphs with the true access graph at the top, leaving only the combining and the noise removal steps. We combine the graphs by simple averaging and obtain a single combined graph.

In order to get rid of the noise in the combined graph, we applied a threshold filter as can be seen in Fig. 6. We used 35 % of the maximum peak value observed in graphs as the threshold value. Note that a simple threshold was sufficient to remove noise terms since they are not common between graphs.

Now we convert scaled time slots of the filtered graph to real time slot indexes. We do so by dividing them with the spy process resolution ratio, obtaining the Fig. 7. In the figure, the top and the bottom graphs represent the true access indexes and the measured graph, respectively. Also, note that even if additional noise peaks are observed in the obtained graph, it is very unlikely that two graphs monitoring consecutive table positions have noise peaks at the same time slot. Therefore, we can filter out the noise stemming from the prefetching by combining two graphs that belong to consecutive table positions. Thus, the resulting indexes are the corresponding timing slots for look-up table positions.

The very last step of the leakage analysis is finding the intersections of two graphs that monitor consecutive sets. By doing so, we obtain accesses to a single

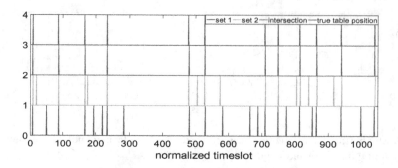

Fig. 8. Combination of two sets

Table 2. Successfully recovered peaks on average in an exponentiation

Average number of traces/set	4000
Average number of correct graphs/set	10
Wrong detected peaks	7.19 %
Missdetected peaks	0.65 %
Correctly detected peaks	92.15 %

table position as seen in Fig. 8 with high accuracy. At the same time, we have total of three positions in two graphs. Therefore, we also get the positions of the neighbors. A summary of the result of the leakage analysis is presented in Table 2. We observe that more than 92 % of the recovered peaks are in the correct position. However, note that by combining two different sets, the wrong peaks will disappear with high probability, since the chance of having wrong peaks in the same time slot in two different sets is very low.

8   Recovering RSA Keys with Noise

We divide the section in two different scenarios, i.e., the scenario where the identity and public key of the target is known (targeted co-location) and the scenario where we have no information about the public key (bulk key recovery).

8.1   Targeted Co-location: The Public Key Is Known

In this case we assume that the attacker implemented a targeted co-location against a known server, and that she has enough information about the public key parameters of the target. The leakage analysis described in the previous section recovers information on the CRT version of the secret exponent d, namely $d_p = d \mod (p-1)$ and $d_q = d \mod (q-1)$. A noise-free version of either one can be used to trivially recover the factorization of $N = pq$, since $\gcd(m - m^{ed_p}, N) = p$ for virtually any m [13].

In cases where the noise on d_p and d_q is too high for a direct recovery with the above-mentioned method, their relation to the known public key can be exploited if the used public exponent e is small [20].

Almost all RSA implementations currently use $e = 2^{16} + 1$ due to the heavy performance boost over a random and full size e. For CRT exponents it holds that $ed_p = 1 \mod (p - 1)$ and hence $ed_p = k_p(p - 1) + 1$ for some $1 \leq k_p < e$ and similarly for d_q, yielding $k_p p = ed_p + k_p - 1$ and $k_q p = ed_q + k_q - 1$.

Algorithm 1. Windowed RSA Key Recovery with Noise

---

  for k_p **from** 1 **to** $e - 1$ **do**
      Compute $k_q = (1 - k_p)(k_p N - k_p + 1)^{-1} \pmod{e}$
      while $i < |wp|$ **do**
         Process windows $wp[i], wp[i + 1]$
         Introduce shifts; vary $ip[i]]$ up max_{zeros}
         for each d_p variation **do**
            Compute $X = \sum_{j=0}^{i+1} wp[j] 2^{ip[j]}$
            Identify wq that overlap with $wp[i], wp[i + 1]$
            Compute $Y = \sum_{j=0}^{i+1} wq[j] 2^{iq[j]}$
            if $\delta(X, Y, t){=}0$ **then**
               Update wp, ip, wq, iq
               Create thread for $i + 1$
            end if
            if if no check succeeded **then**
               too many failures: abandon thread.
               if max_{zeros} achieved **then**
                  $i = i - 1$
               end if
               Update ip, wq, iq
               Create thread for i
            end if
         end for
      end while
  end for

Multiplying both equations gives us a key equation which we will exploit in two ways

$$k_p k_q N = (ed_p + k_p - 1)(ed_q + k_q - 1). \tag{5}$$

If we consider Eq. (5) modulo e, the unknowns d_p and d_q disappear and we obtain $k_p k_q N = (k_p - 1)(k_q - 1) \pmod{e}$. Therefore given k_p we can recover k_q and vice versa by solving this linear equation. Since $1 \leq k_p < e$ represents an exhaustible small space we can simply try all values for k_p and compute corresponding k_q as shown above.

Next, assume we are given the first t bits of d_p and d_q, e.g. $a = d_p \mod 2^t$ and $b = d_q \mod 2^t$. For each k_p we check whether $\delta(a, b, t) = 0$ where

$$\delta(a, b, t) = k_p k_q N - (ea + k_p - 1)(eb + k_q - 1) \pmod{2^t}$$

This means we have a simple technique to check the correctness of the least-significant t bits of d_p, d_q for a choice of k_p. We can

- **Check parts** of d_p and d_q by verifying if the test $\delta(d_p(t), d_q(t), t) = 0$ holds for $t \in [1, \lceil \log(p) \rceil]$.
- **Fix alignment and minor errors** by shifting and varying $d_p(t)$ and $d_q(t)$, and then sieving working cases by checking if $\delta(d_p(t), d_q(t), t) = 0$,
- **Recover parts** of d_q given d_p (and vice versa) by solving the error equation $\delta(d_p(t), d_q(t), t) = 0$ in case the data is missing or too noisy to correct.

Note that the algorithm may need to try all 2^{16} values of k_p in a loop. Further, in the last case where we recover a missing data part using the checking equation we need to speculatively continue the iteration for a few more steps. If we observe too many mistakes we may early terminate the execution thread without reaching the end of d_p and d_q.

To see how this approach can be adapted into our setting, we need to consider the error distribution observed in d_p and d_q as recovered by cache timing. Furthermore, since the sliding window algorithm was used in the RSA exponentiation operation, we are dealing with variable size (1–5 bit) *windows* with contents wp, wq, and window positions ip, iq for d_p and d_q, respectively.

The windows are separated by 0 strings. We observed:

- The window wp contents for d_p had no errors and were in the correct order. There were slight misalignments in the window positions ip with extra or missing zeros in between.
- In contrast, d_q had not only alignment problems but also few windows with incorrect content, extra windows, and missing windows (overwritten by zeros). The missing windows were detectable since we do not expect unusually long zero strings in a random d_q.
- Since the iterations proceed from the most significant windows to the least we observed more errors towards the least significant words, especially in d_q.

Algorithm 1 shows how one can progressively error correct d_p and d_q by processing groups of consecutive ℓ windows of d_p. The algorithm creates new execution threads when an assumption is made, and kills a thread after assumptions when too many checks fail to produce any matching on different windows. However, then the kill threshold has to be increased and the depth of the computation threads and more importantly the number of variations that need to be tested increases significantly. In this case, the algorithm finds the correct private key in the order of microseconds for a noise-free d_p and needs 4 s for our recovered d_p.

8.2   Bulk Key Recovery: The Public Key Is Unknown

In this scenario, the attacker spins multiple instances and monitors the LLC, looking in all of them for RSA leakages. If viable leakages are observed, the attacker might not know the corresponding public key. However, she can build up a database of public keys by mapping the entire IP range of the targeted Amazon EC2 region and retrieve all the public keys of hosts that have the TLS port open. The attacker then runs the above described algorithm for each of the recovered private keys and the entire public key database. Having the list of 'neighboring' IPs with an open TLS port also allows the attacker to initiate TLS handshakes to make the servers use their private keys with high frequency.

In the South America Amazon EC2 region, we have found 36000+ IP addresses with the TLS port open (shown in more detail in [25]) using nmap. With a public key database of that size, our algorithm takes between less than a second (for noise-free d_ps) and 30 CPU hours (noisy d_ps) to check each private key with the public key database. This approach recovers the public/private key pair, and consequently, the identity of the key owner.

9   Countermeasures

Libgcrypt 1.6.3 Update: Libgcrypt recently patched this vulnerability by making the sliding window multiplication table accesses indistinguishable from each other. Thus, an update to the latest version of the library avoids the leakage exploited in this work albeit only for ciphers using sliding window exponentiation.

Single-Tenant Instances: Although more expensive, in most cloud services, users have the option of having the whole physical machine to themselves, preventing co-location with potentially malicious users.

Live Migration: In a highly noisy environment like the commercial cloud, an attacker would need many traces to conduct a side-channel attack. In the live migration scenario, the attacker would have to perform the attack in the time period when the attacker and the victim share the physical machine.

10   Conclusion

In conclusion, we show that even with advanced isolation techniques, resource sharing still poses security risk to public cloud customers that do not follow the best security practices. The cross-VM leakage is present in public clouds and can be a practical attack vector for data theft. Therefore, users have a responsibility to use latest improved software for their critical cryptographic operations. Even further, we believe that smarter cache management policies are needed both at the hardware and software levels to prevent side-channel leakages.

Acknowledgments. This work is supported by the National Science Foundation, under grants CNS-1318919 and CNS-1314770.

References

1. Fix Flush and Reload in RSA. https://lists.gnupg.org/pipermail/gnupg-announce/2013q3/000329.html
2. Intel   Xeon   2670–v2.   http://ark.intel.com/es/products/75275/Intel-Xeon-Processor-E5-2670-v2-25M-Cache-2_50-GHz
3. OpenSSL fix flush and reload ECDSA nonces. https://git.openssl.org/gitweb/?p=openssl.git;a=commitdiff;h=2198be3483259de374f91e57d247d0fc667aef29
4. Transparent Page Sharing: Additional management capabilities and new default settings. http://blogs.vmware.com/security/vmware-security-response-center/page/2
5. Acıiçmez, O.: Yet another microarchitectural attack: exploiting I-cache. In: Proceedings of the 2007 ACM Workshop on Computer Security Architecture
6. Acıiçmez, O., Koç, Ç.K., Seifert, J.-P.: Predicting secret keys via branch prediction. In: Abe, M. (ed.) CT-RSA 2007. LNCS, vol. 4377, pp. 225–242. Springer, Heidelberg (2006)
7. Bates, A., Mood, B., Pletcher, J., Pruse, H., Valafar, M., Butler, K.: Detecting co-residency with active traffic analysis techniques. In: Proceedings of the 2012 ACM Workshop on Cloud Computing Security Workshop
8. Benger, N., van de Pol, J., Smart, N.P., Yarom, Y.: "Ooh Aah.. Just a Little Bit" : a small amount of side channel can go a long way. In: Batina, L., Robshaw, M. (eds.) CHES 2014. LNCS, vol. 8731, pp. 75–92. Springer, Heidelberg (2014)
9. Bernstein, D.J.: Cache-timing attacks on AES (2004). http://cr.yp.to/papers.html#cachetiming
10. Bernstein, D.J., Chang, Y.-A., Cheng, C.-M., Chou, L.-P., Heninger, N., Lange, T., van Someren, N.: Factoring RSA keys from certified smart cards: coppersmith in the wild. In: Sako, K., Sarkar, P. (eds.) ASIACRYPT 2013, Part II. LNCS, vol. 8270, pp. 341–360. Springer, Heidelberg (2013)
11. Bhattacharya, S., Mukhopadhyay, D.: Who watches the watchmen?: utilizing performance monitors for compromising keys of RSA on Intel platforms. In: Güneysu, T., Handschuh, H. (eds.) CHES 2015. LNCS, vol. 9293, pp. 248–266. Springer, Heidelberg (2015)
12. Brumley, D., Boneh, D.: Remote timing attacks are practical. In: Proceedings of the 12th USENIX Security Symposium, pp. 1–14 (2003)
13. Campagna, M.J., Sethi, A.: Key recovery method for CRT implementation of RSA. Cryptology ePrint Archive, Report 2004/147. http://eprint.iacr.org/
14. Liu, F., Yarom, Y., Ge, Q., Heiser, G., Lee, R.B.: Last level cache side channel attacks are practical, September 2015
15. Gandolfi, K., Mourtel, C., Olivier, F.: Electromagnetic analysis: concrete results. In: Koç, Ç.K., Naccache, D., Paar, C. (eds.) CHES 2001. LNCS, vol. 2162, pp. 251–261. Springer, Heidelberg (2001)
16. Genkin, D., Pachmanov, L., Pipman, I., Tromer, E.: Stealing keys from PCs using a radio: cheap electromagnetic attacks on windowed exponentiation. In: Güneysu, T., Handschuh, H. (eds.) CHES 2015. LNCS, vol. 9293, pp. 207–228. Springer, Heidelberg (2015)
17. Genkin, D., Shamir, A., Tromer, E.: RSA key extraction via low-bandwidth acoustic cryptanalysis. In: Garay, J.A., Gennaro, R. (eds.) CRYPTO 2014, Part I. LNCS, vol. 8616, pp. 444–461. Springer, Heidelberg (2014)
18. Gruss, D., Spreitzer, R., Mangard, S.: Cache.: template attacks: automating attacks on inclusive last-level caches. In: 24th USENIX Security Symposium, pp. 897–912. USENIX Association (2015)

19. Gullasch, D., Bangerter, E., Krenn, S.: Cache games - bringing access-based cache attacks on AES to practice. In: SP 2011, pp. 490–505
20. Hamburg, M.: Bit level error correction algorithm for RSA keys. Personal Communication. Cryptography Research Inc. (2013)
21. Heninger, N., Durumeric, Z., Wustrow, E., Halderman, J.A.: Mining your Ps and Qs: detection of widespread weak keys in network devices. In: Presented as Part of the 21st USENIX Security Symposium (USENIX Security 2012), Bellevue, WA. USENIX, pp. 205–220 (2012)
22. Hu, W.-M.: Lattice scheduling and covert channels. In: Proceedings of the 1992 IEEE Symposium on Security and Privacy
23. Hund, R., Willems, C.,Holz, T.: Practical timing side channel attacks against kernel space ASLR. In: Proceedings of the 2013 IEEE Symposium on Security and Privacy, pp. 191–205
24. İnci, M.S., Gülmezoglu, B., Eisenbarth, T., Sunar, B.: Co-location detection on the cloud. In: COSADE (2016)
25. İnci, M.S., Gülmezoglu, B., Irazoqui, G., Eisenbarth, T., Sunar, B.: Cache attacks enable bulk key recovery on the cloud (extended version) (2016). http://v.wpi. edu/wp-content/uploads/Papers/Publications/bulk_extended.pdf
26. Irazoqui, G., Eisenbarth, T., Sunar, B.: S$A: a shared cache attack that works across cores and defies VM sandboxing and its application to AES. In: 36th IEEE Symposium on Security and Privacy, S&P (2015)
27. Irazoqui, G., Eisenbarth, T., Sunar, B.: Systematic reverse engineering of cache slice selection in Intel processors. In: Euromicro DSD (2015)
28. Irazoqui, G., Eisenbarth, T., Sunar, B.: Cross processor cache attacks. In: Proceedings of the 11th ACM Symposium on Information, Computer and Communications Security, ASIA CCS 2016. ACM (2016)
29. Irazoqui, G., İnci, M.S., Eisenbarth, T., Sunar, B.: Know thy neighbor: crypto library detection in cloud. Proc. Priv. Enhancing Technol. 1(1), 25–40 (2015)
30. Irazoqui, G., İnci, M.S., Eisenbarth, T., Sunar, B.: Wait a minute! a fast, cross-VM attack on AES. In: RAID, pp. 299–319 (2014)
31. Irazoqui, G., İnci, M.S., Eisenbarth, T., Sunar, B.: Lucky 13 strikes back. In: Proceedings of the 10th ACM Symposium on Information, Computer and Communications Security, ASIA CCS 2015, pp. 85–96 (2015)
32. Kocher, P.C., Jaffe, J., Jun, B.: Differential power analysis. In: Wiener, M. (ed.) CRYPTO 1999. LNCS, vol. 1666, pp. 388–397. Springer, Heidelberg (1999)
33. Kocher, P.C.: Timing attacks on implementations of Diffie-Hellman, RSA, DSS, and other systems. In: Koblitz, N. (ed.) CRYPTO 1996. LNCS, vol. 1109, pp. 104–113. Springer, Heidelberg (1996)
34. Libgcrypt: The Libgcrypt reference manual. http://www.gnupg.org/ documentation/manuals/gcrypt/
35. Lipp, M., Gruss, D., Spreitzer, R., Mangard, S. ARMageddon : last-level cache attacks on mobile devices. CoRR abs/1511.04897 (2015)
36. Maurice, C., Scouarnec, N.L., Neumann, C., Heen, O., Francillon, A.: Reverse engineering intel last-level cache complex addressing using performance counters. In: RAID 2015 (2015)
37. Oren, Y., Kemerlis, V.P., Sethumadhavan, S., Keromytis, A.D.: The spy in the sandbox : practical cache attacks in javascript and their implications. In: Proceedings of the 22nd ACM SIGSAC Conference on Computer and Communications Security, New York, NY, USA, CCS 2015, pp. 1406–1418. ACM (2015)

38. Osvik, D.A., Shamir, A., Tromer, E.: Cache attacks countermeasures.: the case of AES. In: Proceedings of the 2006 The Cryptographers' Track at the RSA Conference on Topics in Cryptology, CT-RSA 2006

39. Page, D.: Theoretical use of cache memory as a cryptanalytic side-channel (2002)

40. Ristenpart, T., Tromer, E., Shacham, H., Savage, S.: Hey you, get off of my cloud: exploring information leakage in third-party compute clouds. In: Proceedings of the 16th ACM Conference on Computer and Communications Security, CCS 2009, pp. 199–212

41. Suzaki, K., Iijima, K., Toshiki, Y., Artho, C.: Implementation of a memory disclosure attack on memory deduplication of virtual machines. IEICE Trans. Fundam. Electron., Commun. Comput. Sci. **96**, 215–224 (2013)

42. Varadarajan, V., Zhang, Y., Ristenpart, T., Swift, M.: A placement vulnerability study in multi-tenant public clouds. In: 24th USENIX Security Symposium (USENIX Security 2015), Washington, D.C., August 2015, pp. 913–928. USENIX Association

43. Wu, Z., Xu, Z., Wang, H.: Whispers in the hyper-space: high-speed covert channel attacks in the cloud. In: USENIX Security Symposium, pp. 159–173 (2012)

44. Xu, Z., Wang, H., Wu, Z.: A measurement study on co-residence threat inside the cloud. In: 24th USENIX Security Symposium (USENIX Security 2015), Washington, D.C., August 2015, pp. 929–944. USENIX Association

45. Yarom, Y., Falkner, K.: FLUSH+RELOAD: a high resolution, low noise, L3 cache side-channel attack. In: 23rd USENIX Security Symposium (USENIX Security 2014), pp. 719–732

46. Yarom, Y., Ge, Q., Liu, F., Lee, R.B., Heiser, G.: Mapping the Intel last-level cache. Cryptology ePrint Archive, Report 2015/905 (2015). http://eprint.iacr.org/

47. Zhang, Y., Juels, A., Oprea, A., Reiter, M.K.: HomeAlone : co-residency detection in the cloud via side-channel analysis. In: Proceedings of the 2011 IEEE Symposium on Security and Privacy

48. Zhang, Y., Juels, A., Reiter, M. K., Ristenpart, T.: Cross-tenant side-channel attacks in paas clouds. In: Proceedings of the 2014 ACM SIGSAC Conference on Computer and Communications Security

49. Zhang, Y., Juels, A., Reiter, M.K., Ristenpart, T.: Cross-VM side channels and their use to extract private keys. In: Proceedings of the 2012 ACM Conference on Computer and Communications Security

Physical Unclonable Functions

Strong Machine Learning Attack Against PUFs with No Mathematical Model

Fatemeh Ganji$^{(\boxtimes)}$, Shahin Tajik, Fabian Fäßler, and Jean-Pierre Seifert

Security in Telecommunications, Technische Universität Berlin and Telekom
Innovation Laboratories, Berlin, Germany
{fganji,stajik,jpseifert}@sec.t-labs.tu-berlin.de,
fabian.faessler@campus.tu-berlin.de

Abstract. Although numerous attacks revealed the vulnerability of different PUF families to non-invasive Machine Learning (ML) attacks, the question is still open whether all PUFs might be learnable. Until now, virtually all ML attacks rely on the assumption that a mathematical model of the PUF functionality is known a priori. However, this is not always the case, and attention should be paid to this important aspect of ML attacks. This paper aims to address this issue by providing a provable framework for ML attacks against a PUF family, whose underlying mathematical model is unknown. We prove that this PUF family is inherently vulnerable to our novel PAC (Probably Approximately Correct) learning framework. We apply our ML algorithm on the Bistable Ring PUF (BR-PUF) family, which is one of the most interesting and prime examples of a PUF with an unknown mathematical model. We practically evaluate our ML algorithm through extensive experiments on BR-PUFs implemented on Field-Programmable Gate Arrays (FPGA). In line with our theoretical findings, our experimental results strongly confirm the effectiveness and applicability of our attack. This is also interesting since our complex proof heavily relies on the spectral properties of Boolean functions, which are known to hold only asymptotically. Along with this proof, we further provide the theorem that *all* PUFs must have some challenge bit positions, which have larger influences on the responses than other challenge bits.

Keywords: Machine learning · PAC learning · Boosting technique · Fourier analysis · Physically Unclonable Functions (PUFs)

1 Introduction

Nowadays, it is broadly accepted that Integrated Circuits (ICs) are subject to overbuilding and piracy due to the adaption of authentication methods relying on insecure key storage techniques [24]. To overcome the problem of secure key storage, Physically Unclonable Functions (PUFs) have been introduced as promising solutions [15,30]. For PUFs, the manufacturing process variations lead eventually to instance-specific, and inherent physical properties that can generate virtually

© International Association for Cryptologic Research 2016
B. Gierlichs and A.Y. Poschmann (Eds.): CHES 2016, LNCS 9813, pp. 391–411, 2016.
DOI: 10.1007/978-3-662-53140-2_19

unique *responses*, when the instance is given some *challenges*. Therefore, PUFs can be utilized as either device fingerprints for secure authentication or as a source of entropy in secure key generation scenarios. In this case, there is no need for permanent key storage, since the desired key is generated instantly upon powering up the device. Regarding the instance-specific, and inherent physical properties of the PUFs, they are assumed to be *unclonable* and *unpredictable*, and therefore trustworthy and robust against attacks [26]. However, after more than a decade of the invention of PUFs, the design of a really unclonable physical function is still a challenging task. Most of the security schemes relying on the notion of PUFs are designed based on a "design-break-patch" rule, instead of a thorough cryptographic approach.

Along with the construction of a wide variety of PUFs, several different types of attacks, ranging from non-invasive to semi-invasive attacks [18,19,33,39], have been launched on these primitives. Machine learning (ML) attacks are one of the most common types of non-invasive attacks against PUFs, whose popularity stems from their characteristics, namely being cost-effective and non-destructive. Moreover, these attacks require the adversary to *solely* observe the input-output (i.e., so called *challenge-response*) behavior of the targeted PUF. In this attack scenario, a relatively small subset of challenges along with their respective responses is collected by the adversary, attempting to come up with a model describing the challenge-response behavior of the PUF. In addition to heuristic learning techniques, e.g., what has been proposed in [33,34], the authors of [12–14] have proposed the probably approximately correct (PAC) learning framework to ensure the delivery of a model for prespecified levels of accuracy and confidence. One of the key results reported in [12–14] is that knowing about the mathematical model of the PUF functionality enables the adversary to establish a proper *hypothesis representation* (i.e., mathematical model of the PUF), and then try to PAC learn this representation. This gives rise to the question of whether a PUF can be PAC learned without prior knowledge of a precise mathematical model of the PUF.

Bistable Ring PUFs (BR-PUF) [7] and Twisted Bistable Ring PUFs (TBR-PUF) [37] are examples of PUFs, whose functionality cannot be easily translated to a precise mathematical model. In an attempt, the authors of [37,41] suggested simplified mathematical models for BR-PUFs and TBR-PUFs. However, their models do not precisely reflect the physical behavior of these architectures.

In this paper, we present a sound mathematical machine learning framework, which enables us to PAC learn the BR-PUF family (i.e., including BR- and TBR-PUFs) without knowing their precise mathematical model. Particularly, our framework contributes to the following novel aspects related to the security assessment of PUFs in general:

Exploring the inherent mathematical properties of PUFs. One of the most natural and commonly accepted mathematical representation of a PUF is a Boolean function. This representation enables us to investigate properties of PUFs, which are observed in practice, although they have not been precisely and mathematically described. One of these properties exhaustively studied in our paper is related to the "silent" assumption that each and every bit of a challenge has equal influence on the respective response of a PUF. We prove that this assumption is invalid for all PUFs. While this phenomenon has been already occasionally observed in practice and is most often attributed to implementation imperfections, we will give a rigorous mathematical proof on the existence of influential bit positions, which holds for every PUF.

Strong ML attacks against PUFs without available mathematical model. We prove that even in a worst case scenario, where the internal functionality of the BR-PUF family cannot be mathematically modeled, the challenge-response behavior of these PUFs can be PAC learned for given levels of accuracy and confidence.

Evaluation of the applicability of our framework in practice. In order to evaluate the effectiveness of our theoretical framework, we conduct extensive experiments on BR-PUFs and TBR-PUFs, implemented on a commonly used Field Programmable Gate Array (FPGA).

2   Notation and Preliminaries

This section serves as brief introduction into the required background knowledge and known results to understand the approaches taken in this paper. For some more complex topics we will occasionally refer the reader to important references.

2.1   PUFs

Note that elaborate and formal definitions as well as formalizations of PUFs are beyond the scope of this paper, and for more details on them we refer the reader to [3,4]. In general, PUFs are physical input to output mappings, which map given *challenges* to *responses*. Intrinsic properties of the physical primitive embodying the PUF determine the characteristics of this mapping. Two main classes of PUFs, namely strong PUFs and weak PUFs have been discussed in the literature [16]. In this paper we consider the strong PUFs, briefly called PUFs. Here we focus only on two characteristics of PUFs, namely unclonablity and unpredictability (i.e., so called unforgeability). Let a PUF be described by the mapping $f_{\text{PUF}} : \mathcal{C} \to \mathcal{Y}$, where $f_{\text{PUF}}(c) = y$. In this paper, we assume that the issue with noisy responses (i.e., the output is not stable for a given input) must have been resolved by the PUF manufacturer. For an *ideal* PUF, unclonablity means that for a given PUF f_{PUF} it is virtually impossible to create another physical mapping $g_{\text{PUF}} \neq f_{\text{PUF}}$, whose challenge-response behavior is *similar* to f_{PUF} [3].

Moreover, an ideal PUF is *unpredictable*. This property of PUFs is closely related to the notion of learnability. More precisely, given a single PUF f_{PUF} and a set of challenge response pairs (CRPs) $U = \{(c, y) \mid y = f_{\text{PUF}}(c) \text{ and } c \in \mathcal{C}\}$, it is (almost) impossible to predict $y' = f_{\text{PUF}}(c')$, where c' is a random challenge so that $(c', \cdot) \notin U$. In this paper we stick to this (simple, but) classical definition of unpredictability of a PUF, and refer the reader to [3,4] for more refined definitions.

2.2   Boolean Functions as representations of PUFs

Defining PUFs as mappings (see Sect. 2.1), the most natural mathematical model for them are Boolean functions over the finite field $\mathbb{F}_2$. Let $V_n = \{c_1, c_2, \ldots, c_n\}$ denote the set of Boolean attributes or variables, where each attribute can be *true* or *false*, commonly denoted by "1" and "0", respectively. In addition, $C_n = \{0,1\}^n$ contains all binary strings with n bits. We associate each Boolean attribute c_i with two *literals*, i.e., c_i, and $\bar{c}_i$ (complement of c_i). An *assignment* is a mapping from V_n to $\{0,1\}$, i.e., the mapping from each Boolean attribute to either "0" or "1". In other words, an assignment is an n-bits string, where the ith bit of this string indicates the value of c_i (i.e., "0" or "1").

An assignment is mapped by a Boolean formula into the set $\{0,1\}$. Thus, each Boolean attribute can also be thought of as a formula, i.e., c_i and $\bar{c}_i$ are two possible formulas. If by evaluating a Boolean formula under an assignment we obtain "1", it is called a *positive example* of the "concept represented by the formula" or otherwise a *negative example*. Each Boolean formula defines a respective Boolean function $f : C_n \to \{0,1\}$. The conjunction of Boolean attributes (i.e., a Boolean formula) is called a *term*, and it can be true or false ("1" or "0") depending on the value of its Boolean attributes. Similarly, a *clause* that is the disjunction of Boolean attributes can be defined. The number of literals forming a term or a clause is called its size. The size 0 is associated with only the term **true**, and the clause **false**.

In the related literature several representations of Boolean functions have been introduced, e.g., juntas, Monomials (M_n), Decision Trees (DTs), and Decision Lists (DLs), cf. [29, 31].

A Boolean function depending on solely an unknown set of k variables is called a k-junta. A monomial $M_{n,k}$ defined over V_n is the conjunction of at most k clauses each having only one literal. A DT is a binary tree, whose internal nodes are labeled with a Boolean variable, and each leaf with either "1" or "0". A DT can be built from a Boolean function in this way: for each assignment a unique path form the root to a leaf should be defined. At each internal node, e.g., at the ith level of the tree, depending on the value of the ith literal, the labeled edge is chosen. The leaf is labeled with the value of the function, given the respective assignment as the input. The *depth* of a DT is the maximum length of the paths from the root to the leafs. The set of Boolean functions represented by decision trees of depth at most k is denoted by k-DT. A DL is a list L that contains r pairs $(f_1, v_1), \ldots, (f_r, v_r)$, where the Boolean formula f_i is a term and $v_i \in \{0,1\}$ with $1 \leq i \leq r - 1$. For $i = r$, the formula f_r is the constant function $v_r = 1$. A Boolean function can be transformed into a decision list, where for a string $c \in C_n$ we have $L(c) = v_j$, where j is the smallest index in L so that $f_j(c) = 1$. k-DL denotes the set of all DLs, where each f_i is a term of maximum size k.

Linearity of Boolean Functions. Here, our focus is on *Boolean linearity*, which must not be confused with the linearity over other domains different from $\mathbb{F}_2$.

A linear Boolean function $f : \{0,1\}^n \rightarrow \{0,1\}$ features the following equivalent properties, cf. [29]:

- $\forall c, c' \in \{0,1\}^n : f(c + c') = f(c) + f(c')$
- $\exists a \in \{0,1\}^n : f(c) = a \cdot c$.

Equivalently, we can define a linear Boolean function f as follows. There is some set $S \subseteq \{1, \ldots, n\}$ such that $f(c) = f(c_1, c_2, \ldots, c_n) = \sum_{i \in S} c_i$.

Boolean linearity or linearity over $\mathbb{F}_2$ is closely related to the notion of correlation immunity. A Boolean function f is called k-**correlation immune**, if for any assignment c chosen randomly from $\{0,1\}^n$ it holds that $f(c)$ is independent of any k-tuple $(c_{i_1}, c_{i_1}, \ldots, c_{i_k})$, where $1 \leq i_1 < i_2 < \cdots < i_k \leq n$. Now let $\deg(f)$ denote the degree of the $\mathbb{F}_2$-polynomial representation of the Boolean function f. It is straightforward to show that such representation exists. Siegenthaler proved the following theorem, which states how correlation immunity can be related to the degree of f.

Theorem 1. (Siegenthaler Theorem [29,38]) *Let* $f : \{0,1\}^n \rightarrow \{0,1\}$ *be a Boolean function, which is k-correlation immune, then* $\deg(f) \leq n - k$.

Average Sensitivity of Boolean Functions. The Fourier expansion of Boolean functions serves as an excellent tool for analyzing them, cf. [29]. In order to define the Fourier expansion of a Boolean function $f : \mathbb{F}_2^n \rightarrow \mathbb{F}_2$ we should first define an encoding scheme as follows. $\chi(0_{\mathbb{F}_2}) := +1$, and $\chi(1_{\mathbb{F}_2}) := -1$. Now the Fourier expansion of a Boolean function can be written as

$$f(c) = \sum_{S \subseteq [n]} \hat{f}(S) \chi_S(c),$$

where $[n] := \{1, \ldots, n\}$, $\chi_S(c) := \prod_{i \in S} c_i$, and $\hat{f}(S) := \mathbf{E}_{c \in \mathcal{U}}[f(c)\chi_S(c)]$. Here, $\mathbf{E}_{c \in \mathcal{U}}[\cdot]$ denotes the expectation over uniformly chosen random examples. The **influence of variable** i **on** $f : \mathbb{F}_2^n \rightarrow \mathbb{F}_2$ is defined as

$$\text{Inf}_i(f) := \Pr_{c \in \mathcal{U}}[f(c) \neq f(c^{\oplus i})],$$

where $c^{\oplus i}$ is obtained by flipping the i-th bit of c. Note that $\text{Inf}_i(f) = \sum_{S \ni i}(\hat{f}(S))^2$, cf. [29]. Next we define the **average sensitivity** of a Boolean function f as

$$\text{I}(f) := \sum_{i=1}^{n} \text{Inf}_i(f).$$

2.3   Our Learning Model

The Probably Approximately Correct (PAC) model provides a firm basis for analyzing the efficiency and effectiveness of machine learning algorithms. We briefly introduce the model and refer the reader to [23] for more details. In the

PAC model the learner, i.e., the learning algorithm, is given a set of *examples* to generate with high probability an approximately correct hypothesis. This can be formally defined as follows. Let $F = \cup_{n \geq 1} F_n$ denote a *target concept class* that is a collection of Boolean functions defined over the *instance space* $C_n = \{0,1\}^n$. Moreover, according to an arbitrary probability distribution D on the instance space C_n each example is drawn. Assume that hypothesis $h \in F_n$ is a Boolean function over C_n, it is called an ε-approximator for $f \in F_n$, if

$$\Pr_{c \in_D C_n} [f(c) = h(c)] \geq 1 - \varepsilon.$$

Let the mapping $size : \{0,1\}^n \to \mathbb{N}$ associate a natural number $size(f)$ with a target concept $f \in F$ that is a measure of complexity of f under a target representation, e.g., k-DT. The learner is a polynomial-time algorithm denoted by A, which is given labeled examples $(c, f(c))$, where $c \in C_n$ and $f \in F_n$. The examples are drawn independently according to distribution D. Now we can define strong and weak PAC learning algorithms.

Definition 1. *An algorithm* A *is called a* **strong** *PAC learning algorithm for the target concept class F, if for any $n \geq 1$, any distribution D, any $0 < \varepsilon, \delta < 1$, and any $f \in F_n$ the follwing holds. When* A *is given a polynomial number of labeled examples, it runs in time polynomial in n, $1/\varepsilon$, $size(f)$, $1/\delta$, and returns an ε-approximator for f under D, with probability at least $1 - \delta$.*

The weak learning framework was developed to answer the question whether a PAC learning algorithm with constant but insufficiently low levels of ε and δ can be useful at all. This notion is defined as follows.

Definition 2. *For some constant $\delta > 0$ let algorithm* A *return with probability at least $1 - \delta$ an $(1/2 - \gamma)$-approximator for f, where $\gamma > 0$.* A *is called a* **weak** *PAC learning algorithm, if $\gamma = \Omega(1/p(n, size(f))$ for some polynomial $p(\cdot)$.*

The equivalence of weak PAC learning and strong PAC learning has been proved by Freund and Schapire in the early nineties in their seminal papers [9,35]. For that purpose *boosting* algorithms have been introduced.

Definition 3. *An algorithm* B *is called a boosting algorithm if the following holds. Given any $f \in F_n$, any distribution D, $0 < \varepsilon, \delta < 1$, $0 < \gamma \leq 1/2$, a polynomial number of labeled examples, and a weak learning algorithm* WL *returning an $(1/2 - \gamma)$-approximator for f, then* B *runs in time, which is polynomial in n, $size(f)$, $1/\gamma$, $1/\varepsilon$, $1/\delta$ and generates with probability at least $1 - \delta$ an ε-approximator for f under D.*

The construction of virtually all existing boosting algorithms is based primarily on the fact that if WL is given examples drawn from any distribution D', WL returns a $(1/2 - \gamma)$-approximator for f under D'. At a high-level, the skeleton of all such boosting algorithms is shown in Algorithm 1.

Algorithm 1. Canonical Booster

Require: Weak PAC learner WL, $0 < \varepsilon, \delta < 1$, $0 < \gamma \leq 1/2$, polynomial number of examples, i that is the number of iterations
Ensure: Hypothesis h that is an ε-approximator for f

1: $D_0 = D$, use WL to generate an approximator h_0 for f under D_0
2: $k = 1$
3: **while** $k \leq i - 1$ **do**
4:     Build a distribution D_k consisting of examples, where the previous approximators $h_0, \cdots, h_{k-1}$ can predict the value of f poorly
5:     use WL to generate an approximator h_k for f under D_k
6:     $k = k + 1$
7: **od**
8: Combine the hypotheses $h_0, \cdots, h_{i-1}$ to obtain h, where each h_i is an $(1/2 - \gamma)$-approximator for f under D_i, and finally h is an ε-approximator for f under D
9: **return** h

2.4 Non-linearity of PUFs Over $\mathbb{F}_2$ and the Existence of Influential Bits

Section 2.2 introduced the notion of Boolean linearity. Focusing on this notion and taking into account the definition of PUFs mentioned in Sect. 2.1, now we prove the following theorem that is our first important result. For all PUFs, when represented as a Boolean function, it holds that their degree as $\mathbb{F}_2$-polynomial is strictly greater than one. This will then lead us to the following dramatic consequence. *There exists no PUF, in which all of its challenge bits have an equal influence.*

Theorem 2. *For every PUF $f_{PUF} : \{0,1\}^n \rightarrow \{0,1\}$, we have $\deg(f_{PUF}) \geq 2$. Consequently, for every PUF it holds that not all bit positions within respective challenges are equally influential in generating the corresponding response.*

Proof: Towards contradiction assume that f_{PUF} is Boolean linear over $\mathbb{F}_2$ and unpredictable. From the unpredictability of f_{PUF} it follows that the adversary has access to a set of CRPs $U = \{(c,y) \mid y = f_{\mathrm{PUF}}(c) \text{ and } c \in \mathcal{C}\}$, which are chosen uniformly at random, however, the adversary has only a negligible probability of success to predict a new random challenge $(c', \cdot) \notin U$ (as he cannot apply f_{PUF} to this unseen challenge). Note that the size of U is actually polynomial in n. Now, by the definition of linearity over $\mathbb{F}_2$, cf. Sect. 2.2, we deduce that the only linear functions over $\mathbb{F}_2$ are the Parity functions, see also [29,38]. However, there are well-known algorithms to PAC learn Parity functions in general [8,20]. Thus, now we simply feed the right number of samples from our CRP set U into such a PAC learner. For the right parameter setting, the respective PAC algorithm delivers then with high probability an ε-approximator h for our PUF f_{PUF} such that $\Pr[f(c') = h(c')] \geq 1 - \varepsilon$. This means that with high probability, the response to every randomly chosen challenge can be calculated in polynomial time. This is of course a contradiction to the definition of f_{PUF}, being a PUF. Hence, f_{PUF} cannot be linear over $\mathbb{F}_2$. In other words, for every PUF f_{PUF} we have $\deg(f_{\mathrm{PUF}}) \geq 2$. Moreover, in conjunction with the above mentioned Siegenthaler Theorem, we deduce that every PUF is at most an $n - 2$-correlation immune function, which indeed means that not all of its challenge bits have an equal influence on the respective PUF response.   ■

Theorem 2 states that every PUF has some challenge bits, which have some larger influence on the responses than other challenge bits. We call these bits "loosely" as *influential bits*[1].

3   PUF Architectures

In this section, we explain the architectures of two intrinsic silicon PUFs, namely the BR- and TBR-PUFs, whose internal mathematical models are more complicated than other intrinsic PUF constructions. In an attempt, we apply simple models to describe the functionality of these PUFs. However, we believe that these models cannot completely reflect the real characteristics of the BR-PUF family, and their concrete, yet unknown model should be much more complex.

3.1   Memory-Based PUFs

BR-PUFs can be thought of as a combination of memory-based and delay-based PUFs. Memory-based PUFs exploit the settling state of digital memory circuits, e.g., SRAM cells [16,21] consisting of two inverters in a loop (see Fig. 1a) and two transistors for read and write operation. Due to manufacturing process variations the inverters have different electrical gains, when the cell is in the metastable condition. In the metastable condition the voltage of one of the inverters is equal to V_m, where V_m is an invalid logic level. Moreover, the invertes have different propagation delays due to the differences in their output resistance and load capacitance. One can model the SRAM cell architecture as a linear amplifier with gain G, when $V_{initial}$ is close to the metastable voltage V_m [40], see Fig. 1b. In order to predict the metastable behavior, we have [40]

$$V_{initial}(0) = V_m + V(0),$$

(a)   (b)

Fig. 1. (a) The logical circuit of an SRAM cell. (b) The small signal model of bistable element in metastability

---

[1] Note that the existence of such influential bits has been also noticed by several other experimental research papers. However, none of them has been able to correctly and precisely pinpoint the mathematical origin of this phenomenon.

where $V(0)$ is a small signal offset from the metastable point. To derive $V(t)$ we can write the equation of the circuit as follows.

$$\frac{G \cdot V(t) - V(t)}{R} = C \cdot \frac{dV(t)}{dt}.$$

By solving this equation, we obtain $V(t) = V(0) \cdot e^{t/\tau_s}$, where $\tau_s = RC/G - 1$, c.f. [40]. The time required to reach a stable condition increases as $V_{initial}$ approaches the metastable point and $V(0)$ approaches 0. On the other hand, it can approach infinity, if $V(0) = 0$, however, in practice this is not the case due to the presence of noise. Nevertheless, there is no upper bound on the settling time of the SRAM cell to one of the stable states. Therefore, the settling state of the SRAM cells cannot be predicted after power-on. One can thus use the logical addresses of SRAM cells as different challenges and the state of the SRAM cells after power-on as PUF responses.

3.2 Bistable Ring PUF

SRAM PUFs are believed to be secure against modeling attacks. This can be explained by the fact that knowing the state of one SRAM PUF after power-on does not help the attacker to predict the response of other SRAM cells. However, in contrast to delay-based PUFs, e.g., arbiter PUFs [25], the challenge space of an SRAM PUF is not exponential. Therefore, if an adversary gets access to the initial values stored in the SRAM cells, the challenge-response behavior of the SRAM PUF can be emulated. In order to combine the advantages offered by delay-based PUFs and memory-based PUFs, namely, exponential challenge space and the unpredictability, a new architecture called BR-PUF was introduced by [7]. A BR-PUF consists of n stages (n is an even number), where each stage consists of two NOR gates, one demultiplexer and one multiplexer, see Fig. 2. Based on the value of the ith bit of a

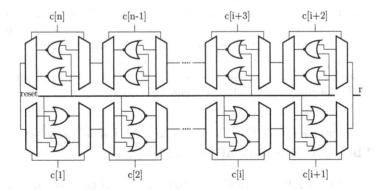

Fig. 2. The schematic of a BR-PUF with n stages. The response of the PUF can be read between two arbitrary stages. For a given challenge, the reset signal can be set low to activate the PUF. After a transient period, the BR-PUF might be settled to an allowed logical state.

challenge applied to the ith stage, one of the NOR gates is selected. Setting the reset signal to low, the signal propagates in the ring, which behaves like an SRAM cell with a larger number inverters. The response of the PUF is a binary value, which can be read from a predefined location on the ring between two stages, see Fig. 2.

The final state of the inverter ring is a function of the gains and the propagation delays of the gates. According to the model of the SRAM circuit in the metastable state provided in Sect. 3.1, one might be able to extend the electrical model and analyze the behavior of the inverter ring. Applying a challenge, the ring may settle at a stable state after a oscillation time period. However, for a specific set of challenges the ring might stay in the metastable state for an infinite time, and the oscillation can be observed in the output of the PUF.

The analytical models of the metastable circuits introduced in Sect. 3.1 are valid for an ASIC implementation and respective simulations. Although few simulation results of BR-PUF are available in the literature, to the best of our knowledge there are no results for a BR-PUF implemented on an ASIC, and experimental results have been limited to FPGA implementations. In this case, the BR-PUF model can be further simplified by considering the internal architecture of the FPGAs. The NOR gates of the BR-PUF are realized by dedicated Lookup Tables (LUTs) inside an FPGA. The output of the LUTs are read from one of the memory cells of the LUT, which have always stable conditions. Hence, it can be assumed that there is almost no difference in the gains of different LUTs. As a result, the random behavior of the BR-PUF could be defined by the delay differences between the LUTs.

3.3 Twisted Bistable Ring PUF

Although the mathematical model of the functionality of a BR-PUF is unknown, it has been observed that this construction is vulnerable to bias and simple linear approximations [37]. Hence, the TBR-PUF, as an enhancement to BR-PUFs, has been introduced [37]. Similar to BR-PUFs, a TBR-PUF consists of n stages (n is an even number), where each stage consists of two NOR gates. In contrast to BR-PUF, where for a given challenge only one of the NOR gates in each stage is selected, all $2n$ gates are selected in a TBR-PUF. This can be achieved by placing two multiplexers before and two multiplexers after each stage and having feedback lines between different stages, see Fig. 3. As all NOR gates are always in the circuit, the challenge specific bias can be reduced.

4   PAC Learning of PUFs Without Prior Knowledge of Their Mathematical Model

When discussing the PAC learnability of PUFs as a target concept, two scenarios should be distinguished. First, the precise mathematical model of the PUF functionality is known, and hence, a hypothesis representation is known to learn the PUF. This scenario has been considered in several studies, e.g., [12–14], where different hypothesis representations have been presented for each individual PUF

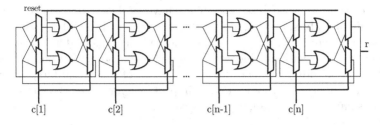

Fig. 3. The schematic of a TBR-PUF with n stages. The response of the PUF is read after the last stage. For a given challenge, the reset signal can be set low to activate the PUF. After a transient period, the BR-PUF might be settled to an allowed logical state.

family. Second, due to the lack of a precise mathematical model of the respective PUF functionality, to learn the PUF a more sophisticated approach is required. Therefore, the following question arises: is it possible to PAC learn a PUF family, even if we have no mathematical model of the physical functionality of the respective PUF family? We answer this question at least for the BR-PUF family. Our roadmap for answering this question, more specifically, the steps taken to prove the PAC learnability of BR-PUF family in the second scenario, is illustrated in Fig. 4. While theoretical insights into the notions related to the first two blocks have been presented in Sect. 2.4, which are valid for all PUF families, Sect. 4.1 provides more specific results for the BR-PUF family (i.e., According to these new insights, in Sect. 4.2 we eventually prove that BR-PUF family (which lack a precise mathematical model) can nevertheless be PAC learned (see last two blocks in Fig. 4).

Fig. 4. Our roadmap for proving the PAC learnability of BR-PUF family, whose mathematical model is unknown

4.1   A Constant Upper Bound on the Number of Influential Bits

First, we reflect the fact that our Theorem 2 is in line with the empirical results obtained by applying heuristic approaches, which are reported in [37, 42]. Although here we compare their results for BR- and TBR-PUFs with our results, our proof of having influential bits in PUF families in general, speaks for itself, and is one of the novel aspects of this paper.

In an attempt to assess the security of BR-PUFs, Yamamoto et al. have implemented BR-PUFs on several FPGAs to analyze the influence of challenge bits on the respective responses [42]. They have explicitly underlined the existence of influential bits, and found so called prediction rules. Table 1 summarizes their results, where for each type of the rules (monomials of different sizes) we report only the one with the highest estimated response prediction probability. In addition to providing evidence for the existence of influential bits, the size of the respective monomials is of particular importance for us. As shown in Table 1, their size is surprisingly small, i.e., only five.

Table 1. Statistical analysis of the 2048 CRPs, given to a 64-bit BR-PUF [42]. The first column shows the rule found in the samples, whereas the second column indicates the estimated probability of predicting the response.

Rule	Est. Pr.
$(c_1 = 0) \rightarrow y = 1$	0.684
$(c_9 = 0) \wedge (c_6 = 1) \rightarrow y = 1$	0.762
$(c_{25} = 0) \wedge (c_{18} = 1) \wedge (c_1 = 0) \rightarrow y = 1$	0.852
$(c_{27} = 0) \wedge (c_{25} = 0) \wedge (c_{18} = 1) \wedge (c_6 = 1) \rightarrow y = 1$	0.932
$(c_{53} = 0) \wedge (c_{51} = 0) \wedge (c_{45} = 0) \wedge (c_{18} = 1) \wedge (c_7 = 0) \rightarrow y = 1$	1

Similarly, the authors of [37] translate the influence of the challenge bits to the weights needed in artificial neural networks that represent the challenge-response behavior of BR-PUFs and the TBR-PUFs. They observed that there is a pattern in these weights, which models the influence of the challenge bits. It clearly reflects the fact that there are influential bits determining the response of the respective PUF to a given challenge. From the results presented in [37], we conclude that there is at least one influential bit, however, the precise number of influential bits has not been further investigated by the authors.

Inspired by the above results from [37,42], we conduct further experiments. We collect 30000 CRPs from BR-PUFs and TBR-PUFs implemented on Altera Cyclone IV FPGAs. In all of our PUF instances at least one influential bit is found, and the maximum number of influential bits (corresponding to the size of the monomials) is just a constant value in all cases. For the sake of readability, we present here only the results obtained for one arbitrary PUF instance.

Our results shown in Table 2 are not only aligned with the results reported in [37,42], but also reflect our previous theoretical findings. We could conclude this section as follows. There is at least one influential bit determining the response of a BR-PUF (respectively, TBR-PUF) to a given challenge. However, for the purpose of our framework their existence is not enough, and we need an upper bound on the number of influential bits.

Looking more carefully into the three different datasets, namely our own and the data reported in [37,42], we observe that the total number of influential bits is always only a very small value. Motivated by this commonly observed phenomenon, we compute for our PUFs (implemented on FPGAs) the average

Table 2. Our statistical analysis of the 30000 CRPs, given to a 64-bit BR-PUF. The first column shows the rule found in the sample, whereas the second column indicates the estimated probability of predicting the response.

Rule	Est. Pr.
$(c_{61} = 1) \rightarrow y = 1$	0.71
$(c_{11} = 1) \rightarrow y = 1$	0.72
$(c_{29} = 1) \rightarrow y = 1$	0.725
$(c_{39} = 1) \rightarrow y = 1$	0.736
$(c_{23} = 1) \rightarrow y = 1$	0.74
$(c_{46} = 1) \rightarrow y = 1$	0.745
$(c_{50} = 1) \rightarrow y = 1$	0.75
$(c_{61} = 1) \wedge (c_{23} = 1) \rightarrow y = 1$	0.82
$(c_{61} = 1) \wedge (c_{11} = 0) \rightarrow y = 1$	0.80
$(c_{23} = 1) \wedge (c_{46} = 1) \rightarrow y = 1$	0.86
$(c_{39} = 1) \wedge (c_{50} = 1) \rightarrow y = 1$	0.85
$(c_{61} = 1) \wedge (c_{11} = 1) \wedge (c_{29} = 1) \rightarrow y = 1$	0.88
$(c_{50} = 1) \wedge (c_{23} = 1) \wedge (c_{46} = 1) \rightarrow y = 1$	0.93
$(c_{50} = 1) \wedge (c_{23} = 1) \wedge (c_{46} = 1) \wedge (c_{39} = 0) \rightarrow y = 1$	0.97
$(c_{50} = 1) \wedge (c_{23} = 1) \wedge (c_{11} = 0) \wedge (c_{39} = 0) \wedge (c_{29} = 1) \rightarrow y = 1$	0.98
$(c_{50} = 1) \wedge (c_{23} = 1) \wedge (c_{46} = 1) \wedge (c_{39} = 0) \wedge (c_{29} = 1) \rightarrow y = 1$	0.99
$(c_{50} = 1) \wedge (c_{23} = 1) \wedge (c_{46} = 1) \wedge (c_{39} = 0) \wedge (c_{29} = 1) \wedge (c_{11} = 0) \rightarrow y = 1$	0.994
$(c_{50} = 1) \wedge (c_{23} = 1) \wedge (c_{46} = 1) \wedge (c_{39} = 0) \wedge (c_{29} = 1) \wedge (c_{61} = 0) \rightarrow y = 1$	0.995
$(c_{50} = 1) \wedge (c_{23} = 1) \wedge (c_{46} = 1) \wedge (c_{39} = 0) \wedge (c_{29} = 1) \wedge (c_{61} = 1) \wedge (c_{11} = 0) \rightarrow y = 1$	1

sensitivity of their respective Boolean functions[2]. Averaging over many instances of our BR-PUFs, we obtain the results shown in Table 3 (TBR-PUFs scored similarly). This striking result[3] lead us to the following plausible heuristic.

"Constant Average Sensitivity of BR-PUF family": *for all practical values of n it holds that the average sensitivity of a Boolean function associated with a physical n-bit PUF from the BR-PUF family is only a constant value.*

---

[2] As explained in Sect. 2.2, for a Boolean function f, the influence of a variable and the total average sensitivity can be calculated by employing Fourier analysis. However, in practice this analysis is computationally expensive. Instead, it suffices to simply approximate the respective average sensitivity. This idea has been extensively studied in the learning theory-related and property testing-related literature (see [22], for a survey). Here we describe how the average sensitivity of a Boolean function, representing a PUF, can be approximated. We follow the simple and effective algorithm as explained in [32]. The central idea behind their algorithm is to collect enough random pairs of labeled examples from the Boolean function, which have the following property: $(c, f(c))$ and $(c^{\oplus i}, f(c^{\oplus i}))$, i.e., the inputs differ on a single Boolean variable.

[3] Note that it is a known result and being folklore, cf. [29], that randomly chosen n-bit Boolean functions have an expected average sensitivity of exactly $n/2$.

Table 3. The average sensitivity of n-bit BR-PUFs.

n	The average sensitivity
4	1.25
8	1.86
16	2.64
32	3.6
64	5.17

Finally, some relation between the average sensitivity and the strict avalanche criterion (SAC) can be recognized, although we believe that the average sensitivity is a more direct metric to evaluate the security of PUFs under ML attacks.

4.2   Weak Learning and Boosting of BR-PUFs

The key idea behind our learning framework is the provable existence of influential bits for any PUF and the constant average sensitivity of BR-PUFs in our scenario. These facts are taken into account to prove the existence of weak learners for the BR-PUF family. We start with the following theorem (Theorem 3) proved by Friedgut [11].

Theorem 3. *Every Boolean function $f : \{0,1\}^n \rightarrow \{0,1\}$ with $\mathrm{I}(f) = k$ can be ε-approximated by another Boolean function h depending on only a constant number of Boolean variables K, where $K = \exp\left((2 + \sqrt{2\varepsilon \log_2(4k/\varepsilon)/k})\frac{k}{\varepsilon}\right)$, and $\varepsilon > 0$ is an arbitrary constant.*

We explain now how Theorem 3 in conjunction with the results presented in Sect. 4.1 help us to prove the existence of a weak learner (Definition 2) for the BR-PUF family.

Theorem 4. *Every PUF from the BR-PUF family is weakly learnable.*

Proof: For an arbitrary PUF from the BR-PUF family, consider its associated but unknown Boolean function that is denoted by f_{PUF} (i.e., our target concept). Our weak learning framework has two main steps. In the first step, we identify a (weak) approximator for f_{PUF}, and in the second step this approximator is PAC learned (in a strong sense). Still, we can guarantee only that the total error of the learner does not exceed $1/2 - \gamma$, where $\gamma > 0$, as we start with a weak approximator of f_{PUF}. The first step relies on the fact that Theorem 2 ensures the existence of influential bits for f_{PUF}, while we can also upper bound $\mathrm{I}(f_{\mathrm{PUF}})$ by some small constant value k due to the Constant Average Sensitivity heuristic. According to the Theorem 3 there is a Boolean function h that is an ε-approximator of f_{PUF}, which depends only on a constant number of Boolean variables K since k and ε are constant values, independent of n. However, note that h depends on an unknown set of K variables. Thus, our Boolean function

h is a so called K-junta function, cf. [29]. More importantly, for constant K it is known that the K-junta function can be PAC learned by a trivial algorithm within $O\left(n^K\right)$ steps, cf. [2,5,6]. This PAC algorithm is indeed our algorithm WL that weakly learns f_{PUF}. Carefully choosing the parameters related to our approximators as well as the PAC learning algorithm, we ensure that WL returns a $1/2 - \gamma$-approximator for f_{PUF} and some $\gamma > 0$. ∎

Applying now the canonical booster introduced in Sect. 2.3 to our WL proposed in the proof of Theorem 4 and according to Definition 3, our weak learning algorithm can be transformed into an efficient and strong PAC learning algorithm.

Corollary 1. *BR-PUFs are strong PAC learnable, regardless of any mathematical model representing their challenge-response behavior.*

5 Results

5.1 PUF Implementation

We implement BR and TBR-PUFs with 64 stages on an Altera Cyclone IV FPGA, manufactured on a 60nm technology [1]. It turns out that most PUF implementations are highly biased towards one of the responses. Therefore, we apply different manual routing and placement configurations to identify PUFs with a minimum bias in their responses. However, it is known that by reducing the bias in PUF responses, the number of noisy responses increases [27].

Finding and resolving the noisy responses are two of the main challenges in the CRP measurement process. In almost all PUF constructions it can be predicted, at which point in time a generated response is valid and can be measured. For instance, for an arbiter PUF one can estimate the maximum propagation delay (evaluation period) between the enable point and the arbiter. After this time period the response is in a valid logical level (either "0" or "1") and does not change, and afterwards by doing majority voting on the responses generated for a given challenge the stable CRPs can be collected. However, in the case of BR-PUF family, for a given challenge the settling time of the response to a valid logical level is not known a priori, see Fig. 5. Furthermore, it is not known whether the response to a given challenge would

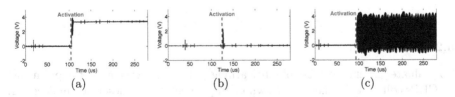

(a)   (b)   (c)

Fig. 5. The settling time of the BR-PUF response: (a) the PUF response after a transient time reaches a stable logical state "1". (b) after a transient time the PUF response is "0". (c) the PUF response does not settle and oscillates for an undefined time period.

not be unstable after observing the stable response during some time period
(see Sect. 3.1). Therefore, the majority voting technique cannot be employed for
BR-PUFs and TBR-PUFs. To deal with this problem, for a given challenge we
read the response of the PUF at different points in time, where at each point
in time 11 measurements are conducted additionally. We consider a response
being stable, if it is the same at all these different measurement time points.
Otherwise, the response is considered being unstable, and the respective CRP is
excluded from our dataset.

In order to observe the impact of the existing influential bits on our PUF
responses, first we apply a large set of challenges chosen uniformly at random, and then measure their respective responses. Afterwards, for both possible
responses of the PUF (i.e., "0" and "1") we count the number of challenge bits,
which are set to either "0" or "1", see Fig. 6. It can be seen that some challenge
bits are more influential towards a certain response. These results are the basis
for our statistical analysis presented in Sect. 4.1. We also repeat this experiment
in the scenario, where the response of the PUF is unstable — in this case we
observe almost no influential challenge bits. The most important conclusion that
we can draw from these experiments is that a PUF with stable responses has
at least one influential bit, which can already predict with low probability the
response of the PUF to a respective challenge.

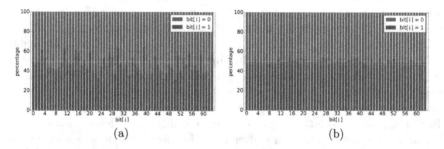

(a)   (b)

Fig. 6. The impact of the influential bits on the responses of the PUF: (a) the response
of the PUF is "0". (b) unstable responses. Here the y-axis shows the percentage of the
challenges, whose bits are set to either "0" or "1", whereas the x-axis shows the bit
position.

5.2   ML Results

To evaluate the effectiveness of our learning framework, we conduct experiments
on CRPs collected from our PUF, whose implementation is described in Sect. 5.1.
As discussed and proved in Sect. 4, having influential bits enables us to define a
prediction rule, where this rule can serve as a hypothesis representation, which
fulfills the requirements of a weak learner. The algorithm WL proposed in the
proof of the Theorem 4 relies on the PAC learnability of K-juntas, where K is a

small constant. However, it is known that every efficient algorithm for learning K-DTs (i.e., the number of leaves is 2^K) is an efficient algorithm for learning K-juntas, see, e.g., [28]. Furthermore, it is known that DLs generalize K-DTs [31]. Moreover, a monomial $M_{n,K}$ is a very simple type of a K-junta, where only the conjunction of the relevant variables is taken into account. Therefore, for our experiments we decide to let our weak learning algorithms deliver DLs, Monomials, and DTs.

To learn the challenge-response behavior of BR- and TBR-PUFs using these representations, we use the open source machine learning software Weka [17]. One may argue that more advanced tools might be available, but here we only aim to demonstrate that publicly accessible, and off-the-shelf software can be used to launch our proposed attacks. All experiments are conducted on a MacBook Pro with 2.6 GHz Intel Core i5 processor and 10GB of RAM. To boost the prediction accuracy of the model established by our weak learners, we apply the Adaptive Boosting (AdaBoost) algorithm [10]; nevertheless, any other boosting framework can be employed as well. For Adaboost, it is known that the error of the final model delivered by the boosted algorithm after T iteration is theoretically upper bounded by $\prod_{t=1}^{T} \sqrt{1 - 4\gamma^2}$, c.f. [36]. To provide a better understanding of the relation between K, the number of iterations, and the theoretical bound on the error of the final model, a corresponding graph[4] is shown in Fig. 7.

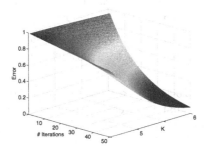

Fig. 7. The relation between the theoretical upper bound on the error of the final model returned by Adaboost, the number of iterations, and K. The graph is plotted for $k = 2$, $\varepsilon' = 0.01$, and $n = 64$. Here, $\varepsilon' = 0.01$ denotes the error of the K-junta learner.

Our experiments in Weka consist of a training phase and a testing phase. In the training phase a model is established from the training data based on the chosen representation. Afterwards, the established model is evaluated on the test set, which contains an unseen subset of CRPs. The size of the training sets in our

---

[4] Note that at first glance the graph may seem odd as after a few iterations the error is close to 1, although we start from a weak learner, whose error rate is strictly below 0.5. As explained in [36, pp. 57–60], and shown in their Fig. 3.1, this is due to Adaboosts's theoretical worst-case analysis, which is only asymptotically (in T) meaningful.

Table 4. Experimental results for learning 64-bit BR-PUF and TBR-PUF, when $m = 100$. The accuracy $(1 - \varepsilon)$ is reported for three weak learners. The first row shows the accuracy of the weak learner, whereas the other rows show the accuracy of the boosted learner.

# boosting iterations	BR-PUF			TBR-PUF		
	M_n	DT	DL	M_n	DT	DL
0 (no boosting)	54.48 %	66.79 %	67.24 %	65.18 %	72.29 %	74.84 %
10	67.12 %	74.25 %	76.99 %	76.96 %	79.22 %	81.36 %
20	77.53 %	80.53 %	80.89 %	82.05 %	85.73 %	86.71 %
30	81.32 %	83.13 %	83.14 %	84.93 %	88.34 %	89.4 %
40	82.65 %	83.91 %	84.6 %	88.11 %	89.67 %	90.22 %
50	82.65 %	85.62 %	85.5 %	90.05 %	89.69 %	91.58 %

Table 5. Experimental results for $m = 1000$ (the same setting as for the Table 4).

# boosting iterations	BR-PUF			TBR-PUF		
	M_n	DT	DL	M_n	DT	DL
0 (no boosting)	63.73 %	75.69 %	84.59 %	64.9 %	75.6 %	84.34 %
10	81.09 %	85.49 %	94.2 %	79.9 %	87.12 %	95.05 %
20	89.12 %	91.08 %	96.64 %	88.28 %	91.57 %	97.89 %
30	93.24 %	93.24 %	97.50 %	93.15 %	93.9 %	98.75 %
40	95.69 %	94.28 %	97.99 %	96.73 %	95.05 %	99.13 %
50	96.80 %	95.04 %	98.32 %	98.4 %	95.96 %	99.37 %

experiments are 100 and 1000, whereas the test set contains 30000 CRPs. Our experiments demonstrate that the weak learning of our test set always results in the delivery of a model with more than 50 % accuracy as shown in the first rows of Tables 4 and 5.

By boosting the respective models with AdaBoost, the accuracy is dramatically increased, see Tables 4 and 5. It can be observed that after 50 iterations of Adaboost applied to the weak model generated from 100 CRPs, the prediction accuracy of the boosted model is increased to more than 80 % for all three representations. By increasing the number of samples to 1000 CRPs, the prediction accuracy is further increased up to 98.32 % for learning the BR-PUFs, and 99.37 % for learning the TBR-PUFs under DL representations. It is interesting to observe that the simplest representation class, i.e., Monomials clearly present the greatest advantage given by the boosting technique. As explained in [36] this is due to avoiding any overfitting tendency.

6   Conclusion

As a central result, which speaks for itself, we have proved that in general the responses of all PUF families are not equally determined by each and every bit of their respective challenges. Moreover, the present paper has further addressed the issue of strong PAC learning of the challenge-response behavior of PUFs, whose functionality lacks a precise mathematical model. We have demonstrated that representing BR- and TBR-PUFs by Boolean functions, we are able to precisely describe the characteristics of these PUFs as observed in practice. This fact results in developing a new and generic machine learning framework that strongly PAC learns the challenge-response behavior of the BR-PUF family. The effectiveness and applicability of our framework have also been evaluated by conducting extensive experiments on BR-PUFs and TBR-PUFs implemented on FPGAs, similar to experimental platforms used in the most relevant literature.

Last but not least, although our strong PAC learning framework has its own novelty value, we feel that our Theorem 3 and the precise mathematical description of the characteristics of BR-PUFs and TBR-PUFs are the most important aspects of our paper. We strongly believe that this description can help to fill the gap between the mathematical design of cryptographic primitives and the design of PUFs in real world. As an evidence thereof, we feel that the Siegenthaler Theorem and the Fourier analysis that are well-known and widely used in modern cryptography may provide special insights into the physical design of secure PUFs in the future.

Acknowledgements. We would like to thank Prof. Dr. Frederik Armknecht for the fruitful discussion as well as pointing out the Siegenthaler's paper. Furthermore, the authors greatly appreciate the support that they received from Helmholtz Research School on Security Technologies.

References

1. Altera: Cyclone IV Device Handbook. Altera Corporation, San Jose (2014)
2. Angluin, D.: Queries and concept learning. Mach. Learn. **2**(4), 319–342 (1988)
3. Armknecht, F., Maes, R., Sadeghi, A., Standaert, O.X., Wachsmann, C.: A formalization of the security features of physical functions. In: 2011 IEEE Symposium on Security and Privacy (SP), pp. 397–412 (2011)
4. Armknecht, F., Moriyama, D., Sadeghi, A.R., Yung, M.: Towards a unified security model for physically unclonable functions. In: Sako, K. (ed.) CT-RSA 2016. LNCS, vol. 9610, pp. 271–287. Springer, Heidelberg (2016)
5. Arvind, V., Köbler, J., Lindner, W.: Parameterized learnability of k-juntas and related problems. In: Hutter, M., Servedio, R.A., Takimoto, E. (eds.) ALT 2007. LNCS (LNAI), vol. 4754, pp. 120–134. Springer, Heidelberg (2007)
6. Blum, A.L., Langley, P.: Selection of relevant features and examples in machine learning. Artif. Intell. **97**(1), 245–271 (1997)
7. Chen, Q., Csaba, G., Lugli, P., Schlichtmann, U., Rührmair, U.: The bistable ring PUF: a new architecture for strong physical unclonable functions. In: 2011 IEEE International Symposium on Hardware-Oriented Security and Trust (HOST), pp. 134–141. IEEE (2011)
8. Fischer, P., Simon, H.U.: On learning ring-sum-expansions. SIAM J. Comput. **21**(1), 181–192 (1992)

9. Freund, Y.: Boosting a weak learning algorithm by majority. Inf. Comput. **121**(2), 256–285 (1995)

10. Freund, Y., Schapire, R.E.: A decision-theoretic generalization of on-line learning and an application to boosting. J. Comp. Syst. Sci. **55**(1), 119–139 (1997)

11. Friedgut, E.: Boolean functions with low average sensitivity depend on few coordinates. Combinatorica **18**(1), 27–35 (1998)

12. Ganji, F., Tajik, S., Seifert, J.P.: Let me prove it to you: RO PUFs are provably learnable. In: The 18th Annual International Conference on Information Security and Cryptology (2015)

13. Ganji, F., Tajik, S., Seifert, J.-P.: Why attackers win: on the learnability of XOR arbiter PUFs. In: Conti, M., Schunter, M., Askoxylakis, I. (eds.) TRUST 2015. LNCS, vol. 9229, pp. 22–39. Springer, Heidelberg (2015)

14. Ganji, F., Tajik, S., Seifert, J.P.: PAC learning of arbiter PUFs. J. Cryptographic Eng. Spec. Sect. Proofs **2014**, 1–10 (2016)

15. Gassend, B., Clarke, D., Van Dijk, M., Devadas, S.: Silicon physical random functions. In: Proceedings of the 9th ACM Conference on Computer and Communications Security, pp. 148–160 (2002)

16. Guajardo, J., Kumar, S.S., Schrijen, G.-J., Tuyls, P.: FPGA intrinsic PUFs and their use for IP protection. In: Paillier, P., Verbauwhede, I. (eds.) CHES 2007. LNCS, vol. 4727, pp. 63–80. Springer, Heidelberg (2007)

17. Hall, M., Frank, E., Holmes, G., Pfahringer, B., Reutemann, P., Witten, I.H.: The WEKA data mining software: an update. ACM SIGKDD Explor. Newslett. **11**(1), 10–18 (2009)

18. Helfmeier, C., Boit, C., Nedospasov, D., Seifert, J.-P.: Cloning physically unclonable functions. In: 2013 IEEE International Symposium on Hardware-Oriented Security and Trust (HOST), pp. 1–6 (2013)

19. Helfmeier, C., Nedospasov, D., Tarnovsky, C., Krissler, J.S., Boit, C., Seifert, J.-P.: Breaking and entering through the silicon. In: Proceedings of the 2013 ACM SIGSAC Conference on Computer and Communications Security, pp. 733–744. ACM (2013)

20. Helmbold, D., Sloan, R., Warmuth, M.K.: Learning integer lattices. SIAM J. Comput. **21**(2), 240–266 (1992)

21. Holcomb, D.E., Burleson, W.P., Fu, K.: Initial SRAM state as a fingerprint and source of true random numbers for RFID tags. In: Proceedings of the Conference on RFID Security, vol. 7 (2007)

22. Kalai, G., Safra, S.: Threshold phenomena and influence: perspectives from mathematics, computer science, and economics. In: Computational Complexity and Statistical Physics, Santa Fe Institute Studies on the Sciences of Complexity, pp. 25–60 (2006)

23. Kearns, M.J., Vazirani, U.V.: An Introduction to Computational Learning Theory. MIT Press, Cambridge (1994)

24. Koushanfar, F.: Hardware metering: a survey. In: Tehranipoor, M., Wang, C. (eds.) Introduction to Hardware Security and Trust, pp. 103–122. Springer, New York (2012)

25. Lee, J.W., Lim, D., Gassend, B., Suh, G.E., Van Dijk, M., Devadas, S.: A technique to build a secret key in integrated circuits for identification and authentication applications. In: 2004 Symposium on VLSI Circuits. Digest of Technical Papers, pp. 176–179 (2004)

26. Maes, R.: Physically Unclonable Functions: Constructions, Properties and Applications. Springer, Heidelberg (2013)

27. Maes, R., van der Leest, V., van der Sluis, E., Willems, F.: Secure key generation from biased PUFs. In: Güneysu, T., Handschuh, H. (eds.) CHES 2015. LNCS, vol. 9293, pp. 517–534. Springer, Heidelberg (2015)
28. Mossel, E., O'Donnell, R., Servedio, R.A.: Learning functions of k relevant variables. J. Comp. Syst. Sci. **69**(3), 421–434 (2004)
29. O'Donnell, R.: Analysis of Boolean Functions. Cambridge University Press, Cambridge (2014)
30. Pappu, R., Recht, B., Taylor, J., Gershenfeld, N.: Physical one-way functions. Science **297**(5589), 2026–2030 (2002)
31. Rivest, R.L.: Learning decision lists. Mach. Learn. **2**(3), 229–246 (1987)
32. Ron, D., Rubinfeld, R., Safra, M., Samorodnitsky, A., Weinstein, O.: Approximating the influence of monotone boolean functions in $O(\sqrt{n})$ query complexity. ACM Trans. Comput. Theory (TOCT) **4**(4), 11 (2012)
33. Rührmair, U., Sehnke, F., Sölter, J., Dror, G., Devadas, S., Schmidhuber, J.: Modeling attacks on physical unclonable functions. In: Proceedings of the 17th ACM Conference on Computer and Communications Security, pp. 237–249 (2010)
34. Saha, I., Jeldi, R.R., Chakraborty, R.S.: Model building attacks on physically unclonable functions using genetic programming. In: 2013 IEEE International Symposium on Hardware-Oriented Security and Trust (HOST), pp. 41–44. IEEE (2013)
35. Schapire, R.E.: The strength of weak learnability. Mach. Learn. **5**(2), 197–227 (1990)
36. Schapire, R.E., Freund, Y.: Boosting: Foundations and Algorithms. MIT Press, Cambridge (2012)
37. Schuster, D., Hesselbarth, R.: Evaluation of bistable ring PUFs using single layer neural networks. In: Holz, T., Ioannidis, S. (eds.) Trust 2014. LNCS, vol. 8564, pp. 101–109. Springer, Heidelberg (2014)
38. Siegenthaler, T.: Correlation-immunity of nonlinear combining functions for cryptographic applications (Coresp.). IEEE Trans. Inf. Theory **30**(5), 776–780 (1984)
39. Tajik, S., Dietz, E., Frohmann, S., Seifert, J.-P., Nedospasov, D., Helfmeier, C., Boit, C., Dittrich, H.: Physical characterization of arbiter PUFs. In: Batina, L., Robshaw, M. (eds.) CHES 2014. LNCS, vol. 8731, pp. 493–509. Springer, Heidelberg (2014)
40. Weste, N.H.E., Harris, D.: CMOS VLSI Design: A Circuits and Systems Perspective, 4th edn. Addison Wesley, Boston (2010)
41. Xu, X., Rührmair, U., Holcomb, D.E., Burleson, W.P.: Security evaluation and enhancement of bistable ring PUFs. In: Mangard, S., Schaumont, P. (eds.) Radio Frequency Identification. LNCS, vol. 9440, pp. 3–16. Springer, Heidelberg (2015)
42. Yamamoto, D., Takenaka, M., Sakiyama, K., Torii, N.: Security evaluation of Bistable Ring PUFs on FPGAs using differential and linear analysis. In: 2014 Federated Conference on Computer Science and Information Systems (FedCSIS), pp. 911–918 (2014)

Efficient Fuzzy Extraction of PUF-Induced Secrets: Theory and Applications

Jeroen Delvaux[1,2(✉)], Dawu Gu[2], Ingrid Verbauwhede[1], Matthias Hiller[3], and Meng-Day (Mandel) Yu[1,4,5]

[1] KU Leuven, ESAT/COSIC and iMinds, Kasteelpark Arenberg 10, B-3001 Leuven, Belgium
{jeroen.delvaux,ingrid.verbauwhede}@esat.kuleuven.be
[2] Shanghai Jiao Tong University, CSE/LoCCS, 800 Dongchuan Road, Shanghai 200240, China
dwgu@sjtu.edu.cn
[3] Chair of Security in Information Technology, Technical University of Munich, Munich, Germany
matthias.hiller@tum.de
[4] Verayo Inc., San Jose, USA
myu@verayo.com
[5] CSAIL, MIT, Cambridge, USA

Abstract. The device-unique response of a *physically unclonable function* (PUF) can serve as the root of trust in an embedded cryptographic system. *Fuzzy extractors* transform this noisy non-uniformly distributed secret into a stable high-entropy key. The overall efficiency thereof, typically depending on error-correction with a binary $[n, k, d]$ block code, is determined by the universal and well-known $(n - k)$ bound on the min-entropy loss. We derive new considerably tighter bounds for PUF-induced distributions that suffer from, e.g., bias or spatial correlations. The bounds are easy-to-evaluate and apply to large non-trivial codes, e.g., BCH, Hamming and Reed-Muller codes. Apart from an inherent reduction in implementation footprint, the newly developed theory also facilitates the analysis of state-of-the-art error-correction methods for PUFs. As such, we debunk the reusability claim of the reverse fuzzy extractor. Moreover, we provide proper quantitative motivation for debiasing schemes, as this was missing in the original proposals.

Keywords: Fuzzy extractor · Secure sketch · Min-entropy · Physically unclonable function · Coding theory

1 Introduction

Cryptography relies on reproducible uniformly distributed secret keys. Obtaining affordable physically secure key-storage in embedded non-volatile memory is hard though. Harvesting entropy from *physically unclonable functions* (PUFs) comprehends an alternative that lowers the vulnerability during the power-off

© International Association for Cryptologic Research 2016
B. Gierlichs and A.Y. Poschmann (Eds.): CHES 2016, LNCS 9813, pp. 412–431, 2016.
DOI: 10.1007/978-3-662-53140-2_20

state. Unfortunately, PUF responses are corrupted by noise and non-uniformities are bound to occur. A *fuzzy extractor* [11] provides an *information-theoretically secure* mechanism to convert PUF responses into high-quality keys. The essential building block for handling noisiness is the *secure sketch*, providing error-correction with most frequently a binary $[n, k, d]$ block code. Associated public helper data reveals information about the PUF response though; the system provider should hence quantify how much min-entropy remains. So far, the conservative $(n - k)$ upper bound on the min-entropy loss has been applied. Unfortunately, the residual min-entropy is underestimated, implying that more PUF response bits than necessary have to be used. Expensive die area is hence blocked by PUF circuits that are not strictly required to obtain the desired security level, i.e., symmetric key length.

1.1 Contribution

The novelty of our work is twofold:

- First, we derive new bounds on the secure sketch min-entropy loss for PUF-induced distributions with practical relevance. Our bounds are considerably tighter than the well-known $(n - k)$ formula, hereby improving the implementation efficiency of PUF-based key generators. The discrepancy is showcased for two predominant PUF imperfections, i.e., biased and spatially correlated response bits. It is important to note that a variety of commonly used codes is covered, e.g., BCH and Reed-Muller codes, regardless of their algebraic complexity. Furthermore, a large variety of distributions could be supported. Therefore, our scope reaches considerably further than related work in [8,22], focussing on simple repetition codes and biased distributions only. As in the latter works, our bounds are easy-to-evaluate and able to support large codes.
- Second, the newly developed theory is applied to state-of-the-art error-correction methods for PUFs. As such, we reveal a fundamental flaw in the reverse fuzzy extractor, proposed by Van Herrewege et al. [28] at Financial Crypto 2012. The latter lightweight primitive is gaining momentum and has also been adopted in the CHES 2015 protocol of Aysu et al. [1]. We debunk the main security claim that repeated helper data exposure does not result in additional min-entropy loss. Furthermore, we contribute to the motivation of debiasing schemes such as the *index-based syndrome* (IBS) proposal of Yu et al. [30], and the CHES 2015 proposal of Maes et al. [22]. The latter proposals assume that a stand-alone sketch cannot handle biased distributions. We eliminate the need for an educated guess that originates from the extrapolation of repetition code insights and/or the application of the overly conservative $(n - k)$ bound.

1.2 Organization

The remainder of this manuscript is organized as follows. Section 2 introduces notation and preliminaries. Section 3 derives new tight bounds on the secure sketch min-entropy loss. Section 4 elaborates applications of the newly developed theory. Section 5 concludes the work.

2   Preliminaries

2.1   Notation

Binary vectors are denoted with a bold lowercase character, e.g., x. All vectors are row vectors. All-zeros and all-ones vectors are denoted with 0 and 1 respectively. Binary matrices are denoted with a bold uppercase character, e.g., H. A random variable and its corresponding set of outcomes are denoted with an uppercase *italic* and calligraphic character respectively, e.g., X and $\mathcal{X}$. Variable assignment is denoted with an arrow, e.g., $x \leftarrow X$. Custom-defined procedure names are printed in a sans-serif font, e.g., Hamming weight $\mathsf{HW}(x)$ and Hamming distance $\mathsf{HD}(x, \widetilde{x})$. The probability of an event A is denoted as $\mathbb{P}(A)$. The expected value of a function $g(X)$ of random variable X is denoted as $\mathbb{E}_{x \leftarrow X}[g(X)]$. The probability density function and cumulative distribution function of a standard normal distribution $N(0, 1)$ are denoted as $\mathsf{f}_{\mathsf{norm}}(\cdot)$ and $\mathsf{F}_{\mathsf{norm}}(\cdot)$ respectively. For a binomial distribution with n trials and success probability p, we use $\mathsf{f}_{\mathsf{bino}}(\cdot; n, p)$ and $\mathsf{F}_{\mathsf{bino}}(\cdot; n, p)$ respectively.

2.2   Min-Entropy Definitions

The *min-entropy* of a random variable X is as defined in (1). Consider now a pair of possibly correlated random variables: X and P. The *conditional min-entropy* [11] of X given P is as defined in (2). Terms with $\mathbb{P}(P = p) = 0$ are evaluated as 0. Both definitions quantify the probability that an attacker guesses $x \leftarrow X$ first time right, on a logarithmic scale. We emphasize that min-entropy is a more conservative notion than Shannon entropy and therefore often preferred within cryptology.

$$\mathbb{H}_\infty(X) = -\log_2\left(\max_{x \in \mathcal{X}} \mathbb{P}(X = x)\right). \tag{1}$$

$$\widetilde{\mathbb{H}}_\infty(X|P) = -\log_2\left(\mathbb{E}_{p \leftarrow P}\left[\max_{x \in \mathcal{X}} \mathbb{P}((X = x)|(P = p))\right]\right). \tag{2}$$

2.3   Physically Unclonable Functions

A prominent category of PUFs, suitable for key generation in particular, consists of an array of identically designed cells. Each cell produces a single bit, or occasionally a few bits. This includes memory-based designs, such as the SRAM PUF [16], as well as the coating PUF [25] and a subset of the large number of ring oscillator-based designs, e.g., [29]. The most prominent entropy-degrading effects for such PUFs are bias and spatial correlations. Bias comprehends an imbalance between the number of zeros and ones. Spatial correlations implicate that neighboring cells might influence each other.

We describe a parameterized probability distribution for the error rate of individual PUF response bits $\widetilde{x}(i)$, with $i \in [1, n]$. Experimental validation on various PUF circuits, e.g., in [10,20], labelled the model as accurate. Two hidden random variables are incorporated: the normalized manufacturing variability $V_i \sim N(0, 1)$, drawn only once for each response bit, and additive noise $N_{ij} \sim N(0, \sigma_N)$, drawn for each evaluation j of a given response bit. A response bit $\widetilde{x}(i)$ evaluates to 1 if $(v_i + n_{ij}) > t$ and 0 otherwise, with threshold t a fixed parameter. Bias corresponds to a nonzero t. Spatial correlations can be incorporated via a multivariate normal distribution $(V_1 \ldots V_n) \sim N(\mathbf{0}, \boldsymbol{\Sigma})$, with $\boldsymbol{\Sigma}$ the symmetric $n \times n$ covariance matrix.

For ease of analysis, we consider the response bits $x(i)$ obtained by thresholding $v_i > t$ as a reference. In practice, these nominal values can be approximated via a majority vote among noisy replicas $\widetilde{x}(i)$, possibly accelerated via circuit techniques [4,30]. Bias parameter b, defined as the probability $\mathbb{P}(x(i) = 1)$, then equals $\mathsf{F}_{\mathsf{norm}}(-t)$. Zero bias corresponds to $b = 0.5$. The error rate p_E of a response bit $\widetilde{x}(i)$ with respect to its reference, i.e., the probability $\mathbb{P}(x(i) \neq \widetilde{x}(i))$, then equals $\mathsf{F}_{\mathsf{norm}}(-|v_i - t|/\sigma_N)$.

2.4 Secure Sketch and Fuzzy Extractor Definitions

Secure sketches operate on a metric space $\mathcal{X}$ with distance function dist. For PUFs, we can restrict our attention to binary vectors $x \in \{0, 1\}^{1 \times n}$ and the Hamming distance HD therebetween. An attacker knows the probability distribution of $x \leftarrow X$. Consider a noisy version $\widetilde{x}$ of sample x. A secure sketch [11] is a pair of efficient and possibly randomized procedures: the sketching procedure $p \leftarrow \mathsf{SSGen}(x)$, with helper data $p \in \mathcal{P}$, and the recovery procedure $\widehat{x} \leftarrow \mathsf{SSRep}(\widetilde{x}, p)$. There are two defining properties:

- *Correctness.* If $\mathsf{HD}(x, \widetilde{x}) \leq t$, correctness of reconstruction is guaranteed, i.e., $\widehat{x} = x$. If $\mathsf{HD}(x, \widetilde{x}) > t$, there is no guarantee whatsoever.
- *Security.* Given a certain lower bound h_{in} on the ingoing min-entropy, i.e., $\mathbb{H}_\infty(X) \geq h_{\mathsf{in}}$, a corresponding lower bound h_{out} on the residual min-entropy, i.e., $\widetilde{\mathbb{H}}_\infty(X|P) \geq h_{\mathsf{out}}$, can be imposed. Often, but not necessarily, this condition can be satisfied regardless of h_{in}. Or stated otherwise, there is a certain upper bound on the min-entropy loss $\Delta\mathbb{H}_\infty = \mathbb{H}_\infty(X) - \widetilde{\mathbb{H}}_\infty(X|P)$.

A slightly modified notion brings us to the *fuzzy extractor* [11]. Output $k \in \mathcal{K}$ is then required to be nearly-uniform, given observation $p \leftarrow P$, and is therefore suitable as a secret key. There is a proven standard method to craft a fuzzy extractor from a secure sketch. In particular, a *randomness extractor* could derive a key from the secure sketch output, i.e., $k \leftarrow \mathsf{Ext}(x)$. *Universal hash functions* [7] are good randomness extractors, according to the *(generalized) leftover hash lemma* [2,13]. Unfortunately, their min-entropy loss is quite substantial. In practice, key generators therefore often rely on a cryptographic hash function that is assumed to behave as a *random oracle*. The latter idealized heuristic results in zero min-entropy loss.

2.5   Coding Theory

A *binary code* C is a bijection from a message space M to a codeword space $W \subseteq \{0,1\}^{1 \times n}$. The *minimum distance* d is the minimum number of bits in which any two distinct codewords differ. A procedure $w \leftarrow \mathsf{Encode}(m)$ maps a message $m \in M$ to a codeword $w \in W$. A procedure $\widehat{w} \leftarrow \mathsf{Correct}(\widetilde{w})$ corrects up to $t = \lfloor \frac{d-1}{2} \rfloor$ errors for any noise-corrupted codeword $\widetilde{w} = w \oplus e$, with $\mathsf{HW}(e) \leq t$. Equation (3) expresses the Hamming bound [18]. The equality holds for *perfect codes* only, implicating that any vector in $\{0,1\}^{1 \times n}$ is within distance t of a codeword. All other codes are subject to the inequality.

$$\sum_{i=0}^{t} \binom{n}{i} |M| \leq 2^n. \tag{3}$$

A binary $[n, k, d]$ *block code* C restricts the message length $k = \log_2(|M|)$ to an integer. For a linear block code, any linear combination of codewords is again a codeword. A $k \times n$ *generator matrix* G, having full rank, can then implement the encoding procedure, i.e., $w = m \cdot G$. For any translation $\tau \in \{0,1\}^{1 \times n}$ and linear code C, the set $\{\tau \oplus w : w \in W\}$ is referred to as a *coset*. Two cosets are either disjoint or coincide. Therefore, the vector space $\{0,1\}^{1 \times n}$ is fully covered by 2^{n-k} cosets, referred to as the *standard array*. The minimum weight vector ϵ in a coset is called the *coset leader*. In case of conflict, i.e., a common minimum $\mathsf{HW}(\epsilon) > t$, an arbitrary leader can be selected. The minimum distance d of a linear code equals the minimum Hamming weight of its nonzero codewords. A linear code C is *cyclic* if every circular shift of a codeword is again a codeword belonging to C.

2.6   The Code-Offset Secure Sketch

Several secure sketch constructions rely on a binary code C. For ease of understanding, we focus on the code-offset method of Dodis et al. [11] exclusively. Nevertheless, equivalencies in the extended version of this manuscript (Cryptology ePrint Archive, Report 2015/854) prove that all results apply to six other constructions equally well. The code C that instantiates the code-offset method in Fig. 1 is not necessarily linear. Even more, it is not required be a block code either. Linear codes (BCH, Hamming, repetition, etc.) remain the most frequently used though due to their efficient decoding algorithms [18]. Correctness of reconstruction is guaranteed if $\mathsf{HD}(x, \widetilde{x}) \leq t$, with t the error-correcting capability of the code.

Min-entropy loss can be understood as a *one-time pad* imperfection. Sketch input x is masked with a random codeword w, i.e., an inherent entropy deficiency: $\mathbb{H}_\infty(W) = \log_2(|M|) < n$. For linear codes in particular, we highlight a convenient interpretation using cosets. Helper data p then reveals in which coset reference x resides. It can be seen easily that p is equal to a random vector in the same coset as x. The residual min-entropy in (2) hence reduces to (4) for linear codes, with ϵ a coset leader. We emphasize that the min-entropy

$p \leftarrow \mathsf{SSGen}(x)$	$\hat{x} \leftarrow \mathsf{SSRep}(\tilde{x}, p)$
Random $w \in \mathcal{C}$	$\tilde{w} \leftarrow \tilde{x} \oplus p = w \oplus e$
$p \leftarrow x \oplus w$	$\hat{x} \leftarrow p \oplus \mathsf{Correct}(\tilde{w})$

Fig. 1. The code-offset secure sketch, having an n-bit reference input x.

loss $\Delta\mathbb{H}_\infty$ does not depend on the decoding method, simply because the helper data is not affected. For $[n, k, d]$ block codes in particular, the well-known upper bound $\Delta\mathbb{H}_\infty \leq (n - k)$ holds, as proven in [11]. More generally, this extends to $\Delta\mathbb{H}_\infty \leq n - \log_2(|\mathcal{M}|)$.

$$\widetilde{\mathbb{H}}_\infty(X|P) = -\log_2\left(\mathbb{E}_{\epsilon \leftarrow E}\left[\max_{w \in \mathcal{W}} \mathbb{P}((X = \epsilon \oplus w)|(E = \epsilon))\right]\right). \tag{4}$$

3 Tight Bounds on the Min-Entropy Loss

Currently, secure sketch implementations rely on the $(n - k)$ upper bound on the min-entropy loss, e.g., [23]. Unfortunately, this leads to an overly conservative design when instantiating security parameters accordingly. We develop a graphical framework that produces tight bounds on $\widetilde{\mathbb{H}}_\infty(X|P)$ for typical PUF-induced distributions. The critical *first-order* effects of bias and spatial correlations are captured. Both lower and upper bounds are supported. The lower bounds are of primary interest for a conservative system provider, entertaining the worst-case scenario. We considerably improve upon the $(n - k)$ bound, i.e., the leftmost inequality in (5). We also improve upon the rather trivial upper bounds [11] that comprehend the rightmost inequality in (5).

$$\underbrace{\max(\mathbb{H}_\infty(X) - (n - \log_2(|\mathcal{M}|)), 0)}_{\text{worst-case}} \leq \widetilde{\mathbb{H}}_\infty(X|P) \leq \underbrace{\min(\log_2(|\mathcal{M}|), \mathbb{H}_\infty(X))}_{\text{best-case}}.$$
$$\tag{5}$$

Our lower and upper bounds combined define a relatively narrow interval in which the exact value of $\widetilde{\mathbb{H}}_\infty(X|P)$ is enclosed. We considerably extend related work in [8,22] as follows. First, we cover a variety of codes, regardless of their algebraic complexity. Prior work focussed on repetition codes only. Although frequently used as the inner code of a concatenated code [5], full-fledged key generators [23] typically rely on non-trivial codes, e.g., BCH codes [18]. Second, our techniques may be applied to a variety of distributions, while prior work covered biased distributions only. Our bounds remain easy-to-evaluate and are able to handle large codes. Although derived for the code-offset sketch of Dodis et al. [11] in particular, the extended version of this manuscript establishes the equivalence with six other constructions.

3.1   Distributions

Our work is generic in the sense that a large variety of distributions X could be covered. We only require that $\mathcal{X} = \{0,1\}^{1 \times n}$ can be partitioned in a limited number of subsets φ_j, with $j \in [1, J]$, so that all elements of φ_j have the same probability of occurrence q_j. Formally, $\mathbb{P}(X = x) = q_j$ if and only if $x \in \varphi_j$. These probabilities are strictly monotonically decreasing, i.e., $q_1 > q_2 > \ldots > q_J$. Occasionally, $q_J = 0$. The ingoing min-entropy is easily computed as $\mathbb{H}_\infty(X) = -\log_2(q_1)$.

We determine bounds on $\widetilde{\mathbb{H}}_\infty(X|P)$. The runtime of the corresponding algorithms is roughly proportional to J. The crucial observation is that even a very small J might suffice to capture realistic PUF models. Below, we describe a parameterized distribution X for both biased and spatially correlated PUFs. Both distributions are to be considered as proof-of-concept models, used in showcasing the feasibility of a new research direction. In case a given PUF is not approximated accurately enough, one can opt for an alternative and possibly more complicated *second-order* distribution. As long as J is limited, bounds can be evaluated in milliseconds-minutes on a standard desktop computer.

- *Biased distribution.* We assume response bits to be independent and identically distributed (i.i.d.) so that $\mathbb{P}(X(i) = 1) = b$, with $i \in [1, n]$ and a real-valued $b \in [0, 1]$. For $b = \frac{1}{2}$, this corresponds to a uniform distribution. The latter bias model comprehends a very popular abstraction in PUF literature. The min-entropy loss of various other helper data methods has been analyzed as such, e.g., *soft-decision decoding* [8,21] as well as *IBS* [15,30] and von Neumann [22, 27] debiasing. Therefore, our results enable adequate comparison with related methods, all using a common baseline distribution.
- *Correlated distribution.* We assume response bits to be distributed so that $\mathbb{P}(X(i) = X(i+1)) = c$, with $i \in [1, n-1]$ and a real-valued $c \in [0, 1]$. This extends to (6) for larger neighborhoods. There is no bias, i.e., $\mathbb{P}(X(i) = 1) = \frac{1}{2}$. For $c = \frac{1}{2}$, the latter model corresponds to a uniform distribution. Although spatial correlations are frequently encountered in experimental work, e.g., byte-level dependencies for the SRAM PUFs in [1,14], these are often neglected in information theoretic work due to their complexity. We hope that our results may help turn the tide on this.

$$\mathbb{P}(X(i) = X(j)) = \sum_{u=0}^{\lfloor |i-j|/2 \rfloor} f_{\text{bino}}(2u; |i-j|, 1-c), \quad \text{with } i, j \in [1, n]. \quad (6)$$

Figure 2 specifies the subsets φ_j for both distributions. For the biased distribution, we partition according to $\mathsf{HW}(x)$. This corresponds to a binomial distribution with $j-1$ successes for n Bernoulli trials, each having success probability $b_\star = \min(b, 1-b)$. For the correlated distribution, we partition according to $\mathsf{HD}(x(1:n-1), x(2:n))$, i.e., the number of transitions in x. Inputs in subset φ_j exhibit $j-1$ transitions and obey either one out of two forms, i.e., $x = (0\|1\|0\|\ldots)$ and $x = (1\|0\|1\|\ldots)$. A related observation is that if

$\boldsymbol{x} \in \varphi_j$, then so is its ones' complement, i.e., $\overline{\boldsymbol{x}} \in \varphi_j$. This explains the factors 2 and $\frac{1}{2}$ everywhere. Set size $|\varphi_j|$ is further determined with *stars and bars* combinatorics [12]. In particular, we separate n indistinguishable stars into j distinguishable bins by adding $j - 1$ out of $n - 1$ bars.

j	$\lvert\varphi_j\rvert$	q_j	j	$\lvert\varphi_j\rvert$	q_j
1	1	$(1 - b_\star)^n$	1	2	$\frac{1}{2}(1 - c_\star)^{n-1}$
2	n	$b_\star(1 - b_\star)^{n-1}$	2	$2(n-1)$	$\frac{1}{2}c_\star(1 - c_\star)^{n-2}$
...	...	...	...	...	...
j	$\binom{n}{j-1}$	$(b_\star)^{j-1}(1 - b_\star)^{n-j+1}$	j	$2\binom{n-1}{j-1}$	$\frac{1}{2}(c_\star)^{j-1}(1 - c_\star)^{n-j}$
...	...	...	...	...	...
n	n	$(b_\star)^{n-1}(1 - b_\star)$	$n-1$	$2(n-1)$	$\frac{1}{2}(c_\star)^{n-2}(1 - c_\star)$
$n+1$	1	$(b_\star)^n$	n	2	$\frac{1}{2}(c_\star)^{n-1}$

Fig. 2. Subsets φ_j for a biased and correlated distribution X, left and right respectively. We define $b_\star = \min(b, 1 - b)$ and $c_\star = \min(c, 1 - c)$.

We treat the degenerate case $b = c = \frac{1}{2}$, i.e., a uniform distribution, separately. There is only one set then. Formally, $J = 1$, $|\varphi_1| = 2^n$ and $q_1 = 1/2^n$. As proven by Reyzin [24], the min-entropy loss of a secure sketch is maximal for a uniformly distributed input, making this a case of special interest.

3.2   Generic Bounds

Equation (7) holds for the code-offset construction of Dodis et al. [11], given that a codeword is selected fully at random during enrollment.

$$\mathbb{P}((P = \boldsymbol{p})|(X = \boldsymbol{x})) = \begin{cases} 1/|\mathcal{M}|, & \text{if } \exists \boldsymbol{w} : \boldsymbol{p} = \boldsymbol{x} \oplus \boldsymbol{w} \\ 0, & \text{otherwise.} \end{cases} \tag{7}$$

Equation (8) applies Bayes' rule to the definition of conditional min-entropy in (2) and fills in (7). The 0 case is resolved by switching variables for the max operator. A direct exhaustive evaluation of the resulting formula requires up to $2^n|\mathcal{M}|$ operations.

$$\widetilde{\mathbb{H}}_\infty(X|P) = -\log_2\left(\sum_{\boldsymbol{p}\in\mathcal{P}} \mathbb{P}(P = \boldsymbol{p}) \max_{\boldsymbol{x}\in\mathcal{X}} \frac{\mathbb{P}(X = \boldsymbol{x})\mathbb{P}((P = \boldsymbol{p})|(X = \boldsymbol{x}))}{\mathbb{P}(P = \boldsymbol{p})}\right)$$

$$= -\log_2\left(\frac{1}{|\mathcal{M}|} \sum_{\boldsymbol{p}\in\mathcal{P}} \max_{\boldsymbol{w}\in\mathcal{W}} \mathbb{P}(X = \boldsymbol{p} \oplus \boldsymbol{w})\right). \tag{8}$$

For linear codes, the workload can be reduced substantially. With a similar derivation as before, we rewrite (4) as shown in (9). Up to 2^n operations suffice.

Nevertheless, direct evaluation is only feasible for small codes. We emphasize that our bounds are able to handle large codes, as is typically the case for a practical key generator.

$$\widetilde{\mathbb{H}}_\infty(X|P) = -\log_2\Big(\sum_{\epsilon\in\mathcal{E}} \max_{w\in\mathcal{W}} \mathbb{P}(X = \epsilon \oplus w)\Big). \tag{9}$$

Equation (8) iterates over all p's and selects each time the most likely x that is within range, via the addition of a codeword $w \in \mathcal{W}$. We now reverse the roles, as shown in Fig. 3. We iterate over all x's, from most likely to least likely, i.e., from φ_1 to φ_J. Within a certain φ_j, the order of the x's may be chosen arbitrarily. Subsequently, we assign p's to each x, as represented by the black squares, until the set $\mathcal{P}$ of size 2^n is depleted. For each assigned p, we assume that the corresponding x is the most likely vector, according to (8). Let s_j^p denote the number of black squares assigned to set φ_j. The residual min-entropy is then easily computed as in (10).

$$\widetilde{\mathbb{H}}_\infty(X|P) = -\log_2\Big(\frac{1}{|\mathcal{M}|} \sum_{j=1}^{J} s_j^p q_j\Big). \tag{10}$$

Both linear and non-linear codes are supported by former graphical representation. Nevertheless, we elaborate linear codes as a special case due to their practical relevance. Figure 4 swaps the order of iteration in (9). Only one row suffices, i.e., each column of helper data vectors p in Fig. 3 is condensed to a single square. Black and white squares are now assigned to cosets, as represented by their coset leaders ϵ. Let s_j^ϵ denote the number of black squares assigned to set φ_j. The residual min-entropy is then easily computed as in (11), hereby dropping denominator $|\mathcal{M}|$ compared to (10), given that $s_j^p = 2^k \cdot s_j^\epsilon$.

$$\widetilde{\mathbb{H}}_\infty(X|P) = -\log_2\Big(\sum_{j=1}^{J} s_j^\epsilon q_j\Big). \tag{11}$$

In the worst-case scenario, the most likely x's all map to unique p's, without overlap, resulting in a lower bound on $\widetilde{\mathbb{H}}_\infty(X|P)$. For a linear code, this would be the case if the first 2^{n-k} x's all belong to different cosets. In the best-case scenario, our sequence of x's exhibits maximum overlap in terms of p, resulting in an upper bound on $\widetilde{\mathbb{H}}_\infty(X|P)$. For a linear code, this would be the case if the first 2^k x's all map to the same coset, and this repeated for all 2^{n-k} cosets. Algorithms 1 and 2 comprehend a literal transcript of Fig. 3 and compute the lower bound and upper bound respectively. Auxiliary variables s^p and s^x accumulate black and gray squares respectively. To maintain generality, we abstain from special case algorithms for linear codes, although it would result in a few simplifications.

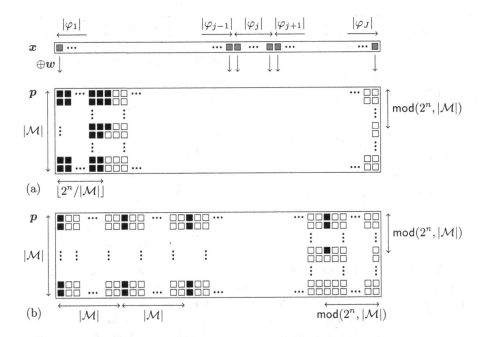

Fig. 3. Reversal of the roles in (8). (a) A lower bound on $\widetilde{\mathbb{H}}_\infty(X|P)$. (b) An upper bound on $\widetilde{\mathbb{H}}_\infty(X|P)$. Black squares represent terms that contribute to $\widetilde{\mathbb{H}}_\infty(X|P)$, one for each $p \in \mathcal{P}$. White squares represent non-contributing terms, overruled by the max operator. In general, there are few black squares but many white squares, 2^n versus $(|\mathcal{M}| - 1)2^n$ to be precise. For block codes, i.e., $|\mathcal{M}| = 2^k$, the last column of black squares is completely filled.

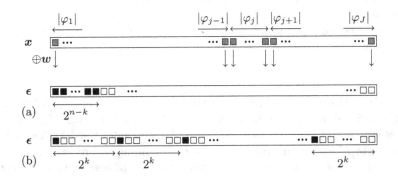

Fig. 4. Reversal of the roles in (9), as applied to linear codes. (a) A lower bound on $\widetilde{\mathbb{H}}_\infty(X|P)$. (b) An upper bound on $\widetilde{\mathbb{H}}_\infty(X|P)$. Black squares represent terms that contribute to $\widetilde{\mathbb{H}}_\infty(X|P)$, one for each $\epsilon \in \mathcal{E}$. White squares represent non-contributing terms, overruled by the max operator.

Algorithm 1. BoundWorstCase	**Algorithm 2.** BoundBestCase
Input: List $\langle|\varphi_j|, q_j\rangle$	**Input:** List $\langle|\varphi_j|, q_j\rangle$
Output: Lower bound on $\widetilde{\mathbb{H}}_\infty(X\|P)$	**Output:** Upper bound on $\widetilde{\mathbb{H}}_\infty(X\|P)$
$j, q, s^p \leftarrow 0$	$j, q, s^p, s^x \leftarrow 0$
while $s^p < 2^n$ **do**	**while** $s^p < 2^n$ **do**
$\quad j \leftarrow j+1$	$\quad j \leftarrow j+1$
$\quad s_j^p \leftarrow \min(|\varphi_j|\|\mathcal{M}|, 2^n - s^p)$	$\quad s^x \leftarrow s^x + |\varphi_j|$
$\quad s^p \leftarrow s^p + s_j^p$	$\quad s_j^p \leftarrow \lceil(s^x - s^p)/|\mathcal{M}|\rceil|\mathcal{M}|$
$\quad q \leftarrow q + s_j^p \cdot q_j$	$\quad s_j^p \leftarrow \min(\max(s_j^p, 0), 2^n - s^p)$
$\widetilde{\mathbb{H}}_\infty(X\|P) \leftarrow -\log_2(q/|\mathcal{M}|)$	$\quad s^p \leftarrow s^p + s_j^p$
	$\quad q \leftarrow q + s_j^p \cdot q_j$
	$\widetilde{\mathbb{H}}_\infty(X\|P) \leftarrow -\log_2(q/|\mathcal{M}|)$

Algorithms 1 and 2 may now be applied to a variety of distributions. For a uniform distribution, the lower and upper bound both evaluate to $\widetilde{\mathbb{H}}_\infty(X|P) = log_2(|\mathcal{M}|)$, regardless of other code specifics. Or simply k, for block codes in particular. The min-entropy loss is hence exactly $(n-k)$, given that $\mathbb{H}_\infty(X) = n$. Reyzin's proof [24] therefore implicates that the general-purpose $(n-k)$ bound cannot be tightened any further. Although results are fairly presentable already for the biased and correlated distributions, we further tighten these bounds first.

3.3   Tighter Bounds

Tighter bounds can be obtained by leveraging code properties more effectively. Algorithms 3 and 4 generalize Algorithms 1 and 2 respectively. In the former case, an additional input imposes an upper bound on the accumulated number of black squares, i.e., $\forall j, (s_1^p + s_2^p + \ldots + s_j^p) \leq (u_1^p + u_2^p + \ldots + u_j^p)$. In the latter case, an additional input imposes a lower bound on the accumulated number of black squares, i.e., $\forall j, (s_1^p + s_2^p + \ldots + s_j^p) \geq (l_1^p + l_2^p + \ldots + l_j^p)$. We now provide several examples.

Worst-Case Bounds. We further tighten the lower bound on $\widetilde{\mathbb{H}}_\infty(X|P)$ for the correlated distribution. The improvement applies to linear codes that have the all-ones vector $\mathbf{1}$ of length n as a codeword. This includes Reed-Muller codes of any order [18]. This also includes many BCH, Hamming and repetition codes, on the condition that these are cyclic and having d odd, as easily proven hereafter. Consider an arbitrary codeword with Hamming weight d. XORing all 2^n circular shifts of this codeword results in the all-ones codeword, which ends the proof. As mentioned before, each set φ_j of the correlated distribution can be partitioned in pairs $\{\boldsymbol{x}, \overline{\boldsymbol{x}}\}$, with $\overline{\boldsymbol{x}}$ the ones' complement of $\boldsymbol{x}$. Paired inputs belong to the same coset, i.e., maximum overlap in terms of helper data $\boldsymbol{p}$. Therefore, we impose the cumulative upper bound in (12).

$$u_j^p = |\mathcal{M}| \frac{|\varphi_j|}{2} = 2^{k-1} |\varphi_j|. \tag{12}$$

Algorithm 3. BoundWorstCase2	**Algorithm 4.** BoundBestCase2
Input: List $\langle|\varphi_j|, q_j, u_j^p\rangle$	**Input:** List $\langle|\varphi_j|, q_j, l_j^p\rangle$
Output: Lower bound on $\widetilde{\mathbb{H}}_\infty(X\|P)$	**Output:** Upper bound on $\widetilde{\mathbb{H}}_\infty(X\|P)$
$j, q, s^p, u^p \leftarrow 0$	$j, q, s^p, s^x, l^p \leftarrow 0$
while $s^p < 2^n$ **do**	**while** $s_{1:j}^p < 2^n$ **do**
$\quad j \leftarrow j + 1$	$\quad j \leftarrow j + 1$
$\quad u^p \leftarrow u^p + u_j^p$	$\quad s^x \leftarrow s^x + |\varphi_j|$
$\quad s_j^p \leftarrow \min(|\varphi_j| |\mathcal{M}|, u^p - s^p)$	$\quad l^p \leftarrow l^p + l_j^p$
$\quad s_j^p \leftarrow \min(s_j^p, 2^n - s^p)$	$\quad s_j^p \leftarrow \lceil (s^x - s^p)/|\mathcal{M}|\rceil |\mathcal{M}|$
$\quad s^p \leftarrow s^p + s_j^p$	$\quad s_j^p \leftarrow \max(s_j^p, l^p - s^p, 0)$
$\quad q \leftarrow q + s_j^p \cdot q_j$	$\quad s_j^p \leftarrow \min(s_j^p, 2^n - s^p)$
$\widetilde{\mathbb{H}}_\infty(X\|P) \leftarrow -\log_2(q/|\mathcal{M}|)$	$\quad s^p \leftarrow s^p + s_j^p$
	$\quad q \leftarrow q + s_j^p \cdot q_j$
	$\widetilde{\mathbb{H}}_\infty(X\|P) \leftarrow -\log_2(q/|\mathcal{M}|)$

For instance, consider linear/cyclic $[n, k = 1, d = n]$ repetition codes, i.e., having generator matrix $\boldsymbol{G} = \boldsymbol{1}$, with n odd. Algorithms BoundWorstCase2 and BoundBestCase then converge to the exact result $\widetilde{\mathbb{H}}_\infty(X|P) = 1$, not depending on parameter c. This is the best-case scenario, given the universal bound $\widetilde{\mathbb{H}}_\infty(X|P) \leq k$. Figure 5 illustrates the former with squares for $n = 5$. The result also holds if the repetition code is neither linear/cyclic nor odd. As long as $\boldsymbol{w}_1 \oplus \boldsymbol{w}_2 = \boldsymbol{1}$, the elements of each φ_j can be paired into cosets. Although the term coset is usually preserved for linear codes, translations of a non-linear repetition code are either disjunct or coincide and still partition the space $\{0, 1\}^{1 \times n}$. As a side note, the result offers another [8] refutation of the *repetition code pitfall* of Koeberl et al. [17], a work that overlooks that $(n - k)$ is an upper bound only.

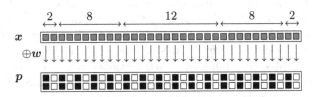

Fig. 5. The exact residual min-entropy $\widetilde{\mathbb{H}}_\infty(X|P)$ for the correlated distribution and an $[n = 5, k = 1, d = 5]$ repetition code.

Best-Case Bounds. We improve the upper bound on $\widetilde{\mathbb{H}}_\infty(X|P)$ for both the biased and correlated distribution. In particular, we take minimum distance d into account. The main insight is that two slightly differing inputs $\boldsymbol{x}_u \neq \boldsymbol{x}_v$ do not overlap in terms of helper data $\boldsymbol{p}$. More precisely, if $\mathsf{HD}(\boldsymbol{x}_u, \boldsymbol{x}_v) \in [1, d-1]$, then $\{\boldsymbol{x}_u \oplus \boldsymbol{w} \mid \boldsymbol{w} \in \mathcal{W}\} \cap \{\boldsymbol{x}_v \oplus \boldsymbol{w} \mid \boldsymbol{w} \in \mathcal{W}\} = \varnothing$. For the biased distribution, the following holds: $\mathsf{HD}(\boldsymbol{x}_u, \boldsymbol{x}_v) \in [1, d-1]$ if $\boldsymbol{x}_u \neq \boldsymbol{x}_v$ and $\boldsymbol{x}_u, \boldsymbol{x}_v \in (\varphi_1 \cup \varphi_2 \cup \ldots \cup \varphi_{t+1})$. Or stated otherwise, the elements of the first $t+1$ sets all result in unique $\boldsymbol{p}$'s. Therefore, we can impose the constraint given in (13). Figure 6 depicts the squares.

$$l_j^{\boldsymbol{p}} = \begin{cases} |\varphi_j||\mathcal{M}|, & \text{if } j \in [1, t+1] \\ 0, & \text{otherwise} \end{cases}. \tag{13}$$

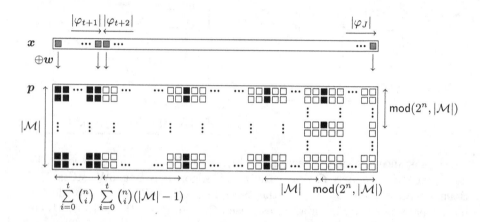

Fig. 6. A tightened upper bound on $\widetilde{\mathbb{H}}_\infty(X|P)$ for the biased distribution, hereby making use of (13).

There is an interesting observation for perfect codes in particular. As clear from the Hamming bound in (3), all unique $\boldsymbol{p}$'s are covered by the first $t+1$ sets exclusively. BoundWorstCase and BoundBestCase2 hence produce the same output, implying that the residual min-entropy is evaluated exactly, as further simplified in (14). Delvaux et al. [8] derived the same formula for $[n, k = 1, d = n]$ repetition codes with n odd. The scope of their result is hence extended from perfect repetition codes to perfect codes in general. As a side note, the formula was originally adopted to debunk the aforementioned *repetition code pitfall* [17]. Maes et al. [22] later presented a similar contribution at CHES 2015, differing in its use of Shannon entropy rather than min-entropy.

$$\widetilde{\mathbb{H}}_\infty(X|P) = -\log_2\left(\sum_{j=1}^{t+1} |\varphi_j| \cdot q_j\right) = -\log_2(\mathsf{F}_{\mathsf{bino}}(t; n, \min(b, 1-b))). \tag{14}$$

Also for the correlated distribution, distance d might be incorporated to tighten the upper bound on $\widetilde{\mathbb{H}}_\infty(X|P)$. First of all, we assign $|\mathcal{M}|$ unique $\boldsymbol{p}$'s to one out of two elements in φ_1. For ease of understanding, assume $\boldsymbol{x} = \boldsymbol{0}$, comprehending the first case in (15). For each set φ_j, with $j \in [2, n]$, we then count the number of inputs $\boldsymbol{x} \in \varphi_j$ such that $h = \mathsf{HW}(\boldsymbol{x}) \leq t$. The latter constraint guarantees all assigned $\boldsymbol{p}$'s to be unique. We distinguish between two forms, $\boldsymbol{x} = (\boldsymbol{0}\|\boldsymbol{1}\|\boldsymbol{0}\|\ldots)$ and $\boldsymbol{x} = (\boldsymbol{1}\|\boldsymbol{0}\|\boldsymbol{1}\|\ldots)$, resulting in two main terms. For each form, we apply *stars and bars* combinatorics twice. In particular, we assign h indistinguishable stars, i.e., ones, to distinguishable bins and independently also for $n - h$ zeros. Note that $l_j^{\boldsymbol{p}} = 0$ for $j > 2t + 1$. To ensure formula correctness, one may verify numerically that $l_1^{\boldsymbol{p}} + l_2^{\boldsymbol{p}} + \ldots + l_{2t+1}^{\boldsymbol{p}}$ equals the left hand side of the Hamming bound in (3).

$$
l_j^{\boldsymbol{p}} = \begin{cases} |\mathcal{M}|, & \text{if } j = 1 \\ |\mathcal{M}|\left(\sum_{h=\lfloor j/2\rfloor}^{t} \binom{h-1}{\lfloor j/2\rfloor-1}\binom{n-h-1}{\lceil j/2\rceil-1}\right. \\ \left. + \sum_{h=\lceil j/2\rceil}^{t} \binom{h-1}{\lceil j/2\rceil-1}\binom{n-h-1}{\lfloor j/2\rfloor-1}\right), & \text{otherwise.} \end{cases}
$$
(15)

3.4 Numerical Results

Figure 7 presents numerical results for various BCH codes. We focus on small codes, as these allow for an exact exhaustive evaluation of the residual min-entropy using (8) and/or (9). As such, the tightness of various bounds can be assessed adequately. Figure 7(d) nevertheless demonstrates that our algorithms support large codes equally well, in compliance with a practical key generator. Note that only half of the bias interval $b \in [0, 1]$ is depicted. The reason is that all curves mirror around the vertical axis of symmetry $b = \frac{1}{2}$. The same holds for the correlated distribution with parameter c.

Especially the lower bounds perform well, which benefits a conservative system provider. The best lower bounds in Fig. 7(a), (b) and (c) visually coincide with the exact result. The gap with the $(n - k)$ bound is the most compelling around $b, c \approx 0.7$, where the corresponding curves hit the horizontal axis $\widetilde{\mathbb{H}}_\infty(X|P) = 0$. Also our upper bounds are considerably tighter than their more general alternatives in (5). Nevertheless, the latter bounds remain open for further improvement, with the exception of Fig. 7(b). An $[n = 7, k = 4, d = 3]$ code is perfect and lower and upper bounds then converge to the exact result for a biased distribution.

4 Applications

The newly developed theory of Sect. 3 facilitates the design and analysis of error-correction methods for PUFs, as exemplified in twofold manner. First, we point out a fundamental security flaw in the reverse fuzzy extractor [28]. Second, we provide a motivational framework for debiasing schemes [15,22,26,27,30].

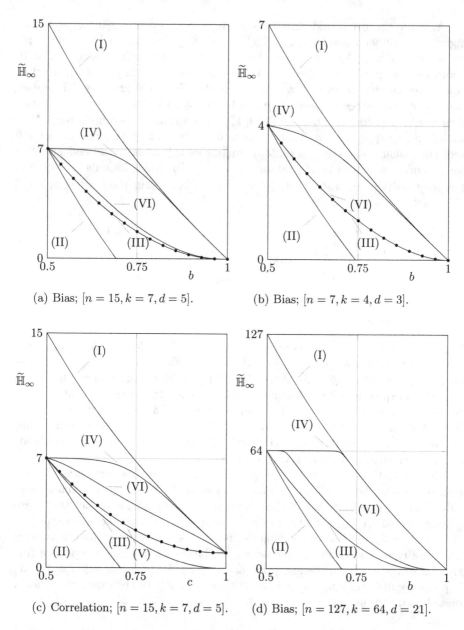

(a) Bias; $[n = 15, k = 7, d = 5]$.   (b) Bias; $[n = 7, k = 4, d = 3]$.

(c) Correlation; $[n = 15, k = 7, d = 5]$.   (d) Bias; $[n = 127, k = 64, d = 21]$.

Fig. 7. The secure sketch min-entropy loss for various BCH codes. Dots correspond to an exact exhaustive evaluation of (8)/(9). The legend of the curves is as follows. (I) The ingoing min-entropy $\mathbb{H}_\infty(X) = -\log_2(q_1)$. (II) The lower bound $\widetilde{\mathbb{H}}_\infty(X|P) = \max(\mathbb{H}_\infty(X) - (n-k), 0)$. (III) The lower bound on $\widetilde{\mathbb{H}}_\infty(X|P)$ according to BoundWorstCase. (IV) The upper bound on $\widetilde{\mathbb{H}}_\infty(X|P)$ according to BoundBestCase. (V) The lower bound on $\widetilde{\mathbb{H}}_\infty(X|P)$ according to BoundWorstCase2. (VI) The upper bound on $\widetilde{\mathbb{H}}_\infty(X|P)$ according to BoundBestCase2.

4.1   A Fundamental Security Flaw in Reverse Fuzzy Extractors

The reverse fuzzy extractor, as proposed by Van Herrewege et al. [28] at Financial Crypto 2012, improves the lightweight perspectives of PUF-based authentication protocols. The construction was therefore also adopted in the CHES 2015 protocol of Aysu et al. [1]. Instead of a single helper data exposure only, $p \leftarrow \mathsf{SSGen}(\widetilde{x})$ is regenerated and transferred with each protocol run by a resource-constrained PUF-enabled device. A receiving resource-rich server, storing reference response x, can hence reconstruct $\widetilde{x} \leftarrow \mathsf{SSRec}(x, p)$ and establish a shared secret as such. The footprint of the device is reduced due to the absence of the heavyweight SSRec procedure.

We debunk the main security claim that repeated helper data exposure does not result in additional min-entropy loss. The revealed flaw is attributed to the misuse of a reusability proof of Boyen [6]. For the code-offset sketch with linear codes, the exposure of $p_1 \leftarrow \mathsf{SSGen}(x)$ and $p_2 \leftarrow \mathsf{SSGen}(x \oplus e)$, with perturbation e known and fully determined by the attacker, is provably equivalent. The latter helper data reveals that x belongs to an identical coset $\{p_1 \oplus w : w \in \mathcal{W}\} = \{p_2 \oplus e \oplus w : w \in \mathcal{W}\}$. However, perturbation e is determined by PUF noisiness rather than by the attacker and its release hence reveals new information. Given a sequence of protocol runs, the attacker can approximate all individual bit error rates p_E as well as the coset to which reference x belongs.

Figure 8 quantifies the residual min-entropy of X with the exclusion and inclusion of revealed bit error rates p_E respectively. In the latter case, we rely on a Monte Carlo evaluation of (16), as enabled by choosing a small $[n = 15, k = 7, d = 5]$ BCH code, given that an analytical approach is not so very straightforward. Exposure of p_E boils down to knowledge of threshold discrepancy $|v(i) - t|$. For the biased distribution, the situation is identical to the flaw in the *soft-decision decoding* scheme of Maes et al. [21]. As pointed out by Delvaux of al. [8], there is a bit-specific bias $b_i = \mathbb{P}(r(i) = 1) = \mathsf{f_{norm}}(t + |v(i) - t|)/(\mathsf{f_{norm}}(t+|v(i)-t|)+\mathsf{f_{norm}}(t-|v(i)-t|))$. For each x in the coset corresponding to p, we then compute $\mathbb{P}(X = x) = \prod_{i=1}^{n}(x(i)b_i + (1 - x(i))(1 - b_i))$. Similarly, for the spatially correlated distribution, we compute $\mathbb{P}(X = x) = \mathsf{f_{norm}}(v, 0, \Sigma)$, with covariance matrix Σ exclusively depending on correlation parameter c, as detailed in the extended version of this manuscript.

$$\widetilde{\mathbb{H}}_\infty(X|P) = -\log_2\Big(\mathbb{E}_{v \leftarrow V} \max_{w \in W} \mathbb{P}(V = t + (1 - 2w)|v - t| \mid |v - t|\Big). \quad (16)$$

The revealed flaw differs from existing attacks by Delvaux et al. [9] and Becker [3] that apply to the original protocol [28] exclusively. The latter attacks comprehend the modeling of the highly correlated arbiter PUF via repeated helper data exposure; a preemptive fix can be found in the PhD thesis of Maes [19]. The newly revealed flaw is more fundamentally linked to the reverse fuzzy extractor primitive and applies to all existing protocols so far [1,19,28]. Observe in Fig. 8 that the overly conservative $(n-k)$ bound would compensate for

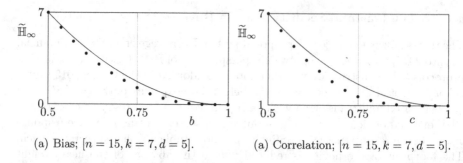

(a) Bias; $[n = 15, k = 7, d = 5]$.   (a) Correlation; $[n = 15, k = 7, d = 5]$.

Fig. 8. The residual min-entropy $\widetilde{\mathbb{H}}_\infty(X|P)$ for a BCH code. The solid lines that exclude revealed bit error rates are computed with BoundWorstCase2; Fig. 7 confirms the visual overlap with the exact result. Dots that include revealed bit error rates correspond to Monte Carlo evaluations of size 10^6.

the additional unanticipated min-entropy loss. However, this somewhat defeats the purpose in light of the original lightweight intentions, and this observation might not necessarily hold for every possible distribution. Further theoretical work may determine to which extent and at which cost reverse fuzzy extractors can be repaired. A potential fix already exists for biased distributions, as illustrated later-on.

4.2   Motivation for Debiasing Schemes

Debiasing schemes transform a biased PUF-induced distribution into a uniform distribution. A considerable fraction of the response bits is discarded in order to restore the balance between 0 and 1. Indices of retained bits are stored as helper data. A subsequent secure sketch, known to have an exact min-entropy loss of $(n-k)$ bits for uniform inputs, still corrects the errors. A first debiasing proposal is the *index-based syndrome* (IBS) scheme of Yu et al. [30], further generalized by Hiller et al. [15]. Second, several variations of the von Neumann debiasing algorithm can be applied. This was first proposed by van der Leest et al. [26], and later also by Van Herrewege in his PhD thesis [27]. Most recently, Maes et al. [22] presented an optimization of the von Neumann algorithm that applies to repetition codes in particular.

Prior debiasing proposals conjectured that a stand-alone sketch cannot handle biased distributions well. This conclusion originates from the extrapolation of repetition code insights and/or application of the $(n-k)$ bound. The precise entropy loss behavior for larger codes, e.g., a BCH $[n = 127, k = 64, d = 21]$ code as in Fig. 7, was an educated guess so far. Our newly derived bounds clearly resolve this motivational uncertainty, in addition to making stand-alone sketches more competitive. For low-bias situations, the $(n-k)$ bound already resulted in a competitive sketch [22]; the new bounds can only improve hereupon. We emphasize that modern high-quality PUFs tend to have a low bias. Notable cases of a high bias can typically be attributed to an avoidable asymmetry in the circuit.

Nevertheless, for high-bias situations, the new bounds clearly indicate the need of debiasing schemes. The benefit is amplified by choosing a sketch with a k-bit output, several of which are listed in the extended version of this manuscript. The uniform output is then directly usable as a key, hereby eliminating the Hash function and its additional min-entropy loss in case the leftover hash lemma is applied.

Finally, we highlight that one of the von Neumann debiasing schemes in [22] was claimed to be reusable. This claim holds, despite overlooking the misuse of Boyen's proof and stating that a stand-alone sketch is reusable. A side effect of retaining pairs of alternating bits only, i.e., 01 and 10, is that the imbalance in error rates between 0 and 1 cannot be observed in the helper data. The scheme is considerably less efficient than other von Neumann variants though, showing that reusability comes at a price.

5   Conclusion

Secure sketches are the main workhorse of modern PUF-based key generators. The min-entropy loss of most sketches is upper-bounded by $(n - k)$ bits and designers typically instantiate system parameters accordingly. However, the latter bound tends to be overly pessimistic, resulting in an unfortunate implementation overhead. We showcased the proportions for a prominent category of PUFs, with bias and spatial correlations acting as the main non-uniformities. New considerably tighter bounds were derived, valid for a variety of popular but algebraically complex codes. These bounds are unified in the sense of being applicable to seven secure sketch constructions. Deriving tighter alternatives for the $(n - k)$ bound counts as unexplored territory and we established the first significant stepping stone. New techniques may have to be developed in order to tackle more advanced *second-order* distributions. Elaborating a wider range of applications would be another area of progress. We hope to have showcased the potential by debunking the main security claim of the reverse fuzzy extractor and by providing proper quantitative motivation for debiasing schemes.

Acknowledgment. The authors greatly appreciate the support received. The European Union's Horizon 2020 research and innovation programme under grant number 644052 (HECTOR). The Research Council of KU Leuven, GOA TENSE (GOA/11/007), the Flemish Government through FWO G.0550.12N and the Hercules Foundation AKUL/11/19. The national major development program for fundamental research of China (973 Plan) under grant number 2013CB338004. Jeroen Delvaux is funded by IWT-Flanders grant number SBO 121552. Matthias Hiller is funded by the German Federal Ministry of Education and Research (BMBF) in the project SIBASE through grant number 01IS13020A.

References

1. Aysu, A., Gulcan, E., Moriyama, D., Schaumont, P., Yung, M.: End-to-end design of a PUF-based privacy preserving authentication protocol. In: Güneysu, T., Handschuh, H. (eds.) CHES 2015. LNCS, vol. 9293, pp. 556–576. Springer, Heidelberg (2015)
2. Barak, B., Dodis, Y., Krawczyk, H., Pereira, O., Pietrzak, K., Standaert, F.-X., Yu, Y.: Leftover hash lemma, revisited. In: Rogaway, P. (ed.) CRYPTO 2011. LNCS, vol. 6841, pp. 1–20. Springer, Heidelberg (2011)
3. Becker, G.T.: On the pitfalls of using arbiter-PUFs as building blocks. IEEE Trans. CAD Integr. Circuits Syst. 34(8), 1295–1307 (2015)
4. Bhargava, M., Mai, K.: An efficient reliable PUF-based cryptographic key generator in 65nm CMOS. In: Design, Automation & Test in Europe Conference & Exhibition, DATE 2014, Dresden, Germany, 24–28 March 2014, pp. 1–6 (2014)
5. Bösch, C., Guajardo, J., Sadeghi, A.-R., Shokrollahi, J., Tuyls, P.: Efficient helper data key extractor on FPGAs. In: Oswald, E., Rohatgi, P. (eds.) CHES 2008. LNCS, vol. 5154, pp. 181–197. Springer, Heidelberg (2008)
6. Boyen, X.: Reusable cryptographic fuzzy extractors. In: Proceedings of the 11th ACM Conference on Computer and Communications Security, CCS 2004, Washington, DC, USA, 25–29 October 2004, pp. 82–91 (2004)
7. Carter, L., Wegman, M.N.: Universal classes of hash functions. J. Comput. Syst. Sci. 18(2), 143–154 (1979)
8. Delvaux, J., Gu, D., Schellekens, D., Verbauwhede, I.: Helper data algorithms for PUF-based key generation: overview and analysis. IEEE Trans. CAD Integr. Circ. Syst. 34(6), 889–902 (2015). http://dx.doi.org/10.1109/TCAD.2014.2370531
9. Delvaux, J., Peeters, R., Gu, D., Verbauwhede, I.: A survey on lightweight entity authentication with strong PUFs. ACM Comput. Surv. 48(2), 26 (2015)
10. Delvaux, J., Verbauwhede, I.: Fault injection modeling attacks on 65nm arbiter and RO sum PUFs via environmental changes. IEEE Trans. Circuits Syst. 61–I(6), 1701–1713 (2014)
11. Dodis, Y., Ostrovsky, R., Reyzin, L., Smith, A.: Fuzzy extractors: how to generate strong keys from biometrics and other noisy data. SIAM J. Comput. 38(1), 97–139 (2008)
12. Feller, W.: An Introduction to Probability Theory and Its Applications, vol. 1, 3rd edn. Wiley, New York (1968)
13. Håstad, J., Impagliazzo, R., Levin, L.A., Luby, M.: A pseudorandom generator from any one-way function. SIAM J. Comput. 28(4), 1364–1396 (1999)
14. Van Herrewege, A., van der Leest, V., Schaller, A., Katzenbeisser, S., Verbauwhede, I.: Secure PRNG seeding on commercial off-the-shelf microcontrollers. In: TrustE 2013, Proceedings of the 2013 ACM Workshop on Trustworthy Embedded Devices, pp. 55–64 (2013)
15. Hiller, M., Merli, D., Stumpf, F., Sigl, G.: Complementary IBS: application specific error correction for PUFs. In: 2012 IEEE International Symposium on Hardware-Oriented Security and Trust, HOST 2012, 3–4 June 2012, pp. 1–6 (2012)
16. Holcomb, D.E., Burleson, W.P., Fu, K.: Power-up SRAM state as an identifying fingerprint and source of true random numbers. IEEE Trans. Comput. 58(9), 1198–1210 (2009)
17. Koeberl, P., Li, J., Rajan, A., Wu, W.: Entropy loss in PUF-based key generation schemes: the repetition code pitfall. In: 2014 IEEE International Symposium on Hardware-Oriented Security and Trust, HOST 2014, Arlington, VA, USA, 6–7 May 2014, pp. 44–49 (2014)

18. MacWiliams, F.J., Sloane, N.J.A.: The Theory of Error Correcting Codes. North-Holland Mathematical Library (Book 16). North Holland Publishing Co., New York (1977)
19. Maes, R.: Physically unclonable functions: constructions, properties and applications. Ph.D. thesis, KU Leuven (2012). Ingrid Verbauwhede (promotor)
20. Maes, R.: An accurate probabilistic reliability model for silicon PUFs. In: Bertoni, G., Coron, J.-S. (eds.) CHES 2013. LNCS, vol. 8086, pp. 73–89. Springer, Heidelberg (2013)
21. Maes, R., Tuyls, P., Verbauwhede, I.: A soft decision helper data algorithm for SRAM PUFs. In: ISIT 2009, IEEE International Symposium on Information Theory, pp. 2101–2105 (2009)
22. Maes, R., van der Leest, V., van der Sluis, E., Willems, F.: Secure key generation from biased PUFs: extended version. J. Cryptogr. Eng. 6(2), 121–137 (2016)
23. Maes, R., Van Herrewege, A., Verbauwhede, I.: PUFKY: a fully functional PUF-based cryptographic key generator. In: Prouff, E., Schaumont, P. (eds.) CHES 2012. LNCS, vol. 7428, pp. 302–319. Springer, Heidelberg (2012)
24. Reyzin, L.: Entropy loss is maximal for uniform inputs. Technical report BUCS-TR-2007-011, Department of Computer Science, Boston University, September 2007
25. Tuyls, P., Schrijen, G.-J., Škorić, B., van Geloven, J., Verhaegh, N., Wolters, R.: Read-proof hardware from protective coatings. In: Goubin, L., Matsui, M. (eds.) CHES 2006. LNCS, vol. 4249, pp. 369–383. Springer, Heidelberg (2006)
26. van der Leest, V., Schrijen, G.-J., Handschuh, H., Tuyls, P.: Hardware intrinsic security from D flip-flops. In: Proceedings of the Fifth ACM Workshop on Scalable Trusted Computing, STC 2010, pp. 53–62 (2010)
27. Van Herrewege, A.: Lightweight PUF-based key and random number generation. Ph.D. thesis, KU Leuven, 2015. Ingrid Verbauwhede (promotor)
28. Van Herrewege, A., Katzenbeisser, S., Maes, R., Peeters, R., Sadeghi, A.-R., Verbauwhede, I., Wachsmann, C.: Reverse fuzzy extractors: enabling lightweight mutual authentication for PUF-enabled RFIDs. In: Keromytis, A.D. (ed.) FC 2012. LNCS, vol. 7397, pp. 374–389. Springer, Heidelberg (2012)
29. Yu, H., Leong, P.H.W., Hinkelmann, H., Möller, L., Glesner, M., Zipf, P.: Towards a unique FPGA-based identification circuit using process variations. In: FPL 2009, International Conference on Field Programmable Logic and Applications, pp. 397–402 (2009)
30. Yu, M., Devadas, S.: Secure and robust error correction for physical unclonable functions. IEEE Des. Test Comput. 27(1), 48–65 (2010)

Run-Time Accessible DRAM PUFs
in Commodity Devices

Wenjie Xiong[1](✉), André Schaller[2], Nikolaos A. Anagnostopoulos[2],
Muhammad Umair Saleem[2], Sebastian Gabmeyer[2],
Stefan Katzenbeisser[2], and Jakub Szefer[1]

[1] Yale University, New Haven, CT, USA
{wenjie.xiong,jakub.szefer}@yale.edu
[2] Technische Universität Darmstadt and CASED, Darmstadt, Germany
{schaller,anagnostopoulos,gabmeyer,
katzenbeisser}@seceng.informatik.tu-darmstadt.de,
muhammadumair.saleem@stud.tu-darmstadt.de

Abstract. A Physically Unclonable Function (PUF) is a unique and
stable physical characteristic of a piece of hardware, which emerges due
to variations in the fabrication processes. Prior works have demonstrated
that PUFs are a promising cryptographic primitive to enable secure key
storage, hardware-based device authentication and identification. So far,
most PUF constructions require addition of new hardware or FPGA
implementations for their operation. Recently, intrinsic PUFs, which can
be found in commodity devices, have been investigated. Unfortunately,
most of them suffer from the drawback that they can only be accessed
at boot time. This paper is the first to enable the run-time access of
decay-based intrinsic DRAM PUFs in commercial off-the-shelf systems,
which requires no additional hardware or FPGAs. A key advantage of
our PUF construction is that it can be queried during run-time of a
Linux system. Furthermore, by exploiting different decay times of individual DRAM cells, the challenge-response space is increased. Finally,
we introduce lightweight protocols for device authentication and secure
channel establishment, that leverage the DRAM PUFs at run-time.

1 Introduction

Continued miniaturization and cost reduction of processors and System-on-Chip
designs have enabled the creation of almost ubiquitous smart devices, from smart
thermostats and refrigerators, to smartphones and embedded car entertainment
systems. While there are numerous advantages to the proliferation of such smart
devices, they create new security vulnerabilities [1,6,8,12]. One major concern is
that they often lack the implementation of sufficient security mechanisms [34,46].
Critical challenges in securing these devices are to provide robust device authentication and identification mechanisms, and means to store long-term cryptographic keys in a secure manner that minimizes the chances of their illegitimate
extraction or access.

© International Association for Cryptologic Research 2016
B. Gierlichs and A.Y. Poschmann (Eds.): CHES 2016, LNCS 9813, pp. 432–453, 2016.
DOI: 10.1007/978-3-662-53140-2_21

A classic approach to device identification is to embed cryptographic keys in each device by burning them in at manufacturing time. However, this solution comes with potential pitfalls, such as increased production complexity as well as rather limited protection against key extraction attempts [2]. In order to address these issues, researchers have proposed Physically Unclonable Functions (PUFs). PUFs leverage the unique behavior of a device due to manufacturing variations as a hardware-based fingerprint. A PUF instance is extremely difficult to replicate, even by the manufacturer. Hence, PUFs have been proposed as cryptographic building blocks in security primitives and protocols for: authentication and identification [18,40,43], hardware-software binding [9,10,19,31,33], remote attestation [20,37], and secret key storage [44,45]. So far, most types of PUFs in digital electronic systems (such as arbiter PUFs [7,40]) require addition of dedicated circuits to the device and thus increase manufacturing costs and hardware complexity. Consequently, there is great interest in so-called intrinsic PUFs [9], which are PUFs that are already inherent to a device.

Intrinsic PUFs are considered an attractive low-cost security anchor, as they provide PUF instances within standard hardware that can be found in commercial off-the-shelf devices [26,42], without requiring any hardware modifications. The most prominent example of an intrinsic PUF is a PUF based on Static Random-Access Memory (SRAM) [19,25,31,35,38], which draws its characteristics from the startup values of bi-stable SRAM memory cells. SRAM PUFs are known to have good PUF characteristics [14]. However, PUF measurements must be extracted during a very early boot stage (before the SRAM is used). Consequently, the derived key can only be used at this time, or must be saved to a different memory region, which may cause security problems. Recently, a new error-based SRAM PUF, which can be accessed at run-time, was proposed [3]. However, to query the PUF, the supply voltage needs to be lowered to induce errors in SRAM cells, requiring special hardware in the processor.

Most recently, PUF-like behavior has been found in Dynamic Random-Access Memory (DRAM) [28]. One approach to extract unique DRAM behavior induced by manufacturing variations relies on startup tendencies of DRAM cells [41]. Another approach to extract DRAM PUFs is to leverage the unique decay characteristics of DRAM cells. In [16], authors exploit the fact that charges of individual DRAM cells, if not refreshed, decay over time in a unique manner. PUF responses[1] can be generated by initializing the DRAM cells with a specific value, disabling DRAM refresh cycles and letting the cells decay for a defined *decay time*. As a result of this decay, a DRAM chip exhibits unique bit flips at unique locations, which in their entirety can be used as a PUF response by reading the DRAM content after the decay time elapsed. However, current state of the art requires custom hardware or FPGA-based platforms [16,41], in order to modify the DRAM refresh mechanism such that DRAM PUF extraction is possible.

This paper is the first to extract DRAM PUFs from commercial systems, requiring no special hardware modifications or FPGA setup, and to provide a

---

[1] In the rest of the paper we will use the terms PUF response and PUF measurement interchangeably.

practical solution to query DRAM PUFs during run-time on a Linux system. Our decay-based DRAM PUF allows for repeated access, which overcomes the limitation of previous intrinsic memory-based PUFs that were available at device startup only. Moreover, the capacity of DRAM is magnitudes larger than SRAM, allowing to draw many more bits in order to derive larger cryptographic key material, or to segment DRAM into several logical PUFs. Furthermore, DRAM is an excellent candidate for an intrinsic PUF as DRAM is an integral part of today's commodity platforms and can be found in many "smart" devices, such as smartphones or smart thermostats. Recent use of embedded DRAM [4, 29] in low-cost microprocessors will further increase the availability of DRAM as part of mobile and embedded computing platforms.

1.1   Related Work on DRAM PUFs

The earliest approach to exploit manufacturing variations of DRAM cells for identification and random number generation was reported in [28,29], in which an embedded DRAM chip was designed to generate fingerprints to mitigate hardware counterfeiting. In subsequent work [16,22,27], the decay of external DDR3 modules was evaluated through memory controllers in FPGAs and was used for identification and key storage. Other work has focused on the design of a circuit exploiting the variation in write reliability of DRAM cells [11], and presented an authentication scheme based on signatures generated using such variations. Unlike our work, all previous research required dedicated circuits to be designed or FPGAs to be used. To the best of our knowledge, this is the first work to present an approach to enable the usage of intrinsic DRAM PUF instances on commodity devices at run-time. Further, we provide a system-level solution for querying the DRAM PUF while a Linux OS is running on same hardware and is actively using DRAM chip wherein the PUF is located.

1.2   Contributions

- We extract decay-based DRAM PUF instances from unmodified commodity devices, including the PandaBoard and the Intel Galileo platforms. Two approaches are presented: (i) accessing the PUF at device startup using a customized firmware, and (ii) querying the PUF with a kernel module, while the Linux OS is running on the same hardware and is actively using the DRAM chip wherein the PUF is located.
- Through extensive experiments, we show that DRAM PUFs exhibit robustness, reliability, and in particular allow usage of the decay time as part of the PUF challenge.
- We introduce new metrics for evaluating DRAM PUFs, based on the Jaccard index, and show they are significantly better suited for the decay-based DRAM PUF evaluation over the classic Hamming-distance based metrics.
- Finally, we exploit time-dependent decay characteristics of DRAM cells in the design of PUF-enhanced protocols. In particular, we show protocols for device identification and authentication that draw their security from the time-dependent decay of DRAM cells.

1.3 Paper Organization

The remainder of the paper is organized as follows. Section 2 presents background on DRAM and introduces our DRAM PUFs. Section 3 describes our experimental setup and the implementation of software needed to realize the DRAM PUFs. Section 4 contains our evaluation of DRAM PUFs characteristics. Section 5 describes lightweight protocols for device authentication and secure channel establishment. Section 6 presents open research issues. Section 7 concludes the paper.

2 Extracting DRAM PUFs from Commodity Devices

In a DRAM cell, a single data bit is stored in a capacitor and can be accessed through a transistor, as shown in Fig. 1. DRAM cells are grouped in arrays, where each row of the array is connected to a horizontal word-line. Cells in the same column are connected to a bit-line. All bit-lines are coupled to sense-amplifiers that amplify small voltages on bit-lines to levels such that they can be interpreted as logical zeros or ones. In order to access a row, all the bit-lines will be *precharged* to half the supply voltage $V_{DD}/2$; subsequently the word-line is *enabled*, connecting every capacitor in that row with its bit-line. The sense amplifier will then drive the bit-line to V_{DD} or $0\,V$, depending on the charge on the capacitor. The amplifiers are usually shared by two bit-lines [15], of which only one can be accessed at the same time. This structure makes the two bit-lines complementary, which results in two kinds of cells: true cells and anti-cells. True cells store the value 1 as V_{DD} and 0 as $0\,V$ in the capacitor, whilst anti-cells store the value 0 as V_{DD} and 1 as $0\,V$.

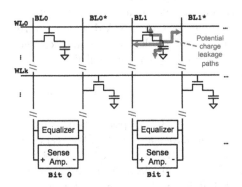

Fig. 1. A single DRAM cell consists of a capacitor and a transistor, connected to a word-line (WL) and a bit-line (BL or BL*); arrows indicate leakage paths for dissipation of charges that lead to PUF behavior.

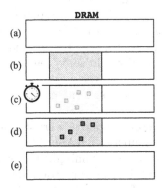

Fig. 2. Five steps required for run-time access of a DRAM PUF. Only during steps (b)–(d) the memory associated with the PUF is not usable for other processes.

DRAM cells require periodic refresh of the stored charges, as otherwise the capacitors lose its charge over time, which is referred to as DRAM cell decay or leakage. The hardware memory controller takes care of periodic refresh, whose interval is defined by the vendor and is usually 32 ms or 64 ms. Without this periodic refresh, some of the cells will slowly decay to 0, while others decay to 1, depending on whether they are a true cell or an anti-cell. Because of the manufacturing variations among DRAM cells, some cells decay faster than others, which can be exploited as a PUF.

2.1   Decay-Based PUFs in DRAM

The process of exploiting the unique decay behavior of DRAM cells to extract a PUF measurement is summarized in Fig. 2. The starting point (a) comprises the DRAM module being configured for ordinary use, where the memory controller periodically refreshes all of the cells' content. In a first step (b), the memory region defined by starting address ($addr$) and size ($size$) is reserved, e.g., using memory ballooning introduced in Sect. 2.2. Furthermore, the refresh for the PUF region is disabled and the initialization value ($initval$) is written to the region. Next, (c) for a given decay time (t), the memory region containing the PUF is not accessed to let the cells decay. (d) After the decay time has expired, the memory content is read in order to extract the PUF measurement. At the end, (e) the normal operating condition of the memory is restored and the memory region is made available to the operating system (OS) again.

We introduce here the concept of logical DRAM PUFs, which are memory regions within a DRAM module that are used for obtaining the PUF measurements. For a particular DRAM, each logical PUF is determined by: (i) $addr$, the starting address of the logical PUF, and (ii) $size$, its size. A typical DRAM memory can be divided into thousands or more logical PUFs.

To get a challenge/response, two additional parameters are needed. First, an initial value ($initval$), which is written into the cells in the DRAM region before any decay. Second, the desired decay time (t) that will cause enough charge to have leaked in some cells such that their stored logical bits will flip. As the decay time and the positions of the flipped bits are unique for individual DRAM regions, the "pattern" of flipped bits for a given decay time t can serve as the PUF response.

In order to derive a cryptographic key from the PUF response using a minimum number of DRAM cells, the entropy within a logical DRAM PUF response needs to be maximized. The value stored in a DRAM cell before it decays, $initval$, plays an important role, as some DRAM cells decay to 0 and some to 1. Thus, for example, if a cell decays to 0, but its initial value is set to 0, the decay effect cannot be observed. If the physical layout of the DRAM module is known (i.e., the distribution of the true cells and anti-cells, and hence the individual decay directions), it is possible to construct an initialization pattern that maximizes the number of observable bit flips in the PUF response. However, the physical layout is rarely known. Furthermore, the optimal initialization value would need to be part of the challenge, or have to be stored on the device.

In our evaluation, we use a fixed initialization value $initval = 0$ to all cells. The entropy of our measurements thus can be further improved.

Overall, the challenge of a DRAM PUF can be defined as a tuple (id, t), where id denotes the logical PUF instance ($addr$ and $size$) and t denotes the decay time after which the memory content is read. We will not specify the $initval$ as we assume it is fixed.

Although SRAM and DRAM PUFs are both considered weak PUFs [30], the DRAM PUF presented in this paper offers multiple challenges due to the ability to vary decay times t. Given two PUF measurements m_x and m_{x+1}, taken at corresponding decay times t_x and t_{x+1} ($t_{x+1} \geq t_x$), both m_{x+1} and m_x can serve as PUF responses. With increasing decay times t, the number of DRAM cells flipping is monotonically increasing. Thus, m_{x+1} consists of a number of $newly$ flipped bits as well as the majority[2] of bits that already flipped in m_x. In general, if $t_x \leq t_{x+1}$ and $addr_x = addr_{x+1}$, $size_x = size_{x+1}$, we observe $m_x \subseteq m_{x+1}$, up to noise. However, note that it is not possible to measure responses for several decay times $t_0, t_1, ..., t_n$ at once. In particular, reading the PUF response at one decay time will cause the memory to be refreshed (the cells are re-charged as the data is read from DRAM cells into row buffers). Querying a PUF response with different decay time thus requires one to restart the experiment.

2.2   Run-Time DRAM PUF Access

Deactivating DRAM refresh for PUF access during device operation is a non-trivial task: when DRAM refresh cycles are disabled, critical data (such as data belonging to the OS or user-space programs) will start to decay and the system will crash. In our experiments, the Intel Galileo board with Yocto Linux crashes about a minute after DRAM refresh is disabled. Therefore, we present a customized solution which allows us to refresh critical code, but leaves PUF areas untouched. This solution is based on two techniques dubbed *selective DRAM refresh* and *memory ballooning*. The former allows for selectively refreshing the memory regions occupied by the OS and other critical applications so that they run normally and do not crash. Memory ballooning, on the other hand, safely reserves the memory region that corresponds to a logical PUF without corrupting critical data and also protects the memory region from OS and user-space programs accesses, to let the cells decay during PUF measurement.

Selective DRAM Refresh. On some devices, such as the PandaBoard, DRAM consists of several physical modules or logical segments, where the refresh of each module/segment can be controlled individually. In this case, the PUF can be allocated in a different memory segment from the OS and user-space programs. When querying the PUF, only the refresh of the segment holding the PUF is deactivated, while the other segments remain functional.

---

[2] Due to noise, the set of flipping cells for a fixed time t_x will not be completely stable. Nevertheless, our experiments in Sect. 4 show very low amounts of noise.

On other devices, e.g., the Intel Galileo, the refresh rate can only be controlled at the granularity of the entire DRAM[3]. Refresh at segment granularity is not possible. However, memory rows can be refreshed implicitly once they are accessed due to a read or a write operation. When a word line is selected because of a memory access, the sense amplifier drives the bit-lines to either the full supply voltage V_{DD} or back down to $0\,V$, depending on the value that was in the cell. In this way, the capacitor charge is restored to the value it had before the charges leaked. Using the above principle, even if refresh of the whole memory is disabled, selective memory rows can be refreshed by issuing a read to a word within each of the selected memory rows. This functionality can be implemented in a kernel module by reading a word within each memory row to be refreshed (Sect. 3).

Ballooning System Memory. To query a chosen logical PUF, the DRAM portion given by *addr* and *size* is overwritten by the respective initialization value (*initval*) and refresh is deactivated. To prohibit applications from accessing the PUF and thus implicitly refreshing them, we use memory ballooning concepts developed for virtual machines [47]. Memory ballooning is a mechanism for reserving a portion of the memory so as to prevent the memory region from being used by the kernel or any application. This approach allows to specify the physical address (*addr*) and size (*size*) of the memory region that will be reserved, i.e., the PUF. Once PUF memory is "ballooned", DRAM refresh can be disabled and selective refresh enabled for the non-PUF memory region. After PUF access is finished, the balloon can be deflated and the memory restored to normal use.

2.3 Security Assumptions

DRAM PUFs differ from classic memory-based PUFs, as they can be evaluated during run-time. An attacker, who wants to evaluate the PUF has less capabilities in doing so due to the fact that disabling and enabling DRAM refresh includes writing to hardware registers, a task which can only be performed by the kernel. An attacker thus requires root privileges. Furthermore, accessing the memory dedicated to the PUF is restricted to the kernel as well. Thus, a crucial security assumption is that firmware and operating system are trusted and an attacker never gains root privileges.

An attacker may try to change the ambient temperature in order to influence the bit flip characteristics, but a legitimate user can compensate the temperature effect by adjusting the decay time (as discussed in Sect. 4). The attacker could also try to adapt the "rowhammering" approach presented in [17], i.e., inducing random bit flips into DRAM cells by repeatedly accessing adjacent rows.

---

[3] Although the test boards do have multiple DRAM modules, DRAM refresh cannot be disabled individually. In particular, on the Galileo board, one DRAM chip is used to store the most significant 8 bits of every 16 bits, while the other chip is used to store the least significant 8 bits of every 16 bits. Disabling refresh on a single chip is not possible, as half of each memory word would be lost.

However, he or she would not succeed, as DRAM PUFs allocate a continuous chunk of memory. Rowhammering would only apply at the borders of the PUF area. Using voltage variations in order to manipulate PUF behavior, as done in [11,28], is out of scope of this paper, as we are focussing on intrinsic PUFs on commodity hardware where such voltage control is not possible.

3   Implementation and Performance

We implemented and tested our DRAM PUF construction on two popular platforms, the PandaBoard ES Revision B3 and the Intel Galileo Gen 2. The Panda-Board houses a TI OMAP 4460 System-on-Chip (SoC) module that implements 1 GB of DDR2 memory from ELPIDA in a Package-on-Package (PoP) configuration, which operates at 1.2 V. The Intel Galileo has an Intel Quark SoC X1000 SoC with two 128 MB DDR3 from Micron, operating at 1.5 V. The two physical DRAM modules are accessed in parallel and located on the same PCB as the processor.

We implemented two different approaches to query the PUF. The first approach uses a modified firmware in order to obtain PUF measurements during the boot phase. Second, we implemented a kernel module-based solution that enables PUF queries during run-time of a Linux operating system. The firmware solution is easy to implement and was used to take most of the measurements from the Intel Galileo. The kernel module-based solution was used for obtaining measurements on the PandaBoard platform and for gathering temperature stability measurements on the Galileo. The kernel module thus also serves as a general proof-of-concept of the run-time accessibility of the proposed DRAM PUF. We present implementation details of both approaches in the following.

3.1   Firmware-Based PUF Access

The firmware is the first code to be executed upon device start. During the DRAM initialization phase, the firmware itself does not require the use of DRAM. This makes it ideal for gathering PUF measurements.

In the case of the Galileo platform, we modified the Quark EDKII firmware. PUF measurement code was inserted just before DRAM refresh is enabled in order to access the PUF, comprising the following steps: writing the initial value (*initval*) to the specific logical PUF (as defined by *addr* and *size*), waiting for the decay time *t* to elapse, and then reading back the PUF response via the console. After the PUF response is retrieved, normal firmware execution and eventual boot of the OS can resume. The firmware patch consists of about 60 lines of C code. Most of the code implements initializing the PUF parameters and accessing the PUF memory region. The PUF response is read and printed to the console for later analysis.

On the PandaBoard, the implementation is similar: DRAM is initialized with *initval*, the auto-refresh of the memory controller is disabled, and after decay time *t*, the memory content is sent over UART to a workstation. Our firmware patch for the PandaBoard consists of about 50 lines of C code.

3.2   Linux Kernel Module-Based PUF Access

In order to be able to access the DRAM PUF during run-time, we implemented a kernel module for each platform, which can be inserted at run-time. The kernel module is designed to work in three phases: (1) Upon loading, the kernel module overwrites the cells in the desired logical PUF region by the *initval*. (2) The kernel module then modifies the memory controller via writes to configuration registers to disable DRAM refresh, while memory holding the OS and application is selectively refreshed. (3) After the decay time of t seconds elapsed, memory refresh is enabled again and the PUF response is read out.

On the PandaBoard, DRAM can be accessed using two individual external memory interfaces (EMIF), with each EMIF covering 512 MB. Thus, memory interfaced by the first EMIF can be used by the kernel and user space applications, while memory covered by the second EMIF can be used exclusively as DRAM PUF. In case of the PandaBoard, in order to implement this configuration, the interleaving mechanism that alternately maps subsequent logical addresses to physical addresses from both modules must first be disabled within the bootloader. Next, measurements can be obtained by turning off the refresh rate of the module that implements the logical PUFs and reading the memory contents after the decay time t, while the kernel and user space applications are residing functional on the other DRAM module. The kernel module takes about 100 lines of C code in total.

On the Intel Galileo, the refresh of the whole DRAM has to be disabled as it is not possible to control refresh at granularity smaller than a DRAM module. Consequently, the kernel module must selectively refresh memory used by the kernel and applications. The kernel module schedules selective refresh tasks[4] every N ms, where N is the desired refresh rate. For selective refresh, the module loops over all memory addresses that need to be refreshed, issuing a read to a memory word in every DRAM row. The kernel module takes about 300 lines of C code in total.

During a PUF query, the OS and other applications can operate normally, but some CPU resources must be spent on selective memory refresh. If the size of the memory region is too large, the CPU core will spend the majority of its time refreshing the defined memory area, leaving little resources to user space applications. Furthermore, if the time required to refresh the whole memory region is much longer then the required refresh period, critical portions of code and data may have decayed before they can be accessed by the kernel module.

Table 1 shows the time required to perform selective refresh of memory regions of various sizes, ranging from 32 MB up to 128 MB. We see that selective refresh takes between 7.6 ms and 21.2 ms for a single run. The last two columns in Table 1 show the CPU time spent on selective refresh, assuming 64 ms and 200 ms refresh rates. For an active memory size of 128 MB, the system will spend 33 % of CPU time on selective refresh, when a target refresh period of 64 ms is

---

[4] A key feature of Linux, the so-called `workqueues`, allowing tasks to be scheduled at specific time intervals, is used for this purpose.

Table 1. Time needed to perform memory reads (i.e. the selective refresh) to refresh varying sizes of memory regions on the Intel Galileo board with DDR3 memory.

Memory size	Selective refresh time	%CPU time (64 ms refresh period)	%CPU time (200 ms refresh period)
32 MB	7.6 ms	12 %	4 %
64 MB	12.1 ms	19 %	6 %
128 MB	21.2 ms	33 %	10 %

selected. However, at room temperature, the 64 ms refresh period, picked by most vendors, is very conservative, and our experiments suggest that even with a refresh rate of 200 ms our setup is stable. Previous work on DRAM retention time support our results [21]. Thus, depending on the operating conditions and required stability guarantees, the selective refresh period can be increased, allowing larger DRAM to be refreshed, or leaving more CPU resources for computation. In our setup, we were able to reduce the memory footprint of Yocto Linux, commonly used on Intel Quark devices, down to 32 MB without any special modifications.[5] At 32 MB, only 7.6 ms are needed for selective refresh at 64 ms, making more than 87 % CPU time available for other applications. These numbers demonstrate that selective refresh is viable for realistic code sizes.

4   Evaluation of DRAM PUF Characteristics

We measured the PUF instances on the Intel Galileo and PandaBoard, as described in Sect. 3. We performed measurements using four different Panda-Boards and five Intel Galileo devices. Furthermore, given the large amount of memory present, we measured two 32 KB logical PUFs on each device, resulting in eight different logical PUFs for the PandaBoard as well as ten logical PUFs for the Intel Galileo. Each logical PUF was measured at five different decay times t, with 50 measurements each. Based on these measurements we evaluated robustness, uniqueness, and randomness, as well as time and temperature dependency, and stability of the DRAM PUFs.

The characteristics of the DRAM PUFs are different compared to the SRAM PUFs. Rather than being considered as an array of bits, a DRAM PUF response mainly comprises the positions of flipped bits in a memory region. Thus, classic metrics that are used to evaluate memory-based PUFs, which are usually based on fractional Hamming distances, do not properly reflect the properties of the DRAM PUFs. This effect is particularly noticeable when evaluating the uniqueness of PUF instances. In case of the SRAM PUF, uniqueness is expressed due to differences in the startup values of all SRAM cells amongst different devices.

---

[5] One required change is disabling or limiting the journaling service. Other options available are to reduce the size of the journal so it does not take much memory, or using persistent storage for the journal.

Table 2. Metrics of logical PUF instances measured at different decay times.

Decay time	Device family	Min. J_{intra}	Max. J_{inter}	Fractional entropy H_t/N	Avg. decay rate	Max. fractional intra-HD	Min. fractional inter-HD
120 s	PandaBoard	0.4634	0.0102	0.0271	0.0041	0.0045	0.0038
	IntelGalileo	0.7712	0.0038	0.0062	0.0009	0.0003	0.0012
180 s	PandaBoard	0.4382	0.0168	0.0754	0.0102	0.0083	0.0139
	IntelGalileo	0.8361	0.0044	0.0169	0.0024	0.0005	0.0032
240 s	PandaBoard	0.4087	0.0258	0.0893	0.0159	0.0101	0.0244
	IntelGalileo	0.6261	0.0049	0.0250	0.0041	0.0020	0.0057
300 s	PandaBoard	0.4222	0.0405	0.1478	0.0202	0.0123	0.0238
	IntelGalileo	0.7944	0.0055	0.0353	0.0061	0.0013	0.0080
360 s	PandaBoard	0.3484	0.0342	0.1440	0.0234	0.0206	0.0279
	IntelGalileo	0.8276	0.0072	0.0541	0.0093	0.0022	0.0124

Consequently, uniqueness is measured using the fractional Hamming distance between startup values taken from different PUF instances (inter-Hamming Distance, inter-HD). However, in case of the DRAM PUF it is rather the location, i.e., the indices, of the cells that flip, which is the root cause for the uniqueness. If one would apply the *fractional* inter-Hamming Distance, the whole 32 KB measurement would be considered, including those cells that did not flip within the observed time period, resulting in a very low value, which does not capture uniqueness to the full extent.

Thus, we propose new metrics to evaluate robustness and uniqueness of the DRAM PUF that are based on the Jaccard index [13]. The Jaccard index is a well known metric to quantify the similarity of two sets of different size: the index results in a value of zero if both sets share no common elements and a value of one if both sets are identical. A summary of our results is shown in Table 2. Only for comparison to the case of SRAM PUFs we also give numbers for the classic fractional Hamming-distance based metrics.

Uniqueness. In order to evaluate the uniqueness of the PUF, we consider the set of indices of DRAM cells that flipped due to decay among different PUFs. In particular, based on two measurements m_1, m_2 that were obtained from two different logical PUFs for the same decay time t, we construct two corresponding sets v_1 and v_2 that store the indices of the flipped cells. Uniqueness is measured by the Jaccard index $J_{inter}(v_1, v_2)$:

$$J_{inter}(v_1, v_2) = \frac{|v_1 \cap v_2|}{|v_1 \cup v_2|}. \tag{1}$$

For an ideal PUF, the value of $J_{inter}(v_1, v_2)$ should be close to zero, indicating that two logical PUFs rarely share flipped bits. Indeed, as Table 2 shows, our DRAM PUFs depict an almost perfect behavior with the Intel Galileo having a

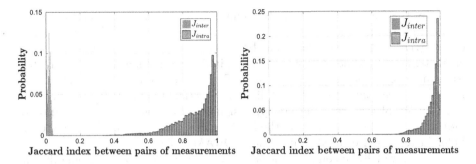

Fig. 3. Distribution of J_{intra} and J_{inter} values for (left) the PandaBoard and (right) the Intel Galileo.

maximum of $J_{inter} = 0.0072$ at $t = 360\,$s. The PandaBoard shows larger values with a maximum value of 0.0405 at $t = 300\,$s which, however, is still close to the optimal value of zero.

Robustness. In order to quantify the inherent noise in the PUF measurements and consequently PUF robustness, we computed the Jaccard index $J_{intra}(v_1, v_2)$ between two sets containing the indices of flipped bits in two measurements of the *same* logical PUF at identical decay times. An ideal PUF should show values close to one, indicating that responses are stable.

Figure 3 displays the distributions of $J_{intra}(v_1, v_2)$ and $J_{inter}(v_1, v_2)$ of all measurements, corresponding to identical decay times, for both device types. A clear divide between the two distributions indicates that individual devices can be distinguished perfectly, while the PUF response is stable over subsequent measurements.

Again, for comparison, we also provide data on the fractional intra-Hamming Distance (intra-HD) in Table 2, i.e., the Hamming distance between subsequent measurements. In comparison to SRAM PUFs, the Hamming distance values are much smaller due to the lower number of bit flips within the DRAM PUF. Nevertheless, except for one case, also the minimum inter-HD is multiply larger than the maximum intra-HD, indicating close to perfect separability.

Entropy. In order to generate cryptographic keys from the PUF response, PUF measurements must exhibit sufficient entropy. We estimate the Shannon entropy of DRAM PUF responses as follows. We again consider the set v of indices of DRAM cells that flipped after time t. Denote with k the cardinality of v and with N the total number of DRAM cells. Assuming that the flipped bits are distributed uniformly, as confirmed by our experiments, the probability of observing one set v is: $P(v) = 1/\binom{N}{k}$. The Shannon entropy of the DRAM PUF for a given decay time can thus be calculated using

$$H_t = log_2 \binom{N}{k}. \tag{2}$$

Note, that simply observing the number of bits decaying after time t has elapsed, is not sufficient for determining k, as the bit decay will be due to two effects: (i) short-term noise that must be corrected and (ii) stable long-term decay characteristics. In order to approximate k, indicating the stable PUF character-istics, multiple measurements for a single PUF can be averaged in order to elim-inate the noise component. Table 2 lists the fractional entropy H_t/N computed this way. We observe that the entropy is significantly bigger on the PandaBoard, indicating more bit flips than on the Intel Galileo. This is most likely due to the different technologies used to implement DRAM cells.

It is noteworthy to compare the entropy that can be extracted from different PUF implementations. While SRAM PUFs usually show min-entropy values of around 0.7–0.9 bits per cell, the entropy of the proposed DRAM PUF is one order of magnitude smaller. This can be explained as follows: whilst within SRAM the majority of cells have a unique startup pattern, in case of DRAM only some cells will flip during the observed decay time. However, this lower entropy can be easily compensated by the magnitudes higher (usually a thousand times) amount of DRAM cells available.

Decay Dependency on Time and Temperature. Figure 4 shows the decay rate as a function of decay time for both the PandaBoard and Intel Galileo. All measure-ments were taken at ambient room temperature with DRAM chips operating at around 40 °C. Every data point shows the average of all logical PUFs. We see that the decay rate significantly increases with time on the Galileo. The Panda-Board shows an s-like decay that has a steep beginning and saturates towards $t = 360$ s.

This plot allows us to estimate the number of time-dependent challenges that a logical PUF can provide. In order to allow for unique identification at any given decay time, the set of decay times $t_1, t_2, ..., t_n$ must be chosen such that the corresponding measurements show a minimum number of *new* bits flips, referred to as ϵ_{bits}, which is greater than the inherent noise. Given ϵ_{bits}, the set of viable decay times (and thus the challenges of a logical PUF) can be

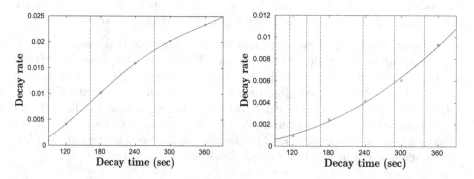

Fig. 4. Time-dependency of decay rate for DRAM modules on the (left) PandaBoard and the (right) Intel Galileo at room temperature.

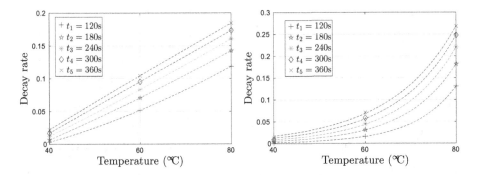

Fig. 5. Relation between the temperature and the decay rate measured on (left) the PandaBoard and (right) the Intel Galileo.

chosen accordingly. We used the maximum noise level previously observed for each respective decay time t in order to get a conservative approximation of the maximum number of challenges per logical PUF. We experimentally determined the maximum number of decay times to be $n = 7$ for the Intel Galileo and $n = 2$ for the PandaBoard. The number assumes a maximum decay time $t_n \leq 360\,\mathrm{s}$ and possible challenges are indicated by vertical red lines in Fig. 4. The smaller number for the PandaBoard is mainly due to higher noise. In particular, we observe that for the PandaBoard the J_{intra} values can be comparably low, i.e. $J_{intra} = 0.3484$ at $t = 360\,\mathrm{s}$. However, given J_{inter} is a magnitude different from J_{intra}, unique identification ability is preserved.

A second factor influencing the decay rate of DRAM cells is temperature. In Fig. 5 we show the dependency between temperature and decay rate for DRAM modules on the Intel Galileo and the PandaBoard. In order to control the temperature, we used a metal ceramic heater to heat the surface of DRAM modules to the desired temperature and took the measurements.

Although temperature affects the decay rate significantly, it does not change the decay characteristics much; instead, it affects decay time: We observed that by using a carefully chosen smaller decay time $t'_{T'} < t$ at a larger temperature $T' > T$, the same PUF response can be obtained as with decay time t at temperature T. In our experiments, we derive the following dependency for the Intel Galileo boards:

$$t'_{T'} = t * e^{-0.0662*(T'-T)}. \tag{3}$$

Hence, if the PUF is evaluated at a different temperature than during enrollment, this can be compensated through adapting the decay time according to Eq. (3). In order to support this statement, we calculated the noise J_{intra} between an enrollment measurement at room temperature ($40\,°\mathrm{C}$) and a measurement taken at a different temperature by adjusting decay time. For this purpose, we created reference measurements at room temperature with decay times $t_x = \{120\,\mathrm{s},\ 180\,\mathrm{s},\ 240\,\mathrm{s},\ 300\,\mathrm{s},\ 360\,\mathrm{s}\}$. In a next step, we used equivalent decay times $t'_{T'}$ that correspond to temperatures $T' = \{40\,°\mathrm{C}, 50\,°\mathrm{C}, 60\,°\mathrm{C}\}$

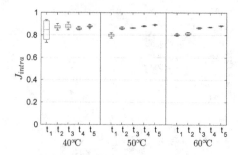
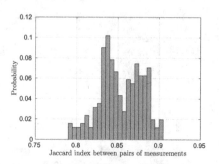

Fig. 6. J_{intra} values (i.e., similarity) of enrollment measurements taken at room temperature and measurements at higher temperatures $T' = \{40\,^{\circ}\text{C}, 50\,^{\circ}\text{C}, 60\,^{\circ}\text{C}\}$, with adjusted decay times t'.

Fig. 7. Distribution of J_{intra} of enrollment, reconstruction measurements pairs taken from the same logical PUF instances on Intel Galileo over four months.

and measured the PUF accordingly. As shown in Fig. 6, for all measurements, J_{intra} lies within the usual noise level. Thus, differences in temperature can be accommodated by adjusting decay time accordingly.

Stability over Time. During extended lifetime of devices, DRAM aging effects will begin to take place. Existing work on SRAM PUFs has explored aging effects [23,25,32,38]. We are aware of limited work on aging-related effects in DRAM cells with regard to security [36]. Figure 7 shows the histogram of J_{intra} values for measurements of an Intel Galileo, taken 4 months apart. Three logic PUFs were measured, and results are combined. Note that the measurements also include the noise introduced by temperature changes in our lab. J_{intra} values were computed of measurement pairs that comprise an enrollment and a reconstruction measurement each. The values are similar to the J_{intra} results shown in Table 2, suggesting sufficient stability of DRAM PUFs over a long-term usage time period.

5 Lightweight Protocols for Device Authentication and Secure Channel Establishment

In the this section we propose two novel PUF-based protocols that draw their security from the time-dependent decay characteristics of a DRAM PUF instance when queried at different decay times. Both protocols involve two parties, a client $\mathcal{C}$ and server $\mathcal{S}$. Whilst the first protocol authenticates $\mathcal{C}$ towards an honest $\mathcal{S}$, the second protocol establishes a secure channel between $\mathcal{C}$ and $\mathcal{S}$. The protocols leverage PUF instances extracted from DRAM modules and thus require $\mathcal{C}$ to own a device $\mathcal{D}$ that implements a DRAM PUF during the course of the protocol. For the sake of clarity, we will refer to the PUF instance on the client's device as $\mathcal{C}$ itself. Further, we omit the full specification parameters of the logical PUF instance to be queried. Instead of stating all parameters $(addr, size)$ in every protocol, we refer to one logical PUF instance as id.

Adversary and Threat Model. Our adversary model for the protocols considers a passive attacker, who is able to observe the network traffic between client and server and who can capture transmitted messages, in particular previous PUF measurements that were sent by the client. Furthermore, we consider the Fuzzy Extractor construction, in particular the ECC parameters as well as the Helper Data, to be public and thus known by the attacker.

Enrollment. An enrollment phase precedes both protocols, which is assumed to be conducted at a trusted party $\mathcal{SYS}$, such as a manufacturer or a system integrator. For each logical PUF instance, during the enrollment phase, $\mathcal{SYS}$ queries the PUF n times in order to get a set of measurements $\mathcal{M} = \{m_{id,0}, m_{id,1}, ..., m_{id,n}\}$ at a defined set of decay times $\mathcal{T} = \{t_0, t_1, ..., t_n\}$, i.e., $m_{id,x} = PUF(id, t_x)$. Decay times $t_0, t_1, ..., t_n$ are carefully chosen such that $t_0 < t_1 < ... < t_n$ and for every tuple of subsequent decay times the number of newly introduced bit flips in PUF measurements is always greater than a security parameter ϵ_{bits}. The parameter ϵ_{bits} can be changed to adjust security and usability of the protocol (see the end of this section).

To generate keys for the secure channel establishment protocol, $\mathcal{SYS}$ chooses a set $\mathcal{K} = \{k_{id,0}, k_{id,1}, ..., k_{id,n}\}$ containing uniformly distributed keys and uses a Fuzzy Extractor to create a set of Helper Data $\mathcal{W} = \{w_{id,0}, w_{id,1}, ..., w_{id,n}\}$, such that $(k_{id,x}, w_{id,x}) = GEN(m_{id,x})$, where $GEN(\cdot)$ denotes the generation function of the Fuzzy Extractor. While the current Fuzzy Extractor constructions [5,24] might leak entropy from the helper data in case of biased PUF, we assume there is a construction tailored for DRAM PUFs. Eventually, $\mathcal{T}$, $\mathcal{M}$ $\mathcal{W}$ and $\mathcal{K}$ will be given to $\mathcal{S}$, whilst the device will be handed to $\mathcal{C}$ in a secure manner.

Device Authentication. In order to authenticate the client $\mathcal{C}$ towards an honest server $\mathcal{S}$, the server chooses the smallest decay time t_x not previously used for logical PUF id in a run of the authentication protocol. Next, $\mathcal{S}$ transmits id and t_x to $\mathcal{C}$, who uses it as input to his or her PUF to retrieve a measurement $m'_{id,x}$, which is sent back to $\mathcal{S}$. $\mathcal{S}$ checks if $m'_{id,x}$ is close enough to a stored measurement $m_{id,x}$. This is done by checking whether the Jaccard index of $m'_{id,x}$ and $m_{id,x}$ is larger than a given threshold ϵ_{auth}, defined based on the noise of measurement m_x. This authentication protocol is depicted on the left side of Fig. 8. Note that for subsequent authentication trials, decay times are monotonically increasing.

The authentication is designed to be lightweight for the client in terms of computational overhead and memory footprint. It does not require $\mathcal{C}$ to store any long-term Helper Data or perform expensive decoding that is usually part of the key reconstruction process performed by classical Fuzzy Extractors. This is especially useful in the context of highly resource-constrained low-cost devices that have to be authenticated towards a server repeatedly.

Secure Channel Establishment. Using similar ideas, a secure channel can be established between $\mathcal{C}$ and $\mathcal{S}$, see Fig. 8 (right side). Again, $\mathcal{S}$ sends the smallest, not previously used decay time t_x for logical PUF id, this time along with the corresponding Helper Data $w_{id,x}$. The client evaluates his PUF instance id using

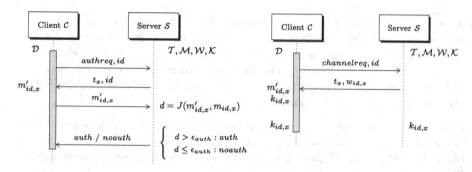

Fig. 8. Sequence diagram of (left) the device authentication protocol and (right) the secure channel establishment protocol.

t_x in order to retrieve $m'_{id,x}$, which is used in combination with $w_{id,x}$ to reconstruct $k'_{id,x} = REC(m'_{id,x}, w_{id,x})$. If the measurement m'_x was obtained using the correct logical PUF, the resulting key $k'_{id,x}$ will be identical to the key $k_{id,x}$ stored at the server in $\mathcal{K}$. Thus, both parties $\mathcal{C}$ and $\mathcal{S}$ will share the same key. In contrast to the authentication protocol depicted above, secure channel establishment is less lightweight, as it requires the evaluation of the Fuzzy Extractor on the client.

On the Choice of Security Parameters. Following our threat model, the attacker can obtain all previously used PUF measurements m_x by eavesdropping the authentication protocol, the security of the protocol is inherently based on the number of *newly* flipped bits ϵ_{bits} that emerge between measurements for subsequent decay times t_x, t_{x+1}. The value of ϵ_{bits}, and correspondingly the decay times, must be chosen in a way that a new PUF measurement has enough new entropy, even if the attacker knows the previous measurements.

In order to forge authentication or to derive the session key, the attacker has to guess the PUF measurement corresponding to the next unused decay time. In order to do so, the best strategy, without the knowledge of the physical PUF characteristics, is to randomly guess where the bit flips in the subsequent measurement will occur, knowing the previous measurement m_x. Suppose that the attacker guesses M new bit flips. Then, he can use these M flips together with the bit flips in the old response m_x as his guess of the new PUF measurement m_{x+1}. In the next paragraphs we estimate the probability of success for such a strategy. This allows us to fix the security parameter ϵ_{bits}, such that the probability of a successful guess is small.

We estimate the success probability as follows. The space of potential new bit flips is of size N, which is the number of bits that did not flip in m_x. Out of the remaining N bits, the attacker can guess M bits and combine them with m_x in order to generate m'_{x+1}. Note that the attacker does not need to guess the exact pattern m_{x+1}. Instead, the attacker will be successful, if the guessed measurement m'_{x+1} is a noisy version of the true measurement, i.e., m'_{x+1} lies within the error-correction bounds of the Fuzzy Extractor.

The probability that an attacker guesses M random bits and l of them happen to be real new bit flips of the subsequent measurement is $\frac{\binom{\epsilon_{bits}}{l}\binom{N-\epsilon_{bits}}{M-l}}{\binom{N}{M}}$. Note that in this case, the Jaccard index of the attacker's guess and the true measurement is $J(m'_{x+1}, m_{x+1}) = \frac{l+|m_x|}{\epsilon_{bits}+M-l+|m_x|}$, where $|m_x|$ is the number of bit flips in the previous measurement m_x. Assuming the authentication and key generation is successful if $J(m'_{x+1}, m_{x+1}) > \Delta$, the attacker will only be successful if l is greater than $\frac{(\epsilon_{bits}+M)*\Delta}{1+\Delta} - \frac{|m_x|*(1-\Delta)}{1+\Delta}$. Thus, the probability for an attacker to make a successful guess is:

$$P_M = \sum_{l=\lceil \frac{(\epsilon_{bits}+M)*\Delta}{1+\Delta} - \frac{|m_x|*(1-\Delta)}{1+\Delta} \rceil}^{\epsilon_{bits}} \frac{\binom{\epsilon_{bits}}{l}\binom{N-\epsilon_{bits}}{M-l}}{\binom{N}{M}}. \tag{4}$$

The attacker can chose any M, which will maximize the success probability P_M. If N is large and M is between $M_{min} = \epsilon_{bits} * \Delta - (1 - \Delta)|m_x|$ and $M_{max} = \frac{\epsilon_{bits}+(1-\Delta)*|m_x|}{\Delta}$, P_M is monotonically decreasing with M.[6] Hence, the attacker can choose $M = M_{min}$ to maximize the success probability.

In order to provide 128-bit security, $P = \max_M\{P_M\}$ must be smaller than 2^{-128}. Given Formula 4 and PUF characteristics, one can fix N and Δ, then derive ϵ_{bits} for different $|m_x|$, and subsequently estimate the feasible decay time. For the Intel Galileo, as a conservative estimation, the space of potential new bit flips is of size $N = 30\,\mathrm{KB}$ (assuming that out of a 32 KB logical PUF, less than 2 KB are flipping in m_x), and the threshold is $\Delta = 0.6$. To set $|m_0|$, a point where the decay is larger than the noise should be found. To be conservative, minimum max intra-HD is used as a reference for $|m_0|$.[7] Hence, we set $|m_0| = 80$, and then we can get $\epsilon_{bits1} = 73$, and $|m_1| = |m_0| + \epsilon_{bits2} = 153$. Then with $|m_1|$, we can get $\epsilon_{bits2} = 122$ and thus $|m_2| = 275$, etc. Consequently, in the Galileo, a 32 KB logical PUF can provide 7 challenges, each with the decay time shorter than 360 s.

6   Open Research Topics

This novel work on run-time accessible DRAM PUFs still leaves a number of open research issues and questions that need to be addressed. This creates opportunities for the community to refine and further improve the concept of DRAM PUFs.

Temperature dependency of the DRAM cell decay allows physical attackers to control the decay rate by adjusting the ambient temperature. For example, heating a DRAM chip may "speed up" the decay rate, shortening the time needed for an attacker to observe certain bits flip. Further investigation on the temperature dependence is needed and counter-measures need to be developed to thwart such attacks.

---

[6] $P_M > 0$ when M is between $\epsilon_{bits} * \Delta - (1 - \Delta)|m_x|$ and $\frac{\epsilon_{bits}+(1-\Delta)*|m_x|}{\Delta}$.

[7] If the PUF characteristic is better understood for $t < 120\,s$, a smaller $|m_0|$ may be chosen.

Voltage dependency of the DRAM cell decay was not considered in this paper, as commodity devices usually give no control over DRAM voltages. However, voltage dependency could be another viable characteristic used for the run-time accessible DRAM PUFs, if future commodity devices provide interfaces that allow for fine-grained control of DRAM voltages.

Readout time of the DRAM PUFs is in the order of minutes. This can be seen as a disadvantage, although in many cases it can be compensated by the advantage of being able to access the DRAM PUFs at run-time. Use cases that allow for such relatively long readout times need to be better understood. At the same time, improving the readout time is critical in order to broaden the applicability of DRAM PUFs.

Security assumptions, e.g., the trusted firmware and the operating system, may be considered as too strong. While these are also required for the other PUFs in commodity devices, one may look for solutions requiring a smaller trusted computing base.

Fuzzy Extractor constructions are needed that are either specifically tailored towards heavily biased PUF responses, found in decay-based DRAM PUFs, or that use the introduced Jaccard distances. Classic Fuzzy Extractors are based on Hamming distance-related metrics and are not secure for heavily biased PUFs. Thus, new constructions for biased PUFs, such as [24,39], should be developed.

7   Conclusion

In this work we presented intrinsic PUFs that can be extracted from Dynamic Random-Access Memory (DRAM) in commodity devices. An evaluation of the DRAM PUFs found on unmodified, commodity devices, in particular the Panda-Board and Intel Gallileo, showed their robustness, uniqueness, randomness, as well as stability over period of at least few months. Moreover, in contrast to existing DRAM and SRAM PUFs, we demonstrate a system model that is able to query the PUF instance directly during run-time using a Linux kernel module, based on the ideas of *selective DRAM refresh* and *memory ballooning*. We further presented protocols for device authentication and identification that draw their security from time-dependent decay characteristics of our DRAM PUF. Our intrinsic DRAM PUFs overcome two limitations of the popular intrinsic SRAM PUFs: they have the ability to be accessed at run-time, and have an expanded challenge-response space due to use of decay time t as part of the challenge. Consequently, our work presents a new alternative for device authentication by leveraging DRAM in commodity devices.

Acknowledgements. This work has been co-funded by the DFG as part of project P3 within the CRC 1119 CROSSING. This work was also partly funded by CASED. The authors would like to thank Kevin Ryan and Ethan Weinberger for their help with building the heater setup used in the experiments, and Intel for donating the Intel Galileo boards used in this work. The authors would also like to thank anonymous CHES reviewers, and especially our shepherd, Roel Maes, for numerous suggestions and guidance in making the final version of this paper.

References

1. Hacking DefCon 23's IoT Village Samsung fridge. https://www.pentestpartners. com/blog/hacking-defcon-23s-iot-village-samsung-fridge/. Accessed Feb 2016
2. Armknecht, F., Maes, R., Sadeghi, A.R., Sunar, B., Tuyls, P.: Memory leakage-resilient encryption based on physically unclonable functions. In: Sadeghi, A.-R., Naccache, D. (eds.) Towards Hardware-Intrinsic Security, pp. 135–164. Springer, Heidelberg (2010)
3. Bacha, A., Teodorescu, R.: Authenticache: harnessing cache ECC for system authentication. In: Proceedings of International Symposium on Microarchitecture, pp. 128–140. ACM (2015)
4. Batra, P., Skordas, S., LaTulipe, D., Winstel, K., Kothandaraman, C., Himmel, B., Maier, G., He, B., Gamage, D.W., Golz, J., et al.: Three-dimensional wafer stacking using Cu TSV integrated with 45 nm high performance SOI-CMOS embedded DRAM technology. J. Low Power Electron. Appl. **4**, 77–89 (2014)
5. Dodis, Y., Reyzin, L., Smith, A.: Fuzzy extractors: how to generate strong keys from biometrics and other noisy data. In: Cachin, C., Camenisch, J.L. (eds.) EUROCRYPT 2004. LNCS, vol. 3027, pp. 523–540. Springer, Heidelberg (2004)
6. Foster, I., Prudhomme, A., Koscher, K., Savage, S.: Fast and vulnerable: a story of telematic failures. In: USENIX Workshop on Offensive Technologies (2015)
7. Gassend, B., Clarke, D., Van Dijk, M., Devadas, S.: Delay-based circuit authentication and applications. In: Proceedings of the ACM Symposium on Applied Computing, pp. 294–301. ACM (2003)
8. Greenberg, A.: Hackers remotely kill a jeep on the highway–with me in it. Wired (2015). https://www.wired.com/2015/07/hackers-remotely-kill-jeep-highway/. Accessed 08 July 16
9. Guajardo, J., Kumar, S.S., Schrijen, G.-J., Tuyls, P.: FPGA intrinsic PUFs and their use for IP protection. In: Paillier, P., Verbauwhede, I. (eds.) CHES 2007. LNCS, vol. 4727, pp. 63–80. Springer, Heidelberg (2007)
10. Guajardo, J., Kumar, S.S., Schrijen, G.J., Tuyls, P.: Brand and IP protection with physical unclonable functions. In: IEEE International Symposium on Circuits and Systems, pp. 3186–3189 (2008)
11. Hashemian, M.S., Singh, B., Wolff, F., Weyer, D., Clay, S., Papachristou, C.: A robust authentication methodology using physically unclonable functions in DRAM arrays. In: Proceedings of the Design, Automation and Test in Europe Conference, pp. 647–652 (2015)
12. Hernandez, G., Arias, O., Buentello, D., Jin, Y.: Smart nest thermostat: a smart spy in your home. Black Hat USA (2014)
13. Jaccard, P.: Etude comparative de la distribution orale dans une portion des Alpes et du Jura. Impr. Corbaz (1901)
14. Katzenbeisser, S., Kocabaş, Ü., Rožić, V., Sadeghi, A.-R., Verbauwhede, I., Wachsmann, C.: PUFs: myth, fact or busted? A security evaluation of physically unclonable functions (PUFs) cast in silicon. In: Prouff, E., Schaumont, P. (eds.) CHES 2012. LNCS, vol. 7428, pp. 283–301. Springer, Heidelberg (2012)
15. Keeth, B.: DRAM Circuit Design: Fundamental and High-Speed Topics. Wiley, Hoboken (2008)
16. Keller, C., Gurkaynak, F., Kaeslin, H., Felber, N.: Dynamic memory-based physically unclonable function for the generation of unique identifiers and true random numbers. In: IEEE International Symposium on Circuits and Systems, pp. 2740–2743. IEEE (2014)

17. Kim, Y., Daly, R., Kim, J., Fallin, C., Lee, J.H., Lee, D., Wilkerson, C., Lai, K., Mutlu, O.: Flipping bits in memory without accessing them: an experimental study of DRAM disturbance errors. In: ACM SIGARCH Computer Architecture News, pp. 361–372 (2014)

18. Kocabaş, Ü., Peter, A., Katzenbeisser, S., Sadeghi, A.-R.: Converse PUF-based authentication. In: Camp, L.J., Volkamer, M., Reiter, M., Zhang, X., Katzenbeisser, S., Weippl, E. (eds.) Trust 2012. LNCS, vol. 7344, pp. 142–158. Springer, Heidelberg (2012)

19. Kohnhäuser, F., Schaller, A., Katzenbeisser, S.: PUF-based software protection for low-end embedded devices. In: Conti, M., Schunter, M., Askoxylakis, I. (eds.) TRUST 2015. LNCS, vol. 9229, pp. 3–21. Springer, Heidelberg (2015)

20. Kong, J., Koushanfar, F., Pendyala, P.K., Sadeghi, A.R., Wachsmann, C.: PUFatt: embedded platform attestation based on novel processor-based PUFs. In: ACM/EDAC/IEEE Design Automation Conference, pp. 1–6 (2014)

21. Liu, J., Jaiyen, B., Kim, Y., Wilkerson, C., Mutlu, O.: An experimental study of data retention behavior in modern DRAM devices: implications for retention time profiling mechanisms. In: ACM SIGARCH Computer Architecture News, pp. 60–71 (2013)

22. Liu, W., Zhang, Z., Li, M., Liu, Z.: A trustworthy key generation prototype based on DDR3 PUF for wireless sensor networks. Sensors 14, 11542–11556 (2014)

23. Maes, R., van der Leest, V.: Countering the effects of silicon aging on SRAM PUFs. In: IEEE International Symposium on Hardware-Oriented Security and Trust, pp. 148–153 (2014)

24. Maes, R., van der Leest, V., van der Sluis, E., Willems, F.: Secure key generation from biased PUFs. In: Güneysu, T., Handschuh, H. (eds.) CHES 2015. LNCS, vol. 9293, pp. 517–534. Springer, Heidelberg (2015)

25. Maes, R., Rožić, V., Verbauwhede, I., Koeberl, P., Van der Sluis, E., Van der Leest, V.: Experimental evaluation of physically unclonable functions in 65 nm CMOS. In: Proceedings of the ESSCIRC, pp. 486–489 (2012)

26. Phone as a Token - turn your phone into an authentication token. https://www.intrinsic-id.com/technology/phone-as-a-token/. Accessed Feb 2016

27. Rahmati, A., Hicks, M., Holcomb, D.E., Fu, K.: Probable cause: the deanonymizing effects of approximate DRAM. In: Proceedings of the International Symposium on Computer Architecture, pp. 604–615 (2015)

28. Rosenblatt, S., Chellappa, S., Cestero, A., Robson, N., Kirihata, T., Iyer, S.S.: A self-authenticating chip architecture using an intrinsic fingerprint of embedded DRAM. IEEE J. Solid-State Circuits 48, 2934–2943 (2013)

29. Rosenblatt, S., Fainstein, D., Cestero, A., Safran, J., Robson, N., Kirihata, T., Iyer, S.S.: Field tolerant dynamic intrinsic chip ID using 32 nm high-K/metal gate SOI embedded DRAM. IEEE J. Solid-State Circuits 48, 940–947 (2013)

30. Rührmair, U., Sölter, J., Sehnke, F.: On the foundations of physical unclonable functions. IACR Cryptology ePrint Archive 2009, p. 277 (2009)

31. Schaller, A., Arul, T., van der Leest, V., Katzenbeisser, S.: Lightweight anti-counterfeiting solution for low-end commodity hardware using inherent PUFs. In: Holz, T., Ioannidis, S. (eds.) Trust 2014. LNCS, vol. 8564, pp. 83–100. Springer, Heidelberg (2014)

32. Schaller, A., Škorić, B., Katzenbeisser, S.: On the systematic drift of physically unclonable functions due to aging. In: Proceedings of the International Workshop on Trustworthy Embedded Devices, pp. 15–20. ACM (2015)

33. Scheel, R.A., Tyagi, A.: Characterizing composite user-device touchscreen physical unclonable functions (pufs) for mobile device authentication. In: Proceedings of the International Workshop on Trustworthy Embedded Devices, pp. 3–13. ACM (2015)
34. Schneier, B.: The internet of things is wildly insecure—and often unpatchable. Wired (2014). http://www.wired.com/2014/01/theres-no-good-way-to-patch-the-internet-of-things-and-thats-a-huge-problem/. Accessed 08 July 2016
35. Schrijen, G.J., van der Leest, V.: Comparative analysis of SRAM memories used as PUF primitives. In: Proceedings of the Conference on Design, Automation and Test in Europe, pp. 1319–1324. EDA Consortium (2012)
36. Schroeder, B., Pinheiro, E., Weber, W.D.: DRAM errors in the wild: a large-scale field study. In: ACM SIGMETRICS Performance Evaluation Review, pp. 193–204 (2009)
37. Schulz, S., Sadeghi, A.R., Wachsmann, C.: Short paper: lightweight remote attestation using physical functions. In: Proceedings of the ACM Conference on Wireless Network Security, pp. 109–114 (2011)
38. Selimis, G., Konijnenburg, M., Ashouei, M., Huisken, J., De Groot, H., Van der Leest, V., Schrijen, G.J., Van Hulst, M., Tuyls, P.: Evaluation of 90 nm 6T-SRAM as Physical Unclonable Function for secure key generation in wireless sensor nodes. In: IEEE International Symposium on Circuits and Systems, pp. 567–570 (2011)
39. Skoric, B.: A trivial debiasing scheme for helper data systems. Cryptology ePrint Archive, Report 2016/241 (2016)
40. Suh, G.E., Devadas, S.: Physical unclonable functions for device authentication and secret key generation. In: Proceedings of the Design Automation Conference, pp. 9–14 (2007)
41. Tehranipoor, F., Karimina, N., Xiao, K., Chandy, J.: DRAM based intrinsic physical unclonable functions for system level security. In: Proceedings of the Great Lakes Symposium on VLSI, pp. 15–20 (2015)
42. Intrinsic-ID to Showcase TrustedSensor IoT Security Solution at InvenSense Developers Conference. https://www.intrinsic-id.com/intrinsic-id-to-showcase-trusted sensor-iot-security-solution-at-invensense-developers-conference/. Accessed Feb 2016
43. Tuyls, P., Batina, L.: RFID-tags for anti-counterfeiting. In: Pointcheval, D. (ed.) CT-RSA 2006. LNCS, vol. 3860, pp. 115–131. Springer, Heidelberg (2006)
44. Tuyls, P., Schrijen, G.J., Willems, F., Ignatenko, T., Skoric, B.: Secure key storage with PUFs. In: Tuyls, P., Skoric, B., Kevenaar, T. (eds.) Security with Noisy Data-On Private Biometrics, Secure Key Storage and Anti-Counterfeiting, pp. 269–292. Springer, London (2007)
45. Tuyls, P., Škorić, B.: Secret key generation from classical physics: physical unclonable functions. In: Mukherjee, S., Aarts, R.M., Roovers, R., Widdershoven, F., Ouwerkerk, M. (eds.) AmIware Hardware Technology Drivers of Ambient Intelligence, pp. 421–447. Springer, Netherlands (2006)
46. Viega, J., Thompson, H.: The state of embedded-device security (spoiler alert: it's bad). IEEE Secur. Priv. 10, 68–70 (2012)
47. Waldspurger, C.A.: Memory resource management in VMware ESX server. In: ACM SIGOPS Operating Systems Review, pp. 181–194 (2002)

Side Channel Countermeasures II

On the Multiplicative Complexity of Boolean Functions and Bitsliced Higher-Order Masking

Dahmun Goudarzi[1,2(✉)] and Matthieu Rivain[1]

[1] CryptoExperts, Paris, France
{dahmun.goudarzi,matthieu.rivain}@cryptoexperts.com
[2] ENS, CNRS, INRIA and PSL Research University, Paris, France

Abstract. Higher-order masking is a widely used countermeasure to make software implementations of blockciphers achieve high security levels against side-channel attacks. Unfortunately, it often comes with a strong impact in terms of performances which may be prohibitive in some contexts. This situation has motivated the research for efficient schemes that apply higher-order masking with minimal performance overheads. The most widely used approach is based on a polynomial representation of the cipher s-box(es) allowing the application of standard higher-order masking building blocks such as the ISW scheme (Ishai-Sahai-Wagner, Crypto 2003). Recently, an alternative approach has been considered which is based on a bitslicing of the s-boxes. This approach has been shown to enjoy important efficiency benefits, but it has only been applied to specific blockciphers such as AES, PRESENT, or custom designs. In this paper, we present a generic method to find a Boolean representation of an s-box with efficient bitsliced higher-order masking. Specifically, we propose a method to construct a circuit with low *multiplicative complexity*. Compared to previous work on this subject, our method can be applied to any s-box of common size and not necessarily to small s-boxes. We use it to derive higher-order masked s-box implementations that achieve important performance gain compared to optimized state-of-the-art implementations.

1 Introduction

One of the most widely used strategy to protect software implementations of blockciphers against side-channel attacks consists in applying *secret sharing* at the implementation level. This strategy also known as (*higher-order*) *masking* notably achieves provable security in the *probing security model* [ISW03] and in the *noisy leakage model* [PR13, DDF14]. While designing a higher-order masking scheme for a given blockcipher, the main issue is the secure and efficient computation of the s-box. Most of the proposed solutions (see for instance [RP10, CRV14, CPRR15]) are based on a polynomial representation of the s-box over the finite field $\mathbb{F}_{2^n}$ (where n is the input bit-length), for which the field multiplications are secured using the *ISW scheme* due to Ishai et al. [ISW03].

An alternative approach has recently been put forward which consists in applying higher-order masking at the Boolean level by bitslicing the s-boxes within a

© International Association for Cryptologic Research 2016
B. Gierlichs and A.Y. Poschmann (Eds.): CHES 2016, LNCS 9813, pp. 457–478, 2016.
DOI: 10.1007/978-3-662-53140-2_22

cipher round [GLSV15, GR16]. In the bitsliced higher-order masking paradigm, the ISW scheme is applied to secure bitwise AND instructions which are significantly more efficient than their field-multiplication counterparts involved in polynomial schemes. Moreover, such a strategy allows to compute all the s-boxes within a cipher round at the same time, which results in important efficiency gains. To the best of our knowledge, bitsliced higher-order masking has only been applied to specific blockciphers up to now. In [GLSV15], Grosso *et al.* introduce new blockciphers with LS-designs tailored to efficient masked computation in bitslice. The approach has also been used by Goudarzi and Rivain in [GR16] to get fast implementations of two prominent blockciphers, namely AES and PRESENT, masked at an order up to 10. However, no generic method to apply this approach to *any* blockcipher has been proposed so far. In contrast several generic methods have been published for the polynomial setting [CGP+12, CRV14, CPRR15]. Therefore, and given the efficiency benefits of bitsliced higher-order masking approach, defining such a generic method is an appealing open issue.

Finding a Boolean representation of an s-box that yields an efficient computation in the bitsliced masking world merely consists in finding a circuit with low *multiplicative complexity*. The multiplicative complexity of Boolean functions has been studied in a few previous papers [MS92, BPP00, TP14]. In particular, optimal circuits have been obtained for some small (3-bit/4-bit/5-bit) s-boxes using SAT solvers [CMH13, Sto16]. However no general (heuristic) method has been proposed up to now to get an efficient decomposition for any s-box, and in particular for n-bit s-boxes with $n \geq 6$.

In this paper, we introduce a new heuristic method to decompose an s-box into a circuit with low multiplicative complexity. Our proposed method follows the same approach as the CRV and *algebraic decomposition* methods used to get efficient representations in the polynomial setting [CRV14, CPRR15]. We also introduce the notion of *parallel multiplicative complexity* to capture the fact that several AND gates might be bundled in a single instruction, enabling further gain in the bitslice setting [GR16]. Eventually, we describe ARM implementations of bitsliced higher-order-masked s-box layers using our decomposition method and we compare them to optimized versions of the CRV and algebraic decomposition methods. Our results show a clear superiority of the bitslice approach when the masking order exceeds a certain threshold.

The paper is organized as follows. Section 2 gives some preliminaries about Boolean functions and higher-order masking. We then introduce the notion of (parallel) multiplicative complexity and discuss previous results as well as our contribution in Sect. 3. Section 4 presents our heuristic method in a general setting as well as some s-box-specific improvements. Finally, Sect. 5 describes our implementations and the obtained performances.

2 Preliminaries

2.1 Boolean Functions

Let $\mathbb{F}_2$ denote the field with 2 elements and let n be a positive integer. A *Boolean function* f with n variables is a function from $\mathbb{F}_2^n$ to $\mathbb{F}_2$. The set of such functions is denoted $\mathcal{F}_n$ in this paper. Any Boolean function $f \in \mathcal{F}_n$ can be seen as a multivariate polynomial over $\mathbb{F}_2[x_1, x_2, \ldots, x_n]/(x_1^2 - x_1, x_2^2 - x_2, \ldots, x_n^2 - x_n)$:

$$f(x) = \sum_{u \in \{0,1\}^n} a_u \, x^u, \tag{1}$$

where $x = (x_1, x_2, \ldots, x_n)$, $x^u = x_1^{u_1} \cdot x_2^{u_2} \cdot \ldots \cdot x_n^{u_n}$, and $a_u \in \mathbb{F}_2$ for every $u \in \{0,1\}^n$. The above representation is called the *Algebraic Normal Form* (ANF).

For any family $f_1, f_2 \ldots, f_m \in \mathcal{F}_n$, the set $\langle f_1, f_2 \ldots, f_m \rangle = \{\sum_{i=0}^m a_i f_i \mid a_i \in \mathbb{F}_2\}$ is called the *span* of the f_i's (or the space *spanned* by the f_i's), which is a $\mathbb{F}_2$-vector space. Let $\mathcal{M}_n$ denote the set of *monomial functions* that is $\mathcal{M}_n = \{x \mapsto x^u \mid u \in \{0,1\}^n\}$. Then, the set of Boolean functions with n variables can be defined as the span of monomial functions, that is $\mathcal{F}_n = \langle \mathcal{M}_n \rangle$.

Let n and m be two positive integers, and let S be a function mapping $\mathbb{F}_2^n$ to $\mathbb{F}_2^m$. Such a function can be seen as a vector of Boolean functions, *i.e.* $S(x) = (f_1(x), f_2(x) \ldots, f_m(x))$ and is hence called a *vectorial (Boolean) function* also known as an $(n \times m)$ s-box in cryptography. The Boolean functions $f_1, f_2, \ldots, f_m \in \mathcal{F}_n$ are then called the *coordinate functions* of S.

2.2   Higher-Order Masking

Higher-order masking consists in sharing each internal variable x of a cryptographic computation into d random variables x_1, x_2, $\ldots$, x_d, called *the shares* and satisfying $x_1 + x_2 + \cdots + x_d = x$, for some group operation $+$, such that any set of $d - 1$ shares is randomly distributed and independent of x. In this paper, the considered masking operation will be the bitwise addition. It has been formally demonstrated that in the noisy leakage model, where the attacker gets noisy information on each share, the complexity of recovering information on x grows exponentially with the number of shares [CJRR99, PR13]. This number d, called *the masking order*, is hence a sound security parameter for the resistance of a masked implementation.

The main issue while protecting a blockcipher implementation with masking is the secure computation of the nonlinear layer applying the s-boxes to the cipher state. The prevailing approach consists in working on the polynomial representation of the s-box over the field $\mathbb{F}_{2^n}$, which is secured using the ISW scheme [ISW03] for the field multiplications [RP10, CGP+12]. The most efficient polynomial evaluation method in this paradigm is due to Coron et al. [CRV14]. The polynomial representation can also be decomposed in functions of lower algebraic degree as recently proposed by Carlet *et al.* in [CPRR15]. In the quadratic case, these functions can then be efficiently secured using the CPRR scheme [CPRR14].

2.3   Bitsliced Higher-Order Masking

A variant of polynomial methods is to apply masking at the Boolean level using bitslicing (see for instance [DPV01, GLSV15, BGRV15]). In [GR16], the authors apply this approach to get highly efficient implementations of AES and PRESENT with masking order up to 10. In their implementations, bitslice is applied at the s-box level. Specifically, based on a Boolean circuit for an s-box S, one can perform ℓ parallel evaluations of S in software by replacing each gate of the circuit with the corresponding bitwise instruction, where ℓ is the bit-size of the underlying CPU architecture. It results that the only nonlinear operations in the parallel s-box processing are bitwise AND instructions between ℓ-bit registers which can be efficiently secured using the ISW scheme. Such an approach achieves important speedup compared to polynomial methods since (i) ISW-based ANDs are substantially faster than ISW-based field multiplications in practice, (ii) all the s-boxes within a cipher round are computed in parallel. The authors of [GR16] propose an additional optimization. In their context, the target architecture (ARM) is of size $\ell = 32$ bits, whereas the number of s-boxes per round is 16 (yielding 16-bit bitslice registers). Therefore, they suggest to group the ANDs by pair in order to perform a single ISW-based 32-bit AND where the standard method would have performed two ISW-based 16-bit AND. This roughly decreases the complexity by a factor up to two.[1]

3   Multiplicative Complexity of Boolean Functions

We shall call Boolean circuit any computation graph composed of $\mathbb{F}_2$-multiplication nodes (AND gates), $\mathbb{F}_2$-addition nodes (XOR gates), and switching nodes (NOT gates). Informally speaking, the multiplicative complexity of a Boolean function is the minimum number of $\mathbb{F}_2$-multiplication gates required by a Boolean circuit to compute it. This notion can be formalized as follows:

Definition 1. *The multiplicative complexity* $C(f_1, f_2, \ldots, f_m)$ *of a family of Boolean functions* $f_1, f_2, \ldots, f_m \in \mathcal{F}_n$, *is the minimal integer* t *for which there exist Boolean functions* $g_i, h_i \in \mathcal{F}_n$ *for* $i \in [\![1, t]\!]$ *such that:*

$$\begin{cases} g_1, h_1 \in \langle 1, x_1, x_2, \ldots, x_n \rangle \\ \forall i \in [\![2, t]\!] : g_i, h_i \in \langle 1, x_1, x_2, \ldots, x_n, g_1 \cdot h_1, \ldots, g_{i-1} \cdot h_{i-1} \rangle \end{cases} \quad (2)$$

and

$$f_1, f_2, \ldots, f_m \in \langle 1, x_1, x_2, \ldots, x_n, g_1 \cdot h_1, \ldots, g_t \cdot h_t \rangle. \quad (3)$$

It is easy to see that any set of Boolean functions $\{f_1, f_2, \ldots, f_m\} \subseteq \mathcal{F}_n$ has multiplicative complexity satisfying

$$C(f_1, f_2, \ldots, f_m) \leq C(\mathcal{M}_n) = 2^n - (n + 1). \quad (4)$$

Moreover, a counting argument shows that there exists $f \in \mathcal{F}_n$ such that

$$C(f) > 2^{\frac{n}{2}} - n. \quad (5)$$

---

[1] Packing the operands and depacking the result implies a linear overhead in the number of shares, whereas the number of quadratic operations (the ISW-ANDs) are divided by a factor up to 2.

In [BPP00], Boyar *et al.* provide a constructive upper bound for any Boolean function:

Theorem 1 ([BPP00]). *For every $f \in \mathcal{F}_n$, we have*

$$C(f) \leq \begin{cases} 2^{\frac{n}{2}+1} - \frac{n}{2} - 2 & \text{if } n \text{ is even,} \\ 3 \cdot 2^{\frac{n-1}{2}} - \frac{n-1}{2} - 2 & \text{otherwise.} \end{cases} \tag{6}$$

The particular case of Boolean functions with 4 and 5 variables has been investigated by Turan and Peralta in [TP14]. They give a complete characterization of affine-equivalence classes of these functions and they show that every $f \in \mathcal{F}_4$ has $C(f) \leq 3$ and every $f \in \mathcal{F}_5$ has $C(f) \leq 4$.

Other works have focused on the multiplicative complexity of particular kinds of Boolean functions. In [MS92], Mirwald and Schnorr deeply investigate the case of functions with quadratic ANF. In particular they show that such functions have multiplicative complexity at most $\lfloor \frac{n}{2} \rfloor$. Boyar *et al.* give further upper bounds for symmetric Boolean functions in [BPP00].

3.1 Multiplicative Complexity of S-Boxes

The multiplicative complexity of an s-box $S : x \mapsto (f_1(x), f_2(x) \dots, f_m(x))$ is naturally defined as the multiplicative complexity of the family of its coordinate functions. We shall also call multiplicative complexity of a given circuit the actual number of multiplication gates involved in the circuit, so that the multiplicative complexity of a circuit gives an upper bound of the multiplicative complexity of the underlying s-box.

The best known circuit for the AES s-box in terms of multiplicative complexity is due to Boyar *et al.* [BMP13]. This circuit achieves a multiplicative complexity of 32 which was obtained by applying logic minimization techniques to the compact representation of the AES s-box due to Canright [Can05] (and saving 2 multiplications compared to the original circuit).

In [CMH13], Courtois *et al.* use SAT-solving to find the multiplicative complexity of small s-boxes. Their approach consists in writing the Boolean system obtained for a given s-box and a given (target) multiplicative complexity t as a SAT-CNF problem, where the unknowns of the system are the coefficients of the g_i and h_i in Definition 1. For each value of t, the solver either returns a solution or a proof that no solution exists, so that the multiplicative complexity is the first value of t for which a solution is returned. They apply this approach to find Boolean circuits with the smallest multiplicative complexity for a random 3×3 s-box (meant to be used in CTC2 [Cou07]), the 4×4 s-box of PRESENT, and for several sets of 4×4 s-boxes proposed for GOST [PLW10]. These results have recently been extended by Stoffelen who applied the Courtois *et al.* approach to find optimal circuits for various 4×4 and 5×5 s-boxes [Sto16].

The main limitation of the SAT-solving approach is that it is only applicable to small s-boxes due to the combinatorial explosion of the underlying SAT problem, and getting the decomposition of an s-box of size *e.g.* $n = 8$ seems out of reach. Moreover, the method is not generic in the sense that the obtained decomposition stands for a single s-box and does not provide an upper bound for the multiplicative complexity of s-boxes of a given size.

3.2 Our Results

We give new constructive upper bounds for the multiplicative complexity of s-boxes. As a first result, we extend Theorem 1 to s-boxes (see proof in the full version):

Theorem 2. *For every* $S \in \mathcal{F}_n^m$, *we have:*

$$C(S) \leq \min_{k \in [\![1,n]\!]} (m2^k + 2^{n-k} + k) - (m + n + 1). \tag{7}$$

When $m = n$, *the min is achieved by* $k = \lfloor \frac{n - \log_2 n}{2} \rceil$ *for most* $n \in \mathbb{N}$, *which gives* $C(S) \leq B_n$ *with*

$$B_n \approx \sqrt{n}\, 2^{\frac{n}{2}+1} - \left(\frac{3n + \log_2 n}{2} + 1 \right). \tag{8}$$

We further introduce in this paper a heuristic decomposition method achieving lower multiplicative complexity. Our general result is summarized in the following Theorem:

Theorem 3. *For every* $S \in \mathcal{F}_n^m$, *we have* $C(S) \leq C_{n,m}$ *with*

$$C_{n,m} \approx \sqrt{m}\, 2^{\frac{n}{2}+1} - m - n - 1. \tag{9}$$

And in particular

$$C_{n,n} = \begin{cases} 17 & \text{for } n = 5 \\ 31 & \text{for } n = 6 \\ 50 & \text{for } n = 7 \end{cases} \quad \text{and} \quad C_{n,n} = \begin{cases} 77 & \text{for } n = 8 \\ 122 & \text{for } n = 9 \\ 190 & \text{for } n = 10 \end{cases} \tag{10}$$

In the above theorem, $C_{n,m}$ denote the multiplicative complexity of the generic method presented in Sect. 4. We also propose non-generic improvements of this method that might give different results depending on the s-box. Table 1 summarizes the multiplicative complexities obtained by the two above theorems and the non-generic improved method for $n \times n$ s-boxes with $n \in [\![4, 10]\!]$. For the latter, the figures represent what we hope to achieve for a random s-box (that we were able to achieve for some tested s-boxes).

Table 1. Multiplicative complexities of $n \times n$ s-boxes.

n	4	5	6	7	8	9	10
Theorem 2	8	16	29	47	87	120	190
Our generic method ($C_{n,n}$)	8	17	31	50	77	122	190
Our improved method ($C_{n,n}^*$)	7	13	23	38	61	96	145

3.3 Parallel Multiplicative Complexity

We introduce hereafter the notion of *parallel multiplicative complexity* for Boolean functions and s-boxes. We consider circuits with multiplication gates that can process up to k multiplications in parallel. The k-parallel multiplicative complexity of an s-box is the least number of k-parallel multiplication gates required by a circuit to compute it. We formalize this notion hereafter:

Definition 2. *The k-parallel multiplicative complexity $C^{(k)}(f_1, f_2, \ldots, f_m)$ of a family of Boolean functions $f_1, f_2, \ldots, f_m \in \mathcal{F}_n$, is the minimal integer t for which there exist Boolean functions $g_i, h_i \in \mathcal{F}_n$ for $i \in [\![1, tk]\!]$ such that:*

$$\begin{cases} g_1, h_1, g_2, h_2, \ldots, g_k, h_k \in \langle 1, x_1, x_2, \ldots, x_n \rangle , \\ \forall i \in [\![1, t-1]\!] : g_{ik+1}, h_{ik+1}, \ldots, g_{(i+1)k}, h_{(i+1)k} \\ \qquad \in \langle 1, x_1, x_2, \ldots, x_n, g_1 \cdot h_1, \ldots, g_{ik} \cdot h_{ik} \rangle \end{cases} \tag{11}$$

and

$$f_1, f_2, \ldots, f_m \in \langle 1, x_1, x_2, \ldots, x_n, g_1 \cdot h_1, \ldots, g_{tk} \cdot h_{tk} \rangle . \tag{12}$$

The main motivation for introducing this notion comes from the following scenario. Assume we want to perform m s-box computations in bitslice on an ℓ-bit architecture, where $\ell > m$. Then we have to pick a circuit computing the s-box and translate it in software by replacing Boolean gates with corresponding bitwise instructions. Since each bitsliced register contains m bits (m versions of the same input or intermediate bit), one can perform up to $k = \lceil \ell/m \rceil$ multiplication gates with a single ℓ-bit AND instruction (modulo some packing of the operands and unpacking of the results). If the used circuit has a k-parallel multiplicative complexity of t, then the resulting bitsliced implementation involve t bitwise AND instructions. This number of AND instructions is the main efficiency criterion when such an implementation is protected with higher-order masking which makes the k-parallel multiplicative complexity an important parameter for an s-box in this context.

The authors of [GR16] show that the AES circuit of Boyar *et al.* can be fully parallelized at degree 2, *i.e.* its 2-parallel multiplicative complexity is 16. In the full version of this paper, we further show that a sorted version of this circuit can achieve k-parallel multiplicative complexity of 9, 7 and 6 for $k = 4$, $k = 8$, and $k = 16$ respectively.

The decomposition method introduced in this paper has the advantage of being highly parallelizable. Table 2 summarizes the obtained k-parallel multiplicative complexity $C_{n,n}^{(k)}$ for $n \times n$ s-boxes for $k \in \{2, 4\}$. Note that we always have $C_{n,n}^{(k)} \in \{\lceil \frac{C_{n,n}}{k} \rceil, \lceil \frac{C_{n,n}}{k} \rceil + 1\}$ which is almost optimal.

4 A Heuristic Decomposition for S-Boxes

In this section, we introduce a heuristic decomposition method for s-boxes that aim to minimize the number of $\mathbb{F}_2$ multiplications. The proposed method follows the same approach than the CRV decomposition over $\mathbb{F}_{2^n}[x]$. We first describe the proposed heuristic for a single Boolean function before addressing the case of s-boxes.

Table 2. Parallel multiplicative complexities of our method for $n \times n$ s-boxes.

n	4	5	6	7	8	9	10
$C_{n,n}$	8	17	31	50	77	122	190
$C_{n,n}^{(2)}$	4	9	16	25	39	62	95
$C_{n,n}^{(4)}$	2	5	9	13	20	31	48

4.1 Decomposition of a Single Boolean Function

Let f be a Boolean function. The proposed decomposition simply consists in writing f as:

$$f(x) = \sum_{i=0}^{t-1} g_i(x) \cdot h_i(x) + h_t(x) \tag{13}$$

where $g_i, h_i \in \langle \mathcal{B} \rangle$, for some basis of functions $\mathcal{B} = \{\phi_j\}_{j=1}^{|\mathcal{B}|}$. Assume that all the $\phi_j(x)$, $\phi_j \in \mathcal{B}$, can be computed with r multiplications. Then the total multiplicative complexity of the above decomposition is of $r + t$. We now explain how to find such a decomposition by solving a linear system.

Solving a Linear System. As in the CRV method, we first sample t random functions g_i from $\langle \mathcal{B} \rangle$. This is simply done by picking $t \cdot |\mathcal{B}|$ random bits $a_{i,j}$ and setting $g_i = \sum_{\phi_j \in \mathcal{B}} a_{i,j} \phi_j$. Then we search for a family of $t + 1$ Boolean functions $\{h_i\}_i$ satisfying (13). This is done by solving the following system of linear equations over $\mathbb{F}_2$:

$$A \cdot c = b \tag{14}$$

where $b = (f(e_1), f(e_2), \dots, f(e_n))^\mathsf{T}$ with $\{e_i\} = \mathbb{F}_2^n$ and where A is a matrix defined as the concatenation of $t + 1$ submatrices:

$$A = (A_0 | A_1 | \cdots | A_t) \tag{15}$$

with

$$A_i = \begin{pmatrix} \phi_1(e_1) \cdot g_i(e_1) & \phi_2(e_1) \cdot g_i(e_1) & \cdots & \phi_{|\mathcal{B}|}(e_1) \cdot g_i(e_1) \\ \phi_1(e_2) \cdot g_i(e_2) & \phi_2(e_2) \cdot g_i(e_2) & \cdots & \phi_{|\mathcal{B}|}(e_2) \cdot g_i(e_2) \\ \vdots & \vdots & \ddots & \vdots \\ \phi_1(e_{2^n}) \cdot g_i(e_{2^n}) & \phi_2(e_{2^n}) \cdot g_i(e_{2^n}) & \cdots & \phi_{|\mathcal{B}|}(e_{2^n}) \cdot g_i(e_{2^n}) \end{pmatrix} \tag{16}$$

for $0 \leq i \leq t-1$, and

$$
A_t = \begin{pmatrix}
\phi_1(e_1) & \phi_2(e_1) & \cdots & \phi_{|\mathcal{B}|}(e_1) \\
\phi_1(e_2) & \phi_2(e_2) & \cdots & \phi_{|\mathcal{B}|}(e_2) \\
\vdots & \vdots & \ddots & \vdots \\
\phi_1(e_{2^n}) & \phi_2(e_{2^n}) & \cdots & \phi_{|\mathcal{B}|}(e_{2^n})
\end{pmatrix}
\tag{17}
$$

It can be checked that the vector c, solution of the system, gives the coefficients of the h_i's over the basis $\mathcal{B}$. A necessary condition for this system to have a solution whatever the target vector b (*i.e.* whatever the Boolean function f) is to get a matrix A of full rank. In particular, the following inequality must hold:

$$
(t+1)|\mathcal{B}| \geq 2^n.
\tag{18}
$$

Another necessary condition to get a full-rank matrix is that the *squared basis* $\mathcal{B} \times \mathcal{B} = \{\phi_i \cdot \phi_k \mid \phi_i, \phi_k \in \mathcal{B}\}$ spans the entire space $\mathcal{F}_n$. A classic basis of the vector space is the set of monomials $\mathcal{M}_n$. Therefore, we suggest to take a basis $\mathcal{B}$ such that $\mathcal{M}_n \subseteq \mathcal{B} \times \mathcal{B}$. Let

$$
\mathcal{B}_0 = \{x \mapsto x^u, u \in \mathcal{U}\}
$$
$$
\text{with } \mathcal{U} = \{(u_1, \ldots, u_\ell, 0, \ldots, 0)\} \cup \{(0, \ldots, 0, u_{\ell+1}, \ldots, u_n)\} \tag{19}
$$

where $\ell = \lceil \frac{n}{2} \rceil$ and where $u_i \in \{0,1\}$ for every $i \in [\![1,n]\!]$. Then, we clearly have $\mathcal{B}_0 \times \mathcal{B}_0 = \mathcal{M}_n$. We hence suggest taking $\mathcal{B} \supseteq \mathcal{B}_0$, with $\mathcal{B}$ possibly larger than $\mathcal{B}_0$ since restraining ourselves to $\mathcal{B} = \mathcal{B}_0$ could be non-optimal in terms of multiplications for the underlying decomposition method. Indeed, (18) shows that the more elements in the basis, the smaller t, *i.e.* the less multiplications $g_i \cdot h_i$. We might therefore derive a bigger basis by iterating $\mathcal{B} \leftarrow \mathcal{B} \cup \{\phi_j \cdot \phi_k\}$, where ϕ_j and ϕ_k are randomly sampled from $\mathcal{B}$ until reaching a basis $\mathcal{B}$ with the desired cardinality.

We then have $r = |\mathcal{B}| - n - 1$, where we recall that r denotes the number of multiplications to derive $\mathcal{B}$, and since $x \mapsto 1, x \mapsto x_1, \ldots, x \mapsto x_n \in \mathcal{B}$ requires no multiplications. By construction, we have $|\mathcal{B}| \geq |\mathcal{B}_0| = 2^\ell + 2^{n-\ell} - 1$, implying $r \geq 2^\ell + 2^{n-\ell} - (n+2)$. Let $C_n = r + t$ denote the number of multiplications achieved by our decomposition method. Then, by injecting C_n in (18) we get:

$$
(C_n - r + 1)(n + 1 + r) \geq 2^n,
\tag{20}
$$

that is:

$$
C_n \geq r + \frac{2^n}{n+1+r} - 1.
\tag{21}
$$

It can be checked that the value of r minimizing the above bound is $2^{\frac{n}{2}} - (n-1)$. However, r must satisfy $r \geq 2^\ell + 2^{n-\ell} - (n+2)$ where $\ell = \lceil \frac{n}{2} \rceil$, which is always greater than $2^{\frac{n}{2}} - (n-1)$ for $n \geq 2$. That is why we shall define the optimal value of the parameter r (for the single-Boolean-function case) as:

$$r_{opt} = 2^{\ell} + 2^{n-\ell} - (n+2) = \begin{cases} 2^{\frac{n}{2}+1} - (n+2) & \text{if } n \text{ even,} \\ 3 \cdot 2^{\frac{n-1}{2}} - (n+2) & \text{if } n \text{ odd,} \end{cases} \tag{22}$$

which amounts to taking $\mathcal{B} = \mathcal{B}_0$. The corresponding optimal value for t is then defined as:

$$t_{opt} = \left\lceil \frac{2^n}{r_{opt} + n + 1} \right\rceil - 1 \tag{23}$$

which gives $t_{opt} \approx 2^{\frac{n}{2}-1}$ for n even, and $t_{opt} \approx \frac{1}{3} 2^{\frac{n+1}{2}}$ for n odd.

Table 3. Optimal and achievable parameters for a single Boolean function.

n	4	5	6	7	8	9	10
Optimal parameters							
(r,t)	(2,2)	(5,2)	(8,4)	(15,5)	(22,8)	(37,10)	(52,16)
$\|\mathcal{B}\|$	7	11	15	23	31	47	63
C_n	4	7	12	20	30	46	68
Achievable parameters							
(r,t)	(2,3)	(5,3)	(9,5)	(16,6)	(25,9)	(41,11)	(59,17)
$\|\mathcal{B}\|$	7	11	16	24	34	51	70
C_n	5	8	14	22	34	52	78

In Table 3, we give the optimal values for (r,t) as well as the corresponding size of the basis $\mathcal{B}$ and multiplication complexity C_n for $n \in [\![4, 10]\!]$. We also give the parameter values that we could actually achieve in practice to get a full-rank system. We observe a small gap between the optimal and the achievable parameters, which results from the heuristic nature of the method (since we cannot prove that the constructed matrix A is full-rank).

4.2   S-Box Decomposition

Let $S: x \mapsto (f_1(x), f_2(x), \ldots, f_m(x))$ be an s-box. We can apply the above heuristic to each of the m coordinate functions f_i to get a decomposition as follows:

$$f_i(x) = \sum_{j=0}^{t-1} g_j(x) \cdot h_{i,j}(x) + h_{i,t}(x), \tag{24}$$

for $1 \leq i \leq m$. Here the g_j's are randomly sampled from $\langle \mathcal{B} \rangle$ until obtaining a full-rank system, which is then used to decompose every coordinate function f_i. The total number of multiplications is $C_{n,m} = r + m \cdot t$. Then, (18) gives:

$$C_{n,m} \geq r + m \left(\frac{2^n}{n+1+r} - 1 \right). \tag{25}$$

It can be checked that the value of r minimizing the above bound is $\sqrt{m2^n}-n-1$. We hence define

$$r_{opt} = \left\lfloor \sqrt{m2^n} \right\rceil - n - 1, \tag{26}$$

which minimizes (25) for every $n \in [\![2,10]\!]$ and every $m \in [\![1,n]\!]$. Moreover, this value satisfies the constraint (18) *i.e.* $r_{opt} \geq 2^\ell + 2^{n-\ell} - (n+2)$ for every $m \geq 4$, and in practice we shall only consider s-boxes with $m \geq 4$. The corresponding optimal value t_{opt} is then defined w.r.t. r_{opt} as in (23), which satisfies

$$t_{opt} = \left\lceil \frac{2^{\frac{n}{2}}}{\sqrt{m}} \right\rceil - 1 \tag{27}$$

for every $n \in [\![2,10]\!]$ and every $m \in [\![1,n]\!]$. We hence get

$$C_{n,m} \geq r_{opt} + m \cdot t_{opt} \approx \sqrt{m}\, 2^{\frac{n}{2}+1} - (n+m+1). \tag{28}$$

In Table 4, we give the optimal values for the parameters (r,t) as well as the corresponding size of the basis $\mathcal{B}$ and multiplication complexity $C_{n,n}$ for $n \times n$ s-boxes with $n \in [\![4,10]\!]$. We also give the parameter values that we could actually achieve in practice to get a full-rank system.

Table 4. Optimal and achievable parameters for an $n \times n$ s-box.

n	4	5	6	7	8	9	10
Optimal parameters							
(r,t)	(3,1)	(7,2)	(13,3)	(22,4)	(36,5)	(58,7)	(90,10)
$|\mathcal{B}|$	8	13	20	30	45	68	101
$C_{n,n}$	7	17	31	50	76	121	190
Achievable parameters							
(r,t)	(4,1)	(7,2)	(13,3)	(22,4)	(37,5)	(59,7)	(90,10)
$|\mathcal{B}|$	9	13	20	30	46	69	101
$C_{n,n}$	8	17	31	50	77	122	190

In comparison to the single-Boolean-function case, the optimal size of the basis $\mathcal{B}$ for the s-box decomposition is significantly bigger. This comes from the fact that a bigger basis implies a lower t for each of the m coordinate functions (*i.e.* decrementing t implies decreasing $C_{n,m}$ by m). We also observe a very close gap (sometimes null) between the optimal and the achievable parameters. This tightness, compared to the single-Boolean-function case, is most likely due to the fact that we use a bigger basis.

4.3 Improvements

We present hereafter some improvements of the above method which can be applied to get a decomposition with better multiplicative complexity for a given s-box. In comparison to the above results, the obtained system and the associated multiplicative complexity depend on the target s-box and are not applicable to all s-boxes.

Basis Update. Our first improvement of the above method is based on a dynamic update of the basis, each time a coordinate function $f_i(x)$ is computed.[2] Indeed, the term $g_j(x) \cdot h_{i,j}(x)$ involved in the computation of $f_i(x)$ can be reused in the computation of the following $f_{i+1}(x), \ldots, f_n(x)$. In our decomposition process, this means that the $g_j \cdot h_{i,j}$ functions can be added to the basis for the decomposition of the next coordinate functions $f_{i+1}, \ldots, f_n$. Basically, we start with some basis $\mathcal{B}_1 \supseteq \mathcal{B}_0$, where $\mathcal{B}_0$ is the minimal basis as defined in (19). Then, for every $i \geq 1$, we look for a decomposition

$$f_i(x) = \sum_{j=0}^{t_i-1} g_{i,j}(x) \cdot h_{i,j}(x) + h_{i,t_i}(x), \qquad (29)$$

where $t_i \in \mathbb{N}$ and $g_{i,j}, h_{i,j} \in \langle \mathcal{B}_i \rangle$. Once such a decomposition has been found, we carry on with the new basis $\mathcal{B}_{i+1}$ defined as:

$$\mathcal{B}_{i+1} = \mathcal{B}_i \cup \{g_{i,j} \cdot h_{i,j}\}_{j=0}^{t_i-1}. \qquad (30)$$

Compared to the former approach, we use different functions $g_{i,j}$ and we get a different matrix A for every coordinate function f_i. On the other hand, for each decomposition, the basis grows and hence the number t_i of multiplicative terms in the decomposition of f_i might decrease. In this context, we obtain a new condition for every i that is:

$$t_i \geq \frac{2^n}{|\mathcal{B}_i|} - 1. \qquad (31)$$

The lower bound on t_i hence decreases as $\mathcal{B}_i$ grows. The total multiplicative complexity of the method is then of:

$$C_{n,m}^* = r + \sum_{i=1}^{m} t_i, \qquad (32)$$

where $r = |\mathcal{B}_1| - (n+1)$ is the number of multiplications required to derive the initial basis $\mathcal{B}_1$. From the above inequality, we can define the optimal sequence of t_i and $s_i = |\mathcal{B}_i|$ as:

$$t_1 = \psi_n(s_1) \quad \text{and} \quad \begin{cases} s_{i+1} = s_i + t_i \\ t_{i+1} = \psi_n(s_{i+1}) \end{cases} \quad \text{for every } i > 1 \qquad (33)$$

where $\psi_n \colon x \mapsto \left\lceil \frac{2^n}{x} \right\rceil - 1$. The sequence (s_i, t_i) is fully determined by the cardinality of the original basis $s_1 = |\mathcal{B}_1|$, and we have:

$$\begin{cases} s_i = (\psi_n + \mathrm{Id})^{(i-1)}(s_1) \\ t_i = \psi_n \circ (\psi_n + \mathrm{Id})^{(i-1)}(s_1) \end{cases} \qquad (34)$$

---

[2] A similar idea is used in [BMP13] to construct an efficient circuit for the inversion in $\mathbb{F}_{16}$.

for every $i \geq 1$, where Id denote the identity function. The obtained optimal complexity is then:

$$C_{n,m}^* = s_1 - (n+1) + \sum_{i=1}^{m} \psi_n \circ (\psi_n + \mathrm{Id})^{(i-1)}(s_1)$$

$$= (\psi_n + \mathrm{Id})^{(m)}(s_1) - (n+1) .$$

By definition of ψ_n, the obtained functions $(\psi_n + \mathrm{Id})^{(i)}$ are sums of continued fractions with ceiling, for which we do not have an analytic expression.

Table 5. Optimal parameters with basis-update improvement.

n	$|\mathcal{B}_1|$	r	$t_1, t_2, \ldots, t_n$	$C_{n,n}^*$
4	7	2	2,1,1,1	7
5	11	5	2,2,2,1,1	13
	12	6	2,2,1,1,1	13
6	15	8	4,3,2,2,2,2	23
	16	9	3,3,2,2,2,2	23
7	23	15	5,4,3,3,3,3,2	38
8	31	22	8,6,5,5,4,4,4,3	61
	32	23	7,6,5,5,4,4,4,3	61
	33	24	7,6,5,5,4,4,3,3	61
	34	25	7,6,5,4,4,4,3,3	61
9	47	37	10,8,7,7,6,6,5,5,5	96
	48	38	10,8,7,7,6,5,5,5,5	96
	49	39	10,8,7,6,6,5,5,5,5	96
10	63	52	16,12,11,10,9,8,7,7,7,6	145
	64	53	15,12,11,10,9,8,7,7,7,6	145
	65	54	15,12,11,9,9,8,7,7,7,6	145

In Table 5, we give the optimal parameters $s_1 = |\mathcal{B}_1|$ and corresponding $r = s_1 - (n+1)$, $t_1, t_2, \ldots, t_n$, and $C_{n,n}^*$ for $n \times n$ s-boxes with $n \in [\![4, 10]\!]$. When the optimal multiplicative complexity is obtained for several values of s_1, we give all the obtained set of parameters. We observe that the optimal multiplicative complexity is always achieved by starting with the minimal basis *i.e.* by taking $\mathcal{B}_1 = \mathcal{B}_0$. It can also be obtained by taking s_1 up to $|\mathcal{B}_0| + 3$ depending on the values of n.

The achievable counterpart of Table 5 only exists with respect to a given s-box since the functions $g_{i,j} \cdot h_{i,j}$ added to the basis at each step depend on the actual s-box. But while focusing on a given s-box, we can still improve the method as we show hereafter.

Rank Drop. Our second improvement is based on the observation that even if the matrix A is not full-rank, the obtained system can still have a solution for some given s-box. Specifically, if A is of rank $2^n - \delta$ then we should get a solution for one s-box out of 2^δ in average. Hence, instead of having t_i satisfying the condition $(t_i + 1)|\mathcal{B}| \geq 2^n$, we allow a rank drop in the system of equations, by taking $t_i \geq \frac{2^n - \delta}{|\mathcal{B}_i|} - 1$ for some integer δ for which solving 2^δ systems is affordable. We hence hope to get smaller values of t_i by trying 2^δ systems. Note that heuristically, we can only hope to achieve the above bound if δ is (a few times) lower than the maximal rank 2^n (*e.g.* $\delta \leq \frac{2^n}{4}$). We can then define the (theoretical) optimal sequence (s_i, t_i) and the corresponding multiplicative complexity $C^*_{n,m}$ from $s_1 = |\mathcal{B}_1|$ as in (33) and (35) by replacing the function ψ_n for $\psi_{n,\delta} \colon x \mapsto \lceil \frac{2^n - \delta}{x} \rceil - 1$. As an illustration, Table 6 provides the obtained parameters for a δ up to 32. We see that the rank-drop improvement (theoretically) saves a few multiplications.

Table 6. Optimal parameters with basis-update and rank-drop improvements.

n	δ	$|\mathcal{B}_1|$	r	$t_1, t_2, \ldots, t_n$	$C^*_{n,n}$
4	4	7	2	1,1,1,1	6
5	8	11	5	2,1,1,1,1	11
	8	12	6	1,1,1,1,1	11
6	16	15	8	3,2,2,2,1,1	19
	16	16	9	2,2,2,2,1,1	19
7	32	23	15	4,3,3,2,2,2,2	33
	32	24	16	3,3,3,2,2,2,2	33
8	32	31	22	7,5,5,4,4,3,3,3	56
	32	32	23	6,5,5,4,4,3,3,3	56
9	32	47	37	10,8,7,6,6,5,5,5,4	93
	32	48	38	9,8,7,6,6,5,5,5,4	93
10	32	63	52	15,12,11,9,9,8,7,7,7,6	143
	32	64	53	15,12,10,9,9,8,7,7,7,6	143
	32	65	54	15,12,10,9,8,8,7,7,7,6	143
	32	66	55	15,12,10,9,8,8,7,7,6,6	143
	32	67	56	14,12,10,9,8,8,7,7,6,6	143

In practice, we observe that the condition $(t_i + 1)|\mathcal{B}_i| \geq 2^n - \delta$ is not always sufficient to get a matrix A of rank $2^n - \delta$. We shall then start with $t_i = \psi_{n,d}(|\mathcal{B}_i|)$ and try to solve $\alpha \cdot 2^\delta$ systems, for some constant α. In case of failure, we increment t_i and start again until a solvable system is found. The overall process is summarized in Algorithm 1.

The execution time of Algorithm 1 is dominated by the calls to a linear-solving procedure (Step 6). The number of trials is in $o(n\,\alpha\,2^\delta)$, where the

---

Algorithm 1. Improved method with exhaustive search

Input: An s-box $S \equiv (f_1, f_2, \ldots, f_m)$, parameters $s_1 = |\mathcal{B}_1|$, α, and δ
Output: A basis $\mathcal{B}_1$ and the functions $\{h_{i,j}\}_{i,j}$ and $\{g_{i,j}\}_{i,j}$
1. $i = 1$; $t_1 = \psi_{n,\delta}(s_1)$
2. **do** $\alpha \cdot 2^\delta$ **times:**
3.   **if** $i = 1$ **then** randomly generate $\mathcal{B}_1 \supseteq \mathcal{B}_0$ with $|\mathcal{B}_1| = s_1$
4.   randomly sample t_i functions $g_{i,j} \in \langle \mathcal{B}_i \rangle$
5.   compute the corresponding matrix A
6.   **if** $A \cdot c = b_{f_i}$ has a solution **then**
7.   store the corresponding functions $\{h_{i,j}\}_j$ and $\{g_{i,j}\}_j$
8.   **if** $i = n$ **then return** $\mathcal{B}_1, \{h_{i,j}\}_{i,j}, \{g_{i,j}\}_{i,j}$
9. $\mathcal{B}_{i+1} = \mathcal{B}_i \cup \{h_{i,j} \cdot g_{i,j}\}_j$; $t_{i+1} = \psi_{n,\delta}(|\mathcal{B}_{i+1}|)$; i++
10.   **goto** Step 2
11.   **endif**
12. **enddo**
13. t_i++; **goto** Step 2

---

constant in the $o(\cdot)$ is the average incrementation of t_i (*i.e.* the average number of times Step 13 is executed per i). In our experiments, we observed that the optimal value of $t_1 = \psi_{n,\delta}(s_1)$ is rarely enough to get a solvable system for f_1. This is because we start with the minimal basis as in the single-Boolean-function case. We hence have a few incrementations for $i = 1$. On the other hand, the next optimal t_i's are often enough or incremented a single time.

We used Algorithm 1 to get the decomposition of various $n \times n$ s-boxes for $n \in [\![4, 8]\!]$, namely the eight 4×4 s-boxes of Serpent [ABK98], the s-boxes S_5 (5×5) and S_6 (6×6) of SC2000 [SYY+02], the 8×8 s-boxes S_0 and S_1 of CLEFIA [SSA+07], and the 8×8 s-box of Khazad [BR00]. The obtained results are summarized in Table 7. Note that we chose these s-boxes to serve as examples for our decomposition method. Some of them may have a mathematical structure allowing more efficient decomposition (*e.g.* the CLEFIA S_0 s-box is based on the inversion over $\mathbb{F}_{256}$ and can therefore be computed with a 32-multiplication circuit as the AES).

We observe that Algorithm 1 achieves improved parameters compared to the optimal ones with basis update and without the rank-drop improvement (see Table 5) for $n \in \{4, 5, 6\}$. For $n = 8$, we only get parameters close to the optimal ones for the basis update ($C_{n,n}^* = 62$ instead of 61). This can be explained by the fact that when n increases the value of δ becomes small compared to 2^n and the impact of exhaustive search is lowered. Thus Algorithm 1 can close the gap and (almost) achieve optimal parameters even in presence of a minimal starting basis, however it does not go beyond.

4.4 Parallelization

The proposed decomposition method is highly parallelizable. In practice, most SPN blockciphers have a nonlinear layer applying 16 or 32 s-boxes and most processors are based on a 32-bit or a 64-bit architecture. Therefore we shall

Table 7. Achieved parameters for several s-boxes.

	$|\mathcal{B}_1|$	r	$t_1, t_2, \ldots, t_n$	$C_{n,n}^*$
$n = 4$				
Serpent S_1–S_5	7	2	1, 1, 1, 1	6
Serpent S_6, S_7	7	2	1, 2, 1, 1	7
$n = 5$				
SC2000 S_5	11	5	2, 1, 1, 1, 1	11
	12	6	1, 1, 1, 1, 1	11
$n = 6$				
SC2000 S_6	15	8	4, 2, 2, 2, 2, 1	21
	16	9	3, 2, 2, 2, 2, 1	21
$n = 8$				
Khazad & CLEFIA (S_0, S_1)	31	22	11, 6, 5, 4, 4, 4, 3, 3	62
	33	24	9, 6, 5, 4, 4, 4, 3, 3	62
	32	23	10, 6, 5, 4, 4, 4, 3, 3	62

focus our study on the k-parallel multiplicative complexity of our method for $k \in \{2, 4\}$.

General Method. In the general method (without improvement) described in Sect. 4.2, the multiplications between the g_j's and the $h_{i,j}$'s can clearly be processed in parallel. Specifically, they can be done with exactly $\lceil \frac{m \cdot t}{k} \rceil$ k-multiplications. The multiplications involved in the minimal basis $\mathcal{B}_0 = \{x \mapsto x^u, u \in \mathcal{U}\}$ can also be fully parallelized at degree $k = 2$ and $k = 4$ for every $n \geq 4$. In other words, the k-multiplicative complexity for deriving $\mathcal{B}_0$ equals $\lceil \frac{r_0}{k} \rceil$ for $k \in \{2, 4\}$ where $r_0 = C(\mathcal{B}_0) = |\mathcal{B}_0| - (n + 1)$ (see Sect. 4.1). One just has to compute x^u by increasing order of the Hamming weight of $u \in \mathcal{U}$ (where $\mathcal{U}$ is the set defined in (19)), then taking the lexicographical order inside a Hamming weight class. As an illustration, the 4-parallel evaluation of $\mathcal{B}_0$ is given for $n \in \{4, 6, 8\}$ in Table 8.

Once all the elements of $\mathcal{B}_0$ have been computed, and before getting to the multiplicative terms $g_j \cdot h_{i,j}$, we have to update it to a basis $\mathcal{B} \supseteq \mathcal{B}_0$ with target cardinality (see Table 4). This is done by feeding the basis with $|\mathcal{B}| - |\mathcal{B}_0|$ products of random linear combinations of the current basis. In order to parallelize this step, these new products are generated 4-by-4 from previous elements of the basis. We could validate that, by following such an approach, we still obtain full-rank systems with the achievable parameters given in Table 8. This means that for every $n \in [\![4, 10]\!]$, the k-multiplicative complexity of the general method is $\lceil \frac{r}{k} \rceil + \lceil \frac{m \cdot t}{k} \rceil$. The obtained results (achievable parameters) are summarized in Table 9.

Improved Method. The parallelization of the improved method is slightly more tricky since all the multiplicative terms $g_{i,j} \cdot h_{i,j}$ cannot be computed in parallel. Indeed, the resulting products are fed to the basis so that they are

Table 8. Parallel evaluation of $\mathcal{B}_0$ for $n \in \{4, 6, 8\}$.

$n = 4$	$n = 6$	
$x_1x_2 \leftarrow x_2 \cdot x_1$	$x_1x_2 \leftarrow x_2 \cdot x_1$	$x_4x_6 \leftarrow x_6 \cdot x_4$
$x_3x_4 \leftarrow x_4 \cdot x_3$	$x_1x_3 \leftarrow x_3 \cdot x_1$	$x_5x_6 \leftarrow x_6 \cdot x_5$
	$x_2x_3 \leftarrow x_3 \cdot x_2$	$x_1x_2x_3 \leftarrow x_3 \cdot x_1x_2$
	$x_4x_5 \leftarrow x_5 \cdot x_4$	$x_4x_5x_6 \leftarrow x_6 \cdot x_4x_5$

$n = 8$		
$x_1x_2 \leftarrow x_2 \cdot x_1$	$x_2x_4 \leftarrow x_4 \cdot x_2$	$x_5x_8 \leftarrow x_8 \cdot x_5$
$x_1x_3 \leftarrow x_3 \cdot x_1$	$x_3x_4 \leftarrow x_4 \cdot x_3$	$x_6x_7 \leftarrow x_7 \cdot x_6$
$x_1x_4 \leftarrow x_4 \cdot x_1$	$x_5x_6 \leftarrow x_6 \cdot x_5$	$x_6x_8 \leftarrow x_8 \cdot x_6$
$x_2x_3 \leftarrow x_3 \cdot x_2$	$x_5x_7 \leftarrow x_7 \cdot x_5$	$x_7x_8 \leftarrow x_8 \cdot x_7$
$x_1x_2x_3 \leftarrow x_3 \cdot x_1x_2$	$x_5x_6x_7 \leftarrow x_7 \cdot x_5x_6$	$x_1x_2x_3x_4 \leftarrow x_4 \cdot x_1x_2x_2$
$x_1x_2x_4 \leftarrow x_4 \cdot x_1x_2$	$x_5x_6x_8 \leftarrow x_8 \cdot x_5x_6$	$x_5x_6x_7x_8 \leftarrow x_8 \cdot x_5x_6x_7$
$x_1x_3x_4 \leftarrow x_4 \cdot x_1x_3$	$x_5x_7x_8 \leftarrow x_8 \cdot x_5x_7$	
$x_2x_3x_4 \leftarrow x_4 \cdot x_2x_3$	$x_6x_7x_8 \leftarrow x_8 \cdot x_6x_7$	

Table 9. Parallel multiplicative complexity of our general method an $n \times n$ s-box.

n	4	5	6	7	8	9	10
(r, t)	(4,1)	(7,2)	(13,3)	(22,4)	(37,5)	(59,7)	(90,10)
$|\mathcal{B}|$	9	13	20	30	46	69	101
$C_{n,n}$	8	17	31	50	77	122	190
$C_{n,n}^{(2)}$	4	9	16	25	39	62	95
$C_{n,n}^{(4)}$	2	5	9	13	20	31	48

potentially involved in the linear combinations producing the next functions $g_{i+1,j}, h_{i+1,j}, \ldots, g_{m,j}, h_{m,j}$. In order to fully parallelize our improved method we customize Algorithm 1 as follows. We keep a counter q of the number of products added to the basis. Each time a new f_{i+1} is to be decomposed, if the current counter q is not a multiple of k, then the first q_0 products $g_{i+1,j} \cdot h_{i+1,j}$ will be bundled with the last q_1 products $g_{i,j} \cdot h_{i,j}$ in the parallel version of our improved decomposition, where

$$\begin{cases} q_0 = (k - q) \bmod k \\ q_1 = q \bmod k \end{cases} \tag{35}$$

We must then ensure that the functions $\{g_{i+1,j}, h_{i+1,j}\}_{j=0}^{q_0-1}$ are independent of the few last products $\{g_{i,j} \cdot h_{i,j}\}_{j=t_i-q_1}^{t_i-1}$. This can be done at no cost for the $g_{i+1,j}$'s which can be generated without the last q_1 products, and this add a constraint on the linear system for the first q_0 searched $h_{i+1,j}$ functions. However, we observed in our experiments that for small values of k such as $k \in \{2, 4\}$, this constraint has a negligible impact on Algorithm 1. We could actually obtain the exact same parameters than in Table 7 for all the tested s-boxes (Serpent, SC2000, CLEFIA, and Khazad) for a parallelization degree of $k = 2$, except for the s-box S_3 of Serpent that requires 1 more multiplication.

5   Implementations

This section describes our implementations of a bitsliced s-box layer protected with higher-order masking based on our decomposition method. Our implementations evaluate 16 $n \times n$ s-boxes in parallel where $n \in \{4, 8\}$, and they are developed in generic 32-bit ARM assembly. They take n input sharings $[\boldsymbol{x}_1]$, $[\boldsymbol{x}_2], \ldots, [\boldsymbol{x}_n]$ defined as

$$[\boldsymbol{x}_i] = (\boldsymbol{x}_{i,1}, \boldsymbol{x}_{i,2}, \ldots, \boldsymbol{x}_{i,d}) \ \text{ such that } \ \sum_{j=1}^{d} \boldsymbol{x}_{i,j} = \boldsymbol{x}_i \qquad (36)$$

where $\boldsymbol{x}_i$ is a 16-bit register containing the i-th bit of the 16 s-box inputs. Our implementations then output n sharings $[\boldsymbol{y}_0], [\boldsymbol{y}_1], \ldots, [\boldsymbol{y}_n]$ corresponding to the bitsliced output bits of the s-box. Since we are on a 32-bit architecture with 16-bit bitsliced registers, we use a degree-2 parallelization for the multiplications. Namely, the 16-bit ANDs are packed by pairs and replaced by 32-bit ANDs which are applied on shares using the ISW scheme as explained in [GR16].

The computation is then done in three stages. First, we need to construct the shares of the elements of the minimal basis $\mathcal{B}_0$, specifically $[\boldsymbol{x}^u]$ for every $u \in \mathcal{U}$, where $\boldsymbol{x}^u$ denote the bitsliced register for the bit x^u, and where $\mathcal{U}$ is the set defined in (19). This first stage requires $r_0/2$ 32-bit ISW-ANDs, where $r_0 = 2$ for $n = 4$ and $r_0 = 22$ for $n = 8$ (see Table 8).

Once the first stage is completed, all the remaining multiplications are done between linear combinations of the elements of the basis. Let us denote by $[\boldsymbol{t}_i]$ the sharings corresponding to the elements of the basis which are stored in memory. After the first stage we have $\{[\boldsymbol{t}_i]\} = \{[\boldsymbol{x}^u] \mid u \in \mathcal{U}\}$. Each new $\boldsymbol{t}_i$ is defined as

$$\left(\sum_{j<i} a_{i,j} \boldsymbol{t}_j \right) \odot \left(\sum_{i<j} b_{i,j} \boldsymbol{t}_j \right) \qquad (37)$$

where $\odot$ denote the bitwise multiplication, and where $\{a_{i,j}\}_j$ and $\{b_{i,j}\}_j$ are the binary coefficients obtained from the s-box decomposition (namely the coefficients of the functions $g_{i,j}$ and $h_{i,j}$ in the span of the basis). The second stage hence consists in a loop on the remaining multiplications that

1. computes the linear-combination sharings $[\boldsymbol{r}_i] = \sum_{j<i} a_{i,j}[\boldsymbol{t}_j]$ and $[\boldsymbol{s}_i] = \sum_{j<i} b_{i,j}[\boldsymbol{t}_j]$
2. refreshes the sharing $[\boldsymbol{r}_i]$
3. computes the sharing $[\boldsymbol{t}_i]$ such that $\boldsymbol{t}_i = \boldsymbol{r}_i \odot \boldsymbol{s}_i$

where the last step is performed for two successive values of i at the same time by a call to a 32-bit ISW-AND. The sums in Step 1 are performed on each share independently. The necessity of the refreshing procedure in Step 2 is explained in [GR16] since an ISW multiplication of two linear combinations of the same sharings can introduce a security flaw (see for instance [CPRR14]). As in [GR16], this refreshing is implemented from an ISW multiplication with $(1,0,0,\ldots,0)$.

Once all the basis sharings $[t_i]$ have been computed, the third stage simply consists in deriving each output sharing $[y_i]$ as a linear combination of the $[t_i]$, which is refreshed before being returned.

We compare our results with the optimized implementations from [GR16] of the CRV method [CRV14] and the algebraic decomposition (AD) method [CPRR15]. These implementations compute four s-boxes in parallel for $n = 8$ and eight s-boxes in parallel for $n = 4$ on a 32-bit ARM architecture. Table 10 summarizes the obtained performances in clock cycles with respect to the masking order d. It is worth noticing that packing and unpacking the bitslice registers for the parallelization of the ISW-ANDs implies a linear overhead in d. For $d \in [\![2,20]\!]$, this overhead is between 4 % and 6 % of the overall s-box computations for $n = 8$, and between 7 % and 11 % for $n = 4$ (and this ratio is asymptotically negligible). For $d = 2$, the overhead slightly exceeds the gain, but for every $d \geq 3$, parallelizing the ISW-ANDs always results in an overall gain of performances.

Table 10. Performances in clock cycles.

	CRV [GR16]	AD [GR16]	Our implementations
	$4 \times 4/\!/$ s-boxes	$4 \times 4/\!/$ s-boxes	$16/\!/$ s-boxes
$n = 8$	$2576\,d^2 + 5476\,d + 2528$	$2376\,d^2 + 3380\,d + 5780$	$656\,d^2 + 19786\,d + 5764$
	$2 \times 8/\!/$ s-boxes	$2 \times 8/\!/$ s-boxes	$16/\!/$ s-boxes
$n = 4$	$337\,d^2 + 563\,d + 434$	$564\,d^2 + 270\,d + 660$	$59\,d^2 + 1068\,d + 994$

We observe that our implementations are asymptotically faster than the optimized implementations of CRV and AD methods (3.6 times faster for $n = 8$ and 5.7 times faster for $n = 4$). However, we also see that the linear coefficient is significantly greater for our implementations, which comes from the computation of the linear combinations in input of the ISW-ANDs (*i.e.* the sharings $[r_i]$ and $[s_i]$). As an illustration, Figs. 1 and 2 plots the obtained timings with respect to d. We see that for $n = 4$, our implementation is always faster than the optimized AD and CRV. On the other hand, for $n = 8$, our implementation is slightly slower for $d \leq 8$. We stress that our implementations could probably be improved by optimizing the computation of the linear combinations.

The RAM consumption and code size of our implementations are given in Table 11 and compared to those of the CRV and AD implementations from [GR16]. We believe these memory requirements to be affordable for not-too-constrained embedded devices. In terms of code size, our implementations are always the best. This is especially significant for $n = 8$ where CRV and AD needs

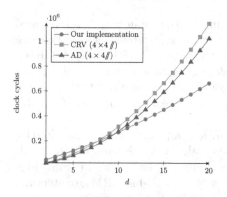 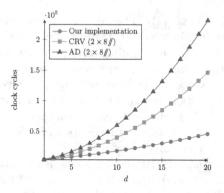

Fig. 1. Timings for $n = 8$.   **Fig. 2.** Timings for $n = 4$.

Table 11. Code sizes and RAM consumptions.

	CRV [GR16]	AD [GR16]	Our implementations
$n = 8$	$4 \times 4 /\!/$ s-boxes	$4 \times 4 /\!/$ s-boxes	$16 /\!/$ s-boxes
Code size	27.5 KB	11.2 KB	4.6 KB
RAM	$80d$ bytes	$188d$ bytes	$644d$ bytes
$n = 4$	$2 \times 8 /\!/$ s-boxes	$2 \times 8 /\!/$ s-boxes	$16 /\!/$ s-boxes
Code size	3.2 KB	2.6 KB	2.2 KB
RAM	$24d$ bytes	$64d$ bytes	$132d$ bytes

a high amount of storage for the lookup tables of the linearized polynomials
(see [GR16]). On the other hand, we observe a big gap between our implementations and those from [GR16] regarding the RAM consumption. Our method
is indeed more consuming in RAM because of all the $[t_i]$ sharings that must be
stored while such a large basis is not required for the CRV and AD methods,
and because of some optimizations in the computation of the linear combinations
(see the full version). .

References

[ABK98] Anderson, R., Biham, E., Knudsen, L.: Serpent: a proposal for the
         advanced encryption standard. NIST AES Propos. (1998)
[BGRV15] Balasch, J., Gierlichs, B., Reparaz, O., Verbauwhede, I.: DPA, bitslicing
         and masking at 1 GHz. In: Güneysu, T., Handschuh, H. (eds.) CHES 2015.
         LNCS, vol. 9293, pp. 599–619. Springer, Heidelberg (2015)
[BMP13] Boyar, J., Matthews, P., Peralta, R.: Logic minimization techniques with
         applications to cryptology. J. Cryptol. **26**(2), 280–312 (2013)
[BPP00] Boyar, J., Peralta, R., Pochuev, D.: On the multiplicative complexity of
         Boolean functions over the basis $(\wedge, \oplus, \mathbf{1})$. Theor. Comput. Sci. **235**(1),
         43–57 (2000)

[BR00]   Barreto, P., Rijmen, V.: The Khazad legacy-level block cipher. In: First
          Open NESSIE Workshop (2000)
[Can05]   Canright, D.: A very compact S-box for AES. In: Rao, J.R., Sunar, B.
          (eds.) CHES 2005. LNCS, vol. 3659, pp. 441–455. Springer, Heidelberg
          (2005)
[CGP+12] Carlet, C., Goubin, L., Prouff, E., Quisquater, M., Rivain, M.: Higher-
          order masking schemes for S-boxes. In: Canteaut, A. (ed.) FSE 2012.
          LNCS, vol. 7549, pp. 366–384. Springer, Heidelberg (2012)
[CJRR99] Chari, S., Jutla, C.S., Rao, J.R., Rohatgi, P.: Towards sound approaches
          to counteract power-analysis attacks. In: Wiener, M. (ed.) CRYPTO 1999.
          LNCS, vol. 1666, pp. 398–412. Springer, Heidelberg (1999)
[CMH13]   Courtois, N., Mourouzis, T., Hulme, D.: Exact logic minimization and
          multiplicative complexity of concrete algebraic and cryptographic circuits.
          Adv. Intell. Syst. 6(3–4), 43–57 (2013)
[Cou07]   Courtois, N.T.: CTC2 and fast algebraic attacks on block ciphers revisited.
          Cryptology ePrint Archive, Report 2007/152 (2007). http://eprint.iacr.
          org/2007/152
[CPRR14] Coron, J.-S., Prouff, E., Rivain, M., Roche, T.: Higher-order side channel
          security and mask refreshing. In: Moriai, S. (ed.) FSE 2013. LNCS, vol.
          8424, pp. 410–424. Springer, Heidelberg (2014)
[CPRR15] Carlet, C., Prouff, E., Rivain, M., Roche, T.: Algebraic decomposition for
          probing security. In: Gennaro, R., Robshaw, M.J.B. (eds.) CRYPTO 2015.
          LNCS, vol. 9215, pp. 742–763. Springer, Heidelberg (2015)
[CRV14]   Coron, J.-S., Roy, A., Vivek, S.: Fast evaluation of polynomials over
          binary finite fields and application to side-channel countermeasures. In:
          Batina, L., Robshaw, M. (eds.) CHES 2014. LNCS, vol. 8731, pp. 170–
          187. Springer, Heidelberg (2014)
[DDF14]   Duc, A., Dziembowski, S., Faust, S.: Unifying leakage models: from prob-
          ing attacks to noisy leakage. In: Nguyen, P.Q., Oswald, E. (eds.) EURO-
          CRYPT 2014. LNCS, vol. 8441, pp. 423–440. Springer, Heidelberg (2014)
[DPV01]   Daemen, J., Peeters, M., Van Assche, G.: Bitslice ciphers and power analy-
          sis attacks. In: Schneier, B. (ed.) FSE 2000. LNCS, vol. 1978, pp. 134–149.
          Springer, Heidelberg (2001)
[GLSV15] Grosso, V., Leurent, G., Standaert, F.-X., Varıcı, K.: LS-designs: bitslice
          encryption for efficient masked software implementations. In: Cid, C.,
          Rechberger, C. (eds.) FSE 2014. LNCS, vol. 8540, pp. 18–37. Springer,
          Heidelberg (2015)
[GR16]   Goudarzi, D., Rivain, M.: How fast can higher-order masking be in soft-
          ware? Cryptology ePrint Archive (2016). http://eprint.iacr.org/
[ISW03]   Ishai, Y., Sahai, A., Wagner, D.: Private circuits: securing hardware
          against probing attacks. In: Boneh, D. (ed.) CRYPTO 2003. LNCS, vol.
          2729, pp. 463–481. Springer, Heidelberg (2003)
[MS92]   Mirwald, R., Schnorr, C.P.: The multiplicative complexity of quadratic
          Boolean forms. Theor. Comput. Sci. 102(2), 307–328 (1992)
[PLW10]   Poschmann, A., Ling, S., Wang, H.: 256 bit standardized crypto for 650
          GE – GOST revisited. In: Mangard, S., Standaert, F.-X. (eds.) CHES
          2010. LNCS, vol. 6225, pp. 219–233. Springer, Heidelberg (2010)
[PR13]   Prouff, E., Rivain, M.: Masking against side-channel attacks: a formal
          security proof. In: Johansson, T., Nguyen, P.Q. (eds.) EUROCRYPT 2013.
          LNCS, vol. 7881, pp. 142–159. Springer, Heidelberg (2013)

[RP10]   Rivain, M., Prouff, E.: Provably secure higher-order masking of AES. In: Mangard, S., Standaert, F.-X. (eds.) CHES 2010. LNCS, vol. 6225, pp. 413–427. Springer, Heidelberg (2010)

[SSA+07]   Shirai, T., Shibutani, K., Akishita, T., Moriai, S., Iwata, T.: The 128-bit blockcipher CLEFIA (extended abstract). In: Biryukov, A. (ed.) FSE 2007. LNCS, vol. 4593, pp. 181–195. Springer, Heidelberg (2007)

[Sto16]   Stoffelen, K.: Optimizing S-box implementations for several criteria using sat solvers. In: Fast Software Encryption (2016)

[SYY+02]   Shimoyama, T., Yanami, H., Yokoyama, K., Takenaka, M., Itoh, K., Yajima, J., Torii, N., Tanaka, H.: The block cipher SC2000. In: Matsui, M. (ed.) FSE 2001. LNCS, vol. 2355, pp. 312–327. Springer, Heidelberg (2002)

[TP14]   Turan Sönmez, M., Peralta, R.: The multiplicative complexity of Boolean functions on four and five variables. In: Eisenbarth, T., Öztürk, E. (eds.) LightSec 2014. LNCS, vol. 8898, pp. 21–33. Springer, Heidelberg (2015)

Reducing the Number of Non-linear Multiplications in Masking Schemes

Jürgen Pulkus[1]([✉]) and Srinivas Vivek[2]([✉])

[1] Giesecke and Devrient, Munich, Germany
Juergen.Pulkus@gi-de.com
[2] University of Bristol, Bristol, UK
sv.venkatesh@bristol.ac.uk

Abstract. In recent years, methods to securely mask S-boxes against side-channel attacks by representing them as polynomials over finite binary fields have become quite efficient. A good cost model for this is to count how many non-linear multiplications are needed. In this work we improve on the current state-of-the-art generic method published by Coron–Roy–Vivek at CHES 2014 by working over slightly larger fields than strictly needed. This leads us, for example, to evaluate DES S-boxes with only 3 non-linear multiplications and, as a result, obtain 25 % improvement in the running time for secure software implementations of DES when using three or more shares.

On the theoretical side, we prove a logarithmic upper bound on the number of non-linear multiplications required to evaluate any d-bit S-box, when ignoring the cost of working in unreasonably large fields. This upper bound is lower than the previous lower bounds proved under the assumption of working over the field $\mathbb{F}_{2^d}$, and we show this bound to be sharp. We also achieve a way to evaluate the AES S-box using only 3 non-linear multiplications over $\mathbb{F}_{2^{16}}$.

Keywords: Side-channel countermeasure · Masking · Probing security · Block cipher · Software implementation · Polynomial evaluation

1 Introduction

Side-channel attacks are a realistic and serious threat for cryptographic implementations [Koc96, KJJ99]. These attacks have the potential to leak one or more sensitive intermediate variables that would otherwise be unavailable in a black-box execution of a cryptographic primitive. Block ciphers are typical targets of such attacks. Secret sharing, a.k.a. *masking*, is a popular technique to protect block cipher implementations against leakage of one or more sensitive intermediate variables. Depending on how a sensitive variable is split into shares, processed and then re-combined, and the formal leakage model used for security analysis, there are several generic higher-order masking schemes that can secure block cipher computations, with the secrets shared into as many shares as we desire [ISW03, GM11, PR11, CGP+12, BFGV12, Cor14, BFG15]. Indeed, these schemes can be used to secure any circuit.

© International Association for Cryptologic Research 2016
B. Gierlichs and A.Y. Poschmann (Eds.): CHES 2016, LNCS 9813, pp. 479–497, 2016.
DOI: 10.1007/978-3-662-53140-2_23

The most popular among existing generic masking schemes for block cipher implementations are those where the secrets are additively shared. This is in part due to the effectiveness, efficiency and simplicity of additive masking [CJRR99, ISW03, PR13, DDF14, DFS15, BFG15]. Over binary fields this type of masking has also been called as *Boolean masking*. In fact, the very first generic higher-order masking scheme, due to Ishai, Sahai and Wagner [ISW03] (henceforth referred to as the *ISW method*), is based on additive masking. Their method can be used to secure arbitrary Boolean circuits in the so-called *probing model*, where an adversary can choose to leak, say, t intermediate variables and the scheme is secure so long as the number of shares $s \geq 2t + 1$. Though working with Boolean circuits is probably well-suited to hardware implementations, representing a computation as a Boolean circuit will lead to huge overheads in software implementations. Nonetheless, this method and the probing security framework introduced in their work formed the basis for most of the later masking schemes. Rivain and Prouff [RP10] adapted the ISW method to secure AES by representing its S-box as an arithmetic circuit over $\mathbb{F}_{2^8}$.

CGPQR Method. Carlet *et al.* [CGP+12] adapted the ISW method to secure software implementations of arbitrary block ciphers over binary finite fields $\mathbb{F}_{2^n}$ (hereafter referred to as the *CGPQR method*). For an additive masking scheme processing $\mathbb{F}_2$-linear or affine functions in the presence of shares is straightforward. Hence the main challenge is to securely process non-linear functions. Since in a block cipher the only non-linear operations are the S-box table lookups, the technique used in the CGPQR method to securely mask such table lookups is to first represent a d-to-r-bit S-box function ($d \geq r$) as a univariate polynomial over a binary finite field $\mathbb{F}_{2^d}$. Then this polynomial is evaluated in the presence of shares using the following operations: *addition* (of two polynomials over $\mathbb{F}_{2^d}$), *scalar multiplication* (i.e., multiplication of a polynomial by a constant from $\mathbb{F}_{2^d}$), *squaring* (of a polynomial over $\mathbb{F}_{2^d}$), and multiplications of two distinct polynomials (a.k.a. *non-linear multiplications*). While additions, scalar multiplications and squarings are $\mathbb{F}_2$-linear operations, the non-linear multiplications, as the name suggests, are *not* $\mathbb{F}_2$-linear. To process a non-linear multiplication in the CGPQR method, an adaptation of the technique used in the ISW method to mask (non-linear) AND gates is utilised. The overhead caused by the CGPQR method (relative to unshared evaluation), in terms of both the time and the randomness required, to securely mask a non-linear multiplication is $\mathcal{O}(s^2)$, where s is the number of input shares. For a linear or affine function the overhead is only $\mathcal{O}(s)$.

Relation to Polynomial Evaluation. One of the relatively well-understood approaches to analysing and improving the efficiency of the CGPQR method is to investigate the problem of evaluating polynomials over binary finite fields. The goal is to minimise the number of non-linear multiplications needed to evaluate a polynomial over $\mathbb{F}_{2^d}$, while *ignoring* the cost of additions, scalar multiplications and squarings. As the works of Carlet *et al.* [CGP+12], Roy and Vivek [RV13], and Coron, Roy and Vivek [CRV14, CRV15] demonstrate, this cost model of minimising the non-linear multiplications while evaluating an S-box polynomial has turned out to be a reasonably effective way to model the overall cost of processing a block cipher in software implementations, as long as one makes sure that the use of linear operations is not made "unreasonably" large.

In [CGP+12], two methods to evaluate arbitrary polynomials over $\mathbb{F}_{2^d}$ are presented that are tailored to the non-linear cost model: the *cyclotomic-class* method (having complexity $\Omega(2^d/d)$) and the *parity-split* method (having proven complexity $\mathcal{O}(2^{d/2})$). These two methods were applied to various S-box polynomials to understand their complexity in terms of non-linear multiplications. In [RV13], improved evaluation techniques for various specific S-box polynomials were presented. In particular, it was shown that the 6-to-4-bit DES S-boxes can be evaluated with 7 non-linear multiplications, while 8-bit (i.e., 8-to-8-bit) CAMELLIA and CLEFIA S-boxes can be evaluated with 15 or 16 non-linear multiplications. The work of [RV13] also initiated a formal analysis of this cost model and established lower bounds on the necessary number of non-linear multiplications required to evaluate any polynomial over $\mathbb{F}_{2^d}$. In particular, they showed that, under certain representation over $\mathbb{F}_{2^6}$, the DES S-box polynomials need at least 3 non-linear multiplications to evaluate them, while the PRESENT S-box polynomial over $\mathbb{F}_{2^4}$ needs at least 2 non-linear multiplications.

CRV Method. In [CRV14, CRV15], Coron et al. proposed an improved method (henceforth referred to as the *CRV method*) to evaluate arbitrary polynomials over $\mathbb{F}_{2^d}$. Their method has a heuristic worst-case complexity of $\mathcal{O}(2^{d/2}/\sqrt{d})$ non-linear multiplications. They also show that the complexity of $\mathcal{O}(2^{d/2}/\sqrt{d})$ is optimal for any method to evaluate arbitrary polynomials over $\mathbb{F}_{2^d}$. Currently, w.r.t. the non-linear multiplications cost model, the CRV method is the most efficient way to implement the CGPQR countermeasure.

In the CRV method, a d-to-r-bit S-box S is represented by a polynomial $P(X) \in \mathbb{F}_{2^d}[X]$ that is actually computed in the process. The d-bit and the r-bit strings are identified with the elements of $\mathbb{F}_{2^d}$. The polynomial $P(X)$ satisfies the property that its evaluation on the elements of $\mathbb{F}_{2^d}$ produces output elements of $\mathbb{F}_{2^d}$ that agree in the lower-order r-bits with the corresponding S-box outputs. Briefly the CRV method for a generic d-to-r-bit S-box is as follows:

Step 1: Pre-compute a collection of monomials L in $\mathbb{F}_{2^d}[X]$ (a) that is closed w.r.t. squaring (because squarings are free) (b) has the property that $L \cdot L$ generates all the monomials X^i $(i = 0, 1, \ldots, 2^d - 1)$.

Step 2: Consider the following relation over $\mathbb{F}_{2^d}[X]$:

$$P(X) = \sum_{i=1}^{t-1} p_i(X) \cdot q_i(X) + p_t(X) \quad \mathrm{mod}\ X^{2^d} + X \qquad (1)$$

for some chosen parameter t, where the polynomials $p_i(X)$ and $q_i(X)$ have monomials only from the set L, and the polynomials $q_i(X)$ are randomly chosen but the values of $P(X)$ and the coefficients of $p_i(X)$ are *unknown*. Next they write down a set of $r \cdot 2^d$ linear equations over $\mathbb{F}_2$ (in the unknown bits), corresponding to each S-box output bit, by evaluating the above relation at the elements

Table 1. Comparison of the worst-case complexity of generic methods for various d-to-r-bit S-boxes.

(d, r)	$(4, 4)$	$(5, 5)$	$(6, 4)$	$(6, 6)$	$(7, 7)$	$(8, 8)$
Cyclotomic class method [CGP+12]	3	5	11	11	17	33
Parity-split method [CGP+12]	4	6	10	10	14	22
CRV method [CRV15]	2	4	4	5	7	10
Our method (over $\mathbb{F}_{2^8}$)	**2**	**3**	**3**	**4**	**6**	**10**
Our method (over $\mathbb{F}_{2^{16}}$)	**2**	**3**	**3**	**3**	**4**	**6**

of $\mathbb{F}_{2^d}$. Finally, the unknown bits are obtained by solving the resulting linear system over $\mathbb{F}_2$ whose matrix has dimension $r \cdot 2^d \times d \cdot t \cdot |L|$, which is approximately $r \cdot 2^d \times r \cdot 2^d$. The total number of non-linear multiplications required is about $t - 1 + |L|/d$.

It is shown in [CRV15] that any 4-bit S-box can be evaluated with 2 non-linear multiplications in the worst case (which is optimal), any 6-bit S-box with at most 5, any 6-to-4-bit S-box (in particular, DES S-boxes) with at most 4, any 8-bit S-box with at most 10 non-linear multiplications (cf. Table 1). As, in a block cipher, the time required for S-box table lookups grows quadratically with the number of shares, seemingly marginal reductions in the count of non-linear multiplications per S-box evaluation indeed lead to significant gains in the overall execution time, as demonstrated in [Cor14, CRV15].

One obvious approach to improve the CRV method is to simultaneously solve for the unknown coefficients of both the set of polynomials $p_i(X)$ and $q_i(X)$ (including $P(X)$) in Step 2 of the CRV method described above, instead of linearising (1) by choosing random polynomials $q_i(X)$. This results in $r \cdot 2^d$ multivariate homogeneous quadratic equations over $\mathbb{F}_2$ in approximately $d \cdot 2^d$ variables. To our knowledge, determining the roots of such a system of equations seems infeasible with current techniques even for small values of $d = 6$ or $d = 8$. Hence it is of interest to find alternative ways to reduce the parameters of the CRV method (particularly, the parameters t and L) that affect the total number of non-linear multiplications for the S-box polynomials. This is one of the main themes of this paper.

1.1   Our Contribution

We give an improved generic method to reduce the number of non-linear multiplications required to evaluate various S-box polynomials. Our method may be viewed as an extension of the CRV method (cf. page 3). While in the CRV method and other previous works the inputs/outputs of a d-to-r-bit S-box are naturally identified with the elements of $\mathbb{F}_{2^d}$, we instead encode them in fields $\mathbb{F}_{2^n}$, where $n \geq d$. Our heuristic analysis seems to suggest that the complexity of the CRV method improves by a factor of two in the limiting case, though both the methods have the same heuristic asymptotic (worst-case) complexity of $\mathcal{O}(2^{d/2}/\sqrt{d})$ non-linear multiplications.

From a technical point of view, apart from the problem of encoding mentioned above, the main and the only other difference between our method and the CRV method is in the selection of the following two parameters: L (the pre-computed monomial list) and t (the number of summands in the decomposition in (1)). Once these parameters are carefully determined, then the remaining steps to obtain a decomposition of the form (1) by setting up a linear system of equations is exactly the same. Since in the matrix step of the CRV method (cf. page 3) we heuristically need $n \cdot t \cdot |L| \approx r \cdot 2^d$, it is evident that we could end up with smaller values of t, and hence a reduction in the total number of non-linear multiplications required. Some technical hurdles arise due to the fact that we would not gain anything if we insist, as in the CRV method, that the pre-computed set of monomials L must span all monomials in $\mathbb{F}_{2^n}[X]$. Our generic method and its analysis is presented in Sect. 2.

Our method leads to improvements for most of the S-boxes found in practice. Table 1 lists the (worst-case) cost of processing *arbitrary* d-to-r-bit S-boxes using our method over $\mathbb{F}_{2^8}$ and $\mathbb{F}_{2^{16}}$, and compares these with those of the previous methods. In particular, any 6-to-4 bit S-box, including all the DES S-boxes, now need at most 3 non-linear multiplications to evaluate them instead of the previous best of 4 non-linear multiplications required by the CRV method that works over $\mathbb{F}_{2^6}$ in this case (cf. Table 2). We discuss how to select suitable parameters for various S-box dimensions in Sect. 2.2.

Table 2. Expected and observed (worst-case) complexity $M_{d,r,n}$ of evaluating d-to-r-bit S-boxes over $\mathbb{F}_{2^n}$ (cf. (11)).

d	4			5			6						7			8	
r	4			5			4			6			7			8	
n	4	8	16	5	8	16	4	8	16	6	8	16	7	8	16	8	16
Estimated $M_{d,r,n}$	3	0	0	4	2	0	4	2	1	5	3	1	7	6	3	10	5
Observed $M_{d,r,n}$	2	2	2	4	3	3	4	3	3	5	4	3	7	6	4	10	6

We have made a proof-of-concept implementation in software of our improved method for DES. As Table 5 suggests, the CGPQR method combined with our technique outperforms the CGPQR+CRV method by around 25 % in the overall processing time of the block cipher when there are 3 shares, and even better when there are greater numbers of shares. Our implementation also needs less (RAM) memory and fewer calls to a Pseudo Random Generator (PRG) (that outputs bytes) than the CRV method. We believe that since it is convenient to manipulate bytes in a software implementation, working over $\mathbb{F}_{2^8}$ instead of $\mathbb{F}_{2^6}$ or $\mathbb{F}_{2^7}$ should not cause any noticeable overhead. This reasoning is also confirmed by our above implementation, the details of which are presented in Sect. 2.3. Our improvements obtained by working over $\mathbb{F}_{2^{16}}$ could possibly be interesting for microprocessors such as ARM with Neon core [Lim13] that has a SIMD instruction to perform several parallel multiplications of two degree-7 polynomials over $\mathbb{F}_2$ represented as bytes. This instruction can be used to perform parallel multiplications in $\mathbb{F}_{2^{16}}$ with considerably less overhead than on a sequential processor thanks to Barrett reduction [Bar86, WVGX15]. But the downside is that the number of calls to a PRG is still double compared to the case of $\mathbb{F}_{2^8}$. Besides, note that such processors can also be targets of side-channel attacks [GMPT15].

Finally, in Sect. 3, we analyse the advantage and the limitations of using larger fields $\mathbb{F}_{2^n}$ $(n \geq d)$ to encode the input/output bit-strings of d-to-r-bit S-boxes as arbitrary subspaces in $\mathbb{F}_{2^n}$. Note that since additive masking is $\mathbb{F}_2$-linear, the set of encodings must be an ($\mathbb{F}_2$-linear) subspace of $\mathbb{F}_{2^n}$ (when viewed as an $\mathbb{F}_2$-vector space). We *prove* a logarithmic upper bound of $\lceil \log_2 d \rceil$, which is also optimal, on the complexity of evaluating d-to-r-bit S-boxes, when working over some huge field extension of $\mathbb{F}_{2^d}$. We stress that this result does not contradict the exponential lower bound results of [CRV15] as they hold over the (smaller field) $\mathbb{F}_{2^d}$. Using the techniques introduced to obtain the above results, we achieve a way to evaluate the AES S-box using only 3 non-linear multiplications over $\mathbb{F}_{2^{16}}$, instead of 4 non-linear multiplications over $\mathbb{F}_{2^8}$. We then generalise the lower bound results of [CRV15] to determine a lower bound on the exact complexity of generic d-to-r-bit S-boxes when working over any specified field $\mathbb{F}_{2^n}$ $(n \geq d)$.

1.2 Related Works

Another generic masking scheme based on the additive masking is by Coron [Cor14]. This countermeasure is a generalisation of the table-recomputation technique [CJRR99, SP06] to the higher-order setting. As shown in [CRV15], the CGPQR method combined with the CRV method outperforms this countermeasure, both asymptotically and in practice, w.r.t. time and memory complexity, and also the randomness required.

As far as the CGPQR method is concerned, there are other interesting approaches to improving its efficiency than by minimising the number of non-linear multiplications. One such way was introduced by Coron et al. [CPRR13] and further considered by Grosso et al. [GPS14]. This approach is based on the observation that certain types of non-linear multiplications are more than efficient than the rest. Hence the efficiency can be gained by trading the costlier non-linear multiplications for more efficient ones. Recently, Carlet et al. [CPRR15] introduced techniques based on the algebraic decomposition of a non-linear function as a sequence of low algebraic-degree functions. The CGPQR method combined with their technique outperforms the CGPQR+CRV method in many realistic scenarios.

It must be stressed that the above approaches to making the CGPQR method more efficient are not mutually exclusive of one another but, indeed, complementary. In fact, the improvements w.r.t. the non-linear multiplications cost model have motivated the approaches of [GPS14, CPRR15]. Finally, we would like to note that the relative simplicity of the non-linear multiplications cost model has made it amenable to a rigorous analysis, in particular, the lower bound results in [RV13, CRV15], while relatively little is known about the other cost models. Also, this cost model and its variant where the circuit depth w.r.t. non-linear multiplications also matters have found applications in fully homomorphic encryption and multi-party computation settings [GHS12a, GHS12b, ARS+15]. We do not consider such applications in this work, and hence, prefer to work in the non-linear multiplications cost model.

2   Improved Generic Method for S-Boxes

Consider a d-to-r-bit S-box, where $d \geq r$. We identify the d-bit and the r-bit strings with the elements of $\mathbb{F}_{2^n}$ ($r, d \leq n$) in the "usual" way. That is, let $\mathbb{F}_{2^n} = \mathbb{F}_2[Y]/(g(Y) \cdot \mathbb{F}_2[Y])$, where $g(Y) \in \mathbb{F}_2[Y]$ is an irreducible polynomial over $\mathbb{F}_2$ with $\deg(g) = n$ that is used to represent $\mathbb{F}_{2^n}$. A d-bit string is encoded as follows

$$\mathsf{E}_{d,n} : \{0,1\}^d \rightarrow \mathbb{F}_{2^n},$$

$$\langle b_{d-1}, b_{d-2}, \ldots, b_0 \rangle \mapsto \sum_{i=0}^{d-1} b_i\, Y^i.$$

An element of $\mathbb{F}_{2^n}$ is decoded to a d-bit string by dropping its corresponding higher-degree coefficients

$$\mathsf{D}_{n,d} : \mathbb{F}_{2^n} \rightarrow \{0,1\}^d,$$

$$\sum_{i=0}^{n-1} b_i\, Y^i \mapsto \langle b_{d-1}, b_{d-2}, \ldots, b_0 \rangle .$$

The functions $\mathsf{E}_{r,n} : \{0,1\}^r \rightarrow \mathbb{F}_{2^n}$ and $\mathsf{D}_{n,r} : \mathbb{F}_{2^n} \rightarrow \{0,1\}^r$ are similarly defined, as are $\mathsf{E}_{n,n} : \{0,1\}^n \rightarrow \mathbb{F}_{2^n}$ and $\mathsf{D}_{n,n} : \mathbb{F}_{2^n} \rightarrow \{0,1\}^n$.

Remark 1. The composition map $\mathsf{D}_{d,d} \circ \mathsf{E}_{d,n} : \mathbb{F}_{2^d} \rightarrow \mathbb{F}_{2^n}$ is a group homomorphism w.r.t. addition. But, in general, this map is not homomorphic w.r.t. multiplication.

We say that a polynomial $P(X) \in \mathbb{F}_{2^n}[X]$ evaluates a d-to-r bit S-box S if the trailing r bits of its evaluation on the encodings of every d-bit string matches with the output of S. Formally,

$$S(i) = \mathsf{D}_{n,r}\left(P\left(\mathsf{E}_{d,n}(i)\right)\right), \qquad \forall i \in \{0,1\}^d. \tag{2}$$

Our goal is to find a polynomial representation for a given S-box whose evaluation requires as small a number of non-linear multiplications as possible.

Let C_α^n denote the *cyclotomic class* of α w.r.t n ($n \geq 1, 0 \leq \alpha < 2^n$) [CGP+12, RV13], that is, $C_0^n = \{0\}$, $C_{2^n-1}^n = \{2^n - 1\}$ and

$$C_\alpha^n := \left\{ \alpha \cdot 2^i \pmod{2^n - 1} : i = 0, 1, \ldots, n-1 \right\} \text{ for } 0 < \alpha < 2^n - 1.$$

For any subset $\Lambda \subseteq \{0, 1, \ldots, 2^n - 1\}$, let X^Λ denote the set $X^\Lambda := \{X^i : i \in \Lambda\} \subseteq \mathbb{F}_{2^n}[X]$. Define $X^\Lambda \cdot X^\Lambda := \{X^i \cdot X^j : i, j \in \Lambda\}$. Finally, $\mathcal{P}(X^\Lambda) \subseteq \mathbb{F}_{2^n}[X]$ denotes the set of all polynomials (of degree at most $2^n - 1$) that have their monomials only from X^Λ.

2.1 Our Method

Our method is a variant of the CRV method [CRV15]. The main difference is that we allow $n \geq d$, which requires a change in the way the pre-computed list of monomials is chosen. Our method is summarised in Algorithm 1.

Step 1. Choose a collection $\mathcal{T}'$ of ℓ cyclotomic classes w.r.t. d:

$$\mathcal{T}' = \left\{ C_{\alpha_1=0}^d, C_{\alpha_2=1}^d, C_{\alpha_3}^d, \ldots, C_{\alpha_\ell}^d \right\}. \tag{3}$$

Let

$$L' = \bigcup_{C_{\alpha_i}^d \in \mathcal{T}'} C_{\alpha_i}^d. \tag{4}$$

Now "lift" the above collection of cyclotomic classes w.r.t. d to a collection w.r.t. n. That is, for every $C_{\alpha_i}^d$, we choose $C_{\alpha_i}^n$ for *some* representative $\alpha_i \in C_{\alpha_i}^d$. Define

$$\mathcal{T} = \left\{ C_{\alpha_1=0}^n, C_{\alpha_2=1}^n, C_{\alpha_3}^n, \ldots, C_{\alpha_\ell}^n \right\}. \tag{5}$$

Let

$$L = \bigcup_{C_{\alpha_i}^n \in \mathcal{T}} C_{\alpha_i}^n. \tag{6}$$

Note that we will be using only the collection $\mathcal{T}$ and the set L in the decomposition step of our method (cf. (8)).

Heuristic 1. We assume that it is possible to choose a $\mathcal{T}$ as specified above (for any ℓ "sufficiently smaller" than 2^d) in such a way that:

1. each cyclotomic class (except C_0^n) in $\mathcal{T}$ has (maximal) length n,
2. X^L can be computed using only $\ell - 2$ non-linear multiplications,
3. $X^{\{0,1,2,\ldots,X^{2^d-1}\}} \subseteq X^{L'} \cdot X^{L'} \subseteq \mathbb{F}_{2^d}[X]$. We refer to this property by saying that $X^{L'}$ spans the set $\{1, X, X^2, \ldots, X^{2^d-1}\}$ in $\mathbb{F}_{2^d}[X]$.

The first two heuristics above are also used in the CRV method. The difference is in the third heuristic (Heuristic 1.3). Note that the condition is only on the set L', not L. Note that in the CRV method it is required that X^L spans $\{1, X, X^2, \ldots, X^{2^n-1}\}$ in $\mathbb{F}_{2^n}[X]$ (in their case $n = d$). But as we prescribe only the values on $\mathbb{F}_{2^d}$, not on all of $\mathbb{F}_{2^n}$ we do not need such a strong condition. Indeed if we use this (stronger) condition from the CRV method, then we cannot expect any improvement over the CRV method (it will actually be worse since we are working in a bigger field).

Remark 2. In general, X^L does *not* span $\{1, X, X^2, \ldots, X^{2^n-1}\}$ nor $\{1, X, X^2, \ldots, X^{2^d-1}\}$ in $\mathbb{F}_{2^n}[X]$.

So we will make another assumption that turns out to be true experimentally for instances of practical relevance.

Heuristic 2. Corresponding to any d-to-r-bit S-box S, there exists a polynomial in $\mathcal{P}(X^L \cdot X^L) \subseteq \mathbb{F}_{2^n}[X]$ that evaluates S.

The CRV method does not need to make the above assumption as the condition is implied by Heuristic 1.3 when $n = d$.

Remark 3. As noted in [RV13, Proof of Theorem 1], if $d|n$, then the cyclotomic classes C_u^n "lie above" C_z^d for every $u \in C_z^d$. That is, $(\delta \mod 2^d - 1) \in C_z^d$ for every $\delta \in C_v^n$ and every $v \in C_z^d$.

Note that
$$|L| = 1 + n \cdot (\ell - 1). \tag{7}$$
We would like to choose as small a value for ℓ as possible but still satisfying Heuristic 1.3 (as we shall soon see, that ℓ must satisfy another (relatively milder) condition in Heuristic 4). We use the following heuristic from the CRV method for choosing a value of ℓ.

Heuristic 3. There exists a collection of cyclotomic classes $\mathcal{T}'$ (w.r.t. d) satisfying Heuristic 1.3 such that $\ell \approx \sqrt{\frac{2^d}{d}}$.

Step 2. Then, as in the CRV method [CRV15, Sect. 4.3], we choose $t-1$ random polynomials $q_i(X) \overset{\$}{\leftarrow} \mathcal{P}(X^L) \subseteq \mathbb{F}_{2^n}[X]$, for some parameter t to be determined later, that have their monomials only from X^L. Then we try to find t polynomials $p_i(X) \in \mathcal{P}(X^L)$ such that

$$P(X) = \sum_{i=1}^{t-1} p_i(X) \cdot q_i(X) + p_t(X) \mod X^{2^n} + X \tag{8}$$

evaluates S.

Note that Heuristic 3 guarantees that the decomposition of (8) exists for every d-to-r-bit S-box S for some $t \leq |L| \cdot (|L| - 1)$. But we need to find as small a value of t as possible for a chosen L.

The unknown coefficients of the polynomials $p_i(X)$ are obtained by evaluating $P(X)$ at $\mathsf{E}_{d,n}(j) \ \forall j \in \{0,1\}^d$ and then writing the resulting set of linear equations over $\mathbb{F}_2$ instead of $\mathbb{F}_{2^n}$. That is, we obtain a system of linear equations over $\mathbb{F}_2$ with each equation corresponding to an output bit of $S(j)$. Note that the unknowns in these equations correspond to the (unknown) n "bits" of the unknown coefficients (from $\mathbb{F}_{2^n}$) of $p_i(X)$. Denote the resulting system of linear equations as

$$A \cdot c = b, \tag{9}$$

where the matrix A over $\mathbb{F}_2$ will have $r \cdot 2^d$ rows and $t \cdot |L| \cdot n$ columns, the $\mathbb{F}_2$-vector c corresponds to the unknown bits of the (to-be-determined) coefficients of $p_i(X)$, and the $\mathbb{F}_2$-vector b corresponds to the bits of the outputs of the S-box S. We can solve the above linear equation for any b if A has rank $r \cdot 2^d$. We make the following assumption, similar to the CRV method, that says that if the number of columns exceed the number of rows, then the matrix A has full rank $r \cdot 2^d$.

Heuristic 4. The condition $t \cdot |L| \cdot n \geq r \cdot 2^d$ suffices for A to have (full) rank $r \cdot 2^d$.

Once the solution vector c is computed, then the unknown coefficients (from $\mathbb{F}_{2^n}$) of the polynomials $p_i(X)$, and hence the polynomial $P(X)$, are readily obtained. This completes the description of our method.

Remark 4. If the matrix A has full rank $(r \cdot 2^d)$ for a randomly chosen set of polynomials $q_i(X) \in \mathcal{P}(X^L)$, then this same set of polynomials will yield the decomposition of (8) for any d-to-r-bit S-box.

Algorithm 1. Our method to evaluate generic S-boxes

Input: A d-to-r-bit S-box table S.

Output: Polynomials $p_i(X), q_i(X) \in \mathbb{F}_{2^n}[X]$ such that $P(X) = \sum\limits_{i=1}^{t-1} p_i(X) \cdot q_i(X) + p_t(X)$ satisfies (2).

1: Choose a collection $\mathcal{T}$ of ℓ cyclotomic classes w.r.t. some $n \geq d$ that satisfies Heuristics 1 and 3.
2: Compute X^L, where $L \leftarrow \bigcup\limits_{C \in \mathcal{T}} C$.
3: Choose t such that $t \cdot |L| \cdot n \geq r \cdot 2^d$.
4: For $1 \leq i \leq t$, choose $q_i(X) \overset{\$}{\leftarrow} \mathcal{P}\left(X^L\right)$.
5: Set up a linear system of equations over $\mathbb{F}_2$, $A \cdot c = b$, to solve for the $\mathbb{F}_2$-vector c that corresponds to the unknown coefficients of the polynomials $p_i(X)$ (cf. (9)).
6: Construct the polynomials $p_i(X)$ from the solution vector c.

Complexity Analysis. The number of non-linear multiplications required to pre-compute the set X^L is $\ell - 2$, and the number required in (8) is $t - 1$. Hence in total the number of non-linear multiplications required is

$$M_{d,r,n} = \ell - 2 + t - 1 = \ell + t - 3. \tag{10}$$

From Heuristic 4, we get the condition

$$t \geq \frac{r \cdot 2^d}{|L| \cdot n}.$$

By substituting from (10) and (7) in the above inequality, we get

$$M_{d,r,n} \geq \ell - 3 + \frac{r \cdot 2^d}{(1 + n \cdot (\ell - 1)) \cdot n}.$$

Since, from Heuristic 3, we can set $\ell \approx \sqrt{\frac{2^d}{d}}$, we obtain from the above inequality

$$M_{d,r,n} \approx \sqrt{\frac{2^d}{d}} - 3 + \frac{r \cdot 2^d}{n \cdot \left(1 + n \cdot \left(\sqrt{\frac{2^d}{d}} - 1\right)\right)} \tag{11}$$

Note that if $d = r = n$, then we recover an estimate close to that found in [CRV15, Sect. 2.2]. If $n \gg \sqrt[4]{2^d \cdot d \cdot r^2}$, then

$$M_{d,r,\infty} \approx \sqrt{\frac{2^d}{d}}.$$

Hence in the limiting case the complexity of our method is half that of the CRV method.

Numerical Experiments. In Table 2, we compare the estimate of (11) (on rounding up to the successive integer) with the observed complexity for various cases of practical interest. It turns out that the observed values are close to the estimated values.

Remark 5. Experiments tend to indicate that the value of t *cannot* be made arbitrarily small with increasing values of n. The resulting ranks of the matrices seem to saturate after a certain value of n. This, of course, has to do with the structure of the pre-computed set X^L. But the dependency is currently unclear, and hence we are unable to give a lower bound on the value of t, unlike the case of ℓ.

Linear Operations. An upper bound on the number of additions (over $\mathbb{F}_{2^n}$) required by our method to evaluate the polynomial $P(X)$ in (8) is $(2t - 1) \cdot (|L| - 1) + (t - 1)$ since each of the polynomials $p_i(X)$ and $q_i(X)$ have at most $|L|$ non-zero coefficients. Since, from Heuristic 4, we have $t \cdot |L| \approx \frac{r \cdot 2^d}{n}$, an upper bound on the number of additions is about $\frac{r \cdot 2^{d+1}}{n}$. Note that working in bigger fields can lead to smaller numbers of additions, though each such field addition operation now takes a greater number of bit operations.

The number of scalar multiplications (over $\mathbb{F}_{2^n}$) that is required is at most $(2t - 1) \cdot (|L|) \approx \frac{r \cdot 2^{d+1}}{n}$, while the number of squarings (over $\mathbb{F}_{2^n}$) that is required is $n \cdot (\ell - 1) \approx n \cdot \sqrt{\frac{2^d}{d}}$.

2.2   Concrete Parameters for Various S-Boxes

Table 3 suggests how to choose the parameters t and L in Algorithm 1 for various d-to-r-bit S-box dimensions depending on the choice of n. If these parameters of Algorithm 1 are chosen as indicated, then the number of non-linear multiplications required to evaluate any S-box of given dimension is upper bounded as specified by Table 2. For the special case of $d = r = n$ the parameters are as suggested in [CRV15, Appendix B] except for the case $d = r = n = 8$.

As Remark 4 suggests, once a chosen set of random polynomials $q_i(X)$ in Algorithm 1 yields the decomposition of (8) for a given d-to-r-bit S-box, then the same set of $q_i(X)$ will yield a decomposition for any other S-box of the same dimension. In practice, we have observed that a randomly chosen set of polynomials $q_i(X)$ almost always yield the decomposition of (8).

2.3   Software Implementation of DES

We have performed a software implementation of the CGPQR method [CGP+12] combined with our technique for the DES block cipher [oST93] that needs only 3 non-linear multiplications over $\mathbb{F}_{2^8}$. Note that DES uses eight 6-to-4-bit S-boxes. We used the C implementation of the CGPQR method combined with

Table 3. Choosing parameters l, t and L for evaluating d-to-r-bit S-boxes over $\mathbb{F}_{2^n}$, where L is always the union of the first l elements of $\{C_0^n, C_1^n, C_3^n, C_7^n, C_{29}^n, C_{87}^n\}$

d	4		5		6					7			8	
r	4		5		4		6			7			8	
n	4	8	5	8	4	8	6	8	16	7	8	16	8	16
l	3	3	4	4	4	4	4	4	4	5	5	5	6	6
t	2	2	3	2	3	2	4	3	2	5	4	2	7	3
$|L|$	9	17	16	25	19	25	19	25	49	29	33	65	41	81

the improvements of [RV13, CRV15] that is publicly available from [Cor13]. For a fair comparison, we have compared our improvement only with the CGPQR method combined with the improvements of [RV13] (that needs 7 non-linear multiplications) and the CRV method (that needs 4 non-linear multiplications) [CRV15], both of which are analysed in the non-linear multiplication cost model. The results are presented in Table 5.

We decomposed the DES S-boxes as

$$P_{\mathrm{DES}}(X) = p_1(X) \cdot q_1(X) + p_2(X),$$

where $p_1, q_1, p_2 \in \mathcal{P}(X^L) \subseteq \mathbb{F}_{2^8}[X]$, $L = C_0^8 \cup C_1^8 \cup C_3^8 \cup C_7^8$, and the coefficients of q_1 are randomly chosen from $\mathbb{F}_{2^8}$ (cf. Table 3 and Algorithm 1). Table 4 describes a polynomial q_1 that will yield the above decomposition for each of the 8 S-boxes of DES.

Table 4. A polynomial q_1 that could be used in common for all the DES S-boxes. The irreducible polynomial used to represent $\mathbb{F}_{2^8}$ is $a^8 + a^4 + a^3 + a + 1$.

$$
\begin{aligned}
&(a^2) \cdot x^{224} + (a^7 + a^6 + a^5 + a^4 + a^2 + 1) \cdot x^{193} + (a^7 + a^4 + a + 1) \cdot x^{192} + (a^7 + \\
&a^5 + a^3 + a^2 + a + 1) \cdot x^{131} + (a^6 + a^3 + 1) \cdot x^{129} + (a^7 + a^5 + a) \cdot x^{128} + (a^6 + \\
&a^5 + a^4 + a) \cdot x^{112} + (a^7 + a^5 + a^4 + a^2 + a) \cdot x^{96} + (a^7 + a^5 + a^4 + a^3 + a^2 + 1) \cdot \\
&x^{64} + (a^5 + a^4) \cdot x^{56} + (a^7 + a^6 + a^3 + a^2 + a) \cdot x^{48} + (a^6 + a^3 + a^2 + a) \cdot x^{32} + \\
&(a^6 + a^3 + 1) \cdot x^{28} + (a^5 + a) \cdot x^{24} + (a^7 + a^5 + a^4 + a^3 + a + 1) \cdot x^{16} + (a^7 + a^6 + \\
&a^5 + a^4 + a + 1) \cdot x^{14} + (a^5 + a^4 + a^3) \cdot x^{12} + (a^7 + a^4 + a + 1) \cdot x^8 + (a^3 + 1) \cdot \\
&x^7 + (a^7 + a^4 + a + 1) \cdot x^6 + (a^6 + a^4 + a^3) \cdot x^4 + (a^6 + a^5 + a^4 + a^3 + a^2 + a + \\
&1) \cdot x^3 + (a^7 + a^3 + a) \cdot x^2 + (a^6 + a^4 + a^3 + a^2 + a) \cdot x + (a^7 + a^3 + a^2 + a + 1)
\end{aligned}
$$

The experiments were performed on a DELL LATITUDE E55450 laptop (with CORE i3 processor and 64-bit architecture) running CentOS 7 in a virtual machine with 4 GB allotted memory. For efficiency, we have tabulated the computation of all the linear polynomials that appear in the evaluation of DES S-boxes (cf. [CRV15, Remark 3]). Note that these polynomials need to be stored only in the ROM. In Table 5, the parameter t' refers to the order of security in

Table 5. Comparison of secure masked implementations of DES.

Method	t'	n'	Rand $\times 10^3$	RAM Mem (bytes)	Time (ms)	PF
Unprotected					0.005	1
CGPQR+RV	1	3	2752	72	0.290	58
CGPQR+CRV	1	3	1600	40	0.093	18
CGPQR+this work	1	3	1216	34	0.068	13
CGPQR+RV	2	5	9152	118	0.538	107
CGPQR+CRV	2	5	5312	64	0.175	35
CGPQR+this work	2	5	4032	54	0.133	26
CGPQR+RV	3	7	19200	164	0.824	164
CGPQR+CRV	3	7	11136	88	0.293	58
CGPQR+this work	3	7	8448	74	0.214	42
CGPQR+RV	4	9	32896	210	1.188	237
CGPQR+CRV	4	9	19072	112	0.455	91
CGPQR+this work	4	9	14464	94	0.323	64

the full security model of [ISW03], and $n' = 2t' + 1$ is the number of shares. The RAM memory usage (in bytes) that is reported is only for the S-box computations and the total CPU time for a DES encryption is measured in milliseconds. The penalty factor (PF) is the ratio of the total execution time for a given method to that of an unprotected implementation. The total number of calls made to the PRG that outputs random bytes is 1000 times the reported quantity.

3   The Power of Using Bigger Fields and Its Limitations

In this section we ignore the higher cost of field operations when using a bigger field, so that we can gain some understanding of what can and what cannot be achieved by working with bigger fields.

As in our general cost model linear maps are for free, the domain $\mathbb{F}_2^d$ of our d-to-r-bit S-box table can be chosen to be any fixed d-dimensional subspace of the field $\mathbb{F}_{2^n}$ seen as a vector space over $\mathbb{F}_2$. When passing from using the field $\mathbb{F}_{2^n}$ for the non-linear multiplications to some extension field $\mathbb{F}_{2^{n'}}$ containing $\mathbb{F}_{2^n}$, one can therefore assume that the table is defined on a subspace $\mathbb{F}_2^d$ of $\mathbb{F}_{2^n}$, and use the same sequence of non-linear multiplications as for $\mathbb{F}_{2^n}$, but now viewed as products of polynomials over $\mathbb{F}_{2^{n'}}$ instead. So switching to an extension field never increases the number of non-linear multiplications.

Any two finite fields $\mathbb{F}_{2^n}$ and $\mathbb{F}_{2^d}$ of characteristic 2 are contained in some bigger field with $\mathbb{F}_{2^{lcm(n,d)}}$ being the minimal one. Hence we can assume in this section that d *divides* n and that the table is defined on the *subfield* $\mathbb{F}_{2^d}$ of $\mathbb{F}_{2^n}$.

Since, for a polynomial $f(X) = \sum_{0 \le i \le \deg f} f_i X^i \in \mathbb{F}_{2^n}[X]$, we are only interested in the values on a subspace $\mathbb{F}_2^d \le \mathbb{F}_{2^n}$, we can reduce it modulo

$p(X) := \prod_{z \in \mathbb{F}_2^d}(X - z)$ without changing these. So we can work with polynomials of degree $< 2^d$ instead of 2^n as is the case when the table is defined on all of $\mathbb{F}_{2^n}$. However, in general, the polynomial p does not have a nice structure. But if $\mathbb{F}_2^d = \mathbb{F}_{2^d}$ is the unique subfield of order 2^d of $\mathbb{F}_{2^n}$, then $p(X) = X^{2^d} + X$ and the equation $x^{2^d} = x$ for all elements $x \in \mathbb{F}_{2^d}(\leq \mathbb{F}_{2^n})$ implies

$$f(x) = \sum_{0 \leq i \leq \deg f} f_i x^i = f_0 + \sum_{0 < j < 2^d} \left(\sum_{i = j \bmod 2^d - 1} f_i \right) x^j.$$

Working over a bigger field than in the original CRV method has two benefits. The cyclotomic classes over $\mathbb{F}_{2^n}$ have sizes up to n, and hence more elements than the possible d over $\mathbb{F}_2^d$, so that one gathers more degrees of freedom per non-linear multiplication in Step 1.[1] Additionally some extra power is given by being able to choose the coefficients of the polynomials in Step 2 from a bigger field:

Lemma 1. *Given $2k$ polynomials $f_i, g_i \in \mathbb{F}_{2^n}[X]$ $(0 \leq i < k)$ there exists an extension field $\mathbb{F}_{2^{n'}}$ of $\mathbb{F}_{2^n}$ and elements $a_i, b_i \in \mathbb{F}_{2^{n'}}$ such that for every i the function $x \mapsto f_i(x) \cdot g_i(x)$ defined on $\mathbb{F}_{2^n}$ is an $\mathbb{F}_2$-linear image of the single non-linear product $h := (\sum_i a_i \cdot f_i(X)) \cdot (\sum_i b_i \cdot g_i(X)) \in \mathbb{F}_{2^{n'}}[X]$, i.e. there are $\mathbb{F}_2$-linear functions $\lambda_i : \mathbb{F}_{2^{n'}} \to \mathbb{F}_{2^n}$ with $\lambda_i \circ h(x) = f_i(x) \cdot g_i(x)$ for all $x \in \mathbb{F}_{2^n}$.*

In particular, any finite number of independent non-linear multiplications over any finite field can be replaced by a single non-linear multiplication over a bigger field when restricting the maps to the smaller field.

Proof. Take a prime $q > k^2$ not dividing n, and set $n' = q \cdot n$. For any element $z \in \mathbb{F}_{2^{n'}} \setminus \mathbb{F}_{2^n}$ the set $\{1, z, z^2, \dots, z^{k^2-1}\}$ is linearly independent over $\mathbb{F}_{2^n}$ (otherwise it would span a proper intermediate field between $\mathbb{F}_{2^n}$ and $\mathbb{F}_{2^{n'}}$, but this extension has prime degree). Hence there exist $\mathbb{F}_{2^n}$-linear and therefore $\mathbb{F}_2$-linear maps $\lambda_i : \mathbb{F}_{2^{n'}} \to \mathbb{F}_{2^n}$ with $\lambda_i(\sum_{0 \leq j < k^2} c_j z^j) = c_{i+ki}$ when all $c_j \in \mathbb{F}_{2^n}$. For $a_i := z^i$ and $b_i := z^{ki}$ we get

$$\left(\sum_{0 \leq i < k} a_i \cdot f_i(X) \right) \cdot \left(\sum_{0 \leq j < k} b_j \cdot g_j(X) \right) = \sum_{0 \leq i,j < k} z^{i+kj}(f_i(X) \cdot g_j(X)).$$

Since, for $x \in \mathbb{F}_{2^n}$, we have also $f_i(x)g_j(x) \in \mathbb{F}_{2^n}$, the claim is proved.

Remark 6. The technique in the proof of Lemma 1 can be used to evaluate the non-linear part of the S-box of AES given by the monomial X^{254} (over $\mathbb{F}_{2^8}$) with 3 non-linear multiplications over $\mathbb{F}_{2^{16}}$. The first non-linear multiplication is spent to get X^3, the second to multiply $X^2 + z \cdot X^3$ by $(X^3)^4$, where z is any element of $\mathbb{F}_{2^{16}} \setminus \mathbb{F}_{2^8}$. From the result $X^{14} + z \cdot X^{15}$, one can $\mathbb{F}_2$-linearly extract the functions $x \mapsto x^{14}$ and $x \mapsto x^{15}$ defined over the subfield $\mathbb{F}_{2^8}$, which enables one to finally obtain $X^{254} = X^{14} \cdot (X^{15})^{16}$.

---

[1] Lemma 2 generalizes this statement about monomials to polynomials.

Corollary 1. With l non-linear multiplications, *all* monomial functions $x \mapsto x^k$ defined on $\mathbb{F}_{2^d}$ with Hamming weight $k \leq 2^l$ can be obtained in parallel. In particular, for some huge extension field $\mathbb{F}_{2^n}$ of $\mathbb{F}_{2^d}$ *all* functions $\mathbb{F}_{2^d} \to \mathbb{F}_{2^n}$, including d-to-r-bit S-boxes, require just $\lceil \log_2 d \rceil$ non-linear multiplications.

The bound given in Corollary 1 is sharp: as the linear functions have *algebraic degree*[2] 1 and the algebraic degree of a product is at most the sum of the algebraic degrees of its factors, the function $f : \mathbb{F}_{2^d} \to \mathbb{F}_{2^n}$ given by monomial $X^{2^d - 1}$ that maps 0 to 0 and the rest of $\mathbb{F}_{2^d}$ to 1 has algebraic degree d.

For judging the usefulness of the result of a specific non-linear multiplication we have (denoting the space of functions from Z to Y as Y^Z for sets Y and Z):[3]

Lemma 2. *For $f : Z \to \mathbb{F}_{2^n}$ the set $F := \{g \circ f \mid g : \mathbb{F}_{2^n} \to \mathbb{F}_{2^n} \text{ is } \mathbb{F}_2\text{-linear}\}$ is an $\mathbb{F}_{2^n}$-subspace of $\mathbb{F}_{2^n}^Z$ whose dimension over $\mathbb{F}_{2^n}$ equals the dimension over $\mathbb{F}_2$ of the $\mathbb{F}_2$-subspace of $\mathbb{F}_{2^n}$ generated by the image of f.*

Proof. F is the image of the $\mathbb{F}_{2^n}$–linear map $\varphi : g \mapsto g \circ f$ from the set $\mathrm{End}_{\mathbb{F}_2}(\mathbb{F}_{2^n})$ of $\mathbb{F}_2$-linear maps $\mathbb{F}_{2^n} \to \mathbb{F}_{2^n}$ to the set $\mathbb{F}_{2^n}^Z$ of functions $Z \to \mathbb{F}_{2^n}$. $\mathrm{End}_{\mathbb{F}_2}(\mathbb{F}_{2^n}) = \mathbb{F}_{2^n}^* \otimes_{\mathbb{F}_2} \mathbb{F}_{2^n}$ has dimension n over $\mathbb{F}_{2^n}$ (with $*$ denoting the dual $\mathbb{F}_2$-vector space). The kernel of φ is the $\mathbb{F}_{2^n}$-subspace of $\mathbb{F}_2$-linear maps whose restriction to the image of f in $\mathbb{F}_{2^n}$ is 0. This is the tensor product with $\mathbb{F}_{2^n}$ (over $\mathbb{F}_2$) of the annihilator ($\leq \mathbb{F}_{2^n}^*$) of the image $\{f(x) \mid x \in Z\}$ of f in $\mathbb{F}_{2^n}$, proving the claim.

Example 1. For monomials X^α the dimension of the set F from Lemma 2 is the cardinality of the cyclotomic class containing α. For example, in the field $\mathbb{F}_{64}$ the cyclotomic classes of $9 = 1001_2$ and $21 = 10101_2$ have order 3 resp. 2, so the dimension of the corresponding F over $\mathbb{F}_{64}$ is 3 resp. 2. On the other hand, the images under $f(x) = x^9$ resp. $g(x) = x^{21}$ of the multiplicative group $\mathbb{F}_{64}^\times \cong Z_{63}$ have order 7 resp. 3, and are therefore the multiplicative groups of the subfields $\mathbb{F}_8$ resp. $\mathbb{F}_4$. Their dimensions over $\mathbb{F}_2$ are 3 resp. 2 as claimed by the lemma.

A criterion for having enough degrees of freedom in Step 2 is given by:

Lemma 3. *Let F be $\mathbb{F}_{2^n}$-subspace of $\mathbb{F}_{2^n}[X]/(X^{2^n} + X)$ that is closed under taking squares. Then the $\mathbb{F}_{2^n}$-subspace $\langle F \cdot F \rangle_{\mathbb{F}_{2^n}}$ generated by the products of pairs of elements of F contains F, is also closed under taking squares and has dimension at most $\dim F + \binom{\dim F}{2}$.*

Proof. As squaring is a field automorphism, only the statement about the dimensions needs to be proved. But this follows from the commutativity of multiplication as for any base (f_i) of F the set $(f_i \cdot f_j)_{i \leq j}$ generates $\langle F \cdot F \rangle_{\mathbb{F}_{2^n}}$.

The remainder of this section is devoted to proving a lower worst-case bound for the number of non-linear multiplications over $\mathbb{F}_{2^n}$ needed for functions from $\mathbb{F}_2^d$ to $\mathbb{F}_2^r$ with $d, r \leq n$ but not necessarily $d \mid n$. The proof is an adaption of [CRV14, Proposition 3] to our situation with minor improvements.

---

[2] For a polynomial $f = \sum_l f_l \cdot X^l$ this is $\max \{\text{Hamming weight}(l) \mid f_l \neq 0\}$.

[3] Corresponding to choosing L in Algorithm 1 as the union of cyclotomic classes that have as many elements as possible to get as many degrees of freedom as possible for the linear equation system being constructed.

Proposition 1. *For $d, r \leq n$ and fixed subspaces $\mathbb{F}_2^d, \mathbb{F}_2^r \leq \mathbb{F}_{2^n}$ there is a function $f : \mathbb{F}_2^d \to \mathbb{F}_2^r$ that cannot be represented by any polynomial in $\mathbb{F}_{2^n}[X]$ that requires less than $\frac{\sqrt{r(2^d - 1 - d) + (d + \frac{r-n}{2})^2} - (d + \frac{r-n}{2})}{n}$ non-linear multiplications for evaluation.*

In case of $n = r = d$ this term simplifies to $\sqrt{\frac{2^n - 1}{n}} - 1$.

Proof. Without loss of generality, we may look only at functions that map 0 to 0: the only monomial not fixing zero is 1, and on $\mathbb{F}_{2^n} \setminus \{0\}$ the monomial $X^{2^n - 1}$ is constant 1. This allows us to work with linear functions where the authors of [CRV14] used affine functions instead. Starting with $z_0 = id\,|_{\mathbb{F}_2^d}$ one can get all $\mathbb{F}_2$-linear functions $\mathbb{F}_2^d \to \mathbb{F}_{2^n}$ without using any non-linear multiplication. Having obtained $z_0, \ldots, z_j$ using exactly j non-linear multiplications, one can choose $\mathbb{F}_2$-linear maps $\lambda_{0,j}, \lambda'_{0,j} : \mathbb{F}_2^d \to \mathbb{F}_{2^n}$ and $\lambda_{1,j}, \lambda'_{1,j}, \ldots, \lambda_{j,j}, \lambda'_{j,j} : \mathbb{F}_{2^n} \to \mathbb{F}_{2^n}$ to get

$$z_{j+1} = \left(\sum_{i=0}^{j} \lambda_{i,j} \circ z_i \right) \cdot \left(\sum_{i=0}^{j} \lambda'_{i,j} \circ z_i \right).$$

(Adding a constant to either factor changes z_{j+1} by a summand that can be represented already by the z_i with $i \leq j$). With the help of $z_0, \ldots, z_k$ we then can evaluate

$$f = \sum_{0 \leq i \leq k} \lambda_i \circ z_i$$

for $\mathbb{F}_2$-linear maps $\lambda_0 : \mathbb{F}_2^d \to \mathbb{F}_2^r$ and $\lambda_1, \ldots, \lambda_k : \mathbb{F}_{2^n} \to \mathbb{F}_2^r$ without further non-linear multiplication. Conversely, any $f : \mathbb{F}_2^d \to \mathbb{F}_2^r$ fixing 0 that can be evaluated using at most k non-linear multiplications is of this form.

In total we have to choose $2k$ $\mathbb{F}_2$-linear maps from $\mathbb{F}_2^d$ to $\mathbb{F}_{2^n}$, $2 \sum_{i=0}^{k-1} i = k(k - 1)$ from $\mathbb{F}_{2^n}$ to $\mathbb{F}_{2^n}$, one from $\mathbb{F}_2^d$ to $\mathbb{F}_2^r$ and k from $\mathbb{F}_{2^n}$ to $\mathbb{F}_2^r$ giving us $((2^n)^d)^{2k} \cdot ((2^n)^n)^{k(k-1)} \cdot (2^r)^d \cdot ((2^r)^n)^k = 2^{2ndk + n^2 k(k-1) + rd + rnk}$ choices. As there are $(2^r)^{2^d - 1} = 2^{r(2^d - 1)}$ functions from $\mathbb{F}_2^d$ to $\mathbb{F}_2^r$ mapping 0 to 0, to get enough functions we need

$$2ndk + n^2 k(k - 1) + rd + rnk \geq r(2^d - 1).$$

This is via $(nk)^2 + (2d + r - n)nk \geq r(2^d - 1) - rd$ and $(nk + (d + \frac{r-n}{2}))^2 = (nk)^2 + (2d + r - n)nk + (d + \frac{r-n}{2})^2 \geq r(2^d - 1 - d) + (d + \frac{r-n}{2})^2$ equivalent to

$$k \geq \frac{\sqrt{r(2^d - 1 - d) + (d + \frac{r-n}{2})^2} - (d + \frac{r-n}{2})}{n}.$$

Remark 7. As the images of the z_js in the proof of Proposition 1 can span at most a $(2^d - 1)$-dimensional $\mathbb{F}_2$-subspace of $\mathbb{F}_{2^n}$, Lemma 2 shows that for $n \geq 2^d - 1$ the $\lambda_{i,j}, \lambda'_{i,j}$ and λ_i with $i > 0$ have to be defined only on these $(2^d - 1)$-dimensional subspaces reducing the degrees of freedom for obtaining the next z_j resp. f. With $n' := \max\{n, 2^d - 1\}$ the number of choices reduces to $2^{2ndk + nn'k(k-1) + rd + rn'k}$, but as one gets better lower bounds by using the algebraic degree, we do not expand upon this.

Acknowledgements. We would like to thank Jean-Sébastien Coron and Johann Großschädl for pointing out possible applications of our improvements to ARM Neon processors and also for pointing out [GMPT15]. Thanks to Jake Longo Galea for clarifying the work of [GMPT15]. We are also thankful to Carolyn Whitnall, Srinivas Karthik and the anonymous reviewers of CHES 2016 for many helpful comments.

Srinivas Vivek's work has been supported in part by the European Union's H2020 programme under grant agreement number ICT-644209.

References

[ARS+15] Albrecht, M.R., Rechberger, C., Schneider, T., Tiessen, T., Zohner, M.: Ciphers for MPC and FHE. In: Oswald, E., Fischlin, M. (eds.) EURO-CRYPT 2015. LNCS, vol. 9056, pp. 430–454. Springer, Heidelberg (2015)

[Bar86] Barrett, P.: Implementing the Rivest Shamir and Adleman public key encryption algorithm on a standard digital signal processor. In: Odlyzko, A.M. (ed.) CRYPTO 1986. LNCS, vol. 263, pp. 311–323. Springer, Heidelberg (1987)

[BFG15] Balasch, J., Faust, S., Gierlichs, B.: Inner product masking revisited. In: Oswald, E., Fischlin, M. (eds.) EUROCRYPT 2015. LNCS, vol. 9056, pp. 486–510. Springer, Heidelberg (2015)

[BFGV12] Balasch, J., Faust, S., Gierlichs, B., Verbauwhede, I.: Theory and practice of a leakage resilient masking scheme. In: Wang, X., Sako, K. (eds.) ASIACRYPT 2012. LNCS, vol. 7658, pp. 758–775. Springer, Heidelberg (2012)

[CGP+12] Carlet, C., Goubin, L., Prouff, E., Quisquater, M., Rivain, M.: Higher-order masking schemes for S-boxes. In: Canteaut, A. (ed.) FSE 2012. LNCS, vol. 7549, pp. 366–384. Springer, Heidelberg (2012)

[CJRR99] Chari, S., Jutla, C.S., Rao, J.R., Rohatgi, P.: Towards sound approaches to counteract power-analysis attacks. In: Wiener, M. (ed.) CRYPTO 1999. LNCS, vol. 1666, pp. 398–412. Springer, Heidelberg (1999)

[Cor13] Jean-Sébastien Coron (2013). https://github.com/coron/htable/

[Cor14] Coron, J.-S.: Higher order masking of look-up tables. In: Nguyen, P.Q., Oswald, E. (eds.) EUROCRYPT 2014. LNCS, vol. 8441, pp. 441–458. Springer, Heidelberg (2014)

[CPRR13] Coron, J.-S., Prouff, E., Rivain, M., Roche, T.: Higher-order side channel security and mask refreshing. In: Moriai, S. (ed.) FSE 2013. LNCS, vol. 8424, pp. 410–424. Springer, Heidelberg (2014)

[CPRR15] Carlet, C., Prouff, E., Rivain, M., Roche, T.: Algebraic decomposition for probing security. In: Gennaro, R., Robshaw, M. (eds.) CRYPTO 2015. LNCS, vol. 9215, pp. 742–763. Springer, Heidelberg (2015)

[CRV14] Coron, J.-S., Roy, A., Vivek, S.: Fast evaluation of polynomials over binary finite fields and application to side-channel countermeasures. In: Batina, L., Robshaw, M. (eds.) CHES 2014. LNCS, vol. 8731, pp. 170–187. Springer, Heidelberg (2014)

[CRV15] Coron, J.-S., Roy, A., Vivek, S.: Fast evaluation of polynomials over binary finite fields and application to side-channel countermeasures. J. Cryptographic Eng. 5(2), 73–83 (2015)

[DDF14] Duc, A., Dziembowski, S., Faust, S.: Unifying leakage models: from probing attacks to noisy leakage. In: Nguyen, P.Q., Oswald, E. (eds.) EUROCRYPT 2014. LNCS, vol. 8441, pp. 423–440. Springer, Heidelberg (2014)

[DFS15]   Dziembowski, S., Faust, S., Skorski, M.: Noisy leakage revisited. In: Oswald, E., Fischlin, M. (eds.) EUROCRYPT 2015. LNCS, vol. 9057, pp. 159–188. Springer, Heidelberg (2015)

[GHS12a] Gentry, C., Halevi, S., Smart, N.P.: Homomorphic evaluation of the AES circuit. IACR Cryptology ePrint Archive 2012:99 (2012)

[GHS12b] Gentry, C., Halevi, S., Smart, N.P.: Homomorphic evaluation of the AES circuit. In: Safavi-Naini, R., Canetti, R. (eds.) CRYPTO 2012. LNCS, vol. 7417, pp. 850–867. Springer, Heidelberg (2012)

[GM11]   Goubin, L., Martinelli, A.: Protecting AES with Shamir's secret sharing scheme. In: Takagi, T., Preneel, B. (eds.) CHES 2011. LNCS, vol. 6917, pp. 79–94. Springer, Heidelberg (2011)

[GMPT15] Longo, J., De Mulder, E., Page, D., Tunstall, M.: SoC it to EM: electromagnetic side-channel attacks on a complex system-on-chip. In: Güneysu, T., Handschuh, H. (eds.) CHES 2015. LNCS, vol. 9293, pp. 620–640. Springer, Heidelberg (2015)

[GPS14]   Grosso, V., Prouff, E., Standaert, F.-X.: Efficient masked S-boxes processing – a step forward –. In: Pointcheval, D., Vergnaud, D. (eds.) AFRICACRYPT. LNCS, vol. 8469, pp. 251–266. Springer, Heidelberg (2014)

[ISW03]   Ishai, Y., Sahai, A., Wagner, D.: Private circuits: securing hardware against probing attacks. In: Boneh, D. (ed.) CRYPTO 2003. LNCS, vol. 2729, pp. 463–481. Springer, Heidelberg (2003)

[KJJ99]   Kocher, P.C., Jaffe, J., Jun, B.: Differential power analysis. In: Wiener, M. (ed.) CRYPTO 1999. LNCS, vol. 1666, pp. 388–397. Springer, Heidelberg (1999)

[Koc96]   Kocher, P.C.: Timing attacks on implementations of Diffie-Hellman, RSA, DSS, and other systems. In: Koblitz, N. (ed.) CRYPTO 1996. LNCS, vol. 1109, pp. 104–113. Springer, Heidelberg (1996)

[Lim13]   ARM Limited. NEON Programmer's Guide (2013)

[NO14]   Nguyen, P.Q., Oswald, E.: EUROCRYPT 2014. LNCS, vol. 8441. Springer, Heidelberg (2014)

[OF15]   Oswald, E., Fischlin, M.: EUROCRYPT 2015. LNCS, vol. 9056. Springer, Heidelberg (2015)

[oST93]   National Institute of Standards and Technology. FIPS 46-3: Data EncryptionStandard, March 1993. http://csrc.nist.gov

[PR11]   Prouff, E., Roche, T.: Higher-order glitches free implementation of the AES using secure multi-party computation protocols. In: Preneel, B., Takagi, T. (eds.) CHES 2011. LNCS, vol. 6917, pp. 63–78. Springer, Heidelberg (2011)

[PR13]   Prouff, E., Rivain, M.: Masking against side-channel attacks: a formal security proof. In: Johansson, T., Nguyen, P.Q. (eds.) EUROCRYPT 2013. LNCS, vol. 7881, pp. 142–159. Springer, Heidelberg (2013)

[PT11]   Preneel, B., Takagi, T.: CHES 2011. LNCS, vol. 6917. Springer, Heidelberg (2011)

[RP10]   Rivain, M., Prouff, E.: Provably secure higher-order masking of AES. In: Mangard, S., Standaert, F.-X. (eds.) CHES 2010. LNCS, vol. 6225, pp. 413–427. Springer, Heidelberg (2010)

[RV13]   Roy, A., Vivek, S.: Analysis and improvement of the generic higher-order masking scheme of FSE 2012. In: Bertoni, G., Coron, J.-S. (eds.) CHES 2013. LNCS, vol. 8086, pp. 417–434. Springer, Heidelberg (2013)

[SP06] Schramm, K., Paar, C.: Higher order masking of the AES. In: Pointcheval, D. (ed.) CT-RSA 2006. LNCS, vol. 3860, pp. 208–225. Springer, Heidelberg (2006)

[Wie99] Wiener, M.J.: CRYPTO 1999. LNCS, vol. 1666. Springer, Heidelberg (1999)

[WVGX15] Wang, J., Vadnala, P.K., Großschädl, J., Xu, Q.: Higher-order masking in practice: a vector implementation of masked AES for ARM NEON. In: Nyberg, K. (ed.) CT-RSA 2015. LNCS, vol. 9048, pp. 181–198. Springer, Heidelberg (2015)

Faster Evaluation of SBoxes via Common Shares

Jean-Sébastien Coron[1]([✉]), Aurélien Greuet[2], Emmanuel Prouff[3],
and Rina Zeitoun[2]

[1] University of Luxembourg, Luxembourg City, Luxembourg
jean-sebastien.coron@uni.lu
[2] Oberthur Technologies, Colombes, France
{a.greuet,r.zeitoun}@oberthur.com
[3] Sorbonne Universités, UPMC Univ Paris 06, CNRS, INRIA,
Laboratoire d'Informatique de Paris 6 (LIP6), Équipe PolSys, 4 place Jussieu,
75252 Paris Cedex 05, France

Abstract. We describe a new technique for improving the efficiency of the masking countermeasure against side-channel attacks. Our technique is based on using common shares between secret variables, in order to reduce the number of finite field multiplications. Our algorithms are proven secure in the ISW probing model with $n \geqslant t + 1$ shares against t probes. For AES, we get an equivalent of 2.8 non-linear multiplications for every SBox evaluation, instead of 4 in the Rivain-Prouff countermeasure. We obtain similar improvements for other block-ciphers. Our technique is easy to implement and performs relatively well in practice, with roughly a 20 % speed-up compared to existing algorithms.

1 Introduction

Side-Channel Attacks. Side-channel analysis is a class of cryptanalytic attacks that exploit the physical environment of a cryptosystem to recover some *leakage* about its secrets. It is often more efficient than a cryptanalysis mounted in the so-called *black-box model* where no leakage occurs. In particular, *continuous side-channel attacks* in which the adversary gets information at each invocation of the cryptosystem are especially threatening. Common attacks as those exploiting the running-time, the power consumption or the electromagnetic radiations of a cryptographic computation fall into this class. Many implementations of block ciphers have been practically broken by continuous side-channel analysis and securing them has been a longstanding issue for the embedded systems industry.

The Masking Countermeasure. A sound approach to counteract side-channel attacks is to use *secret sharing* [Bla79, Sha79], often called *masking* in the context of side-channel attacks. This approach consists in splitting each sensitive

---

E. Prouff—Part of this work has been done at Safran Identity and Security, and while the author was at ANSSI, France.

B. Gierlichs and A.Y. Poschmann (Eds.): CHES 2016, LNCS 9813, pp. 498–514, 2016.
DOI: 10.1007/978-3-662-53140-2_24

variable x of the implementation into n shares such that $x = x_1 \oplus \cdots \oplus x_n$, where n is called the *sharing order*, such that x can be recovered from these shares but no information can be recovered from fewer than n shares. It has been shown that the complexity of mounting a successful side-channel attack against a masked implementation increases exponentially with the order [CJRR99, PR13, DDF14]. Starting from this observation, the design of efficient *secure schemes* for different ciphers has become a foreground issue. When specified *at order n*, such a scheme aims at specifying how to update the sharing of the internal state throughout the processing while ensuring that (1) the final sharing corresponds to the expected ciphertext, and (2) the n-th order security property is satisfied.

The ISW Probing Model. Ishai, Sahai and Wagner [ISW03] initiated the theoretical study of securing circuits against an adversary who can probe a fraction of its wires. They showed how to transform any circuit of size $|C|$ into a circuit of size $\mathcal{O}(|C| \cdot t^2)$ secure against any adversary who can probe at most t wires. The ISW constructions consists in secret-sharing every variable x into $x = x_1 \oplus x_2 \oplus \cdots \oplus x_n$ where $x_2, \ldots, x_n$ are uniformly and independently distributed bits, with $n \geqslant 2t + 1$ to get security against t probes. Processing a XOR gate is straightforward as the shares can be xored separately. The processing of an AND gate $z = xy$ is based on writing:

$$z = xy = \left(\bigoplus_{i=1}^{n} x_i \right) \cdot \left(\bigoplus_{i=1}^{n} y_i \right) = \bigoplus_{1 \leqslant i, j \leqslant n} x_i y_j \tag{1}$$

where the cross-products $x_i y_j$ are first computed and then randomly recombined to get an n-sharing of the output z. This construction, called *ISW gadget* in the rest of this paper, enables, in its general form, to securely evaluate a multiplication at the cost of n^2 multiplications, $2n(n-1)$ additions and $n(n-1)/2$ random values. Its complexity is therefore $\mathcal{O}(n^2)$, which implies that the new circuit with security against t probes has $\mathcal{O}(|C| \cdot t^2)$ gates.

A proof of security in the ISW framework is usually simulation based: one must show that any set of t probes can be perfectly simulated without the knowledge of the original variables of the circuit. In [ISW03] and subsequent work this is done by progressively generating a subset I of input shares such that the knowledge of those input shares is sufficient to simulate all the t probes. For example, in the above AND gate, if the adversary would probe $x_i \cdot y_j$, one would put both indices i and j in I, so that the simulator would get the input shares x_i and y_j, and therefore could simulate the product $x_i \cdot y_j$. More generally in the ISW construction every probe adds at most two indices in I, which implies $|I| \leqslant 2t$. Therefore if the number of shares n is such that $n \geqslant 2t + 1$, then $|I| < n$, which implies that only a proper subset of the input shares is required for the simulation; those input shares can in turn be generated as independently uniformly distributed bits. Therefore, the knowledge of the original circuit variables is not required to generate a perfect simulation of the t probes, hence these probes do not bring any additional information to the attacker (since he could perform that simulation by himself).

Existing Work. In the last decade, several masking countermeasures have been proposed for block-ciphers together with security proofs in the ISW probing model, based on the original notion of private circuits introduced in [ISW03]. Except [Cor14] which extends the original idea of [KJJ99] to any order, the other proposals are based on the ISW gadget recalled above. The core idea of the latter works is to split the processing into a short sequence of field multiplications and $\mathbb{F}_2$-linear operations, and then to secure these operations independently, while ensuring that the local security proofs can be combined to prove the security of the entire processing. When parametrized at order n, as recalled above the complexity of the ISW gadget for the field multiplication is $\mathcal{O}(n^2)$, but only $\mathcal{O}(n)$ for $\mathbb{F}_2$-linear operations.[1] Therefore, an interesting problem is to minimize the number of field multiplications required to evaluate an SBox.

In the Rivain-Prouff countermeasure [RP10], the authors showed how to adapt the ISW circuit construction to a software implementation of AES, by working in $\mathbb{F}_{2^8}$ instead of $\mathbb{F}_2$. Namely as illustrated in Fig. 1, the non-linear part $S(x) = x^{254}$ of the AES SBox can be evaluated with only 4 non-linear multiplications over $\mathbb{F}_{2^8}$, and a few linear squarings. Each of those 4 multiplications can in turn be evaluated with the previous ISW gadget based on Eq. (1), by working over $\mathbb{F}_{2^8}$ instead of $\mathbb{F}_2$.

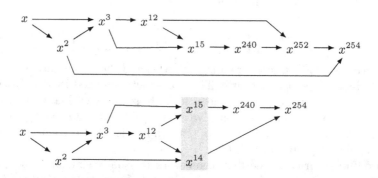

Fig. 1. (a) Sequential computation of x^{254} as used in [RP10,BBD+15a]. (b) Alternative computation of x^{254}; the multiplications $x^{14} = x^{12} \cdot x^2$ and $x^{15} = x^{12} \cdot x^3$ can be computed in parallel [GHS12].

The Rivain-Prouff countermeasure was later extended by Carlet et al. to any look-up table [CGP+12]. Namely any given k-bit SBox can be represented by a polynomial $\sum_{i=0}^{2^k-1} a_i x^i$ over $\mathbb{F}_{2^k}$ using Lagrange's interpolation theorem. Therefore one can mask any SBox by securely evaluating this polynomial using

---

[1] A function f is $\mathbb{F}_2$-linear if it satisfies $f(x \oplus y) = f(x) \oplus f(y)$ for any pair (x, y) of elements in its domain. This property must not be confused with $\mathbb{F}_{2^m}$-linearity of a function, where m divides n and is larger than 1, which is defined such that $f(ax \oplus by) = af(x) \oplus bf(y)$, for every $a, b \in \mathbb{F}_{2^m}$. An $\mathbb{F}_{2^m}$-linear function is $\mathbb{F}_2$-linear but the converse is false in general.

n-shared multiplications as in the Rivain-Prouff countermeasure. To improve efficiency, one must look for operations sequences (*e.g.* SBox representations) that minimize the number of field multiplications which are not $\mathbb{F}_2$-linear[2] (this kind of multiplication shall be called *non-linear* in this paper). This problematic has been tackled out in [CGP+12, RV13] and [CRV14] and led to significantly reduce the number of multiplications needed to evaluate any function defined over $\mathbb{F}_{2^k}$ for $k \leqslant 10$ (*e.g.* the AES SBox can be evaluated with only 4 multiplications, and only 4 multiplications are needed for the DES SBoxes).

Recently, a sequence of works continued to improve the original work [ISW03] and led, in particular, to exhibit a new scheme enabling to securely evaluate any function of algebraic degree 2 at the cost of a single multiplication (with the ISW gadget). The application of this work to the AES SBox led the authors of [GPS14] to describe a scheme which can be secure at any order n and is a valuable alternative to the scheme proposed in [RP10]. In parallel, some schemes [BGN+14, NRS11, PR11] have been proposed which remain secure in the probing model even in presence of so-called glitches [MS06] and the recent work [RBN+15] has investigated relations between these schemes and the ISW construction.

Refined Security Model: t-SNI Security. Since in this paper we are interested in efficiency improvements, we would like to use the optimal $n = t + 1$ number of shares instead of $n = 2t + 1$ as in the original ISW countermeasure. For $n \geqslant 2t + 1$ shares the security proof for the single ISW multiplication gadget easily extends to the full circuit [ISW03]; however for $n \geqslant t + 1$ shares only one must be extra careful. For example, for the Rivain-Prouff countermeasure, it was originally claimed in [RP10] that only $n \geqslant t + 1$ shares were required, but an attack of order $\lceil (n-1)/2 \rceil + 1$ was later described in [CPRR13]; the security proof in [RP10] with $n \geqslant t + 1$ shares actually applies only when the ISW multiplication is used in isolation, but not for the full block-cipher.

To prove security with $n \geqslant t + 1$ shares only for the full block-cipher, a refined security model against probing attacks was recently introduced in [BBD+15a], called t-SNI security. As shown in [BBD+15a], this stronger definition of t-SNI security enables to prove that a gadget can be used in a full construction with $n \geqslant t + 1$ shares, instead of $n \geqslant 2t + 1$ for the weaker definition of t-NI security (corresponding to the original ISW security proof). The authors show that the ISW multiplication gadget does satisfy this stronger t-SNI security definition. They also show that with some additional mask refreshing, the Rivain-Prouff countermeasure for the full AES can be made secure with $n \geqslant t + 1$ shares. Due to its power and simplicity, the t-SNI notion appears to be the "right" security definition against probing attacks. Therefore, in this paper, we always prove the security of our algorithms under this stronger t-SNI notion, so that our algorithms can be used within a larger construction (typically a full block-cipher) with $n \geqslant t + 1$ shares only.

---

[2] A multiplication over a field of characteristic 2 is $\mathbb{F}_2$-linear if it corresponds to a Frobenius automorphism, *i.e.* to a series of squarings.

Our Contribution. Our goal in this paper is to further improve the efficiency of the masking countermeasure. As recalled above, until now the strategy followed by the community has been to reduce the number of calls to the ISW multiplication gadget. In this paper, we follow a complementary approach consisting in reducing the complexity of the ISW multiplication gadget itself. Our core idea is to use common shares between the inputs of multiple ISW multiplication gadgets, up to the first $n/2$ shares; in that case, a given processing performed in the first ISW gadget can be re-used in subsequent gadgets.

Consider for example the alternative evaluation circuit for x^{254} in AES used in [GHS12], as illustrated in Fig. 1. It still has 4 non-linear multiplications as in the original circuit [RP10], but now the two multiplications $x^{14} \leftarrow x^{12} \cdot x^2$ and $x^{15} \leftarrow x^{12} \cdot x^3$ can be evaluated in parallel, moreover with a common operand x^{12}. Let denote by $d \leftarrow c \cdot a$ and $e \leftarrow c \cdot b$ those two multiplications with common operand c. In the ISW multiplication gadget, one must compute all cross-products $c_i \cdot a_j$ and $c_i \cdot b_j$ for all $1 \leqslant i, j \leqslant n$. Now if we can ensure that half of the shares of a and b are the same, that is $a_j = b_j$ for all $1 \leqslant j \leqslant n/2$, then the products $c_i \cdot a_j$ and $c_i \cdot b_j$ for $1 \leqslant j \leqslant n/2$ are the same and can be computed only once; see Fig. 2 for an illustration. This implies that when processing the second multiplication gadget for $e \leftarrow c \cdot b$, we only have to compute $n^2/2$ finite field multiplications instead of n^2. For two multiplications as above, this saves the equivalent of 0.5 multiplication.

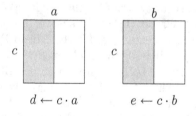

Fig. 2. When half of the shares in a and b are the same, the multiplications corresponding to the left-hand blocks are the same. This saves the equivalent of 0.5 multiplications out of 2.

To ensure that the two inputs have half of their shares in common, we introduce a new gadget called CommonShares with complexity $\mathcal{O}(n)$, taking as input two independent n-sharings of data and outputting two new n-sharings, but with their first $n/2$ shares in common. Obviously this must be achieved without degrading the security level; we show that this is indeed the case by proving the security of the full SBox evaluation in the previous t-SNI model, with $n \geqslant t + 1$ shares. Note that we cannot have more than $n/2$ shares in common between two variables a and b, since otherwise there would be a straightforward attack with fewer than n probes: namely if $a_i = b_i$ for all $1 \leqslant i \leqslant k$, then we can probe the $2(n-k)$ remaining shares a_i and b_i for $k+1 \leqslant i \leqslant n$; if $k > n/2$ this gives strictly less than n shares, whose xor gives the secret variable $a \oplus b$. Hence having half of the shares in common is optimal.

More generally, the 16 SBoxes of AES can be processed in parallel, and therefore each of the 4 non-linear multiplications in x^{254} can be processed in parallel. As opposed to the previous case those multiplications do not share any operand, but we show that by using a generalization of the CommonShares algorithm between m operands instead of 2, for every multiplication in the original circuit one can still save the equivalent of roughly $1/4$ multiplication. This also applies to other block-ciphers as well, since in most block-ciphers the SBoxes are applied in parallel. One can therefore apply the technique from [CRV14] based on fast polynomial evaluation, and using our CommonShares algorithm between the inputs of the evaluated polynomials, we again save roughly $1/4$ of the number of finite field multiplications. Our results for various block-ciphers are summarized in Table 1, in which we give the equivalent number of non-linear multiplications for a single SBox evaluation, for various block-ciphers; we refer to Sect. 5 for a detailed description. Finally, we show in the full version of this paper [CGPZ16] how to apply our common shares technique to the Threshold Implementations (TI) approach for securing implementation against side channel attacks, even in the presence of glitches.

Table 1. Equivalent number of non-linear multiplications for a single SBox evaluation, for various block-ciphers.

Methods	SBox					
	AES	DES	PRESENT	SERPENT	CAMELLIA	CLEFIA
Parity-Split [CGP+12]	4	10	3	3	22	22
Roy-Vivek [RV13]	4	7	3	3	15	15,16
[CRV14]	4	4	2	2	10	10
Our Method	**2.8**	**3.1**	**1.5**	**1.5**	**7.8**	**7.8**

Practical Implementation. A practical implementation of our common shares technique is described in Sect. 7, for the n-shared evaluation of x^{254} in AES, on ATmega1284P (8-bit AVR microcontroller) and ARM Cortex M0 (32-bit CPU). We obtain that our technique is relatively practical: for a large number of shares, we get roughly a 20 % speed improvement compared to the Rivain-Prouff countermeasure (but only roughly 5 % compared to the quadratic evaluation technique in [GPS14]).

2   Security Definitions

Given a variable $x \in \mathbb{F}_{2^k}$ and an integer n, we say that the vector $(x_1, \ldots, x_n) \in (\mathbb{F}_{2^k})^n$ is an n-sharing of x if $x = \bigoplus_{i=1}^{n} x_i$. We recall the security definitions from [BBD+15a], which we make slightly more explicit. For simplicity we only provide the definitions for a simple gadget taking as input a single variable x (given by n shares x_i) and outputting a single variable y (given by n shares y_i). We provide the generalization to multiple inputs and outputs the full version of this paper [CGPZ16]. Given a vector $(x_i)_{1 \leqslant i \leqslant n}$, we denote by $x_{|I} := (x_i)_{i \in I}$ the sub-vector of shares x_i with $i \in I$.

Definition 1 (t-NI Security). *Let G be a gadget taking as input $(x_i)_{1 \leqslant i \leqslant n}$ and outputting $(y_i)_{1 \leqslant i \leqslant n}$. The gadget G is said t-NI secure if for any set of t_1 intermediate variables and any subset $\mathcal{O}$ of output indices, there exists a subset I of input indices with $|I| \leqslant t_1 + |\mathcal{O}|$, such that the t_1 intermediate variables and the output variables $y_{|\mathcal{O}}$ can be perfectly simulated from $x_{|I}$.*

Definition 2 (t-SNI Security). *Let G be a gadget taking as input $(x_i)_{1 \leqslant i \leqslant n}$ and outputting $(y_i)_{1 \leqslant i \leqslant n}$. The gadget G is said t-SNI secure if for any set of t_1 intermediate variables and any subset $\mathcal{O}$ of output indices such that $t_1 + |\mathcal{O}| \leqslant t$, there exists a subset I of input indices with $|I| \leqslant t_1$, such that the t_1 intermediate variables and the output variables $y_{|\mathcal{O}}$ can be perfectly simulated from $x_{|I}$.*

The t-NI security notion corresponds to the original security definition in the ISW probing model; it allows to prove the security of a full construction with $n \geqslant 2t + 1$ shares. The stronger t-SNI notion allows to prove the security of a full construction with $n \geqslant t + 1$ shares only [BBD+15a]. The difference is that in the stronger t-SNI notion, the size of the input shares subset I can only depend on the number of internal probes t_1, and must be independent of the number of output variables $|\mathcal{O}|$ that must be simulated (as long as the condition $t_1 + |\mathcal{O}| \leqslant t$ is satisfied). Intuitively, this provides an "isolation" between the output shares and the input shares of a given gadget, and for composed constructions this enables to easily prove that a full construction is t-SNI secure, based on the t-SNI security of its components.

3   The Rivain-Prouff Countermeasure

In this section we recall the Rivain-Prouff countermeasure [RP10] for securing AES against high-order attacks. It can be seen as an extension to $\mathbb{F}_{2^k}$ of the original ISW countermeasure [ISW03] described in $\mathbb{F}_2$. The Rivain-Prouff countermeasure is proved t-SNI secure in [BBD+15a]; therefore it can be used to protect a full block-cipher against t probes with $n \geqslant t + 1$ shares, instead of $n \geqslant 2t + 1$ shares in the original ISW probing model.

3.1   The Rivain-Prouff Multiplication

The Rivain-Prouff countermeasure is based on the SecMult operation below, which is similar to the ISW multiplication gadget but over $\mathbb{F}_{2^k}$ instead of $\mathbb{F}_2$. The SecMult algorithm enables to securely compute a product $c = a \cdot b$ over $\mathbb{F}_{2^k}$,

Algorithm 1. SecMult

Require: shares a_i satisfying $\bigoplus_{i=1}^{n} a_i = a$, shares b_i satisfying $\bigoplus_{i=1}^{n} b_i = b$
Ensure: shares c_i satisfying $\bigoplus_{i=1}^{n} c_i = a \cdot b$

1: **for** $i = 1$ to n **do**
2:     $c_i \leftarrow a_i \cdot b_i$
3: **end for**
4: **for** $i = 1$ to n **do**
5:     **for** $j = i + 1$ to n **do**
6:        $r \leftarrow \mathbb{F}_{2^k}$ $\triangleright$ referred by $r_{i,j}$
7:        $c_i \leftarrow c_i \oplus r$ $\triangleright$ referred by $c_{i,j}$
8:        $r \leftarrow (a_i \cdot b_j \oplus r) \oplus a_j \cdot b_i$ $\triangleright$ referred by $r_{j,i}$
9:        $c_j \leftarrow c_j \oplus r$ $\triangleright$ referred by $c_{j,i}$
10:     **end for**
11: **end for**
12: **return** $(c_1, \ldots, c_n)$

---

from an n-sharing of a and b, and outputs an n-sharing of c. Here we use the linear memory version from [Cor14], using similar notations as in [BBD+15a].

It is shown in [BBD+15a] that the SecMult algorithm is t-SNI secure with $n \geqslant t+1$ shares. For completeness we provide a proof of Lemma 1 in the full version of this paper [CGPZ16]; our proof is essentially the same as in [BBD+15a]. In the full version of this paper [CGPZ16], we also provide a slightly different, more modular proof in which we separate the computation of the matrix elements $v_{ij} = a_i \cdot b_j$ from the derivation of the output shares c_i.

Lemma 1 (t-SNI of SecMult). *Let $(a_i)_{1\leqslant i\leqslant n}$ and $(b_i)_{1\leqslant i\leqslant n}$ be the input shares of the SecMult operation, and let $(c_i)_{1\leqslant i<n}$ be the output shares. For any set of t_1 intermediate variables and any subset $|\mathcal{O}| \leqslant t_2$ of output shares such that $t_1 + t_2 < n$, there exist two subsets I and J of indices with $|I| \leqslant t_1$ and $|J| \leqslant t_1$, such that those t_1 intermediate variables as well as the output shares $c_{|\mathcal{O}}$ can be perfectly simulated from $a_{|I}$ and $b_{|J}$.*

3.2 Mask Refreshings

To obtain security against t probes with $n \geqslant t+1$ shares instead of $n \geqslant 2t+1$, the previous SecMult algorithm is usually not sufficient; one must also use a mask refreshing algorithm. The following RefreshMask operation is used in [BBD+15a] to get the t-SNI security of a full construction.

The following lemma is proven in [BBD+15a], showing the t-SNI security of RefreshMask. In the full version of this paper [CGPZ16] we also provide a modular proof, using the same approach as in Lemma 1; namely the above RefreshMask algorithm can be viewed as a SecMult with multiplication by 1, with shares $(1, 0, \ldots, 0)$; therefore the same proof technique applies.

Lemma 2 (t-SNI of RefreshMask). *Let $(a_i)_{1\leqslant i\leqslant n}$ be the input shares of the RefreshMask operation, and let $(c_i)_{1\leqslant i\leqslant n}$ be the output shares. For any set of*

Algorithm 2. RefreshMask

Input: $a_1, \ldots, a_n$
Output: $c_1, \ldots, c_n$ such that $\bigoplus_{i=1}^{n} c_i = \bigoplus_{i=1}^{n} a_i$
1: **For** $i = 1$ **to** n **do** $c_i \leftarrow a_i$
2: **for** $i = 1$ **to** n **do**
3:     **for** $j = i + 1$ **to** n **do**
4:         $r \leftarrow \{0, 1\}^k$
5:         $c_i \leftarrow c_i \oplus r$
6:         $c_j \leftarrow c_j \oplus r$
7:     **end for**
8: **end for**
9: **return** $c_1, \ldots, c_n$

---

t_1 *intermediate variables and any subset* $|\mathcal{O}| \leqslant t_2$ *of output shares such that* $t_1 + t_2 < n$, *there exists a subset* I *of indices with* $|I| \leqslant t_1$, *such that the* t_1 *intermediate variables as well as the output shares* $c_{|\mathcal{O}}$ *can be perfectly simulated from* $a_{|I}$.

3.3   Application to the Computation of x^{254} in $\mathbb{F}_{2^8}$

To compute $y = x^{254}$ over $\mathbb{F}_{2^8}$ with 4 multiplications, the following sequence of operation is used in [RP10], including two RefreshMask operations.

Algorithm 3. SecExp254

Input: shares $x_1, \ldots, x_n$ satisfying $x = \bigoplus_{i=1}^{n} x_i$
Output: shares $y_1, \ldots, y_n$ such that $\bigoplus_{i=1}^{n} y_i = x^{254}$
1: **For** $i = 1$ **to** n **do** $z_i \leftarrow x_i^2$ $\triangleright \bigoplus_i z_i = x^2$
2: $(z_i)_{1 \leqslant i \leqslant n} \leftarrow$ RefreshMask$((z_i)_{1 \leqslant i \leqslant n})$
3: $(y_i)_{1 \leqslant i \leqslant n} \leftarrow$ SecMult$((z_i)_{1 \leqslant i \leqslant n}, (x_i)_{1 \leqslant i \leqslant n})$ $\triangleright \bigoplus_i y_i = x^3$
4: **For** $i = 1$ **to** n **do** $w_i \leftarrow y_i^4$ $\triangleright \bigoplus_i w_i = x^{12}$
5: $(w_i)_{1 \leqslant i \leqslant n} \leftarrow$ RefreshMask$((w_i)_{1 \leqslant i \leqslant n})$
6: $(y_i)_{1 \leqslant i \leqslant n} \leftarrow$ SecMult$((y_i)_{1 \leqslant i \leqslant n}, (w_i)_{1 \leqslant i \leqslant n})$ $\triangleright \bigoplus_i y_i = x^{15}$
7: **For** $i = 1$ **to** n **do** $y_i \leftarrow y_i^{16}$ $\triangleright \bigoplus_i y_i = x^{240}$
8: $(y_i)_{1 \leqslant i \leqslant n} \leftarrow$ SecMult$((y_i)_{1 \leqslant i \leqslant n}, (w_i)_{1 \leqslant i \leqslant n})$ $\triangleright \bigoplus_i y_i = x^{252}$
9: $(y_i)_{1 \leqslant i \leqslant n} \leftarrow$ SecMult$((y_i)_{1 \leqslant i \leqslant n}, (z_i)_{1 \leqslant i \leqslant n})$ $\triangleright \bigoplus_i y_i = x^{254}$
10: **return** $y_1, \ldots, y_n$

Using the two previous lemmas, one can prove the t-SNI security of Sec-Exp254; we refer to [BBD+15a] for the proof.

Lemma 3 (t-SNI of x^{254}). *Let* $(x_i)_{1 \leqslant i \leqslant n}$ *be the input shares of* ExpSec254, *and let* $(y_i)_{1 \leqslant i \leqslant n}$ *be the output shares. For any set of* t_1 *intermediate variables and any subset* $|\mathcal{O}| \leqslant t_2$ *of output shares such that* $t_1 + t_2 < n$, *there exists a subset* I *of indices with* $|I| \leqslant t_1$, *such that those* t_1 *intermediate variables as well as the output shares* $y_{|\mathcal{O}}$ *can be perfectly simulated from* $x_{|I}$.

As explained in [BBD+15a], since the SecExp254 operation has the t-SNI property, it can be used to secure a full AES against t probes with $n \geqslant t + 1$ shares.

4 Secure Computation of 2 Parallel Multiplications with Common Operand, and Application to AES

In this section we show a first efficiency improvement of the Rivain-Prouff countermeasure for AES recalled in the previous section. Namely, we show that when two finite-field multiplications $d \leftarrow c \cdot a$ and $e \leftarrow c \cdot b$ have the same operand c, we can save $n^2/2$ field multiplications in SecMult by making sure that the inputs a and b have half of their shares in common; we then show how to apply this technique to the evaluation of the AES SBox, by using an alternative evaluation circuit for x^{254}.

Arithmetic Circuit with Depth 3 for x^{254}. The original arithmetic circuit for computing $y = x^{254}$ over $\mathbb{F}_{2^8}$ from [RP10] and recalled in Sect. 3.3 has 4 multiplicative levels, with a total of 4 non-linear multiplications. Below we use an alternative circuit with only 3 multiplicative levels, still with 4 multiplications, as described in [GHS12]; see Fig. 1 for an illustration.

- Level 1: compute $x^3 = x \cdot x^2$ (1 mult) and then $x^{12} = (x^3)^4$.
- Level 2: compute $x^{14} = x^{12} \cdot x^2$ (1 mult) and $x^{15} = x^{12} \cdot x^3$ (1 mult), and then $x^{240} = (x^{15})^{16}$.
- Level 3: compute $x^{254} = x^{240} \cdot x^{14}$ (1 mult).

Multiplications with Common Shares. In the arithmetic circuit above, the multiplications $x^{14} \leftarrow x^{12} \cdot x^2$ and $x^{15} \leftarrow x^{12} \cdot x^3$ can be computed in parallel; moreover they have one operand x^{12} in common. More generally, assume that we must compute two multiplications with a common operand c:

$$d \leftarrow c \cdot a$$
$$e \leftarrow c \cdot b$$

The SecMult algorithm will compute the cross-products $c_i \cdot a_j$ and $c_i \cdot b_j$ for all $1 \leqslant i, j \leqslant n$. Now assume that half of the shares of a and b are the same, that is $a_j = b_j$ for all $1 \leqslant j \leqslant n/2$. In that case the products $c_i \cdot a_j$ for $1 \leqslant j \leqslant n/2$ have to be computed only once, and therefore when processing $e \leftarrow c \cdot b$, we only have to compute $n^2/2$ multiplications instead of n^2; see Fig. 2 for an illustration. For an arithmetic circuit with 4 multiplications as above, this saves the equivalent of 0.5 multiplication.

4.1 The CommonShares Algorithm

The CommonShares algorithm below ensures that the output shares a'_i and b'_i corresponding to a and b are the same on the first half, that is $a'_i = b'_i$ for all $1 \leqslant i \leqslant n/2$. In the rest of the paper, for simplicity we assume that n is even.

Algorithm 4. CommonShares

Require: shares a_i satisfying $\bigoplus_{i=1}^n a_i = a$, shares b_i satisfying $\bigoplus_{i=1}^n b_i = b$
Ensure: shares a_i' and b_i' satisfying $\bigoplus_{i=1}^n a_i' = a$ and $\bigoplus_{i=1}^n b_i' = b$, with $a_i' = b_i'$ for all $1 \leqslant i \leqslant n/2$
1: **for** $i = 1$ **to** $n/2$ **do**
2:     $r_i \xleftarrow{\$} \mathbb{F}_{2^k}$
3:     $a_i' \leftarrow r_i, \ a_{n/2+i}' \leftarrow (a_{n/2+i} \oplus r_i) \oplus a_i$ $\triangleright \ a_i' \oplus a_{n/2+i}' = a_i \oplus a_{n/2+i}$
4:     $b_i' \leftarrow r_i, \ b_{n/2+i}' \leftarrow (b_{n/2+i} \oplus r_i) \oplus b_i$ $\triangleright \ b_i' \oplus b_{n/2+i}' = b_i \oplus b_{n/2+i}$
5: **end for**
6: **return** $(a_i')_{1 \leqslant i \leqslant n}$ and $(b_i')_{1 \leqslant i \leqslant n}$

It is easy to see that we still get as output an n-sharing of the same variables a and b, since for each $1 \leqslant i \leqslant n/2$ we have $a_i' \oplus a_{n/2+i}' = a_i \oplus a_{n/2+i}$, and similarly for b. As explained previously, we cannot have more than $n/2$ shares in common between a and b, since otherwise there would be a straightforward attack with fewer than n probes: namely if $a_i = b_i$ for all $1 \leqslant i \leqslant k$, then we can probe the $2(n-k)$ remaining shares a_i and b_i for $k+1 \leqslant i \leqslant n$; if $k > n/2$ this gives strictly less than n shares, whose xor gives the secret variable $a \oplus b$. Hence having half of the shares in common is optimal.

The following Lemma shows the security of the CommonShares algorithm; as will be shown later, for this algorithm we only need the weaker t-NI security property (instead of t-SNI).

Lemma 4 (t-NI of CommonShares). *Let $(a_i)_{1 \leqslant i \leqslant n}$ and $(b_i)_{1 \leqslant i \leqslant n}$ be the input shares of the algorithm CommonShares, and let $(a_i')_{1 \leqslant i \leqslant n}$ and $(b_i')_{1 \leqslant i \leqslant n}$ be the output shares. For any set of t_1 intermediate variables and any subsets of indices $I, J \subset [1,n]$, there exists a subset $S \subset [1,n]$ with $|S| \leqslant |I| + |J| + t_1$, such that those t_1 variables as well as the output shares $a_{|I}'$ and $b_{|J}'$ can be perfectly simulated from $a_{|S}$ and $b_{|S}$.*

Proof. The proof intuition is as follows. If for a given i with $1 \leqslant i \leqslant n/2$ the adversary requests only one of the variables $r_i, a_{n/2+i} \oplus r_i, b_{n/2+i} \oplus r_i, a_{n/2+i}'$ or $b_{n/2+i}'$, then such variable can be perfectly simulated without knowing any of the input shares $a_i, b_i, a_{n/2+i}$ and $b_{n/2+i}$, thanks to the mask r_i. On the other hand, if two such variables (or more) are requested, then we can provide a perfect simulation from the 4 previous input shares, whose knowledge is obtained by adding the two indices i and $n/2 + i$ in S. Therefore we never add more than one index in S per probe (or per output index in I or J), which implies that the size of the subset S of input shares is upper-bounded by $|I| + |J| + t_1$, as required.[3]

---

[3] Note that the proof would not work without the masks r_i; namely with $r_i = 0$ we would need to know both a_i and $a_{n/2+i}$ to simulate $a_{n/2+i}'$; hence with t probes we would need at least $n \geqslant 2t + 1$ shares, which would make CommonShares useless.

More precisely, we describe hereafter the construction of the set $\mathcal{S} \subset [1, n]$ of input shares, initially empty. For every probed input variable a_i and b_i (for any i), we add i to $\mathcal{S}$. For all $1 \leqslant i \leqslant n/2$, we let t_i be the number of probed variables among $a_{n/2+i} \oplus r_i$ and $b_{n/2+i} \oplus r_i$. We let:

$$\lambda_i := t_i + |\{i, n/2 + i\} \cap I| + |\{i, n/2 + i\} \cap J|,$$

We then add $\{i, n/2 + i\}$ to $\mathcal{S}$ if $\lambda_i \geqslant 2$. This terminates the construction of $\mathcal{S}$. By construction of $\mathcal{S}$, we must have $|\mathcal{S}| \leqslant |I| + |J| + t$ as required.

We now show that the output shares $a'_{|I}$ and $b'_{|J}$ and the t_1 intermediate variables of Algorithm CommonShares can be perfectly simulated from $a_{|\mathcal{S}}$ and $b_{|\mathcal{S}}$. This is clear for the probed input variables a_i and b_i. For all $1 \leqslant i \leqslant n/2$, we distinguish two cases. If $\lambda_i \geqslant 2$, then $\{i, n/2+i\} \in \mathcal{S}$, so we can let $r_i \leftarrow \mathbb{F}_{2^k}$ as in the real algorithm and simulate all output and intermediate variables from the knowledge of a_i, $a_{n/2+i}$, b_i and $b_{n/2+i}$. If $\lambda_i = 1$, then if $t_i = 0$, then only a single output variable among a'_i, b'_i, $a'_{n/2+i}$ and $b'_{n/2+i}$ must be simulated. Since each of those variables is masked by r_i, we can simulate this single output variable by generating a random value in $\mathbb{F}_{2^k}$. Similarly, if $t_i = 1$, then only one of the two intermediate variables among $a_{n/2+i} \oplus r_i$ and $b_{n/2+i} \oplus r_i$ is probed (while no output variable must be simulated), and therefore we can also simulate such variable by generating a random value in $\mathbb{F}_{2^k}$. This terminates the proof of Lemma 4.   □

4.2   The CommonMult Algorithm

To perform the two multiplications with the same operand $d \leftarrow c \cdot a$ and $e \leftarrow c \cdot b$, instead of doing two independent SecMult, we define the following CommonMult algorithm below.

Algorithm 5. CommonMult

Input: shares satisfying $c = \bigoplus_{i=1}^{n} c_i$, $a = \bigoplus_{i=1}^{n} a_i$ and $b = \bigoplus_{i=1}^{n} b_i$.
Output: d_i such that $\bigoplus_{i=1}^{n} d_i = c \cdot a$, and e_i such that $\bigoplus_{i=1}^{n} e_i = c \cdot b$
  1: $(a'_i)_{1 \leqslant i \leqslant n}, (b'_i)_{1 \leqslant i \leqslant n} \leftarrow$ CommonShares$((a_i)_{1 \leqslant i \leqslant n}, (b_i)_{1 \leqslant i \leqslant n})$
  2: $(d_i)_{1 \leqslant i \leqslant n} \leftarrow$ SecMult$((c_i)_{1 \leqslant i \leqslant n}, (a'_i)_{1 \leqslant i \leqslant n})$
  3: $(e_i)_{1 \leqslant i \leqslant n} \leftarrow$ SecMult$((c_i)_{1 \leqslant i \leqslant n}, (b'_i)_{1 \leqslant i \leqslant n})$
  4: **return** $(d_i)_{1 \leqslant i \leqslant n}$ and $(e_i)_{1 \leqslant i \leqslant n}$.

The algorithm first calls the previous CommonShares subroutine, to ensure that half of the shares of a and b are the same. It then applies the previous SecMult algorithm twice to securely compute the two multiplications. Then the multiplications $c_i \cdot a_j$ for $1 \leqslant j \leqslant n/2$ performed in the first SecMult can be re-used in the second SecMult, so this saves $n^2/2$ multiplications. More precisely, for the SecMult computation performed at Line 3, we don't have to compute again the products $c_i \cdot b'_j$ for $1 \leqslant j \leqslant n/2$, since those products have already been computed at Line 2 with $c_i \cdot a'_j$, since $a'_j = b'_j$ for all $1 \leqslant j \leqslant n/2$. However reusing at Line 3 the products already computed at Line 2 requires to store $\mathcal{O}(n^2)$ values. In the full version of this paper [CGPZ16] we describe a different version of the CommonMult algorithm above, where the matrix elements $c_i \cdot a_j$ are computed on the fly and then used in both SecMult, with memory complexity $\mathcal{O}(n)$ instead of $\mathcal{O}(n^2)$.

The following Lemma shows that the CommonMult algorithm is t-SNI secure in the ISW model, with $n \geqslant t+1$ shares. We provide the proof in the full version of this paper [CGPZ16].

Lemma 5 (t-SNI of CommonMult). *Let $(a_i)_{1 \leqslant i \leqslant n}$, $(b_i)_{1 \leqslant i \leqslant n}$ and $(c_i)_{1 \leqslant i \leqslant n}$ be the input shares of the CommonMult operation, and let $(d_i)_{1 \leqslant i \leqslant n}$ and $(e_i)_{1 \leqslant i \leqslant n}$ be the output shares. For any set of t_1 intermediate variables and any subsets $|\mathcal{O}_1| \leqslant t_2$ and $|\mathcal{O}_2| \leqslant t_2$ of output shares such that $t_1 + t_2 < n$, there exist two subsets I and J of indices such that $|I| \leqslant t_1$ and $|J| \leqslant t_1$, and those t_1 intermediate variables as well as the output shares $d_{|\mathcal{O}_1}$ and $e_{|\mathcal{O}_2}$ can be perfectly simulated from $a_{|J}$, $b_{|J}$ and $c_{|I}$.*

4.3   Application to AES SBoxes

We are now ready to describe the full computation of $y = x^{254}$ based on the CommonShares algorithm; the algorithm SecExp254' is described below; it is a variant of Algorithm 3.

Algorithm 6. SecExp254'

Input: shares $x_1, \ldots, x_n$ satisfying $x = \bigoplus_{i=1}^{n} x_i$
Output: shares $y_1, \ldots, y_n$ such that $\bigoplus_{i=1}^{n} y_i = x^{254}$
1: **For** $i = 1$ to n **do** $z_i \leftarrow x_i^2$ $\triangleright \bigoplus_i z_i = x^2$
2: $(x_i)_{1 \leqslant i \leqslant n} \leftarrow$ RefreshMask$((x_i)_{1 \leqslant i \leqslant n})$
3: $(y_i)_{1 \leqslant i \leqslant n} \leftarrow$ SecMult$((z_i)_{1 \leqslant i \leqslant n}, (x_i)_{1 \leqslant i \leqslant n})$ $\triangleright \bigoplus_i y_i = x^3$
4: **For** $i = 1$ to n **do** $w_i \leftarrow y_i^4$ $\triangleright \bigoplus_i w_i = x^{12}$
5: $(w_i)_{1 \leqslant i \leqslant n} \leftarrow$ RefreshMask$((w_i)_{1 \leqslant i \leqslant n})$
6: $(z_i)_{1 \leqslant i \leqslant n}, (y_i)_{1 \leqslant i \leqslant n} \leftarrow$ CommonMult$((w_i)_{1 \leqslant i \leqslant n}, (z_i)_{1 \leqslant i \leqslant n}, (y_i)_{1 \leqslant i \leqslant n})$ $\triangleright$
$\bigoplus_i z_i = x^{14}, \quad \bigoplus_i y_i = x^{15}$
7: **For** $i = 1$ to n **do** $y_i \leftarrow y_i^{16}$ $\triangleright \bigoplus_i y_i = x^{240}$
8: $(y_i)_{1 \leqslant i \leqslant n} \leftarrow$ SecMult$((y_i)_{1 \leqslant i \leqslant n}, (z_i)_{1 \leqslant i \leqslant n})$ $\triangleright \bigoplus_i y_i = x^{254}$
9: **return** $y_1, \ldots, y_n$

The following Lemma proves the t-SNI security of our new algorithm; therefore our new algorithm achieves exactly the same security level as Algorithm 3. That is, it can be used in the computation of a full block-cipher, with $n \geqslant t+1$ shares against t probes. We provide the proof in the full version of this paper [CGPZ16].

Lemma 6 (t-SNI of x^{254}). *Let $(x_i)_{1 \leqslant i \leqslant n}$ be the input shares of the x^{254} operation, and let $(y_i)_{1 \leqslant i \leqslant n}$ be the output shares. For any set of t_1 intermediate* *variables and any subset* $|\mathcal{O}| \leqslant t_2$ *of output shares such that* $t_1 + t_2 < n$, *there exists a subset* I *of indices with* $|I| \leqslant t_1$, *such that those* t_1 *intermediate variables as well as the output shares* $y_{|\mathcal{O}}$ *can be perfectly simulated from* $x_{|I}$.

Finally, we summarize in Table 2 the complexities of the above algorithms. Table 2 shows that our new algorithm for x^{254} saves $n^2/2$ multiplications, with the same security level as in the original algorithm.

Table 2. Complexity of CommonMult and SecExp254'; for simplicity we omit the $\mathcal{O}(n)$ terms.

	# add	# mult	# rand
SecMult (Algorithm 1)	$2n^2$	n^2	$n^2/2$
RefreshMask (Algorithm 2)	n^2	-	$n^2/2$
SecMult × 2	$4n^2$	$2n^2$	n^2
CommonMult (Algorithm 5)	$4n^2$	$3n^2/2$	n^2
SecExp254 (Algorithm 3)	$10n^2$	$4n^2$	$3n^2$
SecExp254' (Algorithm 6)	$10n^2$	$7n^2/2$	$3n^2$

5   Parallel Multiplications with Common Shares

In the previous section, we have shown that by using a different arithmetic circuit for x^{254}, two multiplications in $\mathbb{F}_{2^8}$ could be processed in parallel, moreover with a common operand, and then by using half common shares we could save the equivalent of $1/2$ multiplication out of 4 in the evaluation of an AES SBox.

In the full version of this paper [CGPZ16], we consider the case of parallel multiplications that do not necessarily share an operand. Previously we have focused on a single evaluation of an AES SBox, but in AES the 16 SBoxes can actually be processed in parallel, and therefore each of the 4 multiplications in x^{254} can be processed in parallel. As opposed to the previous case those multiplications do not share any operand, but we show that by using a generalization of the CommonShares algorithm between m operands instead of 2, for every multiplication one can still save the equivalent of roughly $1/4$ multiplication.

6   Parallel Computation of Quadratic Functions

In [CPRR15], the authors propose a generalization of an idea originally published in [CPRR13] to securely process any function h of algebraic degree[4] 2, with

---

[4] The *algebraic degree* of a function h is the integer value $\max_{a_i \neq 0}(\mathrm{HW}(i))$ where the a_i's are the coefficients of the polynomial representation of h and where $\mathrm{HW}(i)$ denotes the Hamming weight of i.

application to the secure evaluation of SBoxes. The algorithm is based on the following equation:

$$h\left(\sum_{i=1}^{n} x_i\right) = \sum_{1\leqslant i < j \leqslant n} \left(h(x_i + x_j + s_{ij}) + h(x_i + s_{ij}) + h(x_j + s_{ij}) + h(s_{ij})\right)$$
$$+ \sum_{i=1}^{n} h(x_i) + ((n+1) \bmod 2) \cdot h(0) \qquad (2)$$

which holds for any $s_{ij} \in \mathbb{F}_{2^k}$. From the above equation, any function h of algebraic degree 2 can be securely processed with n-th order security.

In the full version of this paper [CGPZ16], we recall the algorithm from [CPRR15] for the secure evaluation of the quadratic function $h(x)$, and its application to AES. We then show how to use our common shares technique for we provide for m parallel evaluations of $h(x)$.

7 Implementation

We have done a practical implementation of our algorithms for the AES SBox. More precisely we have implemented the n-shared evaluation of x^{254} in four different ways:

- RP10: using the Rivain-Prouff algorithm, as described in Algorithm 3;
- CM: using our common shares technique, as described in Algorithm 6;
- GPS14: using quadratic functions, as described in the full version of this paper [CGPZ16];
- GPS14CS: using quadratic functions and common shares, as explained in the full version of this paper [CGPZ16];

Table 3. Performances comparison of the RP10, CM, GPS14 and GPS14CS algorithms, on the ATmega and ARM platforms.

	8 shares				16 shares			
	RP10	CM	GPS14	GPS14CS	RP10	CM	GPS14	GPS14CS
ATmega	20360	18244	11076	12447	70966	57644	39554	40086
ARM	20333	18156	13796	13156	77264	65556	54133	50560

	32 shares				Ratio for 8,16 and 32 shares	
	RP10	CM	GPS14	GPS14CS	CM/RP10	GPS14CS/GPS14
ATmega	268.10^3	209.10^3	152.10^3	147.10^3	0.9, 0.81, 0.78	1.1, 1, 0.97
ARM	303.10^3	251.10^3	215.10^3	200.10^3	0.89, 0.85, 0.83	0.95, 0.93, 0.93

For portability, the code is written in C, except the field multiplication in $\mathbb{F}_{2^8}$ which is written in assembly for ATmega1284P (8-bit AVR microcontroller) and for ARM Cortex M0 (32-bit CPU). Performance is evaluated using simulators (AVR Studio for ATmega, Keil uVision for ARM). We assume that the random generation of one byte takes 1 cycle. This assumption is reasonable: there are at least several dozens of cycles between two 1-byte random number requests; on chips embedding hardware RNG, this is often enough to get a random value by a single memory access, without waiting. We give the average number of cycles to compute one AES SBox among 16 SBoxes in Table 3.

Those implementation results show that our common shares technique is relatively practical: for a large number of shares, we get roughly a 20 % speed improvement compared to the Rivain-Prouff countermeasure (but only roughly 5 % compared to the quadratic evaluation technique in [GPS14]).

Acknowledgments. We wish to thank Sonia Belaïd who applied the EasyCrypt verification tool [BBD+15b] on our AES SBox algorithm with common shares, at order $n = 6$.

References

[BBD+15a] Barthe, G., Belaïd, S., Dupressoir, F., Fouque, P.-A., Grégoire, B.: Compositional verification of higher-order masking: application to a verifying masking compiler. Cryptology ePrint Archive, Report 2015/506 (2015). http://eprint.iacr.org/

[BBD+15b] Barthe, G., Belaïd, S., Dupressoir, F., Fouque, P.-A., Grégoire, B., Strub, P.-Y.: Verified proofs of higher-order masking. In: Oswald, E., Fischlin, M. (eds.) EUROCRYPT 2015. LNCS, vol. 9056, pp. 457–485. Springer, Heidelberg (2015)

[BGN+14] Bilgin, B., Gierlichs, B., Nikova, S., Nikov, V., Rijmen, V.: Higher-order threshold implementations. In: Sarkar, P., Iwata, T. (eds.) ASIACRYPT 2014, Part II. LNCS, vol. 8874, pp. 326–343. Springer, Heidelberg (2014)

[Bla79] Blakely, G.R.: Safeguarding cryptographic keys. In: National Computer Conference, vol. 48, pp. 313–317. AFIPS Press, New York (1979)

[CGP+12] Carlet, C., Goubin, L., Prouff, E., Quisquater, M., Rivain, M.: Higher-order masking schemes for S-Boxes. In: Canteaut, A. (ed.) FSE 2012. LNCS, vol. 7549, pp. 366–384. Springer, Heidelberg (2012)

[CGPZ16] Coron, J.-S., Greuet, A., Prouff, E., Zeitoun, R.: Faster evaluation of Sboxes via common shares. Cryptology ePrint Archive, Report 2016/572 (2016). http://eprint.iacr.org/. Full version of this paper

[CJRR99] Chari, S., Jutla, C.S., Rao, J.R., Rohatgi, P.: Towards sound approaches to counteract power-analysis attacks. In: Wiener, M. (ed.) CRYPTO 1999. LNCS, vol. 1666, pp. 398–412. Springer, Heidelberg (1999)

[Cor14] Coron, J.-S.: Higher order masking of look-up tables. In: Nguyen, P.Q., Oswald, E. (eds.) EUROCRYPT 2014. LNCS, vol. 8441, pp. 441–458. Springer, Heidelberg (2014)

[CPRR13] Coron, J.-S., Prouff, E., Rivain, M., Roche, T.: Higher-order side channel security and mask refreshing. In: Moriai, S. (ed.) FSE 2013. LNCS, vol. 8424, pp. 410–424. Springer, Heidelberg (2014)

[CPRR15] Carlet, C., Prouff, E., Rivain, M., Roche, T.: Algebraic decomposition for probing security. In: Gennaro, R., Robshaw, M. (eds.) CRYPTO 2015, Part I. LNCS, vol. 9215, pp. 742–763. Springer, Heidelberg (2015)

[CRV14] Coron, J.-S., Roy, A., Vivek, S.: Fast evaluation of polynomials over binary finite fields and application to side-channel countermeasures. In: Batina, L., Robshaw, M. (eds.) CHES 2014. LNCS, vol. 8731, pp. 170–187. Springer, Heidelberg (2014)

[DDF14] Duc, A., Dziembowski, S., Faust, S.: Unifying leakage models: from probing attacks to noisy leakage. In: Nguyen, P.Q., Oswald, E. (eds.) EURO-CRYPT 2014. LNCS, vol. 8441, pp. 423–440. Springer, Heidelberg (2014)

[GHS12] Gentry, C., Halevi, S., Smart, N.P.: Homomorphic evaluation of the AES circuit. In: Safavi-Naini, R., Canetti, R. (eds.) CRYPTO 2012. LNCS, vol. 7417, pp. 850–867. Springer, Heidelberg (2012)

[GPS14] Grosso, V., Prouff, E., Standaert, F.-X.: Efficient masked S-Boxes processing – a step forward –. In: Pointcheval, D., Vergnaud, D. (eds.) AFRICACRYPT. LNCS, vol. 8469, pp. 251–266. Springer, Heidelberg (2014)

[ISW03] Ishai, Y., Sahai, A., Wagner, D.: Private circuits: securing hardware against probing attacks. In: Boneh, D. (ed.) CRYPTO 2003. LNCS, vol. 2729, pp. 463–481. Springer, Heidelberg (2003)

[KJJ99] Kocher, P.C., Jaffe, J., Jun, B.: Differential power analysis. In: Wiener, M. (ed.) CRYPTO 1999. LNCS, vol. 1666, pp. 388–397. Springer, Heidelberg (1999)

[MS06] Mangard, S., Schramm, K.: Pinpointing the side-channel leakage of masked AES hardware implementations. In: Goubin, L., Matsui, M. (eds.) CHES 2006. LNCS, vol. 4249, pp. 76–90. Springer, Heidelberg (2006)

[NRS11] Nikova, S., Rijmen, V., Schläffer, M.: Secure hardware implementation of nonlinear functions in the presence of glitches. J. Cryptology 24(2), 292–321 (2011)

[PR11] Prouff, E., Roche, T.: Higher-order glitches free implementation of the AES using secure multi-party computation protocols. In: Preneel, B., Takagi, T. (eds.) CHES 2011. LNCS, vol. 6917, pp. 63–78. Springer, Heidelberg (2011)

[PR13] Prouff, E., Rivain, M.: Masking against side-channel attacks: a formal security proof. In: Johansson, T., Nguyen, P.Q. (eds.) EUROCRYPT 2013. LNCS, vol. 7881, pp. 142–159. Springer, Heidelberg (2013)

[RBN+15] Reparaz, O., Bilgin, B., Nikova, S., Gierlichs, B., Verbauwhede, I.: Consolidating masking schemes. In: Gennaro, R., Robshaw, M. (eds.) CRYPTO 2015, Part I. LNCS, vol. 9215, pp. 764–783. Springer, Heidelberg (2015)

[RP10] Rivain, M., Prouff, E.: Provably secure higher-order masking of AES. In: Mangard, S., Standaert, F.-X. (eds.) CHES 2010. LNCS, vol. 6225, pp. 413–427. Springer, Heidelberg (2010)

[RV13] Roy, A., Vivek, S.: Analysis and improvement of the generic higher-order masking scheme of FSE 2012. In: Bertoni, G., Coron, J.-S. (eds.) CHES 2013. LNCS, vol. 8086, pp. 417–434. Springer, Heidelberg (2013)

[Sha79] Shamir, A.: How to share a secret. Commun. ACM 22(11), 612–613 (1979)

Hardware Implementations

FourQ on FPGA: New Hardware Speed Records for Elliptic Curve Cryptography over Large Prime Characteristic Fields

Kimmo Järvinen[1], Andrea Miele[2], Reza Azarderakhsh[3], and Patrick Longa[4(✉)]

[1] Department of Computer Science, Aalto University, Espoo, Finland
kimmo.jarvinen@aalto.fi
[2] Intel Corporation, Santa Clara, USA
andrea.miele@intel.com
[3] Department of Computer Engineering,
Rochester Institute of Technology, Rochester, USA
rxaeec@rit.edu
[4] Microsoft Research, Redmond, USA
plonga@microsoft.com

Abstract. We present fast and compact implementations of FourQ (ASIACRYPT 2015) on field-programmable gate arrays (FPGAs), and demonstrate, for the first time, the high efficiency of this new elliptic curve on reconfigurable hardware. By adapting FourQ's algorithms to hardware, we design FPGA-tailored architectures that are significantly faster than any other ECC alternative over large prime characteristic fields. For example, we show that our single-core and multi-core implementations can compute at a rate of 6389 and 64730 scalar multiplications per second, respectively, on a Xilinx Zynq-7020 FPGA, which represent factor-2.5 and 2 speedups in comparison with the corresponding variants of the fastest Curve25519 implementation on the same device. These results show the potential of deploying FourQ on hardware for high-performance and embedded security applications. All the presented implementations exhibit regular, constant-time execution, protecting against timing and simple side-channel attacks.

Keywords: Elliptic curves · FourQ · FPGA · Efficient hardware implementation · Constant-time · Simple side-channel attacks

1 Introduction

With the growing deployment of elliptic curve cryptography (ECC) [15,24] in place of traditional cryptosystems such as RSA, compact, high-performance ECC-based implementations have become crucial for embedded systems and hardware applications. In this setting, field-programmable gate arrays (FPGAs)

A. Miele—This work was performed while the second author was a post-doctoral researcher at EPFL, Lausanne, Switzerland.

B. Gierlichs and A.Y. Poschmann (Eds.): CHES 2016, LNCS 9813, pp. 517–537, 2016.
DOI: 10.1007/978-3-662-53140-2_25

offer an attractive option in comparison to classical application-specific integrated circuits (ASICs), thanks to their great flexibility and faster prototyping at reduced development costs. Examples of efficient ECC implementations on FPGAs are Güneysu and Paar's implementations of the standardized NIST curves over prime fields [11] and Sasdrich and Güneysu's implementations of Curve25519 [28,29]. There is also a plethora of FPGA implementations based on binary curves, which are particularly attractive for hardware platforms (see, e.g., [1,2,13,14,18,26,31]). Prime fields are by far the preferred option in software implementations mainly because efficient integer arithmetic is readily supported by instruction sets of processors. Therefore, efficient hardware implementations of ECC over large prime characteristic fields are needed to provide compatibility with software. In this work, we focus on elliptic curves defined over large prime characteristic fields.

At ASIACRYPT 2015, Costello and Longa [6] proposed a new elliptic curve called FourQ, which provides approximately 128 bits of security and supports highly-efficient scalar multiplications by uniquely combining a four-dimensional decomposition [8] with the fastest twisted Edwards explicit formulas [12] and the efficient Mersenne prime $p = 2^{127} - 1$. In particular, by performing experiments on a large variety of software platforms, they showed that, when computing a standard variable-base scalar multiplication, FourQ is more than 5 times faster than the standardized NIST P-256 curve and between 2 and 3 times faster than the popular Curve25519 [5].

In this work, we propose an efficient architecture for computing scalar multiplications using FourQ on FPGAs. Our architecture, which leverages the power of the embedded multipliers found in modern FPGA's DSP blocks (similarly to many prior works [11,19–23,27–29]), supports all the necessary operations to perform FourQ's 4-way multi-scalar multiplication, including point validation, scalar decomposition and recoding, cofactor clearing (if required by a given protocol) and the final point conversion to affine coordinates. Based on this architecture, we designed two *high-speed* variants: a single-core architecture intended for constrained, low latency applications, and a multi-core architecture intended for high-throughput applications. Moreover, we also explore the possibility of avoiding the use of FourQ's endormorphisms and present an implementation variant based on the Montgomery ladder [25], which might be suitable for constrained environments. All the proposed architectures exhibit a fully regular, constant-time execution, which provides protection against timing and simple side-channel attacks (SSCA) [16,17]. To our knowledge, these are the first implementations of FourQ on an FPGA in the open literature.

When compared to the most efficient FPGA implementations in the literature, our implementations show a significant increase in performance. For example, in comparison to the state-of-the-art FPGA implementation of Curve25519 by Sasdrich and Güneysu [28,29], our single-core architecture is approximately 2.5 times faster in terms of computing time ($157\,\mu s$ versus $397\,\mu s$), and our multi-core architecture is capable of computing (at full capacity) 2 times as many scalar multiplications per second as their multi-core variant (64730 scalar multiplications per second versus 32304 scalar multiplications per second). Even when comparing the case without endomorphisms, our FourQ-based FPGA implementation is faster: the laddered variant is about 1.3 times faster than Curve25519 in terms of computing time. All these results were obtained on the same Xilinx Zynq-7020 FPGA model used by [29].

The paper is organized as follows. In Sect. 2, the relevant mathematical background and general architectural details of the proposed design are provided. In Sect. 3, the field arithmetic unit (called "the core") is presented. In Sect. 4, we describe the scalar unit consisting of the decomposition and recoding units. In Sect. 5, *three* architecture variants are detailed: single-core, multi-core and the Montgomery ladder implementation. We present the performance analysis and carry out a detailed comparison with relevant work in Sect. 6. Finally, we conclude the paper and give directions for future work in Sect. 7.

2   Preliminaries: FourQ

FourQ is a high-performance elliptic curve recently proposed by Costello and Longa [6]. Given the quadratic extension field $\mathbb{F}_{p^2} = \mathbb{F}_p(i)$ with $p = 2^{127} - 1$ and $i^2 = -1$, FourQ is defined as the complete twisted Edwards [4] curve given by

$$\mathcal{E}/\mathbb{F}_{p^2} : \, - x^2 + y^2 = 1 + dx^2 y^2, \tag{1}$$

where $d := 125317048443780598345676279555970305165 \cdot i + 4205857648805777768770$.

The set of $\mathbb{F}_{p^2}$-rational points lying on Eq. (1), which includes the neutral point $\mathcal{O}_{\mathcal{E}} = (0, 1)$, forms an additive abelian group. The cardinality of this group is given by $\#\mathcal{E}(\mathbb{F}_{p^2}) = 392 \cdot \xi$, where ξ is a 246-bit prime, and thus, the group $\mathcal{E}(\mathbb{F}_{p^2})[\xi]$ can be used in cryptographic systems.

The fastest set of explicit formulas for the addition law on $\mathcal{E}$ are due to Hisil et al. [12] using the so-called *extended twisted Edwards coordinates*: any tuple $(X : Y : Z : T)$ with $Z \neq 0$ and $T = XY/Z$ represents a projective point corresponding to an affine point $(x, y) = (X/Z, Y/Z)$. Since d is non-square over $\mathbb{F}_{p^2}$, this set of formulas is also *complete* on $\mathcal{E}$, i.e., they work without exceptions for any point in $\mathcal{E}(\mathbb{F}_{p^2})$.

Since FourQ is a degree-2 $\mathbb{Q}$-curve with complex multiplication [10,30], it comes equipped with two efficiently computable endomorphisms, namely, ψ and ϕ. In [6], it is shown that these two endomorphisms enable a four-dimensional decomposition $m \mapsto (a_1, a_2, a_3, a_4) \in \mathbb{Z}^4$ for any integer $m \in [0, 2^{256} - 1]$ such that $0 \leq a_i < 2^{64}$ for $i = 1, 2, 3, 4$ (which is optimal in the context of multi-scalar multiplication) and such that a_1 is odd (which facilitates efficient, side-channel protected scalar multiplications); see [6, Proposition 5] for details about FourQ's decomposition procedure. This in turn induces a four-dimensional scalar multiplication with the form

$$[m]P = [a_1]P + [a_2]\phi(P) + [a_3]\psi(P) + [a_4]\phi(\psi(P)),$$

for any point $P \in \mathcal{E}(\mathbb{F}_{p^2})[\xi]$.

2.1 Scalar Multiplication Execution

Assume that the decomposition procedure in [6, Proposition 5] is applied to a given input scalar m. To execute the 4-way multi-scalar multiplication with protection against timing and SSCA attacks, one can follow [6] and use the method proposed by Faz et al. [7]: the multi-scalars a_i are recoded to a representation $b_i = \sum_{i=0}^{64} b_i[j] \cdot 2^j$ with $b_i[j] \in \{-1, 0, 1\}$ for $i = 1, 2, 3, 4$, such that $b_1[j] \in \{-1, 1\}$ and $b_1[64] = 1$, and such that the recoded digits for a_2, a_3 and a_4 are "sign-aligned" with the corresponding digit from a_1, i.e., $b_i[j] \in \{0, b_1[j]\}$ for $i = 2, 3, 4$. It follows that this recoding produces exactly 65 "signed digit-columns", where a signed digit-column is defined as the value $d_j = b_1[j] + b_2[j] \cdot 2 + b_3[j] \cdot 2^2 + b_4[j] \cdot 2^3$ for $j = 0, ..., 64$. If one then precomputes the eight points $T[u] = P + u_0\phi(P) + u_1\psi(P) + u_2\phi(\psi(P))$ for $0 \le u < 8$, where $u = (u_2, u_1, u_0)_2$, scalar multiplication—scanning the digit-columns from left to right—consists of an initial point loading and a single loop of 64 iterations, where each iteration computes one doubling and one addition with the point from $T[\,]$ corresponding to the current digit-column. Given that digit-columns are signed, one needs to negate the precomputed point before addition in the case of a negative digit-column.

Next, we recap details about the coordinate system strategy used in [6]. Costello and Longa [6] utilize *four* different point representations for $(X : Y : Z : T)$: $\mathbf{R_1} : (X, Y, Z, T_a, T_b)$, such that $T = T_a \cdot T_b$, $\mathbf{R_2} : (X+Y, Y-X, 2Z, 2dT)$, $\mathbf{R_3} : (X+Y, Y-X, Z, T)$ and $\mathbf{R_4} : (X, Y, Z)$. In the main loop of scalar multiplication, point doublings are computed as $\mathbf{R_1} \leftarrow \mathbf{R_4}$ and point additions as $\mathbf{R_1} \leftarrow \mathbf{R_1} \times \mathbf{R_2}$, where precomputed points are stored using $\mathbf{R_2}$. Note that converting point addition results from $\mathbf{R_1}$ to $\mathbf{R_4}$ (as required by inputs to point doublings) is for free: one simply ignores coordinates T_a, T_b.

2.2 High-Level Design of the Proposed Architecture

Our core design follows the same methodology described above and computes Fourℚ's scalar multiplication as in [6, Algorithm 2]. However, there is a slight variation: since the negative of a precomputed point $(X + Y, Y - X, 2Z, 2dT)$ is given by $(Y - X, X + Y, 2Z, -2dT)$, we precompute the values $-2dT$ and store each precomputed point using the tuple $(X + Y, Y - X, 2Z, 2dT, -2dT)$. This representation is referred to as $\mathbf{R_5}$. During scalar multiplication, we simply read coordinates in the right order and assemble either $(X + Y, Y - X, 2Z, 2dT)$ (for positive digit-columns) or $(Y - X, X + Y, 2Z, -2dT)$ (for negative digit-columns). This approach completely eliminates the need for point negations during scalar multiplication at the cost of storing only 8 extra elements in $\mathbb{F}_{p^2}$. The slightly modified scalar multiplication algorithm is presented in Algorithm 1.

In Algorithm 2, we detail the conversion of the multi-scalars to digit-columns d_i. During a scalar multiplication, the 3-least significant bits of these digits (values "v_i") are used to select one out of eight points from the precomputed table. The top bit (values "s_i") is then used to select between the coordinate

---

Algorithm 1. FourQ's scalar multiplication on $\mathcal{E}(\mathbb{F}_{p^2})[\xi]$ (adapted from [6]).

Input: Point $P \in \mathcal{E}(\mathbb{F}_{p^2})[\xi]$ and integer scalar $m \in [0, 2^{256})$.
Output: $[m]P$.
   Compute endomorphisms:
  1: Compute $\phi(P)$, $\psi(P)$ and $\psi(\phi(P))$.
   Precompute lookup table:
  2: Compute $T[u] = P + [u_0]\phi(P) + [u_1]\psi(P) + [u_2]\psi(\phi(P))$ for $u = (u_2, u_1, u_0)_2$ in
     $0 \le u \le 7$. Write $T[u]$ in coordinates $(X + Y, Y - X, 2Z, 2dT, -2dT)$.
   Scalar decomposition and recoding:
  3: Decompose m into the multi-scalar (a_1, a_2, a_3, a_4) as in [6, Proposition 5].
  4: Recode (a_1, a_2, a_3, a_4) into $(d_{64}, \ldots, d_0) = (\overline{s_{64}v_{64}}, \ldots, \overline{s_0v_0})$ using Algorithm 2.
    Write $m_i = 1$ if $s_i = 1$ and $m_i = -1$ if $s_i = 0$ for $i = 0, \ldots, 63$.
   Main loop:
  5: $Q = T[v_{64}]$
  6: **for** $i = 63$ to 0 **do**
  7:    $Q = [2]Q$
  8:    $Q = Q + m_i \cdot T[v_i]$
  9: **return** Q

---

value $2dT$ (if the bit is 1) and $-2dT$ (if the bit is 0), as described above for a point using representation $\mathbf{R_5}$.

The structure of Algorithm 1 leads to a natural division of operations in our ECC processor. The processor consists of two main building blocks: (a) a scalar unit and (b) a field arithmetic unit. The former carries out the scalar decomposition and recoding (steps 3 and 4 in Algorithm 1), and the latter—referred simply as "the core"—is responsible for computing the endomorphisms, precomputation, and the main loop through a fixed series of operations over $\mathbb{F}_{p^2}$. We describe these units in detail in Sects. 3 and 4.

3   Field Arithmetic Unit

The field arithmetic unit ("the core") performs operations in $\mathbb{F}_{p^2}$. The architecture of the core is depicted in Fig. 1. It consists of datapath (see Sect. 3.1), control logic (see Sect. 3.2), and memory. The memory is a 256×127-bit simple dual-port RAM that is implemented using BlockRAM (36 Kb) resources from the FPGA device. We chose to have a 127-bit wide memory in order to minimize the overhead during memory reading and writing. This requires the use of 4 BlockRAMs which provide storage space for up to 128 $\mathbb{F}_{p^2}$ elements. As a result, storing the negative coordinate values $-2dT$ of the precomputed points as described in Sect. 2.2 comes essentially for free.

3.1   Datapath

The datapath computes operations in $\mathbb{F}_p$ and it thus operates on 127-bit operands. The datapath supports basic operations that allow the implementation of field

---

Algorithm 2. Fourℚ's multi-scalar recoding (adapted from [6]).

Input: Four positive integers $a_i = (0, a_i[63], \ldots, a_i[0])_2 \in \{0,1\}^{65}$ less than 2^{64} for $1 \leq i \leq 4$ and with a_1 odd.
Output: $(d_{64}, \ldots, d_0)$ with $0 \leq d_i < 16$.
1: $s_{64} = 1$
2: **for** $j = 0$ to 63 **do**
3:    $v_j = 0$
4:    $s_j = a_1[j+1]$
5:    **for** $i = 2$ to 4 **do**
6:       $v_j = v_j + (a_i[0] \ll (i-2))$
7:       $c = (a_1[j+1] \mid a_i[0]) \wedge a_1[j+1]$
8:       $a_i = (a_i \gg 1) + c$
9:    $v_{64} = a_2 + 2a_3 + 4a_4$
10: **return** $(d_{64}, \ldots, d_0) = (\overline{s_{64}v_{64}}, \ldots, \overline{s_0v_0})$.

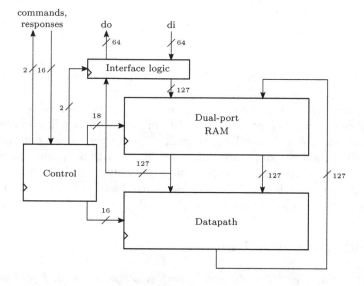

Fig. 1. Architectural diagram of the core.

multiplication, addition and subtraction. A field multiplication is performed (a) by computing a 127×127-bit integer multiplication, (b) by adding the lower and higher halves of the multiplication result to perform the first part of the reduction modulo $p = 2^{127} - 1$ and (c) by finalizing the reduction by adding the carry from the first addition. Addition and subtraction in $\mathbb{F}_p$ are computed (a) by adding/subtracting the operands and (b) by adding/subtracting the carry/borrow-bit in order to perform the modular reduction. The operations in $\mathbb{F}_{p^2}$ are implemented as a series of operations in $\mathbb{F}_p$ managed by the control logic; see Sect. 3.2. The datapath consists of two separate paths: (a) multiplier path and (b) adder/subtractor path. The datapath is shown in Fig. 2.

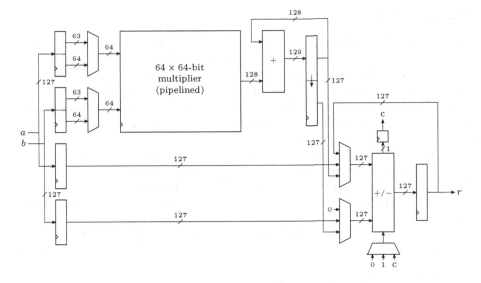

Fig. 2. The datapath for operations in $\mathbb{F}_p$.

The multiplier path is built around a pipelined 64×64-bit multiplier that is implemented using 16 hardwired multipliers (DSP blocks). The integer multiplications $a \times b$ are computed via the schoolbook algorithm. It requires four 64×64-bit partial multiplications $a_i \times b_j$ with $i, j \in \{0, 1\}$ such that $a = a_1 2^{64} + a_0$ and $b = b_1 2^{64} + b_0$. The partial multiplications are computed directly with the pipelined multiplier by selecting the operands from the input registers with two multiplexers. Results of the partial multiplications are accumulated into the upper half of a 256-bit register by using a 128-bit adder in the order $(i, j) = (0, 0), (0, 1), (1, 0), (1, 1)$. The register is shifted down by 64 bits after $(0, 0)$ and $(1, 0)$. The pipelined multiplier has *seven* pipeline stages (designed such that it matches the 128-bit adder's critical path delay).

The adder/subtractor path computes additions and subtractions as well as modular reductions over the integer multiplication results. It is built around a 127-bit adder/subtractor and multiplexers for selecting the inputs, i.e., operands and carry/borrow-bit. The value stored in the output register is the only output of the entire datapath.

The adder/subtractor path can be used for other operations while the multiplier path is performing a multiplication whenever reduction and read/write patterns of the multiplication permits it. This was achieved by including a separate set of input registers into the adder/subtractor path. In addition, the adder/subtractor path also allows accumulating the resulting value in its output register. All this allows computing most additions and subtractions required during scalar multiplication essentially for free.

3.2   Control Logic

The control logic controls the datapath and memory and, as consequence, implements all the hierarchical levels required by scalar multiplications on FourQ. The control logic consists of a program ROM that includes instructions for the datapath and memory addresses, a small finite state machine (FSM) that controls the read addresses of the program ROM, and a recoder for recoding the instructions in the program ROM to control signals for the datapath and memory.

Field operations. consist of multiple instructions that are issued by the control logic, as discussed in Sect. 3.1. Because of the pipelined multiplier, multiplications in $\mathbb{F}_p$ take several clock cycles (20 clock cycles including memory reads and writes). Fortunately, pipelining allows computing independent multiplications simultaneously and thus enables efficient operations over $\mathbb{F}_{p^2}$.

Let $a = (a_0, a_1), b = (b_0, b_1) \in \mathbb{F}_{p^2}$. Then, results (c_0, c_1) of operations in $\mathbb{F}_{p^2}$ are given by

$$
\begin{aligned}
a + b &= (a_0 + b_0, a_1 + b_1) \\
a - b &= (a_0 - b_0, a_1 - b_1) \\
a \times b &= (a_0 \cdot b_0 - a_1 \cdot b_1, (a_0 + a_1) \cdot (b_0 + b_1) - a_0 \cdot b_0 - a_1 \cdot b_1) \\
a^2 &= ((a_0 + a_1) \cdot (a_0 - a_1), 2a_0 \cdot a_1) \\
a^{-1} &= (a_0 \cdot (a_0^2 + a_1^2)^{-1}, -a_1 \cdot (a_0^2 + a_1^2)^{-1})
\end{aligned}
$$

where operations on the right are in $\mathbb{F}_p$. Operations in $\mathbb{F}_{p^2}$ are directly computed using the equations above: multiplication requires three field multiplications, two field additions and three field subtractions, whereas squaring requires only two field multiplications, two field additions and one field subtraction. Field inversions are computed via Fermat's Little Theorem ($a^{-1} = a^{p-2} = a^{2^{127}-3}$) using 138 multiplications in $\mathbb{F}_p$.

An example of how the control logic implements $c = a \times b$ with $a = (a_0, a_1)$ and $b = (b_0, b_1) \in \mathbb{F}_{p^2}$ using the datapath is shown in Fig. 3. The multiplication begins by computing $t_1 = a_0 \cdot b_0$ in $\mathbb{F}_p$ followed by $t_2 = a_1 \cdot b_1$. The additions $t_3 = a_0 + a_1$ and $t_4 = b_0 + b_1$ are interleaved with these multiplications. As soon as they are ready and the multiplier path becomes idle, the last multiplication $t_3 \leftarrow t_3 \cdot t_4$ is computed. The multiplication $a \times b$ ends with three successive subtractions $c_0 = t_1 - t_2$ and $c_1 = t_3 - t_1 - t_2$. The operation sequence was designed to allow the interleaving of successive multiplications over $\mathbb{F}_{p^2}$. A preceding multiplication $f = d \times e$ and subsequent multiplications $g \times h$ and $i \times j$ are depicted in gray color in Fig. 3. A multiplication finishes in 45 clock cycles but allows the next multiplication to start after only 21 clock cycles. For every other multiplication one must use t_5 in place of t_3 in order to avoid writing to t_3 before it is read. This operation sequence also allows interleaving further additions/subtractions in $\mathbb{F}_p$ with the interleaved multiplications. E.g., if we read operands from the memory in line 14, then we can compute an addition followed by a reduction in lines 16 and 17 and write the result back in line 18. There is also a variant

#	Memory			Regs.	Multiplier						Add/sub	
	R_A	R_B	W	Regs.	m.in	m.1	m.2$\cdots$m.5	m.6	m.7	Acc.	Regs.	Res.
1	a_0	b_0				$t_5^1 \cdot t_4^0$	$\ldots$	$d_1^1 \cdot e_1^1$		$+$		
2					t_5^1,t_4^1		$\ldots$		$d_1^1 \cdot e_1^1$	sft.		
3				a_0,b_0		$t_5^1 \cdot t_4^1$	$\ldots$	$t_5^0 \cdot t_4^0$		$+$		
4	a_0	a_1			a_0^0,b_0^0		$\ldots$		$t_5^0 \cdot t_4^0$	clr.		R-1$(d_1 \cdot e_1)$
5	b_0	b_1			$a_0^0 \cdot b_0^0$		$\ldots$	$t_5^0 \cdot t_4^1$		$+$		R-2$(d_1 \cdot e_1)$
6			t_2		a_0^0,b_0^1		$\ldots$	$t_5^1 \cdot t_4^1$	$t_5^0 \cdot t_4^1$	sft.	a_0,a_1	
7					a_0^1,b_0^0	$a_0^0 \cdot b_0^1$	$\ldots$		$t_5^1 \cdot t_4^0$	$+$	b_0,b_1	a_0+a_1
8	a_1	b_1				$a_0^1 \cdot b_0^0$	$\ldots$	$t_5^1 \cdot t_4^1$		$+$		R(a_0+a_1)
9			t_3		a_0^1,b_0^0		$\ldots$		$t_5^1 \cdot t_4^1$	sft.		b_0+b_1
10	t_1	t_2		a_1,b_1	$a_0^1 \cdot b_0^0$		$\ldots$	$a_0^0 \cdot b_0^0$		$+$		R(b_0+b_1)
11			t_4		a_1^0,b_0^1		$\ldots$		$a_0^0 \cdot b_0^0$	clr.	t_1,t_2	R-1$(t_5 \cdot t_4)$
12						$a_0^0 \cdot b_0^1$	$\ldots$	$a_0^0 \cdot b_0^1$		$+$		R-2$(t_5 \cdot t_4)$
13			t_5		a_0^0,b_1^1		$\ldots$	$a_0^0 \cdot b_0^0$	$a_0^0 \cdot b_0^1$	sft.		
14					a_1^0,b_1^0	$a_0^0 \cdot b_1^1$	$\ldots$	$a_0^0 \cdot b_0^0$		$+$		t_1-t_2
15	t_3	t_4				$a_1^0 \cdot b_1^0$	$\ldots$	$a_0^0 \cdot b_0^0$		$+$		R(t_1-t_2)
16			f_0		a_1^1,b_1^0		$\ldots$		$a_0^0 \cdot b_0^1$	sft.		
17	t_5	t_1		t_3,t_4		$a_1^1 \cdot b_1^1$	$\ldots$	$a_1^0 \cdot b_0^0$		$+$		
18					t_3^0,t_4^0		$\ldots$		$a_1^0 \cdot b_0^1$	clr.		R-1$(a_0 \cdot b_0)$
19		t_2			t_3^0,t_4^1		$\ldots$	$a_1^0 \cdot b_0^1$		$+$	t_5,t_1	R-2$(a_0 \cdot b_0)$
20			t_1		t_3^0,t_4^1	$t_3^0 \cdot t_4^1$	$\ldots$	$a_1^0 \cdot b_0^1$	$a_1^0 \cdot b_0^1$	sft.		t_5-t_1
21					t_3^1,t_4^0	$t_3^1 \cdot t_4^0$	$\ldots$	$a_1^1 \cdot b_1^1$	$a_1^0 \cdot b_0^0$	$+$	t_2	R(t_5-t_1)
22	g_0	h_0				$t_3^1 \cdot t_4^0$	$\ldots$	$a_1^1 \cdot b_1^1$		$+$		$R-t_2$
23					t_3^1,t_4^1		$\ldots$		$a_1^1 \cdot b_1^1$	sft.		R$(R-t_2)$
24			f_1	g_0,h_0		$t_3^1 \cdot t_4^1$	$\ldots$	$t_3^0 \cdot t_4^0$		$+$		
25	g_0	g_1			g_0^0,h_0^0		$\ldots$	$t_3^0 \cdot t_4^1$	$t_3^0 \cdot t_4^0$	clr.		R-1$(a_1 \cdot b_1)$
26	h_0	h_1			$g_0^0 \cdot h_0^0$		$\ldots$	$t_3^1 \cdot t_4^0$	$t_3^0 \cdot t_4^1$	$+$		R-2$(a_1 \cdot b_1)$
27			t_2		g_0^0,h_0^1		$\ldots$	$t_3^1 \cdot t_4^1$	$t_3^0 \cdot t_4^0$	sft.	g_0,g_1	g_0+g_1
28					g_0^1,h_0^0	$g_0^0 \cdot h_0^1$	$\ldots$		$t_3^1 \cdot t_4^0$	$+$	h_0,h_1	h_0+h_1
29	g_1	h_1			$g_0^1 \cdot h_0^0$		$\ldots$	$t_3^1 \cdot t_4^1$		$+$		R(g_0+g_1)
30			t_5		g_0^1,h_0^0		$\ldots$		$t_3^1 \cdot t_4^1$	sft.		h_0+h_1
31	t_1	t_2		g_1,h_1	$g_0^1 \cdot h_0^0$		$\ldots$	$g_0^0 \cdot h_0^0$		$+$		R(h_0+h_1)
32			t_4		g_1^0,h_1^1		$\ldots$		$g_0^0 \cdot h_0^0$	clr.		R-1$(t_3 \cdot t_4)$
33						$g_1^0 \cdot h_1^0$	$\ldots$	$g_0^0 \cdot h_0^1$		$+$	t_1,t_2	R-2$(t_3 \cdot t_4)$
34			t_3		g_1^0,h_1^1		$\ldots$	$g_0^1 \cdot h_0^0$	$g_0^0 \cdot h_0^1$	sft.		
35					g_1^1,h_1^0	$g_1^0 \cdot h_1^1$	$\ldots$	$g_1^1 \cdot h_1^0$	$g_0^1 \cdot h_0^0$	$+$		t_1-t_2
36	t_5	t_4			$g_1^1 \cdot h_1^1$		$\ldots$	$g_1^1 \cdot h_1^0$		$+$		R(t_1-t_2)
37			c_0		g_1^1,h_1^1		$\ldots$		$g_0^1 \cdot h_0^1$	sft.		
38	t_3	t_1		t_5,t_4		$g_1^1 \cdot h_1^1$	$\ldots$	$g_1^0 \cdot h_1^0$		$+$		
39					t_5^0,t_4^0		$\ldots$		$g_1^0 \cdot h_1^1$	clr.		R-1$(g_0 \cdot h_0)$
40		t_2			t_5^0,t_4^1		$\ldots$	$g_1^0 \cdot h_1^1$		$+$	t_3,t_1	R-2$(g_0 \cdot h_0)$
41			t_1		t_5^0,t_4^1	$t_5^0 \cdot t_4^1$	$\ldots$	$g_1^0 \cdot h_1^1$	$g_1^0 \cdot h_1^1$	sft.		t_3-t_1
42					t_5^1,t_4^0	$t_5^1 \cdot t_4^0$	$\ldots$	$g_1^1 \cdot h_1^1$	$g_1^0 \cdot h_1^0$	$+$	t_2	R(t_3-t_1)
43	i_0	j_0				$t_5^1 \cdot t_4^0$	$\ldots$	$g_1^1 \cdot h_1^1$		$+$		$r-t_2$
44					t_5^1,t_4^1		$\ldots$		$g_1^1 \cdot h_1^1$	sft.		R$(r-t_2)$
45			c_1	i_0,j_0		$t_5^1 \cdot t_4^1$	$\ldots$	$t_5^0 \cdot t_4^0$		$+$		

Fig. 3. Use of the datapath for (successive) multiplications in $\mathbb{F}_{p^2}$.

of the multiplication sequence which completes the multiplication after 38 clock cycles by computing the final subtractions faster, but it does not allow efficient interleaving.

Latencies and throughputs of field operations are collected in Table 1.

The program ROM. includes hand-optimized routines (fixed sequences of instructions) for all the operations required for computing scalar multiplications on FourQ. The program ROM consists of 8015 lines of instructions (13-bit

Table 1. Latencies and throughputs of operations in $\mathbb{F}_p$ and $\mathbb{F}_{p^2}$.

Operation	Latency	Throughput
Addition/subtraction in $\mathbb{F}_p$	6	1/2
Multiplication/squaring in $\mathbb{F}_p$	20	1/7
Inversion in $\mathbb{F}_p$ [a]	2760	—
Addition/subtraction in $\mathbb{F}_{p^2}$	8	1/4
Multiplication in $\mathbb{F}_{p^2}$ (max. throughput)	45	1/21
Multiplication in $\mathbb{F}_{p^2}$ (min. latency)	38	1/31
Squaring in $\mathbb{F}_{p^2}$	28	1/16
Inversion in $\mathbb{F}_{p^2}$	2817	—

[a] 126 squarings and 12 multiplications in $\mathbb{F}_p$.

addresses). Each line is 25 bits wide: 3 bits for the multiplier path, 5 bits for the adder/subtractor path, one bit for write enable and two 8-bit memory addresses for the RAM. Execution of each instruction line takes one clock cycle. We tested implementing the program ROM both using distributed memory and BlockRAM blocks. The latter resulted in slightly better timing results arguably because of an easier place-and-route process. Accordingly, we chose to implement the program ROM using 6 BlockRAM blocks.

There are in total *seven* separate routines in the program ROM. Given a basepoint $P = (x, y)$ and following Algorithm 1, *initialization* (lines 1–14) assigns $X \leftarrow x$, $Y \leftarrow y$, $Z \leftarrow 1$, $T_a \leftarrow x$ and $T_b \leftarrow y$ (i.e., it maps the affine point P to representation $\mathbf{R_1}$; see Sect. 2.1). *Precomputation* (lines 15–4199) produces the table T containing 8 points using the endormorphisms and point additions. Precomputed points are stored using representation $\mathbf{R_5}$. *Initialization of the main loop* (lines 4200–4214) initializes the point accumulator by loading a point from the table T using the first digit of the recoded multi-scalar and by mapping it to representation $\mathbf{R_4}$. In the *main loop* (lines 4215–4568), point doublings $Q \leftarrow [2]Q$ and additions $Q \leftarrow Q + T[d_i]$ are computed using the representations $\mathbf{R_1} \leftarrow \mathbf{R_4}$ and $\mathbf{R_1} \leftarrow \mathbf{R_1} \times \mathbf{R_2}$, respectively. As explained in Sect. 2.1, converting precomputed points from representation $\mathbf{R_5}$ to $\mathbf{R_2}$ is simply done by reading values from memory in the right order. The main loop consists of 64 iterations and significant effort was devoted to optimizing its latency. *Affine conversion* (lines 4569–7437) maps the resulting point in representation $\mathbf{R_1}$ to affine coordinates by computing $x = X/Z$ and $y = Y/Z$. The bulk of this computation consists of an inversion in $\mathbb{F}_p$. *Point validation* (lines 7438–7561) checks if the basepoint $P = (x, y)$ is in $\mathcal{E}(\mathbb{F}_{p^2})$, i.e., it verifies that $-x^2 + y^2 - 1 - dx^2y^2 = 0$. *Cofactor clearing* (lines 7562–8014) kills the cofactor by computing $392P$. This is done with an $\mathbf{R_2} \leftarrow \mathbf{R_1}$ map (lines 7562–7643) followed by eight point doublings (lines 7644–7799) and two point additions (lines 7800–8014).

The control FSM. sets the address for the program ROM depending on the phase of the scalar multiplication. The FSM includes a counter and hardcoded

---

Algorithm 3. Truncated multiplication algorithm.

Input: integers $X = X_{10}, X_9, \ldots, X_0$ in radix 2^{24}, $Y = Y_{11}, X_{10}, \ldots, Y_0$ in radix 2^{17}.
Output: $Z_H = \lfloor X \cdot Y / 2^{256} \rfloor \bmod 2^{64}$ or $Z_L = X \cdot Y \bmod 2^{64}$.

1:   $Z_H \leftarrow 0, Z_L \leftarrow 0$
2:   **for** $i = 0$ to 11 (**or** 3) **do**
3:      $T \leftarrow 0$
4:      **for** $j = 0$ to 10 (**or** 2) **do**
5:        $T \leftarrow T + ((Y_i \cdot X_j) \ll 24j)$
6:      $Z_H \leftarrow (Z_H \gg 17) + T$
7:      **if** $i < 4$ **then**
8:        $Z_L \leftarrow (Z_L \gg 17) + ((Z_H \bmod 2^{16}) \ll 51)$
9:   $Z_H \leftarrow (Z_H \gg 68) \bmod 2^{64}$
10: $Z_L \leftarrow Z_L \bmod 2^{64}$
11: **return** Z_H, Z_L

---

pointers to the routines in the program ROM. The value of the counter is used as the address to the program ROM. Depending on the operation, the FSM sets the counter to the address of the first line of the appropriate routine and, then, lets the counter count up by one every clock cycle until it reaches the end pointer of that routine. After that, the FSM jumps to the next routine or to the wait state (line 0 is no-operation).

The instruction recoder. recodes instructions from the program ROM to control signals for the datapath. The memory addresses from the program ROM are fed into an address recoding circuit, which recodes the address if it is needed to access a precomputed point (otherwise, it passes the address unchanged). The address from the program ROM simply specifies the coordinate of the precomputed point and the recoding unit replaces this placeholder address with a real RAM memory address by recoding it using the value and sign of the current digit-column d_i of the scalar.

4   Scalar Unit

This unit is in charge of decomposing the input scalar m into four 64-bit multi-scalars a_1, a_2, a_3, a_4, which are then recoded to a sequence of digit-columns $(d_{64}, \ldots, d_0)$ with $0 \leq d_i < 16$. These digits are used during scalar multiplication to extract the precomputed points that are to be added. In our design, this unit is naturally split into the decompose and recode units, which are described below.

4.1   Decompose Unit

The decompose unit computes the multi-scalar values a_1, a_2, a_3 and a_4 as per [6, Proposition 5]. The inputs to the decompose unit are the four curve constants ℓ_1, ℓ_2, ℓ_3 and ℓ_4 and the four basis values b_1, b_2, b_3 and b_4, which are stored in a

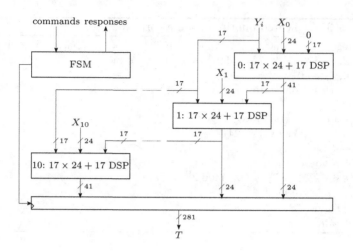

Fig. 4. Architecture of the 17×264-bit row multiplier using DSPs.

ROM, and the 256-bit input scalar m, which is stored in a register. The core of
the decompose unit is a *truncated multiplier*: on input integers $0 \leq X < 2^{256}$ and
$0 \leq Y < 2^{195}$, it calculates the integer $Z_H = \lfloor X \cdot Y/(2^{256}) \rfloor \bmod 2^{64}$. This oper-
ation is needed to compute each of the four values $\widetilde{\alpha_1}$, $\widetilde{\alpha_2}$, $\widetilde{\alpha_3}$ and $\widetilde{\alpha_4}$ from
[6, Proposition 5] modulo 2^{64}. The truncated multiplier computes Z_H as
described in Algorithm 3. In addition, this multiplier can be adapted to computations with the form $Z_L = XY \bmod 2^{64}$ by simply reducing the two for-loop
counters in Algorithm 3 from 11 to 3 and from 10 to 2, respectively. Thus, we
reuse the truncated multiplier for the 14 multiplications modulo 2^{64} that are
needed to produce the final values a_1, a_2, a_3 and a_4 as per [6, Proposition 5].

The main building block of the truncated multiplier is a 17×264-bit *row*
multiplier that is used to compute the product of $Y_j \cdot X$ for some $j \in [0, 11]$
(lines 4–5 of Algorithm 3). The row multiplier is implemented using a chain of
11 DSPs as shown in Fig. 4. Note that the DSP blocks available on the Xilinx
Zynq FPGA family allow 17×24 unsigned integer multiplication plus addition
of the result with an additional 47-bit unsigned integer. In order to comply with
the operand size imposed by the DSP blocks, we split the input integer X into
24-bit words and the input Y into into 17-bit words (the most significant words
are zero-padded). Both X and Y are then represented as $X_{10}, X_9, \ldots, X_0$ in
radix 2^{24} and $Y_{11}, X_{10}, \ldots, Y_0$ in radix 2^{17}, respectively.

The row multiplier computes the full 17×264-bit product after 11 clock
cycles. Its 281-bit result is then added to the 281-bit partial result right-shifted
by 17 bits (line 6 of Algorithm 3). This operation is performed by an *adder-*
shifter component. In our current design, the addition has been split into 3
steps to reduce the critical path. Finally, a shift register outputs the result (line
9 of Algorithm 3).

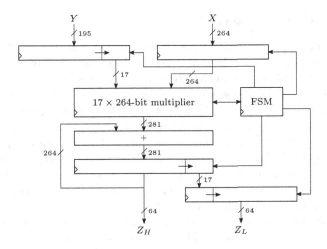

Fig. 5. Architecture of the truncated multiplier.

The high level architecture of the truncated multiplier unit is depicted in Fig. 5. An FSM drives the various components to execute the control statements of Algorithm 3.

The remaining part of the decompose unit is an FSM that first drives the truncated multiplier to compute the four values $\widetilde{\alpha_1}$, $\widetilde{\alpha_2}$, $\widetilde{\alpha_3}$ and $\widetilde{\alpha_4}$ in four separate runnings, using as inputs the constants stored in ROM and the scalar m. For these computations, the multiplier produces outputs Z_H running for the maximum number of loop iterations according to Algorithm 3. Subsequently, the FSM drives the truncated multiplier to compute products modulo 2^{64} (by running it for a reduced number of loop iterations, as explained above) and to accumulate the results Z_L to produce the output values a_1, a_2, a_3 and a_4 in 24 steps.

4.2 Recode Unit

The recode unit is very simple, as the operations it performs are just bit manipulations and 64-bit additions. The unit is designed as an FSM performing 64 iterations according to Algorithm 2, where each iteration is split into 6 steps (corresponding to 6 states of the FSM). The first 4 states implement lines 3 to 8 of Algorithm 2, whereas the last 2 states implement line 9.

5   Architectures

We designed *three* variants of our architecture in order to provide a full picture of its capabilities compared to other designs presented in the literature.

5.1   Single-Core Architecture

Our single-core architecture is the simplest possible architecture for Algorithm 1. It combines one instance of the scalar unit with one instance of the core. Most ECC hardware architectures in the literature are single-core architectures.

The interface of the single-core architecture is such that the host connects to the architecture through a 64-bit interface (this can be easily modified) by writing and reading values to and from the RAM. The host can issue three instructions: point validation, cofactor clearing, and scalar multiplication. Point validation computes the field operations required for computing $-x^2 + y^2 - 1 - dx^2y^2$ and the host reads the result and checks if it is zero. The need for cofactor clearing depends on the protocol and, hence, it is not included in the main scalar multiplication instruction. The scalar multiplication instruction initiates (a) the scalar unit to decompose and recode the scalar and (b) the core to begin the precomputation and all the other subsequent routines. The scalar unit computes its operations at the same time that the core computes the precomputation. Hence, scalar decomposition and recoding do not incur in any latency overhead. Once an instruction is issued, the architecture raises a busy signal which remains high as long as the operation is in process.

5.2   Multi-core Architecture

Our multi-core architecture aims at improving throughput (operations per second). It includes one scalar unit and N instances of the core. The multi-core architecture is shown in Fig. 6. It is conceptually similar to the multi-core architecture presented by Sasdrich and Güneysu for Curve25519 in [29]. In their case, multiple cores share a common inverter unit (inversions modulo $2^{255} - 19$ are more expensive than inversions in $\mathbb{F}_{p^2}$), which is used *after* scalar multiplication. In our case the common resource is the scalar unit, which is used *at the beginning* of scalar multiplication and is computed *simultaneously* with it.

The multi-core architecture is designed so that it acts as a FIFO (first-in-first-out), which is straightforward to implement because all the operations have constant latencies. The architecture has a *busy* signal which is high when the scalar unit is computing or when all the cores are busy (or have results that have not been read by the host). The host can issue new instructions only when the busy signal is low. The cores are used cyclically so that whenever a scalar multiplication instruction is issued, the turn is given to the next core. There is also a *done* signal which is high when there are results which have not been read by the host. Reading is also performed cyclically so that the turn is handed to the next core only when the host acknowledges that it has read the previous results. This cyclic writing and reading operate independently of each other, and the interface allows reading and writing different cores. Thanks to the cyclic utilization of the cores, the interface is transparent to the host who does not need to take care of which core is actually performing the computations; in fact, that is not even visible to the host.

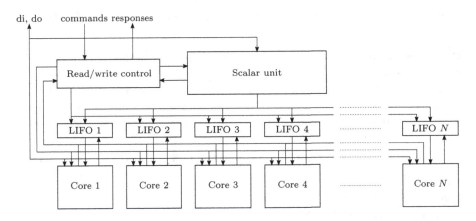

Fig. 6. The multi-core architecture with one scalar unit and N cores.

The scalar unit writes digits to a LIFO (last-in-first-out) buffer[1] attached to each core. This way a core can proceed with a scalar multiplication independently of the scalar unit as soon as the scalar unit has finished decomposing and recoding a scalar. The scalar unit can then process other scalars while the previous cores are computing scalar multiplications. In this paper, we only consider situations in which a single scalar unit serves N cores. If $N > 14$, then the scalar unit becomes the bottleneck for throughput and, therefore, multiple scalar units could be required.

5.3 Architecture Using the Montgomery Ladder

The architectures above can be easily modified to compute scalar multiplications on FourQ without utilizing the endomorphisms. This option might be beneficial in some resource-constrained applications. To demonstrate this, we designed a modification of the single-core architecture. The main difference is that the scalar unit is no longer needed, which results in a significant reduction in the size of the architecture. Changes in the core are small and are strictly limited to the control logic. In particular, the program ROM reduces in size because of a shorter program and smaller address space (fewer temporary variables in use). The architecture accepts both 256-bit and 246-bit (reduced modulo ξ) scalars, and also supports cofactor clearing.

The size of the memory remains the same even though the memory requirements of the Montgomery ladder are relatively smaller than the single-core architecture using endormorphisms (which requires a precomputed point table). The reason for this is that the number of BlockRAMs is dictated by the width (in our case, 127 bits). Using smaller width would lead to a decrease in BlockRAM

---

[1] The scalar unit outputs digits in the order $d_0, d_1, \ldots, d_{64}$ and the core uses them in a reversed order (see Algorithm 1).

Table 2. Summary of resource requirements in Xilinx Zynq-7020 XC7Z020CLG484-3.

Component	LUTs		Regs.		Slices		BRAMs		DSPs	
Single-core design										
Core	869	(1.6 %)	1637	(1.5 %)	490	(3.7 %)	10	(7.1 %)	16	(7.3 %)
Scalar unit	3348	(6.3 %)	2771	(2.6 %)	1226	(9.2 %)	0	(0.0 %)	11	(5.0 %)
Total	4217	(7.9 %)	4413	(4.1 %)	1691	(12.7 %)	10	(7.1 %)	27	(12.3 %)
Multi-core design ($N = 11$)										
Core (min.)	902	(1.7 %)	1616	(1.5 %)	417	(3.1 %)	10	(7.1 %)	16	(7.3 %)
⋮	⋮	⋮	⋮	⋮	⋮	⋮	⋮	⋮	⋮	⋮
Core (max.)	1001	(1.9 %)	1630	(1.5 %)	511	(3.8 %)	10	(7.1 %)	16	(7.3 %)
Scalar unit	3422	(6.4 %)	3029	(2.8 %)	1201	(9.0 %)	0	(0.0 %)	11	(5.0 %)
Total	13595	(25.6 %)	20924	(19.7 %)	5697	(42.8 %)	110	(78.6 %)	187	(85.0 %)
Single-core design, Montgomery ladder										
Core	1068	(2.0 %)	1638	(1.5 %)	522	(3.9 %)	7	(5.0 %)	16	(7.3 %)
Total	1069	(2.0 %)	1894	(1.8 %)	565	(4.2 %)	7	(5.0 %)	16	(7.3 %)

requirements but also to a lower performance. Because BlockRAMs are not the critical resource, we opted for keeping the current memory structure.

We derived hand-optimized routines for the scalar multiplication initialization and the double-and-add step using the formulas from [25]. The accumulator is initialized with $Q = (X : Z) = (1 : 0)$. One double-and-add step of the Montgomery ladder takes 228 clock cycles. Because we have an either 256-bit or 246-bit scalar, a scalar multiplication involves 256 or 246 double-and-add steps, which take exactly 58368 or 56088 clock cycles, respectively. A final conversion to extract x from $(X : Z)$ takes 2855 clock cycles. The total cost of scalar multiplication (without cofactor clearing) is 61235 or 58967 cycles for 256-bit and 246-bit scalars, respectively. Cofactor clearing is computed with nine double-and-add steps followed by an extraction of x from $(X : Z)$ and takes 4932 cycles.

6   Results and Analysis

The three architectures from Sect. 5 were compiled with Xilinx Vivado 2015.4 to a Xilinx Zynq-7020 XC7Z020CLG484-3 FPGA, which is an all programmable system-on-chip for embedded systems. All the given results were obtained after place-and-route. Table 2 presents the area requirements of the designs. Table 3 collects latencies, timings and throughputs of the different operations supported by the designs.

The single-core design requires less than 13 % of all the resources available in the targeted Zynq-7020 FPGA. Timing closure was successful with a clock constraint of 190 MHz (clock period of 5.25 ns). Hence, one scalar multiplication (without cofactor clearing) takes 156.52 µs, which means 6389 operations per

Table 3. Performance characteristics of the designs in a Xilinx Zynq-7020 XC7Z020CLG484-3 FPGA, excluding interfacing with the host.

Operation	Latency (clocks)	Time (μs) @190 MHz	@175 MHz	Throughput (ops) 1×190 MHz	11×175 MHz
Initialization	14	0.07	0.08	—	—
Point validation	124	0.65	0.71	—	—
Cofactor clearing	1760	9.26	10.06	—	—
Precomputation	4185	22.03	23.91	—	—
Scalar multiplication, init	15	0.08	0.09	—	—
Double-and-add	354	1.86	2.02	—	—
Affine conversion	2869	15.10	16.39	—	—
Mont. ladder, init. (256-bit)	12	0.06	—	—	—
Mont. ladder, init. (246-bit)	24	0.13	—	—	—
Mont. ladder, cofact. clr	4932	25.96	—	—	—
Mont. ladder, double-and-add	228	1.20	—	—	—
Mont. ladder, x-coord	2855	15.03	—	—	—
Scalar decomp. and recoding	1984	10.44	11.33	95766	88206
Scalar mult. (w/o cofact. clr.)^a	29739	156.52	169.94	6389	64730
Scalar mult. (w/ cofact. clr.)^b	31499	165.78	179.99	6032	61113
Scalar mult. (Mont. ladder)^c	58967	310.35	—	3222	—

^{a} Init.+Prec.+Scalar mult. init.+ 64 × double-and-add + affine conv.
^{b} Init.+Cofactor clr.+Prec.+Scalar mult. init.+ 64 × double-and-add + affine conv.
^{c} Mont. ladder, init. (246-bit) + 246 × Mont. ladder, double-and-add + Mont. ladder, x-coord.

second. Using Vivado tools, we analyzed the power consumption of the single-core with signal activity from post-synthesis functional simulations of ten scalar multiplications. The power estimate was 0.359 W (with high confidence level), and the energy required by one scalar multiplication was about 56.2 μJ.

The multi-core design was implemented by selecting the largest N that fitted in the Zynq-7020 FPGA. Since the DSP blocks are the critical resource and there are 220 of them in the targeted FPGA, one can estimate room for up to 13 cores. However, Vivado was unable to place-and-route a multi-core design with $N = 13$. In practice, the largest number of admissible cores was $N = 11$ (85 % DSP utilization). Even in that case timing closure was successful only with a clock constraint of 175 MHz (clock period of 5.714 ns). This results in a small increase in the computing time for one scalar multiplication, which then takes 169.94 μs (without cofactor clearing). Throughput of the multi-core design is 64730 operations per second, which is more than ten times larger than the single-core's throughput. Hence, the multi-core design offers a significant improvement for high-demand applications in which throughput is critical.

The single-core design based on the Montgomery ladder is significantly smaller than the basic single-core design mainly because there is no scalar unit. The area requirements reduce to only 7.3 % of resources (DSP blocks) at the

Table 4. Comparison of FPGA-based designs of about 256-bit prime field ECC.

Ref.	Device	Curve	N	Resources	Time (μs)	T-put (ops)
[9]	Stratix-2	any 256-bit	1	9177 ALM, 96 DSP	680	1471
[11]	Virtex-4	NIST P-256	1	1715 LS, 32 DSP, 11 BRAM	495	2020
[11]	Virtex-4	NIST P-256	16	24574 LS, 512 DSP, 176 BRAM	n/a	24700
[19]	Virtex-5	NIST P-256	1	1980 LS, 7 DSP, 2 BRAM	3951	253
[20]	Virtex-5	any 256-bit	1	1725 LS, 37 DSP, 10 BRAM	376	2662
[22]	Virtex-2	any 256-bit	1	15755 LS, 256 MUL	3836	261
[23]	Virtex-2	any 256-bit	1	3529 LS, 36 MUL	2270	441
[27]	Virtex-5	NIST P-256	1	4505 LS, 16 DSP	570	1754
[29]	Zynq-7020	Curve25519	1	1029 LS, 20 DSP, 2 BRAM	397	2519
[29]	Zynq-7020	Curve25519	11	11277 LS, 220 DSP, 22 BRAM	397	32304
This work	Zynq-7020	FourQ, Mont	1	565 LS, 16 DSP, 7 BRAM	310	3222
This work	Zynq-7020	FourQ, End	1	1691 LS, 27 DSP, 10 BRAM	157	6389
This work	Zynq-7020	FourQ, End	11	5697 LS, 187 DSP, 110 BRAM	170	64730

expense of an increase in the computing time of scalar multiplication, which in this case takes $310.35\,\mu s$ (with a 246-bit scalar). Throughput becomes 3222 operations per second, which is about half of the single-core design with fast endomorphisms.

Table 4 compares our implementations with different FPGA-based designs for prime field ECC with approximately 128 bits of security. The large variety of implementation platforms (also from different vendors), elliptic curves and design features (e.g., inclusion of side-channel countermeasures or support for multiple primes) make a fair comparison extremely difficult. Nevertheless, the table reveals that all of our designs compute scalar multiplications faster (in terms of computation time) than any other published FPGA-based designs.

The most straightforward comparison can be done against Sasdrich and Güneysu's implementations using Curve25519 [29] (cases without DPA countermeasures) because the designs use the same FPGA and share several similarities in terms of optimization goals and approach. Our single-core architecture is 2.67 times faster in latency and 2.54 times faster in computation time and throughput. In terms of DSP blocks (the critical resource), our architecture requires 27 and [29] requires 20. Therefore, our implementation has about 1.88 times better speed-area ratio than [29]. In the case of the multi-core architecture, we obtain a throughput that is 2 times larger than that from [29]. This speedup is achieved despite the fact that the maximum clock frequency dropped to 175 MHz in our case and we were unable to utilize all of the DSP blocks because the place-and-route failed; Sasdrich and Güneysu [29] reported results with 100 % utilization with no reduction in clock frequency, without providing a technical justification.

Even the variant without endomorphisms is faster than the design from [29]. In this case, the speedup comes from the use of a different architecture and a simpler arithmetic in $\mathbb{F}_{p^2}$ over a Mersenne prime; the simpler inversion alone saves more than 10000 clock cycles. Our architecture computes scalar multiplications on FourQ with 1.35 times faster latency compared to [29], but because of the lower clock frequency, throughput and computation time are only 1.28 times faster. These results showcase FourQ's great performance even when endomorphisms are not used (e.g., in some applications with very strict memory constraints).

7   Conclusions

We presented *three* FPGA designs for the recently proposed elliptic curve FourQ. These architectures are able to compute one scalar multiplication in only 157 μs or, alternatively, with a maximum throughput of up to 64730 operations per second by applying parallel processing in a single Zynq-7020 FPGA. The designs are the fastest FPGA implementations of elliptic curve cryptography over large prime characteristic fields at the 128-bit security level. This extends the software results from [6] by showing that FourQ also offers significant speedups in hardware when compared to other elliptic curves with similar strength such as Curve25519 or NIST P-256.

Our designs are inherently protected against SSCA and timing attacks. Recent horizontal attacks (such as horizontal collision correlations [3]) can break SSCA-protected implementations by exploiting leakage from partial multiplications. Our designs compute these operations with a large 64-bit word size in a highly pipelined and parallel fashion. Nevertheless, resistance against these attacks, and other attacks that apply to scenarios in which an attacker can exploit traces from multiple scalar multiplications (e.g., differential power analysis), require further analysis. Future work involves the inclusion of strong countermeasures against such attacks.

Acknowledgments. Kimmo Järvinen's work was supported in part by the Intel Institute for Collaborative Research in Secure Computing.

Reza Azarderakhsh's work was supported by the National Science Foundation under award No. CNS-1464118 and and by the US Army Research Laboratory under award No. W911NF-16-1-0204-(68023-CS). The views and conclusions contained in this document are those of the authors and should not be interpreted as representing the official policies, either expressed or implied, of the U.S. Army Research Laboratory, or the U.S. Government. The U.S. Government is authorized to reproduce and distribute reprints for Government purposes notwithstanding any copyright notation hereon.

References

1. Azarderakhsh, R., Reyhani-Masoleh, A.: Efficient FPGA implementations of point multiplication on binary Edwards and generalized Hessian curves using Gaussian normal basis. IEEE Trans. Very Large Scale Integr. (VLSI) Syst. **20**(8), 1453–1466 (2012)
2. Azarderakhsh, R., Reyhani-Masoleh, A.: Parallel and high-speed computations of elliptic curve cryptography using hybrid-double multipliers. IEEE Trans. Parallel Distrib. Syst. **26**(6), 1668–1677 (2015)
3. Bauer, A., Jaulmes, E., Prouff, E., Reinhard, J.R., Wild, J.: Horizontal collision correlation attack on elliptic curves. Crypt. Commun. **7**(1), 91–119 (2015)
4. Bernstein, D.J., Birkner, P., Joye, M., Lange, T., Peters, C.: Twisted Edwards curves. In: Vaudenay, S. (ed.) AFRICACRYPT 2008. LNCS, vol. 5023, pp. 389–405. Springer, Heidelberg (2008)
5. Bernstein, D.J.: Curve25519: new Diffie-Hellman speed records. In: Yung, M., Dodis, Y., Kiayias, A., Malkin, T. (eds.) PKC 2006. LNCS, vol. 3958, pp. 207–228. Springer, Heidelberg (2006)
6. Costello, C., Longa, P.: FourQ: four-dimensional decompositions on a Q-curve over the Mersenne prime. In: Iwata, T., et al. (eds.) ASIACRYPT 2015. LNCS, vol. 9452, pp. 214–235. Springer, Heidelberg (2015). https://eprint.iacr.org/2015/565
7. Faz-Hernández, A., Longa, P., Sánchez, A.H.: Efficient and secure algorithms for GLV-based scalar multiplication and their implementation on GLV-GLS curves (extended version). J. Cryptographic Eng. **5**(1), 31–52 (2015)
8. Gallant, R.P., Lambert, R.J., Vanstone, S.A.: Faster point multiplication on elliptic curves with efficient endomorphisms. In: Kilian, J. (ed.) CRYPTO 2001. LNCS, vol. 2139, pp. 190–200. Springer, Heidelberg (2001)
9. Guillermin, N.: A high speed coprocessor for elliptic curve scalar multiplications over $\mathbb{F}_p$. In: Mangard, S., Standaert, F.-X. (eds.) CHES 2010. LNCS, vol. 6225, pp. 48–64. Springer, Heidelberg (2010)
10. Guillevic, A., Ionica, S.: Four-dimensional GLV via the Weil restriction. In: Sako, K., Sarkar, P. (eds.) ASIACRYPT 2013, Part I. LNCS, vol. 8269, pp. 79–96. Springer, Heidelberg (2013)
11. Güneysu, T., Paar, C.: Ultra high performance ECC over NIST primes on commercial FPGAs. In: Oswald, E., Rohatgi, P. (eds.) CHES 2008. LNCS, vol. 5154, pp. 62–78. Springer, Heidelberg (2008)
12. Hisil, H., Wong, K.K.-H., Carter, G., Dawson, E.: Twisted Edwards curves revisited. In: Pieprzyk, J. (ed.) ASIACRYPT 2008. LNCS, vol. 5350, pp. 326–343. Springer, Heidelberg (2008)
13. Järvinen, K., Skyttä, J.: On parallelization of high-speed processors for elliptic curve cryptography. IEEE Trans. Very Large Scale Integr. (VLSI) Syst. **16**(9), 1162–1175 (2008)
14. Järvinen, K., Skyttä, J.: Optimized FPGA-based elliptic curve cryptography processor for high-speed applications. Integr. VLSI J. **44**(4), 270–279 (2011)
15. Koblitz, N.: Elliptic curve cryptosystems. Math. Comput. **48**, 203–209 (1987)
16. Kocher, P.C.: Timing attacks on implementations of Diffie-Hellman, RSA, DSS, and other systems. In: Koblitz, N. (ed.) CRYPTO 1996. LNCS, vol. 1109, pp. 104–113. Springer, Heidelberg (1996)
17. Kocher, P.C., Jaffe, J., Jun, B.: Differential power analysis. In: Wiener, M. (ed.) CRYPTO 1999. LNCS, vol. 1666, pp. 388–397. Springer, Heidelberg (1999)

18. Loi, K.C.C., Ko, S.B.: High performance scalable elliptic curve cryptosystem processor for Koblitz curves. Microprocess. Microsyst. **37**(4–5), 394–406 (2013)
19. Loi, K.C.C., Ko, S.B.: Scalable elliptic curve cryptosystem FPGA processor for NIST prime curves. IEEE Trans. Very Large Scale Integr. (VLSI) Syst. **23**(11), 2753–2756 (2015)
20. Ma, Y., Liu, Z., Pan, W., Jing, J.: A high-speed elliptic curve cryptographic processor for generic curves over GF(p). In: Lange, T., Lauter, K., Lisoněk, P. (eds.) SAC 2013. LNCS, vol. 8282, pp. 421–437. Springer, Heidelberg (2014)
21. McIvor, C.J., McLoone, M., McCanny, J.V.: An FPGA elliptic curve cryptographic accelerator over $GF(p)$. Proc. Irish Signals Syst. Conf. **2004**, 589–594 (2004)
22. McIvor, C.J., McLoone, M., McCanny, J.V.: Hardware elliptic curve cryptographic processor over $GF(p)$. IEEE Trans. Circuits Syst. I Regul. Pap. **55**(9), 1946–1957 (2006)
23. Mentens, N.: Secure and efficient coprocessor design for cryptographic applications on FPGAs. Ph.D. thesis, Katholieke Universiteit Leuven, July 2007
24. Miller, V.S.: Use of elliptic curves in cryptography. In: Williams, H.C. (ed.) CRYPTO 1985. LNCS, vol. 218, pp. 417–426. Springer, Heidelberg (1986)
25. Montgomery, P.L.: Speeding the Pollard and elliptic curve methods of factorization. Math. Comput. **48**(177), 243–264 (1987)
26. Rebeiro, C., Roy, S.S., Mukhopadhyay, D.: Pushing the limits of high-speed $GF(2^m)$ elliptic curve scalar multiplication on FPGAs. In: Prouff, E., Schaumont, P. (eds.) CHES 2012. LNCS, vol. 7428, pp. 494–511. Springer, Heidelberg (2012)
27. Roy, D.B., Mukhopadhyay, D., Izumi, M., Takahashi, J.: Tile before multiplication: an efficient strategy to optimize DSP multiplier for accelerating prime field ECC for NIST curves. In: Proceedings of the 51st Annual Design Automation Conference–DAC 2014, pp. 177: 1–177: 6. ACM (2014)
28. Sasdrich, P., Güneysu, T.: Efficient elliptic-curve cryptography using Curve25519 on reconfigurable devices. In: Goehringer, D., Santambrogio, M.D., Cardoso, J.M.P., Bertels, K. (eds.) ARC 2014. LNCS, vol. 8405, pp. 25–36. Springer, Heidelberg (2014)
29. Sasdrich, P., Güneysu, T.: Implementing Curve25519 for side-channel-protected elliptic curve cryptography. ACM Trans. Reconfigurable Technol. Syst. 9(1), (2015). Article 3
30. Smith, B.: Families of fast elliptic curves from Q-curves. In: Sako, K., Sarkar, P. (eds.) ASIACRYPT 2013, Part I. LNCS, vol. 8269, pp. 61–78. Springer, Heidelberg (2013)
31. Sutter, G.D., Deschamps, J.P., Imaña, J.L.: Efficient elliptic curve point multiplication using digit-serial binary field operations. IEEE Trans. Industr. Electron. **60**(1), 217–225 (2013)

A High Throughput/Gate AES Hardware Architecture by Compressing Encryption and Decryption Datapaths
— Toward Efficient CBC-Mode Implementation

Rei Ueno[1(✉)], Sumio Morioka[2], Naofumi Homma[1], and Takafumi Aoki[1]

[1] Tohoku University, Aramaki Aza Aoba 6–6–05, Aoba-ku,
Sendai-shi 980-8579, Japan
ueno@aoki.ecei.tohoku.ac.jp
[2] Central Research Laboratories, NEC Corporation, Athene, Odyssey Business Park,
West End Road, South Ruislip, Middlesex HA4 6QE, UK

Abstract. This paper proposes a highly efficient AES hardware architecture that supports both encryption and decryption for the CBC mode. Some conventional AES architectures employ pipelining techniques to enhance the throughput and efficiency. However, such pipelined architectures are frequently unfit because many practical cryptographic applications work in the CBC mode, where block-wise parallelism is not available for encryption. In this paper, we present an efficient AES encryption/decryption hardware design suitable for such block-chaining modes. In particular, new operation-reordering and register-retiming techniques allow us to unify the inversion circuits for encryption and decryption (i.e., SubBytes and InvSubBytes) without any delay overhead. A new unification technique for linear mappings further reduces both the area and critical delay in total. Our design employs a common loop architecture and can therefore efficiently perform even in the CBC mode. We also present a shared key scheduling datapath that can work on-the-fly in the proposed architecture. To the best of our knowledge, the proposed architecture has the shortest critical path delay and is the most efficient in terms of throughput per area among conventional AES encryption/decryption architectures with tower-field S-boxes. We evaluate the performance of the proposed and some conventional datapaths by logic synthesis results with the TSMC 65-nm standard-cell library and NanGate 45- and 15-nm open-cell libraries. As a result, we confirm that our proposed architecture achieves approximately 53–72 % higher efficiency (i.e., a higher bps/GE) than any other conventional counterpart.

Keywords: AES · Hardware architectures · Unified encryption/decryption architecture · CBC mode

© International Association for Cryptologic Research 2016
B. Gierlichs and A.Y. Poschmann (Eds.): CHES 2016, LNCS 9813, pp. 538–558, 2016.
DOI: 10.1007/978-3-662-53140-2_26

1   Introduction

Cryptographic applications have been essential for many systems with secure communications, authentication, and digital signatures. In accordance with the rapid increase in Internet of Things (IoT) applications, many cryptographic algorithms are required to be implemented in resource-constrained devices and embedded systems with a high throughput and efficiency. Since 2001, many hardware implementations for AES have been proposed and evaluated for CMOS logic technologies. Studies of AES design are important from both practical and academic perspectives since AES employs an SPN structure and the major components (i.e., an 8-bit S-box and permutation used in ShiftRows and MixColumns) followed by many other security primitives.

AES encryption and decryption are commonly used in block-chaining modes such as CBC, CMAC, and CCM (e.g., for SSL/TLS, IEEE802.11 wireless LAN, and IEEE802.15.4 wireless sensor networks). Therefore, AES architectures that efficiently perform both encryption and decryption in the above block-chaining modes are highly demanded. However, many conventional architectures employ pipelining techniques to enhance the throughput and efficiency [13,15,17], although such block-wise parallelism is not available in the above block-chaining modes. For example, the highest throughput of 53 Gbps was achieved in the previous best encryption/decryption architecture [17], but it only worked in the ECB mode. In addition, these previous studies assumed offline key scheduling owing to the difficulty of on-the-fly scheduling. On-the-fly key scheduling should be implemented in most resource-constrained devices because an offline key scheduling implementation requires additional memory to store expanded round keys. Thus, it is valuable to investigate an efficient AES architecture with on-the-fly key scheduling without any pipelining technique.

In this paper, we present a new round-based AES architecture for both encryption and decryption with on-the-fly key scheduling, which achieves the lowest critical path delay (the least number of serially connected gates in the critical path) with less area overhead compared to conventional architectures with tower-field S-boxes. Our architecture employs new operation-reordering and register-retiming techniques to unify the inversion circuits for encryption and decryption without any selectors. In addition, these techniques make it possible to unify the affine transformation and linear mappings (i.e., the isomorphism and constant multiplications) to reduce the total number of logic gates. The proposed and conventional AES encryption/decryption datapaths are synthesized and evaluated with the TSMC standard-cell and NanGate open-cell libraries. The evaluation results show that our architecture can perform both (CBC-) encryption and decryption more efficiently. For example, the throughput per gate of the proposed architecture in the NanGate 15-nm process is 72 % larger than that of the best conventional architecture.

The rest of this paper is organized as follows: Sect. 2 introduces related works on AES hardware architectures, especially those with round-based encryption and decryption. Section 3 presents a new AES hardware architecture based on our operation-reordering, register-retiming, and affine-transformation unification techniques. Section 4 evaluates the proposed datapath by the logic synthesis compared with conventional round-based datapaths. Section 5 discusses variations of the proposed architecture. Finally, Sect. 6 contains our conclusion.

2   Related Works

2.1   Unified AES Datapath for Encryption and Decryption

Architectures that perform one round of encryption or decryption per clock cycle without pipelining are the most typical for AES design and are called round-based architectures in this paper. Round-based architectures can be implemented more efficiently in terms of throughput per area than other architectures by utilizing the inherent parallelism of symmetric key ciphers. For example, the byte-serial architecture [16,18] is intended for the most compact and low-power implementations such as in RFID but is not intended for the high throughput and efficiency. In contrast, round-based architectures are suitable for a high throughput per gate, which leads to a low-energy implementation [29].

To design such round-based encryption/decryption architectures in an efficient manner, we consider how to unify the resource-consuming components such as the inversion circuits in SubBytes/InvSubBytes for the encryption and decryption datapaths. There are two conventional approaches for designing such unified datapaths. The first approach is to place two distinct datapaths for encryption and decryption and select one of the datapaths with multiplexers as in [15]. Figure 1 shows an overview of the datapath flow in [15], where the inversion circuit is shared by both paths, and additional multiplexers are used at the input and output of the encryption and decryption paths. In [15], a reordered decryption operation was introduced as shown in Fig. 2. The intermediate value is stored in a register after InvMixColumns instead of AddRoundKey. Such register retiming was suitable for pipelined architectures. The main drawbacks of such approaches are the false critical path delay and the required area and delay overheads caused by three multiplexers. The critical path of the datapath in Fig. 1 is denoted in bold, which would never be active because it passes from the decryption path to the encryption path. This false critical path reduces the maximum operation frequency owing to logic synthesis due to the false longest logic chain. The overhead caused by the multiplexers is also nonnegligible for common standard-cell-based designs.

The second approach is to unify the circuits of the functions SubBytes, ShiftRows, and MixColumns with their inverse functions, respectively. Figure 3 shows the datapath in [29] where encryption and decryption paths are combined using the second approach, where the reordering technique is given in Fig. 4. The order of the decryption operations is changed to be the same as that of the encryption operations. Note that the order of (Inv)SubBytes and (Inv)ShiftRows can be changed without any overhead, and the datapath in [29] changes the order of SubBytes and ShiftRows in the encryption. The reordering of AddRoundKey and InvMixColumns utilizes the linearity of InvMixColumns as follows: $MC^{-1}(M_r + K_r) = MC^{-1}(M_r) + MC^{-1}(K_r)$, where MC^{-1} is

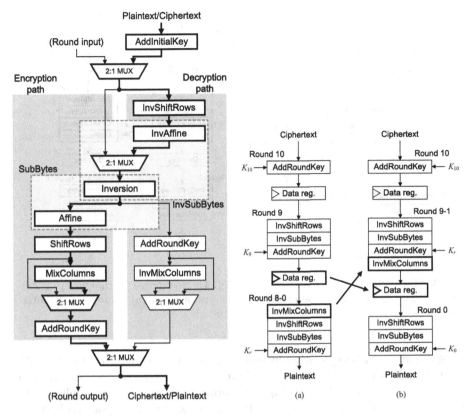

Fig. 1. Conventional parallel datapath in [15].

Fig. 2. Register-retiming techniques in [15]: (a) original and (b) resulting decryption flows.

the function InvMixColumns, and M_r and K_r are the intermediate value after InvShiftRows and the round key at the r-th round, respectively. Here, InvMix-Columns requires the round keys, whereas MixColumns and InvMixColumns can be unified to reduce the area. Therefore, this type of architecture requires an additional InvMixColumns to compute $MC^{-1}(K_r)$ for decryption. In addition, the false path and multiplexer overhead exist because each function and its inverse function are implemented in a partially serial manner with multiplexers like SubBytes and InvSubBytes in Fig. 1, where the critical path consists of Affine, Inversion, InvAffine, and an additional multiplexer.

The architecture in [17] employs a reordering technique similar to [29]. The major difference is the intermediate value stored in the register. The architecture in [14] also employs the same approach that combines the encryption and decryption datapaths, but does not change the order of AddRoundKey and InvMixColumns to remove InvMixColumns to compute $MC^{-1}(K_r)$. As a result, an additional selector is required to unify MixColumns and InvMixColumns.

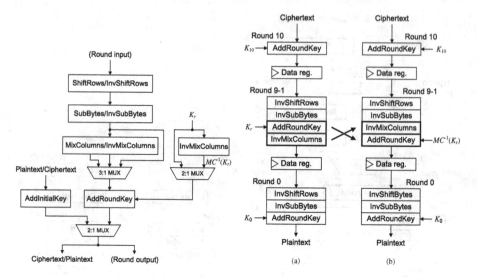

Fig. 3. Conventional datapath in [29], where encryption and decryption paths are combined.

Fig. 4. Reordering technique in [29]: decryption flows (a) before and (b) after reordering.

As described above, sharing inversion circuits is essential for designing efficient AES hardware. Although a hardware T-box architecture such as that in [20] is also useful for a high-throughput implementation, it is not applicable to the above shared datapath owing to the lack of sharable components between the encryption and decryption paths.

2.2   Inversion Circuit Design and Tower-Field Arithmetic

The design of the inversion circuit used in (Inv)SubBytes has a significant impact on the performance of AES implementations. Many inversion circuit designs have been proposed. There are two major approaches using direct mapping and tower-field arithmetic. Inversion circuits based on direct mapping such as table-lookup, Binary Decision Diagram (BDD), and Positive-Polarity Reed-Muller (PPRM) [15,19,20] are faster but larger than those based on a tower field. On the other hand, tower-field arithmetic enable us to design more compact and more area-time efficient inversion circuits in comparison with direct mapping. Therefore, we focus on inversion circuits based on tower-field arithmetic in this paper.

The performance of tower-field-based inversion circuits varies with the field towering and Galois field (GF) representation. After the introduction of tower-field inversion over $GF(((2^2)^2)^2)$ based on a polynomial basis (PB) by Satoh et al. [29], Canright reduced the gate count using a normal basis-(NB-)based $GF(((2^2)^2)^2)$, which has been known as the smallest for a long time [7], Nogami et al. showed that a mixture of a PB and an NB was useful for a more efficient design [23]. On the other hand, Rudra et al., Joen et al., and Mathew et al.

designed inversion circuits using PB-based $GF((2^4)^2)$, which have a smaller critical path delay than those based on $GF(((2^2)^2)^2)$ [12, 17, 27]. Nekado et al. showed that a redundantly represented basis (RRB) was useful for an efficient design [21]. Recently, Ueno et al. designed an inversion circuit based on the combination of an NB, an RRB, and a polynomial ring representation (PRR), which is known as the most area-time efficient inversion [31]. In addition, a logic minimization technique was applied to Canright's S-box, which resulted in a more compact S-box [6].

To embed such a tower-field-based inversion circuit in AES hardware, an isomorphic mapping between the AES field and the tower field is required because the inversion and MixColumns are performed over the AES field (i.e., PB-based $GF(2^8)$ with an irreducible polynomial $x^8 + x^4 + x^3 + x + 1$). Typically, the input into the inversion circuit (in the AES field) is initially mapped to the tower field by the isomorphic mapping. After the inversion operation over the tower field, an inverse isomorphic mapping (and affine transformation) are applied [29]. On the other hand, some architectures perform all of the AES subfunctions (i.e., SubBytes as well as ShiftRows, MixColumns, and AddRoundKey) over the tower field, where isomorphic mapping and its inverse mappings are performed at the timings of the data (i.e., plaintext and ciphertext) input and output, respectively [10, 16–18, 27]. In other words, the cost of field conversion is suppressed when the conversion is performed only once during encryption or decryption. However, the cost of constant multiplications in MixColumns over a tower field is worse than that over the AES field while inversion is efficiently performed over the tower field. More precisely, in tower-field architectures, such linear mappings including constant multiplications usually require $3T_{XOR}$ delay, where T_{XOR} indicates the delay of an XOR gate [21]. The XOR gate count used in (Inv)MixColumns over a tower field is also worse than that over AES field.

3   Proposed Architecture

This section presents a new round-based AES architecture that unifies the encryption and decryption paths in an efficient manner. The key ideas for reducing the critical path delay are summarized as follows: (1) to merge linear mappings such as MixColumns and isomorphic mappings as much as possible by reordering subfunctions, (2) to minimize the number of selectors to unify the encryption and decryption paths by the above merging and a register retiming, and (3) to perform isomorphic mapping and its inverse mappings only once in the pre- and post-round datapaths. We can reduce the number of linear mappings to at most one for each round operation as the effect of (1). Moreover, we can reduce the number of selectors to only one (4-to-1 multiplexer) in the unified datapath as the effect of (2) while the inversion circuit is shared by the encryption and decryption paths. From the idea of (3), we can remove the isomorphic mapping and its inverse mappings from the critical path. Figure 5 shows the overall architecture that consists of the round function and key scheduling parts. Our architecture performs all of the subfunctions over a tower field for

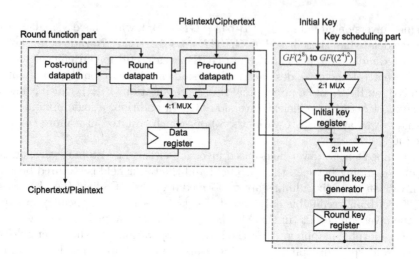

Fig. 5. Overall architecture of proposed AES hardware.

both the round function and key scheduling parts and therefore applies iso-morphic mappings between the AES and tower fields in the datapaths of the pre- and post-round operations, which are represented as the blocks "Pre-round datapath" and "Post-round datapath" in Fig. 5. "Round datapath" performs one round operation for either encryption or decryption.

3.1   Round Function Part

The proposed architecture employs a unified datapath for encryption and decryp-tion as in [15] and applies new operation-reordering and register-retiming tech-niques to address the conventional issues of a false critical path and additional multiplexers. Using our operation-reordering technique and then merging linear mappings, we can reduce the number of linear mappings on the critical path of the round datapath to at most one. Our reordering technique also allows to unify the linear mappings and affine transformation in a round. The unifica-tion of these mappings can drastically reduce the critical path delay and the XOR-gate count of linear mappings, even in a tower-field architecture.

The new operation reordering is derived as follows. First, the original round operation of AES encryption is represented by the following equation:

$$m_{i,j}^{(r+1)} = u_{-i}S(m_{0,i+j}^{(r)}) + u_{1-i}S(m_{1,i+j}^{(r)}) + u_{2-i}S(m_{2,i+j}^{(r)}) + u_{3-i}S(m_{3,i+j}^{(r)}) + k_{i,j}^{(r)}$$
$$= \sum_{e=0}^{3}(u_{e-i}S(m_{e,i+j}^{(r)})) + k_{i,j}^{(r)}, \tag{1}$$

where $m_{i,j}^{(r)}$ and $k_{i,j}^{(r)}$ are the i-th row and j-th column intermediate value and round key at the r-th round, except for the final round. Note that the sub-scripts of each variable are a member of $\mathbb{Z}/4\mathbb{Z}$. The function S indicates the 8-bit S-box, and $u_0, u_1, u_2,$ and u_3 are the coefficients of the matrix of MixColumns and respectively given by $\beta, \beta + 1, 1$, and 1, where β is the indeterminate of $GF(2^8)$ satisfying $\beta^8 + \beta^4 + \beta^3 + \beta + 1 = 0$. We can rewrite Eq. (1) by decomposing S into inversion and affine transformation as follows:

$$m_{i,j}^{(r+1)} = \sum_{e=0}^{3}(u_{e-i}(A((m_{e,i+j}^{(r)})^{-1}) + c)) + k_{i,j}^{(r)}, \tag{2}$$

where A is the linear mapping of the affine transformation, and $c \ (= \beta^6 + \beta^5 + \beta + 1)$ is a constant. In the case of tower-field architectures, Eq. (2) is represented by

$$m_{i,j}^{(r+1)} = \sum_{e=0}^{3}(u_{e-i}(A(\Delta'((\Delta(m_{e,i+j}^{(r)}))^{-1})) + c)) + k_{i,j}^{(r)}, \tag{3}$$

where Δ is the isomorphic mapping from the AES field to a tower field, and Δ' is the inverse isomorphic mapping.

The linear mappings, which include an isomorphism and constant multiplications over the GF, are performed by the constant multiplication of the corresponding matrix over $GF(2)$. Therefore, we can merge such mappings to reduce the critical path delay and the number of XOR gates. In addition, we consider the variable $d_{i,j}^{(r)}$ of the tower field derived from $m_{i,j}^{(r)}$. Substituting $m_{i,j}^{(r)}$ with $\Delta'(d_{i,j}^{(r)}) \ (= m_{i,j}^{(r)})$, we can merge the linear mappings as follows:

$$d_{i,j}^{(r+1)} = \sum_{e=0}^{3}(U_{e-i}((d_{e,i+j}^{(r)})^{-1})) + \Delta(c) + \Delta(k_{i,j}^{(r)}), \tag{4}$$

where $U_e(x) = \Delta(u_e(A(\Delta'(x))))$. Note that an arbitrary linear mapping L satisfies $L(a + b) = L(a) + L(b)$. Thus, the linear mappings of a round in Eq. (4) can be merged into at most one, even with a tower-field S-box, whereas the linear mappings in Eq. (3) cannot be.

On the other hand, the corresponding equation for AES decryption with tower-field arithmetic is given by

$$d_{i,j}^{(r-1)} = \sum_{e=0}^{3}(\Delta(v_{e-i}(\Delta'((\Delta(A'(\Delta'(\Delta(d_{e,j-i}^{(r)}))) + \Delta(c'))^{-1} + \Delta(k_{e,j-i}^{(r)}))))), \tag{5}$$

where A' indicates the linear mapping of the inverse affine transformation. The coefficients v_0, v_1, v_2, and v_3 are respectively given by $\beta^3 + \beta^2 + \beta, \beta^3 + \beta + 1, \beta^3 + \beta^2 + 1$, and $\beta^3 + 1$, and $c' \ (= \beta^2 + 1)$ is a constant. Here, the linear mappings cannot be merged into one because they are performed both before and after the inversion operation. In addition, if we construct an encryption/decryption datapath based on Eqs. (4) and (5), the inversion circuit cannot be shared by encryption and decryption without a selector because the timings of the inversion operations are different from each other. Therefore, we consider a register retiming to store the intermediate value $s_{i,j}^{(r)}$ given after the inverse affine transformation over the

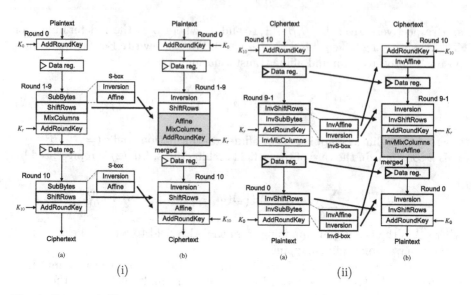

Fig. 6. Proposed (i) encryption and (ii) decryption flows (a) before and (b) after reordering and register-retiming.

tower-field. Here, $s_{i,j}^{(r)}$ is given by $s_{i,j}^{(r)} = \Delta(A'(\Delta'(d_{i,j}^{(r)}))) + \Delta(c')$. In the decryption, we store $s_{i,j}^{(r)}$ in the data register instead of $d_{i,j}^{(r)}$. Using $s_{i,j}^{(r)}$ and $s_{i,j}^{(r-1)}$, we rewrite Eq. (5) as follows:

$$s_{i,j}^{(r-1)} = \sum_{e=0}^{3}(V_{e-i}(\left(s_{e,j-i}^{(r)}\right)^{-1} + \Delta(k_{e,j-i}^{(r)}))) + \Delta(c'), \tag{6}$$

where $V_e(x) = \Delta(A'(v_e(\Delta'(x))))$.

Our round datapath is constructed with a minimal critical path delay according to Eqs. (4) and (6). Here, we further reorder the sequence of operations (i.e., subfunctions) to share inversion circuits without additional selectors and to unify the linear mappings. Figure 6 shows the proposed reordering technique. We first decompose SubBytes into the inversion and (Inv)Affine. In the encryption, Affine, MixColumns, and AddRoundKey can be merged by exchanging Affine and ShiftRows. In the decryption, the inversion circuit is located at the beginning of the round by exchanging the inversion and InvShiftRows. Thus, additional selectors for sharing the inversion circuit are not required thanks to the operation-reordering and register-retiming techniques. This is because both inversion operations are performed at the beginning of the round, which means that the data register output can be directly connected to the inversion circuit.

Figure 7 illustrates the proposed round function datapath with the unification of linear mappings. Our architecture employs only one 128-bit 4-in-1 multiplexer, whereas conventional ones employ several 128-bit multiplexers. For example, the

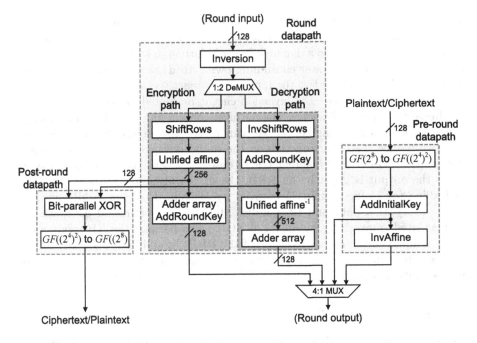

Fig. 7. Proposed round function part.

datapath in [14] employs seven 128-bit multiplexers[1]. Fewer selectors can reduce the critical path delay and circuit area and solve the false critical path problem. Unified affine and Unified affine^{-1} in Fig. 7 perform the unified linear mappings (i.e., $U_0, \ldots, U_3$ and $V_0, \ldots, V_3$) and constant addition. The number of linear mappings on the critical path is at most one in our architecture, whereas that of the conventional architectures is not. We can also suppress the overhead of constant multiplication over the tower field by the unification. Adder arrays in Fig. 7 consist of four 4-input 8-bit adders in MixColumns or InvMixColumns. In the encryption, the factoring technique for MixColumns and AddRoundKey [21] is available for Unified affine, which makes the circuit area smaller without a delay overhead. As a result, the data width between Unified affine and Adder array in Encryption path is reduced from 512 to 256 bits because the calculations of U_1 and U_3 are not performed in Encryption path. In addition, Adder array and AddRoundKey are unified in Encryption path because both of them are composed of 8-bit adders[2]. On the other hand, since there is no factoring technique for InvMixColumns without delay overheads, the data width from Unified affine^{-1} to Adder array in Decryption path is 512 bits. Finally, an inactive path can be disabled using a demultiplexer since our datapath is fully parallel after the inversion circuit. Thanks to the disabling, a multiplexer and AddRoundKey

---

[1] The selectors in SubBytes/InvSubBytes are included in the seven multiplexers.

[2] Some architectures such as [14,29] unify AddInitialKey and AddRoundKeys. We did not unify them to avoid increasing the number of selectors.

are unified as Bit-parallel XOR. (The addition of $\Delta(c)$ in Unified affine should be active only when encryption.) In addition, the demultiplexer would suppress power consumption due to a dynamic hazard. Although tower-field inversion circuits are known to be power-consuming owing to dynamic hazards [19], these hazards can be terminated at the input of the inactive path.

Our datapath employs the inversion circuit presented in [31] because it has the highest area-time efficiency among inversion circuits including one using a logic minimization technique [6]. We can merge the isomorphic mappings in order to reduce the linear function on the round datapath to only one, even if the inversion circuit has different GF representations at the input and output. Since the output is given by an RRB, the data width from Inversion to Unified affine (or Unified affine^{-1}) is given by 160 bits. However, AddRoundKey in the decryption path and Bit-parallel XOR in the post-round datapath are implemented respectively by only 128 XOR gates because the NB used as the input is equal to the reduced version of the RRB. In addition, a 1:2 DeMUX is implemented with NOR gates thanks to the redundancy, whereas nonredundant representations require AND gates.

3.2   Key Scheduling Part

The on-the-fly key scheduling part is shared by the encryption and decryption processes. For the encryption, the key scheduling part first stores the initial key in the initial key register (in Fig. 5) and then generates the round keys during the following clock cycles. For the decryption, the final round key should be calculated from the initial key and stored in the initial key register in advance. The key scheduling part then generates the round keys in the reverse order by the round key generator (in Fig. 5). However, conventional key scheduling datapaths such those as in [14,29] are not applicable to our round datapath because they have a loop with a false path and/or a longer true critical path than our datapath.

To address the above issue, we introduce a new architecture for the key scheduling datapath. For on-the-fly implementation, the subkeys are calculated for each of the four subkeys (i.e., 128 bits) in a clock cycle. Therefore, the on-the-fly key scheduling for the encryption is expressed as

$$\begin{cases} k_0^{(r+1)} = k_0^{(r)} + KeyEx(k_3^{(r)}) \\ k_1^{(r+1)} = k_0^{(r)} + k_1^{(r)} + KeyEx(k_3^{(r)}) \\ k_2^{(r+1)} = k_0^{(r)} + k_1^{(r)} + k_2^{(r)} + KeyEx(k_3^{(r)}) \\ k_3^{(r+1)} = k_0^{(r)} + k_1^{(r)} + k_2^{(r)} + k_3^{(r)} + KeyEx(k_3^{(r)}) \end{cases}, \qquad (7)$$

where $k_0^{(r)}, k_1^{(r)}, k_2^{(r)}$, and $k_3^{(r)}$ are a 32-bit subkey at the r-th round and $KeyEx$ is the key expansion function that consists of a round constant addition, RotWord, and SubWord. The inverse key scheduling for the decryption is represented by

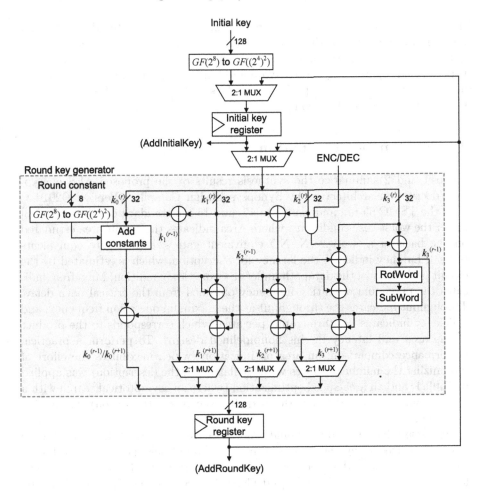

Fig. 8. Proposed key scheduling part.

$$\begin{cases} k_0^{(r-1)} = k_0^{(r)} + KeyEx(k_2^{(r)} + k_3^{(r)}) \\ k_1^{(r-1)} = k_0^{(r)} + k_1^{(r)} \\ k_2^{(r-1)} = k_1^{(r)} + k_2^{(r)} \\ k_3^{(r-1)} = k_2^{(r)} + k_3^{(r)} \end{cases} \qquad (8)$$

Figure 8 shows the proposed key scheduling datapath architecture, where the $KeyEx$ components are unified for encryption and decryption. Note here that most of adders (i.e., XOR gates) for computing $k_1^{(r+1)}$, $k_2^{(r+1)}$, and $k_3^{(r+1)}$ should be non-integrated to make the critical path shorter than that of the round function part. The input key is initially mapped to the tower field, and all of the computations (including AddRoundKey) are performed over the tower field. The ENC/DEC signal controls the input to RotWord and SubWord using a 32-bit AND gate. The upper 2-in-1 multiplexer selects an initial key or a final round key as the input to

Initial key register, the middle 2-in-1 multiplexer selects a key stored in Initial key register or a round key as the input to Round key generator, and the lower 2-in-1 multiplexers select encryption or decryption path. The round constant addition is performed separately from RotWord and SubWord to reduce the critical path delay. As a result, the critical path delay of the key scheduling part becomes shorter than that of the round function part.

4   Performance Evaluation

Tables 1 and 2 summarize the synthesis results of the proposed AES encryption/decryption architecture by Synopsys Design Compiler (Version D2010-3) with the TSMC 65-nm and NanGate 45- and 15-nm standard-cell libraries [2, 3] under the worst-case conditions, where Area indicates the circuit area estimated on the basis of a two-way NAND equivalent gate size (i.e., gate equivalents (GEs)); Latency indicates the latency for encryption, which is estimated by the circuit path delay of the datapath under the worst low condition; Max. freq. indicates the maximum operation frequency obtained from the critical path delay; Throughput indicates the throughput at the maximum operation frequency; and Efficiency indicates the throughput per area, which corresponds to the product of the area and latency in this nonpipelined design[3]. To perform a practical performance comparison, an area optimization (which maximizes the effort of minimizing the number of gates without flattening the description) was applied in Table 1, and an area-speed optimization (where an asymptotical search with a set of timing constraints was performed after the area optimization) was applied in Table 2.

In these tables, the conventional representative datapaths [14, 15, 17, 29] were also synthesized using the same optimization conditions. The source codes for these syntheses were described by the authors referring to [14, 15, 17, 29], except for the source codes of Satoh's and Canright's S-boxes in [7, 29] that can be obtained from their websites [1, 8]. For a fair comparison, the datapaths of [15, 17] were adjusted to the round-based nonpipelined architecture corresponding to the proposed datapath. Note that only the inversion circuit over a PB-based $GF((2^4)^2)$ in [17] was not described faithfully according to the paper[4]. Latency and Throughput were calculated assuming that the datapath of [15] requires 10 clock cycles to perform each encryption or decryption and the others require 11

---

[3] Design Compiler generated a static power consumption report for each architecture. However, the report dose not consider the effect of glitches while tower-field inversion circuits are known to include non-trivial glitches [19]. Therefore, we did not mention the power consumption report to avoid misleading.

[4] According to [17], the $GF(2^4)$ inversion in the circuit can be implemented with a $T_{XOR} + 3T_{NAND}$ delay, where T_{XOR} and T_{NAND} are the delays of the XOR and NAND gates, respectively. However, there is no detailed description to realize such a circuit. Therefore, using the best of our knowledge, we described the circuit by a direct mapping based on the PPRM expansion, which is an algebraic normal form frequently used for designing GF arithmetic circuits [19, 28].

Table 1. Synthesis results for proposed and conventional AES hardware architectures with area optimization

	Area (GE)	Latency (ns)	Max. freq. (MHz)	Throughput (Gbps)	Efficiency (Kbps/GE)
TSMC 65-nm					
Satoh et al. [29]	13, 671.75	78.10	140.85	1.64	119.88
Lutz et al. [15]	20, 380.50	68.50	145.99	1.87	91.69
Liu et al. [14]	12, 538.75	85.25	129.03	1.50	119.75
Mathew et al. [17]	20, 639.50	97.68	112.61	1.31	63.49
This work	15, 242.75	46.97	234.19	2.73	178.78
NanGate 45-nm					
Satoh et al. [29]	12, 560.99	31.57	348.43	4.05	322.78
Lutz et al. [15]	20, 000.66	20.30	492.61	6.31	315.26
Liu et al. [14]	11, 829.34	34.43	319.49	3.72	314.28
Mathew et al. [17]	17, 573.33	41.80	263.16	3.06	174.25
This work	13, 814.69	16.94	649.35	7.56	546.96
NanGate 15-nm					
Satoh et al. [29]	14, 526.01	4.36	2, 524.17	29.37	2, 022.04
Lutz et al. [15]	23, 391.49	4.57	2, 185.84	25.44	1, 087.37
Liu et al. [14]	13, 847.25	4.74	2, 321.05	27.01	1, 950.46
Mathew et al. [17]	21, 361.00	5.32	2, 066.93	24.05	1, 125.95
This work	15, 468.97	2.65	4, 144.22	48.22	3, 117.44

clock cycles. This is because the initial key addition and first-round computation are performed with one clock cycle for [15]. Area was calculated without the initial key, round key, and data registers to compare the datapaths more clearly. Note also that the key scheduling parts of [15,17] were implemented with the one presented in this paper because there is no description for the key scheduling parts. (For [15], the isomorphic mapping from $GF(2^8)$ to $GF((2^4)^2)$ was removed for applying to the round function part.)

The results in Table 1 show that our datapath achieves the lowest latency (i.e., highest throughput) compared with the conventional ones with tower-field inversion circuits owing to the lower critical path delay. Moreover, the circuit area is not the largest owing to fewer selectors. Note that the latency is consistent with the throughput because these circuits are not pipelined. Although all operations are translated to the tower field in our architecture, the area and delay overheads of MixColumns and InvMixColumns are suppressed by the unification technique. In addition, even with a tower-field S-box, our architecture has an advantage with regard to the latency over Lutz's one with table-lookup-based inversion, as indicated in Table 2. As a result, our architecture is more efficient in terms of the throughput per area than any conventional architecture. More precisely, the proposed datapath is approximately 53–72 % more efficient than any conventional architecture under the conditions of the three CMOS processes. The results also suggest that the proposed architecture would perform an AES encryption or decryption with the smallest energy. Moreover, the cutoff of an inactive path by a demultiplexer would further reduce the power

Table 2. Synthesis results for proposed and conventional AES hardware architectures with area-speed optimization

	Area (GE)	Latency (ns)	Max. freq. (MHz)	Throughput (Gbps)	Efficiency (Kbps/GE)
TSMC 65-nm					
Satoh et al. [29]	14,516.50	56.87	193.42	2.25	155.05
Lutz et al. [15]	22,883.25	33.90	294.99	3.78	165.00
Liu et al. [14]	13,970.50	60.17	182.82	2.13	152.27
Mathew et al. [17]	23,298.49	65.45	168.07	1.96	83.94
This work	15,807.00	34.10	322.58	3.75	237.47
NanGate 45-nm					
Satoh et al. [29]	13,386.67	24.42	450.45	5.24	391.55
Lutz et al. [15]	22,417.01	14.40	694.44	8.89	396.52
Liu et al. [14]	12,443.66	28.27	389.11	4.53	363.86
Mathew et al. [17]	19,243.67	31.90	344.83	4.01	208.51
This work	14,582.99	13.53	813.01	9.46	648.73
NanGate 15-nm					
Satoh et al. [29]	16,924.74	3.31	3,322.26	38.66	2,284.17
Lutz et al. [15]	25,692.49	2.08	4,799.85	61.44	2,391.28
Liu et al. [14]	15,768.43	3.65	3,014.14	35.07	2,224.29
Mathew et al. [17]	23,789.48	4.03	2,729.18	31.76	1,334.95
This work	17,232.00	1.80	6,117.70	71.19	4,131.14

consumption caused by a dynamic hazard, but this could not be evaluated by the logic synthesis and still remains for the future study.

The performance of the architecture in [17] was relatively lower for our experimental conditions because its critical path includes InvMixColumns to compute $MC^{-1}(K_r)$ and therefore becomes longer than those of other designs. In addition, InvMixColumns over a tower-field is more area-consuming than that over an AES field. This suggests that the architecture in [17] is not suitable for an on-the-fly key scheduling implementation. The architectures in [14,29] have smaller areas than the proposed architecture; however, our architecture has a higher throughput. The increasing ratio of the throughput is larger than that of the circuit area because the architectures in [14,29] use InvMixColumns to compute $MC^{-1}(K_r)$ and require several additional selectors, respectively.

The above comparative evaluation was done with the proposed and some conventional but representative datapaths. There are other previous works focusing on efficiency (i.e., throughput per gate) by round-based architectures. However, such previous works do not provide a concrete implementation and/or exhibit better performance than the abovementioned conventional datapaths. For example, a hardware AES implementation with a short critical path was presented in [21], which employed an RRB to reduce the critical path delay of SubBytes/InvSubBytes and MixColumns/InvMixColumns. However, we could not evaluate the efficiency by ourselves because of the lack of a detailed description. Another AES encryption/decryption architecture with a high throughput was presented in [14]. However, the architecture had a lower throughput/area efficiency compared to the architecture in [29] according to that paper. Moreover, AES architectures that support either encryption or decryption such as in [20,32] are not evaluated in this paper.

5   Discussion

The proposed design employs a round-based architecture without block-wise parallelism such as pipelining. The modes of operations with block-wise parallelism (e.g., the ECB and CTR modes) are also available owing to the trade-off between the area and the throughput by pipelining [11]. A simple way to obtain a pipelined version of the proposed architecture is to unroll the rounds and insert pipeline registers between them. The datapath can be further pipelined by inserting registers into the round datapath. The proposed datapath can be efficiently pipelined by placing the pipeline register at the output of the inversion with a good delay balance between the inversion and the following circuit. For example, the synthesis results for the proposed datapath using the area-speed optimization with the NanGate 45-nm standard-cell library indicated that the inversion circuit had a delay of 0.63 ns, and the remainder had a delay of 0.67 ns. As a result, pipelining would achieve a throughput of 17.37 Gbps, which is nearly twice that without pipelining. Thus, the proposed datapath is also suitable for such a pipelined implementation.

Another discussion point is how the proposed architecture can be resistant to side-channel attacks. A masking countermeasure would be based on a masked tower-field inversion circuit [9,25] such as that in [24]. The major features of the countermeasure are to replace the inversion with a masked inversion and to duplicate other linear operations. Such a countermeasure can also be applied to the proposed datapath. In addition, hiding countermeasures, such as WDDL [30], which replaces the logic gates with a complementary logic style, would also be applicable, and the hardware efficiency would be proportionally lower with respect to the results in Tables 1 and 2.

More sophisticated countermeasures such as threshold implementation (TI) and generalized masking schemes (GMSs) [4,5,18,22,26] would also be applicable to the proposed datapath in principle in the same manner as other conventional ones. On the other hand, such countermeasures, especially against higher-order DPAs, require a considerable area overhead and more random bits compared with the aforementioned countermeasures. When applying such countermeasures, the area overhead would be critical for some applications. In addition, TI- and GMS-based inversion circuits should be pipelined to reduce the resulting circuit area (i.e., the number of shares). To divide the circuit delay equally, it would be better to insert pipeline register at the middle of Encryption and Decryption path in Fig. 7.

6   Conclusion

This paper presented a new efficient round-based AES architecture that supports both encryption and decryption. An efficient AES datapath with a lower latency (or higher throughput per gate) is suitable for some practical modes of operation, such as CBC and CCM, because pipelined parallelism cannot be applied to such modes. The proposed datapath utilizes new operation-reordering and register-retiming techniques to unify critical components (i.e., inversion and linear matrix operations) with fewer additional selectors. As a result, our datapath has the lowest critical path delay compared to conventional ones with tower-field S-boxes. The proposed and conventional AES hardware were designed on the basis of compatible round-based architectures and evaluated using logic synthesis with TSMC 65-nm and NanGate 45- and 15-nm CMOS standard-cell libraries under the worst-case conditions. The synthesis results suggested that the proposed architecture was approximately 53–72 % more efficient than the best conventional architecture in terms of the throughput per area, which would also indicate that the proposed architecture can perform encryption/decryption with the lowest energy.

The performance evaluation was performed at the design stage of the logic synthesis; therefore, the power consumption and latency considering place and route were not evaluated. A detailed evaluation after the place and route is planned as future work. However, the post-synthesis results would be proportional to the presented synthesis results because the proposed and conventional architectures employ the same or similar hardware algorithms (e.g., tower-field inversion) and do not have any extra global wires that have an impact on the critical path. The design of efficient and side-channel-resistant AES hardware based on the proposed datapath is also planned for future work.

Acknowledgment. This work has been supported by JSPS KAKENHI Grant No. 25240006.

Appendix: An Example Set of Linear Mappings and a Unified Affine

This appendix provides an example set of matrices for linear operations, i.e., an isomorphic mapping, an inverse isomorphic mapping, an affine transformation over the tower field, inverse affine transformation over the tower field, $U_0, U_1, U_2, U_3, V_0, V_1, V_2$, and V_3. In this study, we employ the tower-field inversion circuit in [31]. In the following formulae, the least-significant bits are in the upper-left corner.

The conversion matrices of the isomorphic mapping and its inverse mapping (denoted by δ and δ', respectively) are given by

$$
\delta = \begin{pmatrix}
0\,1\,0\,1\,1\,1\,0\,0 \\
1\,0\,1\,0\,0\,0\,1\,1 \\
1\,0\,0\,1\,0\,0\,0\,1 \\
0\,0\,0\,0\,0\,1\,0\,0 \\
0\,1\,1\,0\,1\,1\,0\,0 \\
1\,0\,1\,0\,1\,0\,0\,0 \\
1\,1\,1\,0\,0\,0\,0\,1 \\
0\,0\,1\,1\,0\,0\,0\,1
\end{pmatrix}, \quad
\delta' = \begin{pmatrix}
1\,1\,0\,1\,1\,0\,0\,1\,1\,0 \\
0\,1\,0\,1\,0\,0\,1\,0\,1\,0 \\
0\,1\,0\,0\,1\,1\,0\,1\,1\,1 \\
1\,0\,0\,0\,1\,0\,1\,1\,1\,1 \\
1\,0\,0\,1\,0\,0\,0\,1\,0\,1 \\
1\,0\,0\,0\,1\,0\,0\,0\,0\,0 \\
1\,1\,1\,1\,0\,1\,1\,0\,0\,0 \\
1\,1\,0\,0\,0\,0\,1\,0\,0\,1
\end{pmatrix}. \tag{9}
$$

The isomorphic mapping using δ performs conversion from the AES field to the tower field used in [31] (i.e., an NB-based $GF((2^4)^2)$). The inverse isomorphic mapping using δ' performs conversion from the RRB-based $GF((2^4)^2)$ to the AES field. The affine and inverse affine matrices over the tower field (denoted by ϕ and ϕ', respectively) are given by

$$
\phi = \begin{pmatrix}
1\,1\,1\,0\,1\,0\,0\,1\,1\,0 \\
1\,0\,0\,0\,1\,0\,0\,1\,1\,0 \\
1\,1\,0\,1\,1\,1\,0\,1\,0\,0 \\
1\,0\,0\,0\,1\,1\,0\,1\,1\,1 \\
1\,0\,0\,1\,0\,1\,0\,0\,0\,1 \\
1\,1\,0\,1\,1\,0\,1\,0\,0\,1 \\
1\,0\,0\,1\,0\,1\,1\,1\,1\,0 \\
1\,1\,0\,1\,1\,0\,1\,1\,0\,0
\end{pmatrix}, \quad
\phi' = \begin{pmatrix}
0\,0\,0\,1\,0\,1\,1\,0 \\
1\,1\,0\,1\,0\,1\,1\,0 \\
0\,1\,0\,1\,1\,0\,0\,0 \\
0\,0\,1\,1\,1\,0\,1\,1 \\
0\,0\,1\,0\,0\,0\,0\,1 \\
0\,1\,0\,1\,0\,1\,0\,1 \\
0\,0\,1\,0\,1\,1\,1\,0 \\
0\,1\,0\,1\,0\,0\,0\,0
\end{pmatrix}. \tag{10}
$$

The input and output of the linear mapping represented by ϕ are given by the RRB- and NB-based $GF((2^4)^2)$, respectively. The input and output of the linear mapping represented by ϕ' are given by the NB-based $GF((2^4)^2)$. The constants $\Delta(c)$ and $\Delta(c')$ are given by $\beta^5 + \beta^3 + \beta^2$ and $\beta^7 + \beta^4 + \beta^2$, respectively. Let ψ_e and ψ'_e be the matrices representing U_e and V_e, respectively ($0 \le e \le 3$). The matrices ψ_0, ψ_1, ψ_2, and ψ_3 are given by

$$
\psi_0 = \begin{pmatrix}
1\,1\,1\,1\,0\,0\,1\,1\,1 \\
0\,0\,1\,1\,0\,1\,0\,1\,0\,0 \\
1\,1\,0\,1\,1\,0\,1\,1\,1\,1 \\
1\,1\,0\,1\,1\,1\,0\,0\,0\,1 \\
1\,0\,0\,1\,0\,0\,0\,0\,1\,1 \\
1\,0\,1\,1\,1\,0\,0\,0\,0\,0 \\
1\,1\,1\,0\,1\,0\,1\,0\,1\,0 \\
0\,1\,0\,0\,1\,0\,1\,0\,0\,1
\end{pmatrix}, \quad
\psi_1 = \begin{pmatrix}
0\,0\,0\,1\,1\,0\,1\,0\,0\,1 \\
1\,0\,1\,1\,1\,1\,0\,0\,1\,0 \\
0\,0\,0\,0\,0\,1\,1\,0\,1\,1 \\
0\,1\,0\,1\,0\,0\,0\,1\,1\,0 \\
0\,0\,0\,0\,0\,1\,0\,0\,1\,0 \\
0\,1\,1\,0\,0\,0\,1\,0\,0\,1 \\
0\,1\,1\,1\,1\,1\,0\,1\,0\,0 \\
1\,0\,0\,1\,0\,0\,0\,1\,0\,1
\end{pmatrix}, \tag{11}
$$

$$
\psi_2 = \psi_3 = \phi. \tag{12}
$$

respectively. The matrices ψ_0', ψ_1', ψ_2', and ψ_3' are given by

$$
\psi_0' = \begin{pmatrix}
0 & 0 & 0 & 0 & 0 & 0 & 1 & 1 & 0 & 0 \\
0 & 0 & 1 & 0 & 1 & 0 & 0 & 1 & 0 & 1 \\
0 & 1 & 0 & 0 & 1 & 1 & 1 & 0 & 1 & 1 \\
1 & 0 & 0 & 0 & 1 & 1 & 1 & 0 & 1 & 1 \\
1 & 1 & 0 & 0 & 0 & 0 & 0 & 1 & 0 & 1 \\
0 & 0 & 1 & 0 & 1 & 0 & 0 & 0 & 1 & 1 \\
1 & 1 & 0 & 1 & 1 & 0 & 0 & 0 & 1 & 1 \\
1 & 1 & 0 & 1 & 1 & 1 & 1 & 1 & 1 & 0
\end{pmatrix},\
\psi_1' = \begin{pmatrix}
0 & 0 & 0 & 0 & 0 & 1 & 1 & 0 & 1 & 1 \\
0 & 0 & 0 & 1 & 1 & 0 & 0 & 0 & 1 & 1 \\
1 & 1 & 0 & 0 & 0 & 0 & 1 & 0 & 0 & 1 \\
0 & 1 & 1 & 1 & 1 & 0 & 1 & 0 & 0 & 1 \\
1 & 0 & 1 & 1 & 1 & 0 & 0 & 0 & 1 & 1 \\
0 & 0 & 0 & 1 & 1 & 1 & 1 & 1 & 1 & 0 \\
0 & 1 & 0 & 0 & 1 & 1 & 1 & 1 & 1 & 0 \\
0 & 1 & 0 & 0 & 1 & 0 & 1 & 0 & 1 & 0
\end{pmatrix},
\tag{13}
$$

$$
\psi_2' = \begin{pmatrix}
1 & 0 & 1 & 1 & 1 & 1 & 1 & 1 & 1 & 0 \\
0 & 1 & 0 & 1 & 0 & 1 & 1 & 1 & 1 & 0 \\
1 & 0 & 0 & 0 & 1 & 1 & 1 & 0 & 1 & 1 \\
0 & 1 & 1 & 1 & 1 & 1 & 0 & 1 & 0 & 0 \\
1 & 1 & 0 & 0 & 0 & 1 & 0 & 1 & 1 & 1 \\
1 & 0 & 0 & 0 & 1 & 1 & 0 & 0 & 0 & 1 \\
1 & 1 & 0 & 0 & 0 & 0 & 0 & 1 & 0 & 1 \\
1 & 0 & 0 & 0 & 1 & 0 & 0 & 0 & 0 & 0
\end{pmatrix},\
\psi_3' = \begin{pmatrix}
0 & 0 & 1 & 1 & 0 & 0 & 1 & 1 & 1 & 1 \\
1 & 0 & 0 & 0 & 1 & 1 & 1 & 1 & 1 & 0 \\
0 & 0 & 1 & 0 & 1 & 1 & 0 & 0 & 0 & 1 \\
1 & 0 & 0 & 1 & 0 & 1 & 1 & 1 & 0 & 1 \\
0 & 0 & 1 & 0 & 1 & 0 & 0 & 0 & 0 & 0 \\
1 & 0 & 0 & 1 & 0 & 0 & 1 & 0 & 0 & 1 \\
1 & 1 & 0 & 0 & 0 & 0 & 0 & 1 & 1 & 0 \\
0 & 0 & 1 & 1 & 0 & 1 & 0 & 1 & 0 & 0
\end{pmatrix}.
\tag{14}
$$

References

1. Cryptographic hardware project. http://www.aoki.ecei.tohoku.ac.jp/crypto/
2. NanGate FreePDK15 open cell library, January 2016. http://www.nangate.com/?page_id=2328
3. NanGate FreePDK45 open cell library, January 2016. http://www.nangate.com/?page_id=2325
4. Bilgin, B., Gierlichs, B., Nikova, S., Nikov, V., Rijmen, V.: Higher-order threshold implementations. In: Sarkar, P., Iwata, T. (eds.) ASIACRYPT 2014, Part II. LNCS, vol. 8874, pp. 326–343. Springer, Heidelberg (2014)
5. Bilgin, B., Gierlichs, B., Nikova, S., Nikov, V., Rijmen, V.: Trade-offs for threshold implementations illustrated on AES. IEEE Trans. Comput. Aided Des. Integr. Syst. **34**(7), 1188–1200 (2015)
6. Boyer, J., Matthews, P., Peralta, P.: Logic minimization techniques with applications to cryptology. J. Cryptology **47**, 280–312 (2013)
7. Canright, D.: A very compact S-box for AES. In: Rao, J.R., Sunar, B. (eds.) CHES 2005. LNCS, vol. 3659, pp. 441–455. Springer, Heidelberg (2005)
8. Canright, D.: http://faculty.nps.edu/drcanrig/
9. Canright, D., Batina, L.: A very compact "Perfectly Masked" S-Box for AES. In: Bellovin, S.M., Gennaro, R., Keromytis, A.D., Yung, M. (eds.) ACNS 2008. LNCS, vol. 5037, pp. 446–459. Springer, Heidelberg (2008)
10. Hammad, I., El-Sankary, K., El-Masry, E.: High-speed AES encryptor with efficient merging techniques. IEEE Embed. Syst. Lett. **2**, 67–71 (2010)
11. Hodjat, A., Verbauwhede, I.: Area-throughput trade-offs for fully pipelined 30 to 70 Gbits/s AES processors. IEEE Trans. Comput. **50**(4), 366–372 (2006)
12. Jeon, Y., Kim, Y., Lee, D.: A compact memory-free architecture for the AES algorithm using resource sharing methods. J. Circ. Syst. Comput. **19**(5), 1109–1130 (2010)

13. Lin, S.Y., Huang, C.T.: A high-throughput low-power AES cipher for network applications. In: The 12th Asia and South Pacific Design Automation Conference (ASP-DAC 2007), pp. 595–600. IEEE (2007)
14. Liu, P.C., Chang, H.C., Lee, C.Y.: A 1.69 Gb/s area-efficient AES crypto core with compact on-the-fly key expansion unit. In: 41st European Solid-State Circuits Conference (ESSCIRC 2009), pp. 404–407. IEEE (2009)
15. Lutz, A., Treichler, J., Gürkaynak, F., Kaeslin, H., Basler, G., Erni, A., Reichmuth, S., Rommens, P., Oetiker, P., Fichtner, W.: 2Gbit/s hardware realizations of RIJN-DAEL and SERPENT: a comparative analysis. In: Kaliski, B.S., Koç, Ç.K., Paar, C. (eds.) CHES 2002. LNCS, vol. 2523, pp. 144–158. Springer, Heidelberg (2002)
16. Mathew, S., Satpathy, S., Suresh, V., Anders, M., Himanshu, K., Amit, A., Hsu, S., Chen, G., Krishnamurthy, R.K.: 340 mV-1.1V, 289 Gbps/W, 2090-gate nanoAES hardware accelerator with area-optimized encrypt/decrypt $GF(2^4)^2$ polynomials in 22 nm tri-gate CMOS. IEEE J. Solid-State Circ. **50**, 1048–1058 (2015)
17. Mathew, S.K., Sheikh, F., Kounavis, M.E., Gueron, S., Agarwal, A., Hsu, S.K., Himanshu, K., Anders, M.A., Krishnamurthy, R.K.: 53 Gbps native $GF(2^4)^2$ composite-field AES-encrypt/decrypt accelerator for content-protection in 45 nm high-performance microprocessors. IEEE J. Solid-State Circ. **46**, 767–776 (2011)
18. Moradi, A., Poschmann, A., Ling, S., Paar, C., Wang, H.: Pushing the limits: a very compact and a threshold implementation of AES. In: Paterson, K.G. (ed.) EUROCRYPT 2011. LNCS, vol. 6632, pp. 69–88. Springer, Heidelberg (2011)
19. Morioka, S., Satoh, A.: An optimized S-Box circuit architecture for low power AES design. In: Kaliski, B.S., Koç, Ç.K., Paar, C. (eds.) CHES 2002. LNCS, vol. 2523, pp. 172–186. Springer, Heidelberg (2002)
20. Morioka, S., Satoh, A.: A 10 Gbps full-AES crypto design with a twisted-BDD S-box architecture. IEEE Trans. Very Large Scale Integr. (VLSI) Syst. **12**, 686–691 (2004)
21. Nekado, K., Nogami, Y., Iokibe, K.: Very short critical path implementation of AES with direct logic gates. In: Hanaoka, G., Yamauchi, T. (eds.) IWSEC 2012. LNCS, vol. 7631, pp. 51–68. Springer, Heidelberg (2012)
22. Nikova, S., Rijmen, V., Schläffer, M.: Secure hardware implementation of nonlinear functions in the presence of glithces. J. Cryptology **24**, 292–321 (2011)
23. Nogami, Y., Nekado, K., Toyota, T., Hongo, N., Morikawa, Y.: Mixed bases for efficient inversion in $\mathbb{F}_{((2^2)^2)^2}$ and conversion matrices of SubBytes of AES. In: Mangard, S., Standaert, F.-X. (eds.) CHES 2010. LNCS, vol. 6225, pp. 234–247. Springer, Heidelberg (2010)
24. Okamoto, K., Homma, N., Aoki, T., Morioka, S.: A hierarchical formal approach to verifying side-channel resistant cryptographic processors. In: Hardware-Oriented Security and Trust (HOST), pp. 76–79. IEEE (2014)
25. Oswald, E., Mangard, S., Pramstaller, N., Rijmen, V.: A side-channel analysis resistant description of the AES S-Box. In: Gilbert, H., Handschuh, H. (eds.) FSE 2005. LNCS, vol. 3557, pp. 413–423. Springer, Heidelberg (2005)
26. Reparaz, O., Bilgin, B., Nikova, S., Gierlichs, B., Verbauwhede, I.: Consolidating masking schemes. In: Gennaro, R., Robshaw, M. (eds.) CRYPTO 2015. LNCS, vol. 9215, pp. 764–783. Springer, Heidelberg (2015)
27. Rudra, A., Dubey, P.K., Jutla, C.S., Kumar, V., Rao, J.R., Rohatgi, P.: Efficient Rijndael encryption implementation with composite field arithmetic. In: Koç, Ç.K., Naccache, D., Paar, C. (eds.) CHES 2001. LNCS, vol. 2162, pp. 171–184. Springer, Heidelberg (2001)

28. Sasao, T.: AND-EXOR expressions and their optimization. In: Sasao, T. (ed.) Logic Synthesis and Optimization. The Kluwer International Series in Engineering and Computer Science, vol. 212, pp. 287–312. Kluwer Academic Publishers (1993)

29. Satoh, A., Morioka, S., Takano, K., Munetoh, S.: A compact Rijndael hardware architecture with S-Box optimization. In: Boyd, C. (ed.) ASIACRYPT 2001. LNCS, vol. 2248, pp. 239–254. Springer, Heidelberg (2001)

30. Tiri, K., Verbauwhede, I.: A logic level design methodology for a secure DPA resistant ASIC or FPGA implementation. In: Design, Automation and Test in Europe Conference and Exhibition (DATE), vol. 1, pp. 246–251 (2004)

31. Ueno, R., Homma, N., Sugawara, Y., Nogami, Y., Aoki, T.: Highly efficient $GF(2^8)$ inversion circuit based on redundant GF arithmetic and its application to AES design. In: Güneysu, T., Handschuh, H. (eds.) CHES 2015. LNCS, vol. 9293, pp. 63–80. Springer, Heidelberg (2015)

32. Verbauwhede, I., Schaumont, P., Kuo, H.: Design and performance testing of a 2.29-GB/s Rijndael processor. IEEE J. Solid-State Circ. **38**, 569–572 (2003)

Efficient High-Speed WPA2 Brute Force Attacks Using Scalable Low-Cost FPGA Clustering

Markus Kammerstetter[1](✉), Markus Muellner[1], Daniel Burian[1],
Christian Kudera[1], and Wolfgang Kastner[2]

[1] Secure Systems Lab Vienna, Automation Systems Group, Institute of Computer
Aided Automation, Vienna University of Technology, Vienna, Austria
{mk,mmuellner,dburian,ckudera}@seclab.tuwien.ac.at
[2] Automation Systems Group, Institute of Computer Aided Automation,
Vienna University of Technology, Vienna, Austria
k@auto.tuwien.ac.at

Abstract. WPA2-Personal is widely used to protect Wi-Fi networks
against illicit access. While attackers typically use GPUs to speed up the
discovery of weak network passwords, attacking random passwords is
considered to quickly become infeasible with increasing password length.
Professional attackers may thus turn to commercial high-end FPGA-
based cluster solutions to significantly increase the speed of those attacks.
Well known manufacturers such as Elcomsoft have succeeded in creating
world's fastest commercial FPGA-based WPA2 password recovery system, but since they rely on high-performance FPGAs the costs of these
systems are well beyond the reach of amateurs. In this paper, we present
a highly optimized low-cost FPGA cluster-based WPA-2 Personal password recovery system that can not only achieve similar performance at
a cost affordable by amateurs, but in comparison our implementation
would also be more than 5 times as fast on the original hardware. Since
the currently fastest system is not only significantly slower but proprietary as well, we believe that we are the first to present the internals of
a highly optimized and fully pipelined FPGA WPA2 password recovery
system. In addition, we evaluated our approach with respect to performance and power usage and compare it to GPU-based systems.

Keywords: FPGA · WPA2 · Security · Brute force · Attacks

1 Introduction

Today's Wi-Fi networks are commonly protected with the well known WPA2
protocol defined in the IEEE 802.11 standard documents [6]. The WPA2-
Personal variant is designed for smaller networks and uses a pre-shared key
(i.e., a Wi-Fi password) to derive the necessary key material for authentication,
encryption and integrity protection. The Wi-Fi password needs to be at least 8
characters long and the key material is mainly derived through the salted key

© International Association for Cryptologic Research 2016
B. Gierlichs and A.Y. Poschmann (Eds.): CHES 2016, LNCS 9813, pp. 559–577, 2016.
DOI: 10.1007/978-3-662-53140-2_27

derivation function PBKDF2 [8] in combination with the SHA1 hashing algorithm [1] in HMAC configuration [2]. Due to the computational complexity of the key derivation function and the use of the Wi-Fi's SSID as cryptographic salt, brute force attacks are very hard to conduct in the presence of random passwords with increasing length. Incurring significant costs well outside of what amateurs can afford, professional attackers can turn to commercial high-end FPGA-based cluster solutions achieving WPA-2 password guessing speeds of 1 million guesses per second and more [10]. In this paper, we focus on the WPA2-Personal key derivation function and low-cost FPGA cluster based attacks affordable by amateurs. Especially considering second-hand FPGA boards that have been used for cryptocurrency mining, those boards are now available at low cost and can be repurposed to mount attacks on cryptographic systems. In the first part, we use a top-down approach to present WPA2-Personal security at a high level and we subsequently break it down to low-level SHA1 computations. In the second part, we use a bottom-up approach to show how these computations can be addressed in hardware with FPGAs and we present how our solution can be integrated into a scalable low-cost system to conduct WPA-2 Personal brute force attacks. We evaluate our system with respect to performance and power usage and we compare it to results we obtained from GPUs. The extended version of our paper [9] also includes a real-world case study highlighting the practical impact. Specifically, the contributions presented in this paper are as follows:

- We present a highly optimized design of a scalable and fully pipelined FPGA implementation for efficient WPA2 brute force attacks that brings the performance of today's highly expensive professional systems to the low-cost FPGA boards affordable by amateurs.
- Our implementation on Kintex-7 devices indicates that on the same hardware, our implementation is more than 5 times as fast in comparison to what is currently marketed to be world's fastest FPGA-based WPA2 password recovery system [4,10].
- We implemented and evaluated our approach on three different low-cost FPGA architectures including an actual FPGA cluster with 36 Spartan 6 LX150T devices located on repurposed cryptocurrency mining boards.
- We evaluate our system with respect to the power consumption and performance in comparison to GPU clusters, showing that FPGAs can achieve comparable or higher performance with considerably less power and space requirements.

2   Related Work

Since WPA2 is commonly used, there are several publications and projects dealing with WPA2 security and brute force attacks in particular. For instance in [11], Visan covers typical CPU and GPU accelerated password recovery approaches with state-of-the-art tools like aircrack-ng[1] or Pyrit[2]. He considers a

---
[1] http://www.aircrack-ng.org.
[2] https://code.google.com/p/pyrit.

time-memory tradeoff usable for frequent Wi-Fi SSIDs and provides a performance overview of common GPUs and GPU cluster configurations. In that respect, oclHashcat[3] and the commercial Wireless Security Auditor software[4] need to be mentioned which are both password recovery frameworks with GPU acceleration and WPA2 support. Unlike these GPU-based approaches, our system comprises of a highly optimized and scalable FPGA implementation allowing higher performance at lower costs and power consumption in comparison. In [7], Johnson et al. present an FPGA architecture for the recovery of WPA and WPA2 keys. Although WPA support is mentioned, their implementation seems to support WPA2 only which is comparable to our system. However, while our implementation features multiple fully pipelined and heavily optimized cores for maximum performance, Johnson et al. present a straight-forward and mostly sequential design leading to a significantly less performance in comparison. In [5], Güneysu et al. present the RIVYERA and COPACOBANA high-performance FPGA cluster systems for cryptanalysis. They provide details on exhaustive key search attacks for cryptographic algorithms such as DES, Hitag2 or Keeloq and have a larger cluster configuration than we had available for our tests. Yet, in contrast to our work, they do not cover WPA2 or exhaustive key search attacks on WPA2 in their work. As a result, it would be highly interesting to evaluate our FPGA implementation on their machines. Finally, Elcomsoft's commercial Distributed Password Recovery[5] software needs to be mentioned due to its support for WPA2 key recovery attacks on FPGA clusters [4,10] and its claim to be world's fastest FPGA-based password cracking solution [3]. Although there is practically no publicly available information on the internals of their WPA2 implementation, in [10] performance data are provided. In contrast to their work, we do not only disclose our design, architecture and optimizations of our FPGA implementation, but we also claim that on the same professional FPGA hardware our implementation would be more than 5 times as fast. In comparison to the professional system, our system can achieve similar speeds on the low-cost repurposed cryptocurrently mining hardware available to amateurs.

3   WPA2-Personal Handshake and Key Derivation

In WPA2-Personal, Station and Access Point (AP) mutually authenticate against each other with the 4-way handshake depicted in Fig. 1a. To start the mutual authentication process, the AP generates a 32 byte random ANonce and sends it to the Station. Similarly, the Station generates a 32 byte random SNonce and uses both nonces as well as the password to derive the PMK (Pairwise Master Key) and the Pairwise Transient Key (PTK) with the help of the WPA2-Personal key derivation (Fig. 1b). The nonces ensure that the handshake cannot by replayed by an attacker at a later time. Afterwards, the Station sends the SNonce back to the AP and utilizes the PTK truncated to the first 128 bits (Key

---

[3] http://hashcat.net/oclhashcat.

[4] https://www.elcomsoft.com/ewsa.html.

[5] https://www.elcomsoft.com/edpr.html.

Confirmation Key - KCK) to compute a Message Integrity Code (MIC) over the packet data. At this point, the AP can compare the received MIC with the computed one to validate that the Station is authentic and has knowledge of the password. To prove to the Station that the AP knows the password, the Station sends a message including ANonce and the corresponding MIC code. Since the Station can only compute the correct MIC code if it knows the PTK, the AP can use this information for authentication. On success, the Station completes the handshake by sending a usually empty, but signed (MIC) message back to the AP.

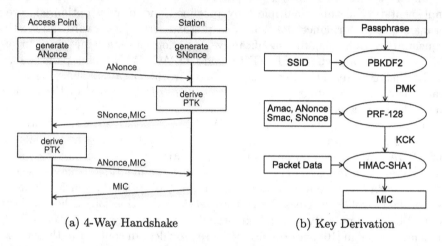

(a) 4-Way Handshake   (b) Key Derivation

Fig. 1. WPA2-personal handshake and key derivation

During key derivation (Fig. 1b), PMK is computed from the password and the SSID as cryptographic salt through the PBKDF2 [8] key derivation function with HMAC-SHA1 at its core. The PTK and its truncated variant denoted KCK are computed through the HMAC-SHA1 based pseudo random function PRF-128. Likewise, also the computation of the MIC integrity code relies on HMAC-SHA1.

3.1   Breaking it Down to SHA1 Computations

Internally, the PBKDF2 key derivation function employed in WPA2-Personal utilizes 4,096 HMAC-SHA1 iterations to obtain 160 bit hash outputs (Fig. 2). Since the WPA2 Pairwise Master Key PMK needs to be 256 bits long, two PBKDF2 rounds are necessary. Their output is concatenated, but from the second iteration the output is truncated to 96 bits to achieve a 256 bit result. In both PBKDF2 iterations the password is used as key while the SSID of the Wi-Fi network concatenated with a 32 bit counter value serves as input. In the first iteration, the counter value is one while in the second iteration it is two. Consequently within both PBKDF2 iterations, there are 8,192 HMAC-SHA1 iterations required to compute the PMK. In the first PBKDF2 round the xor-transformation is applied on the password and the inner pad ipad. The result is a 512 bit block serving as input to the SHA1 hash function in initial state. The output is the HMAC inner state. Since the SSID may be no longer than 32 bytes, the hashing of the SSID and the PBKDF2 round counter can be done together with the SHA1 finalization so that only one SHA1 iteration is necessary.

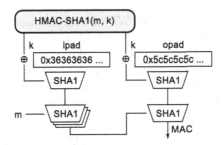

Fig. 2. PBKDF2 core with SHA1 rounds in HMAC construction

In the next step, the outer HMAC state is computed by hashing the xor of the password and the outer pad opad. Afterwards, the previously finalized 160 bit digest is hashed and finalized with the outer state. At this point the MAC is ready. The second PBKDF2 iteration is computed in the same way with the difference that the round counter value is set to two instead of one. Since the password does not change during PBKDF2 iterations, the inner and outer HMAC states stay the same allowing us to use cached states instead of having to compute the states again. With that optimization in mind, it is required to compute at least $2 + 4{,}096 * 2$ SHA1 iterations for the first PBKDF2 round and $4{,}096 * 2$ SHA1 iterations for the second round (i.e., 16,386 SHA1 iterations in total) to obtain the PMK. This computational effort, the use of the SSID as salt for key derivation and the security of the innermost SHA1 cryptographic hash function are the main reasons why WPA2-Personal key derivation is very strong against typical exhaustive key search attacks. Once the PMK is available, the KCK is derived by applying a 128 bit Pseudo Random Function (PRF). Internally, it just uses HMAC-SHA1 again with the PMK as key. The hashed message is made up of the string "Pairwise key expansion", a terminating zero byte, an arithmetically sorted tuple of the AP and Station addresses as well as another sorted tuple of their nonces (i.e., ANonce and SNonce) including a finalizing zero byte. The PTK is the resulting MAC and it is truncated to the first 128 bits to obtain the KCK. If the PMK is available, the computation of the KCK takes 5 SHA1 iterations as due to the length of the PMK the finalization of the inner HMAC state can not be combined with the hashing of the PMK. Whenever AP or Station would like to compute a MIC, they can do so by utilizing HMAC-SHA1 on the message with KCK as key. The result of the computation truncated to the first 128 bits is the MIC. The computational effort depends on the length of the message. However, considering the messages from the 4-way WPA2-Personal handshake, a total of 5 SHA1 iterations is required to compute the MIC since, similar to the KCK computation, the finalization of the inner HMAC state requires one additional iteration. A more detailed description of the key derivation is available in the extended version of our paper [9].

3.2   Attacking the 4-Way Handshake

If an attacker wants to determine the WPA2-Personal password, a 4-way WPA2-Personal handshake between a Station and AP needs to be obtained first. This can either be done passively or with the help of an active de-authentication attack where the attacker spoofs the source address of the AP and sends de-authentication frames to the Station. Since those frames are not authenticated, the Station will falsely believe that the de-authentication request came from the genuine AP and will follow the request. However at a later time, it will re-authentication and thus give the attacker the opportunity to intercept the handshake. As soon as the attacker has the handshake, passwords can be guessed offline by deriving the key material for the PMK and the KCK and computing the MIC for one of the observed packets in the handshake. If the observed MIC is the same as the computed MIC for a password candidate, the attacker has found the correct password for the network. However, since a WPA2-Personal password needs to have a minimum length of 8 characters and for each password candidate a total of at least $16,386 + 5 + 5 = 16,396$ SHA1 iterations are necessary to compute the corresponding MIC over a handshake packet, exhaustive password guessing attacks are considered to be increasingly infeasible with higher password complexity and length. In the subsequent chapters, we show that the high computational effort can be addressed with special purpose FPGA hardware so that a high number of real-world WPA2-Personal protected networks with random passwords can be broken within days.

4   FPGA Implementation

Assuming familiarity with FPGA design in general, SHA1 [12] is especially well suited for FPGA implementation due to the following reasons:

1. The algorithm has practically no memory requirements.
2. The rotate and shift operations utilized in SHA1 can be realized through FPGA interconnects with minimal time delay.
3. Algebraic logic functions (xor, and, or, not, etc.) require minimal effort and can efficiently utilize the FPGAs LUTs.

The most expensive operation are SHA1's additions due to the long carry chain between the adders. To implement the algorithm, a surrounding state machine is required to control which inputs should be supplied to the logic in different rounds. Considering that SHA1 has 80 rounds and we would like to achieve maximum performance, there are two design options: Either the SHA1 algorithm is implemented sequentially or in a fully pipelined way. The advantage of a sequential implementation is that the FPGA can be completely filled up with relatively small SHA1 cores. However, the disadvantage is that each of those cores would require its own state machine which takes up a significant amount of space. In comparison, a fully pipelined implementation does not require an internal state machine as each of the SHA1 rounds is implemented in its own logic block. While this is a significant advantage enabling parallel processing, the drawback is that a fully pipelined implementation has much higher space and routing requirements. When using multiple cores (each containing a full pipeline), only an integer number of cores can be placed so that a significant amount of unused space might be left on the FPGA. In our implementation, we also experimented with filling up this space with sequential cores but refrained from it due to the negative effect on the overall design complexity and the lower achievable clock speeds. Due to the typically higher performance that can be achieved through pipelining and the property that we get one full SHA1 computation output per clock cycle per core, we targeted a heavily optimized and fully-pipelined approach. However, while pipelining alone has a considerable performance impact in comparison to a sequential approach, the key of obtaining maximum design performance are the optimizations. Our overall FPGA design is illustrated in Fig. 3 and has the following components: A global brute force search state machine, a shared password generator and an FPGA device specific number of brute force cores, each comprising a WPA2-Personal state machine with password verifier and a SHA1 pipeline.

Global Brute Force State Machine. The task of the global brute force state machine is to constantly supply all brute force cores with new password candidates and check whether one of them found the correct password. Due to the insignificant speed impact and the advantage of lower design complexity we chose an iterative approach. Since our SHA1 pipeline comprises of 83 stages, we can concurrently test 83 passwords per brute force core. With our iterative approach, we enable the password generator and consecutively fill all brute force cores with passwords. Once all cores have been filled, the password generator is paused and we iteratively wait until all cores have completed. At that point, the password filling process is restarted. If a core finds the correct password or the password generator has reached the last password, the state machine jumps into the idle state and can accept the next working block. The penalty for this iterative approach is 83 clock cycles per core since once a brute force core has finished, we could immediately fill it with a new password. However, in comparison to the long run time of each core the impact is insignificant.

Password Generator. The password generator (Fig. 3b) is realized as a fast counter. Whenever the FPGA is idle, it can accept a new working block comprising of all necessary data including the actual start password (start_password) and how many passwords (n) should be tested. Initially starting at the start password, whenever the password generator is enabled (`enable`) it will output a new password (`current_password`) and the current password number (`count`) in each clock cycle. In case no more passwords can be fed into the brute force cores, the generator can be paused at any time by disabling the `enable` input. Ultimately, it will output new passwords until n passwords have been reached and assert the `done` signal to indicate that all passwords within the current working block have been generated.

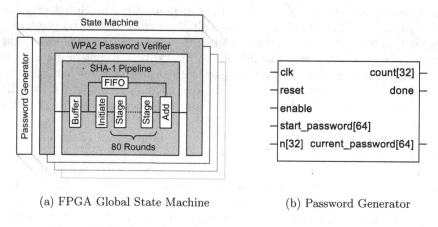

(a) FPGA Global State Machine   (b) Password Generator

Fig. 3. FPGA global state machine and password generator block

During the optimizations of our cryptographic cores in the design, at some point the long carry chain in the password counter became the clock speed limiting critical path. We were able to address the issue by parallelizing the counter and implementing the password carry with static multiplexers outside the sequential logic block. The sequential logic block can be seen as typical register transfer logic (RTL). With the clock signal, the old counter value is fetched from the source register, increased and finally output to the destination register. The path in between accounts for the delay. Since we need to have a carry overflow at the last valid password character (e.g., 'Z') we need a set of multiplexers that eventually reset the characters at each position of the password string. However, if this multiplexer based reset logic is within the sequential path it will also increase the time delay. By statically implementing the reset logic outside this sequential path we were able to balance the overall worst-case delays and achieved a password counter implementation that no longer accounted for the critical path in our overall design. Another password generator optimization approach we considered is utilizing multiple clock domains. The general idea is that the overall design naturally spends most of its time computing SHA1 iterations. At that time the password generator is disabled. We could thus use a less critical slower clock to generate the passwords and output them to clock synchronizing FIFO buffers directly placed next to the input of the SHA1 pipelines. As soon as a SHA1 pipeline requires a new password input, it can utilize its fast clock to drain the FIFO buffer which would in turn enable the password generator to refill the corresponding buffer at its slower clock. The advantages of this approach would be the following: First, the complexity of the password generator design can be further increased without negatively impacting the critical path. Second, the big advantage is the routing of the bus signals from the password generator to all the cores. Considering that the password generator is located at the center of the design and the passwords need to be distributed across the entire FPGA to all brute force cores, there is a significant impact on the time-driven routing complexity and the interconnect delays that negatively impact the maximum clock speed of the overall design. By leveraging a slower clock, the passwords would be already located in the FIFO buffers next to the SHA1 pipelines of each core but they could still be read with the fast clock the SHA1 pipelines are operating on. However, since with our previously mentioned password generator optimization the critical path was no longer within the password generator domain, we did not implemented the approach. It will be covered in future work.

WPA2-Personal State Machine with Password Verifier. Each brute force core has a WPA-2 Personal state machine with a password verifier. It is the most complex state machine in the overall design. Its task is to compute the MIC code for each password candidate with the help of the SHA1 pipeline in its center. Each computed MIC is compared with the MIC from the WPA2-Personal 4-way handshake to determine whether the password candidate was correct or not. Figure 4 shows all necessary states and state transitions.

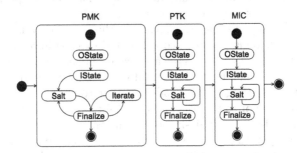

Fig. 4. WPA2-personal FPGA states

The state machine is divided into three WPA2-Personal key derivation phases: PMK computation (1), PTK computation (2), and MIC computation (3). The computation of the PMK has the highest computation effort due to the 2 PBKDF2 rounds with 4,096 iterations requiring 16,386 SHA1 iterations in total. Initially, 83 password candidates and the network's SSID are fed into the SHA1 pipeline to compute the corresponding HMAC outer and inner states (OState and IState). Since these states do not change over the PBKDF2 iterations, the HMAC state computation needs to be done only once. In the first

PBKDF2 round, the SSID and the PBKDF2 round counter with value 1 are used as salt. After that, there are 4,095 more iterations in which the digest output is used as input. At that point, the second PBKDF2 round is computed by first computing the salt with an increased round counter value (2) and subsequently performing 4,095 iterations to obtain the PMK.

SHA1 Pipeline. In each brute force core, the SHA1 pipeline occupies a large amount of space due to the high number of pipeline stages. While SHA1 has 80 rounds and a fully pipelined implementation would thus have an equal number of pipeline stages, we heavily optimized our pipeline to allow higher clock frequencies and consequently achieve more performance. The SHA1 pipeline is the key limiting factor of how fast our password guessing attacks can be conducted. Within the brute force cores, each of our SHA1 pipelines has 83 stages due to the optimizations we performed. Each core can thus compute 83 password candidates in parallel. The optimization approaches we applied are described in the following.

The first stage of the SHA1 pipeline is a buffer stage so that the delays of the different input logic blocks within the WPA-2 Personal state machine are not added to the pipeline's input logic and thereby do not increase the overall time delay of the critical path. The second stage denoted 'Initiate' is an optimization of the 4 required (expensive) additions in each SHA1 round. Instead of having all 4 additions in one stage, the structure of the SHA1 algorithm allows us to split up the required 4 sequential additions into two rounds with 2 additions each, thereby significantly improving the maximum clock speed. Since the SHA1 expansion steps require only a small amount of logic, another optimization is to do multiple message expansion steps in a single pipeline stage so that it is not needed in the following few stages. As a result, the source data is not accessed in each stage and shift register inference is boosted causing lower flip-flop fan-out as well as less power usage and lower area requirements. Another approach we took is the pipeline stage denoted 'Add' after the SHA1 rounds. After the last SHA1 round, the resulting digest is added either to the constant initialization vector (first iteration) or to the previous digest for subsequent iterations. Due to these expensive additions, the design performance can be improved if they are carried out in a separate pipeline stage. Instead of forwarding the initial digest through all stages to the final addition stage, we leverage a FIFO-based delay line utilizing the FPGAs Block-RAM resources. This avoids excessive interconnect routing through all stages and thus makes the design smaller, reduces the number of critical paths and allows us to achieve higher clock frequencies more easily.

Additional FPGA Design Optimizations. In the WPA2-Personal state machine, we directly use the output from the password generator and compute the HMAC OState state first. At the same time, we store the password candidates in a Block-RAM buffer for later IState computation. After that, we no longer work with the passwords but use password offsets instead. The result is a lower design density as no more additional interconnects are required for the password in later stages. A similar approach is used to avoid excessive interconnects and design density. Instead of having large buses, we either use Block-RAMs directly or form RAM-based delay lines to keep the IState and OState states as well as the computed PMKs and PTKs in memory. Instead of one large WPA2-Personal state multiplexer directly controlling all SHA1 pipeline inputs and outputs, we make use of several smaller and less complex multiplexers. Once again, this reduces overall design complexity and allows us to achieve higher clock speeds more easily. The top-level design needs to communicate with the outside world. Each time a new working block is added, all necessary Wi-Fi and WPA2-Personal data needs to be transferred and subsequently forwarded to all brute force cores. The result is a very broad bus spreading all over the FPGA design and causing severe design congestion. Since in our design only the password candidates and the SSID are required early within the WPA2-Personal state machine, we transfer the rest of the data over a small 16 bit bus leveraging inferred shift registers. This significantly reduces the complexity of the interconnects between the shared global state machine and the brute force cores across the FPGA. To lower the amount of input and output data exchanged with the outside world, we use a minimized Wi-Fi and WPA2-Personal data set that only includes the variable data fields from the captured handshake. All other data is not only fixed within the FPGA, but also kept locally in the cores. In addition, the FPGA does not output the correct password, but a numeric offset from the start password instead. To avoid design congestion and to push the design to the highest clock speed possible, we make use of custom parameters within the Xilinx design tools for synthesis, mapping and routing such as the minimum inferred shift register size, register balancing or the number of cost tables. In addition, we use floor planning to support the mapper, placer and router in achieving higher clock rates. Floor planning is important to place critical components requiring a fast interconnect in between next to each other. In general, we were able to obtain the highest speed improvements by utilizing a star like topography: The password generator is distributed over the very center of the FPGA and the brute force cores are surrounding it. In addition we also used floor planning to avoid the placement of time critical components in FPGA areas that are hard to reach through interconnects. Consequently, we carefully placed critical components like the SHA1 pipelines in a way that those regions do not negatively impact the routing delay. In our FPGA implementations, we use a slow clock for communication with the outside world and a fast clock for computation at the same time. In our Spartan-6 implementation, the speed of the fast clock can be adjusted dynamically during runtime by programming the clock multiplier. In contrast, our Artix-7 implementation includes an automatic clock scaling mechanism to adjust the fast clock frequency with the device core temperature. Both approaches allow the FPGA design to run at high speeds without the danger of overheating.

4.1   Overall System Design

Targeting FPGAs well in the range of amateurs, we implemented and practically evaluated our system on Xilinx Spartan-6 and Xilinx Artix-7 FPGAs. The Spartan-6 FPGAs are located on low-cost repurposed cryptocurrency mining boards. For comparison purposes, we created a full implementation for the more expensive Xilinx Kintex-7 XC7K410T FPGAs utilized in Elcomsoft's system as well, but could not practically test it since we did not have one of these FPGAs at hand. The overall system design for the Spartan-6 FPGAs is visible in Fig. 5 and based on ZTEX FPGA boards[6]. The Artix-7 design is similar but has only one XC7A200T FPGA on the board.

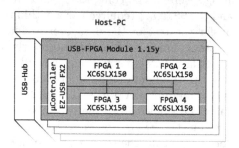

Fig. 5. System overview (Spartan 6 System)

The system comprises of a PC with a host software and several FPGA boards connected via the USB 2.0 high-speed interface. Each FPGA board has a fast EZ-USB FX2 micro-controller with custom firmware to interface with the FPGAs. Our custom host software utilizes the ZTEX SDK to allow easy communication with the micro-controller and the FPGAs. The host software accepts a configuration file that includes all necessary Wi-Fi and WPA-2 Personal handshake data. At startup, it enumerates all connected FPGA boards, uploads the micro-controller firmware if necessary and configures the FPGAs with our bit stream. The software makes use of several threads. Apart from the main program, there is a thread to generate password working blocks for the FPGAs and additional threads for each FPGA board. The password working blocks are kept in a pool with constant size. The device threads can supply working blocks to FPGAs and mark them as being processed. If an FPGA has finished a block, it is removed from the pool and the generator automatically creates a new working block. If for some reason an FPGA fails, the block sent to the FPGA is still in the pool and just needs to be unmarked so that the next free FPGA can process it instead. The micro-controller firmware is responsible for USB communication with the host and communication with the FPGAs.

---

[6] http://www.ztex.de.

5   Evaluation

We performed multiple evaluations with regard to our design performance, the power usage and performance in comparison to GPUs. We evaluated the performance and the power usage of our design on multiple FPGAs and FPGA boards. The first FPGA we targeted was a Spartan-6 XC6SLX150T-3 device. Four of these FPGAs can be found on the Ztex 1.15y board visible on the left of Fig. 6. The second FPGA we used for our evaluation was an Artix-7 XC7A200T-2 device on the Ztex 2.16 board visible on the right of the picture. For both FPGAs, we created an optimized implementation and a configuration bit stream that can be uploaded to the device. The main difference between the bit streams is the FPGA type, the maximum clock frequency and most importantly the number of brute force cores we were able to fit onto the device.

Fig. 6. Ztex 1.15y board (left), Ztex 2.16 board (right)

To evaluate the performance and the power requirements, we used the obtained timing and power reports by utilizing the Xilinx timing and power analysis tools. In addition to these results, we conducted practical measurements on the FPGA boards. At first, we measured the idle wattage of each unconfigured board at the power supply to determine the idle power usage. In the next step, we used a generated WPA2-Personal handshake with our software to mount a brute force attack on each of our FPGA boards. We used large password working packages resulting in a 30 s runtime per FPGA to avoid I/O bottlenecks. By measuring the wattage again during operation, we were able to determine the overall power consumption. To reduce the influence of the power consumption caused by losses in the power supplies or components other than the FPGA, we obtained the power consumption of our FPGA implementation through the difference between the overall idle consumption and the consumption during operation. In Sect. 5.1, we use the same method to determine the power consumption of GPUs to get results that can be compared to the FPGA power consumption. To obtain brute force performance measurements as well, we let each system run for at least 1 hour and computed the performance by measuring the number of password guesses during that time. The result is the average number of password guesses per second. In addition to these evaluations, we executed the implementation on our FPGA cluster with 36 Spartan-6 XC6SLX150T FPGAs located on 9 Ztex 1.15y FPGA boards. The cluster setup allowed us to perform measurements on a larger setup and to determine how well our design scales with an increasing number of FPGAs. Using the power and performance measuring methodology from above, we obtained measurement results for the cluster as well. To allow comparison with the commercial Elcomsoft password recovery system [4,10], we created an implementation and a configuration bitstream for the more expensive Kintex-7 XC7K410T-3 devices as well. However, since we did not have a board with this type of Kintex-7 FPGA, we can provide the Xilinx development tool's timing and power analysis results only.

5.1 GPU Comparison

To measure performance and power requirements of GPUs, we utilized cud-aHashcat[7] v1.36 to mount brute force attacks on the same WPA2-Personal handshake we used previously to test our FPGA implementations. We executed the tool on machines with different Nvidia GPUs (GeForce GTX 750 Ti, GeForce GTX770 Windforce OC, GRID K520) and measured the performance in passwords per second as well as the power consumption. We applied the same power measurement methodology as during our FPGA evaluation. For the Amazon EC2 GPU cloud machines with GRID K520 GPUs, we were unable to obtain power measurements. The specific machine configurations and results are described in detail in Sect. 6.

6 Results and Discussion

The results for our FPGA performance and power evaluation are visible in Table 1. In the System and FPGA column the table shows on which systems we conducted our tests and how many FPGAs there are on the corresponding board and/or in the overall system. The FPGA device types are visible in the Type column whereat the name before the hyphen is the Xilinx device name and the number after the hyphen indicates the device speed grade (the higher the better). The Cost column provides an approximate cost estimate per FPGA in US$ we obtained by looking up the devices at common Xilinx distributors

Table 1. Performance and power results of our implementations for different FPGA devices and systems/boards

System	FPGAs	Type	Cost	Cores	Tool W	Tool MHz	Meas. W	Act. MHz	calc pwd/s	pwd/s	pwd/s W
Ztex 1.15y	1	XC6SLX150T-3	175	2	4.281	187	6.99*	180	21,956	21,871	3,128*
Ztex 1.15y	4	XC6SLX150T-3	700	8	17.124	187	27.96	180	87,826	87,461	3,128
9x Ztex 1.15y	36	XC6SLX150T-3	2,400	72	154.116	187	254	180	790,436	741,200	2,918
Ztex 2.16	1	XC7A200T-2	213	8	10.458	180	11.04	180	87,826	87,737	7,947
N/A	1	XC7K410T-3	2,248	16	25.634	216	N/A	N/A	210,783	N/A	N/A
N/A	48	XC7K410T-3	107,904	768	1,230.432	216	N/A	N/A	10,117,584	N/A	N/A

---

[7] http://hashcat.net/oclhashcat.

such as Digi-key[8]. However while the cost for 9 new Ztex 1.15y would be appoximately 6,300 US\$, we considered our 9 second-hand Ztex 1.15y boards previously used for cryptocurrency mining instead. We were able to obtain these boards for 2,400 US\$ which we believe is what amateurs could do as well, depending on how much boards they would like to acquire and how much they are willing to spend. The `Cores` column shows how many cores we were able to fit onto the device to achieve maximum performance. While more cores per device generally increase the performance, it can also cause the maximum clocking speed to drop significantly due to mapping, placement and routing issues. The table presents the implementations allowing us to achieve the maximum performance per device. The `Tool W` and `Tool MHz` columns present the design tool's power and timing analysis results. For the Spartan-6 FPGAs, we used the Xilinx ISE Suite 14.7 whereas for the newer 7-series devices Artix-7 and Kintex-7, we used Vivado Design Suite 2015.1. In general, it appeared that the newer Vivado tools produced better results, but since it doesn't support older model 6-series devices, we were unable to use it for our Spartan-6 implementations. The `Meas. W` and `Act. MHz` columns present the results for the power measurements we conducted on the FPGA boards/systems and the actual clock speed we used to run the devices. The `calc pwd/s` and `pwd/s` columns provide the WPA2-Personal performance in passwords per second whereas the first one indicates the calculated and theoretic maximum performance of our implementation whereas the latter one shows the actual measured average performance per board and/or system. In the last column `pwd/s W`, we use our actual power and performance measurements to determine how much brute force speed can be achieved per Watt which is especially important when scaling up our implementation to larger FPGA cluster systems. In the following, we discuss the results of our implementations on a per-device basis.

Spartan-6 Results. We used the Xilinx Spartan-6 XC6SLX150T-3 FPGA as the target for our first implementation due to the availability of a high-performance FPGA cluster with 36 of these devices at our lab. The implementation on the Spartan-6 turned out to be especially challenging for multiple reasons. We had to deal with long design tool runs (3 h of more) each time we made modifications to the design. Since the effects of many of our optimizations could not be tested through simulations alone, the duration of the design tool runs significantly slowed down the development. In addition, the internal switch boxes and types of slices in the Spartan-6 architecture are not well suited for more complex and larger implementations in comparison to newer 7-series devices. An important factor to achieve routable designs was our use of FPGA floor planning. Our optimized 2 core implementation visible in Fig. 7a is able to run at up to 187 MHz leading to the highest performance we were able to achieve on this device. The picture shows the ready-to-upload placed and routed design. On the left and right the 2 brute force cores are clearly visible. In between the password generator and the global state machine are located. Although the dark

---

[8] http://www.digikey.com.

areas indicate that there would be sufficient space for an additional core, our experiments showed that this would lead to lower performance due design congestion. The first 3 rows in Table 1 present the results we obtained through this implementation. Due to cooling requirements, we ran the design with a reduced clock speed of 180 MHz. Our measurements indicate that in this configuration, our implementation requires a total of 27.96 W for all 4 FPGAs on the Ztex 1.15y board. The power measurements per Spartan-6 FPGA are marked with an asterisk to indicate that we were unable to measure them directly, but rather derived the measurement results from our power measurements for the entire Ztex 1.15y board with its 4 FPGAs. Our results show that our approach scales well and can be easily run in a cluster configuration producing a performance of 790,436 password guesses per second on our cluster. The difference between the calculated maximum performance and the measured performance is mainly due to the I/O times between the PC, the microcontroller and the FPGAs. In addition, our Spartan-6 implementation includes a dynamic frequency scaling mechanism slowing down the FPGAs in case of device temperatures getting too high. With better cooling inside the cluster, we believe that the gap between the theoretic performance and the measured performance could be made smaller.

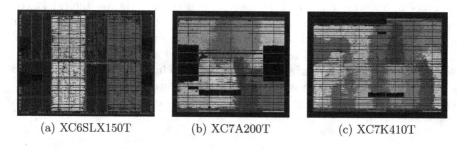

(a) XC6SLX150T   (b) XC7A200T   (c) XC7K410T

Fig. 7. Placed and routed FPGA designs

Artix-7 Results. Starting from our already highly optimized Spartan-6 design we ported our implementation to the newer 7-series Artix-7 XC7A200T-2 FPGA. Since device internals such as the clocks or PLLs are different from the Spartan-6 architecture, we had to adapt our implementation accordingly. The ability to read the device's core temperature from within the FPGA implementation was especially interesting. It allowed us to implement frequency scaling mechanisms directly on the FPGA not only preventing possible damage due to overheating, but also ensuring that each device always runs at the maximum performance possible. Our ready-to-upload placed and routed design is visible in Fig. 7b. Through floorplaning all of the cores have a small path to the center where the small block with the global state machine and the password generator are located. The implementation can be run at up to 180 MHz to achieve a theoretic maximum of 87,826 password guesses per second. With a measured performance of 87,737 password guesses per second, our results show that a single XC7A200T-2 device achieves not only more performance than 4 of the older model Spartan-6 XC6SLX150T-3 FPGAs altogether, but it also requires just 11.04 Watt during operation.

Kintex-7 Results. In contrast to the low-cost Artix-7 FPGAs, Kintex-7 FPGAs are larger and allow higher performance but are also significantly more expensive. Although we didn't have any of those FPGAs at hand, we created an implementation for the Kintex-7 XC7K410T FPGA for two reasons. First, Elcomsoft's marketed to be world's fastest FPGA-based WPA2 password recovery system relies on these FPGAs just the same and even provides performance figures for it [10]. Our targeting of the same FPGAs thus allows direct performance comparison between their implementation and ours. Their document indicates that on the PicoComputing SC5/M505-48 cluster with 48 XC7K410T FPGAs their implementation is able to produce 1,988,360 passwords guesses per second [10]. Assuming that their implementation targets WPA2 employing SHA1 instead of WPA1 employing the much less complex MD5 algorithm, our implementation could achieve up to 10,117,584 passwords per second on the same hardware and would thus be more than 5 times as fast. Second, we wanted to obtain performance data for larger FPGAs as well. Although expensive, we believe that Kintex-7 FPGAs are well in the price range for professional attackers allowing them to achieve significantly more brute force attack performance per FPGA in comparison to low-cost FPGAs such as the Artix-7. Our ready-to-upload placed and routed design is visible in Fig. 7c. It comprises 16 cores running at up to 216 MHz. Similar to our Artix-7 implementation, the password generator and the global state machine are located in the center. At the same time, the image suggests that with an increasing number of cores, the centralized state machine and password generator becomes a bottleneck due to the long bus interconnects reaching to the outside cores. We believe that this problem could be easily addressed by including FIFOs for the password candidates in each of the brute force cores.

6.1 GPU Results and Comparison

The results of our GPU evaluation (Sect. 5.1) are visible in Table 2. We performed the performance measurements by running cudaHashcat v1.36 on different systems and measuring the power consumption as the difference between idle and busy WPA2 computations to get results independent from other components in the system. The table shows the different GPU configurations (System) we used for our tests. The pwd/s column shows the performance in passwords per second and the W column indicates the power consumed by the GPU during runtime in Watt. The performance per Watt is visible in the pwd/s W column. In addition to running GPU measurements on our own machines, we also conducted measurements on dedicated Amazon Elastic Cloud (EC2) GPU machines as well. While we could measure the performance on the machines just the same, we were unable to obtain power measurements. Although using a high number of GPU cloud machines appears promising to achieve high brute force attack performance, the limiting factor is the cost. Although our combined experiments on the dedicated Amazon EC2 machines took no longer than an hour, the costs we accumulated for our tests were already US$ 14.92. Since realistic brute force attacks might take considerably longer, the costs for an attacker would be far lower for acquiring a powerful GPU system instead of using the Amazon EC2 GPU nodes. In comparison to the results we obtained from our FPGA implementation, it is visible that GPUs can achieve the performance of a state-of-the-art low-cost FPGA (i.e., Artix-7), but their power consumption and performance per Watt is more than 10 times as high. At the same time, the performance achievable with a single larger FPGA such as the Kintex-7 XC7K410T is no longer in the range of GPUs. Considering high-speed attacks with clusters, we believe that the scalability for FPGA-based attacks is better due to the small size of FPGAs, their lower power consumption and the high performance they can produce.

Table 2. Performance and power results on GPUs

System	pwd/s	W	pwd/s W
GeForce GTX750 Ti	52,446	106	495
GeForce GTX770 OC	62,420	184	339
Amazon EC2 - GRID K520	30,370	N/A	N/A
Amazon EC2 - GRID K520 x4	109,073	N/A	N/A

7   Conclusion and Future Work

In this paper, we demonstrated that WPA2 passwords can be attacked at high speed rates not only by expensive professional FPGA cluster solutions but similar speeds can be achieved by amateurs on a low budget as well, especially when considering second hand FPGA boards previously used for cryptocurrently mining. We specifically targeted low-cost FPGA devices, conducted implementations on 3 different FPGA architectures and evaluated our results with regard to performance and power. Our GPU evaluation suggests that FPGAs can not only achieve higher speeds at significantly less power, but they can also be used to easily create small and afforable FPGA clusters in the reach of amateurs. A case study highlighting the practical impact of our attacks as well as a more detailed description of our approach is available in the extended version of our paper [9]. However, we believe that besides the speedup we achieved it is more important to consider that the WPA2-Personal brute force performance achievable on professional systems is now becoming feasible on the low-cost systems amateurs can afford as well. As counter measure, users need to increase the length of their passwords, the password should be random and it should utilize a large character set to increase password entropy. In future work, we are looking forward to evaluate the security of other cryptographic systems as well. In that regard, we plan to design and implement a powerful low-cost FPGA cluster similar to COPACOBANA [5] but with low-cost 7-series devices instead.

Acknowledgments. The research was funded by the Austrian Research Funding Agency's (FFG) KIRAS security research program through the $(SG)^2$ project under national FFG grant number 836276, the AnyPLACE project under EU H2020 grant number 646580, and the IT security consulting company Trustworks KG who also provided the FPGA boards and the cluster.

References

1. Eastlake 3rd, D., Jones, P.: US Secure Hash Algorithm 1 (SHA1). RFC 3174 (Informational), September 2001. Updated by RFCs 4634, 6234
2. Eastlake 3rd, D., Hansen, T.: US Secure Hash Algorithms (SHA and SHA-based HMAC and HKDF). RFC 6234 (Informational), May 2011
3. Elcomsoft: ElcomSoft and Pico Computing Demonstrate World's Fastest Password Cracking Solution. https://www.elcomsoft.com/PR/Pico_120717_en.pdf. Accessed 13 Nov 2015
4. Elcomsoft Blog: Accelerating Password Recovery: The Addition of FPGA (2012). http://blog.elcomsoft.com/2012/07/accelerating-password-recovery-the-addition-of-fpga. Accessed 13 Nov 2015
5. Güneysu, T., Kasper, T., Novotný, M., Paar, C., Wienbrandt, L., Zimmermann, R.: High-performance cryptanalysis on RIVYERA and COPACOBANA computing systems. In: Vanderbauwhede, W., Benkrid, K. (eds.) High-Performance Computing Using FPGAs, pp. 335–366. Springer, New York (2013). http://dx.doi.org/10.1007/978-1-4614-1791-0_11
6. IEEE-Inst.: 802.11-2012 - IEEE Standard for Information technology-Telecommunications and information exchange between systems Local and metropolitan area networks-Specific requirements Part 11: wireless LAN Medium Access Control (MAC) and Physical Layer (PHY) Specifications. Technical report, IEEE Std 802.11^{TM}-2012, IEEE-Inst (2012). http://ieeexplore.ieee.org/servlet/opac?punumber=6178209
7. Johnson, T., Roggow, D., Jones, P.H., Zambreno, J.: An FPGA architecture for the recovery of WPA/WPA2 keys. J. Circ. Syst. Comput. **24**(7) (2015). http://dx.doi.org/10.1142/S0218126615501054
8. Kaliski, B.: PKCS #5: Password-Based Cryptography Specification Version 2.0. RFC 2898 (Informational), September 2000. http://www.ietf.org/rfc/rfc2898.txt
9. Kammerstetter, M., Muellner, M., Burian, D., Kudera, C., Kastner, W.: Efficient high-speed WPA2 brute force attacks using scalable low-cost FPGA clustering (extended version). http://arxiv.org/pdf/1605.07819v1.pdf. Accessed 25 May 2016
10. PicoComputing Inc.: SC5-4U Overview. http://picocomputing.com/brochures/SC5-4U.pdf. Accessed 13 Nov 2015
11. Visan, S.: WPA/WPA2 password security testing using graphics processing units. J. Mob. Embed. Distrib. Syst. **5**(4), 167–174 (2013)
12. U.S. Department of Commerce National Institute of Standards, Technology: FIPS PUB 180-2, Secure Hash Standard (SHS), U.S. Department of Commerce/National Institute of Standards and Technology (2002)

Fault Attacks

EnCounter: On Breaking the Nonce Barrier in Differential Fault Analysis with a Case-Study on PAEQ

Dhiman Saha$^{(\boxtimes)}$ and Dipanwita Roy Chowdhury

Crypto Research Lab, Department of Computer Science and Engineering,
IIT Kharagpur, Kharagpur, India
{dhimans,drc}@cse.iitkgp.ernet.in

Abstract. This work exploits internal differentials within a cipher in the context of Differential Fault Analysis (DFA). This in turn overcomes the nonce barrier which acts as a natural counter-measure against DFA. We introduce the concept of *internal differential fault analysis* which requires only one faulty ciphertext. In particular, the analysis is applicable to parallelizable ciphers that use the counter-mode. As a proof of concept we develop an internal differential fault attack called EnCounter on PAEQ which is an AES based parallelizable authenticated cipher presently in the second round of on-going CAESAR competition. The attack is able to uniquely retrieve the key of three versions of full-round PAEQ of key-sizes 64, 80 and 128 bits with complexities of about 2^{16}, 2^{16} and 2^{50} respectively. Finally, this work addresses in detail the instance of fault analysis with varying amounts of partial state information and also presents the first analysis of PAEQ.

Keywords: Fault analysis · Authenticated encryption · PAEQ · Internal differential · AESQ · Nonce · AES

1 Introduction

The popularity of cryptanalyzing a cipher by observing its behavior under the influence of faults is mainly attributed to the ease of such fault induction and overhead in incorporating a counter-measure. Among different types of fault based cryptanalysis, Differential Fault Analysis (DFA) [1–7] has garnered particular attention of the side-channel research community since it has been one of the most effective side-channel attacks on symmetric-key constructions. DFA puts in the hand of an attacker an interesting ability: *The possibility of performing a differential analysis starting from an intermediate state of the cipher.* This ability could be fatal in case of iterated symmetric-key designs since it is equivalent to cryptanalyzing a round-reduced version of the cipher. However, classical DFA has a specific requirement known as the *replaying criterion* which states that the attacker must be able to induce faults while **replaying** a previous fault-free run of the algorithm. In this scenario, the introduction of a *nonce* constraint comes in as a direct contradiction to the ability to replay.

© International Association for Cryptologic Research 2016
B. Gierlichs and A.Y. Poschmann (Eds.): CHES 2016, LNCS 9813, pp. 581–601, 2016.
DOI: 10.1007/978-3-662-53140-2_28

The notion of nonce-based encryption was formalized by Rogaway in [8] where the security proofs relied on the pre-condition of the *uniqueness of the nonce* in every instantiation of the cipher. Thus, it can be easily inferred why nonces provide an in-built protection against DFA. Usage of nonces to counter fault attacks are already available in Public-Key literature. The famous Bellcore attack [9,10] on RSA-CRT signatures can be prevented if the message is padded with a random nonce which is recoverable only when verifying a correct signature. It was shown by Coron et al. [11] that in some limited setting these nonces can be tackled. However, the techniques used rely on theoretical constructs which may not be applicable to their private-key counterparts. Though there have also been attempts to mount DFA attacks on symmetric-key designs in the presence of a nonce, the solutions are very specific to the underlying cipher. Such an instance can be found in [12], where the authors studied the impact of the nonce constraint on the fault-attack vulnerability of authenticated cipher APE [13] and demonstrated the idea of *faulty collisions* to overcome it.

This work tries to address the nonce barrier in a more general setting by totally bypassing the replaying criterion which amplifies the scope of the ideas presented here. This is made possible by a DFA strategy that no longer requires a fault-free run of the cipher. Instead the strategy needs only one multi-block plaintext and faulty ciphertext pair to mount an attack. The nonce constraint is no longer a threat to DFA if the analysis relies on a single faulty ciphertext. The idea of using single faulty ciphertext stems from the prospect of using internal differentials within the cipher. This type of analysis is well-studied and has been successfully used in cryptanalysis of symmetric-key designs [14,15]. We explore the possibility of deploying this in the context of DFA. In particular, we look at parallelizable authenticated encryption (AE) schemes that use the counter mode of operation to separate the branches. The parallel branches of these schemes provide a good platform for injecting faults and studying the fault propagation in the internal difference of the branches. The main idea is to nullify very low hamming distance between the inputs of the parallel branches using a primary fault and subsequently employ internal differential fault analysis using a secondary fault. To undertake a case-study we select PAEQ which is among the 30 Round-2 candidates in the on-going CAESAR [16] competition on authenticated ciphers. PAEQ meets the basic criteria for analysis since it is parallelizable and uses the counter mode. Moreover, the underlying permutation follows AES [17] very closely which provides an edge in terms of fault analysis. In this work, we present the first analysis of PAEQ in form of an internal difference based fault attack called ENCOUNTER on full-round paeq-64, paeq-80 and paeq-128 using a 4-round distinguishing property. Two byte faults are required to be injected in one of the parallel branches during the encryption phase of PAEQ. ENCOUNTER uses only *one 255-block known plaintext and corresponding faulty ciphertext* to significantly reduce the average key-search space of the three versions of PAEQ. Finally, one might be tempted to believe that classical differential fault analysis results on AES would *suffice* to analyze an AE scheme like PAEQ which is inherently AES based. However, there is a fundamental difference given the fact that the output here is truncated giving an attacker access to only partial information of the state. Thus the current work provides an instance of a fault based analysis of partially specified states.

Our Results

- Introduce the concept of internal differential fault analysis (IDFA) in the context of parallelizable ciphers in the counter mode
- Showcase that IDFA requires only one run of the algorithm thereby overcoming the *nonce barrier* of DFA.
- Present a 4-round internal differential distinguisher for PAEQ.
- Use the distinguisher to develop the ENCOUNTER attack on full-round PAEQ using only two faults in the same instance of PAEQ
- Reduces average key-space of primary PAEQ variants to practical limits viz., paeq-64: 2^{64} to 2^{16}, paeq-80: 2^{80} to 2^{16}, paeq-128: 2^{128} to 2^{50}.
- Present instances of fault analysis of an AES based design with various types of partially specified internal states.

The rest of the paper is organized as follows. Section 2 provides a brief description of PAEQ. The notations used is the work are given in Sect. 3. The concept of internal differential fault analysis is introduced in Sect. 4. A 4-round distinguisher of PAEQ is showcased in Sect. 5. Section 6 introduces the notion of fault quartets. The ENCOUNTER attack on PAEQ is devised in Sect. 7 and its complexity analysis is furnished in Subsect. 7.5. The experimental results are presented in Sect. 8 while the concluding remarks are given in Sect. 9.

2   The Design of PAEQ

PAEQ which stands for *Parallelizable Authenticated Encryption based on Quadrupled AES* was introduced by Biryukov and Khovratovich in ISC 2014 [18] along with a new generic mode of operation PPAE (Parallelizable Permutation-based Authenticated Encryption). It was also submitted to the on-going CAESAR competition for authenticated cipher and is presently one of the 30 round 2 candidates. The design of PAEQ was mainly driven by simplicity and to achieve a security level equal to the key-length. Hence the authors argued in favor of a permutation based design. It is fully parallelizable and on-line and offers a security level up to 128 bits and higher (up to $w/3$, $w \leftarrow$ width of internal permutation) and equal to the key length. An interesting aspect of the PPAE mode of operation (denoted PPAE$_f$) is that *the inputs to the internal permutation f are only linked by counters.* This property makes PAEQ a prime candidate to apply the concept of fault based internal differentials proposed in this work. Next we touch upon PPAE$_f$ and the internal permutation of PAEQ called AESQ.

2.1   PPAE Mode of Operation

$PPAE_f$ (illustrated in Algorithm 1) can be instantiated with an n-bit permutation
f. The inputs to the permutation are formatted as $(D_i\|counter\|N\|K)$ for each
plaintext block and $(D_i\|counter\|AD\text{-}block\|K)$ for processing associated data
(AD) where $D_i \leftarrow$ domain separator, $N \leftarrow$ nonce and $K \leftarrow$ key. The plaintext
and AD are divided into blocks of size $n - k - 16$ and $n - 2k - 16$, respectively,
where k is the key-size. Incomplete last blocks are padded using the byte-length
of the block and domain separators are changed accordingly. Plaintext processing
and authentication calls f twice while AD data is authenticated using a single
call. Partial authentication data from all branches are passed to a final call to f,
the output of which is optionally truncated to get the tag. The entire operation
is depicted in Fig. 1. An interested reader can refer to [18,19] for details.

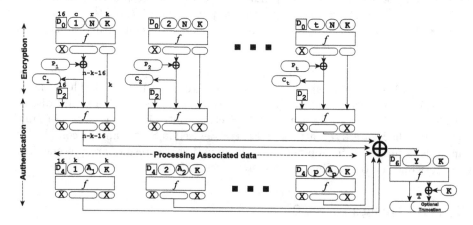

Fig. 1. Encryption and authentication with PAEQ

2.2   The Internal Permutation: AESQ

AESQ operates on a 512-bit internal state which can be subdivided into 128-bit
substates. Before going into details we introduce some definitions.

Definition 1 (Word). *Let* $\mathbb{T} = \mathbb{F}[x]/(x^8 + x^4 + x^3 + x + 1)$ *be the field* $\mathbb{F}_{2^8}$ *used
in the* AES MixColumns *operation. Then a **word** is defined as an element of* $\mathbb{T}$.

A **word** is just a **byte** redefined to account for the field arithmetic. In this work,
we will come across *partially specified states/substates* where certain words might
have unknown values. To capture this scenario, we use the symbol 'X' to represent
unknown words. Thus, to be precise a **word** is an element of $\mathbb{T} \cup \{\,`\mathtt{X}\text{'}\,\}$.

Definition 2 (Substate, State). *The internal **state** of the* AESQ *permutation
is defined as a 4-tuple of substates where each substate is a* (4×4)*-word matrix.*

Algorithm 1. $\text{PPAE}_f(P, N, K, A, n)$

Input: $\begin{cases} P \leftarrow \text{Plaintext}, & N \leftarrow \text{Nonce}, \quad |N| = r, \quad K \leftarrow \text{Key}, \quad |K| = k \\ A \leftarrow \text{Associated Data}, & f \leftarrow \text{Internal permutation}, \quad n \leftarrow \text{Internal state size} \end{cases}$

Output: $C, T \rightarrow$ Ciphertext and Tag

1: $D_i = (k, (r+i) \mod 256), \ i = 1, 2, \cdots, 6 \ \triangleright$ Generating 2-byte domain separators
2: $\{P_1, P_2, \cdots, P_t\} \leftarrow P \quad |P_i| = (n - k - 16)$ bits
3: $\{A_1, A_2, \cdots, A_p\} \leftarrow A \quad |A_i| = (n - 2k - 16)$ bits
4: **if** $(|P_t| < n - k - 16)$ **then** $P_t \leftarrow P_t||a||a \cdots ||a \qquad \triangleright a = |P_t|/8$ and $|a| = 1$ byte
5: **if** $(|A_p| < n - 2k - 16)$ **then** $A_p \leftarrow A_p||b||b \cdots ||b \qquad \triangleright b = |A_p|/8$ and $|b| = 1$ byte
6: $Y = 0 \hspace{7cm} \triangleright |Y| = n - k - 16$
7: **for** $i = 1$ **to** t **do**
8: $\quad V_i \leftarrow D_0||R_i||N||K \quad \triangleright \begin{cases} R_i \leftarrow \text{Branch Index}, R_i = i, |R_i| = n - k - r - 16 \\ D_0 \leftarrow D_1 \text{ for incomplete last block} \end{cases}$
9: $\quad W_i \leftarrow f(V_i); \ C_i \leftarrow W_i[17 \cdots (n-k)] \oplus P_i$
10: $\quad X_i \leftarrow D_2||C_i||W_i[(n-k+1) \cdots n] \quad \triangleright D_2 \leftarrow D_3$ for incomplete last block
11: $\quad Y_i \leftarrow (f(X_i))[17 \cdots (n-k)]; \ Y \leftarrow Y \bigoplus Y_i$
12: **for** $i = 1$ **to** p **do** $\hspace{4cm} \triangleright$ Binding Associated Data
13: $\quad X_i' \leftarrow D_4||R_i||A_i||K \qquad \triangleright \begin{cases} R_i = i, \ |R_i| = k \\ D_4 \leftarrow D_5 \text{ for incomplete last block} \end{cases}$
14: $\quad Y_i' \leftarrow (f(X_i'))[17 \cdots (n-k)]$
15: $\quad Y \leftarrow Y \bigoplus Y_i'$
16: $T \leftarrow f(D_6||Y||K) \oplus (0^{n-k}||K)$
17: $C = \{C_1, C_2, \cdots, C_t\} \hspace{2.5cm} \triangleright$ Truncate C_t for incomplete last plaintext block

A state is denoted by s, while each substate is represented by $s^m = [s_{i,j}^m]$ where $s_{i,j}^m$ are the elements of s^m and m denotes the **substate index**. We denote a column of $[s_{i,j}^m]$ as $s_{*,j}^m$ while a row is referred to as $s_{i,*}^m$.

$$s^m = [s_{i,j}^m], \text{ where } \begin{cases} s_{i,j} \in \mathbb{T} \cup \{'X'\} \\ 0 \le i, j < 4; \ m \in \{1, 2, 3, 4\} \end{cases} \qquad s = (s^1, s^2, s^3, s^4)$$

AESQ is a composition of 20 round functions with a Shuffle operation (denoted by $\mathscr{S}$, Refer Table 1) after every 2 rounds. Each round-function is denoted by $\mathcal{R}_r$ where the index r denotes the rth round of AESQ. Every round applies on the internal state a composition of four bijective functions which are basically the standard AES round operations SubBytes, ShiftRows, MixColumns, AddRoundConstants applied individually on each substate. In the context, of a state we denote these functions as β_r, ρ_r, μ_r and α_r respectively. The reference to a substate is addressed by including the substate index in notation. For example, to refer to the MixColumns on the second substate in $\mathcal{R}_{17}$ we use μ_{17}^2. Similarly, when considering a substate in $\mathcal{R}_r$ we refer to the round function applied individually to the substate as $\mathcal{R}_r^m$ by including the substate index in the notation. This implies that for an internal state s the output of the rth round of AESQ is $\mathcal{R}_r(s) = \mathcal{R}_r^1(s^1)||\mathcal{R}_r^2(s^2)||\mathcal{R}_r^3(s^3)||\mathcal{R}_r^4(s^4)$.

Table 1. Column mapping under Shuffle ($\mathscr{S}$)

	s^1				s^2				s^3				s^4			
From	$s^1_{*,0}$	$s^1_{*,1}$	$s^1_{*,2}$	$s^1_{*,3}$	$s^2_{*,0}$	$s^2_{*,1}$	$s^2_{*,2}$	$s^2_{*,3}$	$s^3_{*,0}$	$s^3_{*,1}$	$s^3_{*,2}$	$s^3_{*,3}$	$s^4_{*,0}$	$s^4_{*,1}$	$s^4_{*,2}$	$s^4_{*,3}$
To	$s^1_{*,3}$	$s^4_{*,3}$	$s^3_{*,2}$	$s^2_{*,2}$	$s^1_{*,1}$	$s^4_{*,1}$	$s^3_{*,0}$	$s^2_{*,0}$	$s^1_{*,2}$	$s^4_{*,2}$	$s^3_{*,3}$	$s^2_{*,3}$	$s^1_{*,0}$	$s^4_{*,0}$	$s^3_{*,1}$	$s^2_{*,1}$

$$\text{AESQ} = \mathscr{S} \circ \mathcal{R}_{20} \circ \mathcal{R}_{19} \circ \cdots \circ \mathscr{S} \circ \mathcal{R}_2 \circ \mathcal{R}_1$$
$$\mathcal{R}_r = \alpha_r \circ \mu_r \circ \rho_r \circ \beta_r; \quad \mathcal{R}_r^m = \alpha_r^m \circ \mu_r^m \circ \rho_r^m \circ \beta_r^m$$

Round-reduced AESQ permutation is denoted by AESQ^n where $n = 2k, 1 \leq k \leq 9$. Thus $\text{AESQ}^n = \mathscr{S} \circ \mathcal{R}_n \circ \mathcal{R}_{n-1} \circ \cdots \circ \mathscr{S} \circ \mathcal{R}_2 \circ \mathcal{R}_1$. Since n is even, it implies that we consider reductions in steps of two-rounds and AESQ^n always ends in the $\mathscr{S}$ operation. Finally, the round constant for substate m in round r of AESQ is given by: $rc_r^m = ((r-1) * 4 + m)$. In α_r^m, rc_r^m is added to all words of row $s_{1,*}^m$.

2.3 Handling Partially Specified States/Substates

As mentioned earlier in this work we have to handle states or substates that may have multiple unknown values. We now define how the operations $\beta_r^m, \rho_r^m, \mu_r^m$ and α_r^m behave in case of a partially specified substate $s^m = [s_{i,j}^m]$. Here SBOX denotes the AES Substitution box and M_μ denotes the MixColumns matrix. ρ_r^m does not rely on values of s^m and just shifts the positions of unknown values.

$$s_{i,j}^m \xrightarrow{\beta_r^m} \begin{cases} \text{X} & \text{if } s_{i,j}^m = \text{X} \\ \text{SBOX}(s_{i,j}^m) & \text{Otherwise} \end{cases} \quad\Big|\quad s_{*,j}^m \xrightarrow{\mu_r^m} \begin{cases} M_\mu \times s_{*,j}^m & \text{if } \forall i, s_{i,j}^m \neq \text{X} \\ \{\text{X}, \text{X}, \text{X}, \text{X}\}^T & \text{Otherwise} \end{cases} \quad\Big|\quad s_{i,j}^m \xrightarrow{\alpha_r^m} \begin{cases} s_{i,j}^m & \text{if } i \neq 1 \\ s_{i,j}^m \oplus rc_r^m & \text{if } s_{i,j}^m \neq \text{X} \\ \text{X} & \text{Otherwise} \end{cases}$$

3   Notations

Definition 3 (Diagonal). *A **diagonal** of a substate ($s^m = [s_{i,j}^m]$) is the set of words which map to the same column under the Shift-Row operation.*

$$d_k^m = \{s_{i,j}^m : \rho^m(s_{i,j}^m) \in s_{*,k}^m\}, \text{ where } k = (j - \sigma(i)) \bmod 4; \sigma = \{0, 1, 2, 3\} \quad (1)$$

Definition 4 (Differential State). *A **differential state** is defined as the element-wise XOR between an internal state $s = (s^1, s^2, s^3, s^4)$ and the corresponding state $s' = (s'^1, s'^2, s'^3, s'^4)$ belonging to a different branch of PAEQ.*

$$\delta = (\delta^1, \delta^2, \delta^3, \delta^4) = ((s^1 \oplus s'^1), (s^2 \oplus s'^2), (s^3 \oplus s'^3), (s^4 \oplus s'^4))$$

Definition 5 (Column Vector). *A **Column Vector**, is a set of columns where each element is a candidate for one particular column of a substate.*

Definition 6 (State/Substate Vector). *A **Substate Vector**, identified by $[s^m]^v$, is a set of substates where each element is a prospective candidate for substate s^m. A **State Vector** of state s is the cross-product of its substate vectors.*

4   Internal Differential Fault Analysis

In this work, for the first time, we explore the idea of using internal differentials to mount fault based attacks. Though the concept of internal differentials is well-known in cryptanalysis [14,15], the idea has never been applied in fault based Side Channel Analysis. Our research reveals that the best crypto-primitives to mount such a type of attack are the ones that employ a parallel mode of operation. In principle, internal differentials exploit self-symmetric structures present within a construction. In the parallel mode of operation all parallel branches are structurally similar exhibiting nice instances of such self-symmetry. We look at inputs of such branches. Parallelizable ciphers using the counter mode are generally characterized by the common property that the inputs to the parallel branches only differ in the counter value. Thus, the hamming distance of the inputs are quite low. More interestingly, we can find branches in which *the bit positions where the inputs differ are very localized.*[1] This localization can be fatal from the perspective of fault analysis since a fault injection in the counter could possibly lead to a collision in the counter values. So the faulty counter could become equal to a fault-free counter and since the inputs differ only in the counter value this would give us two branches with the same input. This forms a pre-condition for deploying internal differentials analysis since under this scenario, we could inject a second fault in the internal state of any of these two identical branches and study how the fault diffuses in internal difference of the corresponding states. The problem now reduces to classical DFA and hence we may apply standard techniques pertaining to differential fault analysis. Figure 2 depicts the concept visually in a very generic sense.

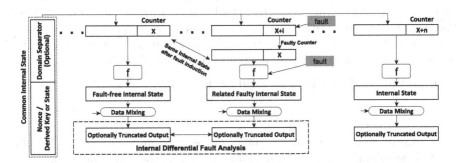

Fig. 2. Generic model for using internal differentials in fault analysis of parallelizable ciphers in the counter mode.

An interesting aspect of this strategy is that it requires *only one multi-block ciphertext with a single faulty block* thereby making the analysis independent of the effect of a nonce which prohibits usage of standard DFA. One could argue regarding the viability of the first fault in terms of achieving the counter collision.

---

[1] For instance, the differing bits could be localized within a byte.

However, in this work we introduce the concept of *Fault Quartets* (Refer Sect. 6) which can use a round-reduced distinguisher of the underlying cipher to locate the fault-free branch corresponding to a faulty branch due to the first fault under reasonable assumptions. Building upon these ideas a practical IDFA attack is mounted on PAEQ. Though the specifics rely on the underlying construction, the overall notion of IDFA can be adapted to other ciphers which meet the properties discussed earlier. In the next section we develop a four-round distinguisher of PAEQ based on internal differentials arising from counter values.

5   An Internal Differential Distinguisher for 4-Round PAEQ

In this section we showcase a 4-round internal differential distinguisher which surfaces due to low Hamming-distance between inputs to various parallel branches of the first call to the AESQ permutation during the encryption phase. Here we deal with AESQ reduced to 4-rounds. We start devising the distinguisher by making the following observation which is due to the PPAE mode of operation.

Observation 1. *Two parallel branches of PAEQ with the same domain separator differ only in the counter value.*

Based on Observation 1, we first choose any branch of PAEQ in the encryption phase with counter value i. We next find a branch with counter value j such that their corresponding c-bit[2] binary representations differ in exactly one[3] byte. The main idea is to restrict the internal-difference to a byte and later study its diffusion from $\mathcal{R}_1$ to $\mathcal{R}_4$. The differential propagation in an AES round is quite well-known. However, the presence of quadruple AES instantiations in AESQ and the inclusion of $\mathscr{S}$ operation that mixes the substates make the analysis interesting. Here, we are particularly interested in studying how the bytes belonging to the same column become interrelated as the difference diffuses.

Four Round Differential Propagation in AESQ:

- $\mathcal{R}_1$: Difference spreads to entire column, and the bytes are related by factors governed by the MixColumns matrix.
- $\mathcal{R}_2$: Entire substate affected; columns of the substate are related by factors.
- $\mathscr{S}$: One column of each substate affected; factor relations unaffected.
- $\mathcal{R}_3$: All substates affected. All columns exhibit byte inter-relations due to μ_3.
- $\mathcal{R}_4$: All substates still affected with all relations destroyed due to β_4
- $\mathscr{S}$: Columns permute.

This process is illustrated in Fig. 3a. After every round the corresponding byte inter-relations are given. Recall that here we are dealing with a differential state (Definition 4). Here, the numbers in a particular column indicate the factor by

---

[2] Recall, the counter is of size $c = n - k - 16$ bits.
[3] For instance, $i = 5$ and $j = 8$ differ only in the least significant byte.

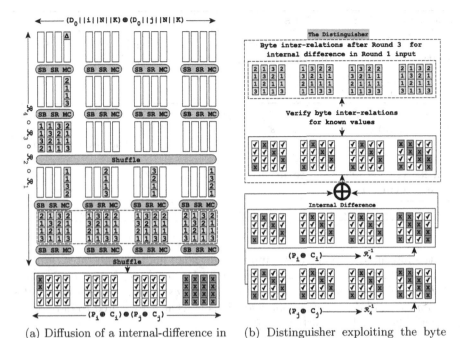

(a) Diffusion of a internal-difference in the first substate in 4 rounds of AESQ. SB $\leftrightarrow \beta_r^m$, SR $\leftrightarrow \rho_r^m$, MC $\leftrightarrow \mu_r^m$

(b) Distinguisher exploiting the byte inter-relations after $\mathcal{R}_3$.

Fig. 3. A demonstration of the 4-round distinguishing strategy using paeq-128. A $\checkmark$ denotes a known value while a X denotes an unknown value.

which the byte-wise differences in that column are related. In the first substate $\{2, 1, 1, 3\}$ imply that differences are of the form $\{2 \times f, 1 \times f, 1 \times f, 3 \times f\}$ where $f \in \mathbb{T} \setminus \{0\}$. The byte inter-relations after $\mathcal{R}_3$ translates into the following observation:

Observation 2. *The byte inter-relations after $\mathcal{R}_r$ due to a difference in $\mathcal{R}_{r-2}$ input is invariant based on which substate the initial difference was located.*[4]

The implication of Observation 2 is that there is a bijective relation between byte inter-relations after $\mathcal{R}_3$ and substate where we had the initial internal difference in $\mathcal{R}_1$ input. As there are four substates so we have four unique byte inter-relations (Fig. 6) after $\mathcal{R}_3$. We can now present the proposed distinguisher in Algorithm 2 which passes with probability 1 for PAEQ if $n = 4$.

Remark 1. DISTINGUISHER(P, C, i, j, n) will fail for any $n > 4$ because Observation 2 only holds for three rounds while the last round is handled by inversion to get a meet-in-the-middle scenario to verify the byte inter-relations (Fig. 3). Moreover, it might also fail if i and j differ in more than one byte since in that

---

[4] It is understood that $r > 2$ and $2|(r - 1)$.

Algorithm 2. DISTINGUISHER (P, C, i, j, n)

Input: $\begin{cases} P, C \rightarrow 1 \text{ known plaintext-ciphertext } (P = P_1||\cdots||P_t, C = C_1||\cdots||C_t) \\ (i \neq j) < t \rightarrow \text{Branch indexes which differ in one byte}^a \\ n \rightarrow \text{Total number of AESQ rounds considered} \end{cases}$

Output: 0/1

1: $s \leftarrow \mathscr{S}^{-1}(P_i \oplus C_i) \quad s' \leftarrow \mathscr{S}^{-1}(P_j \oplus C_j)$
2: $s \leftarrow \mathcal{R}_n^{-1}(s) \qquad\quad s' \leftarrow \mathcal{R}_n^{-1}(s')$
3: $\delta = s \oplus s'$ ▷ The internal difference
4: **Result** $\xleftarrow{\text{Verify Byte Inter-relations (Fig. 6)}} \delta$
5: **if Result** == **TRUE then return** 1
6: **else return** 0

---

^{a} $i, j \neq t$ since the last block might have a different domain separator in which case Observation 1 will not hold.

---

case the internal difference in $\mathcal{R}_1$ input might span multiple substates. *Finally,* DISTINGUISHER *constitutes a general 3-round differential characteristic which will hold for any 3 consecutive rounds of* AESQ *as long as the starting states have an internal difference of one byte.* This is what is exploited to develop an internal differential fault attack on PAEQ.

From the above remark we get the impression that if *somehow* we could get a one-byte internal difference in $\mathcal{R}_{17}$ then the 4-round distinguishing property could be verified from $\mathcal{R}_{20}$ i.e. the full AESQ permutation. In order to achieve this scenario we introduce the concept of **Fault Quartets** in the next section.

6 The Fault Quartet

Definition 7. *A fault quartet ($\mathcal{Q}_{i,j}$) is a configuration of four internal states of the* AESQ *belonging to two different branches i and j of an instance of* PAEQ *in the encryption phase. It is uniquely identified by the ordered pair of the branch indexes (i,j). $\mathcal{Q}_{i,j}$ is of the following form and has the following constraints:*

$$\mathcal{Q}_{i,j} = \{s, s^{\#}, t, t^{\#}\} \tag{2}$$

where $\begin{cases} s, t \rightarrow \text{ branch input states, } s^{\#} = \text{AESQ}^{16}(s), \ t^{\#} = \text{AESQ}^{16}(t) \\ \text{Constraint 1}: s \oplus t = \mathbf{0} \\ \text{Constraint 2}: s^{\#} \text{ and } t^{\#} \text{ have an internal difference of one byte.} \end{cases}$

To generate a fault quartet, we take a plaintext of 255 blocks[5] and induce two random byte faults during the encryption phase of PAEQ. The first fault, called the **equalizer** is injected in the last byte of the counter of any branch i. The second fault called the **differentiator** is injected anywhere in the input of $\mathcal{R}_{17}$ of AESQ in the same branch. The **equalizer** achieves the first constraint

---

[5] Last block is a complete block (i.e., block-size = $n - k - 16$) due to Observation 1.

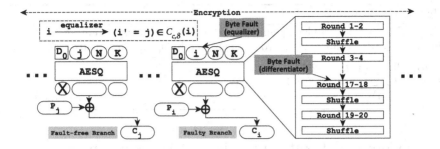

Fig. 4. Fault injection in PAEQ

of $\mathcal{Q}_{i,j}$ which states that the input states must have no internal difference while the `differentiator` induces a one-byte internal difference between the outputs of $\mathcal{R}_{16}$ which constitutes the second constraint. Figure 4 demonstrates the fault injection. The following observation accounts for the choice of a 255-block message above.

Observation 3. *The number of the plaintext blocks required to guarantee[6] the existence of a fault quartet with the* `equalizer` *fault injected in the **last byte** of the counter of any branch is 255 with a **complete** last block.*

The complete block at the end ensures that all inputs to AESQ have the same domain separator. The choice of 255 implies that all of these differ only in the **last byte** of the counter. Due to `equalizer` fault the counter value of branch i changes to j which is equal to the counter value of any[7] one of the remaining 254 fault-free branches. Thus, this outlines the condition to guarantee that a fault quartet is generated. But how would one find such a quartet since neither the input states nor the output of of AESQ[16] is visible to an adversary. This is addressed next where we give an algorithm to find such a quartet.

Finding $\mathcal{Q}_{i,j}$: Finding a fault-quartet translates into finding the branch-index ordered pair (i, j) where i corresponds to the branch of PAEQ where the faults have been introduced and the j corresponds to the fault-free branch. This is done by Algorithm 3 using the distinguisher developed earlier as a sub-routine. One can recall that due to the `differentiator` there will be a one-byte internal difference between branch i and j in the input of $\mathcal{R}_{17}$. Thus distinguishing property can be verified from $\mathcal{R}_{20}$ i.e., the full AESQ permutation.

$\mathcal{Q}_{i,j}$ gives us the opportunity to exploit the distinguishing property of PAEQ in the last four rounds of AESQ. With these concepts we are in a position to finally introduce the ENCOUNTER attack which exploits the property further to recover the entire internal state of AESQ thereby revealing the key.

---

[6] With a probability of $\frac{255}{256}$.
[7] Except for the case when $j = 0$ when it matches none of the remaining branches.

Algorithm 3. FINDQ (P, C, i)

Input: $P, C \to$ One 255-block plaintext-ciphertext; $i \to$ Index of faulty-branch
Output: $(i, j) \to$ Branch-index ordered pair identifying the fault quartet $\mathcal{Q}_{i,j}$

1: **for all** $j \in \{1, 2, \cdots, 255\} \setminus \{i\}$ **do**
2:     **if** (DISTINGUISHER$(P, C, i, j, 20) == 1$) **then**
3:         **return** (i, j) ▷ This line is reached exactly once

7   EnCounter: Fault Analysis of PAEQ using Internal Differentials

The EnCounter attack proceeds in two phases: InBound and OutBound. The InBound phase is common to all PAEQ variants while the OutBound phase varies. In this work we focus on paeq-64, paeq-80 and paeq-128 which constitute the primary set of PAEQ family as specified by the designers. We first provide a high-level description of the attack and then delve into the details.

High-level Description of EnCounter

→ Fault-Injection: Run PAEQ on a plaintext with 255 complete blocks. Inject the equalizer and differentiator faults in any branch i.
→ Find Fault-Quartet: Use FINDQ to get index of the fault-free branch.
→ InBound Phase: Invert states from output of AESQ for both branches and reconstruct internal differential state after $\mathcal{R}_{19}$. Guess diagonal of differentiator fault to get a set of four column vectors for the state after β_{19}.
→ OutBound Phase: Recovers candidates for all substates at the end of $\mathcal{R}_{20}$ for the fault-free branch using the column vectors from InBound phase. Return them is the form of substate vectors.
→ Complete Attack: Repeat InBound phase for every guess of the diagonal and consequently OutBound too. Accumulate substate vectors from every guess. Their cross-product gives the reduced state-space for the state after $\mathcal{R}_{20}$. Inverting every candidate state and verifying the known part of the input reveals the correct key.

7.1   The Fault Model

Firstly, as EnCounter is an IDFA attack it needs only a single run of PAEQ. Secondly, it is based on a **random byte** fault model requiring 2 faults: equalizer and differentiator, induced in any branch of AESQ while encrypting the plaintext. equalizer targets the *last byte* of the counter while differentiator targets *any* byte at the input of $\mathcal{R}_{17}$ (Fig. 4). While classical DFA generally deals with single block messages, IDFA uses a single multi-block message as it targets parallelizable ciphers. In the context of EnCounter the plaintext itself is a 255-block message. After fault injection the attacker uses faulty and fault-free blocks of the same ciphertext and corresponding plaintext blocks to mount the attack. Assuming the faulty branch to be i, faulty ciphertext block C_i^* is identified below.

$$\text{ENCOUNTER Input} \begin{cases} P = P_1||P_2|| \cdots ||P_i|| \cdots ||P_j|| \cdots ||P_{255} \\ C = C_1||C_2|| \cdots ||C_i^*|| \cdots ||C_j|| \cdots ||C_{255}||\text{Tag}^* \end{cases}$$

7.2 The INBOUND Phase

As the name suggests the INBOUND phase tries to invert the the faulty and fault-free branches using the observable part of the output. A pictorial abstraction of the process is provided in Fig. 5 for early reference. After identifying the fault-free branch using FINDQ, the attacker separately inverts the partially known output[8] of AESQ for both branches up to the input of $\mathcal{R}_{20}$. He then computes the internal difference of the states which gives him a partially specified differential state. This state, by virtue of fault diffusion, has a special property that the differences in individual columns are related. These relations are given in Fig. 6 and help to recover the complete differential state. Further, by Obervation 2 the verified byte inter-relations will also *reveal the substate* where the differentiator fault got injected.

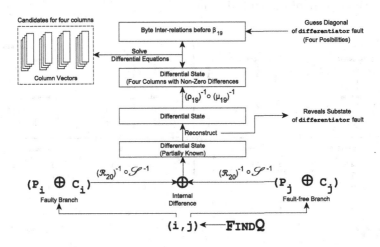

Fig. 5. The INBOUND phase. Returns candidates for columns after β_{19}.

The attacker inverts the reconstructed state up to input of ρ_{19}. Again, due to fault diffusion every substate of this state has exactly one column with non-zero related differences (Refer Fig. 3a). However, the relations differ based on the location of differentiator fault. By virtue of the *Diagonal Principle*[9] [7] which

---

[8] Computed using the XOR of plaintext and ciphertext blocks.

[9] Faults injected in the same diagonal of an AES state in round r input lead to the same byte interrelations at the end of round $(r + 1)$.

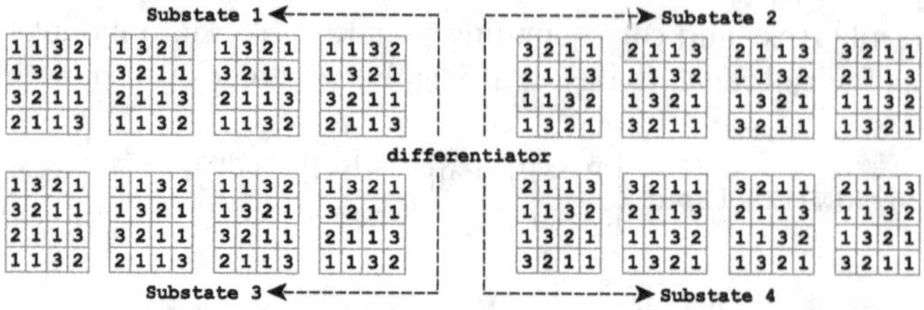

Fig. 6. Byte inter-relations after $\mathcal{R}_{19} \leftrightarrow$ Location of differentiator fault.

is a well-known result of DFA on AES, we know that for a particular substate there can be four kinds of relations based on the diagonal where the differentiator was injected. Figure 7 shows all these possible byte inter-relations based on the source of the byte-fault at the input of $\mathcal{R}_{17}$.

The attacker already knows which quadrant to look at in Fig. 7 since he knows the substate location of differentiator. However, he has no idea about the source diagonal and has to resort to *guessing*. So like classical DFA using the input and output difference of β_{19}, the attacker solves differential equations to generate candidates for the four columns which are stored in column vectors. At the end of INBOUND phase the attacker has a set of four column vectors for the particular guess of the fault diagonal.

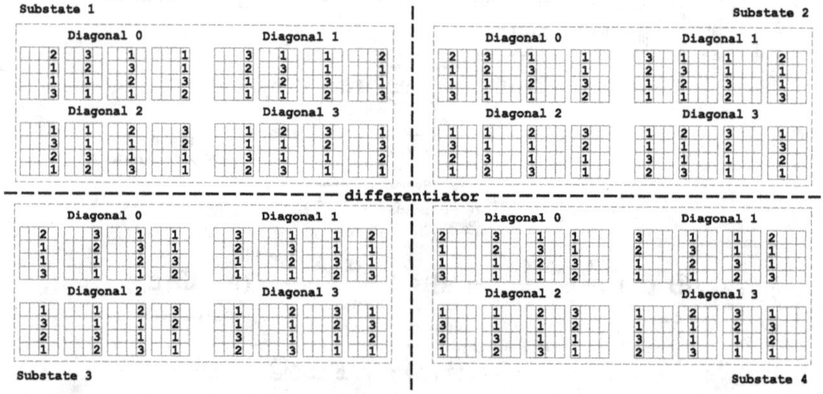

Fig. 7. Byte inter-relations at $\mathcal{R}_{19}$ input vs location of differentiator fault. Each quadrant corresponds to a source substate. For each substate, the relations correspond to a source diagonal.

7.3 The OUTBOUND Phase

Unlike the INBOUND phase, the OUTBOUND phase works only on the fault-free branch of AESQ specifically on the partial state at the end of $\mathcal{R}_{20}$. Additionally, the column vectors generated above are also used. Let us look at the nature of

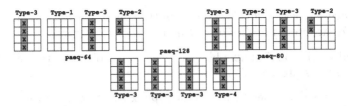

Fig. 8. The classification of substates observed in the internal state after $\mathscr{S}^{-1}(P_j \oplus C_j)$ based on number of unknown bytes.

the substate in the state determined by $\mathscr{S}^{-1}(P_j \oplus C_j)$. This is captured by Fig. 8 for PAEQ variants analyzed in this work.

There are four types of substates with varying number of unknown bytes. The primary aim of this phase is to reduce the search space for these substates. A Type-1 substate is left unaltered since it has no unknown byte. Type-2 and Type-3 are equivalent in the sense that both have three completely known columns while Type-4 can be converted to the same form by guessing 2 bytes of the first column. Thus for the rest of the analysis we assume that we are dealing with a substate with only one unknown column. We now describe how the attacker produces candidates for such a substate. Again Fig. 9 visually illustrates this process for easy reference. Let us consider the mth substate.

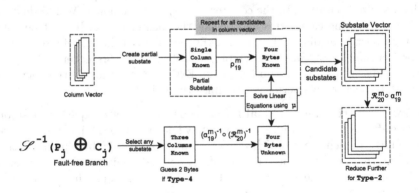

Fig. 9. The OUTBOUND phase. Returns candidates for substates after $\mathcal{R}_{20}$.

1. The substate is inverted up to **output** of μ_{19}^m. At this point the substate bears a property that every column has exactly one *unknown* byte.
2. Any column from the corresponding column vector[10] is used to form a partial substate which is propagated forward up to the **input** of μ_{19}^m. At this point the substate has exactly one *known* byte in every column.
3. The attacker exploits linear relations between the partial input and partial output of μ_{19}^m to uniquely retrieve the substate. The recovered substate is propagated forward up to the end of $\mathcal{R}_{20}$.

---

[10] Recall that the column vector corresponds to the state after β_{19}.

4. The process repeated for all columns in the column vector and all computed substates are stored in the corresponding substate vectors.

At the end of the OUTBOUND phase we have a set of substate vectors for all substates of the state after $\mathcal{R}_{20}$.

Remark 2. Unlike a Type-3 substate, a Type-2 substate has two extra known bytes in the fourth column which can be exploited. Thus, substate vector is reduced by comparing candidates with respect to these two bytes and eliminated if unmatched. *This should lead to large scale reduction of candidates.* As regards a Type-4 substate 2 bytes need to be guessed to make it like a Type-3. Thus we have to repeat the process of candidate generation 2^{16} times.

7.4   The Complete Attack

At the outset ENCOUNTER repeats the INBOUND phase four times for different diagonals positions of differentiator. Every iteration returns four column vectors one for each substate of the state after β_{19}. The OUTBOUND phase then follows, iterating over different types of substates $\in \mathscr{S}^{-1}(P_j \oplus C_j)$ from the fault-free branch j returning corresponding substate candidates in substate vectors. The cross-product of the substate vectors forms the state vector which constitutes the reduced state-space for $\mathscr{S}^{-1}(P_j \oplus C_j)$. The last step is to invert every candidate state to get the input of branch j. Here, we can exploit the knowledge of the domain separator D_0, the counter value j and the nonce N. This helps to eliminate all wrong candidates and reveals the master key $\mathcal{K}$. It must be noted that for a particular diagonal guess in INBOUND phase if the size of any substate vector returned by OUTBOUND is empty, all substate vectors generated for that guess are discarded. Algorithm 4 presents ENCOUNTER at an abstract level. In the next subsection, we perform a complexity analysis.

Remark 3. **Retrieving diagonal for paeq-64:** In case of paeq-64 since second substate after $\mathcal{R}_{20}$ (Refer Fig. 8) is completely known (Type-1), it can be inverted two rounds to reach input of $\mathcal{R}_{19}^2$ for both branches i, j. The byte inter-relations in the internal-difference of these inputs is verified against the ones given in Fig. 7. This reveals the fault diagonal of differentiator. Thus as a special case, for paeq-64 the diagonal guess can be avoided.

7.5   Complexity Analysis

Here we are mainly interested in getting the size of set $\mathcal{S}$ since from Algorithm 4 it is evident that AESQ^{-1} constitutes the most expensive operation of ENCOUNTER and the number of calls is bounded by $|\mathcal{S}|$. Equation 3 gives the upper bound on the size of $\mathcal{S}$ assuming that $s \leftarrow \mathscr{S}^{-1}(P_j \oplus C_j)$.

$$|\mathcal{S}| \leq \sum_d |([s]^v)_d| = \sum_d \left(\prod_{x=1}^{4} |[s^x]^v| \right)_d \tag{3}$$

Algorithm 4. ENCOUNTER(P, C, i)

Input: $\begin{cases} P, C \leftarrow \text{One known plaintext-ciphertext with 255 complete blocks} \\ i \leftarrow \text{Index of faulty-branch} \end{cases}$

Output: $\mathcal{K} \leftarrow$ The Master Key

1: $(i, j) \leftarrow \text{FINDQ}\,(P, C, i)$ ▷ Locate Fault-quartet $\mathcal{Q}_{i,j}$

2: $\mathcal{S} \leftarrow \varnothing$

3: **for** $d \xleftarrow{\text{Guess}}$ Fault diagonal **do**   ▷ Location of **differentiator**

4:      Four Column Vectors $\xleftarrow{\text{INBOUND}} \Big(P_i \oplus C_i, P_j \oplus C_j, d \Big)$

5:      Four Substate Vectors $\xleftarrow{\text{OUTBOUND}} \Big(P_j \oplus C_j, \text{Column Vectors} \Big)$

6:      **if** $\Big(\text{Any Substate Vector} = \varnothing \Big)$ **then Go to** 3

7:      State Vector $\xleftarrow{\text{Cross-Product}}$ Four Substate Vectors

8:      $\mathcal{S} \leftarrow \Big(\mathcal{S} \bigcup \text{State Vector} \Big)$ ▷ Reduced state-space

9: **for all** $e \in \mathcal{S}$ **do** $(D_x || j_x || N_x || \mathcal{K}) \leftarrow \text{AESQ}^{-1}(\mathscr{S}(e))$

10:      **if** $(D_x || j_x || N_x) == (D_0 || j || N)$ **then return** $\mathcal{K}$

Table 2. Substate vector sizes in terms of Type-3 substate vector size

GetType(s^x)	Type-1	Type-2	Type-3	Type-4
$\|[s^x]^v\|$ (Refer Remark 2)	1	$p \ll q$	q	$r \leq 2^{16} \times q$

It implies that it suffices to study the sizes of substate vectors. It was seen in OUTBOUND phase that Type-2 and Type-4 substates are related to Type-3. Accordingly, the sizes of the corresponding substate vectors can be expressed in terms of a Type-3 substate vector. This is furnished in Table 2 where q denotes the size of a Type-3 substate vector while p and r denote sizes of Type-2 and Type-4 substate vectors respectively. Table 3 enumerates the theoretical upper bounds of the complexities individually identifying sizes of the substate vectors.

8 Experimental Results

Computer simulations of ENCOUNTER were performed over 1000 randomly chosen nonces, keys. The results for paeq-64/80 are shown in the form of bar diagrams in Figs. 10 and 11 respectively. The bars segregate the substate vectors in terms of their sizes (the value at the base) with the frequency of occurrence given at the top. The figures mainly show that in the average case q is concentrated around 2^8. It was mentioned in Remark 2 that in the presence of additional information p could be further reduced such that $p \ll q$. This is confirmed by the results which show that $p = 1$ with a few exceptions when $p = 2$. Table 3 summaries the results while the details are given below:

– paeq-64: By Remark 3 we know that the diagonal for **differentiator** can be recovered thereby avoiding the guessing step in Algorithm 4 and reducing the complexity by a factor of four. So the final experimentally verified size of $\mathcal{S}$ for paeq-64 stands at $72292 \approx 2^{16.14}$.

- **paeq-80**: During simulation it was found that for `Type-2` substates OUTBOUND phase returned empty substate vectors for a wrong guess of faulty diagonal. This made Step 6 of Algorithm 4 to be TRUE reducing $|\mathcal{S}|$ by four times. So the final verified size $72578 \approx 2^{16.14}$ is very close to `paeq-64`.
- **paeq-128**: It has three `Type-3` substates contributing around 2^{24} while a `Type-4` substate is supposed to contribute over $2^{16} \times 2^{8}$. Finally, the complexity is increased four times due to diagonal guess. Thus the *estimated* value of $|\mathcal{S}|$ is around 2^{50}.

Table 3. ENCOUNTER Complexities

PAEQ	Substate vector size $s = \mathcal{S}^{-1}(P_j \oplus C_j)$				Theoretical complexity($|\mathcal{S}|$)	Experimental result($\approx |\mathcal{S}|$)
	$|[s^1]^v|$	$|[s^2]^v|$	$|[s^3]^v|$	$|[s^4]^v|$		
paeq-64	q (Type-3)	1 (Type-1)	q (Type-3)	p (Type-2)	$q^2 p(\ll q^3)$	$2^{16.14}$
paeq-80	q (Type-3)	p (Type-2)	q (Type-3)	p (Type-2)	$4p^2 q^2(\ll 4q^4)$	$2^{16.14}$
paeq-128	q (Type-3)	q (Type-3)	q (Type-3)	r (Type-4)	$4q^3 r(\le 2^{18} q^4)$	2^{50}(estd.)

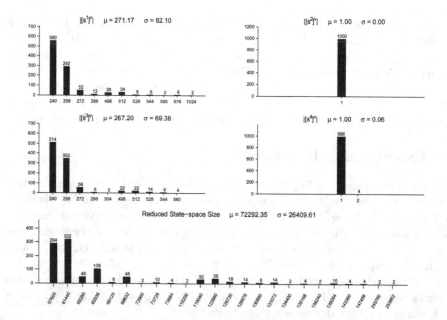

Fig. 10. Bar diagram for sizes of substate vectors and reduced state-space for 1000 experiments on `paeq-64` with mean (μ) and standard-deviation (σ) indicated.

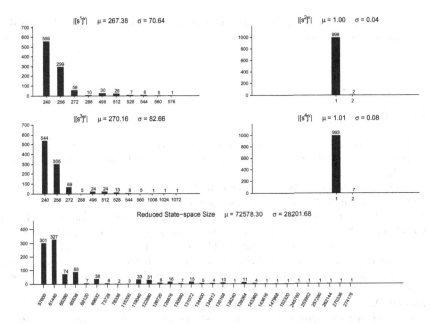

Fig. 11. Bar diagram for sizes of substate vectors and reduced state-space for 1000 experiments on **paeq-80** with mean (μ) and standard-deviation (σ) indicated.

9   Conclusion

This work introduces the notion of fault analysis using internal differentials. Parallelizable ciphers using the counter mode are found to be good targets for such kind of analysis though the real attack relies on the underlying construction. A 4-round distinguisher for authenticated cipher **PAEQ** is demonstrated. Using this the idea of fault quartets is proposed which can locate the fault-free branch corresponding to a faulty branch. Finally, an internal differential fault attack **EnCounter** is devised against **PAEQ** using just two random byte faults with only a single faulty ciphertext and the corresponding plaintext. The attack reduces the key-space of **paeq-64**, **paeq-80** and **paeq-128** to around 2^{16}, 2^{16} and 2^{50} respectively. The ability to mount an attack using a single faulty run of the cipher makes IDFA independent of the effect of nonce thereby breaking the *nonce barrier* of DFA. Moreover, the fault analysis presented here is of particular interest since it deals with internal states that are partially specified which deviates it from classical DFA. Finally, this work constitutes the first analysis of CAESAR candidate **PAEQ**.

Acknowledgement. We would like to thank the anonymous reviewers for their invaluable comments and Orr Dunkelman for helping us in preparing the final version of the paper.

References

1. Biham, E., Shamir, A.: Differential fault analysis of secret key cryptosystems. In: Kaliski Jr., B.S. (ed.) CRYPTO 1997. LNCS, vol. 1294, pp. 513–525. Springer, Heidelberg (1997)
2. Giraud, C.: DFA on AES. In: Dobbertin, H., Rijmen, V., Sowa, A. (eds.) AES 2005. LNCS, vol. 3373, pp. 27–41. Springer, Heidelberg (2005)
3. Dusart, P., Letourneux, G., Vivolo, O.: Differential fault analysis on A.E.S. IACR Cryptology ePrint Archive, 2003:10 (2003). http://eprint.iacr.org/2003/010
4. Piret, G., Quisquater, J.-J.: A differential fault attack technique against SPN structures, with application to the AES and KHAZAD. In: Walter, C.D., Koç, Ç.K., Paar, C. (eds.) CHES 2003. LNCS, vol. 2779, pp. 77–88. Springer, Heidelberg (2003)
5. Moradi, A., Shalmani, M.T.M., Salmasizadeh, M.: A generalized method of differential fault attack against AES cryptosystem. In: Goubin, L., Matsui, M. (eds.) CHES 2006. LNCS, vol. 4249, pp. 91–100. Springer, Heidelberg (2006)
6. Mukhopadhyay, D.: An improved fault based attack of the advanced encryption standard. In: Preneel, B. (ed.) AFRICACRYPT 2009. LNCS, vol. 5580, pp. 421–434. Springer, Heidelberg (2009)
7. Saha, D., Mukhopadhyay, D., Chowdhury, D.R.: A diagonal fault attack on the advanced encryption standard. IACR Cryptology ePrint Archive, 2009:581 (2009). http://eprint.iacr.org/2009/581
8. Rogaway, P.: Nonce-based symmetric encryption. In: Roy, B., Meier, W. (eds.) FSE 2004. LNCS, vol. 3017, pp. 348–359. Springer, Heidelberg (2004)
9. Boneh, D., DeMillo, R.A., Lipton, R.J.: On the importance of eliminating errors in cryptographic computations. J. Cryptol. **14**(2), 101–119 (2001)
10. Joye, M., Lenstra, A.K., Quisquater, J.-J.: Chinese remaindering based cryptosystems in the presence of faults. J. Cryptol. **12**(4), 241–245 (1999)
11. Coron, J.-S., Joux, A., Kizhvatov, I., Naccache, D., Paillier, P.: Fault attacks on RSA signatures with partially unknown messages. In: Clavier, C., Gaj, K. (eds.) CHES 2009. LNCS, vol. 5747, pp. 444–456. Springer, Heidelberg (2009)
12. Saha, D., Kuila, S., Chowdhury, D.R.: EscApe: diagonal fault analysis of APE. In: Progress in Cryptology - INDOCRYPT 2014 - 15th International Conference on Cryptology in India, New Delhi, India, December 14–17, 2014, pp. 197–216 (2014)
13. Andreeva, E., Bilgin, B., Bogdanov, A., Luykx, A., Mennink, B., Mouha, N., Wang, Q., Yasuda, K.: PRIMATEs v1.02. Submission to the CAESAR Competition (2014). http://competitions.cr.yp.to/round2/primatesv102.pdf
14. Peyrin, T.: Improved differential attacks for ECHO and Grøstl. In: Rabin, T. (ed.) CRYPTO 2010. LNCS, vol. 6223, pp. 370–392. Springer, Heidelberg (2010)
15. Dinur, I., Dunkelman, O., Shamir, A.: Collision attacks on up to 5 rounds of SHA-3 using generalized internal differentials. In: Moriai, S. (ed.) FSE 2013. LNCS, vol. 8424, pp. 219–240. Springer, Heidelberg (2014)
16. CAESAR: Competition for Authenticated Encryption: Security, Applicability, and Robustness. http://competitions.cr.yp.to/caesar.html

17. Daemen, J., Rijmen, V.: The Design of Rijndael: AES - The Advanced Encryption Standard. Information Security and Cryptography. Springer, Heidelberg (2002)
18. Biryukov, A., Khovratovich, D.: PAEQ: parallelizable permutation-based authenticated encryption. In: Chow, S.S.M., Camenisch, J., Hui, L.C.K., Yiu, S.M. (eds.) ISC 2014. LNCS, vol. 8783, pp. 72–89. Springer, Heidelberg (2014)
19. Khovratovich, D., Biryukov, A.: PAEQ v1. Submission to the CAESAR Competition (2014). http://competitions.cr.yp.to/round1/paeqv1.pdf

Curious Case of Rowhammer: Flipping Secret Exponent Bits Using Timing Analysis

Sarani Bhattacharya$^{(\boxtimes)}$ and Debdeep Mukhopadhyay

Department of Computer Science and Engineering, Indian Institute of Technology, Kharagpur, Kharagpur 721302, India
{sarani.bhattacharya,debdeep}@cse.iitkgp.ernet.in

Abstract. Rowhammer attacks have exposed a serious vulnerability in modern DRAM chips to induce bit flips in data which is stored in memory. In this paper, we develop a methodology to combine timing analysis to perform the hammering in a controlled manner to create bit flips in cryptographic keys which are stored in memory. The attack would require only user level privilege for Linux kernel versions before 4.0 and is unaware of the memory location of the key. An intelligent combination of timing *Prime + Probe* attack and *row-buffer collision* is shown to induce bit flip faults in a 1024 bit RSA key on modern processors using realistic number of hammering attempts. This demonstrates the feasibility of fault analysis of ciphers using purely software means on commercial x86 architectures, which to the best of our knowledge has not been reported earlier. The attack is also relevant for the newest Linux kernel in a Cross-VM environment where the VMs having root privilege are not denied to access the pagemap.

Keywords: Rowhammer · Fault attack · *Prime + Probe* · Bit flip

1 Introduction

Rowhammer is a term coined for disturbances observed in recent DRAM devices in which repeated row activation causes the DRAM cells to electrically interact among themselves [1–4]. This results in bit flips [2] in DRAM due to discharging of the cells in the adjacent rows. DRAM cells are composed of an access transistor and a capacitor which stores charge to represent a bit. Since capacitors loose their charge with time, DRAM cells require to be refreshed within a fixed interval of time referred to as the refresh interval. DRAM comprises of two dimensional array of cells, where each row of cells have its own wordline and for accessing each row, its respective wordline needs to be activated. Whenever some data is requested, the cells in the corresponding row are copied to a direct-mapped cache termed Row-buffer. If same row is accessed again, then the contents of row-buffer is read without row activation. However, repeatedly activating a row causes cells in adjacent rows to discharge themselves and results in bit flip.

© International Association for Cryptologic Research 2016
B. Gierlichs and A.Y. Poschmann (Eds.): CHES 2016, LNCS 9813, pp. 602–624, 2016.
DOI: 10.1007/978-3-662-53140-2_29

The authors in [2] show that rowhammer vulnerability exists in majority of the recent commodity DRAM chips and is most prevalent for sub 40 nm memory technology. DRAM process technology over the years have seen continuous reduction in the size of each cell and cell density has also increased to a great extent reducing the cost per bit of memory. Smaller cells hold less charge and this makes them even more vulnerable. Moreover, the increased cell density has a negative impact on DRAM reliability [2] as it introduces electromagnetic coupling effects and leads to such disturbance errors.

In [5], it was first demonstrated that rowhammer not only has issues regarding memory reliability but also are capable of causing serious security breaches. DRAM vulnerability causing bit flips in Native Client (NaCl) program was shown to gain privilege escalation, such that the program control escapes x86 NACL sandbox and acquires the ability to trigger OS syscall. The blog also discusses about how rowhammer can be exploited by user-level programs to gain kernel privileges. In [5], the bit flips are targeted at a page table entry which after flip points to a physical page of the malicious process, thus providing read-write access to cause a kernel privilege escalation. A new approach for triggering rowhammer with x86 non-temporal store instruction is proposed in [6]. The paper discusses an interesting approach by using `libc's` `memset` and `memcpy` functions and the threats involved in using non-temporal store instructions for triggering rowhammer. A vivid description of the possible attack scenarios exploiting bit flips from rowhammer are also presented in the paper.

A javascript based implementation of the rowhammer attack, Rowhammer.js [7] is implemented using an optimal eviction strategy and claims to exploit rowhammer bug with high accuracy without using `clflush` instruction. Being implemented in javascript, it can induce hardware faults remotely. But, in order to mount a successful fault attack on a system the adversary should have the handle to induce fault in locations such that the effect of that fault is useful in making the attack successful. Another variant of rowhammer exists, termed as double-sided-rowhammer [8]. This variant chooses three adjacent rows at a time, targeting bit blips at the middle row by continuously accessing the outer rows for hammering. The existing implementation [8] is claimed to work in systems having a specific DRAM organization. In all of the existing works, precisely inducing bit flip in the data used by a co-residing process has not been attempted. None of the previous works attempted to demonstrate a practical fault analysis attack using rowhammer. The address mappings to various components of the LLC and DRAM being functions of physical address bits, inducing bit flip in a data residing in an unknown location of DRAM seems to be a challenging task.

In this paper, we illustrate a software driven fault attack on public key exponentiation by inducing a bit flip in the secret exponent. It is well known from [9], theoretically if any fault is induced while public key exponentiation is taking place, then a single faulty signature is enough to leak the secret exponent in an unprotected implementation. However, to inflict the fault using rowhammer on the secret exponent to lead to a usable faulty signature requires further investigation. While [5] was able to successfully induce rowhammer flips in the DRAM to cause a fault in a page table entry, the challenge to induce faults to perform a fault attack on a cipher, requires a better understanding of the location of the secret key in the corresponding row of a bank of the DRAM. More recent developments of rowhammering, like double-sided-rowhammer [8], while increasing the probability of a bit flip, cannot be directly applied to the current scenario, as the row where the secret resides can be in any arbitrary location in the target bank. The chance of the memory location for the secret key lying between the rows of the allocated memory for rowhammer is low. In this scenario a double-sided-rowhammer will reduce the probability of a successful exploitable fault. Hence, it is imperative to ascertain the location of the secret exponent before launching the rowhammer. Our novelty is to combine *Prime + Probe* attack and row-buffer collision, detected again through timing channel, to identify the target bank where the secret resides.

We combine knowledge of reverse engineering of LLC slice and DRAM addressing with timing side-channel to determine the bank in which secret resides. We precisely trigger rowhammer to address in the same bank as the secret. This increases probability of bit flip in the secret exponent and the novelty of our work is that we provide series of steps to improve the controllability of fault induction. The overall idea of the attack involves three major steps. The attacker successfully identifies an *eviction set* which is a set of data elements which maps to the same cache set and slice as that of the secret exponent by timing analysis using *Prime + Probe* methodology. This set essentially behaves as an alternative to clflush statement of x86 instruction set. The attacker now observes timing measurements to DRAM access to determine the DRAM bank in which the secret resides in. The variation in timing is observed due to the row-buffer conflict forced by the adversary, inducing bit flips by repeated row activation in the particular bank where the secret is residing. Elements which map to same bank but separate rows are accessed continuously to observe a successful bit flip.

The organization of the paper is as follows:- The following Sect. 2 provides a brief idea on Cache and DRAM architecture and also the rowhammer bug. In Sect. 3, we provide the algorithm using timing observations to determine the LLC set, slice and also the DRAM banks in which the secret maps to. Section 4 provides the experimental validation for a successful bit flip in the secret exponent in various steps. Section 5 discusses the existing hardware and software driven countermeasures to the rowhammer problem. Section 6 provides a detailed discussion on the assumptions and limitations of our attack model on bigger range of systems. The final section concludes the work we present here.

2   Preliminaries

In this section, we provide a background on some key-concepts, which include some DRAM details, the rowhammer bug and details of cache architecture which have been subjected to attack.

2.1   Dynamic Random Access Memory

Dynamic Random-Access Memory (DRAM) is a Random-Access Memory in which each unit of charge is stored in a capacitor and is associated with an access transistor, together they constitute a *cell* of DRAM. The DRAM cells are organized in rows and columns. The access transistor is connected to the wordline of a row, which when enabled, connects the capacitor to the bitline of the column and allows reading or writing data to the connected row. The reading or writing to cells in a row is done through *row-buffer* which can hold charges for a single row at a time. There are three steps that are performed, when data is requested to be read from a particular row:

Opening Row - The wordline connected to the row is enabled, which allows the capacitors in the entire row to get connected to the bitlines. This results in the charge of each cell to discharge through the bitlines to the row-buffer.

Reading or Writing to cells - The row-buffer data is read or written by the memory controller by accessing respective columns.

Closing Row - The wordline of the respective row is disabled, before some other row is enabled.

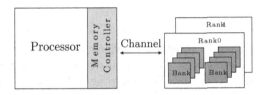

Fig. 1. DRAM architecture [2]

DRAM Architecture. DRAM is hierarchically composed of Channels, Rank and Banks. The physical link between the memory controller and the DRAM module is termed as *channel*. Inside the channel, the physical memory modules connected to the motherboard are named as *Dual Inline Memory Module (DIMM)* which typically comprises of one or two *ranks* as in Fig. 1. Each rank is further comprised of multiple *banks*, as for example, 8 banks exist in a DDR3 rank. Each bank is a two-dimensional collection of cells having typically 2^{14} to 2^{17} rows and a row-buffer. Any row in a particular bank can only be read and written by involving the row-buffer. The latency in DRAM access when two access request concurrently map to same channel, rank, bank but different row is termed as *row-buffer conflict*. The channel, rank, bank and the row index where a data element is going to reside, is decided as functions of physical address of the concerned data element.

The capacitors in each cell of DRAM discharges with time. The capacitor can hold charge upto a specific interval of time before it completely looses its charge. This interval is termed as *retention time*, which is guaranteed to be 64 ms in DDR3 DRAM specifications [10]. But it is shown, that repeated row activation over a period of time leads to faster discharge of cells in the adjacent rows [2].

2.2   The Rowhammer Bug

Persistent and continuous accesses to DRAM cells, lead the neighboring cells of the accessed cell to electrically interact with each other. The phenomenon of flipping bits in DRAM cells is termed as the *rowhammer* bug [1,2]. As described in Sect. 2.1, accessing a byte in memory involves transferring data from the row into the bank's row-buffer which also involves discharging the row's cells. Repeated discharging and recharging of the cells of a row can result in leakage of charge in the adjacent rows. If this can be repeated enough times, before automatic refreshes of the adjacent rows (which usually occur every 64 ms), this disturbance error in DRAM chip can cause bit flips.

```
Code-hammer
{
  mov (X), %eax   // read from address X
  mov (Y), %ebx   // read from address Y
  clflush (X)     // flush cache for address X
  clflush (Y)     // flush cache for address Y
  jmp Code-hammer
}
```

In [2], a code snippet is provided in which the program generates a read to DRAM on every data access. The *mov* instructions generate access request to DRAM at X and Y locations. The following `clflush` instructions evict the data elements from all levels of cache. However, if X and Y point to different rows in the same bank, code-hammer will cause X and Y's rows to be repeatedly activated. This may lead to disturbance error in the adjacent cells of the accessed rows, resulting in flipping bits in the adjacent row cells.

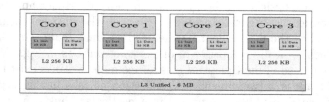

Fig. 2. Cache architecture in Intel Ivy Bridge [11]

In the next subsection, we summarize some key concepts of cache architecture in modern processors.

2.3   Cache Memory Architecture

In recent processors, there exists a hierarchy of cache memories where the size of each cache level increases as we move to its higher level, but their access times

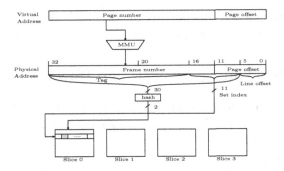

Fig. 3. Cache memory indexing [12]

increases. L3 or Last Level Cache (LLC) is shared across processor cores, takes larger time and is further divided into slices such that it can be accessed by multiple cores concurrently. Figure 2 illustrates the architectural specification for a typical Intel Ivy-Bridge architecture [11]. In Intel architecture, the data residing in any of the lower levels of cache are included in the higher levels as well. Thus are inclusive in nature. On a LLC cache miss, the requested element is brought in the cache from the main memory, and the cache miss penalty is much higher compared to the lower level cache hits.

Requested data are brought from the main memory in the cache in chunks of cache lines. This is typically of 64 Bytes in recent processors. The data requested by the processor is associated with a virtual address from the virtual address space allocated to the running process by the Operating System. The virtual address can be partitioned into two parts: the lower bits in Fig. 3 is the offset within the page typically represented by $log_2(page\_size)$ bits, while the remaining upper bits forms the *page_number*. The *page_number* forms an index to *page table* and translates to physical *frame number*. The frame number together with the offset bits constitute the physical address of the element. The translation of virtual to physical addresses are performed at run time, thus physical addresses of each elements are most likely to change from one execution to another.

The physical address bits decide the cache sets and slices in which a data is going to reside. If the cache line size is of b bytes, then least significant $log_2(b)$ bits of the physical addresses are used as index within the cache line. If the target system is having k processor cores, the LLC is partitioned into k slices each of the slice have c cache sets where each set is m way associative.

The $log_2(k)$ bits following $log_2(b)$ bits for cache line determines the cache set in which the element is going to reside. Because of associativity, m such cache lines having the identical $log_2(k)$ bits reside in the same set. The slice addressing in modern processors is implemented computing a complex Hash function. Recently, there has been works which reverse engineered [12,13] the LLC slice addressing function. Reverse engineering on Intel architectures has been attempted in [13] using timing analysis. The functions differ across different architectures and each of these functions are documented via successful reverse engineering in [12,13].

In the following sections, we use this knowledge of underlying architecture to build an attack model which can cause successful flips in a secret value.

3   Combining Timing Analysis and Rowhammer

In this section we discuss the development of an algorithm to induce bit flip in the secret exponent by combining timing analysis and DRAM vulnerability.

3.1   Attack Model

In this paper, we aim to induce bit fault in the secret exponent of the public key exponentiation algorithm using rowhammer vulnerability of DRAM with increased controllability. The secret resides in some location in the cache memory and also in some unknown location in the main memory. The attacker having user-level privileges in the system, does not have the knowledge of these locations in LLC and DRAM since these location are decided by mapping of physical address bits. The threat model assumed throughout the paper allows adversary to send known ciphertext to the algorithm and observe its decrypted output.

Let us assume that the adversary sends input plaintext to the encryption process and observes the output of the encryption. Thus the adversary gets hold of a valid plaintext-ciphertext pair, which will be used while checking for the bit flips. The adversary has the handle to send ciphertext to the decryption oracle, which decrypts the input and sends back the plaintext. The decryption process constantly polls for its input ciphertexts and sends the plaintext to the requesting process. The adversary aims to reproduce bit flip in the exponent and thus first needs to identify the corresponding bank in DRAM in which the secret exponent resides. Let us assume, that the secret exponent resides in some bank say, bank A. Though the decryption process constantly performs exponentiation with accesses to the secret exponent, but such access requests are usually addressed from the cache memory itself since they result in a cache hit. In this scenario it is difficult for the adversary to determine the bank in which the secret resides because the access request from the decryption process hardly results in main memory access.

According to the DRAM architecture, the channel, rank, bank and row addressing of the data elements depend on the physical address of the data elements. In order to perform rowhammering on the secret exponent, precise knowledge of these parameters need to be acquired, which is impossible for an adversary since the adversary does not have the privilege to obtain the corresponding physical addresses to the secret. This motivates the adversary to incorporate a spy process which probes on the execution of the decryption algorithm and uses timing analysis to successfully identify the channel, rank and even the bank where the secret gets mapped to.

The adversary introduces a spy process which runs everytime, before each decryption is requested. The spy process issues accesses to data elements of the eviction set, which eventually flushes the existing cache lines with its own data requests and fills the cache. Thus during the next request to the decryption process, the access to the secret exponent results in a cache miss and the corresponding access request is addressed from the bank A of main memory. Effectively, a spy process running alternate to the decryption process, makes arbitrary data accesses to ensure that every access request from the decryption process is addressed from the corresponding bank of the main memory.

3.2   Determining the Eviction Set

As mentioned before, the attack model is assumed to be such that the adversary has access to a system where the decryption is running. The decryption algorithm performs exponentiation involving the secret exponent and initially the adversary aims to determine the cache sets in which the secret exponent bits maps to. The adversary is oblivious of the virtual address space used by the decryption engine and thus involves a spy process which uses *Prime + Probe* [11,14,15] cache access methodology to identify the target sets. The execution scenario of the decryption and the adversarial processes running concurrently on the same system are depicted in Fig. 4. In this context, the spy process targets the Last Level cache (LLC) since it is shared within all cores of the system. The adversary sends input to the decryption engine which performs decryption on request, otherwise remains idle. Figure 4 illustrates the following steps.

1. **Step 1:** The adversary starts the spy process, which initially allocates a set of data elements and consults its own pagemap to obtain the corresponding physical addresses for each element. The kernel allows userspace programs to access their own pagemap (`/proc/self/pagemap`)[1] to examine the page tables and related information by reading files in */proc*. The virtual pages are

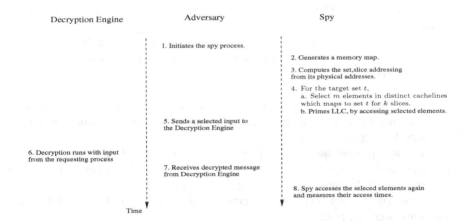

Fig. 4. Steps to determine cache sets shared by secret exponent

---

[1] For all Linux kernels before version 4.0, the versions released from early 2015 requires administrator privilege to consult pagemap, refer to Sect. 6.2.

mapped to physical frames and this mapping information is utilized by the spy process in the following steps.

2. **Step 2:** Once the physical addresses are obtained, the Last level cache set number and their corresponding LLC slice mappings are precomputed by the spy with the address mapping functions as explained in Sect. 2.3. Let us suppose, that the target system is having k processor cores, thus the LLC is partitioned into k slices, each of the slice have c cache sets where each set is m way associative. All elements belonging to the same cache line are fetched at a time.

   - If the cache line size is of b bytes, then least significant $log_2(b)$ bits of the physical addresses are used as index within the cache line.
   - As described in Sect. 2.3, the $log_2(k)$ bits following these $log_2(b)$ bits determine the cache set in which the element is going to reside.
   - Because of associativity, m such cache lines having identical $log_2(k)$ bits reside in the same set.
   - In modern processors, there exists one more parameter that determines which slice the element belongs to. Computing the Hash function reverse engineered in [12,13], we can also compute the slice in which a cache set gets mapped. The functions are elaborated in the experimental Sect. 4.1.

   Thus, at the end of this step, the spy simulates the set number and slice number of each element in its virtual address space.

   Repeat the following steps for all of the c sets in the LLC.

3. **Priming Target set t:** The spy primes the target Set t and becomes idle. This is the most crucial step for the entire procedure since the success of correctly determining the cache sets used by spy process entirely depends on how precisely the existing cache lines have been evicted from the cache by the spy in the Prime phase. In order to precisely control the eviction of existing cache lines from set t, a selection algorithm is run by the spy which selects an *eviction set* of $m * k$ elements each belonging to set t from its defined memory map.

   - Thus the selection algorithm selects elements belonging to distinct cache lines for each of the k cache slices where their respective physical addresses maps to the same set t. These selected data elements constitutes the *eviction set* for the set t.
   - In addition to this, since each set of a slice is m way associative, the selection algorithm selects m such elements corresponding to each k cache slice belonging to set t.
   - The spy process accesses each of these $m * k$ selected memory elements repeatedly in order to ensure that the cache replacement policy has evicted all the previously existing cache lines.

   This essentially ensures that the target set t of all slices is only occupied with elements accessed by the spy.

4. **Decryption Runs:** The adversary sends the chosen ciphertext for decryption and waits till the decryption engine sends back the message. In this decryption process, some of the cache lines in a particular set where the secret maps, gets evicted to accommodate the cache line of the secret exponent.

5. **Probing LLC:** On getting the decrypted output the adversary signals the spy to start probing and timing measurements are noted. In this probing step, the spy process accesses each of the selected m elements (in Prime phase) of eviction set t for all slices and time to access each of these elements are observed.

The timing measurements will show a variation when the decryption algorithm shares same cache set as the target set t. This is because, after the priming step the adversary allows the decryption process to run. If the cache sets used by the decryption is same as that of the spy, then some of the cache lines previously primed by the spy process gets evicted during the decryption. Thus, when the spy is again allowed to access the same elements, if it takes longer time to access then it is concluded that the cache set has been accessed by the decryption as well. On the other hand, if the cache set has not been used by the decryption, then the time observed during probe phase is less since no elements primed by spy have been evicted in the decryption phase.

Determining the LLC Slice Where the Secret Maps. The *Prime + Probe* timing analysis elaborated in the previous discussion successfully identifies the LLC set in which the cache line containing the secret exponent resides. Thus at the end of the previous step we obtain an *eviction set* of $m * k$ elements which map to the same set as the secret in all of the k slices. Now, this time the adversary can easily identify the desired LLC slice by iteratively running the same *Prime + Probe* protocol separately for each of the k slices with the selected m elements for that particular slice. The timing observations while probing will show significant variation for a set of m elements which corresponds to the same slice where the secret maps. Thus we further refine the size of *eviction set* from $m * k$ to m elements.

3.3 Determining the DRAM Bank that the Secret Maps

In this section, we describe a timing side channel analysis performed by the adversary to successfully determine the bank of the DRAM in which the secret exponent maps to. In the previous section, a timing analysis is elaborated which finally returns an *eviction set* of m elements which maps to the same set as well as the same slice as the secret exponent. Thus, if the adversary allows the spy and the decryption engine to run in strict alternation, then the decryption engine will always encounter a cache miss for the secret exponent, and the access request shall always result in a main memory access. As described in Sect. 2.1, DRAMs are primarily partitioned into channel, ranks and banks where each bank access is serviced through a buffer termed as row-buffer. Concurrent accesses to different rows in the same DRAM bank results in row-buffer conflict and automatically leads to higher access time. The functions which decide the channel, rank and bank mapping from the physical addresses are not disclosed by the architecture manufacturers. In some recent works, reverse engineering of these unknown mappings have been targeted. A successful deployment of a high speed covert channel has also been reported [16].

In this paper, we illustrate a timing analysis of accessing separate DRAM banks using this knowledge of reverse engineering and the following steps highlight how this is achieved. In order to exploit timing variation occurring due to the row-buffer collision, accesses requested from the decryption process as well as the adversarial spy process must result in main memory accesses. Intuitively, DRAM access time will increase only if addresses map to the same bank but to a different row. Thus to observe row-buffer conflict between the decryption and adversarial spy the major challenges are:

- To ensure that every access to secret exponent by the decryption process results in LLC cache miss and thus automatically result in main memory access. This is elaborated in the previous subsection, as to how the spy determines the *eviction set* and selectively accesses those elements to evict existing cache lines from the set. Let the spy generates an eviction set C with data elements in distinct cache lines mapping to the same set and slice as the secret.
- This suggests that before each decryption run, the spy has to fill the particular cache set by accessing elements in eviction set C.
- In addition to this, row-buffer conflict and access time delay can only be observed if two independent processes concurrently request data residing in the same bank but in different rows. In order to produce a row-buffer conflict with the secret exponent requested by the spy, the adversary has to produce concurrent access requests to the same bank.

The adversary allows the spy process to mmap a chunk of memory and the spy refers to its own pagemap to generate the physical addresses corresponding to each memory element. Following the functions reverse engineered in [16,17] the spy pre-computes the channel, rank and bank addressing for the corresponding physical addresses. As illustrated in Fig. 5, the timing analysis has to be

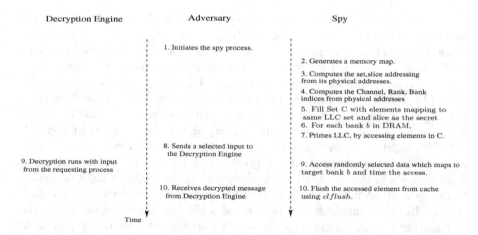

Fig. 5. Steps to determine the DRAM bank in which secret maps

performed by accessing elements from each bank. After each access request by the spy, the elements are flushed deliberately from the cache using clflush.

The adversary sends an input to the decryption engine and waits for the output to be received. While it waits for the output, the spy process targets one particular bank, selects a data element which maps to the bank and accesses the data element. This triggers concurrent accesses from the spy and the decryption to the DRAM banks. Repeated timing measurements are observed for each of the DRAM bank accesses by the spy, and this process is iterated for elements from each DRAM bank respectively.

3.4 Performing Rowhammer in a Controlled Bank

In the previous subsections, we have discussed how the adversary performs timing analysis to determine cache set collision and subsequently use it to determine DRAM bank collisions to identify where the secret data resides. In this section, we aim to induce fault in the secret by repeatedly toggling DRAM rows belonging to the same DRAM bank as the secret.

Inside the DRAM bank, the cells are two-dimensionally aligned in rows and columns. The row index in which any physical address maps is determined by the most significant bits of the physical address. Thus it is absolutely impossible for an adversary to determine the row index of the secret exponent. Thus rowhammer to the secret exponent has to be performed with elements which map to the same DRAM bank as the secret, but on different row indices until and unless the secret exponent is induced with a bit flip.

The original algorithm for rowhammer in [2], can be modified intelligently to achieve this precise bit flip. The algorithm works in following steps:

- A set of addresses are chosen which map to different row but the same bank of DRAM.
- The row indices being a function of the physical address bits are simulated while execution. Elements of random row indices are selected and accessed repeatedly by the adversary to induce bit flips in adjacent rows.
- The detection of bit flip in secret can be done easily, if and only if the output of decryption differs.

The rowhammering attempts required to produce a suitable bit flip on the secret depends on the total number of rows in a bank, since the adversary has no handle to know in which row in the bank the secret exponent is residing. Neither it has handle to place its own mmap-ed data deliberately adjacent to the secret, such that it can easily exploit the rowhammer bug. Thus the adversary can only select those elements which belong to the same bank as secret and access them repeatedly to induce bit flips in the secret. To increase the probability of bit flip in the secret exponent, the adversary needs to mmap multiple times to generate data which belong to different rows.

4   Experimental Validation for Inducing Bit Flips on Secret

In this section we present the validation of our previous discussion through experiments. Our experiments are framed with the following assumptions:

- We target an 1024 bit RSA implementation using square and multiply as the underlying exponentiation algorithm. We have used the standard GNU-MP big integer library (version number 2:5.0.2+dfsg-2) for our implementation. The adversary sends a chosen ciphertext for decryption which involves an exponentiation using the secret exponent.
- The experimentations are performed considering the address bit mappings of Intel Ivy Bridge micro-architecture. These are the line of processors based on the 22 nm manufacturing process. The experiments are performed on Intel Core i5-3470 processor running Ubuntu 12.04 LTS with the kernel version of 3.2.0-79-generic.
- The adversary is assumed to have user-level privileges to the system where decryption process runs. It uses mmap to allocate a large chunk of data and accesses its own pagemap (/proc/self/pagemap) to get the virtual to physical address mappings. The Linux kernel version for our experimental setup being older than version 4.0, we did not require administrator privileges to perform the entire attack.

4.1   Identifying the Cache Set

The experiments being performed on RSA, the 1024 bit exponent resides in consecutive 1024 bit locations in memory. Considering the cache line size as 64 bytes, 1024 bits of secret maps to 2 cache lines. As described in Sect. 2.3, 11 bits of physical address from $b_6, b_7, \cdots b_{16}$ refer to the Last Level cache set. Moreover, the papers [12,13] both talk about reverse engineering of the cache slice selection functions. The authors in paper [13], used *Prime + Probe* methodology to learn the cache slice function, while the authors in [12] monitored events from the performance counters to build the cache slice functions. Though it has been observed that the LLC slice functions reported in these two papers are not same.

In our paper, we devised a *Prime + Probe* based timing observation setup and wished to identify the target cache set and slice which collides with the secret. Thus we were in the lines of [13] and used the function from [13] in our experiments for *Prime + Probe* based timing observations. As illustrated in the following section, the timing observations using functions from [13] can correctly identify the target cache slice where the secret maps to. Reverse engineering of Last Level Cache (LLC) slice for Intel Ivy Bridge Micro-architecture in [13] uses the following function:

$$b_{17} \oplus b_{18} \oplus b_{20} \oplus b_{22} \oplus b_{24} \oplus b_{25} \oplus b_{26} \oplus b_{27} \oplus b_{28} \oplus b_{30} \oplus b_{32}.$$

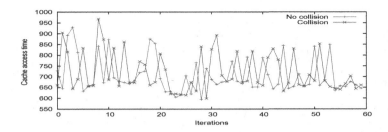

Fig. 6. Timing observations for cache set collision

But the architectural specification described in [13], documented that their selected system for Ivy Bridge architecture has LLC size of $3MB$. In our experimental setup, instead of $3MB$ we had $6MB$ LLC with is divided among 4 cores. Thus we adopted the functions documented for Haswell, and the function worked successfully. The functions used for slice selection are:

$$h_0 = b_{17} \oplus b_{18} \oplus b_{20} \oplus b_{22} \oplus b_{24} \oplus b_{25} \oplus b_{26} \oplus b_{27} \oplus b_{28} \oplus b_{30} \oplus b_{32}$$
$$h_1 = b_{18} \oplus b_{19} \oplus b_{21} \oplus b_{23} \oplus b_{25} \oplus b_{27} \oplus b_{29} \oplus b_{30} \oplus b_{31} \oplus b_{32}$$

Our host machine has LLC with 12 way associativity and having 4 cache slices each consisting of 2048 sets. The adversary `mmaps` a large chunk of memory, and consults its own pagemap to obtain the physical addresses corresponding to each element in the memory map. Using the equations mentioned above, the adversarial process simulates the cache set and slice in which their respective physical address points to. The experimental setup being 12-way associative, the selection algorithm for each set and slice selects the *eviction set* with 12 elements belonging to distinct cache lines and mapping to the same set for a particular slice. The host machine having 4 LLC slice for 4 cores selects the eviction set having altogether $12 * 4 = 48$ data elements in distinct cache lines mapped to same set and all 4 slices.

In our experimental setup, the adversary runs the *Prime + Probe* cache access methodology over each of the 2048 sets in each of the LLC slices. Each of the 2048 sets are targeted one after another. The cycle starts with priming a set with elements from eviction set and then allowing the decryption to happen and again observing the timings required for accessing selected elements from the set. The timing observations from the probe phase on 2 such LLC sets are illustrated in Fig. 6. The sets are chosen such that one of them is having a collision with the secret exponent and the other set does not have any collision. The variation of timing in these two sets is apparent in Fig. 6, where the set which observes a collision observes higher access time to the other set. The average access time of the these two sets during the probe phase differs by approximately 80 clock cycles. This implies that the LLC cache set having collision with the secret exponent cache line can be identified from the other sets which does not have collision with the decryption algorithm.

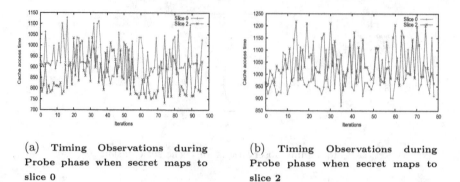

(a) Timing Observations during Probe phase when secret maps to slice 0

(b) Timing Observations during Probe phase when secret maps to slice 2

Fig. 7. Timing observations for LLC slice collision

4.2 Alternative Strategy to Determine the Target Cache Set

In the previous subsection, we observed that timing observations obtained by repeating the $m * k$ accesses to the individual set on all k slices is sufficient for identification of the target cache set. Though in [7], it has been stated that only $m * k$ accesses may not be sufficient to guarantee the existing cache lines to be evicted from the cache. In this context, we argue that the cache eviction sets are identified in [7] so that accessing the elements of this set in a predetermined order results in an equivalent effect of clflush to induce rowhammer flips. Since to exhibit successful bit flips, hammering of rows needs to satisfy various preconditions, it was crucial for authors in [7] to generate an optimal eviction set.

In our paper the conditions are little less stringent, since we are using clflush to induce bit flips. In addition to this, we constrain the hammering to the target bank. The identification of this bank has a series of experiments to be performed. In this scenario, we claimed that accessing the near-optimal eviction set of $m * k$ accesses for each cache set for all k slices repeatedly will result in eviction of secret from the respective cache set and result in DRAM accesses of the secret key. In addition, we have again performed our experiments by implementing the optimal eviction set as described in [7]. The results we obtain in Fig. 8a can be compared with Fig. 6. The separation of timing and identification of collision set from the non-collision set definitely improves upon accessing the eviction set with parameters defined in [7].

4.3 Identifying the LLC Slice

Once the cache set is identified, the variation from timing observations for different LLC slices leak the information of which LLC slice the secret maps to. In the same experimental setup as in the previous section, we identify the slice in which the actual secret resides, using timing analysis with the slice selection function. Since we have already identified the LLC cache set with which the

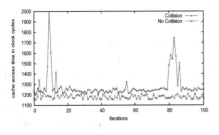 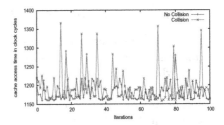

(a) **Timing Observation of Cache set Collision from optimal eviction set**

(b) **Timing Observation of Cache slice Collision using equations in [12]**

Fig. 8. Timing observations for LLC set and slice collision

secret collides, 12 data elements belonging to each slice of the particular set are selected. *Prime + Probe* timing observations are noted for the set of 12 elements for each slice. The slice observing collision with the secret exponent will suffer from cache misses in the probe phase and thus have higher access time to other slices.

We illustrate the timing observations for two scenarios in Fig. 7a and b. In Fig. 7a, the secret is mapped to LLC slice 0, while in Fig. 7b, the secret gets mapped to LLC slice 2. In both of the figures, access time for probing elements for the cache slice for which the secret access collides is observed to be higher than the other cache slice which belongs to the same set but do not observe cache collision. Thus because of collision of accesses of both the processes to the same slice, the spy observed higher probe time for slice 0, than slice 2 in Fig. 7a. On the contrary, in a different run, the secret exponent got mapped to LLC slice 2, which in Fig. 7b shows higher probe time than slice 0. Thus we can easily figure out the cache slice for the particular set for which both the decryption and the spy process accesses actually collides.

We also extended our experiment with the reverse engineered cache slice functions from [12]. Figure 8b shows the timing observations when we use the slice selection functions for a 4-core processor. The functions [12] are:

$$o_0 = b_6 \oplus b_{10} \oplus b_{12} \oplus b_{14} \oplus b_{16} \oplus b_{17} \oplus b_{18} \oplus b_{20} \oplus b_{22} \oplus b_{24} \oplus b_{25} \oplus b_{26} \oplus b_{27} \oplus b_{28} \oplus b_{30} \oplus b_{32} \oplus b_{33}$$

$$o_1 = b_{07} \oplus b_{11} \oplus b_{13} \oplus b_{15} \oplus b_{17} \oplus b_{19} \oplus b_{20} \oplus b_{21} \oplus b_{22} \oplus b_{23} \oplus b_{24} \oplus b_{26} \oplus b_{28} \oplus b_{29} \oplus b_{31} \oplus b_{33} \oplus b_{34}$$

Similar to our previous observations, Fig. 8b shows that we were able to identify the target cache slice from the timing observations using cache slice reverse engineering functions from [12].

Determining the LLC set and slice in which secret maps, actually gives the control to the adversary to flush the existing cache lines in these locations, and thus everytime the decryption process have to access the main memory. In simple words, accesses made by the adversary to this particular LLC set and slice acts as an alternative to `clflush` instruction being added to the decryption process.

4.4   Identifying the DRAM Bank

From the previous subsections, we identified particularly the LLC set and the slice mappings for the decryption process. Thus if the adversary selects data elements which belong to same set as well slice as to the secret exponent, and alternatively primes the LLC before running each decryption, each time the decryption process will encounter a cache miss and which will eventually get accessed from the main memory. This aids the adversary to identify the respective bank of DRAM, where the secret exponent is mapped. For the 1024-bit RSA exponentiation secret key, the channel, rank and bank mappings of DRAM will be decided by the equations reverse engineered in [16,17]. In our experimental setup, there exists 2 channel, 1 DIMM per channel, 2 ranks per DIMM, 8 banks per rank and 2^{14} rows per bank.

– The DRAM bank equations for Ivy Bridge [16] is decided by the physical address bits: $ba_0 = b_{14} \oplus b_{18}$, $ba_1 = b_{15} \oplus b_{19}$, $ba_2 = b_{17} \oplus b_{21}$,
– Rank is decided by $r = b_{16} \oplus b_{20}$ and the
– Channel is decided by, $C = b_7 \oplus b_8 \oplus b_9 \oplus b_{12} \oplus b_{13} \oplus b_{18} \oplus b_{19}$.
– The DRAM row index is decided by physical address bits $b_{18}, \cdots, b_{31}$.

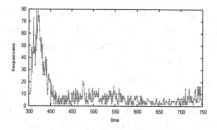 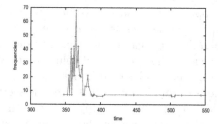

(a) **Timing Observations in clock cycles for DRAM bank collision**

(b) **Timing Observations in clock cycles of separate DRAM bank access**

Fig. 9. Timing observations for Row-buffer collision during DRAM bank accesses

In the same experimental setup as previous, the adversary targets each bank at a time and selects elements from the memory map for which the physical addresses map to that particular bank. The following process is repeated to obtain significant timing observations:

1. The spy primes the LLC and requests decryption by sending ciphertext.
2. While the spy wait for the decrypted message, it selects an element for the target bank from the memory map, `clflush`'es it from cache, and accesses the element. The `clflush` instruction removes the element from all levels of cache, and the following access to the element is addressed from the respective bank of the DRAM.
3. The time to DRAM bank access is also noted.

It is important to note that, there is no explicit synchronization imposed upon the the two concurrent processes in their software implementation. The decryption and the spy both requests a DRAM bank access. If the target bank matches with the bank in which the secret is mapped, then we expect to have higher access time. Figure 9a and b are the timing observations noted by the spy process while it accesses elements selected from the target bank. Figure 9a refers to the the case where the higher access times are observed due to the row-buffer collision as the bank accessed by the spy is same as the secret mapped bank. While Fig. 9b refers to the situation where the elements accessed by the spy are from an arbitrary different bank than the bank where secret maps. In both of the figures, the significant high peak has been observed in timing range of $350 - 400$ clock cycles. While in Fig. 9a, the row-buffer collision is apparent because there are significant number of observations which have timings greater than the region where the peak is observed. Had there been an absolute synchronization of two processes accessing the same DRAM bank, each access to DRAM bank, by either of the two process would have suffered from row-buffer collision. Thus in our scenario, we claim that in majority of cases, though the accesses are addressed from the same bank they seldom result in row-buffer collision, which justifies the peak around 350–400 clock cycles. From this we conclude that detection of row-buffer collision can only be identified over a significant number of timing observations. The DRAM bank which shows such higher access times is identified to be the bank where secret data resides.

4.5   Inducing Bit Flip Using Rowhammer

In the previous section, we have illustrated that how the adversary is able to distinguish the bank in which the secret exponent resides. The software implementation of the induction of bit flip is performed by repeated access to the elements of the same bank. The following pseudo-code is used to hammer rows in specific banks After each access to the element it is deliberately flushed from the cache using the `clflush` instruction by the adversary.

```
Code-hammer-specific-bank
{
  Select set of 10 data elements mapping to specific bank
  Repeat
  {
    Access all elements of the set
    Clflush each element of the set
  }
  jmp Code-hammer-specific-bank
}
```

A statistic over observations of bit flips in respective banks is reported in Fig. 10. The bar graph shows the number of bit flip instances we were able to observe for respective banks of a single Dual In-line Memory Module (DIMM). The bit faults that we have observed in our experiments are bit-reset faults.

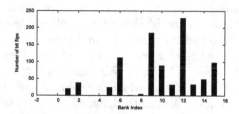

Fig. 10. Number of bit flips observed in all banks of a single DIMM

The row index of the location of the secret in the DRAM bank is determined by the physical address bits of the secret. Thus this implies that the secret exponent can sit in any of the rows in the target bank. Accordingly, we restricted our hammering attempts in the target bank and we selected random accesses to the target bank which eventually resulted in bit flips. Thus we slightly modified our setup such that the code iteratively runs until and unless the decryption output changes, which signifies that secret exponent bits have been successfully flipped. The fault attack in [9] requires a single faulty signature to retrieve the secret. Thus, bit flip introduced in the secret exponent by the rowhammer in a specific bank can successfully reveal the secret by applying fault analysis techniques in [9]. The probability of bit flip is $1/2^{14}$, since there are 2^{14} rows in a particular bank. Interestingly, the size of the secret key has an effect on the probability of bit flip in the secret exponent. In other words, we can say that the probability of bit flip in the secret exponent will be more if the secret exponent size is larger.

5   Possible Countermeasures

There has been various countermeasures of rowhammer attacks proposed in literature. In [2], seven potential system level mitigation techniques were proposed which range from designing secure DRAM chips, enforcing ECC protection on them, increasing the refresh rate, identification of victim cells and retiring them and refreshing vulnerable rows (for which the adjacent rows are getting accessed frequently). As mentioned in [2], each of these solutions suffers from the trade-off between feasibility, cost, performance, power and reliability. In particular, the solution named as Probabilistic Adjacent Row Activation (PARA) has the least overhead among the solutions proposed in [2]. The memory controller in PARA is modeled such that every time a row closes, the controller decides to refresh its adjacent rows with probability p (typically $1/2$). Because of its probabilistic nature, the approach is low overhead as it does not require any complex data structure for counting the number of row activations.

Another hardware level mitigation is reported in [5], where it is mentioned that the LPDDR4 standard for the DRAM incorporated two features for the hardware level mitigation such as Targeted Row Refresh (TRR) and Maximum Activate Count (MAC). Among which, it is reported that TRR technique is getting deployed in the next generation DDR4 memory units [18,19]. TRR incorporates a special module which can track the frequently made row-activations and can selectively refresh the rows adjacent to these aggressor rows. All of the above discussed protections have to be incorporated in hardware, but this does not eliminate the threat from rowhammer attacks since many of the manufacturers refer to these as optional modules.

There are few attempts which provide software level protection from rowhammer attacks. The `clflush` instruction was responsible for removing the target element from the cache and that resulted in DRAM accesses. In order to stop the security breaches from NaCl sandbox escape and privilege escalation [5], Google NaCl sandbox was recently patched to disallow applications from using the `clflush` instruction. The other software level mitigation is to double the refresh rate from 64 ms to 32 ms by changing the BIOS settings, or alternatively upgrading own BIOS with a patched one. It has been reported in [20], that system manufacturers such as HP, Lenovo and Apple have already considered updating the refresh rate. But both of the techniques such as doubling refresh rate and removing access to `clflush` instruction as a prevention technique has been proved to be ineffective in [20]. The paper illustrates a case study of introducing bit flips inspite of having refresh interval as low as 16 ms and the method does not use the `clflush` instruction. The paper also propose an effective, low cost software based protection mechanism named ANVIL. Instead [20] propose a two-step approach which observe the LLC cache miss statistics from the performance counters for a time interval, and examines if the number of cache misses crosses the predetermined threshold. If there are significantly high number of cache misses, then the second phase of evaluation starts, which samples the DRAM accesses of the suspected process and identifies if rows in a particular DRAM bank is getting accessed. If repeated row activation in same bank is detected, then ANVIL performs a selective refresh on the rows which are vulnerable.

6   Further Discussion

The present paper's main focus is to show that targeted faults can be inflicted by rowhammer. As a consequence, we have cited the example of a fault analysis on RSA, which is not protected by countermeasures. One of the objectives of this paper, is to show that fault attacks are serious threats even when triggered using software means. This makes the threat more probable as opposed to a fault injection by hardware means: like voltage fluctuations etc. Thus, this emphasizes more the need for countermeasures, at the software level.

Having said that, even standard libraries like OpenSSL use fault countermeasures, but they are not fully protected against these class of attacks. For example, in Black Hat 2012 [21], a hardware based fault injection was shown to be of threat to OpenSSL based RSA signature schemes. It was reported that the initial signature is verified by the public key exponent, however in case of a fault, another signature is generated and this time it is not verified [21]. The final signature is not verified because it is widely assumed that creating a controlled fault on a PC is impractical. More so, the faults are believed to be accidental computational errors, rather than malicious faults. Hence, the probability of inflicting two successive faults is rather low in normal computations! However, in case of rowhammer, as the fault is created in the key, repeating the process would again result in a wrong signature and thus get released.

Hence, the objective of the current paper is to highlight that inflicting controlled faults are more probable through software techniques than popularly believed, and hence ensuring that verification should be a compulsory step before releasing signatures.

6.1   Assumptions of the Proposed Attack

In our proposed attack, we assumed that the secret decryption exponent resides in a particular location of the DRAM and the decryption oracle continuously polls for input ciphertexts. In addition we also assume that the secret resides in the same location in the DRAM through out the duration of the attack and is not page-swapped by other running processes.

6.2   Limitations and Practicality of Our Attack

In this paper, the access to pagemap is assumed to be available at user privilege level since our setup has 3.2.0-79-generic version of Linux kernel. But from early 2015, for versions of kernel 4.0 onwards, the access to this pagemap has been restricted to processes with root privileges. However, the attack would still be relevant in a cross-VM environment as in [22], where the users of the co-located VMs actually have the administrator privilege and can consult the pagemap for the required virtual to physical address translation. In such a scenario, the attacker is assumed to be mounted on a VM which is co-resident to the VM which hosts the decryption oracle. Timing information obtained from *Prime + Probe* methodology in this experimental setup along with the reverse engineering knowledge can be used to precisely induce fault in the secret of the co-resident VM. Our paper primarily focuses on the vulnerability analysis of rowhammer in context to Linux kernels, but the vulnerability may be equally or more relevant in context to other operating systems where the access to a data structure such as pagemap (in context to Linux kernels) is not restricted only to administrator privileges. Moreover, the attack in its original form might be relevant in customized embedded system applications, thus it would be an interesting exercise to ascertain the security impact of rowhammer in such applications.

7   Conclusion

In this paper, we claim to illustrate in steps a combination of timing and fault analysis attack exploiting vulnerability of recent DRAM's disturbance error to induce a bit flip targeting the memory bank shared by the secret. This is a practical fault model and uses *Prime + Probe* cache access attack methodology to narrow down the search space where the adversary is supposed to induce flip. The experimental results illustrate that the timing analysis shows significant variation and leads to the identification of LLC set and slices. In addition row-buffer collision has been exploited to identify the DRAM bank which holds the secret. The worst case complexity of inducing fault by repeated hammering of rows in the specific memory bank typically is same as the number of rows in bank. The proposed attack finds most relevance in cross-VM setup, where the co-located VMs share the same underlying hardware and thus root privileges are usually granted to the attack instance.

Acknowledgements. We would like to thank the anonymous reviewers for their valuable comments and suggestions. We would also like to thank Prof. Berk Sunar for his insightful feedback and immense support. This research was supported in part by the TCS Research Scholarship Program in collaboration with IIT Kharagpur. This work was also supported in part by the Challenge Grant from IIT Kharagpur, India and Information Security Education Awareness (ISEA), Deity, India.

References

1. Wikipedia: Rowhammer wikipedia page (2016). https://en.wikipedia.org/wiki/Row-hammer
2. Kim, Y., Daly, R., Kim, J., Fallin, C., Lee, J.-H., Lee, D., Wilkerson, C., Lai, K., Mutlu, O.: Flipping bits in memory without accessing them: an experimental study of DRAM disturbance errors. In: ACM/IEEE 41st International Symposium on Computer Architecture, ISCA 2014, Minneapolis, MN, USA, June 14–18, 2014, pp. 361–372. IEEE Computer Society (2014)
3. Huang, R.-F., Yang, H.-Y., Chao, M.C.-T., Lin, S.-C.: Alternate hammering test for application-specific drams and an industrial case study. In: Groeneveld, P., Sciuto, D., Hassoun, S. (eds.) The 49th Annual Design Automation Conference 2012, DAC 2012, San Francisco, CA, USA, June 3–7, 2012, pp. 1012–1017. ACM (2012)
4. Kim, D.-H., Nair, P.J., Qureshi, M.K.: Architectural support for mitigating row hammering in DRAM memories. Comput. Archit. Lett. **14**(1), 9–12 (2015)
5. Seaborn, M., Dullien, T.: Exploiting the DRAM rowhammer bug to gain kernel privileges (2015). http://googleprojectzero.blogspot.in/2015/03/exploiting-dram-rowhammer-bug-to-gain.html
6. Qiao, R., Seaborn, M.: A new approach for rowhammer attacks. In: HOST 2016 (2016)
7. Gruss, D., Maurice, C., Mangard, S.: Rowhammer.js a remote software-induced fault attack in javascript. CoRR, abs/1507.06955 (2015)
8. Seaborn, M., Dullien, T.: Test DRAM for bit flips caused by the rowhammer problem (2015). https://github.com/google/rowhammer-test,2015
9. Boneh, D., DeMillo, R.A., Lipton, R.J.: On the importance of checking cryptographic protocols for faults. In: Fumy, W. (ed.) EUROCRYPT 1997. LNCS, vol. 1233, pp. 37–51. Springer, Heidelberg (1997)
10. JEDEC. Standard No. 79-3F. DDR3 SDRAM Specification (2012)

11. Yarom, Y., Falkner, K.: FLUSH+RELOAD: A high resolution, low noise, L3 cache side-channel attack. In: Fu K., Jung, J. (eds.) Proceedings of the 23rd USENIX Security Symposium, San Diego, CA, USA, August 20–22, 2014, pp. 719–732. USENIX Association (2014)

12. Maurice, C., Le Scouarnec, N., Neumann, C., Heen, O., Francillon, A.: Reverse engineering intel last-level cache complex addressing using performance counters. In: Bos, H., et al. (eds.) RAID 2015. LNCS, vol. 9404, pp. 48–65. Springer, Heidelberg (2015). doi:10.1007/978-3-319-26362-5_3

13. Irazoqui, G., Eisenbarth, T., Sunar, B.: Systematic reverse engineering of cache slice selection in intel processors. In: 2015 Euromicro Conference on Digital System Design, DSD 2015, Madeira, Portugal, 26–28 August 2015, pp. 629–636. IEEE Computer Society (2015)

14. Osvik, D.A., Shamir, A., Tromer, E.: Cache attacks and countermeasures: the case of AES. In: Pointcheval, D. (ed.) CT-RSA 2006. LNCS, vol. 3860, pp. 1–20. Springer, Heidelberg (2006)

15. Liu, F., Yarom, Y., Ge, Q., Heiser, G., Lee, R.B.: Last-level cache side-channel attacks are practical. In: 2015 IEEE Symposium on Security and Privacy, SP 2015, San Jose, CA, USA, 17–21 May 2015, pp. 605–622. IEEE Computer Society (2015)

16. Pessl, P., Gruss, D., Maurice, C., Mangard, S.: Reverse engineering intel DRAM addressing and exploitation. CoRR, abs/1511.08756 (2015)

17. Hund, R., Willems, C., Holz, T.: Practical timing side channel attacks against kernel space ASLR. In: 2013 IEEE Symposium on Security and Privacy, SP 2013, Berkeley, CA, USA, 19–22 May 2013, pp. 191–205. IEEE Computer Society (2013)

18. JEDEC Solid State Technology Association: Low Power Double Data Rate 4 (LPDDR4) (2015)

19. Micron Inc. DDR4 SDRAM MT40A2G4, MT40A1G8, MT40A512M16 Data sheet, 2015 (2015)

20. Aweke, Z.B., Yitbarek, S.F., Qiao, R., Das, R., Hicks, M., Oren, Y., Austin, T.M.: ANVIL: software-based protection against next-generation rowhammer attacks. In: Conte, T., Zhou, Y. (eds.) Proceedings of the Twenty-First International Conference on Architectural Support for Programming Languages and Operating Systems, ASPLOS 2016, Atlanta, GA, USA, 2–6 April 2016, pp. 743–755. ACM (2016)

21. Bertacco, V., Alaghi, A., Arthur, W., Tandon, P.: Torturing openSSL

22. Inci, M.S., Gülmezoglu, B., Irazoqui, G., Eisenbarth, T., Sunar, B.: Cache attacks enable bulk key recovery on the cloud. IACR Cryptology ePrint Archive: 2016/596

A Design Methodology for Stealthy Parametric Trojans and Its Application to Bug Attacks

Samaneh Ghandali[1(✉)], Georg T. Becker[2], Daniel Holcomb[1],
and Christof Paar[1,2]

[1] University of Massachusetts Amherst, Amherst, USA
{samaneh,dholcomb}@umass.edu, Christof.Paar@rub.de
[2] Horst Görtz Institut for IT-Security, Ruhr-Universität Bochum, Bochum, Germany
Georg.Becker@ruhr-uni-bochum.de

Abstract. Over the last decade, hardware Trojans have gained increasing attention in academia, industry and by government agencies. In order to design reliable countermeasures, it is crucial to understand how hardware Trojans can be built in practice. This is an area that has received relatively scant treatment in the literature. In this contribution, we examine how particularly stealthy Trojans can be introduced to a given target circuit. The Trojans are triggered by violating the delays of very rare combinational logic paths. These are parametric Trojans, i.e., they do not require any additional logic and are purely based on subtle manipulations on the sub-transistor level to modify the parameters of the transistors. The Trojan insertion is based on a two-phase approach. In the first phase, a SAT-based algorithm identifies rarely sensitized paths in a combinational circuit. In the second phase, a genetic algorithm smartly distributes delays for each gate to minimize the number of faults caused by random vectors.

As a case study, we apply our method to a 32-bit multiplier circuit resulting in a stealthy Trojan multiplier. This Trojan multiplier only computes faulty outputs if specific combinations of input pairs are applied to the circuit. The multiplier can be used to realize bug attacks, introduced by Biham et al. In addition to the bug attacks proposed previously, we extend this concept for the specific fault model of the path delay Trojan multiplier and show how it can be used to attack ECDH key agreement protocols.

Our method is a general approach to path delay faults. It is a versatile tool for designing stealthy Trojans for a given circuit and is not restricted to multipliers and the bug attack.

1 Introduction

Hardware Trojans have gained increasing attention in academia, industry and government agencies over the last ten years or so. There is a large body of research concerned with various methods for detecting Trojans, cf., e.g., [14].

The research was partially supported by NSF Grant CNS-1421352

B. Gierlichs and A.Y. Poschmann (Eds.): CHES 2016, LNCS 9813, pp. 625–647, 2016.
DOI: 10.1007/978-3-662-53140-2_30

On the other hand, there is scant treatment in literature about how to design Trojans. Nevertheless, Trojan detection and design are closely related: in order to design effective detection mechanisms and countermeasures, we need an understanding of how Hardware Trojans can be built. This holds in particular with respect to Trojans that are specifically designed to avoid detection. The situation is akin to the interplay of cryptography and cryptanalysis.

There are several different ways that hardware Trojans can be inserted into an IC [14]. The insertion scenarios that have drawn the most attention in the past are hardware Trojans introduced during manufacturing by an untrusted semiconductor foundry. One of the main motivations behind this is the fact that the vast majority of ICs world wide are fabricated abroad, and a foundry can possibly be pressured by a government agency to maliciously manipulate the design. However, we note that a similar situation can exist in which the original IC designer is pressured by her own government to manipulate all or some of the ICs, e.g., those that are used in overseas products. Similarly, 3rd party IP cores are another possible insertion point.

The primary setting we consider is modification during manufacturing, but the method also carries over to the other scenarios mentioned above. The Trojan will be inserted by modifying a few gates at the sub-transistor level during manufacturing, so that their delay values increase. The goal is to select and chose the delays such that only for extremely rare input combinations these delays add up to a path delay fault. There are many possible ways to increase the delays in practice in stealthy ways. Since not a single transistor is removed or added to the design and the changes to the individual gates are minor, the Trojan is very difficult to detect post-manufacturing using reverse-engineering, visual inspection, side-channel profiling or most other known detection methods. Due to the extremely rare trigger conditions, it is also highly unlikely that the Trojan will be detected during functional testing. Even full reverse-engineering of the IC will not reveal the presence of the backdoor. Similarly, since the actual Trojan will be inserted in the last step of the design flow, the Trojan will not be present at higher abstraction levels such as the netlist. Accordingly, this type of Trojan is also very interesting for the scenario of stealthy, government-mandated backdoors. The number of engineers that are aware of the Trojan would be reduced to a minimum since even the designers of the Trojan-infested IP core would not be aware that such a backdoor has been inserted into the product. This can be crucial to eliminate the risk of whistle blowers revealing the backdoor. In summary, our method overcomes two major problems a Trojan designer faces, namely making the Trojan detection resistant and to provide a very rare trigger condition.

1.1   Related Work

The power of hardware Trojans was first demonstrated by King *et al.* in 2008 by showing how a Hardware Trojan inserted into a CPU can enable virtually unlimited access to the CPU by an external attacker [15]. The Trojan presented by King *et al.* was a Trojan inserted into the HDL code of the design. Similarly,

Lin *et al.* presented a Hardware Trojan that stealthily leaks out the cryptographic key using a power side-channel [18]. This Hardware Trojan was also inserted at the netlist or HDL level, similarly to the Hardware Trojans that were designed as part of a student Hardware Trojan challenge at ICCD 2011 [19]. How to build stealthy Trojans at the layout-level was demonstrated in 2013 by Becker *et al.* which showed how a Hardware Trojan can be inserted into a cryptographically secure PRNG or a side-channel resistant SBox only by manipulating the dopant polarity of a few registers [4]. Another idea proposed in the literature is the idea of building Hardware Trojans that are triggered by aging [23]. Such Trojans are inactive after manufacturing and only become active after the IC has been in operation for a long time. Kumar *et al.* proposed a parametric Trojan [17] that triggers probabilistically with a probability that increases under reduced supply voltage.

Compared to research concerned with the design of Hardware Trojans, considerably more results exist related to different Hardware Trojan detection mechanisms and countermeasures. Most research focuses on detecting Hardware Trojans inserted during manufacturing. In many cases, a golden model is used that is supposed to be Trojan free to serve as a reference. One important question is how to get to a Trojan-free golden model. One approach proposed is to use visual reverse-engineering of a few chips to ensure that these chips were not manipulated. For this the layout is compared to SEM images of the chip. In [3] methods of how to automatically do this are discussed. Please note that not all Hardware Trojans are directly visibly in black-and-white SEM images. For example, to detect the dopant-level Hardware Trojans additional steps are needed, e.g., the method presented by Sugawara *et al.* [24]. One motivation of our work is that we might achieve an even higher degree of stealthiness by only slowing down transistors as opposed to completely changing transistors as has been done in [4]. Such parametric changes can be done cleverly to make visual reverse-engineering very difficult as discussed in Sect. 3. Another approach to Trojan detection uses power profiles that are used to compare the chip-under-test with previously recorded side-channel measurement of the golden chip. The most popular approach uses power side channels, first proposed by Agrawal *et al.* [2]. The idea to build specific Trojan detection circuitry has also been proposed, e.g., in [20]. However, these approaches usually suffer from the problem that a Trojan can also be inserted into such detection circuitry. Preventing Hardware Trojans inserted at the HDL level by third party IP cores has been discussed, e.g., in [13] and [26]. Efficient generation of test patterns for Hardware Trojans triggered by a rare input signals is the focus of work by Chakraborty *et al.* in [8] and Saha *et al.* in [21].

1.2   Our Contribution

The main contributions of this paper can be summarized as follows:

- We introduce a new class of parametric hardware Trojans, the Path Delay Trojans. They posses the two desirable features that they are (i) very stealthy and thus difficult to detect with most standard methods and (ii) have very rare trigger conditions.

- We present an automation flow for inserting the proposed style of Trojan. We propose an efficient, SAT solver-based path selection algorithm, which identifies suitably rare paths within a given target circuit. We also propose a second algorithm, based on genetic algorithms, for distributing the necessary delay along the rare path. The key requirement is to minimize the effect of the added delay on the remaining circuit.
- As a case study for the effectiveness of the proposed method, a Trojan multiplier is designed. We were able to identify a rare path and perform specific delay modification in a 32-bit multiplier circuit model in such a way that the faulty behavior only occurs for very few combinations of two consecutive input values. We note that the input space of the multiplier is $(2^{32})^2 = 2^{64}$ so that most random input values occur very rarely during regular operation.
- We show how the Trojan multiplier can used for realizing the bug attack by Biham et al. [5,6] and propose a related attack on the ECDH key agreement protocol. We provide probabilities for this new bug attack variant. A precomputation phase reduces the attack complexity and makes the attacks practical for real-world scenarios. We show that the attacker can engineer the failure probability to the desired level by increasing the introduced propagation delay of the Trojan.

2   Overview of the Proposed Method

This work implements Trojan functionality in a given target circuit by using path delay faults (PDF), without modification to logic circuit, to induce inaccurate results for extremely rare inputs. Before describing the details of our method, we first define the notion of a viable delay-based Trojan in the unmodified HDL of the circuit as follows. A viable delay-based trojan must posses the following two properties.

Triggerability. For secret inputs, which are known to the attacker, cause an error with certainty or relatively high probability.

Stealthiness. For randomly chosen inputs, cause an error with extremely low probability.

As shown in Fig. 1, our method of creating triggerable and stealthy delay-based Trojans consists of two phases: *path selection* and *delay distribution*. We give an overview of each phase here, and give detailed descriptions in Sect. 4.

Path Selection: The path selection phase finds a rarely sensitized path from the primary inputs of a combinational circuit to the primary outputs. The algorithm chooses the path incrementally by adding gates to extend a subpath backward toward inputs and forward toward outputs. The selection of which gates to include is guided by controllability and observability metrics so that the path will be rarely sensitized. To ensure that the selected path can be triggered,

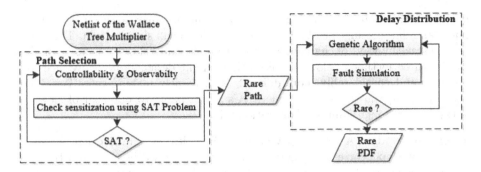

Fig. 1. Flowchart of the proposed method for creating a stealthy PDF (path delay faults).

a SAT-based check is performed to ensure that the path remains sensitizable each time a gate is added. In addition to ensuring that the path is sensitizable, the SAT-based check also provides the Trojan designer with a specific input combination that will sensitize the path. This input combination will later serve as the trigger for the Trojan. Details of the path selection are given in Sect. 4.1.

Delay Distribution: After a rarely sensitized path is selected, the overall delay of the path must be increased so that a delay fault will occur when the path is sensitized; this is required for the Trojan to be triggerable. However, any delay added to gates on the selected path may also cause delay faults on intersecting paths, which would cause more frequent errors and compromise stealthiness. Our delay distribution heuristic addresses this problem by smartly choosing delays for each gate to minimize the number of faults caused by random vectors. At the same time, the approach ensures that the overall path delay is sufficient for the fault to occur when the trigger vectors are applied. Details of delay distribution are given in Sect. 4.2.

3   Delay Insertion

Delay faults occur when the total propagation delay along a sensitized circuit path exceeds the clock period. Our algorithm causes delay faults by increasing the delay of gates on a chosen path. While the approach is compatible with any mechanism for controlling gate delays, in this section we provide background on practical methods that a Trojan designer might use to implement slow gates. In static CMOS logic, a path delay fault is not triggered by a single input vector, but instead is triggered by a sequence of two input vectors applied on consecutive cycles. The physical reason for delay being caused by a pair of inputs is that delay depends on the charging or discharging of capacitances, and the initial states of these capacitances in the second vector are determined as final states from the first vector. Assuming the capacitances need to be charged or discharged along a path, as is the case in delay faults, the delay of each gate depends on how

quickly it can charge or discharge some amount of capacitance on its output
node, and diminishing the ability of a gate to do so will slow it down. There are
several stealthy ways of changing a circuit to make gates slower. As an example,
we list three methods below. We note that circuit designers typically face the
opposite and considerably more difficult task, namely making gates fast. The
ever-shrinking feature size of modern ICs is amenable to our goal of slowing
gates down through minuscule alterations (Fig. 2).

Decrease Width. A gate library typically includes several drive strengths for
each gate type, corresponding to different transistor widths. A narrow transistor is slower to charge a load capacitance because transistor current is linear
in channel width. A straightforward way to increase delay is to replace a gate
with a weaker variant of the same gate, or to create a custom cell variant
with an extremely narrow channel. A limitation to using a downsized gate is
that an attacker who delayers the chip could potentially observe the sizing
optically, depending on how much the geometry has been altered.

Raise Threshold. A second way of increasing gate delay is to increase threshold voltages of selected transistors through doping or body biasing. Dual-Vt
design is common in ICs and allows transistors to be designated as high or
low threshold devices; low threshold devices are fast and used where delay
is critical, and high threshold devices are slow and used elsewhere to reduce
static power. Typically no more than two threshold levels are used on a single chip because creating multiple thresholds through doping requires additional process steps, but in principle an arbitrary number of thresholds can
be created. Body biasing, changing the body-source voltage of MOSFETs, is
another way to change threshold and delay [16]; specifically, a reverse body
bias (i.e., body terminal at lower voltage than source) raises threshold voltage and slows down a device. Regardless whether the mechanism is doping or
body biasing, a raised threshold voltage will cause transistors to turn on later
when an input switches, and to conduct less current when turned on, so the
output capacitance connected to the transistor will be charged or discharged

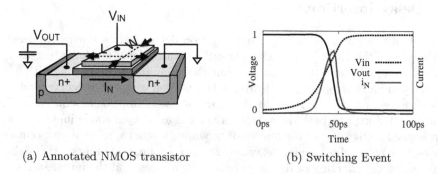

(a) Annotated NMOS transistor   (b) Switching Event

Fig. 2. Propagating an input transition to an output transition requires current to
charge or discharge a capacitor. Decreasing width or increasing length of MOSFETs
are two ways of reducing switching current and increasing propagation delay.

more slowly. Both, changing to dopant concentrations and body biasing, are difficult to detect, even with invasive methods.

Increase Gate Length. Delay of chosen gates can be increased by gate length biasing. Lengthening the gate of transistor causes a reduction in current, and therefore increases delay [11]. Again, the likelihood of detection depends on the degree of the alteration.

We note that the methods sketched above (and other slow-down alterations) can be combined such that each manipulation is relatively minor and, thus, more difficult to detect.

4 Finding a Trojan Path

Fundamentally, the challenge in designing and validating triggerable and stealthy delay-based Trojans is that timing and logical sensitization cannot be decoupled. Regardless of the type of path sensitization considered, the probability of causing an error is not a well-defined concept until after delays are assigned. Therefore, when designing a candidate Trojan, path selection and delay assignment must both be considered. We will use a heuristic for this which combines logical path selection and delay distribution along a chosen path.

4.1 Phase I: Rare Path Selection

In this phase we try to select a path among huge number of paths existing in the netlist of a multiplier circuit, in such a way that random inputs will very rarely sensitize the path. The rareness is a first step towards ensuring stealthiness of the Trojan.

Controllability and Observability: Before giving our algorithm, we introduce several preliminaries. First, we note that every node in the circuit has a controllability metric and an observability metric associated with the 0 value and the 1 value. Controllability and observability are common metrics used in testing. Controllability of a 0 or 1 value on a circuit node is an estimate of the probability that a random input vector would induce that value on that node. Observability of a 0 or 1 value on a node is an estimate of the probability with which that value would propagate to some output signal when a random vector is applied. For rareness, we seek a path that includes low controllability nodes and low observability nodes, as this would indicate that the values on the path rarely occur randomly, and when they do occur they are usually masked from reaching the outputs. We estimate controllability using random simulation, and observability using random fault injection [12].

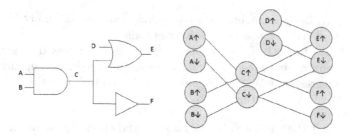

Fig. 3. Circuit and corresponding timing graph.

Timing Graph: The propagation delays of logic paths in combinational VLSI circuits are typically represented using weighted DAGs called timing graphs. Each node in a circuit will have two nodes in the timing graph, representing rising and falling transitions on the node; we use the terms transition and node interchangeably when discussing timing graphs. A directed edge between two nodes exists if the transition at the tail of the edge can logically propagate to the one at the head. The edges that exist in the timing graph therefore depend on the logic function of each gate in the circuit (see Fig. 3).

For example, an AND gate with inputs A and B, and output X, will have an edge from $A \uparrow$ to $X \uparrow$, from $A \downarrow$ to $X \downarrow$, from $B \uparrow$ to $X \uparrow$, and from $B \downarrow$ to $X \downarrow$, but will not have an edge from $A \uparrow$ to $X \downarrow$ because a rising transition on an AND gate input cannot induce a falling output. In timing analysis, e.g. STA, the edge weights of a timing graph represent propagation delay, but for our purpose of path selection, the delays are ignored and we utilize only the connectivity of the timing graph.

Selecting a Path Through Timing Graph: Our path selection technique seeks to find a path π through the timing graph of the circuit that is rarely sensitized. Note that the delays are not considered in this phase of the work. Path π is initialized to contain a single hard to sensitize transition somewhere in the middle of the circuit. More formally, the starting point for the path search is a rising or falling transition on a single node such that the product of its 0 and 1 controllability values is the lowest among all nodes in the circuit. This initial single-node path π is then extended incrementally backward until reaching the primary inputs (PIs), and extended incrementally forward until reaching the primary outputs (POs). The backward propagation is given in Algorithm 1, and the forward propagation is given in Algorithm 2.

First we explain the backward propagation heuristic in Algorithm 1. Starting from the first transition (i.e. the tail) on the current path π, we repeatedly try to extend the path back toward the PIs by prepending one new transition to the path. To select such a transition, the algorithm creates a list of candidate transitions that can be be prepended to the path. In the timing graph, these candidates are predecessor nodes to the current tail of π. The list of candidate nodes is then sorted according to $diffj$, the difficulty of creating the necessary conditions to justify the transition. See Table 3 in the appendix for the formula used to compute $diffj$ for each transition on each gate type. Note that our difficulty metric is weighted to always prefer robust sensitization first, and only resort to non-robust sensitization when there are no robustly sensitizable nodes in the list of candidates. Whenever a node is prepended to π to create a candidate path π' (line 5) the sensitizability of π' is checked by calling *check-sensitizability* function. In this function SAT-based techniques [9] are used to check sensitizability of a path and to find a vector pair that justifies and propagates a transition along the path (line 6). If the SAT solver returns SAT, then path π' is known to be a subpath of a sensitizable path from PIs to POs. Because the candidates are visited in order of preference, there is no need to check other candidates after finding a first candidate that produces a sensitizable path. At this point, the algorithm updates π to be π' and the algorithm exits the for loop having extended the path by one node. If this newly added tail node is not a PI, then the algorithm will again try to extend it backwards.

Algorithm 1. Extend path backward to PIs while trying to maximize difficulty of justification while ensuring that path will remain sensitizable.

Require: A sensitizable subpath π in timing graph of circuit.
Ensure: A longer sensitizable subpath π in timing graph that starts at a PI
1: **while** $tail(\pi) \notin PIs$ **do**
2:     $candidates \leftarrow (\forall n | n \in pred(tail(\pi)))$ {transitions that can be prepended to π}
3:     $candidates.order(diffj)$ {Order candidates by difficulty of justification}
4:     **for** $n' \in candidates$ **do**
5:         $\pi' \leftarrow (n', \pi)$ {Create a candidate path by prepending current path}
6:         **if** check-sensitizability$(\pi') = SAT$ **then**
7:             $\pi \leftarrow \pi'$ {candidate accepted, update path π with new tail}
8:             Exit for loop
9:         **end if**
10:     **end for**
11: **end while**

The forward propagation algorithm (Algorithm 2) is similar to the aforementioned backward propagation algorithm, except that it adds nodes to the head of the path until reaching POs. At each step of the algorithm, a list of candidates is again formed. In this case, the candidates are successors of the head of the path (line 2) instead of predecessors of the tail, and they are ordered according to difficulty of propagation (line 3) instead of difficulty of justification (see Table 4 in Appendix A). Each time a new candidate path is created by adding a candidate node to the existing path, a sat check is again performed to ensure that the nodes are only added to π if it remains sensitizable (line 6).

Algorithm 2. Extend path forward to POs while trying to maximize difficulty of propagation while ensuring that path will remain sensitizable.

Require: A sensitizable subpath π in timing graph of circuit.
Ensure: A longer sensitizable subpath π in timing graph that ends at a PO
1: **while** $head(\pi) \notin POs$ **do**
2:      $candidates \leftarrow (\forall n | n \in succ(head(\pi)))$ {transitions that can be appended to π}
3:      $candidates.order(diffp)$ {Order candidates by difficulty of propagation}
4:      **for** $n' \in candidates$ **do**
5:          $\pi' \leftarrow (\pi, n')$ {Create a candidate path by appending to current path}
6:          **if** check-sensitizability$(\pi') = SAT$ **then**
7:              $\pi \leftarrow \pi'$ {candidate accepted, update path π with new head}
8:              Exit for loop
9:          **end if**
10:    **end for**
11: **end while**

4.2   Phase II: Delay Distribution

Once a path is selected, we must increase the delay of the path so that the total path delay will exceed the clock period and an error will occur when the path is sensitized. Yet, we must be careful in choosing where to add delay on the path, because the gates along the chosen path are also part of many other intersecting or overlapping paths. Any delay added to the chosen path therefore may cause errors even when the chosen path is not sensitized. To ensure stealthiness, we must minimize the probability of this by smartly deciding where to add delays along the path.

We use a genetic algorithm to decide the delay of each gate that will cause the Trojan to be stealthy. Genetic algorithm is an optimization technique that tries to minimize a cost function by creating a population of random solutions, and repeatedly selecting the best solutions in the population and combining and mutating them to create new solutions; the quality of each solution is evaluated according to a fitness function. We use the genetic algorithm function **ga** in Matlab [1], and do not utilize any special modifications to the genetic algorithm implementation. Our interaction with the **ga** function is limited to providing constraints that restrict the allowed solution space, and a fitness function for evaluating solutions. We describe these constraints and fitness function here.

Constraint on Total Path Delay. Given a chosen path π comprising gates $(p_0, p_1, \ldots, p_n)$ and assuming a target path delay of D, the genetic algorithm decides the delay of each gate on the path. Our first constraint therefore specifies that the sum of assigned delays along the path is equal to the target path delay D. To cause an error, D must exceed the clock period, and we later show advantages of using different values of D.

$$D = \sum_{i=0}^{n} d_i \tag{1}$$

Constraint on Delay of Each Gate. Next we provide the genetic algorithm with a hint that helps it to discover reasonable delays for each gate. In this step, we use d_i' to represent the nominal delay of the ith gate on chosen path π, and s_i to represent the a slack metric associated with the same gate. Each slack parameter s_i describes how much delay can be added to the corresponding gate without causing the path to exceed the clock period. Because the targeted path delay D does exceed the clock period, gate delays are allowed to exceed their computed slack. The slack for each gate is computed as a function of the nominal delay of the gate, data dependency, and the clock period [10,25]. The following equation shows the constraint on delay of gate i, where c is a constant.

$$d_i' + s_i - c \leq d_i \leq d_i' + s_i + c \qquad (2)$$

Fitness Function. Simply stated, the cost function that we want to minimize is the probability of causing an error when random input vectors are applied to the circuit. Because there is no simple closed-form expression for this, we use random simulation to evaluate the cost of any delay assignment. When the genetic algorithm in Matlab needs to evaluate the cost of a particular delay assignment, it does so by executing a timing simulator. The timing simulator, in our case ModelSim, applies random vectors to the circuit-under-evaluation and a golden copy of the circuit and compares the respective outputs to count the number of errors that occur. These errors are caused by the delay assignments in the circuit-under-evaluation. The cost that is returned from the simulator is the percentage of inputs that caused an error for this delay assignment. As the genetic algorithm proceeds through more and more generations of solutions, the quality of the solutions improve. Matlab's genetic algorithm implementation comes with a stopping criterion, so we simply allow the algorithm to run until completion.

5   Experimental Results

We now evaluate the effectiveness of our method of designing Trojans, using a 32×32 Wallace tree multiplier as a test case. The circuit has a nominal critical path of length 128, and the delay of this path is 2520 ps.

5.1   Evaluation of Phase I (Path Selection)

To evaluate the ability of our path selection algorithm (Sect. 4.1) to find a rare path, we compare the stealthiness of the path selected by the algorithm against the stealthiness of 750 randomly chosen paths. For each of these paths, we seek to find how often an error would occur under random inputs if the path delay is increased. We measure this by uniformly increasing the delay of each gate on the path such that the total delay of the path is 5040 ps, which is twice the delay of the nominal critical path. After the delay modification, 10,000 random vectors are applied and the number of error-causing vectors is counted. The histogram of Fig. 4 shows the result; the x-axis represents error rates, and the y-axis shows how many of the paths have each error rate. The result shows that a majority of paths would cause frequent errors if their delay is increased, and these paths are thus unsuitable for stealthy Trojans. The rare path (RP) selected by our algorithm caused an error for only 4 of 10,000 vectors. By comparison, the best of the random paths caused an error in 174 of 10,000 vectors. In this experiment, the path chosen by the path selection algorithm is 43x less likely to cause an error than the best of 750 random paths. Note that this experiment is conservative in that the amount of additional delay added is very large, and the delay is not smartly distributed along the path to minimize detection.

5.2   Evaluation of Phase II (Delay Distribution)

To evaluate the effectiveness of our delay distribution method, we apply the proposed method (Sect. 4.2) on 10 paths from the multiplier. These 10 paths are the rare path chosen by the path selection algorithm, and 9 paths randomly selected from the set of all paths that caused less than 10 % error rates in Fig. 4. For each of these paths, we use the genetic algorithm to optimally allocate a total delay of 3276 ps (i.e. 1.3 times of the delay of the nominal critical path) over the path, and then evaluate the error probability using random simulation with 5,000,000 vectors. Figure 5 shows the error probability of each path before and after applying our proposed delay distribution method. In each case, the optimization step reduces the probability of causing an error by at least 3.5x. For the rare path (RP), just one error in 5,000,000 vectors is caused after delay

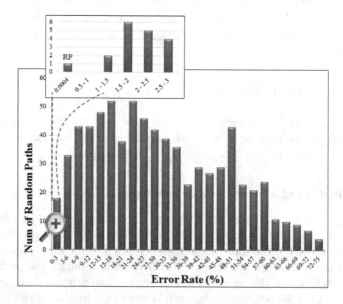

Fig. 4. Fault simulation of rare path and 750 random paths of 32 × 32 Wallace tree multiplier.

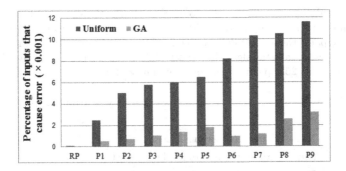

Fig. 5. Error probability of circuit before and after optimizing delay assignment of rare path and 9 other paths in a 32×32 Wallace tree multiplier.

distribution. This result shows that, for a given total path delay, optimizing the delay assignment along the path can reduce the probability of having an error when random vectors are applied. It is important to note that this improvement in stealthiness comes from minimizing the side effects of the added delay, and does not impact triggerability when vectors are applied that actually sensitize the entire chosen path.

5.3   Overall Evaluation

We evaluate our overall methodology comprising path selection and delay distribution on the 32×32 Wallace Tree multiplier circuit. Instead of assuming a particular clock frequency, here we examine whether it is possible to add delay to the chosen rare path such that the circuit will (1) exceed the nominal critical path delay of 2520 ps when the applied input sensitizes the rare path, and (2) always have delay of less than 2520 ps otherwise. We first distribute delay uniformly over the path, and then apply the same total delay to the path but distribute it using the genetic algorithm (Sect. 4.2). The results are shown in Table 1. Despite simulating 260 million random vectors, we are unable to randomly discover any vectors in which the circuit delay exceeds 2520 ps. Yet, when applying a vector pair produced by our SAT-based sensitization check, we observe that the chosen path delay does exceed 2520 ps. As simulating 260 million vectors on a circuit this size already used more than 240 h of computation on an AMD Opteron (TM) Processor running at 2.3 GHz with 8 cores and 64 GB RAM, it will become quite expensive to check increasing numbers of vectors beyond 260 million. This highlights a significant challenge: given a space of 2^{128} possible vector pairs that might cause an error, it is very hard to estimate the probability of an error that is sufficiently rare. If the probability of error is around or above roughly 2^{-26}, then random simulation will suffice to find a few errors and estimate the error probability. If the probability of error is below roughly 2^{-98} it would be possible to use SAT to exhaustively enumerate all 2^{30} vectors that would cause an error. Unfortunately, for very interesting region of error probabilities between 2^{-26} and 2^{-98} there is no clear solution for estimating the error probabilities.

Table 1. Probability of exceeding the nominal critical path delay in a 32 × 32 Wallace Tree Multiplier after adding delay to the rare path. When uniformly distributing the delay over the path, the longest delay exceeds 2520 ps for 57 of 200,000 random applied vectors. After using genetic algorithm (Sect. 4.2) to distribute the delay, the circuit delay never exceeds 2520 ps in 260 million random vectors.

	Delay distribution	
	Uniform	GA
Num. of times exceeding 2520 ps	57	0
Num. of random vectors applied	200,000	260M
Prob. of exceeding 2520 ps	0.0003	$< 2^{-26}$

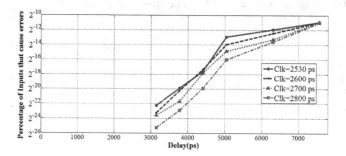

Fig. 6. Increasing the rare path delay increases the probability of causing an error when random vectors are applied. This delay is allocated to gates according to the delay distribution algorithm. The results are shown for different clock periods.

When the amount of delay added to the rare path is increased, and the probability of error grows above 2^{-26}, the error probability can feasibly be estimated with random simulation. In this regime, we can evaluate the tradeoff of delay and trigger probability. For example, when the chosen path is given a total delay of 3150 ps allocated using genetic algorithm for delay distribution, and the circuit is operated at a clock period of 2800 ps (as might be reasonable for a nominal critical path of 2520 ps) an erroneous output occurs with probability of roughly 2^{-24} (once every 16 million multiplications) when random inputs are applied. The overall tradeoff is shown in Fig. 6 for different clock periods. One can exploit this tradeoff to create a desired error probability by increasing or decreasing the total amount of delay added to the chosen path.

6   Bug Attack on ECDH with a Trojan Multiplier

The main motivation of choosing a multiplier as our case study is the bug attack paper by Biham *et al.* [5,6]. They showed how several public key implementations can be attacked if the used multiplier computes a faulty response for some rare inputs. The real-world implications of bug attacks were first demonstrated by Brumley *et al.* in 2012 when they showed how a software bug in an implementation of the reduction step of an elliptic curve group operation in OpenSSL could be exploited to recover private ECDH-TLS server keys [7]. Note that while they exploited a software bug as opposed to a hardware bug and a modular reduction as opposed to a multiplication, the attack idea itself is the same as in the original bug attack paper [5].

6.1   Fault Model of the Trojan Multiplier

The Trojan Multiplier introduced in the precious Section has a different fault model than the one assumed in [5]. In particular, the output of the Trojan Multiplier does not only depend on the current input but also on the previous inputs, i.e., it has a state. We define the multiplication of two 32-bit numbers a_1, b_1 with our Trojan Multiplier as $\tilde{y} = MUL_{a_0,b_0}(a_1, b_1)$ where a_0, b_0 is the previous input pair to the multiplier. The list F of quadruples (a_0, b_0, a_1, b_1) are all input sequences for which the Trojan Multiplier computes a faulty response:

$$\text{For all } (a_0, b_0, a_1, b_1) \in F : \tilde{y} = MUL_{a_0,b_0}(a_1, b_1) \neq y = a_1 \cdot b_1$$
$$\text{For all } (a_0, b_0, a_1, b_1) \notin F : \tilde{y} = MUL_{a_0,b_0}(a_1, b_1) = y = a_1 \cdot b_1 \tag{3}$$

Outputs computed with the Trojan Multiplier are always represented with a tilde. An ECC scalar multiplication of point $Q \in E$ with an integer k is denoted as $R = k \cdot Q$. An elliptic curve scalar multiplication using the Trojan Multiplier is denoted with an $\odot$, i.e., $\tilde{R} = k \odot Q$. In the following we assume that an attacker has knowledge of the Trojan Multiplier or access to a chip with the Trojan Multiplier such that the attacker knows for which inputs $\tilde{R} \neq R$.

The attack complexity strongly depends on the probability that a multiplication results in a faulty response. In order to be able to compute this probability we make following definitions:

1. $P_{M(a_1,b_1)}$: Probability that for two random 32-bit integers a_1, b_1 there exits at least one pair of 32-bit integers a_0, b_0 such that $\tilde{y} = MUL_{a_0,b_0}(a_1, b_1)$ computes a faulty response
2. $P_{M(a_1)}$: Probability that for a random 32-bit integers a_1 there exits at least one triplet of 32-bit integers a_0, b_0, b_1 such that $\tilde{y} = MUL_{a_0,b_0}(a_1, b_1)$ computes a faulty response. Probability $P_{M(b_1)}$ is defined in the same fashion.
3. $P_{M(a_0,b_0|a_1,b_1)}$: Probability that for two random 32-bit integers a_0, b_0 and two given integers a_1, b_1 the multiplication $\tilde{y} = MUL_{a_0,b_0}(a_1, b_1)$ computes a faulty response if there exists at least one other input pair a_0', b_0' for which $\tilde{y} = MUL_{a_0',b_0'}(a_1, b_1)$ computes a faulty response
4. $P_{M(a_0|a_1,b_1=b_0)}$: Probability that for a random 32-bit integers a_0, and two given integers a_1, b_1 the multiplication $\tilde{y} = MUL_{a_0,b_0}(a_1, b_1)$ with $b_0 = b_1$ computes a faulty response if there exists at least one other input pair a_0', b_0' for which $\tilde{y} = MUL_{a_0',b_0'}(a_1, b_1)$ computes a faulty response

Furthermore, we make following assumptions regarding these probabilities for the Trojan Multiplier :

1. $P_{M(a_1)} \approx P_{M(b_1)}$ and $P_{M(a_1,b_1)} = P_{M(a_1)} \cdot P_{M(b_1)}$
2. $P_{M(a_0,b_0|a_1,b_1)} \approx 0.09$
3. $P_{M(a_0|a_1,b_1=b_0)} \approx 0.18$

Assumption (1) follows from the fact that both inputs have the same impact on the propagation path of the signal. Hence it is reasonable that both values are equally important to determine if a multiplication fails. Assumption (2) is based on experimental results in which 892 out of 10,000 multiplication failed when a_0 and b_0 are changed randomly while keeping a_1, b_1 constant. Assumption (3) is based on a similar experiment in which 1813 out of 10,000 multiplication failed when a_0 was changed randomly and b_0 was fixed to $b_0 = b_1$ and a_1 was kept constant as well.

6.2   Case Study: An ECDH Implementation with Montgomery Ladder

For our case study we assume a 255-bit ECDH key agreement with a static public key. Furthermore, we assume the implementation uses the Montgomery Ladder scalar multiplication. The ECDH key agreement works as follows: Given are a standardized public curve E (e.g. Curve25519) and the point $G \in E$. The private key of the server is a 255 bit integer k_s and the corresponding public key is $Q_s = k_s \cdot G$. The key agreement is started by the client by choosing a random 255-bit integer k_c and computing $Q_c = k_c \cdot G$. The client sends Q_c to the server and computes the shared key $R = k_s \cdot Q_s$. The server computes the shared secret key R using Q_c and his secret key k_s by computing $R = k_S \cdot Q_c$. Usually, the key agreement is followed by a handshake to ensure that both the client and the server are now in possession of the same shared session key R.

The general idea of the bug attack is that the attacker makes a key guess of the first l bits of the secret key K_s. Then the attacker searches for a point $Q = m \cdot G$ such that the scalar multiplication $\tilde{R} = k_s \odot Q$ results in a failure if, and only if, the most significant bits of k_s are indeed the l bits the attacker guessed. The attacker then sends Q to the server and completes the ECDH key exchange protocol by making a handshake with the shared key $R = m \cdot Q_s$. If this handshake fails, the expected multiplication error in the Trojan Multiplier has occurred and hence, the attacker knows that his key guess is correct. This way more and more bits of the key are recovered consecutively. In the Montgomery Ladder scalar multiplication only one bit of the key is processed in each ladder step and the attack works as follows:

1. Input: Elliptic curve E with point $G \in E$ and public server key $Q_s \in E$
2. Initialization: Set $k = 1_{(2)}$
3. Repeat for key bit 2 to 255:
   (a) Define $k_0 = k||0_{(2)}$ [Append a zero to the key k]
   (b) Define $k_1 = k||1_{(2)}$ [Append a one to the key k]
   (c) Repeatedly choose a value m and compute $Q = m \cdot G$ until:
   $(\tilde{P}_i = k_i \odot Q) \neq (P_i = k_i \cdot Q)$ for $i \in \{0,1\}$
   $(\tilde{P}_j = k_j \odot Q) = (P_j = k_j \cdot Q)$ for $j \neq i$, $j \in \{0,1\}$

(d) Send Q to the server and complete handshake with $R = m \cdot Q_s$
(e) If handshake failed, set $k = k_i$, else set $k = k_j$

The attack described above is a straight forward adaption of the bug attack from [7]. However, in the Trojan multiplier scenario the attack can be improved significantly by adding a precomputation step. The main idea is to not use randomly generated points Q in step 3.c) but to use points Q in which the x-coordinate Q_x contains a b_1 for which the Trojan Multiplier $\tilde{y} = MUL_{a_0,b_0}(a_1,b_1)$ has a high chance to return a faulty response. That is, b_1 is one of the inputs for which the Trojan Multiplier fails. In each step of the Montgomery Ladder algorithm the projective coordinate Z_2 is computed with $Z_2 \leftarrow Z_2 \cdot Q_x$[1] Hence, Q_x, and therefore also b_1, is used in every ladder step. Furthermore, the value Z_2 is different depending on the currently processed key bit. Our improved attack targets this 255-bit integer multiplication $Z_2 \cdot Q_x$ to find a Q such that $(\tilde{P}_i \neq P_i)$ while $(\tilde{P}_j \neq P_j)$ as needed in step 3.c) of the attack algorithm.

Unfortunately, the attacker cannot freely choose Q since the attacker needs to know m such that $Q = m \cdot G$ to finish the handshake. Instead of computing suitable points for each attack, we propose to search for t suitable points Q during a precomputation step as described below:

1. Input: Elliptic curve E with point $G \in E$
2. Initialization: $m = 1$, $Q = G$
3. Repeat t times:
   (a) $m = m + 1$, $Q = Q + G$
   (b) If Q_x contains b_1, store m and Q in list L

To compute the probability that the 255-bit integer multiplication $Z_2 \cdot Q_x$ fails the used multiplication algorithm is important. We assume that the schoolbook multiplication is used. One 255-bit schoolbook multiplication consists of 64 multiplications of which 8 have b_1 as an operand. Since one of these multiplication is a 31-bit multiplication and we assume that only 32-bit multiplications can trigger the Trojan, 7 32-bit multiplications with b_1 that can trigger the Trojan are performed in each ladder step. Furthermore, due to the FOR loops in the schoolbook multiplication, in 6 of these 7 multiplications $b_0 = b_1$, i.e., the second operand in the multiplication remains unchanged. Note that $P_{M(a_0|a_1,b_1=b_0)} \approx 0.18$ and hence this is actually not a problem but rather helpful. The average number A_Q of points Q that need to be tested until a failure occurs for key bit 1 or 0 is therefore:

$$A_Q = \frac{1}{2} \cdot \frac{1}{P_{M(a_1)} \cdot P_{M(a_0|a_1,b_1=b_0)} \cdot 6 + P_{M(a_1)} \cdot P_{M(a_0,b_0|a_1,b_1)} \cdot 1}$$

Let us assume that the attacker tries to find a point Q for key bit i. Since the attacker searches for a fault in the last Montgomery Ladder step, for every point Q the attacker needs to compute $i - 2$ Montgomery Ladder steps (for the first

---

[1] See Appendix B of the IACR ePrint version for the Montgomery Ladder algorithm.

Table 2. Attack complexity of the proposed improved bug attack using the Trojan multiplier assuming a 256 bit curve.

$P_{M(a_1,b_1)}$	2^{-64}	2^{-48}	2^{-32}
Precomputation complexity (point additions)	$2^{66.8}$	$2^{50.8}$	$2^{34.8}$
Storage requirement	14 PB	55 TB	215 GB
Attack complexity (scalar multiplications)	$2^{30.8}$	$2^{22.8}$	$2^{14.8}$
Attack complexity (montgomery ladder steps)	$2^{46.8}$	$2^{38.8}$	$2^{30.8}$

key bit no step is needed) and then two Montgomery Ladder steps for key bit 1 and 0 respectively to check if the multiplication fails. Hence, in total the attacker needs an average of A_M Montgomery Ladder steps to recover a 255 bit key:

$$A_M = \sum_{i=2}^{255} (i \cdot A_Q) = \frac{255^2 + 255}{2} \cdot A_Q \approx 2^{16} \cdot A_Q$$

To compute t points Q during the precomputation such that b_1 is in Q_x the attacker needs in average

$$A_P = t \cdot \frac{1}{P_{M(b_1)}}$$

point additions. We chose $t = 16 \cdot A_Q$ which results in a failure probability of ca. $3.3 \cdot 10^{-8}$ which should be small enough for all reasonable attack scenarios. Table 2 summarizes the attack complexity for our improved bug attack with precomputation for different parameters for the Trojan Multiplier. To put these numbers into perspective, the hardware implementation of curve25519 presented in [22] can compute roughly $2^{39.3}$ Montgomery Ladder steps per second on a Xilinx Zynq 7020 FPGA. Hence, especially for a failure probability of $P_{M(a_1,b_1)} = 2^{-48}$ the attack complexity of 2^{39} Montgomery ladder steps (and 2^{50} point additions that only need to be done once) is quite practical in a real-world scenario. On the other hand, the probability that the Trojan is triggered unintentionally during normal operation is about 2^{-37} which is low enough to not cause problems (see Appendix B for details).

7   Conclusion

This paper introduced a new type of parametric hardware Trojans based on rarely-sensitized path delay faults. While hardware Trojans using parametric changes (i.e. that only modify the performance/parameters of gates) have been proposed before, the previously proposed parametric hardware Trojans cannot be triggered deterministically. They are instead either triggered after time by aging [23], triggered randomly under reduced voltage [17] or are always on and can leak keys using a power side-channel [4]. In contrast, the proposed parametric hardware Trojan in this paper can be triggered by applying specific input sequences to the circuit. Hence, this paper introduces the first trigger-based hardware Trojan that is realized solely by small and stealthy parametric changes. To achieve this, a SAT-based algorithm is presented which efficiently searches a combinational circuit for paths that are extremely rarely sensitized. A genetic algorithm is then used to distribute delays over all the gates on the path so that a path delay fault occurs when trigger inputs are applied, while for other inputs the timing criteria are met. In this way, a faulty response is computed only for a very small subset of input combinations.

To demonstrate the usefulness of the proposed technique, a 32-bit multiplier is modified so that, for some multiplications, faulty responses are computed. These faults can be so rare that they do not interfere with normal operations but can still be used by the Trojan designer for a bug attack against public key algorithms. As a motivating example, we showed how this can be achieved for ECDH implementations. Please note that while we used a multiplier as our case study, the general idea of path delay Trojans and the tool-flow and algorithms presented in this paper are not restricted to multipliers. Hence, this work shows that by only making extremely stealthy parametric changes to a design, a malicious factory could insert backdoors to leak out secret keys.

A   Difficulty of Justification and Propagation Tables

Table 3. Computation of $diffj$ for different gate types. In the case of 2-input gates, we assume without loss of generality that input A is the on-path input and B is the off-path input. The first two columns show the output transition, and the input transition that we are trying to justify for this output transition. Columns 3–6 show the values that the on-path input (A) and off-path input (B) must take in the first and second cycles to justify the desired transition. The final column shows the formula to compute $diffj$ in terms of the controllability of the inputs.

	Output trans	Input trans	A		B		$Diffj$
			v(1)	v(2)	v(1)	v(2)	
X = AND(A,B)	$X \downarrow$	$A \downarrow$	1	0	1	1	$C_1(A) * C_0(A) * C_1^2(B)$
	$X \uparrow$	$A \uparrow$	0	1	-	1	$C_0(A) * C_1(A) * C_1(B)$
X = OR(A,B)	$X \downarrow$	$A \downarrow$	1	0	-	0	$C_1(A) * C_0(A) * C_0(B)$
	$X \uparrow$	$A \uparrow$	0	1	0	0	$C_0(A) * C_1(A) * C_0^2(B)$
X = XOR(A,B)	$X \downarrow$	$A \downarrow$	1	0	0	0	$C_1(A) * C_0(A) * C_0^2(B)$
	$X \downarrow$	$A \uparrow$	0	1	1	1	$C_0(A) * C_1(A) * C_1^2(B)$
	$X \uparrow$	$A \uparrow$	0	1	0	0	$C_0(A) * C_1(A) * C_0^2(B)$
	$X \uparrow$	$A \downarrow$	1	0	1	1	$C_1(A) * C_0(A) * C_1^2(B)$
X = BUFF(A)	$X \downarrow$	$A \downarrow$	1	0	-	-	1
	$X \uparrow$	$A \uparrow$	0	1	-	-	1
X = INV(A)	$X \downarrow$	$A \uparrow$	0	1	-	-	1
	$X \uparrow$	$A \downarrow$	1	0	-	-	1

Table 4. Computation of $diffp$ for different gate types. In the case of 2-input gates, we assume without loss of generality that input A is the on-path input and B is the off-path input. The first two columns show the output transition, and the input transition that we are trying to propagate for this on-path input transition. Columns 3–6 show the values that the output (X) and off-path input (B) must take in the first and second cycles to propagate the desired transition. The final column shows the formula to compute $diffp$ in terms of the controllability of the off-path input and observability of output.

	Output trans	Input trans	X		B		$Diffp$
			v(1)	v(2)	v(1)	v(2)	
X = AND(A,B)	X ↓	A ↓	1	0	1	1	$OB_1(X) * OB_0(X) * C_1^2(B)$
	X ↑	A ↑	0	1	-	1	$OB_0(X) * OB_1(X) * C_1(B)$
X = OR(A,B)	X ↓	A ↓	1	0	-	0	$OB_1(X) * OB_0(X) * C_0(B)$
	X ↑	A ↑	0	1	0	0	$OB_0(X) * OB_1(X) * C_0^2(B)$
X = XOR(A,B)	X ↓	A ↓	1	0	0	0	$OB_1(X) * OB_0(X) * C_0^2(B)$
	X ↓	A ↑	1	0	1	1	$OB_1(X) * OB_0(X) * C_1^2(B)$
	X ↑	A ↑	0	1	0	0	$OB_0(X) * OB_1(X) * C_0^2(B)$
	X ↑	A ↓	0	1	1	1	$OB_0(X) * OB_1(X) * C_1^2(B)$
X = BUFF(A)	X ↓	A ↓	1	0	-	-	$OB_1(X) * OB_0(X)$
	X ↑	A ↑	0	1	-	-	$OB_0(X) * OB_1(X)$
X = INV(A)	X ↓	A ↑	1	0	-	-	$OB_1(X) * OB_0(X)$
	X ↑	A ↓	0	1	-	-	$OB_0(X) * OB_1(X)$

B   Montgomery Ladder

To be able to compute the exact attack complexity the details of the Montgomery Ladder are important to determine how many manipulations are performed in each step. Algorithms 3 and 4 describe the details of the assumed Montgomery Ladder implementation.

Computing the Failure Probability of a Scalar Multiplication. In this subsection we describe how the failure probability of a Montgomery Ladder

---

Algorithm 3. MONTGOMERY LADDER

Input: A 255-bit scalar s and the x-coordinate Q_x of $Q \in E$
Output: c-coordinate P_x of point $P \in E$ with $P = s \cdot Q$
1 $X_1 \leftarrow 1; Z_1 \leftarrow 0; X_3 \leftarrow Q_x ; Z_2 \leftarrow 1$
2 **for** $i \leftarrow 254$ *downto 0* **do**
3 $\quad$ $b \leftarrow$ bit i of s
4 $\quad$ $c \leftarrow$ bit $i-1$ of s for $i < 254$ else $c \leftarrow 0$
5 $\quad$ **if** $b \oplus c = 1$ **then**
6 $\quad\quad$ Swap(X_1, X_2)
7 $\quad\quad$ Swap(Z_1, Z_2)
8 $\quad$ $(X_1, Z_1, X_2, Z_2) \leftarrow LADDERSTEP(Q_x, X_1, Z_1, X_2, Z_2)$
9 $P_x \leftarrow X_1/Z_1$
10 **return** P_x

Algorithm 4. LADDERSTEP OF THE MONTGOMERY LADDER (FOR CURVE 25519)

Input: Q_x, X_1, Z_1, X_2, Z_2
Output: X_1, Z_1, X_2, Z_2

1   $T_1 \leftarrow X_2 + Z_2$ 11 $Z_1 \leftarrow Z_1 + X_1$
2   $X_1 \leftarrow X_2 - Z_2$ 12 $Z_1 \leftarrow T_2 \cdot Z_1$
3   $Z_2 \leftarrow X_1 + Z_1$ 13 $X_1 \leftarrow Z_2 \cdot X_1$
4   $X_1 \leftarrow X_1 - Z_1$ 14 $Z_2 \leftarrow T_1 - X_2$
5   $T_1 \leftarrow T_1 \cdot Z_2$ 15 $Z_2 \leftarrow Z_2 \cdot Z_2$
6   $X_2 \leftarrow X_2 \cdot Z_2$ 16 $Z_2 \leftarrow Z_2 \cdot Q_x$
7   $Z_2 \leftarrow Z_2 \cdot Z_2$ 17 $X_2 \leftarrow T_1 + X_2$
8   $X_1 \leftarrow X_1 \cdot X_1$ 18 $X_2 \leftarrow X_2 \cdot X_2$
9   $T_2 \leftarrow Z_2 - X_1$ 19   **return** X_1, Z_1, X_2, Z_2
10   $Z_1 \leftarrow T_2 \cdot a24$

---

scalar multiplication with schoolbook multiplication on the Trojan Multiplier can be compute. To compute the probability that the computation fails we fist compute the probability that a computation does not fail. As noted previously, in a 255-bit schoolbook integer multiplications with 32-bit word size, 64 multiplications are performed. From this 64 multiplications, 49 multiplications are the multiplications of two 32-bit numbers, while 6 are 32-bit times 31-bit multiplications and one 31-bit times 31-bit multiplications. We again assume that only 32-bit multiplications can result in a faulty response. In 42 multiplications the second operand is the same as in the previous multiplications and hence the probability that such a multiplication fails is:

$$P_{M(a_1, a_b)} \cdot P_{M(a_0 | a_1, b_1 = b_0)}$$

For 7 multiplications the failure probability is:

$$P_{M(a_1, a_b)} \cdot P_{M(a_0, b_1 | a_1, b_1)}$$

The probability that *no* failure occurs during one Montgomery Ladder step is therefore:

$$\left(1 - P_{M(a_1, a_b)}\right)^{42} \cdot \left(1 - P_{M(a_0, b_1 | a_1, b_1)}\right)^7$$

A 255-bit scalar multiplication requires 254 Montgomery Ladder steps. Hence the probability that a failure occurs is given by:

$$1 - \left(\left(1 - P_{M(a_1, a_b)}\right)^{42} \cdot \left(1 - P_{M(a_0, b_1 | a_1, b_1)}\right)^7\right)^{254}$$

References

1. Genetic Algorithm. http://www.mathworks.com/discovery/genetic-algorithm.html. Accessed 01 Feb 2016
2. Agrawal, D., Baktir, S., Karakoyunlu, D., Rohatgi, P., Sunar, B.: Trojan detection using IC fingerprinting. In: IEEE Symposium on Security and Privacy (SP 2007), pp. 296–310 (2007)
3. Bao, C., Forte, D., Srivastava, A.: On reverse engineering-based hardware Trojan detection. IEEE Trans. Comput.-Aided Des. Integr. Circ. Syst. **35**(1), 49–57 (2016)
4. Becker, G.T., Regazzoni, F., Paar, C., Burleson, W.P.: Stealthy dopant-level hardware Trojans. In: Bertoni, G., Coron, J.-S. (eds.) CHES 2013. LNCS, vol. 8086, pp. 197–214. Springer, Heidelberg (2013)
5. Biham, E., Carmeli, Y., Shamir, A.: Bug attacks. In: Wagner, D. (ed.) CRYPTO 2008. LNCS, vol. 5157, pp. 221–240. Springer, Heidelberg (2008)
6. Biham, E., Carmeli, Y., Shamir, A.: Bug attacks. J. Cryptology 1–31 (2015). http://dx.doi.org/10.1007/s00145-015-9209-1
7. Brumley, B.B., Barbosa, M., Page, D., Vercauteren, F.: Practical realisation and elimination of an ECC-related software bug attack. In: Dunkelman, O. (ed.) CT-RSA 2012. LNCS, vol. 7178, pp. 171–186. Springer, Heidelberg (2012)
8. Chakraborty, R.S., Wolff, F., Paul, S., Papachristou, C., Bhunia, S.: *MERO*: a statistical approach for hardware Trojan detection. In: Clavier, C., Gaj, K. (eds.) CHES 2009. LNCS, vol. 5747, pp. 396–410. Springer, Heidelberg (2009)
9. Eggersgl, S., Wille, R., Drechsler, R.: Improved SAT-based ATPG: more constraints, better compaction. In: IEEE/ACM International Conference on Computer-Aided Design (ICCAD), pp. 85–90 (2013)
10. Ghandali, S., Alizadeh, B., Navabi, Z.: Low power scheduling in high-level synthesis using dual-Vth library. In: 16th International Symposium on Quality Electronic Design (ISQED), pp. 507–511 (2015)
11. Gupta, P., Kahng, A.B., Sharma, P., Sylvester, D.: Gate-length biasing for runtime-leakage control. IEEE Trans. Comput.-Aided Des. Integr. Circ. Syst. **25**(8), 1475–1485 (2006)
12. Heragu, K., Agrawal, V., Bushnell, M.: FACTS: fault coverage estimation by test vector sampling. In: Proceedings of IEEE VLSI Test Symposium, pp. 266–271 (1994)
13. Hicks, M., Finnicum, M., King, S.T., Martin, M.M., Smith, J.M.: Overcoming an untrusted computing base: detecting and removing malicious hardware automatically. In: IEEE Symposium on Security and Privacy (SP 2010), pp. 159–172 (2010)
14. Karri, R., Rajendran, J., Rosenfeld, K., Tehranipoor, M.: Trustworthy hardware: identifying and classifying hardware Trojans. Computer **10**, 39–46 (2010)
15. King, S.T., Tucek, J., Cozzie, A., Grier, C., Jiang, W., Zhou, Y.: Designing and implementing malicious hardware. In: Proceedings of the 1st USENIX Workshop on Large-scale Exploits and Emergent Threats (LEET 08), pp. 1–8 (2008)
16. Kulkarni, S.H., Sylvester, D.M., Blaauw, D.T.: Design-time optimization of post-silicon tuned circuits using adaptive body bias. IEEE Trans. Comput. Aided Des. Integr. Circ. Syst. **27**(3), 481–494 (2008)
17. Kumar, R., Jovanovic, P., Burleson, W., Polian, I.: Parametric Trojans for fault-injection attacks on cryptographic hardware. In: 2014 Workshop on Fault Diagnosis and Tolerance in Cryptography (FDTC), pp. 18–28. IEEE (2014)

18. Lin, L., Kasper, M., Güneysu, T., Paar, C., Burleson, W.: Trojan side-channels: lightweight hardware Trojans through side-channel engineering. In: Clavier, C., Gaj, K. (eds.) CHES 2009. LNCS, vol. 5747, pp. 382–395. Springer, Heidelberg (2009)
19. Rajendran, J., Jyothi, V., Karri, R.: Blue team red team approach to hardware trust assessment. In: IEEE 29th International Conference on Computer Design (ICCD 2011), pp. 285–288, October 2011
20. Rajendran, J., Jyothi, V., Sinanoglu, O., Karri, R.: Design and analysis of ring oscillator based design-for-trust technique. In: 29th IEEE VLSI Test Symposium (VTS 2011), pp. 105–110 (2011)
21. Saha, S., Chakraborty, R.S., Nuthakki, S.S., Mukhopadhyay, D.: Improved test pattern generation for hardware Trojan detection using genetic algorithm and Boolean satisfiability. In: Güneysu, T., Handschuh, H. (eds.) CHES 2015. LNCS, vol. 9293, pp. 577–596. Springer, Heidelberg (2015)
22. Sasdrich, P., Güneysu, T.: Implementing Curve25519 for side-channel-protected elliptic curve cryptography. ACM Trans. Reconfigurable Technol. Syst. (TRETS) 9(1), 3 (2015)
23. Shiyanovskii, Y., Wolff, F., Rajendran, A., Papachristou, C., Weyer, D., Clay, W.: Process reliability based Trojans through NBTI and HCI effects. In: NASA/ESA Conference on Adaptive Hardware and Systems (AHS 2010), pp. 215–222 (2010)
24. Sugawara, T., Suzuki, D., Fujii, R., Tawa, S., Hori, R., Shiozaki, M., Fujino, T.: Reversing stealthy dopant-level circuits. In: Batina, L., Robshaw, M. (eds.) CHES 2014. LNCS, vol. 8731, pp. 112–126. Springer, Heidelberg (2014)
25. Tang, X., Zhou, H., Banerjee, P.: Leakage power optimization with dual-Vth library in high-level synthesis. In: 42nd Annual Design Automation Conference (DAC 2005), pp. 202–207 (2005)
26. Waksman, A., Sethumadhavan, S.: Silencing hardware backdoors. In: IEEE Symposium on Security and Privacy (SP 2011), pp. 49–63 (2011)

Author Index

Anagnostopoulos, Nikolaos A.   432
Aoki, Takafumi   538
Azarderakhsh, Reza   517

Batina, Lejla   301
Battistello, Alberto   23
Becker, Georg T.   625
Bhattacharya, Sarani   602
Bilgin, Begül   194
Boit, Christian   147
Bos, Joppe W.   215
Boss, Erik   171
Bruinderink, Leon Groot   323
Burian, Daniel   559

Chou, Tung   280
Chowdhury, Dipanwita Roy   581
Coron, Jean-Sébastien   23, 498

Danger, Jean-Luc   3
De Cnudde, Thomas   194
Del Pozo, Santos Merino   40
Delvaux, Jeroen   412
Dugardin, Margaux   3
Durvaux, François   40

Eisenbarth, Thomas   368

Fäßler, Fabian   391

Gabmeyer, Sebastian   432
Ganji, Fatemeh   391
Genkin, Daniel   346
Ghandali, Samaneh   625
Goudarzi, Dahmun   457
Greuet, Aurélien   498
Grosso, Vincent   61, 171
Gu, Dawu   412
Guajardo, Jorge   85
Guilley, Sylvain   3
Gulmezoglu, Berk   368
Güneysu, Tim   171

Heninger, Nadia   346
Hiller, Matthias   412
Holcomb, Daniel   625
Homma, Naofumi   538
Hubain, Charles   215
Hülsing, Andreas   323

İnci, Mehmet Sinan   368
Irazoqui, Gorka   368

Jain, Shalabh   85
Järvinen, Kimmo   517

Kammerstetter, Markus   559
Kastner, Wolfgang   559
Katzenbeisser, Stefan   432
Kudera, Christian   559

Lange, Tanja   323
Leander, Gregor   171
Lohrke, Heiko   147
Longa, Patrick   517
López, Julio   259

Michiels, Wil   215
Miele, Andrea   517
Moradi, Amir   171
Morioka, Sumio   538
Muellner, Markus   559
Mukhopadhyay, Debdeep   602

Najm, Zakaria   3
Nikov, Ventzislav   194
Nikova, Svetla   194
Nürnberger, Stefan   106

Oliveira, Thomaz   259

Paar, Christof   625
Poussier, Romain   61
Prouff, Emmanuel   23, 498
Pulkus, Jürgen   479

Renes, Joost   301
Reparaz, Oscar   194
Rijmen, Vincent   194
Rioul, Olivier   3
Rivain, Matthieu   457
Rodríguez-Henríquez, Francisco   259
Rossow, Christian   106

Saha, Dhiman   581
Saleem, Muhammad Umair   432
Schaller, André   432
Schneider, Tobias   171
Schwabe, Peter   301
Seifert, Jean-Pierre   147, 391
Smith, Benjamin   301
Srivastava, Ankur   127
Standaert, François-Xavier   40, 61
Sunar, Berk   368
Szefer, Jakub   432

Tajik, Shahin   147, 391
Teuwen, Philippe   215

Ueno, Rei   538

Verbauwhede, Ingrid   412
Vivek, Srinivas   479

Xie, Yang   127
Xiong, Wenjie   432

Yarom, Yuval   323, 346
Yener, Bülent   237
Yu, Meng-Day (Mandel)   412

Zeitoun, Rina   23, 498
Zonenberg, Andrew   237

Printed in the United States
By Bookmasters